International Handbook of Metacognition and Learning Technologies

Springer International Handbooks of Education

VOLUME 26

For further volumes:
http://www.springer.com/series/6189

Roger Azevedo • Vincent Aleven
Editors

International Handbook of Metacognition and Learning Technologies

Editors
Roger Azevedo
Department of Educational
and Counselling Psychology
McGill University
Montreal, QC, Canada

Vincent Aleven
Human-Computer Interaction Institute
Carnegie Mellon University
Pittsburgh, PA, USA

ISBN 978-1-4419-5545-6 ISBN 978-1-4419-5546-3 (eBook)
DOI 10.1007/978-1-4419-5546-3
Springer New York Heidelberg Dordrecht London

Library of Congress Control Number: 2013934001

Printed on acid-free paper

Springer is part of Springer Science+Business Media (www.springer.com)

Preface

This is the first international handbook on the topic of metacognition and learning technologies. We are proud to have been invited by Springer to coedit such an important two-volume international handbook. The handbook represents the best cutting-edge interdisciplinary research from leading scholars across the globe. The ubiquity and widespread use of learning technologies across various settings (e.g., classrooms, informal settings, and research laboratories) necessitate a theoretically guided and empirical basis for their use for learning and instruction. It has become clear in recent years that learners' self-regulatory and metacognitive processes are a key influence on their learning outcomes with computer-based learning environments. A deep understanding of the relations between self-regulation, metacognition, the design of learning environment, and learning outcomes is therefore highly desirable from both a scientific and a practical perspective. This fundamental requirement has led dozens of interdisciplinary researchers to focus on understanding, measuring, supporting, and fostering metacognition and self-regulated learning in individual and collaborative groups. As such, the timely publication of this handbook is critical since it is the first to document the most influential interdisciplinary research on the topic from researchers in the fields of educational psychology, learning sciences, computing sciences, artificial intelligence (AI), cognitive psychology, human–computer interaction (HCI), educational technology, educational data mining, engineering, mathematics education, science education, teacher education, and literacy.

We hope that the handbook will be viewed as a standard of scholarship for conceptual, theoretical, empirical, and applied research in the several areas related to learning technologies and metacognition. This handbook is targeted as a resource; as such it should appeal to a broad interdisciplinary audience, including researchers, professors, graduate and upper-level undergraduate students, instructional designers, curriculum developers, teachers, and anyone else interested in learning about learning technologies and metacognition. Our handbook can be used as the primary textbook for a graduate-level course in metacognition and learning technologies. It can also be used as a supplement for graduate courses on cognition, metacognition, learning, learning sciences, theories of learning and instruction, human–computer interaction, artificial intelligence (AI) in education, educational technology, and measuring complex cognitive, metacognitive, motivational, and affective processes prior to, during, and following learning and problem solving.

The *International Handbook of Metacognition and Learning Technologies* has 46 chapters thematically structured across seven sections: Models and Components of Metacognition, Assessing and Modeling Metacognitive Knowledge and Skills, Scaffolding Metacognition and Learning with Hypermedia and Hypertext, Intelligent Tutoring Systems and Tutorial Dialogue Systems, Multi-Agent Systems to Measure and Foster Metacognition and Self-Regulated Learning, Individual and Collaborative Learning in Classroom Settings, and Motivation and Affect: Key Processes in Metacognition and Self-Regulated Learning. Each section contains a varying number of chapters, ranging from four to nine, written by leading scholars in each topic area. The difference in the number of chapters across each section is representative of the focus of research in the area of metacognition and learning technologies. For example, there are nine chapters in the section on scaffolding metacognition and learning with hypermedia and hypertext because this area has traditionally been a dominant area of research. By contrast, there are only five chapters in the motivation and affect section because this area of research has been emerging more recently; it is our opinion that it stands to contribute immensely to our understanding of the role of metacognition and learning technologies.

Our greatest challenge was assembling the finest collection of contributors to the handbook. We as editors are extremely impressed with the quality and diversity of the chapters that are collected in this handbook. It is our profound hope that the readers of this handbook will find the chapters as stimulating and gratifying as we found them when assembling the handbook. Happy reading! Please don't forget to monitor as you read.

Montreal, QC, Canada — Roger Azevedo
Pittsburg, PA, USA — Vincent Aleven

Acknowledgements

We wish to acknowledge Marie Sheldon, Bill Tucker, and Melissa James at Springer for their encouragement and support in putting this handbook together. We also thank Lana Karabachian for her editorial assistance.

Montreal, QC, Canada — Roger Azevedo
Pittsburg, PA, USA — Vincent Aleven

About the Authors

Philip C. Abrami, Ph.D., is a Concordia University Research Chair and the Director of the Centre for the Study of Learning and Performance. His current work focuses on research integrations and primary investigations in support of applications of educational technology in distance and higher education, in early literacy, and in the development of higher-order thinking skills.

Vincent Aleven is an Associate Professor in the Human–Computer Interaction Institute at Carnegie Mellon University. He has 20 years of experience in research and development of advanced learning technologies based on cognitive and metacognitive theory, including intelligent tutoring systems, game-based learning, and simulation-based learning. Aleven is a member of the Executive Committee of the Pittsburgh Science of Learning Center (PSLC). Within the PSLC, he is a coleader of the research thrust entitled "Metacognition and Motivation." He is an Associate Editor of the *International Journal of Artificial Intelligence in Education* and is a member of the editorial boards of the *Journal of Educational Psychology, Learning and Instruction,* and *Metacognition and Learning.*

Katerina Avramides is a Research Fellow at the London Knowledge Lab. She has a B.Sc. in Psychology and Artificial Intelligence from the University of Nottingham, a M.Sc. in Human-Centred Computer Systems, and Ph.D. in Informatics from the University of Sussex. Her research focuses on the design of technology to support learning in formal and informal learning contexts. Her work has explored the development of high-order thinking skills, the role of motivation and affect in learning, and the development of social communication skills.

Roger Azevedo is a Professor of Educational Psychology at McGill University (Montreal, Canada). He is also a Senior Canada Research Chair in the area of Metacognition and Advanced Learning Technologies. His main research areas include examining the role of cognitive, metacognitive, affective, and motivational self-regulatory processes during learning with computer-based learning environments. He has designed and developed several computer-based learning environments for learning and training in several science and medicine domains. He is the Director of the Laboratory for the Study of Metacognition and Advanced Learning Technologies (http://www.smartlaboratory.ca/). He has published over 200 peer-reviewed papers, book chapters, refereed conference proceedings, and special issues of journals in the areas of educational, learning, and cognitive sciences. He is the editor of the *Metacognition and Learning* journal and he also serves of the editorial board of several top-tiered educational psychology and instructional science journals (*Educational Psychologist, Educational Psychology Review*). He is a Fellow of the American Psychological Association and the recipient of the prestigious Early Faculty Career Award from the National Science Foundation. His interdisciplinary research on advanced learning technologies is currently funded by NSF, NIH, IES, the Social Sciences and Humanities Research Council of Canada (SSHRC), and the Canadian Foundation for Innovation (CFI).

Ryan S.J.d. Baker holds the Julius and Rosa Sachs Distinguished Lectureship at Columbia University Teachers College. His research, at the intersection of educational data mining and learner–computer interaction, focuses on studying students' robust learning, engagement, and affect. He is the founding President of the International Educational Data Mining Society, and is an Associate Editor of the *Journal of Educational Data Mining.* He graduated from Carnegie Mellon University in 2005, with a Ph.D. in Human–Computer Interaction. He has received five Best Paper, Best Oral Presentation, or Best Student Paper Awards.

Maria Bannert holds a chair in Instructional Media at the University of Wuerzburg (Germany), Department of Human-Computer-Media. Her research covers several areas in educational psychology, in particular the use of information technologies in universities and for adult training. Her actual research focus is on self-regulated hypermedia learning, its integration with theories of metacognition and motivation, its empirically based description and intervention models, as well as its successful application in real life settings. She works as reviewer for the German National Science Foundation (DFG) and for several scientific international journals. Furthermore, she is a consultant on e-learning projects and involved in a number of research and R&D projects.

Carole R. Beal is a Professor in the School of Information: Science, Technology and Arts at the University of Arizona. Her research centers on the development of technology-based math and science learning tools for middle and high school students, and the evaluation of these tools in authentic classroom contexts. She has a particular focus on designing learning systems to engage students who are members of groups traditionally under-represented in the sciences, including students with visual impairments. Her research projects have been supported by DARPA, the National Science Foundation and the U.S. Department of Education.

Matthew L. Bernacki is a postdoctoral researcher at the Learning Research and Development Center at the University of Pittsburgh and a member of the Pittsburgh Science of Learning Center's Metacognition and Motivation thrust. He received his Ph.D. in Educational Psychology at Temple University and completed graduate training in Experimental Psychology at Saint Joseph's University in Philadelphia, Pennsylvania. His research investigates how self-regulated learning theory can be applied to learning with educational technology and his recent work examines the metacognitive and motivational processes that underlie student learning.

Kirsten Berthold studied Psychology with a minor in Educational Science in Kiel (Germany), Lund (Sweden), and Freiburg (Germany). In 2003 she graduated with a diploma in psychology from the University of Freiburg (Germany). Afterwards she worked there as a scientific assistant. In 2006, she received her doctoral degree from the University of Freiburg. From 2006 to 2007 she was a postdoctoral fellow at the Swiss Federal Institute of Technology Zurich (Switzerland). As an assistant professor, she spent the 2 following years at the University of Freiburg (Germany) before becoming "junior professor" (new rank with full academic freedom and with an option for tenure track in the German academic system) of Educational Psychology at the University of Bielefeld (Germany). In October 2011, she became a full professor of Educational Psychology at the University of Bielefeld (Germany). Her main research interests are instructional explanations, self-explanations, training interventions to foster transfer across domains, learning with multiple representations, contrasting of examples, cognitive and metacognitive learning strategies in learning journals, and the integration of motivational aspects in instructional design approaches.

Gautam Biswas is a Professor of Computer Science, Computer Engineering, and Engineering Management in the EECS Department and a Senior Research Scientist at the Institute for Software Integrated Systems (ISIS) at Vanderbilt University. He conducts research in Intelligent Systems with primary interests in modeling, simulation, and analysis of complex embedded systems, and intelligent learning environments for STEM education. He is also working on developing innovative educational data mining techniques for studying students' learning behaviors. Dr. Biswas is an associate editor of the *IEEE Transactions on Systems, Man, and Cybernetics, Prognostics and Health Management, Educational Technology and Society,* and *Metacognition and Learning* journals.

Rainer Bromme is a Professor (Educational Psychology) in the Department of Psychology (University of Münster, Germany). From 1990 to 1995, he was a Professor of Educational Psychology at the University of Frankfurt. From 1979 to 1990, he was a Senior Researcher at the Institute for Research in Mathematics Education (IDM) at the University of Bielefeld. His research interests are in Cognition and Teaching/Learning processes, especially as they relate to communication and cooperation between experts and laypersons, digital literacy, and the development of knowledge and understanding in Science and Mathematics. Since 2009 he is the Coordinator of the German research program "Science and the Public—The public understanding of conflicting scientific evidence," funded by the German research foundation (DFG; http://www.scienceandthepublic.de).

François Bouchet is a postdoctoral researcher at the Faculty of Education at McGill University (Montreal, Canada) and a member of the Laboratory for the Study of Metacognition and Advanced Learning Technologies. He received his Ph.D. and Master's degrees in Computer Science at University Paris-Sud 11, and graduated in Engineering from ESIEA. In his research, he has been investigating natural language requests to assistant conversational agents and designing agent cognitive architectures embedding personality and emotions. His recent work focuses on data mining multiple channels of data collected with an agent-based ITS and analyzing emotional response from its users to improve its adaptivity.

Susan Bull leads the Artificial Intelligence in Education research in the School of Electronic, Electrical and Computer Engineering, at the University of Birmingham, UK. Much of this work is in the area of Open Learner Models and aims to help promote metacognitive activities in learning, including self-reflection, monitoring, and planning. The work also considers skills related to collaborative learning and peer help. This work focuses on both the more traditional, as well as emerging social and other new technologies, and applies not only to learners but also to professors and lecturers, teachers, parents, and other stakeholders in the education process.

Eva M. Bures is an associate professor at Bishop's University's School of Education and a faculty member of the Center for the Study of Learning and Performance. She earned a B.A. in French Literature at Reed College and a Ph.D. in Educational Technology at Concordia University. Her research explores supporting student-centered learning and assessment through computer-based technologies. Her work focuses on improving the quality of online dialogue and student learning through the intersection of instructional design techniques with features embedded in the interface. Her work also explores how to use electronic portfolios as an alternative assessment approach, primarily at the K-11 level and with preservice and in-service teachers.

Winslow Burleson is an Assistant Professor of Human–Computer Interaction at Arizona State University, where he directs the Motivational Environments research group (http://www.hci.asu.edu). He has authored 80 scientific publications and 10 patents. He received the AIED 2009 and UMUAI: Journal of Personalization Research 2011 Best Papers. He holds a Ph.D. from the MIT Media Lab, an MSE from Stanford, and a B.A. from Rice. He worked with MIT's Life Long Kindergarten, Harvard Business School's Entrepreneurial Management Unit, IBM Research, NASA-SETI Institute, Space Telescope Science Institute, and UNICEF. NSF, NASA-JPL, Deutsche Telekom, iRobot, LEGO, Microsoft, and Motorola support his research. He frequently serves on NASA, NAE, NAS, and NSF committees.

Roberto Carneiro is President of the Study Centre on Peoples and Cultures and Dean of the Institute for Distance Learning of the Portuguese Catholic University (UCP). Carneiro has led European and National research projects dealing with his main fields of expertise: Education, Human Resources, Economics of Education, Future and Foresight Studies, ICT impacts on Society and Culture, and Migrations. He has extensive international experience with development agencies, and served as a member of the UNESCO International Commission on Education in the twenty-first Century. He was President of the Editorial Board of *e-Learning Papers* and chairs the Editorial Board of the *European Journal of Education.* A former Portuguese Minister of Education, Carneiro is an Honorary Doctor in Education/Presentation Fellow of King's College (University of London).

Amanda Carr is a Lecturer in Psychology at the University of Roehampton where she is a member of the Centre for Research in Cognition, Emotion and Interaction. She has a Bachelor's degree and Ph.D. in Psychology, both from the University of Sussex. Her research concerns the role that social-cognitive processes play in motivation and learning. In particular, she is interested in the influence of mastery and performance goals on children's behavior in individual and collaborative learning contexts.

Jennifer King Chen is a doctoral student in the Education in Math, Science and Technology program at the University of California, Berkeley. She studies how instruction designed to scaffold the use and development of metacognitive skills can help students to learn from dynamic visualizations and generate scientific explanations. Jennifer is a National Science Foundation Graduate Research Fellow. Prior to graduate school, she was a curriculum developer with the Great Explorations in Math and Science (GEMS) group at the Lawrence Hall of Science. She also worked for several years as a scientific researcher in the fields of astrophysics and cardiovascular medicine.

Jennifer L. Chiu is an Assistant Professor of Science, Technology, Engineering and Mathematics (STEM) Education in the Curry School of Education at the University of Virginia. She investigates how students learn from technology-enhanced curricula in authentic classroom settings, how students monitor their understanding in computer-based environments, and how to support student learning with dynamic visualizations through generative activities and instructional design patterns. Formerly, Chiu was an engineer and high school math and science teacher. She currently teaches undergraduate and graduate courses in STEM education.

Geraldine Clarebout is a Professor at the K.U. Leuven (Belgium). She is a member of the Center for Instructional Psychology and Technology, and a member of the Interdisciplinary Research team on Technology, Educational, and Communication. She got her Ph.D. at the K.U. Leuven with a dissertation on the enhancement of tool use in open learning environments. Her current research interests relate to the use of instructional interventions, blended learning, and mobile learning. She teaches courses on educational technology at the graduate and undergraduate level.

Mihaela Cocea is a Lecturer in the School of Computing at the University of Portsmouth, UK. She received her Ph.D. in Computer Science in 2011 from Birkbeck College, University of London and her M.Sc. by Research in Learning Technologies in 2008 from National College of Ireland. Her research expertise lies at the intersection of computer science, psychology and education; she is interested in intelligent systems, with a focus on artificial intelligence techniques for user modeling, knowledge management, and decision making. In 2010 she was awarded the Best Student Paper award at The 14th International Conference on Knowledge-Based and Intelligent Information & Engineering Systems.

Cristina Conati is an Associate Professor of Computer Science at the University of British Columbia. She received her M.Sc. (1996) and Ph.D. (1999) in Artificial Intelligence from the University of Pittsburgh. Conati's research areas include User-Adaptive Interaction, Intelligent Tutoring Systems, User Modeling, and Affective Computing. She published over 60 refereed articles, and received awards from the International Conferences on User Modeling, AI in Education, Intelligent User Interfaces, as well as the *Journal of User Modeling and User-Adapted Interaction.* Conati is Associate Editor of the I*nternational Journal of AI in Education, IEEE Transactions in Affective Computing,* and *ACM Transactions on Interactive Intelligent Systems.*

A.T. Corbett is an Associate Research Professor in the Human–Computer Interaction Institute and codirector of the Pittsburgh Advanced Cognitive Tutor Center at Carnegie Mellon University. He received a B.A. in Psychology from Brown University and a Ph.D. in Psychology from the University of Oregon. Over the past 25 years he has brought his interests in memory, learning, and problem solving to the development and evaluation of cognitive tutors for programming, mathematics, and genetics. This research has included a special focus on student modeling of learning and performance and the use of student models to improve learning outcomes.

Lara-Jeane Costa is a doctoral student in the Educational Psychology, Measurement, and Evaluation program at the University of North Carolina at Chapel Hill. Her research focuses on cognition and quantitative methods. She has examined the development of writing skills in school-aged children as well as the mechanisms that influence self-regulated learning in college students. Lara is also interested in understanding the neurological basis of cognitive development and how it influences students' learning.

Ilian Cruz-Panesso is a doctoral candidate in the Learning Sciences program at McGill University (Canada, Montreal) and is a research assistant at the Advanced Technologies for Learning in Authentic Settings (ATLAS) Laboratory. Ms. Cruz-Panesso received a B.S. in Psychology from Universidad Javeriana Colombia-Cali and her M.A. in Learning Sciences from McGill University. Her research interests include individual and team problem solving with applications to medical education, development of simulation-based learning environments, and team-based training. Ms. Cruz-Panesso research has mainly looked at military trauma teams. She has established learning curves for team training and ways to scaffold team performance in simulation-based environments.

Nada Dabbagh is a Professor of Instructional Design and Technology and director of the Division of Learning Technologies in the College of Education and Human Development at George Mason University in Fairfax, Virginia. Her research explores the pedagogical ecology of technology mediated learning environments with the goal of understanding the social and cognitive consequences of learning systems design. Dr. Dabbagh has an extensive publication record and has presented her research at over 100 scholarly venues participating as keynote and invited speaker at international, national, and regional conferences.

Bridget Dalton is an Assistant Professor of Language, Literacy, and Culture at Vanderbilt University. Her research interests include digital literacies, comprehension, multimodal composition, and students who experience difficulty with literacy. Prior to joining Vanderbilt, she served as Chief Officer of Literacy and Technology at CAST, designing and studying universally designed e-Texts with embedded supports for comprehension and expression. Dalton served as coeditor of the International Reading Association's online journal, *Reading Online*, and has published numerous articles and chapters on technology and literacy. She earned her doctorate in reading, language, and learning disabilities at Harvard University.

Kristin R. Dellinger is a doctoral student in the Educational Psychology, Measurement, and Evaluation program at the University of North Carolina at Chapel Hill. Her research interests include self-regulated learning and cognitive neuroscience. Specifically, she is interested in the study of learning and memory, in typically developing humans, from both philosophical and theoretical perspectives. Her current work focuses on the role of neural and behavioral mechanisms of cognitive control and their relationship to working memory and self-regulated learning.

Giuliana Dettori has been doing research for the Italian National Research Council since 1978. She is currently at the Institute for Educational Technology in Genoa, Italy. Her research interests include self-regulated learning, narrative learning, and the mediating role of ICT in education, in relation to both face-to-face and distance settings. She is teaching in the Ph.D. school "ICT for Human and Social Sciences" at Genoa University, has authored over 200 papers at the international and national level, is carrying out editorial collaboration with many journals and conferences, and has been responsible in her institute for international and national projects.

Sidney K. D'Mello is an Assistant Professor in the departments of Computer Science and Psychology at the University of Notre Dame His primary research interests are in the affective, cognitive, and learning sciences. More specific interests include emotional processing, affective computing, artificial intelligence in education, human–computer interaction, speech recognition and natural language understanding, and computational models of human cognition. He has published over 100 journal papers, book chapters, and conference proceedings in these areas. D'Mello has edited two books on Affective Computing and was the general chair and program cochair for the 2011 Affective Computing and Intelligent Interaction conference. He is an associate editor for *IEEE Transactions on Affective Computing* and serves as an advisory editor for the *Journal of Educational Psychology.* D'Mello received his Ph.D. in Computer Science from the University of Memphis in 2009. He also holds a M.S. in Mathematical Sciences and a B.S. in Electrical Engineering.

Melissa Duffy is a doctoral student in the Educational Psychology program (Learning Sciences Stream) at McGill University. She received her B.A. in Psychology from Saint Mary's University and her M.A. in Educational Psychology from McGill University. Her research focuses on the links between epistemic beliefs, achievement motivation, and metacognitive processes involved in self-regulated learning. As a member of the Laboratory for the Study of Metacognition and Advanced Learning Technologies, Melissa has explored these facets of learning within computer-based learning environments.

John Dunlosky is a Professor of Psychology at Kent State University. He received his Ph.D. from the University of Washington. He has contributed empirical and theoretical work on memory and metacognition, and a major aim of his research program is to develop techniques to improve people's self-regulated learning. A fellow of the Association for Psychological Science, he is a founder of the International Association for Metacognition and has served as an Associate Editor for the *Journal of Experimental Psychology (JEP): Learning, Memory and Cognition.*

Catherine Eberbach completed a Ph.D. in Cognitive Studies in Education at the University of Pittsburgh and is currently a Research Associate at Rutgers University. Her research interests include the development and practice of scientific observation in everyday and disciplinary-rich learning contexts, as well as the design of learning environments to facilitate learning trajectories associated with understanding complex biological phenomena.

Jan Elen is a professor in the Center for Instructional Psychology and Technology at the K.U.Leuven (Belgium). He received his Ph.D. from the K.U.Leuven with a dissertation on the transition from description to prescription in instructional design. He teaches in the domains of Educational Psychology and Educational Technology both at the graduate and the undergraduate level. His current research interests relate to the theoretical and empirical underpinnings of instructional design models, the actual use of instructional interventions by students, serious gaming in mathematics, and the integration of research into higher education. He is one of the editors of the fourth edition of the *Handbook of Research on Educational Communications and Technology.*

Reza Feyzi-Behnagh is a doctoral student in Educational Psychology, Learning Sciences stream at McGill University, Montréal, Canada. He is a member of the Laboratory for the Study of Metacognition and Advanced Learning Technologies at McGill University. Reza is interested in studying how students self-regulate while learning about complex science topics. Specifically, he is interested in using trace data, such as eye-tracking and physiological measures in order to investigate learners' cognitive and metacognitive processes.

Kate Forbes-Riley is a Senior Research Associate with the Learning Research and Development Center at the University of Pittsburgh. She obtained a Ph.D. in Computational Linguistics in 2003, and an M.S.E. in Computer and Information Science in 2001, at the University of Pennsylvania. She also holds a B.A. in Linguistics from Dartmouth College. Her current research concerns prediction and adaptation to user affective and metacognitive states in spoken dialogue tutorial systems, and her research interests center on (para-) linguistic aspects of discourse and dialogue.

Doris Holzberger graduated from University of Koblenz-Landau, Germany, in 2010. In her Diploma-thesis, she analyzed influences of metacognition on teaching and learning behavior within a computer-mediated tutoring environment at the California State University, Chico. Doris Holzberger is currently working on her Ph.D. at the University of Frankfurt, Germany. She is studying aspects of teacher competence and is, in particular, interested in the effects of teacher motivation on their instructional behavior. For her longitudinal analysis of teachers' self-efficacy beliefs on instructional quality, she received the 2011 Student Research Excellence Award from the special interest group motivation and emotion.

Timothy Gallant is completing his Master of Arts in Educational Technology at Concordia University. His interests lie in ontology development and methodologies to uncover the nature of interactions in online communities of practice.

Xun Ge is an Associate Professor with the Program of Instructional Psychology and Technology, Department of Educational Psychology at the University of Oklahoma. She earned her Ph.D. in Instructional Systems from the Pennsylvania State University in 2001. Dr. Ge's primary research interest involves designing and developing instructional scaffolds, learning technologies, and open learning environments to support students' ill-structured problem solving and self-regulated learning. Her other related research includes computer-supported collaborative learning and virtual learning communities. Dr. Ge has been teaching graduate courses of instructional design and technology, including multimedia learning, computers as cognitive tools, and designing open-ended learning environments.

Peter Gerjets is a Full Professor at the Knowledge Media Research Center in Tuebingen, Germany, where he heads the Hypermedia Research Lab. He has a background in applied Cognitive Psychology and Educational Psychology. His main research interests are related to individual learning in multi- and hypermedia environments with a focus on cognitive processes underlying hypermedia learning, information evaluation during Web search, learner control, cognitive load measurement, eye tracking, learning with dynamic visualizations, and multi-touch interaction.

Jill Größling, Ph.D., M.Sc., completed her Ph.D. thesis on "Discovery experimenting—Learning effects of strategy use" in 2010 at the University of Duisburg-Essen. She serves as a Research Fellow at the department of Instructional Psychology (University of Duisburg-Essen) since 2010. Her research interests include theoretical and methodical questions in research on learning and instruction (e.g., self-regulated and computer-based learning, classroom management, and the development of trainings).

Ashok K. Goel is a Professor of Computer Science & Cognitive Science in the School of Interactive Computing at Georgia Institute of Technology. He is Director of the school's Design & Intelligence Laboratory, and a Codirector of the institute's Center for Biologically Inspired Design. He conducts research into functional reasoning, analogical reasoning, visual reasoning and meta-reasoning as fundamental processes of creativity, design, and learning. His research has been supported by NSF, DARPA, ONR, DHS and IES, and he has been a consultant to NCC and NEC. Goel was Chair of the Eighth ACM Conference on Creativity and Cognition, and is an Associate Editor of *IEEE Intelligent Systems.*

Art Graesser is a Full Professor in the Department of Psychology, an Adjunct Professor in Computer Science, and Codirector of the Institute for Intelligent Systems at the University of Memphis. In 1977 Dr. Graesser received his Ph.D. in Psychology from the University of California at San Diego. He is currently a Senior Research Fellow at the University of Oxford. Graesser's primary research interests are in cognitive science, discourse processing, and the learning sciences. More specific interests include knowledge representation, question asking and answering, tutoring, text comprehension, inference generation, conversation, reading, education, memory, emotions, artificial intelligence, and human–computer interaction. In addition to publishing over 400 articles in journals, books, and conference proceedings, he has written 2 books and edited 9 books. He has designed, developed, and tested cutting-edge software in learning, language, and discourse technologies, including AutoTutor, Coh-Metrix, HURA Advisor, SEEK Web Tutor, MetaTutor, ARIES, Question Understanding Aid (QUAID), QUEST, and Point & Query.

Jeffrey A. Greene is an Assistant Professor of Educational Psychology at the University of North Carolina at Chapel Hill. Greene's research focuses upon student cognition, regulation and beliefs in science and history domains. Specifically, he studies self-regulated learning, or how students' knowledge, beliefs, and characteristics interact with their ability to actively and adaptively monitor and control their learning, motivation, behavior and context. He also examines epistemic and ontological cognition, or how students think about knowledge and knowing, and the ways in which those views influence learning.

Thomas D. Griffin earned his Ph.D. in Psychology, with an emphasis in Measurement and Statistics. He is currently an Assistant Research Professor at the University of Illinois at Chicago. His lines of research focus on how people self-regulate their comprehension of and their personal belief/theory formation about complex scientific topics. He examines factors that prompt learners to shift their metacognitive monitoring from their shallow understanding and memory of scientific texts to monitoring their deeper comprehension of complex causal systems. He also examines how value-based dispositions related to epistemology, affect, and reasoning impact comprehension and belief formation on controversial science topics.

Cornelia S. Grosse received the Diploma degree in Psychology from the Albert-Ludwigs-University, Freiburg, Germany, in 2001. From 2001 to 2004 she was a research assistant at the University of Freiburg, Department of Educational Psychology, working with Prof. Dr. Alexander Renkl, and received her doctoral degree in 2004. From 2005 to 2009 she worked as lecturer at the University of Bremen, Germany. Since 2010 she is supported by a postdoctoral research grant from the University of Bremen. Her research interests include teaching and learning, cognitive learning processes, learning from worked examples, and acquisition of mathematical skills.

Allyson F. Hadwin (Ph.D., Simon Fraser University) is an Associate Professor in Educational Psychology at the University of Victoria and codirector of the Technology Integration and Evaluation (TIE) research lab. Her research focuses on: (a) the regulation of learning in collaborative and solo task contexts, and (b) the ways technologies can be used to support regulated learning. She uses multiple methodologies to explore the dynamic and social nature of regulated learning as it evolves over time and through interaction with others. Hadwin is the President of the Canadian Association for Educational Psychology (2010–2012) and recent recipient of the Award for Excellence in Teaching. She is an active member of the Canadian Society for the Study of Education, American Educational Research Association, and European Association for Research on Learning and Instruction.

Jason Harley received his B.A. in Psychology and his M.A. in Educational Psychology at McGill University. Jason is currently a Ph.D. student in Educational Psychology, supervised by Dr. Roger Azevedo. Jason's research interests include emotional measurement, analysis, and theory, intelligent tutoring systems, agent-based learning environments, co-regulation, serious games, and CAMM (cognitive, affective, metacognitive, and motivational) processes. Jason's current research investigates learners' dynamic and unfolding discrete and co-occurring emotional responses to pedagogical agents' prompts and feedback.

Arnon Hershkovitz is a postdoctoral research fellow in the Learning Sciences at Worcester Polytechnic Institute. His research focuses on using data mining and machine-learning methodologies for exploring the relationships between student attributes, and affective states and engagement during learning. He is the Web Chair of the *Journal of Educational Data Mining*. He graduated from Tel Aviv University (Israel) with a Ph.D. in Science Education (2011). He holds an M.A. in Applied Mathematics, and a B.A. in Mathematics and Computer Science (both from the Technion—Israel Institute of Technology).

Cindy E. Hmelo-Silver is a Professor of Educational Psychology at the Graduate School of Education, Rutgers University. She is currently coeditor of the *Journal of the Learning Sciences*, formerly associate editor of *Journal of Research in Science Teaching,* and serves on the editorial board of the *International Journal of Computer Supported Collaborative Learning* and the *Interdisciplinary Journal of Problem-based Learning*. She has edited several books and has published widely in the areas of problem-based learning, science education and the learning sciences. Dr. Hmelo-Silver's research focuses on collaborative knowledge construction and technology support for complex learning.

Yuan-Jin Hong is a Ph.D. Candidate in the Department of Educational and Counseling Psychology at McGill University and is currently working under Dr. Susanne Lajoie in the ATLAS laboratory. His research foci are quite varied, the primary area being self-regulated learning. Other areas of interest include emotion and cognition in technology-rich learning environments, preservice teacher education, in-service teacher professional development, and transformative learning for intercultural awareness and personal growth. Yuan-Jin

Hong's current research involves the examination of how self-regulated learning, computer-supported collaborative learning, and critical analysis skills interrelate among undergraduate medical students participating in a journal club activity.

Sameer Honwad, Ph.D., is a fellow at the Center for Play, Science and Technology Learning (SciPlay) at the New York Hall of Science. His research interests focus on how to bridge science learning between formal and informal learning environments. He is particularly interested in how people apply science while making decisions in their everyday lives. Along with SciPlay, he is also actively involved in the mountain project initiative (http://www.dolcelab.org/mountain). As a part of this project his research examines the role of indigenous knowledge systems in environmental issue based decision-making processes in village communities of the Himalayas.

Roland Hübscher is an Associate Professor in Information Design at Bentley University. He received a Ph.D. in Computer Science from the University of Colorado at Boulder. His research in Educational Technology started with a postdoctoral position at the EduTech Institute at the Georgia Institute of Technology. He has been on the Computer Science faculty at Auburn University before joining Bentley University. His research centers on the design of intelligent user interfaces for learning environments. Specifically, he focuses on issues, such as adaptive support, knowledge representation, visualization, and data mining.

Einat Idan has a M.A. degree in Educational Technology from Concordia University and a B.A. in Education and Literature from the Hebrew University of Jerusalem. She is the lead Instructional Designer at the Centre for the Study of Learning and Performance at Concordia University. Her work over the last 5 years has presented such diverse challenges as early literacy curricula, self-regulated learning, electronic white board interaction, biodiversity, and ill-structured problems. She has presented findings in international conferences and cowritten articles and chapters in various publications.

Halszka Jarodzka holds a Master of Science in Psychology (2007) and a Ph.D. (2011) from Tuebingen University, Germany. Her Ph.D. thesis focused on characteristics and training of visual expertise in biological and medical domains, and during her Ph.D. research she worked at the eye-tracking laboratory at Lund University (Sweden), the medical department of Aarhus University (Denmark), and the Center for Learning Sciences and Technologies (the Netherlands). In July 2010 she joined the Open University of the Netherlands as an Assistant Professor, where she pursues her investigations of visual expertise and her research interest in methodological aspects of eye-tracking.

Lai Jiang is a Researcher and Coordinator in the Institute of Tropical Medicine, Antwerp, Belgium. She received her Ph.D. at the Katholieke Universiteit Leuven, Belgium. Her research deals with the effects of support in learning environments. A particular point of interest relates to learners' use of scaffolds/tools in computer-based environments. She has expertise in the analysis of data to look deeply into students' cognitive operations of different tools/scaffolds. Her research is devoted to gaining an in-depth understanding of the comprehensive interactions between learner-related variables and characteristics of learning environments.

Ton de Jong is Professor of Educational Psychology at the University of Twente, the Netherlands. He specializes in inquiry learning (mainly in science learning) supported by technology. He was project manager of several EC projects and several national projects, including the ZAP project, in which interactive simulations for psychology were developed. ZAPs are sold worldwide. For ZAP and SimQuest he has won a number of international prizes. He published over 100 journal articles and book chapters and is on the editorial board of 7 ISI journals. In 2006 he published a paper in *Science* on inquiry learning with computer simulations.

Rebecca Jordan is an Associate Professor of Citizen Science and Environmental Education in the Department of Ecology, Evolution, and Natural Resources, as well as the Director of the Program in Science Learning, in the School of Environmental and Biological Sciences at Rutgers University. She is interested in researching the role of behavior in socio-ecological systems. Her research program includes studying learning in animal (including human) systems and with this she has devoted considerable effort to investigating public understanding of science.

David A. Joyner is a doctoral student at the Georgia Institute of Technology. He works in the Design and Intelligence Laboratory in the School of Interactive Computing investigating ways in which to teach and facilitate model-based reasoning and scientific inquiry in middle-school classrooms. His forthcoming Ph.D. proposal will propose an environment and software tutor for interactively teaching students these skills.

Norma A. Juarez Collazo is a Ph.D. student at the K.U.Leuven at the Center of Instructional Psychology and Technology. Her main research interests focus on exploring the functionality of tools in computer-based learning environments and the types of cognitive, metacognitive and motivational variables that may influence quantity and quality of tool use.

Judy Kay is Professor of Computer Science at the University of Sydney, leading the CHAI (Computer Human Adapted Interaction) research group, which aims to create advanced technologies for human–computer interaction, personalization, and pervasive and mobile interaction. Her personalization research aims to empower people to harness and control the large amounts of data from their digital footprints, to support lifelong and life-wide learning. She is Immediate Past President of the International Artificial Intelligence in Education Society (IAIED).

John S. Kinnebrew is a Researcher at the Institute for Software Integrated Systems at Vanderbilt University and received his Ph.D. in Computer Science from Vanderbilt University. His research interests include educational data mining, coordination in multi-agent systems, and autonomous planning and scheduling. He is currently involved in four computer-based learning environment projects, where his research focuses on the use of machine learning and data mining techniques to assess learning behaviors, including metacognition and self-regulated learning strategies, from activity traces of student interaction in learning environments.

Anastasia Kitsantas is a Professor in the Educational Psychology Program in the College of Education and Human Development at George Mason University. Her research interests focus on the role of self-regulation on learning and performance across diverse areas of functioning, including academics, athletics, and health. She is the coauthor or author of 1 book and over 100 scholarly publications, many of which are directed toward the training of self-regulation.

K.R. Koedinger is Professor of Human–Computer Interaction and Psychology at Carnegie Mellon. His research has contributed new principles and techniques for the design of educational software and has produced basic cognitive science research results on the nature of mathematical thinking and learning. Dr. Koedinger is a cofounder of Carnegie Learning (http://www.carnegielearning.com) and the CMU Director of the Pittsburgh Science of Learning Center (http://www.learnlab.org). The center leverages cognitive and computational approaches to support researchers in investigating the instructional conditions that cause robust student learning.

Hermann Koerndle is Professor of Psychology of Learning and Instruction at Dresden University of Technology, Germany. He has an extensive background in both cognitive psychology and man–machine interaction. Hermann Koerndle received his Ph.D. at Oldenburg University, worked at Regensburg University in the field of applied psychology, then at the Technical University of Aachen in the field of man–machine interaction. Since October 1993 he is at Dresden University where he is currently engaged in (a) research on the factors in and effects of technology-enhanced interactive learning tasks, and (b) research on open-ended authoring tools in various instructional contexts.

Bracha Kramarski is an Associate Professor and the head of the Mathematical Training department in Bar-Ilan University. Her research deals with metacognition and SRL in mathematics education and teachers' professional education with advanced technology environments. She developed in her Ph.D. an innovative method called IMPROVE for learning mathematics, based on metacognitive and SRL principles, cooperative learning, and feedback-corrective theories. Her research is published in prestigious journals. Recently she was invited by the OECD to write a paper on the impact of mathematics education on twenty-first century skills based on the IMPROVE research. Prof. Kramarski was the principal investigator and research director for PISA 2000, 2006 in Israel.

Susanne P. Lajoie received her Doctorate from Stanford University in 1986. She is a Canadian Research Chair in Advanced Technologies for Learning in Authentic Settings (ATLAS) and directs the ATLAS group at McGill University. She is a Fellow of the American Psychological Association as well as an Inaugural Fellow of the American Educational Research Association. Dr. Lajoie uses a cognitive approach to identify learning trajectories that help novice learners become more skilled in the areas of science, statistics, and medicine. She has designed effective computer-based learning environments in these domains based on her research findings.

Arun Lakhana is a Systems Engineer who works in the field of Information Development. He also studies Educational Technology at Concordia University. Lakhana is interested in human factors and cybernetics, and he is exploring the psychometric construct of Ambiguity Tolerance.

Ronald Landis, Ph.D., is the Nambury S. Raju Professor of Psychology in the College of Psychology at Illinois Institute of Technology. Dr. Landis has primary research interests in the areas of structural equation modeling, multiple regression, and other issues associated with measurement and the prediction of performance. He currently serves as Associate Editor for the *Journal of Business and Psychology* and is on the editorial boards of *Personnel Psychology, Organizational Research Methods, Journal of Management, Human Performance,* and *Journal of Applied Psychology.*

James C. Lester is Professor of Computer Science at North Carolina State University. His research in intelligent tutoring systems, computational linguistics, and intelligent user interfaces focuses on intelligent game-based learning environments, affective computing, and tutorial dialogue. He received his B.A., M.S., and Ph.D. degrees in Computer Science from the University of Texas at Austin, and his B.A. degree in History from Baylor University. He has served as Program Chair for the ACM International Conference on Intelligent User Interfaces and the International Conference on Intelligent Tutoring Systems. He is Editor-in-Chief of the *International Journal of Artificial Intelligence in Education.*

Detlev Leutner, Ph.D., Dipl.-Psych., completed his Ph.D. thesis on mathematical achievement structures in 1985 and his Habilitation on adaptive instructional systems in 1992, both at RWTH Aachen University of Technology. He served as Professor for Psychological Methods at Gießen University and as Professor for Instructional Psychology at Erfurt University. Since 2002 he is Professor for Instructional Psychology at Duisburg-Essen University. His research interests include basic and applied research on learning and instruction (e.g., self-regulated learning, learning strategies, learning styles, problem-solving competencies, science teaching, early mathematics, learning with multimedia, computer-based training, driver licensing, stress prevention).

Marcia C. Linn is a Professor at the Graduate School of Education, University of California, Berkeley. She is a member of the National Academy of Education, and a Fellow of American Association for the Advancement of Science (AAAS), American Psychological Association, and Association for Psychological Science. She was elected President of the International Society of the Learning Sciences, Chair of the AAAS Education Section, and member of the AAAS Board. She received the National Association for Research in Science Teaching Award for Lifelong Distinguished Contributions to Science Education and the Council of Scientific Society Presidents first award for Excellence in Educational Research.

Diane Litman is Professor of Computer Science, Senior Scientist with the Learning Research and Development Center, and faculty with the Graduate Program in Intelligent Systems, all at the University of Pittsburgh. She has been working in the field of artificial intelligence since she received her Ph.D. in Computer Science from the University of Rochester. Before joining the University of Pittsburgh, she was a member of the Artificial Intelligence Principles Research Department, AT&T Labs—Research (formerly Bell Laboratories). Dr. Litman's research focuses on enhancing educational technology through the use of spoken language processing, affective computing, and machine learning and other statistical methods.

Rose Luckin has a Bachelor's degree in Computer Science and Artificial Intelligence and a Ph.D. in Cognitive Science, both from University of Sussex. She is Professor of Learner Centered Design at the London Knowledge Lab. Her research explores how to scaffold learning across multiple technologies, locations, subjects, and times. Luckin has taught in a range of sectors, including schools, and Further and Higher Education. In her book "Re-designing Learning Contexts," (Routledge, 2010), Luckin explores the meaning of *Context*, it's relationship to learning, and the manner in which we can develop technology rich contextualized learning activities that meet each learners needs.

Valentina Lupi earned her degree in Languages at the University of Genoa (Italy) in 1995, then (1996–2000) studied Linguistic and Theatre Translation at the Sophia-Antipolis University in Nice (France), and later earned a Ph.D. in "Languages, Cultures, and ICT" at the University of Genoa (2006–2008). She is currently a French teacher in a junior high school. She has been teaching in the teacher training school of the University of Genoa and collaborates with researchers of the University of Genoa and of the Institute for Educational Technology of CNR. Her current research focuses on the mediation of ICT to learn foreign languages, applying task-based activities to trigger creativity.

Griet Lust is a Ph.D. student at the K.U.Leuven at the Center of Instructional Psychology and Technology at the K.U.Leuven (Belgium). Her main research interest is on the use of tools in blended learning environment with a high interest towards ecological settings and the influence of students' self-regulation skills with respect to tool use.

Samuel Mamane is a Montreal native currently studying Medicine at McGill University. He grew up in Montreal and after completing his Bachelor of Science in Physiology in 2008, he chose to pursue a career in Medicine. He joined the ATLAS research team in January 2010 and has played a role in case development for BioWorld, and as a medical liaison for data interpretation. As he completes his medical degree, he is seeking a career in Internal Medicine. He is particularly interested in the field of Medical Education and hopes to contribute to further research in this field.

Jessica Marschner, Ph.D., Dipl.-Psych., completed her Ph.D. thesis on "Supporting scientific discovery learning by adaptive feedback" in 2011 at Duisburg-Essen University. Since 2010 she is a research assistant for Research on Learning and Instruction at Ruhr-University Bochum. Her research interests include applied research on learning and instruction (e.g., self-regulated learning, support of learning processes, training of self-regulation competencies).

Moffat Mathews is a Ph.D. candidate at Computer Science and Software Engineering department at the University of Canterbury. He is also the manager of the Intelligent Computer Tutoring Group and project development leader on a number of diverse projects focused on building Intelligent Systems for learning and rehabilitation. His primary research focus is on providing adaptive pedagogical strategies during runtime in Intelligent Tutoring Systems. His current emphasis is on using these techniques to try to cognitively rehabilitate stroke patients when using an Intelligent System. He is also working on mobile technologies to create second generation Audience Response Systems.

Christoph Mengelkamp is a Lecturer for Instructional Media at the University of Wuerzburg (Germany), Department of Human-Computer-Media. He graduated in Psychology at the University of Koblenz-Landau, and then worked as a researcher at the Center for Educational Research in different national and international projects developing diagnostic instruments and evaluating learning environments. Afterwards he worked at the Department of General and Educational Psychology, University of Koblenz-Landau, mainly in the field of text-picture comprehension. He received his Ph.D. for studies about metacognitive judgments and learning. Beyond metacognition he is interested in learning with interactive animations and pedagogical assessment.

Elizabeth Meyer is an Assistant Professor in the School of Education at California Polytechnic State University in San Luis Obispo, CA. She is the author of Gender, Bullying, and Harassment: Strategies to End Sexism and Homophobia in Schools (Teachers College Press, 2009) and Gender and Sexual Diversity in Schools (Springer, 2010). Her research has been published in journals, such as *Gender and Education, The Clearinghouse,* and *Computers and Education.* She completed her M.A. at the University of Colorado, Boulder and her Ph.D. at McGill University. She blogs regularly for *Psychology Today,* and you can follow her on twitter: @lizjmeyer.

Tova Michalsky is a Senior Lecturer in Bar-Ilan University. She was the head of the Preservice Biology Teachers in Practice Training Program at Bar-Ilan University. Her research deals with SRL on science education and teachers' professional education with advanced technology environments. She developed the innovative MINT method, a digital higher-order thinking skills learning environment for teaching science inquiry under SRL guidance. Dr. Michalsky is an expert in designing courses for enhancing higher-order thinking skills for preservice teachers. She also designed for the Israeli Ministry of Education challenging tasks based on PISA's conceptual framework. Her work has been published in prestigious journals.

Antonija Mitrovic is Professor and Head of Department of Computer Science and Software Engineering at the University of Canterbury,

New Zealand. Her research focuses on student modeling in constraint-based Intelligent Tutoring Systems. She is the leader of the Intelligent Computer Tutoring Group (ICTG) which has developed many constraint-based ITSs over the last 15 years, as well as the ASPIRE authoring system. Prof. Mitrovic was the local chair of the AIED 2011 conference. Prof. Mitrovic is the associate editor of the RPTEL and COMSIS journals, as well as the member of editorial boards of the UMUAI, AIED, TICL, and JUCS journals. She received the Distinguished Research Award from APSCE in 2011 and the AAEE Engineering Education Excellence Award in 2007.

Inge Molenaar is a Researcher at the Research Institute of Child Development and Education of the University of Amsterdam. Dr. Molenaar has published on computerized scaffolding of self- and social-regulated learning in refereed journal articles and several edited books. Her current work focuses on finding new ways to measure metacognitive activities during learning with process and analysis of multiple data streams. Moreover, she has a strong interest in the effect of computerized agents on human–human interaction to identify how young students learn self-regulatory skills both from intelligent agents and each other.

Daniel C. Moos is an Assistant Professor in the Education Department at Gustavus Adolphus College, St. Peter, Minnesota (USA). His research broadly considers the relationship between cognitive, metacognitive and motivational processes in learning. Most recently, he has focused on the role of metacognitive calibration and its effect on motivation in learning with emerging technology. His research also extends to teacher preparation and the relationship between self-regulated learning and instructional practices.

Bradford W. Mott is a Research Scientist in the Department of Computer Science at North Carolina State University. He received the B.S., M.C.S., and Ph.D. degrees in Computer Science from North Carolina State University. He oversees research and development on several advanced learning technology projects, including Crystal Island, an intelligent game-based learning environment that was first launched as part of his dissertation research. Prior to joining NC State, he led development efforts on Gamebryo, a cross-platform 3D game engine used extensively in the digital entertainment and training industries, for the Nintendo Wii at Emergent Game Technologies.

Laura Naismith is a doctoral student in the Department of Educational and Counseling Psychology at McGill University in Montreal, Canada and a member of the ATLAS laboratory. Her dissertation examines the influence of emotion on medical students' attention to feedback in a computer-based learning environment. Previously, she worked with subject specialists in the Centre for Learning, Innovation and Collaboration (CLIC) at the University of Birmingham in the UK to develop a needs-driven research program in Educational Technology with funding from Microsoft UK Ltd. Naismith trained as a systems design engineer at the University of Waterloo in Canada.

Susanne Narciss is a Professor at the Department of Psychology of Learning and Instruction at Dresden University of Technology. She received her Ph.D.

from Heidelberg University in 1993, and then moved to Dresden University. Her current interests include (a) motivation and meta-cognition in self-regulated learning, (b) technology-enhanced learning and instruction, and (c) research on the factors in and effects of informative tutoring feedback (ITF). Her work on ITF was considered cutting-edge research by the American Association on Educational Communication and Technology (AECT). Her AECT-handbook-chapter *Feedback strategies for interactive learning tasks* received the AECT-Distinguished Development Award 2007.

Timothy J. Nokes-Malach is an Assistant Professor of Psychology and a Research Scientist at the Learning Research and Development Center at the University of Pittsburgh. He received his Ph.D. from the University of Illinois at Chicago and postdoctoral training at the Beckman Institute at the University of Illinois at Urbana-Champaign. His research focuses on human learning, problem solving, knowledge transfer, and most recently on the effects of motivation and social interaction on those processes. His work has been supported with grants from the Pittsburgh Science of Learning Center, the National Science Foundation, and the Department of Education's Institute of Education Sciences.

Maria Opfermann is an Assistant Professor at the Department of Instructional Psychology at the University of Duisburg-Essen, Germany. She has a background in Educational Psychology with a focus on Instructional Psychology and received her Ph.D. in 2008 with her thesis focusing on the role of instructional design and individual learner characteristics in multimedia and hypermedia learning. In line with this, her main research interests focus on learning with multimedia and the role of cognitive load and its measurement. In addition, current studies focus on different ways of instructional support to foster self-regulated learning with multimedia.

Marily Oppezzo received her doctoral training in the School of Education of Stanford University. She also earned a Master's degree in Nutritional Science and is a Registered Dietitian. Her Ph.D. thesis demonstrated that simply taking a walk outdoors doubles highly structured creativity compared to several control conditions, including being pushed in a wheel chair outdoors or walking on a treadmill. Her recent studies investigate the most effective strategies for empowering people to motivate themselves to maintain difficult behavior changes that include academic and health-related goals.

Annemarie Sullivan Palincsar is the Jean and Charles Walgreen Jr. Chair of Reading and Literacy, Associate Dean for academic affairs and a Teacher Educator at the University of Michigan. Her research focuses on the design of learning environments that support self-regulation in learning activity, especially for children who experience difficulty learning in school. Palincsar has served as a member of: the National Academy's Research Council on the Prevention of Reading Difficulty in Young Children; the OERI/RAND Reading Study Group, and the National Research Council's Panel on Teacher Preparation. She recently coedited the journal, *Cognition and Instruction*. She completed her doctorate at the University of Illinois, Champaign-Urbana.

Stephanie Pieschl is a postdoctoral research fellow in the Department of Psychology at the "Westfälische Wilhelms-Universität" in Münster, Germany. Pieschl also earned her Diploma as well as a Doctorate of Philosophy at Münster University. As an Educational Psychologist her main research interests concern self-regulated learning, metacognitions, and epistemological beliefs regarding learning with computer-based learning environments. Pieschl has also served as co-coordinator of the Special Interest Group "Metacognition" of the European Association for Research on Learning and Instruction for 4 years. In recent years she has also been interested in issues of media literacy or lack thereof.

Eric Poitras is currently completing the requirements of a doctoral degree in Educational Psychology with specialization in the Learning Sciences at McGill University. He obtained his B.A. at the University of Moncton, NB, and his M.A. at McGill University under the supervision of Dr. Susanne Lajoie and is a member of the ATLAS laboratory. His research aims to evaluate the design of a metacognitive tool called the MetaHistoReasoning tool in terms of enhancing learning through historical inquiry.

Antje Proske is a research assistant at the department of Psychology of Learning and Instruction at Dresden University of Technology. She received her Ph.D. in Psychology (2006) on the development and evaluation of interactive training tasks in academic writing. She was actively involved in several joint projects of the German funding program "New Media in Education" dealing with the question of how to support efficient Web-based learning in various instructional contexts (http://www.studierplatz2000.tu-dresden.de). Her current research interests include the development and experimental investigation of computer-based scaffolding for academic writing and self-regulated learning, as well as the construction of interactive learning tasks.

Sadhana Puntambekar is a Professor in the Learning Sciences program in the Educational Psychology department at University of Wisconsin-Madison. Her expertise is in scaffolding student learning in classroom context, especially examining the distributed nature of scaffolding in which several agents, resources and technologies work in a coordinated way to help students learn. In recent years, her research has focused on the CoMPASS project that integrates digital text with design-based science learning, in which she is examining metacognitive strategies in learning from non-linear scientific text, integration of text in design-based science classrooms, and scaffolding of student learning.

John Ranellucci received a B.A. in psychology from Concordia University, a M.Ed. in Educational Psychology at McGill, and is currently a doctorate candidate at McGill and is a member of the ATLAS laboratory. His research interests focus on motivation, emotion, and self-regulated learning.

Katherine A. Rawson is an Associate Professor of Psychology at Kent State University (Ph.D. from University of Colorado, Boulder). Her research program includes empirical and theoretical work on cognitive skill acquisition, text comprehension, metacomprehension, and study strategies that promote durable and efficient student learning. She is a 2010 recipient of the US

Presidential Early Career Award for Scientists and Engineers and a Kavli Frontiers Fellow (National Academy of Sciences). She currently serves as an Associate Editor for *Memory & Cognition* and for *Memory*.

Alexander Renkl studied Psychology in Aachen and Marburg (Germany) and finished his diploma degree in 1987. From 1988 to 1990 he worked as a graduate student at the Max-Planck Institute of Psychological Research, Munich (Germany), and received his doctoral degree from the University of Heidelberg in 1991. As Assistant Professor, he spent several years (1991–1997) at the University of Munich before he became a Full Professor of Educational Psychology at the University of Education in Schwäbisch Gmünd (Germany). Presently, he is working at the University of Freiburg as Professor of Educational and Developmental Psychology. His main research areas are cognitive learning processes, learning from examples, learning and communicating with new media, and learning by journal writing.

Falko Rheinberg was born 1945. He received his Master's degree in psychology in 1972, followed by a doctoral degree in Philosophy in 1977. He completed his Habilitation at the University of Bochum, Germany in 1983, where he held the position of Assistant Professor between 1972 and 1983. During this time, he conducted research on how teachers' achievement evaluation has an effect on students' motivation to learn (Reference Norm Orientation). From 1983 to 1994, he was a Professor of Educational Psychology at the University of Heidelberg, Germany. His research focused on motivational training in schools and organizations. Between 1994 and 2007, he held the position of Professor of Psychology at the University of Potsdam, Germany, where he was Chair of Psychology of Motivation, Emotion, and Action. He investigated motivational effects on learning activities, incentives of purpose and action, risk motivation, and flow experience. He retired in 2007.

Ido Roll is a Science Teaching and Learning Fellow at the Carl Wieman Science Education Initiative at the University of British Columbia and a researcher in the Pittsburgh Science of Learning Center. His research focuses on helping students become more capable, curious, and innovative learners. Roll is particularly interested in understanding, promoting, and assessing self-regulation and inquiry learning skills in the context of authentic environments, often using educational technologies. He has published numerous papers in the fields of Education and the Learning Sciences, Cognitive Science, Artificial Intelligence, and Human–Computer Interaction. His work has received several best-paper awards in peer-reviewed conferences.

Jonathan P. Rowe is a doctoral candidate in the department of Computer Science at North Carolina State University. His research focuses on intelligent tutoring systems, user modeling, and interactive narrative in game-based learning environments. He received the M.S. degree in Computer Science from North Carolina State University and the B.S. degree in Computer Science from Lafayette College. He served as a co-organizer for the Fourth Workshop on Intelligent Narrative Technologies. His research has been recognized with Best Paper Awards at the Seventh International Artificial Intelligence and

Interactive Digital Entertainment Conference and the Second International Conference on Intelligent Technologies for Interactive Entertainment.

Spencer Rugaber is a Senior Research Scientist in the College of Computing at the Georgia Institute of Technology. His research interests are in the area of Software Engineering, specifically software modeling and design. Dr. Rugaber received his Ph.D. in Computer Science from Yale University in 1978. He is currently Principal Investigator in several research projects in this area funded by the National Science Foundation, the Institute of Educational Sciences and private industry. He is the author of the article on Program Understanding included in the *Encyclopedia of Computer Science and Technology* and of numerous articles appearing in technical journals and conference proceedings.

Carlos R. Salas is a third year doctoral student in the Cognitive Psychology program at the University of Illinois at Chicago. His general research interests are in metacognition, epistemological beliefs, and science text comprehension. His recent work has used eye-tracking analyses to examine differences in reading strategies and how they impact comprehension of expository science texts. He has also explored how individual differences in epistemological beliefs influence comprehension and argumentation in science, including how learners selectively attend to and utilize evidence-based arguments versus emotional appeals.

Katharina Scheiter is a Full Professor at the Knowledge Media Research Center in Tuebingen, Germany, where she heads the Multimedia Research Lab. She has a background in Applied Cognitive Psychology and Educational Psychology. Her main research interests focus on cognitive processes underlying learning with multimedia and hypermedia, the use of eye tracking in educational research, as well as learning with visualizations. Since 2009, she coordinates the Special Interest Group 2: Comprehension of Text and Graphics of the European Association of Research in Learning and Instruction (EARLI).

Annett Schmeck (nee Schwamborn) is a postdoctoral research scientist at the Department of Instructional Psychology at the University of Duisburg-Essen, Germany. In 2007, Dr. Schmeck received a Diploma of Psychology at the Ruhr-University Bochum. She received her Ph.D. in Educational Psychology in 2010 at the University of Duisburg-Essen, under the advisement of Prof. Dr. Detlev Leutner. Her dissertation focused on the use of provided and learner-generated visualizations as comprehension aids in learning from science texts. Her current work continues this line of research by focusing on the cognitive psychological principles of learning and instruction, and on their application in evaluation and training programs.

Daniel L. Schwartz is a Professor of Education at Stanford University and received his Ph.D. at Teachers College Columbia University. He studies how people's facility for spatial thinking can inform and influence processes of learning, instruction, and assessment. Detailed examples of the work from his lab may be found at: http://www.aaalab.stanford.edu/

Neil H. Schwartz graduated from Arizona State University in Learning, Cognition, and Instruction in 1981. He studies graphics as they influence learning, comprehension, perspective, and persuasion, as well as metacognition—how learners monitor their learning with graphics and text. Dr. Schwartz currently serves as U.S. Coordinator of the International Cognitive Visualization Program—a dual Master's program in Cognitive Visualization—in France, Germany, and the US. He has served as Senior Research Fellow at NASA's Classroom of the Future and Visiting Professor at the University of New England in Australia and the University of Koblenz-Landau in Germany.

Rolf Schwonke studied Psychology in Konstanz (Germany) and Freiburg (Germany) and finished his diploma degree in 2002. From 2002 to 2005 he worked as a graduate student at University of Freiburg, Department of Psychology, and received his doctoral degree from the University of Freiburg in 2005. Since 2005 until present he works as an Assistant Professor at the University of Freiburg. His main research areas are cognitive learning processes, learning from multiple external representations, and learning with new media. His work has been published in a variety of international journals (e.g., *Topics in Cognitive Science, Applied Cognitive Psychology*, and *Computers in Human Behaviour*).

Brianna M. Scott graduated in 2008 with a doctorate in Learning Sciences from Indiana University. Her main research interests center around metacognition, working memory, and academic achievement. Dr. Scott is currently an Assistant Professor of Psychology at the University of Indianapolis, teaching courses on cognitive theory and research methods at the undergraduate and graduate levels. Previously, Dr. Scott worked as an Associate Researcher for the National Collegiate Athletic Association, as well as a Senior Researcher for Rockman et al., an independent evaluation firm.

Kamran Shaikh is a doctoral student in Educational Technology. While completing his studies at Concordia University, he has been involved in pre-service teacher training, priming and arming his students with an arsenal of pedagogical tools and approaches which they may employ in elementary science classrooms. He has a vested interest in technology integration, primarily models of user interaction and the design of technologically enriched learning environments. His research interests include the history and philosophy of science, approaches for elementary and secondary science education, conceptualizations and examinations of technologies and of learning through technology and models of interaction in feedback.

Lucy R. Shores is a Ph.D. student in Educational Psychology at North Carolina State University. Her research focuses on self-regulated learning, human abilities, and cognitive processes, and, specifically, their role in intelligent game-based learning environments. She received the M.S. degree in Computer Science from North Carolina State University in 2010 and the B.A. degree in Computer Science/Psychology from Rhodes College in Memphis, TN in 2008. Lucy is a National Science Foundation Graduate Research Fellow and has authored several peer-reviewed papers, including one nominated for Best Paper Award at the Tenth International Conference on Intelligent Tutoring Systems.

Suparna Sinha is a doctoral student at the Department of Educational Psychology in the Graduate School of Education at Rutgers University. Her research interests have been to observe patterns of students' engagement in computer-supported collaborative learning environments. She aims to investigate influence of students' collaborative engagement on individual transfer of knowledge and skills.

Peter Sleegers is Professor of Educational Sciences at the University of Twente. Dr. Sleegers has published extensively on leadership, innovation and educational policy in refereed journal articles and several edited books. He is a member of the editorial board of *School Improvement and School Effectiveness, Leadership and Policy in Schools, Journal of Educational Administration, Educational Administration Quarterly* and the *Kluwer Series on Studies in Educational Leadership*. Current research projects are studies into the effects of educational leadership on student motivation for school, longitudinal research into sustainability of reforms and design studies into professional learning communities. The work of Dr. Sleegers has been rewarded several times for excellence.

Marcia Sprang, Ph.D., is a Board Certified, Advanced Placement teacher and has a Ph.D. in Chemistry. For 10 years she directed summer workshops for middle and high school teachers in the Placentia-Yorba Linda School District, Orange County, CA, where dozens of IMMEX problem solving simulations were created. She has made presentations at the Ministry of Education, Beijing, China and has directed multiple professional development workshops in urban school districts in Beijing and Shanghai. She has been an investigator on multiple NSF grants and coauthor of multiple publications.

Elmar Stahl is a Full Professor at the University of Education, Institute of Media in Education, in Freiburg, Germany. He received a diploma in Psychology in 1995, his Ph.D. in 2001 and his "Habilitation" in 2006. His current research interests include research on epistemological beliefs, self-regulated learning, and learning by design.

Karl Steffens is Psychologist and Senior Researcher at the University of Cologne/Germany. He obtained his Ph.D. from the University of Bonn and has been working at the universities of Bonn, Cologne, Frankfurt, Erfurt, and Barcelona (Spain). At the University of Barcelona, he conducted research in the field of ICT for a year with a grant from the European Commission (Human Capital and Mobility Programme). In his teaching, he focuses on learning and instruction, technology-enhanced learning, motivation, emotion and personality development. His research activities have centered on technology-enhanced learning and on intercultural communication, with a focus on self-regulated learning in technology enhanced learning environments.

Ron Stevens, Ph.D., is a Professor and a member of the Brain Research Institute at the UCLA School of Medicine. He directs the Internet-based IMMEX problem-solving project which has engaged over 150,000 students and teachers in computational education and professional development activities that span elementary school through medical school. Recently Dr. Stevens received the "Foundations of Augmented Cognition" award from the Augmented Cognition Society. His interests include using machine learning tools and electroencephalography (EEG) to model the neurodynamics of military and business teams.

Christopher A. Stewart is a 11th and 12th grade World History teacher at North Lakes Academy High School in Forest Lake, MN (USA). His research interests include self-regulation in Social Studies classrooms, with an emphasis on how motivation in learning World History is affected by emerging technologies, such as hypermedia.

Amber Chauncey Strain is a Ph.D. student in the Department of Psychology and the Institute for Intelligent Systems at the University of Memphis. She has a B.S. in Psychology from Middle Tennessee State University, and an M.S. in Cognitive Psychology from the University of Memphis. Her research interests include the broad areas of cognitive and educational psychology, cognitive science, emotions, and emotion regulation during learning. Specifically, her interests include self-regulated learning, the causal influence of emotions on self-regulation, and the role of emotion regulation strategies on affective, metacognitive, and cognitive processes during complex learning.

Brian Sulcer is a Staff Engineer in the Institute for Software Integrated Systems (ISIS) at Vanderbilt University. He has built interesting things with software for more than 15 years across many different platforms. His recent work has been on Web-based learning environments and data visualization tools to support their use.

Sarah A. Sullivan is a Ph.D. candidate in the Learning Sciences area of the Educational Psychology department at the University of Wisconsin-Madison. Her research focuses on understanding the strategies that adolescents use to comprehend and learn from information presented in multiple text-based resources. In particular, her work involves examining the metacognitive strategies and self-regulated behaviors exhibited by adolescents learning from multiple digital texts presented in hypermedia environments within the context of scientific inquiry. With her research, her goal is to inform our understanding of the new skills required by the changing definitions of literacy and comprehension in the digital age.

Roger S. Taylor is an Assistant Professor in the Psychology Department at the State University of New York, Oswego campus. His research is focused on science education, educational technology, and the relationships between students' learning and their emotional (or affective) states. This line of research includes the goals of refining psychological theory and developing educational applications, such as emotionally adaptive learning environments.

Hubertina Thillmann, Ph.D., Dipl.-Psych., completed her Ph.D. thesis on "Self-regulated learning by experimenting—from assessment to support" in 2008 at Duisburg-Essen University. She served as research assistant for Instructional Psychology at Duisburg-Essen University from 2007 to 2009.

Since 2009 she is research assistant for Research on Learning and Instruction at Ruhr-University Bochum. Her research interests include theoretical and methodical questions in research on learning and instruction (e.g., self-regulated learning and metacognition, motivation and self-regulation of motivation, strategy knowledge and strategy use, computer-based learning).

Gregory Trevors is a doctoral student in Educational Psychology, Learning Sciences stream at McGill University, Montréal, Canada. He is a member of the Laboratory for the Study of Metacognition and Advanced Learning Technologies at McGill University. His studies have focused on students' science conceptions and epistemic beliefs. Trevors is interested in using trace methodologies to study the cognitive, metacognitive, and motivational processes involved in changing these conceptions and beliefs.

Banu Binbaşaran Tüysüzoğlu is an Independent Writer and Game Developer who graduated from the University of North Carolina with a Master of Arts degree in Educational Psychology, Measurement, and Evaluation. Her thesis was an investigation of the role of metacognitive behavior in self-regulated learning. Specifically, she investigated the relationship between monitoring (e.g., judgments of learning) and control (e.g., strategy change). Besides cognition and learning, she is interested in the cognitive neuroscience of learning.

Kathryn Urbaniak is an M.A. Educational Technology student and research assistant at Concordia University with a passion for media. She graduated with a B.A. (Hons) in Business Studies in 1998 and P.G. Dip. in Information Technology in 2000. Kathryn has worked in new media project management and software development in her native Scotland. Her teaching experience includes teaching in 4 different countries and facilitating online learning with participants from more than 40 countries over the past 7 years.

Carla van Boxtel is Professor of Historical Culture and Education at Erasmus University Rotterdam and senior researcher at the Research Institute Child Development and Education of the University of Amsterdam. She leads the Dutch Center for Social Studies Education. Dr. van Boxtel has published extensively on the learning and teaching of history and the effects of collaborative learning tasks and visual representations on the quality of student interaction and learning outcomes. She coauthored with Dr. Jannet van Drie an article about historical reasoning that was awarded the EARLI Outstanding Publication Award in 2009.

Tamara van Gog is Associate Professor of Educational Psychology at the Institute of Psychology of the Erasmus University Rotterdam, The Netherlands. She holds a Master's degree in Developmental and Educational Psychology from Tilburg University (2001) and a Ph.D. in Educational Technology from the Open University of the Netherlands (2006). Her research focuses mainly on instructional design for example-based learning and learning from dynamic visualizations (e.g., video and animations), on self-assessment and self-regulated learning, and on uncovering cognitive processes using verbal reports and eye tracking. Tamara is a member of The Young Academy of the Royal Netherlands Academy of Arts and Sciences.

Wouter van Joolingen is Professor of Dynamical Modeling in Educational Settings at the Department of Instructional Technology of the University of Twente. He specializes in the use of models in early science education. His work includes the use of creative techniques, such as drawing to create computational models, as well as the use of computer simulation in classroom settings. The work focuses on understanding learners' behavior in such open learning environments as well as the design of adaptive support for such complex but fruitful learning tasks.

Swaroop S. Vattam is a Ph.D. candidate in Computer Science at the Georgia Institute of Technology. He works in the Design & Intelligence Laboratory in the School of Interactive Computing, where he is investigating analogical reasoning and creativity in the context of biologically inspired design. His forthcoming Ph.D. thesis investigates mediated analogy (i.e., analogical problem solving mediated by external information environments). The insights from his investigations are applied to explain some of the serious challenges associated with the task of seeking bio-inspiration and to design knowledge-based systems that support this task.

Marcel V.J. Veenman studied Cognitive Psychology at the University of Amsterdam. In 1993, he obtained a Ph.D. in Amsterdam with a thesis on the relation between metacognitive and intellectual abilities. Since then he is affiliated with Leiden University in the Netherlands, where he teaches developmental and educational psychology. Main research interests concern conceptions of metacognition, validity issues in metacognitive assessment, developmental processes in metacognition, and the relation between metacognition and giftedness. He authored over a hundred articles, chapters, and books on metacognition. From 2006 to 2011, was the founding editor of *Metacognition and Learning*, an international journal published by Springer.

Vivek Venkatesh is Director of Graduate Programs in Educational Technology and Assistant Professor at the Department of Education at Concordia University in Montréal, Canada. Venkatesh specializes in the design and development of instruction in online learning environments as well as methodologies for evaluation of learning across both scholastic and training contexts. His research projects in the last decade, which have been funded by the governments of both Québec and Canada, span the fields of technology integration, information retrieval, educational psychology, and cognitive science.

Regina Vollmeyer was born in 1962. She earned a Master's degree in psychology from the University of Heidelberg, Germany, in 1989, and a Ph.D. from the University of Mainz, Germany, in 1992. From 1992 to 1994, she was a postdoctoral researcher at the University of California, Los Angeles. In 2002, she completed her Habilitation at the University of Potsdam, Germany. Between 1995 and 2004, she was an Assistant Professor at the University of Potsdam, Germany. In 2004, she was appointed Professor of Educational Psychology at the University of Frankfurt, Germany. Her research areas are motivational effects on learning, problem solving, and self-regulated learning.

Anne Wade (M.L.I.S.) has served as Manager and Information Specialist at the Center for the Study of learning and Performance for many years and coordinated the ePEARL research and development. Her expertise is in information literacy, self regulated learning, and educational technology.

Jennifer Wiley earned her Ph.D. in Cognitive Psychology from the University of Pittsburgh. She is currently an Associate Professor of Psychology with a courtesy appointment in Computer Science at the University of Illinois at Chicago. She has two main lines of research. One main area is in supporting subject matter learning from reading and writing activities. In this work she has focused on contexts that benefit metacomprehension accuracy, as well as the understanding of text and diagrams. Her other main line of research explores individual differences and their role in analytic and creative problem solving.

Philip H. Winne (Ph.D., Stanford University) is Professor and Canada Research Chair in Self-Regulated Learning and Educational Technologies at Simon Fraser University. He has published more than 140 scholarly articles and chapters on how learners transform information into knowledge and regulate learning processes; and software for gathering and analyzing data about learning. A Fellow of the American Educational Research Association, American Psychological Association, Association for Psychological Science and Canadian Psychological Association, he was awarded the Robbie Case Memorial Award for outstanding contributions to Educational Psychology in Canada. He served as President of the Canadian Educational Researchers Association, Canadian Association for Educational Psychology, and Division 15—Educational Psychology of the American Psychological Association.

Joachim Wirth, Ph.D., Dipl.-Psych., completed his Ph.D. on self-regulation of learning processes at Humboldt-University Berlin in 2003. He worked as research assistant for Instructional Psychology at Duisburg-Essen University from 2002 to 2008. Since 2008 he is Full Professor for Research on Learning and Instruction at Ruhr-University Bochum. His research interests cover among others self-regulated learning and problem solving, teaching and learning with multimedia, teacher knowledge and competences, as well as computer-based learning environments and computer-based assessment.

Jeffrey Wiseman is a Core Member of the McGill Centre for Medical Education, an Associate of the McGill Faculty of Education ATLAS laboratory and an Associate Professor at the McGill Faculty of Medicine. He is Director of McGill's Internal Medicine Clerkship as well as of a Clinical Teaching Ward. His research interests include the role of emotions in clinical reasoning, inter-professional education, simulations, technology-rich learning environments and how implicit power relations impact on medical practice-based learning.

Nicola Yuill has a Bachelor's degree in Social Psychology with Cognitive Studies and a Ph.D. in Developmental Psychology, from the University of Sussex. She is senior lecturer in developmental psychology and manager of the Children and Technology Lab (http://www.sussex.ac.uk/psychology/chatlab).

She is interested in how technology can be used to understand and support children working and playing together, at school and at home, in typical and atypical development, with peers, with parents, and with teachers. An underlying theme of this work is the role of social interaction and collaboration in learning and development, and how technology supports mechanisms of collaboration.

Amna Zuberi is a Ph.D. student in Education at Concordia University. Her research interests focus on the interplay between Educational Technology and Educational Studies—centered on how learners conceptualize their use of technologies and the pedagogical mechanisms in technology education which prepare them to create and navigate critically. She has also been involved in numerous projects investigating self-regulated learning and metacognition to uncover factors involved in encouraging student learning in online environments.

Contents

Contributors

Philip C. Abrami Centre for the Study of Learning and Performance, Concordia University, Montreal, QC, Canada

Vincent Aleven Human-Computer Interaction Institute, Carnegie Mellon University, Pittsburgh, PA, USA

Pittsburgh Science of Learning Center, Pittsburgh, PA, USA

Katerina Avramides The London Knowledge Lab, Institute of Education, London, UK

Roger Azevedo, Ph.D. Laboratory for the Study of Metacognition and Advanced Learning Technologies, Department of Educational and Counselling Psychology, McGill University, Montreal, QC, Canada

Maria Bannert University of Wuerzburg, Educational Media, Wuerzburg, Germany

Carole R. Beal School of Information Science, University of Arizona, Tucson, AZ, USA

Matthew L. Bernacki Learning Research and Development Center, University of Pittsburgh, Pittsburgh, PA, USA

Kirsten Berthold Department of Psychology, University of Freiburg, Freiburg, Germany

Gautam Biswas Department of EECS and ISIS, Vanderbilt University, Nashville, TN, USA

François Bouchet Laboratory for the Study of Metacognition and Advanced Learning Technologies, Department of Educational and Counselling Psychology, McGill University, Montreal, QC, Canada

Rainer Bromme Westfälische Wilhelms-Universität Münster, Muenster, Germany

Susan Bull Electronic, Electrical and Computer Engineering, University of Birmingham, Birmingham, UK

Eva M. Bures Center for the Study of Learning and Performance, Bishop's University School of Education, Lennoxville, QC, Canada

Winslow Burleson Arizona State University, Tempe, AZ, USA

Roberto Carneiro Institute for Distance Learning, Universidade Católica Portuguesa, Lisbon, Portugal

Amanda Carr (nee Harris) Department of Applied Social Sciences, Canterbury Christ Church University, Canterbury, UK

Jennifer King Chen Education in Mathematics, Science, and Technology, University of California, Berkeley, CA, USA

Jennifer L. Chiu Science, Technology, Engineering and Math (STEM) Education, Curry School of Education, University of Virginia, Charlottesville, VA, USA

Geraldine Clarebout Center for Medical Education, Faculty of Medicine, University of Leuven, Leuven, Belgium

Mihaela Cocea School of Computing, University of Portsmouth, Portsmouth, Hampshire, UK

Norma A. Juarez Collazo Center for Instructional Psychology and Technology, University of Leuven, Leuven, Belgium

Cristina Conati, M.Sc., Ph.D. Department of Computer Science, University of British Columbia, Vancouver, BC, Canada

A.T. Corbett Human–Computer Interaction Institute, Carnegie Mellon University, Pittsburgh, PA, USA

Pittsburgh Advanced Cognitive Tutor Center, Carnegie Mellon University, Pittsburgh, PA, USA

Lara-Jeane Costa Educational Psychology, Measurement, and Evaluation Program, University of North Carolina, Chapel Hill, NC, USA

Ilian Cruz-Panesso Advanced Technologies for Learning in Authentic Settings (ATLAS), Department of Educational and Counselling Psychology, McGill University, Montreal, Canada

Nada Dabbagh Instructional Design and Technology, George Mason University, Fairfax, VA, USA

Bridget Dalton University of Colorado Boulder, Boulder, CO, USA

Ryan S.J.d. Baker Columbia University Teachers College, New York, NY, USA

A.M.J.B. de Caravalho Human-Computer Interaction Institute, CMU Carnegie Mellon University, Pittsburgh, PA, USA

Ton de Jong Institute for Teacher Education and Science, Communication, Faculty of Behavioral Sciences, University of Twente, Enschede, The Netherlands

Kristin R. Dellinger Educational Psychology, Measurement, and Evaluation Program, University of North Carolina, Chapel Hill, NC, USA

Giuliana Dettori Institute for Educational Technology—CNR, Genoa, Italy

Sidney K. D'Mello University of Notre Dame, Notre Dame, UN, USA

Melissa Duffy Laboratory for the Study of Metacognition and Advanced Learning Technologies, Department of Educational and Counselling Psychology, McGill University, Montreal, QC, Canada

John Dunlosky Kent State University, Kent, OH, USA

Catherine Eberbach Rutgers University, New Brunswick, NJ, USA

Jan Elen Center for Instructional Psychology and Technology, University of Leuven, Leuven, Belgium

Kate Forbes-Riley Learning Research and Development Center, University of Pittsburgh, Pittsburgh, PA, USA

Doris Holzberger University of Frankfurt, Frankfurt, Germany

Reza Feyzi-Behnagh Laboratory for the Study of Metacognition and Advanced Learning Technologies, Department of Educational and Counselling Psychology, McGill University, Montreal, QC, Canada

Timothy Gallant Topic Map Laboratory—Learning for Life Centre, Department of Education, Concordia University, Montréal, QC, Canada

Xun Ge Department of Educational Psychology, Jeannine Rainbolt College of Education, at the University of Oklahoma, Norman, OK, USA

Peter Gerjets Knowledge Media Research Center, Tuebingen, Germany

Jill Gößling, Ph.D., M.Sc. Department of Instructional Psychology, Duisburg-Essen University, Essen, Germany

Ashok K. Goel Design & Intelligence Laboratory, School of Interactive Computing, Georgia Institute of Technology, Atlanta, GA, USA

Art Graesser University of Memphis, Memphis, TN, USA

Jeffrey A. Greene Educational Psychology, Measurement, and Evaluation Program, University of North Carolina, Chapel Hill, NC, USA

Thomas D. Griffin University of Illinois at Chicago, Chicago, IL, USA

Cornelia S. Grosse Department of Psychology, University of Freiburg, Freiburg, Germany

Allyson F. Hadwin University of Victoria, Victoria, BC, Canada

Jason Harley Laboratory for the Study of Metacognition and Advanced Learning Technologies, Department of Educational and Counselling Psychology, McGill University, Montreal, QC, Canada

A. Hershkovitz Learning Sciences at Worcester Polytechnic Institute, Worcester, MA, USA

Cindy E. Hmelo-Silver Graduate School of Education, Rutgers University, New Brunswick, NJ, USA

Yuan-Jin Hong Advanced Technologies for Learning in Authentic Settings (ATLAS), Department of Educational and Counselling Psychology, McGill University, Montreal, Canada

Sameer Honwad, Ph.D. Center for Play, Science and Technology Learning (SciPlay), Rutgers University, New Brunswick, NJ, USA

Roland Hübscher, Ph.D. Information Design, Bentley University, Waltham, MA, USA

Einat Idan Centre for the Study of Learning and Performance, Concordia University, Montreal, QC, Canada

Halszka Jarodzka, Ph.D. Center for Learning Sciences and Technologies, Open University of The Netherlands, Heerlen, The Netherlands

Lai Jiang Institute for Tropical Medicine, Antwerp, Belgium

Rebecca Jordan Department of Ecology, Evolution, and Natural Resources, School of Environmental and Biological Sciences, Rutgers University, New Brunswick, NJ, USA

David A. Joyner Design and Intelligence Laboratory, School of Interactive Computing, Georgia Institute of Technology, Atlanta, GA, USA

Judy Kay School of Information Technologies, University of Sydney, Sydney, NSW, Australia

John S. Kinnebrew Department of EECS and ISIS, Vanderbilt University, Nashville, TN, USA

Anastasia Kitsantas Educational Psychology, George Mason University, Fairfax, VA, USA

K.R. Koedinger Pittsburgh Science of Learning Center, Pittsburgh, PA, USA

Human-Computer Interaction and Psychology, Carnegie Mellon University, Pittsburgh, PA, USA

Hermann Koerndle Psychology of Learning and Instruction, Technische Universität Dresden, Dresden, Germany

Bracha Kramarski, Ph.D. School of Education, Bar-Ilan University, Ramat-Gan, Israel

Susanne P. Lajoie Advanced Technologies for Learning in Authentic Settings (ATLAS), Department of Educational and Counselling Psychology, McGill University, Montreal, Canada

Arun Lakhana Topic Map Laboratory—Learning for Life Centre, Department of Education, Concordia University, Montréal, QC, Canada

Ronald Landis Illinois Institute of Technology, College of Psychology Chicago, IL, USA

James C. Lester North Carolina State University, Raleigh, NC, USA

Detlev Leutner, Ph.D. Department of Instructional Psychology, Duisburg-Essen University, Essen, Germany

Marcia C. Linn Education in Mathematics, Science, and Technology, University of California, Berkeley, CA, USA

Diane Litman Learning Research and Development Center, University of Pittsburgh, Pittsburgh, PA, USA

Rose Luckin The London Knowledge Lab, Institute of Education, London, UK

Valentina Lupi Junior High School "Don Milani-Colombo", Genoa, Italy

Griet Lust Center for Instructional Psychology and Technology, University of Leuven, Leuven, Belgium

Samuel Mamane Advanced Technologies for Learning in Authentic Settings (ATLAS), Faculty of Medicine, McGill University, Montreal, Canada

Jessica Marschner, Ph.D. Department of Research on Learning and Instruction, Ruhr-University Bochum, Bochum, Germany

M. Mathews Intelligent Computer Tutoring Group (ICTG), Department of Computer Science and Software Engineering, University of Canterbury, Christchurch, New Zealand

Christoph Mengelkamp University of Wuerzburg, Educational Media, Wuerzburg, Germany

Elizabeth Meyer School of Education, California Polytechnic State University, San Luis Obispo, CA, USA

Tova Michalsky, Ph.D. School of Education, Bar-Ilan University, Ramat-Gan, Israel

A. Mitrovic Intelligent Computer Tutoring Group (ICTG), Department of Computer Science and Software Engineering, University of Canterbury, Christchurch, New Zealand

Inge Molenaar Behavioural Science Institute, University of Amsterdam, Amsterdam, The Netherlands

Daniel C. Moos Department of Education, Gustavus Adolphus College, Saint Peter, MN, USA

Bradford W. Mott North Carolina State University, Raleigh, NC, USA

Laura Naismith Advanced Technologies for Learning in Authentic Settings (ATLAS), Department of Educational and Counselling Psychology, McGill University, Montreal, Canada

Susanne Narciss Psychology of Learning and Instruction, Technische Universität Dresden, Dresden, Germany

Timothy J. Nokes-Malach Learning Research and Development Center, University of Pittsburgh, Pittsburgh, PA, USA

Andrew Olney University of Memphis, Memphis, TN, USA

Maria Opfermann Department of Instructional Psychology, Duisburg-Essen University, Essen, Germany

Marily Oppezzo, Ph.D. School of Education, Stanford University, Stanford, CA, USA

Annemarie Sullivan Palincsar University of Michigan, Ann Arbor, MI, USA

Stephanie Pieschl Westfälische Wilhelms-Universität Münster, Muenster, Germany

Eric Poitras Advanced Technologies for Learning in Authentic Settings (ATLAS), Department of Educational and Counselling Psychology, McGill University, Montreal, Canada

Antje Proske Psychology of Learning and Instruction, Technische Universität Dresden, Dresden, Germany

Sadhana Puntambekar Learning Sciences Program, Educational Psychology Department, University of Wisconsin, Madison, WI, USA

John Ranellucci Advanced Technologies for Learning in Authentic Settings (ATLAS), Department of Educational and Counselling Psychology, McGill University, Montreal, Canada

Katherine A. Rawson Kent State University, Kent, OH, USA

Alexander Renkl Department of Psychology, University of Freiburg, Freiburg, Germany

Falko Rheinberg University of Potsdam, Postdam, Germany

Jennifer L. Robison North Carolina State University, Raleigh, NC, USA

Ido Roll Carl Wieman Science Education Initiative, University of British Columbia, Vancouver, BC, Canada

Pittsburgh Science of Learning Center, Pittsburgh, PA, USA

Jonathan P. Rowe North Carolina State University, Raleigh, NC, USA

Spencer Rugaber School of Computer Science, Georgia Institute of Technology, Atlanta, GA, USA

Carlos R. Salas University of Illinois at Chicago, Chicago, IL, USA

Katharina Scheiter Knowledge Media Research Center, Tuebingen, Germany

Annett Schmeck Department of Instructional Psychology, Duisburg-Essen University, Essen, Germany

Daniel L. Schwartz, Ph.D. School of Education, Stanford University, Stanford, CA, USA

Neil H. Schwartz Department of Psychology, California State University, Chico, CA, USA

International Cognitive Visualization Program, Chico, USA; Grenoble, France; Landau, Germany

Rolf Schwonke Department of Psychology, University of Freiburg, Freiburg, Germany

Brianna M. Scott University of Indianapolis, Indianapolis, IN, USA

Kamran Shaikh Topic Map Laboratory—Learning for Life Centre, Department of Education, Concordia University, Montréal, QC, Canada

Lucy R. Shores North Carolina State University, Raleigh, NC, USA

Suparna Sinha Department of Educational Psychology, Rutgers University, New Brunswick, NJ, USA

Peter Sleegers Department of Education Organization and Management, University of Twente, Enschede, The Netherlands

Marcia Sprang Placentia-Yorba Linda Unified School District, Anaheim, CA, USA

Elmar Stahl University of Education, Freiburg, Germany

Karl Steffens Department of Didactics and Educational Research, University of Cologne, Cologne, Germany

Ron Stevens UCLA IMMEX Project, Brain Research Institute, UCLA School of Medicine, Culver City, CA, USA

Christopher A. Stewart North Lakes Academy Charter School, MN, USA

Amber Chauncey Strain University of Memphis, Memphis, TN, USA

Brian Sulcer Department of EECS and ISIS, Vanderbilt University, Nashville, TN, USA

Sarah A. Sullivan, Ph.D. Learning Sciences Program, Educational Psychology Department, University of Wisconsin, Madison, WI, USA

Roger S. Taylor Department of EECS and ISIS, Vanderbilt University, Nashville, TN, USA

Hubertina Thillmann, Ph.D. Department of Research on Learning and Instruction, Ruhr-University Bochum, Bochum, Germany

Gregory Trevors Laboratory for the Study of Metacognition and Advanced Learning Technologies, Department of Educational and Counselling Psychology, McGill University, Montreal, QC, Canada

Banu Binbaşaran Tüysüzoğlu Educational Psychology, Measurement, and Evaluation Program, University of North Carolina, Chapel Hill, NC, USA

Kathryn Urbaniak Topic Map Laboratory—Learning for Life Centre, Department of Education, Concordia University, Montréal, QC, Canada

Carla van Boxtel Radboud University Nijmegen, Postbus, HE Nijmegen, The Netherlands

Tamara van Gog Educational Psychology, Institute of Psychology, Erasmus University Rotterdam, Rotterdam, The Netherlands

Wouter van Joolingen Institute for Teacher Education and Science Communication, Faculty of Behavioral Sciences, University of Twente, Enschede, The Netherlands

Swaroop S. Vattam, Ph.D. Design and Intelligence Laboratory, School of Interactive Computing, Georgia Institute of Technology, Atlanta, GA, USA

Marcel V.J. Veenman Department of Developmental and Educational Psychology, Institute for Psychological Research, Leiden University, Leiden, The Netherlands

Vivek Venkatesh Centre for the Study of Learning and Performance, Concordia University, Montréal, QC, Canada

Regina Vollmeyer Institute of Psychology, Johann Wolfgang Goethe-University Frankfurt, Frankfurt, Germany

Anne Wade Center for the Study of Learning and Performance, Concordia University, Montreal, QC, Canada

Jennifer Wiley University of Illinois at Chicago, Chicago, IL, USA

Philip H. Winne Simon Fraser University, Burnaby, BC, Canada

Joachim Wirth, Ph.D. Department of Research on Learning and Instruction, Ruhr-University Bochum, Bochum, Germany

Jeffrey Wiseman Advanced Technologies for Learning in Authentic Settings (ATLAS), Faculty of Medicine, McGill University, Montreal, Canada

Nicola Yuill School of Psychology, University of Sussex, Brighton, UK

Amna Zuberi Topic Map Laboratory—Learning for Life Centre, Department of Education, Concordia University, Montréal, QC, Canada

1 Metacognition and Learning Technologies: An Overview of Current Interdisciplinary Research

Roger Azevedo and Vincent Aleven

Abstract
This international handbook is the first compendium focused specifically on cutting-edge interdisciplinary research on metacognition and learning technologies. It presents current interdisciplinary research from the cognitive, educational, and computational sciences on learning with educational technologies. The topic is of key importance to researchers and educators because there is a wealth of empirical data indicating that learners of all ages have difficulty learning about complex topics in areas such as science and math. A major challenge for learners lies in monitoring and controlling key cognitive and metacognitive processes during learning. To synthesize current research, all handbook authors were asked to address the following in their individual chapters: (1) describe the context in which a particular learning technology is used to support or foster learners' metacognition and self-regulated learning, (2) explain the conceptual and theoretical framework of cognition and metacognition, (3) provide evidence regarding the system's effectiveness in detecting, modeling, tracking, and fostering learners' metacognitive and self-regulatory behaviors, (4) discuss design implications for metacognitive tools to support metacognition and SRL, and (5) critically examine theoretical, methodological, analytical, and instructional challenges when using learning technologies for metacognition and SRL. The handbook is divided into five sections: (1) models and components of metacognition, (2) assessment and modeling metacognitive knowledge and skills, (3) scaffolding metacognition and learning with hypermedia and hypertext, (4) ITSs and dialogue systems, and (5) multi-agent systems to measure and foster metacognition and SRL.

R. Azevedo, Ph.D. (✉)
Laboratory for the Study of Metacognition and Advanced Learning Technologies, Department of Educational and Counselling Psychology, McGill University, 3700 McTavish Street, Montreal, QC, Canada H3A 1Y2
e-mail: roger.azevedo@mcgill.ca

V. Aleven
Human-Computer Interaction Institute, Carnegie Mellon University, 5000 Forbes Ave, Pittsburgh, PA 15213, USA
e-mail: aleven@cs.cmu.edu

R. Azevedo and V. Aleven (eds.), *International Handbook of Metacognition and Learning Technologies*, Springer International Handbooks of Education 26, DOI 10.1007/978-1-4419-5546-3_1,

This international handbook presents cutting-edge interdisciplinary research on metacognition and learning technologies within specific tasks and learning contexts. Current psychological and educational research on learning with advanced technologies provides a wealth of empirical data, indicating that learners of all ages have difficulty learning about complex topics in areas such as science and math. Learning with advanced technologies requires students to analyze the learning situation, set meaningful learning goals, and determine which strategies to use. During learning, students need to assess whether the strategies are effective in meeting the learning goal while they evaluate their emerging understanding of the topic and continuously determine whether any particular learning strategy is effective for a given learning goal. In addition, they need to modify their plans, goals, strategies, and effort in relation to internal conditions (e.g., cognitive standards) and contextual conditions (e.g., scaffolding from a human tutor) while using a particular learning technology. Further, depending on the learning task, they need to reflect on their learning. Collectively, these processes involve metacognitive monitoring and control, and are sometimes also called self-regulated learning (SRL).

Traditionally, researchers have used or developed their own discipline-specific frameworks, models, and theories to account for the various metacognitive and self-regulatory processes used by humans while using learning technologies to comprehend complex materials. Recently, several researchers have extended these theories and models by advancing models of metacognition and SRL that describe the influence of mediating processes related to students' learning of these complex topics and domains. These new models have been advanced to account for the various *phases* (e.g., planning, metacognitive monitoring, strategy use, and reflection) and *areas* (e.g., cognitive, affect/motivation, behavior, and context) of learning. However, these emerging frameworks pose significant conceptual, theoretical, empirical, and educational challenges for understanding students' learning with advanced learning technologies.

A large variety of learning technologies are becoming widespread at a very rapid pace, such as distributed online or hybrid courses, open online repositories of educational materials, hypermedia environments, games, simulations, virtual worlds, intelligent tutoring systems (ITSs), tutorial dialogue systems, electronic portfolios, and peer review systems. The list goes on and on. As a practical matter, the better we understand how learners learn with these technologies, and what challenges they encounter, the more likely it is that instructional designers and developers of technology-enhanced learning will create learning environments that benefit learners and help them learn better, instead of being just a cheaper delivery vehicle for "old" instructional methods. A particularly enticing perspective is that these learning environments will not only help learners acquire deep conceptual knowledge of complex topics, or robust cognitive skill, but will also help them become better learners across domains by allowing them to acquire, internalize, share (with other human and nonhuman agents), and practice key metacognitive and self-regulatory skills.

The study of self-regulation and metacognition in computer-based learning environments (CBLEs) is timely and important, for a number of reasons. First, it is becoming increasingly clear that the way learners monitor and regulate their learning in CBLEs is a major influence on their learning outcomes. At the same time, CBLEs can be very taxing in terms of the amount of self-regulation that they require. It is important, therefore, that these environments are designed with a good understanding of the challenges that learners face. It is good to see described in this handbook many CBLEs that are designed to scaffold aspects of SRL (e.g., metacognitive knowledge versus metacognitive skills). Even better, many systems are designed to foster important self-regulatory or metacognitive skills and we are beginning to see systems that assess and adapt to learners' SRL and metacognition so as to help them become more effective learners.

CBLEs are excellent platforms to study metacognition and self-regulation for a number of methodological and practical reasons. First, they offer unprecedented opportunities for fine-grained data gathering at a large scale with very frequent "sampling" (i.e., multiple data points in a single minute) over longer periods of time. Often, systems can gather data in an unobtrusive manner, which has many practical advantages. This trend toward unobtrusive, automated data gathering and analysis of log data from systems is very compatible with the recent methodological emphasis on trace-based methodologies for studying SRL. It is also very compatible with the recent theoretical emphasis on event-based approaches and models of SRL. This is not to say that meaningful analysis of trace data or log data from CBLEs to study SRL is straightforward. There are many challenges due to the inherent uncertainty in any process that infers unobservable mental processes from behavioral data. Adding to this fundamental challenge, there is a growing trend toward using interdisciplinary research methods and analytical techniques with multichannel data (e.g., log files, eye tracking, physiological measures) to capture the complex nature of SRL and metacognitive processes. Nonetheless, interesting progress is being made, and it is good to see connections between SRL research and the burgeoning field of educational data mining.

In addition to these methodological reasons, CBLEs are also an attractive platform for studying SRL when viewed from a practical perspective. There is great natural variety in the types of self-regulatory processes that learners may employ in these environments. Therefore, they offer researchers the opportunity to observe and study these processes. As a research strategy, researchers studying SRL or metacognition can vary the design of the environments in order to study the influence of particular strategies. For example, researchers may vary the amount of learner control in an environment as a way of making certain metacognitive monitoring and control strategies more likely or less likely to occur. They may then observe the frequency of these strategies and its relation with learning outcomes. This approach to research may yield interesting insights into how system design, self-regulation, and learning outcomes are related. However, it is important to note that data on SRL and metacognitive processes must be analyzed vis-à-vis the context in which they are collected and analyzed.

The current state of research and educational applications of metacognition and learning technologies poses several challenges that are addressed in this handbook. *Theoretically*, we document the assumptions and complexity of various models, frameworks, and theories of metacognition and how they relate to our understanding of learning with technologies. This is a critical step in understanding how different fields conceptualize metacognition, the specificity and granularity of these models, the accuracy with which these models can be used to predict learning, and the relation between metacognition and other key learning processes (e.g., cognition, motivation, and affect). *Empirically*, we summarize the different types of data that researchers collect when they seek to understand the nature of metacognitive processes used during learning with advanced technologies. The foci will be on the methods used to collect, measure, and interpret data on metacognition and learning technologies. This is a critical aspect of the handbook since the inclusion of data from different disciplines will allow researchers to critically examine how various methods and analytical approaches can be used to understand the complex nature and dynamics of metacognitive knowledge and regulatory strategies used during learning with technology. *Methodologically*, this handbook also addresses how the use of educational technologies enables novel ways of studying metacognition, for example it makes possible a dramatic shift toward capturing, storing, analyzing, and making inferences based on highly detailed behavioral data. The availability of large stores of data also brings with it the challenge of analyzing the data; as such the handbook also contains chapters on novel data analysis techniques. Likewise, novel techniques have been developed and are described for analyzing the metacognitive data stream in a moment-by-moment fashion in order for the system to react adaptively to individual students' metacognition. *Educationally*, this handbook serves as a repository of theoretically driven and empirically based examples of effective ways that learning technologies can be used to enhance learning for students of all ages and in various tasks and domains. These examples can be used by professionals in science and math education, classroom teachers, industry, etc. This timely volume will present innovative interdisciplinary research and stands to contribute to numerous fields and areas of research and instruction.

Brief Overview of Chapters in Each Section

The two-volume international handbook contains 46 chapters contributed by an international group of leading researchers. We organized the chapters thematically into seven different sections.

To ensure uniformity across chapters, we asked each contributing author or group of authors to address (as much as possible) the following questions found below.

1. Provide an overview of the context in which a particular learning technology is used to study and foster students' metacognitive or SRL. This should include a brief description of the type of learning technology used (e.g., hypermedia, multimedia, ITS, microworld, hybrid system), the level (e.g., developmental, expert) of the target audience, and the domain or topic being addressed. Describe how the features of the learning technology have been designed to study and support metacognitive processing and SRL (e.g., adaptive help-seeking behavior, explicit scaffolding techniques, questioning techniques, etc.), and their individual and combined role in supporting students' learning of the task/topic/domain.
2. Provide an overview of the metacognitive (or SRL) theoretical/conceptual framework and the underlying assumptions. This should include the model or framework assumptions, and an explanation of how the particular theory/model addresses students' metacognitive SRL processes (e.g., which specific phases and areas are being targeted).
3. Describe how effective their existing learning technology is in detecting, tracing, modeling, and fostering learners' metacognitive and self-regulatory behaviors, by summarizing their empirical findings. This should emphasize the nature of the measurement tools and analytical techniques used in the research.
4. Discuss the implications for the design of metacognitive tools to support metacognition and learning. Which of these components or aspects of metacognition and SRL can and should be modeled and why?
5. Examine the theoretical, methodological, analytical, and instructional challenges. For example, discuss limitations of current methodologies, theoretical models, analytical methods and assumptions, etc.

The first section focuses on *models and components of metacognition*. As such, we have five chapters that focus on a diverse set of models and components. A common theme in these chapters is the design and evaluation of specific instructional interventions that are grounded in theoretical work focused on particular models of metacognition, often including monitoring. Thus, in this work, theoretical development and practical application are closely intertwined, which has many advantages. In fact, close ties (and bidirectional influence) between theory and practical applications are found in much of the work reported in this handbook.

The chapter by Griffin, Wiley, and Salas explains an empirically grounded and detailed theoretical framework for understanding the distinction between metacognitive knowledge and metacognitive monitoring. Particular emphasis is placed on the importance of improving the relative accuracy of metacognitive monitoring skills; typical instruction in study strategies may not be sufficient to improve monitoring. The chapter by Kramarski and Michalsky describes the results of eight controlled experimentations examining different conditions for implementation of the IMPROVE self-questioning prompts in Web-based learning environments (Web-LEs) from two perspectives, first for students' learning in the classroom, and second for preservice teachers' learning during their professional preparation. The IMPROVE method aims to support key aspects of self-regulation targeting learning processes. By contrast the chapter by Pieschl, Stahl, and Bromme raises two important issues regarding the metacognitive self-regulation of learning with technologies. First, adaptation to the external context is a core component of SRL. Second, learner characteristics play an important role in SRL and adaptation. As such, their empirical work emphasizes epistemic beliefs as an exemplary learner characteristic and they demonstrate the importance of this learner characteristic in terms of the deployment of various cognitive, metacognitive self-regulatory processes. Rawson and Dunlosky provide an overview of the retrieval-monitoring-feedback (RMF) technique, a learning technology designed to promote both durable and efficient student learning of key concepts from course material. This is a carefully designed technique that involves core concepts from cognitive psychology and metacomprehension research. The RMF program uses the student's monitoring judgments to schedule subsequent practice trials for each item. The technique has shown to yield relatively impressive levels of long-term retention of key concepts and it can be used to support learning for materials from many different topic domains and promises to benefit a wide range of learners. Lastly, the chapter by N. Schwartz and colleagues takes the position that learning and thinking are synergistic actions of the way people develop knowledge to adapt to the world. As such, they propose a conceptualization of metacognition as a closed-loop model of biased competition by proposing that the actions are collateral cognitive operations sharing a unitary outcome of performance, with metacognition functioning as an integral operator in the actions. They propose a model from evidence originating in neuroscience and cognitive psychology to show that metacognitive monitoring and control are reciprocal functions of the same neurologic processes that excite and inhibit, in a recursive fashion, the regions of the brain responsible for two types of activities involved in learning. These are activities involved in processing information relative to the goals of a task and other activities involved in processing the original activities deployed to seek goal attainment. They conclude their chapter by explaining how the model explains the results of research investigating the effects of metacognition on performance in CBLEs.

The *assessment and modeling metacognitive knowledge and skills* is the focus of the second section of the handbook, which contains five chapters. All chapters describe innovative assessment methods that can be used in conjunction with CBLEs; some of these methods are also applicable in other types of learning environments (i.e., without computers), whereas others depend critically on the automated logging that CBLEs provide. Interestingly, most work in this section is grounded in SRL or metacognitive theory. As is typical of all sections in the handbook, this section highlights a range of theoretical and methodological perspectives, as well as different types of CBLEs. Interestingly, the section also highlights the use of a range of different types of data in the study of SRL. Many projects featured in this section created automated methods for assessment, which in the future can be used to make CBLEs adapt to individual learners.

This section starts with Baker and colleagues' chapter on why students "game the system," a malaptive self-regulatory strategy, in which learners try to circumvent the hard work of learning, somewhat ironically by taking advantage of features of the system that aim to support learning (e.g., using hints to get answers without understanding). This work leverages machine-learned models of student gaming, termed "detectors," which can infer student gaming from students' interaction with educational software recorded in log files. These detectors are developed using a combination of human observation and annotation, and educational data mining. They applied the detectors to large data sets and analyzed the detectors' predictions. They used the detectors to discover and study the factors associated with gaming behavior, which can then be remedied through adaptive scaffolding. The chapter by Greene and colleagues focuses on a pervasive issue that shows that the lack of instructional scaffolding and high degree of user control inherent to most hypermedia-learning environments (HLEs) make them difficult learning environments, especially for learners who lack the ability to appropriately self-regulate their learning. In order to address this issue, they introduce a two-tiered (i.e., the micro and macro level) approach to analyzing SRL data derived from think-aloud protocols. This approach turns out to be informative in terms of the domain-, task-specific self-regulatory processes that should be scaffolded in particular HLEs. They also report findings from a number of their research studies that illustrate how analyzing data at both tiers results in a comprehensive understanding of how learners self-regulate in HLEs, and how the nature and quality of that self-regulation interact with internal and external conditions. Opfermann and colleagues' chapter also focuses on the benefits of hypermedia and requirements of hypermedia environments by presenting and detailing about how theories and models of SRL can serve as a framework for their research on the effectiveness of HLEs. In particular, they focus on multilevel componential and theoretical approaches, and analyses of cognitive, metacognitive, learner characteristics and cognitive load interact during learning with HLEs. The chapter by van Gog and Jarodzka discusses the use of eye tracking to assess cognitive and metacognitive processes and cognitive load in CBLEs. They discuss the benefits and limitations of eye tracking for studying such processes during learning and problem solving. In addition, they also provide examples of how eye tracking can be used to improve the design of instruction with CBLEs and discuss opportunities and challenges provided by eye-tracking technology. Finally, Veenman's chapter ends this section by emphasizing how metacognitive skills are considered to be an organized set of metacognitive self-instructions for the monitoring of and control over cognitive activity. These self-instructions can be represented as a production system of condition-action rules. He discusses how in computerized learning tasks, online traces of learner activities can be unobtrusively stored in log files. He also emphasizes the need to capture the dynamic change in metacognitive processes over time, and how progressive patterns of metacognitive activity can be identified in logged traces through time-series analysis.

The third section focuses on *scaffolding metacognition and learning with hypermedia and hypertext*. The nine chapters presented in this section highlight the widespread focus placed on the use of nonlinear learning systems by several researchers, of which hypertext and hypermedia are prime examples. In these environments, learners typically study a complex web of related and challenging concepts. These environments lend themselves well to the study of SRL and metacognition, as learners working in these environments face a challenging self-regulation problem and exhibit a wide range of self-regulatory processes. At the same time, these environments are known to be challenging to learners due to the open-endedness and complexity in both the targeted learning materials and the learning environment itself. A common theme in this section is therefore the design and evaluation of various methods to scaffold learners working in complex, nonlinear learning environments. The nine chapters focus on a diverse set of systems and types of scaffolding. As is the case in other sections of the handbook, the work presented in this section has a strong grounding in theories of SRL and metacognition.

The first chapter, by Bannert and Mengelkamp, provides evidence and discusses appropriate scaffolding (e.g., reflection prompts, metacognitive prompts, training and metacognitive prompts) for metacognitive reflection when learning with modern CBLEs. Specifically, it focuses on prompting metacognitive and SRL skills during hypermedia learning. They end their chapter by proposing implications for the design of metacognitive support to improve hypermedia learning. The chapter by Clarebout and colleagues discusses the relationship between metacognition and the use of tools. Being able to determine when the use of a tool would be beneficial for one's learning is seen as a metacognitive skill. Different assumptions are made with respect to this relationship between metacognitive knowledge (including instructional conceptions) and tool usage. They report on a series of studies in which different instruments were used to measure metacognitive knowledge and metacognitive skills to provide empirical underpinning for these assumptions. Dabbagh and Kitsantas' chapter reviews research that examined whether tools and features of learning management systems (LMSs), referred to in this research as Web-based pedagogical tools (WBPT), can be used to support and promote specific processes of student SRL, such as goal setting, help seeking, and self-monitoring, in online and distributed learning contexts. Five categories of WBPT are described, including administrative tools, content creation and delivery tools, collaborative and communication tools, learning tools, and assessment tools. In addition, they present findings from several studies and demonstrate how WBPT can be used to support a number of self-regulatory processes, and that college instructors and faculty can use WBPT to design effective learning tasks that promote student SRL. Ge's chapter presents a Web-based, database-driven cognitive support system for scaffolding self-regulation in the process of ill-structured problem solving. Of particular interest are the mechanisms of question prompts, expert view, and peer review in supporting self-monitoring, self-regulation, and self-reflection during ill-structured problem solving. She summarizes findings from several empirical studies on the effects of various support mechanisms conducted in several different knowledge domains (e.g., instructional design, education, and pharmacy). Her findings show that the cognitive support system has a positive influence on self-monitoring and self-regulation, which subsequently facilitates ill-structured problem-solving processes. The chapter by Lajoie and colleagues focuses on medical students' metacognitive and self-regulatory behaviors during medical diagnosis using BioWorld, a technology-rich learning environment. The system offers an authentic problem-based environment where students solve clinical cases and receive expert feedback. Their team focuses on the evaluation of key system features (e.g., the evidence table and visualization maps) to determine whether they promote metacognitive monitoring and evaluation. Learning outcomes, based on novice/expert comparisons, are compared to other key measures of medical reasoning and problem solving (e.g., diagnostic accuracy, confidence, and case summaries). They present guidelines to foster key metacognitive and self-regulatory processes in medical problem-solving tasks. Narciss and colleagues' chapter summarizes the rationale and findings of several studies conducted by her team on rich open-ended Web-LEs as learning technology in higher education. Their Web-LEs include a combination of scaffolds to support cognitive and metacognitive learning activities with university students and across various topics (e.g., introductory psychology). They close their chapter by discussing the limitations, challenges, and implications of using log-file data for investigating SRL with rich Web-LEs. The chapter by Puntambekar and colleagues emphasizes the difficulties experienced by learners when self-regulating their learning in order to make navigation decisions that align with their goals with hypertext environments. This chapter presents their extensive work in helping students learn from hypertext using the CoMPASS hypertext system in middle school science classes in physics. The system detects students' self-regulated behavior with log files. The logs are used to analyze student navigation behavior and create clusters of navigation patterns. In turn, these patterns are used to inform an algorithm that provides adaptive real-time navigation prompts in order to scaffold metacognition and SRL. Venkatesh and colleagues' chapter explores learner metacognition and self-regulation in information retrieval environments equipped with a powerful indexing technology called Topic Maps. Their mixed-method studies describe academic self-regulatory processes associated with graduate learners' understandings of ill-structured academic writing tasks and attempt to relate them to learners' metacognitive ability to judge their own performance on iterations of these writing tasks. Their findings are critical in highlighting the novel intra-sample statistical analyses used to uncover relationships between academic performance, metacognition, and task understanding. The last chapter in this section is by Winne and Hadwin and focuses on reviewing their model of SRL and identifying three obstacles learners face when they strive to effectively self-regulate learning autonomously. As such, they provide an overview of the nStudy software system, a Web application that offers learners a wide array of tools for identifying and operating on information they study. The system is designed to be a "laboratory" for learners and researchers alike to explore learning skills, metacognition, and SRL as researchers collect rich logs of fine-grained, time-stamped trace data that reflect the cognitive and metacognitive events in SRL.

ITSs and dialogue systems are the focus of the fourth section of the handbook. Whereas hypertext and hypermedia systems (featured in the previous section) focus primarily on helping learners study and understand a complex set of interrelated concepts, ITSs typically focus on "learning by doing" or problem-solving practice. Dialogue systems are systems that interact with learners in natural language (e.g., English), in ways strongly reminiscent of human tutors. Typically, these dialogues revolve around a task to be solved that requires strong conceptual knowledge. Learning with ITSs and dialogue systems tends to involve a different range of self-regulatory and metacognitive processes, than those reported in the chapters in the previous section, although there is substantial overlap. The type of scaffolding offered also differs. The seven chapters presented in this fourth section present a variety of intelligent systems designed to measure, foster, and support various processes related to metacognition and SRL across several school domains, such as math and science and age groups. In addition, a couple of chapters also focus on specific metacognitive and SRL processes (help seeking and self-explanations), learning processes (e.g., use of multiple representations), and system features (e.g., open learner models) that can foster the development of metacognition and SRL. As in other sections, there is great variety in the systems studied and the theoretical perspectives taken. A trend that can be discerned is that these types of systems tend to focus on particular metacognitive strategies within larger theoretical frameworks.

The first chapter by Aleven focuses on help-seeking behavior of students during tutored problem solving with an ITS, the Geometry Cognitive Tutor. As is typical of ITSs, this system provides step-by-step guidance with complex problems, including on-demand help (as well as step-by-step feedback). Help-seeking behavior is a key metacognitive process that can be initiated by learners and ITSs in order to foster and support problem solving. He discusses several key theories, including the ACT-R theory of cognition and learning, the Knowledge-Learning-Instruction theoretical framework focused on learning from instruction, SRL theories, and educational psychology theories of help seeking. As a first step toward theoretical integration, he reviews his work and that of his colleagues on rule-based modeling of help seeking, which integrates cognitive and metacognitive aspects within a single modeling framework. The rule-based model has been used to provide students with feedback on their help-seeking behavior. Beal's chapter describes and provides evidence of how AnimalWatch, an ITS, provides students with instruction in algebra readiness problem solving, including basic computation, fractions, variables and expressions, basic statistics, and simple geometry. Students solve word problems that include authentic environmental science content. As they do so, they can access a range of multimedia resources that provide instructional scaffolding, such as video lessons and worked examples. The system enhances students' motivation by providing learners with choices about what science topic they would like to learn about, and when they would like to navigate between different modules in the system. She summarizes several classroom evaluation studies, which have found positive effects on study-specific measures of problem solving. The chapter by Bull and Kay emphasizes the role of open learner models (OLMs), which allow systems to maintain a model of the learner's understanding as he or she interacts with an e-learning environment, which allows adaptation to the learner's educational needs. An OLM makes the machine's representation of the learner available to him or her. Typically, the state of the learner's knowledge (as inferred by the system based on the learner's performance over a series of problems) is presented in some form, ranging from a simple overall mastery score to a detailed display of how much and what the learner appears to know, his or her misconceptions, and progress through a course. This means that an OLM provides a suitable interface onto the learner model for use by the learner and in some cases for others who support his or her learning, including peers, parents, and teachers. As such, their chapter considers some of the similarities between the goals of supporting and encouraging metacognition in ITSs and learning in general, and the benefits of opening the learner model to the user. Conati's chapter describes her team's research on providing computer-based support for the metacognitive skill of self-explanation. The distinguishing element of their work is that they aim to provide support for self-explanation that is student adaptive (i.e., tailored to the specific needs and traits of each individual). She demonstrates her approach by illustrating how they built such models for two different ITSs: one that helps college students self-explain worked-out solutions of physics problems, and one that supports self-explanation during interaction with an interactive simulation for mathematical functions. Interestingly, they were able to design a method (not unlike Baker and colleagues' detectors) that automatically detects spontaneous, internal self-explanations, which are not expressed by the learner by means of overt, observable actions in the tutor's user interface. The chapter by Litman and Forbes-Riley focuses on ITSpoke, a dialogue system for qualitative physics, which engages students in a spoken natural language dialogue about challenging physics concepts. Specifically, their work focused on the hypothesis that automatically responding to student uncertainty (as detected in the student's speech) over and above correctness is one method for increasing both student learning and self-monitoring abilities. They tested this hypothesis using spoken data from both wizarded and fully automated versions of their tutorial dialogue system, where tutor responses to uncertain and/or incorrect student answers were manipulated. They present data on several metacognitive metrics that are significantly correlated with student learning. These results suggest that monitoring and responding to student uncertainty have the potential to improve students' cognitive and metacognitive abilities. Renkl and colleagues' chapter focuses on the use of multiple representations when using learning technologies. In fact, modern learning technologies (e.g., hypermedia systems, ITSs) usually provide information in multiple forms, such as text, "realistic" pictures, formal graphs of various kinds, or algebraic equations in order to foster learning. They argue that learners usually make suboptimal use of such multiple external representations. In this chapter, they present results from a series of experiments with older students (senior high school and up) that analyzed the effects of two metacognitive intervention procedures (i.e., self-explanation prompts and "instruction for use"—information on how to use multiple representations) that have shown to foster conceptual understanding and procedural skills. The last chapter in this section by Stevens and colleagues focuses on how learning trajectories have been developed for thousands of students who solved a series of online chemistry problem-solving simulations using quantitative measures of the efficiency and the effectiveness of their problem-solving approaches. Their analyses showed that the poorer problem solvers, as determined by item response theory analysis, were modifying their strategic efficiency as rapidly as the better students, but did not converge on effective outcomes. This trend was also observed at the classroom level with the more successful classes simultaneously improving both their problem-solving efficiency and effectiveness. They present evidence that placing students in collaborative groups increased both the efficiency and effectiveness of the problem-solving process, while providing pedagogical text messages increased problem-solving effectiveness, but at the expense of problem solving efficiency.

The four chapters found in the fifth section of the handbook focus on *multi-agent systems to measure and foster metacognition and SRL*. Animated pedagogical agents have a relatively long history in CBLEs and learning sciences research, but have only recently been applied to the modeling and scaffolding of self-regulatory and metacognitive processes. These agents are arguably a way of imbuing systems with personality, or multiple personalities, in an effort to make the interactions with the system take on a slightly more social nature, and make them more memorable, motivating, and engaging. Typically, the agent is visible in the interface (sometimes as a "talking head," sometimes displayed "head to toe") and produces speech output. Typically, the agent takes on the role of a tutor, sometimes a tutor specialized in particular aspects of learning (e.g., monitoring learners' metacognitive judgements, assessing learners' use of learning strategies, modeling key metacognitive and regulatory skills). Sometimes, the pedagogical agent takes on the role of a learning companion or of a student to be tutored (teachable agents). The social aspects of pedagogical agents may make them particularly well suited for supporting metacognition and self-regulation, as the social processes involved with these agents are a way of externalizing covert metacognitive and SRL skills for learners. The four chapters in this section represent contemporary cutting-edge work on the use of animated pedagogical agents embedded in hybrid intelligent systems (e.g., ITS, games, hypermedia) to detect, track, model, and foster middle school, high school, and college students' metacognition and SRL.

The first chapter by Azevedo and colleagues emphasizes the importance of using multichannel trace data to examine the complex roles of cognitive, affective, and metacognitive (CAM) self-regulatory processes deployed by students during learning with multi-agent systems, such as MetaTutor. In MetaTutor, four different pedagogical agents are responsible for modeling, tracking, and scaffolding key metacognitive and regulatory processes and skills used by students while they learn about challenging biology topics. They argue and provide extensive evidence that tracing these processes as they unfold in real time is key to understanding how they contribute both individually and together to learning and problem solving. By treating SRL as an event, they provide empirical evidence from five different kinds of trace data, including concurrent think-alouds, eye tracking, note taking and drawing, log files, and facial recognition, to exemplify how these diverse sources of data help understand the complexity of CAM processes and their relation to learning. Kinnebrew and colleagues' chapter on Betty's Brain, a CBLE that helps students learn science by constructing causal concept map models, is based on the Learning by Teaching paradigm, where the system has students take on the role and responsibilities of being the teacher to a virtual student named Betty. They provide evidence of classroom studies conducted with elementary school children and discuss the generation of hidden Markov models (HMMs) that capture students' aggregated behavior patterns, which form the basis for analyzing students' metacognitive strategies in the system. They also provide ample evidence on the use of sophisticated computational methods to analyze SRL behaviors. These methods stand to contribute to our existing conceptions and framework of metacognition and SRL, and are related to the work presented in Section 2, on assessing and modeling metacognitive knowledge and skills. Indeed, the kinds of assessment methods discussed in Section 2 can (and increasingly, do) form the foundation for the pedagogical agents discussed in the current section, who in order to interact effectively must assess student metacognition. The chapter by Lester and colleagues presents their extensive evidence on narrative-centered learning environments (e.g., CRYSTAL ISLAND) that provide engaging, story-centric virtual spaces that afford opportunities for discreetly embedding pedagogical guidance for content knowledge and problem-solving skill acquisition. Students' abilities to self-regulate learning significantly impacts performance in these environments and are critical for academic achievement and lifelong learning. Their chapter explores the relationship between narrative-centered learning environments and self-regulation for science learning. Empirical support from a series of studies with hundreds of middle school students provides evidence that narrative-centered learning environments are particularly well suited for simultaneously promoting learning, engagement, and self-regulation. The last chapter by Oppezzo and Schwartz emphasizes that producing lasting changes to metacognition, or the more encompassing construct of SRL, has strong parallels to producing behavior change. As such, they discuss and illustrate how techniques and theories of behavior change can inform the design of instruction intended to support the development and transfer of SRL. They present a four-stage model of behavior change and use it to critique their own work on Teachable Agents. They also discuss the successes of the Teachable Agents in achieving SRL goals and improving learning for each stage of the model.

Individual and collaborative learning in classroom settings is the theme of the nine chapters in Section 6 of the handbook. Again, the number of chapters in this section reflects the interest and empirical work in the area of individual and group learning with various learning technologies by research from various fields. As in other sections, the work is often firmly grounded in SRL theory, as well as other theoretical frameworks from the learning and educational sciences, reading comprehension, literacy, science education, and complex systems. In addition, the work in the current section pays careful attention to practical and theoretical issues that come up as technology-based scaffolds for SRL are embedded in classroom contexts. Interestingly, we see a variety of technologies represented, ranging from electronic portfolios to systems that support scientific inquiry and discovery learning to a toolkit for modeling biological processes, each with its own needs for metacognitive scaffolding. Many of these systems have been used in actual classrooms, underlining the relevance, to real educational settings and contexts, of the work featured in the current handbook. This theme runs throughout the handbook: Many chapters in other sections of the handbook also feature work carried out in real educational contexts.

The first chapter by Abrami and colleagues describes how they have developed, tested, and disseminated to schools an *E*lectronic *P*ortfolio *E*ncouraging *A*ctive and *R*eflective *L*earning (ePEARL). ePEARL is designed to be faithful to predominant models of self-regulation, as it scaffolds and supports learners and their educators from grade one through grade 12 and beyond. The system encourages learners to engage in the cyclical phases and subphases of forethought, performance, and self-reflection. In a series of studies, they have explored the positive impacts of ePEARL on the enhancement of students' SRL skills, their literacy skills, and changes in teaching while simultaneously researching classroom implementation fidelity and teacher professional development. Chiu and colleagues view metacognition and cognition as interacting processes that together promote coherent understanding. As such, their chapter proposes that the use of the knowledge integration pattern to design instructional scaffolding encourages the interplay between these two processes. They present and discuss several findings that indicate that instructional activities designed using the knowledge integration pattern promote student learning from dynamic visualizations by helping to overcome deceptive clarity. The chapter by Dalton and Palincsar describes the empirical and theoretical roots of the *Reading to Learn* program of research, which was designed to investigate the metacognition and learning of upper elementary students in supportive e-text environments. They present their findings, using various instructional manipulations (e.g., static, interactive, interactive diagram/coaching) designed to provide both procedural and conceptual support. Their chapter includes a critique on the methods used in the intervention studies and a proposal for future research. Goel and colleagues' chapter describes the Aquarium Construction Toolkit (ACT) project which is an ongoing collaboration among learning, cognitive, computing, and biological scientists focusing on learning functional models of ecosystems in middle school science. The system is an interactive learning environment for stimulating and scaffolding construction of Structure–Behavior–Function (SBF) models to reason about classroom aquaria. The authors summarize the results from the deployment of ACT in several middle school science classrooms with several hundred middle school students. They found significant improvements in students' ability to identify the structure, behaviors, and functions of classroom aquaria, as well as their appropriation of SBF modeling by some middle school teachers for modeling other natural systems. Lastly, they describe SRL in ACT while looking ahead and outlining the design of a metacognitive ACT. The chapter by Molenaar and colleagues describes a new method for the computerized scaffolding of SRL in CBLEs with avatars. The system works with an attention management system that registers the attentional focus of learners with the intention to adjust scaffolding to students' current activities. They provide evidence that their scaffolding system enhances group performance and students' metacognitive knowledge and that differential effects are most likely explained by a combination of quantitative and qualitative differences in the metacognitive activities triggered by problematizing scaffolds compared with structuring scaffolds. Thillmann and colleagues' chapter presents new assessment methods for different aspects of metacognition and SRL. They argue that metacognitive knowledge about strategies and metacognitive regulation of strategies are two distinct components of metacognition that make different demands on their respective assessment method. Also, they contend that metacognitive knowledge about and metacognitive regulation of strategy use should be assessed with regard to the same strategies, in order to be able to relate both measures and to localize specific deficiencies. They exemplify their arguments using two CBLEs for scientific discovery learning by illustrating two kinds of assessment methods, including a test format that intends to assess metacognitive knowledge about scientific discovery strategies and log files to assess metacognitive regulation of the use of these strategies during SRL with the CBLEs. Their results reveal that the relationship between metacognitive knowledge and metacognitive regulation of the actual use of the same strategy is moderated by current motivation. The chapter by van Joolingen and de Jong discusses the use of models of inquiry processes, such as the Scientific Discovery and Dual Search (SDDS) model and the inquiry cycle for the generation of support on the regulation of these processes. Based on their extensive research, they argue that such scaffolding must be adaptive as too much scaffolding can actually hinder learning. Further, in order to make scaffolding adaptive, the system needs to gather information about the learners' task progress. They discuss a few ways of using less obtrusive methods for obtaining learner information, and present an example of how such information can be used to support learners in monitoring their progress. Carneiro and Steffens' chapter focuses on the challenges of using digital technologies since these technologies offer an almost unlimited access to information and a wide variety of tools for information processing and communication. It has also become clear that managing these resources requires a new kind of literacy, digital literacy, and that part of this digital literacy is the capacity to regulate one's own learning. As such, their chapter examines recent theoretical approaches to SRL with digital technologies. They also expand on research and implementation policies for technology-enhanced learning in Europe and present two examples of research on SRL: Taconet, a community of European researchers that grew out of a project on this topic, and the New Opportunities Initiative (NOI), a large-scale program implemented by the Portuguese Government to empower low-skilled workers in which the use of digital technologies and SRL play a vital role. Lastly, the chapter by Dettori and Lupi describes the use of audio technology and metacognition to improve pronunciation in the learning of a second language (L2). They describe a methodological approach to guide L2 learners to observe their utterances and become aware of their pronunciation errors, with the support of peer collaboration and metacognitive prompts. Identifying pronunciation errors is not easy because it requires good self-observation, evaluation, and reflection skills.

The last section of the handbook is on *motivation and affect as key processes in metacognition and SRL.* While motivation has long been emphasized in theories and models of SRL, the inclusion of affect and its interrelations with cognitive, metacognitive, and motivational aspects of self-regulation is more novel. (We do not mean to say that affect has been entirely ignored by SRL researchers; only that it has been less emphasized than cognitive, metacognitive, and motivational realms.) The six chapters presented in this last section of the handbook represent some of the best research in the areas of motivation and emotions that has already had an impact in several fields from educational psychology to affective computing. These chapters represent a growing awareness that motivation and emotions are a key and integral part of understanding cognitive and metacognitive self-regulation. Recent advances in affective computing and CBLEs make this work particularly timely. This work is yielding automated methods for detecting learners' affective state as they interact with learning technologies. One theme in the chapters reviewed here is on how these detectors can lead to useful scaffolds for self-regulation in CBLEs, making these environments more adaptive to individual learners and ultimately more effective. As before, we can point to interesting cross-connections with other sections of the handbook, for instance, the work on automated assessment of metacognitive and self-regulatory skills featured in Section 2. We as editors feel it is imperative that we continue to conduct interdisciplinary research on the role of cognitive, metacognitive, motivational, and affective processes prior to, during, and following learning and problem solving with CBLEs. The work featured in this handbook section points the way.

The first chapter is by Bernacki and colleagues on overcoming the weaknesses of using self-report questionnaires to measure motivation by proposing to capture motivational states during learning and problem solving. They hypothesize and illustrate that motivation can change during an activity or curricular unit. Therefore, without temporally fine-grained assessment (i.e., without frequent sampling), dynamic relations between motivation, cognitive, and metacognitive processes cannot be observed and studied. They describe a method for collecting fine-grained assessments of motivational variables during learning mathematics with ITS and examine their association with cognitive and metacognitive behaviors. The utility of their method for assessing motivation and use of these assessments to test hypotheses of SRL and motivation are discussed. Burleson's chapter emphasizes the importance of understanding the affective state of a learner in determining when and how best to provide appropriate support. He describes an Affective Learning Companion built upon an Affective Agent Research Platform with the goal of discovering when, at various points in the problem-solving process, a student encounters optimal flow experiences or nonoptimal Stuck experiences. Using theories from metacognition and motivation, the goal is to help students become aware of their emotional states, and to develop metacognitive strategies to use this awareness to persevere in the face of frustration. The findings focus on gender differences in meta-affective skills, experiences of several affective states, goal orientations, and intrinsic-motivation. The chapter by Carr and colleagues describes the team's extensive research with the Ecolab software, an interactive learning environment for 10–11-year-old learners designed to help children learn about food chains and food webs. Their chapter discusses the results of their recent work on achievement goal orientation and help seeking within the Ecolab environment. They situate the results within the broader landscape of previous studies and discuss the evolutionary approach they have adopted to design metacognitive learning tools. This methodology has been built up over a series of empirical studies with the Ecolab software that have demonstrated that children who achieved above-average learning gains use a high level of system help. Focusing specifically on the relationships between young learners' metacognition (e.g., help-seeking behavior) and their achievement goal orientations, they extend their research on metacognitive software scaffolding and the influence of goal orientation on children's learning. D'Mello and colleagues' chapter argues that complex learning of difficult subject matter with educational technologies involves a coordination of cognitive, metacognitive, and affective processes. Their chapter describes several key theories of affect, meta-affect, and affect regulation during learning followed by a summary of their empirical research that focuses on identifying the affective states that spontaneously emerge during learning with educational technologies, how affect relates to learning outcomes, and how affect can be regulated. They provide extensive evidence across a large number of studies using a variety of educational technologies, different learning contexts, a number of student populations, and diverse methodologies to track affect. Lastly, they describe and evaluate an affect-sensitive version of AutoTutor, a fully automated ITS that detects and helps learners regulate their negative affective states (frustration, boredom, confusion) in order to increase engagement, task persistence, and learning gains. They conclude by discussing future directions of research on affect, meta-affect, and affect regulation during learning with educational technologies. The chapter by Moos and Stewart emphasizes the need to extend research on SRL and hypermedia to extend beyond the use of cognitively based theoretical models of SRL. As such, they argue that future contributions to this theory to the field of hypermedia learning need additional empirical research that systematically considers theoretically grounded constructs of motivation within SRL. The premise of their chapter is that motivation offers a potential explanation of individual differences in how students respond to negative feedback loops during hypermedia learning. They also highlight methodological and theoretical challenges, including the identification of specific motivation constructs (e.g., outcome expectations, incentives, efficacy expectations, attributions, and utility) that align with existing SRL theoretical frameworks. The last chapter, by Vollmeyer and Rheinberg, focuses on their paradigm using microworlds with their biology-lab task. They introduce their cognitive-motivational process model which specifies variables that help to describe SRL. For example, initial motivation (probability of success, interest, anxiety, and challenge) affects performance through mediating variables, such as strategies and motivation during learning, while metacognition, especially planning, could be included as a further mediating variable. They present their findings and discuss which aspects of metacognition could be integrated into the model without risking an overlap with the construct of motivation.

We are deeply impressed with the conceptual, theoretical, empirical, and educational work presented here, including its relevance to educational practice, and the promise it holds for future developments both in research and practice. The seven sections found in this handbook represent the most impressive cutting-edge work conducted by colleagues around the world. The work is innovative and inspirational: Not only do we see areas that traditionally have dominated research on metacognition and learning technologies, such as the extensive work on hypertext and hypermedia environments and ITSs and dialogue systems (see Sections 3 and 4), but we also see the huge promise from other emerging areas represented by the chapters on multi-agent systems, and motivation and emotions found in sections five and seven of the handbook. As seen in the first two sections of the handbook, the conceptual and theoretical work on models, components, assessment, and modeling of metacognition and SRL remains strong. This line of work is very much needed, because the emergence of novel learning technologies continues to challenge our ability to understand how they can potentially impact learners. Lastly, the section on individual and collaborative learning in classroom settings represents a burgeoning area of research across various disciplines using a plethora of theoretical frameworks and models. It deals successfully with the individual and collaborative nature of metacognition and SRL in authentic classroom contexts.

Future Directions

As editors, we are extraordinarily pleased to have captured a collection of the most impressive interdisciplinary work in the area of metacognition and learning technologies. Despite the efforts represented in this handbook, there is still more work to be done. We conclude this introductory chapter by highlighting a few specific issues that, we believe, necessitate further work in the areas of conceptual, theoretical, empirical, methodological, analytical, and educational issues.

First, there is a great need for theoretical clarity, including better definitions and descriptions of the components of metacognition and SRL. The challenge lies in the widespread proliferation of terms, constructs, mechanisms, and processes that are found in the literature. In addition, more theoretical work needs to be conducted so that current theoretical frameworks, models, and conceptualizations of metacognition and SRL can deal with important issues such as level of granularity, comprehensiveness, descriptiveness, dynamic processes and feedback loops, and the role of context. For example, some models are too abstract or provide high-level descriptions of a few key metacognitive processes without specifying how the recursive nature of dynamic metacognitive and SRL processes may impact how a learner self-regulates and ultimately learns with the learning technology. Such a specification should include a learners' cognitive architecture, learning technology, and other contextual factors.

Second, more research is needed to examine the complex interactions between cognitive, metacognitive, motivational, and emotional processes. The complex interactions amongst these key processes are critical in determining their role, influence, and impact on one's ability to monitor and regulate during learning with CBLEs. These issues are associated with a third issue—one of learning and instruction—namely, the fact that most models of learning and instruction provide very abstract, macro-level descriptions of learning, which make it difficult for researchers and designers to build systems that adequately scaffold and foster metacognition and SRL. For example, imagine a learner using a hypermedia system to develop a deep conceptual understanding of a complex physical system. During learning, the learner indicates that he or she is not interested in the topic, does not value the need to learn about it, and has demonstrated low self-efficacy in using effective learning strategies. In addition, he or she demonstrates an abundance of prolonged negative affective states during learning associated with confusion and frustration, rarely showing any enjoyment during learning. While the motivational and affective processes clearly indicate a lack of engagement in the task, he or she also has low prior knowledge of the domain, cannot seem to set relevant goals for the tasks, and repeatedly demonstrates that he or she is not capable of assessing his or her emerging understanding of the most appropriate content to use. These learner characteristics (whether transient or more stable) are inferred in real time from data collected with various sensors, so the question becomes—"When and how does the system intervene and offer scaffolding and feedback?" We do not know the answer to this question yet, because we lack theories and models of instruction that provide instructional prescriptions to handle the complex nature of cognitive, metacognitive, motivational, and affective processes during learning. The scenario provided raises the following questions: When does the system intervene, how does the system intervene, who or what should intervene (e.g., a peer, a teacher, a pedagogical agent, etc.), should the system intervene (at all), and what should the system offer (e.g., feedback, prompting, modeling, scaffolding)? If we are to design effective systems, general principles and guidelines need to be developed that help instructional designers (and systems) address these challenging questions.

Another key area that needs further attention is the measurement of metacognitive and self-regulatory processes. As seen in several chapters and sections throughout the handbook, researchers are making strides in the measurement of key cognitive, metacognitive, motivational, and affective processes. Measurement of a wide range of these processes is crucial as we strive to understand the nature of these processes prior to, during, and following learning with CBLEs. We are beginning to see the emergence of multi-method, multichannel approaches to capture the complex nature, deployment, and use of these processes during learning. Analytical techniques from educational mining and machine learning are currently being used and can contribute in many important ways. For example, patterns emerging from thousands of data points can be used to challenge current conceptions of metacognition and SRL. Further, they can provide descriptive accounts of adaptive and maladaptive SRL behavior, which are interesting from a theoretical perspective, but can also be used by the system to foster metacognition and learning (e.g., by recognizing maladaptive behaviors in real time and providing an adequate response). In addition, we need to expand our methodologies by using longitudinal studies to capture and understand the qualitative and quantitative changes in the acquisition, internalization, and use of metacognitive and regulatory processes over extended periods of time. We also need to continue to build and use our learning technologies as both research and learning tools. Naturally, the adoption of new methods and research designs will necessitate new analytical and statistical techniques, since current techniques are constantly challenged by the nature of the data collected in the area of metacognition and learning. For example, use of concurrent think-aloud data may be limited when data is non-normally distributed. For example, based on a learner's verbosity, such data may yield few coded SRL processes and therefore violates assumptions of normalcy, thus limiting the use of inferential statistics. By contrast, log-file data is excellent in collecting fine-grained temporal data at the millisecond data in an unobtrusive manner. However, this data needs to be augmented with other data since making inferences about the presence of metacognitive processes is challenging. Researchers continually face the challenge to temporally collect and align multichannel theoretically derived data. This data needs to be captured, coded, scored, and interpreted in real time and post hoc, so we can advance the field by contributing to our theories and models, and so we can ultimately improve metacognition and self-regulation with learning technologies. These are just a few of the critical issues that need to be addressed in order to continue to make progress in our challenging interdisciplinary area of research.

In sum, we are encouraged by the advancement we (researchers working in the field of metacognition and learning technologies) have made thus far and are excited about the work that lies ahead of us!

Part I

Models and Components of Metacognition

Supporting Effective Self-Regulated Learning: The Critical Role of Monitoring

2

Thomas D. Griffin, Jennifer Wiley, and Carlos R. Salas

Abstract

This chapter explicates an empirically grounded and detailed theoretical framework for understanding the various components of self-regulated learning. A key distinction is articulated between metacognitive knowledge and metacognitive monitoring. It is argued that it is the accurate monitoring of learning experiences that is critical for effective self-regulation during learning, and that various accuracy measures for judgments of learning differ in how well they assess this construct of monitoring accuracy. Particular emphasis is placed on the importance of improving the relative accuracy of metacognitive monitoring skills, and that typical instruction in study strategies may not be sufficient to improve monitoring. The results of studies and manipulations that have resulted in superior monitoring accuracy are reviewed, and the implications for the development of learning technologies are discussed. A key observation is that in order to provide the opportunity for the development of effective regulatory skills, learning environments need to be careful not to deprive students of the opportunity to engage in self-regulation or monitoring of their own understanding.

Supporting Effective Self-Regulated Learning: The Critical Role of Monitoring

Imagine that a student has several homework assignments to complete in one night including reading several passages for biology and a set of readings in social studies. The readings for biology are on vision, taste, and the auditory system. The readings in social studies are a textbook passage on taxation without representation and two essays about the Boston Tea Party, one from an American perspective and one from a British perspective. For most daily schoolwork, students find themselves in situations such as this where they must regulate and monitor their own study behaviors. They must make important decisions such as when to read, what to read, how to read, and how much to read. Critical to this process is the ability to discriminate which readings

T.D. Griffin • J. Wiley (✉) • C.R. Salas
University of Illinois at Chicago, Chicago, IL, USA
e-mail: jwiley@uic.edu

R. Azevedo and V. Aleven (eds.), *International Handbook of Metacognition and Learning Technologies*, Springer International Handbooks of Education 26, DOI 10.1007/978-1-4419-5546-3_2,

have been understood well and which have not. This requires readers to actively and consciously monitor their ongoing learning progress in order to compare to a goal state or in relation to their progress on other tasks competing for their limited time and resources. Only with accurate monitoring will a student engage in effective self-regulated learning (SRL). Given the importance of monitoring to SRL, it is of great interest to find contexts that may improve the monitoring skills of students as they learn from text. However, pursuit of this goal requires clarity about what exactly the phenomenon of monitoring is and how it relates to the other components of SRL.

Monitoring and Its Place in SRL

Within literature on SRL, there are researchers who use similar terminology to refer to different constructs. This creates some confusion and potentially leads to incorrect inferences about what factors, individual differences, contexts, manipulations, and interventions influence particular aspects of SRL. Hacker (1998) commented on two different approaches to "monitoring." One approach, used primarily by cognitive psychologists, focuses upon learners' monitoring of ongoing learning via having students make overt judgments of their current level of understanding (judgments of learning, or JOLs) and comparing these to objective measures of the quality of their mental representations. The correspondence between these subjective and objective measures of learning is referred to monitoring accuracy or, more specifically, metamemory accuracy when the learning goal is memory (usually of word-pairs) and metacomprehension accuracy when the learning goal is comprehension (usually of texts). The focus of this research approach is to determine which conditions support accurate monitoring.

In contrast, another approach, used primarily by educational researchers, tends to use terms like "comprehension monitoring" more broadly to incorporate several kinds of monitoring, such as monitoring of goals, use and monitoring of strategies, as well as monitoring of learning. This approach generally attempts to improve SRL by supporting the use of particular learning and study strategies and utilizes assessments such as self-report scales of strategy knowledge and use, rather than focusing on accurate monitoring of ongoing learning.

The basis for both of these approaches to SRL was present in the original notion of metacognition put forth by Flavell (1979) 30 years ago, and both foci are still reflected in modern models of SRL. Flavell's original construct of metacognition was defined as "one's knowledge of one's own cognitive processes and products or anything related to them." The key components from Flavell's original theory of metacognition are depicted in Fig. 2.1. In Flavell's framework, metacognitive processes are designed to optimize one's cognitive *actions* in pursuit of learning *goals*. There are two major factors that determine the coordination of actions and goals. The first is the application of preexisting metacognitive *knowledge* about particular tasks, strategies, or a learner's abilities that can be used to select cognitive actions to increase learning. The second are metacognitive reactions to *experiences* of subjective internal states that occur as a result of the cognitive actions one executes and that reflect how learning is progressing. Metacognitive knowledge and experiences are distinct. Knowledge influences actions that in turn impact learning outcomes and can produce subjective experiences. However, as depicted by the recursive loop in Fig. 2.1, it is the internal metacognitive *experiences* associated with current attempts to learn that learners must monitor in order to judge their actual learning progress and make online revisions to their cognitive actions (i.e., regulation). Otherwise they will be guided only by incomplete and often erroneous prior knowledge. Later theories articulated that this experience monitoring process occurs at another level of awareness, the "meta" level of processing, because the subjective experiences that are being reflected on are the result of the cognitive processes or actions that students engage in at the "object" level (Fischer & Mandl, 1984; Nelson & Narens, 1990; for a recent discussion, see Griffin, Wiley, & Thiede, 2008). Consistent with Flavell, this model depicts monitoring as the processing of one's own ongoing cognitive states

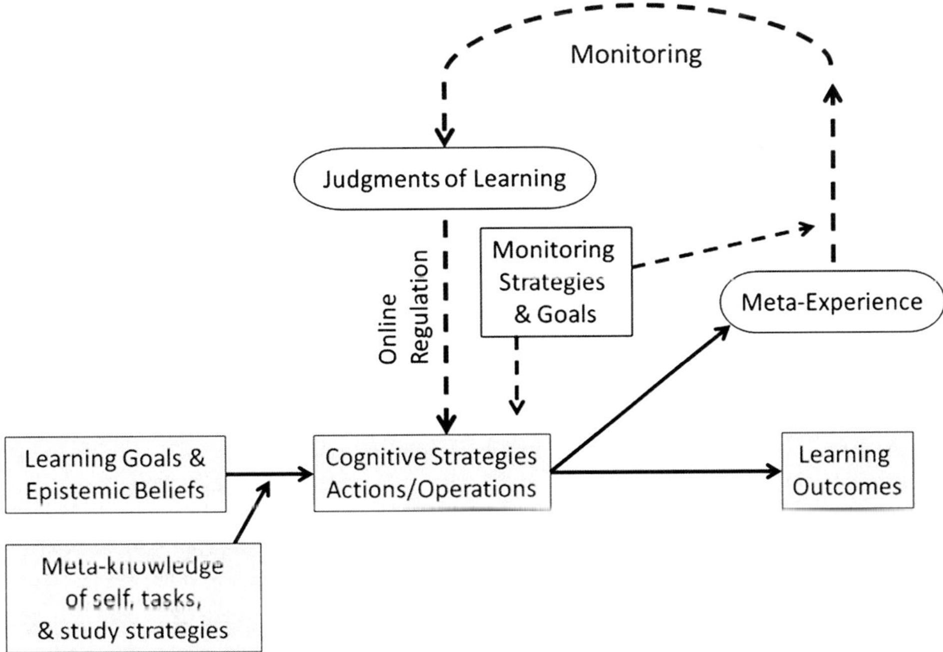

Fig. 2.1 Components of the self-regulated learning process

(i.e., experiences), and regulation as the outcome of that processing whereby self-assessments of learning progress are used to alter the lower-level cognitive processing. Meanwhile, the implementation of strategies intended to improve learning occurs on the "object" level, as it represents a direct cognitive action. So while metacognitive knowledge contributes to cognitive processing, only monitoring of the ongoing learning experience has the quality of processing information about cognitive processes that defines *meta*cognitive processing. Figure 2.1 depicts knowledge states and processes that do not necessarily entail meta-level processing as the solid lines and boxes. The dashed lines and ovals entail meta-level processing where the learner is processing information about their own cognitive states.

Similarly, Flavell (1979) points out a critical distinction between *cognitive strategies* that are used to increase learning versus *metacognitive strategies* that are deliberately used to produce experiences that can be monitored to self-assess learning progress. Metacognitive strategies are essentially self-tests to evaluate learning. "Cognitive strategies are invoked to *make* cognitive progress, metacognitive strategies to *monitor* it" (Flavell, p. 909). Sometimes the entire distinction between cognitive and metacognitive strategy use rests in the learner's intended purpose for using a strategy. The same activity (e.g., asking oneself questions at the end of a chapter) could be employed as either type of strategy. If it is employed to deepen learning, it is a cognitive strategy. But if it is employed so that the learner can monitor and pay deliberate attention to the resulting subjective experiences to assess learning progress (such as the ease with which they answered the various questions), then it is a metacognitive strategy.

The fact that certain strategies direct learners to attend to the meta-level experiences resulting from self-testing actions is depicted in the center of the model as a moderating influence on the action-experience relationship. We refer to these as *monitoring strategies* to highlight the direct monitoring role served by only a subset of strategies, distinct from the object-level cognitive processing role of most strategies explored in SRL research. Only these experience monitoring strategies are part of the regulatory loop.

Influences of Metacognitive Knowledge on SRL

A common approach to improving SRL is to focus upon learners' awareness and use of study strategies. In a review of 201 empirical studies published from 2003 to 2007 in the major education journals on metacognition and SRL, Dinsmore, Alexander, and Loughlin (2008) reported that definitions of both constructs typically employ terms like monitoring and control. However, few of the studies actually assessed monitoring accuracy. Instead, most studies investigated awareness or use of study strategies, usually assessed with self-report measures.

Commonly used self-report inventories of metacognitive knowledge (Mokhtari & Reichard, 2002; Pintrich, Wolters, & Baxter, 2000), including the Metacognitive Awareness Inventory (MAI; Schraw & Dennison, 1994) are dominated by items that assess general study strategies ("I summarize," "I read instructions carefully," and "I try to break studying down into smaller steps"), general self-beliefs ("I am good at remembering information"), and beliefs about contexts that impact learning ("I learn more when I am interested in the topic"). Learners receive higher scores when they report always using the same normatively preferred strategy, which means they are not actually regulating strategy use to specific contexts. Most of these scales have either no items (Moore, Zabrucky, & Commander, 1997) or very few items within a much larger scale (Mokhtari & Reichard, 2002; Pintrich et al., 2000) that explicitly assess monitoring strategies and goals. The MAI is somewhat of an exception with a few items designed to assess monitoring strategies, such as "I ask myself questions about how well I am doing while I am learning something new" and "I ask myself how well I've accomplished my goals." However, these items are typically analyzed as part of larger subscales that tap general information processing and study strategies, such as "I periodically review to help me understand important relationships" and "I summarize what I've learned." In addition, these subscales are typically analyzed as components of even broader latent constructs such as "Regulation of Cognition" which are combinations of many things including pre-task planning strategies, such as "I set specific goals before I begin a task" (Schraw & Dennison, 1994).

Some research has found that learners who score higher on these instruments do show superior text comprehension (Schraw & Dennison, 1994). Also, direct instruction in strategic reading has been shown to produce both changes in responses to these strategy inventories and improved comprehension or learning outcomes (Caverly, Nicholson, & Radcliffe, 2004; Pressley, 2002; Zimmerman, 2002). However, some critics have questioned whether these strategy inventories reflect actual strategy use since these self-reports have not been verified against converging measures of actual learning behaviors (Cromley & Azevedo, 2006).

The bottom pathway from left to right in Fig. 2.1 represents the direct influence that metacognitive knowledge can have on learning outcomes by impacting initial strategy selection during planning. This can entail generally effective strategies such as "summarize after reading" or context-dependent beliefs like "I learn more easily when interested" that interact with other a priori factors such knowledge about the task, topic, context, and beliefs about learning to determine strategy selection. In this model, metacognitive knowledge acts as an object-level cognitive process that directly impacts learning. This means that any observed relation between strategy use and learning outcomes can occur completely outside the regulatory loop, and the presence of such a relation cannot be used to determine whether monitoring is accurate or even if experiences are being monitored.

In fact, strong a priori commitment to a strategy that is generally effective could yield above average learning gains while also undermining online monitoring and regulation in certain situations where the strategy is suboptimal, resulting in inefficiency and costly use of resources. If strategy selection is based purely on a priori information, there is no opportunity for accurate monitoring of ongoing learning to play a role in SRL. Further, monitoring of actual learning outcomes in relation to strategy use is a critical source of information for updating and revising strategy knowledge in order to improve the efficacy of strategy choice on future learning trials. The exclusive reliance on a priori metacognitive knowledge will stagnate the long-term development of more accurate strategy knowledge because feedback from monitored learning outcomes is the presumed primary means by which errors in strategy knowledge are revised (Flavell, 1979; Winne & Hadwin, 1998).

The fact that many forms of strategy knowledge can have a direct effect on learning or an effect on strategy choice only in the planning stage is at least implicit in most models of SRL (e.g., Hacker, 1998; Nelson & Narens, 1990; Pintrich et al., 2000). For example, despite the highly recursive nature of Winne and Hadwin's (1998, Figure 12.1) SRL model, the arrows of influence show that preexisting knowledge of tasks and strategies can influence operations, cognitive products, and then performance without engaging the "monitoring" and "control" components at the heart of the model. This simply means that even though learners may have some awareness of task demands and may match this to a known strategy, once this initial plan is implemented, its influence on outcomes, products, and comprehension can occur without any online experience monitoring or responsive regulation.

Thus, a key point is that strategies that directly improve learning may or may not evoke metacognitive experiences that are useful for accurate monitoring. Students who are aware of these strategies or who report using them may be more effective learners, but these results will necessarily be unable to address whether they are better at online monitoring or regulation of their learning. Accurate online monitoring is important not only for revising strategies that have failed but also simply for knowing when the strategy needs to be repeated, due perhaps to idiosyncratic influences such as a brief distraction that limited its benefits. A priori strategy selection does not allow the learner to adapt to the numerous idiosyncratic contextual factors that foster and hinder comprehension processes as they actually occur. Judgments of learning that are based only in prelearning assumptions are not truly judgments of learning and cannot be used to modify and improve the initial strategies selected based upon those same assumptions.

Influences of Epistemic Beliefs on SRL

Similar issues can be raised about the burgeoning literature on learners' *epistemic beliefs* about the nature of knowledge and the process of knowing (with respect to the certainty, complexity, source, and potential revision of 'true justified' knowledge) and its influence on SRL (e.g., see Hofer & Sinatra, 2010). Research on *epistemic metacognition* has been shaped by models that construe epistemic beliefs as a type of general and abstract metacognitive knowledge (e.g., Hofer, 2004; Kitchener, 1983; Kuhn, 1999). However, rather than integrating epistemic beliefs into traditional models of SRL, this literature has largely attempted to construct a parallel model that repurposes monitoring as being in the service of "monitoring what [one] believe[s] to be true" and "monitoring and judging epistemic claims" for their truth status (Hofer, 2004, pp. 48–49) rather than monitoring of learning progress. Similarly, evaluative strategies are said to be regulated, such as by checking for internal logical inconsistencies in order to evaluate an argument's validity (Richter & Schmid, 2010) and generally increasing or decreasing one's efforts in evaluating a claim's veracity (Hofer, 2004).

In contrast to these parallel models of epistemic metacognition, Winne and Hadwin (1998) integrate epistemic beliefs into their more traditional SRL model as a component of metacognitive knowledge, where these beliefs serve as *cognitive conditions* that can foster use of certain learning strategies. For example, a belief that true knowledge is acquired effortlessly may promote the use of less effortful strategies. This expands upon and attaches an epistemic label to several kinds of general and abstract beliefs that Flavell (1979) also incorporated into the original model as part of metacognitive knowledge. Due to their level of abstraction and generality, epistemic beliefs might best be construed as determinants of learning goals that interact with knowledge of particular strategies to determine actual strategy use and cognitive actions.

The model in Fig. 2.1 depicts the effects of epistemic beliefs on learning as occurring via initial strategy selection without any impact on the metacognitive monitoring loop. Consistent with this suggestion, several recent studies have shown effects of epistemic beliefs on both the initial selection of more effective strategies (Bromme, Pieschl, & Stahl, 2010; Stahl, Pieschl, & Bromme, 2006) and on learning outcomes (e.g., Mason, Boldrin, & Ariasi, 2010; Muis & Franco, 2010). As with the study strategy literature, audiences might be misled to infer effects of epistemic beliefs on comprehension monitoring by the confusing use of traditional metacognitive terms employed in discussions of these findings. For example, Stahl and colleagues (2006) have described the effects of epistemic beliefs on learners' importance ratings of certain strategies for certain tasks in terms of superior *monitoring* and *calibration*. Mason et al. (2010, p. 85) have inferred superior *self-regulation* from pre-task self-reported general strategies. Muis (2008) has discussed *monitoring* effects in reference to engaging in behaviors that appear to reflect monitoring attempts, but these were not analyzed separately from non-monitoring behaviors. Most of these outcome measures do not reflect attempts to monitor ongoing learning progress or regulation in response to monitoring, and none reflect the accuracy of learners' monitoring. The potential effect of epistemic beliefs on actual comprehension monitoring and online regulation is still awaiting empirical confirmation.

In summary, this model highlights how metacognitive knowledge of context, goals, beliefs, and study strategies can influence learning and even regulation at the planning and selection stages without impacting monitoring of ongoing learning via reflection on experiences. Metacognitive knowledge serves to inform learners *what* strategies they should employ, but it is separate from the metacognitive processing that involves online monitoring of experience which can inform a learner *when* strategies are effective and when they need to be regulated, reapplied, or revised.

Experience Monitoring and Metacomprehension Accuracy

As posed above, a central element in models of SRL is the self-regulatory loop – the part of the model where a reader reflects on their own processing and alters their learning or study behaviors as a result. The regulatory loop depends on self-evaluation or judgments of learning (JOLs). Self-evaluation judgments, in turn, rely on cues. The quality of self-evaluation judgments depends largely on the quality of the cues that are used for the basis of these judgments. Such reasoning has been unpacked most extensively by Koriat in his cue-utilization theory. Koriat (1997) has discussed two classes of cues that learners use to draw inferences about their learning and future performance. One set are cues that are tied to the learner's internal online subjective experiences that reflect their cognitive processing in the specific situation. Because Koriat has been mainly concerned with judgments of learning during memorization tasks, he calls these mnemonic cues. These cues include the subjective sense of ease or fluency during learning (Benjamin & Bjork, 1996; Dunlosky & Nelson, 1992).

The other kinds of cues are tied to objective features of the learning situation that are either *intrinsic* to the materials and task demands (e.g., relatedness of word-pairs, memory of details versus conceptual application) or *extrinsic* to the task or stimuli, but instead related to the context (e.g., how many times items were studied or what strategy was used). These knowledge-based cues bypass the monitoring of subjective experience. Instead, people may make judgments based on their perceptions of the general effectiveness of certain strategies.

Although the cue-utilization theory was developed with reference to metamemory monitoring of rather simple materials like word-pairs, it can be adapted to metacomprehension of complex texts. Such an adaption is reflected in the model by Griffin, Jee, and Wiley (2009) that distinguishes heuristic from representation-based cues that can be used for self-evaluation. Representation-based cues, like mnemonic cues, are tied to subjective online experiences that reflect processing during learning and the quality of the mental representation that a learner has actually formed. Heuristic cues are those based in a priori general assumptions about topic interest, domain knowledge, ability, and text and task features. The model proposes that these heuristic cues (which comprise metacognitive knowledge) may have modest predictive validity because they refer to things that can have some influence on learning, but they are insensitive to idiosyncrasies of the specific learning situation and can therefore be erroneous. For example, the heuristic knowledge that one is good at multiple-choice tests may predict higher than average overall performance on such tests, but will be of no help in predicting whether one will do better on a test about the Irish potato famine versus a test about earthquakes. In addition to capturing Koriat's key distinction between cue types and providing a reason why mnemonic cues are generally more valid, this heuristic-representation distinction maps rather clearly onto Flavell's (1979) knowledge-experience distinction. The subjective experiences that readers need to monitor are those that arise from processes of building a mental representation of the meaning of a text. However, when metacognitive knowledge is used as a heuristic that directly influences judgments of learning, then it bypasses the active monitoring process and use of representation cues. In essence, the judgments are no longer about learning, but are merely performance predictions based on a priori knowledge of factors that may or may not have some impact on whatever learning actually occurred.

Measures of Monitoring Accuracy

In the metacomprehension literature, a standard approach has been developed to assess the accuracy of these self-evaluations and the ability of students to monitor their ongoing comprehension processes (Glenberg & Epstein, 1985; Maki, 1998). In the typical metacomprehension paradigm, participants read a series of texts on a variety of topics, then rate their comprehension of each text, and complete a test for each text. Following the lead of metamemory research on paired associate learning (Nelson, 1984), a person's monitoring accuracy is operationalized as the intraindividual correlation between a person's comprehension ratings and actual test performances across the set of texts. More accurate self-evaluation or greater monitoring accuracy is indexed by stronger correlations. A standard term for this predictive accuracy measure is *relative metacomprehension accuracy*. This relative accuracy paradigm targets ongoing active monitoring of actual learning progress independent from either the level of progress itself (Nelson, 1984) or the learner's ability to make heuristic guesses about average progress based on general a priori beliefs about themselves or the task (Griffin et al., 2009).

In addition, this paradigm attempts to tap into the kinds of decisions a student must make as they decide among homework activities. If a student does not accurately differentiate well-learned material from less-learned material, time could be wasted studying material that is already well learned while no time would be devoted to material that has not yet been adequately learned. Students will also fail to realize when current study strategies are not working and new ones are needed. Consistent with this proposition, relative monitoring accuracy has been demonstrated to relate positively to self-regulated learning outcomes (Thiede, Anderson, & Therriault, 2003).

There are several reasons why relative accuracy has become the standard for determining monitoring accuracy. The other measures of metacognitive judgments (i.e., confidence bias, absolute accuracy) differ from relative accuracy in important ways. A central premise of research on metacognitive monitoring and SRL is the recognition that students do not have unlimited time to engage in study, and principled decisions need to be made about what should be studied or restudied for efficient self-regulated learning. Only measures of relative metacomprehension accuracy address this aspect of SRL.

Beyond this ecologically valid feature of the relative accuracy paradigm, a major reason for the increasing dominance of the relative accuracy paradigm in metacomprehension research is because it represents a measure of monitoring that is not heavily dependent upon average test performance (Nelson, 1984; Yates, 1990). Other methods used to assess monitoring accuracy simply compute the difference between judgments of learning and objective performance. As such, they are just as dependent upon how well a learner generally performs as they are on their skill in monitoring that performance. These methods include *absolute accuracy* which computes the unsigned absolute difference and *confidence bias* which computes the signed difference (Maki, 1998). Two people with poor monitoring skills who both just use a midpoint-of-the-scale heuristic can have drastically different absolute accuracy or confidence bias just because of differences in performance. Not only will the readers differ in accuracy despite no differences in their monitoring process, but one could have extremely high accuracy even though neither are actually monitoring at all and both are merely using a general anchoring heuristic. With relative accuracy, both readers would wind up with a poor accuracy score close to a correlation of zero, which would validly reflect the fact that they failed to monitor. In addition, since average performance levels often reflect relatively stable individual differences and can be systematically impacted by features of the learning context, all of these non-metacognitive factors will systematically produce differences in absolute accuracy and confidence bias, even when there are no differences in either the judgments themselves or the psychological processes that give rise to them. Differences on these measures may not reflect anything about metacognitive processes or skills.

Confidence bias brings even more interpretive problems, because it is not a linear measure of degree of accuracy but rather of the amount of directional bias in whatever errors exist. A score of zero reflects a lack of directional bias, and positive scores reflect more overconfidence errors while negative scores reflect more under-confidence errors (see Yates, 1990). One person with a higher score than another can be either less under-confident or more overconfident and either less accurate or more accurate depending on where each of these two people being compared happen to be in relation to the zero point. Group means for confidence bias reflect whether more people were over or under confident and do not represent the average level of accuracy of individuals. As a result, differences in this measure reflect neither monitoring nor accuracy.

One benefit of relative accuracy that has not been previously emphasized is that the independence of relative accuracy from average performance makes it the only measure of accuracy that necessarily reflects the actual monitoring of ongoing learning. Because it is not dependent upon average performance, high relative accuracy cannot be achieved by the use of heuristic meta-knowledge, even when that knowledge is accurate. Instead, high relative accuracy requires active attention to the ongoing learning process and its variable outcomes. Whether a reader has accurate knowledge about their own general skill in science learning might greatly impact both their absolute accuracy and their confidence bias, but this heuristic will be of little relevance in predicting their understanding of a text on volcanoes relative to their understanding of a text on evolution. This positive feature of relative accuracy makes it a superior measure of a students' ability to actually monitor ongoing learning processes which is the heart of the self-regulation processes in SRL. Absolute accuracy and confidence bias measures are not capable of discriminating real monitoring from either performance effects or the reliance on heuristic judgments that bypass monitoring processes in predicted overall performance levels.

As shown in Fig. 2.1, knowledge of and use of study strategies that determine what actions and operations are enacted play a very different role in SRL than experience monitoring. Study strategies are largely object-level constructs that guide actions which may or may not happen to evoke attention to meta-level experiences as represented by the regulatory loop. Yet, a number of researchers have used terminology such as metacognitive monitoring to refer to monitoring of one's strategy use. Even when increased knowledge of study strategies has positive effects on learning, it may not affect the regulation process. In fact, if learners become overly confident in their existing strategy-outcome beliefs, they may rely more heavily on these beliefs at the expense of monitoring subjective experience. Thus, theoretically, strategy instruction cannot be assumed to lead to better monitoring of learning progress and in fact could harm it.

In addition to a lack of theoretical basis to generally assume a positive effect of strategy knowledge or use on monitoring accuracy, there is a lack of empirical support. The few studies in the metacognitive knowledge literature that have measured JOLs have operationalized accuracy with the problematic measures of absolute accuracy or confidence bias (e.g., Schraw & Dennison, 1994), while failing to account for the non-monitoring influences of average performance and heuristic cues that plague these measures. Learning environments cannot be presumed to have improved monitoring processes unless improvements in JOL accuracy can be demonstrated independent from any effects on performance itself. And, unless a measure of relative accuracy is employed, then claims of benefits in monitoring skills are unwarranted.

Improving Monitoring Accuracy with a Valid Cues Approach

Both models and data suggest that accurate metacognitive monitoring of ongoing learning is central to effective regulation of study (e.g., Metcalfe, 2002; Nelson & Narens, 1990; Thiede, Griffin, Wiley, & Redford, 2009; Winne & Hadwin, 1998; Zimmerman, 2002). Because accurate monitoring is so critical for effective SRL, it is of great concern that the typical finding from the metacomprehension literature is that levels of monitoring accuracy are quite low. Several independent reviews have reported that the mean intraindividual correlation between comprehension ratings and test performance across numerous studies is only about +0.27 (Dunlosky & Lipko, 2007; Lin & Zabrucky, 1998; Maki, 1998). A recent comprehensive review of all published studies of relative monitoring accuracy for learning from text done in the last 30 years arrived at the same figure of 0.27 for the average among baseline conditions (Thiede et al., 2009). This review also showed that the majority of manipulations have little effect in improving this accuracy. The above analysis of cue validity suggests that in order to be accurate, students need to be monitoring cues directly related to reading experiences and not just relying on heuristic bases for their judgments. However, there are many levels on which one can attempt to monitor their reading processes, and only some of these are predictive of comprehension. When considering learning from text, we must bear in mind that a text can be processed at several levels from surface memory of the exact words to constructing a conceptual model of the meaning of the text (Graesser, Millis, & Zwaan, 1997; Kintsch, 1998). To make accurate judgments of comprehension, readers need to reflect specifically on experiences that correspond to the level of representation the learning task requires. Because it is a person's situation model that largely determines his or her performance on tests of comprehension (Kintsch, 1998; McNamara et al., 1996), metacomprehension monitoring will be most accurate when situation-model level cues are utilized (Rawson, Dunlosky, & Thiede, 2000; Wiley, Griffin, & Thiede, 2005). For example, Thiede, Griffin, Wiley, and Anderson (2010) observed that most readers self-report that they base their judgments of learning upon heuristic judgment cues related to text features (e.g., "the text was long") or upon beliefs about their own skill and familiarity with the topic. Readers' reported use of representation cues was largely limited to how much of the text they could remember. Both the reliance on heuristic and immediate memory cues were associated with poor monitoring accuracy, while those few readers who did self-report relying upon situation-model-level cues (like the ability to explain a causal process described in the text to someone else) tended to have superior monitoring accuracy. The assumption that monitoring accuracy can be improved by shifting readers to rely more upon valid situation-model cues is the foundation for our work described below.

Instantiating a Relative Accuracy Paradigm

In these studies, our goal has been attempting to find conditions that improve readers' ability to accurately judge their own level of comprehension from text using a standard relative accuracy paradigm. The texts are approximately 1,000 words long and are on science topics such as the vision system. Sets of five to six texts on different topics are generally used. Students read all texts, then they are asked to judge their level of comprehension for each text ("How many items do you think you will get correct on a 5 item test?"), and then they take comprehension tests in the same order as reading. The comprehension tests consist of five multiple-choice items tapping inferences that follow from each text.

Design Considerations for Texts

Wiley et al. (2005) pointed out that the design of the expository texts and comprehension tests are both critical to examining metacomprehension accuracy. Only texts that have clearly distinguishable surface and situation-model representations and only test questions that can be answered using just one or the other representation will lead to interpretable results. Thus, we use explanatory science texts for which the situation model is not entirely explicit within the surface model of the text. Since creating the situation model for a text involves generating inferential connections, it is important to construct texts that can test whether the reader is making connections beyond what is explicitly stated. Our own texts typically describe a complex causal relation (e.g., the relation between continental and ocean plates and the emergence of volcanoes). For example, a well-developed situation model for the volcano text would contain inferential links such as "the least likely place for a volcano is in the center of a plate." The key here is that this connection needs to be constructed by the reader. The text itself does not contain this statement. Based on previous research (Kintsch, 1998), we believe that comprehension is best represented by a person's situation model for a text, and the quality of reader's understanding of a text can best be discerned by assessing whether the person can recognize causal inferences implied by a text (Trabasso & Wiley, 2005; Wiley & Myers, 2003). When the test performance being predicted reflects the quality of a reader's situation model, then the accuracy of the monitoring judgments represents meta*comprehension,* as opposed to meta*memory* for explicitly stated idea units within a text. Although readers must also comprehend explicitly stated ideas, researchers must take care to create tests that require actual understanding of those ideas rather than mere memory for words.

Design Considerations for Tests

We also have specific considerations for the design of our comprehension tests. One important feature is that they contain more than one or two items. Weaver (1990) addressed the weaknesses associated with assessing comprehension monitoring with limited items per text. In particular, he argued that a one-item test does not provide a reliable measure of comprehension. Moreover, using a one-item test creates an issue of content coverage, where computed monitoring accuracy is highly contingent upon the arbitrary overlap between what portion of the text the test covers and what portion the readers emphasized in their judgment. Thus, it is important to use tests with multiple items that assess comprehension of the majority of the content presented in the text.

Perhaps more important, the tests must also provide a valid measure of comprehension (i.e., tap the situation model of the text). With these concerns in mind, we have developed multiple-choice tests (following Royer, Carlo, Dufrense, & Mestre, 1996 and Wiley & Voss, 1999) that directly tap understanding of text content by asking students to verify inferences that follow from the texts. Performance on the inference tests that we have developed reliably correlates with other learning assessments, including performance on "how" and "why" essay questions (Sanchez & Wiley, 2006; Wiley et al., 2009), as well as with performance on the Nelson Denny (Griffin et al., 2008).

Design Considerations for Judgments

The valid cues approach suggests that the more strongly a cue is diagnostic of the mental representation that will determine test performance, the more valid and predictive of performance it will be. An extreme illustration of this point is that postdictions are generally very accurate (Maki & Serra, 1992; Pierce & Smith, 2001). A postdiction is when a person simply predicts future performance based on a prior test that assesses the same mental representation. The cues that are generated by the initial test with the same items are directly diagnostic for later performance, which explains the postdiction superiority effect. However, note that providing learners with the actual test questions and the experience of answering them circumvents the need for engaging in monitoring of the learning experience. Postdiction judgments are more accurate because they do not rely upon the metacognitive system and do not require any actual metacognitive monitoring which is what learners struggle with. For this reason, predictive judgments are more useful as a measure of online monitoring processes. It is also useful if the judgments are made in the same metric as the test scores.

Supporting Access to Valid Comprehension Cues

In earlier work (Thiede et al., 2003), having students engage in delayed generation tasks (keyword listing or summaries) after reading produced unprecedented levels of metacomprehension accuracy compared to an immediate generation control group. Because both groups engaged in generation, an implication was that the delay itself was responsible. However, Thiede, Dunlosky, Griffin, and Wiley (2005) conducted a series of follow-up studies that independently manipulated delay and generation tasks. Simply delaying judgments did nothing to accuracy and neither did having readers perform non-generative tasks at a delay, such as reading a list of keywords or being prompted to "think about the text." The key to producing better monitoring accuracy was in making readers perform a specific type of generative self-test. In this case, these generation tasks (summary or keyword listing) only yielded benefits when performed at a delay. This is because these tasks can be done using surface memory when performed immediately, but the surface representation decays with a delay while the situation model is more robust over time (Kintsch, Welsch, Schmalhofer, & Zimny, 1990). It was not delaying judgments themselves but being directed to perform a delayed generation task as a self-test that increased readers' access to the appropriate representation cues and improved monitoring accuracy.

Griffin et al. (2008) provided further evidence that certain types of self-testing targeted toward situation-model cues can increase accuracy. One study employed self-explanation as the type of self-test designed to increase access to valid cues. Readers who engaged in a self-explanation task while reading had significantly higher metacomprehension accuracy than those who simply reread. Self-explanation requires readers to simultaneously construct and self-test their situation model by asking themselves how certain ideas fit together with the theme of the text (Chi, 2000; Wiley & Voss, 1999). Accuracy improved even without delaying judgments. Self-explanation directly involves the situation model, making the timing less relevant to what cues are accessed by it, unlike keyword lists and summaries that could be based largely in a surface representation when performed immediately. Another important aspect of this study was that there was actually no effect of self-explanation on test performance itself. One should not view the lack of learning gains in this study as conflicting with other research on self-explanation, since these students received neither training in how to self-explain nor did they have the opportunities for restudy that have supported better learning in other studies (Chi, 2000; McNamara, 2004). Instead, the lack of effects on performance allows for the conclusion that self-explanation had its effect on monitoring, since performance was not affected but accuracy was improved.

Another study reported by Griffin et al. (2008) has shown that simple rereading can improve metacomprehension accuracy, but only for readers with limited attentional resources or low comprehension skill. These effects were interpreted as demonstrating that readers with limited or taxed attentional resources during a single reading can use a second reading to attend to important online experience-based representation cues. Without the resources to attend to these cues during a first reading, readers are forced to rely more heavily on heuristic cues. Together these studies from the first phase of our research program suggest that the key factor in utilizing valid representation cues is having access to these cues, both by being able to attend to them when available and making them more available by employing self-tests designed to target the appropriate level of representation. This work utilizing delayed generation, rereading, and self-explanation has been successful at producing uncommon levels of monitoring accuracy, raising intraindividual correlations between judgments and performance from the usual 0.27 to above 0.6 in most cases.

Supporting the Selection of Valid Comprehension Cues

The interventions previously described direct readers to engage in cognitive actions designed to evoke certain metacognitive experiences and make valid representation cues more accessible. Although this increase in accessibility makes valid cue use more likely, optimal cue use will also require readers to actively discriminate and select among those cues available to them. If texts and tests require students to gain conceptual understanding, for example, of scientific processes and phenomena from expository text, then it is important to prompt students to override the "reading for memory" setting evident in their self-reported selection of memory cues over situation-model cues (Thiede et al., 2010). Readers need to realize that their goal for reading is to try to understand how or why a phenomena or process occurs and that the questions they will be asked will depend on making connections and causal inferences across sentences, in order to engage in monitoring of the most relevant experiences. This influence of cue selection on monitoring is depicted in Fig. 2.1 as the arrow from *monitoring goals* that intersects the link between *experiences* and *monitoring*. In terms of Winne and Hadwin (1998), we suggest that in order to engage in effective SRL, learners need meta-knowledge of standards on which their learning can be evaluated. In terms of the present model, learners' monitoring goals need to reflect the appropriate level of understanding or type of learning, so that they can selectively attend to and make use of those metacognitive experiences that reflect this level of understanding.

Thus, in a second series of experiments, we attempted to shape the selection of valid cues by influencing learners' test expectancies with an explicit statement about the inferential nature of the final test items they should expect and the need to make connections between different parts of a text. Readers were also given practice texts and tests with inference items to set the expectation. This manipulation has been highly effective in improving relative monitoring accuracy (Thiede, Wiley, & Griffin, 2011). In additional studies, we have found that when combining this test-expectancy manipulation with a self-explanation instruction, the two interventions had independent effects, suggesting that both cue accessibility and cue selection are determining accuracy and are distinct contributors to cue use (Wiley et al., 2008).

Negative Effects of Providing Feedback

It is critical to note that in the above test-expectancy studies, students were not provided with any performance feedback on the practice tests. The effects of test expectancy were assessed by a transfer paradigm in which monitoring goals had to be generalized from the practice trials and applied to new texts and tests.

Given that attention to internal experiences defines metacognitive monitoring, externally provided performance feedback during practice tests may short-circuit effective monitoring of ongoing learning by shifting readers' attention from internal to external cues. Overt judgments of learning will no longer be based in inferences derived from the experience monitoring process, but rather based in the externally provided information, such as simply anchoring all future judgments on the numerical score one received on the previous tests. When external feedback is predictive of future performance, such as when the future tests are on the same material, the accuracy of JOLs may increase even though readers are no longer truly monitoring. However, when accurate JOLs depend upon actual meta-level monitoring because the feedback on past performance is not related to future performance, then JOL accuracy could be harmed by feedback.

An example of such a scenario is when learners' might receive feedback on their performance on one set of texts, but later need to monitor their learning for a new set of texts on different topics. On the one hand, the practice tests provide a basis for abstracting a transferable expectancy they can use to guide their monitoring during future texts, but on the other hand the concrete numerical performance scores on the practice tests may become the basis for future judgments on other texts, without regard to the fact that they are about different topics and thus require an independent judgment. In other words, the readers might merely transfer the concrete numerical performance scores from one text to another rather than the more abstract concept about the general nature of the type of test and level of comprehension required.

We tested this scenario by employing the same test-expectancy paradigm previously described, but added two feedback conditions. Both feedback conditions were identical to the inference test-expectancy condition, except they also gave readers performance feedback (i.e., number of questions answered correctly) for the practice inference tests. One of the feedback conditions also reminded readers of their JOLs in relation to their actual practice performance. If feedback undermines experience monitoring, then the benefits of having a valid monitoring goal created by inference test expectancy should disappear when that expectancy is accompanied by prior performance feedback. The results supported this hypothesis, revealing that the notably improved monitoring accuracy by providing inference test expectancies ($r=0.49$) versus control ($r=0.15$) was completely eliminated by simply adding feedback on practice test performance ($r=0.21$). Apparently, readers focused upon the external concrete practice feedback and failed to transfer an expectancy about the more general nature of the tests. We do not know whether the participants in this study actually failed to engage in monitoring due to the feedback or whether they simply failed to use the cues derived from that monitoring when making their judgments. But, it is clear that readers were unduly influenced by their past performance scores when predicting future performance, even though those scores had little relevance. Obviously, feedback can have a number of positive effects on learning. The point here is that the development of accurate monitoring skills may be best aided by practice tests that are not accompanied by concrete numerical performance feedback.

Implications for the Design of Learning Technologies

This chapter has attempted to explicate an empirically grounded and detailed theoretical framework for understanding the various related but distinct components of SRL. The emphasis has been upon the importance of accurate metacognitive monitoring for engaging in effective regulation of learning. Understanding these conceptual and theoretical issues is critical for those who seek to develop instructional environments to foster the development of self-regulation skills. In particular, we highlight a few observations about the implications of this approach for the design of learning environments.

Regulation Is a Process of Making Decisions

Effective self-regulated learning involves decisions about what to read next, what to reread, and what strategies to apply as you are reading. If you take those decisions away from the learner, then you rob them of the opportunity to develop skills in regulating their learning. Learning environments may not be able to support both the most efficient learning at the cognitive level and the development of regulatory skills at the metacognitive level simultaneously. Conditions that aid learning of content (such as by matching difficulty of the learning task to each student's ability or prescribing strategy use) may lead to improvements in learning for that unit when the student is supported by the system. However, they may obviate the need for the student to grapple with difficulties and make their own choices about what to study next and how to study it, which may have negative consequences for their ability to engage in effective SRL in new, unsupported contexts.

More often, the strategies that are supported by learning technologies are study strategies that more directly support learning. Learning environments designed to foster students' knowledge of effective study strategies should avoid breeding excessive confidence in the global efficacy of specific strategies. Rather, students could be taught a repertoire of strategies, made aware that strategy effectiveness is context dependent, and prompted to always monitor their learning progress and reassess effectiveness of each strategy in each particular learning context. This decision process would help to support reflection and regulation skills, especially if coupled with instruction in strategy use explicitly for the purpose of monitoring, such as self-testing or self-explanation.

Regulation Is a Process of Self-Evaluation

If you give feedback, then readers no longer need to self-evaluate. As we have shown above, giving feedback can be problematic for monitoring accuracy. Dictating the use of a particular learning strategy also obviates the need for self-evaluation. To support SRL, learning environments need to support self-testing and online monitoring strategies. Theoretically, the only types of strategy knowledge and use that should directly impact monitoring are those that explicitly direct learners' attention toward metacognitive processing, such as attending to the ease with which one can summarize information or answer self-generated questions as an indicator of comprehension. However, these *metacognitive* monitoring strategies are not well represented on the most commonly used inventories. They also do not seem to be the type of strategies that are taught or supported in most learning technology environments. Indeed many intelligent tutoring and cognitive tutoring systems remove the need to monitor one's own level of performance and regulate actions as the learning technology is often designed to monitor students' learning for them.

Final Thoughts

Accurately monitoring one's current state of understanding during a cognitive task is a central feature of effective control and self-regulation that impacts learning for both that task and potentially for future tasks. Monitoring one's "experiences of puzzlement or failure," such as a "sense that you do not yet know a certain chapter in your text well enough," is critical for creating new subgoals, applying alternate strategies, and revising one's metacognitive knowledge about the effectiveness of the strategies (Flavell, p. 908). In other words, the monitoring of the dynamic and changing states of one's learning progress is what tells a reader *when* they need to intensify, reduce, stop, or alter the cognitive learning strategies being employed and is what informs the learner what strategies should be modified, deleted, or added to the strategy knowledge base for use on future tasks. Without this monitoring of actual learning, a learner is not engaging the heart of self-regulated learning. Further, without studies that directly assess the accuracy of this monitoring, it is difficult to draw conclusions about which learning technologies may improve the monitoring skills needed for effective SRL. To provide the opportunity for the development of effective regulatory skills, learning environments need to be careful not to deprive students of the opportunity to monitor their own understanding.

References

Benjamin, A. S., & Bjork, R. A. (1996). Retrieval fluency as a metacognitive index. In L. M. Reder (Ed.), *Implicit memory and metacognition* (pp. 309–38). Hillsdale, NJ: Erlbaum.

Bromme, R., Pieschl, S., & Stahl, E. (2010). Epistemological beliefs are standards for adaptive learning. *Metacognition and Learning, 5*, 7–26.

Caverly, D. G., Nicholson, S. A., & Radcliffe, R. (2004). The effectiveness of strategic reading instruction for college developmental readers. *Journal of College Reading and Learning, 35*, 25–46.

Chi, M. T. H. (2000). Self explaining expository texts: The dual processes of generating inferences and repairing mental models. In R. Glaser (Ed.), *Advances in instructional psychology* (pp. 161–238). Hillsdale, NJ: Erlbaum.

Cromley, J. G., & Azevedo, R. (2006). Self-report of reading comprehension strategies: What are we measuring? *Metacognition and Learning, 1*, 229–247.

Dinsmore, D. L., Alexander, P. A., & Loughlin, S. M. (2008). Focusing the conceptual lens on metacognition, self-regulation, and self-regulated learning. *Educational Psychology Review, 20*, 429–444.

Dunlosky, J., & Lipko, A. R. (2007). Metacomprehension: A brief history and how to improve its accuracy. *Current Directions in Psychological Science, 16*, 228–232.

Dunlosky, J., & Nelson, T. O. (1992). Importance of the kind of cue for judgments of learning (JOL) and the delayed-JOL effect. *Memory & Cognition, 20*, 374–380.

Fischer, P. M., & Mandl, H. (1984). Learner, text variables, and the control of text comprehension and recall. In H. Mandl, N. L. Stein, & T. Trabasso (Eds.), *Learning and comprehension of text* (pp. 213–254). Hillsdale, NJ: Erlbaum.

Flavell, J. H. (1979). Metacognition and cognitive monitoring: A new area of cognitive developmental inquiry. *American Psychologist, 34*, 906–911.

Glenberg, A. M., & Epstein, W. (1985). Calibration of comprehension. *Journal of Experimental Psychology: Learning, Memory, and Cognition, 11*, 702–718.

Graesser, A. C., Millis, K. K., & Zwaan, R. A. (1997). Discourse comprehension. *Annual Review of Psychology, 48*, 163–189.

Griffin, T. D., Jee, B. D., & Wiley, J. (2009). The effects of domain knowledge on metacomprehension accuracy. *Memory & Cognition, 37*, 1001–13.

Griffin, T. D., Wiley, J., & Thiede, K. W. (2008). Individual differences, rereading, and self explanation: Concurrent processing and cue validity as constraints on metacomprehension accuracy. *Memory & Cognition, 36*, 93–103.

Hacker, D. J. (1998). Self-regulated comprehension during normal reading. In D. J. Hacker, J. Dunlosky, & A. C. Graesser (Eds.), *Metacognition in educational theory and practice* (pp. 165–191). Mahwah, NJ: Erlbaum.

Hofer, B. K. (2004). Epistemological understanding as a metacognitive process: thinking aloud during online searching. *Educational Psychologist, 39*, 43–56.

Hofer, B. K., & Sinatra, G. M. (2010). Epistemology, metacognition, and self-regulation: musings on an emerging field. *Metacognition and Learning, 5*, 113–120.

Kintsch, W. (1998). *Comprehension: A paradigm for cognition*. New York: Cambridge University Press.

Kintsch, W., Welsch, D., Schmalhofer, F., & Zimny, S. (1990). Sentence memory: A theoretical analysis. *Journal of Memory and Language, 29*, 133–159.

Kitchener, K. S. (1983). Cognition, metacognition, and epistemic cognition: a three-level model of cognitive processing. *Human Development, 26*, 106–116.

Koriat, A. (1997). Monitoring one's own knowledge during study: A cue-utilization approach to judgments of learning. *Journal of Experimental Psychology. General, 126*, 349–370.

Kuhn, D. (1999). A developmental model of critical thinking. *Educational Research, 28*, 16–26.

Lin, L., & Zabrucky, K. M. (1998). Calibration of comprehension: Research and implications for education and instruction. *Contemporary Educational Psychology, 23*, 345–391.

Maki, R. H. (1998). Test predictions over text material. In D. J. Hacker, J. Dunlosky, & A. C. Graesser (Eds.), *Metacognition in educational theory and practice* (pp. 117–144). Hillsdale, NJ: Erlbaum.

Maki, R. H., & Serra, M. (1992). Role of practice tests in the accuracy of test predictions on text material. *Journal of Educational Psychology, 84*, 200–210.

Mason, L., Boldrin, A., & Ariasi, N. (2010). Epistemic metacognition in context: evaluating and learning online information. *Metacognition and Learning, 5*, 67–90.

McNamara, D. S. (2004). Self-explanation reading training. *Discourse Processes, 38*, 1–30.

McNamara, D. S., Kintsch, E., Songer, N. B., & Kintsch, W. (1996). Are good texts always better? *Cognition and Instruction, 14*, 1–43.

Metcalfe, J. (2002). Is study time allocated selectively to a region of proximal learning? *Journal of Experimental Psychology. General, 131*, 349–363.

Mokhtari, K., & Reichard, C. A. (2002). Assessing student's metacognitive awareness of reading strategies. *Journal of Educational Psychology, 94*, 249–259.

Moore, D., Zabrucky, K., & Commander, N. E. (1997). Validation of the metacomprehension scale. *Contemporary Educational Psychology, 22*, 457–471.

Muis, K. R. (2008). Epistemic profiles and self-regulated learning. *Contemporary Educational Psychology, 33*, 177–208.

Muis, K. R., & Franco, G. (2010). Epistemic profiles and metacognition: support for the consistency hypothesis. *Metacognition and Learning, 5*, 27–45.

Nelson, T. O. (1984). A comparison of current measures of feeling-of-knowing accuracy. *Psychological Bulletin, 95*, 109–133.

Nelson, T. O., & Narens, L. (1990). Metamemory: A theoretical framework and new findings. In G. H. Bower (Ed.), *The psychology of learning and motivation* (Vol. 26, pp. 125–141). New York: Academic.

Pierce, B. H., & Smith, S. M. (2001). The postdiction superiority effect in metacomprehension of text. *Memory & Cognition, 29*, 62–67.

Pintrich, P. R., Wolters, C., & Baxter, G. (2000). Assessing metacognition and self-regulated learning. In G. Schraw & J. Impara (Eds.), *Issues in the measurement of metacognition* (pp. 43–97). Lincoln, NE: Buros Institute of Mental Measurement.

Pressley, M. (2002). Metacognition and self-regulated comprehension. In A. Farstrup & S. J. Samuels (Eds.), *What research has to say about reading instruction* (3rd ed., pp. 184–200). Newark, De: International Reading Association.

Rawson, K. A., Dunlosky, J., & Thiede, K. W. (2000). The rereading effect: Metacomprehension accuracy improves across reading trials. *Memory & Cognition, 28*, 1004–1010.

Richter, T., & Schmid, S. (2010). Epistemological beliefs and epistemic strategies in self- regulated learning. *Metacognition and Learning, 5*, 47–65.

Royer, J. M., Carlo, M. S., Dufrense, R., & Mestre, J. (1996). The assessment of levels of domain expertise while reading. *Cognition and Instruction, 14*, 373–408.

Sanchez, C., & Wiley, J. (2006). Effects of working memory capacity on learning from illustrated text. *Memory & Cognition, 34*, 344–355.

Schraw, G., & Dennison, R. S. (1994). Assessing metacognitive awareness. *Contemporary Educational Psychology, 19*, 460–475.

Stahl, E., Pieschl, S., & Bromme, R. (2006). Task complexity, epistemological beliefs, and metacognitive calibration: An exploratory study. *Journal of Educational Computing Research, 35*, 319–338.

Thiede, K. W., Anderson, M. C. M., & Therriault, D. (2003). Accuracy of metacognitive monitoring affects learning of texts. *Journal of Educational Psychology, 95*, 66–73.

Thiede, K. W., Dunlosky, J., Griffin, T. D., & Wiley, J. (2005). Understanding the delayed keyword effect on metacomprehension accuracy. *Journal of Experiment Psychology: Learning, Memory and Cognition, 31*, 1267–1280.

Thiede, K. W., Griffin, T. D., Wiley, J., & Anderson, M. (2010). Poor metacomprehension accuracy as a result of inappropriate cue use. *Discourse Processes, 47*, 331–362.

Thiede, K. W., Griffin, T. D., Wiley, J., & Redford, J. S. (2009). Metacognitive monitoring during and after reading. In D. J. Hacker, J. Dunlosky, & A. C. Graesser (Eds.), *Handbook of metacognition and self-regulated learning* (pp. 85–106). Mahwah, NJ: Erlbaum.

Thiede, K. W., Wiley, J., & Griffin, T. D. (2011). Test expectancy affects metacomprehension accuracy. *British Journal of Educational Psychology, 81*, 264–273.

Trabasso, T., & Wiley, J. (2005). Goal plans of action and inferences during comprehension of narratives. *Discourse Processes, 39*, 129–164.

Weaver, C. A. (1990). Constraining factors in calibration of comprehension. *Journal of Experimental Psychology: Learning, Memory, and Cognition, 16*, 214–222.

Wiley, J., Goldman, S., Graesser, A., Sanchez, C. A., Ash, I. K., & Hemmerich, J. (2009). Source evaluation, comprehension, and learning in internet science inquiry tasks. *American Educational Research Journal, 46*, 1060–1106.

Wiley, J., Griffin, T., & Thiede, K. W. (2005). Putting the comprehension in metacomprehension. *The Journal of General Psychology, 132*, 408–428.

Wiley, J., Griffin, T. D., & Thiede, K. W. (2008). To understand your understanding you must understand what understanding means. In V. Sloutsky, B. Love, & K. McRae (Eds.), *Proceedings of the 30th annual conference of the Cognitive Science Society*. Cognitive Science Society: Austin, TX.

Wiley, J., & Myers, J. L. (2003). Availability and accessibility of information and causal inferences from scientific text. *Discourse Processes, 36*, 109–129.

Wiley, J., & Voss, J. F. (1999). Constructing arguments from multiple sources. *Journal of Educational Psychology, 91*, 301–311.

Winne, P. H., & Hadwin, A. F. (1998). Studying as self-regulated learning. In D. J. Hacker, J. Dunlosky, & A. C. Graesser (Eds.), *Metacognition in educational theory and practice* (pp. 277–304). Mahwah, NJ: Erlbaum.

Yates, J. F. (1990). *Judgment and decision making*. Englewood Cliffs, NJ: Prentice-Hall.

Zimmerman, B. J. (2002). Becoming a self-regulated learner: An overview. *Theory into Practice, 41*, 64–72.

Student and Teacher Perspectives on IMPROVE Self-Regulation Prompts in Web-Based Learning

3

Bracha Kramarski and Tova Michalsky

Abstract

This chapter describes the results of eight controlled experimentations examining different conditions for implementation of the IMPROVE self-questioning prompts (Kramarski & Mevarech, 2003; Mevarech & Kramarski, 1997) in web-based learning environments from two perspectives, first for students' learning in the classroom, and second for preservice teachers' learning during their professional preparation. The IMPROVE method aims to support key aspects of self-regulation targeting learning processes. In evaluating the effect of the IMPROVE prompts, we focused our efforts on assessing progress at high levels of conceptual understanding in the learning domain, referring to mathematical or scientific reasoning among students and teachers alike and also referring to designing traditional and technology-based lessons among the teachers. Thus, we assessed whether learners performed well not only on immediate posttests with items similar to training, but also on tests measuring near and far transfer. In addition, we assessed acquisition of self-regulated learning (SRL) that included offline aptitude questionnaires and online process measures during real-time forum discussions. In this chapter we critically discuss the findings and raise directions for practical implications and future inquiry.

Student and Teacher Perspectives on IMPROVE Self-Regulation Prompts in Web-Based Learning

This chapter reviews our recent research series examining different conditions for implementation of the IMPROVE self-questioning prompts (Kramarski & Mevarech, 2003; Mevarech & Kramarski, 1997) in Web-based learning environments (WBLEs). The IMPROVE method

B. Kramarski, Ph.D. (✉) • T. Michalsky, Ph.D.
School of Education, Bar-Ilan University, Ramat-Gan 52900, Israel
e-mail: bracha.kramarski@biu.ac.il; tova.michalsky@biu.ac.il

R. Azevedo and V. Aleven (eds.), *International Handbook of Metacognition and Learning Technologies*, Springer International Handbooks of Education 26, DOI 10.1007/978-1-4419-5546-3_3,

aims to support key aspects of self-regulation targeting learning processes. We focused on the different conditions' impact on learning in two domain contents—mathematics and science—and on acquisition of the targeted self-regulated learning (SRL) skills. We describe the results of eight controlled experimentations performed in the context of real educational settings from two perspectives, first for students' learning in the classroom and second for preservice teachers' learning during their professional preparation. Our studies followed educators' and researchers' call for SRL support to facilitate effective student learning in self-directed open-ended WBLEs (Pintrich, 2000; Zimmerman, 2000) as well as for teachers' ability to promote these processes among students (e.g., Putnam & Borko, 2000; Randi & Corno, 2000).

We have defined four goals for effective support of SRL skills, where each builds on the previous one. The first goal is for learners (students and teachers) to advance their SRL skills within WBLEs while receiving IMPROVE prompts. Ideally, this advancement will lead to better learning gains in the domain targeted by the supported environment, which comprises the second goal of SRL support. The third goal is for learners to internalize the SRL knowledge and skills and thus to demonstrate better SRL in subsequent instruction using a similar environment (near transfer). Our fourth goal is that learners will improve their future domain-level learning (far and long-term transfer) based on the SRL they internalized.

In evaluating the effect of the IMPROVE prompts, we focused our efforts on assessing progress at high levels of conceptual understanding in the learning domain, referring to mathematical or scientific reasoning among students and teachers alike and also referring to designing traditional and technology-based lessons among the teachers (e.g., Kramarski, 2008; Kramarski & Revach, 2009). Thus, we assessed whether learners performed well not only on immediate posttests with items highly similar to training but also on tests measuring near and far transfer. Furthermore, we designed complementary means for assessing SRL, including offline aptitude questionnaires and online process measures during real-time learning. SRL assessment issues are very important, in light of SRL's complex structure and researchers' emphases on the need for measurements and methods to characterize unfolding patterns of engagement in online based SRL, in terms of tactics and strategies that constitute SRL (e.g., Greene & Azevedo, 2010; Veenman, 2007; Winne & Perry, 2000).

Next, we present the theoretical framework for our research and then a synthesis of our main studies (see Table 3.1 for a summary). Finally, we critically discuss the findings, propose practical implications, and raise directions for future inquiry.

Theoretical Framework

Web-Based Learning Environments

Standards of mathematics and science education have emphasized the importance of engaging students in meaningful learning as part of a coherent curriculum for developing conceptual understanding (Programme for International Student Assessment—PISA, 2003). These standards raise challenges for learning environments to engage students in multilayered processes of learning and teaching.

Researchers have explored a variety of WBLE alternatives as means of enhancing conceptual understanding in mathematics and science in different age groups (e.g., Azevedo, 2005; Kramarski & Michalsky, 2009a, 2010). WBLEs are computer-based tools that consist of nodes of information inter-connected using hyperlinks. Such environments contain multiple representations of information including video, audio, diagrams, text, and animations (Azevedo, 2005; Azevedo & Jacobson, 2008). WBLEs offer several unique advantages for promoting meaningful conceptual learning. Their linked structure affords opportunities "to seek rather than to comply, to experiment rather than to accept, to evaluate rather than to accumulate, and to interpret rather than to adopt" (Hannafin & Land, 1997, p. 175). Such opportunities for learning arise not only at the individual level but also at the social level, where

Table 3.1 Summary of eight studies in both perspectives (student and teacher)

	Authors (year)	Design	Treatment	Measures
Students' perspective	(A) Kramarski and Mizrachi (2006)	86 seventh-grade students Four online instructional methods: Online + META F2F + META Online F2F 4 weeks Mathematics problem-solving context	IMPROVE prompts on an index card Practicing in pairs	Pre/post Mathematics tasks: Authentic online tasks (PISA, 2003) Authentic pencil and paper (near transfer) Standard pencil and paper (far transfer) SRL self-report questionnaires: General: problem-solving strategies Specific: online problem solving
	(B) Zion et al. (2005)	407 tenth-grade students Two ALN groups and two F2F groups: MINT ALN F2F + META F2F 12 weeks Scientific online inquiry context	IMPROVE prompts on an index card Practicing in pairs	Pre/post General scientific ability and domain-specific inquiry skills in microbiology
	(C) Michalsky et al. (2007)	212 tenth-grade students Two ALN groups: ALN + META ALN 12 weeks Scientific inquiry context	IMPROVE prompts on an index card Practicing in pairs	RL (Schraw & Dennison, 1994) Knowledge of cognition self-report (pre/post) Regulation of cognition self-reflective scale (pre/mid/post)
	(D) Kramarski and Gutman (2006)	65 ninth-grade students Two e-learning (EL) environments: EL + IMPROVE EL 5 weeks Mathematics formal context	Three kinds of prompts on the computer screen: IMPROVE prompts Explanation and feedback prompts Prompts to practice in pairs	Pre/post Mathematical, procedural, and conceptual knowledge and transfer SRL self-report questionnaire: strategy use and self-monitoring

(continued)

Table 3.1 (continued)

	(E) Kramarski and Dudai (2009)	100 ninth-grade students Two metacognitive online discussion methods: Self-explanation guidance (SEG) Group feedback guidance (GFG) Control group 5 weeks Mathematics inquiry context	Both groups received IMPROVE prompts SEG group received self-explanation electronic pop-ups GFG group received group feedback pop-ups Practicing in groups of four students	Pre/post Mathematics tasks: Online inquiry task (PISA, 2003) Paper and pencil tasks (near transfer) Far transfer for the formal context and skills (posing a problem) Mathematical feedback SRL tasks: Self-report scale on cognitive and metacognitive aspects Metacognitive feedback: planning, monitoring, and evaluation (Schraw & Dennison, 1994)
Teachers' perspective	(F) Kramarski and Michalsky (2009a)	194 preservice teachers Four instructional methods: EL + SRL F2F + SRL EL F2F One-semester course (56 h) Pedagogical online context	IMPROVE prompts directed to pedagogical skills embedded in electronic screens Practicing in pairs	Pre/post Pedagogical knowledge: comprehension and design skills (transfer) SRL: self-reported MSLQ questionnaire Perceptions of student- versus teacher-centered learning: metaphors
	(G) Kramarski and Michalsky (2010)	95 preservice teachers Two instructional hypermedia methods: HYP + META HYP One-semester course (56 h) Pedagogical context	IMPROVE prompts embedded in electronic pop-ups Practicing in pairs	Pre/post TPCK: comprehension and design skills SRL: Self-reported MSLQ questionnaire (student's perspective) Online self-reflections (students and teacher's perspectives)
	(H) Kramarski and Michalsky (2010)	144 preservice teachers Three instructional online methods Planning Monitoring Evaluation One-semester course (56 h) Pedagogical context	IMPROVE prompts embedded in electronic pop-ups Practicing in pairs	Pre/post TPCK: comprehension and design skills SRL: self-reported MSLQ questionnaire (student's perspective) Self-reported metacognitive awareness index (teacher's perspective)

Meta metacognitive, *F2F* face-to-face, *ALN* asynchronous learning network, *MINT* metacognitive-guided inquiry within ALN technology, *MSLQ* Motivated Strategies for Learning Questionnaire, *TPCK* technological pedagogical content knowledge individual group members reciprocally influence each other in forum discussions. Forums serve as virtual communities in practice (Wenger, 1998, 2007), enabling the sharing of knowledge and opinions with others in the group as well as the chance to argue in favor of one's opinion. Learners must therefore explain their own thinking to other group members and also adapt their own thinking to others' proposed solutions, which in turn may facilitate a more sophisticated conceptual understanding (e.g., Hadwin, Oshige, Gress, & Winne, 2010; Kramarski & Dudai, 2009). Unfortunately, alongside these benefits, research (e.g., Azevedo & Jacobson, 2008; Kramarski & Mizrachi, 2006) has indicated that learners also often experience cognitive overload and disorientation in such environments, thus precluding realization of WBLEs' full potential for effective learning. To offset this overload, researchers suggested the need to foster SRL skills in WBLEs (e.g., Azevedo, 2005; Kramarski & Dudai, 2009).

Self-Regulated Learning

In recent years, research has focused on the importance of SRL in academic achievement. According to Zimmerman (2000, p. 14): "Self-regulation refers to self-generated thoughts, feelings, and actions that are planned and cyclically adapted to the attainment of personal goals." In general, self-regulated learners are proactive learners in processing academic skills such as setting goals, selecting and deploying strategies, and self-monitoring one's effectiveness, rather than merely responding reactively to events that occur due to impersonal forces (Zimmerman, 2008). Zimmerman (2000) developed a cyclical model of self-regulation based on implementation of various self-regulation processes in three cyclical phases within an environmental context: forethought (e.g., planning), action and performance (e.g., monitoring), and self-reflection (e.g., evaluation).

Researchers have also begun to direct increasing attention to individual self-regulation at the social level, where individual group members influence each other through co-regulation, a process known as shared reciprocal regulation (e.g., King, 1991). Researchers emphasized that co-regulation should be viewed as an essential part of a group's work when peers or other group participants act as external regulators. Through critically examining others' reasoning and participating in resolving disagreements, students learn to monitor their own thinking, which in turn improves their conceptual reasoning (Azevedo, 2005; Hadwin et al., 2010; Kramarski & Dudai, 2009).

Research has demonstrated that students have difficulties in adopting SRL processes at both the individual and social levels (e.g., Arvaja, Salovaara, Hakkinen, & Jarvela, 2007; Azevedo, 2005; Janssen, Erkens, Kirschner, & Kanselaar, 2012; Kramarski & Gutman, 2006; Kramarski & Dudai, 2009).

Students often do not realize that they should regulate their ideas and do not know how to regulate effectively (e.g., setting goals). Consequently, students are not spontaneously open to sharing regulation with other group members (Janssen et al., 2012; Kramarski & Dudai, 2009; Kramarski & Mevarech, 2003). In light of these difficulties, Zimmerman (2000, 2008) suggested that multi-component training is necessary to help learners better interpret the SRL phases in a learning environment context.

IMPROVE Self-Questioning Prompts

Prompts enable learners to focus attention on their own thoughts and to understand their own activities during learning and teaching (Bannert, 2006; Davis, 2003; White, Frederiksen, & Collins, 2009; White & Frederiksen, 1998). Prompts differ in format, delivery method, goal, timing, and specificity (Davis, 2003). They may occur in a text, on an index card, or on a computer interface (static or dynamic), or they may be delivered by a human tutor or peer, teacher, or artificial agent (e.g., pedagogical agent). Prompts can be directed to the content, to the problem-solving process (e.g., strategy use), or to specific metacognitive strategies (e.g., self-explanation; Aleven & Koedinger, 2002; Kramarski & Dudai, 2009).

The IMPROVE metacognitive method (Introducing new concepts; Metacognitive questioning; Practicing in small groups; Reviewing; Obtaining mastery; Verification; and Enrichment and remediation; Kramarski & Mevarech, 2003; Mevarech & Kramarski, 1997) aims to support key aspects of self-regulation by actively using four self-questioning prompts targeting learning processes: *comprehension, connection, strategy, and reflection. Comprehension* questions help learners understand the task's or problem's goals or main idea (e.g., "What is the problem/task?"). *Connection* questions prompt learners to understand the task's deeper-level relational structures by focusing on prior knowledge and by articulating thoughts and self-explanations (e.g., "What is the difference/similarity?" and "How do I justify my conclusion?"). *Strategy* questions encourage learners to plan and select appropriate strategies and to monitor and control their effectiveness (e.g., "What is the strategy?" and "Why?"). *Reflection* questions play an important role in helping learners to evaluate their problem-solving processes by encouraging learners to consider various perspectives and values regarding their solutions and processes (e.g., "Does the solution make sense?" and "Am I satisfied from the way I faced the task?"). Students are encouraged to use these questions before, during and after their problem-solving process, and in their discussions in small groups (traditional settings or online). Students are asked to answer them in writing (paper and pencil or electronic screen; see the following sections for the way students were prompted to use them).

The IMPROVE method is grounded in the SRL theoretical framework. The questions direct learners' thoughts and actions throughout the cyclical SRL phases of the solution process (Zimmerman, 2000, 2008). The method is also grounded in socio-cognitive theories of learning (Bandura, 1986; Pintrich, 2000; Vygotsky, 1978; Zimmerman, 2000), which extend the view of SRL to encompass not only the individual aspect but social aspects as well (Hadwin et al., 2010).

Initially, IMPROVE research focused on traditional learning environments for school students in the mathematical domain and showed strong positive effects of IMPROVE support compared to non-metacognitive support (Kramarski & Mevarech, 2003; Mevarech & Kramarski, 1997). Outcomes emerged for conceptual understanding (i.e., mathematics reasoning and transfer) and for metacognitive knowledge (i.e., specific problem-solving strategies). Following these positive effects, we adapted the IMPROVE model to WBLEs in both the mathematics and science domains for both school students and for preservice teachers' professional development. First, we will present the studies on the students' perspective and then on the teachers' perspective. Both kinds of studies raise one main question: Under what conditions can learners (students and teachers) be promoted effectively with the SRL model based on IMPROVE self-questioning?

Integrating IMPROVE Self-Questioning Prompts for Students in WBLEs

This section summarizes two lines of research in the mathematics and science domains about school students learning within WBLEs, as presented in the first part of Table 3.1. The first line of research (studies A, B, and C) compared WBLEs with traditional human learning environments comprising cooperative and face-to-face (F2F) discussions while referring students to IMPROVE prompts on an index card. The Kramarski and Mizrachi (2006) study investigated the effects of 4 weeks of online discussion on 86 seventh graders' mathematical literacy and SRL, by comparing four learning conditions with and without metacognitive support: online +META, online alone, F2F+META, and F2F alone. Students were assessed by (a) pre-/post-mathematical authentic (i.e., real-life) problem-solving tasks presented online, similar to those they practiced (PISA, 2003), and (b) transfer measures referring to standard tasks that were not practiced on the Web and were presented in a different format (paper and pencil—far transfer). In addition, students completed two kinds of SRL self-reports, assessing general SRL for problem solving (Kramarski & Mevarech, 2003) and specific SRL in online discussions (i.e., motivation, reasoning, and communication).

Analytical analysis (i.e., repeated measures and MANCOVA) showed that students who were exposed to online discussions with IMPROVE self-questions (online+META) attained the highest levels of general SRL (i.e., problem solving) and of specific SRL (i.e., online discussions) compared to students in the other three learning conditions. They also outperformed the other groups in their ability to solve online tasks, transfer tasks, and justify their reasoning. Interestingly, the specific SRL of the online+META group increased, whereas the specific SRL of the online alone group decreased. Differences were especially salient for motivation to perform online problem-solving activities. Findings from Kramarski and Mizrachi (2006) suggest that integrating IMPROVE self-questioning prompts in online discussions may serve as a springboard for enhancing students' mathematical literacy and SRL.

The other two studies in this group (B and C) obtained similar conclusions from a 12-week scientific inquiry among 407 tenth graders. The Zion, Michalsky, and Mevarech (2005) study compared the effects of four learning methods on students' scientific inquiry skills: (a) metacognitive-guided inquiry within asynchronous learning networked technology (MINT), (b) an asynchronous learning network (ALN) with no metacognitive guidance, (c) metacognitive-guided inquiry embedded within F2F interaction, and (d) F2F interaction with no metacognitive guidance. The study examined general scientific ability and domain-specific inquiry skills in microbiology.

Analytical analysis (i.e., repeated measures and MANCOVA) indicated that the MINT research group significantly outperformed the other three, while the F2F alone group acquired the lowest mean scores. No significant differences were found between the F2F groups with and without metacognitive guidance. The authors concluded that the MINT makes significant contributions to students' achievements in designing experiments and drawing conclusions. No transfer measures were implemented in this study, and no SRL measures were reported.

In a follow-up study, Michalsky, Zion, and Mevarech (2007) investigated metacognitive awareness among 212 tenth-grade science students exposed to IMPROVE self-questions in ALN versus F2F. Metacognitive awareness was assessed by two self-report measurements based on Schraw and Dennison (1994), one a pre-/post-paper and pencil test focusing on students' knowledge about cognition and the other an online open questionnaire focusing on students' regulation of cognition, which was implemented three times, once after each online scientific inquiry solution. Analytical analysis (i.e., repeated measures and MANCOVA) indicated that the ALN+META students significantly outperformed their F2F+META counterparts on both knowledge about cognition and regulation of cognition. These results were strengthened by a qualitative analysis of the latter measure on 10 students under the two instructional methods. The improvement in regulation of cognition in the ALN+META online questionnaire clearly indicated the crucial effects of the metacognitive support on the progress and success of the scientific inquiry processes. The authors concluded that ALN with metacognitive self-questioning is a promising learning environment, holding great potential for enhancing metacognitive awareness among students.

The second line of studies (D and E on Table 3.1) investigated the beneficial effects of electronic prompts (i.e., static self-questions on the screen) on students' SRL and mathematical outcomes in WBLEs. Kramarski and Gutman (2006) investigated 65 ninth-grade students during 5 weeks of e-learning with electronic prompts based on IMPROVE self-questioning (EL+IMPROVE) versus e-learning without SRL prompts (EL alone). Both groups practiced the linear function unit in a socio-computer setting (working in pairs), but neither was exposed to planned forum discussions. In the electronic unit, the EL+IMPROVE group received IMPROVE self-questioning prompts (comprehension, connection, strategy, and reflection) embedded in the task, and they answered the electronic prompts onscreen. In addition, the EL+IMPROVE participants were encouraged to think about good mathematical explanations (e.g., "What is a good mathematical explanation?") and metacognitive feedback (e.g., "What is the difference between the present expression and the expression that you found?"), and they received feedback on their final results. Students in the EL environment only received a computer-generated feedback to their final result. Study D evaluated each group with (a) pre-/post-mathematical measures (Kramarski & Mizrachi, 2006) on procedural knowledge (standard tasks), explanations (formal, daily, computational, and drawing), and far transfer knowledge (real-life context); and (b) SRL measures of strategy use and self-monitoring (Kramarski & Mevarech, 2003).

Analytical analysis (i.e., repeated measures, MANCOVA, and correlations) showed that students exposed to IMPROVE prompts in e-learning (EL+IMPROVE) significantly outperformed the EL students in mathematical procedural and transfer tasks and in providing logical mathematical arguments. We also found that the EL+IMPROVE students outperformed their peers in using self-monitoring strategies but not in the use of problem-solving strategies. Further analysis indicated significant correlations between using self-monitoring strategies and mathematical performance on transfer tasks, particularly in the EL+IMPROVE group. Our findings support the conclusion about the beneficial effects of integrating self-questioning prompts in WBLE for enhancing domain outcomes and to strengthen SRL. However, the study provided data on mixed types of self-questioning prompts (IMPROVE, explanation, and feedback) in a socio-computer environment for students' self-reported SRL, which did not provide insight about the differential effects of the explanation and feedback prompts for online self-/co-regulation. These issues were addressed by the following study (E).

Kramarski and Dudai (2009) investigated effects of co-regulation support in online mathematical forum discussions among two experimental groups and a control group (100 ninth graders during 5 weeks). The experimental groups were exposed to different group-metacognitive prompts, based on the IMPROVE model for self-explanation guidance (SEG) and group feedback guidance (GFG). These groups were compared to a control group (CONT) that practiced mathematical problem solving in a socio-computer setting without metacognitive support. Students participated in forums of small groups (four students). Prompts appeared in automatic pop-up screens as shown in Appendix 1 (Fig. 3.1 for IMPROVE prompts that were provided to the two experimental groups, Fig. 3.2 for SEG prompts, and Fig. 3.3 for GFG prompts). The SEG questions focused on the individual regulation perspective, encouraging students to provide an elaborated explanation (why) for their thinking and to suggest a clear conclusion in forum discussions. The GFG questions encouraged students to take a social perspective (group regulation) and to provide elaborated feedback to all group participants in the forum discussions. Study E measured mathematical ability and SRL in complementary ways within one comprehensive experimental framework: as analyzed from different online and offline measures in mathematics (online problem solving, mathematical feedback, and transfer test in the formal context) and in SRL (metacognitive feedback and self-report questionnaire).

Mixed quantitative (repeated measures and MANCOVA) and qualitative analyses showed that GFG students outperformed SEG students in most mathematical and SRL measures and the control students in all measures. In addition, SEG students outperformed the control students in mathematical problem solving but not on mathematical transfer ability or SRL. The study suggested that providing online metacognitive feedback (based on IMPROVE self-questioning) in the GFG group enabled students to act as better external regulators at a social level and to share multidimensional perspectives regarding solution processes that may challenge them to try to solve new problems. In contrast, the SEG approach enabled students to regulate their processes at the individual level, which helped them only in the solution of familiar tasks but not in their transfer ability to new tasks. These conclusions support the importance of the social-cognitive aspect in the SRL process (e.g., Pintrich, 2000; Zimmerman, 2000).

Discussion of the Studies on the Students' Perspective

These studies showed that prompting SRL with IMPROVE self-questioning in WBLE can lead to effective learning of mathematics and science and can strengthen SRL among school students ages 13–15. Our findings suggest that IMPROVE questions offer a powerful tool for making problem solving explicit in four aspects: (a) knowing *what* to do (i.e., comprehension questions), (b) looking for the *big* picture (i.e., connection questions), (c) finding *how* and *when* to do (i.e., strategy questions), and (d) focusing on *things to think* about (i.e., reflection questions).

In general, these five studies on students used conceptual and transfer measures for domain learning, as well as various SRL measures (self-report and forum discussions) that were implemented online and immediately at the end of the study.

Integrating IMPROVE Self-Questioning Prompts for Preservice Teachers in WBLEs

This section presents three of our recent studies in an ongoing project of SRL support in mathematics and science domains for preservice teachers' professional development (studies F, G, and H on Table 3.1). Before these studies, no research systematically investigated teachers' professional development with SRL support, based on the same model to which students were exposed.

The first study (Kramarski & Michalsky, 2009a) observed teachers' professional growth along three dimensions: SRL, pedagogical knowledge, and perceptions of teaching and learning. Examining teachers' perceptions enabled a holistic view of teachers' professional development because prior perceptions often serve as a lens through which preservice teachers view the new pedagogical knowledge being taught (e.g., Pajares, 1992). We examined 194 preservice teachers' professional growth over a one-semester course (56 h), comparing four learning environments: e-learning supported by SRL (EL+SRL) or alone (EL) and F2F discussions supported by SRL (F2F+SRL) or alone (F2F). In study F, the IMPROVE prompts were extended to pedagogical skills (e.g., identifying learning objectives and planning didactic materials). In the EL environment, the IMPROVE self-questions were displayed as automatic pop-ups during the practice of each pedagogical skill.

Three pre-/post-measures were administered. A self-reported SRL questionnaire (Motivated Strategies for Learning Questionnaire—MSLQ; Pintrich, Smith, Garcia, & McKeachie, 1991) assessed self-perceptions of regulatory behavior (i.e., cognition, metacognition, and motivation). Pedagogical knowledge was measured by comprehension skills for analyzing pedagogical events and by design of teaching units (not practiced in the study) to assess transfer ability. Participants' perceptions of teaching and learning were assessed through a metaphor questionnaire comprising four perceptions of teaching and learning along the continuum from teacher-centered activity (transmitting information) to student-centered activity (self-construction of knowledge).

Statistical analyses (repeated measures and MANCOVA) showed that preservice teachers in both SRL-supported conditions outperformed their unsupported peers on all professional growth measures. Moreover, findings revealed that EL+SRL teachers were the highest on SRL ability (cognition, metacognition, motivation), pedagogical knowledge (comprehension and transfer of designing a learning unit), and student-centered learning perceptions (self-construction of knowledge). Despite these beneficial findings, we suggested caution in interpreting the data because SRL skills were self-reported and referred to teachers' own learning regulation (i.e., the learners' perspective) and not to their teaching regulation ability in technology environments (i.e., teachers' perspective). These issues were addressed by studies G and H.

Kramarski and Michalsky (2010) undertook a more comprehensive, holistic examination of preservice teachers' professional development in technology uses than the previous study (Kramarski & Michalsky, 2009a). Study G expanded the use of the IMPROVE model to incorporate two perspectives of SRL for preservice teachers: as a learner and as a teacher. We investigated pedagogical uses of hypermedia termed "technological pedagogical content knowledge" (TPCK; Angeli & Valanides, 2009), in which components of technology (T) and pedagogical content knowledge (PCK) should be developed concurrently via technology-rich lessons designed "toward transformation of these contributing knowledge bases into something new" (Angeli & Valanides, 2009, p. 5). In that study, like the previous one, practice of TPCK consisted of comprehension and design skills. The TPCK comprehension skills constitute basic skills such as analyzing technology pedagogical events. Design skills in TPCK require higher-order thinking that places the learner at the center of the learning process (i.e., to explore or collaborate with others). Comprehension tasks reflected the learner's perspective (preservice teachers' own learning), whereas design tasks reflected the teachers' perspective (based on students' learning).

We examined 95 preservice teachers' professional development over a one-semester course (56 h), comparing two hypermedia environments: HYP+META versus HYP. The four types of IMPROVE metacognitive questions were displayed onscreen as automatic pop-ups at certain times during the practice of TPCK tasks and online discussions (see Appendix 2 for examples). The study aimed to compare the differential effects of HYP+META versus HYP, first on the preservice teachers' TPCK skills and second on their SRL in both perspectives, as learner and as teacher.

Four measures were administered in study G at two testing intervals (pretest/posttest). Two measures assessed both TPCK skills (comprehension and design; Kramarski & Michalsky, 2009a). The other two measures assessed SRL dimensions: the MSLQ self-report on teachers' learning regulation (Pintrich et al., 1991), tapping cognition, metacognition, and motivation and online self-reflections regarding the online TPCK comprehension and design tasks. Participants received two reflection scores—for the learner and teacher perspectives—which we assessed with four rubrics for planning, monitoring, debugging, and evaluation of the process (Schraw & Dennison, 1994).

Mixed quantitative (repeated measures, MANCOVA, and correlations) and qualitative analyses showed that HYP+META was more effective in developing TPCK (both for comprehension and design skills) and fostering SRL (both on self-report and online self-reflections), compared to HYP without explicit SRL support. Furthermore, the findings of our study (2010) demonstrated a higher level of self-reflections on the comprehension task (learner's perspective), whereas preservice teachers continued to demonstrate relative difficulties in reflecting on the design task (teacher's perspective). Our findings support other conclusions that designers of preservice teacher instructional programs should invest more explicit metacognitive support focusing directly on the perspective (as learner or as teacher) taken by the teacher (Putnam & Borko, 2000; Randi & Corno, 2000).

The third study (Kramarski & Michalsky, 2009b) aimed to investigate which learning phase (Zimmerman, 2000) would be most effective for implementing the IMPROVE self-questioning prompts in order to develop preservice teachers' SRL (both learner and teacher perspectives) and TPCK. We addressed this question through a quasi-experiment comparing three kinds of self-questioning prompts: provided before, during, and immediately after receiving the TPCK task in WBLE. The study was conducted during a one-semester course (56 h) and included 144 first-year preservice teachers randomly assigned to one of three metacognitive groups: planning, monitoring, or evaluation. During practice in the WBLE, each group was prompted with questions (based on the

IMPROVE model) adapted to the three SRL phases. The planning group was prompted with the *comprehension* questions to focus on the TPCK task *before* solving or designing it (the planning phase). The monitoring group was prompted with the *strategy* questions *during* the action and performance of the TPCK task. The *evaluation* group was prompted with the *reflection* questions at the end of the process to evaluate their problem solving and design of TPCK activities. Prompts appeared as pop-ups screens, and the preservice teachers were asked to answer prompts online, in the pop-up box.

This study (H in Table 3.1) assessed preservice teachers' SRL in both perspectives (learner's and teacher's) using two complementary self-report measures: the MSLQ questionnaire (Pintrich et al., 1991) to assess cognition, metacognition, and motivation in learning; and the MAI questionnaire (Metacognitive Awareness Index; Schraw & Dennison, 1994) for assessing self-regulation along the teaching phases (planning, monitoring the action and performance, and evaluating the process). In addition, we examined TPCK with comprehension and design tasks similarly to both studies described earlier.

Analysis (repeated measures and MANCOVA) showed that prompting preservice teachers with reflection questions in the evaluation phase (after) had a synergic effect on the entire SRL process in terms of learning (cognitive, metacognitive strategies, and motivation) and in terms of teaching (planning, monitoring, and evaluation), which in turn affected the TPCK of the comprehension and design of lessons. In contrast, the monitoring group (during) gained the lowest scores in both SRL measures and TPCK skills. Our findings support theoretical models that reflection plays an important role in acquisition of learning (e.g., Zimmerman, 2000, 2008) and teaching (e.g., Schön, 1983) competences. Despite these interesting findings, we suggest caution in interpreting the data because they were gathered as self-perceived data only at the beginning and end of the process; thus, we cannot draw conclusions on the pattern of SRL in both perspectives along the course of the study.

Discussion of Studies from the Teachers' Perspective

Similar to the students' studies, we found that integrating the IMPROVE self-questioning model in WBLEs is a promising learning approach for preservice teachers (in the mathematics and science domains), carrying great potential for enhancing SRL (both perspectives) and TPCK. We explained the findings based on the fact that the four IMPROVE questions (comprehension, connection, strategy use, and reflection) could help teachers "to (a) think *what* learning/teaching steps they need to take in their work; (b) identify *which* content of a task is suitable for teaching in a technology context; (c) decide *how* they should transform the content to make it teachable to their students; and (d) find out *how* tool affordances could support constructing meanings with learner-centered pedagogy; and (e) *why*" (Kramarski & Michalsky, 2010, p. 16).

Despite our promising findings for implementing the IMPROVE model in both perspectives (student and teacher), we recognize some limitations in achieving our goals as discussed in the following section.

General Discussion: Limitations, Implications, and Future Research

The two-perspective research series (student and teacher) described here revealed promising effects regarding four goals for effective support of SRL skills with the IMPROVE method: attaining conceptual understanding, SRL, near transfer, and far transfer, where each builds on the previous one. Despite these effects, we recognize three main limitations in achieving our goals referring to (a) the transfer goal, (b) methodological and analytical methods, and (c) implementing instructional challenges.

The main limitation of the presented studies involves learners' attainment of transfer. Our studies were directed mainly to near and far transfer of IMPROVE to gain conceptual understanding, but these studies did not examine long-term transfer as regards fading, which would assess the interventions' lasting effects when students were no longer exposed to IMPROVE prompts. The fading effects of scaffolding tools (i.e., the IMPROVE prompts) play a critical role in any intervention (Puntambekar & Hubscher, 2005). In particular, the studies on preservice teaching ability were based on measures assessed during teachers' preparation phase (i.e., designing a lesson) and not during real class practice. We suggest that future research should follow up on teachers' professional development in authentic class settings by observing and interviewing teachers at the in-service stage who previously underwent preservice training with the IMPROVE model, and then examining these data's links to students' learning outcomes. Such links can serve as an indicator of long-term transfer.

Another limitation refers to methodological and analytical methods for analyzing the data in our studies. As mentioned earlier, the IMPROVE method is based on socio-cognitive SRL models. Thus, in our studies, students and preservice teachers practiced peer-assisted learning on online forums. However, their regulation of learning was assessed individually (e.g., Kramarski & Dudai, 2009; Kramarski & Michalsky, 2009a, 2009b, 2010). The need to use other methods to assess co-regulation in authentic settings is obvious. Future research based on mixed methods (quantitative and qualitative) and complementary means to assess SRL as an aptitude (questionnaires) and as an event (real time) may shed further light on SRL prompts' effects on co-regulation and academic performance along the course of the study and their lasting effects (Azevedo, 2005; Greene & Azevedo, 2010; Veenman, 2007; Zimmerman, 2008).

Finally, the presented studies did not sufficiently focus on instructional challenges using different formats of IMPROVE prompts. In our studies, we distinguished between various formats of IMPROVE self-questioning prompts as provided in index cards, electronic pop-ups, and human delivery in WBLEs. However, no research thus far has scrutinized the effects of these various formats in comparison to other kinds of prompts such as dynamic pedagogical agents, while examining automatic delivery versus delivery following a request for help or while comparing formats' different timing conditions for the learning phases (Zimmerman, 2000). We are now conducting some ongoing studies that address these issues.

In conclusion, our research series (on students and teachers) described here makes an important contribution to theoretical research and raises practical implications regarding learning and teaching with WBLEs. Our studies call for further scrutiny of how students' and teachers' SRL in mathematics, science, and TPCK emerge in the context of self-/co-regulatory learning environments. This call for research reflects the urgency of the new goals outlined for student learning and teacher training in the mathematics and science domains (e.g., PISA, 2003). The TPCK of preservice teachers who learn in WBLEs is a relatively new topic that has not yet been investigated. Integrating the same SRL support based on the IMPROVE model into different learning subjects for both students' learning and teachers' TPCK frameworks should be a continuing goal.

Appendix 1

Self-Questioning Prompts Provided to the Two Experimental Groups

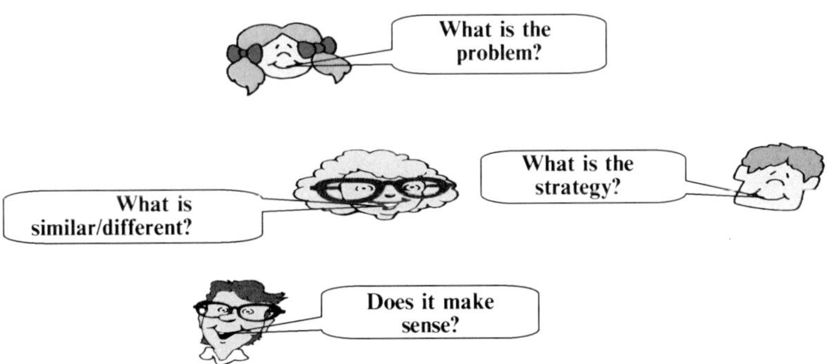

Fig. 3.1 The IMPROVE metacognitive self-questioning prompts: comprehension, connection, strategy, and reflection

Fig. 3.2 Self-questioning that provides self-explanation guidance (SEG): expressions, arguments, conclusions, and clarity

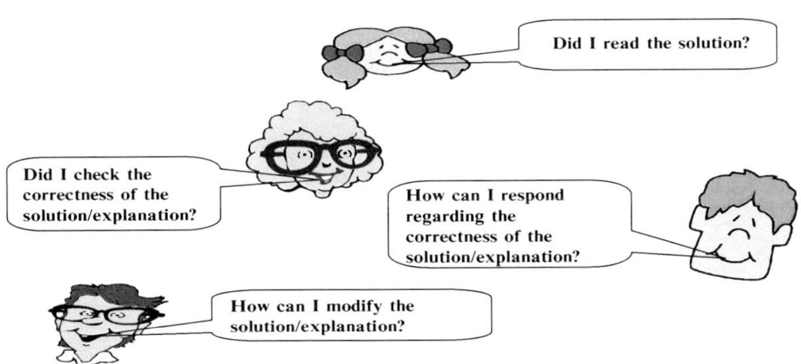

Fig. 3.3 Self-questioning that provides group feedback guidance (GFG): read, check, respond, and modify friends' answers and explanations

Appendix 2

Screen Shots for Comprehension Task (Student's Perspective) and for Design Task (Teacher's Perspective)

Comprehension Task (Student's Perspective)

Dan and Yael are asked to analyze the video-recorded lesson: "On the dangers of smoking." Dan claims that the lesson incorporates high-order thinking skills in a technological environment, whereas Yael claims that the lesson is not appropriate for teaching in heterogenic class. Look over the lesson and refer to Dan's and Yael's opinions. Bring examples from the lesson. In the forum, present your opinion and refer to the opinions of two colleagues.

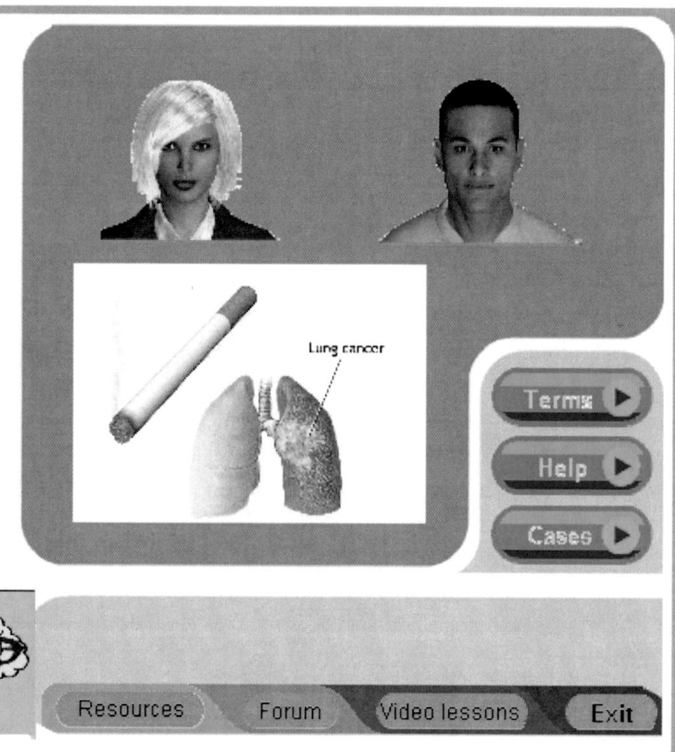

Design Task (Teacher's Perspective)

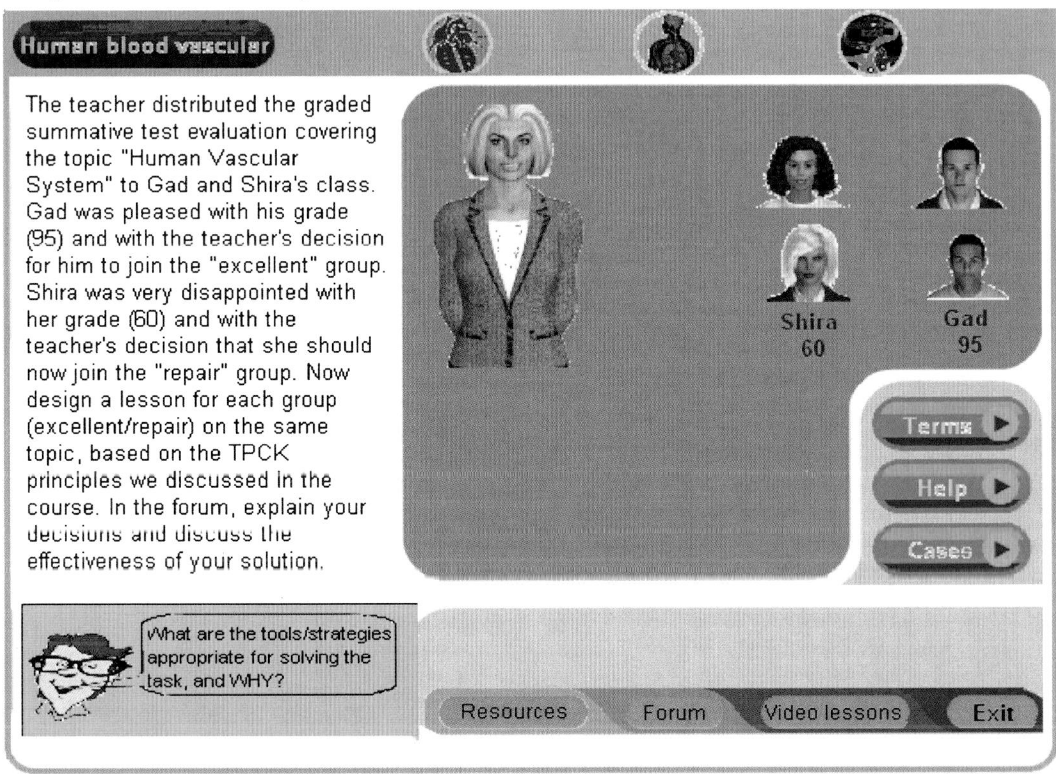

Human blood vascular
The teacher distributed the graded summative test evaluation covering the topic "Human Vascular System" to Gad and Shira's class. Gad was pleased with his grade (95) and with the teacher's decision for him to join the "excellent" group. Shira was very disappointed with her grade (60) and with the teacher's decision that she should now join the "repair" group. Now design a lesson for each group (excellent/repair) on the same topic, based on the TPCK principles we discussed in the course. In the forum, explain your decisions and discuss the effectiveness of your solution.
Shira 60
Gad 95
Terms
Help
Cases
What are the tools/strategies appropriate for solving the task, and WHY?
Resources
Forum
Video lessons
Exit

References

Aleven, V., & Koedinger, K. R. (2002). An effective metacognitive strategy: Learning by doing and explaining with a computer-based cognitive tutor. *Cognitive Science, 26*, 147–179.

Angeli, C., & Valanides, N. (2009). Epistemological and methodological issues for the conceptualization, development, and assessment of ICT-TPCK: Advances in technological pedagogical content knowledge (TPCK). *Computers in Education, 52*(1), 154–168.

Arvaja, M., Salovaara, H., Hakkinen, P., & Jarvela, S. (2007). Combining individual and group-level perspectives for studying collaborative knowledge construction in context. *Learning and Instruction, 17*, 448–459.

Azevedo, R. (2005). Using hypermedia as a metacognitive tool for enhancing student learning? The role of self-regulated learning. *Educational Psychologist, 40*(4), 199–209.

Azevedo, R., & Jacobson, M. (2008). Advances in scaffolding learning with hypertext and hypermedia: A summary and critical analysis. *Educational Technology Research and Development, 56*(1), 93–100.

Bandura, A. (1986). *Social foundations of thought and action: A social cognitive theory*. Englewood Cliffs, NJ: Prentice-Hall.

Bannert, M. (2006). Effects of reflection prompts when learning with hypermedia. *Journal of Educational Computing Research, 4*, 359–375.

Davis, E. A. (2003). Prompting middle school science students for productive reflection: Generic and directed prompts. *The Journal of the Learning Sciences, 12*(1), 91–142.

Greene, J. A., & Azevedo, R. (2010). The measurement of learners' self-regulated cognitive and metacognitive processes while using computer-based learning environments [Special issue]. *Educational Psychologist, 45*(4), 1–9.

Hadwin, H. F., Oshige, M., Gress, C. L. Z., & Winne, P. H. (2010). Innovative ways for using gStudy to orchestrate and research social aspects of self-regulated learning. *Computers in Human Behavior, 26*, 794–805.

Hannafin, M. J., & Land, S. M. (1997). The foundations and assumptions of technology-enhanced student-centered learning environments. *Instructional Science, 25*(3), 167–202.

Janssen, J., Erkens, G., Kirschner, P. A., & Kanselaar, G. (2012). Task-related and social regulation during online collaborative learning. *Metacognition and Learning, 7*(2), 25–43.

King, E. (1991). Effects of training in strategic questioning on children's problem-solving performance. *Journal of Educational Psychology, 83*(3), 307–317.

Kramarski, B. (2008). Promoting teachers' algebraic reasoning and self-regulation with metacognitive guidance. *Metacognition and Learning, 3*(2), 83–99.

Kramarski, B. (2011). Developing and assessing self-regulation through sharing feedback in online mathematical problem solving. In G. Dettori & D. Persico (Eds.), *Fostering self-regulated learning through ICTs* (pp. 232–247). Hershey: IGI Global.

Kramarski, B., & Dudai, V. (2009). Group-metacognitive support for online inquiry in mathematics with differential self-questioning. *Journal of Educational Computing Research, 40*(4), 365–392.

Kramarski, B., & Gutman, M. (2006). How can self-regulated learning be supported in mathematical e-learning environments? *Journal of Computer Assisted Learning, 22*, 24–33.

Kramarski, B., & Mevarech, Z. R. (2003). Enhancing mathematical reasoning in the classroom: Effects of cooperative learning and metacognitive training. *American Educational Research Journal, 40*(1), 281–310.

Kramarski, B., & Michalsky, T. (2009a). Investigating preservice teachers' professional growth in self-regulated learning environments. *Journal of Educational Psychology, 101*(1), 161–175.

Kramarski, B., & Michalsky, T. (2009b). Three metacognitive approaches to training pre-service teachers in different learning phases of technological pedagogical content knowledge. *Special issue: Educational Research and Evaluation: An International Journal on Theory and Practice, 15*(5), 465–490.

Kramarski, B., & Michalsky, T. (2010). Preparing preservice teachers for self-regulated learning in the context of technological pedagogical content knowledge. *Learning and Instruction, 20*, 434–447.

Kramarski, B., & Mizrachi, N. (2006). Online discussion and self-regulated learning: Effects of four instructional methods on mathematical literacy. *The Journal of Educational Research, 99*(4), 218–230.

Kramarski, B., & Revach, T. (2009). The challenge of self-regulated learning in mathematics teachers' professional training. *Educational Studies in Mathematics, 72*(3), 379–399.

Mevarech, Z. R., & Kramarski, B. (1997). IMPROVE: A multidimensional method for teaching mathematics in heterogeneous classrooms. *American Educational Research Journal, 34*(2), 365–395.

Michalsky, T., Zion, M., & Mevarech, Z. R. (2007). Developing students' metacognitive awareness in asynchronous learning networks in comparison to face-to-face discussion groups. *Journal of Educational Computing Research, 36*, 421–450.

Pajares, F. (1992). Teachers' beliefs and educational research: Cleaning up a messy construct. *Review of Educational Research, 62*, 307–332.

Pintrich, P. R. (2000). Multiple goals, multiple pathways: The role of goal orientation in learning and achievement. *Journal of Educational Psychology, 92*, 544–555.

Pintrich, P. R., Smith, D. A. F., Garcia, T., & McKeachie, W. J. (1991). *A manual for the use of the motivational strategies learning questionnaire (MSLQ)*. Ann Arbor, MI: University of Michigan, National Center for Research to Improve Postsecondary Teaching and Learning.

Programme for International Student Assessment—PISA. (2003). *Literacy skills for the world of tomorrow: Further results from PISA 2000*. Paris: Author.

Puntambekar, S., & Hubscher, R. (2005). Tools for scaffolding students in a complex learning environment: What have we gained and what have we missed? *Educational Psychologist, 40*(1), 1–12.

Putnam, R. T., & Borko, H. (2000). What do new views of knowledge and thinking have to say about research on teacher learning? *Educational Research, 29*(1), 4–15.

Randi, J., & Corno, L. (2000). Teacher innovations in self-regulated learning. In P. Pintrich, M. Boekaerts, & M. Zeidner (Eds.), *Handbook of self-regulation* (pp. 651–685). San Diego: Academic.

Schön, D. A. (1983). *The reflective practitioner: How professionals think in action*. New York: Basic Books.

Schraw, G., & Dennison, R. S. (1994). Assessing metacognitive awareness. *Contemporary Educational Psychology, 19*, 460–475.

Veenman, M. V. J. (2007). The assessment and instruction of self-regulation in computer-based environments: A discussion. *Metacognition and Learning, 2*, 177–183.

Vygotsky, L. S. (1978). *Mind in society: The development of higher psychological processes*. Cambridge, MA: Harvard University Press (Original work published in 1934).

Wenger, E. (1998). *Communities of practice: Learning, meaning and identity*. Cambridge, UK: Cambridge University Press.

Wenger, E. (2007). Communities of practice: A brief introduction. http://www.ewenger.com/theory/. Accessed 5 Oct 2010.

White, B., & Frederiksen, J. R. (1998). Inquiry, modeling, and metacognition: Making science accessible to all students. *Cognition and Instruction, 16*(1), 3–118.

White, B., Frederiksen, J. R., & Collins, A. (2009). The interplay of scientific inquiry and metacognition: More than a marriage of convenience. In D. J. Hacker, J. Dunlosky, & A. C. Graesser (Eds.), *Handbook of metacognition in education* (pp. 175–205). New York: Routledge.

Winne, P. H., & Perry, N. E. (2000). Measuring self-regulated learning. In M. Boekaerts, P. Pintrich, & M. Zeidner (Eds.), *Handbook of self-regulation* (pp. 532–566). San Diego: Academic.

Zimmerman, B. J. (2000). Attainment of self-regulated learning: A social cognitive perspective. In M. Boekaerts, P. Pintrich, & M. Zeidner (Eds.), *Handbook of self-regulation: Research and applications* (pp. 13–39). Orlando, FL: Academic.

Zimmerman, B. J. (2008). Investigating self-regulated and motivation: Historical background, methodological development, and future prospects. *American Educational Research Journal, 45*(1), 166–183.

Zion, M., Michalsky, T., & Mevarech, Z. R. (2005). The effects of metacognitive instruction embedded within an asynchronous learning network on scientific inquiry skills. *International Journal of Science Education, 27*(8), 957–983.

4 Adaptation to Context as Core Component of Self-Regulated Learning: The Example of Complexity and Epistemic Beliefs

Stephanie Pieschl, Elmar Stahl, and Rainer Bromme

Abstract

In this chapter we raise two important issues regarding the metacognitive self-regulation of learning with technologies: First, adaptation to the external context is a core component of self-regulated learning. Empirical research regarding task complexity and text complexity – two exemplary external conditions – shows that learners systematically adapt their whole self-regulated learning process within a hypermedia learning environment to these contextual conditions. Therefore, careful construction and evaluation of learning tasks and learning content is warranted. In this context communicating and teaching the demands of complex learning scenarios deserves special attention. Second, learner characteristics play an important role in self-regulated learning and adaptation. Empirical research regarding epistemic beliefs – one exemplary learner characteristic – shows that learners with absolutistic beliefs will plan and execute different learning processes than those with sophisticated beliefs; these differences are especially pronounced under conditions of high complexity. Given the general superiority of the learning and adaptation processes of more sophisticated learners such beliefs should be a learning goal of their own and should be explicitly addressed in learning scenarios.

Theoretical Framework

In our research about metacognition, epistemic beliefs, and learning with computer-based learning environments (CBLE), we rely on multiple theoretical frameworks. The COPES model of studying (Winne & Hadwin, 1998) depicts self-regulated learning (SRL) from an information processing perspective, focusing predominantly on cognitive and metacognitive processes. It is a well-suited umbrella for our research because it considers contextual

S. Pieschl (✉) • R. Bromme
Westfälische Wilhelms-Universität Münster, Fliednerstr. 21, 48149 Muenster, Germany
e-mail: pieschl@uni-muenster.de

E. Stahl
University of Education, Kunzenweg 21, 79117 Freiburg, Germany

R. Azevedo and V. Aleven (eds.), *International Handbook of Metacognition and Learning Technologies*, Springer International Handbooks of Education 26, DOI 10.1007/978-1-4419-5546-3_4,

variables such as the complexity of the learning content as well as the role of learner characteristics such as epistemic beliefs. In line with the general COPES model but elaborating certain complementary aspects, we have more specific assumptions about metacognitive calibration, for example, regarding complexity (Bromme, Pieschl, & Stahl, 2010; Pieschl, 2008, 2009) and about the function of epistemic beliefs in SRL (Bromme et al., 2010; Greene, Muis, & Pieschl, 2010). These will be elaborated subsequently but can be best understood against the backdrop of the COPES model.

Learning according to the COPES model occurs in four weakly sequenced and recursive stages: (1) task definition, (2) goal setting and planning, (3) enactment, and (4) adaptation. In the task definition stage, a student generates her own perception about what the studying task is and what constraints and resources are in place. Consequently, the student generates idiosyncratic goals and constructs a plan for addressing that study task. In the enactment stage the previously created plan of study tactics is carried out. The adaptation stage pertains to fine-tuning of strategies within the actual learning task as well as to long-term adaptations based on the study experience. All four stages are embedded in the same general cognitive architecture with five constituents whose acronym gave the model its name: conditions (C), operations (O), products (P), evaluations (E), and standards (S). Conditions pertain to external task conditions or task demands (e.g., task complexity) as well as to internal cognitive conditions or learner characteristics (e.g., epistemic beliefs). Conditions influence the whole learning process via operations and standards. Operations include all cognitive processes (tactics, strategies) that learners utilize to solve a learning task. In each learning stage, these operations create internal (e.g., mental model) or external products (e.g., observable behavior). Students' goals are represented as multivariate profiles of standards that can be described as a profile of different criteria that a student sets for the learning task (e.g., targeted level of understanding). Evaluations occur during the whole learning process when a student metacognitively monitors her learning process, namely, the (intermediate) products of her learning process, against her standards. When she notices discrepancies she is able to perform metacognitive control by executing fix-up operations (e.g., rereading).

Within the COPES framework it is possible to model how students might adapt their SRL process to important external conditions and how learner-related internal conditions might impact these adaptations. The COPES model specifies how conditions interact with other parts of the cognitive COPES architecture within all phases of self-regulated learning. However, this model is not specified with regard to specific predictions for specific conditions. In line with this model we acknowledge that a multitude of external conditions might be relevant for all kinds of learning scenarios and that a multitude of internal conditions might influence SRL. However, we focus on two specific examples in our research program: Regarding external conditions, we focus on learners' adaptation to the complexity of the learning content, operationalized as adaptation to task complexity or text complexity. Regarding learner-related internal conditions, we focus on epistemic beliefs.

SRL and Calibration to Complexity

Complexity of the learning material is one of the most influential external contextual demands to which learners should adapt their self-regulated learning process. As an example we illustrate how an ideal self-regulated learner might adapt her learning to task complexity according to the COPES model (Winne & Hadwin, 1998): This learner is confronted with two tasks, task A is simple vocabulary learning task and task B is complex task of writing an argumentative essay. This learner would correctly diagnose task complexity in the task definition stage, namely, task A is simple and task B is complex. In the subsequent stage of goal setting and planning, she would set corresponding learning goals and plan to execute corresponding learning strategies, namely, for task A simple goals and strategies and for task B complex goals and strategies of deep elaboration. She would also generate corresponding standards for metacognitively monitoring her whole learning process, namely, simple standards for task A and complex standards for task B. In the enactment stage, she would enact the previously planned learning strategies and constantly and diligently monitor her learning process against her standards, thus carefully self-regulating her learning within both tasks. As a result, the products of learning would correspond to the given complexity of the task, namely, a simple memory trace for task A—vocabulary is memorized—while task B might require the construction of a complex mental model and a complex written essay.

We define task complexity in line with Bloom's revised taxonomy of educational objectives (Anderson et al., 2001). Within this taxonomy, tasks are classified with regard to the complexity of the underlying cognitive operations (in ascending order): (1) remember, (2) understand, (3) apply, (4) analyze, (5) evaluate, and (6) create (from now on referred to as Bloom-categories). These cognitive processes are assumed to be ordered on a single dimension from simple to complex (hierarchy assumption), and each class of behaviors is presumed to include all the behaviors of the less complex classes (cumulative hierarchy assumption). Note that task complexity in this sense does not equal task difficulty. As an illustration consider the following example: The question "What is the capital of Germany?" (Berlin) is a simple remember task and might be quite easy for German citizens (probably 95% correct answers). The same type of question with less familiar content such as "What is the capital of Mongolia?" (Ulan Bator) is more difficult (probably 20% correct answers) but not more complex.

To determine the extent of learners' adaptation to task complexity, we use a method transferred from traditional research on calibration (for more information see Pieschl, 2009). In this context the accuracy of learners' judgments (e.g., regarding their confidence) is investigated by determining how closely these judgments match learners' performance on the corresponding criterion tasks (e.g., a multiple-choice test). Such calibration can be measured on an absolute level, for example, with the bias score that denotes the absolute fit between judgments and performance or on a relative level, for example, with intraindividual correlations that denote the covariation of judgments and performance. We transfer the latter idea as well as the methodology of relative calibration to relate task complexity to learners' SRL. More specifically, we give learners tasks of different Bloom-categories and capture their SRL for each task. If learners' SRL covaries positively with task complexity, we conclude that such a learner is well-calibrated with regard to task complexity: for example, if a learner uses more complex SRL processes for more complex tasks. The same idea and methodology can also be applied to investigate learners' calibration with regard to other external conditions, for example, text complexity.

SRL and Epistemic Beliefs

Epistemic beliefs are internal conditions that strongly influence learners' self-regulated learning process (Winne & Hadwin, 1998). Epistemic beliefs are learners' personal beliefs about the nature of knowledge and knowing. Thus, epistemology involves questions pertaining to the origin, nature, form, limits, and methods of human knowledge and questions about the processes by which such knowledge is verified and justified (for an overview see Hofer & Pintrich, 2002). One important theoretical assumption is that learners' epistemic beliefs develop from strongly absolutistic towards more sophisticated epistemologies. The term absolutistic is used to indicate that a person believes, for example, that knowledge is certain, an accumulation of facts, and can be transferred (effectively) by a person in a position of authority. Persons with a sophisticated perspective on the other hand believe that knowledge is relative, contextual, and a complex network. They accept uncertainty and changeability of truth and the notion that knowledge is rather construed than given.

Based on the COPES model (Winne & Hadwin, 1998) and elaborations (Muis, 2007), we assume that epistemic beliefs act as general knowledge structures through which the content to be learnt is apprehended, in other words, a learner automatically and probably without conscious awareness perceives all learning content through their personal "lens" of epistemic beliefs (Bromme et al., 2010). With more sophisticated epistemic beliefs, we assume that more flexible apprehension is possible. However, whether a learner acts on these perceptions might be highly context-dependent. For example, in certain contexts learners might not execute deep elaboration strategies even though they would be able to do so. This latter idea is consistent with context-sensitive epistemic beliefs (Bromme, Kienhues, & Stahl, 2008; Elby & Hammer, 2001; Greene et al., 2010). As an example we illustrate how epistemic beliefs might influence how learners calibrate their SRL to task complexity according to the COPES model and elaborations (Bromme et al., 2010; Winne & Hadwin, 1998). Imagine two learners: learner A has absolutistic epistemic beliefs in simple, stable, and certain knowledge and learner B has more sophisticated epistemic beliefs in complex, tentative, and uncertain knowledge. First, consider potential main effects of epistemic beliefs. According to the COPES model, conditions directly influence learners' standards and operations. If we apply this general model to the case of epistemic beliefs, we can conclude that learner A might set superficial standards for SRL ("The goal is achieved if I have memorized the facts"; "I will complete this task in a short time") compared to learner B ("I have to deeply understand the subject-matter in order to apply it"; "I will need much time to complete the task"). Additionally, learner A might enact simple and often superficial learning tactics and strategies for task completion (memorizing) compared to learner B who might plan complex strategies of deeper elaboration (critically evaluating). Second, consider potential interactions with task complexity, namely, how epistemic beliefs might impact calibration to task complexity. If learners are confronted with the complex evaluate task requiring written arguments and counterarguments about a controversial topic, this task might be interpreted in multiple ways. The sophisticated learner B might attempt to verify each argument by searching for additional information, whereas the absolutistic learner A might take each argument at face value or might not even search for information contradicting her position given that she believes that there should be only one truth. For a very simple remember task like a factual question on the other hand, these potential differences might not be observable. Learner A might approach this task with simple strategies because she has a general bias to underestimate task complexity. Learner B also might plan simple strategies, but because this learner more adequately diagnoses task complexity. Therefore, we hypothesize that students with more sophisticated epistemic beliefs are better at flexibly and accurately diagnosing task complexity because their epistemic beliefs act as a more adequate and flexible apprehension structure (Bromme et al., 2010). Therefore, ideal self-regulated learners with sophisticated epistemic beliefs should demonstrate better calibration to task complexity.

To summarize these arguments: First, we argue that adaptation to context is a core component of SRL and that this adaptation can be captured by applying the idea and methodology of calibration to this issue. Learners who flexibly adapt their SRL to task complexity are well-calibrated with regard to task complexity. Second, we argue that epistemic beliefs play an important role in SRL, but not in all contexts equally. Rather, learners with more sophisticated beliefs in complex and tentative knowledge should be able to more flexibly apprehend the learning content. Therefore, these learners should show superior calibration with regard to complexity (Bromme et al., 2010). Both of these arguments have important implication for material construction and evaluation in educational research as well as in educational practice.

An Illustrative Example: Learning About Genetic Fingerprinting

We describe our learning material in detail as an illustrative example of how our theoretical assumptions outlined above could be investigated further. This includes the development and systematic formative evaluation of our hypermedia environment as well as of corresponding learning tasks of different complexity. We acknowledge that other learning technologies and tasks might be equally well suited and that it might even be possible to investigate these issues in traditional learning scenarios. In this line of argumentation, the learning content is more important than the technological implementation. But in line with our emphasis on context, we concede that the technology itself also might suggest assumptions about the epistemology of the underlying domain.

We chose the topic of genetic fingerprinting—a colloquial term for DNA (deoxyribonucleic acid) analysis—which is usually taught in German high schools but also at the University level for a multitude of reasons: First, tasks on all levels of complexity (Bloom-categories) can be constructed easily. On the one hand genetic fingerprinting involves well-proven facts that can be used to construct simple remember tasks, for example about the structure of DNA. On the other hand, some issues within the topic of genetic fingerprinting are discussed controversially even within the scientific community. For example, it is still not possible to sequence a whole human genome in a short period of time. Thus all statements regarding matches and non-matches between two DNA profiles, for example in forensic cases, can only give probabilistic answers. For these issues more complex tasks are feasible. Second, these properties of genetic fingerprinting also allow for different interpretations of tasks and learning materials. For example, if learners possess the absolutistic epistemic belief that knowledge consists of separate and certain facts, they might concentrate on factual aspects such as the structure of DNA. On the other hand, if learners think that knowledge consists of a complex network of interrelated and uncertain bits of knowledge (sophisticated view), they might pay more attention to the problems involved in genetic fingerprinting. And third, the topic of genetic fingerprinting is perceived as inherently interesting by learners, mostly because of the forensic cases discussed in mass media.

How Does Our Hypermedia Environment Help Studying SRL?

We opted for maximal control of our learning material and constructed our own hypermedia environment about genetic fingerprinting. This hypermedia environment consists of 106 pages, which are directly linked by 193 hyperlinks. Additionally, each page can be accessed from all locations within the environment by advanced navigational features such as opening the table of contents and clicking on any selected page. Each page mainly contains text and within these texts all technical terms are hyperlinked to an explanatory glossary. Most pages also contain illustrative or instructional photos, pictures, or tables. Apart from this general description our hypermedia environment possesses specific features that enable the investigation of our theoretical assumptions:

First, the pages of the main part of our hypermedia environment are linked in a hierarchical structure, more specifically the pages of the content chapters about three different methods of DNA analysis: mtDNA analysis (14 pages; sequence of the mitochondrial genome; see Fig. 4.1), STR analysis (18 pages; number of short tandem repeats at specific noncoding loci), and Y-STR analysis (17 pages; same method applied to the male Y-chromosome). This means that short and easily comprehensible pages are on the top introductory level 1 (simple learning material), moderately complex pages are on level 2 (moderately complex learning material), and detailed, more scientific pages written for experts are on the deepest levels 3 (complex learning material). This hierarchical structure can be navigated by direct hyperlinks that are labeled according to a family tree metaphor, namely "parent" links lead to superordinate pages, "children" links to subordinate pages, and "sibling" links to neighboring pages on the same hierarchical level. Due to this hierarchical structure we can investigate if and how learners adapt their SRL to the complexity of the learning material. Furthermore, if learners are working on specific learning tasks the depth of their navigation gives us first hints about their depth of elaboration.

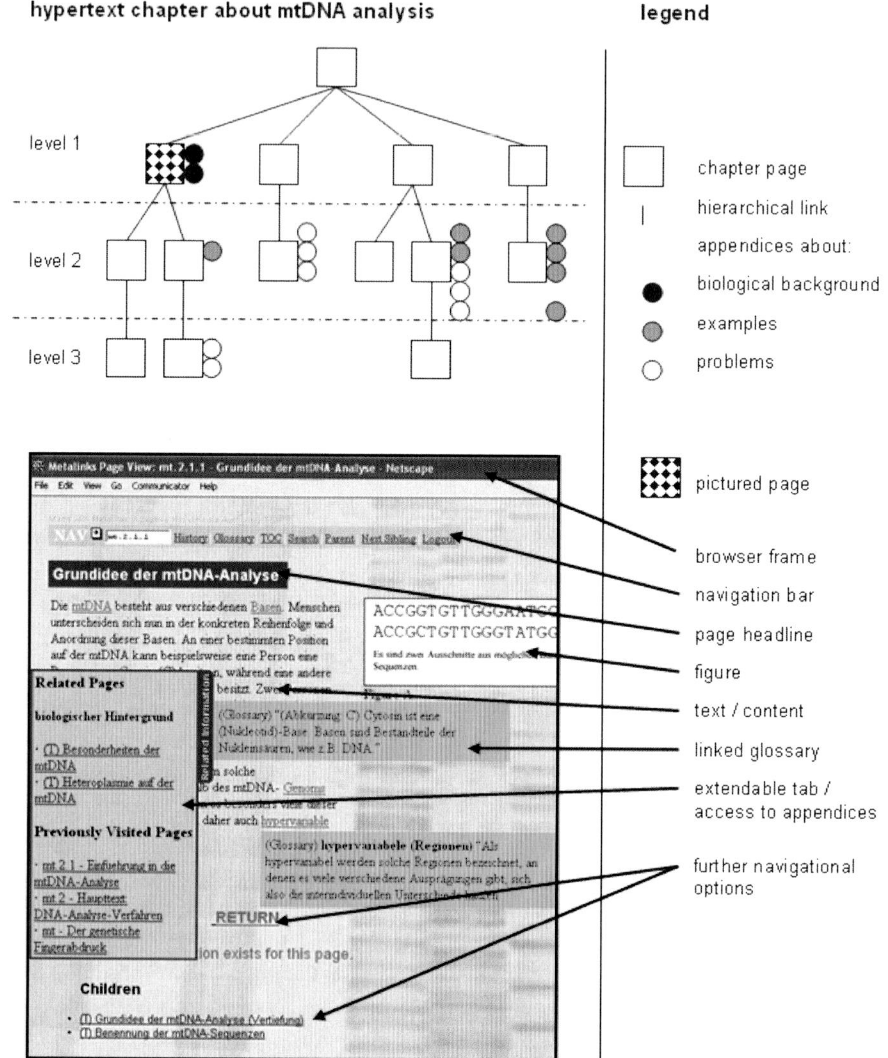

Fig. 4.1 Visualization of the hierarchical hypertext structure for the chapter on mtDNA analysis (*top*) and sample hypertext page (*bottom*)

Second, the hypertext encompasses additional pages in three thematic appendices with more biological background that go beyond the topic of genetic fingerprinting, additional examples (e.g., forensic case studies), and information highlighting potential problems or uncertainties regarding methods of DNA analysis. Especially the problem appendices are interesting because they potentially facilitate the evaluation and justification of specific methods and procedures. Therefore, we assume that learners with more sophisticated epistemic beliefs who think, for example, that knowledge is tentative would more frequently access such information. These appendix pages are accessible not only from the table of contents but also from the main hypertext pages and are explicitly labeled (see Fig. 4.1, bottom) and additionally learners have a visual representation of the structure of the hypertext (see Fig. 4.1, top). Therefore, we assume that accessing these pages is deliberate.

Third, the authoring software MetaLinks (Murray, 2003) that was used to create the hypermedium automatically generates logfiles about all learners' actions. This trace data details learners' ongoing navigation. More specifically, it tracks the date and time of each user action including the navigational commands used and the hypertext pages that were accessed by these commands. Such data that directly records the task solution process has many advantages over self-report instruments, for example researchers can draw conclusions about learners' SRL processes. Learners' self-reports about their metacognitions and learning strategies often show little relation to their ongoing SRL process (Jamieson-Noel & Winne, 2003). Therefore, it might be beneficial if researchers use traces, data about actual studying events recorded while individuals engage in learning, to directly observe learners' SRL processes over time (Greene et al., 2010).

Material Development and Evaluation

For investigating learners' adaptation to context, more specifically to task complexity and text complexity, it is paramount to construct adequate learning material and tasks and systematically evaluate their correspondence with theoretical assumptions.

Models of text comprehension (e.g., Kintsch, 1998) underline that levels of comprehension are not only dependent on the text itself but also on learner characteristics (e.g., prior domain knowledge) and reading strategies. Therefore, text complexity can hardly be thoroughly determined by examining the text alone. However, in general, simple texts are characterized by short sentences with known words, high structure, conciseness, and stimulating additions to enhance readers' motivation (e.g., Langer, Schulz von Thun, & Tausch, 1990). More complex texts on the other hand are characterized by longer sentences, the use of unknown technical terms, less obvious structure, more detailed elaborations, and the absence of stimulating additions. We created texts for different levels of complexity for our hypermedium adhering to these criteria. Additionally, we had test readers evaluate pages of our hypertext with regard to text complexity. This series of pilot studies also tested whether the texts were comprehensible for laypersons. In the first pilot study, students of psychology ($n=24$) had to evaluate the complexity of 31 printed texts developed for the chapter on mtDNA analysis. Results show that students judged texts intended for the simplest level 1 in the hypertext significantly simpler than those intended for level 2. Those in turn were judged significantly simpler than those intended for level 3. However, students still indicated a number of comprehension problems. Therefore, the texts were revised to be more comprehensible for laypersons. In the second pilot study students of psychology ($n=29$) had to evaluate the complexity of 13 selected hypertext pages from the hypertext chapter of mtDNA analysis. Furthermore, more objective indicators of comprehension such questions about the content of the hypertext were administered. Results indicate that participants judged hypertext pages on more complex hierarchical levels o be significantly more complex, that they needed more time to process more complex hypertext pages, and that they provided significantly fewer correct answers to multiple-choice questions about the content of more complex pages. Therefore, we concluded that our hierarchical hypertext levels did indeed systematically vary in text complexity.

We constructed tasks of different complexity in accordance with Bloom's revised taxonomy of educational objectives (Anderson et al., 2001; see above). Tasks for each Bloom-category were constructed in a cyclic process. First, two content experts extensively searched through textbooks about molecular biology and corresponding websites and extracted relevant tasks. Furthermore, these experts were introduced to Bloom' revised taxonomy and constructed several tasks representing all Bloom-categories. As a result, a pool of approximately 100 tasks was established, containing molecular biology tasks as well as very specific tasks for the topic of genetic fingerprinting. Second, the two content experts as well as three content novices, all deeply familiar with the revised Taxonomy, independently categorized this pool of learning tasks according to the Bloom-categories. For 39 tasks all five raters immediately agreed, for a further 25 tasks only one of the five raters diverged. For the remaining tasks divergence in categorizations was discussed by all five raters and led to rephrasing or deletion of tasks. As result a pool of 86 learning tasks was retained. Third, six tasks for each Bloom-category were chosen by the content experts, resulting in a total of 36 learning tasks. These tasks were used in a pilot study (Stahl, Pieschl, & Bromme, 2006) where students ($n=72$) had to classify these tasks into the correct Bloom-categories. In all subsequent studies those tasks were selected that were judged to be best matched to the Bloom-categories. Due to our careful construction and evaluation of these tasks and due to the results of our pilot study we concluded that our tasks did indeed systematically vary in complexity.

Empirical Results

Calibration with Regard to Complexity

Task complexity has a high impact on SRL. For simple learning tasks, students in general demonstrate effective SRL, for example more metacognitive awareness, better learning strategies, and more complete information search (Pressley & Ghatala, 1988; Rouet, 2003; Veenman & Elshout, 1999), but such simple tasks are detrimental for achieving deeper understanding (Gall, 2006). For complex learning tasks, students in general demonstrate less adequate SRL, for example less metacognitive awareness, fewer learning strategies, and fragmentary information search (Pressley & Ghatala, 1988; Rouet, 2003; Veenman & Elshout, 1999), but these complex tasks foster superior conceptual understanding (Gall, 2006).

Only few studies directly measure learners' calibration to task complexity. Results show that during the first phases of SRL learners demonstrate good calibration regarding task complexity, they systematically adapt their task definitions, goals, and plans to task complexity (Pieschl, 2008; Stahl et al., 2006; Stallmann, 2007). For example, Pieschl (2008) confronted learners ($n=102$) with one task from each Bloom-category in random order. For each task, students had to imagine they had to solve the task with a hypermedia system on genetic fingerprinting and then had to answer a questionnaire about their task definitions, goals, and plans. Results show significant intraindividual correlations between the Bloom-categories and learners' responses on all scales. For example, learners indicate that they would not plan deep processing learning strategies such as "elaborating deeply" for simple tasks but consider those of ascending importance for more complex tasks ($G=0.54$; Goodman-Kruskal Gamma correlation). On the other hand they consider superficial processing learning strategies such as "memorizing" quite important for simple tasks but of decreasing importance for more complex tasks ($G=-0.55$). Results of studies focusing on the enactment stages of learning show a similar pattern of results. Learners systematically adapt their SRL to task complexity (Pieschl, Stahl, Murray, & Bromme, 2012; Pieschl, Bromme, Porsch, & Stahl, 2008). For example, Pieschl et al. (2012) confronted learners ($n=129$) with multiple tasks from different Bloom-categories, three of which were analyzed: A = remember, B = evaluate, and C = remember. These tasks had to be solved with the hypermedia system on genetic fingerprinting. Computer-generated logfiles were collected and learners had to answer a standardized questionnaire about their task-specific SRL processes. Results of a logfile analysis show that learners access more hypertext pages for complex tasks and spend more time on these kinds of tasks. Furthermore, the questionnaire data shows that they judge complex tasks to be more complex, are less satisfied with this kind of task, and they report deeper processing for this kind of task.

Text complexity also has a high impact on SRL. However, these effects seem to be highly learner-dependent. In general, readers tend to use strategies of deeper elaboration for more complex texts (Veenman & Beishuizen, 2004), but text complexity might be detrimental for less knowledgeable readers (Salmerón, Kintsch, & Canas, 2006). Furthermore, most results indicate that metacognitive awareness might be better for texts of at least moderate difficulty than for simple texts (Weaver & Bryant, 1995).

Only few studies directly measure learners' calibration to text complexity. Results show that learners demonstrate calibration regarding text complexity. For example, Pieschl, Stahl, and Bromme (2008) gave advanced students of biology ($n = 25$) and of humanities ($n = 26$) 1 h time to learn as much as possible about mtDNA analysis with the hypermedia system about genetic fingerprinting. Computer-generated logfiles were collected, learners had to give comprehensibility ratings for each accessed hypertext page, and subsequently learners had to answer a knowledge test. Results show that learners spend less time on simple hypertext pages than on more complex pages, access a higher percentage of simple hypertext pages than of complex pages, and judge the simpler pages' comprehensibility higher than that of the complex pages.

To summarize, the empirical results reviewed above show consistent and strong effects of complexity, for example regarding task and text complexity: Regarding task complexity according to Bloom's revised taxonomy, complex tasks are considered more complex and are considered to afford more metacognitive planning, reflection and cognitive enactment. Further, they take longer to solve and more hypertext pages are accessed to solve them. Regarding text complexity, more complex hypertext pages are considered more complex and take longer to process. These effects are not only consistent across different phases of SRL but also across different methods (questionnaires, stimulated-recall interviews, think-aloud protocols, or navigation logfiles). Learners systematically adapt their whole SRL to complexity. Therefore, we conclude that adaptation to context such as complexity is a core component of self-regulated learning.

The Influence of Epistemic Beliefs

Epistemic beliefs are systematically related to SRL, for example on learners' goal orientation (Bråten & Strømsø, 2004), responses to learning strategy questionnaires (Cano, 2005), reading strategies (Kardash & Howell, 2000), help-seeking behavior (Bartholomé, Stahl, Pieschl, & Bromme, 2006), or written argumentation (Mason & Scirica, 2006). In general, these studies show superior SRL processes and outcomes for learners with sophisticated epistemic beliefs, namely, main effects of epistemic beliefs.

Only few studies directly investigate the interaction between epistemic beliefs and external conditions such as complexity. For example, Pieschl et al. (2008) experimentally manipulated learners' topic-specific epistemic beliefs and tested the effects on calibration to task complexity. More specifically, advanced students of biology ($n = 14$) and students of humanities ($n = 21$) were assigned to two matched subsamples that were either confronted with a neutral factual introduction to genetic fingerprinting (control group; sample: "A gene is the basic unit of genetic information") or with one that was enriched with comments about the epistemological nature of the presented facts (experimental group; sample: "*According to the present state of knowledge*, a gene *can be considered* the basic unit of genetic information"; comments in italics). The CAEB questionnaire (connotative aspects of epistemological beliefs; Stahl & Bromme, 2007) was administered before and after this manipulation and showed that the manipulation was successful. In the main part of the experiment, the learners were confronted with five tasks from different Bloom-categories: A = remember, B = remember, C = evaluate, D = understand, and E = remember. During this phase, students were asked every 2 min "What are you currently thinking about?" to capture their concurrent thoughts and computer-generated logfiles were collected. Furthermore, two in-depth retrospective stimulated-recall interviews were conducted with each student, about a remember task and about the evaluate task. Results indicate significant calibration to task complexity on all SRL indicators. Regarding epistemic beliefs, we found main and interaction effects consistent with our assumptions. For example, logfiles indicate that learners in the experimental group spend more time on task across all tasks (main effect) and that the difference between the experimental and the control group was most pronounced for the complex evaluate task (interaction). A similar effect was detected for learners' concurrent thoughts (answers to the prompting question: "What are you currently thinking about?") classified as planning: Learners in the experimental group uttered more planning thoughts across all tasks (main effect) and the difference between the experimental and the control group was most pronounced for the complex evaluate task (interaction). Similar effects were found in the task definition, goal setting, and planning phases of SRL (Stahl et al., 2006). However, effects are less consistent for high school students (Stallmann, 2007), and no effects were found under less reflective conditions (Bromme et al., 2010).

To summarize, the empirical results reviewed above show (mostly) consistent effects of epistemic beliefs. In general, more sophisticated beliefs are related to better SRL processes and outcomes. Additionally, epistemic beliefs seem to be most relevant under highly complex conditions. For example, only for a complex evaluate task did more sophisticated learners need significantly more time and execute significantly more planning. And only for the most complex hierarchical hypertext pages did more sophisticated learners access more hypertext pages and execute shorter, more precise searches within these pages (Pieschl et al., 2008). Learners' SRL processes were significantly impacted by their epistemic beliefs. Therefore, we conclude that epistemic beliefs play an important role in SRL, especially under conditions of high complexity.

Challenges and Implications

In this chapter we exclusively focused on the external condition of task and text complexity and on the internal condition of epistemic beliefs. But these are certainly not the only conditions relevant to SRL nor might they be the most relevant in all learning scenarios. This implies that our conclusions are limited to these exemplary conditions and that it is necessary to determine relevant external and internal criteria for any given learning situation.

Furthermore, our approach of combining logfile data with other data sources exemplifies methodological challenges of multimethod approaches. First, logfiles offer rich information about not only the number of navigational actions but also the sequence of actions. We need new statistical and graphical ways of representing this data such as graph theory (Winne, Jamieson-Noel, & Muis, 2002). Additionally, it is an open question, which level of granularity offers meaningful insight. Fine-grained methods that also entail sequence information such as path diagrams or time series analyses offer rich insights but also have strong limitations, mostly regarding the comparability and interpretation of results (McEneaney, 2001). Therefore, we decided to use aggregate measures such as time or number of accessed pages per task. These large-grained measures offer no information about the sequence of actions or the different navigational commands used to execute these actions (Richter, Naumann, & Noller, 2003). Therefore, these measures are limited because part of the wealth of information is systematically ignored. Second, if logfiles are analyzed as stand-alone measure conclusions about the cognitive processes behind the actions can be made only very carefully. For example, if a learner accesses an appendix page about problems we cannot be sure if she intended to find further information about the validity of the information presented in the base page, if she accessed this page by accident, or out of curiosity. We hypothesized that learners with more sophisticated epistemic beliefs would more frequently access appendix pages about problems but the data did not confirm this hypothesis. However, we cannot conclude that learners with more sophisticated epistemic beliefs were not concerned with validating the learning content. They might have used other criteria for validation or they might not have found the problem appendices in the hypertext due to the structure of the hypertext on genetic fingerprinting. Only if logfile information is combined with other data sources such as think-aloud protocols, interviews, or questionnaire data can we be more certain in our interpretations. Combining different data sources, however, implies a different set of limitations and also depends on interpretations that are to some degree subjective. Despite these limitations of our research methods and analytical procedures we strongly recommend the use of such multiple methods because only such methods can yield in-depth insights into ongoing learning processes.

The results of our empirical research have implications for the theoretical frameworks as well as for educational practice. Regarding the calibration to complexity, results show consistent effects indicating that adaptation to complexity is indeed a core component of SRL. However, while we diagnosed a significant and systematic covariation of SRL processes with task complexity, the absolute adequacy of this adaptation is questionable. It might have only small detrimental effects to overestimate the complexity of simple tasks. For example, a learner might access multiple hypertext pages to verify one's own answer instead of only accessing the one relevant target page. One disadvantageous side effect would be that this learner had less time for other tasks and thus the efficiency of learning might suffer. However, underestimating the complexity of complex tasks is more detrimental for learning. It might result in failure to achieve adequate internal (e.g., mental model) or external (e.g., essay) products of learning. For example, within our empirical studies the logfiles show that most students did not access all relevant pages for the more complex tasks. Thus their understanding of the subject matter can only be fragmentary and incomplete. Furthermore, students themselves explicitly reported that they noticed this problem, for example: "I have given a very brief answer […] but you could write much more about this topic […], ten pages." However, we do not know if these problems are due to the fact that learners misperceived the complexity of this task, to the fact that learners adopted inadequate goals and plans, or to the fact that they were not able to execute adequate operations, for example because of the experimental time constraints, because of the complex navigation option within the hypertext, or because of their limited cognitive capacity. Because of these issues students might have enacted less adaptation to task complexity than they were capable of or than they would have enacted in their natural learning setting (Bromme et al., 2010; Pieschl et al., 2012).

Regarding epistemic beliefs, results clearly show the importance of this learner characteristic in all phases of SRL; more sophisticated epistemic beliefs are generally associated with superior SRL processes, better learning outcomes, and more adaptation to complexity. However, results also show partly inconsistent effects. Therefore, effects of epistemic beliefs do not seem as clear-cut as theoretically assumed. One challenge in this context is the valid and reliable measurement of epistemic beliefs. Theoretically assumed dimensions of epistemic beliefs can often not be detected empirically and are controversially discussed (Bromme, 2005). Besides these challenges of measurement, research on epistemic beliefs so far is mostly limited to correlational data. This means that we cannot determine if epistemic beliefs are causally responsible for specific SRL processes or vice versa. This issue can only be determined by experimental studies (Pieschl et al., 2008). Furthermore, it is an open issue on which levels of granularity epistemic beliefs exist. Keeping the above mentioned limitations in mind, we tentatively conclude that epistemic beliefs impute and constrain learners' assumptions about the learning content and thus can be conceptualized as general knowledge apprehension structures that can help overcome the learning paradox (Bromme et al., 2010). In this sense, more sophisticated beliefs allow for more adequate apprehension of learning content and thus for better calibration. However, these general structures do not seem to exert the same influence in all situations but may be activated or deactivated by specific contextual factors (Bromme et al., 2008; Elby & Hammer, 2001; Greene et al., 2010). Epistemic beliefs seem to be most relevant and influential in complex learning scenarios.

For educational practice this implies that the use of complex tasks and complex information sources requires special attention. In these cases students will differ in their perception of these learning scenarios as well as in all subsequent SRL phases depending on their learner characteristics such as epistemic beliefs. One way to deal with these differences is to provide adequate scaffolding, for example by eliciting an adequate understanding of the task or by stimulating adequate goals for the task. In this context, it might be especially beneficial to also explicitly address the epistemic nature of the learning task and content as we could demonstrate that epistemic beliefs can be manipulated this way (Pieschl et al., 2008). This kind of learning support could also result in superior calibration to task complexity.

References

Anderson, L. W., Krathwohl, D. R., Airasian, P. W., Cruikshank, K. A., Mayer, R. E., Pintrich, P. R., et al. (2001). *A taxonomy for learning, teaching, and assessing. A revision of Bloom's taxonomy of educational objectives*. New York: Longman.

Bartholomé, T., Stahl, E., Pieschl, S., & Bromme, R. (2006). What matters in help-seeking? A study of help effectiveness and learner-related factors. *Computers in Human Behavior, 22*, 113–129.

Bråten, I., & Strømsø, H. I. (2004). Epistemological beliefs and implicit theories of intelligence as predictors of achievement goals. *Contemporary Educational Psychology, 29*, 371–388.

Bromme, R. (2005). Thinking and knowing about knowledge: A plea for and critical remarks on psychological research programs on epistemological beliefs. In M. Hoffman, J. Lenhard, & F. Seeger (Eds.), *Activity and sign - Grounding mathematics education* (pp. 191–201). New York: Springer.

Bromme, R., Kienhues, D., & Stahl, E. (2008). Knowledge and epistemological beliefs: An intimate but complicate relationship. In M. S. Khine (Ed.), *Knowing, knowledge, and beliefs: Epistemological studies across diverse cultures* (pp. 423–444). New York: Springer.

Bromme, R., Pieschl, S., & Stahl, E. (2010). Epistemological beliefs are standards for adaptive learning: A functional theory about epistemological beliefs and metacognition. *Metacognition and Learning, 5*(1), 7–26.

Cano, F. (2005). Epistemological beliefs and approaches to learning: Their change through secondary school and their influence on academic performance. *British Journal of Educational Psychology, 75*, 203–221.

Elby, A., & Hammer, D. (2001). On the substance of a sophisticated epistemology. *Science Education, 85*(5), 554–567.

Gall, J. (2006). Orienting tasks and their impact on learning and attitudes in the use of hypertext. *Journal of Educational Multimedia and Hypermedia, 15*(1), 5–29.

Greene, J. A., Muis, K. R., & Pieschl, S. (2010). The role of epistemic beliefs in students' self-regulated learning with computer-based learning environments: Conceptual and methodological issues. *Educational Psychologist, 45*(4), 245–257.

Hofer, B. K., & Pintrich, P. R. (2002). *Personal epistemology. The psychology of beliefs about knowledge and knowing*. Mahwah, NJ: Erlbaum.

Jamieson-Noel, D., & Winne, P. H. (2003). Comparing self-reports to traces of studying behavior as representations of students' studying and achievement. *Zeitschrift für Pädagogische Psychologie, 17*(3/4), 159–171.

Kardash, C. M., & Howell, K. L. (2000). Effects of epistemological beliefs and topic-specific beliefs on undergraduates' cognitive and strategic processing of dual-positional text. *Journal of Educational Psychology, 92*(3), 524–535.

Kintsch, W. (1998). *Comprehension: A paradigm for cognition*. New York, NY: Cambridge University Press.

Langer, I., Schulz von Thun, F., & Tausch, R. (1990). *Sich verständlich ausdrücken - Anleitungstexte, Unterrichtstexte, Vertragstexte, Amtstexte, Versicherungstexte, Wissenschaftstexte, u.a. [To express oneself comprehensible—instructional texts, bureaucratic texts, etc.]* (4th ed.). München: Ernst Reinhard, GmbH & Co, Verlag.

Mason, L., & Scirica, F. (2006). Prediction of students' argumentation skills about controversial topics by epistemological understanding. *Learning and Instruction, 16*(5), 492–509.

McEneaney, J. E. (2001). Graphic and numerical methods to assess navigation in hypertext. *International Journal of Human-Computer Studies, 55*, 761–786.

Muis, K. R. (2007). The role of epistemic beliefs in self-regulated learning. *Educational Psychologist, 42*(3), 173–190.

Murray, T. (2003). MetaLinks: Authoring and affordances for conceptual and narrative flow in adaptive hyperbooks. *Journal of Artificial Intelligence in Education, 13*, 199–233.

Pieschl, S. (2008). To calibrate or not to calibrate? Conditions and processes of metacognitive calibration during hypermedia learning. URN: urn:nbn:de:hbz:6–14569461694. http://nbn-resolving.de/urn:nbn:de:hbz:6–14569461694. Accessed on 10 June 2011.

Pieschl, S. (2009). Metacognitive calibration - an extended conceptualization and potential applications. *Metacognition and Learning, 4*(1), 3–31.

Pieschl, S., Bromme, R., Porsch, T., & Stahl, E. (2008). *Epistemological sensitisation causes deeper elaboration during self-regulated learning. International perspectives in the learning sciences: Cre8ting a learning world. Proceedings of the Eighth International Conference for the Learning Sciences - ICLS 2008* (Vol. 2, pp. 213–220). London: Lulu Enterprises.

Pieschl, S., Stahl, E., & Bromme, R. (2008). Epistemological beliefs and self-regulated learning with hypertext. *Metacognition and Learning, 1*, 17–37.

Pieschl, S., Stahl, E., Murray, T., & Bromme, R. (2012). Is adaptation to task complexity really beneficial for performance? *Learning and Instruction, 22*, 281–289. doi:10.1016/j.learninstruc.2011.08.005.

Pressley, M., & Ghatala, E. S. (1988). Delusions about performance on multiple-choice comprehension tests. *Reading Research Quarterly, 24*(4), 454–464.

Richter, T., Naumann, J., & Noller, S. (2003). LOGPAT: A semi-automatic way to analyze hypertext navigation behavior. *Swiss Journal of Psychology, 62*(2), 113–120.

Rouet, J.-F. (2003). What was I looking for? The influence of task specificity and prior knowledge on students' search strategies in hypertext. *Interacting with Computers, 15*, 409–428.

Salmerón, L., Kintsch, W., & Canas, J. (2006). Reading strategies and prior knowledge in learning from hypertext. *Memory & Cognition, 34*(5), 1157–1171.

Stahl, E., & Bromme, R. (2007). The CAEB: An instrument for measuring connotative aspects of epistemological beliefs. *Learning and Instruction, 17*(6), 773–785.

Stahl, E., Pieschl, S., & Bromme, R. (2006). Task complexity, epistemological beliefs and metacognitive calibration: An exploratory study. *Journal of Educational Computing Research, 35*(4), 319–338.

Stallmann, F. (2007). The influence of epistemological beliefs and academic self-concept on metacognitive calibration in German 12th graders. Unpublished diploma thesis, University of Muenster, Muenster, Germany.

Veenman, M., & Beishuizen, J. (2004). Intellectual and metacognitive skills of novices while studying texts under conditions of text difficulty and time constraints. *Learning and Instruction, 14*(6), 621–640.

Veenman, M., & Elshout, J. J. (1999). Changes in the relationship between cognitive and metacognitive skills during the acquisition of expertise. *European Journal of Psychology of Education, 15*(4), 509–523.

Weaver, C. A., & Bryant, D. S. (1995). Monitoring of comprehension: The role of text difficulty in metamemory for narrative and expository text. *Memory & Cognition, 23*(1), 12–22.

Winne, P. H., & Hadwin, A. F. (1998). Studying as self-regulated learning. In D. J. Hacker, J. Dunlosky, & A. C. Graesser (Eds.), *Metacognition in educational theory and practice* (pp. 277–304). Mahwah, NJ: Erlbaum.

Winne, P. H., Jamieson-Noel, D., & Muis, K. R. (2002). Methodological issues and advances in researching tactics, strategies, and self-regulated learning. In P. R. Pintrich & M. L. Maehr (Eds.), *New directions in measures and methods* (pp. 121–155). Oxford, UK: Elsevier Sciences.

Retrieval-Monitoring-Feedback (RMF) Technique for Producing Efficient and Durable Student Learning

5

Katherine A. Rawson and John Dunlosky

Abstract

In this chapter, we overview the *Retrieval-Monitoring-Feedback* (RMF) technique, a learning technology designed to promote both durable and efficient student learning of key concepts from course material. In the RMF technique, key concepts are first presented for initial study followed by RMF trials. Phase 1 of each RMF trial involves retrieval practice, in which the concept term is presented as a cue and the student attempts to type the correct definition into the computer. In Phase 2 of each trial, the student then monitors the quality of the retrieved response using computer-generated feedback, which helps students evaluate whether their response includes the key ideas comprising the definition. In Phase 3, the correct answer is presented intact for a self-paced restudy opportunity. The RMF program uses the student's monitoring judgments to schedule subsequent practice trials for each item. Recent research has shown that the RMF technique can yield relatively impressive levels of long-term retention of key concepts. The RMF technique can be used to support learning for materials from many different topic domains and promises to benefit a wide range of learners.

Overview of Context

A primary goal of education is the acquisition of durable knowledge, not just a transient increase in the familiarity of information. In many school settings, students learn information that must be remembered months later, such as on standardized tests and for advanced courses that follow an introductory course on a topic. Accordingly, discovering how to support students' learning of key concepts in a manner that ensures long-term retention is a major challenge for teachers and researchers. Overcoming this challenge will not be trivial, given current mandates that students demonstrate competence across many content areas before advancing in school. Thus, students must not only learn important class materials in a way to promote long-term retention but they must also do

K.A. Rawson (✉) • J. Dunlosky
Kent State University, Kent, OH, USA
e-mail: krawson1@kent.edu

R. Azevedo and V. Aleven (eds.), *International Handbook of Metacognition and Learning Technologies*, Springer International Handbooks of Education 26, DOI 10.1007/978-1-4419-5546-3_5,

so efficiently, so as to allow time to learn all of the important content.

Learning Technology: Retrieval-Monitoring-Feedback Technique

To help meet this challenge, we are currently developing a metacognitive intervention to improve the *durability* and *efficiency* of students' learning of key concepts, which often provide the foundational knowledge that is requisite for mastering more advanced content. Our intervention capitalizes on well-established principles in memory research (e.g., Pyc & Rawson, 2009; Roediger & Karpicke, 2006a) and on recent advances from research on metacognitive monitoring (Dunlosky & Lipko, 2007; Lipko, Dunlosky, Hartwig, Rawson, Swan, & Cook, 2009). More specifically, our intervention, which we refer to as the *Retrieval-Monitoring-Feedback* (RMF) technique, is founded on two principles: (a) The durability of learning can be improved by spaced *retrieval practice,* and (b) the efficiency of learning can be improved if the scheduling of practice is based on accurate *monitoring* of learning that involves appropriate *feedback.*

We begin with a brief summary of the RMF technique, which will help set the stage for the next sections. First, key concepts are presented one at a time on a computer screen. As an example of a key concept from Introductory Psychology, "The *self-serving bias* is the tendency to attribute positive outcomes to our own traits or characteristics (internal causes) but negative outcomes to factors beyond our control (external causes)." Students study each item at their own pace. Next, items are presented for RMF trials, with each trial consisting of three phases. As illustrated in Fig. 5.1, Phase 1 of each RMF trial involves *retrieval practice*, in which the concept is presented in question form (e.g., "What is the self-serving bias?"), and the student attempts to type the correct definition into the computer. In Phase 2 of each trial, the student then *monitors* the quality of the retrieved response using computer-generated *feedback*, which helps students evaluate whether their response expresses the key ideas comprising the definition. In Phase 3, the correct answer is presented intact for a self-paced restudy opportunity. Importantly, the RMF program uses the student's monitoring judgments to schedule the next RMF trial for that concept. If the student judges that the response is incorrect, it will be scheduled for another RMF trial later in that study session. If the student judges that the response is correct, the program keeps track of how many times each item has been judged as correctly recalled. Once an item reaches a prespecified criterion, the program drops it from further practice. The RMF technique continues for a given session until all concepts have reached criterion.

In the remainder of this chapter, we explore the promise of the RMF technique for helping students to learn efficiently and to retain important concepts over meaningful periods of time. We first consider the target audience and topic domains for the RMF technique, and then we discuss the general frameworks of self-regulated learning that inspired its development. Finally, we describe this technique in more detail, discuss evidence relevant to its promise, and end with discussion of some limitations and future directions.

Target Audience and Topic Domains

A strength of the RMF technique is that it can be used by many students of differing ages and abilities and for many topic domains and materials. Given that the RMF technique has been developed to improve students' learning of key concepts, it can be used to facilitate learning in any course or topic domain in which the content includes key concepts, facts, or definitions. The broad applicability of the RMF technique partly arises from the fact that many content courses at most grade levels require learning of these kinds of materials. For example, fifth graders studying astronomy will need to learn the definitions of *atmosphere*, *orbit*, and *lunar eclipse*; eighth graders studying measurement and statistics will need to learn the meaning of *independent events* and *probability*; and college students in a social psychology course will need to learn the phenomena to which the terms *self-serving bias* and *just-world hypothesis* refer.

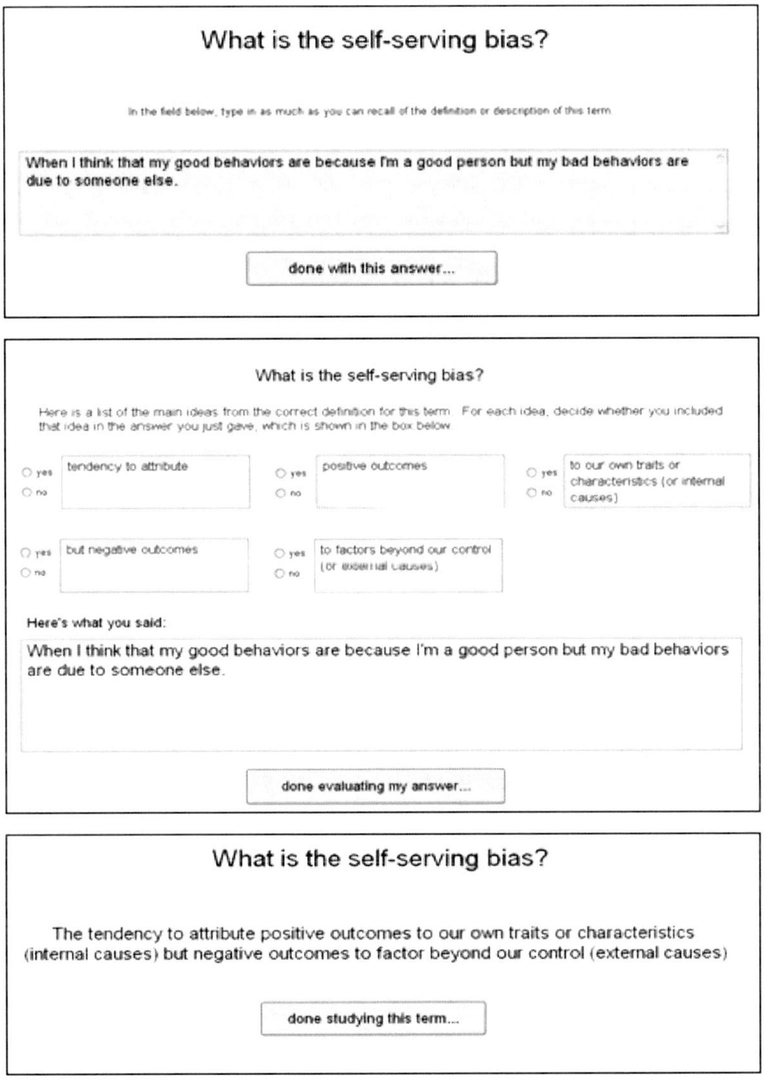

What is the self-serving bias?
In the field below, type in as much as you can recall of the definition or description of this term
When I think that my good behaviors are because I'm a good person but my bad behaviors are due to someone else.
done with this answer...
What is the self-serving bias?
Here is a list of the main ideas from the correct definition for this term. For each idea, decide whether you included that idea in the answer you just gave, which is shown in the box below
yes
no
tendency to attribute
yes
no
positive outcomes
yes
no
to our own traits or characteristics (or internal causes)
yes
no
but negative outcomes
yes
no
to factors beyond our control (or external causes)
Here's what you said:
When I think that my good behaviors are because I'm a good person but my bad behaviors are due to someone else.
done evaluating my answer...
What is the self-serving bias?
The tendency to attribute positive outcomes to our own traits or characteristics (internal causes) but negative outcomes to factor beyond our control (external causes)
done studying this term...

Fig. 5.1 Illustrations of the three phases involved in each Retrieval-Monitoring-Feedback (RMF) practice trial. The *top panel* illustrates the retrieval phase, the *middle panel* illustrates the monitoring with feedback phase, and the *bottom panel* illustrates the restudy phase. See text for details

Our assumption concerning the broad applicability of the RMF technique is further bolstered by research that establishes that its key components—accurate monitoring and the positive benefits of retrieval practice—can be applied across a wide range of materials. Retrieval practice boosts learning for foreign language vocabulary, definitions, maps, facts, and text materials (e.g., Agarwal, Karpicke, Kang, Roediger, & McDermott, 2008; Carpenter & Pashler, 2007; Carpenter, Pashler, Wixted, & Vul, 2008; Chan, 2009; Pyc & Rawson, 2010; Roediger & Karpicke, 2006a). Thus, all of these materials will benefit from the retrieval practice provided by the first phase of RMF trials (see Fig. 5.1). Also, when students use an appropriate monitoring technique, they can accurately monitor their learning of key concepts in many different topic domains. The monitoring technique illustrated in Fig. 5.1 uses idea-unit feedback that allows students to accurately evaluate the quality of what they retrieve during the retrieval phase (for details, Improving Monitoring of Ongoing Learning).

The RMF technique also promises to benefit a wide range of learners, because learners of many ages profit from retrieval practice and can monitor their learning accurately under the right conditions. Concerning the former, prior research has shown that retrieval practice can improve memory for preschool-age children, grade-school students, college students, and older adults (e.g., Fritz, Morris, Nolan, & Singleton, 2007; Logan & Balota, 2008; Pyc & Rawson, 2011; Rea & Modigliani, 1985). Under the conditions supported by the RMF technique (discussed in greater detail below), learners at least as young as middle-school age are very accurate at monitoring their learning (Lipko et al., 2009; Schneider & Lockl, 2008). Thus, the RMF technique can be applied to materials from many different domains, and students of most ages should also be able to take advantage of the technique.

Conceptual Framework: Key Components of Self-Regulated Learning

The RMF technique was designed to achieve both efficient learning and durable learning by helping students to effectively regulate their learning. The technique supports effective regulation by helping students to accurately monitor their learning (to produce efficient learning) and to schedule retrieval practice of the to-be-learned materials both within and across study sessions (to produce durable learning). To understand why accurate monitoring and effective scheduling of practice are vital, we briefly consider general theoretical frameworks of self-regulated learning (SRL). These frameworks assume that students use their ongoing monitoring of learning in an attempt to control their learning (Dunlosky & Ariel, 2011; Nelson & Narens, 1990; Winne & Hadwin, 1998; for overviews, see Dunlosky & Metcalfe, 2009; Zimmerman & Schunk, 2001). More specifically, students presumably monitor their learning to figure out what they still need to learn and then control their subsequent study strategies and schedules accordingly.

To illustrate the relevance of these metacognitive processes to effective learning, consider two hypothetical students. When preparing for an upcoming exam, a student may judge that she understands a concept well and thus decide to stop studying it. Preparing for the same exam, another student may judge that he has not yet mastered a key concept and thus decide to study that concept again during another study session. In both cases, the students are relying on their monitoring to decide how to control their learning. Because of this interplay between students' monitoring and control processes (Flavell, 1979; Nelson & Narens, 1990), SRL frameworks predict that the accuracy of monitoring will influence both the efficiency and durability of learning. For instance, if the first student inaccurately judged that she would remember the concept on the test (when in fact she had not yet learned it well enough to remember it later), then her decision to not study it further would lead to minimal durability for that concept. For the second student, if he inaccurately judged that he would not retain the concept (when in fact he had learned it well enough to remember it later), then his decision to study it further would be inefficient—his time would have been better spent learning other concepts. The importance of accurate monitoring for effective learning has been empirically established (Dunlosky, Hertzog, Kennedy, & Thiede, 2005), consistent with the core assumptions of SRL frameworks.

The efficiency and durability of learning also depends on effective control. In the examples above, even if both students perfectly monitored their learning, poor control decisions could compromise both the durability and efficiency of learning. Unfortunately, research suggests that students do not spontaneously use the most appropriate study strategies or schedules of practice. For example, students often report passively rereading textbook chapters and lecture notes (e.g., Amlund, Kardash, & Kulhavy, 1986; Carrier, 2003; Feldt & Ray, 1989; Kornell & Bjork, 2007). In one self-report study, 65% of the students said they reread textbook chapters to prepare for exams (the most frequently reported strategy), in comparison to only 19% reporting that they used testing as a study strategy (Carrier, 2003). However, passive rereading—especially when done in massed fashion the night before an exam—is an inferior strategy for achieving durable learning (e.g., Cull, 2000; Cull, Shaughnessy, & Zechmeister, 1996; Fritz, Morris, Bjork, Gelman, & Wickens, 2000; Rawson & Kintsch, 2005).

A much more effective study strategy involves *retrieval practice*, in which a student attempts to retrieve concepts from memory sometime after they have been studied. Retrieval practice is particularly effective when it is repeated with intervening time and material between repetitions (i.e., *spaced* practice) and when it is combined with subsequent restudy opportunities. The benefits of spaced retrieval practice have been repeatedly replicated in laboratory experiments (for a review, see Roediger & Karpicke, 2006b). However, the benefit of retrieval practice for durable learning depends critically on the amount and timing of practice (e.g., Cepeda, Coburn, Rohrer, Wixted, Mozer, & Pashler, 2009; Pyc & Rawson, 2009; Rawson & Dunlosky, 2011). Unfortunately, recent research suggests that even when students use retrieval practice to study, they may not spontaneously adopt an effective amount or timing of retrieval practice (e.g., Kornell & Bjork, 2007, 2008).

Detailed Introduction of the RMF Technique

Inspired by the general SRL frameworks, the RMF technique combines two key components—spaced retrieval practice and metacognitive monitoring with feedback—in a straightforward fashion. A student first studies the to-be-learned concepts. Afterwards, he or she attempts to retrieve each concept, followed by monitoring with feedback (Fig. 5.1). The feedback provides students with information that they can use to judge the quality of their response. Because judgments based on the particular form of feedback provided in the RMF technique are highly accurate (as described further below), a student's judgments can be used to tailor the schedule of further practice for each particular concept. For instance, concepts judged as not correctly recalled are slated for another spaced retrieval attempt within that particular study session. Concepts judged as correctly recalled a sufficient number of times are slated to receive RMF trials in a future study session or are dropped entirely from study. To obtain durable learning, concepts must be scheduled for sufficient practice both within and across sessions, and to obtain efficient learning, concepts must be dropped from study as soon as possible both within a given session and across sessions.

Currently, we are implementing the RMF technique using a computer program that (1) presents the key concepts for initial study, (2) prompts students to make retrieval attempts of each key concept, (3) provides feedback, (4) prompts students to judge their learning of the concepts, (5) provides a restudy opportunity, and (6) uses the monitoring judgments to schedule subsequent practice that is tailored for each student and for each concept. Accordingly, the RMF technique is sensitive to the differing abilities of individual students and to the varying difficulty of individual concepts. In summary, the key components of the RMF technique involve (1) eliciting accurate monitoring judgments, which in turn (2) permits tailored scheduling of retrieval practice for durable and efficient learning. Each of these components is described further below, along with a brief summary of research involved in the development of the RMF technique.

Improving Monitoring of Ongoing Learning

A student who accurately evaluates his or her own learning progress will be able to isolate just those materials that require further practice (for a review, see Dunlosky et al., 2005). Concerning the extent to which students can accurately evaluate the quality of their own responses when recalling key concepts, college students are often good at identifying when a correct answer is correct, but they have difficulty in accurately evaluating commission errors (i.e., when a response is made but it is entirely incorrect). For instance, Rawson and Dunlosky (2007) had college students study key concepts and then attempt to recall each one. After a given recall attempt, students scored their response using a three-point scale, including no credit, partial credit, and full credit (for analyses,

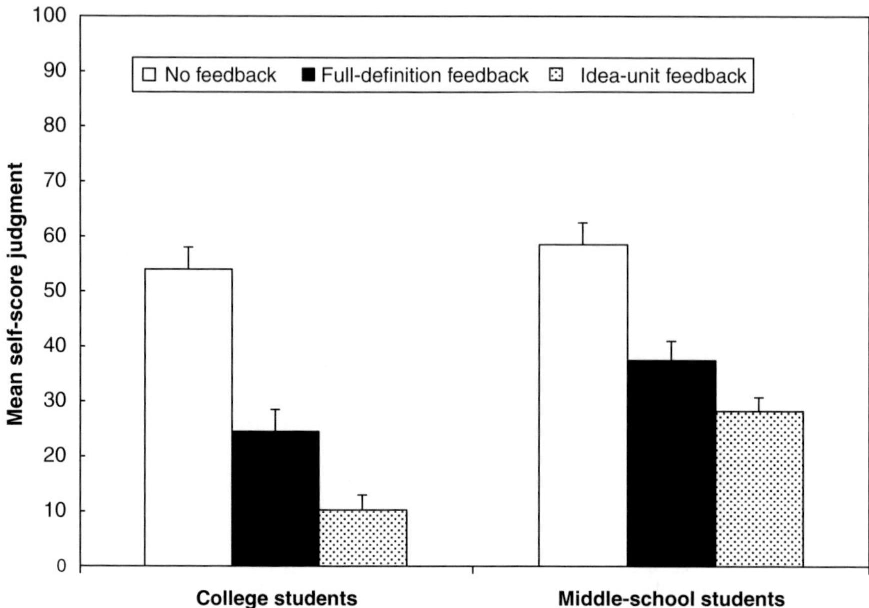

Fig. 5.2 Mean self-score judgment made for commission errors (with standard errors of the mean), using different kinds of feedback; see text for details. For college students, the *leftmost* two values are from Rawson and Dunlosky (2007), and the value for idea-unit feedback is from Dunlosky et al., (2011, Experiment 1). Note that full-definition feedback was also examined in Dunlosky et al., (2011) and the corresponding value (Mean = 28) is nearly identical to the value above from Rawson and Dunlosky (2007). Outcomes from middle-school students are from Lipko et al. (2009, Experiment 2)

we assigned values of 0, 50, and 100 to these three judgments). Unfortunately, when students made commission errors, they rated them as partially correct or fully correct 83% of the time. As Fig. 5.2 (open bars) illustrates, college students' mean self-score judgments for commission errors were well above 0, the objectively appropriate score for these responses. Notably, this situation involved no feedback; students were merely shown their response and were asked to score it. In another group, students received the full definition as feedback so that they could compare it to their response while they scored it. Although providing the full definition as feedback reduced overconfidence, surprisingly, it did not reduce it entirely—students still rated commission errors as partially or fully correct 43% of the time (Rawson & Dunlosky, 2007), and mean self-score judgments were still significantly greater than 0 (see Fig. 5.2, filled bars).

More recently, we have developed a form of feedback for the RMF technique that supports even better levels of accuracy for judging the learning of key concepts (Dunlosky, Hartwig, Rawson & Lipko, 2011; Lipko et al., 2009). Instead of receiving the entire definition as feedback, students are presented with the definition broken down into its constituent idea units and are asked to evaluate whether each idea from the correct definition is contained in their response. For instance, as illustrated in the middle panel of Fig. 5.1, the correct definition of *self-serving bias* is parsed into five idea units. The student compares his or her response (shown concurrently at the bottom of the screen) to each idea unit, marking those believed to be contained in the response. Importantly, college students show high levels of monitoring accuracy when making these idea-unit judgments, and doing so helps them to evaluate the quality of their response. In one study (Dunlosky et al., 2011), we asked students to self-score their own responses after making idea-unit judgments, and students correctly assigned self-score ratings of "no credit" to their commission errors 82% of the time. Although mean self-score ratings for commission errors were not quite at 0

(Fig. 5.2, shaded bars), overconfidence in these errors was dramatically reduced.

Improving monitoring accuracy for commission errors is of obvious importance, given that commission errors rated as completely correct by students may be prematurely dropped from further practice by the RMF program. The same concern holds for student responses that are only partially correct, which is a common kind of response when students are learning new concepts. Fortunately, the improvements in monitoring accuracy demonstrated for commission errors also obtain for partially correct responses. In one study (Dunlosky et al., 2011, Experiment 1), students who received full-definition feedback judged that 46% of their partially correct response should receive full credit, whereas students who used idea-unit feedback judged that only 13% of their partially correct answers should receive full credit. These outcomes indicate that making idea-unit judgments can also help students to judge when a response is only partially correct.

Given that the aforementioned studies involved college students, an important question arises: How accurately can younger students assess their learning of newly studied key concepts? This question pertains to the development of monitoring skills that are central to the RMF technique. Perhaps surprisingly, not much is known about the age at which monitoring skills involved in evaluating one's learning of complex materials reach a level comparable to that of adults (for an excellent review of the development of metamemory skills for learning simple materials, see Schneider & Lockl, 2008). Recently, we evaluated whether middle-school students would also benefit from feedback as they evaluated their recall responses for science concepts (Lipko et al., 2009). Middle-school students studied key concepts from course materials. After all of the concepts had been studied, students attempted to recall each one and then scored the quality of their own response as described above. Just like college students, grade-school students often scored commission errors as either partially or fully correct when no feedback was provided. Most important, as shown in the right-hand side of Fig. 5.2, middle-school students' overconfidence was reduced when they received full-definition feedback and was further reduced with idea-unit feedback. Thus, idea-unit feedback may help younger learners as well as adult learners better evaluate their learning of key concepts, which in turn can be used to control schedules of retrieval practice.

Using Accurate Monitoring to Control Schedules of Retrieval Practice

The RMF program uses students' monitoring judgments to schedule practice of concepts both within and across sessions in a manner that will lead to durable retention. In so doing, research aimed at developing the RMF technique provides important extensions of prior work on retrieval practice. For example, the majority of previous research on retrieval practice has involved relatively simple verbal materials, such as word lists, paired associates, or question prompts that require 1–2 word responses. Although these materials are similar to some kinds of information that students are expected to learn (e.g., the paired associates used in past research often included foreign language vocabulary words with their English translations), much of the information students are expected to learn involves material that is more linguistically and conceptually complex. Thus, it is important to establish that spaced retrieval practice effects generalize to more complex verbal material.

In a typical experiment on spaced retrieval practice, all items within a condition are treated identically. For instance, all items assigned for spaced retrieval might be presented for three retrieval attempts, regardless of whether each item is correctly recalled or not. This experimental technique has been valuable for establishing the benefits of spaced retrieval practice over various control conditions. Nevertheless, this particular technique is unlikely to fulfill all the requirements of an effective learning technology, because (a) it does not ensure that all items obtain a durable level of learning and (b) it would not be efficient (and likely not even possible) for students to practice retrieving every concept the same number of times during every study session, given the amount of materials that students must learn.

Thus, tailored schedules of practice are preferable for both durability and efficiency. However, for retrieval practice with key concepts, tailoring schedules of practice to the learning status of individual items for each student depends critically on having an accurate means of tracking online when items have been correctly recalled. Whereas single-word responses (such as those involved in the materials used in most prior research) can be accurately scored via computer, automated technologies are not currently available for reliably scoring sentence-length responses. Fortunately, this end can be met by using students' evaluations of their own learning online, given the high levels of judgment accuracy observed when students use the idea-unit feedback provided in the RMF technique. Thus, accurate monitoring affords extension of prior research on retrieval practice by allowing investigation of how best to tailor schedules of retrieval practice.

One outstanding issue concerns which schedule of RMF practice (both within a study session and across sessions) will yield the most durable learning while using the least amount of time. The bulk of our research to develop the RMF technique for key concepts has addressed this issue by answering three questions. First, how many times does a given concept need to be correctly recalled during a study session so that the likelihood of recalling it during the next session is high? The answer to this question will set the parameter for how many correct RMF trials to schedule for a concept during the initial learning session. Second, how many times does a concept need to be correctly recalled across study sessions so that it will be retained across a long retention interval? The answer to this question will set the parameter for the number of subsequent relearning sessions in which a given concept will receive RMF practice. And third, which combination of parameter settings (for initial learning criterion and relearning criterion) will not only lead to the highest levels of retention but will also involve the fewest number of RMF trials? All else equal, the parameter settings that require the fewest numbers of RMF trials to obtain a given level of retention yield the most efficient learning.

We acknowledge that what constitutes an acceptable level of retention is somewhat arbitrary and may change as a function of student and teacher goals. In our research, the criterion test has involved gist recall of each concept, and our benchmark was to identify parameter values for initial learning and relearning criteria that would support at least 50% recall (as well as rapid relearning of those items not initially recalled correctly) after a retention interval of several weeks. To identify these parameter values, we have conducted numerous large-scale studies that systematically vary the number of RMF trials (both within and across sessions) that occur for each concept.

To highlight the importance of exploring criterion-based practice schedules, we provide a brief historical account of some of our earlier research. Our initial attempts to explore the efficacy of retrieval practice for learning key concepts occurred prior to discovery of the idea-unit feedback technique that supports high levels of monitoring accuracy, and thus our early research involved fixed schedules of practice like those used in most prior research. For example, one early study was intended to explore the number of retrieval practice trials that would be needed to obtain adequate retention after a 2-day retention interval, which is a typical interval between two study sessions in the RMF program. Students performed either one or three retrieval attempts for each key concept during the initial learning session and then completed a final cued recall test 2 days later. Much to our surprise, tripling the number of retrieval attempts produced only a small and nonsignificant improvement in performance (24% vs. 19%), and performance overall was disappointingly low after such a short retention interval. Despite several attempts to improve performance in follow-up research, generally by having students restudy using strategies that would presumably support conceptual processing (e.g., paraphrasing, comparing and contrasting), none of these processing-based interventions boosted recall in a meaningful manner.

As hindsight now makes clear, the limitation was that we were examining the influence of the number of retrieval practice *trials* per concept (regardless of whether a concept was correctly recalled during the retrieval phase) and not the number of trials that yielded *correct recall* of the concept. Our most recent research takes advantage of the idea-unit judgments to systematically vary the number of correct RMF trials both within and across sessions and has shown substantially more impressive levels of retention. Outcomes from these studies are reported in detail elsewhere (e.g., Rawson & Dunlosky, 2011), but here we briefly describe some of the key generalizations and their implications for developing the RMF technique.

First, as the number of correct RMF trials during an initial study session increases, recall performance 2 days later increases. However, the returns from each additional correct RMF trial diminish (cf. Pyc & Rawson, 2009), with four or more correct RMF trials yielding relatively minimal incremental benefit given the additional amount of time required to achieve these higher initial criterion levels. Second, we have also explored the durability and efficiency achieved by increasing the number of relearning sessions that take place after initial learning. In brief, each relearning session involves RMF trials until concepts are correctly recalled once. How many relearning sessions are needed to obtain long-term retention? Mimicking the qualitative pattern found for initial learning criterion, the effects of relearning criterion also show a pattern of diminishing returns: As the number of relearning sessions increases, so too does performance on long-term retention tests 1–4 months later but with smaller and smaller incremental gains from each next relearning session. Most important, combining effective parameter values for initial learning criterion and relearning criterion has produced impressive levels of retention. For example, an initial learning criterion of three correct RMF trials combined with four subsequent relearning sessions produced recall near 60% 1 month later and near 40% 4 months later. Furthermore, after the 4-month recall test, students completed RMF trials until they had correctly recalled each concept once, and the rate of this relearning was significantly faster than initial learning. The implication is that even after a summer break, students can prepare for advanced classes on a given topic by quickly relearning core concepts using the RMF technique.

Unfortunately, few studies have investigated the degree to which grade-school students benefit from spaced retrieval practice and restudy. The few studies that have been reported (e.g., Metcalfe, Kornell, & Son, 2007; Rea & Modigliani, 1985) demonstrate that grade-school students can benefit from self-testing and restudy, but they also have used simple materials with single-word responses. Given these limitations of the existing literature, our ongoing research exploring the RMF technique with younger learners is promising. Younger students do benefit from tailored schedules of retrieval practice with key concepts and can achieve relatively high levels of recall performance after a 1-month retention interval, although we have not yet identified parameter values (for the number of correct RMF trials within and between sessions) that yield the most efficient and durable learning. However, exploration of these parameters for younger students—and for any population of learners and tasks—is possible using the straightforward empirical techniques described for our research with college students.

Challenges and Implications

The implications of the RMF technique are far reaching for teachers and students, because the technique provides a means to help students efficiently master class materials. The RMF technique is meant to supplement classroom instruction. Our vision is that teachers will be able to input key concepts into the program, which can then be made available on the Internet, so that students can log in and interact with the program to learn course content in an efficient manner (e.g., logging in for RMF practice two times a week). One benefit of the RMF technique derives from its broad applicability. Any student learning any set of materials can use it to their benefit as long as three goals are met: (1) Students can practice retrieving the to-be-learned materials, (2) a monitoring technique is available that the students can use to obtain high levels of monitoring accuracy, and (3) the schedule of RMF trials (both within and across sessions) that efficiently yields the desired level of retention has been identified. In this chapter, we focused on the application of the RMF technique to learning key concepts, which provide foundational concepts for many content domains. For these concepts, our research has begun to meet these goals—we have discovered a monitoring technique that supports accurate monitoring and are beginning to identify parameter values to schedule RMF trials in a manner that supports efficient and durable learning.

Nevertheless, many challenges remain for using the RMF technique for learning key concepts as well as applying this technique to other materials. Concerning the former, idea-unit judgments do help students to identify when they cannot yet correctly recall the gist of a concept from memory. That is, these judgments help students identify commission errors; students rarely mistake them for correctly recalled concepts when using idea-unit judgments, and hence, these concepts will not be prematurely dropped from practice. One difficulty arises in that idea-unit judgments sometimes lead to underconfidence for correct recalls (but not always, see Lipko et al., 2009). That is, when students correctly recall a concept, they do not always realize that their response is correct (in terms of the idea-unit interface shown in Fig. 5.1, when a response is actually correct, students sometimes do not check "yes" for all the idea units). Such underconfidence can lead to inefficient learning, because students should not waste time studying concepts that have already been learned well enough.

However, we believe this limitation is the lesser of two evils—namely, students are merely at risk for overlearning some concepts (due to some underconfidence in correct responses), which seems better than being at risk for underlearning (due to overconfidence in commission errors). Even so, this underconfidence in correct responses may be easy to minimize, because currently the RMF program provides very little in the way of guidance for how students should make the idea-unit judgments. We suspect that more detailed instructions and practice with the judgments could reduce students' underconfidence without producing overconfidence.

Note that a strength of the RMF technique is that it provides students with external support for making idea-unit judgments. That is, teachers will input the key term concepts and their idea units into the RMF program, which then uses this input during the monitoring phase of an RMF trial. Nevertheless, a potential limitation is that students may not be able to use the technique without the teacher's input and the RMF interface. Fortunately, recent research from our laboratory has demonstrated that college students can parse concept definitions into idea units and use them to accurately judge their recall responses (Dunlosky et al., 2011). The students often do not develop the same idea units as do teachers, but the student-generated idea units work just as well for attaining high levels of monitoring accuracy. Thus, idea-unit feedback can be applied by students even when the program is not available. Of course, the RMF program also keeps track of the retrieval history of each concept so that it can make appropriate control decisions about whether (and when) to schedule concepts for subsequent RMF trials. In principle, students could keep track of their progress, but even here external support may be needed to do so.

Finally, although we believe that the RMF technique will likely be widely applicable, we also admit that advances in metacognitive and cognitive technology are still required to apply the technique in some domains. For instance, researchers still have not discovered how students can achieve high levels of accuracy at judging their comprehension of lengthier text materials (but see Thiede et al., 2009). We also do not know the most efficient and durable schedules of practice for many kinds of materials and learning goals. Discovering these effective schedules is largely an empirical challenge that can be met using standard techniques of cognitive psychology. Thus, although the RMF technique currently cannot be applied in some domains, applying it more broadly can be achieved by conducting investigations to better understand students' metacognitive and learning abilities in any target domain.

Acknowledgements The research reported here was supported by the Institute of Education Sciences, US Department of Education, through Grant # R305A080316 to Kent State University. The opinions expressed are those of the authors and do not represent views of the Institute or the US Department of Education.

References

Agarwal, P. K., Karpicke, J. D., Kang, S. H. K., Roediger, H. L., III, & McDermott, K. B. (2008). Examining the testing effect with open- and closed-book tests. *Applied Cognitive Psychology, 22*, 861–876.

Amlund, J. T., Kardash, C. M., & Kulhavy, R. W. (1986). Repetitive reading and recall of expository texts. *Reading Research Quarterly, 21*, 49–58.

Carpenter, S. K., & Pashler, H. (2007). Testing beyond words: Using tests to enhance visuospatial map learning. *Psychonomic Bulletin & Review, 14*, 474–478.

Carpenter, S. K., Pashler, H., Wixted, J. T., & Vul, E. (2008). The effects of tests on learning and forgetting. *Memory & Cognition, 36*, 438–448.

Carrier, L. M. (2003). College students' choices of study strategies. *Perceptual and Motor Skills, 96*, 54–56.

Cepeda, N. J., Coburn, N., Rohrer, D., Wixted, J. T., Mozer, M. C., & Pashler, H. (2009). Optimizing distributed practice: Theoretical analysis and practical implications. *Experimental Psychology, 56*, 236–246.

Chan, J. C. K. (2009). When does retrieval induce forgetting and when does it induce facilitation? Implications for retrieval inhibition, testing effect, and text processing. *Journal of Memory and Language, 61*, 153–170.

Cull, W. (2000). Untangling the benefits of multiple study opportunities and repeated testing for cued recall. *Applied Cognitive Psychology, 14*, 215–235.

Cull, W. L., Shaughnessy, J. J., & Zechmeister, E. B. (1996). Expanding understanding of the expanding-pattern-of-retrieval mnemonic: Toward confidence in applicability. *Journal of Experimental Psychology: Applied, 2*, 365–378.

Dunlosky, J & Ariel, R. (2011). Self-regulated learning and the allocation of study time. In B. Ross (Ed.), *Psychology of Learning and Motivation, 54*, 103–140.

Dunlosky, J., Hartwig, M., Rawson, K. A., & Lipko, A. R. (2011). Improving college students' evaluation of text learning using idea-unit standards. *Quarterly Journal of Experimental Psychology, 64*, 467–484.

Dunlosky, J., Hertzog, C., Kennedy, M., & Thiede, K. (2005). The self-monitoring approach for effective learning. *Cognitive Technology, 10*, 4–11.

Dunlosky, J., & Lipko, A. (2007). Metacomprehension: A brief history and how to improve its accuracy. *Current Directions in Psychological Science, 16*, 228–232.

Dunlosky, J., & Metcalfe, J. (2009). *Metacognition*. Beverly Hills, CA: Sage.

Feldt, R. C., & Ray, M. (1989). Effect of test expectancy on preferred study strategy use and test performance. *Perceptual and Motor Skills, 68*, 1157–1158.

Flavell, J. H. (1979). Metacognition and cognitive monitoring: A new area of cognitive-developmental inquiry. *American Psychologist, 34*, 906–911.

Fritz, C. O., Morris, P. E., Bjork, R. A., Gelman, R., & Wickens, T. D. (2000). When further learning fails: Stability and change following repeated presentation of text. *British Journal of Psychology, 91*, 493–511.

Fritz, C. O., Morris, P. E., Nolan, D., & Singleton, J. (2007). Expanding retrieval practice: An effective aid to preschool children's learning. *The Quarterly Journal of Experimental Psychology, 60*, 991–1004.

Kornell, N., & Bjork, R. A. (2007). The promise and perils of self-regulated study. *Psychonomic Bulletin & Review, 14*, 219–224.

Kornell, N., & Bjork, R. A. (2008). Optimising self-regulated study: The benefits—and costs—of dropping flashcards. *Memory, 16*, 125–136.

Lipko, A. R., Dunlosky, J., Hartwig, M. K., Rawson, K. A., Swan, K., & Cook, D. (2009). Using standards to improve middle-school students' accuracy at evaluating the quality of their recall. *Journal of Experimental Psychology: Applied, 15*, 307–318.

Logan, J. M., & Balota, D. A. (2008). Expanded vs. equal interval spaced retrieval practice: Exploring different schedules of spacing and retention interval in younger and older adults. *Aging, Neuropsychology, and Cognition, 15*, 257–280.

Metcalfe, J., Kornell, N., & Son, L. K. (2007). A cognitive-science based programme to enhance study efficacy in a high and low risk setting. *European Journal of Cognitive Psychology, 19*, 743–768.

Nelson, T. O., & Narens, L. (1990). *The psychology of learning and motivation* (Vol. 26, pp. 125–141). New York: Academic.

Pyc, M. A., & Rawson, K. A. (2009). Testing the retrieval effort hypothesis: Does greater difficulty correctly recalling information lead to higher levels of memory? *Journal of Memory and Language, 60*, 437–447.

Pyc, M. A., & Rawson, K. A. (2010). Why testing improves memory: Mediator effectiveness hypothesis. *Science, 330*, 335.

Pyc, M. A., & Rawson, K. A. (2011). Costs and benefits of dropout schedules of test-restudy practice: Implications for student learning. *Applied Cognitive Psychology, 25*, 87–95.

Rawson, K., & Dunlosky, J. (2007). Improving students' self-evaluation of learning for key concepts in textbook materials. *European Journal of Cognitive Psychology, 19*, 559–579.

Rawson, K. A., & Dunlosky, J. (2011). Optimizing schedules of retrieval practice for durable and efficient learning: How much is enough? *Journal of Experimental Psychology: General, 140*, 283–302.

Rawson, K. A., & Kintsch, W. (2005). Rereading effects depend on time of test. *Journal of Educational Psychology, 97*, 70–80.

Rea, C. P., & Modigliani, V. (1985). The effect of expanded versus massed practice on the retention of multiplication facts and spelling lists. *Human Learning: Journal of Practical Research and Applications, 4*, 11–18.

Roediger, H. L., III, & Karpicke, J. D. (2006a). Test enhanced learning: Taking memory tests to improve long-term retention. *Psychological Science, 17*, 249–255.

Roediger, H. L., III, & Karpicke, J. D. (2006b). The power of testing memory: Basic research and implications for educational practice. *Perspectives on Psychological Science, 1*, 181–210.

Schneider, W., & Lockl, K. (2008). Procedural metacognition in children: Evidence for developmental trends. In R. A. Bjork & J. Dunlosky (Eds.), *Handbook of metamemory and memory* (pp. 391–409). UK: Taylor & Francis.

Thiede, K. W., Griffin, T. D., Wiley, J., & Redford, J. S. (2009). Metacognitive monitoring during and after reading. In D. Hacker, J. Dunlosky, & A. Graesser (Eds.), *Handbook of metacognition in education* (pp. 85–106). Psychology Press: NY.

Winne, P. H., & Hadwin, A. F. (1998). Studying as self-regulated learning. In D. J. Hacker, J. Dunlosky, & A. C. Graesser (Eds.), *Metacognition in educational theory and practice* (pp. 277–304). Hillsdale, NJ: LEA.

Zimmerman, B. J., & Schunk, D. H. (Eds.). (2001). *Self-regulated learning and academic achievement: Theoretical perspectives* (2nd ed.). Mahwah, NJ: Erlbaum.

Metacognition: A Closed-Loop Model of Biased Competition–Evidence from Neuroscience, Cognition, and Instructional Research

6

Neil H. Schwartz, Brianna M. Scott, and Doris Holzberger

Learning without thought is labor lost.
~Confucius

Abstract

In this chapter, we take the position that self-regulation and metacognition reveal an undeniable conceptual core that assumes individuals make efforts to monitor their thoughts and actions, and try to gain some control over them. In the neurosciences, the higher-order processes of monitoring and control are referred to as "executive control processes"—processes that should be evident as neurological activity within known neuroanatomical locations. From this vantage point, we closely examine two predominant cognitive models of working memory—Cowan's embedded processing model and Baddeley's model containing a central executive component. We conclude that the former is the best fit with research from neuroscience and explains most efficiently the findings of metacognition in instruction. Thus, we offer a model of monitoring and control as a reciprocal function of the same neurologic processes that excite and inhibit, in a recursive fashion, the regions of the brain responsible for two types of activities involved in learning—the activities involved in processing the information itself relative to the goals of a task and the activities involved in processing (evaluating and correcting) the original activities deployed to seek goal attainment, activities that are metacognitive.

N.H. Schwartz (✉)
Department of Psychology, California State University,
Chico, CA 95929-0234, USA

International Cognitive Visualization Program,
Chico, USA; Grenoble, France; Landau, Germany
e-mail: nschwartz@csuchico.edu

B.M. Scott
University of Indianapolis,
Indianapolis, IN, USA

D. Holzberger
University of Frankfurt, Frankfurt, Germany

R. Azevedo and V. Aleven (eds.), *International Handbook of Metacognition and Learning Technologies*, Springer International Handbooks of Education 26, DOI 10.1007/978-1-4419-5546-3_6,

Learning and thinking are synergistic actions of the way people develop knowledge to adapt to the world. The actions are collateral cognitive operations that share a unitary outcome of performance. And yet, it is not entirely clear how the operations actually take place—either at the neurological level of the brain, the metaphoric level of the mind, or the action-oriented level of behavior. In this chapter, we will build a case for metacognition as an integral operator in learning and thought. We will put forth a position that thinking is best characterized by the metacognitive operations learners deploy when they attempt to learn—the planning, monitoring, and evaluating learners do to regulate their learning processes. We will support our case at the level of the neuroanatomical structures of the brain, the metaphorical architecture of human cognition, and relevant features of instruction. We focus on these three levels because of the following: (1) There is a rich literature on frontal lobe involvement specifically targeted to explain learners' ability to think and learn, (2) decades of research on human cognitive architecture has been closely examined in the context of the neurological involvement of frontal lobe activation, and (3) learning and thinking are inextricably combined under the auspices of instruction. Finally, we will inventory the role of metacognition in some of our work and selected works of others.

Differentiating Metacognition from Self-Regulated Learning

Metacognition and self-regulation are not synonymous terms. Individually, the concepts have a long, independent history with distinct theoretical bases (e.g., Bandura, 1977; Flavell, 1979); however, over the last few decades, the concepts have been blurred by inconsistent use and theoretical ambiguity, in addition to the necessary and inevitable revisions the concepts require to evolve theoretically over time. This led Dinsmore, Alexander, and Loughlin (2008) to review 255 articles published over the last 5 years, asking the question: "Should we expect to hold current generations to the conceptions first framed by Flavell, Bandura, and others, or is it assumed that alternative and contemporary conceptions are warranted?"

Dinsmore et al. (2008) conclude that metacognition is rooted in the theoretical foundation of Jean Piaget and centers around cognition and matters of the mind. Flavell, working from a Piagetian theoretical base, was responsible for conceptualizing metacognition as "thinking about thinking" (Dinsmore et al., 2008), a definition that still stands 40 years later. Further, metacognition is conceptualized as being comprised of two factors: *knowledge* (what individuals know about their own cognition and cognition in general) and *monitoring/regulation* (the set of activities that help students control their learning) (e.g., Flavell, 1979; Schraw & Moshman, 1995). Of most importance is the focus on endogenous characteristics (Moshman, 1982)—that is, metacognition is within the realm of the mind with much less concern over the human–environment interaction. Metacognition deals primarily with reflective abstraction of new or existing cognitive structures.

Self-regulation, on the other hand, originates from Bandura's (1977) writings emphasizing the person-environment interaction, the importance of emotional and behavioral regulation, and the regulation of motivation. In short, Dinsmore et al. (2008) describe self-regulation as "the reciprocal determinism of the environment on the person, mediated through behavior. Person variables include the distinct self processes that interact with the environment through one's actions" (p.393). Thus, self-regulation consists of the "higher order control of lower order processes responsible for the planning and execution of behavior"—in addition to emotional control (Banfield, Wyland, Macrae, Munte, & Heatherton, 2004; Efklides, 2006).

We chose to start from Schraw, Crippen, and Hartley's (2006) definition of self-regulation as consisting of three main components: cognition, metacognition, and motivation. It is within this framework that we examine the overlapping conceptual space between self-regulation and metacognition. We are most interested in the individual's ability to monitor his or her own thinking, with or without environmental interaction. This monitoring action fits within the "multidimensional conceptual space of self-regulated action" that Kaplan (2008) put forward. This conceptual space, Kaplan (2008) contends, is the abstract "umbrella" under which metacognition and self-regulation stand. The commonalities between self-regulation and metacognition reveal an undeniable conceptual core binding the constructs, namely, that individuals make efforts to monitor their thoughts and actions and to act accordingly to gain some control over them. It is, in effect, a marriage between self-awareness and intention to act that aligns these bodies of work (Dinsmore et al., 2008). In short, metacognition and self-regulation are not mutually exclusive; rather, they are "subtypes of the same general phenomenon of self-regulated action" (Kaplan, 2008).

The question becomes, then, not what is different between these concepts but which subcomponent one is interested in studying. Thus, the distinction between self-regulation and metacognition is less important to the conceptual center of this chapter; one's ability to monitor and control their thinking, regardless of theoretical roots, is of the utmost importance when examining the connection to cognitive architecture and the underlying neurological connections.

The Neuroanatomy of Executive Control

Fernandez-Duque, Baird, and Posner (2000) suggested that metacognition could benefit from a cognitive neuroscience perspective where metacognitive regulation is examined in terms of the processes of executive control. The rationale for such a position is based on the work of Shimamura (2000) and others (c.f. Bench, Frith, Grasby, & Griston, 1993; Rugg, Fletcher, Chua, & Dolan, 1999) who have successfully mapped the concept of executive function onto specific mental operations, anchoring the operations within specific anatomical structures of the brain. Indeed, if Kaplan (2008) is correct that individuals monitor their thoughts and actions—exerting some control over them—then monitoring and control should be evident as neurological activity within known neuroanatomical locations. Alternatively, describing the activity of specific brain locations implicated in metacognition helps delineate and define specific metacognitive functions.

Nelson and Narens (1990) suggested that metacognitive regulation is principally a *coordinating* activity made up of both bottom-up and top-down processes—cognitive monitoring and cognitive control, respectively. Monitoring is responsible for such processes as error detection, attention, and source monitoring in memory retrieval; control is seen in conflict resolution, error correction, inhibitory control, planning, and resource allocation. The coordination is accomplished via a reciprocal influence at two levels of analysis—an object level and a meta-level. Metacognitive *monitoring* involves the flow of information from the object level to the meta-level where judgments of learning and feelings of knowing are evaluated by the learner; metacognitive *control* refers to the learner's regulation of information processing where attention is monitored and cognitive strategies are deployed to manage learning performance. The point is that there is a strong relationship between metacognition in terms of monitoring and control and brain-based executive functions. In fact, there is now "incontrovertible evidence suggesting a trend toward a cognitive neuroscience perspective for many if not all aspects of human cognition" (Shimamura, 2000, p. 320) including metacognitive monitoring and control (Shimamura, 2008). That is, the spatial resolution of event-related fMRI has become so precise that the ability to identify regions of brain activation has become extremely impressive, allowing for replicable patterns of activation to be observed across laboratories. This means that it is now possible to observe the metacognitive functions that were originally derived from theory, as in vivo brain tissue activation in the context of behavioral activity within carefully controlled experiments of thinking and learning.

In the neurosciences, the higher-order processes of metacognitive monitoring and control are referred to as "executive control processes." We now know that separate, albeit interactive, frontal areas of the brain are critically involved in these processes (c.f. Cummings, 1994; Pannu, Kaszniak, & Rapcsak, 2005). In fact, recent evidence from neuroscience has led to the conclusions that (1) there is a strong correlation between indices of frontal lobe structural integrity and metamemory accuracy and (2) the combination of frontal lobe dysfunction and poor memory severely restricts metamemory processes. The term metamemory is used here to note the synergistic effect of monitoring and control processes on successful memory functions. Specifically, patients with damage to the frontal lobe show impairments in metacognitive monitoring associated with feelings of knowing an answer, before the answer is given, and evaluation—the kind of evaluation in which learners must evaluate contextual information such as remembering when or where some event occurred or who presented the information (Nolde, Johnson, & D'Esposito, 1998; Rugg et al., 1999).

Other judgments and feelings are also good indices of metacognitive monitoring–for example, feelings of knowing judgments, ease of learning, tip-of-the-tongue feelings and retrospective confidence judgments, and global predictions and postdictions. Indeed, all these indices have been used to provide evidence with neurological patients that the prefrontal cortex is an essential region for performance and reflects the *monitoring* function of metacognition. For example, in patients with Korsakoff's syndrome, Moscovitch and Melo (1997) found that frontal lobe lesions or dysfunction results in a common occurrence of confabulation, because of a breakdown in search mechanisms and poor metacognitive monitoring. Schnyer et al. (2004) had learners with specific frontal lobe damage learn sentences and make judgments of feelings of knowing and retrospective confidence of the last word in each of several sentences. The learners performed poorer than normal controls on their feeling of knowing judgments. In fact, lesion analysis revealed an overlapping region of the right medial prefrontal cortex in the learners with frontal damage who performed the poorest on the task. Finally, Pannu et al. (2005) examined differences in performance between patients with frontal lobe damage and healthy controls during a learning task in which the participants were asked to make feeling of knowing and retrospective confidence judgments in a face-name retrieval task. The two groups performed similarly when the faces were either extremely familiar or extremely unfamiliar, but quite different when the faces were of intermediate familiarity. Pannu et al. (2005) explained that the patients with damage to the right ventral medial prefrontal cortex monitored more poorly, suggesting that the "monitoring mechanism is engaged most critically when decisions are difficult" (p. 112).

By the same token, executive functions of the frontal cortex are involved in metacognitive *control* as well. Nagel (2009) found that high-level reasoning is an index of strategic behavior controlled by neural activity in the medial prefrontal cortex when learners believe they are controlling their cognition in the presence of a human rather than a machine. McGlynn and Kaszniak (1991) observed impairment in metacognitive control process associated with the allocation of time when learners with Huntington's disease had to search memory for answers to general information questions. Huntington's disease is an inherited degenerative disorder in which dysfunction exists in the frontal-subcortical circuits of the brain (Cummings, 1994). Finally, metacognitive control has been observed in neuroimaging studies of the Stroop effect, where learners must resolve the conflict between the name of a color and the color in which the name is printed by *inhibiting* an incorrect response when the word and its color are incongruent. The neuroimaging data consistently reveal activation of the anterior cingulate within the prefrontal cortex (c.f. Carter, Mintun, & Cohen, 1995).

In gist, Fernandez-Duque et al. (2000) summed up the neurological evidence this way:

> Neuroimaging studies have shown activation of a network of frontal areas in tasks of executive control. The activated areas usually include the anterior cingulated and supplementary motor area, the orbitofrontal cortex, the dorsolateral prefrontal cortex, and portions of the basal ganglia and the thalamus. The tasks that activate these areas typically require subjects to deal with conflict, error, or emotion, therefore demanding effortful cognitive processing (Bush et al., 1998; Bush, Luu, & Posner, 2000). These mental abilities may be the building blocks that metacognitively-sophisticated thinkers use in their achievement of complex tasks, such as problem solving, strategy selection, and decision making.

Based on the evidence above, we believe that knowledge of the neurological underpinnings of metacognition is important because it leads to testable hypotheses of instruction. Consider recent work by Fugelsang and Dunbar (2005) on conceptual change. Fugelsang and Dunbar used fMRI to investigate the patterns of neurological activation when students were acquiring new scientific knowledge. The question was whether the students would change their relatively naïve understanding of scientific concepts when given new information either consistent or inconsistent with theory plausible to their previously held beliefs; the second question was whether different parts of the brain would be activated under the two plausibility conditions. What the researchers found bears directly on instruction. When given data consistent with their previous scientific understanding, the students showed activation of neural networks in the caudate and parahippocampal gyrus (C and PG)—networks well known to be involved in learning. However, when presented with data inconsistent with their previously held beliefs, activation was seen in the anterior cingulated cortex and the dorsolateral prefrontal cortex, with no activation of the C and PG. This suggests that when new information fits in well with information students already know, learning networks are activated, but when information does not make good sense in terms of students' existing knowledge, students activate neural networks that actually *inhibit* the development of new learning. The finding has implications for our purposes here because it attests to the influence of students' executive control on the ways teachers and instructional designers might approach their delivery of instruction.

Working Memory: The Link Between Metacognition and Executive Control

One of the best ways to make sense of neurologically based executive processes in terms of metacognitive monitoring and control is to examine both levels in the context of a single model. After all, a single model permits each to be explained relative to the other using a framework common to both. We chose Baddeley's model of working memory (Baddeley, 2003) for such a purpose, because the model has had a substantial influence in generating research of human cognitive processing. Indeed, Jonides et al. (2008) pointed out that "between the years 1980 and 2006, of the 16,154 papers that cited 'working memory' in their titles or abstracts, fully 7,339 included citations to Alan Baddeley" (p. 195).

Baddeley's model of working memory (Baddeley, 2003) is an extension of the tripartite model of human cognitive architecture originally proposed by Broadbent (1953) and later developed by Atkinson and Shiffrin (1968). Designed to explain the dynamic functions of in vivo thinking, the model of working memory can be used to account for the executive control processes investigated within the neurosciences and the concept of metacognition evolving from studies of cognition and cognitive performance. *In short, we outline the model here because it is an effective framework with which to map the overlap of each and explain the importance of metacognition in instruction.*

Working memory, as described by Baddeley (2000), is a four-component model comprised of two slave systems—the visuospatial sketchpad and the phonological loop—an episodic buffer and a central executive. The sketchpad is assumed to hold visuospatial information for further processing and is believed to be fractionable into separate visual, spatial, and possibly kinesthetic components. The phonological loop is assumed to hold verbal and acoustic information using a temporary store and an articulatory rehearsal system. The episodic buffer is postulated to be a limited capacity system providing temporary storage of information in the form of multimodal codes and capable of binding information from the other components, and from long-term memory, into a unitary episodic representation. Finally, the central executive is conceived as the part of the model capable of "retrieving information from the episodic buffer in the form of conscious awareness, reflecting on that information and, where necessary, manipulating and modifying it" (Baddeley, 2000, p. 420). Baddeley, Allen, and Hitch (2010) contend that executive control is at the "heart of working memory" (p. 223).

The Role of the Central Executive in Working Memory

Baddeley's (2000) concept of the central executive implicates the two hallmark features of metacognition, namely, monitoring and control. In effect, the central executive was postulated to be the component responsible for determining whether attention is necessary for deployment under conditions when a person is required to learn, solve a problem, or act in an unfamiliar way. Routine actions such as reciting the alphabet or driving a car are automatic and place only a light demand on attention, but when routine action is impossible, a *supervisory attention system* (SAS) (Shallice, 1988) is probably deployed capable of reflecting on alternative plans of action and biasing behavior in the direction of the actions most likely to lead to a goal.

However, there was a problem with the central executive as originally explained using the SAS. The central executive was conceived purely as an attentional allocation and deployment system, but evidence from a number of investigations suggested that this could not entirely be the case. Data from studies examining people's capacity to focus attention, divide attention between two or more sources, switch attention between tasks, and link information between working and long-term memory failed to entirely support the central executive in this capacity (Baddeley et al., 2010). Investigations *did* support the attentional focus function (c.f. Logie, Gilhooly, & Wynn, 1994). Empirical results also supported the assumption that the central executive was likely responsible for dividing attention between two or more sources (Logie, della Sala, Wynn, & Baddeley, 2000). But, the other two functions were not unequivocally supported by research. Specifically, task switching seemed to be better considered a result of a number of different processes rather than a single executive process (Saeki & Saito, 2004), and the linking function was probably better conceptualized in terms of a working memory component entirely different than the central executive. Thus, Baddeley et al. (2010) proposed an episodic buffer, the nature of which they described as "a buffer in the sense that it is a limited capacity temporary store that forms an interface between a range of systems all having different basic memory codes; having a multi-dimensional coding system; [and] episodic in the sense that it is capable of holding episodes, and integrating chunks of information that then became accessible to conscious awareness" (p. 229).

And yet, there are serious questions as to how the episodic buffer functions in conjunction with the central executive, whether the episodic buffer and the central executive are clearly responsible for different cognitive functions, whether the two can be anchored in different or complementary neurological functions of the brain, and whether metacognition can be explained in terms of both components at both a neurological and cognitive level. It is certainly conceivable that the central executive may be responsible for metacognitive monitoring, and the episodic buffer may be responsible for metacognitive control. *If this is true, then brain activation associated with the central executive might be expected to be principally attentional, and brain activation associated with the episodic buffer might be based on composite operations of specific brain systems acting to control the integration of information.*

Implicating the Episodic Buffer in Metacognitive Control

Repovs and Baddeley (2006) postulated that the episodic buffer was the working memory component responsible for creating and manipulating novel representations, creating a mental modeling space that enables the consideration of possible outcomes, and provides the basis for planning future action. Thus, the episodic buffer would seem to be the part of working memory responsible for more integrative processing during learning.

However, if the episodic buffer were the section where information is integrated (where "binding" takes place), two things would have to be evident. One, the central executive and the episodic buffer sections should have relatively independent actions on information during processing, and two, the brain regions activated for the two working memory sections and their respective actions (e.g., attention and binding, respectively) should be different. Unfortunately, neither the first nor the second condition appears to be the case. The two components do not appear to have entirely independent actions (Chein & Feiz, 2010), the actions are not contained in separate and unrelated regions of the brain (c.f. Baddeley, Allen, & Hitch, 2010), and evidence from functional neuroimaging studies provides little, if any, support for the buffer's binding function (Allen, Baddeley, & Hitch, 2006; Rossi-Arnaud, Pieroni, & Baddeley, 2006). Instead, there is substantial evidence that the "concept of specialized buffers do not adequately map onto neural architecture at all. Findings appear more consistent with a system in which active maintenance involves the recruitment of the same circuitry that represents the information itself, with different circuits for different types of information" (D'Esposito, 2007, p. 764).

In addition, compartmentalization of working memory into components consisting of a central executive *and* an episodic buffer is based on research that is very complex and hotly debated, and there is evidence that, as sovereign entities, there is no need for a central executive and episodic buffer to actually exist. As Rawley and Constantinidis (2009) explained, it is true that Baddeley's working memory components refer to functional rather than anatomical units, but there should be a functional neurology to the subsystems, and there does not appear to be. In fact, with regard to the central executive, the prefrontal cortex should be most actively involved when the central executive is activated, if the central executive is responsible for controlling and coordinating information through the slave systems and the episodic buffer. However, "physiologic evidence indicates that prefrontal neurons in area 46 represent spatial and object attributes of visual memoranda in correspondence to the visual-spatial sketchpad (Rao, Rainer, & Miller, 1997) while at the same time providing neural correlates of executive functions such as rule execution and category classification (Freedman, Riesenhuber, Poggio, & Miller, 2001; Wallis, Anderson, & Miller, 2001)" (Rawley & Constantinidis, 2009, p. 133). The problem is apparently the same for the other subsystems. All of the subsystems appear to activate multiple brain areas, including both the prefrontal and anterior cingulate cortices (Smith and Jonides, 1999).

Thus, an episodic buffer is not a utilitarian concept with which to explain metacognitive monitoring or control.

Implicating the Central Executive in Metacognitive Monitoring

According to Repovs and Baddeley (2006), the central executive has always been the "most important but least understood and least empirically studied component of the multi-component working memory model" (p. 12). However, based on a careful and exhaustive review of the evidence, Baddeley and his colleagues also contended that "in complex cognitive abilities, the central executive seems to be mostly involved as a source of attentional control, enabling the focusing of attention, the division of attention between concurrent tasks, and as one component of attentional switching" (Repovs & Baddeley, 2006, pp. 14–15). Thus, the role of the central executive seems to be the functional component of working memory principally responsible for the allocation, deployment, and maintenance of attention during learning.

There is also evidence that the central executive is predominantly responsible for attentional processes. In the time-based-resource-sharing (TBRS) model proposed by Barrouillet and Valérie (2010), information in working memory is maintained by a rapid switching between brief processing and storage, allowing for memory traces to be constantly refreshed by attention. Raye, Johnson, Mitchell, Greene, and Johnson (2007) point out that this recursive refreshing involves the left dorsolateral prefrontal cortex. The same is true for the embedded processing model of working memory (Cowan, 1999). While structurally different from Baddeley and colleagues' four-component model and wherein a central executive is not postulated per se, the embedded processing model nevertheless does postulate the operation of a central controller. Most importantly, the controller is purported to supervise the preservation of information in working memory by iteratively subjecting it to a recursion of attentional focus (Cowan, 1999)—a reactivation strategy that Lewandowsky and Oberauer (2008) refer to as "attentional refreshing." Finally, Chein and Feiz (2010) provide neuroimaging and corroborating behavioral evidence to support the central controller.

Thus, attention is manipulated by some sort of attention controller—a controller that is moderated by the individual, necessary for other cognitive processes to be deployed, and grounded in areas of the brain known to be involved in attentional focus. As Barrouillet and Valérie (2010) point out: "processing most often requires the selection, activation, and maintenance of goals and sub-goals, the selection of relevant information, the retrieval from long-term memory of related items of knowledge, the planning and monitoring of adapted strategies, and response selection, *all activities known as requiring attention*" (italics added) (p. 356). Thus, the evidence suggests that the allocation, deployment, and maintenance of this attention are executive functions grounded in the neurological activity (principally, but not exclusively) of the prefrontal cortex. If attention can be assumed to be integral to monitoring per se, then the central controller is likely responsible for what is postulated to be the monitoring function of metacognition.

At the same time, most agree that attention directed top-down (e.g., internal representation to behavioral action) is based on information held in working memory (c.f. Bundesen, 1990). Thus, from a top-down approach, using visual stimuli as an example, Lavie and colleagues (Forster & Lavie, 2007; Lavie, 2005) demonstrated that one's ability to filter out irrelevant stimuli during selection of visual stimuli depends on the processing load in working memory. As the load increases, fewer resources are available to support the efficient selection of targets relative to the rejection of distracters. The net effect is an increase of the interference from distracters under conditions of high working memory load. On the other hand, there is a decrease of the interference effect of distracters even when the complexity of a visual display is high. This suggests that the allocation of attention is selectively deployed-- and is based on a biased competition model of attention (Desimone & Duncan, 1995). That is, stimuli compete for selection at multiple levels of representation, with the winner gaining control of both perceptual and response systems. Thus, working memory acts to bias the competition for attention to favor objects that fit the goals of the task. Soto, Hodsoll, Rotshtein, and Humphreys (2008) suggest that prefrontal cells are implicated in this attention-biasing effect by being involved in prioritizing the relevant goals for tasks. Thus, "attentional refreshing," "recursion of attentional focus," "biased competition," and other ways of describing the allocation of attention are voluntary processes of cognitive engagement learners use to *monitor* the deployment of other cognitive processes.

Implicating the Central Executive in Metacognitive Monitoring and Control

The evidence above suggests that the prefrontal cortex is of critical importance in the monitoring function of the central executive. However, without an episodic buffer, it must have a controlling function as well—to be able to control "when behavior must be guided and controlled by internal states and intentions, when automatic responses have to be suppressed, and when tasks require the establishment of new or rapidly changing mappings between perception and action" (Wolters & Raffone, 2008, p. 2). Indeed, the prefrontal cortex is well positioned to coordinate processing in the rest of brain because it is strongly interconnected with reciprocal connections to virtually all other neocortical and subcortical brain regions (Constantinidis & Procyk, 2004; Rawley & Constantinidis, 2009).

The evidence from neuroscience suggests that the prefrontal cortex *does* control behavior, but it does so by *modulating* rather than simply *transmitting* neural impulses.

According to Wolters and Raffone (2008), "simple adaptive behavior rests on a cycle of perception, action, and perception-of-action results," but the prefrontal cortex allows an "internalization of this loop, freeing the organism of the restrictions of being aware of, or acting upon, physically present objects or situations only." This means that the prefrontal cortex can orchestrate other brain regions in the manipulation of internal representations, independent of the present environment; it can maintain physically absent information in an active state by recurrent connections between itself and the rest of the cortex, and it can redirect actions of monitoring, attention, and control by activating and or inhibiting particular motor programs. More importantly, its capacity for recurrent connections with memory systems, in addition to its mechanisms for combining information within neural loops, allows for the formation and updating of future goal states and ways of achieving them. Taken together, the functions of the prefrontal cortex are clearly involved in cognitive control, relative to the regulation and influence of other brain regions.

But, the prefrontal cortex is responsible for cognitive control by virtue of three interdependent functions—maintenance, attentional control, and integration (Wolters & Raffone, 2008)—the same functions erroneously believed to be associated with an episodic buffer. Maintenance refers to the process of actively holding a limited amount of task-relevant information supplied by a preceding event; attentional control is the top-down selective activation of the representations of task relevant stimuli and their corresponding responses; integration is the combination and reorganization of information from different sources in the service of controlling the execution of a task. Maintenance is the result of neurological patterns of activation borne from specific external inputs oscillating in a recurrent loop between multiple networks of prefrontal and other cortical cells in regions of the brain that are specialized for the nature of the input (Ranganath et al., 2004). Attentional control seems to operate in a biasing and competitive fashion where neuronal responses of the prefrontal cortex bias neuronal responses in posterior parts of the brain, creating a competition of activation and suppression for the task-relevant and task-irrelevant stimuli, respectively, required for task performance (Miller & Cohen, 2001). Integration appears to be a hierarchically arranged deployment of control, cascading down from superordinate prefrontal cortical modules specialized for large-scale integration, to subordinate modules that are relatively specialized for processing simple tasks (Koechlin, Ody, & Kouneiher, 2003).

As D'Esposito (2007) explained it, there appear to be a least two types of these top-down signals—one that serves to enhance and another that serves to suppress task-relevant information. Both are important for our discussion here because enhancement and suppression mechanisms may actually exist to control both cognitive *and* metacognitive functions (Knight, Staines, Swick, & Chao, 1999). After all, it is well documented that excitatory and inhibitory mechanisms are pervasively interleaved throughout the nervous system, in spinal reflexes, cerebellar outputs, and basal ganglia movement control networks, etc.—indeed, at multiple levels throughout the entire neuroaxis. That means "by generating contrast via both enhancements and suppressions… top–down signals bias the likelihood of successful representation of relevant information in a competitive system" (D'Esposito, 2007, p. 768). In short, the top-down function and the biasing effect within the context of a competitive system could be a compelling way to think about a neurological explanation of metacognitive monitoring and control.

Working Memory and Metacognitive Monitoring and Control

Based on the evidence above, we conclude that it is not necessary to involve a central executive and episodic buffer as two distinct components of the working memory system to explain metacognition. Rather, it is necessary only to implicate a central executive controller of some kind that regulates attention and deploys operations of activation and suppression of internally stored and externally perceived input to reach a behavioral goal. In short, metacognition is certainly "in the brain," but it is not in the central executive and episodic buffers of Baddeley and his colleagues' working memory model.

So, just where would metacognition likely be?

We suggest that metacognition is manifest within the function of cognitive—and hence neuroanatomical—activity of the brain best represented by the model of embedded processes (Cowan, 1999), the operations of which we have described in the evidence above (see Fig. 6.1).

To be specific, metacognitive monitoring and control are probably reciprocal functions of the same neurological processes that excite and inhibit, in a recursive fashion, the regions of the brain responsible for two types of activities involved in learning—the activities involved in

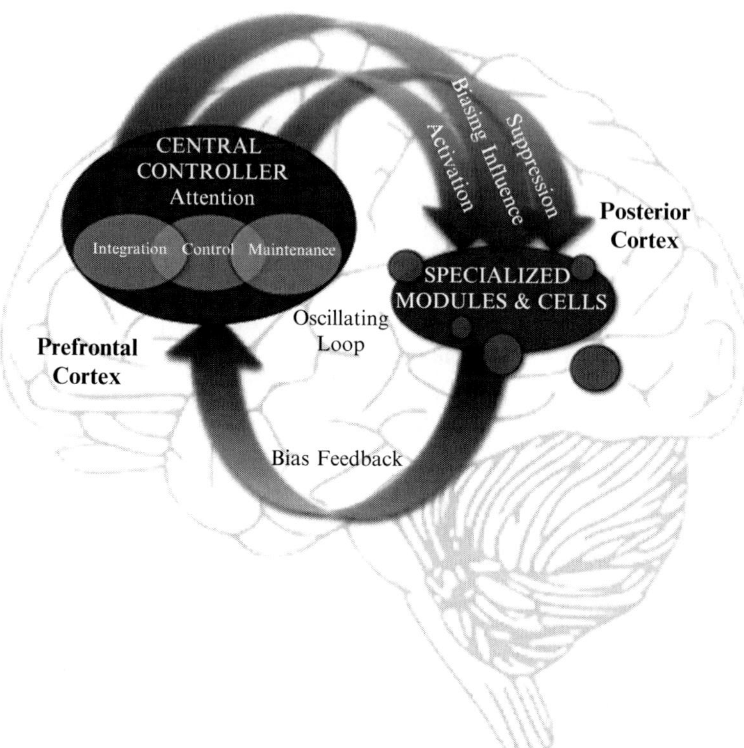

Fig. 6.1 Interdependent top-down function of cognitive control

processing the information itself relative to the goals of a task and the activities involved in processing (evaluating and correcting) the original activities deployed to seek goal attainment—activities that are metacognitive. We believe that the monitoring function is probably principally attentional, and the control function is principally strategic. Thus, attention is probably allocated to evaluate the degree to which an individual is closer to the goal—a matching-to-sample function; the strategies are activated to change the person's processing approach (and hence the corresponding brain activation) in meeting the goal. This alternating procedure is probably an interleaved activation of excitatory and inhibitory mechanisms based on two sources of information and two sources of goals, exchanged in a recursive fashion depending upon the degree to which the goal is being met. One source of information is composed of the stimuli that comprise the task in the context of the original task demands; the other is the information composed of the internal representation of the assessment of the correspondence between task demand and task success and the information about effective strategies for obtaining the success. In effect, we suggest that there may be no difference in the mechanisms operating between cognitive and metacognitive processing when one considers activation of regions of the brain. Instead, it is the nature of the information being processed in the system that differentiates the two.

We believe the operations of active cognition and metacognitive monitoring and control probably look something like the patterns shown in Fig. 6.2. That is, learners begin the process of learning by first directing their attention to two types of external information. One is the to-be-learned material; the other is the learning goal—in essence, the instructions with which the to-be-learned material is to be processed. This directed attention is an operation of the central controller where the learner seeks to differentiate between task-relevant and task-irrelevant stimuli in the external learning environment in order to find the stimuli having the highest probability of further processing utility. Once the differentiation is made, the central controller maintains

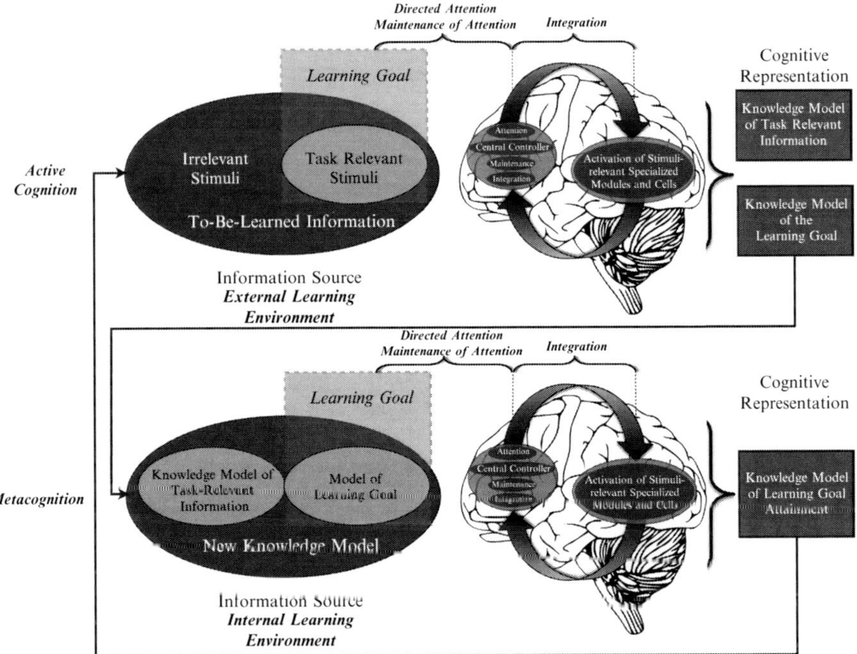

Fig. 6.2 Metacognitive monitoring and control: a closed neurocognitive loop

attention on the task-relevant stimuli and the learning goal while concomitantly redirecting attention to the internally stored stimuli activated among the modules and cells distributed in the posterior cortex that are germane to the task. At the same time, while attention is being switched between directing and maintaining the two sources of stimuli—external and internal—the central controller is also engaged in the integration of these stimuli into new knowledge models: one model of the to-be-learned information and the other model representing the learning goal. In short, the direction of attention among relevant stimuli inside and out, the maintenance of that attention on the stimuli inside and out, and the integration of those stimuli inside and out are oscillating processes of active cognition which lead to the development of the new models of knowledge.

However, the function of active cognition in this oscillating process is improved when learners report competence in their general use of metacognitive skills and when metacognitive activities are activated and supported within learners during the learning process. Thus, the question becomes how metacognition can possibly operate when active cognition seems to be sufficient for processing, but metacognition enhances performance beyond the outcomes of the tightly interleaved active cognition operations.

Our position is that metacognition must be comprised of the same processes as active cognition, but with attention and integration allocated to a different source of information. That source is no longer exclusively external per se but rather originates from the internal cognitive environment instead—from the new model of the task-relevant information borne from the information intended to be learned and the personalized model of the learning goal that was constructed during active cognition. This suggests that active cognition and metacognition form a closed loop, where metacognition is comprised of the same operations of the central controller in the prefrontal cortex and the posterior cortex's activation of relevant models and cells, but at this point, oscillating to construct a knowledge model of learning goal attainment. That means that the cognitive system must negotiate, by attentional switching, three models of knowledge during the learning phase—one model that targets the to-be-learned material, one that targets the learning goal, and the third that monitors and controls whether the first two models are sufficiently formed to reach the learning goal.

Once the process begins, the system must balance attentional direction and maintenance between both sources of information along with an integration of each. Thus, active cognition and metacognition use the same resources, activate the same gross neuroanatomical regions, and balance the same operations to resolve the learning process until the final metacognitively constructed knowledge model of goal attainment is complete.

Metacognition and Learning

If we are correct in our appraisal of the way metacognition works, then we should be able to interpret why manipulations of metacognition may, or may not, be instructionally successful. After all, we stated earlier that students' executive control should exert an influence on the ways teachers and instructional designers might approach their delivery of instruction.

The literature on metacognition in learning and instruction is substantial. Thus, we sampled 28 investigations published between 2002 and 2009, with the intention of building a corpus of work from which to determine if our model is heuristically valuable. Half of the investigations addressed the degree to which learners actually deploy their metacognitive skills during the time in which they learn; the other half reported the results of conditions in which metacognitive operations were instructionally scaffolded. All of the investigations were situated in learning environments that were delivered on computers via arrangements of hypermedia.

What we generally discovered is that learners learn more when their metacognitive skills are well developed. The finding occurs with surprising regularity and is consistent across multiple types of manipulations of learning materials (c.f. Azevedo, 2005; Graesser, McNamara, & VanLehn, 2005; Hartley & Bendixen, 2003; Schwartz, Anderson, Hong, Howard, & McGee, 2004; Schwartz, Oppy, & Gust, 1999; Scott & Schwartz, 2007; Veenman, Prins, & Elshout, 2002). For example, Graesser et al. (2005) noted that there are well-documented difficulties among learners when they do not possess adequate proficiencies in metacognitive skills; poor inquiry learning behavior and lower levels of comprehension characterize the difficulties. Azevedo (2005) reported that students who lack key metacognitive skills learn very little from hypermedia when learning environments are open ended. And, Hartley and Bendixen (2003) found that learners make better use of comprehension aids during learning within hypermedia environments, but only when the learners possess metacognitive skills that are high.

There are other supporting investigations as well. Veenman et al. (2002) could predict learners' acquisition of high-quality conceptual knowledge from the degree to which the learners had effective metacognitive skills, and Scott and Schwartz (2007) and Schwartz et al. (2004, 1999) found that learners could navigate more effectively within, and learn more from, hypermedia environments when the learners' metacognitive skills were high. Thus, learners with better-developed metacognitive skills do, in fact, learn better, and the evidence is apparent among multiple indices of performance.

And yet, not all learners have sufficiently well-developed metacognitive skills (c.f. Bannert, 2006), nor do all learners actually deploy those skills even if the skills are well developed (c.f. Azevedo, Guthrie, & Seibert, 2004). Manlove, Lazonder, and de Jong (2007), for example, found that learners typically show very few instances of metacognitive regulatory control operations during inquiry work in computer-based learning environments. Azevedo and Cromley (2004) and Bannert, Hildebrand, and Mengelkamp (2009) reported that learners rarely use metacognitive monitoring when negotiating complex hypermedia learning environments, in addition to failing to plan or activate their prior knowledge or use other effective knowledge acquisition strategies that would benefit their performance. Finally, Azevedo and Hadwin (2005) found that when learners learn about complex topics in computer-based learning environments without external metacognitive supports, their use of metacognitive control operations is very poor, and they fail to gain a conceptual understanding of the target instructional topics. Thus, the evidence is very clear that the failure to use metacognitive skills results in poor learning performance.

But, the failure to deploy metacognitive skills is puzzling when it is clear that metacognition works to benefit learning performance. Thus, we questioned whether metacognitive operations scaffolded during instruction actually lead to better performance. Scaffolded instruction refers to the types of computer-based tools designed to detect, trace, monitor, and foster metacognitive skills (Azevedo, 2002); they are the human or nonhuman learning agents whose roles are designed to lead learners to strategic learning activities that result in better performance (Azevedo, Cromley, & Seibert, 2004).

According to the preponderance of the empirical evidence, scaffolding does work (c.f. Azevedo & Cromley, 2004; Azevedo & Hadwin, 2005; Azevedo & Jacobson, 2008; Bannert, 2006, 2009; Graesser et al., 2005; Manlove et al., 2007). When learners' metacognitive processes are augmented via computer-based training systems and instructional strategies, metacomprehension accuracy and transfer task performance improve (Cuevas, Fiore, Bowers, & Salas, 2004). Also, learners learning with reflection prompts in computer-based learning environments show better performance on transfer tasks and make navigation decisions that are more strategic (Bannert, 2006). Finally, Rouet and Le Bigot (2007) found evidence that training learners on meta-textual knowledge, hypertext navigation strategies, and methods to acquire problem-relevant information leads the learners to spend more time visiting relevant sections of the hypertext and write better essays containing more critical and more deeply processed information. The point is that teaching, prompting, and facilitating learners' use of metacognitive skills result in improved learning performance.

So, why is it that some learners do not seem to develop metacognitive skills, why do some learners fail to deploy the skills on their own even when the skills have already been developed, and why is it that scaffolds work to incur skill deployment?

We believe that the resources incurred to develop and deploy metacognitive skills are demanding. After all, learners must construct two knowledge models as we described above. Then, they must broker those models with the development of a third—the metacognitively constructed model built to negotiate learning goal attainment. This forces attentional direction and maintenance to be split across three large knowledge models of separate but related domains. It also forces integration within and between the three models—a heavy resource-consuming task of concomitant cognitive and metacognitive operations. Unless one or more of the models is well consolidated among the modules distributed in the posterior cortex, it is not at all surprising that learners economize their efforts in building any one of the three. Since the metacognitive model is, by definition, always secondary to the other two, it is quite likely that the model either does not initially get built or, more likely, is built incompletely. In the first case, it would necessarily fail to be deployed; in the second case, its partial construction would occlude and/or seriously compromise the construction of either or both of the primary cognitively constructed models. This would explain why learners (1) learn very little from hypermedia when the environments are open ended, (2) navigate within those environments more inefficiently, and (3) fail to plan or activate prior knowledge and other effective knowledge acquisition strategies that would benefit their performance. In short, the inadequacies become apparent because the monitoring and control processes comprising the learning goal attainment model never get adequately constructed. If construction is attempted, on the other hand, the central controller would be expected to be overtaxed and fatigued, accounting in part for the failure of learners to gain a conceptual understanding of target instructional topics.

This is exactly the reason why we believe metacognitive scaffolds actually work. When metacognitive scaffolds are available, learners make use of the scaffolded strategies. These scaffolds either incur the construction of a metacognitive model while relieving the central controller's attention allocation and maintenance function of the controlling processes themselves, or they provide learners the learning control functions during primary knowledge model construction. In either case, both would lead to better performance on transfer tasks, better and more strategic navigation decisions in hypermedia, and more critically and deeply processed information following the learning phase.

Concluding Remarks

We began this chapter by stating that learning and thinking are synergistic actions of the way people develop knowledge to adapt to the world. We suggested that the actions are collateral cognitive operations sharing a unitary outcome of performance, with metacognition functioning as an integral operator. Assuming that metacognition is within the realm of the mind with much less concern over the human–environment interaction, we sought to find where metacognition might be operating at two levels—one, the metaphorical level of cognition and, two, the neuroanatomical level of the brain. At the level of cognition, we discovered that metacognition does not fit well within the model of working memory described by Baddeley and his colleagues (e.g., Baddeley & Hitch, 2000). Instead, it is much better explained by the embedded processing model of Cowan (Cowan, 1999). At the level of neuroanatomy, based on an examination of the neurological processes forthcoming from fMRI research, we discovered that metacognition seems to be a reciprocal function of the same neurological processes that reciprocally excite and inhibit the regions of the brain responsible for the activities involved in processing the to-be-learned material relative to the goals of a task and the activities involved in evaluating and correcting the original activities deployed to seek goal attainment. Taken together, both the embedded processing model and the neuroanatomical functions underlying it lead to the conclusion that processes of metacognition and active cognition form a closed loop of operations occurring in the same areas of the brain. The construction of cognitive models (and hence neural processes) is derived from a biased competition of limited resources that lead to new learning.

References

Allen, R., Baddeley, A., & Hitch, G. J. (2006). Is the binding of visual features in working memory resource-demanding? *Journal of Experimental Psychology. General, 135*(2), 298–313.

Atkinson, R. C., & Shiffrin, R. M. (1968). Human memory: A proposed system and its control processes. In K. W. Spence (Ed.), *The psychology of learning and motivation: Advances in research and theory* (pp. 89–195). New York: Academic.

Azevedo, R. (2002). Beyond intelligent tutoring systems: Using computers as METAcognitive tools to enhance learning? *Instructional Science, 30*, 31–45.

Azevedo, R. (2005). Using hypermedia as a metacognitive tool for enhancing student learning? The role of self-regulated learning. *Educational Psychologist, 40*(4), 199–209.

Azevedo, R., & Cromley, J. G. (2004). Does training on self-regulated learning facilitate Students' learning with hypermedia? *Journal of Educational Psychology, 93*(3), 523–535.

Azevedo, R., Cromley, J. G., & Seibert, D. (2004). Does adaptive scaffolding facilitate students' ability to regulate their learning with hypermedia? *Contemporary Educational Psychology, 29*, 344–370.

Azevedo, R., Guthrie, J. T., & Seibert, D. (2004). The role of self-regulated learning in fostering students' conceptual understanding of complex systems with hypermedia. *Journal of Educational Computing Research, 30*, 87–111.

Azevedo, R., & Hadwin, A. F. (2005). Scaffolding self-regulated learning and metacognition—Implications for the design of computer-based scaffolds. *Instructional Science, 33*, 367–379.

Azevedo, R., & Jacobson, M. J. (2008). Advances in scaffolding learning with hypertext and hypermedia: A summary and critical analysis. *Educational Technology Research and Development, 56*, 93–100.

Baddeley, A. D. (2000). The episodic buffer: A new component of working memory? *Trends in Cognitive Science, 4*, 417–423.

Baddeley, A. (2003). Working memory and language: An overview. *Journal of Communication Disorders, 36*(3), 189–208.

Baddeley, A. D., & Hitch, G. J. (2000). Development of working memory: Should the Pascual-Leone and the Baddeley and Hitch models be merged? *Journal of Experimental Child Psychology, 77*(2), 128–137.

Baddeley, A., Allen, R. J., & Hitch, G. J. (2010). Investigating the episodic buffer. *Psychologica Belgica, 50*(3–4), 223–243.

Bandura, A. (1977). *Social learning theory*. Oxford, England: Prentice-Hall.

Banfield, J., Wyland, C. L., Macrae, C. N., Munte, T. F., & Heatherton, T. F. (2004). The cognitive neuroscience of self-regulation. In R. F. Baumeister & K. D. Vohs (Eds.), *The handbook of self-regulation* (pp. 63–83). New York: Guilford.

Bannert, M. (2006). Effects of reflection prompts when learning with hypermedia. *Journal of Educational Computing Research, 35*(4), 359–375.

Bannert, M. (2009). Promoting self-regulated learning through prompts. *Zeitschrift für Pädagogische Psychologie, 23*(2), 139–145.

Bannert, M., Hildebrand, M., & Mengelkamp, C. (2009). Effects of a metacognitive support device in learning environments. *Computers in Human Behavior, 25*, 829–835.

Barrouillet, P. C., & Valérie. (2010). Working memory and executive control: A time-based resource-sharing account. *Psychologica Belgica, 50*, 353–382.

Bench, C. J., Frith, C. D., Grasby, P. M., & Friston, K. J. (1993). Investigations of the functional anatomy of attention using the Stroop test. *Neuropsychologia, 31*(9), 907–922. doi:10.1016/0028-3932(93)90147-R.

Broadbent, D. E. (1953). *Perception and communication*. Pergamon Press.

Bundesen, C. (1990). A theory of visual attention. *Psychology Review, 97*, 523–547.

Bush, G., Luu, P., & Posner, M. I. (2000). Cognitive and emotional influences in anterior cingulate cortex. *Trends in Cognitive Sciences, 4*(6), 215–222.

Bush, G., Whalen, P. J., Rosen, B. R., Jenike, M. A., McInerney, S. C., & Rauch, S. L. (1998). The counting stroop: An interference task specialized for functional neuroimaging. Validation study with functional MRI. *Human Brain Mapping, 6*, 270–282.

Carter, C. S., Mintun, M., & Cohen, J. D. (1995). Inference and facilitation effects during selective attention: An H215O PET study of stroop task performance. *NeuroImage, 2*, 264–272.

Chein, J. M., & Feiz, A. F. (2010). Evaluating models of working memory through the effects of concurrent irrelevant information. *Journal of Experimental Psychology. General, 139*(1), 117–137.

Constantinidis, C., & Procyk, E. (2004). The primate working memory networks. *Cognitive, Affective and Behavioral Neuroscience, 4*, 444–465.

Cowan, N. (1999). An embedded-process model of working memory. In A. Miyake & P. Shah (Eds.), *Models of working memory: Mechanisms of active maintenance and executive control* (pp. 62–101). Cambridge, UK: Cambridge University Press.

Cuevas, H. M., Fiore, S. M., Bowers, C. A., & Salas, E. (2004). Fostering constructive cognitive and metacognitive activity in computer-based complex task training environments. *Computers in Human Behavior, 20*, 225–241.

Cummings, M. (1994). Frontal-subcortical circuits and neuropsychiatric disorders. *The Journal of Neuropsychiatry and Clinical Neurosciences, 6*, 358–370.

D'Esposito, M. (2007). From cognitive to neural models of working memory. *Philosophical Transactions of the Royal Society of London B, 363*, 761–772.

Desimone, R., & Duncan, J. (1995). Neural mechanisms of selective visual attention. *Annual Review of Neuroscience, 18*, 193–222.

Dinsmore, D. L., Alexander, P. A., & Loughlin, S. M. (2008). Focusing the conceptual lens on metacognition, self-regulation, and self-regulated learning. *Educational Psychology Review, 20*, 391–409.

Efklides, A. (2006). Metacognition and affect: What can metacognitive experiences tell us about the learning process? *Educational Research Review, 1*, 3–14.

Fernandez-Duque, D., Baird, J. A., & Posner, M. I. (2000). Executive attention and metacognitive regulation. *Consciousness and Cognition, 9*(2), 288–307.

Flavell, J. H. (1979). Metacognition and cognitive monitoring: A new area of cognitive-developmental inquiry. *American Psychologist, 34*, 906–911.

Forster, S., & Lavie, N. (2007). High perceptual load makes everybody equal: Eliminating individual differences in distractibility with load. *Psychological Science, 18*, 377–382.

Freedman, D. J., Riesenhuber, M., Poggio, T., & Miller, E. K. (2001). Categorical representation of visual stimuli in the primate prefrontal cortex. *Science, 291*, 312–316.

Fugelsang, J. A., & Dunbar, K. N. (2005). Brain-based mechanisms underlying complex causal thinking. *Neuropsychologia, 43*(8), 1204–1213.

Graesser, A. C., McNamara, D. S., & VanLehn, K. (2005). Scaffolding deep comprehension strategies through point and query, AutoTutor, and iSTART. *Educational Psychologist, 40*(4), 225–234.

Hartley, K., & Bendixen, L. D. (2003). The use of comprehension aids in a hypermedia environment: Investigating the impact of metacognitive awareness and epistemological beliefs. *Journal of Educational Multimedia and Hypermedia, 12*(3), 275–289.

Jonides, J., Lewis, R. L., Nee, D. E., Lustig, C. A., Berman, M. G., & Moore, K. S. (2008). The mind and brain of short-term memory. *Annual Review of Psychology, 59*, 193–224.

Kaplan, A. (2008). Clarifying metacognition, self-regulation, and self-regulated learning: What's the purpose? *Educational Psychology Review, 20*, 477–484.

Knight, R. T., Staines, W. R., Swick, D., & Chao, L. L. (1999). Prefrontal cortex regulates inhibition and excitation in distributed neural networks. *Acta Psychologica, 101*, 159–178.

Koechlin, E., Ody, C., & Kouneiher, F. (2003). The architecture of cognitive control in the human prefrontal cortex. *Science, 302*, 1181–1185.

Lavie, N. (2005). Distracted and confused?: Selective attention underload. *Trends in Cognitive Science, 9*, 75–82.

Lewandowsky, S., & Oberauer, K. (2008). The word-length effect provides no evidence for decay in short-term memory. *Psychonomic Bulletin & Review, 15*(5), 875–888. doi:10.3758/PBR.15.5.875.

Logie, R. H., Della Sala, S., Wynn, V., Baddeley, A. D. (2000). *Division of attention in Alzheimer's disease*. Paper presented at the Psychonomics Society meeting, Los Angeles, CA.

Logie, R. H., Gilhooly, K. J., & Wynn, V. (1994). Counting on working memory in mental arithmetic. *Memory & Cognition, 22*, 395–410.

Manlove, S., Lazonder, A. W., & de Jong, T. (2007). Software scaffolds to promote regulation during scientific learning. *Metacognition and Learning, 2*, 141–155. doi:10.1007/s11409-007-9012-y.

McGlynn, S. M., & Kaszniak, A. W. (1991). When metacognition fails: Impaired awareness of deficit in Alzheimer's disease. *Journal of Cognitive Neuroscience, 3*(2), 184–189.

Miller, E. K., & Cohen, J. D. (2001). An integrative theory of prefrontal cortex function. *Annual Review of Neuroscience, 24*, 167–202.

Moscovitch, M., & Melo, B. (1997). Strategic retrieval and the frontal lobes: Evidence from confabulation and amnesia. *Neuropsychologia, 35*(7), 1017–1034.

Moshman, D. (1982). Exogenous, endogenous, and dialectical constructivism. *Developmental Review, 2*(4), 371–384. doi:10.1016/0273-2297(82)90019-3.

Nagel, C. (2009). Neural correlates of depth of strategic reasoning in medial prefrontal cortex. ******PNAS, 106*(23), 9163–9168.

Nelson, T., & Narens, N. (1990). Metamemory: A theoretical framework and new findings. *Psychology of Learning and Motivation, 26*, 125–301.

Nolde, S. F., Johnson, M. K., & D'Esposito, M. (1998). Left prefrontal activation during episodic remembering: An event-related fMRI study. *Neuroreport, 9*(15), 3509–3514.

Pannu, J. K., Kaszniak, A. W., & Rapcsak, S. Z. (2005). Metamemory for faces following frontal lobe damage. *Journal of the International Neuropsychological Society, 11*, 668–676.

Ranganath, C., Yonelinas, A. P., Cohen, M. X., Dy, C. J., Tom, S. M., & D'Esposito, M. (2004). Dissociable correlates of recollection and familiarity within the medial temporal lobes. *Neuropsychologia, 42*(1), 2–13.

Rao, S. C., Rainer, G., & Miller, E. K. (1997). Integration of what and where in the primate prefrontal cortex. *Science, 276*(5313), 821–824.

Rawley, J. B., & Constantinidis, C. (2009). Neural correlates of learning and working memory in the primate posterior parietal cortex. *Neurobiology of Learning and Memory, 91*(2), 129–138.

Raye, C. L., Johnson, M. K., Mitchell, K. J., Greene, E. J., & Johnson, M. R. (2007). Refreshing: A minimal executive function. *Cortex, 43*, 135–145.

Repovs, G., & Baddeley, A. (2006). The multi-component model of working memory: Explorations in experimental cognitive psychology. *Neuroscience, 139*(1), 5–21.

Rossi-Arnaud, C., Pieroni, L., & Baddeley, A. (2006). Symmetry and binding in visuo-spatial working memory. *Neuroscience, 139*(1), 393–400.

Rouet, J.-F., & Le Bigot, L. (2007). Effects of academic training on metatextual knowledge and hypertext navigation. *Metacognition and Learning, 2*, 157–168. doi:10.1007/s11409-007-9011-z.

Rugg, M. D., Fletcher, P. C., Chua, P. M. L., & Dolan, R. J. (1999). The role of the prefrontal cortex in recognition memory and memory for source: An fMRI study. *NeuroImage, 10*(5), 520–529.

Saeki, E., & Saito, S. (2004). Effect of articulatory suppression on task switching performance: Implications of models of working memory. *Memory, 12*, 257–271.

Schnyer, D. M., Verfaellie, M., Alexander, M. P., LaFleche, G., Nicholls, L., & Kaszniak, A. W. (2004). A role for right medial prefrontal cortex in accurate feeling-of-knowing judgments: Evidence from patients with lesions to frontal cortex. *Neuropsychologia, 42*(7), 957–966.

Schraw, G., Crippen, K. J., & Hartley, K. (2006). Promoting self-regulation in science education: Metacognition as part of a broader perspective on learning. *Research in Science Education, 36*, 111–139.

Schraw, G., & Moshman, D. (1995). Metacognitive theories. *Educational Psychology Review, 7*(4), 351–371.

Schwartz, N. H., Anderson, C., Hong, N., Howard, B., & McGee, S. (2004). The influence of metacognitive skills on learners' memory of information in a hypermedia environment. *Journal of Educational Computing Research, 31*(1), 77–93.

Schwartz, N. H., Oppy, B., & Gust, K. (1999). Learning and the web: The role of metacognition and configurational knowledge in comprehension and problem solving. *Proceedings of Metacognition: Products and Processes*. France: Universite Blaise Pascal, Clermont-Ferrand.

Scott, B., & Schwartz, N. H. (2007). Navigational spatial displays: The role of metacognition as cognitive load. *Learning and Instruction, 17*, 89–105.

Shallice, T. (1988). *From neuropsychology to mental structure*. Cambridge: Cambridge University Press.

Shimamura, A. P. (2000). The role of prefrontal cortex in dynamic filtering. *Psychobiology, 28*(2), 207–218.

Shimamura, A. P. (2008). A Neurocognitive approach to metacognitive monitoring and control. In J. Dunlosky & R. Bjork (Eds.), *Handbook of memory and metacognition*. Mahwah, NJ: Erlbaum.

Smith, E. E., & Jonides, J. (1999). Storage and executive processes in the frontal lobes. *Science, 283*(5408), 1657–1661.

Soto, D., Hodsoll, J., Rotshtein, P., & Humphreys, G. (2008). Automatic guidance of attention from working memory. *Trends in Cognitive Sciences, 12*(9), 342–348.

Veenman, M. V. J., Prins, F. J., & Elshout, J. J. (2002). Initial inductive learning in a complex computer simulated environment: The role of metacognitive skills and intellectual ability. *Computers in Human Behavior, 18*, 327–341.

Wallis, J. D., Anderson, K. C., & Miller, E. K. (2001). Single neurons in prefrontal cortex encode abstract rules. *Nature, 411*(6840), 953–956.

Wolters, G., & Raffone, A. (2008). Coherence and recurrency: Maintenance, control and integration in working memory. *Cognitive Processing, 9*(1), 1–17. doi:10.1007/s10339-007-0185-8.

Part II

Assessing and Modeling Metacognitive Knowledge and Skills

Modeling and Studying Gaming the System with Educational Data Mining

7

Ryan S.J.d. Baker, A.T. Corbett, I. Roll, K.R. Koedinger, V. Aleven, M. Cocea, A. Hershkovitz, A.M.J.B. de Caravalho, A. Mitrovic, and M. Mathews

Abstract

In this chapter, we will discuss our work to understand why students game the system. This work leverages models of student gaming, termed "detectors", which can infer student gaming in log files of student interaction with educational software. These detectors are developed using a combination of human observation and annotation, and educational data mining. We then apply the detectors to large data sets, and analyze the detectors' predictions, using discovery with models methods, to study the factors associated with gaming behavior. Within this chapter, we will discuss the work to develop these detectors, and what we have discovered through these analyses based on these detectors. We will discuss evidence for how gaming the system impacts learning and evidence for why students choose to game. We will also discuss attempts to address gaming the system through adaptive scaffolding.

R.S.J.d. Baker (✉) • A. Hershkovitz
Columbia University Teachers College,
New York, NY, USA
e-mail: ryan@educationaldatamining.org

A.T. Corbett
Human-Computer Interaction Institute, Carnegie Mellon University, Pittsburgh, PA, USA

Pittsburgh Advanced Cognitive Tutor Center, Carnegie Mellon University, Pittsburgh, PA, USA

I. Roll
Carl Wieman Science Education Initiative, University of British Columbia, Vancouver, BC, Canada

Pittsburgh Science of Learning Center, Pittsburgh, PA, USA

K.R. Koedinger
Pittsburgh Science of Learning Center, Pittsburgh, PA, USA

Human-Computer Interaction and Psychology, Carnegie Mellon University, Pittsburgh, PA, USA

V. Aleven
Human-Computer Interaction Institute, Carnegie Mellon University, 5000 Forbes Avenue, Pittsburgh, PA 15213, USA

Pittsburgh Science of Learning Center, Pittsburgh, PA, USA

M. Cocea
School of Computing, University of Portsmouth, Portsmouth, Hampshire, UK

A.M.J.B. de Caravalho
Human-Computer Interaction Institute, CMU Carnegie Mellon University, Pittsburgh, PA 15213, USA

A. Mitrovic • M. Mathews
Intelligent Computer Tutoring Group (ICTG), Department of Computer Science and Software Engineering, University of Canterbury, Christchurch, New Zealand

R. Azevedo and V. Aleven (eds.), *International Handbook of Metacognition and Learning Technologies*, Springer International Handbooks of Education 26, DOI 10.1007/978-1-4419-5546-3_7,

Introduction

In recent years, there has been increasing awareness that students using interactive learning technologies often "game the system," defined as attempting to succeed in an educational task by systematically taking advantage of properties and regularities in the system used to complete that task, rather than by thinking through the material (Baker, Corbett, Koedinger, et al., 2006). Examples of gaming the system include misusing help features of educational software to obtain answers (Aleven, McLaren, Roll, & Koedinger, 2006), systematic guessing (Baker, Corbett, Koedinger, & Wagner, 2004), intentional rapid mistakes (Murray & VanLehn, 2005), spam postings in graded newsgroups (Cheng & Vassileva, 2005), and point cartels in collaborative games (Magnussen & Misfeldt, 2004). Analogous behaviors also occur within wholly human classrooms, where students ask teachers and teachers-aides repeatedly for answers (Nelson-Le Gall, 1985).

Gaming the system occupies an interesting place within self-regulated learning (SRL) and metacognition. In some ways, it can be considered as a behavior that requires sophisticated metacognition, involving—to quote Hacker (1999) discussing Flavell (1976)—"active monitoring and consequent regulation and orchestration of cognitive processes to achieve cognitive goals." Qualitative and quantitative analysis has suggested that students actively choose which problem steps to game on, with some students explicitly gaming specific poorly known material and other students gaming well-known material (cf. Baker, Corbett, & Koedinger, 2004). To the degree that students game the system precisely on the material that they do not know, the choice to game appears to explicitly involve "knowledge of one's knowledge" (cf. Hacker, 1999). Gaming clearly involves a substantial degree of self-regulation (Zimmerman, 2000) as well, inasmuch as the student appears to consciously choose to game as opposed to other strategies, such as attempting to seek help or answer using their knowledge (cf. Aleven et al., 2006).

However, while gaming appears to involve self-regulation, it is open to question whether gaming can be considered a strategy within SRL (cf. Butler & Winne, 1995). Many students who game the system appear not to be trying to learn at all during their gaming behavior (there are exceptions, which are discussed in this chapter). Hence, gaming the system could potentially be viewed as self-regulated behavior with the goal of avoiding learning, rather than SRL. There are several forms of self-regulation driven towards avoiding learning or effort, including self-handicapping (Midgley & Urdan, 2002) and off-task behavior (cf. Fisher & Ford, 1998). It is not clear that gaming is a form of self-handicapping, and gaming and off-task behavior appear to emerge from different motivation, at least in part (Baker, 2007b). Nonetheless, it may be valuable to conceptualize gaming in this fashion—as a self-regulated behavior but not as a strategy for SRL. Alternatively, gaming the system could be viewed as a tactic or a strategy emerging from low motivation during self-regulation, a possibility implicit within models of SRL that incorporate motivation (e.g., Winne & Hadwin, 1998). Interestingly, the one model of metacognition or SRL which explicitly incorporates gaming behaviors is Aleven and colleagues' (2006) model of help-seeking within tutors. Within this model, gaming is conceptualized as a "metacognitive bug," a cognitive rule that represents an ineffective or maladaptive form of help-seeking.

However, there is increasing evidence that gaming is more than simply an ineffective or maladaptive form of help-seeking. First of all, as we discuss in this chapter, there are multiple ways that students game. For instance, some students appear to game on time-consuming steps that they already know, potentially to spend more time on what they need to learn (Baker, Corbett, & Koedinger, 2004). Other students game in order to obtain answers more quickly, and then self-explain those answers (Shih, Koedinger, & Scheines, 2008). Gaming in these fashions may therefore be a strategy within sophisticated self-regulatory behavior (cf. Winne & Hadwin, 1998). Secondly, there is recent evidence that the triggers of gaming the system include features of the design of intelligent tutors (discussed in this chapter), and the student emotion immediately prior to gaming (Baker, D'Mello, Rodrigo, & Graesser, 2010). As such, it appears that gaming emerges from relatively complex self-regulatory processes, involving several factors, including an assessment of the current situation and the student's emotion.

In this chapter, we discuss our work to understand why students game the system. This work leverages models of student gaming, termed "detectors," which can infer student gaming in log files of student interaction with educational software. These detectors are developed using a combination of human observation and annotation, and educational data mining (Baker & Yacef, 2009; Romero & Ventura, 2010). We then apply the detectors to large data sets, and analyze the detectors' predictions, using discovery with model methods (Baker & Yacef, 2009), to study the factors associated with gaming behavior. Within this chapter, we discuss the work to develop these detectors, and what we have discovered through these analyses based on these detectors. We discuss evidence for how gaming the system impacts learning and evidence for why students choose to game. We also discuss attempts to address gaming the system through adaptive scaffolding.

Contexts of Detector Development and Use

Gaming the system has been studied in a variety of learning systems (Baker, Corbett, Koedinger, & Wagner, 2004; Baker, D'Mello, et al., 2010; Baker, Mitrovic, & Mathews, 2010; Beal, Qu, & Lee, 2006; Beck, 2005; Gobel, 2008; Johns & Woolf, 2006; Muldner, Burleson, Van de Sande, & VanLehn, 2011; Murray & VanLehn, 2005; Walonoski & Heffernan, 2006a). In this chapter, we focus on the research into gaming the system within Cognitive Tutors, though we briefly discuss research in other learning systems as well. A key advance that has supported research on gaming the system in recent years has been the advent of models that assess whether a student is gaming, often termed "detectors" (e.g., Aleven et al., 2006; Baker, Corbett, & Koedinger, 2004; Baker, Corbett, Roll, & Koedinger, 2008; Baker, Mitrovic et al., 2010; Beal et al., 2006; Beck, 2005; Johns & Woolf, 2006; Muldner et al., 2011; Walonoski & Heffernan, 2006a). Cognitive Tutors were the first type of learning environment for which gaming detector development occurred; they are also the environment for which gaming detectors have been most thoroughly validated, and for which gaming detectors have been used in the largest number of "discovery with models" analyses.

Cognitive Tutors are a popular type of interactive learning environment now used by around half a million students a year in the USA, in particular for high school Algebra and Geometry (Koedinger & Corbett, 2006). Cognitive Tutor curricula combine conceptual instruction delivered by a teacher with problem-solving where each student works one on one with a cognitive tutoring system which chooses exercises and feedback based on a running model of which skills the student possesses (Koedinger & Corbett, 2006). Within this chapter, we focus on students' online problem-solving. We discuss results from the Middle School Mathematics Cognitive Tutor, shown in Fig. 7.1, and the Algebra Tutor, shown in Fig. 7.2. In its original version, the Middle School Tutor was used by the U.S. middle school students, who are typically between approximately 11 and 14 years old. The Middle School Tutor has become Bridge to Algebra, and is now in use in high schools and middle schools across the USA (we refer to it by its original name, as this was the version used in the research presented in this chapter). The Algebra Tutor is typically used in the U.S. high schools, where students typically range from 14 to 18 years old.

Cognitive Tutor learning environments are designed to promote learning by doing. Within the Cognitive Tutor environments discussed within this chapter, each student individually completes mathematics problems. The Cognitive Tutor environment breaks down each mathematics problem into the steps of the process used to solve the

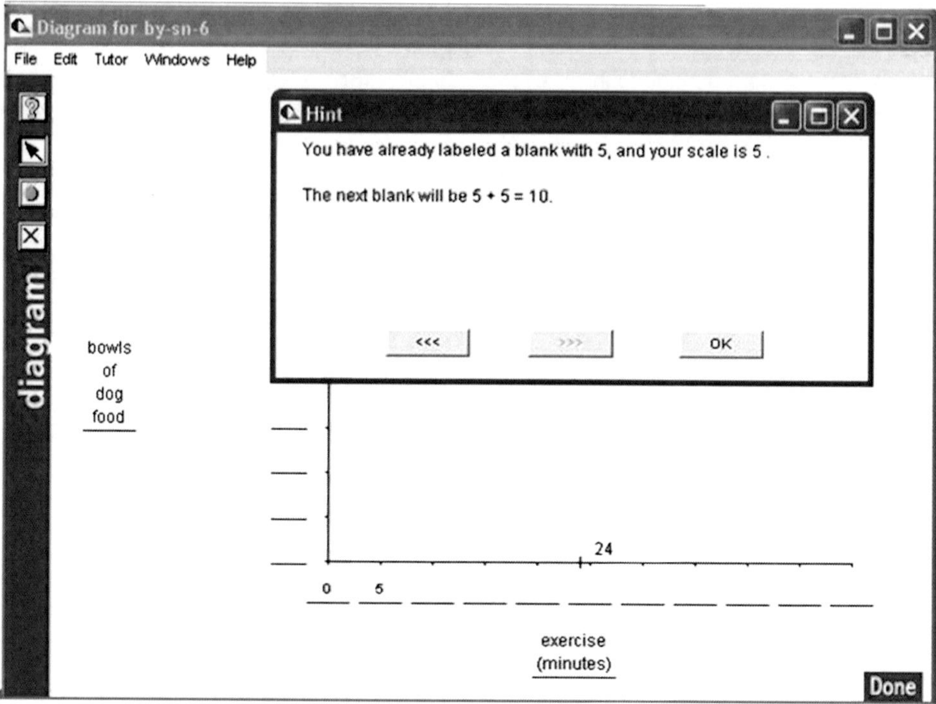

Fig. 7.1 A screenshot from the Cognitive Tutor for Middle School Mathematics

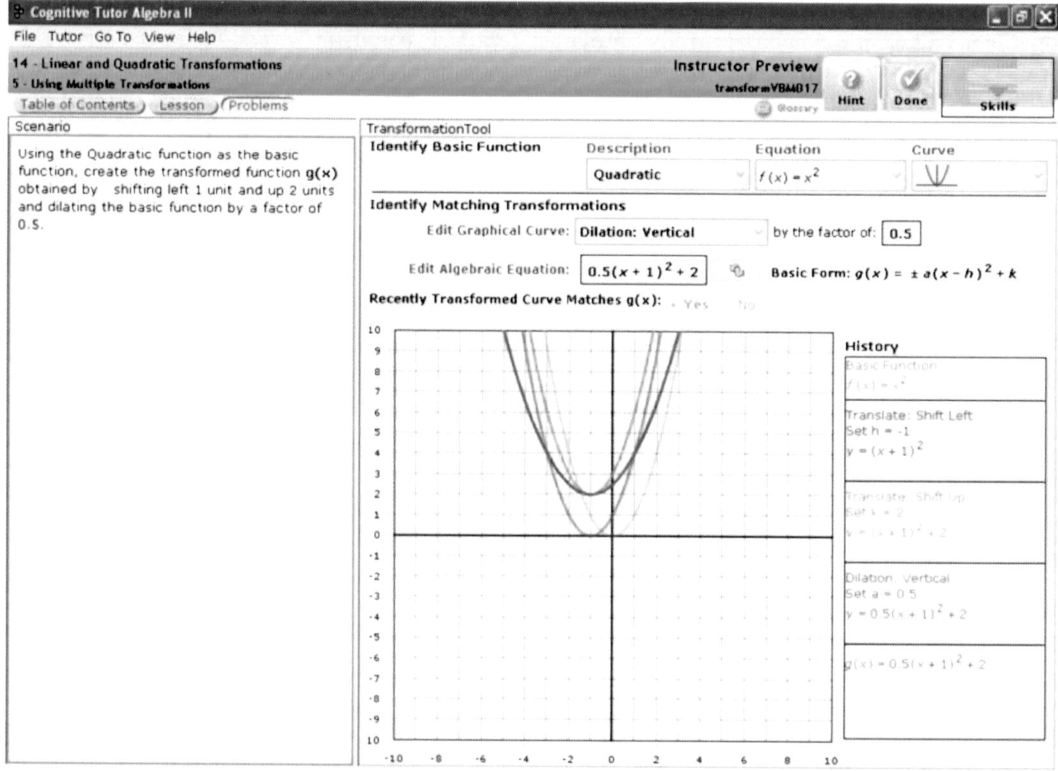

Fig. 7.2 A screenshot from the Algebra Cognitive Tutor

problem, making the student's thinking visible. As a student works through a problem, a running cognitive model assesses whether the student's answers map to correct understanding or to a known misconception (cf. Anderson, Corbett, Koedinger, & Pelletier, 1995). If the student's answer is incorrect, the answer turns red; if the student's answers are indicative of a known misconception, the student is given a "buggy message" indicating how their current knowledge differs from correct understanding. Cognitive Tutors also have multistep hint features; a student who is struggling can ask for a hint. He or she first receives a conceptual hint, and can then request further hints, which become more and more specific until the student is given the answer. The hints are context-sensitive and tailored to the exact problem step the student is working on. As the student works through the problems in a specific curricular area, the system uses Bayesian Knowledge-Tracing (Corbett & Anderson, 1995) to determine which skills that student is having difficulty with, calculating the probability that the student knows each skill based on that student's history of responses within the tutor. Using these estimates of student knowledge, the tutoring system gives each student problems which are relevant to the skills which he or she is having difficulty with. Cognitive Tutor material is typically structured into independent lessons, each of which covers a set of related skills and concepts. Year-long courses are composed of sequences of lessons, where the knowledge in later lessons generally builds upon the knowledge in previous lessons.

Detector Development

Detectors of gaming the system can be developed in several ways. While many researchers have utilized knowledge engineering to develop detectors of gaming the system (cf. Aleven et al., 2006; Gong, Beck, Heffernan, & Forbes-Summers, 2010; Johns & Woolf, 2006; Muldner et al., 2011), our research group has emphasized machine learning/data mining approaches, in order to support more thorough model validation. We believe that comprehensive validation is essential when using detectors to support research in the complex phenomena found in metacognition and SRL; without high confidence in a detector's validity and generalizability, it is difficult to have confidence in the results obtained from analyzing a detector's output. Within this section, we present our work to develop and validate detectors of gaming the system. A fuller discussion of the trade-offs between machine learning and knowledge engineering approaches for modeling student behaviors, such as gaming the system, can be found in Baker (2010).

Our approach to developing gaming detectors is as follows. We first use human labeling methods to gather "ground truth" labels of students or actions judged to be gaming the system. We then use data mining methods to distill these labels into reusable detectors of gaming. We then validate these models at multiple levels, including generalizability to new students and lessons, and temporal precision. We discuss these steps, as well as some challenges that need to be met for these detectors to be maximally useful for the field.

Human Labeling Methods

Within our research, we have used two methods for humans to label gaming the system. The first is *quantitative field observations* (Baker, Corbett, Koedinger, & Wagner, 2004; Karweit & Slavin, 1982). Quantitative field observations are repeated observations of students (in this case, whether they are gaming the system or not), conducted according a predefined coding scheme and observation method. Within our observations of gaming the system, each observation lasted 20 s, and was conducted using peripheral vision. That is, the observers stood diagonally behind or in front of the student being observed and avoided looking at the student directly (cf. Baker, Corbett, Koedinger, & Wagner, 2004), in order to make it less clear when an observation was occurring. If two distinct behaviors were seen during an observation, only the first behavior observed was coded. Any behavior by a student other than the student currently being observed was not coded. Observations are in some cases carried out by single observers and other times by observational pairs. Inter-rater reliability on assessments of gaming using this method have been calculated at over 0.7 across several studies involving different coders (Baker, Corbett, & Wagner, 2006; Baker, D'Mello, et al., 2010; Rodrigo et al., 2008). Another benefit of quantitative field observation is that it can be used for a variety of constructs (including affect as well as behavior—cf. Baker, D'Mello, et al., 2010; Rodrigo et al., 2008). The method's key disadvantages are that it is time-consuming, and it has historically been challenging to synchronize exactly between field observations and log files. (Our research group has recently developed a handheld observation application which synchronizes to the same time server as the software logs; we believe that this will substantially reduce challenges to synchronization.)

The second method we have used for humans to label gaming the system is *text replays* (Baker, Corbett, & Wagner, 2006; Baker & de Carvalho, 2008; Baker, Mitrovic, et al., 2010). Text replays represent a segment of student behavior from the log files in a textual ("pretty-printed") form. A sequence of actions of a preselected duration (in terms of time or length) is shown in a textual format that gives information about the actions and their context. In the example shown in Fig. 7.3, the coder sees each action's time (relative to the first action in the clip), the problem context, the input entered, the relevant skill (production), and how the system assessed the action (correct, incorrect, a help request, or a "bug"/misconception). The coder can then choose one of a set of behavior categories (in this study, gaming or not gaming), or indicate that something has gone wrong, making it impossible to code the clip. Text replays give relatively limited information, compared to quantitative field observations; however, text replays are very quick to classify, between two and ten times faster than quantitative field observations (Baker, Corbett, & Wagner, 2006; Baker & de Carvalho, 2008), and can be generated automatically from existing log files, enabling retrospective analysis. Inter-rater reliability has been found to be comparable to quantitative field observations, ranging between 0.58 and 0.80 (Baker, Corbett, & Wagner, 2006; Baker, D'Mello, et al., 2010), though it typically requires multiple rounds of training to get convergent categorization (Baker, D'Mello, et al., 2010; Sao Pedro, Baker, Montalvo, Nakama, & Gobert, 2010).

Educational Data Mining Methods Used

All of our detectors of gaming are based upon a distillation of features of students' actions within the tutoring software. For Cognitive Tutors, for each student action recorded in the log files, a set of 26 features describing that student action were distilled. These features included the following (an exhaustive list is given in Baker, Corbett, et al., 2008):

- Details about the action
  - The tutoring software's assessment of the action—Was the action correct, incorrect and indicating a known bug (procedural misconception), incorrect but not indicating a known bug, or a help request?
  - The type of interface widget involved in the action.
  - Was this the student's first attempt to answer or obtain help on this problem step?
- Knowledge assessment
  - The tutor's assessment, after the action, of the probability that the student knows the skill involved in this action, derived using the Bayesian knowledge tracing algorithm in Corbett and Anderson (1995).
  - Whether the action involved a skill which students, on the whole, knew before starting the tutor lesson, or failed to learn during the tutor lesson.
- Time
  - How long the action took, both in absolute time and in standard deviations faster or slower than the mean time taken by all students on this problem step, across problems (e.g., unitized time).
  - Unitized time across the last 3, or 5, actions.

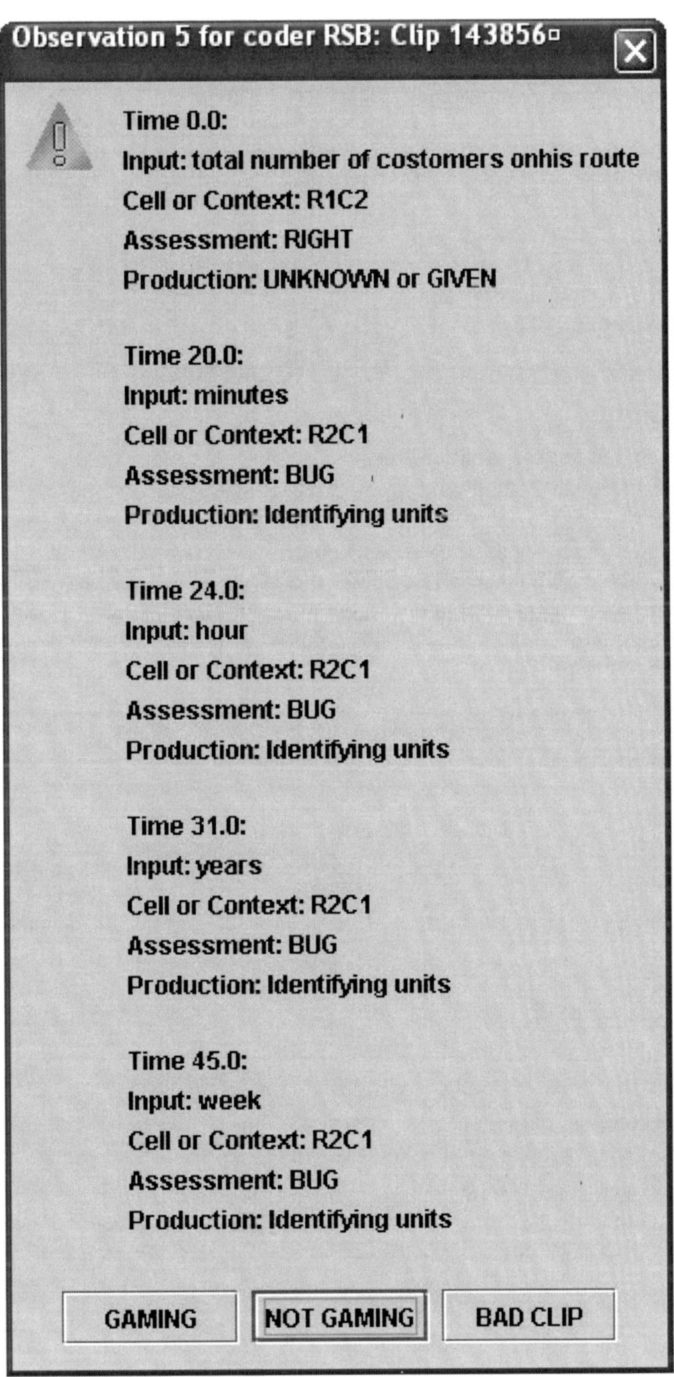

Observation 5 for coder RSB: Clip 143856
Time 0.0:
Input: total number of costomers onhis route
Cell or Context: R1C2
Assessment: RIGHT
Production: UNKNOWN or GIVEN
Time 20.0:
Input: minutes
Cell or Context: R2C1
Assessment: BUG
Production: Identifying units
Time 24.0:
Input: hour
Cell or Context: R2C1
Assessment: BUG
Production: Identifying units
Time 31.0:
Input: years
Cell or Context: R2C1
Assessment: BUG
Production: Identifying units
Time 45.0:
Input: week
Cell or Context: R2C1
Assessment: BUG
Production: Identifying units
GAMING
NOT GAMING
BAD CLIP

Fig. 7.3 A text replay of student gaming behavior

- Previous interaction
  - The total number of times the student has gotten this specific problem step wrong or asked for help, across all problems (includes multiple attempts within one problem).
  - How many recent actions involved this problem step, help requests, or errors?

Our research group has used two primary methods to develop detectors of gaming the system for Cognitive Tutors: Latent Response

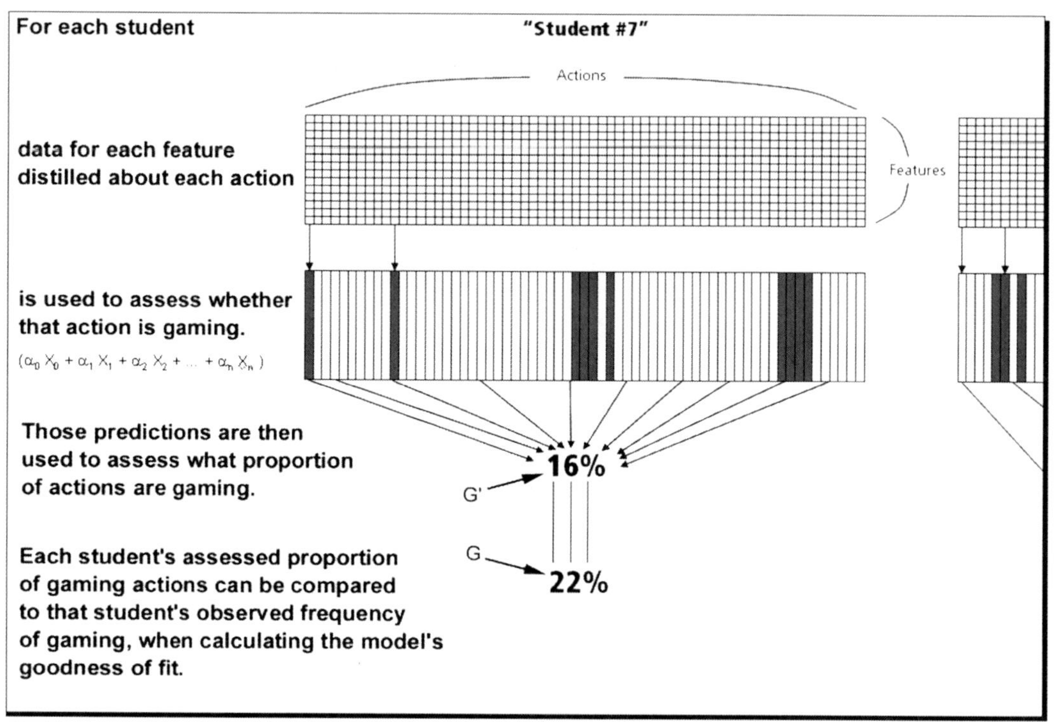
For each student
"Student #7"
Actions
data for each feature
distilled about each action
Features
is used to assess whether
that action is gaming.
$(\alpha_0 X_0 + \alpha_1 X_1 + \alpha_2 X_2 + \ldots + \alpha_n X_n)$
Those predictions are then
used to assess what proportion
of actions are gaming.
G'
16%
Each student's assessed proportion
of gaming actions can be compared
to that student's observed frequency
of gaming, when calculating the model's
goodness of fit.
G
22%

Fig. 7.4 The architecture of a gaming detector based on a Latent Response Model

Models (Maris, 1995) and J48 Decision Trees (an open-source variant published by Witten and Frank, 2005, of the C4.5 algorithm developed by Quinlan, 1993). J48 Decision Trees were first used to detect gaming the system by Walonoski and Heffernan (2006a). Recent work on detecting gaming the system in SQL-Tutor has also used step regression (Baker, Mitrovic, et al., 2010), an approach similar to the internal step function in our Latent Response Model approach discussed below.

Latent Response Models have the advantage of easily and naturally integrating multiple data sources, at different grain-sizes, into a single model. They can be used when data is not well synchronized. A detector of gaming, in the framework used here, has one observable level and two hidden ("latent") levels. The model's overall structure is shown in Fig. 7.4. In a gaming detector's outermost/observable layer, the gaming detector assesses how frequently each of n students is gaming the system; those assessments are labeled $G'0, \ldots, G'n$. The gaming detector's assessments for each student can then be compared to the observed proportions of time each student spent gaming the system, $G0, \ldots, Gn$ (the metrics used will be discussed within the next section). The proportion of time each student spends gaming is assessed as follows: First, the detector makes a (binary) assessment as to whether each individual student action (denoted $P'm$) is an instance of gaming. From these assessments, $G'0, \ldots, G'n$ are derived by taking the percentage of actions which are assessed to be instances of gaming, for each student. An action is assessed to be gaming or not, by a function on parameters composed of the features drawn from each action's characteristics. An assessment Hm as to whether action m is an instance of gaming is computed as $Hm = a0 \cdot X0 + a1 \cdot X1 + a2 \cdot X2 + \ldots + a\,n \cdot Xn$, where ai is a parameter value and Xi is the data value for the corresponding parameter, for this action, in the log files. The value given by the linear combination is the first hidden level and top layer in Fig. 7.4. Each assessment Hm is then thresholded using a step function, such that if Hm £ 0.5, H′m=0; otherwise H′m=1. The set of thresholded values makes up the second hidden level and middle layer in Fig. 7.4. This gives us a set of classifications H′m for each action within the tutor, which are then used to create the assessments of each student's proportion of gaming, G′0, …, G′n. These assessments of each student's proportion of gaming, which make up the observable level of the model (the bottom layer in Fig. 7.2), are compared to the observed values of gaming during model fitting and validation. Within the model framework, the best model is selected out of the large space of possible models, using a combination of Fast Correlation-Based Filtering (Yu & Liu, 2003) and Forward Selection (Ramsey & Schafer, 1997).

J48 decision trees, the second method used to detect gaming in Cognitive Tutors, are a standard data mining method. As such, J48 has a single level of hierarchy and can be used when specific actions are known to involve gaming the system or to not involve gaming the system, requiring text replays or good synchronization of field observations. In the case of text replays, we label segments of behavior as gaming or not gaming; if a segment is labeled as involving gaming, every action in the segment is labeled as gaming. It is worth noting that these labels of individual actions cannot be considered perfectly accurate, since the observer labeled a clip as "gaming" if any of the actions in the clip involved gaming. Therefore, actions at the beginning or end of clips may not in all cases be instances of gaming. This suggests that, within text replay data, a 100% perfect match between our classifier's labels of individual actions and those actions' labels is not necessary (or desirable). This limitation could be addressed by having observers explicitly label which actions in a clip are gaming, but would have the cost of reducing the method's speed. J48 decision trees are a good approach for noisy data of this nature, as the pruning step of this algorithm addresses noise in the data and reduces over-fitting.

Validation Methods and Effectiveness

In order to validate the effectiveness of a detector of the types discussed here, and its appropriateness for different types of use, it is important to analyze its generalizability at multiple levels. Four types of generalizability are particularly important for a detector that will be used in "discovery with models" analyses. First, a detector should be able to accurately determine which students game, even for entirely new students. This is important, because it enables the detector to be used with new students, for instance at run-time, or in larger data sets than the original training set. In order to do this, it is necessary to train a detector with one group of students and test it with a different group of students. Cross-validation is a systematic method for splitting up a data set into groups and testing model generalizability across groups (Efron & Gong, 1983). However, one limitation is that many existing tools for data mining, such as Weka (Witten & Frank, 2005), do not support student-level cross-validation, only supporting cross-validation at the grain-size of individual data points. Another tool, RapidMiner (Mierswa, Wurst, Klinkenberg, Scholz, & Euler, 2006), does not directly support student-level or lesson-level cross-validation, but its "batch cross-validation" functionality makes it possible to conduct student-level or lesson-level cross-validation through predefining student batches outside of the data mining software. Student-level cross-validation has been conducted for gaming detectors based on Latent Response Models (e.g., Baker, Corbett, et al., 2008) and J48 Decision Trees. Latent Response Models appear to achieve the goal of detecting which students game more successfully than J48 Decision Trees (Baker & de Carvalho, 2008).

Second, a detector should be able to accurately determine exactly when a student games. This is important, because it enables inference about the context and antecedents and immediate consequences of gaming behavior. Determining exactly when each student games is not possible without synchronized observations or text replays, since exact labels are needed. In Baker and de Carvalho (2008), Latent Response Models were compared to J48 Decision Trees in terms of ability to determine this, and J48 Decision Trees performed significantly better. There was evidence that the Latent Response Model identified gaming on the correct skills, but identified gaming the system later than it actually occurred.

Third, a detector should be able to transfer to new classrooms and schools. This is important because some behaviors may differ in important ways between students across different classroom cultures. This type of validation is generally rare because of the difficulty of collecting and labeling data sets that span significant numbers of classrooms. Latent Response Models of gaming the system have been validated in this fashion (Baker, Corbett, Koedinger, & Roll, 2005).

Fourth, a detector should be able to transfer to new tutor lessons or related tutors. This is important because many modern intelligent tutoring systems, including Cognitive Tutors, cover a significant number of topics that necessarily differ in presentation and user interaction, over the course of a semester or a year (cf. Koedinger & Corbett, 2006). It is important for analyses spanning across these topics to be based on detectors validated to be accurate across all of the interaction contexts where the detectors are applied. Latent Response Models of gaming the system have been validated in this fashion (Baker, Corbett, et al., 2008).

"Harmful" Gaming and "Non-harmful" Gaming

One finding in the development of detectors of gaming the system which has not been fully explained is the possible split between "harmful" and "non-harmful" forms of gaming, defined as forms of gaming behavior associated with differential learning outcomes. In specific, "harmful" forms of gaming can be conceptualized as gaming associated with poor performance on the posttest (e.g., the failure to learn), whereas "non-harmful" forms of gaming are not associated with poor posttest performance (Baker, Corbett, & Koedinger, 2004). Within a Cognitive Tutor for middle school mathematics, a replicable split (replicable across lessons) has been found between gaming students who perform poorly on the posttest, and gaming students who nonetheless still perform well on the posttest. This split is sufficiently strong that detectors can be trained to detect students in either category, not detecting students in the other category (Baker, Corbett, et al., 2008); in at least one data set the attempt to detect both groups only succeeded in detecting gaming students who perform poorly on the posttest (Baker, Corbett, & Koedinger, 2004). This split appears to be between gaming that occurs on poorly known skills (harmful gaming) and gaming that occurs on well-known skills (non-harmful gaming), thus far, this split has failed to replicate within other systems and populations, including middle school students using Math ASSISTments (Walonoski & Heffernan, 2006a), high school students using a Cognitive Tutor for Algebra (Baker & de Carvalho, 2008), and college students using SQL-Tutor (Baker, Mitrovic, et al., 2010). It is not clear what aspect of the middle school mathematics Cognitive Tutor or its population leads to the split in types of gaming, but it is an important area of future research.

A third type of gaming, not explicitly studied in our research, is the beneficial form of gaming discovered by Shih et al. (2008) in high school students using a Cognitive Tutor for Geometry. In this behavior, a student clicks through hints in order to receive the answer to a problem step, but then stops and self-explains the step before proceeding. This behavior is associated with positive learning gains, and is likely to be a way of turning tutoring into a worked example. We view this behavior as a positive metacognitive strategy that is only related to gaming the system at a surface level.

Challenges

One of the key challenges to studying gaming (or metacognitive behavior in general) at scale is generalizability. Even though the generalizability of gaming detectors has been validated across students, and across tutor lessons, all validation has been within the context of specific intelligent tutors. Gaming detectors have been developed through the process discussed here for multiple intelligent tutors, including Cognitive Tutors for Algebra (Baker & de Carvalho, 2008) and middle school mathematics (Baker, Corbett, et al., 2008; Baker, Walonoski, et al., 2008), and a constraint-based tutor for SQL (Baker, Mitrovic, et al., 2010). However, the detectors developed for Cognitive Tutors have had relatively little obviously in common, feature-wise, with the detectors of gaming for SQL-Tutor. The features distilled from log data have themselves had fairly little in common between tutors. This lack of commonality limits the broader generalization of gaming research, as the entire process of labeling data, distilling data features, developing a detector, and validating generalizability must be undertaken for any new learning system. Our research group is currently attempting to address this limitation, by building gaming detectors for multiple learning systems for which there exists data in a standardized format in the Pittsburgh Science of Learning Center DataShop (Koedinger et al., 2010). The hope is that by studying generalizability across learning systems within data collected in the same standardized format, we can learn whether gaming the system has common features across learning systems that can be used as the basis of gaming detection that generalizes across learning systems.

Another key challenge is balancing between detecting exactly when a student is gaming, and detecting which students game. Our initial investigations (Baker & de Carvalho, 2008) appear to suggest that J48 Decision Trees are more successful at detecting the exact moment of gaming, while Latent Response Models are more successful at detecting exactly which students game. Both of these goals are clearly important. One immediate takeaway message is that the selection of algorithm should be based upon which of these goals is more important for model usage. For instance, analyzing the different rates of gaming across schools depends on higher accuracy as to which students game, whereas analyzing the antecedents and consequents of gaming behavior depends upon higher accuracy as to exactly when students game. Interventions, in general, are probably more important to target towards the right students than towards the right moments. In the long term, it will be valuable to develop modeling approaches that optimize simultaneously on both of these goals, or at least balance between accuracy on the two goals.

Use in "Discovery with Models" Analyses

In this section we discuss the utilization of gaming detectors in "discovery with models" analyses. Discovery with models is defined as taking a model of a phenomenon developed via prediction, clustering, or knowledge engineering, and then using this model as a component in another type of analysis (Baker & Yacef, 2009). We will present two discovery with models analyses, which establish the potential of this class of research method to support the development of future models and theories of SRL and metacognition.

Studying Why Gaming Leads to Poorer Learning

A negative association between gaming the system and learning has been seen in most of the studies investigating this relationship (Aleven et al., 2006; Baker, Corbett, & Koedinger, 2004; Baker, Corbett, Koedinger, & Wagner, 2004; Baker, Corbett, Koedinger, et al., 2006; Walonoski & Heffernan, 2006a), though exceptions exist (e.g., Gobel, 2008). However, up until the publication of a discovery with models analysis of this relationship (e.g., Cocea, Hershkovitz, & Baker, 2009), it was not clear what mechanism might be leading to this relationship. Cocea et al. (2009) examined whether this relationship was the result of gaming leading to less learning within individual problem steps, an immediate harmful impact due to gaming. In order to analyze these possibilities, a validated Latent Response Model of gaming was applied to data from four tutor lessons (scatterplots, geometry, percents, and probability), drawn from a middle school Cognitive Tutor mathematics curriculum (Koedinger & Corbett, 2006).

We assessed whether gaming the system was associated with immediate poorer learning, by setting up a logistic regression model similar to the approach in Beck's (2006) learning decomposition method, where learning over time is assessed in terms of events that occur in the student's learning process. Performance on a given skill at a given time was predicted based on the number of steps on this skill where the student previously engaged in gaming behavior; we distinguish between "harmful gaming" (HG) steps and "non-harmful gaming" (NHG) steps. Within the model, harmful gaming was statistically significantly associated with less learning ($p<0.01$), at the step-by-step grain-size. Surprisingly, NHG was also associated with less learning at the step-by-step grain-size, though only to about half the degree of harmful gaming, and only marginally significantly ($p=0.054$). In other words, student performance improves less over time if the student games the system, as compared to the other potential learning strategies the student could have used. Off-task behavior, by contrast, was not associated with poorer immediate performance improvement. Complete details on this analysis are given in Cocea and colleagues (2009).

Studying Why Students Game the System

Discovery with models methods were also used to study why students game the system. Broadly, two classes of hypothesis have been advanced for why students game the system. First, researchers have hypothesized that some individual difference leads students to game the system (Arroyo & Woolf, 2005; Baker, Walonoski, et al., 2008; Beal, Qu, & Lee, 2008; Martínez Mirón, du Boulay, & Luckin, 2004). Second, researchers have hypothesized that aspects of software design lead students to game the system (Magnussen & Misfeldt, 2004; Baker et al., 2009). Discovery with models analyses have been used to study both of these possibilities within Cognitive Tutors.

Baker and colleagues (Baker, Walonoski, et al., 2008) applied gaming detectors to two data sets of usage of the middle school mathematics Cognitive Tutor. The students in these data sets had also completed questionnaires measuring a range of moti-vational and attitudinal constructs, including grit (Duckworth, Peterson, Matthews, & Kelly, 2007), performance goals (Dweck, 2000), anxiety, negative attitudes towards mathematics, and negative attitudes towards computers. Though some constructs were statistically significantly associated with gaming the system (specifically, grit, negative attitudes towards mathematics, and negative attitudes towards computers), none accounted for more than 5% of the variance in how much a student gamed ($r^2<0.05$). A similar pattern, with significant but weak correlations between learner characteristics and gaming frequency, was found in other learning systems (Arroyo & Woolf, 2005; Baker, Walonoski, et al., 2008). Beal and colleagues (2008) also reported statistically significant relationships between learner characteristics and gaming frequency, but did not report the magnitude of the correlations or other measures of effect size.

Following on this research, Baker (2007a) attempted to determine whether these prior results were the result of investigating the wrong learner characteristics, by assessing the overall predictive power of knowing which student was gaming the system. In doing so, this analysis treated the student as a proxy for the combination of all explanations stemming from learner characteristics. This analysis applied the Latent Response Model gaming detector validated to transfer across students and tutor lessons (Baker, Corbett, et al., 2008) to every action by a set of students during the use of the middle school mathematics Cognitive Tutor, a data set of 240 students using 35 Cognitive Tutor lessons during the course of a school year. Within this data set, the student predicted 16% of the variance in gaming whereas the lesson predicted 55% of the variance in gaming. Recent results within the

Andes system and ASSISTments attempting to predict gaming the system by student and problem have obtained a strong opposite result, with student predicting gaming significantly better than problem (Gong et al., 2010; Muldner et al., 2011). It is not yet clear why such contradictory results have been obtained; in particular, it is possible that the difference stems from the difference between the learning systems or the difference in the definition of gaming (the definitions of gaming used in the Gong et al., 2010 and Muldner et al., 2011 analyses were knowledge-engineered, and to the best of our knowledge have not yet been validated against human labels of gaming).

Following up on the apparent strong relationship between the lesson and the amount of gaming in Cognitive Tutors, Baker and colleagues (2009) investigated which specific differences between lessons predicted gaming. In this case, automated gaming detection was not used, in case specific lessons might be mis-predicted, biasing the model. Although overall generalizability of the gaming detector across lessons has been validated (e.g., Baker, Corbett, et al., 2008), it is still possible that generalization might fail for a specific lesson. If that lesson exemplified a specific set of rare lesson features, those features could be spuriously predicted to lead to gaming (or to reduce gaming). Hence, instead, text replay labels of gaming were used. A set of 79 features of tutor lessons were developed and applied to 22 lessons in a Cognitive Tutor for Algebra. Then, Principal Component Analysis was used to group the 79 features into six components. One component was predictive of gaming, predicting 29% of the variance in gaming. Two additional features were added through forward selection. The eventual best model predicting gaming through lesson features predicted 56% of the variance in gaming, roughly five times the degree of variance in gaming predicted by any prior study predicting gaming with specific student individual differences. The lesson features that predicted gaming the system, either as part of the component or as individual features, included the following:

- The same number is used for multiple constructs [more gaming].
- Hints do not lead to better future performance [more gaming].
- Hints are abstract [more gaming].
- Toolbar icons are unclear [more gaming].
- Lack of interest-increasing text in problem statements [more gaming].
- Lack of problem statement [less gaming].
- Directional feedback given [less gaming].
- Hints request that student perform some action [more gaming].
- Location of the first problem step is not directly indicated and does not follow standard conventions (e.g., being the top-left cell of a worksheet) [more gaming].

Overall, many of these lesson features can be interpreted in the following fashion: lesson features that could be expected to cause boredom or confusion are associated with more gaming. This finding accords with work studying the affective antecedents of gaming behavior (e.g., Baker, D'Mello, et al., 2010). However, many other features that also might have been expected to cause boredom or confusion were not associated with more gaming (a full list of the lesson features can be found in Baker et al., 2009). Hence, the factors mediating the relationship between lesson features and gaming are still not fully understood. However, the relationship between gaming and specific lesson features seems established, at least within Cognitive Tutors.

Potential to Contribute to Future Models and Theories of Self-Regulated Learning and Metacognition

This work has the potential to contribute to future models and theories of SRL and metacognition in at least two ways.

First, this work establishes key findings about gaming the system, a behavior that appears to involve sophisticated metacognition and self-regulation (as discussed in the introduction), but which appears to have the goal of avoiding learning rather than being an SRL behavior. Research in the last 5 years has indicated that gaming behaviors are found in a wide variety of learning systems, and analogues can also be seen even in wholly human classrooms as well (e.g., Nelson-Le Gall, 1985). Depending on how and when students game, the impacts on learning appear to differ. Current theories of metacognition and SRL do not explicitly incorporate gaming the system and similar disengaged behaviors (e.g., off-task behavior and carelessness), with the exception of Aleven and colleagues' (2006) help-seeking model. That model does an excellent job of integrating gaming into consideration of complex phenomena. However, that model's conceptualization of gaming as metacognitive bugs does not appear to fully represent the complex self-regulation and metacognition that appear to be associated with gaming, including consideration of the current learning situation (inferable from the relations between tutor design features and gaming), and the student's current emotions. As such, models of SRL and motivation which incorporate gaming will need to explicitly model the motivation, affective, and situational factors which precede gaming behavior, as well as how gaming (in its various forms) influences learning. This type of linkage is present, at a high level, in existing models of SRL (cf. Winne & Hadwin, 1998). The work presented here represents a step towards making these links concrete and specific, towards models of SRL are increasingly precise.

Second, this work serves as an example for how educational data mining methods can be integrated into future research in SRL and metacognition. Increasingly, research into metacognition and motivation in interactive learning environments leverages models of student behavior (examples relevant to gaming behavior include Aleven et al., 2006; Beal et al., 2008; Beck, 2005; Gong et al., 2010; Muldner et al., 2011; Shih et al., 2008). However, the work presented here goes to a further degree than most other work in attempting to validate construct validity (through connecting to a significant volume of human labels of the constructs of interest) and generalizability (through cross-validating models across contexts as well as students). A fuller discussion of the benefits of using human labels and generalizability analysis in development of student metacognitive models is out of the scope of this chapter, but one such discussion can be found in Baker (2010). In general, the endeavor of using student models to computationally study student metacognition will be facilitated by improving the reliability and validity of our models.

Design Implications: How to Reduce Gaming

As we improve our understanding of why students game the system, we can begin to think about developing learning environments that adapt in a relevant and purposeful way to gaming when it occurs. In recent years, there have been a number of attempts to develop systems that adapt to gaming in a productive and constructive fashion, or to address gaming by preventing it from ever occurring.

The first way that developers of educational software attempted to address gaming was by attempting to eliminate gaming by making it more difficult to game. For instance, both Cognitive Tutors and AnimalWatch adopted the strategy of putting delays between hint messages (e.g., Beck, 2005; Murray & VanLehn, 2005). Each time a student received a hint, the option to request the next hint was grayed out for several seconds. However, Murray and VanLehn (2005) found that students simply found alternate ways to game the system.

A second approach towards reducing gaming was to give students feedback on the metacognition associated with gaming (according to the model in Aleven et al., 2006), as soon as gaming behavior was recognized (Roll, Aleven, McLaren, & Koedinger, 2007). This feedback suggested that a student who games help should slow down and read the hints more carefully, and that a student who responds too quickly (a proxy for guessing behaviors) should slow down and either request a hint or try to figure out the answer. This system was successful at reducing students' degrees of these behaviors as they used the tutoring system, and led to long-term positive changes in help-seeking behavior (Roll, Aleven,

McLaren, & Koedinger, 2011), but had no impact on domain learning (Roll et al., 2007, 2011).

Based on the low success of this generation of gaming interventions at improving domain learning (despite the success of both interventions at changing student behavior), a second generation of gaming interventions attempted to address gaming through introducing more complex interactions intended to impact students' awareness of gaming by communicating gaming's prevalence via visualizations or attempting to mitigate its effects through cognitive interventions.

Within this second generation of gaming interventions, Walonoski and Heffernan (2006b) placed visualizations about gaming behavior over the last 20 min on-screen, for viewing by students and teachers. These visualizations had a bar travelling from left to right; the visualizations indicated the passage of time from left to right, gaming behavior by color (red indicating certain gaming, yellow indicating possible gaming, and green indicating no gaming), and the correctness (at the cognitive level) of the action from top to bottom. Placing the mouse pointer over a point on the graph gave greater detail about that action. This system was successful at reducing students' degrees of gaming behavior as they used the tutoring system; domain learning was not measured.

A second project, Arroyo and colleagues (2007), gave visualizations of student correctness between problems rather than during problems. These visualizations showed overall correctness rather than directly showing gaming (the two constructs are, of course, closely related). Along with the visualizations were textual messages (when gaming had occurred) about how correctness could be raised by avoiding gaming strategies. This system was successful at reducing students' degrees of gaming behavior as they used the tutoring system, and was also found to improve domain learning.

A third project, Baker and colleagues (Baker, Corbett, Koedinger, et al., 2006), combined feedback on how to use the software appropriately (as in Roll et al., 2007, but the feedback was substantially less sophisticated), with an attempt to give students another way to learn material missed by gaming. This intervention involved a pedagogical agent named Scooter the Tutor, shown in Fig. 7.5. When students did not game, Scooter remained in the background, occasionally giving a positive message; when the student gamed the system, Scooter first displayed negative emotion and gave metacognitive messages similar to those in Roll and colleagues (2007), and then gave supplementary exercises which involved using the same skills or concepts bypassed via gaming. Scooter was successful at reducing students' degrees of gaming behavior as they used the tutoring system, and was also found to improve domain learning. However, the very students who benefited from Scooter's interventions reported strongly disliking Scooter.

Each of these interventions was successful in reducing gaming, and two were successful in improving domain learning. However, none of these interventions were successful in a broader sense: none were adopted and applied at a wider scale by software developers, even within the three projects that originally developed them. One possible explanation for this puzzling lack of uptake is that all three of these interventions required significant development and made the interaction between the student and the educational software substantially more complex. This may be a general limitation for interventions intended to solve single problems in metacognition or address single problematic behaviors: the intervention cannot be larger in scope and complexity than the problem's perceived level of importance justifies to software developers.

The recent research on which features of intelligent tutoring systems lead to gaming, described earlier in this chapter, provides a possible avenue for addressing gaming the system in a more lightweight fashion. Knowing the features that predict gaming creates the possibility that changing these features will reduce students' propensity to game the system (this is not guaranteed, of course, as correlation does not imply causation), and perhaps also improve learning. Research into this possibility is an important area of future works.

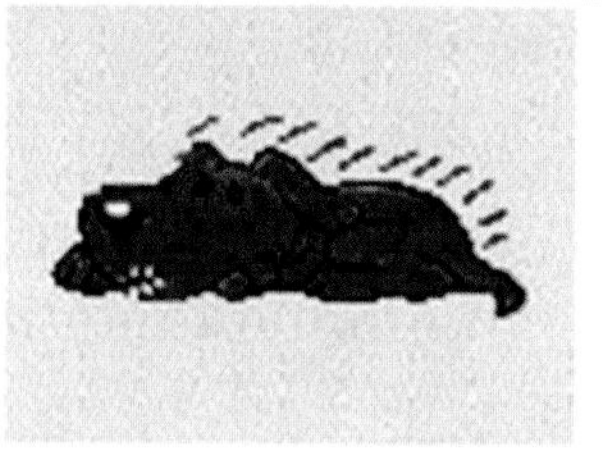

Why do we need to know the
largest value of height
in this part of the problem?
To help pick a scale for the axis
To help pick the last label of the axis
To help pick the first label of the axis
To help pick which point to plot first

Fig. 7.5 Scooter the Tutor—looking happy when the student has not been gaming harmfully (*top-left*), giving a supplementary exercise to a gaming student (*right*), and looking angry when the student is believed to have been gaming heavily, or attempted to game Scooter during a supplementary exercise (*bottom-left*)

Conclusions

In this chapter, we have talked about our work to model and study gaming the system using educational data mining methods (Baker & Yacef, 2009; Romero & Ventura, 2010). Our work has leveraged the development of automated detectors of gaming behavior for Cognitive Tutors and other interactive learning environments. Our detector development has relied upon first using human labeling methods to gather "ground truth" labels of students or actions judged to be gaming the system, then using data mining methods to distill these labels into reusable detectors of gaming, and finally validating these models at multiple levels.

We then discuss two "discovery with models" analyses where these detectors are leveraged in order to analyze research questions of interest. Gaming detectors have supported the analysis of why students game the system, and how gaming the system impacts learning. In specific, these analyses show that gaming the system is associated with less learning, in an immediate fashion—a different pattern than was found for off-task behavior, where learning was only reduced in the aggregate. In addition, these analyses discover a set of nine features of tutor lessons that are associated with differences in the prevalence of gaming the system.

We also discuss ongoing work, both in our research group and other research groups, to develop software that remediates gaming the system. Thus far, this work has had only partial success. We discuss how the discovery with models analyses presented earlier in the chapter may have the potential to influence the design of educational software that effectively prevents gaming in a nonintrusive fashion. If successful, this program of research will form a key example of how to design for effective student behavior, in a fashion that either stimulates metacognition which leads to more effective learning strategies or alternatively by addressing the negative learning outcomes potentially stemming from students' ineffective or counterproductive self-regulation during learning.

In the long term, studying gaming and related phenomena using discovery with models methods has the potential to significantly improve our field's understanding of the metacognitive and motivational processes that occur during learning with interactive learning technologies, in turn leading to software more effectively tuned to students' educational needs.

References

Aleven, V., McLaren, B. M., Roll, I., & Koedinger, K. R. (2006). Toward meta-cognitive tutoring: A model of help seeking with a cognitive tutor. *International Journal of Artificial Intelligence in Education, 16*, 101–130.

Anderson, J. R., Corbett, A. T., Koedinger, K. R., & Pelletier, R. (1995). Cognitive tutors: Lessons learned. *The Journal of the Learning Sciences, 4*(2), 167–207.

Arroyo, I., Ferguson, K., Johns, J., Dragon, T., Meheranian, H., & Fisher, D. (2007). Repairing disengagement with non-invasive interventions. In J. Greer, R. Luckin, & K. Koedinger (Eds.), *Proceedings of the 13th International Conference on Artificial Intelligence in Education* (pp. 195–202). Amsterdam, Netherlands: Ios Press.

Arroyo, I., & Woolf, B. (2005). Inferring learning and attitudes from a Bayesian Network of log file data. In U. Hoppe, F. Verdejo, & J. Kay (Eds.), *Proceedings of the 12th International Conference on Artificial Intelligence in Education* (pp. 33–40). Amsterdam, Netherlands: Ios Press.

Baker, R. S. J. d. (2007a). Is gaming the system state-or-trait? Educational data mining through the multi-contextual application of a validated behavioral model. In R. Baker, J. Beck, B. Berendt, A. Kroner, E. Menasalvas, & S. Weibelzahl (Eds.), *Complete on-line Proceedings of the Workshop on Data Mining for User Modeling at the 11th International Conference on User Modeling* (pp. 76–80). Pittsburgh, PA: International Working Group on Educational Data Mining.

Baker, R. S. J. d. (2007b). Modeling and understanding students' off-task behavior in intelligent tutoring systems. In M. Rosson & D. Gilmore (Eds.), *Proceedings of ACM CHI 2007 Conference on Human Factors in Computing Systems* (pp. 1059–1068). Washington, DC: Association for Computing Machinery.

Baker, R. S. J. d. (2010). Mining data for student models. In R. Nkmabou, R. Mizoguchi, & J. Bourdeau (Eds.), *Advances in intelligent tutoring systems* (pp. 341–356). Secaucus, NJ: Springer.

Baker, R. S., Corbett, A. T., & Koedinger, K. R. (2004a). Detecting student misuse of intelligent tutoring systems. In J. Lester, R. Vicari, & F. Paraguacu (Eds.), *Proceedings of the 7th International Conference on Intelligent Tutoring Systems* (pp. 531–540). Heidelberg, Germany: Springer.

Baker, R. S. J. d., Corbett, A. T., Koedinger, K. R., Evenson, S. E., Roll, I., & Wagner, A. Z. (2006). Adapting to when students game an intelligent tutoring system. In M. Ikeda, K. Ashley, & T. Chan (Eds.), *Proceedings of the 8th International Conference on Intelligent Tutoring Systems* (pp. 392–401). Heidelberg, Germany: Springer.

Baker, R. S., Corbett, A., Koedinger, K., & Roll, I. (2005). Detecting when students game the system, across tutor subjects and classroom cohorts. In L. Ardissono, P. Brna, & A. Mitrovic (Eds.), *Proceedings of the 10th International Conference on User Modeling* (pp. 220–224). Heidelberg, Germany: Springer.

Baker, R. S., Corbett, A. T., Koedinger, K. R., & Wagner, A. Z. (2004b). Off-task behavior in the cognitive tutor classroom: When students "game the system". In E. Dykstra-Erickson & M. Tscheligi (Eds.), *Proceedings of ACM CHI 2004 Conference on Human Factors in Computing Systems* (pp. 383–390). Washington, DC. Association for Computing Machinery.

Baker, R. S. J. d., Corbett, A. T., Roll, I., & Koedinger, K. R. (2008). Developing a generalizable detector of when students game the system. *User Modeling and User-Adapted Interaction, 18*(3), 287–314.

Baker, R. S. J. d., Corbett, A. T., & Wagner, A. Z. (2006). Human classification of low-fidelity replays of student actions. In C. Heiner, R. Baker, & K. Yacef (Eds.), *Proceedings of the Educational Data Mining Workshop at the 8th International Conference on Intelligent Tutoring Systems* (pp. 29–36). Pittsburgh, PA: International Working Group on Educational Data Mining.

Baker, R. S. J. d., & de Carvalho, A. M. J. A. (2008). Labeling student behavior faster and more precisely with text replays. In R. Baker, T. Barnes, & J. Beck (Eds.), *Proceedings of the 1st International Conference on Educational Data Mining* (pp. 38–47). Pittsburgh, PA: International Working Group on Educational Data Mining.

Baker, R. S. J. d., de Carvalho, A. M. J. A., Raspat, J., Aleven, V., Corbett, A. T., & Koedinger, K. R. (2009). Educational software features that encourage and discourage "gaming the system". In V. Dimitrova, R. Mizoguchi, B. du Boulay, & A. Graesser (Eds.), *Proceedings of the 14th International Conference on Artificial Intelligence in Education* (pp. 475–482). Amsterdam, Netherlands: Ios Press.

Baker, R. S. J. d., D'Mello, S. K., Rodrigo, M. M. T., & Graesser, A. C. (2010). Better to be frustrated than bored: The incidence, persistence, and impact of learners' cognitive-affective states during interactions with three different computer-based learning environments. *International Journal of Human Computer Studies, 68*(4), 223–241.

Baker, R. S. J. d., Mitrovic, A., & Mathews, M. (2010). Detecting gaming the system in constraint-based tutors. In P. de Bra, A. Kobsa, & D. Chin (Eds.),

Proceedings of the 18th Annual Conference on User Modeling, Adaptation, and Personalization (pp. 267–278). Heidelberg, Germany: Springer.

Baker, R., Walonoski, J., Heffernan, N., Roll, I., Corbett, A., & Koedinger, K. (2008). Why students engage in "gaming the system" behavior in interactive learning environments. *Journal of Interactive Learning Research, 19*(2), 185–224.

Baker, R. S. J. d., & Yacef, K. (2009). The state of educational data mining in 2009: A review and future visions. *Journal of Educational Data Mining, 1*(1), 3–17.

Beal, C. R., Qu, L., & Lee, H. (2006). Classifying learner engagement through integration of multiple data sources. In Y. Gil & R. Mooney (Eds.), *Proceedings of the 21st National Conference on Artificial Intelligence* (pp. 2–8). Washington, DC: Association for the Advancement of Artificial Intelligence.

Beal, C. R., Qu, L., & Lee, H. (2008). Mathematics motivation and achievement as predictors of high school students' guessing and help-seeking with instructional software. *Journal of Computer Assisted Learning, 24*, 507–514.

Beck, J. (2005). Engagement tracing: Using response times to model student disengagement. In U. Hoppe, F. Verdejo, & J. Kay (Eds.), *Proceedings of the 12th International Conference on Artificial Intelligence in Education (AIED 2005)* (pp. 88–95). Amsterdam, Netherlands: Ios Press.

Beck, J. E. (2006). Using learning decomposition to analyze student fluency development. In C. Heiner, R. Baker, & K. Yacef (Eds.), *Proceedings of the workshop on Educational Data Mining at the 8th International Conference on Intelligent Tutoring Systems* (pp. 21–28). Pittsburgh, PA: International Working Group on Educational Data Mining.

Butler, D. L., & Winne, P. (1995). Feedback and self-regulated learning: A theoretical synthesis. *Review of Educational Resarch, 65*(3), 245–281.

Cheng, R., & Vassileva, J. (2005). Adaptive reward mechanism for sustainable online learning community. In U. Hoppe, F. Verdejo, & J. Kay (Eds.), *Proceedings of the 12th International Conference on Artificial Intelligence in Education* (pp. 152–159). Amsterdam, Netherlands: Ios Press.

Cocea, M., Hershkovitz, A., & de Baker, R. S. J. (2009). The impact of off-task and gaming behaviors on learning: Immediate or aggregate? In V. Dimitrova, R. Mizoguchi, B. du Boulay, & A. Graesser (Eds.), *Proceedings of the 14th International Conference on Artificial Intelligence in Education* (pp. 507–514). Amsterdam, Netherlands: Ios Press.

Corbett, A. T., & Anderson, J. R. (1995). Knowledge tracing: Modeling the acquisition of procedural knowledge. *User Modeling and User-Adapted Interaction, 4*, 253–278.

Duckworth, A. L., Peterson, C., Matthews, M. D., & Kelly, D. R. (2007). Grit: Perseverance and passion for long-term goals. *Journal of Personality and Social Psychology, 92*, 1087–1101.

Dweck, C. S. (2000). *Self-theories: Their role in motivation, personality, and development*. Philadelphia, PA: Psychology Press.

Efron, B., & Gong, G. (1983). A leisurely look at the bootstrap, the jackknife, and cross-validation. *The American Statistician, 37*(1), 36–48.

Fisher, S. L., & Ford, J. K. (1998). Differential effects of learner effort and goal orientation on two learning outcomes. *Personnel Psychology, 51*(2), 397–420.

Flavell, J. H. (1976). Metacognitive aspects of problem solving. In L. B. Resnick (Ed.), *The nature of intelligence*. Hillsdale, NJ: Lawrence Erlbaum Associates.

Gobel, P. (2008). Student off-task behavior and motivation in the CALL classroom. *International Journal of Pedagogies and Learning, 4*(4), 4–18.

Gong, Y., Beck, J., Heffernan, N. T., & Forbes-Summers, E. (2010). The fine-grained impact of gaming (?) on learning. In V. Aleven, J. Kay, & J. Mostow (Eds.), *Proceedings of the 10th International Conference on Intelligent Tutoring Systems* (pp. 194–203). Heidelberg, Germany: Springer.

Hacker, D. J. (1999). Definitions and empirical foundations. In D. J. Hacker, J. Dunlosky, & A. C. Graesser (Eds.), *Metacognition in educational theory and practice* (pp. 1–24). Mahway, NJ: Erlbaum.

Johns, J., & Woolf, B. (2006). A dynamic mixture model to detect student motivation and proficiency. In Y. Gil & R. Mooney (Eds.), *Proceedings of the 21st National Conference on Artificial Intelligence (AAAI-06)* (pp. 163–168). Washington, DC: Association for the Advancement of Artificial Intelligence.

Karweit, N., & Slavin, R. E. (1982). Time-on-task: Issues of timing, sampling, and definition. *Journal of Experimental Psychology, 74*(6), 844–851.

Koedinger, K. R., de Baker, R. S. J., Cunningham, K., Skogsholm, A., Leber, B., & Stamper, J. (2010). A data repository for the EDM community: The PSLC DataShop. In C. Romero, S. Ventura, M. Pechenizkiy, & R. S. J. de Baker (Eds.), *Handbook of educational data mining* (pp. 43–56). Boca Raton, FL: CRC Press.

Koedinger, K. R., & Corbett, A. T. (2006). Cognitive tutors: Technology bringing learning sciences to the classroom. In R. K. Sawyer (Ed.), *The Cambridge handbook of the learning sciences*. New York: Cambridge University Press.

Magnussen, R., & Misfeldt, M. (2004). Player transformation of educational multiplayer games. In M. Sicart & J. Smith (Eds.), *Proceedings of other players*. Copenhagen, Denmark: IT University of Copenhagen.

Maris, E. (1995). Psychometric latent response models. *Psychometrika, 60*(4), 523–547.

Martínez Mirón, E. A., du Boulay, B., & Luckin, R. (2004). Goal achievement orientation in the design of an ILE. In C. Frasson & K. Porayska-Pomsta (Eds.), *Proceedings of the ITS2004 Workshop on Social and Emotional Intelligence in Learning Environments* (pp. 72–78). Maceio, Brazil: Federal University of Alagoas.

Midgley, C., & Urdan, T. (2002). Academic self-handicapping and achievement goals: A further examination. *Contemporary Educational Psychology, 26*(1), 61–75.

Mierswa, I., Wurst, M., Klinkenberg, R., Scholz, M., & Euler, T. (2006). Yale: Rapid prototyping for complex data mining tasks. In L. Ungar, M. Craven, & D. Gunopulos (Eds.), *Proceedings of the 12th ACM SIGKDD International Conference on Knowledge Discovery and Data Mining* (pp. 935–940). Washington, DC: Association for Computing Machinery.

Muldner, K., Burleson, W., Van de Sande, B., & VanLehn, K. (2011). An analysis of students' gaming behaviors in an intelligent tutoring system: Predictors and impact. *User Modeling and User-Adapted Interaction, 21*(1–2), 99–135.

Murray, R. C., & VanLehn, K. (2005). Effects of dissuading unnecessary help requests while providing proactive help. In U. Hoppe, F. Verdejo, & J. Kay (Eds.), *Proceedings of the 12th International Conference on Artificial Intelligence in Education* (pp. 887–889). Amsterdam, Netherlands: Ios Press.

Nelson-Le Gall, S. (1985). Help-seeking behavior in learning. *Review of Research in Education, 12*, 55–90.

Quinlan, J. R. (1993). *C4.5: Programs for machine learning*. San Francisco, CA: Morgan Kaufmann.

Ramsey, F. L., & Schafer, D. W. (1997). *The statistical sleuth: A course in methods of data analysis*. Belmont, CA: Duxbury Press.

Rodrigo, M. M. T., Rebolledo-Mendez, G., de Baker, R. S. J., du Boulay, B., Sugay, J. O., & Lim, S. A. L. (2008). The effects of motivational modeling on affect in an intelligent tutoring system. In Y. Yano (Ed.), *Proceedings of 16th International Conference on Computers in Education*. Jhongli, Taiwan: Asia-Pacific Society for Computers in Education.

Roll, I., Aleven, V., McLaren, B. M., & Koedinger, K. R. (2007). Designing for metacognition—Applying cognitive tutor principles to the tutoring of help seeking. *Metacognition and Learning, 2*(2), 125–140.

Roll, I., Aleven, V., McLaren, B. M., & Koedinger, K. R. (2011). Improving students' help-seeking skills using metacognitive feedback in an intelligent tutoring system. *Learning and Instruction, 21*, 267–280.

Romero, C., & Ventura, S. (2010). Educational data mining: A review of the state-of-the-art. *IEEE Transactions of Systems, Man, and Cybernetics, Part C: Applications and Reviews, 40*(6), 601–618.

Sao Pedro, M. A., de Baker, R. S. J., Montalvo, O., Nakama, A., & Gobert, J. D. (2010). Using text replay tagging to produce detectors of systematic experimentation behavior patterns. In R. Baker, A. Merceron, & P. Pavlik (Eds.), *Proceedings of the 3rd International Conference on Educational Data Mining* (pp. 181–190). Pittsburgh, PA: International Working Group on Educational Data Mining.

Shih, B., Koedinger, K., & Scheines, R. (2008). A response time model for bottom-out hints as worked examples. In R. Baker, T. Barnes, & J. Beck (Eds.), *Proceedings of the 1st International Conference on Educational Data Mining* (pp. 117–126). Pittsburgh, PA: International Working Group on Educational Data Mining.

Walonoski, J. A., & Heffernan, N. T. (2006a). Detection and analysis of off-task gaming behavior in intelligent tutoring systems. In M. Ikeda, K. Ashley, & T. Chan (Eds.), *Proceedings of the 8th International Conference on Intelligent Tutoring Systems* (pp. 382–391). Heidelberg, Germany: Springer.

Walonoski, J. A., & Heffernan, N. T. (2006b). Prevention of off-task gaming behavior in intelligent tutoring systems. In M. Ikeda, K. Ashley, & T. Chan (Eds.), *Proceedings of the 8th International Conference on Intelligent Tutoring Systems* (pp. 722–724). Heidelberg, Germany: Springer.

Winne, P., & Hadwin, P. (1998). Studying as self-regulated learning. In D. J. Hacker, J. Dunlosky, & A. C. Graesser (Eds.), *Metacognition in educational theory and practice* (pp. 277–304). Mahway, NJ: Erlbaum.

Witten, I. H., & Frank, E. (2005). *Data mining: Practical machine learning tools and techniques*. San Francisco, CA: Morgan Kaufmann.

Yu, L., & Liu, H. (2003). Feature selection for high-dimensional data: a fast correlation-based filter solution. In T. Fawcett & N. Mishra (Eds.), *Proceedings of the 20th International Conference on Machine Learning* (pp. 856–863). Washington, DC: Association for the Advancement of Artificial Intelligence.

Zimmerman, B. J. (2000). Attaining self-regulation: A social cognitive perspective. In M. Boekarts, P. R. Pintrich, & M. Zeidner (Eds.), *Handbook of regulation* (pp. 13–39). Amsterdam, Netherlands: Elsevier.

8 A Two-Tiered Approach to Analyzing Self-Regulated Learning Data to Inform the Design of Hypermedia Learning Environments

Jeffrey A. Greene, Kristin R. Dellinger, Banu Binbaşaran Tüysüzoğlu, and Lara-Jeane Costa

Abstract

The research shows that the lack of instructional scaffolding and high degree of user control inherent to most HLEs make them difficult learning environments for learners who lack the ability to appropriately self-regulate their learning. Therefore, developers of HLEs must construct these environments in ways that not only promote knowledge acquisition, but also foster and scaffold SRL skills. This chapter introduces a two-tiered (i.e., the micro- and macro- level) approach to analyzing SRL data derived from think aloud protocols, which can be informative in terms of the domain-, task-specific self-regulatory processes that should be scaffolded in particular HLEs. The two-tiered approach provides a bridge between the SRL data and theory by showing how the *micro-level* learning processes (e.g., judgments of learning) can be used to indicate the degree to which individuals engage in the *macro-level* categories of self-regulation discussed in SRL models. Findings from a number of our research studies illustrate how analyzing data at both tiers results in a comprehensive understanding of how learners self-regulate in HLEs, and how the nature and quality of that self-regulation interacts with internal and external conditions.

If the mere introduction of learning technologies into classrooms was enough to bolster learning, the benefits would have been evident almost immediately. Unfortunately, the influence of technology on learning has been variable and inconsistent (Collins & Halverson, 2010; Jacobson & Azevedo, 2008). Technologies such as the Internet and hypermedia-learning environments (HLEs) allow learners to access nearly the entirety of human knowledge with a few simple search commands, but many individuals often

J.A. Greene (✉) • K.R. Dellinger • B. Binbaşaran Tüysüzoğlu • L.-J. Costa
Educational Psychology, Measurement, and Evaluation Program, University of North Carolina, Chapel Hill, NC, USA
e-mail: jagreene@email.unc.edu

R. Azevedo and V. Aleven (eds.), *International Handbook of Metacognition and Learning Technologies*, Springer International Handbooks of Education 26, DOI 10.1007/978-1-4419-5546-3_8,

fail to translate this knowledge into deep conceptual understanding (Ainsworth, 2006; Gerjets, Scheiter, & Schuh, 2008). Many HLEs lack any instructional scaffolding, thus requiring a high degree of learner control, making them difficult learning environments for individuals who are unable to appropriately define learning tasks, set goals, identify gaps in their knowledge, employ relevant strategies, and monitor and adapt their learning. Individuals' ability to appropriately deploy these self-regulated learning (SRL; Winne & Hadwin, 2008; Zimmerman, 2000) processes is an important predictor of the degree to which HLEs can foster conceptual understanding. Therefore, developers of HLEs must construct these environments in ways that not only disseminate knowledge, but also foster and scaffold SRL skills, lest a large segment of their user base fail to benefit from the technology. Determining which SRL processes to scaffold in HLEs, and how to scaffold effectively, have proven to be difficult challenges (Jacobson & Archodidou, 2000; Jacobson & Azevedo, 2008).

There are a number of reasons why it is such a challenge to determine which SRL processes relate to learning in HLEs. First, individual differences in learners' internal conditions, such as prior knowledge, level of motivation, and self-beliefs, make SRL inherently idiosyncratic (Zimmerman, 2000). The SRL processes that help a particular individual learn may differ greatly from those that are beneficial for another individual. Second, much of SRL processing is domain-, task-, and even HLE-specific: The control-of-variables strategy that might be effective in a science-based HLE may be completely useless in an HLE designed to foster historical understanding. The third reason relates to the challenges associated with collecting SRL data. Effective SRL processing is dynamic and adaptive, occurring as a series of events over the entirety of a learning task (Azevedo, Moos, Johnson, & Chauncey, 2010; Greene & Azevedo, 2010). Therefore, researchers and HLE developers must collect and interpret a large amount of complex data to capture all of the decision-making that occurs during a learning task. Further complicating data collection is the fact that empirical evidence has shown that learners are not accurate reporters of their SRL processing (Winne, Jamieson-Noel, & Muis, 2002). Together, these issues have prompted a move toward using online measures (i.e., measures that capture SRL as it occurs) to study how various SRL processes relate to learning with HLEs. These online measures bring with them their own set of challenges, in particular regarding how the data they generate can be related to models of SRL, and how to use those data to inform embedded scaffolds in HLEs.

The main goal of this chapter is to elucidate a two-tiered approach to analyzing online SRL data. This approach involves examining both the specific behaviors learners enact (e.g., judgments of learning) as well as the broader categories of SRL indicated by these specific behaviors (e.g., monitoring). We believe that analyzing data from both tiers of SRL processing (i.e., specific and broad, or what we call the micro- and macro-level) can lead to informed and effective recommendations for instructional scaffolding within HLEs. To describe and justify this approach, first we present a brief review of the advantages and challenges of using HLEs to promote conceptual understanding. Then, we review a conceptual model of SRL that we feel best aligns with how learners monitor and control their learning with HLEs. From this model we describe a method of capturing SRL processing, including the kinds of micro- and macro-level SRL data that can be difficult to infer from self-report instruments. Then we describe our two-tiered approach to analyzing SRL data, including findings from a number of our research studies that illustrate how such analyses can result in a comprehensive understanding of how individuals successfully self-regulate while using HLEs. Finally, we model how this two-tiered approach can be used by designers of HLEs to determine which SRL processes to scaffold, given the specifics of the domain, the task, and the HLE.

Advantages and Challenges of Hypermedia Learning Environments

HLEs connect a network of informational elements (i.e., nodes) and related topics through hyperlinks. Advantages of HLEs include their ability to disseminate information in multiple representational formats (e.g., audio, video, text, illustration), and their nonlinear, hyperlinked structure, which allows for a great deal of user control. Compared to textbooks and other traditional means of knowledge dissemination, HLEs more effectively foster conceptual understanding because individuals are afforded opportunities to (a) learn at their own pace, (b) freely navigate the network of information, and (c) select the representations that best build upon their prior knowledge (Jacobson & Archodidou, 2000; White & Frederiksen, 2005).

These advantages of HLEs only benefit individuals who have the working memory capacity necessary to work with and integrate multiple representations of information (Gerjets et al., 2008). The working memory subsystem handles the temporary encoding and manipulation of information (Baddeley, 2001), and can be easily overwhelmed when learners have little to no background knowledge about HLE content or how to navigate the many hyperlinks in HLEs. The effect of splitting attention between navigation and processing information may cause individuals to learn only knowledge fragments rather than coherent conceptual understanding (Antonenko & Niederhauser, 2010; Jacobson & Archodidou, 2000).

In most HLEs that lack instructional scaffolding, learners must take responsibility for constructing coherent knowledge of the topic, as opposed to depending upon the conceptually ordered points presented in traditional texts (Antonenko & Niederhauser, 2010). This high degree of user control in HLEs requires learners to adapt and regulate their cognitive and metacognitive processes (i.e., self-regulate their learning) in order to monitor the fit of new information with current knowledge to construct accurate understanding. Learners who fail to self-regulate effectively while using an HLE are unlikely to acquire conceptual understanding (Azevedo & Cromley, 2004; Azevedo, Moos, Greene, Winters, & Cromley, 2008; Greene, Costa, Robertson, Pan, & Deekens, 2010; Shapiro, 2008; White & Frederiksen, 2005).

Models of Self-Regulated Learning

Numerous models of SRL exist (Pintrich, 2000; Winne & Hadwin, 2008; Zimmerman, 2000), but each highlights that effective self-regulators are active participants in their learning, capable of monitoring, controlling, and regulating aspects of their cognition, motivation, behavior, and context to meet task demands and build upon prior knowledge. Winne and Hadwin (2008) characterized SRL as four flexibly sequenced, recursive phases of learning. In the first phase, learners interpret task-relevant internal (e.g., prior knowledge) and external (e.g., academic domain, context, task instructions) conditions to create a definition of the task. Based on this definition, in the next phase learners set goals and derive a plan to meet those goals. The third phase of SRL involves enacting learning strategies to meet goals. The fourth phase occurs when learners realize that significant changes to their cognitive and metacognitive processing are needed in order to effectively complete a task of a similar nature in the future. Within each phase, learners engage in metacognitive monitoring to determine if the result of phase processing (e.g., a task definition, plan, conceptual understanding) is likely to meet whatever standards they believe to be relevant (e.g., the level of conceptual understanding necessary to pass a test). When monitoring indicates a mismatch between the results of phase processing and learners' standards (e.g., realizing that despite having reread a Wikipedia entry numerous times, the learner still does not understand quantum physics enough to complete a homework assignment), effective self-regulators engage in metacognitive control processes to alter how they are learning (e.g., redefining the task, altering plans, enacting different strategies). Thus, skillful self-regulators iterate back and forth between phases until they have an adequate task definition and plan that has led to a level of understanding that they feel matches whatever standards they have set for the task.

In sum, within each phase of learning, effective self-regulators make countless decisions regarding how relevant internal and external conditions influence cognitive processing, whether current cognitive and metacognitive processing is likely to result in learning products that sufficiently meet their standards, and if changes need to be made to their task definition, plans, goals, or strategy use. Thus, unless practiced extensively until automatized, SRL processing can exhaust much of an individual's working memory, leaving few resources for the processing of new information, and subsequent learning. Therefore, even the most availing, intelligently designed HLE will have little effect upon a learner's conceptual understanding if that individual lacks the SRL expertise to select and integrate relevant representations of information (Azevedo, 2005). Given the richness, complexity, and sheer volume of self-regulatory processing that can occur over the course of a learning task, a difficult task awaits the developers who wish to create HLEs that foster, and perhaps even scaffold, SRL processing. Capturing and modeling data regarding how learners do and do not enact cognitive and metacognitive processing within specific HLEs requires copious and careful measurement methodology that must align with SRL models (Azevedo et al., 2010).

Capturing and Modeling Self-Regulated Learning Processing

Particularly in the early years of SRL research, a common way to measure SRL processing was with self-report instruments, such as the Motivated Strategies for Learning Questionnaire (MSLQ; Pintrich, Smith, García, & McKeachie, 1991). Although self-report instruments are relatively easy to administer and have been used in countless studies (see Duncan & McKeachie, 2005 for a review), there are several reasons why they are often inadequate measures of SRL. Self-report instruments rely upon retrospective accounts based on individuals' judgments and memories of their previous behavior, often aggregated over many learning episodes (Veenman, 2007; Winne & Perry, 2000). Much like the stock market, prior performance is not necessarily an accurate indicator of future SRL processing. It may be difficult for learners to make a holistic judgment of their typical SRL processing given its domain-specific and even task-specific nature. Likewise, SRL processing is dynamic, and involves countless monitoring and control decisions that are made among changing internal and external conditions over the course of learning. A single administration of a self-report instrument before or after a learning task would fail to capture any of this valuable contextual information.

In addition, self-report instruments tend to produce data with a restricted range because they typically have closed-ended responses where the learner is forced to choose an answer from a limited number of options (Winne & Perry, 2000). Learner behaviors and experiences that are not listed among the possible responses are therefore missed. Perhaps most concerning, Winne and Jamieson-Noel (2002) provided compelling evidence that learners could be quite variable in their calibration between their perceptions and actual behaviors. Overall, learners tend to be inaccurate when self-reporting their use of study tactics, calling into question the validity of the data provided by these instruments. Therefore, it is unlikely that data from self-report instruments accurately represent learners' self-regulatory processing (Veenman, 2007; Winne & Perry, 2000). Given these concerns, recent attempts to measure SRL have focused upon online, process measurement methodologies, such as think-aloud protocols (TAPs; Ericsson, 2006; Ericsson & Simon, 1993; Greene, Robertson, & Costa, 2011).

Using Think-Aloud Protocols to Capture Self-Regulated Learning

Rather than requiring learners to retrospectively report on their SRL processing, as self-report instruments do, TAPs involve asking learners to verbalize their thinking as they engage in a task. For example, learners might be working with an HLE and verbalize, "I don't understand the words in this paragraph. I think I will click on this hyperlink to learn more." Verbalization allows for researchers to capture self-regulation as it occurs, avoiding the concerns related to self-report instruments, such as when participants misremember their SRL processing. TAPs produce verbalizations that occur as the learner self-regulates, requiring no aggregations or judgments of past performance, and they produce a running account of actual processing decisions over the course of learning. Therefore, they allow researchers to gather data regarding the entire learning experience, rather than simply before or after the task. In addition, TAPs are open-ended with an unlimited response range, thus all verbalized aspects of SRL processing can be captured without researchers having to create a priori lists of potential behaviors.

Numerous researchers (Bannert & Mengelkamp, 2008; Veenman, 2007; Veenman, Prins, & Verheij, 2003) have provided empirical evidence that TAPs are much more accurate measures of individuals' self-regulated learning than self-report instruments, and in turn are better predictors of performance. Importantly, empirical research has shown that asking learners to simply verbalize, but not explain, their thinking does not affect their cognitive processing (see Ericsson & Simon, 1993; Greene et al., 2011; Veenman, Elshout, & Groen, 1993 for reviews). Finally, TAPs allow for a level of detail beyond what is possible with self-report instruments because the researcher can determine exactly how frequently and when during the task specific verbalizations occurred (Azevedo et al., 2010).

Coding Think-Aloud Protocol Data to Model Self-Regulated Learning Processing

TAPs produce a great deal of data, and translating those data into a form that can be interpreted within a SRL framework requires a specific and detailed methodology. For example, during one 15 s period of time, an individual using an HLE to learn about the circulatory system may verbalize the following:

> I want to learn more about the pulmonary arteries, and then I want to go back and look at a picture of the heart to see how these arteries relate to how the blood carries oxygen. So, I will click on this link for pulmonary arteries. I see that *pulmonary arteries carry deoxygenated blood to the lungs* but I thought that arteries always carried oxygenated blood. I don't understand. (words in italics indicate text that was read from the HLE)

Clearly, this hypothetical individual is engaging in numerous acts of SRL, but researchers need a systematic way of identifying those processes among the actual words that are verbalized. Azevedo and colleagues (Azevedo & Cromley, 2004; Azevedo, Guthrie, & Seibert, 2004; Greene & Azevedo, 2009) have developed a coding scheme that enumerates over 35 specific SRL processes that can be inferred from TAP data.

Using Azevedo and colleagues' (2004) scheme, researchers can divide a participant's verbalizations into segments that can each be coded for a specific SRL process. In the above example, the first sentence, "I want to learn more about the pulmonary arteries, and then I want to go back and look at a picture of the heart" would be coded as a *plan*, since the participant stated multiple goals to be addressed. The next statement, "I will click on this link" indicated a *selection of a new information source*. After reading some text, the participant *activated his or her prior knowledge* regarding arteries and blood. The participant then recognized the incongruence between the text and prior knowledge with the statement, "I don't understand," which would be coded as a *judgment of learning*. Overall, coding TAP data involves using the scheme to determine the best SRL process code for each segment, or labeling that segment as not relevant to self-regulation (e.g., asking for a drink of water). Azevedo and colleagues (2004, Table 2) have published a list of SRL process codes and examples of how they can be inferred from verbalization data.

These SRL process codes, inferred from participants' verbalizations, are rich sources of information regarding how learners engage with HLEs. Coded transcriptions of TAP data not only provide accurate descriptions of *what* learners do, but also *when* they do it, *what* occurs before and after each behavior, and *how often* each behavior occurs over the course of a learning task

(Azevedo & Witherspoon, 2009; Greene & Azevedo, 2010). Hypotheses about how these data relate to learning outcomes can be generated from models of SRL (e.g., Winne & Hadwin, 2008; Zimmerman, 2000). However, data collected with TAPs and analyzed using Azevedo and colleagues' scheme provide information about *specific* SRL processes, whereas models of SRL outline predictions about the relations among *broad* categories of self-regulation, such as "monitoring" or "strategy use" and learning outcomes. Therefore, researchers need a means of translating specific SRL process codes from TAP data (e.g., *selecting a new information source, judgment of learning*) into these broader categories.

Two-Tiered Approach to Analyzing Self-Regulated Learning Processing

Azevedo and colleagues (Azevedo et al., 2008; Greene & Azevedo, 2009) have outlined how the specific SRL processes derived from TAPs (e.g., *judgments of learning*), which they term micro-level SRL process data, can be used to indicate the degree to which individuals engage in the broader categories of self-regulation discussed in SRL models (e.g., Winne & Hadwin, 2008). They call these broader categories of SRL (i.e., planning, monitoring, strategy use, interest, and handling task difficulty demands) macro-level SRL processing. Their research has also shown how both micro-level and macro-level SRL process data can be helpful when analyzing how individuals learn complex topics with HLEs, and how various internal and external characteristics influence SRL processing.

Micro-Level SRL Processing Data

Micro-level SRL data are the specific learning processes inferred from TAPs through Azevedo and colleagues' (2004; Greene & Azevedo, 2009) coding scheme. Given that, in general, the quantity of adaptive SRL processing predicts learning (Zimmerman, 2000), analyses of how frequently learners enact various micro-level SRL processes may elucidate which SRL processes are particularly helpful in a given HLE (Azevedo & Cromley, 2004; Greene & Azevedo, 2007; Greene, Moos, Azevedo, & Winters, 2008; Greene, Bolick, & Robertson, 2010; Greene, Costa, & Dellinger, 2011). For example, research has shown that within one particular science-based HLE, frequently *coordinating various information sources* is an adaptive strategy, whereas excessive *note taking* is not (Greene et al., 2008). Thus, analyses of micro-level SRL processing allow researchers to examine domain-, task-, and HLE-specific relations between specific self-regulatory behaviors (e.g., *taking notes*) and learning.

However, it is important to remember that SRL is idiosyncratic, and that internal and external conditions may moderate the efficacy of particular micro-level processes in terms of learning. For example, individuals with low prior knowledge may need to devote a great deal of time to memorizing the declarative knowledge in an HLE before attempting to integrate multiple knowledge representations into conceptual understanding. For these individuals with low prior knowledge, frequent use of strategies, such as taking notes may be highly predictive of significant learning gains. On the other hand, for learners with ample prior knowledge about the content of an HLE, taking notes would be a poor use of their time. Instead, these learners might deploy other strategies (e.g., *coordinating information sources*) that are more appropriate for their level of prior knowledge, and subsequently achieve even more substantial learning gains. In a sample of users with varying degrees of prior knowledge, a statistical analysis using the frequency of deploying various strategies to predict learning outcomes may lead to unclear results; some participants (i.e., low prior knowledge) may take notes often and successfully acquire knowledge, whereas others (i.e., high prior knowledge) may take notes rarely but still show significant learning gains. Clearly, the frequency of micro-level SRL processing alone tells only part of the story regarding how self-regulatory behavior relates to learning. In certain situations, it may be helpful to examine SRL processing at a different, broader level. Greene and Azevedo (2009) argued that in certain situations it may be useful to aggregate frequency data for micro-level SRL process codes into macro-level SRL process data.

Macro-Level SRL Processing

In Azevedo and colleagues' (2004) scheme, each of the micro-level SRL processes can be categorized as an example of one of the five broader categories of macro-level SRL processing (i.e., planning, monitoring, strategy use, managing task difficulty and demands, and interest). Therefore, one way to calculate macro-level SRL processing would be to sum the frequencies of each micro-level SRL process that falls within that category. Macro-level analysis can account for some of the idiosyncratic differences in the efficacy of micro-level SRL processes. As illustrated above, various internal and external conditions, such as prior knowledge, can moderate the degree to which particular SRL processes are availing for individuals. Looking at macro-level SRL processing could explain some of the mixed findings that can result from analyzing frequency data on taking notes with the hypothetical participants described previously. For some participants, deploying a taking notes strategy frequently was an adaptive strategy, whereas for others it was not. By aggregating the frequency of all micro-level SRL processes that are indicative of strategy processing (e.g., taking notes and inferencing) into a single macro-level SRL strategy use score, the analysis could reveal that those participants who used more strategies, regardless of which specific strategies were best given the individuals' idiosyncratic differences, were more likely to acquire conceptual understanding (Greene, Bolick, et al., 2010; Greene, Costa, & Dellinger, 2011; Greene, Costa, Robertson, et al., 2010).

There are other advantages to examining macro-level SRL process data besides the ability to account for idiosyncratic interindividual differences. First, most models of SRL are conceptualized at the macro-level, not the micro-level (Pintrich, 2000; Winne & Hadwin, 2008; Zimmerman, 2000). These models do not directly address micro-level SRL processes; instead they make specific predictions about the relations among broad categories of SRL processing (e.g., planning, strategy use, monitoring), internal and external conditions (e.g., self-beliefs, prior knowledge, task conditions), and learning outcomes. Therefore, to test these relations, researchers need a means of translating TAP data into information about these broad categories of SRL processing, such as Greene and Azevedo's (2009) approach. Second, the large number of micro-level SRL processes that can be deployed over the course of a learning task greatly increase the sample size needed to do quantitative analyses with TAP data. Aggregating to the macro-level can reduce the number of relevant variables, resulting in more power and smaller sample size demands. Finally, moving beyond analyses of the frequency of SRL processing, researchers are beginning to examine *when* individuals use macro-level SRL processes, such as planning, monitoring, and strategy use over the entire course of a learning task (Azevedo & Witherspoon, 2009; Greene & Azevedo, 2010; Moos & Azevedo, 2008). These analyses can help developers of HLEs determine not only what to scaffold, but also which macro-level SRL processes should be prompted in the beginning, middle, and towards the end of a learning task.

Thus, the work of Azevedo, Greene, and colleagues (Azevedo et al., 2004; Greene & Azevedo, 2009) has provided a bridge between TAP data, with its inherent advantages over self-report instruments, and models of SRL. Using their coding scheme, TAPs can be coded for micro-level SRL processing, and the frequency with which learners deploy these processes can then be aggregated to the macro-level, and used to test the relations among SRL processing, internal and external conditions, and learning. Next we illustrate how data and findings from both tiers of analysis (i.e., micro- and macro-level) can be integrated to achieve a more complete understanding of users' SRL in HLEs than could be achieved by looking at either tier on its own.

Two-Tiered Approach to Analyzing Self-Regulated Learning Processing

Certainly, micro- and macro-level SRL process data, captured using TAPs, can be used separately to investigate how individuals self-regulate their learning in HLEs. However, we believe that a two-tiered approach to analyzing SRL processing, moving back and forth between the micro- and macro-levels, is necessary to truly understand how learners self-regulate in domain-, task-, and HLE-specific ways. Examining SRL at both tiers also allows for a more rigorous investigation of how the efficacy of specific processes varies depending upon internal and external characteristics.

At the first tier of analysis, researchers can investigate TAP data to identify the micro-level SRL processes individuals tend to deploy in a specific HLE. Then the researchers can determine which micro-level processes are associated with the acquisition of conceptual knowledge, and which ones are not. For instance, depending upon the HLE, the content, and the task, certain micro-level SRL processes may not be a good use of participants' time, regardless of their individual characteristics. Using a control-of-variables strategy in a history-based HLE is a good example of a context where this specific micro-level SRL process is unlikely to be helpful under any circumstances. These findings can be triangulated with a priori predictions of the important micro-level SRL processes for the HLE and its content, and qualitative analyses of successful learners' self-regulation. Assuming some congruence across multiple methodologies, these analyses should lead to a clear, HLE- and context-specific set of micro-level SRL processes associated with learning. Data regarding these micro-level SRL processes can then be aggregated into macro-level SRL process data.

At the second tier of analysis, macro-level SRL process data can be examined to determine how learners' planning, monitoring, and strategy use interact with internal and external conditions to influence learning. For example, analyses might reveal that individuals with low self-efficacy (Bandura, 2001) benefit greatly from engaging in frequent planning and monitoring, perhaps because these macro-level SRL processes allow them to focus on achieving proximal goals to boost their self-efficacy. Participants with high self-efficacy, on the other hand, might not benefit as much from frequent planning, and instead succeed when they set one distal goal and then enact multiple strategies to achieve that goal. The ways in which self-efficacy, an internal condition, influences SRL processing may be difficult to discern when looking at micro-level data, due to the large number of specific and idiosyncratic self-regulatory processes. However, interactions among self efficacy beliefs and SRL processing may be apparent at the macro-level. Macro-level analyses, in turn, could inform more detailed analyses of TAP data. In terms of the previous example, researchers and HLE developers might discover specific groups of micro-level SRL processes that reflect the achievement of proximal goals (e.g., *setting a goal, coordinating information sources, judging learning to be adequate*). Perhaps frequent achievement of proximal goals, as indicated by particular sets of micro-level SRL processes, are predictive of the kinds of adaptations to internal conditions (e.g., self-efficacy beliefs) that Winne and Hadwin (2008) posit to occur in phase four of their model.

Overall, we believe that an iterative, transactional, mutually informative approach to analyzing SRL processing at both tiers (i.e., micro- and macro-level) affords a tremendous wealth of information regarding how learners self-regulate with HLEs, and how the nature and quality of that self-regulation interacts with internal and external conditions. Such analyses allow for the use of TAP data to investigate the claims made in SRL models. They can also be informative in terms of the domain- and task-specific self-regulatory processes that should be scaffolded in particular HLEs.

Using a Two-Tiered Approach to Self-Regulated Learning Research to Inform Design Principles

Much of our empirical work has been focused upon studying how middle-school, high-school, and undergraduate learners use the Microsoft

Encarta (2007) HLE to learn about the circulatory system, and we have recently begun using the same two-tiered approach in a new HLE focused on historical understanding (Greene, Bolick, et al., 2010; Greene, Costa, & Dellinger, 2011; Greene, Costa, Robertson, et al., 2010). In particular, we have been interested in the role SRL plays as a mediator and a moderator of the relationship between prior knowledge and learning. Taken as a whole, on average participants in our studies do acquire both declarative and conceptual knowledge of the circulatory system while using the HLEs (Greene & Azevedo, 2007, 2009; Greene et al., 2008; Greene, Bolick, et al., 2010; Greene, Costa, & Dellinger, 2010; Greene, Costa, Robertson, et al., 2011). However, two-tiered analyses of micro- and macro-level SRL data have revealed what differentiates participants who experience practically significant learning gains from those who do not. These findings could potentially be used to redesign the HLEs to more actively foster and scaffold SRL processes.

In terms of the acquisition of conceptual understanding, our initial micro-level SRL process data analyses revealed that middle-school and high-school students who engaged in more frequent constructive strategy use (e.g., *coordinating information sources, making inferences*), as opposed to those who deployed more basic information-copying strategies (e.g., *taking notes*), learned more from the HLE in terms of pretest to posttest improvements in their mental model of the circulatory system (Greene & Azevedo, 2007; Greene et al., 2008). Findings from these studies suggest that there were HLE-specific micro-level SRL strategies that were predictive of learning, making them likely targets for scaffolding interventions either embedded within the HLE or provided by an instructor. In particular, participants appeared to need assistance in deploying strategies that force them to reconstruct and integrate what they read or see (e.g., *knowledge elaboration;* Greene et al., 2008; Greene, Bolick, et al., 2010; Greene, Costa, & Dellinger, 2011; Greene, Costa, Robertson, et al., 2010).

Interestingly, our past work at the micro-level tier showed no evidence that the frequency of micro-level SRL monitoring processing (e.g., *feeling of knowing, judgment of learning*) related to the acquisition of conceptual understanding. However, when we aggregated micro-level SRL process data to the macro-level, we did find that the frequency of monitoring behaviors was predictive of learning, above and beyond the influence of prior knowledge (Greene & Azevedo, 2009). These findings suggested that middle-school and high-school learners may need a more broad-based approach to scaffolding their monitoring than they do for scaffolding their strategy use. Our data suggest that interventions designed to scaffold specific micro-level monitoring behaviors (e.g., *feeling of knowing, content evaluation*) may have little effect, but more general prompts to monitor in whatever way the learner feels is most helpful may be beneficial. This finding makes particular sense given the domain and nature of the task. Complex systems in science, like the circulatory system, are often quite abstract and require the integration of multiple representations to fully understand them (Hmelo-Silver & Azevedo, 2006). Learners need to monitor frequently to judge whether they are constructing an accurate representation, but the specific nature of that monitoring (e.g., *feeling of knowing, judgment of learning*) most likely depends upon their internal characteristics, such as prior knowledge.

Our subsequent work with undergraduate students showed that, compared to participants with little prior knowledge, students with a great deal of prior knowledge were more likely to activate that knowledge and engage in integrative strategies, such as knowledge elaboration (Greene, Bolick, et al., 2010; Greene, Costa, & Dellinger, 2011; Greene, Costa, Robertson, et al., 2010). These findings are aligned with other research showing that the quality of prior knowledge predicts the types of strategies learners deploy (e.g., Moos & Azevedo, 2008). Further, the frequency of use of constructive micro-level SRL strategies, such as *coordinating information sources* and *making inferences* predicted learning among undergraduate students, above and beyond the effect of prior knowledge. These findings cohere with our work with middle-school and high-school students, and provide further support for scaffolding advanced strategies within the HLE. In our analyses, we found that successful learners engaged in more macro-level planning and monitoring, in general, than learners who were less successful. Again, looking across both tiers of analysis suggested that for this particular HLE, specific strategies and general monitoring processes should be the focus of scaffolding.

In one of our studies (Greene, Costa, Robertson, et al., 2010) we gathered data regarding two internal conditions: undergraduates' prior knowledge and their beliefs about intelligence (Dweck & Leggett, 1988). The latter data indicated the degree to which the participants viewed intelligence as a fixed quality that cannot be improved, a maladaptive belief, versus believing intelligence to be malleable, an adaptive belief. We found that, on average, the frequency of overall SRL processing moderated the influence of these internal conditions on learning. Frequent use of high-quality SRL macro-level processing increased the positive effects of high prior knowledge, and ameliorated the negative effects of having a maladaptive belief about intelligence. This examination of how internal characteristics (i.e., prior knowledge, implicit theory of intelligence) interacted with SRL processing would not have been possible without Azevedo and colleagues' (2004; Greene & Azevedo, 2009) coding scheme, which allowed us the ability to infer micro-level SRL processing from TAP data, aggregate it to the macro-level, and model its relations with other phenomena according to SRL theory (Winne & Hadwin, 2008). These findings suggest that fostering and scaffolding SRL within HLEs may not just affect learning, but also the degree to which internal characteristics influence the likelihood of participants acquiring deep conceptual understanding of complex science topics.

Finally, we have just begun to apply our two-tiered approach to a HLE designed to foster historical understanding (Greene, Bolick, et al., 2010). This HLE consists of a series of hyperlinked primary and secondary sources regarding a pre-Civil War public uprising in North Carolina. Importantly, there was no embedded scaffolding in the HLE, and participants had to determine on their own how to best select, evaluate, and integrate the numerous sources. Pretest measures showed that a majority of the participants had little to no knowledge of the historical event. Our first tier analysis of high-school students' SRL processing with the HLE revealed little use of sophisticated, constructive micro-level SRL strategies. Rather, most participants took notes or summarized what they were reading. This finding, coupled with participants' frequent expressions of confusion while learning, highlighted for us the importance of basic knowledge when working with historical content in this HLE. Embedded scaffolds for this HLE should target strategies that build declarative knowledge. Macro-level SRL process analyses indicated that planning was a key predictor of the acquisition of declarative knowledge, so prompts to make a thoughtful plan for navigating the HLE also seem warranted.

In sum, we believe that our past research provides an excellent model of how to transform TAPs into micro- and macro-level SRL process data that can inform the design of embedded scaffolds with HLEs. By triangulating findings from multiple tiers of analysis, developers of HLEs can have more confidence that the resources they devote to particular SRL scaffolds are well spent. Given the complexity of SRL models, and the idiosyncratic nature of SRL processing, researchers and developers of HLEs must adopt methods of measurement that accurately capture how learners self-regulate within the environments, and analyze those data in multiple ways to inform the design of scaffolds that make their HLEs effective with all learners, even those who lack the requisite SRL skills to take advantages of the HLEs on their own.

Conclusion

In this chapter we have argued that even the best-designed HLEs, given their considerable cognitive demands (Gerjets et al., 2008), will have limited effectiveness unless learners possess sufficient domain- and task-specific SRL knowledge and abilities. Unfortunately, most learners lack these abilities, therefore what should be two strengths of HLEs, their ability to present multiple representations with a high degree of learner control, become detriments. Scaffolding SRL from within the HLE requires studying how successful and unsuccessful individuals deploy SRL processes over the entire course of their learning. Self-report instruments simply do not capture such data in an accurate or comprehensive manner. TAPs are better aligned with the assumptions of SRL models and allow for rich data that can describe *what* users do, *when* they do it, *how often*, and in what *sequence*. From these data, coding schemes, such as the one developed by Azevedo and colleagues (2004; Greene & Azevedo, 2009) can provide a bridge from TAP data to micro- and macro level inferences regarding SRL processing. Our two-tiered approach to analyzing micro-level and macro-level SRL processing captures the specific activities that predict learning within a particular HLE, while also accounting for the idiosyncratic interindividual differences that are inherent to effective SRL. These findings can be triangulated to reveal what types of scaffolds are most likely to foster effective SRL among users who would otherwise not deploy such behaviors. We believe this approach allows developers of HLEs the information they need to make good decisions regarding how to deploy their resources to foster the particular kinds of SRL processing that will be most effective given their HLE, the content, and the tasks in which learners engage.

References

Ainsworth, S. (2006). DeFT: A conceptual framework for considering learning with multiple representations. *Learning and Instruction, 16*, 183–198.

Antonenko, P. D., & Niederhauser, D. S. (2010). The influence of leads on cognitive load and learning in a hypertext environment. *Computers in Human Behavior, 26*(2), 140–150.

Azevedo, R. (2005). Computer environments as metacognitive tools for enhancing learning. *Educational Psychologist, 40*, 193–197.

Azevedo, R., & Cromley, J. G. (2004). Does training on self-regulated learning facilitate students' learning with hypermedia? *Journal of Educational Psychology, 96*(3), 523–535.

Azevedo, R., Guthrie, J. T., & Seibert, D. (2004). The role of self-regulated learning in fostering students' conceptual understanding of complex systems with hypermedia. *Journal of Educational Computing Research, 30*, 87–111.

Azevedo, R., Moos, D. C., Greene, J. A., Winters, F. I., & Cromley, J. G. (2008). Why is externally-regulated learning more effective than self-regulated learning with hypermedia? *Educational Technology Research and Development, 56*(1), 45–72.

Azevedo, R., Moos, D. C., Johnson, A. M., & Chauncey, A. D. (2010). Measuring cognitive and metacognitive regulatory processes during hypermedia learning: Issues and challenges. *Educational Psychologist, 45*(4), 210–223.

Azevedo, R., & Witherspoon, A. M. (2009). Self-regulated use of hypermedia. In D. J. Hacker, J. Dunlosky, & A. C. Graesser (Eds.), *Handbook of metacognition in education* (pp. 319–339). Mahwah, NJ: Erlbaum.

Baddeley, A. D. (2001). Is working memory still working? *American Psychologist, 56*(11), 851–864.

Bandura, A. (2001). Social cognitive theory. An agentic perspective. *Annual Review of Psychology, 52*, 1–26.

Bannert, M., & Mengelkamp, C. (2008). Assessment of metacognitive skills by means of instruction to think aloud and reflect when prompted. Does the verbalisation method affect learning? *Metacognition and Learning, 3*, 39–58.

Collins, A., & Halverson, R. (2010). The second educational revolution: Rethinking education in the age of technology. *Journal of Computer Assisted Learning, 26*(1), 18–27.

Duncan, T. G., & McKeachie, W. J. (2005). The making of the motivated strategies for learning questionnaire. *Educational Psychologist, 40*(2), 117–128.

Dweck, C. S., & Leggett, E. L. (1988). A social-cognitive approach to motivation and personality. *Psychological Review, 95*, 256–273.

Ericsson, K. A. (2006). Protocol analysis and expert thought: Concurrent verbalizations of thinking during experts' performance on representative tasks. In K. A. Ericsson, N. Charness, R. R. Hoffman, & P. J. Feltovich (Eds.), *The Cambridge handbook of expertise and expert performance* (pp. 223–242). Cambridge, MA: Cambridge University Press.

Ericsson, K. A., & Simon, H. A. (1993). *Protocol analysis: Verbal reports as data*. Cambridge, MA: The MIT Press.

Gerjets, P., Scheiter, K., & Schuh, J. (2008). Information comparisons in example-based hypermedia environments: Supporting learners with processing prompts and an interactive comparison tool. *Educational Technology Research and Development, 56*(1), 73–92.

Greene, J. A., & Azevedo, R. (2007). Adolescents' use of self-regulatory processes and their relation to qualitative mental model shifts while using hypermedia. *Journal of Educational Computing Research, 36*(2), 125–148.

Greene, J. A., & Azevedo, R. (2009). A macro-level analysis of SRL processes and their relations to the acquisition of sophisticated mental models. *Contemporary Educational Psychology, 34*, 18–29.

Greene, J. A., & Azevedo, R. (2010). The measurement of learners' self-regulated cognitive and metacognitive processes while using computer-based learning environments. *Educational Psychologist, 45*(4), 203–209.

Greene, J. A., Bolick, C. M., & Robertson, J. (2010). Fostering historical knowledge and thinking skills using hypermedia learning environments: The role of self-regulated learning. *Computers in Education, 54*, 230–243.

Greene, J. A., Costa, L-J., & Dellinger, K. (2011). Analysis of self-regulated learning processing using statistical models for count data. *Metacognition & Learning, 6*, 275–301. doi: 10.1007/s11409-011-9078-4.

Greene, J. A., Costa, L. C., Robertson, J., Pan, Y., & Deekens, V. (2010). Exploring relations among college students' prior knowledge, implicit theories of intelligence, and self-regulated learning in a hypermedia environment. *Computers in Education, 55*, 1027–1043.

Greene, J. A., Moos, D. C., Azevedo, R., & Winters, F. I. (2008). Exploring differences between gifted and grade-level students' use of self-regulatory learning processes with hypermedia. *Computers in Education, 50*, 1069–1083.

Greene, J. A., Robertson, J., & Costa, L.-J. C. (2011). Assessing self-regulated learning using think-aloud protocol methods. In B. J. Zimmerman & D. Schunk (Eds.), *Handbook of self-regulation of learning and performance* (pp. 313–328). New York: Routledge Publishers.

Hmelo-Silver, C., & Azevedo, R. (2006). Understanding complex systems: Some core challenges. *The Journal of the Learning Sciences, 15*(1), 53–61.

Jacobson, M., & Archodidou, A. (2000). The design of hypermedia tools for learning: Fostering conceptual change and transfer of complex scientific knowledge. *The Journal of the Learning Sciences, 9*(2), 145–199.

Jacobson, M. J., & Azevedo, R. (2008). Advances in scaffolding learning with hypertext and hypermedia: Theoretical, empirical, and design issues. *Educational Technology Research and Development, 56*, 1–3.

Microsoft Corporation. (2007). *Encarta Premium. [Computer Software]*. Redmond, WA: Microsoft Corporation.

Moos, D. C., & Azevedo, R. (2008). Self-regulated learning with hypermedia: The role of prior domain knowledge. *Contemporary Educational Psychology, 33*, 270–298.

Pintrich, P. R. (2000). The role of goal orientation in self-regulated learning. In M. Boekaerts, P. Pintrich, & M. Zeidner (Eds.), *Handbook of self-regulation* (pp. 451–502). San Diego, CA: Academic.

Pintrich, P. R., Smith, D. A. F., García, T., & McKeachie, W. J. (1991). *A manual for the use of the motivated strategies for learning questionnaire (MSLQ)*. Ann Arbor, MI: University of Michigan, National Center for Research to Improve Postsecondary Teaching and Learning.

Shapiro, A. (2008). Hypermedia design as learner scaffolding. *Educational Technology Research and Development, 56*(1), 29–44.

Veenman, M. (2007). The assessment and instruction of self-regulation in computer-based environments: A discussion. *Metacognition and Learning, 2*, 177–183.

Veenman, M. V. J., Elshout, J. J., & Groen, M. G. M. (1993). Thinking aloud: Does it affect regulatory processes in learning. *Tijdschrift voor Onderwijsresearch, 18*, 322–330.

Veenman, M. V. J., Prins, F. J., & Verheij, J. (2003). Learning styles: Self-reports versus thinking-aloud measures. *British Journal of Educational Psychology, 73*(3), 357–372.

White, B., & Frederiksen, J. (2005). A theoretical framework and approach for fostering metacognitive development. *Educational Psychologist, 40*, 211–223.

Winne, P., & Hadwin, A. (2008). The weave of motivation and self-regulated learning. In D. Schunk & B. Zimmerman (Eds.), *Motivation and self-regulated learning: Theory, research, and applications* (pp. 297–314). Mahwah, NJ: Erlbaum.

Winne, P. H., & Jamieson-Noel, D. (2002). Exploring students' calibration of self reports about study tactics and achievement. *Contemporary Educational Psychology, 27*, 551–572.

Winne, P. H., Jamieson-Noel, D., & Muis, K. (2002). Methodological issues and advances in researching tactics, strategies, and self-regulated learning. In P. R. Pintrich & M. L. Maehr (Eds.), *Advances in motivation and achievement: New directions in measures and methods* (Vol. 12, pp. 121–155). Greenwich, CT: JAI.

Winne, P. H., & Perry, N. E. (2000). Measuring self-regulated learning. In M. Boekaerts, P. Pintrich, & M. Zeidner (Eds.), *Handbook of self-regulation* (pp. 531–566). San Diego, CA: Academic.

Zimmerman, B. (2000). Attaining self-regulation: A social cognitive perspective. In M. Boekaerts, P. Pintrich, & M. Zeidner (Eds.), *Handbook of self-regulation* (pp. 13–39). San Diego, CA: Academic.

Hypermedia and Self-Regulation: An Interplay in Both Directions

9

Maria Opfermann, Katharina Scheiter, Peter Gerjets, and Annett Schmeck

Abstract

Rapid technological developments and growing interest in learning approaches other than traditional ones such as ex-cathedra teaching have made hypermedia environments an increasingly popular learning device. Such environments have several advantages, but place demands on learners as well, such as *requiring* substantially more metacognitive and self-regulatory skills compared to structured and guided learning environments. For instance, learners should be able to check whether they learn with an appropriate combination of representations and whether their pace of information retrieval or navigation speed are appropriate. On the other hand, hypermedia environments can also *support* metacognitive and self-regulatory abilities and skills precisely because of their demands. When learners are not only passive recipients of information that is presented to them in bite-sized pieces, but have to take decisions regarding their own learning process, active and constructive learning can be enhanced.

This chapter will first give an introduction on hypermedia, including its benefits and requirements. In a next step, we will go into more detail regarding theories and models of self-regulated learning that served as a framework for our own research on the effectiveness of hypermedia learning environment. This will finally be followed by sections discussing the "interplay in both directions", that is, (a) which importance self-regulatory skills have for hypermedia learning and (b) how hypermedia environments could be designed and used to support self-regulated learning.

M. Opfermann (✉) • A. Schmeck
Department of Instructional Psychology, Duisburg-Essen University, Essen 45117, Germany
e-mail: maria.opfermann@uni-duisburg-essen.de

K. Scheiter • P. Gerjets
Knowledge Media Research Center, Tuebingen, Germany

Hypermedia Learning Environments: What Makes Them So Special?

In everyday language use, hypermedia environments are sometimes mixed with multimedia environments. However, while the term *multimedia* (e.g., Mayer, 2009) can refer to any device

R. Azevedo and V. Aleven (eds.), *International Handbook of Metacognition and Learning Technologies*, Springer International Handbooks of Education 26, DOI 10.1007/978-1-4419-5546-3_9,

that combines verbal (printed or spoken text) and pictorial (static or dynamic visualizations) instructional material in a rather system-controlled fashion, *hypermedia* environments are mainly characterized by their network-like structure storing information fragments in nodes that are connected by hyperlinks, which allows information being retrieved and explored in multiple ways. In this regard, Rouet and Levonen (1996) as well as Jonassen (1996) view hypermedia as an integration of hypertext with multimedia elements. This flexible degree of learner control enables adaptive information utilization (Shapiro & Niederhauser, 2004) and can foster active, constructive, and flexible learning.

The high degree of freedom associated with hypermedia environments encompasses various potentials as well as dangers, summarized, for instance, by Scheiter and Gerjets (2007). For instance, hypermedia structures *mirror the mind*, that is, their hyperlink structure might be compared to the way in which humans store and connect information (Jonassen & Grabinger, 1990). Second, their high level of learner control may lead to *increased interest and motivation*, offering learners the opportunity to exert control over their learning and involving them in several decision-making processes (Alexander & Jetton, 2003; Moos & Azevedo, 2008). Third, the higher the learner control is in such environments, the more *learning can be adapted to personal preferences and cognitive needs*. This, in turn, includes *affordances for active and constructive information processing*. This already points to the importance of self-regulatory skills for hypermedia learning and vice versa. That is, successful learning with hypermedia environments requires such skills, but they can also foster them. When learners are "forced" to continuously evaluate whether the information that they just retrieved helps them to achieve their learning goals and to decide between different information sources, one important aspect of successful self-regulated learning according to researchers such as Winne and Hadwin (1998) and Azevedo (2005) has been documented. Such skills can thus be seen as both prerequisites for and consequences of successful learning with hypermedia.

In the following section, the SRL models of Winne and Hadwin (1998) as well as the one of Azevedo (2005) will be described shortly. This will be followed by a discussion on the roles that aspects of self-regulation as well as other individual learner characteristics and the instructional design of learning environments play with regard to the cognitive load learners experience and accordingly their performance in hypermedia learning environments. This discussion is based on an augmented model of the Cognitive Load Theory (CLT; Chandler & Sweller, 1991; Sweller, van Merriënboer, & Paas, 1998) introduced by Gerjets and Hesse (2004). Especially, the latter two models will serve as a framework for our conceptions of hypermedia learning and how SRL can be supported by as well as foster hypermedia learning.

Self-Regulated Learning: Models and Assumptions

The importance of self-regulative skills for learning with hypermedia and vice versa has been debated in a broad range of papers. For instance, Gerjets and Hesse (2004) describe hypermedia as an instance of advanced multimedia technologies which is characterized by high computational power that allows for active, flexible, goal-oriented, and self-controlled learning. The question remains, however, *what exactly* makes up successful self-regulated learning. One model that describes self-regulation in greater detail is the COPES model of self-regulated learning (Winne, 2001; Winne & Hadwin, 1998). According to the model, self-regulated learning unfolds temporally in at least three of four possible phases:

1. *Task definition,* where learners develop a model of the task, which includes perceptions about features of the task, for instance, the perceived goal—the set of standards by which a task can be judged.
2. *Goal setting and planning,* where learners set their goals for learning and build up plans to approach these goals. This also means that

learners can reframe the goals that they perceived during the first stage, for instance, when their personal standards differ from standards that were perceived for the task.

3. *Enacting study tactics and strategies,* which means that learners apply the tactics and strategies they have been planning in phase 2 of the model. In other words (Winne, 2001, p. 167), "work on the task itself is done." This in turn updates prior knowledge and beliefs, as already during the execution of operations, internal feedback is being generated. That is, the products of current operations are monitored and evaluated (e.g., compared to the standards set up in phase 2), and this may result in dynamically sensitive modifications of plans and tactics. It should be noted in this regard that this can also mean that a student quits learning at this point, when, for instance, he recognizes that there are no study tactics available that are suitable to reach the goals set up in the previous phase.
4. *Metacognitively adapting studying* is an optional phase of self-regulated learning. The adaptations that students carry out here refer to more general changes in the (re-)structuring of existing schemas and learning strategies. That is, they are not adapted with regard to the current task, but with regard to future learning situations as well.

In each of the phases, deliberate changes that students make to their own learning mean that they engage in metacognition. That is, metacognitive monitoring and control are seen as the two events that constitute the focus of interest in the model. According to Winne (2001; Winne & Hadwin, 1998), self-regulated learning can be improved by either enhancing these processes or when learners have access to necessary information. Enhancing metacognitive control or metacognitive monitoring can be implemented by using more valid standards to monitor learning or by improving the ability of learners to recognize when comprehension monitoring should occur. In this regard, hypermedia environments seem a suitable option to both enable access to information and enhance metacognitive processes, for instance, by providing multiple information sources (that can be retrieved in multiple ways according to learners' individual needs) or by means of metacognitive prompting or modeling.

The importance of such metacognitive support features for enhancing self-regulated learning and specifically for learning with hypermedia is central in the work of Azevedo and colleagues (Azevedo, 2005; Azevedo & Cromley, 2004; Azevedo, Cromley, Winters, Moos, & Greene, 2005), which will also be presented and discussed in the next section. According to Azevedo (2005), hypermedia environments, despite their educational potential, have failed to enhance students' learning per se especially with regard to complex science topics. In particular, Azevedo (2005) assumes that students who lack key self-regulatory and metacognitive skills have trouble with the open and in itself complex nature of hypermedia environments. More specifically, learners do not deploy monitoring activities like feeling of knowing or judgment of learning, and they do not engage in planning activities such as goal creation or prior knowledge activation (Azevedo, Greene, & Moos, 2007). These activities, however, are seen as central in hypermedia learning. Following his own criticism with regard to preceding hypermedia research which, according to Azevedo (2005), had not yet addressed how exactly a learner regulates his/her learning with hypermedia, the author introduces a model which is adapted from SRL research and allows a more direct view on the interplay between learner characteristics, cognitive processes, and system structure during hypermedia learning.

In line with other SRL researchers, Azevedo (2005) sees self-regulated learning with hypermedia as a constructive process where recursive cycles of (meta-)cognitive activities take place. In line with Winne (2001), Azevedo also proposes SRL as being a multiphase process where learners need to:

- Analyze the learning situation.
- Set meaningful learning goals.
- Determine which strategies to use and assess whether these strategies are effective to meet the learning goals.
- Monitor and evaluate their understanding.
- Modify plans, goals, strategies, and effort in relation to contextual conditions (which

includes cognitive, motivational and task conditions).

The model of Azevedo and colleagues includes 33 variables summarized under:

- *Planning*, e.g., goal setting, prior knowledge activation, and goal recycling in working memory
- *Monitoring activities*, e.g., feeling of knowing, judgment of learning, monitoring progress towards goals, and self-questioning
- *Learning strategies*, e.g., hypothesizing, coordinating information sources, drawing inferences, and summarizing
- *Handling task difficulties*, e.g., help-seeking behavior
- *Interest in the task or the content domain of the task*

In their model, Azevedo et al. (2007; Azevedo 2005) do not explicitly label any of these 33 variables as effective or ineffective aspects of self-regulated learning with hypermedia; however, Azevedo and Cromley (2004) report that successful learners regulate their learning by using effective strategies, planning their learning by *creating* subgoals, *activating* prior knowledge, *monitoring* emerging understanding, and *planning* their time and effort. On the other hand, less successful learners tend to use effective as well as ineffective strategies equally often, plan their learning by *using* subgoals and *recycling* goals in working memory, and handle task difficulties and demands through engaging in help-seeking behavior. In line with this, several researchers found that learners who possess sophisticated self-regulatory skills are better able to cope with the demands imposed by the complex and multifaceted structure of hypermedia environments (e.g., Schwartz, Andersen, Hong, Howard, & McGee, 2004).

This relation between the structure and demands of a learning environment, learner activities and conceptions, cognitive load experienced by learners, and accordingly performance has also been taken up in the above-mentioned model by Gerjets and Hesse (2004), which can be seen as an augmentation of the Cognitive Load Theory (Chandler & Sweller, 1991; Sweller et al., 1998). This model, preceded by a short summary of the original CLT, will be presented and discussed next.

The Augmented Cognitive Load Theory Model

The original Cognitive Load Theory (CLT; Chandler & Sweller, 1991; Sweller et al., 1998) assumes a direct relation between the instructional design of a learning environment and working memory load, which in turn has an impact on learning performance. More specifically, working memory load is divided into three types that differ with regard to their causes and benefits for learning. *Intrinsic cognitive load* refers to the load that is caused by content- or task-inherent complexity. It depends on prior knowledge and the extent of element interactivity, that is, the number of elements that have to be processed simultaneously during performance of a task. Although intrinsic load needs to be considered by instructional designers, Sweller et al. (1998) emphasize that it cannot be directly modified by the design of a learning environment. The influence capabilities of instructional designers rather refer to optimizing *germane cognitive load* through minimizing *extraneous cognitive load*.

Extraneous cognitive load builds the core of the CLT because it can directly be controlled by instructional designers. It is the type of working memory load imposed by any instructional design and is high when this design is inadequate (e.g., too much task-irrelevant information). Intrinsic cognitive load caused by task complexity and element interactivity and extraneous cognitive load caused by instructional design are supposed to be additive. The less working memory load is claimed by the sum of these two load types, the more capacity is available for learning-relevant processes such as schema construction. Such processes relate to germane cognitive load—the effort concerned with applying higher-level cognitive processes that aid understanding.

Contrary to the assumptions of the original CLT, the augmented model of Gerjets and Hesse (2004), which is depicted in Fig. 9.1, proposes

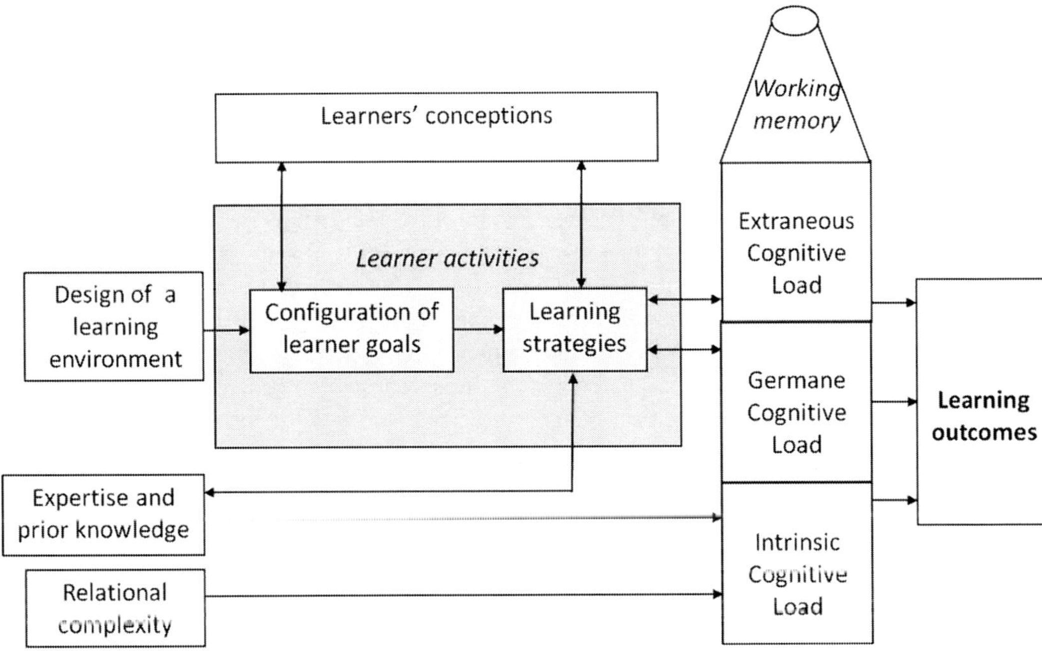

Fig. 9.1 Learner activities and learner conceptions as moderators between instructional design, cognitive load, and learning outcomes (Adapted from Gerjets & Hesse, 2004)

that the relation between the design of a learning environment and learning outcomes such as cognitive load and accordingly performance cannot be seen as a direct one-to-one mapping but that it is mediated by learner activities, which in turn depend on learners' expertise and prior knowledge as well as on the instructional conceptions. These individual prerequisites gain importance with increasing levels of learner control, as is the case in hypermedia learning environments.

In other words, depending on the structure and complexity of such environments and depending on their own individual prerequisites, learners will set goals and make strategic decisions about which contents to access at which sequence. These decisions will result in learning activities, which accordingly lead to specific patterns of cognitive load. These cognitive load patterns, in turn, are seen as being directly responsible for learning outcomes. When, for instance (in line with assumptions of the original CLT), extraneous cognitive load can be kept low so that free capacities can be used for processes related to germane cognitive load (e.g., schema construction), meaningful learning can take place.

To sum up, according to the extended CLT model of Gerjets and Hesse (2004), learners' activities and thus their performance within a hypermedia learning environment are determined by at least two main factors. These are the instructional design of the learning environment on the one hand and individual learner characteristics on the other hand. As for the design side, the learning outcome in a concrete learning situation can be seen as a result of the trade-off between the aforementioned advantages and disadvantages of hypermedia (Scheiter & Gerjets, 2007; Shapiro & Niederhauser, 2004). It is therefore of pivotal importance to design hypermedia environments carefully, which refers to the contents of the environments as well as to the identification of appropriate degrees of learner control. An optimally designed hypermedia environment should thus support learners in setting meaningful goals and deploying appropriate strategies to foster learning.

In this regard, a main difference between effective and ineffective hypermedia learning seems to be that, in the latter case, learners do not seem to engage in SRL activities by themselves. In this regard, Azevedo (2005, p. 203) notes that when learners fail to learn with hypermedia successfully, one might "erroneously conclude that the environments are inherently effective, when in fact what is needed is to foster students' self-regulation while using these powerful but complex learning environments." Azevedo and colleagues (e.g., Azevedo & Cromley, 2004) thus assume that some kind of scaffolding or training might be necessary to help learners display more elaborated SRL strategies and accordingly gain conceptual understanding during hypermedia learning. These studies and other research on self-regulation and hypermedia learning will be presented next.

The Impact of Self-Regulatory Skills for Hypermedia Learning

In traditional learning settings, the importance of self-regulatory skills has been confirmed for areas such as text comprehension and for problem-solving strategies. According to Rouet and Eme (2002) such skills, for instance, knowledge about metacognitive strategies in text comprehension, can also be applied to tasks that are not primarily text-based but *require* sufficient text comprehension. Stadtler (2006) argues that such requirements are met, for instance, by electronic knowledge databases or hypermedia environments, because, in such environments, learners are readers and users of metacognitive strategies at the same time when approaching a high amount of (not only textual) information with differing levels of quality in nonlinear ways. In this regard, research has also investigated the role of self-regulation and metacognition (the latter mainly as one defining constituent of self-regulatory skills) in Web-based or hypermedia learning.

In an early discussion, Cates (1992) states that metacognitive skills are one major factor that enables learners to make the best use of the resources offered by hypermedia. In this regard, Cates (1992) points to a discussion that might be of greater relevance for this chapter. From his point of view, it is unclear whether providing external support features actually stimulates metacognition or rather substitutes for it. According to Cates (1992), there is yet no solution to this discussion; however, the influence of self-regulatory skills for hypermedia learning and vice versa the potential of hypermedia environments for fostering self-regulation cannot be doubted (e.g., Azevedo, 2005).

In a newer study, Bendixen and Hartley (2003), criticizing the lack of research on the relation between self-regulatory skills and hypermedia learning, argue that such skills, in particular metacognitive awareness, come into play when ill-structured problems are presented—and that hypermedia environments share several features with such ill-structured problems. However, using the *Metacognitive Awareness Inventory* (*MAI*; Schraw & Dennison, 1994), Bendixen and Hartley found that neither of the relevant dimensions, *knowledge of cognition* and *regulation of cognition*, contributed significantly to achievement in their hypermedia tutorial. This result was surprising but the authors assume that the ill-structured character of the environment, which might have been a prerequisite for self-regulatory skills to come into play, might not have been given. In fact, their hypermedia tutorial on information about former Yugoslavia was rather structured, as was the form of assessment, namely, the testing of factual knowledge. Taking also into account that learners had only 30 min time to work through the environment, Bendixen and Hartley (2003) argue that some students only might have been able to read the texts and nothing else so that such learning processes would not necessarily have needed to tap into metacognitive resources.

On the other hand, other studies show a rather strong relationship between self-regulatory skills and hypermedia learning. For instance, Bannert (2005a), in an exploratory study, was interested in the spontaneous metacognitive strategy use of students working with a hypermedia environment on psychology and found that such strategies correlated significantly with performance on a transfer task; additionally, metacognitive activities were related to factual knowledge. A correlational study by Nesbit et al. (2006), investigating psychology students' achievement goal orientations and learning strategies in a multimedia environment, showed that goal orientation as assessed with a questionnaire related to study tactics and achievement. In particular, mastery goal orientation was negatively related to the amount of highlighting. The authors see this finding as being in line with expectations as highlighting is assumed to be a less effective study strategy compared to summarizing and other forms of elaboration that are useful for assembling and integrating knowledge.

In one of our own studies (Opfermann, 2008), we aimed at validating the above-mentioned augmented CLT model and investigated whether learners, who differed in regard to (a) attitudes towards mathematics as a learning domain and towards computers as a learning medium, (b) epistemological beliefs, and (c) metacognitive strategy knowledge (indicated before learning took place) and metacognitive activities (reported by learners after learning had taken place), show different strategies with regard to navigational and representational choices and whether they differ with regard to performance and knowledge gains. A hypermedia environment that aimed at conveying knowledge on basic principles of probability theory by means of worked examples was used for high school students (aged about 16 years on average). It was found that, in line with our expectations, attitudes towards mathematics, general epistemological beliefs, and mathematics-related beliefs as well as strategy knowledge influenced the performance of learners. However, this influence seems to appear mainly when learner characteristics are considered as a whole "package" rather than in isolation, and their impact was also found to be more direct and less mediated by learners' information utilization behavior. Contrary to expectations, although strategy knowledge was given, learners did not implement this knowledge in terms of more sophisticated metacognitive activities during learning. It was assumed that this might be due to the fact that learners might not always be aware of or not spontaneously be able to use such strategies during learning. This interpretation would be in line with assumptions by Azevedo and Cromley (2004); Azevedo, Moos, Johnson, and Chauncey (2010); Schnotz, Heiß, and Eckhardt (2005); or Bannert (2003).

Such findings lead Veenman, Wilhelm, and Beishuizen (2004) to conclude that metacognitive training might be needed to foster metacognitive skills in multiple domains as well as transfer or generalizability of such skills. This is in line with the above-mentioned suggestions of Azevedo and Cromley (2004) regarding some kind of scaffolding or training to enhance hypermedia learning. The question how different forms of such instructional support can be implemented in hypermedia environments will thus be focused on in the next section.

How Can Self-Regulated Learning Be Supported in Hypermedia Environments?

With regard to instructional support in general, Bannert (2005b) points out that extensive, long-termed metacognitive training as a form of *direct metacognitive support* should be distinguished from *indirect support* such as metacognitive prompts. Most research investigating the impact of such instructional support for multimedia and hypermedia learning has made use of the latter option—mainly because time restrictions of the short-termed studies did not allow for extensive training.

Schmidt and Ford (2003) investigated the influence of metacognitive instruction on students' work with a learner-controlled computer program that taught them how to create Web pages. Participants in the control group worked with the environment freely without major instructions and could decide whenever they thought they had learned enough to proceed to the posttest. Participants in the experimental group first received a 10-min metacognitive instruction (e.g., how important it is for one's own learning to monitor the own learning progress and to reflect upon what one is doing), which they also had available as a handout throughout the whole learning process. During learning, the experimental group furthermore received metacognitive prompting in form of pop-up windows that asked them to reflect on how well they learned the material. Although Schmidt and Ford (2003) did not find a direct effect of their metacognitive support on any of the learning outcomes, their results were interesting in that they showed that performance avoidance orientation moderated the relationship between interventions and retrospectively reported metacognitive activities, which in turn had an impact on learning outcomes. Overall, metacognitive activities were significantly related to self-efficacy (i.e., learners who reported higher metacognitive activities were also more confident that they could create Web pages after the learning phase) as well as to declarative knowledge and skill-based performance.

A similar but more extensive study was conducted by Bannert (2003), who let two groups of students learn with a Web-based hypertext environment conveying basic concepts of motivational psychology. Learners in the experimental group were made familiar with the importance and usefulness of self-regulation before starting to work with the environment. The information they received was also available as a schematic handout during learning, and students were encouraged to make notes and be geared to this schema throughout the learning phase. However, in contrast to the information given in Schmidt and Ford's study, the information provided here did not only include information on the importance of monitoring one's own learning progress. Rather, students were provided with a model of self-regulated learning that comprised metacognitive activities such as goal setting, planning, monitoring, evaluation, and, if necessary, adaptation of strategies. Additionally, learners in the experimental group received metacognitive prompting in that they were repeatedly reminded to use the provided SRL model for their own learning. Metacognitive activities were assessed by means of verbal protocols. Results show that students in the experimental group expressed significantly higher metacognitive activities on nearly all analyzed dimensions (goal setting, planning, information search, and evaluation). Additionally, they outperformed the control group with regard to transfer tasks. There were, however, no significant differences with regard to factual knowledge and free recall. Bannert (2003) explains some of her findings with the observation that not all learners were able to use the metacognitive schema appropriately. More specifically, learners with little domain-specific prior knowledge struggled with this support feature—which might have been a result of the additional cognitive capacity that was stressed by processing and applying the schema as well as the following metacognitive prompts. This assumption is in line with our own findings, which will be described later in this chapter. In another study, Bannert (2004) left out the instruction phase and "only" prompted learners to display metacognitive activities four times during learning. The first prompt aimed at stimulating their orientation, specification of learning goals, and planning; the second told them to write down relevant links and judge the relevance of the information retrieved; the third aimed at fostering monitoring activities; and the fourth instructed participants to evaluate their learning outcome, for instance, by controlling their comprehension and making summaries. Similar to her previous study, Bannert (2004) found differences between experimental conditions only for transfer tasks. However, Bannert also observed that about half of the participants in the experimental group did not make use of, or better did not comply with, the metacognitive prompts they were given during learning. She thus divided the experimental group into two subgroups: students who complied or did not comply with the prompts. Analysis of performance differences between the groups showed that students who used prompts in a meaningful way outperformed those who did not with regard to both factual knowledge and transfer.

In sum, the results of the above-mentioned studies are in line with earlier findings from Lin and Lehman (1999) who argued that to benefit from instructional support, learners should possess certain prerequisites, because otherwise such support features might lead to cognitive overload.

At first sight, it seems counterintuitive that metacognitive support is only useful for learners who already possess knowledge and self-regulatory skills. Isn't it more logical that learners who lack such abilities receive support to optimize their learning? And if so, how can it be assured that learners with little prior knowledge and little self-regulatory skills benefit from support features such as prompting? According to Schnotz et al. (2005), an important aspect to be considered is the *optional use* of such features, that is, giving students the freedom to decide if and when they retrieve instructional support. In order to enable students with low prior knowledge to benefit from such support, Bannert (2005b) emphasizes the need of extensive metacognitive training for such learners before they are exposed to prompts, which in turn are rather suitable for learners already possessing self-regulatory skills, which only need to be activated. These latter considerations were taken into account by a number of studies conducted by Azevedo and colleagues. For instance, Azevedo and Cromley (2004) found that training students how to regulate their learning according to models of self-regulated learning (e.g., planning, monitoring, and strategic proceeding) led to greater shifts in mental models, higher posttest performance, and higher metacognitive activities such as prior knowledge activation, planning, or monitoring progress towards goals. In later studies (Azevedo et al., 2005, 2007), the effects of several forms of scaffolding were compared. The theoretical background fits well into the discussion about the usefulness of instructional support for learners with differing prerequisites. In particular, Azevedo et al. (2005, 2007) assume that fixed scaffolds such as prompting of predefined subgoals might not be suitable to meet the individual needs of all learners in the same way. In their experiments, they compared such fixed scaffolds with adaptive scaffolding conditions in which learners had access to a human tutor who assisted learners to plan their learning by activating prior knowledge, monitor their emerging understanding and learning progress during learning, and use effective learning strategies. Metacognitive activities were assessed by means of verbal protocols, which were analyzed according to a coding scheme. Results indicate that learners in the adaptive scaffolding condition outperformed those receiving fixed or no scaffolding on several performance measures. Looking at different developmental levels, however, revealed that this effect was especially apparent for middle and high school students, whereas college students also benefited from fixed scaffolding (Azevedo, 2005). Additionally, it was found that younger students also relied more on their tutor when provided with adaptive scaffolding. That is, they were able to follow the metacognitive instructions but did not internalize them. Although this sounds disadvantageous for the acquisition of metacognitive skills, it might well be in line with the assumptions discussed earlier on. That is, by allocating metacognitive strategies to and using them from an external source, younger and more unexperienced learners might have reduced their cognitive load so that they could direct all of their cognitive capacities to learning itself. Once some learning progress was made and schemas were built, it might well have been that metacognitive skills and strategies were internalized. Although these assumptions fit with the findings, they are still subject to empirical validation.

Taken together, research that has aimed at optimizing self-regulated for hypermedia learning by providing metacognitive support has generated mixed results. Instructional support seems to be beneficial under certain, but not all, circumstances. In this regard, Stadtler (2006) summarizes several factors that influence the relation between instructional support and learning outcomes. Such factors are the metacognitive aspects that are meant to be supported, the duration of support (e.g., extensive training versus short-termed intervention), the source of support (e.g., a human tutor or computer), age and prerequisites of learners, as well as characteristics of the learning task and learning environment.

One of our own studies thus investigated whether self-regulated learning in a hypermedia environment can be enhanced by providing learners with two forms of instructional support: a metacognitive modeling video as well as prompting of representational awareness. It was assumed that both support devices would help learners utilizing beneficial SRL strategies that they were either not aware of or not able to display. Additionally, it was assumed that individual learner characteristics would moderate the relationship between support and learning outcomes in that, for instance, learners with less sophisticated self-regulatory skills might benefit from modeling and prompting, whereas learners with sophisticated skills might not need such devices.

Again, findings were partly surprising. Although all participants had significant knowledge gains, these gains were highest for learners who received neither modeling nor prompting and lowest for learners who received both forms of support. An interesting finding was the interaction with knowledge about beneficial metacognitive strategies and displayed activities—for less sophisticated learners (i.e., those who knew little about beneficial strategies and/or did displayed less activities during learning), instructional support was indeed slightly helpful or at least did not impair learning. For sophisticated learners, however, instructional support even appeared to be highly detrimental.

Although initially surprising, the finding that learners benefited most from an environment without additional support features is in line with recent research (e.g., Horz, Winter, & Fries, 2006). One interpretation might be that, regardless of the support form, hypermedia environments have a "novelty" effect and foster learners' motivation because this new form of knowledge acquisition is exciting for them—an assumption that can be supported by findings of Zumbach (2007). However, motivation alone might not be sufficient and can also decrease again, especially when learners realize that they do not possess the self-regulatory skills and the knowledge necessary to learn from a hypermedia environment.

Another explanation refers more directly to the interaction of instructional support with metacognitive strategies and activities observed in our studies. The most plausible explanation for these findings might be that for sophisticated learners, these devices were problematic because they confronted them with strategies and recommendations different from what they had successfully used so far, thereby leading to an increase in extraneous load, because according to the CLT (Sweller et al., 1998), such instructional support would be redundant material for sophisticated learners, unnecessarily stressing working memory resources. Such an interpretation is in line with suggestions such as the ones by Schnotz et al. (2005) who propose instructional support features to be implemented for *optional* use by learners. In such cases, learners themselves could decide whether they need additional modeling or prompting. On the other hand, exactly such decisions could also demand additional cognitive resources for inexperienced learners, leading to disorientation and cognitive overload, because in addition to the already high intrinsic cognitive load, extraneous cognitive load increases due to the instructional demands. An option to overcome this dilemma might be to first assess whether learners possess appropriate self-regulatory skills and accordingly expose them to some self-regulatory training prior to the learning phase.

Finally, an explanation for why the instructional support features did not foster learning in the desired way is rather simple—they might not have been designed optimally. For instance, the feature offering prompting of representational awareness indeed might have provided learners with knowledge about advantages and disadvantages of different representational formats, but this information might need to be connected to further elaborations on how this knowledge can be used. It is also possible that prompting of representational awareness was not beneficial because it was not the kind of prompting that learners would have needed to be supported with regard to their self-regulatory abilities. Especially in addition to the metacognitive modeling video, the prompting of metacognitive awareness might have been more suitable in this context. That is, during watching the modeling video, learners received recommendations such as "I think it might be useful to retrieve examples in a systematic way because this will help me comparing between different categories and being able to solve problems across categories more easily later on"—in line with this, learners could receive metacognitive prompts, for instance, as pop-up windows, that repeatedly remind them of applying such strategies. Instead of being reminders, such prompts could also aim at swaying learners to reflect upon their own learning behavior, for instance, by asking them if they have understood the solution steps before they click on another worked example. Current research shows that these kinds of prompts can be highly effective and helpful especially in hypermedia contexts (e.g., Bannert, 2006).

Furthermore, the design of the modeling video should be reconsidered as well. Other than the video that was successfully implemented in the studies of Stadtler (2006), this video confronted learners with an exemplary good learner who did not speak to learners but rather to herself (e.g., "*I* think *I* should do this…")—a version that might not have had enough affordances for learners to comply with. Furthermore, the video used in Stadtler's research gave more concrete recommendations with regard to the (metacognitively reasonable) use of the learning environment, while recommendations given by the present model were more on a general, abstract level. The video furthermore might have lowered participants' motivation because it was the only feature of the learning environment that they were forced to use.

This latter assumption leads to an important aspect of planning and conducting further research which has rather been neglected so far. Following Scheiter and Gerjets (2007), it may be assumed that sophisticated self-regulatory skills are *necessary but not sufficient* for hypermedia learning. More specifically, motivation and interest might be prerequisites that strongly influence how much effort someone invests in the resource-demanding activation of sophisticated self-regulatory learning strategies.

Conclusion

In this chapter, we have discussed whether metacognitive and self-regulatory skills can be seen as both a necessary prerequisite for and a consequence of successful hypermedia learning. Taken together, results are still very mixed and need to be addressed in future research. Such research should especially take into account:

- That besides instructional design, factors that account for learning behavior and learning success, in line with the augmented CLT model proposed by Gerjets and Hesse (2004), comprise individual characteristics on the side of learners, including metacognitive and self-regulation variables, but also aspects such as epistemological beliefs, motivation, and interest
- That giving learners the freedom to decide which contents they want to access and which help features they want to make use of might be more suitable to foster metacognitive activities (e.g., monitoring) and thus the engagement into deeper learning activities
- That nevertheless just freedom might not be enough to guarantee successful self-regulated learning (just as it is the other way round) and that some kind of guidance or training prior might be advisable before learners are exposed to the complete complexity of the respective hypermedia environment
- That, depending on the domain to be taught, not only the environment itself but also the learning contents will be considered being complex and ill structured so that some support during learning might be beneficial, for instance, in forms of reflecting prompts to help learners organize their (meta-)cognitive processes

Nevertheless, of course, still the most important part of planning and conducting research with hypermedia learning refers to the design of environments, the contents of written or spoken text, the design of animations, the placement of hyperlinks and navigation options, or the inclusion or exclusion of additional help features. These processes, however, should never take place without the consideration of individual prerequisites of learners, so that in the end it can be concluded that the interplay between multimedia/hypermedia environments, metacognitive and self-regulatory skills, instructional support devices, cognitive load, and learning outcomes might be too complex to be reduced to a simple formula or "Do it just like this" recommendations.

References

Alexander, P. A., & Jetton, T. L. (2003). Learning from traditional and alternative texts: New conceptualization for an information age. In A. C. Graesser, M. A. Gernsbacher, & S. R. Goldman (Eds.), *Handbook of discourse processes* (pp. 199–241). Mahwah, NJ: Erlbaum.

Azevedo, R. (2005). Using hypermedia as a metacognitive tool for enhancing student learning? The role of self-regulated learning. *Educational Psychologist, 40*, 199–209.

Azevedo, R., & Cromley, J. (2004). Does training on self-regulated learning facilitate students' learning with hypermedia? *Journal of Educational Psychology, 96*, 523–535.

Azevedo, R., Cromley, J., Winters, F. I., Moos, D. C., & Greene, J. A. (2005). Adaptive human scaffolding facilitates students' self-regulated learning with hypermedia. *Instructional Science, 33*, 381–412.

Azevedo, R., Greene, J. A., & Moos, D. C. (2007). The effect of a human agent's external regulation upon college students' hypermedia learning. *Metacognition and Learning, 2*, 67–87.

Azevedo, R., Moos, D., Johnson, A., & Chauncey, A. (2010). Measuring cognitive and metacognitive regulatory processes during hypermedia learning: Issues and challenges. *Educational Psychologist, 45*, 201–223.

Bannert, M. (2003). Effekte metakognitiver Lernhilfen auf den Wissenserwerb in vernetzten Lernumgebungen. [Effects of metacognitive learning support on knowledge gains in networked learning environments.]. *Zeitschrift für Pädagogische Psychologie, 17*, 13–25.

Bannert, M. (2004). Designing metacognitive support for hypermedia learning. In H. Niegemann, D. Leutner, & R. Brünken (Eds.). *Instructional design for multimedia-learning* (pp. 19–30). Münster: Waxmann.

Bannert, M. (2005a). Designing metacognitive support for hypermedia learning. In T. Okamoto, D. Albert, T. Honda, & F. W. Hesse (Eds.), *The 2nd Joint Workshop of Cognition and Learning through Media-Communication for Advanced e-Learning* (pp. 11–16). Tokyo, Japan: Sophia University.

Bannert, M. (2005b). Explorationsstudie zum spontanen metakognitiven Strategie-Einsatz in hypermedialen Lernumgebungen. [Exploration study on the spontaneous metacognitive strategy use in hypermedia learning environments.]. In C. Artelt & B. Moschner (Eds.), *Lernstrategien und Metakognition: Implikationen für Forschung und Praxis* (pp. 127–151). Münster, Germany: Waxmann.

Bannert, M. (2006). Effects of reflection prompts when learning with hypermedia. *Journal of Educational Computing Research, 4*, 359–375.

Bendixen, L. D., & Hartley, K. (2003). Successful learning with hypermedia: The role of epistemological beliefs and metacognitive awareness. *Journal of Educational Computing Research, 28*, 15–30.

Cates, W. M. (1992). *Considerations in evaluating metacognition in interactive hypermedia/multimedia instruction*. Oral presentation at the meeting of the American Educational Research Association, San Francisco.

Chandler, P., & Sweller, J. (1991). Cognitive load theory and the format of instruction. *Cognition and Instruction, 8*, 293–332.

Gerjets, P., & Hesse, F. W. (2004). When are powerful learning environments effective? The role of learning activities and of students' conceptions of educational technology. *International Journal of Educational Research, 41*, 445–465.

Horz, H., Winter, C., & Fries, S. (2006). Differential effects of situated prompts on learning behaviour in authentic simulations. In G. Clarebout & J. Elen (Eds.), *Avoiding simplicity, confronting complexity: Advances in studying and designing powerful (computer-based) learning environments* (pp. 145–154). Rotterdam, Netherlands: Sense Publishers.

Jonassen, D. H. (1996). *Computers in the classroom. Mindtools for critical thinking*. Upper Saddle River, NJ: Prentice Hall.

Jonassen, D. H., & Grabinger, R. (1990). Problems and issues in designing hypertext/hypermedia for learning. In D. Jonassen & H. Mandl (Eds.), *Designing hypermedia for learning* (pp. 3–26). Berlin, Germany: Springer.

Lin, X., & Lehman, J. (1999). Supporting learning of variable control in a computer-based biology environment: Effects of prompting college students to reflect on their own thinking. *Journal of Research in Science Teaching, 36*, 837–858.

Mayer, R. (2009). *Multimedia learning* (2nd ed.). Cambridge, MA: Cambridge University Press.

Moos, D. C., & Azevedo, R. (2008). Self-regulated learning with hypermedia: The role of prior knowledge. *Contemporary Educational Psychology, 33*, 270–298.

Nesbit, J. C., Winne, P. H., Jamieson-Noel, D., Code, J., Zhou, M., MacAllister, K., et al. (2006). Using cognitive tools in gStudy to investigate how study activities covary with achievement goals. *Journal of Educational Computing Research, 35*, 339–358.

Opfermann, M. (2008). *There's more to it than instructional design—The role of individual learner characteristics for hypermedia learning*. Berlin, Germany: Logos.

Rouet, J. F., & Eme, P. E. (2002). The role of metatextual knowledge in text comprehension: Some issues in development and individual differences. In P. Chambres, M. Izaute, & P. J. Marescaux (Eds.), *Metacognition: Process, function and use* (pp. 121–134). Amsterdam, Netherlands: Kluwer Academic Press.

Rouet, J. F., & Levonen, J. J. (1996). Studying and learning with hypertext: Empirical studies and their implications. In J.-F. Rouet, J. J. Levonen, A. Dillon, & R. J. Spiro (Eds.), *Hypertext and cognition* (pp. 9–23). Mahwah, NJ: Erlbaum.

Scheiter, K., & Gerjets, P. (2007). Learner control in hypermedia environments. *Educational Psychology Review, 19*, 285–307.

Schmidt, A., & Ford, J. K. (2003). Learning within a learner control training environment: The interaction effects of goal orientation and metacognitive instruction on learning outcomes. *Personnel Psychology, 56*, 405–429.

Schnotz, W., Heiß, A., & Eckhardt, E. (2005). Wann sind Lernhilfen in hypermedialen Lernumgebungen erfolgreich? [When is instructional support in hypermedia learning environments successful?]. In A. Schütz, S. Habscheid, W. Holly, J. Krems, & C. G. Voß (Eds.), *Neue Medien im Alltag: Befunde aus den Bereichen Arbeit, Lernen und Freizeit* (pp. 189–203). Lengerich, Germany: Pabst Science Publishers.

Schraw, G., & Dennison, R. S. (1994). Assessing metacognitive awareness. *Contemporary Educational Psychology, 19*, 460–475.

Schwartz, N. H., Andersen, C., Hong, N., Howard, B., & McGee, S. (2004). The influence of metacognitive skills on learners' memory of information in a hypermedia environment. *Journal of Educational Computing Research, 31*, 77–93.

Shapiro, A., & Niederhauser, D. (2004). Learning from hypertext: Research issues and findings. In D. H. Jonassen (Ed.), *Handbook of research on educational communications and technology* (pp. 605–620). Mahwah, NJ: Erlbaum.

Stadtler, M. (2006). *Auf der Suche nach medizinischen Fachinformationen: Metakognition bei der Internetrecherche von Laien. [Searching for medical information: Metacognition in the internet search of novices.]*. Münster, Germany: Waxmann.

Sweller, J., van Merriënboer, J. J. G., & Paas, F. W. C. (1998). Cognitive architecture and instructional design. *Educational Psychology Review, 10*, 251–296.

Veenman, M. V. J., Wilhelm, P., & Beishuizen, J. J. (2004). The relation between intellectual and metacognitive skills from a developmental perspective. *Learning and Instruction, 14*, 89–109.

Winne, P. H. (2001). Self-regulated learning viewed from models of information processing. In B. J. Zimmerman & D. H. Schunk (Eds.), *Self-regulated learning and academic achievement: Theoretical perspectives* (pp. 153–189). Mahwah, NJ: Lawrence Erlbaum Associates.

Winne, P. H., & Hadwin, A. F. (1998). Studying as self-regulated learning. In D. J. Hacker, J. Dunlosky, & A. C. Graesser (Eds.), *Metacognition in educational theory and practice* (pp. 277–304). Mahwah, NJ: Lawrence Erlbaum Associates.

Zumbach, J. (2007). *The role of graphical and text-based argumentation tools in hypermedia learning.* Paper presented at the annual meeting of the European Association for Research on Learning and Instruction (EARLI), Budapest, Hungary.

10 Eye Tracking as a Tool to Study and Enhance Cognitive and Metacognitive Processes in Computer-Based Learning Environments

Tamara van Gog and Halszka Jarodzka

Abstract

This chapter discusses the use of eye tracking to assess cognitive and metacognitive processes and cognitive load in computer-based learning environments. Benefits of eye tracking for studying such processes are discussed (e.g., the very detailed information it provides on where a participant was looking, in what order, and for how long), but also limitations (e.g., that detailed information does not tell one which processes exactly are occurring; this has to be inferred by the researcher). In addition, this chapter provides examples of how eye tracking can be used to improve the design of instruction in computer-based learning environments, both indirectly and directly. For example, an indirect way would be to use the information on experts' or successful performers' viewing patterns to adapt instructions prior to a task (e.g., emphasizing what should be attended to later on) or to adapt the format of the task (e.g., cueing attention). A more direct way would be to display experts' or successful performers' eye movements overlaid onto the instructional materials. In the discussion, the opportunities provided by eye tracking, but also the technical challenges it poses are addressed.

Eye tracking, that is, tracking the movement of the eye ball(s) and relating these movements to a stimulus, allows researchers to determine to what part(s) of the stimulus a person allocated visual attention, for how long, and in what order (Duchowski, 2003; Holmqvist et al., 2011). Depending on the kind of eye-tracking equipment used, the stimulus can be anything ranging from naturalistic scenes (e.g., walking through a supermarket or driving in a car (see Land & Tatler, 2009)) to materials presented on a computer monitor, which is the main focus of this chapter. Determining visual attention allocation can provide researchers with information about the stimulus itself, because salient environmental

T. van Gog (✉)
Educational Psychology, Institute of Psychology, Erasmus University Rotterdam, P.O. Box 1738, Rotterdam 3000 DR, The Netherlands
e-mail: vangog@fsw.eur.nl

H. Jarodzka
Center for Learning Sciences and Technologies, Open University of The Netherlands, Heerlen, The Netherlands

R. Azevedo and V. Aleven (eds.), *International Handbook of Metacognition and Learning Technologies*, Springer International Handbooks of Education 26, DOI 10.1007/978-1-4419-5546-3_10,

features will draw attention automatically (e.g., Stelmach, Campsall, & Herdman, 1997), as well as the viewer's cognitive processes, because attention shifts also occur driven by instructions (e.g., Yarbus, 1967) or by knowledge of the task or the environment (e.g., Jarodzka, Scheiter, Gerjets, & Van Gog, 2010; Underwood, Chapman, Brocklehurst, Underwood, & Crundall, 2003). As such, eye tracking may be a useful tool for detailed study of attention allocation during learning in computer-based environments. In this chapter, we will provide a review of research in which eye tracking was used to study, as well as enhance, (meta)cognitive processes in computer-based learning environments.

A Brief History of Eye Tracking

First used in the nineteenth century, eye-tracking technology has undergone dramatic changes in the last decades, making it more widely available and more easy to use. We will provide a brief overview here based on elaborate reviews of the history of eye tracking, for which the reader is referred to Richardson and Spivey (2004) and Wade and Tatler (2005). The very first studies on eye movements consisted of direct observations of the eyes during reading (e.g., using mirrors). This allowed Javal to distinguish two different types of eye movements: short rapid movements and stops (so-called saccades and fixations). However, this procedure did not allow for objective measurements of the eye movements. At the end of the nineteenth century, Delabarre and Huey addressed this issue by developing rather crude and highly intrusive eye-tracking devices using ceramic lenses with a small hole, to which a wire was attached that "drew" the movement of the eye. A major breakthrough in eye-tracking technology came early in the twentieth century when Dodge started using photography to capture the movements of the eyes, which was far less intrusive and not painful for the participants (people still had to be restrained from moving their heads though). Later *video-based eye trackers* allowed for more freedom of movement and for very precise analysis of the allocation of the eye movements on the stimulus. Most widely used in applied eye- tracking research nowadays is the pupil and corneal reflection method, in which an infrared light source is directed towards the eye, causing a reflection on the cornea captured by an infrared-sensitive video camera. This corneal reflection is the brightest spot on the image, while the pupil is the darkest one. When the eye moves, the pupil does too, but the corneal reflection hardly does. So, by calculating the distance between the pupil and the corneal reflection, the direction of the eye can be calculated, and in combination with parameters of the environment, it can be inferred at which part of the stimulus the eye was directed at different points in time. A wide variety of measures can be obtained by means of eye tracking (see Duchowski, 2003; Holmqvist et al., 2011); we will shortly discuss only a few main measures here that appear in the research discussed in this chapter.

Measures Obtained via Eye Tracking

Two important eye movement measures were already mentioned in the previous section: fixations and saccades. During *fixations*, the eye is (almost completely) still and information can be extracted from a stimulus. As a consequence, the location and duration of fixations provide an indication of what information is attended to and how intensively that information is being processed (relative to other information; cf. eye-mind assumption by Just & Carpenter, 1980). During *saccades*, that is, the rapid eye movements in between fixations, the focus of visual attention is moved to another location, and we are not able to take in visual information—although it seems that under specific circumstances, some information, like motion, can be very roughly processed (Castet & Masson, 2000). Both fixations and saccades occur for all kinds of stimuli. A type of eye movement that occurs only when inspecting dynamic stimuli such as videos or animations is *smooth pursuit*, which occurs when the eye follows moving objects (Dodge, 1903). While fixations and saccades can be easily detected by contemporary eye-tracking software, there are no adequate algorithms yet to detect smooth pursuit, which therefore requires complex calculations on raw gaze data (Holmqvist et al., 2011).

Other measures that can be obtained through eye tracking and that may be relevant in research on computer-based learning are blinks and pupil dilation. *Blinks* of the eye are quite easy to identify, and the frequency of occurrence depends, for instance, on tiredness (e.g., Barbato et al., 2007) or—as will be discussed later—mind wandering (e.g., Smilek, Carriere, & Cheyne, 2010). The dilation of the pupil can, for example, provide information about cognitive load as we will discuss below (e.g., Hyönä, Tommola, & Alaja, 1995; Kahneman & Beatty, 1966, Klingner, Tversky, & Hanrahan, 2010; Van Gerven, Paas, Van Merriënboer, & Schmidt, 2004). It is a difficult measure to use though, as pupil dilation is very sensitive to influences of other factors which need to be carefully controlled (e.g., light changes and changes in the brightness of the stimulus). For more information on these different measures, the reader is referred to Duchowski (2003) and Holmqvist and colleagues (2011).

Studying Cognitive and Metacognitive Processes in Computer-Based Learning Environments

Written text is still a core component of many computer-based learning environments. As mentioned above, early eye-tracking studies focused on reading, and it probably still is one of the most widely studied processes in eye-tracking research. A comprehensive review of eye-tracking research in reading is beyond the scope of this chapter. The reader is referred to Rayner (1998, 2009) for elaborate reviews. Here, we will first discuss some applications of eye tracking for studying cognitive processes in multimedia and hypermedia learning environments. Then, we will address the use of eye tracking to assess cognitive load. Last but not least, we will discuss what eye-tracking research can reveal about metacognitive processes in computer-based learning environments.

Cognitive Processes: Multimedia and Hypermedia Learning

Presentation of Hypertext

Written text in a computer-based learning environment is usually hypertext, that is, it contains hyperlinks to other information which the reader can immediately access (Conklin, 1987). As a consequence, hypertexts have a nonlinear structure which not only allows but also requires the user to determine their own sequence of reading information and therefore carries a risk of disorientation and overload. However, even though hypertexts are nonlinear, they may be preceded by *concept maps* to guide navigation. Amadieu, Van Gog, Paas, Tricot, and Mariné (2009) investigated the effects of a network concept map structure that provides relational links to a hierarchical structure that provides organizational links and cues (and can be considered somewhat more "linear" than network structures). The latter was hypothesized to guide learners' attention towards the main concepts and their semantic relationships. In the network structure, participants with higher prior knowledge spent more time fixating certain key nodes than participants with lower prior knowledge, whereas no such difference occurred in the hierarchical structure. This suggests that a hierarchical structure, in which attention is guided to main concepts, is especially helpful for low-prior-knowledge learners, whereas learners with more prior knowledge can apply that knowledge in searching for relevant concepts in a network structure.

Next to written or spoken textual information, most computer-based learning environments contain visualizations associated with those texts, such as pictures, drawings, diagrams, animations, and videos. The use of text combined with visualizations, however, places certain attentional demands on learners that may or may not be helpful for learning depending on the design. Therefore, the use of eye tracking may have added value in discovering the underlying mechanisms of effects on learning (Van Gog, Kester, Nievelstein, Giesbers, & Paas, 2009) as will be shown in the examples that follow.

Effects of Split Attention or Spatial Contiguity

Research has shown that when providing different mutually referring information sources, such as written text and a graphic, a separate presentation format hampers learning compared to an integrated presentation format. This is known as the split-attention effect or spatial contiguity effect (for a review, see Ayres & Sweller, 2005). However, what exactly causes this effect is unclear. For instance, do learners, when presented with a separate format, fail to integrate both information sources and study them separately one after the other? Or do they try to process them simultaneously and switch between both sources, but lose their last position in the graphic or text as a consequence, leading to unnecessary search, rereading, or both?

Because eye movement data reflect attention and shifts in attention, eye tracking may be very helpful in investigating the underlying mechanisms of the split-attention effect. Hegarty and Just (1993) conducted an eye-tracking study on comprehension of text and diagrams in separated format. They found that readers often switched attention from the text to the diagrams, mostly at the end of sentences or clauses, suggesting that integrations of both representations were made at the level of individual components or groups of components. Using illustrated science textbook passages, Hannus and Hÿonä (1999) found that learners spent by far the most time on the text: Only 6% did they spend on illustrations, and this did not differ between high- and low-ability learners. However, although switching attention between text and pictures was also relatively low in general, high-ability learners did switch more often than low-ability learners. Studying effects of animations with written text, Schmidt-Weigand, Kohert, and Glowalla (2010) also found that learners spent more time reading the text than inspecting the animation and consistently started reading before alternating between text and animation.

Jarodzka, Janssen, Kirschner, and Erkens (submitted) studied this effect in computer-based *testing*. For an authentic arts exam, students completed an electronic version with half of the questions presented in the original separated format and the other half in an integrated format (i.e., within-subject design). Eye tracking was used to estimate the amount of visual search required. Results showed that, in the integrated format, students attended more (indicated by total fixation durations) to additional information provided next to the question text, like pictures and historical background information, and processed this additional information more intensively (indicated by more fixations) than they did when the information was presented in a separated format. By changing the design of such testing environments, students' attention was guided so that they intensively processed *all* given information. Interestingly, however, the integrated format did in this case not lead to higher but to lower test scores. These results suggest that (part of) the additional information given in the tests was redundant, which was useful information for the organization that developed these tests to further improve them.

Under experimental conditions, learners are often "forced" to study material for a certain amount of time. In computer-based learning environments, however, there is usually a large amount of information available (often more than can be studied during the experimental session), and students can decide for themselves which information to consult and for how long. Research on authentic reading behavior suggests that under such circumstances, separate presentation of text and pictures may have even more deleterious effects in that the text may be skipped altogether: In a naturalistic newspaper-reading study, Holsanova, Holmberg, and Holmqvist (2009) found that when text and graphic were presented separately, readers typically read the headline and then switched to the graphic while mostly ignoring the text, whereas when the graphic was integrated with the text, both were processed together.

In sum, it seems that under experimental (learning) conditions people seem to focus on the main text in a separated format (Hannus & Hÿonä, 1999; Jarodzka et al., submitted; Schmidt-Weigand et al., 2010), while under naturalistic (leisure) conditions they mostly focus on pictures (Holsanova et al., 2009). When information is presented in an integrated format, however, all information seems to be processed (Holsanova et al., 2009; Jarodzka et al., submitted).

Effects of Cueing or Signaling

Another well-known effect established by research on multimedia learning is the cueing or signaling effect (for reviews, see De Koning, Tabbers, Rikers, & Paas, 2009; Mayer, 2005) in which the visual saliency of parts of the stimulus material is manipulated to draw the learner's attention. Ozcelik and colleagues used eye tracking to investigate the effect of cueing by means of temporarily changing the color of labels in an otherwise *static* illustration (Ozcelik, Arslan-Arib, & Cagiltay, 2010) or cueing corresponding information in the text and illustration by giving it the same color (Ozcelik, Karakus, Kursun, & Cagiltay, 2009; see also Folker, Sichelschmidt, & Ritter, 2005). They established that such cues indeed successfully guided visual attention and led to more efficient information processing and better learning outcomes.

Increasingly, visual materials provided in computer-based learning environments are *dynamic*, like videos or animations. Cueing that is effective for static presentation formats is not necessarily effective for dynamic formats, and cueing may be even more necessary in dynamic visualizations because (part of) the information may be transient and hence no longer available for processing if it is not attended to at the right moment.

Using dynamic visualizations, De Koning, Tabbers, Rikers, and Paas (2010) showed that spotlight cues in which the important information is made more salient by reducing the saliency of surrounding information (e.g., through darkening) were effective for guiding attention to the cued parts. Boucheix and Lowe (2010) established that continuous cues in which a colored "ribbon" was spreading were more effective than arrow cues for attention guidance in dynamic visualizations. They also showed the importance of temporal aspects of cueing (i.e., guiding attention to the right place at the right time) for attention guidance and learning.

In sum, by using eye tracking, it can be established whether cues in multimedia learning materials indeed are successful at guiding learners' attention.

Effects of Pedagogical Agents

Animated pedagogical agents are often used in multimedia materials in computer-based learning environments (for a review, see Moreno, 2005). Louwerse, Graesser, McNamara, and Lu (2009) applied eye tracking to investigate how learners interact with embodied conversational agents (ECAs), that is, animated humanoid characters that communicate with the learner. They found that learners interact with those agents much as they would with a real human conversational partner, fixating mostly on the agent, or, when multiple agents were present, fixating on the agent that was speaking. This could perhaps explain why the presence of such agents does not always foster learning; when the learner is attending to the agent, she/he may not be attending to the learning content on the screen that the agent is referring to.

Cognitive Load

Eye-tracking data can provide information not only about the processes evoked by different types of materials but also about the *demands* on working memory imposed by those processes (i.e., cognitive load; e.g., Hyönä, Tommola, & Alaja, 1995; Kahneman & Beatty, 1966; Klingner et al., 2010; Van Gerven et al., 2004). For example, Kahneman and Beatty (1966) showed that pupil dilation is associated with working memory load. Participants had to memorize a string of digits or a list of words and report those back (immediate recall) or had to transform a string of digits (add one to each digit). Their data on the digit strings showed that with the presentation of each additional digit, pupil dilation increased, while with reporting back each digit, it decreased. Moreover, pupil dilation increased more steeply with the more demanding tasks of learning word lists or transforming digits than with learning digit strings. Hyönä and colleagues (1995) used pupil dilation to investigate variations in cognitive load during translation tasks. They showed that variations in cognitive load during a translation task were reflected in pupil size: More difficult words to translate resulted in higher levels of pupil dilation than words that were easy to translate. Klingner and colleagues (2010) investigated the effect of auditory versus visual task presentation on pupil dilation with three different tasks and found that while patterns of dilation were similar for auditory and visual presentation for all three tasks, the magnitudes of pupil response were greater for auditory presentation than for visual presentation, suggesting the latter is less cognitively demanding. Van Gerven and colleagues (2004) investigated the usefulness of the pupil response as an indicator of cognitive load in young and aging adults. They used a memory-search task, consisting of two phases. In the encoding phase, participants had to memorize strings of one to six digits (none occurred more than once). In the search phase, participants had to judge whether single-digit probes belonged to the memory set. For both young adults and elderly participants, pupil dilation systematically increased with the length of the string of digits in the encoding phase (i.e., with task difficulty), but in the search phase, pupil dilation was only sensitive to task load variations for the young adults, which suggests this measure may not always be suitable in studies with elderly participants.

Metacognitive Processes

Monitoring Learning and Comprehension

Metacognitive judgments play an important role in self-regulated learning, because such judgments, for example, of whether information has been sufficiently learned or not, affect the allocation of study time and choices about items to select for further studying (Metcalfe, 2009).

Kinnunen and Vauras (1995) assessed children's monitoring of *comprehension* during reading by means of eye tracking. The need for comprehension monitoring was enhanced by causing difficulties in text processing in certain sentences, for example, by adding a nonsense word or a word that made the sentence inconsistent with general knowledge or with a prior sentence. They assumed that comprehension monitoring would be associated with higher reading time and a higher number of regressions (i.e., looking back) to difficult passages in the text. Comprehension was assessed by a text summary provided by the students after reading. Results indeed showed that reading complex sentences lead to higher reading times and more regressions compared to regular sentences. Moreover, this effect was stronger for high-achieving students. Graesser, Lu, Olde, Cooper-Pye, and Whitten (2005) also created a cognitive disequilibrium in participants who read illustrated texts about devices by presenting a breakdown scenario that was assumed to result in question asking, and investigated the relationship between question asking and eye movements. They showed that deep comprehenders tended to formulate better questions and fixate on fault-related components just before or during question formulation. In sum, eye-tracking data can provide detailed insight into the metacognitive process of comprehension monitoring when studying texts.

Roderer and Roebers (2010) conducted an eye-tracking study of confidence judgments. Children were shown easy and difficult Kanji symbols of which they had previously learned the meaning or new ones that they could not recognize. The children were asked to select the correct meaning from four alternatives. Subsequently, a *confidence* rating followed and they were asked to indicate how confident they were of their answer by pointing at one of five smileys (ranging from a very sad looking one to a very happy looking one). In addition to this explicit confidence judgment provided by pointing, the authors measured implicit judgments based on the eye movement data from the phase before the explicit judgment was provided (i.e., looking at the confidence judgment "category" that attracted a maximum of fixation time during confidence scale presentation). They found a high correlation between explicit and implicit confidence judgments, suggesting that eye tracking can be used as a measure of confidence judgments.

Monitoring Information About Other Students' Knowledge in Collaborative Learning

Sangin, Molinari, Nüssli, and Dillenbourg (2008) used eye tracking to investigate how students' monitored and used information about *other students'* knowledge in collaborative learning in a computer-based environment. Participants created concept maps in dyads. One group of participants had an awareness tool available that provided information on the other person's knowledge. Results showed that looking at this knowledge awareness tool (KAT) was positively related to learning. When combined with verbal data from the episodes in which participants looked at the KAT, it was found they looked at the KAT for three reasons: when they were seeking for specific knowledge, when their peers provided information, or when their peers provided cues regarding their existing or nonexisting knowledge.

Self-Explaining

Conati, Merten, Muldner, and Ternes (2005) used eye-tracking data to estimate metacognitive behavior (more specifically, self-explanation), while students performed a task in a computer-based mathematics learning environment. They also asked participants to think aloud. Afterwards, the verbal data were coded in terms of whether or not they contained self-explanations. Then, time on task data (obtained from log files) and eye-tracking data (gaze shifts) were related to each of these episodes that did and did not contain self-explanations. The assumption was that self-explanations would take more time and would be accompanied by gaze shifts between graphs and formulas. Results show that time on task had the highest sensitivity, while eye-tracking data had the highest specificity for predicting self-explanations. In this study, an algorithm was used for analyzing eye-tracking data, which has the benefit over verbal data that it can be analyzed and used *online* (i.e., during learning). Provided eye-tracking data can be coupled to cognitive or metacognitive processes with great sensitivity and specificity, such algorithms could be used to adapt a computer-based learning environment in real time to the learner's cognitive or metacognitive state (e.g., by providing self-explanation prompts when learners do not spontaneously self-explain).

Registering Off-Task Behavior

Mind wandering, that is, a focus of attention on internal processes rather than on processing the external environment, seems to be associated with an increase in eye blinks (Smilek et al., 2010). Smilek and colleagues (2010) had participants read a text during which they were randomly probed ten times by an auditory stimulus to report whether they were on task (i.e., reading) or mind wandering, which could be task related (e.g., thoughts relevant to the text) or unrelated (e.g., thoughts about room temperature or meals). In the 5 s before the probes, participants blinked more when they were mind wandering than when they were on task, and participants made less fixations on the text (even when corrected for blink time). Using a comparable self-report and prompting procedure, Reichle, Reineberg, and Schooler (2010) investigated mindless reading, in which the eyes keep moving across the page but the individual is mind wandering. They found that, compared to normal reading, fixations were longer during mindless reading and were also less affected by characteristics of the text, presumably due to the absence of cognitive processes that normally direct eye movements during reading.

These findings suggest that eye-tracking data may provide interesting information on whether or not participants are on task in computer-based learning environments. A problem of course is that mind wandering may concern task-related thoughts, which are probably highly relevant for learning (e.g., for making inferences beyond the literal text) and that there is (as yet) no way to distinguish such task-relevant episodes of mind wandering from task-unrelated episodes solely based on the eye movement data.

Limitations of Eye Tracking in Studying Cognitive and Metacognitive Processes: Adding Verbal Reports

The studies discussed above show that eye fixation data can provide interesting information about participants' (visual) attention allocation: They tell us where a participant was looking, in what order, and for how long, and how much they were blinking. However, these data require a substantial amount of inferences about underlying cognitive processes, as they do not explain *why* a participant was looking somewhere for a certain amount of time or in a certain order. To reduce the amount of inferences required by the researcher, eye movement data can be complemented with concurrent verbal reports (i.e., thinking aloud; Ericsson & Simon, 1993; for a combination with eye tracking, see, e.g., Van Gog, Paas, & Van Merriënboer, 2005a). The central assumption behind the use of thinking aloud data is "that it is possible to instruct subjects to verbalize their thoughts in a manner that does not alter the sequence and content of thoughts mediating the completion of a task and therefore should reflect immediately available information during thinking" (Ericsson, 2006, p. 227).

However, even if verbalizing thoughts does not alter those thoughts, a potential drawback of asking participants to think aloud during task performance in combination with eye tracking is that this has been suggested to affect their eye movements. For instance, in complex tasks the speech planning process has been shown to alter the allocations of eye movements (e.g., Holsanova, 2008), and, on average, oral reading increases fixation duration and reduces saccade length compared to silent reading for skilled English readers (Rayner, 2009), and concurrent reporting is suspected to slow down task performance (Karpf, 1973) and might therefore lead to more eye movements.

As an alternative to concurrent reports, retrospective verbal reports could be used. However, compared to concurrent reports, retrospective reports tend to suffer from omission of information due to forgetting and from fabulations (e.g., Kuusela & Paul, 2000). Cueing a retrospective report with information from the task performance process might prevent forgetting and fabulation (Van Someren, Barnard, & Sandberg, 1994). Most eye-tracking software allows not only for recording but also for replaying the records of eye movements as an overlay on the stimulus or computer screen recording, and such replays of eye movement records may provide an excellent cue for retrospective reports (Van Gog, Paas, Van Merriënboer, & Witte, 2005b; see also Hansen, 1991; Russo, Johnson, & Stephens, 1989). Van Gog and colleagues found that both concurrent and cued retrospective reporting resulted in quantitatively more information than retrospective reporting without a cue. Interestingly, cued retrospective reporting also resulted in a higher number of metacognitive statements in the protocols than concurrent and retrospective reporting.

Cued retrospective reporting might provide a valuable alternative to concurrent reporting, not just because it cannot affect eye movements as concurrent reporting has been suggested to do but especially for research with novice participants or with instructional materials that make concurrent reporting impossible. For novices, because they have little prior knowledge, tasks often impose a high cognitive load, and as a result, they may stop verbalizing their thoughts during concurrent reporting (Ericsson & Simon, 1993). Indeed, in the study by Van Gog and colleagues (2005b), participants who had lower performance and experienced higher cognitive load on the tasks (i.e., who had lower expertise) also indicated that they preferred cued retrospective reporting over concurrent reporting (reported in

Van Gog, 2006). Not only learners' expertise level but also the type of learning material provided can have consequences for which verbal reporting technique to choose. For instance, instructional materials that are widely used in computer-based learning environments with which concurrent reporting is not possible are animations or videos that contain spoken text.

Cued retrospective reporting has been used, for instance, in problem-solving or information-search tasks in which mouse and keyboard operations were also recorded (Brand-Gruwel, Van Meeuwen, & Van Gog, 2008; Schwonke, Berthold, & Renkl, 2009; Van Gog et al., 2005b), and the replays could therefore cue memory of both overt actions (i.e., via mouse clicks that occurred on the screen) and covert processes (i.e., via the display of eye movements) that occurred during task performance. However, it has also been used with animations or videos in which no overt actions such as mouse clicks were required and the eye movements constituted the sole cue (De Koning et al., 2010; Jarodzka, Scheiter et al., 2010).

Enhancing Cognitive and Metacognitive Processes in Computer-Based Learning Environments

Eye tracking can also be applied to improve the design of components of computer-based learning environments. For example, Buscher, Cutrell, and Morris (2009) recorded the eye movements of participants surfing on several hundreds of Web pages. Based on these data, they developed a model that successfully predicts the saliency of single Web page elements, which can inform designers of (instructional) Web pages. Kammerer and Gerjets (2010) found that the design of a Web search engine influenced the thoroughness of information search. The authors recorded participants' eye movements while they searched information using either a traditional list search engine or a novel search engine, in which search results were presented in a tabular format. Participants searching the tabular format were found to look at more search results, that is, they evaluated the information resulting from the search more thoroughly.

In addition, eye tracking may be used to reveal what the differences are in successful and unsuccessful problem solvers' attention allocation, and this information may then be used to develop cues or instructions to support learners in computer-based environments. For example, Grant and Spivey (2003) showed that participants who were successful at solving Duncker's radiation problem (an insight problem) attended relatively more to a certain area in the picture than unsuccessful problem solvers. In a second experiment, they showed that incorporating a perceptual cue to draw attention to this area led to an increase in successful problem solving. A similar approach was taken by Schwonke and colleagues (2009), using worked examples on probability calculation that consisted of multiple representations (text, tree diagram, and mathematical equation). They showed that conceptual understanding after example study was positively associated with more extensive processing of the tree diagrams and negatively with transitions from text to equations (skipping the diagrams). This suggested that the diagrams played an important role in learning from the worked examples. In a second study, Schwonke and collaborators (2009) provided half of the participants with instruction on how the representations were functionally related, which had a strong effect on learning that was partially mediated by allocation of visual attention to the diagrams.

Next to this indirect route of informing the design of components of computer-based learning environments, eye tracking may also be applied in more direct ways, for instance, in the design of examples. Modelling examples in computer-based learning environments often consist of screen captures of a human model performing a task, and depending on the type of task, the model may also provide a verbal explanation of why she/he is doing what she/he is doing (e.g., McLaren, Lim, & Koedinger, 2008; for a review of research on modelling examples, see Van Gog & Rummel, 2010). Often, the model is an expert on the particular task she/he is demonstrating.

In this case, a problem might arise, especially in examples in which information is transient: Eye-tracking research has shown that with increasing knowledge or expertise on a task, individuals fixate faster and relatively more on relevant information (e.g., Charness, Reingold, Pomplun, & Stampe, 2001; Haider & Frensch, 1999; Jarodzka, Scheiter et al., 2010; Van Gog et al., 2005a). In other words, there might be a discrepancy in attention allocation between the learner and the model, and if the learner does not attend to the right information at the right time, understanding might be compromised, for example, because the information is no longer available for further processing (in case of transience) or because the explanation by the model is more difficult to follow when the learner is not attending to the same information as the model.

Therefore, Van Gog, Jarodzka, Scheiter, Gerjets, and Paas (2009) investigated whether incorporating a display of the eye movements made by the expert model in screen-capture modelling examples with or without spoken explanations could guide students' attention and enhance their learning of a procedural problem-solving task. In contrast to their expectation, they did not find a positive effect of displaying eye movements, although results suggested there might be benefits on transfer. They even found a negative effect when the modelling examples contained both eye movements and spoken explanations, presumably because the verbal explanations were sufficient to guide learners' attention in this task. Using examples of a more perceptual task (learning to classify fish locomotion patterns) with a spoken verbal explanation, in which the verbal explanation was less likely to be sufficient to guide learners' attention, Jarodzka, Van Gog, Dorr, Scheiter, and Gerjets (2013) did find positive effects of displaying the expert model's eye movements in modelling examples on learning.

Not looking at *learning*, but at a direct influence on *performance*, Litchfield, Ball, Donovan, Manning, and Crawford (2010) investigated the effects of seeing another person's eye movements on a visual diagnosis task in medicine: identifying pulmonary nodules (i.e., a lesion in the lung smaller than 3 cm in diameter) in chest X-rays. The "models" in their study did not behave didactically (i.e., their viewing behavior was natural) and did not provide any additional verbal explanation. They found that novices performed better after seeing the "models" searching for nodules.

Such eye movement modelling examples can be constructed and implemented in computer-based learning environments relatively easily, because eye-tracking software nowadays usually allows exporting a screen capture with a display of eye movements as a digital video file. If eye trackers would become cheaper and would become available in classrooms, other direct uses of eye tracking could be conceived of, for instance, in collaborative learning or problem solving. For example, Velichkovsky (1995) conducted a study on real-time cooperative puzzle problem solving by expert-novice pairs, in which the novice controlled the mouse and could observe the expert's eye movements, so the expert could indicate with his gaze what the novice should do.

Another possible application when eye trackers would be more ubiquitous would be to use eye movement records to stimulate reflection. As mentioned above, the findings by Van Gog and colleagues (2005b) showed that reviewing a record of one's own actions and eye movements (during cued retrospective reporting) resulted in a higher number of metacognitive comments (e.g., statements about the adequacy of the learner's own knowledge, actions, or strategies) than concurrent and retrospective reporting. This occurred rather spontaneously, because the instructions for reporting in each condition (concurrent, retrospective, or cued retrospective) were neutral. It also did not occur frequently; even though the difference was significant, the actual number of metacognitive statements in cued retrospective reporting was not very high. However, these findings do suggest that reviewing a record of one's own actions and eye movements may trigger reflective processes, and therefore it has been suggested that such records might be used as explicit tools for reflection (Van Gog, Jarodzka et al., 2009, Van Gog, Kester et al., 2009) or could be implemented to aid self-assessment (Kostons,

Van Gog, & Paas, 2009). Especially combined with additional metacognitive prompts or scaffolds, this might be an effective tool for fostering reflection.

Finally, as mentioned previously, *real-time* analysis of eye movement data could be applied in intelligent tutoring systems or other adaptive learning environments to monitor students engagement in metacognitive behaviors such as self-explaining and to use that information to dynamically adapt the content offered to students (Conati et al., 2005; see also Merten & Conati, 2006; for a discussion of other potential uses of real-time eye movement analysis in tutoring systems, such as error prediction, detection of undesirable solution processes, and identifying when messages are ignored, see Gluck, Anderson, & Douglass, 2000).

Discussion

In sum, eye tracking is not only a useful tool to study (meta)cognitive processes and cognitive load in computer-based learning environments but can also be used indirectly or directly in the design of components of such environments to enhance (meta)cognitive processes and foster learning. Even though eye movement data are still challenging to collect and analyze and often need to be triangulated with another data source such as verbal data to make inferences about associated cognitive processes, they do provide a unique opportunity to study certain kinds of processes in a level of detail that no other data source provides. For example, screen recordings without eye movement data would only provide information on how long the page in its entirety was attended to, not which specific parts of the page received attention. Or in hypermedia environments, screen recordings would only show what hyperlinks are being clicked on, but not which other links have been previously considered but were not opened.

The use of eye tracking to study cognitive processes in computer-based learning environments is increasing rapidly, but there has been much less eye-tracking research on metacognitive processes. The studies discussed in this chapter do highlight some promising areas in which eye tracking may provide useful information on metacognitive processes, such as monitoring one's own comprehension, monitoring information about other people's knowledge in collaborative learning environments, and predicting when students are or are not making self-explanations (thereby providing options for, for instance, adaptive prompting).

The fact that eye-tracking technology is still advancing rapidly will probably stimulate further research on (meta)cognitive processes in computer-based learning environments. In the last decade or so, eye-tracking equipment has become more affordable and much easier to operate. With further technological advances, analysis of eye movement data may become less cumbersome. For example, a major problem when analyzing data on areas of interest (AOI) in videos is that these AOIs often move about, requiring segmentation of the video into very small segments and then computing AOI data and aggregating them over the whole video (see, e.g., Jarodzka, Van Gog et al., 2013), but software solutions are being developed to enable dynamic AOIs (see, e.g., Papenmeier & Huff, 2010). Software features for displaying eye movement data have already come a long way, such as the option to make integrated digital videos of screen recordings and eye movements, and further developments may open up new avenues for the design of learning tasks in computer-based environments.

Acknowledgement During the realization of this work, Tamara van Gog was supported by a Veni grant from the Netherlands Organization for Scientific Research (NWO; # 451-08-003).

References

Amadieu, F., Van Gog, T., Paas, F., Tricot, A., & Mariné, C. (2009). Effects of prior knowledge and concept-map structure on disorientation, cognitive load, and learning. *Learning and Instruction, 19*, 376–386.

Ayres, P., & Sweller, J. (2005). The split-attention principle in multimedia learning. In R. E. Mayer (Ed.), *The Cambridge handbook of multimedia learning* (pp. 135–146). New York: Cambridge University Press.

Barbato, G., De Padova, V., Paolillo, A. R., Arpaia, L., Russo, E., & Ficca, G. (2007). Increased spontaneous eye blink rate following prolonged wakefulness. *Physiology & Behavior, 90*, 151–154.

Boucheix, J.-M., & Lowe, R. K. (2010). An eye tracking comparison of external pointing cues and internal continuous cues in learning with complex animations. *Learning and Instruction, 20*, 123–135.

Brand-Gruwel, S., Van Meeuwen, L., & Van Gog, T. (2008). The use of evaluation criteria when searching the WWW: An eye-tracking study. In A. Maes & S. Ainsworth (Eds.), *Proceedings EARLI Special Interest Group Text and Graphics 'Exploiting the opportunities: Learning with textual, graphical, and multimodal representations'* (pp. 34–37). Tilburg, The Netherlands: Tilburg University.

Buscher, G., Cutrell, E., & Morris, M. R. (2009). What do you see when you're surfing? Using eye tracking to predict salient regions of the web pages. In *Proceedings of the 27th CHI conference* (pp. 21–30). New York: ACM.

Castet, E., & Masson, G. S. (2000). Motion perception during saccadic eye movements. *Nature Neuroscience, 3*, 177–183.

Charness, N., Reingold, E. M., Pomplun, M., & Stampe, D. M. (2001). The perceptual aspect of skilled performance in chess: Evidence from eye movements. *Memory & Cognition, 29*, 1146–1152.

Conati, C., Merten, C., Muldner, K., & Ternes, D. (2005). Exploring eye tracking to increase bandwidth in user modeling. In L. Ardissono, P. Brna, & A. Mitrovic (Eds.), *User modeling 2005: 10th international conference* (pp. 357–367). Berlin: Springer.

Conklin, J. (1987). Hypertext: An introduction and survey. *IEEE Computer, 20*(9), 17–41.

De Koning, B. B., Tabbers, H. K., Rikers, R. M. J. P., & Paas, F. (2009). Towards a framework for attention cueing in instructional animations: Guidelines for research and design. *Educational Psychology Review, 21*, 113–140.

De Koning, B. B., Tabbers, H. K., Rikers, R. M. J. P., & Paas, F. (2010). Attention guidance in learning from a complex animation: Seeing is understanding? *Learning and Instruction, 20*, 111–122.

Dodge, R. (1903). Five types of eye movements in the horizontal meridian plane of the field of regard. *The American Journal of Psychology, 8*, 307–329.

Duchowski, A. T. (2003). *Eye tracking methodology: Theory and practice*. London: Springer.

Ericsson, K. A. (2006). Protocol analysis and expert thought: Concurrent verbalizations of thinking during experts' performance on representative tasks. In K. A. Ericsson, N. Charness, P. J. Feltovich, & R. R. Hoffman (Eds.), *The Cambridge handbook of expertise and expert performance* (pp. 223–241). Cambridge: Cambridge University Press.

Ericsson, K. A., & Simon, H. A. (1993). *Protocol analysis: Verbal reports as data* (revth ed.). Cambridge, MA: MIT Press.

Folker, S., Sichelschmidt, L., & Ritter, H. (2005). Processing and integrating multimodal material: The influence of color-coding. In B. G. Bara, L. Barsalou, & M. Bucciarelli (Eds.), *Proceedings of the 27th Annual Conference of the Cognitive Science Society* (pp. 690–695). Mahwah, NJ: Erlbaum.

Gluck, K. A., Anderson, J. R., & Douglass, S. (2000). Broader bandwidth in student modeling: What if ITS were "Eye"TS? *Intelligent Tutoring Systems—Lecture Notes in Computer Science, 1839*, 504–513.

Graesser, A. C., Lu, S., Olde, B. A., Cooper-Pye, E., & Whitten, S. (2005). Question asking and eye tracking during cognitive disequilibrium: Comprehending illustrated texts on devices when the devices break down. *Memory & Cognition, 33*, 1235–1247.

Grant, E. R., & Spivey, M. J. (2003). Eye movements and problem solving: Guiding attention guides thought. *Psychological Science, 14*, 462–466.

Haider, H., & Frensch, P. A. (1999). Eye movement during skill acquisition: More evidence for the information reduction hypothesis. *Journal of Experimental Psychology: Learning, Memory, and Cognition, 25*, 172–190.

Hannus, M., & Hÿonä, J. (1999). Utilization of illustrations during learning of science textbook passages among low- and high-ability children. *Contemporary Educational Psychology, 24*, 95–123.

Hansen, J. P. (1991). The use of eye mark recordings to support verbal retrospection in software testing. *Acta Psychologica, 76*, 31–49.

Hegarty, M., & Just, M. A. (1993). Constructing mental models of machines from text and diagrams. *Journal of Memory and Language, 32*, 717–742.

Holmqvist, K., Nyström, M., Andersson, R., Dewhurst, R., Jarodzka, H., & Van de Weijer, J. (2011). *Eye tracking a comprehensive guide to methods and measures*. Oxford, UK: Oxford University Press.

Holsanova, J. (2008). *Discourse, vision, and cognition*. Philadelphia: John Benjamins.

Holsanova, J., Holmberg, N., & Holmqvist, K. (2009). Reading information graphics: The role of spatial contiguity and dual attentional guidance. *Applied Cognitive Psychology, 23*, 1215–1226.

Hyönä, J., Tommola, J., & Alaja, A.-M. (1995). Pupil dilation as a measure of processing load in simultaneous interpretation and other language tasks. *The Quarterly Journal of Experimental Psychology. A, Human Experimental Psychology, 48*, 598–612.

Jarodzka, H., Janssen, N., Kirschner, P. A., & Erkens, G. (submitted). Avoiding split attention in computer-based testing: Is neglecting additional information facilitative? Manuscript submitted for publication.

Jarodzka, H., Scheiter, K., Gerjets, P., & Van Gog, T. (2010). In the eyes of the beholder: How experts and novices interpret dynamic stimuli. *Learning and Instruction, 20*, 146–154.

Jarodzka, H., van Gog, T., Dorr, M., Scheiter, K. & Gerjets, P. (2013). Learning to see: Guiding students' attention via a model's eye movements fosters learning. *Learning and Instruction, 25*, 62–70.

Just, M., & Carpenter, P. (1980). A theory of reading: From eye fixations to comprehension. *Psychological Review, 87*, 329–355.

Kahneman, D., & Beatty, J. (1966). Pupil diameter and load on memory. *Science, 154*, 1583–1585.

Kammerer, Y., & Gerjets, P. (2010). How the interface design influences users' spontaneous trustworthiness evaluations of web search results: Comparing a list and a grid interface. In C. Morimoto & H. Instance (Eds.), *Proceedings of the 2010 Symposium on Eye Tracking Research & Applications ETRA'10* (pp. 299–306). New York: ACM.

Karpf, D. (1973). *Thinking aloud in human discrimination learning*. Unpublished doctoral dissertation, State University of New York, New York, USA.

Kinnunen, R., & Vauras, M. (1995). Comprehension monitoring and the level of comprehension in high- and low-achieving primary school children's reading. *Learning and Instruction, 5*, 143–165.

Klingner, J., Tversky, B., & Hanrahan, P. (2010). Effects of visual and verbal presentation on cognitive load in vigilance, memory, and arithmetic tasks. *Psychophysiology, 48*, 323–332.

Kostons, D., Van Gog, T., & Paas, F. (2009). How do I do? Investigating effects of expertise and performance-process records on self-assessment. *Applied Cognitive Psychology, 23*, 1256–1265.

Kuusela, H., & Paul, P. (2000). A comparison of concurrent and retrospective verbal protocol analysis. *The American Journal of Psychology, 113*, 387–404.

Land, M., & Tatler, B. (2009). *Looking and acting: Vision and eye movements in natural behaviour*. Oxford, UK: Oxford University Press.

Litchfield, D., Ball, L. J., Donovan, T., Manning, D. J., & Crawford, T. (2010). Viewing another person's eye movements improves identification of pulmonary nodules in chest x-ray inspection. *Journal of Experimental Psychology. Applied, 16*, 251–262.

Louwerse, M. M., Graesser, A. C., McNamara, D. S., & Lu, S. (2009). Embodied conversational agents as conversational partners. *Applied Cognitive Psychology, 23*, 1244–1255.

Mayer, R. E. (2005). Principles for reducing extraneous processing in multimedia learning: Coherence, signaling, redundancy, spatial contiguity, and temporal contiguity principles. In R. E. Mayer (Ed.), *The Cambridge handbook of multimedia learning* (pp. 183–200). New York: Cambridge University Press.

McLaren, B. M., Lim, S., & Koedinger, K. R. (2008). When and how often should worked examples be given to students? New results and a summary of the current state of research. In B. C. Love, K. McRae, & V. M. Sloutsky (Eds.), *Proceedings of the 30th Annual Conference of the Cognitive Science Society* (pp. 2176–2181). Austin: Cognitive Science Society.

Merten, C., & Conati, C. (2006). Eye-tracking to model and adapt to user meta-cognition in intelligent learning environments. *Proceedings of the 11th international conference on Intelligent user interfaces* (IUI '06), (pp. 39–46). New York: ACM.

Metcalfe, J. (2009). Metacognitive judgments and control of study. *Current Directions in Psychological Science, 18*, 159–163.

Moreno, R. (2005). Multimedia learning with animated pedagogical agents. In R. E. Mayer (Ed.), *The Cambridge handbook of multimedia learning* (pp. 507–523). New York: Cambridge University Press.

Ozcelik, E., Arslan-Arib, I., & Cagiltay, K. (2010). Why does signaling enhance multimedia learning? Evidence from eye movements. *Computers in Human Behavior, 26*, 110–117.

Ozcelik, E., Karakus, T., Kursun, E., & Cagiltay, K. (2009). An eye-tracking study of how color coding affects multimedia learning. *Computers in Education, 53*, 445–453.

Papenmeier, F., & Huff, M. (2010). DynAOI: A tool for matching eye-movement data with dynamic areas of interest in animations and movies. *Behavior Research Methods, 42*, 179–187.

Rayner, K. (1998). Eye movements in reading and information processing: 20 years of research. *Psychological Bulletin, 124*, 372–422.

Rayner, K. (2009). Eye movements and attention in reading, scene perception, and visual search. *The Quarterly Journal of Experimental Psychology, 62*, 1457–1506.

Reichle, E. D., Reineberg, A. E., & Schooler, J. W. (2010). Eye movements during mindless reading. *Psychological Science, 21*(9), 1300–1310.

Richardson, D. C., & Spivey, M. (2004). Eye tracking: Characteristics and methods. In G. Wnek & G. Bowlin (Eds.), *Encyclopedia of biomaterials and biomedical engineering* (pp. 568–572). New York: Marcel Dekker, Inc.

Roderer, T., & Roebers, C. M. (2010). Explicit and implicit confidence judgments and developmental differences in metamemory: An eye-tracking approach. *Metacognition and Learning, 5*, 229–250.

Russo, J. E., Johnson, E. J., & Stephens, D. L. (1989). The validity of verbal protocols. *Memory & Cognition, 17*, 759–769.

Sangin, M., Molinari, G., Nüssli, M. -A., & Dillenbourg, P. (2008). How learners use awareness cues about their peer's knowledge? Insights from synchronized eye-tracking data. *Proceedings of the 8th International Conference on International Conference for the Learning Sciences* (Vol. 2, pp. 287–294). International Society of the Learning Sciences.

Schmidt-Weigand, F., Kohert, A., & Glowalla, U. (2010). A closer look at split visual attention in system- and self-paced instruction in multimedia learning. *Learning and Instruction, 20*, 100–110.

Schwonke, R., Berthold, K., & Renkl, A. (2009). How multiple external representations are used and how they can be made more useful. *Applied Cognitive Psychology, 23*, 1227–1243.

Smilek, D., Carriere, J. S. A., & Cheyne, J. A. (2010). Out of mind, out of sight: Eye blinking as an indicator and embodiment of mind wandering. *Psychological Science, 21*, 786–789.

Stelmach, L. B., Campsall, J. M., & Herdman, C. M. (1997). Attentional and ocular movements. *Journal of Experimental Psychology. Human Perception and Performance, 23*, 823–844.

Underwood, G., Chapman, P., Brocklehurst, N., Underwood, J., & Crundall, D. (2003). Visual attention while driving: Sequences of eye fixations made by experienced and novice drivers. *Ergonomics, 46*, 629–646.

Van Gerven, P. W. M., Paas, F., Van Merriënboer, J. J. G., & Schmidt, H. G. (2004). Memory load and the cognitive pupillary response in aging. *Psychophysiology, 41*, 167–174.

Van Gog, T. (2006). *Uncovering the problem-solving process to design effective worked examples*. Doctoral Dissertation, Open University of The Netherlands, Heerlen, The Netherlands.

Van Gog, T., Jarodzka, H., Scheiter, K., Gerjets, P., & Paas, F. (2009). Attention guidance during example study via the model's eye movements. *Computers in Human Behavior, 25*, 785–791.

Van Gog, T., Kester, L., Nievelstein, F., Giesbers, B., & Paas, F. (2009). Uncovering cognitive processes: Different techniques that can contribute to cognitive load research and instruction. *Computers in Human Behavior, 25*, 325–331.

Van Gog, T., Paas, F., & Van Merriënboer, J. J. G. (2005a). Uncovering expertise-related differences in troubleshooting performance: Combining eye movement and concurrent verbal protocol data. *Applied Cognitive Psychology, 19*, 205–221.

Van Gog, T., Paas, F., Van Merriënboer, J. J. G., & Witte, P. (2005b). Uncovering the problem-solving process: Cued retrospective reporting versus concurrent and retrospective reporting. *Journal of Experimental Psychology. Applied, 11*, 237–244.

Van Gog, T., & Rummel, N. (2010). Example-based learning: Integrating cognitive and social-cognitive research perspectives. *Educational Psychology Review, 22*, 155–174.

Van Someren, M., Barnard, Y., & Sandberg, J. (1994). *The think aloud method: A practical guide to modeling cognitive processes*. Amsterdam: Academic Press.

Velichkovsky, B. M. (1995). Communicating attention: Gaze position transfer in cooperative problem solving. *Pragmatics and Cognition, 3*, 199–224.

Wade, N. J., & Tatler, B. (2005). *The moving tablet of the eye: The origins of modern eye movement research*. Oxford: Oxford University Press.

Yarbus, A. L. (1967). *Eye movements and vision*. New York: Plenum Press.

Assessing Metacognitive Skills in Computerized Learning Environments

11

Marcel V.J. Veenman

Abstract

In this chapter, metacognitive skills are considered to be an organized set of metacognitive self instructions for the monitoring of and control over cognitive activity. These self-instructions can be represented as a production system of condition-action rules. For the assessment of metacognitive skills, however, these covert rules have to be inferred from overt learner behavior during task performance. In computerized learning tasks, on-line traces of learner activities can be unobtrusively stored in logfiles. Prerequisite to logfile assessment is the selection of relevant indicators of metacognitive learning activities on the basis of a rational task analysis, which indicators have to be validated against other on-line measures obtained with, for instance, thinking-aloud protocols. Such analyses of logfiles will allow for the assessment of metacognitive skills as an aptitude, that is, as a relatively stable repertoire of self-instructions. In order to further capture the dynamic change in metacognitive processes over time, progressive patterns of metacognitive activity can be identified in logged traces through time-series analysis. It is argued that the aptitude and dynamic approaches to assessing metacognitive skills are complementary to one another, rather than excluding each other.

Introduction

Metacognition is a relevant predictor of learning outcomes in traditional learning settings (Wang, Haertel, & Walberg, 1990) as well as in computer-based learning environments (Veenman, 2008; Winters, Greene, & Costich, 2008). In conceptions of metacognition, a distinction is often made between knowledge of cognition and regulation of cognition (Brown, 1987; Schraw & Dennison, 1994). Metacognitive knowledge is declarative knowledge about the interplay between person characteristics, task characteristics, and strategy characteristics (Flavell, 1979). Having declarative metacognitive knowledge at one's disposal, however, does not guarantee that

M.V.J. Veenman (✉)
Department of Developmental and Educational Psychology, Institute for Psychological Research, Leiden University, Leiden, The Netherlands
e-mail: veenman@fsw.leidenuniv.nl

R. Azevedo and V. Aleven (eds.), *International Handbook of Metacognition and Learning Technologies*, Springer International Handbooks of Education 26, DOI 10.1007/978-1-4419-5546-3_11,

this knowledge is actually used for the regulation of learning behavior (Veenman, Van Hout-Wolters, & Afflerbach, 2006; Winne, 1996). Metacognitive knowledge may be incorrect or incomplete; the learner may fail to see the usefulness or applicability of that knowledge in a particular situation, or the learner may lack the skills for doing so.

Metacognitive skills refer to procedural knowledge that is required for the regulation of and control over one's learning behavior. Orientation, goal setting, planning, monitoring, checking, evaluation, and recapitulation are manifestations of those skills (Veenman, 2011). These skills directly affect learning behavior and, consequently, learning outcomes. Veenman (2008) estimated that metacognitive skillfulness account for about 40% of variance in learning outcomes for a broad range of tasks. Metacognitive skillfulness is regarded here as an aptitude, which is a relatively stable disposition for how the individual interacts with learning environments (Snow, 1989). This is not to say that metacognitive skills are entirely fixed. Learning experiences, instruction, and training may affect those skills (Pressley & Gaskins, 2006; Veenman, 2011). This chapter addresses issues related to the assessment of metacognitive skills in computer-based learning environments and, in particular, the necessity of validating these assessments through a multi-method approach.

Theoretical Framework

In an attempt to formulate a unifying theory of metacognition, Nelson (1996; Nelson & Narens, 1990) distinguished an "object level" from a "meta-level" in the cognitive system. At the cognitive level, lower-order cognitive activity takes place, usually referred to as *execution* processes. For instance, when solving a math problem, basic reading processes are needed for assessing the problem statement, and calculation processes are needed for producing the outcome. Higher-order *executive* processes of evaluation and planning at the meta-level govern the object level. Two flows of information between both levels are postulated. Information about the state of the object level is conveyed to the meta-level through monitoring processes, while instructions from the meta-level are transmitted to the object level through control processes. Thus, if an error occurs on the object level, a metacognitive monitoring process will give notice of it to the meta-level, and control processes will be activated to resolve the problem.

Nelson's model essentially is a bottom-up process model. Anomalies in task performance trigger monitoring activities, which in turn activate control processes on the meta-level in order to restore cognitive processing at the object level. This model, however, does not clarify how monitoring processes themselves are activated (Dunlosky, 1998). Moreover, Nelson's model ignores the goal-directedness of human problem-solving and learning behavior as it does not allow for spontaneous activation of control processes without prior monitoring activity (Veenman, 2011). Koriath, Ma'ayan, and Nussinson (2006) have shown that causality in the relation between monitoring and control processes is bidirectional. Monitoring processes may elicit control processes, like Nelson emphasized, but control processes can also be activated without prior monitoring and, subsequently, elicit monitoring processes. The question, then, is how these control processes are activated if not by sheer coincidence.

Veenman (2011) extended Nelson's bottom-up model with a top-down approach. Metacognitive skills are perceived as an acquired program of self-instructions for the control over and the regulation of task performance. This program of self-instructions is activated whenever the learner is faced with a task that is familiar to the learner to a certain extent. Either the task has been practiced before or the task resembles another familiar task. These self-instructions can be represented as a production system of condition-action rules (Anderson, 1996; Winne, 2010). For instance, activating prior knowledge can be represented as: If you have read the task assignment, then retrieve all that you know about the topic from memory. Planning could be triggered by the rule: If you have set your goal, then design an action plan for attaining that goal. Even self-induced, intentional monitoring is part of this production system: If you have executed a step from your action plan, then look out for errors in the executed step. This system of self-instructions is acquired through experience and training, much in the same way as the acquisition of cognitive skills (for more details, see Veenman, 2011). The more experienced a learner becomes, the more fine grained the condition-action rules will be with regard to, for instance, the selection of retrieval cues for memory search, the conversion from goal states to action plans, and the recognition of potential errors. In line with Nelson's model, self-instructions from the meta-level evoke various cognitive activities on the object level. However, self-instructions are self-induced, that is, they need not necessarily be triggered by a monitoring process of *anomalies* in task performance. In fact, the monitoring information flow in Nelson's model should be extended with the monitoring of conditions for activating self-instructions at the meta-level, although the latter is not necessarily a conscious process. Recognition of applicable conditions may also be automated to a certain extent in case self-instructions have become proficient metacognitive habits (Veenman et al., 2006). With reading, for instance, many monitoring processes run in the "background" of cognitive processes that are being executed. Proficient readers may not notice them, not even when thinking aloud. In this notion of self-instructions, the monitoring information flow represents the input to the production rule system at the meta-level. In the same vein, the control information flow represents the output of production rules.

What does this notion of self-instructions imply for the assessment of metacognitive skills? The aim of metacognitive assessment is to capture the learner's program of self-instructions at the meta-level. However, metacognitive skills that operate at the meta-level are not directly available for inspection (Veenman, 2011). The production system of self-instructions itself is covert and cannot be assessed, like the program lines of a compiled computer program that cannot be read. Verbalizations of the learner, however, can disclose the input and output of the production system. Thus, the thinking-aloud method gives access to the monitoring and control information flow, and a production rule may be inferred from the relation between input and output information. For instance, we may hear a math learner say that the outcome of a calculation is odd. Yet, we *infer* from its cooccurrence with subsequent recalculation of the problem that a self-instruction for checking the outcomes must have been activated. Such inferences may be flawed, either because the input information is incomplete or because the output information is generated for another reason. When the math learner says "Let's do this again," this output information does not necessarily refer to recalculating the problem. Careful inspection of contingencies between monitoring and control information is warranted.

Most of the control information is gathered from overt operations on the object level. A task assignment is read, a sketch of the problem is drawn, a goal is written down, actions are taken step by step according to a plan, a dictionary is consulted for an unknown word, the flow of cognitive activity is interrupted for checking results, a recalculation is done, and conclusions are formulated. In fact, the execution of metacognitive skills draws heavily on lower-order cognitive processes (Veenman, 2011). From the perspective of the object level, one has to consider the context in which these cognitive processes occur in order to appraise their metacognitive origin. For instance, rereading is not a metacognitive activity as such, but it becomes a metacognitive activity if effortless reading is interrupted by the presence of a difficult word or a complex phrase. Thus, an inference process is required to identify specific cognitive activities at the object level and to tag them as "metacognitive activities." Unfortunately, this inference process is also prone to misinterpretation. Recalculation may be due to the metacognitive self-instruction of checking outcomes, but it may equally result from a learner's sloppiness in note taking. Observation techniques without concurrent thinking aloud or computer registrations of learner activities are more vulnerable to misinterpretations because they only have access to (metacognitive) activities at the object level.

Off-Line vs. Online Assessments

Generally, off-line methods for assessment of metacognitive skills are distinguished from online methods (Veenman, 2005). Off-line assessments concern the learners' self-reports that are gathered *prior to* or *after* task performance. Questionnaires (e.g., MSLQ, Pintrich & De Groot, 1990; MAI, Schraw & Dennison, 1994) and interviews (Zimmerman & Martinez-Pons, 1990) are off-line assessment methods that are frequently being used because they are relatively easy to administer. Off-line self-reports of metacognitive skills, however, suffer from validity problems. A first, fundamental problem concerns the off-line nature of self-reports, which requires learners to reconstruct their earlier performance. This reconstruction process might suffer from memory failure and distortions, especially if experiences from the past have to be retrieved (Veenman, 2011). The second validity problem is embedded in common questions about the relative frequency of certain activities ("How often do/did you…?"). In order to answer these questions, learners have to compare themselves to others (peers, parents, or teachers). The individual reference point chosen, however, may vary from one learner to another or even within a learner from one question to another (Veenman, Prins, & Verheij, 2003). Variation in reference points chosen by learners may yield disparate data. It is much like measuring the temperature with differently scaled thermometers, however, without being able to rescale measurements. Moreover, some learners may produce socially desirable answers.

Online assessments are obtained *during* task performance, that is, they are based on actual performance of the learner. Typical online assessments include observational methods (Whitebread et al., 2009), the analysis of thinking-aloud protocols (Azevedo, Greene, & Moos, 2007; Pressley & Afflerbach, 1995; Veenman, Elshout, & Meijer, 1997), and eye-movement registration (Kinnunen & Vauras, 1995). The essential difference between off-line and online methods is that off-line measures merely rely on learner self-reports, whereas online measures pertain to the coding of actual learner behavior on externally defined criteria by external agencies, such as "blind" judges and observers (Veenman, 2011). The use of a standardized coding system circumvents the validity problems mentioned before. Online assessments also have their limitations. Thinking aloud may not always yield complete protocols, for instance, when processes are highly automated or, conversely, when the task is extremely difficult (Ericsson & Simon, 1993). Observed behavior needs to be interpreted by observers whenever the learner fails to express the reasons for his/her conduct (Veenman, 2011). Similarly, the registration of eye movements only captures the motor activities of the eyes. The meaning of these overt activities is subject to interpretation for which the coding system should provide perspicuous standards.

Research with multi-method designs has shown that off-line measures hardly correspond to online measures. Correlations between off-line and online measures are invariably low ($r = 0.15$ on the average; Bannert & Mengelkamp, 2008; Cromley & Azevedo, 2006; Veenman, 2005, 2011; Veenman et al., 2003), and qualitative analyses show that off-line self-reports do not converge with specific online behaviors (Hadwin, Nesbit, Jamieson-Noel, Code, & Winne, 2007; Winne & Jamieson-Noel, 2002). Apparently, learners do not do what they prospectively say they will do nor do they accurately recollect what they have recently done. Moreover, correlations among off-line measures are often low to moderate, whereas correlations among online measures are moderate to high (Cromley & Azevedo, 2006; Veenman, 2005). Obviously, off-line methods yield rather diverging results, while online methods converge in their assessments of metacognitive skills. Finally, the external validity of assessment methods should be considered (Veenman, 2007). Online assessments are strong predictors of learning outcomes, contrary to off-line assessments. In a review study, Veenman (2005) found that correlations with learning performance range from slightly negative to 0.36 for off-line measures and from 0.45 to 0.90 for online measures. In conclusion, off-line measures suffer from low convergent validity and low external validity, which makes an argument for resorting to online assessment of metacognitive skills (Veenman, 2007). Yet, a majority of studies rely on off-line self-reports for the assessment of metacognition (Dinsmore, Alexander, & Loughlin, 2008; Veenman, 2005), including studies with computer-based learning environments (Gress, Fior, Hadwin, & Winne, 2010; Winters et al., 2008).

Logfile Assessments

Thinking aloud and observation are time-consuming methods because they have to be administered on an individual basis. With the emergence of computer-based learning environments, the online method of tracing metacognitive behaviors of learners in computer logfiles has become available (Greene, & Azevedo, 2010; Hadwin et al., 2007; Kunz, Drewniak, & Schott, 1992; Veenman, Elshout, & Groen, 1993; Veenman, Wilhelm, & Beishuizen, 2004; Winne, 2010). Obviously, the nature of the task should allow for a computerized version, or otherwise it would impair the ecological validity of assessments. The advantage of logfile assessment is that the method is minimally intrusive and that it can be administered to large groups at the same time (Aleven, Roll, McLaren, & Koedinger, 2010; Azevedo, Moos, Johnson, & Chauncey, 2010; Veenman et al., 2006; Winne, 2010). Typically, a logfile contains traces of the learner's overt cognitive activities during task performance on the computer. The frequencies of certain key presses, button pushes, object manipulations, link and screen selections, scrolling, and menu clicks are registered along with time indications. Logfiles do not contain the learner's metacognitive deliberations for enacting those activities, since prompting learners to type in their thoughts would interfere with spontaneous metacognitive processing. Basically, the concrete activities registered in a logfile represent rather raw materials on a low cognitive level, also referred to as "events" (Azevedo et al., 2010; Winne, 2010). In order to lift logfile analysis to a metacognitive level, two steps need to be taken in order to select and validate relevant indicators of metacognition (Veenman, 2007).

A first step in logfile analysis concerns the selection of which cognitive activity may be consequential to metacognitive regulation. This selection of potential indicators of metacognitive skills should be based on a rational analysis of the task at hand, knowledge of the metacognition literature, and common sense. For instance, pushing a particular button at a critical moment in the course of task performance may be such an indicator. The outcome of this selection process, however, is not always entirely successful. Some activities that initially appear to be metacognitive by nature may turn out to be non-metacognitive after all. Hence, a second step is to validate these potential logfile measures with concurrent online assessments, such as think-aloud protocols or systematical observation. This multi-method approach is prerequisite for establishing a firm set of adequate logfile indicators of metacognitive skillfulness (Veenman, 2007; Winters et al., 2008). Selection and validation of indicators need to be done prior to logfile assessments if the coding of learner activities in logfiles is automated. Otherwise, logfiles have to be coded by hand afterwards. Three empirical studies may elucidate the necessity of this two-step procedure.

Veenman and colleagues (1993) assessed the metacognitive skills from logfiles of 40 participants who were either thinking aloud or working silently in a computer-simulated Heat Lab. Participants, novices in the domain of physics, were required to discover principles of calorimetry by designing their own experiments. Several objects of different weights (100 g, 200 g, 1 kg) and materials (gold, copper, glass) could be heated on a burner. The amount of heat transferred to an object was regulated with a time switch and could be read off a joules-meter. Temperature was measured by attaching a thermometer to an object. Thus, the virtual laboratory contained the required means for examining the relationship between heat and temperature depending on weight and material. All activities in Heat Lab were logged. In order to determine which of these activities could be labeled as representing metacognitive skillfulness, a reference group with a similar background was included from an earlier study with Heat Lab

(Veenman et al., 1993). Thinking-aloud protocols of this reference group had been analyzed on the quality of metacognitive skillfulness (i.e., on indications of task orientation, goal setting, planning, monitoring, evaluation, recapitulation, and reflection). Their logfiles were coded on potential positive indicators of metacognitive orientation (frequency of rereading the task assignment and frequency of asking for help with lab operations), positive indicators of planning (frequency of switching on the burner for starting a new experiment, frequency of object manipulations, and the number of unique objects used), as well as negative indicators of planning and monitoring (frequency of *not* measuring either the initial temperature or the final temperature). Although the selection of these indicators was based on a rational task analysis, only three logfile measures appeared to be substantially related to thinking-aloud measures. Frequency of switching the burner on, frequency of *not* measuring the initial temperature, and frequency of *not* measuring the final temperature correlated 0.40, −0.40, and −0.37 with the thinking-aloud measures, while correlations for the other logfile measures were low. Regression analysis confirmed that these three logfile measures each contributed to the prediction of the thinking-aloud measure, whereas the others did not. A composite score of these three logfile measures correlated 0.62 with the thinking-aloud measures. Using the same procedure for obtaining a composite score from logfiles in the main experiment, Veenman and colleagues (1993) showed that participants who were thinking aloud did not differ in metacognitive skillfulness from those who worked silently, $F(1,38)=0.02$. Thinking aloud did not affect metacognitive processes, although it slowed down those processes a bit (cf. Ericsson & Simon, 1993).

In another study, Veenman and colleagues (2004) assessed metacognitive skillfulness from the logfiles of 113 children and adolescents in the age of 9–22 years, who performed four computer-simulated, inductive-learning tasks. Participants completed two biology tasks (a plant-growing task and a food task) as well as two geography tasks (one about the conservation of otter habitats, the other about ageing). In each task, five independent variables with discrete levels (either two or three levels) could be varied, and their effects on the dependent variable could be inspected. The model underlying the relations between the independent and the dependent variables was identical in each task; two independent variables interacted with one another; one variable had a nonlinear effect, and two variables were irrelevant. Each task model corresponded to plausible real-life phenomena. Figure 11.1 shows the interface of the plant-growing task as an example. The task was to find out how different independent variables affected plant growth. Independent variables were (1) giving water, either once or twice a week; (2) using an insecticide or not; (3) putting dead plant leaves in the flowerpot or not; (4) placing the plant either indoors, on a balcony, or in a greenhouse; and (5) size of the flower pot, either large or small. Distinct levels of plant growth as a dependent variable were 5, 10, 15, 20, and 25 cm. Variable 4 had a nonlinear effect, meaning that growing the plant indoors resulted in 5 cm less growth, relative to a balcony or greenhouse. Variable 2 and 3 did not affect plant growth at all. Variable 1 and 5 interacted, as giving water once or twice a week did not matter for a large pot, but it did matter when a small flowerpot was used. In that case, giving water twice a week would reduce plant growth, while giving water once a week would increase growth, relative to growth in the large flowerpot. Within each task, participants performed a series of "experiments." Such an experiment consisted of choosing a value for each of the independent variables, predicting the plant growth as a result of these values, and asking the computer for the actual plant growth. Results of earlier experiments could be inspected by scrolling through the result window at the right side in Fig. 11.1.

During the food task, participants had to find out how eating and drinking habits affected the health status of an imaginary person, called Hans. Independent variables were the consumption of fat, carbohydrates, alcohol, albumen, and supplementary vitamins. In the otter task, the relevance of factors affecting the extinction of otters had to be investigated. Independent variables were extra

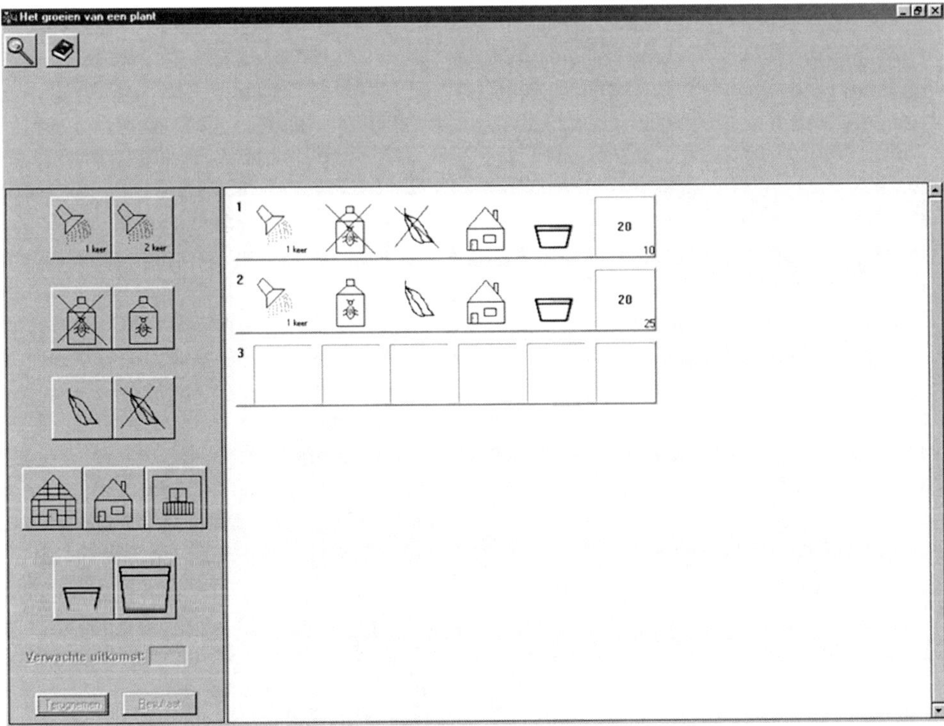

Fig. 11.1 Interface of the plant-growing task (Veenman et al., 2004)

food provision or not, environmental pollution, natural habitat, media exposure, and closing otter areas to the public or not. In the population-ageing task, independent variables that could affect the ageing rate of a population were state of the economy, quality of the educational system, means of living, climate, and general safety. In all cases, two variables interacted, one variable had a nonlinear effect, and two variables were irrelevant to the dependent variable.

The computer program automatically recoded learner activities in the logfiles of each task into several potential indicators of metacognitive skillfulness. Logfile measures included the number of (unique) experiments conducted, the mean number of variables changed per experiment, frequency of scrolling activities, frequency of variable selection activities, the prediction-error rate (mean distance between predicted and actual outcome), and time on task, among others (see Wilhelm, Beishuizen, & Van Rijn, 2005). As participants were required to think aloud during all tasks, logfile measures could be validated against thinking-aloud data. Two judges separately rated 10% of the plant-growing-task protocols and 5% of the otter-task protocols on the quality of metacognitive skillfulness. Protocols were judged on the quality of orientation activities (elaborateness of hypotheses generated before each experiment), systematical behavior (planning a sequence of experiments and avoiding unsystematic variations between subsequent experiments), evaluation (detection and correction of mistakes), and elaboration (drawing conclusions, relating outcomes of experiments, generating explanations, and recapitulating). From the logfile measures, only the mean number of variables changed per experiment, and the frequency of scrolling appeared to be substantially correlated to the thinking-aloud scores. The mean number of variables changed per experiment (VOTAT; Chen & Klahr, 1999) was a negative indicator of think-aloud metacognition. Varying more than one variable at a time represents poor planning behavior (Veenman et al., 1997) and lack of experimental control (Glaser, Schauble, Raghavan, & Zeitz,

1992). Frequency of scrolling back to earlier experiments, on the other hand, was a positive indicator of think-aloud metacognition. Participants use scrolling to check earlier experimental configurations or to relate outcomes of experiments. Scores on both measures were standardized and the sign of the negative indicator was inverted. Composite scores of these two logfile measures correlated 0.85 and 0.84 with the thinking-aloud data of the plant-growing task and the otter task, respectively. Veenman and colleagues (2004) used the composite scores of logfile measures to show that the metacognitive skills of learners develop with age. The mean composite scores of the four age groups (9, 12, 14, and 22 year) revealed a steep linear increment with age, $F(3,109)=38.60$, $p<0.001$. Moreover, composite scores correlated 0.74 with an overall measure of learning performance.

In a recent, unpublished study, Veenman, Van Haaren, and Rens used an adapted version of the plant-growing task to assess the metacognitive skills of gifted secondary-school students. Task complexity was increased to meet the intellectual level of the target group of gifted students. Numerical relations between the variables were made more complex, and a second interaction effect was included: Using insecticides with dead leaves in the pot reduced the growth of the plant, while leaving out any of the two did not affect plant growth. Due to changes in both task settings and target group compared to the original study, a pilot study with five gifted learners needed be carried out to validate logfile measures once more. Think-aloud and logfile data were gathered according to the procedures of Veenman and colleagues (2004). A new posttest with multiple-choice and open-ended questions about the effects of the five independent variables on plant growth was also administered. As expected, VOTAT (converted to positive scores) and the frequency of scrolling activities correlated respectively 0.68 and 0.58 with think-aloud metacognition. However, this time the number of unique experiments, corrected for the total number of experiments, correlated 0.56 with think-aloud metacognition. The number of unique experiments represents coverage of the problem space, consisting of maximal 48 possible experiments. Composite scores of these three logfile measures correlated 0.96 ($p<0.01$) with think-aloud metacognition and 0.90 ($p<0.05$) with posttest learning outcomes.

The first two studies show that a selection of logfile indicators based on a rational task analysis is fallible. Validation of potential indicators is necessary to sift out irrelevant, non-metacognitive activities. Moreover, the third study reveals that additional validation is required when task conditions or participant samples are altered. These studies further show that a limited set of logfile measures may adequately represent a broader range of metacognitive skills assessed from thinking-aloud protocols. Veenman and colleagues (2004) asserted that metacognitive skills during various phases of task performance are highly interdependent. Good orientation leads to good planning and systematical behavior, which in turn allows for more monitoring and evaluative control. This interdependency of metacognitive skills (with intercorrelations of about 0.90; Veenman, 1993) accounts for why a limited set of indicators may adequately represent broad metacognition.

Patterns of Activity in Logfile Assessments

Logfiles assessments often merely capture the quantity of metacognitive activities and not the quality of those activities (Winters et al., 2008). Plain rereading of task assignments, for instance, is not the same as rereading the task assignment consequential to monitoring the understanding of the task. The latter is more goal oriented. One way to access quality is to detect meaningful patterns in the sequence of activities or events. Transition analysis is used to analyze trace data on the sequence and transitions of events (Azevedo et al., 2010; Hadwin et al., 2007). All frequencies of transitions from one event to another are entered in a matrix of all possible events. Inspection of this matrix yields information about the regularity of certain transitions (density) and about the exclusivity of transition starting points (centrality). Transition analysis may be done on group level as well as on the individual level. In the same vein, Biswas, Hogyeong, Kinnebrew, Sulcer, and Roscoe (2010) used a technique of hidden Markov models to detect probability patterns of transitions between (metacognitive) activities over time. Such techniques allow us to detect patterns of contingent events, rather than registering single, isolated ones (Winne, 2010). The metacognitive nature of these patterns, however, remains to be inferred by the researcher.

Researchers in self-regulated learning stress the dynamic nature of metacognitive processes (Azevedo et al., 2010; Greene & Azevedo, 2010; Winne, 2010). Strategy choices and frequency of activities may change over time in interaction with the learning environment. Time-series analysis is a technique for assessing changes in metacognitive functioning. For time-series analyses, either the task is subdivided in distinguishable learning episodes, or a series of highly similar tasks is presented. Repeated assessments over time are analyzed. In the unpublished study of Veenman, Van Haaren, and Rens, eventually 153 students from preuniversity secondary education performed both the plant-growing task and the ageing task in randomized order. Logfile measures were analyzed by means of repeated-measures ANOVA with task order as between-subjects factor. Results show that the total number of experiments, $F(1,151)=36.84$, $p<0.001$, converted VOTAT, $F(1,151)=54.09$, $p<0.001$, and the number of unique experiment, $F(1,151)=26.57$, $p<0.001$, increased between task 1 and task 2, while the scrolling frequency, $F(1,151)=22.80$, $p<0.001$, decreased. Participants became more active and showed more experimental control over time, at the cost of scrolling activities. Perhaps, referring back to previous experiments became less compulsory due to the enhanced experimental control.

Elshout, Veenman, and Van Hell (1993) used time-series analysis to study help-seeking behavior in a computerized learning-by-doing environment. Novice and advanced learners in physics learned to solve a series of 20 complex thermodynamics problems about the relation between volume, pressure, and temperature with the option of asking for help from the computer program. The help facility offered a sequence of steps that would lead the learner through an orientation phase, an execution phase, and an evaluation phase of the problem-solving process. Participants were free to choose a type of help: clue (hint about one specific step), one step (working out of one specific step), student performed (all subsequent steps, but learner executed), or computer demonstrated (working out of all steps, demonstrated by the program). Traces of help requests were logged, while metacognitive skillfulness was assessed from think-aloud protocols. Analysis over the series of 20 problems revealed that metacognitively poor novices preferred the quick and dirty way out by choosing one-step formula with direct access to a working out of the appropriate formula (cf. Aleven et al., 2010). Help requests of metacognitively skilled novices, on the other hand, shifted from merely execution help to orientation help over the 20 problems, thereby matching the help-seeking behavior of advanced learners in the end. These two studies show that time-series analysis of logged traces may capture patterns of change in metacognitive functioning.

Discussion

In the introduction of this chapter, metacognitive skillfulness was defined as an aptitude. Recently, Winne (2010) argued against such an aptitude approach because self-regulation is a dynamic process that unfolds in the course of learning. Self-regulatory processes change in nature and frequency as learning progresses. According to Winne, aptitude measures do not capture the dynamic nature of self-regulation, contrary to computer traces of events that allow for a fine-grained analysis of processes over time. The construct of metacognitive skillfulness is an aptitude indeed, because it represents the availability of self-instructions in learning situations. Assessments of metacognitive skills as an aptitude would provide a static measure of the amount and quality of available skills

(Winne, 2010). Yet, both positions of metacognitive skills as aptitude and as dynamic processes are equally tenable, provided that metacognitive skills are assessed with behavior measures. Studies have shown that learners bring along a rather stable, general repertoire of metacognitive skills when entering various new learning situations (Veenman, 2011). The deployment of this general repertoire, however, must be adapted to task demands and other contextual factors during the learning process, as shown by the studies with time-series analysis. Metacognitive skills are gradually tailored to the task at hand because production rules become more specialized and sensitive to task constraints. Thus, any learning experience may alter the repertoire of production rules for metacognitive self-instruction. Veenman (1993) postulated that a separate set of task- or domain-specific production rules is generated during the acquisition of expertise, alongside the general production rules that serve as default repertoire for novel learning situations. Even general production rules are subject to change due to experience and training, yet at a slow pace (Veenman et al., 2006). Therefore, the notion of metacognitive skills as self-instructions does not preclude a peaceful coexistence of aptitude and dynamic change in learning.

There is ample evidence that online assessments are more valid than off-line assessments of metacognitive skills. Nevertheless, all online assessments make inferences about metacognitive self-instructions, albeit to a different extent. The think-aloud method is a powerful tool for assessing monitoring and control information flows. Yet, protocols may be incomplete and researchers have to fill in the gaps by making inferences about relations between both information flows. The same is true for observations that include the learner's verbalizations. More far-reaching inferences need to be made for observations without verbalization, eye-movement registration, and logfile analysis as these methods only access information about concrete, overt behaviors on the object level of Nelson's model. For two contingent events, the researcher has to infer the causal relation between the two events and their metacognitive nature. First, one needs to infer that the first event represents the condition part of a production rule. Next, one needs to infer that the second event corresponds to the action part of the *same* production rule. Finally, the metacognitive function of the entire production rule has to be inferred. Contingencies in time may offer a plausible but not sufficient reason for making these inferences (cf. Winne, 2010). A further complication is that the conditions for evoking a control event may not become manifest in trace logs, either because the conditions of a production rule are activated by mental operations that are not accessible with trace data or because the tracing system is not sensitive to a particular event. Here is a major challenge that researchers of trace data in computer-based learning environments are facing: extracting an appropriately contextualized (i.e., neither overly general nor overly specific) set of conditions from multiple data points.

Logfile assessment is an unobtrusive method for gaining access to events in detail on the object level, which assessments can be done on a large scale and over extended periods of time. Logfile analysis allows for different levels of granularity in assessment, ranging from tracing the occurrence of separate events to detecting patterns of contingent events. Although scarcely out of the egg, tracing events can be used for attuning feedback and scaffolding of metacognitive functioning to individual needs (Aleven et al., 2010; Azevedo et al., 2010; Gress et al., 2010) and for verifying that these interventions have been successful (Veenman, 2007). However, validation of logfile events with other online assessments is prerequisite to making justified inferences about the metacognitive nature of those events. Ultimate assessments would include different online methods rendering data that are aligned in time and produce converging results. Like a converging lens that directs rays of light to a focal point, even the focal distance may change due to learning experiences. Unfortunately, multi-method research in metacognition is scarce so far (Veenman, 2011; Veenman et al., 2006). Metacognition researchers should sharpen their lenses.

References

Aleven, V., Roll, I., McLaren, B. M., & Koedinger, K. R. (2010). Automated, unobtrusive, action-by-action assessment of self-regulation during learning with an intelligent tutoring system. *Educational Psychologist, 45*, 224–233.

Anderson, J. R. (1996). *The architecture of cognition*. Mahwah, NJ: Erlbaum.

Azevedo, R., Greene, J. A., & Moos, D. C. (2007). The effect of a human agent's external regulation upon college students' hypermedia learning. *Metacognition and Learning, 2*, 67–87.

Azevedo, R., Moos, D. C., Johnson, A. M., & Chauncey, A. D. (2010). Measuring cognitive and metacognitive regulatory processes during hypermedia learning: Issues and challenges. *Educational Psychologist, 45*, 210–223.

Bannert, M., & Mengelkamp, C. (2008). Assessment of metacognitive skills by means of instruction to think aloud and reflect when prompted. Does the verbalization method affect learning? *Metacognition and Learning, 3*, 39–58.

Biswas, G., Hogyeong, J., Kinnebrew, J. S., Sulcer, B., & Roscoe, R. (2010). Measuring self-regulated learning skills through social interactions in a teachable agent environment. *Research and Practice in Technology Enhanced Learning, 5*, 123–152.

Brown, A. (1987). Metacognition, executive control, self-regulation, and other more mysterious mechanisms. In F. E. Weinert & R. H. Kluwe (Eds.), *Metacognition, motivation and understanding* (pp. 65–116). Hillsdale, NJ: Erlbaum.

Chen, Z., & Klahr, D. (1999). All other things being equal: Acquisition and transfer of the control of variables strategy. *Child Development, 70*, 1098–1120.

Cromley, J. G., & Azevedo, R. (2006). Self-report of reading comprehension strategies: What are we measuring? *Metacognition and Learning, 1*, 229–247.

Dinsmore, D. L., Alexander, P. A., & Loughlin, S. M. (2008). Focusing the conceptual lens on metacognition, self-regulation, and self-regulated learning. *Educational Psychology Review, 20*, 391–409.

Dunlosky, J. (1998). Epilogue. Linking metacognitive theories to education. In D. J. Hacker, J. Dunlosky, & A. C. Graesser (Eds.), *Metacognition in educational theory and practice* (pp. 367–381). Mahwah, NJ: Erlbaum.

Elshout, J. J., Veenman, M. V. J., & Van Hell, A. G. (1993). Using the computer as a help tool during learning by doing. *Computers in Education, 21*, 115–122.

Ericsson, K. A., & Simon, H. A. (1993). *Protocol analysis*. Cambridge: MIT Press.

Flavell, J. H. (1979). Metacognition and cognitive monitoring: A new area of cognitive-developmental inquiry. *American Psychologist, 34*, 906–911.

Glaser, R., Schauble, L., Raghavan, K., & Zeitz, C. (1992). Scientific reasoning across different domains. In E de Corte, M. C. Linn, H. Mandl, & L. Verschaffel (Eds.), *Computer-based learning environments and problem solving* (NATO ASI series F, Vol. 84, pp. 345–371). Heidelberg: Springer.

Greene, J. A., & Azevedo, R. (2010). The measurement of learners' self-regulated cognitive and metacognitive processes while using computer-based learning environments. *Educational Psychologist, 45*, 203–209.

Gress, C. L. Z., Fior, M., Hadwin, A. F., & Winne, P. H. (2010). Measurement and assessment in computer-supported collaborative learning. *Computers in Human Behavior, 26*, 806–814.

Hadwin, A. F., Nesbit, J. C., Jamieson-Noel, D., Code, J., & Winne, P. H. (2007). Examining trace data to explore self-regulated learning. *Metacognition and Learning, 2*, 107–124.

Kinnunen, R., & Vauras, M. (1995). Comprehension monitoring and the level of comprehension in high- and low-achieving primary school children's reading. *Learning and Instruction, 5*, 143–165.

Koriath, A., Ma'ayan, H., & Nussinson, R. (2006). The intricate relationships between monitoring and control in metacognition: Lessons for the cause-and-effect relation between subjective experience and behavior. *Journal of Experimental Psychology. General, 135*, 36–69.

Kunz, G. C., Drewniak, U., & Schott, F. (1992). On-line and off-line assessment of self-regulation in learning from instructional text. *Learning and Instruction, 2*, 287–301.

Nelson, T. O. (1996). Consciousness and metacognition. *American Psychologist, 51*, 102–116.

Nelson, T. O., & Narens, L. (1990). Metamemory: A theoretical framework and some new findings. In G. H. Bower (Ed.), *The psychology of learning and motivation* (Vol. 26, pp. 125–173). New York: Academic Press.

Pintrich, P. R., & De Groot, E. V. (1990). Motivational and self-regulated leaning components of classroom academic performance. *Journal of Educational Psychology, 82*, 33–40.

Pressley, M., & Afflerbach, P. (1995). *Verbal protocols of reading: The nature of constructively responsive reading*. Hillsdale, NJ: Erlbaum.

Pressley, M., & Gaskins, I. (2006). Metacognitive competent reading is constructively responsive reading: How can such reading be developed in students? *Metacognition and Learning, 1*, 99–113.

Schraw, G., & Dennison, R. S. (1994). Assessing metacognitive awareness. *Contemporary Educational Psychology, 19*, 460–475.

Snow, R. E. (1989). Aptitude-treatment interaction as a framework for research on individual differences in learning. In P. L. Ackerman, R. J. Sternberg, & R. Glaser (Eds.), *Learning and individual differences*.

Advances in theory and research (pp. 13–59). New York: Freeman.

Veenman, M. V. J. (1993). *Intellectual ability and metacognitive skill: determinants of discovery learning in computerized learning environments. Doctoral dissertation*. Amsterdam: University of Amsterdam.

Veenman, M. V. J. (2005). The assessment of metacognitive skills: What can be learned from multi-method designs? In C. Artelt & B. Moschner (Eds.), *Lernstrategien und metakognition: Implikationen für forschung und praxis* (pp. 75–97). Berlin: Waxmann.

Veenman, M. V. J. (2007). The assessment and instruction of self-regulation in computer-based environments: A discussion. *Metacognition and Learning, 2*, 177–183.

Veenman, M. V. J. (2008). Giftedness: Predicting the speed of expertise acquisition by intellectual ability and metacognitive skillfulness of novices. In M. F. Shaughnessy, M. V. J. Veenman, & C. Kleyn-Kennedy (Eds.), *Meta-cognition: A recent review of research, theory, and perspectives* (pp. 207–220). Hauppage: Nova.

Veenman, M. V. J. (2011). Learning to self-monitor and self-regulate. In R. Mayer & P. Alexander (Eds.), *Handbook of research on learning and instruction* (pp. 197–218). New York: Routledge.

Veenman, M. V. J., Elshout, J. J., & Groen, M. G. M. (1993). Thinking aloud: Does it affect regulatory processes in learning. *Tijdschrift voor Onderwijsresearch, 18*, 322–330.

Veenman, M. V. J., Elshout, J. J., & Meijer, J. (1997). The generality vs. domain-specificity of metacognitive skills in novice learning across domains. *Learning and Instruction, 7*, 187–209.

Veenman, M. V. J., Prins, F. J., & Verheij, J. (2003). Learning styles: Self-reports versus thinking-aloud measures. *British Journal of Educational Psychology, 73*, 357–372.

Veenman, M. V. J., Van Hout-Wolters, B. H. A. M., & Afflerbach, P. (2006). Metacognition and learning: Conceptual and methodological considerations. *Metacognition and Learning, 1*, 3–14.

Veenman, M. V. J., Wilhelm, P., & Beishuizen, J. J. (2004). The relation between intellectual and metacognitive skills from a developmental perspective. *Learning and Instruction, 14*, 89–109.

Wang, M. C., Haertel, G. D., & Walberg, H. J. (1990). What influences learning? A content analysis of review literature. *The Journal of Educational Research, 84*, 30–43.

Whitebread, D., Coltman, P., Pasternak, D. P., Sangster, C., Grau, V., & Bingham, S. (2009). The development of two observational tools for assessing metacognition and self-regulated learning in young children. *Metacognition and Learning, 4*, 63–85.

Wilhelm, P., Beishuizen, J. J., & Van Rijn, H. (2005). Studying inquiry learning with FILE. *Computers in Human Behavior, 21*, 933–943.

Winne, P. H. (1996). A metacognitive view of individual differences in self-regulated learning. *Learning and Individual Differences, 8*, 327–353.

Winne, P. H. (2010). Improving measurements of self-regulated learning. *Educational Psychologist, 45*, 267–276.

Winne, P. H., & Jamieson-Noel, D. (2002). Exploring students' calibrations of self reports about study tactics and achievement. *Contemporary Educational Psychology, 27*, 551–572.

Winters, F. I., Greene, J. A., & Costich, C. M. (2008). Self-regulation of learning with computer-based learning environments: A critical analysis. *Educational Psychology Review, 20*, 429–444.

Zimmerman, B. J., & Martinez-Pons, M. (1990). Student differences in self-regulated learning: Relating grade, sex, and giftedness to self-efficacy and strategy use. *Journal of Educational Psychology, 82*, 51–59.

Part III

Scaffolding Metacognition and Learning with Hypermedia and Hypertext

12 Scaffolding Hypermedia Learning Through Metacognitive Prompts

Maria Bannert and Christoph Mengelkamp

Abstract

The aim of this chapter is to discuss appropriate scaffolding for metacognitive reflection when learning with modern computer-based learning environments. Many researchers assume that prompting students for metacognitive reflection will affect the learning process by engaging students in more metacognitive behaviour leading to better learning performance. After defining basic constructs and assumptions, an overview of research on prompting metacognitive and self-regulated learning skills during hypermedia learning is presented. On the basis of this overview the design and effects of three kinds of metacognitive support (reflection prompts, metacognitive prompts, training & metacognitive prompts) are presented and discussed. In three experiments with university students, the experimental groups are supported by one of the types of metacognitive prompts, whereas the control groups are not supported. Analysis of learning processes and learning outcomes confirms the positive effects of all three types of metacognitive prompts; however their specific influence varies to a significant degree. The results and their explanations are in line with recent theories of metacognition and self-regulated learning. At the end of the chapter implications for the design of metacognitive support to improve hypermedia learning are discussed. Furthermore, implications for investigating metacognitive skills during hypermedia learning will be derived.

Introduction

Recent research in the field of self-regulated learning points out the crucial role of learners' strategic and metacognitive behaviour (e.g. Boekaerts, Pintrich, & Zeidner, 2000; Schunk & Zimmerman, 1998; Winne, 1996, 2001). Thus, successful learning is not a matter of trial and

M. Bannert (✉) • C. Mengelkamp
University of Wuerzburg, Educational Media, WU 97070, Germany
e-mail: maria.bannert@uni-wuerzburg.de

R. Azevedo and V. Aleven (eds.), *International Handbook of Metacognition and Learning Technologies*, Springer International Handbooks of Education 26, DOI 10.1007/978-1-4419-5546-3_12,

error but rather a set and specific sequence of metacognitive activities that has to be performed (e.g. Schnotz, 1998). Ideally, successful students perform different metacognitive activities during learning. First, they analyse the situation before they start processing the information. They will orient themselves by skimming the task description, instruction and resources, will specify the learning goals or even break them down into subgoals, and will plan the ongoing procedure. Based on this analysis the student has to search for relevant information and—especially crucial for self-regulated hypermedia learning—judge whether the information found is really relevant to reach the learning goals. The student then has to extract the information and elaborate it. At the end of the learning activity, the student has to evaluate the learning product, again with respect to the learning goals. These activities are constantly monitored and controlled.

Research of self-regulated learning reveals that many learners have difficulty performing these metacognitive activities spontaneously, which most probably results in lower learning outcomes (Bannert, 2007; Zumbach & Bannert, 2006). So, the key issue of the research project is to develop effective metacognitive instructions, also suggested by other researchers (e.g. Azevedo & Hadwin, 2005; Kramarski & Feldman, 2000). One promising form of instructional support seems to be the use of metacognitive prompts, since they should focus learners' attention on their own thoughts and on understanding the activities in which they are engaged during the course of learning (Lin, 2001; Lin & Lehman, 1999). Hence it is assumed that prompting students to reflect upon their own way of learning will allow them to activate their repertoire of metacognitive knowledge and skills, which will further enhance hypermedia learning and transfer.

Approaches of Metacognition and Metacognitive Instruction

The obvious definition of *metacognition* is that of cognition about cognition, and the function of metacognition is to regulate one's own cognition (Flavell, 1979). More precisely Nelson and Narens (1992) divided cognition into an object level and a meta level. On the meta level a learner builds a mental model of the object level. In multimedia research we use the term mental model to describe analogous mental representations of external representations such as a mental model about a machine (Schnotz & Bannert, 2003). In case of metacognition the mental model is built from the object level, that is, the cognition of the person her/himself. The processes leading to such a mental model of one's own cognition are named *monitoring,* whereas processes that alter the cognition at the object level are named *control.* To sum up, metacognition is defined recursively as cognition about cognition. This implies a mental model of one's own cognition (the meta level) that is acquired and altered during monitoring processes whereas control processes alter the cognition.

In research about metacognition a distinction has been made between metacognitive knowledge and metacognitive skills (e.g. Ertmer & Newby, 1996; Schraw, 2001). On the one hand, *metacognitive knowledge* refers to the individual's declarative knowledge about learning strategies as well as person and task characteristics that are relevant in order to master a specific situation (Flavell & Wellman, 1977). On the other hand, *metacognitive skills* refer to the self-regulation activities taken place in learning and problem solving (Brown, 1978; Veenman, 2005). Some researchers add a third category named *metacognitive experiences* (Efklides, 2008; Flavell, 1979) or *metacognitive judgments and monitoring* (Pintrich, Wolters, & Baxter, 2000). Metacognitive feelings and judgments belong to this category: feelings of knowing, feelings of difficulty, judgments of knowing, judgments of learning, confidence judgments, etc. According to Efklides these feelings and judgments trigger the metacognitive skills, that is, a person feels or judges that there are problems in the learning process and thus begins to use their metacognitive skills. In this research the focus lies on these metacognitive skills of students. There are different processes subsumed to metacognitive skills like goal setting, orientation, planning, strategy selection and use, monitoring the execution of strategies, checking, and reflection (e.g. Pintrich et al., 2000; Veenman, 2005). In this chapter we present results concerning the support of orientation, planning, reflection, and evaluation, and monitoring of strategies using prompts.

In general, *metacognitive support* aims to increase students' learning competence by means of systematic instruction in order to improve significantly his or her learning performance. Reviewing current metacognitive training research (e.g. Schunk & Zimmerman, 1998; Veenman, Van-Hout-Wolters, Afflerbach, 2006; Weinstein, Husman, & Dierking, 2000), there are some general principles for effective metacognitive instruction:

- First of all, metacognitive instruction should be *integrated* in the domain-specific instruction. Thus, metacognitive activities should not be taught separately as an end of itself but embedded in the subject matter.
- Secondly, the application and usefulness of instructed metacognitive strategies have to be *explained*; otherwise students will not use them spontaneously.
- And, last but not least, it is important that *sufficient training time* is allotted in order to implement and automate the metacognitive activities just learned.

Another distinction is made by Friedrich and Mandl (1992) with respect to the level of directness of instructional measures:

- *Direct support* teaches learning strategies explicitly to the students, that is, the strategies are explained and students practice the use of the strategies. Direct metacognitive support is realised by metacognitive training, which focuses explicitly on teaching metacognitive skills and metacognitive knowledge (e.g. Hasselhorn, 1995).
- In contrast *indirect support* measures are embedded into the learning environment, that is, the learning environment is designed in order to promote the use of certain strategies without explaining them explicitly. Metacognitive indirect support offers adequate learning heuristics to the students embedded into the learning environment, which are not explicitly taught. Student's focus lies on knowledge acquisition on a learning domain and not on metacognitive knowledge and skills per se. The integrated learning heuristics, e.g. metacognitive prompts (Bannert, 2009), stimulate students to apply their metacognitive skills adequately.

The decision whether to design direct or indirect metacognitive instruction strongly depends on the student's metacognitive competence. Whereas extensive training is necessary for students lacking metacognitive competence, the so-called *mediation deficit* (e.g. Hasselhorn, 1995), metacognitive prompts seem to be an adequate measure for students already possessing these skills, but who do not perform them spontaneously, the so-called *production deficit*. The target group of this research project are university students who should already possess the metacognitive skills outlined above due to their wide learning experiences (Paris & Newman, 1990; Veenman et al., 2006). Hence, we assume that unsuccessful hypermedia learning of this target group is more a matter of a production deficit than a mediation deficit. Nevertheless, this is ours and the cited author's assumption and not an empirical fact. But if we can show that indirect support fosters learning without teaching the required skills explicitly this would give some support for our assumption. Under this assumption it is reasonable that indirect support combined with a short-term intervention should foster learning effectively without more time-demanding direct support.

The aim of this research approach is to provide metacognitive support to improve self-regulated learning, especially when learning with hypermedia. Although metacognitive knowledge and skills are needed when learning without new learning technology, such technology makes the students' reflective behaviour about their own way of learning more salient (Azevedo, 2005, 2009; Lin, 2001; Lin, Hmelo, Kinzer, & Secules, 1999). For example, in a hypermedia learning environment a successful learner continuously has to decide where to go next and constantly has to evaluate how the information retrieved is related to his/her actual learning goal (Schnotz, 1998). Considering that many students have difficulties in strategic and metacognitive learning behaviour (e.g. Simons & De Jong, 1992), the aim of our research is to provide appropriate scaffolding for metacognitive reflection when learning with hypermedia.

Scaffolding Metacognitive Skills Through Prompts

We define *prompts* as recall and/or performance aids, which vary from general questions (e.g. "what is your plan?") to explicit execution instructions (e.g. "calculate first 2 + 2"; Bannert, 2009). They are all based on the central assumption that students already possess the concept and/or processes, but do not recall or execute them spontaneously. *Instructional prompts* and *instructional prompting* are measures to induce and stimulate cognitive, metacognitive, motivational, volitional, and/or cooperative activities during learning (Bannert, 2009). They may stimulate the recall of concepts and procedures (e.g. by presenting the cognitive prompt: "What are the basic concepts of Skinner's operant learning theory?"), or induce the execution of procedures, tactics, and techniques during learning (e.g. by offering a cognitive prompt: "First, calculate the percentage of different countries, then compare."), or even induce the use of cognitive and metacognitive learning strategies (e.g. by presenting a metacognitive prompt: "Is this in line with my learning goal?") as well as strategies of resource management (e.g. with motivational prompts: "What are the benefits?" or by presenting group coordination prompts, "Decide first who is the editor, the writer, the reviewer").

Instructional prompts differ from prototypical instructional approaches since they do not teach new information, but rather support the recall and execution of student's knowledge and skills. They are often included as support measures in instruction, which is aimed at knowledge acquisition. As illustrated in the few examples presented above instructional prompts include explicit statements that students have to consider during learning and thus differ from worksheets (without such statements) or worked examples.

Paralleling the classification of learning strategies as cognitive learning strategies, metacognitive learning strategies, and resource management strategies (e.g. Weinstein & Mayer, 1986), instructional prompts are classified in this chapter as *cognitive prompts* if they directly support a student's processing of information, for example by stimulating memorising/rehearsal, elaboration, organisation, and/or reduction of learning material (e.g. Nückles, Hübner, & Renkl, 2009). *Metacognitive prompts* are generally intended to support a student's monitoring and control of their information processing by inducing metacognitive and regulative activities, such as orientation, goal specification, planning, monitoring, and control as well as evaluation strategies (Bannert, 2007; Veenman, 1993). *Prompts for resource management* ask the learner to ensure optimal learning conditions, such as to have all necessary learning resources at one's disposal or to organise a well-performing learning group. As our research does not contribute to this issue prompts for resource management are not considered in the following.

To sum up, metacognitive prompts are instructional measures integrated in the learning context that ask students to carry out specific metacognitive activities. In the study of Lin and Lehman (1999) students were prompted at certain times by a pop-up window in a computer simulation, to give reasons for their actions when carrying out experiments in biology. For example, before they started the experiment they first had to answer the question "What is your plan?", "How did you decide that …?", etc. stimulating students to perform planning and monitoring activities, which are major metacognitive skills as introduced above. All metacognitive prompts were explained and their usage was trained several weeks before the experiment was conducted. Lin and Lehman obtained significantly higher far-transfer performance for students learning with those prompts compared to the students of the control group learning without prompts.

In the experiments of Veenman (1993), students were also prompted in a simulation environment to perform several metacognitive regulation activities, e.g. to reflect on the results based on the predictions made before the experiment was conducted. These experiments also showed positive significant learning effects for high-ability learners.

Simons and De Jong (1992) carried out several studies in which students had to practice with certain learning questions, "Do I understand this part?" and "Is this in line with the learning goal?", and learning techniques, e.g. reflection and self-testing. To sum up, they found these learning heuristics effective, especially for older and high-ability students with prior knowledge.

Stark and Krause (2009) investigated the impact of reflective prompts on learning in the domain of statistics using learning material with worked examples. Participants were allowed to decide for each learning task if they wanted to see the worked examples right away or after solving the learning task. Participants in the experimental group were prompted to justify each of their decisions whereas the controls were not prompted. Participants from the prompted group outperformed participants in the control group in solving complex tasks immediately after learning and in a follow-up test but they were not more successful in simple tasks.

Kauffman, Ge, Xie, and Chen (2008) combined cognitive prompts for problem solving with metacognitive prompts for reflection in a Web-based learning environment. Novice students were asked to solve two case studies about classroom management and to present their solution in an e-mail message to a fictive teacher of the class. Problem-solving prompts had an effect on the quality of the solutions and on the quality of writing, whereas prompts for reflection had an effect only for those participants who had received the problem-solving prompts before. Thus, reflection prompts were effective if there was a clear understanding of what participants were asked to reflect on, namely, the problem-solving process that was prompted before.

Stadtler and Bromme (2008) used metacognitive prompts during a search task about medical information in preselected Websites. Laypersons were prompted either to monitor their comprehension or to evaluate the source of the information or both. There were positive effects of monitoring prompts on knowledge about facts and small effects on comprehension. The monitoring prompts may have fostered the detection of comprehension failures and inconsistencies and thus enabled the laypersons to control and optimise their information processing. Evaluation prompts had an effect on the recalled information concerning the sources of the information, that is, participants were more aware of the quality of the information they collected during the task. The results support the conclusion that different metacognitive prompts trigger different learning behaviour.

The effect of prompting over the course of time was investigated in a study by Sitzmann, Bell, Kraiger, and Kanar (2009) in which participants learned about a learning platform over ten sessions in an online learning environment. Participants were randomly assigned to three groups: continuous prompting, prompting in the last five sessions, and no prompting. Participants were prompted concerning their monitoring and evaluation using short questions, which had to be answered on a 5-point-scale (e.g. "Are the study tactics I have been using effective for learning the training material?"). For the continuous prompting group learning performance increased during the first four sessions and then levelled off, whereas for the prompting in the last five sessions group learning performance increased after the prompts were introduced. By contrast, the learning performance of the controls declined over the ten sessions. Results were replicated in a second experiment with different learning material. Additionally, cognitive ability and specific self-efficacy moderated the prompting effects, that is, participants with high cognitive abilities and high specific self-efficacy benefitted more from the prompts than participants with lower cognitive abilities or self-efficacy.

Sitzmann and Ely (2010) prompted their participants while learning about Excel in an online course using metacognitive and motivational/

volitional prompts, e.g. "Do I understand all of the key points of the training material?" or "Am I focusing my mental effort on the training material?" Participants had to answer these questions on a 5-point scale. There were five experimental groups: prompts prior to the training, prompts in all four modules of the training, prompts in the first two modules, prompts in the second two modules, and no prompts. Results showed that participants who were prompted continuously had higher learning outcome and less attrition. This effect was mediated by learning time but surprisingly not by strategy use as measured by a questionnaire. Instead, continuous prompting moderated the effect of learning performance on subsequent strategy use and attrition. That is, continuous prompts prevented learners with low learning performance from dropping out and from reducing their strategy use. Therefore, continuously prompting learners may give them the feeling that they can control their learning, leading to less attrition and more strategy use in subsequent learning phases.

As illustrated by these prompting studies, metacognitive prompts require students to explicitly reflect, monitor, and revise the learning process. They focus students' attention on their own thoughts and on understanding the activities in which they are engaged during the course of learning. Hence it is assumed that prompting students to plan, monitor, and evaluate their own way of learning will allow them to activate their repertoire of metacognitive knowledge and strategies which will as a consequence enhance self-regulated learning and transfer.

Experimental Studies on Metacognitive Prompts

The aim of this research approach is to provide metacognitive support to improve self-regulated learning, especially when learning with hypermedia. The prompting studies outlined above mainly investigate the effects of metacognitive prompts on learning performance by comparing experimentally the effects of metacognitive prompts vs. no prompts (e.g. Veenman, 1993), metacognitive vs. cognitive prompts (Kauffman et al., 2008; Nückles et al., 2009), or metacognitive vs. motivational prompts (e.g. Lin & Lehman, 1999; Sitzmann & Ely, 2010). So far there is little research investigating the effects of different types of metacognitive prompts. Thus, the question of our research is whether different kinds of metacognitive support would lead to different effects in hypermedia learning environments. In particular we asked whether different kinds of metacognitive support will influence the *learning process* by engaging students in different metacognitive behaviour and if they will increase *learning performance.*

Table 12.1 Overview of the three experiments

Experiment	Experimental manipulation
Study 1: Reflection prompts (see Bannert, 2006)	EG = Reflection prompts (n = 24) CG = without (n = 22)
Study 2: Metacognitive prompts (see Bannert, 2005a)	EG = Metacognitive prompts (n = 20) CG = without (n = 20)
Study 3: Training and metacognitive prompts (see Bannert, 2003)	EG = Training + metacognitive prompts (n = 20) CG = without (n = 20)

Design and Effects of Different Types of Metacognitive Prompts

In this research project effects of a range of related types of metacognitive prompts were analysed experimentally using similar design, procedure, and material. In general, the metacognitive support provides prompts stimulating or even suggesting appropriate activities that must be followed by students before, during, and at the end of the learning session. No metacognitive help is offered in the control groups. Three experimental studies (outlined in Table 12.1) were conducted. In this chapter only the main idea, procedures, and results of the different studies will be sketched in order to discuss the main findings with regard to the design and evaluation of effective metacognitive tools supporting self-regulated learning in computer-based leaning environments (CBLEs).

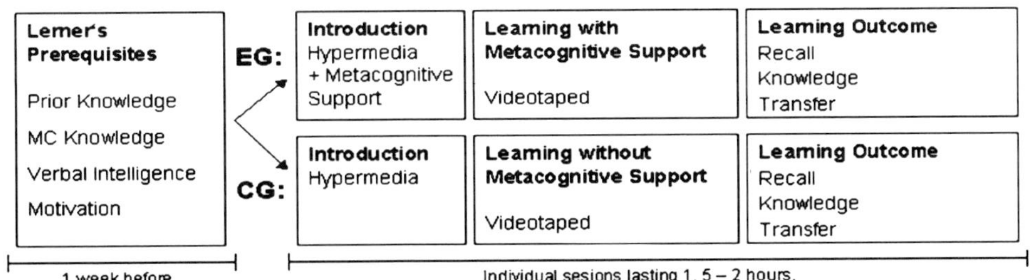

Fig. 12.1 Design and procedure of the experimental studies

Description of Specific Context, Sample, System, and Methods Used

Study 1: Reflection Prompts. 46 undergraduate university students majoring in Psychology and Education participated (mean age = 24.3; *SD* = 5.23; female: 84.8%) Participants were matched according to prior knowledge, metacognitive knowledge, and verbal intelligence and afterwards randomly assigned to one of the two treatments. Students in the experimental group, the so-called *reflection prompting group* (*n* = 24), were prompted by the experimenter to say out loud the reasons why they chose this specific information node. At each navigation step they had to complete the prompted statement "I am choosing this page because …". Students' reasons for node selection were for example "because to get an overview", "because to make a plan", or "because to monitor learning", but also "because I just want to go back" or "because I don't know where I am". Students were completely free in completing the prompted statements. Students in the *control group* (*n* = 22) learned silently, i.e. without such reflection prompting.

Study 2: Metacognitive Prompts. 40 undergraduate university students majoring in Psychology and Education (mean age = 22.13, *SD* = 3.31; female: 67.5%) were randomly assigned to the treatments according to the same learner characteristics as obtained in Study 1. Students in the experimental group, the so-called *metacognitive prompting group* (*n* = 20), were prompted by a pop-up window for metacognitive activities that have to be followed during learning. The metacognitive help was designed to initiate and support orientation, planning, and goal specification activities at the beginning of the learning phase, monitoring and regulation activities during learning, and evaluation activities at the end of learning. Before students started learning, the first prompt requested students to orientate themselves, to specify the learning goals, and to make a plan. During learning (15 min afterwards) they were prompted to judge whether the information they processed was really relevant. They were then prompted to monitor and regulate their learning, e.g. to respond to the prompt "Do I understand the section? Am I still on time?" About 7 min before the end of the learning phase, students were prompted to evaluate their learning outcome, for instance by prompting them to check whether the learning goals were reached. No metacognitive support was offered in the control group (*n* = 20).

Study 3: Training and Metacognitive Prompts. 40 undergraduate university students majoring in different fields (mean age = 22.98, *SD* = 3.63; female: 72.5%) were randomly assigned to the treatments according to the same learner characteristics as obtained in Study 1. Students in the experimental group, the so-called *training and metacognitive prompts group* (*n* = 20), were prompted by pop-up windows for metacognitive activities that had to be followed during learning. In contrast to Study 2, these metacognitive activities were explained in detail, demonstrated, and practiced during a short training period right before the learning session. No metacognitive support was offered to the control group (*n* = 20).

Procedure, Material, and Instruments

Figure 12.1 visualises the general procedure of all three experiments. About 1 week before the

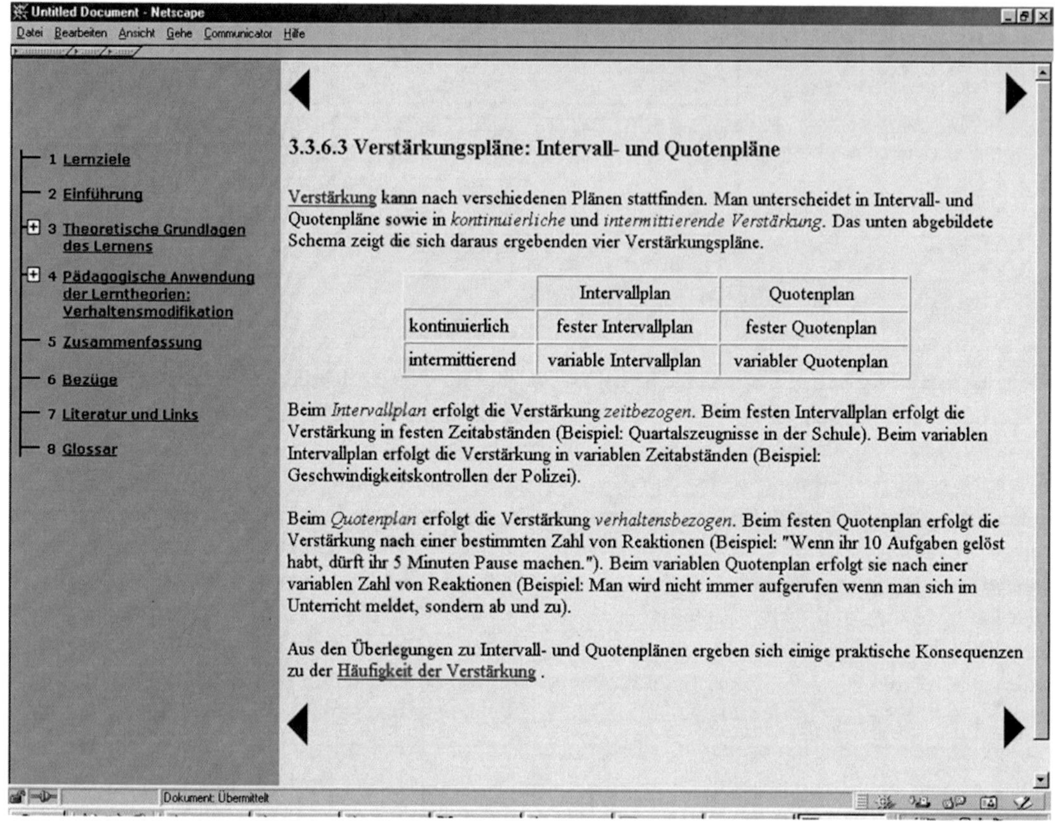

Fig. 12.2 Screen capture of the hypermedia system. The learning content was arranged hierarchically, and participants had three possibilities to navigate throughout the program: (**a**) a hierarchical table of contents placed at the left part of the screen, (**b**) a guided tour with buttons for the next and the previous page, (**c**) associatively via hotwords that were placed in the text

experiment started learner characteristics were obtained by questionnaires. Prior knowledge was measured by a self-developed multiple-choice test, metacognitive knowledge by a modified version of the LIST-questionnaire (Wild, Schiefele, & Winteler, 1992—similar to MSQL, Pintrich, Smith, Garcia, & McKeachi, 1993), verbal intelligence by IST 2000 (Amthauer, Brocke, Liepmann, & Beauducel, 1999), and motivation for achievement and fear of failure by LMT (Hermans, Petermann, & Zielinski, 1978).

All experiments began with an *introduction phase* during which students learned how to navigate the hypermedia program (see Fig. 12.2). Afterwards students in the experimental group of Study 1 were introduced to the method of reflection prompts in a short training period lasting a total of 10 min. All students of Study 2 and Study 3 were introduced to the method of reading and thinking aloud (Ericsson & Simon, 1993). To students of the experimental group of Study 3 metacognitive activities were explained in detail, demonstrated, and practiced in a short training period right before the learning session lasting a total of 20 min. To practice with the different kinds of metacognitive support students in all studies had to carry out several search tasks within another topic of the learning environment.

Following this, the *learning session* began. Students had to learn basic concepts of Learning Theories (Study 1 and 2) or Motivational Psychology (Study 3) within a fixed time interval (30, 35, or 45 min). The experimental groups received metacognitive support as sketched above. Students of all treatment groups were completely free in navigating the hypermedia program during their learning sessions, which were videotaped. In Study 2 and 3 they had to read and think aloud during the whole learning sessions.

Immediately after the learning session, learning outcomes were measured by questionnaires. *Free recall* was measured by counting the basic terms and concepts students wrote down on a blank paper sheet. *Knowledge* attained was measured by a multiple-choice test including 19 or 22 items, each with 1 correct and 3 false alternatives. *Transfer* was measured by asking students to apply the basic concepts and principles just learned to solve prototypical problems in educational settings. Answers of 8 items were rated based on a self-developed rating scheme (interrater agreement—Kappa = 0.74). The experiments were conducted in individual learning sessions, which took about 1.5–2 h.

Comparisons of Different Types of Prompts

Metacognitive Activities During Learning

To test whether metacognitive support increased metacognitive behaviour during learning, for Study 1 the LIST metacognition scale was analysed, which was used retrospectively (see Table 12.2). For Study 2 and 3 the video-protocols were analysed to determine the quality with which the students actually performed different activities (listed in Table 12.2). Here *analysis* subsumes orientation, planning, and goal setting activities, which mainly take place at the beginning of learning. *Searching and judgement* includes strategic searching behaviour and judging information's relevance in respect to the learning goals, *evaluation* refers to activities that are conducted in order to check whether the learning goals are reached, and *regulation* refers to monitoring and controlling activities that took place during learning. Zero points were given when the activity was not performed at all during the learning session, and 2 points were given when it was performed in optimal quality. For instance, with regard to the category "analysis: goal setting activities", a student would receive 2 points if she reflected on learning goals, broke them down into adequate subgoals, and wrote them down. A score of 1 point was given when the activity was performed in a wrong way. For example, a student would be given a score of 1 if she/he reflected on the learning goals very superficially by just repeating the instruction, did not articulate subgoals, and did not write down any learning goals. Interrater agreement of two independent raters was Kappa = 0.83 (due to economical reasons, the Kappa statistic was obtained for a subset of 27 subjects).

As one can see in Table 12.2, the experimental treatments differ only with respect to the online measures obtained in Study 2 and 3, but not for the metacognition scale used in Study 1. In Study 2 and 3 students learning with metacognitive support performed the metacognitive activities significantly better. The biggest effect is obtained for analysis activities (i.e. orientation, goal specification, planning), i.e. students in the experimental prompting groups showed more planning activities, whereas students of the control groups often failed to do so. All differences are significant (t-tests for independent groups), except the activities search and judgement in Study 2 and regulation in Study 3. Thus, students of the experimental groups had higher scores on those measures that they were explicitly instructed to fulfil. With respect to metacognitive training research, this result is far from trivial. Often students in the experimental group fail to carry out the instructed metacognitive activities (see also the section about compliance below). Moreover, students in the (non-instructed) control groups could also show these metacognitive activities spontaneously (Bannert, 2005b).

Learning Performance

Table 12.2 also presents the mean performance scores of recall, knowledge, and transfer tasks for each study. As hypothesised, t-test for independent groups revealed a significant effect for the transfer tasks in Study 1 and 3; however no effects were obtained for recall and knowledge test performance in all studies. A similar result was found in the study of Lin and Lehman (1999),

Table 12.2 Main results of experiments

Study 1: Reflection prompts				
	EG (n=24) M (*SD*)	CG (n=24) M (*SD*)	$t_{(38)}$	d
Metacognitive activities obtained by questionnaire				
Metacognition scale	25.83 (5.85)	25.36 (4.37)	0.306	0.09
Learning performance				
Recall	12.14 (5.39)	11.54 (4.23)	–0.418	–0.13
Knowledge	13.96 (3.19)	14.17 (4.05)	0.196	0.06
Transfer	17.77 (3.84)	20.21 (4.73)	*3.640**	*0.55*
Study 2: Metacognitive prompts				
	EG (n=20) M (*SD*)	CG (n=20) M (*SD*)	$t_{(38)}$	d
Metacognitive activities obtained by process analysis				
Analysis	1.55 (0.50)	0.79 (0.57)	*4.445****	*1.17*
Search and Judgement	1.53 (0.70)	1.24 (0.83)	1.142	0.39
Evaluation	1.70 (0.57)	1.05 (0.97)	*2.522***	*0.76*
Regulation	1.40 (0.60)	0.72 (0.83)	*2.917***	*0.87*
Learning performance				
Recall	15.45 (6.27)	13.90 (7.30)	0.720	0.20
Knowledge	15.65 (3.79)	15.55 (4.62)	0.075	0.00
Transfer	2,323 (5.45)	20.73 (6.17)	1.358	0.43
Study 3: Training and metacognitive prompts				
	EG (n=20) M (*SD*)	CG (n=20) M (*SD*)	$t_{(38)}$	d
Metacognitive activities obtained by process analysis				
Analysis	1.43 (0.60)	1.02 (0.44)	*2.498***	*0.73*
Search and Judgement	1.80 (0.52)	1.35 (0.75)	*2.210**	*0.66*
Evaluation	1.65 (0.49)	1.25 (0.85)	*1.823**	*0.56*
Regulation	1.55 (0.69)	1.30 (0.73)	1.114	0.35
Learning performance				
Recall	11.00 (2.85)	11.65 (3.03)	–0.699	0.02
Knowledge	13.00 (2.64)	13.60 (2.50)	–0,739	0.02
Transfer	23.25 (5.28)	20.05 (5.40)	*1.894**	*0.58*

EG=Learning with metacognitive support; CG=Learning without metacognitive support. Metacognitive activities Study 1 obtained by questionnaire. Metacognitive activities Study 2 and 3 obtained by thinking aloud: max=2, optimal performance; min=0, no performance
$^*p<0.05$, $^{**}p<0.01$, $^{***}p<0.001$, one-tailed

discussed above. They only found a significant effect for far-transfer, and not for near-transfer, tasks. Similarly, Stark and Krause (2009) obtained effects for complex but not for simple tasks. Lin and Lehman's explanation is that solving far-transfer tasks and complex tasks requires deeper understanding and therefore these kinds of tasks are affected the most by metacognitive activities. There was no significant transfer performance effect obtained in Study 2. This unexpected result will be considered in more detail with regard to compliance below.

Compliance and Learning Performance in the Experimental Prompting Groups

Since there is empirical evidence that students often do not use support tools offered in CBLEs as intended (e.g. Clarebout & Elen, 2006) we conducted the following analyses. Video-protocols of three experimental groups were analysed with

Table 12.3 Learning transfer performance by compliance (only experimental groups)

	Complied M (*SD*)	Not complied M (*SD*)	$t_{(18)}$	*d*
Study 1:	(*n*=12)	(*n*=12)		
Reflection prompts	23.08 (4.44)	17.33 (2.99)	*3.719****	*1.92*
Study 2:	(*n*=8)	(*n*=12)		
Metacognitive prompts	26.81 (5.58)	20.83 (3.99)	*2.803**	*1.10*
Study 3:	(*n*=9)	(*n*=11)		
Training and metacognitive prompts	27.00 (3.24)	20.18 (4.64)	*3.718***	*1.29*

Complied = metacognitive support complied; not complied = metacognitive support not complied
*$p<0.05$, **$p<0.01$, ***$p<0.001$, one-tailed

respect to how well the learners complied with the metacognitive support and how well they performed the activity suggested by each prompt. According to this analysis two groups were distinguished within each experimental group, one containing the students who optimally complied with the metacognitive support and one containing the other students who did not comply or complied but not in the intended way. For each group transfer performance was calculated separately. As one can see in Table 12.3, the groups differed significantly with respect to their compliance. Thus, offering metacognitive support is not sufficient; specific care has to be taken that these instructional prompts are performed in the intended manner in order to increase learning outcomes.

But what are the reasons that only half of the experimental groups, or even less than half, complied fully with the prompts? Surely this is due to the rather short introduction, and an extension of the training time would have improved compliance with metacognitive support, as the general principles for effective metacognitive instruction mentioned above suggest. Looking for specific learner characteristics we found that in all studies there were no significant differences in intelligence and motivation between the compliant and the non-compliant students. In Study 2 prior knowledge corresponds with compliance, that is, students who complied optimally had significantly higher prior knowledge. However, this prior knowledge effect did not occur in Study 1, and much more interestingly, because of the similar metacognitive prompting, also did not occur in Study 3. Thus, it seems that the metacognitive support realised in Study 2 requires a certain amount of prior knowledge in order to achieve better learning outcomes. We assume that these metacognitive prompts cause additional cognitive load, which could be partly compensated by sufficient prior knowledge, i.e. a flexible knowledge base (see Valcke, 2002, for a discussion of metacognitive load and prior knowledge). The more direct support in Study 3 (training + metacognitive prompting), however, seems to compensate for low prior knowledge. We assume that the short training based on Cognitive Apprenticeship principles dealing with the metacognitive prompts in advance reduced students' specific cognitive load during learning.

Discussion and Implications for Further Research

Results of our three experimental prompting studies are in accordance with the assumptions derived from the recent research on metacognition sketched above. Participants of the experimental groups supported by metacognitive prompts performed more metacognitive activities during learning. They also showed better transfer performance, especially if they complied with the offered support in the intended way.

But why are the effects found in transfer performance only? We suggest that the processes in metacognition stimulated deep elaboration (cf. Craik & Lockhart, 1972), and that deep elaboration is a prerequisite for solving transfer problems. Firstly, let us define transfer as the solution of a problem in a new situation that was not part of the learning material (cf.

Detterman, 1993). For example, one of our transfer tasks described a situation in which the behaviour of children is reinforced by their parents. As there was no such situation in the learning material (rather, experiments with rats were mentioned), the subjects "behaviour of children" and "parents" were new to the learners. According to the theory of structure mapping and analogies (Gentner, 1983, 1998) transfer requires that relations between elements have to be applied to new elements. In our example the relation between the behaviour of rats and the food, that is, the principle of reinforcement, has to be applied to the behaviour of children and the reinforcers given by the parents. One prerequisite for transfer is a deep understanding of relations between elements mentioned in the learning material rather than encoding the elements in an unrelated manner or associating them loosely to each other. According to our data about the learning process in experiments 2 and 3, analysis and evaluation of the learning content were stimulated by the prompts (see Table 12.2). Therefore the prompts stimulated the processing of the learning content in more depth, that is, more relations were encoded in long-term memory and transfer is more likely.

Design of Metacognitive Prompting Intervention

By means of a comprehensive video analysis it was shown that only half of the supported sample has dealt with the metacognitive support in an optimal manner. Consequently, it has to be investigated why students do not comply with the metacognitive support. Recent research is beginning to address the question why support devices are often ignored or inadequately used by students (e.g. Bannert, Hildebrand, & Mengelkamp, 2009; Clarebout & Elen, 2006).

To prove the basic assumption of students' production deficit as mentioned above (Veenman, van Hout-Wolters, & Afflerbach, 2006; Winne, 1996) further investigation into whether the prompts really affect the assumed quantitative and also qualitative improvements in strategy use are necessary. In this context, researchers in this field need to incorporate more in-depth process analysis procedures in their studies to determine how students are really dealing with the presented prompts (Bannert, 2007b; Greene & Azevedo, 2010; Veenman, 2007). For future research, we suggest that descriptive studies based on multi-method assessment methods (e.g. log-file, eye-movement, thinking aloud, and error analysis) need to be conducted more often. By increasing the sample size of the treatment group more statistical power is available for post hoc analyses that compare students with optimal compliance with prompts—if they are present—with students who fail. This comparison would provide richer insights than experimental studies in which nothing is done to assess the actual strategies that are used during the learning processes. Experiments that focus on outcomes and fail to include process analysis seldom directly answer questions such as whether, why, and in what quality and quantity the manipulated prompts are being utilised by the students that are dealing with them. Missing effects in the learning outcome may also be explained by the students' spontaneous use of strategies in the control group or by undesired or unanticipated effects of the prompting conditions. In brief, we have to further investigate if and how prompts are actually intervening in a student's learning process (Bannert, 2009).

In this study some students reported after learning that they felt restricted in their own way of learning when they had to consider the demanded activities asked by metacognitive support. Most probably these interventions require additional cognitive capacities, which may also be true for tool use in general (e.g. Calvi & deBra, 1997). We assume that metacognitive prompts cause additional cognitive load, which could be partly compensated by sufficient prior knowledge, i.e. a flexible knowledge base (Sweller, van Merrienboer, & Paas, 1998; Valcke, 2002).

Lack of appropriate responses to prompts can possibly be explained by students' individual characteristics. Perhaps students' prior knowledge was too low and, hence, they may be overloaded by additional prompts. Or maybe students' prior knowledge was quite high, so they did not require any strategy support at all. Also students' metacognitive knowledge and skills could have affected the adequate use of prompts. The motivational aspects of learning when paired with meta/cognitive variables is another important consideration on the impact of prompts. In this context, care needs to be taken to ascertain whether students are really convinced that complying with the prompts will improve their learning; otherwise they will not use them (Bannert, 2007b; Veenman et al., 2006). Moreover, although there is usually sufficient training with regard to strategy use in advance, feedback on adequate strategy use is rarely provided for students, which may decrease the quantity of prompt usage and may, moreover, impede the quality of their prompted strategy use. This assumption is partly supplied by the work of Roll, Aleven, McLaren, and Koedinger (2007) who provided immediate feedback on students' help-seeking behaviour with an intelligent tutoring system. There was a lasting improvement on students' help-seeking behaviour and transfer of the behaviour across different learning domains (Roll, Aleven, McLaren, & Koedinger, 2011), though no improvement in domain learning.

This research focused on instructional measures with very short intervention. In further studies we will investigate whether an extension of the training time will improve compliance with the metacognitive support (e.g. Bannert et al., 2009). In addition, other kinds of metacognitive support, such as adaptive metacognitive prompting by means of pedagogical agents (e.g. Azevedo & Witherspoon, 2009), will be developed and evaluated experimentally.

Moreover, one has to point out that the structure of the hypermedia system was well designed. It included a guided tour, a hierarchical navigation menu, an advanced organiser, a summary, and a glossary. Additionally, it was the so-called closed environment, that is, it did not contain links to external nodes. Furthermore, the learning tasks already included specific learning goals so that generally the learning scenarios were not very complex. We assume that greater effects will be obtained for more complex, open-ended environments.

Analytical Techniques and Methodological Approaches

Metacognitive support such as prompts during hypermedia learning can lead to better learning outcomes (in particular, transfer), but there is a significant amount of non-compliance, suggesting that this kind of support might be even more successful if care is taken that these instructional prompts are performed in the intended manner. Maybe this is one major reason why metacognitive instruction often has no positive effects on learning outcome (e.g. Graesser, Wiley, Goldman, O'Reilly, Jeon, & McDaniel, 2007; Manlove, Lazonder, & De Jong, 2007). In future research one has to control whether students who were instructed and trained to apply metacognitive strategies will really apply them in the transfer session.

Finally, it has to be pointed out that without process analysis (by using thinking-aloud methods) a different picture would have emerged. In Study 2 and 3 we asked students to judge their strategic learning activities retrospectively by means of a questionnaire. In accordance with Veenman's review (Veenman, 2005), there was no significant correlation between the scales of questionnaires and the activities obtained by the video analysis. Moreover, no significant correlation was obtained between the questionnaire and learning performance. Even though it is rather time consuming, it is necessary to include process analysis in further research on metacognitive support and self-regulated learning (Bannert & Mengelkamp, 2007; Hofer, 2004; Veenman, 2007).

Recent prompting research is progressing rapidly. Overall, we argue that future research has to conduct more in-depth process analysis that incorporates multi-method assessments and, besides cognitive and metacognitive aspects, to account for individual learner characteristics such as motivation and volition. Prompting research, at present, needs more insight into how students actually deal with learning prompts in order to design more individual support and with that to offer more effective types of prompts to the learners.

Acknowledgement This research was supported by funds from the German Science Foundation (DFG: BA 2044/1-1, BA 2044/5-1).

References

Amthauer, R., Brocke, B., Liepmann, D., & Beauducel, A. (1999). *IST 2000—Intelligenz-Struktur-Test 2000.* Göttingen: Hogrefe.

Azevedo, R. (2005). Using hypermedia as a metacognitive tool for enhancing student learning? The role of self-regulated learning. *Educational Psychologist, 40,* 199–209.

Azevedo, R. (2009). Theoretical, conceptual, methodological, and instructional issues in research on metacognition and self-regulated learning: A discussion. *Metacognition and Learning, 4,* 87–95.

Azevedo, R., & Hadwin, A. F. (2005). Scaffolding self-regulated learning and metacognition: Implications for the design of computer-based scaffolds. *Instructional Science, 33,* 367–379. Special Issue on Scaffolding Self-Regulated Learning and Metacognition: Implications for the Design of Computer-Based Scaffolds.

Azevedo, R., & Witherspoon, A. M. (2009). Self-regulated learning with hypermedia. In D. J. Hacker, J. Dunlosky, & A. C. Graesser (Eds.), *Handbook of metacognition in education* (pp. 319–339). Mahwah, NJ: Routledge.

Bannert, M. (2003). Effekte metakognitiver Lernhilfen auf den Wissenserwerb in vernetzten Lernumgebungen [Effects of metacognitive help devices on knowledge acquistion in networked learning environments]. *Zeitschrift für Pädagogische Psychologie, 17*(1), 13–25.

Bannert, M. (2005a). Designing metacognitive support for hypermedia learning. In T. Okamoto, D. Albert, T. Honda, & F. W. Hesse (Eds.), *The 2nd joint workshop of cognition and learning through media-communication for advanced e-learning* (pp. 11–16). Tokyo, Japan: Sophia University.

Bannert, M. (2005b). Explorationsstudie zum spontanen metakognitiven Strategie-Einsatz in hypermedialen Lernumgebungen [An exploratory study on spontaneous cognitive strategies in hypermedia learning]. In C. Artelt & B. Moschner (Eds.), *Lernstrategien und Metakognition: Implikationen für Forschung und Praxis* (pp. 127–151). Münster: Waxmann.

Bannert, M. (2006). Effects of reflection prompts when learning with hypermedia. *Journal of Educational Computing Research, 4,* 359–375.

Bannert, M. (2007). *Metakognition beil Lernen mit Hypermedien [Metacognition and hypermedia learning].* Münster: Waxmann.

Bannert, M. (2007b). *Metakognition beim Lernen mit Hypermedia. Erfassung, Beschreibung und Vermittlung wirksamer metakognitiver Lernstrategien und Regulationsaktivitäten.* [Metacognition and Learning with Hypermedia]. Münster: Waxmann.

Bannert, M. (2009). Promoting self-regulated learning through prompts: A discussion. *Zeitschrift für Pädagogische Psychologie., 23,* 139–145.

Bannert, M., Hildebrand, M., & Mengelkamp, C. (2009). Effects of Metacognitive Support Device in Learning Environments. *Computers in Human Behavior, 25,* 829–835.

Bannert, M., & Mengelkamp, C. (2007). Assessment of metacognitive skills by means of thinking-aloud instruction and reflection prompts. Does the method affect the learning performance? *Metacognition and Learning, 3,* 39–58.

Boekaerts, M., Pintrich, P. R., & Zeidner, M. (Eds.). (2000). *Handbook of self-regulation.* San Diego, CA: Academic.

Brown, A. L. (1978). Knowing when, where, and how to remember: A problem of metacognition. In R. Glaser (Ed.), *Advances in instructional psychology* (pp. 77–165). Hillsdale, NJ: Erlbaum.

Calvi, L., & De Bra, P. (1997). Proficiency-adapted information browsing and filtering in hypermedia educational systems. *User Modelling & User-Adapted Interaction, 7,* 257–277.

Clarebout, G., & Elen, J. (2006). Tool use in computer-based learning environments: Towards a research framework. *Computers in Human Behavior, 22,* 389–411.

Craik, F. I. M., & Lockhart, R. S. (1972). Levels of processing: A framework for memory research. *Journal of Verbal Learning and Verbal Behaviour, 11,* 671–684.

Detterman, D. K. (1993). The case for the prosecution: Transfer as an epiphenomenom. In D. K. Detterman & R. J. Sternberg (Eds.), *Transfer on trial: Intelligence, cognition, and instruction* (pp. 1–24). Norwood, NJ: Ablex.

Efklides, A. (2008). Metacognition. Defining its facets and levels of functioning in relation to self-regulation and co-regulation. *European Psychologist, 13*(4), 277–287. doi:10.1027/1016-9040.13.4.277.

Ericsson, K. A., & Simon, H. A. (1993). *Protocol analysis: Verbal reports as data.* Cambridge: MIT Press.

Ertmer, P. A., & Newby, T. J. (1996). The expert learner: Strategic, selfregulated, and reflected. *Instructional Science, 24,* 1–24.

Flavell, J. H. (1979). Metacognition and cognitive monitoring: A new area of cognitive-developmental inquiry. *The American Psychologist, 34,* 906–911.

Flavell, J. H., & Wellman, H. M. (1977). Metamemory. In R. Kail & W. Hagen (Eds.), *Perspectives on development of memory and cognition* (pp. 3–31). Hillsdale, NJ: Erlbaum.

Friedrich, H. F., & Mandl, H. (1992). In H. Mandl & H. F. Friedrich (Eds.), *Lern- und Denkstrategien. Analyse und Intervention* (pp. 3–54). Göttingen: Hogrefe.

Gentner, D. (1983). Structure-mapping: A theoretical framework for analogy. *Cognitive Science: A Multidisciplinary Journal, 7,* 155–170.

Gentner, D. (1998). Analogy. In W. Bechtel & G. Graham (Eds.), *A companion to cognitive science* (pp. 107–113). Oxford: Blackwell.

Graesser, A. C., Wiley, J., Goldman, S. R., O'Reilly, T., Jeon, M., & McDaniel, B. (2007). SEEK Web Tutor: Fostering a critical stance while exploring the causes of volcanic eruption. *Metacognition and Learning, 2*, 89–105.

Greene, J. A., & Azevedo, R. (2010). The measurement of learners' self-regulated cognitive and metacognitive processes while using computer-based learning environments'. *Educational Psychologist, 45*(4), 203–209.

Hasselhorn, M. (1995). Kognitives Training: Grundlagen, Begrifflichkeiten und Desirate. In W. Hager (Ed.), *Programme zur Förderung des Denkens bei Kindern* (pp. 14–40). Göttingen: Hogrefe.

Hermans, H., Petermann, F., & Zielinski, W. (1978). *LMT—Leistungsmotivationstest.* Amsterdam: Swets & Zeitlinger.

Hofer, B. (2004). Epistomological understanding as a metacognitive process: Thinking aloud during online searching. *Educational Psychologist, 39*, 43–55.

Kauffman, D. F., Ge, X., Xie, K., & Chen, C.-H. (2008). Prompting in web-based environments: Supporting self monitoring and problem solving skills in college students. *Journal of Educational Computing Research, 38*, 115–137. doi:10.2190/EC.38.2.a.

Kramarski, B., & Feldman, Y. (2000). Internet in the classroom: Effects on reading comprehension, motivation and metacognitive awareness. *Educational Media International, 37*(3), 149–155.

Lin, X. (2001). Designing metacognitive activities. *Educational Technology Research and Development, 49*, 1042–1629.

Lin, X., Hmelo, C., Kinzer, C. K., & Secules, T. (1999). Designing technology to support reflection. *Educational Technology Research and Development, 47*(3), 43–62.

Lin, X., & Lehman, J. D. (1999). Supporting Learning of Variable Corntrol in a Computer-Based Biology Environment: Effects of Prompting College Students to Reflect on their own Thinking. *Journal of Research in Science Teaching, 36*(7), 837–858.

Manlove, S., Lazonder, A. W., & De Jong, T. (2007). Software scaffolds to promote regulation during scientific inquiry learning. *Metacognition and Learning, 2*, 141–155.

Nelson, T. O., & Narens, L. (1990). Metamemory: A theoretical framework and new findings. In G. Bower (Ed.), *The psychology of learning and motivation* (Vol. 26, pp. 125–173). New York: Academic.

Nückles, M., Hübner, S., & Renkl, A. (2009). Enhancing self-regulated Learning by writing learning protocols. *Learning and Instruction, 19*, 259–271.

Paris, S. G., & Newman, R. S. (1990). Developmental aspects of self-regulated learning. *Educational Psychologist, 25*, 87–102.

Pintrich, P. R., Smith, D. A. F., Garcia, T., & McKeachi, W. J. (1993). Reliability and predictive validity of the motivated strategies for learning questionnaire (MSLQ). *Educational and Psychological Measurement, 53*, 801–814.

Pintrich, P. R., Wolters, C. A., & Baxter, G. P. (2000). Assessing metacognition and self-regulated learning. In G. Schraw & J. C. Impara (Eds.), *Issues in the measurement of metacognition* (pp. 43–97). Lincoln, NE: Buros Institute of Mental Measurements.

Roll, I., Aleven, V., McLaren, B., & Koedinger, K. (2007). Designing for metacognition—applying Cognitive Tutor principles to metacognitive tutoring. *Metacognition and Learning, 2*(2–3), 125–140.

Roll, I., Aleven, V., McLaren, B. M., & Koedinger, K. R. (2011). Improving students' help-seeking skills using metacognitive feedback in an intelligent tutoring system. *Learning and Instruction, 21*, 267–280. doi:10.1016/j.learninstruc.2010.07.004.

Schnotz, W. (1998). Strategy-specific information acccess in knowledge acquisition from hypertext. In L. B. Resnick, R. Säljö, C. Pontecorvo, & B. Burge (Eds.), *Discourse, tools, and reasoning. Essays on situated cognition.* Berlin: Springer.

Schnotz, W., & Bannert, M. (2003). Construction and interference in learning from multiple representation. *Learning and Instruction, 13*, 141–156.

Schraw, G. (2001). Promoting general metacognitive awareness. In H. Hartman (Ed.), *Metacognition in learning and instruction. Theory, research and practice* (pp. 3–16). Dordrecht: Kluwer Academic Publishers.

Schunk, D. H., & Zimmerman, B. J. (Eds.). (1998). *Self-regulated learning. From teaching to self-reflective practice.* New York, NY: Guilford.

Simons, P. R. J., & De Jong, F. P. (1992). Self-regulation and computer-assisted instruction. *Applied Psychology: An International Review, 41*, 333–346.

Sitzmann, T., Bell, B. S., Kraiger, K., & Kanar, A. M. (2009). A multilevel analysis of the effect of prompting self-regulation in technology-delivered instruction. *Personnel Psychology, 62*, 697–734. doi:10.1111/j.1744-6570.2009.01155.x.

Sitzmann, T., & Ely, K. (2010). Sometimes you need a reminder: The effects of prompting self-regulation on regulatory processes, learning, and attrition. *The Journal of Applied Psychology, 95*, 132–144.

Stadtler, M., & Bromme, R. (2008). Effects of the metacognitive computer-tool metaware on the web search of laypersons. *Computers in Human Behavior, 24*, 716–737.

Stark, R., & Krause, U.-M. (2009). Effects of reflection prompts on learning outcomes and learning behaviour in statistics education. *Learning Environments Research, 12*, 209–223.

Sweller, J., van Merrienboer, J., & Paas, F. (1998). Cognitive architecture and instructional design. *Educational Psychology Review, 10*(3), 251–296.

Valcke, M. (2002). Cognitive load: updating the theory? *Learning and Instruction, 12*, 147–154.

Veenman, M. V. (1993). *Metacognitive ability and metacognitive skill: Determinants of discovery learning in computeriezed learning environments.* Amsterdam: University of Amsterdam.

Veenman, M. V. (2005). The assessment of metacognitive skills: What can be learned from multi-method designs? In C. Artelt & B. Moschner (Eds.), *Lernstrategien und*

Metakognition: Implikationen für Forschung und Praxis [Learning strategies and metacogntion]. Implications for Research and Practice. Münster: Waxmann.

Veenman, M. V. J. (2007). The assessment and instruction of self-regulation in computer-based environments: a discussion. *Metacognition and Learning, 2*, 177–183.

Veenman, M. J. V., Van Hout-Wolters, B., & Afflerbach, P. (2006). Metacognition and learning: Conceptual and methodological considerations. *Metacognition and Learning, 1*, 3–14.

Weinstein, C. E., Husman, J., & Dierking, D. R. (2000). Self-regulation interventions with a focus on learning strategies. In M. Boekaerts, P. R. Pintrich, & M. Zeidner (Eds.), *Handbook of self-regulation* (pp. 727–747). San Diego, CA: Academic.

Weinstein, C. E., & Mayer, R. E. (1986). The teaching of learning strategies. In M. C. Wittrock (Ed.), *Handbook of research and teaching* (pp. 315–327). New York: Macmillan.

Wild, K. P., Schiefele, U., & Winteler, A. (1992). *LIST. Ein Verfahren zur Erfassung von Lernstrategien im Studium* (Gelbe Reihe: Arbeiten zur Empirischen Pädagogik und Pädagogischen Psychologie, Nr. 20) [LIST. A Questionaire of learning strategies in university students]. Neubiberg: Universität der Bundeswehr, Institut für Erziehungswissenschaft und Pädagogische Psychologie.

Winne, P. H. (1996). A metacognitive view of individual differences in self-regulated learning. *Learning and Individual Differences, 8*, 327–353.

Winne, P. H. (2001). Self-regulated learning viewed from models of information processing. In B. J. Zimmerman & D. H. Schunk (Eds.), *Self-regulated learning and academic achievement: Theoretical perspectives* (2nd ed., pp. 153–189). Mahwah, NJ: Lawrence Erlbaum Associates.

Zumbach, J., & Bannert, M. (2006). Special Issue: Scaffolding cognitive learner control mechanisms in individual and collaborative learning environments. *Journal of Educational Computing Research, 4*.

Metacognition and the Use of Tools 13

Geraldine Clarebout, Jan Elen,
Norma A. Juarez Collazo, Griet Lust, and Lai Jiang

Abstract

In this chapter the relationship between metacognition and the use of tools is addressed. Being able to determine when the use of a tool would be beneficial for one's learning is seen as a metacognitive skill. Different assumptions are made with respect to this relationship between metacognitive knowledge (including instructional conceptions) and tool usage. A series of studies are addressed in which different instruments were used to measure metacognitive knowledge and metacognitive skills to provide empirical underpinning for these assumptions.

Metacognition is a learner characteristic that enables learners to regulate and make optimal choices with respect to their learning process (Dörner & Wearing, 1995; Frensh & Funke, 1995). Flavell (1976) defines it as:

> metacognition refers to one's knowledge concerning one's own cognitive processes and products or anything related to them (….). It refers to the active monitoring and the consequent regulation and orchestration of these processes in relation to cognitive objects or data on which they bear, usually in the service of some concrete goal or objective. (p. 232)

Flavell (1979) makes a distinction between metacognitive knowledge, metacognitive experiences, and metacognitive strategies (i.e., regulatory skills). Metacognitive knowledge refers to knowledge of cognition. It includes knowledge of what and how factors act and interact to affect learning processes, knowledge of how to use available information to achieve a goal, knowledge of what strategies to use for particular purposes, and knowledge of when and where particular cognitive strategies should be used. The aforementioned knowledge can be declarative, procedural, or conditional knowledge (Schraw, 2001; Schraw & Dennison, 1994; Paris, Lipson, & Wixson, 1983). Metacognitive experiences have to do with the conscious awareness of where one

G. Clarebout (✉)
Center for Medical Education, Faculty of Medicine, University of Leuven, Herestraat 49, Box 4000, 3000 Leuven, Belgium
e-mail: geraldine.clarebout@med.kuleuven.be

J. Elen • N.A J. Collazo • G. Lust
Center for Instructional Psychology and Technology, University of Leuven, Dekenstraat 2, Box 3773-3000, Leuven, Belgium
e-mail: geraldine.clarebout@kuleuven-kortrijk.be

L. Jiang
Institute for Tropical Medicine, Antwerp, Belgium

R. Azevedo and V. Aleven (eds.), *International Handbook of Metacognition and Learning Technologies*, Springer International Handbooks of Education 26, DOI 10.1007/978-1-4419-5546-3_13,

stands in a certain cognitive process and what progress one is making to achieving learning goals. These experiences may induce metacognitive strategies that control one's cognitive processes. Metacognitive strategies are "executive" activities—such as planning, monitoring, and evaluation—that one uses to control and regulate one's cognitive processes (Gourgey, 2001; Livingston, 2003).

This chapter focuses on the relationship between metacognitive knowledge and strategies and the use of support devices in computer-based learning environments (CBLEs). Learning environments, and more specifically CLBEs, consist of content, tasks, and different supportive elements (Jonassen, 1999). The supportive elements refer to the devices that foster learning; they support learners to deal with the content and the tasks of the learning environment. These devices can be embedded, meaning that the use is mandatory and out of control of the user, or non-embedded which leaves the use under the learners' control. These non-embedded support devices are referred to as tools (Clarebout & Elen, 2006) and are the focus of this chapter. Depending on the kind of support offered, a distinction is made between information, cognitive, and scaffold tools. Information tools provide the content in a different way, for instance, in a structured or elaborated way. Cognitive tools allow learners to interact with the content and scaffold tools guide the learning efforts. Being able to strategically use tools to learn more efficiently can be considered as a metacognitive strategy (e.g., Greene & Azevedo, 2007; Horz, Winters, & Fries, 2009; Winne & Jamieson-Noel, 2002).

Learner Control, Tools, and Metacognition

In numerous CBLEs, learners have control over the use of tools. When giving learners control over supportive elements, support can be said to be adapted to their needs. Learners receive as much support as they need. This means that possible detrimental effects for learning of either too much or too less support can be avoided. However, giving learners control over the supportive elements assumes that they are good judges of their own learning process and they possess the necessary metacognitive knowledge and skills to determine when and how to use the support. This seems not so evident: Learners often lack the knowledge and skills to regulate their own learning (Butler & Winne, 1995; Clark, 1990; Greene, & Azevedo, 2007; Horz et al., 2009; Winne & Jamieson-Noel, 2002). Indeed, recent reviews and studies indicate that learners often do not use the support offered to them (Aleven, Stahl, Schworm, Fischer, & Wallace, 2003; Azevedo, 2005; Clarebout & Elen, 2006; Narciss, Proske, & Koerndle, 2007; Winne, 2006). Additionally, a number of studies report overuse in an attempt of learners to "game the system" (Aleven & Koedinger, 2000; Bartholomé, Stahl, Pieschl, & Bromme, 2006; Wood & Wood, 1999). Different studies hypothesized that students may not seek adequate support because they lack the necessary metacognitive knowledge and skills. In these studies metacognition has often been the object of support (Jonassen, Beissner, & Yacci, 1993; Narciss et al., 2007; Winters, Greene, & Costich, 2008), but the relationship between metacognition and the use of tools has seldom been the focus of research.

In the studies presented in this chapter, specific attention was given to one aspect of metacognitive knowledge, namely, learners' instructional conceptions about the different support devices (Elen & Lowyck, 1999). Learners' instructional conceptions are a kind of metacognitive knowledge referring to "all ideas and theories that an individual learner holds about (the components of) the learning environment" (Lowyck, Elen, & Clarebout, 2005). Winne (2006) states that the functionality students ascribe to a tool will determine whether and how they use this tool.

The assumption is that in order to be able to make adequate decisions, learners need to know the functionality of tools in general and more specifically how or when the use of these tools may be helpful for their own learning. This also relates to one of the conditions put forwards by Perkins (1985) with respect to grasping learning opportunities, in this case, using support devices.

Perkins indicates that first the opportunity has to be there and second that learners need to know the functionality of the tools at hand. In line with the above reasoning, some studies also suggest that interventions promoting metacognitive strategies and skills need to include aspects that increase metacognitive knowledge (e.g., Schraw & Dennison, 1994; Schwonke, Berthold, & Renkl, 2009).

Based on this theoretical framework, the following assumptions were made:

- *Learners' instructional conceptions influence tool use*: The better learners know the functionality of a tool and how it can contribute to their learning, the more optimal they will use it (including not using it when not needed). The more knowledgeable learners are about the (functionality of the) tools, the more knowledgeable decisions they can make. The more students perceive a tool as functional, the more they will be inclined to adequately use it.
- *Learners' metacognitive skills influence tool usage*: The extent to which learners are able to detect their own learning problems and are capable of regulating their own learning will determine the extent to which they will be inclined to use support devices to solve these problems (Mercier & Frederiksen, 2007). The more they are capable to do this, the more adequate they will use tools. Given that either too much or too less support can be detrimental for learning (Clark, 1990), a third assumption is that for the learners with limited metacognitive skills, the mandatory use of supportive elements, and hence inducing the learners to use the supportive elements, will be beneficial for their learning. While for learners who possess the necessary metacognitive skills, learner control over the supportive elements will be more beneficial than supplanting this decision for them by obliging them to use these elements.

These assumptions were tested in different studies that will be discussed in the next section of this chapter. First the learning environments used in these studies will be described including the participants they aimed at. Next, the different instruments to measure metacognition will be discussed and the results of their use in different studies on the use of tools. Finally, the assumptions are discussed in relation to the results of the studies.

Overview of Empirical Evidence on Metacognition and the Use of Tools

Context

Different studies were carried out in CBLE's. Three of the four studies were a text-based CBLE. Students were asked to read a text on a computer (on obesities/airplanes) and got access to different tools. In the first obesities study (Clarebout & Elen, 2009), students got access to cognitive and scaffold tools, namely, a dictionary, instructional goals, and example questions, and help with interpreting graphics and text. In one version of the environment, additional explanation was offered on the functionality of the support devices before seeing the actual text (e.g., *By clicking on this tool you receive an explanation of the goals that you should achieve by reading this text. By reading these goals, you will be able to gain more insight into what is expected from you*). This intervention aimed at influencing learners' instructional conceptions and hence to make them more knowledgeable about the functionality of the support devices. In the second obesities study (Clarebout, Horz, Elen, & Schnotz, 2010), a German translation was used of the text in the first obesities study and one cognitive tool. This tool gave additional explanation on a graph, where after, students were asked to give an interpretation of this graph in their own words. Two versions were made of the environment, one in which the use of supportive elements was mandatory and hence where the program took over some metacognitive activity. In the other version, students had themselves control of the use of the supportive elements.

A third study with a text-based CBLE was a text on airplanes. Two versions were created, both with a cognitive tool: one with an advanced organizer and one containing three questions.

A final learning environment that was used was an ill-structured CBLE (Clarebout & Elen, 2004) where students were confronted with an ecological problem. Participants were asked to come up with the most environmental-friendly drinking cup for a music festival by considering ecological, financial, and safety aspects. Different tools were available to the learners: information tools (information list containing official documents, videos with opinions of stakeholders), cognitive tools (calculator), and scaffold tools (problem-solving script, reporting script). Additionally, two conditions received advice on the use of these tools. In one condition this advice was given at fixed moments; in the other condition, the advice was given based on the learner's process.

All the CBLEs discussed here were directed towards higher education students and aimed at gaining insight into learners' tool use and factors influencing this tool use.

In order to grasp learner's support device usage, log files were kept and analyzed. These log files allowed to gain insight into the number of times learners consulted a tool and the duration of their consultation. In the problem-solving environment, it was also possible to gain insight into when students consult a tool in their problem-solving process. Next to quantitative data, the log files also registered some more qualitative data. For instance, when students consulted additional explanations on the graph and were asked to give their own interpretation, these interpretations were logged and gave insight into the depth with which learners used the tool and hence formed a measurement of qualitative tool use.

Measurement of Metacognition

Throughout the different studies, different instruments to measure metacognition were used, and they will be addressed in the following, including some empirical results of their use:

ICON questionnaire. In the problem-solving study, students' metacognitive knowledge, more specifically their instructional conceptions, were measured using the ICON questionnaire (Sarfo, Elen, Clarebout, & Louw, 2010). This questionnaire confronts learners with eight statements for each tool. Learners have to indicate the extent to which they agree (from totally disagree to totally agree) that a specific tool can be functional for their problem-solving process [e.g., *According to me, a problem solving script helps students to better understand the content* (Cronbach's alpha = 0.91)]. Strangely enough, the higher students scored on the ICON questionnaire, meaning the more functional they found a tool prior to being confronted with it, the less they used the tool. In the second obesities study, the ICON questionnaire was also used (Cronbach's alpha = 0.93). In this study, no significant relationship was found between learners' instructional conceptions and their tool usage. Interestingly though, a significant correlation was found between learners' instructional conceptions and their internal regulation (see scale below). The more learners were internally regulating their learning process, the more they conceived the tools as being functional for their learning and vice versa.

Perceived usefulness. Based on the questionnaire from Davis and colleagues (Davis, 1989; Davis, Bagozzi, & Warshaw, 1989), perceived usefulness was measured as an indicator of metacognitive knowledge. In contrast to instructional conceptions, learners were already confronted with the learning environment and its tools. Perceived usefulness refers to the extent to which students believe that using a particular tool will enable efficient learning processes and/or increase performance of present learning tasks. Six statements were used to measure this concept (e.g., *studying an available advance organizer/answering questions will enable me to accomplish this learning task more quickly;* Cronbach's alpha = 0.92). This questionnaire was used in the airplane study and revealed a significant effect of perceived usefulness on tool usage. Students who perceive the tools as less useful spent less time on the tools. Students who perceived the usefulness of a tool at medium level spent the most time on the tools.

Regulation scales of Vermunt (1992). To measure learners' metacognitive skills, part of the learning style inventory of Vermunt (1992) was used, namely, the three regulation scales. These scales are internal regulation (e.g., *After each paragraph I try to formulate the learning content in my own words to test my learning process*), external regulation (e.g., *I study according to the instructions given in the study material or provided by the* teacher), and no regulation (e.g., *I notice that it is difficult for me to determine whether I master the subject matter sufficiently*). This questionnaire has been used in a variety of settings and found to be a valid and reliable instrument (Boyle, Duffy, & Duleavy, 2003; Veenman, Prins, & Verhelj, 2003; Schouwenburg, 1996). In the problem-solving study, reliabilities for the internal regulation scale were good (Cronbach's alpha = 0.80) but not for the external regulation (Cronbach's alpha = 0.62) or for the no regulation scale (Cronbach's alpha = 0.68). This was the reason why in the first obesities study, only the internal regulation scale was used (resulting in that study in a Cronbach's alpha = 0.77). The studies could not retrieve a significant relationship between internal regulation and the frequency of tool usage; but it was found that the less learners are inclined to engage in regulation activities, the more time they spent on tools.

Help-seeking behavior measurement. Learners' help-seeking behavior was measured as an indicator of metacognitive skills. Help seeking includes the ability to identify one's own problem and act upon it (Schunk & Zimmerman, 1994). The instrument of Pajares, Cheong, and Oberman (2004) was used. Nine statements measured students' help avoidance behavior (e.g., *I would write down any answer rather than ask for help in class*; Cronbach's alpha = 0.90) and six items measuring students' perceived benefits of help seeking (e.g., *I think asking questions in this class helps me learn;* Cronbach's alpha = 0.86). Results reveal that the more learners avoid help-seeking behavior, the more time they spent on tools. This can be explained by the different nature of help seeking referred to in the instrument of Pajares et al. (2004), and the support learners could request in a CBLE. In the instrument, the help-seeking behaviors are all directed towards humans. One could argue that the less inclined learners are to request help from a teacher, the more they will use the tools in a CBLE.

LIST questionnaire. One of the studies took place in Germany (the second obesities study), which led to the use of a German instrument to measure metacognition to avoid translation issues. The LIST questionnaire (Wild & Schiefele, 1994; Wild, 2000) consists of 48 items that relate to studying learning materials individually (e.g., *I make a list of subject specific expressions and difficult words; the materials I just read are the starting point for my own thoughts.*). Items that were not included related to discussing study materials with others and referring to different contexts (e.g., *I order to study, I remain in the same place*). These statements were not applicable to the task at hand. The scales included in the instruments that were administered were organization, elaboration, critical thinking, memorizing, metacognitive strategies, and effort. These different subscales all showed a good reliability (Cronbach's alphas between 0.73 and 0.84). No relationship was found between metacognitive strategies and the frequency or proportional times spent on tools. However, an interaction effect was found between metacognition and condition on the quality of tool usage. The high metacognitive skilled learners used the tools in significantly less depth in the condition were usage of supportive elements was mandatory as compared to the high metacognitive skilled that had learner control. This difference was not found for the low metacognitive skilled.

Underpinning of the Assumptions

In this part we start with looking at the assumptions that were made and how the different studies can provide empirical evidence for these assumptions.

Assumption 1
Learners' instructional conceptions influence tool usage: the better learners know the functionality of a tool and how it can contribute to their learning, the more optimal they will use it (including not using it when not needed).

In both the problem-solving study and the first obesities study, learners' instructional conceptions were measured. The results are nonconclusive. While in the problem-solving study, the more students conceived of tools as being functional, the less they actually used them; in the first obesities study, no relation was found in terms of tool usage. A possible explanation for these results may be that in the obesities study, the statements did not refer to the specific respondent of the items but to "students" or "learners" in general. Participants may have indicated that indeed tools may be helpful for some learners, but not necessary to themselves. Every item in the questionnaire started with a general explanation on the tool. But it may also be that this explanation was not sufficient for them to imagine the actual tool. Given that in the problem-solving study, the negative effect of instructional conceptions disappeared in the conditions that received fixed advice. The advice provided may have conflicted with students' own conceptions about why they would think the tool would be functional for their own problem-solving process. However, in the first obesities study, this effect was not found, while in one condition, an explanation was given on the functionality of the support devices. It may be that learners need to experience a support device functionality before they can actually express instructional conceptions. In other words, learners may not be able to think about the functionality of a tool before they have actually encountered it. Another argument could be that these instructional conceptions should be measured on a level that connects more to an individual's learning rather than learning in general. This was done in the airplane study. The results of this study revealed that perceived usefulness is related to time spent on tools. However, the relationship is nonlinear. A quadratic trend indicates that students with a medium score on perceived usefulness spent most time on tools. Perceived usefulness was also found to motivate students to optimally use questions. The more students thought questions were useful, the more knowledge students called upon (i.e., activation) and the deeper their understanding (i.e., students were able to give more correct information in their answers).

Assumption 2
Learners' metacognitive skills influence support usage: the extent to which learners are capable of regulating their own learning and are able to detect their own learning problems will determine the extent to which they will be inclined to use tools to solve these problems (Mercier & Frederiksen, 2007).

In the problem-solving study, metacognitive skills were part of a model explaining the variance in frequency of tool use for the fixed advice group. Although this variable did not yield a significant result, removing it from the model reduced the fit of the model significantly. This effect was not found for the time spent on tools. It almost seems that students' metacognitive skills allowed them to compensate for the fixed advice provided in the learning environment. In the first obesities study, no effects were found of metacognitive skills on tool usage. The results of the second obesities study are more in line with the assumptions; learners that possess sufficient metacognitive skills do not use the tools more but use them more in depth if they are given the choice. If the decision when to use a supportive element is taken for them, support provided through these elements is processed in a more superficial way, compared to when learners can decide themselves to use the supportive elements.

Assumption 3
Given that either too much or too less support can be detrimental for learning, a third assumption is that the embeddedness of the supportive elements and the amount of metacognitive skills will interact.

This assumption was mainly tested in the second obesities study, and as already discussed in relation to assumption 2, we could see that embeddedness of supportive elements does matter, especially with respect to the quality of usage. Depending on the presence and kind of advice on tool usage, metacognitive skills seem to play a different role. This was shown in the problem-solving and the first obesities studies. It should be noted though that in these studies, quality of tool usage was not measured.

This third assumption leads to the question whether supportive elements should be mandatory or whether learners should have control. The latter includes the risk that the supportive elements may be less used but to a larger quality if students possess the necessary metacognitive skills.

Conclusion

From a theoretical perspective, it is self-evident that metacognition plays a role in the use of tools. The studies presented here provide some evidence but do also suggest that especially the quality of tool usage seems to be influenced by metacognition, while the quantity expressed by frequency of tool consultation and time spent on the support device have no clear relationship with metacognition. In order to gain more insight into the relationship between metacognition and the quality of tool usage, a clear conceptualization is needed. In these studies, Flavell's definition was used as a starting point. However, when looking at the instruments, it can be questioned whether we actually measured learners' metacognitive knowledge and skills. Metacognitive knowledge was operationalized as students' instructional conceptions or perceived usefulness of the support devices. An extension towards epistemological beliefs and self-efficacy (Bandura, 1997; Moo & Azevedo, 2008) may lead to a more complete profile of a learner's metacognitive knowledge. Additionally, metacognitive skills were measured with self-report questionnaire. It is most likely that learners' answers to these questionnaires provide just an intention of what they will do or measure students' metacognitive knowledge rather than their metacognitive strategies (Winne, 2006). In order to test the relationship between metacognitive skills and support usage, more behavioral data should be collected and examined. For instance, when the learning task is studying a hypertext for which different support devices are available, one could do a pretest in which learners are asked to read a text providing them the normal accessible tools such as highlighting, making notes, taking a summary, and access to a number of links. Using these tools can be seen as an indicator of metacognitive strategies for reading a text (Palincsar & Brown, 1984, 1987). In a next step, the relationship between learners' score on this pretest and their actual tool usage behavior for the learning task could be examined.

In this chapter we focused on the aspect of metacognition, but it may be that not only knowledge about the self, the learning environment, and the relationship between self and learning environments should be considered, but also more motivational "self-related" beliefs should be included. This would refer to Perkins' third condition, namely, that a learner should be motivated to use a learning opportunity. Including motivational variables and considering the interaction with metacognition could probably explain more accurately support usage behavior. Consequently, the term self-regulation may be a more adequate theoretical construct that encompasses more than only metacognitive knowledge and skills to study tool usage (e.g., Pintrich & De Groot, 1990).

Acknowledgement The research described in this chapter was partly funded by a grant of the National Science Foundation—Flanders (FWO-project G0480.09)

References

Aleven, V., & Koedinger, K. R. (2000). Limitations of student control: Do students know when they need help? In G. Gauthier, C. Frasson, & K. VanLehn (Eds.), *Proceedings of the 5th International Conference on Intelligent Tutoring Systems, ITS 2000* (pp. 292–303). Berlin: Springer Verlag.

Aleven, V., Stahl, E., Schworm, S., Fischer, F., & Wallace, R. (2003). Help seeking and help design in interactive learning environments. *Review of Educational Research, 73*, 277–320.

Azevedo, R. (2005). Using hypermedia as a metacognitive tool for enhancing student learning? The role of self-regulated learning. *Educational Psychologis, 40*(4), 199–209.

Bandura, A. (1997). *Self-efficacy: The exercise of control*. New York, NY: Freeman.

Bartholomé, T., Stahl, E., Pieschl, S., & Bromme, R. (2006). What matters in help-seeking? A study of help effectiveness and learner-related factors. *Computers in Human Behavior, 22*(1), 113–129.

Boyle, E. A., Duffy, T., & Duleavy, K. (2003). Learning styles and academic outcomes. The validity and utility of Vermunt's inventory of learning styles in British higher education setting. *British Journal of Educational Psychology, 73*, 267–290.

Butler, D. L., & Winne, P. H. (1995). Feedback and self-regulated learning: A theoretical synthesis. *Review of Educational Research, 65*(5), 245–281.

Clarebout, G., & Elen, J. (2004). STUWAWA: Studying tool use with and without agents. In L. Cantoni & C. McLoughlin (Eds.), *Proceedings of ED-Media 2004. World conference on educational multimedia, hypermedia and telecommunications* (pp. 747–752). Norfolk, VA: AACE.

Clarebout, G., & Elen, J. (2006). Tool use in computer-based learning environments: Towards a research framework. *Computers in Human Behavior, 22*(3), 389–411.

Clarebout, G., & Elen, J. (2009). The complexity of tool use in computer-based learning environments. *Instructional Science: An International Journal of Learning and Cognition, 37*, 475–486.

Clarebout, G., Horz, H., Elen, J., & Schnotz, W. (2010). The relation between self-regulation and the embedding of support devices in learning environments. *Educational Technology Research and Development, 28*(5), 573–587.

Clark, R. E. (1990). When teaching kills learning: Research on mathetmathantics. In H. Mandl, E. De Corte, N. Bennett, & H. F. Friedrich (Eds.), *European research in an international context* (Learning and Instruction, Vol. 2, pp. 1–22). Oxford, NY: Pergamon Press.

Davis, F. D. (1989). Perceived usefulness, perceived ease of use, and user acceptance of information technology. *MIS Quarterly, 13*, 319–340.

Davis, F. D., Bagozzi, R. P., & Warshaw, P. R. (1989). User acceptance of computer technology: A comparison of two theoretical models. *Management Science, 35*(8), 982–1003.

Dörner, D., & Wearing, A. J. (1995). Complex problem solving: Toward a (computersimulated theory). In P. A. Frensch & J. Funke (Eds.), *Complex problem solving. The European perspective* (pp. 65–99). Hillsdale, NJ: Lawrence Erlbaum Associates.

Elen, J., & Lowyck, J. (1999). Metacognitive instructional design. *Journal of Structural Learning and Intelligent Systems, 13*(3–4), 145–169.

Flavell, J. H. (1976). Metacognitive aspects of problem solving. In L. B. Resnick (Ed.), *The nature of intelligence* (pp. 231–235). Hillsdale, NJ: Lawrence Erlbaum Associates.

Flavell, J. H. (1979). Metacognition and cognitive monitoring: A new area of cognitive-developmental inquiry. *The American Psychologist, 34*, 906–911.

Frensh, P. A., & Funke, J. (1995). Definitions, traditions and a general framework for understanding complex problem solving. In P. A. Frensch & J. Funke (Eds.), *Complex problem solving. The European perspective* (pp. 3–25). Hillsdale, NJ: Lawrence Erlbaum Associates.

Gourgey, A. F. (2001). Metacognition in basic skills instruction. In H. J. Hartman (Ed.), *Metacognition in learning and instruction: Theory, research and practice* (pp. 17–32). Boston, MA: Kluwer.

Greene, J. A., & Azevedo, R. (2007). *A macro-level analysis of SRL processes and their relations to the development of sophisticated mental models*. Paper presented at the annual meeting of the American Educational Research Association, Chicago, IL.

Horz, H., Winter, C., & Fries, S. (2009). Differential effects of situated prompts on learning behaviour in authentic simulations. *Computers in Human Behavior, 25*(4), 818–828.

Jonassen, D. H. (1999). Designing constructivist learning environments. In C. M. Reigeluth (Ed.), *Instructional design theories and models. A new paradigm of instructional theory. Vol. 2* (pp. 215–239). Mahwah, NJ: Lawrence Erlbaum Associates.

Jonassen, D. H., Beissner, K., & Yacci, M. (1993). *Structural knowledge: Techniques for representing, conveying, and acquiring structural knowledge*. Hillsdale, NJ: Erlbaum.

Livingston, J. A. (2003). Metacognition: An overview (ERIC Document Reproduction Service No. ED474273).

Lowyck, J., Elen, J., & Clarebout, G. (2005). Instructional conceptions: Analysis from an instructional design perspective. *International Journal of Educational Research, 41*(6), 429–444.

Mercier, J., & Frederiksen, C. (2007). Individual differences in graduate students' help-seeking process in using a computer coach in problem-based learning. *Learning and Instruction, 17*, 184–203.

Moo, D., & Azevedo, R. (2008). Monitoring, planning, and self-efficacy during learning with hypermedia: The impact of conceptual scaffolds. *Computers in Human Behavior, 24*, 1686–1706.

Narciss, S., Proske, A., & Koerndle, H. (2007). Promoting self-regulated learning in web-based learning environments. *Computers in Human Behavior, 23*, 1126–1144.

Pajares, F., Cheong, Y. F., & Oberman, P. (2004). Psychometric analysis of computer science help-seeking scales. *Educational and Psychological Measurement, 64*(3), 496–513.

Palincsar, A. S., & Brown, A. L. (1984). Reciprocal teaching of comprehension-fostering and comprehension-monitoring activities. *Cognition and Instruction, 1*(2), 117–175.

Palincsar, A. S., & Brown, D. S. (1987). Enhancing instructional time through attention to metacognition. *Journal of Learning Disabilities, 20*(2), 66–75.

Paris, S. G., Lipson, M. Y., & Wixson, K. K. (1983). Becoming a strategic reader. *Contemporary Educational Psychology, 8*, 293–316.

Perkins, D. (1985). The fingertip effect: How information-processing technology shapes thinking. *Educational Researcher, 14*, 11–17.

Pintrich, P. R., & De Groot, E. V. (1990). Motivational and self-regulated components of classroom academic performances. *Journal of Educational Psychology, 82*, 33–40.

Sarfo, F., Elen, J., Clarebout, G., & Louw, F. (2010). Innovative instructional intervention and the need for a better insight into instructional conceptions. In M. Zuljan & J. Vogrinc (Eds.), *Facilitating effective student learning through teacher research and innovation* (pp. 151–174). Ljubljana, Slovenia: University of Ljubljana, Faculty of Education.

Schouwenburg, H. C. (1996). Een onderzoek naar leerstijlen [A research on learning styles]. *Tijdschrift voor Onderwijsresearch, 21*(2), 151–161.

Schunk, D. H., & Zimmerman, B. J. (1994). *Self-regulation of learning and performance: Issues and educational applications*. Hillsdale, NJ: Lawrence Erlbaum Associates.

Schraw, G. (2001). Promoting general metacognitive awareness. In H. J. Hartman (Ed.), *Metacognition in learning and instruction: Theory, research and practice* (pp. 3–16). Boston, MA: Kluwer.

Schraw, G., & Dennison, R. S. (1994). Assessing Metacognitive Awareness. *Contemporary Educational Psychology, 19*, 460–475.

Schwonke, R., Berthold, K., & Renkl, A. (2009). How multiple external representations are used and how they can be made more useful. *Applied Cognitive Psychology, 23*, 1227–1243.

Veenman, M. V., Prins, F. J., & Verheij, J. (2003). Learning styles: Self-reports versus thinking-aloud measures. *The British Journal of Educational Psychology, 73*, 357–372.

Vermunt, J. (1992). *Leerstijlen en sturen van leerprocessen in het hoger onderwijs: Naar procesgerichte instructie en zelfstandig denken [Learning styles and coaching learning processes in Higher Education]*. Lisse, The Netherlands: Swets & Zeitlinger.

Wild, K.-P. (2000). *Lernstrategien im Studium. Strukturen und Bedingungen [Learning Strategie in Academic Studies Structures an Conditions]*. Münster: Waxmann.

Wild, K.-P., & Schiefele, U. (1994). Lernstrategien im Studium. Ergebnisse zur Faktorenstruktur und Reliabilität eines neuen Fragebogens [Learning strategies in academic studies. Results about factor structure and reliability of a new questionnaire]. *Zeitschrift für Differentielle und Diagnostische Psychologie, 15*, 185–200.

Winne, P. H. (2006). Meeting challenges to researching learning from instruction by increasing the complexity of research. In J. Elen & R. E. Clark (Eds.), *Handling complexity in learning environments: Research and theory* (pp. 221–236). Amsterdam, NL: Pergamon.

Winne, P. H., & Jamieson-Noel, D. (2002). Exploring students' calibration of self-reports about study tactics and achievement. *Contemporary Educational Psychology, 27*, 551–572.

Winters, F. I., Greene, J. A., & Costich, C. A. (2008). Self-regulation of learning within computer-based learning environments: A critical analysis. *Educational Psychology Review, 20*, 429–444.

Wood, H., & Wood, D. (1999). Help seeking: Learning and contingent tutoring. *Computers in Education, 33*, 153–169.

Using Learning Management Systems as Metacognitive Tools to Support Self-Regulation in Higher Education Contexts

14

Nada Dabbagh and Anastasia Kitsantas

Abstract

The purpose of this chapter is to review research that examined whether tools and features of course or learning management systems, referred to in this research as web-based pedagogical tools (WBPT), can be used to support and promote specific processes of student self-regulated learning such as goal setting, help seeking, and self-monitoring, in online and distributed learning contexts. Five categories of WBPT are described including administrative tools, content creation and delivery tools, collaborative and communication tools, learning tools, and assessment tools. In addition, research designs and data collection instruments of three studies are described. Research findings are summarized showing that WBPT can be used to support a number of self-regulatory processes and that college instructors and faculty can use WBPT to design effective learning tasks that promote student self-regulated learning. Educational implications, limitations, and future directions are also discussed.

Research Context

Technology and Distributed Learning

The growth rate for online enrollments in higher education contexts continues to outpace overall enrollment with more than one in four higher education students taking at least one online course in an academic year (Allen & Seaman, 2010). This is resulting in increased demand for online courses and in a long overdue realization by higher education institutions that online learning is critical and strategic for their continued growth and competitiveness. However, online learning entails much more than delivering a course or academic program online especially if the goal is to support meaningful and effective learning. Research suggests that advances in Internet and Web-based technologies have redefined the boundaries and pedagogies of traditional distance learning and that online learning involves the deliberate

N. Dabbagh (✉)
Instructional Design and Technology, George Mason University, Fairfax, VA, USA
e-mail: ndabbagh@gmu.edu

A. Kitsantas
Educational Psychology, George Mason University, Fairfax, VA, USA
e-mail: akitsant@gmu.edu

R. Azevedo and V. Aleven (eds.), *International Handbook of Metacognition and Learning Technologies*, Springer International Handbooks of Education 26, DOI 10.1007/978-1-4419-5546-3_14,

organization and coordination of distributed forms of interaction and learning activities (Dabbagh, 2004; Dede, 2002). More specifically, online learning has been reconceptualized as learning that is distributed over time and place using various technologies, engaging students in multiple forms of interaction such as learner-learner, learner-group, learner-content, and learner-instructor (Dabbagh & Bannan-Ritland, 2005). This model or framework is referred to in the literature as *distributed learning* and has been the focus of our research for the past 6 years.

Distributed learning is an instructional model that allows instruction and learning to occur independent of time and place as a result of the convergence of technology and education (Oblinger, Barone, & Hawkins, 2001). For example, learning can occur at the same time while learners are in different places through videoconferencing (i.e., synchronously) or at different times in different places through communication technologies such as email or discussion forums (i.e., asynchronously). Hence, the relationship between time, space, and media is an important dynamic in distributed learning. Distributed learning can also be perceived as blended or hybrid learning which has been defined as learning that combines instructional media (e.g., synchronous and asynchronous technologies), instructional methods (e.g., collaborative and individual or didactic and open ended), and instructional delivery modes (e.g., face-to-face and online) (see Graham, Allen, & Ure, 2003; Graham, 2006; Bonk & Graham, 2006).

Research suggests that overall, distributed learning increases students' interest and motivation to learn because it provides more engaging and meaningful learning opportunities than traditional classroom contexts and is adaptive to rapidly changing educational needs (Dabbagh & Bannan-Ritland, 2005; Kitsantas & Dabbagh, 2010; Lovett, Meyer, & Thille, 2008; Maslowski, Visscher, Collis, & Bloemen, 2000; Moore & Head, 2003). For example, Lovett et al. (2008) showed that learning gains of students who participated in an online stand-alone statistics course designed to provide a high-quality learning experience to those who do not have access to an institution or an instructor were at least as good as learning gains of students who participated in the traditional instructor-led statistics course. Additionally, students who participated in the hybrid (blended) statistics course (a combination of online and face-to-face delivery) performed as well or better compared to students in the traditional course and experienced a much more effective and efficient learning experience overall. However, research also indicates that online or distributed learning often requires a large degree of student self-discipline and that the level and type of guidance that should be provided to learners in such contexts is an open instructional design question that needs further research (Collis, 2003; Graham, 2006; Huang & Zhou, 2006). Furthermore, research has shown that college instructors who use learning management systems (LMS) such as Blackboard or Moodle to facilitate online and distributed learning are primarily using LMS features for information dissemination rather than in ways that engage students in meaningful and strategic or self-regulated learning (Apedoe, 2005; Dabbagh, 2005; Morgan, 2003; Oliver, 2001).

Hence, the focus of our research has been to examine the pedagogical potential of LMS particularly as this relates to how LMS features can be used as metacognitive tools to support student self-regulated learning in distributed and online learning contexts. Specifically, we wanted to test whether the different features of LMS such as discussion forum, chat, calendar, and group tools supported specific processes of self-regulated learning such as goal setting, help seeking, self-monitoring, and time management by examining whether students' ratings on these self-regulatory processes varied significantly with their use of different LMS features. We also wanted to examine whether specific processes of self-regulated learning were evoked while students used LMS features to complete complex learning tasks that involve collaborative activities, problem solving, and reflection. Finally, we wanted to find out whether experienced online instructors were deliberately using LMS features to support student self-regulation in distributed and online courses. Finding answers to these questions would enhance students' academic self-regulation and consequently academic achievement and would guide college instructors who use LMS in designing effective learning tasks that promote self-regulated learning. In order to proceed with this research, we developed a conceptual definition of LMS and a pedagogically oriented classification of LMS features and tools which we describe next.

Learning Management Systems

LMS, also known as an "enterprise technology" (Carmean & Brown, 2005) or course management systems (CMS), are defined in this research context as "a collection of Web applications that integrate technological and pedagogical features of the Internet and the Web into a single, template-based authoring and presentation system that facilitates the design, development, delivery, and management of Web-based courses and online [distributed] learning environments" (Dabbagh & Bannan-Ritland, 2005, p. 298). The goal of LMS is to provide a central location or platform for delivery of course content, related information or links, provision of models for assignments, communication between instructors and students, and support for group processes such as the development of shared projects in the form of Web-based products (Dabbagh & Kitsantas, 2004). These instructional and learning activities are supported through the use of specific LMS features or tools, which we referred to in our earlier research as Web-based pedagogical tools (WBPT).

WBPT can be used to facilitate distributed learning interactions in a variety of Web-based formats and pedagogical constructs and can help situate such interactions in authentic contexts supporting meaningful and engaging learning (Berge, 1999; Dede, 1996; Hartley & Bendixen, 2001; Reil & Harasim, 1994). Additionally, several researchers have argued that WBPT can scaffold the acquisition of metacognitive skills and can support students' development of self-regulatory skills that are essential for success in online and distributed learning environments (Dabbagh, 2003; Kitsantas & Chow, 2007; Hollingworth & McLoughlin, 2001). For example, Hollingworth and McLoughlin (2001) argued that while freshmen science students demonstrated many problem-solving skills, they lacked metacognitive skills such as checking, planning, and revising problem solutions. To address this need, they developed an online tutorial using the WebCT LMS to engage students in self-monitoring their own problem-solving approaches in science learning. Preliminary results indicated that the online tutorial which provided access to alternative problem solutions and the ability for students to comment on each others' solutions facilitated the planning and analysis of problems, supported student reflection on many aspects of problem solving, and promoted motivation and self-efficacy beliefs (Hollingworth & McLoughlin, 2005). Additionally, Kitsantas and Chow (2007) found that students enrolled in online and hybrid courses reported higher levels of help-seeking behavior via the use of synchronous and asynchronous technologies and felt less threatened to seek help than those in traditional courses. Research also suggests that WBPT can be used to customize learning content in order to meet individual learner needs, abilities, and goals and to integrate learning and motivational strategies to help students become more self-directed learners (Hartley & Bendixen, 2001; McCombs, 2002). Armed with these preliminary research findings, we initially classified WBPT into four categories: Web-based hypermedia tools, Web-based multimedia tools, content creation and delivery tools, and collaborative and communication tools (Dabbagh & Kitsantas, 2004). However, as LMS features evolved, this classification also evolved to include administrative tools (Kitsantas & Dabbagh, 2004), assessment tools (Dabbagh & Kitsantas, 2005), and learning tools (Dabbagh & Kitsantas, 2009; Kitsantas & Dabbagh, 2010), resulting in five categories of WBPT described next.

Collaborative and Communication Tools

This category of WBPT included asynchronous and synchronous communication tools and group tools. Asynchronous and synchronous communication tools enable one-to-one, one-to-many, and many-to-many learning interactions through a different time-different place mode, whereas synchronous communication tools enable communication in real time (same time-different place). Examples of LMS-embedded asynchronous collaborative and communication tools included email and discussion forums. Examples of LMS-embedded synchronous collaborative and communication tools included chat, electronic whiteboards, and audio and videoconferencing.

Group tools support both asynchronous and synchronous communication to enable groups of students to work and learn as a team. LMS have the capability to support group areas where student teams can share and collaboratively edit course documents to complete group assignments and tasks. Group tools can support formal (e.g., representing the final product of collaborative work) and informal (e.g., work in progress) types of activities. Examples of group tools include group discussion forums, group chat areas, file exchange tools, group posting areas, breakout sessions, and group email.

Content Creation and Delivery Tools

This category of WBPT included tools for instructors that enable them to deliver course content and resources and tools for students that enable them to contribute course content, submit assignments, and interact with course resources. Examples of instructor content creation and delivery tools included a "syllabus" feature, an "assignments" or "activities" feature that allows instructors to develop and post an assignment or class activity, and a "resources" feature that allows instructors to provide Web links for students to explore. Examples of student content creation and delivery tools included a student or group "presentation area" or a "digital dropbox" feature that allows students to post assignments or upload reflection journals and receive feedback from the instructor and peers.

Administrative Tools

This category of WBPT included tools to manage students and student information such as importing the class roster from the institution's registration system, assigning userids and passwords, posting grades, and administering quizzes/tests; tools to add or manage teaching assistants, graders, and course designers and provide guest access; and tools to manage administrative course components such as setting the availability and duration of the course, populating the course calendar, and generating areas for communication and collaboration as described under the collaborative and communication WBPT category.

Learning Tools

This category of WBPT was initially labeled hypermedia tools (Kitsantas & Dabbagh, 2004) and included tools that allow students to explore Web-based resources and create personalized learning experiences. In addition to the use of Web links and search engines to explore and locate information, learning tools enable students to perform tasks such as online bookmarking, note taking, compiling and aggregating content, and using community and social networking tools to create networks based on their learning needs (Kitsantas & Dabbagh, 2010). Examples of learning tools embedded in LMS included a course glossary, course index, a search feature, bookmarking feature, and digital libraries or image databases.

Assessment Tools

This category of WBPT included a variety of tools ranging from supporting the creation of traditional tests to the development of more authentic performance-based assessments such as e-portfolios. LMS-specific assessment tools included test-type tools that support multiple-choice, matching, fill-in-the-blank, and short-answer questions as well as essay tests. In addition, LMS support the development of test questions that include media such as images, video, and audio. Examples of LMS-authentic assessment tools included the capability to create self-assessments, peer assessments, and performance-based assessments using a variety of rubric scales and customized grading schemes.

These five categories of WBPT (see Fig. 14.1) have not been intentionally designed or informed by theories of self-regulation, but they can be used to help learners engage in self-regulated learning

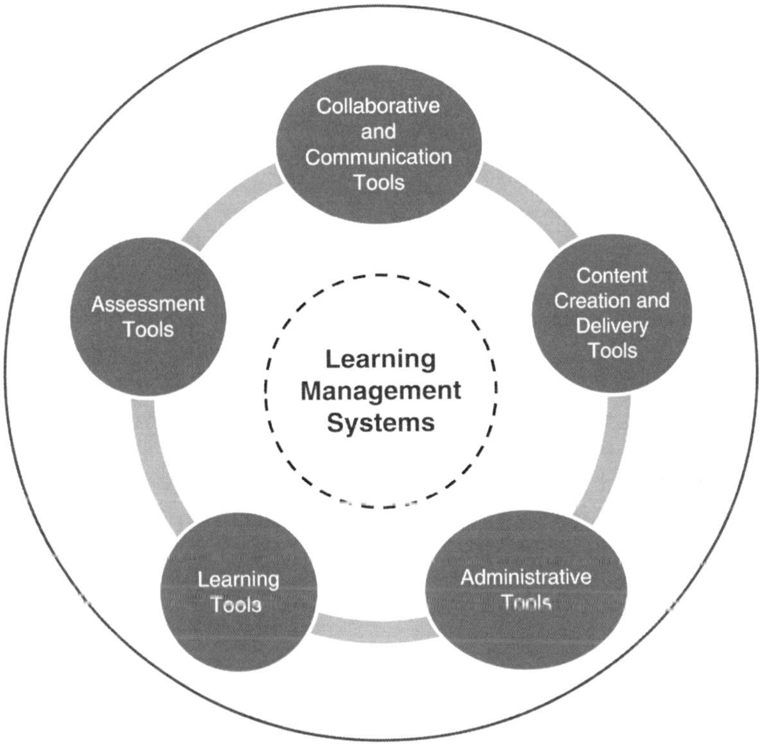

Fig. 14.1 Pedagogical classification of LMS

in a variety of ways. For example, content creation and delivery tools can facilitate the application of task strategies including rehearsing, elaborating, organizing, structuring, and transforming learning content to support meaningful understanding and retention (Dabbagh & Kitsantas, 2004). Content creation and delivery tools can also support meaningful interaction with course content by providing learners with multiple options to view or access the course content resulting in higher intrinsic interest in the material (Dabbagh, 2002). Alternatively, collaborative and communication tools can assist learners in seeking help from social and nonsocial sources when they encounter task difficulties and engage in an active and reflective dialog with peers (Berge, 1999). Collaborative and communication tools can also facilitate the establishment and refinement of individual and group learning goals and promote the development of effective time management to efficiently carry out the responsibilities associated with being an active and accountable member of a group (Dabbagh, 2002).

Given the growth rate in online learning enrollments over the last decade, the ubiquitous use of LMS in higher education to support teaching and learning interactions, and the perceived significance of student self-regulation in distributed and online learning contexts, we wanted to examine whether WBPT can help college students become self-regulated learners and what processes of self-regulation can be supported by WBPT and how. Specifically, we wanted to demonstrate how instructional designers, college faculty, and educators can provide opportunities for student self-regulation using WBPT in order to ensure academic success in these increasingly technology-driven and LMS-supported learning contexts. Hence, our sample population included primarily college students and college faculty. We describe this sample population and associated learning domains next.

Learning Domains and Participants

In the first study (Kitsantas & Dabbagh, 2004), participants were 80 undergraduate and graduate college students (26 male, 54 female) enrolled in five courses taught by five instructors who utilized an LMS to support distributed course events. Participants' ages ranged from 21 to 34 years. The courses were selected because the instructors were utilizing WBPT, namely, administrative tools, collaborative and communication tools, content creation and delivery tools, and hypermedia tools (i.e., learning tools), to support distributed learning. Disciplines or learning domains included instructional technology and advanced instructional design for the graduate courses and advanced composition (business writing) and government (political analysis) for the undergraduate courses. In the second study (Dabbagh & Kitsantas, 2005), participants consisted of 65 graduate college students (22 male, 43 female) enrolled in three courses that supported distributed learning using WBPT. Participants' ages ranged from 22 to 45 years. Learning domains included instructional technology and advanced instructional design. The course instructors utilized primarily collaborative and communication tools, content creation and delivery tools, administrative tools, and assessment tools. In the third study (Dabbagh & Kitsantas, 2009), participants were 12 experienced online course instructors (6 male, 6 female) who utilized an LMS to facilitate undergraduate or graduate online or blended course delivery. Learning domains included operations management, information technology, mathematics education, educational leadership, communities, and management.

Research Questions

Overall, our research examined whether the use of WBPT in online and distributed higher education learning contexts can help support specific self-regulatory processes such as goal setting, help seeking, self-monitoring, self-evaluation, and time management (described later in this chapter). Specifically, we wanted to know whether different categories of WBPT supported different processes of self-regulation. We began with the following question for the first study:

Do students' means on the self-regulatory processes ratings (e.g., goal setting and self-monitoring) vary significantly with their use of the different WBPT (administrative, collaborative and communication, content creation and delivery, and hypermedia tools)?

In the second study, we examined the same variables as in the first study in order to confirm the results, and we added the following question:

Did students perceive WBPT useful in scaffolding strategic learning while completing course assignments?

We wanted to examine student perceptions of the usefulness of WBPT in supporting the completion of course assignments involving specific learning tasks and, more specifically, which self-regulated learning processes were enacted or activated while completing these tasks. For example, we wanted to know which self-regulation processes were activated or supported when students used WBPT to complete course assignments involving (a) collaborative learning tasks such as group projects or activities, (b) exploratory learning tasks such as problem solving (e.g., providing solutions to case studies), or (c) dialogic learning tasks such as articulation and reflection (e.g., engaging in online discourse or writing). In the third study, we shifted our focus to college faculty and examined how experienced online instructors used WBPT to support student self-regulation in distributed and online courses and whether these instructors deliberately used WBPT to facilitate student self-regulation. The overall goal of our research was to better understand the pedagogical potential of WBPT in order to enhance students' academic self-regulation and consequently academic achievement in online and distributed learning contexts and to inform college instructors who use WBPT how to design effective learning tasks that promote student self-regulation.

Theoretical Framework

Self-Regulation: A Social Cognitive Perspective

Self-regulation refers to the degree to which students are able to become metacognitively, motivationally, and behaviorally active participants of their own learning process (Zimmerman, 1989). Specifically, self-regulation involves self-direction and self-motivation, in that the student is able to strategically engage in several different processes that increase the likelihood of accomplishing a goal. However, self-regulation is not an inherent skill that students have; instead, the ability to self-regulate is learned and developed, where instructors must train students how to be self-directed and self-motivated (Zimmerman, 2008). In the context of today's technological world, availability of information, and increasing use of technology in the classroom, it is critical that students learn how to self-regulate their learning to use the online or Web-based material effectively and efficiently (Kitsantas & Dabbagh, 2004). The idea of self-regulation is especially important in distributed, blended, or online learning, because such learning contexts require the student to self-direct their own learning and be self-motivated to engage in those self-directed learning behaviors.

According to Zimmerman (2008), the ability to effectively self-regulate requires the student to be actively engaged in self-regulatory processes including setting goals, using effective strategies, self-monitoring, and self-evaluating during their learning. For example, a student whose goal is to obtain an A on his or her next physics exam will *plan* what steps he or she needs to take in order to obtain the A, select appropriate strategies to attain this goal, self-monitor the effectiveness of these strategies, and self-evaluate to determine the next course of action. Goal setting which refers to a process through which students decide on specific outcomes for learning and identify appropriate strategies to be undertaken in order to accomplish desired goals (Zimmerman, 2000) is one of the key processes of self-regulation. Research indicates that students who set specific as opposed to general goals, and process goals (focus on methods and strategies that can help one master a task) rather than outcome goals (outcomes of learning efforts), show high skill achievement and report positive motivational beliefs for their assigned work (Zimmerman & Kitsantas, 1999; Zimmerman, 2000).

Task strategies are strategies that learners use to accomplish their goals. These strategies are domain specific and may include deep processing elaborative and organizational strategies, such as rewriting notes, selecting main ideas, and/or outlining the text to be learned, and rehearsal strategies for basic memory tasks, such as using mnemonics to remember the key phases of a learning theory. An important strategy for college students is time management, which refers to budgeting time effectively and has been shown to be highly correlated with academic achievement. Research suggests that students who keep careful records of time spent on assigned learning tasks begin to recognize patterns in their own use of study time and develop an appreciation for the value of effective time management and its impact on academic achievement (Zimmerman, 2000; Kitsantas, Winsler, & Huie, 2008).

Self-monitoring, which is defined as one's deliberate attention to an aspect of behavior, is also an important metacognitive process of self-regulated learning because it directs the learners' attention to the task and assists them in evaluating the outcomes of their efforts. For instance, keeping daily records assists the learner in determining how to make appropriate learning adjustments in order to attain his/her goals (Zimmerman & Kitsantas, 1999). Self-evaluation refers to comparing outcomes of performance with a standard or goal (Zimmerman, 2000). As learners monitor their progress towards goal attainment, they make evaluative judgments about their performance and about their self-efficacy for reaching the goal (Zimmerman, 2008). Self-evaluation significantly influences strategic planning for future learning activities. Research studies show that students who self-evaluate their progress display higher skill acquisition and report higher self-efficacy beliefs, intrinsic interest, and self-satisfaction about their performance than students who do not self-evaluate (Zimmerman, 2008). Overall, students who can successfully engage in these self-regulatory processes are more aware of and make a stronger effort to improve the efficacy of their studying. However, how effectively the student is able to control these processes depends on other factors as well, such as motivational beliefs (Zimmerman, 1989; 2008).

Motivational beliefs allow students to persist through difficult tasks and empower them to learn. Specifically, a powerful motivational process is self-efficacy, which is defined as the extent to which students feel confident and equipped enough to accomplish a certain task or goal. A student who is self-regulated would experience more adaptive senses of motivation such as high self-efficacy, expect positive outcomes, adopt a learning goal orientation, and express interest at the particular task at hand (Zimmerman & Kitsantas, 2005). These motivational beliefs form a strong foundation for self-regulated learning and metacognitive monitoring. If a student is not compelled to achieve a difficult task, he or she will most likely not be able to persist through and attain the goals that were set.

In summary, extensive research evidence indicates that high-achieving students (Zimmerman, 2000; Kitsantas, 2002) and experts (Ericsson & Charness, 1994) judiciously use all these self-regulatory processes to enhance their performance. However, without the proper training, students can potentially maladaptively react to their outcomes by engaging in maladaptive strategies such as memorization and rehearsal. Self-regulatory processes can be taught to avoid maladaptive behavior and enhance students' academic study skills (Zimmerman & Kitsantas, 2005; Zimmerman, 2008). For example, with the assistance and guidance of an instructor, students can learn how to evaluate and monitor their own study methods. Once deficiencies are identified, the learner sets specific goals and selects appropriate strategies to attain them. Next, the learner executes the strategy (ies) and monitors its effectiveness. Finally, in order to achieve optimal results, the learner monitors and evaluates outcomes in a reoccurring cycle. However, in distributed and online learning contexts, the physical absence of the instructor coupled with the increased responsibility demanded of learners to achieve learning tasks presents additional difficulties for learners, particularly those with low self-regulatory skills. Consequently, the need to promote effective use of WBPT to support self-regulation processes is paramount. Hence, the goal of this research was to examine whether WBPT can be used to support self-regulated learning and if so, how.

Research Methods

Research Designs

As mentioned earlier, a series of three studies were conducted to examine whether WBPT can be sued to support student self-regulated learning and how. These studies used both quantitative and qualitative methodological approaches. Specifically, in the Kitsantas and Dabbagh (2004) study, an online questionnaire (Web-Supported Self-Regulation Questionnaire, WSSRQ) was administered to 80 college students to examine whether WBPT supported the use of six processes of self-regulation: goal setting, task strategies, self-monitoring, self-evaluation, time planning and management, and help seeking. In the Dabbagh and Kitsantas (2005) study, the WSSRQ was administered to 65 college students in order to confirm the results of the first study. Additionally, qualitative data were collected using a questionnaire (SPU-WBPT) to determine student perceptions of the usefulness of WBPT in scaffolding self-regulated learning while completing courses assignments.

In the third study (Dabbagh & Kitsantas, 2009), an open-ended questionnaire (Evaluating the Instructional Utility of Integrative Learning Technologies) was administered to experienced instructors of online and distributed courses to examine how they utilized WBPT to support student self-regulation. These measures are described in more detail next.

Measurement Tools

Web-Supported Self-Regulation Questionnaire (Kitsantas & Dabbagh, 2004)

This online questionnaire was developed in consultation with experts in the areas of self-regulation and Web-based technologies. The self-regulatory processes used in the scale were adapted from Zimmerman and colleagues research (see Zimmerman, & Martinez-Pons, 1986). Students were asked to rate each of six processes of self-regulation (described above) on a scale from 1 (Strongly Disagree) to 5 (Strongly Agree) in terms of the degree to which WBPT supported the process. The scale included 12 questions addressing the 12 tools or features (grouped in categories) of WBPT utilized in the courses selected for each study. Sample items included "The Discussion Area Helped Me with the Following Processes of Self-regulation" and "The Assignments Feature Helped Me with the Following Processes of Self-regulation." Acceptable reliability coefficients were obtained for each of the questions ranging from $a=0.73$ to 0.93 in the first study (Kitsantas & Dabbagh, 2004) and $a=0.82$ to 0.98 in the second study (Dabbagh & Kitsantas, 2005).

Student Perceptions of the Usefulness of WBPT in Supporting Completion of Course Assignments Questionnaire (SPU-WBPT) (Dabbagh & Kitsantas, 2005)

The purpose of this questionnaire was to elicit student perceptions about the usefulness of WBPT in supporting the completion of course assignments in the courses selected for qualitative analysis and the self-regulation processes that WBPT evoked while completing these assignments. Students were asked to rate the usefulness of WBPT in supporting the completion of each course assignment on a scale from 1 (not useful) to 5 (very useful) and to provide a written explanation for their ratings. Students were also asked to respond to the following two questions: (1) Overall, which [LMS] WebCT tools or features were most useful to you in supporting your learning in this course? Why? and (2) In this class you were exposed to a blended learning environment with both face-to-face and online interactions with the course content and activities. Which interactions overall were more beneficial to your learning? Please explain why.

Evaluating the Instructional Utility of Integrative Learning Technologies Questionnaire (Dabbagh & Kitsantas, 2009)

This questionnaire originally consisted of 34 short-answer items but was condensed to 22 items after pilot testing with a sample of experienced online instructors. The 22 items queried faculty about their use of WBPT (referred to as Integrative Learning Technologies or ILT) to support the six processes of self-regulation used in the WSSRQ. Example items included, "As an instructor what ILT or LMS tools do you use to help your students keep track of their progress on assignments? (Provide a specific example)" and "As an instructor what ILT or LMS tools do you use to help your students set specific goals for what they need to achieve for each course assignment? (Provide a specific example)." The questionnaire also included items that addressed demographics.

Significance of Findings

The results of the first study (Kitsantas & Dabbagh, 2004) revealed significant differences among the self-regulatory processes supported through the use of the four categories of WBPT (administrative tools, collaborative and communication tools, content creation and delivery tools, and hypermedia tools) investigated. Specifically, students reported that collaborative and communication tools were more useful in supporting goal setting, help seeking, and time planning and management; content creation and delivery tools were more useful in supporting self-evaluation, task strategies, and goal setting; hypermedia tools (learning tools) were more useful in supporting task strategies; and administrative tools were more useful in supporting self-monitoring, and help seeking. The results of the second study (Dabbagh & Kitsantas, 2005), as expected, confirmed the results of the first study, namely, that different categories of WBPT supported different processes of self-regulation. More specifically, collaborative and communication tools also supported goal setting; content creation and delivery tools also supported task strategies; and administrative tools also supported self-monitoring which shows consistency across these studies in terms of what WBPT were useful in supporting what self-regulatory processes. Additionally, the qualitative analysis revealed that WBPT were perceived to be highly effective in activating the use of self-regulated learning processes necessary to support specific types of learning tasks required for completion of course assignments. For example, students perceived content creation and delivery tools particularly useful in scaffolding help seeking, task strategies, self-evaluation, and goal setting, while completing course assignments that involve exploratory learning tasks such as problem solving.

These findings have significant implications on the design of distributed learning environments particularly when LMS are used. Implications include the provision of specific WBPT that are more effective than others in supporting certain processes of self-regulated learning. In the absence of face-to-face instructor guidance, these implications are very important. Given that self-regulation has been highly correlated with student academic achievement and motivation, the findings of these studies suggest that learners feel that certain WBPT embedded in LMS assist them to set goals, engage in strategic planning and management, search for effective strategies, self-monitor, and seek needed help. Additionally, strategic learning can greatly impact students' successful engagement in the types of learning tasks required in distributed and online learning contexts (Hartley & Bendixen, 2001).

The results of the third study revealed that overall college instructors reported using specific WBPT to support specific processes of self-regulation. For example, 25 % of participants reported using content creation and delivery tools (e.g., creating and uploading a syllabus checklist or rubric) to support student goal setting and 84 % of participants reported using administrative tools (e.g., the calendar) to support time planning and management. Specifically, instructors used checklists that required students to set specific dates for completion of each online module and each assignment within a course module, thereby encouraging goal-setting behavior. Instructors also used the LMS calendar to assign dates to online activities and assignments so that students can look up these dates for time planning and management. These results confirmed previous findings that different categories of WBPT can be used to support different processes of self-regulation. The results also revealed consistency regarding which categories of WBPT supported which self-regulation processes (see Table 14.1). However, the results of this study also revealed that experienced online instructors did not report deliberately using WBPT to support student self-regulation. In other words, these instructors were not aware that technology can be used to support student self-regulation. These findings underscore the need to train instructors on how to specifically use technology to support student self-regulation in distributed and online learning contexts.

Table 14.1 WBPT-supported self-regulatory processes

WBPT category	Self-regulatory process
Administrative tools	Self-monitoring, help seeking
Collaborative and communication tools	Goal setting, help seeking, time management
Content creation and delivery tools	Self-evaluation, task strategies, goal setting
Learning tools	Task strategies
Assessment tools	Task strategies, self-monitoring, self-evaluation

Clearly, instructors who use WBPT based on principles of self-regulated learning can communicate the value of self-regulation and assist students in setting goals, selecting appropriate strategies to achieve these goals, and collecting and analyzing data about their own learning progress. Additionally, instructors who use

WBPT to help students develop self-regulation skills can instill interest in and motivate students to learn the subject matter which is critical to academic success.

Challenges and Limitations

Several limitations impacting the generalizability of the findings of these studies are noted. First, the classes selected in the first two studies (Kitsantas & Dabbagh, 2004; Dabbagh & Kitsantas, 2005) were blended versus totally online; thus, it is difficult to determine the extent to which students relied on the instructor or the WBPT to scaffold self-regulation. For example, face-to-face interactions may have prevented students from using WBPT exclusively. Second, the results of the first two studies can only be applied to courses that utilize an LMS. Third, since no records were kept regarding students' frequency of using WBPT in these studies, it was not possible to triangulate students' self-reports in the second study with such data. Limitations for the third study (Dabbagh & Kitsantas, 2009) include the small sample size of instructors, subject matter being taught, and the self-report nature of the study. Clearly more research is needed to further verify these findings, particularly using experimental designs, and additional data collection methods such as observation and face-to-face interviews with the target populations. It may be also interesting to determine whether students are self-regulating their learning with or without support from WBPT.

Design Implications and Future Directions

Research has shown that overall, college instructors acknowledge the teaching potential of technology particularly as this relates to promoting student interest in learning and actively engaging students in their learning; however, these instructors generally do not integrate sophisticated technologies into their teaching practice (Brill & Galloway, 2007). Some of the reasons cited include resistance to technology adoption, but more importantly, lack of knowledge of the pedagogical potential of technology and motivation to change traditional teaching practices stand out as critical barriers (Blin & Munro, 2008). Moreover, LMS are increasingly integrating Web 2.0 and social software tools (e.g., weblogs and wikis) and more authentic assessment features (e.g., peer review capabilities, electronic portfolios, and grading rubrics) providing faculty with an even wider and more flexible array of tools to design effective and meaningful learning activities. Additionally, the continual emergence of new learning technologies is constantly challenging the way we teach and learn. For example, students are demanding more engaging learning experiences and instant access to information due to work and life demands (The Horizon Report, 2007). Students are also generating their own content using social media and collaborating through social and professional networking sites such as Facebook and LinkedIn to establish networks of friends and resources (Alexander, 2006). Hence, if faculty wish to gain students' attention, enable strategic learning, and sustain student motivation to learn, they must not only keep up with new technologies but also learn how to deliberately use them to support student self-regulated learning.

Several researchers have developed subject matter-specific technology tutorials or software systems based on self-regulation principles and theories (e.g., Aviram, Ronen, Somekh, Winer, & Sarid, 2008; Hadwin & Winne, 2001; Kramarski & Gutman, 2006; Van den Boom, Paas, van Merrienboer, & van Gog, 2004; Winne, Hadwin, Nesbit, Kumar, & Beaudoin, 2005); however, such tools or systems have not been widely adopted in higher education contexts nor integrated into mainstream LMS despite encouraging research results regarding their effectiveness in promoting student self-regulated learning. Hence, more research is needed to further examine how existing learning technologies can be leveraged to enhance student self-regulation. Specifically, future research should adopt a more encompassing definition of WBPT

Table 14.2 Training students to become self-regulated learners using ILT

Phase	Instructor and student roles
Observation	Instructor uses collaborative and communication tools (e.g., LMS whiteboard or chat features) to model the learning task to students
Provide opportunities for students to observe experts (or the instructor) perform a task	Student observes the instructor and uses learning tools (e.g., notepad) to take notes during the demonstration and begin discriminating appropriate task strategies for this learning task
Emulation	Student uses collaborative and communication tools (e.g., whiteboard or virtual session) or content creation and delivery tools (e.g., creating a Webcast or podcast) to perform a learning task demonstrating awareness of goal setting and task strategies
Provide students with social feedback and encourage them to focus on processes while practicing a task	Instructor uses collaborative and communication tools (e.g., chat or videoconferencing) to coach student
Self -control	Student uses content creation and delivery tools (e.g., Webcast or podcast) to practice performing the task without direct coaching and monitors their own progress
Provide students with opportunities to master the processes while completing a task independently during practice episodes	Instructor uses administrative tools to create areas for supporting practice episodes and collaborative and communication tools (e.g., email) to provide feedback as needed
Self-regulation	Student uses learning tools (e.g., search engines, online bookmarking tools, community and social networking tools) to implement learning strategies to achieve the desired outcomes
Provide students with opportunities to make strategic adjustments when their performance is below expectations	Instructor provides assessment tools (e.g., self-assessment or performance-based assessment) to help students make strategic adjustments

and a viable training model that demonstrates to faculty how to use learning technologies to train students to become self-regulated learners. Towards this effort, Kitsantas and Dabbagh (2010) developed a broader definition of WBPT referred to as Integrative Learning Technologies (ILT). ILT is defined as a dynamic collection or aggregation of Web tools, software applications, and mobile technologies that integrate technological and pedagogical features and affordances of the Internet and the Web to facilitate the design, development, delivery, and management of online and distributed learning (Kitsantas & Dabbagh, 2010). This definition is broad enough to include traditional learning technologies such as LMS as well as emerging learning technologies such as social media and mobile technologies.

Kitsantas and Dabbagh (2010) also developed a model (see Table 14.2) to assist faculty in deliberately applying ILT to train students to become self-regulated learners. This model is based on Zimmerman and colleagues' research (see Zimmerman & Kitsantas, 1999; Zimmerman & Kitsantas, 2005) and consists of four sequential phases: observation, emulation, self-control, and self-regulation. The first two phases focus on social learning experiences that prepare learners to attain higher levels of skill on their own. For example, faculty can model task processes to students and elicit students' enactment of these processes while providing coaching and feedback. In the self-control phase, students learn from self-directed practice to achieve automaticity of task processes, and in the self-regulation phase, students learn to adapt their performance proactively and become independent learners focusing primarily on outcomes. This model of self-regulation has been tested with various learning tasks, and the findings show that it is a powerful tool in helping students become self-regulated learners (Zimmerman & Kitsantas, 1999; 2005). However, can this model be implemented in distributed and online learning contexts? Future research using experimental studies should examine the validity of this model in training students to become self-regulated learners using ILT.

References

Alexander, B. (2006). Web 2.0: A new wave of innovation for teaching and learning? *EDUCAUSE Review, 41(2)*, 32–44. Available from http://www.educause.edu/ir/library/pdf/ERM0621.pdf

Allen, I. E., & Seaman, J. (2010). *Learning on demand: Online education in the United States, 2009*. Babson Survey Research Group and The Sloan Consortium. Available from http://www.sloan-c.org/publications/survey/pdf/learningondemand.pdf

Apedoe, X. S. (2005). The interplay of teaching conceptions and course management system design: Research implications and creative innovations for future designs. In P. McGee, C. Carmean, & A. Jafari (Eds.), *Course management systems for learning: Beyond accidental pedagogy* (pp. 57–68). Hershey, PA: Information Science Publishing.

Aviram, A., Ronen, Y., Somekh, S., Winer, A., & Sarid, A (2008). Self-regulated personalised learning (SRPL): Developing iClass's pedagogical model. *eLearning Papers*, 9. Available form http://www.slideshare.net/elearningpapers/srpl

Berge, Z. L. (1999). *Interaction in post-secondary web-based learning* (pp. 5–11). January-February: Educational Technology.

Blin, F., & Munro, M. (2008). Why hasn't technology disrupted academics' teaching practices? Understanding resistance to change through the lens of activity theory. *Computers in Education, 50*(1), 475–490.

Bonk, C. J., & Graham, C. R. (Eds.). (2006). *Handbook of blended learning: Global perspectives, local designs*. San Francisco, CA: Pfeiffer Publishing.

Brill, J. M., & Galloway, C. (2007). Perils and promises: University instructors' integration of technology in classroom-based practices. *British Journal of Educational Technology, 38*(1), 95–105.

Carmean, C., & Brown, G. (2005). Measure for measure: Assessing course management systems. In P. McGee, C. Carmean, & A. Jafari (Eds.), *Course management systems for learning: Beyond accidental pedagogy* (pp. 1–13). Hershey, PA: Idea Group, Inc.

Collis, B. (2003). Course redesign for blended learning: Modern optics for technical professionals. *International Journal of Continuing Engineering Education and Lifelong Learning, 13*(1/2), 22–38.

Dabbagh, N. (2002). Using a Web-based course management tool to support face-to-face instruction. *The Technology Source, March/April issue*, 2002 (www.technologysource.org).

Dabbagh, N. (2003). Scaffolding: an important teacher competency in online learning. *TechTrends for Leaders in Education and Training, 47*(2), 39–44.

Dabbagh, N. (2004). Distance learning: Emerging pedagogical issues and learning designs. *Quarterly Review of Distance Education, 5*(1), 37–49.

Dabbagh, N. (2005). Pushing the envelope: Designing authentic learning activities using Course Management

Systems. In P. McGee, C. Carmean, & A. Jafari (Eds.), *Course management systems for learning: Beyond accidental pedagogy* (pp. 171–189). Hershey, PA: Information Science Publishing.

Dabbagh, N., & Bannan-Ritland, B. (2005). *Online learning: Concepts, strategies, and application*. Upper Saddle River, N.J.: Pearson, Merrill Prentice Hall.

Dabbagh, N., & Kitsantas, A. (2004). Supporting self-regulation in student-centered web-based learning environments. *International Journal on E-Learning, 3*(1), 40–47.

Dabbagh, N., & Kitsantas, A. (2005). Using web-based pedagogical tools as scaffolds for self-regulated learning. *Instructional Science, 33*(5–6), 513–540.

Dabbagh, N., & Kitsantas, A. (2009). Exploring how experienced online instructors report using integrative learning technologies to support self-regulated learning. *International Journal of Technology in Teaching and Learning, 5*(2), 154–168.

Dede, C. (1996). The evolution of distance education: Emerging technologies and distributed learning. *The American Journal of Distance Education, 10*(2), 4–36.

Dede, C. (2002). Interactive media in an interview with Chris Dede. *Syllabus*, June 2002, 12–14.

EDUCAUSE Learning Initiative & The New Media Consortium (2007). *The Horizon Report 2007 Edition*. Available at: http://www.nmc.org/horizon/2007/report

Ericsson, A. K., & Charness, N. (1994). Expert performance: Its structure and acquisition. *The American Psychologist, 49*, 725–747.

Graham, C. R. (2006). Blended learning systems: Definition, current trends, and future directions. In C. J. Bonk & C. R. Graham (Eds.), *Handbook of blended learning: Global Perspectives, local designs*. San Francisco, CA: Pfeiffer Publishing.

Graham, C. R., Allen, S., & Ure, D. (2003). *Blended learning environments: A review of the research literature*. Provo, UT: Unpublished manuscript.

Hadwin, A. F., & Winne, P. H. (2001). CoNoteS2: A software tool for promoting self-regulation. *Educational Research and Evaluation, 7*(2–3), 313–334.

Hartley, K., & Bendixen, L. D. (2001). Educational research in the Internet age: Examining the role of individual characteristics. *Educational Researcher, 30*(9), 22–26.

Hollingworth, R., & McLoughlin, C. (2001). Developing science students' metacognitive problem solving skills online. *Australian Journal of Educational Technology, 17*(1), 50–63.

Hollingworth, R., & McLoughlin, C. (2005). Developing the metacognitive and problem-solving skills of science students in higher education. In C. McLoughlin & A. Taji (Eds.), *Teaching in the sciences: Learner-centered approaches* (pp. 63–83). Binghamton, NY: Haworth Press.

Huang, R., & Zhou, Y. (2006). Designing Blended Learning Focused on Knowledge Category and Learning Activities. In C. J. Bonk & C. R. Graham (Eds.), *Handbook of blended learning: Global Perspectives, local designs*. San Francisco, CA: Pfeiffer Publishing.

Kitsantas, A. (2002). Test preparation and test performance: A self-regulatory analysis. *The Journal of Experimental Education, 70*(2), 101–113.

Kitsantas, A., & Chow, A. (2007). College students' perceived threat and preference for seeking help in traditional, distributed and distance learning environments. *Computers in Education, 48*(3), 383–395.

Kitsantas, A., & Dabbagh, N. (2004). Promoting self-regulation in distributed learning environments with web-based pedagogical tools: An exploratory study. *Journal on Excellence in College Teaching, 15*(1&2), 119–142.

Kitsantas, A., & Dabbagh, N. (2010). *Learning to learn with Integrative Learning Technologies (ILT): A practical guide for academic success*. Greenwich, CT: Information Age.

Kitsantas, A., Winsler, A., & Huie, F. (2008). Self-regulation and ability predictors of academic success during college: A predictive validity study. *Journal of Advanced Academics, 20*(1), 42–68.

Kramarski, B., & Gutman, M. (2006). How can self-regulated learning be supported in mathematical E-learning environments? *Journal of Computer Assisted Learning, 22*(1), 24–33.

Lovett, M., Meyer, O., & Thille, C. (2008). The Open Learning Initiative: Measuring the effectiveness of the OLI statistics course in accelerating student learning. *Journal of Interactive Media in Education*. Available from http://jime.open.ac.uk/2008/14.

Maslowski, R., Visscher, A. J., Collis, B., & Bloeman, P. P. M. (2000). The formative evaluation of a web-based course-management system within a university setting. *Educational Technology, 40*(30), 5–19.

McCombs, B. L. (2002). *The learner-centered framework on teaching and learning as a foundation for electronically networked communities and cultures*. Retrieved February 13, 2002 from http://www.pt3.org/VQ/teach_learn.php3

Moore, A. H., & Head, J. T. (2003). Philosophy of faculty development at Virginia Tech. In D. G. Brown (Ed.), *Developing faculty to use technology: Programs and strategies to enhance teaching* (pp. 4–5). Hoboken, NJ: Wiley.

Morgan, G. (2003). *Faculty use of course management systems*. Boulder, CO: ECAR Research Publication.

Oblinger, D. G., Barone, C. A., & Hawkins, B. L. (2001). *Distributed education and its challenges: An overview*. Washington, DC: American Council on Education. http://www.acenet.edu/bookstore/.

Oliver, K. (2001). Recommendations for student tools in online course management systems. *Journal of Computing in Higher Education, 13*(1), 47–70.

Reil, M., & Harasim, L. (1994). Research perspectives on network learning. *Journal of Machine-Mediated Learning, 4*(2&3), 91–114.

Van den Boom, G., Paas, F., van Merrienboer, J. G., & van Gog, T. (2004). Reflection prompts and tutor feedback in a web-based learning environment: Effects on students' self-regulated learning competence. *Computers in Human Behavior, 20*(4), 551–567.

Winne, P. H., Hadwin, A. F., Nesbit, J. C., Kumar, V., & Beaudoin, L. (2005). *gStudy: A toolkit for developing computer-supported tutorials and researching learning strategies and instruction (version 2.0) [computer program]*. Burnaby, BC: Simon Fraser University.

Zimmerman, B. J. (1989). A social cognitive view of self-regulated academic learning. *Journal of Educational Psychology, 81*(3), 329–339.

Zimmerman, B. J. (2000). Attaining self-regulation: A social cognitive perspective. In M. Boekaerts, P. R. Pintrich, & M. Zeidner (Eds.), *Handbook of self-regulation: Theory, research, and applications* (pp. 13–39). San Diego: Academic.

Zimmerman, B. J. (2008). Investigating self-regulation and motivation: Historical background, methodological developments, and future prospects. *American Educational Research Journal, 45*(1), 166–183.

Zimmerman, B. J., & Kitsantas, A. (1999). Acquiring writing revision skill: Shifting from process to outcome self-regulatory goals. *Journal of Educational Psychology, 91*, 1–10.

Zimmerman, B. J., & Kitsantas, A. (2005). The hidden dimension of personal competence: Self-regulated learning and practice. In A. J. Elliot & C. S. Dweck (Eds.), *Handbook of Competence and Motivation* (pp. 204–222). New York: Guilford Press.

Zimmerman, B. J., & Martinez-Pons, M. (1986). Development of a structured interview for assessing students' use of self-regulated learning strategies. *American Educational Research Journal, 23*, 614–628.

Designing Learning Technologies to Support Self-Regulation During Ill-Structured Problem-Solving Processes

15

Xun Ge

Abstract

This chapter explicates an empirically grounded and detailed theoretical framework for understanding the various components of self-regulated learning. A key distinction is articulated between metacognitive knowledge and metacognitive monitoring. It is argued that it is the accurate monitoring of learning experiences that is critical for effective self-regulation during learning, and that various accuracy measures for judgments of learning differ in how well they assess this construct of monitoring accuracy. Particular emphasis is placed on the importance of improving the relative accuracy of metacognitive monitoring skills, and that typical instruction in study strategies may not be sufficient to improve monitoring. The results of studies and manipulations that have resulted in superior monitoring accuracy are reviewed, and the implications for the development of learning technologies are discussed. A key observation is that in order to provide the opportunity for the development of effective regulatory skills, learning environments need to be careful not to deprive students of the opportunity to engage in self-regulation or monitoring of their own understanding.

It has been widely recognized that students have difficulty applying knowledge acquired from a classroom setting to a novel situation in a real-world problem-solving context (Feltovich, Spiro, Coulson, & Feltovich, 1996). For this reason, educational researchers have been increasingly emphasizing the importance of creating an open-ended learning environment to engage students in complex, ill-structured problem-solving activities, with the following assumptions: (1) the problem drives the learning; students will learn domain knowledge in the process of solving a problem, which is their learning goal, rather than solving a problem as an application of learning; (2) students will see the meaningfulness and relevance of school knowledge in their day-to-day life; and (3) ill-structured problem-solving activities facilitate knowledge transfer by

X. Ge, Ph.D. (✉)
Department of Educational Psychology, Jeannine Rainbolt College of Education, at the University of Oklahoma, 820 Van Vleet Oval, Norman, OK 73019-2041, USA
e-mail: xge@ou.edu

R. Azevedo and V. Aleven (eds.), *International Handbook of Metacognition and Learning Technologies*, Springer International Handbooks of Education 26, DOI 10.1007/978-1-4419-5546-3_15,

contextualizing knowledge in authentic situations (e.g., Bransford, Brown, & Cocking, 2000; Brown, Collins, & Duguid, 1989; Greeno, Collins, & Resnick, 1996; Jonassen, 1997, 1999).

However, effective learning in an open-ended environment requiring students to solve ill-defined problems demands metacognitive awareness of what is known and what needs to be known about a given topic. Yet, metacognitive strategy use is often dependent on prior domain knowledge. This metacognitive knowledge dilemma presents a challenge to learners (Land, 2000). Azevedo (2005) noted that in some major research on open-ended learning environments, students who had very little metacognitive and self-regulatory skills benefited very little from the environment. It follows that some kind of scaffolding is necessary to scaffold students in ill-structured problem-solving tasks. Without metacognition, students can become overwhelmed in determining what information is important to their needs and what they need to do to refine their knowledge (Land, 2000).

Various instructional design frameworks have been proposed and interactive learning technologies have been developed to address students' learning needs in both cognition and metacognition as a way to scaffold their learning in open-ended learning environments. For example, Ge and Land (2003, 2004) proposed a framework to scaffold ill-structured problem solving using question prompts and peer interactions mediated with technology. Consistently, other researchers (e.g., Lajoie & Azevedo, 2000, 2006) proposed creating technology-rich environments to promote active knowledge transfer and self-monitoring through expert prompting, modeling, and feedback.

The goal of this chapter is to examine how learning technologies can be designed to facilitate self-regulatory activities, which serve as mediators between personal characteristics (e.g., prior knowledge, metacognition, problem-solving competence, and confidence) and contextual characteristics (e.g., open-ended environment, ill-defined problems, etc.) and problem-solving performance in ill-structured tasks (Pintrich, 2000). This chapter first presents a cognitive support system, aiming at scaffolding students' ill-structured problem-solving processes through facilitating their self-monitoring and self-regulation activities. Next, it provides an overview of the theoretical conceptual frameworks underlying the design of the cognitive support system, including sociocultural theory for scaffolding, cognitive theory for ill-structured problem solving, and self-regulated learning theory, followed by an examination of the cognitive and metacognitive functions of the support mechanisms and tools embedded in the cognitive support system. Then, this chapter offers some empirical evidence on the effects of the cognitive support system in supporting self-regulation during ill-structured problem-solving processes. Lastly, this chapter discusses the design implications for learning technologies and future research.

Overview of a Web-Based Cognitive Support System

Based on a critical literature review and empirical findings, a database-driven, Web-based cognitive support system was developed to scaffold complex, ill-structured problem-solving processes through facilitating the development of metacognitive awareness and self-regulatory skills (Ge & Er, 2005; Ge, Planas, & Er, 2010). It is a carefully structured and sequenced scaffolding system, consisting of a case library, the scaffolding mechanisms, and a database. The case library provides students with access to real-world cases related to a content domain under study and requires them to solve complex, ill-structured problems presented by the cases. The scaffolds are mainly characterized by a set of question prompts elicited from content domain experts and representing the mental models of experts for the problem under study. The question prompts are domain-specific, but they can generally be categorized into procedural prompts, elaboration prompts, and reflection prompts, which are discussed specifically in the question prompt section below. The question prompt mechanism is supported with additional social scaffolding mechanisms, including peer review and expert view. The main features, functions

You are a recent graduate from the University of Oklahoma College of Pharmacy. You work as a full-time pharmacist at Phil's Pharmacy, a community pharmacy in Edmond, Oklahoma. Jane Smith comes into your pharmacy to request a refill of her albuterol inhaler. Her complete prescription profile on your computer is as follows:

Name: Jane Smith Sex: Female Age: 23

Allergies: Penicillin Health conditions: Asthma

Medication	Quantity	Directions	Prescriber	Original refills	Remaining refills	Last refill date
Albuterol inhaler	17 gm (200 metered doses)	2 puffs prn asthma	R. Davis, M.D.	11	6	14 days ago

Ms. Smith has had asthma since she was a child. About four months ago, she switched to your pharmacy because it is close to her office. She has been getting her albuterol inhaler filled at your pharmacy every six weeks except for the last two refills, each of which lasted her two weeks. Ms. Smith tells you she's had to use her inhaler more often than usual during the last month. She also mentions that, on several occasions over the last month, she's had to get up at night to use her inhaler for coughing and shortness of breath.

Fig. 15.1 A sample case involving a pharmacy patient, which invited the pharmacy students to propose an appropriate solution during their ill-structured problem-solving task

and their design rationales of the cognitive support system are detailed below.

Case Library

All the cases in the library are indexed, grouped, and searchable with keywords, topics, and levels of difficulty. The database-driven case library is an important component of the cognitive support system because the real-world cases contained in the library serve as anchors (CTGV, 1990), or enabling contexts (Hannafin, Land, & Oliver, 1999), to engage students in an open-ended learning environment to solve ill-structured problems. From the perspective of self-regulated learning, the cases motivate students to set a learning goal to keep them focused. When students perceive the value and relevance of a task, they can attempt to regulate and control those value beliefs (Pintrich, 2000).

Beginning with a description of a specific problem scenario, each of the cases presents a problem-solving task, which invites students to analyze the problem situation and suggest solutions to the problem. A case sets up a context for problem solving and challenges students to seek or generate a solution through manipulating problem space, articulating their reasoning to the problem solutions, and developing a cogent and valid argument to support their proposed solution(s). For example, in a study investigating pharmacy students' problem-solving skills (Ge, Planas, & Er, 2010), the students were provided with a problem scenario, including the prescription profile of a patient who was experiencing a medication problem related to controlling her asthma (see Fig. 15.1). The students were placed in a dilemma here. They were asked to go through the problem-solving steps guided by the question prompts in order to propose an appropriate solution that would both satisfy the patient's needs without compromising their professional standards of practice.

In another study involving preservice teachers (Kauffman, Ge, Xie, & Chen, 2008), the chosen topic for the problem-solving tasks was classroom management, particularly focusing on the issues of flexibility, classroom climate, and effort to limit behaviors. The cases asked the preservice teachers to play the role of an expert in classroom management and to "observe" a teacher's interaction with his students (presented in a dialogue format between the teacher and several student characters). In their simulated roles, the preservice teachers were asked to provide feedback to the classroom teacher via email about the teacher's classroom management skills based on their observations, help the teacher to analyze the problem classroom situation, and suggest ways to improve his classroom management.

All the cases meet the criteria for ill-structured, or ill-defined, problems, which have been identified by researchers (Jonassen, 1997, 1999; Lynch, Ashley, Pinkwart, & Aleven, 2009; Voss & Post, 1988): (a) have vaguely stated goals and constraints, some problem elements missing or unclear; (b) do not have unambiguous right or wrong answers but fall on a range of acceptability; (c) possess multiple solutions, solution paths, or no solutions at all; (d) require learners to justify and defend their solutions by means of argument; (e) possess multiple criteria for evaluating solutions. Given the ill-definedness of these cases, learners are required to reframe or *recharacterize* the problems; and the recharacterization and the resulting solutions are subject to debate (Lynch et al., 2009).

Question Prompts

Question prompts are generated based on subject matter expert reasoning, mental model and processes to model and guide learners through complex, ill-structured problem-solving processes by engaging learners in reflective thinking, monitoring, and evaluation processes. These prompts can be categorized into (a) procedural prompts, (b) elaboration prompts, and (c) reflective prompts, each of which serves different cognitive and metacognitive purposes (Ge & Land, 2004).

Procedural prompts are a set of question prompts, which are designed to guide learners step by step through the entire processes of a specific problem-solving task (e.g., problem representation, developing solutions, constructing arguments, and monitoring and evaluation) while engaging learners in self-monitoring and self-regulation process. Examples of procedural prompts provides an overview of problem-solving steps, for example: *Step 1—identify the problematic situation*, *Step 2—define the problem*, *Step 3—list and evaluate alternative solutions*, *Step 4—choose, justify, and implement a plan*, *Step 5—evaluate the plan*. Each of these steps is followed by elaborative or reflective prompts (Ge, Planas, & Er, 2010). For example, in the case involving the pharmacy patient, the following elaboration prompts were provided for *Step 1—identify the problematic* situation: What *facts* from this case suggest a problem? Is there a standard for comparing these facts? If so, what is (are) the standard(s)? Are the facts out of line? Why or why not? It is assumed that procedural prompts also model an expert's problem-solving approach so that learners will gradually acquire the expert's mental model in their future problem-solving tasks.

Elaborative prompts (e.g., *What is the example of…? Why is it important? How does it affect…?*) are designed to prompt students to articulate their thoughts and elicit explanations (King, 1991). In the case of classroom management for preservice teachers, the students were prompted to think about the following question: "What do you see as the primary problems in Mr. Harrison's tenth grade science class? Why are they occurring? Can there be some other problem(s)? Why or why not? What are they?" It is found that students often propose a solution without solid theoretical support or evidence. This kind of prompt will "force" them to elaborate their thinking and formulate explanations. Elaboration prompts have been proved to direct students' attention to understanding *when* and *why* with college students in a science-related content domain, which facilitated learners' self-monitoring and self-regulation processes (Lin & Lehman, 1999).

Reflection prompts (e.g., *What is our plan? Have our goals changed? To do a good job on this project, we need to …*) are designed to encourage reflection on a meta-level that students do not generally consider (Davis & Linn, 2000). In the pharmacy case, the students were prompted to reflect on the solution, for instance, "How and when will you monitor the implementation of the plan? How will you know if the problem is solved, alleviated, or is getting worse?" Davis and Linn (2000) found that reflection prompts helped students to become autonomous in their knowledge integration. King (1991) found that reflective

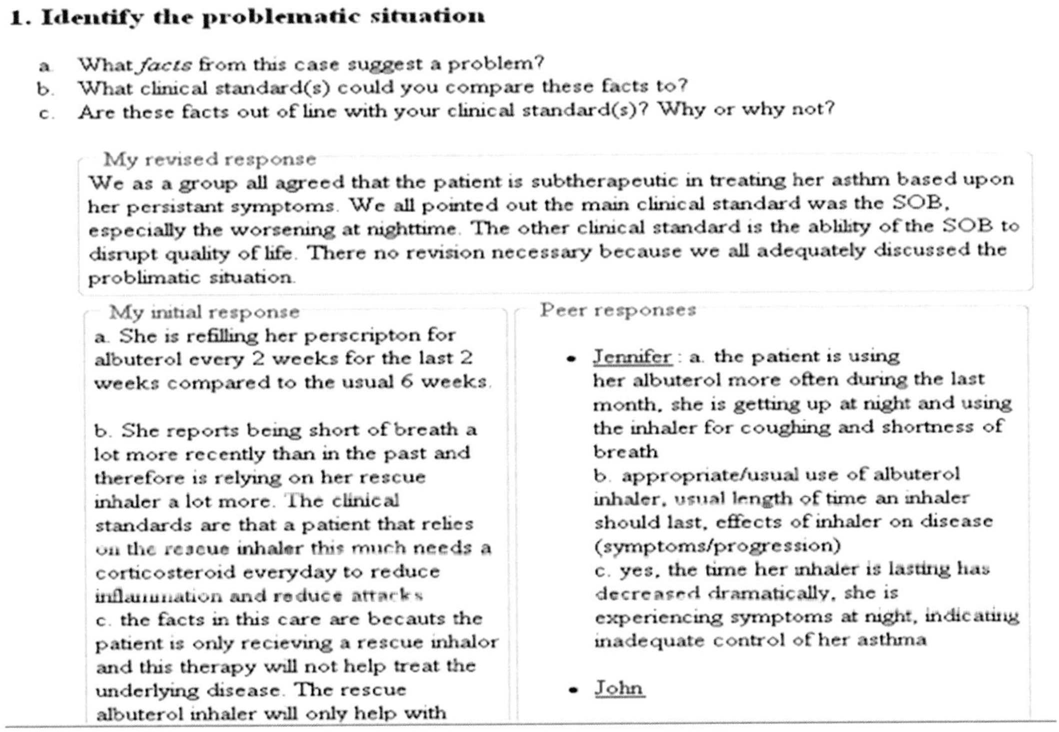

1. Identify the problematic situation

a. What *facts* from this case suggest a problem?
b. What clinical standard(s) could you compare these facts to?
c. Are these facts out of line with your clinical standard(s)? Why or why not?

My revised response
We as a group all agreed that the patient is subtherapeutic in treating her asthm based upon her persistant symptoms. We all pointed out the main clinical standard was the SOB, especially the worsening at nighttime. The other clinical standard is the ablility of the SOB to disrupt quality of life. There no revision necessary because we all adequately discussed the problimatic situation.

My initial response
a. She is refilling her perscripton for albuterol every 2 weeks for the last 2 weeks compared to the usual 6 weeks.

b. She reports being short of breath a lot more recently than in the past and therefore is relying on her rescue inhaler a lot more. The clinical standards are that a patient that relies on the rescue inhaler this much needs a corticosteroid everyday to reduce inflammation and reduce attacks
c. the facts in this care are becauts the patient is only recieving a rescue inhalor and this therapy will not help treat the underlying disease. The rescue albuterol inhaler will only help with

Peer responses

- Jennifer: a. the patient is using her albuterol more often during the last month, she is getting up at night and using the inhaler for coughing and shortness of breath
b. appropriate/usual use of albuterol inhaler, usual length of time an inhaler should last, effects of inhaler on disease (symptoms/progression)
c. yes, the time her inhaler is lasting has decreased dramatically, she is experiencing symptoms at night, indicating inadequate control of her asthma
- John

Fig. 15.2 Question prompts for "Step 1—Identifying the problematic situation" and its associated elaboration prompts, an individual student's initial responses, her peer responses (clicking the name to open or close the peer's response), and her revised responses after reviewing the peers' responses

prompts encouraged student to engage in self-monitoring process during problem solving, such as planning, monitoring, and evaluation. In addition, it is found that reflection prompts serve as a self-evaluation checklist for students to self-assess their learning (Lin, 2001; Rosenshine, Meister, & Chapman, 1996).

Database

Database is used with text boxes that allow students to type, save and retrieve their responses to each of the question prompts. The prompts are a fixed sequence of questions presented to students after they finished reading a case. They are designed to be case-dependent because each case has a different problem context with specific situations and constraints. However, in all the cases the prompts follow the same underlying problem-solving processes by directing students to represent problems, articulate and elaborate their reasoning, develop their solutions, justify and defend their solutions, and monitor and evaluate their solutions. In the earlier version of the system, individual students' initial responses to question prompts, which have been previously saved to the database, are retrieved and made available to them by displaying their responses on the Web page later when students are ready to write their solutions, construct arguments, and evaluate their solutions. In the later version of the system, students can also revise or edit their initial responses that have been saved to the database (see Fig. 15.2 for student's initial and revised responses and peers' responses). In this case, the database system not only serves to store and retrieve data, but also makes students' thinking visible for self-reflection (Davis & Linn, 2000), which scaffolds learners to evaluate and revise their responses, thus facilitating students' self-monitoring and self-regulation. These data can also be made available for peer evaluation in a collaborative problem-solving context and allow students to compare their reasoning with that of an expert regarding a problem-solving task. The affordances of the database have made it possible to develop the peer review and expert view mechanisms (see Ge & Er, 2005; Ge, Planas, & Er, 2010).

Peer Review

The peer review mechanism was designed to enable students to see multiple perspectives from peers' responses to the problem solutions and help them notice things they might not have thought about. By reviewing their peers' thinking, students are supposedly compelled not only to attend more closely to their peers', but also their own ideas, rationales, plans, and solutions for self-reflection. Every student was preassigned by the researchers to a group of three members, who logged into the same group space. Once a student has submitted his/her responses to the question prompts regarding the solutions, he/she will be able to see the other members' responses if the peers have submitted their responses. Figure 15.2 above illustrates the screen of the peer review where an individual student's initial responses, her peers' responses, and her revised responses that have been submitted after viewing the peers' responses. Every student was prompted to revise his/her responses after viewing the peers' responses.

Expert View

Expert modeling is provided by presenting students with an expert's solution to a complex problem. This support mechanism offers students an opportunity to observe an expert's reasoning and compare it with their own reasoning, which may result in disequilibrium (Piaget, 1985). Mediated additionally by reflection prompts, the result of disequilibrium should lead to self-regulation, which will enable students to contemplate and articulate the observable gaps at a deeper level. In addition, the visual display of an expert's problem-solving responses appearing on the same screen as a student's responses (see Fig. 15.3) further fosters students' self-monitoring and self-reflection through identifying gaps between their thinking and an expert's thinking.

The cognitive support system was designed to accommodate various content domains through the system features of categorizing, adding, editing cases by a panel of experts and/or practitioners, who are interested in participating and mentoring students. In addition, the question prompt generator allows instructors, experts, facilitators, or anyone who has the authority, to generate question prompts or make prompt entries by adding, editing or deleting questions that are designed to guide problem solving for a given case. Besides, content domain experts can also enter or edit expert problem solutions into the database for expert view. Therefore, this cognitive support system is easily adaptable by providing an administrative access to instructors or facilitators and to be used for various content domains and allows for generating question prompts that are relevant to the chosen case (see Ge & Er, 2005).

According to Land and Hannafin (2000), a favorable open-ended learning environment should follow the principles of "grounded design" (p. 3), that is, the systematic implementation of processes and procedures for designing technology or a learning environment that are rooted in established theory and research in human learning. The design of this Web-based cognitive support system has followed the principles of grounded design in that it is built upon the foundations and assumptions of socio-cultural theory, cognitive theory for problem solving and self-regulation theory, supported with empirically based and validated strategies and methods from past research, and has continually been tested and refined over time.

4. Choose, justify, and implement a plan of action to solve the problem

a. Which option will you implement as a plan?
b. Why is this plan the best choice?
c. How and when will you implement this plan?

Dr. Planas's response

a. I will implement **Option II** as a plan.

b. I believe this plan is the best choice because it immediately addresses Ms. Smith's primary drug therapy problem, which is the need for additional drug therapy to improve asthma control by preventing asthma symptoms.

c. I will relay to Ms. Smith the importance of Dr. Davis being made aware of her recent increase in asthma symptoms. I will call Dr. Davis' office while Ms. Smith is waiting in the pharmacy. Once on the telephone with Dr. Davis' office, I will identify myself and assertively state the purpose of my call and the need to speak directly with Dr. Davis. Once on the phone with Dr. Davis, I will describe Ms. Smith's current asthma status, her need for additional drug therapy, and my therapy recommendation. I will counsel Ms. Smith on the differences between fluticasone-salmeterol and albuterol (prevention versus treatment) and on the importance of adhering to her new prescription regimen. I will also alert her to common side effects such as increased heart rate and the need to rinse her mouth after use to prevent oral thrush.

My revised response after reviewing peer responses

When a patient presents with worsening symptoms it is very important to treat the disease aggressively. This concept can prevent severe or life threatening attacks and could eventually lead to removal of disease. Therefore, I would talk with the doctor and recommend Advair and Claritin for the patient. I would also evaluate her technique and environmental allergans. The plan will be implemented by first contacting her doctor and giving my recommendation and then when she comes in for her refill and new Rx I will counsel her on the allergans and technique.

My initial response

Both options are needed in this instance due to the progression of the disease. Simply trying to avoid allergens will not drammatically reduce the symptoms. The inflammation of the broncholes must be reduced. In this situation I would recommend the duel therapy as the best choice. This plan needs to be implemented immediatly. This is obviously the patients bad time of the year and one attack could be serious or even deadly.

Peer responses

- Jennifer Mooney
- John Muilenburg
- Stacy Ritter

5. Evaluate the plan

a. How will you know if your plan works?
b. What secondary problems will you watch out for, and how will you do this?

Dr. Planas's response

a. I will know my plan is off to a good start if Dr. Davis accepts my therapy recommendation or prescribes a similar therapy to prevent Ms. Smith's asthma symptoms, and if Ms. Smith agrees to begin the prescribed therapy. I will schedule a follow-up evaluation with Ms. Smith in 2 weeks. At that time, I will ask her how often she has experienced asthma symptoms, including nighttime symptoms; and how often she has used her albuterol inhaler. I will know my plan has worked if Ms. Smith's asthma symptoms have decreased to no more than 2 daytime exacerbations per week and no more than 1 nighttime exacerbation per week. These goals of therapy are consistent with the classification of mild persistent asthma, which is a step down from Ms. Smith previous moderate persistent asthma status.[1]

Fig. 15.3 An expert's view indicated by Dr. Planas's responses for "Step 4—Choose, justify and implement a plan of action to solve the problem" and "Step 5—Evaluate the plan." The individual student's initial and revised responses as well as three peers' responses also appear on the same screen (by clicking on a peer's name, the peer's response will be displayed on the screen)

Theoretical Frameworks and Assumptions

Central to the design of the cognitive support system is Vygotsky's (1978) socio-cultural theory on social interactions and scaffolding. Traditionally, scaffolding is provided through mentoring, modeling and social interactions provided by an adult, a teacher, a domain expert, or a more capable peer. However, with the advancement of technologies, it has become possible that technologies can also be used or designed to provide external support to scaffold learners' problem-solving performance, reflection, and metacognition (Salomon, Globerson, & Guterman, 1989). Pea (1985) argued that tools provide opportunities for learners to amplify and extend their cognitive capabilities, as well as reorganize their thinking process by altering the tasks available to them. However, to harness the power of tools technologies should be designed to provide models, opportunities for higher level thinking, and metacognitive guidance in a learner's zone of proximal development (Lajoie,

1993, 2000; Lajoie & Azevedo, 2006; Land & Hannafin, 2000; Pea, 1985; Salomon, 1993).

In a technology-rich environment, scaffolds can take the form of inexplicit humanlike guidance, such as tools (e.g., cue cards, hints, or prompts) (Scardamalia & Bereiter, 1985; Scardamalia, Bereiter, & Steinbach, 1984) or strategies (e.g., reciprocal teaching and guided peer questioning) (King, 1991; 1992; King & Rosenshine, 1993; Palincsar & Brown, 1984). For the cognitive support system discussed in this chapter, scaffolding is particularly achieved through question prompts, peer review, expert's thinking, and self-reflections.

In addition, the assumption of cognitive apprenticeship further accounts for design of the support mechanisms embedded in the system. According to this assumption, a mentor makes his thinking visible to novices through social dialogues, during which the mentor and a novice engage in the same problem-solving experience (Brown et al., 1989; Collins, Brown, & Newman, 1989), which scaffolds the novice's problem-solving processes. Therefore, an expert's view and students' self-reflection are integrated into the system as parts of the scaffolding mechanisms. However, this support system only models and scaffolds learners' problem-solving processes while it does not address the fading process, which is a limitation discussed at the end. Overall, the social constructivist perspective sets up a theoretical framework for scaffolding ill-structured problem solving, which has guided the design and development of the cognitive support system under discussion.

Ill-Structured Problem Solving, Metacognition, and Self-Regulation

In order to understand how technologies can be designed to scaffold self-regulation and problem solving, we need to first understand the cognitive and metacognitive requirements involved in problem-solving processes (Land, 2000) and how self-monitoring and self-regulation activities can facilitate ill-structured problem-solving processes. Then effective instructional strategies can be selected or developed to scaffold self-regulation activities, which subsequently mediate ill-structured problem-solving processes and performance.

Ill-structured problem solving can be identified as involving four processes (see Ge & Land, 2003; 2004 for a detailed review): (a) problem representation, (b) developing solutions, (c) making justifications and constructing arguments, (d) monitoring and evaluation. The process of making justification and generating arguments and the process of monitoring and evaluation can happen concurrently during the processes of problem representation and developing solutions. In the problem representation process, problem solvers try to define the problem and set the goal for problem solving. This is the initial state of problem solving, which involves examining the interrelationships among different concepts of a problem, isolating major factors causing the problem, identifying constraints, understanding known facts, determining needed information for solving the problem, and recognizing divergent perspectives (Voss & Post, 1988). Problem representation helps problem solvers to generate possible solutions in the later process (Chi & Glaser, 1985). Solution process follows after problem representation when problem solver generates or selects solutions by eliminating the causes of the problem and developing corresponding procedures for implementing them. Since an ill-structured problem often involves multiple solutions and multiple paths to solutions, a problem solver must select the most viable solution and support it with defensible, and cogent argument (Jonassen, 1997; Voss & Post, 1988). Because of the decision-making process involved, making justifications and constructing argument is an essential process and skill in ill-structured problem solving (Jonassen, 1997; Kitchener & King, 1981). This process also compels the problem solver to evaluate his or her solution by examining the selected solution and defending his/her decision against other alternative solutions. Therefore, the monitoring and evaluation process is required in the entire ill-structured problem-solving processes, from problem representation to selecting solutions and defending for the selected solution (Sinnott, 1989).

As indicated from the discussion above, ill-structured problem-solving challenges problem solvers with cognitive and metacognitive demands (Jonassen, 1997). The cognitive demand for solving ill-structured problems involves both domain-specific knowledge (Chi & Glaser, 1985; Voss & Post, 1988; Voss, Wolfe, Lawrence, & Engle, 1991) and structural knowledge (Chi & Glaser, 1985). Problem solvers have to rely on their domain specific knowledge and structural knowledge to understand a problem situation. Metacognition involves both knowledge of cognition and regulation of cognition (Brown, 1987; Pressley & McCormick, 1987). Metacognitive skill is essential in helping problem solvers to relate various problem aspects to their prior knowledge, set goals, select solutions, monitor problem solving process and evaluate solutions, and reflect on their problem-solving processes. It plays an equally or more important role in successfully solving an ill-structured problem, particularly when domain-specific knowledge is limited or absent (Wineburg, 1998). In this chapter, the discussion focuses more on the regulation of cognition within metacognition because self-regulation plays an important role in experts' problem-solving processes (Pressley & McCormick, 1987). Comparing problem solving by experts and novices, researchers found that experts had learned to keep themselves on task and guide their thinking through regulation of complex sequences of procedures that are combined and coordinated with prior knowledge (Zimmerman & Campillo, 2003). When prior knowledge does not fit the new situation, an expert would make self-regulatory adjustments leading to new knowledge, which will then made available for future problem-solving purposes (Zimmerman & Campillo, 2003).

According to Pintrich (2000), self-regulation "is an active, constructive process whereby learners set goals for their learning and then attempt to monitor, regulate, and control their cognition, motivation, and behavior, guided and constrained by their goals and the contextual features in the environment." (p. 453) Pintrich (2000) summarized the shared components of different regulation models into different phases and areas of regulation, which have become a valuable conceptual framework for regulation. The four phases include *forethought, planning and activation*; *monitoring; control; reaction and reflection*, each of which concerns with cognition, motivation/affect, behavior, and context. Pintrich's (2000) framework is similar with Zimmerman and Campillo's (2003) three cyclical self-regulated model underlying problem-solving processes: *forethought phase* (task-analysis and self-motivating beliefs), *performance phase* (self-control, and self-observation), *self-reflection phase* (self-judgment and self-reaction).

Both Pintrich's (2000) and Zimmerman and Campillo's (2003) self-regulated models imply that scaffolding should be provided to direct students to analyze the problem-solving task, set goals, focus on relevant information, activate their prior knowledge, plan for strategy use, and engage in self-monitoring and self-evaluation judgments, all of which are aligned with ill-structured problem-solving processes. Planning and goal setting are essential processes during problem representation (Jonassen, 1997). Further, when ill-structured problems represent states of uncertainty, monitoring one's own cognitive efforts is required in search of solutions, and evaluation is also required to determine the extent to which obtained information may be effective for the solution process and which selected goals may be important in a given situation (Kluwe & Friedrichsen, 1985). This is the time of reflection and reaction, when problem solvers reflect on things like, how the proposed solution would solve the problem, what should be done about any difficulty the selected solution might pose, and evaluate various perspectives and values of the selected solution (Voss et al., 1991). Therefore, it is argued that regulation phases influence problem-solving processes and outcomes. According to the recent work by Lynch et al., (2009), framing/recharacterization is an essential part of the problem-solving process for ill-defined problems. The recharacterization "may include redefining aspects of the problem to relate it to relevant domain rules and concepts; identifying clear solution criteria; reinterpreting essential rules and concepts according to the present goal; and analogizing or distinguishing the current problem from prior cases." (Lynch et al., 2009, p. 259). This process of recharacterization requires problem solvers to constantly monitor, evaluate, and regulate their problem-solving processes until a feasible, viable, and defensible solution is arrived at. Lynch and his colleagues' work (2009) further highlights the importance of the role of the self-regulation in solving ill-defined problems.

Role of Question Prompts in Scaffolding Problem-Solving Through Self-Regulation

When explaining the forethought and planning phase, Pintrich (2000) indicated that activation of prior knowledge of the content area can happen automatically, but it can also be done in a more planful and regulatory manner through various prompts or self-questioning activities. Past research shows that question prompts are an effective instructional strategy for directing students to the most important aspects of a problem, as well as encouraging self-explanation, elaboration, planning, monitoring, and self-reflection, and evaluation (Bransford & Stein, 1993; Chi, Bassok, Lewis, Reimann, & Glaser, 1989; Chi, Leeuw, Chiu, & Lavancher, 1994; King, 1991, 1992; Lin & Lehman, 1999; Palincsar & Brown, 1984; Scardamalia & Bereiter, 1989). Researchers (Chi, Bassok, Lewis, Reimann, & Glaser, 1989; Chi, Leeuw, Chiu, & Lavancher, 1994) found that successful learners tend to generate more working explanations, particularly in response to an awareness of limited understanding. Recent studies reveal that prompting students with questions scaffold their ill-structured problem-solving processes, particularly in problem representation, making justifications, developing solutions, and monitoring and evaluating problem solving (e.g., Ge, Chen, & Davis, 2005; Ge & Land, 2003, 2004). Above all, question prompts proved to be beneficial in developing learners' metacognitive awareness and self-regulatory abilities. Students who were provided with question prompts used them as a checklist to monitor their problem-solving processes, to confirm if they were on the right track, and to check their courses of action (Ge, Chen, & Davis, 2005; Ge & Land, 2003).

In summary, according to a critical review of literature, question prompts play four main functions in facilitating self-monitoring and self-regulation during ill-structured problem solving. First, question prompts direct students to some important information they might have missed. This function is not only particularly important during problem representation when learners' attention is directed to important features of a problem, identifying goals and analyzing factors and constraints, but also important in focusing their attention on particular important information in the other problem-solving processes. Second, questions prompt students to elaborate their thoughts, activate prior knowledge, and elicit relevant explanations, which help students to elaborate the initial state of the problem, make justifications, and generate arguments. Third, question prompts encourage reflection and metacognition that students do not generally consider, which facilitate knowledge integration as well as planning, monitoring and evaluation. Fourth, question prompts guide students' self-monitoring explicitly during their problem-solving processes, such as planning, monitoring and evaluation.

Role of Social Support in Scaffolding Problem-Solving Through Self-Regulation

Peer review: Peer review is an important component of the peer interaction process. In the peer review process, students are compelled to examine their own thinking after reviewing the peers' responses, such as their implicit, unarticulated assumptions, misconceptions, This process also allows students to learn from multiple perspectives and solutions (Ge & Land, 2003; Linn, Bell, & Hsi, 1998). Peer review mechanism supports the performance phase of self-regulation during problem solving (Zimmerman & Campillo, 2003). *Expert view*: Modeling, coaching, and scaffolding are the major characteristics of a cognitive apprenticeship approach (Jonassen, 1999). Research on expert-novice comparison has shown that experts and novices demonstrate different patterns in problem solving (e.g., Anderson, 2000; Bereiter & Scardamalia, 1993; Bransford, Brown, & Cocking, 2000; Dreyfus & Dreyfus, 1986). Expert modeling mechanism supports the performance phase of self-regulation (Zimmerman & Campillo, 2003).

Empirical Studies on the Web-Based Cognitive Modeling System

Different components and versions of the cognitive support system, particularly the mechanism of question prompts, have been tested and studied in the past years in various contexts, content domains, and with different target audiences, including undergraduate students in information science and technology (IST), education, and pharmacy, as well as graduate students in instructional design and technology. Both quantitative and qualitative research methods have been employed to investigate the effects of the cognitive support system on students' ill-structured problem-solving performance in the past years. In all the research contexts, students were provided with one or two cases representing complex, ill-structured problems related to the content domain of the target audience (see Fig. 15.1), and they were asked to analyze the problem, develop solutions, making justifications, and evaluate their solution plan related to the participants' subject domain (see Fig. 15.3 for example).

Experimental Studies

In four experimental studies (i.e., Ge & Land, 2003; Ge, Du, Chen, & Huang, 2005; Ge, Planas, & Er, 2010; Kauffman, Ge, Xie, & Chen, 2008), the participants were assigned to either an experimental group or a control group, and their task was to work on a case in a Web-based learning environment and generate solutions to the ill-structured problem presented by the case, with or without scaffolds depending on the condition they were assigned to (control vs. treatment). Despite the differences in domain and target audiences, these studies shared some commonalities in research method and analytical techniques. All four studies involved the comparisons of a treatment group(s) with a control group in solving one or two ill-structured problem-solving tasks, focusing on the effect of question prompts (independent variable) and measuring problem-solving outcomes in four or five processes (dependent variables): problem representation, generating solutions, constructing argument, and monitoring and evaluation (or variants of these processes depending on a specific domain). At the same time, the variable of monitoring and evaluation was also investigated as the outcome of self-monitoring and self-evaluation. Scoring rubrics were developed to rate each of the students' problem-solving processes. Inferential statistical analysis, such as multivariate analysis of variance and univariate tests were performed in those studies to determine if the use of the cognitive support system led to statistically significant differences between the experimental group and the control group.

In addition, some studies also measured additional dependent variables or investigated the effect of additional independent variables. For example, in Ge and Land's (2003) study question prompts were compared with peer interactions (another independent variable). In Ge, Planas, and Er's (2010) study, the effect of peer review was measured as an additional independent variable. On the other hand, the quality of students' written problem-solving reports was measured as a dependent variable for preservice teachers in the study by Kauffman, Ge, Xie, and Chen (2008). Furthermore, students' perceived competence and confidence were also measured by Ge, Du, Chen, and Huang (2005) when investigating the effect of question prompts on novice instructional designers' problem-solving performance. In all these studies, we only measured the students' problem-solving performance with scaffolding in comparison with the students' problem-solving performance without scaffolding. However, we did not assess the transfer effect of scaffolding on students' subsequent problem-solving performance when scaffolding was withdrawn.

In all these experimental studies, the results invariably showed positive effects of question prompts in scaffolding ill-structured problem-solving processes in problem representation, selecting solutions, making justifications, and evaluating solutions. Kauffman, Ge, Xie, and Chen's (2008) study found that students who received problem-solving prompts (designed to procedurally guide learners through the problem-solving processes) not only showed better problem-solving performance but also wrote with more clarity than the students who did not receive problem-solving prompts. Additionally, the study by Ge, Planas, and Er (2010) showed that simply engaging pharmacy students in revising their problem-solving solution reports improved their performance over time. It suggests that providing learners an opportunity to evaluate and revise their solutions seemed to have offered them time and space to engage in self-reflection and self-regulation activities, which in turn benefited their problem-solving experience. In the same study, however, the peer review mechanism did not show any advantage for the treatment group over the control group. This could be due to the fact that this experiment did not offer peers the opportunity to make comments or suggestions to each other, but only to view each others' solutions. The feedback from this finding had been incorporated to improve the system, the current version of which allows peers to type notes, comments, and suggestions.

Qualitative Studies

Qualitative studies were either carried out independently (Ge, Chen, & Davis, 2005), or as supplemental methods to some of the experimental studies (i.e., Ge & Land, 2003; Ge, Planas, & Er, 2010) presented above. Various methods and techniques, including think-aloud protocols, observations, follow-up interviews, multiple case studies, and content analysis, were carried out to investigate the influence of the system (i.e., Ge, Chen, & Davis, 2005; Ge & Land, 2003; Ge, Planas, & Er, 2010). In the same study involving IST undergraduate students that is described above (Ge & Land, 2003), some individuals were invited to participate in think-aloud protocols when performing an ill-structured problem-solving task by following question prompts while some groups of students were videotaped for their peer interactions. In another study (Ge, Chen, & Davis, 2005), eight graduate students in instructional design and technology received either elaborative prompts or procedural prompts, and they were asked to perform think-aloud protocols, which was followed by interviews. In a recent study of pharmacy students (Ge, Planas, & Er, 2010), both individual responses and reflection notes were analyzed to examine the influence of displaying the expert's thought processes in solving a real-world problem.

It was commonly observed from the qualitative studies that the students who received question prompts were able to: (a) make an intentional effort to identify factors, seek needed information, and analyze constraints during the problem representation process; (b) organize and plan a solution process; (c) make an effort to articulate justifications or arguments during solution process; (d) intentionally evaluate solutions selected, comparing alternatives and justifying the most viable solutions. These findings indicated how question prompts supported reasoning and self-regulation, which in turn influenced problem-solving outcomes. On the other hand, the qualitative findings also revealed the conditions under which question prompts could be either effective, limited, or impeding. For example, in the absence of specific-domain knowledge question prompts were futile in activating a learner' prior knowledge or relevant schema (Ge, Chen, & Davis, 2005); for students who perceived themselves as more competent and confident, question prompts were not only experienced as redundant but also as interfering with their thought flow during their problem-solving processes (Ge, Chen, & Davis, 2005).

The content analysis in Ge, Planas and Er's (2010) study (an experimental study mentioned earlier) showed that students' responses to the first set of question prompts (e.g., "Step 1—Identify the problematic situation") seemed to form a foundation that led to better performance in their responses (i.e., more elaborated, detailed, and specific) to the second set of question prompts (e.g., "Step 2—Define the problem"). In addition, the students in the treatment condition indicated that the peer review process allowed them to see multiple perspectives, different ideas, and different approaches. It is also found that the expert view mechanism served as expert modeling and a standard for the students to compare with their own problem-solving approaches and confirm whether they were on the right track or not. This kind of comparison allowed the students to see where the discrepancies were, and thus helped them to reflect on what must be improved in the future. Most importantly, seeing how an expert solved an ill-structured problem increased the students' confidence in solving similar problems themselves. These findings showed how providing expert modeling may help students engage in self-regulation activities.

Overall, the results from a series of studies (quantitative, qualitative, or mixed) confirmed the positive effects of the cognitive support system in scaffolding problem-solving processes in each of the problem-solving processes (dependent variables): *problem representation*, *generating solutions*, *constructing argument*, and *monitoring and evaluating*. Although some of the experimental studies did not directly measure self-monitoring and self-regulation skills during problem-solving processes, the qualitative data obtained from think-aloud protocols and observations revealed that learners' problem-solving performance was influenced by their execution of self-awareness, self-monitoring, and regulation skills mediated by the scaffolds of question prompts (Ge, Chen, & Davis, 2005; Ge & Land, 2003).

Discussion

A comprehensive review of the work completed in the past years has enabled us to understand what has been achieved and what remains to be resolved in the area of scaffolding ill-structured problem solving through facilitating self-regulation in a technology-rich environment. A number of gaps and challenges have been identified in using the cognitive support system, particularly question prompts, to facilitate self-regulation processes and problem-solving processes and outcomes. For example, one of the research goals that has not been fulfilled is to investigate the transfer effects of self-regulatory and problem-solving skills at different points of intervention as scaffolding is gradually withdrawn over an extended period of time.

One of the challenges is the direct measurement of self-regulation skills. Although empirical findings have confirmed that question prompts embedded in the cognitive support system scaffold problem-solving processes through supporting self-regulation, there have not been direct quantitative indicators to demonstrate the extent or level of self-regulation mediated by question prompts and the mutual influences between self-regulation and ill-structured problem-solving skills.

The second challenge is to examine how to map self-regulatory processes with ill-structured problem-solving processes to generate an integrated conceptual framework that illustrates (a) the interrelationships between self-regulation processes and ill-structured problem-solving processes, and (b) how different areas for regulation (cognition, motivation, behavior, and context) (Pintrich, 2000) interact to support each of the ill-structured problem-solving processes. This kind of conceptual framework will guide instructional design aiming at developing students' self-regulation and ill-structured problem-solving skills.

The third challenge is the measurement of optimal amount or level of scaffolding needed for each individual learner based on one's prior knowledge and metacognition so that proper scaffolding can be provided accordingly within an individual's zone of proximal development. It is expected that the findings of this research will inform instructional design regarding automated scaffolding as to when and how much scaffolding should be provided for different individuals, as well as when scaffolding should be withdrawn.

Design Implications

The empirical studies on the effects of the cognitive support system have led to the evolvement and refinement of the system in a number of ways. For example, the question-prompt generator has been developed for the system, which allows a user, such as an instructor or a subject matter expert, to create protocols for modeling problem solving through writing question prompts for each of the problem-solving processes. Each of these processes is considered a top-level prompt, under which the expert or instructor can generate several sublevel question prompts for elaboration or reflection. This feature allows a teacher or some other authorized user to input prompts according to different problem scenarios and different content domains.

In the future, it is desirable for the system to be capable of adaptively adjusting the level of scaffolding according to (a) learners' prior knowledge and metacognition and (b) learners' progress over time through providing problem-solving tasks of different difficulty levels, based on the results of some kind of automated assessments. Since feedback is an important technique in fostering self-regulation, efforts must be made to enhance the cognitive support system with feedback mechanism, which can be achieved through fixed programmed feedback, expert feedback, and community feedback, even though it is understood that adding this feature might present technical, methodological, and practical challenges for development. In addition, it is hoped that a greater variety of strategies can be incorporated into the design framework of the system to promote self-regulation in all areas (i.e., cognition, motivation/affect, behavior, and context), as proposed by Pintrich (2000).

References

Anderson, J. R. (2000). *Cognitive psychology and its implications* (5th ed.). New York: Worth.

Azevedo, R. (2005). Using hypermedia as a metacognitive tool for enhancing student learning? The role of self-regulated learning. *Educational Psychologist, 40*(4), 199–209.

Bereiter, C., & Scardamalia, M. (1993). *Surpassing ourselves: An inquiry into the nature and implications of expertise*. Chicago: Open Court.

Bransford, J. D., Brown, A. L., & Cocking, R. R. (Eds.). (2000). *How people learn: Brain, mind, experience, and school*. Washington, DC: National Academy Press.

Bransford, J. D., & Stein, B. S. (1993). *The IDEAL problem solver: A guide for improving thinking, learning, and creativity* (2nd ed.). New York, NY: W. H. Freeman.

Brown, A. L. (1987). Metacognition, executive control, self-regulation, and other more mysterious mechanisms. In F. E. Weinert & R. H. Kluwe (Eds.), *Metacognition, motivation, and understanding* (pp. 65–115). Hillsdale, NJ: Lawrence Erlbaum Associates.

Brown, J. S., Collins, A., & Duguid, P. (1989). Situated cognition and the culture of learning. *Educational Researcher, 18*(1), 32–42.

Brown, A. L., & Palincsar, A. S., (1989). Guided, cooperative learning and individual knowledge acquisition. In L. B. Resnick (Ed.), *Knowing, learning, and instruction: Essays in honor of Robert Glaser* (pp. 393–451). Hillsdale, NJ: Lawrence Erlbaum.

Chi, M. T. H., & Glaser, R. (1985). Problem solving ability. In R. J. Sternberg (Ed.), *Human abilities: An information processing approach* (pp. 227–250). New York, NY: W. H. Freeman.

Chi, M., Bassok., M., Lewis, M., Reimann, P., & Glaser, R. (1989). Self-explanations: How students study and use examples in learning to solve problems. *Cognitive Science, 13*, 145–182.

Chi, M. T. H., Leeuw, N. D., Chiu, M., & Lavancher, C. (1994). Eliciting self-explanations improves understanding. *Cognitive Science, 18*, 439–477.

Cognition and Technology Group at Vanderbilt. (1990). Anchored instruction and its relationship to situated cognition. *Educational Researcher, 19*(6), 2–10.

Collins, A., Brown, J. S., & Newman, S. E. (1989). Cognitive apprenticeship: teaching the crafts of reading, writing, and mathematics. In L. B. Resnick (Ed.), *Knowing, learning, and instruction: essays in honor of Robert Glaser*. Hillsdale, NJ: Lawrence Erlbaum Associates.

Davis, E. A., & Linn, M. (2000). Scaffolding students' knowledge integration: Prompts for reflection in KIE. *International Journal of Science Education, 22*(8), 819–837.

Dreyfus, H. L., & Dreyfus, S. E. (1986). *Mind over Machine: The power of human intuition and expertise in the era of the computer*. New York, NY: The Free Press.

Feltovich, P. J., Spiro, R. J., Coulson, R. L., & Feltovich, J. (1996). Collaboration within and among minds: Mastering complexity, individuality and in groups. In T. Koschmann (Ed.), *CSCL: Theory and practice of an emerging paradigm* (pp. 25–44). Mahwah, NJ: Lawrence Erlbaum Associates.

Ge, X., Chen, C. H., & Davis, K. A. (2005). Scaffolding novice instructional designers' problem-solving processes using question prompts in a web-based learning environment. *Journal of Educational Computing Research, 33*(2), 219–248.

Ge, X., Du, J., Chen, C., & Huang, K. (2005). *The effects of question prompts in scaffolding ill-structured problem solving in a Web-based learning environment.* Paper presented at the annual meeting of Association of Educational Communications and Technology, Orlando, FL.

Ge, X., & Er, N. (2005). An online support system to scaffold complex problem solving in real-world contexts. *Interactive Learning Environments, 13*(3), 139–157.

Ge, X., & Land, S. M. (2003). Scaffolding students' problem-solving processes in an ill-structured task using question prompts and peer interactions. *Educational Technology Research and Development, 51*(1), 21–38.

Ge, X., & Land, S. M. (2004). A conceptual framework for scaffolding ill-structured problem-solving processes using question prompts and peer interactions. *Educational Technology Research and Development, 52*(2), 5–22.

Ge, X., Planas, L. G., & Er, N. (2010). A cognitive support system to scaffold students' problem-based learning in a Web-based learning environment. *Interdisciplinary Journal of Problem based Learning, 4*(1), 30–56.

Greeno, J. G., Collins, A., & Resnick, L. B. (1996). Cognition and learning. In D. C. Berliner & R. C. Calfee (Eds.), *Handbook of Educational Psychology* (pp. 15–46). New York: Macmillan.

Hannafin, M., Land, S., & Oliver, K. (1999). Open learning environments: Foundations, methods, and models. In C. M. Reigeluth (Ed.), *Instructional-design theories and models: A new paradigm of instructional theory* (Vol. 2, pp. 115–140). Mahwah, NJ: Lawrence Erlbaum Associates.

Jonassen, D. H. (1997). Instructional design models for well-structured and ill-structured problem-solving learning outcomes. *Educational Technology Research and Development, 45*(1), 65–94.

Jonassen, D. H. (1999). Designing constructivist learning environments. In C. M. Reigeluth (Ed.), *Instructional design theories and models* (A new paradigm of instructional technology, Vol. 2, pp. 215–239). Mahwah, NJ: Lawrence Erlbaum Associates.

Kauffman, D., Ge, X., Xie, K., & Chen, C. (2008). Prompting in web-based environments: Supporting self-monitoring and problem solving skills in college students. *Journal of Educational Computing Research, 38*(2), 115–137.

King, A. (1991). Effects of training in strategic questioning on children's problem-solving performance. *Journal of Educational Psychology, 83*(3), 307–317.

King, A. (1992). Facilitating elaborative learning through guided student-generated questioning. *Educational Psychologist, 27*(1), 111–126.

King, A., & Rosenshine, B. (1993). Effect of guided cooperative questioning on children's knowledge construction. *Journal of Experimental Education, 61*(2), 127–148.

Kitchener, K. S., & King, P. M. (1981). Reflective judgment: Concepts of justification and their relationship to age and education. *Journal of Applied Developmental Psychology, 2*, 89–116.

Kluwe, R. H., & Friedrichsen, G. (1985). Mechanism of control and regulation in problem solving. In J. Kuhl & J. Beckmann (Eds.), *Action control: From cognition to behavior* (pp. 183–218). New York, NJ: Springer.

Lajoie, S. P. (1993). Computer environments as cognitive tools for enhancing learning. In S. P. Lajoie & S. J. Derry (Eds.), *Computer as cognitive tools* (pp. 261–288). Hillsdale, NJ: Lawrence Erlbaum Associates.

Lajoie, S. P. (Ed.). (2000). *Computers as cognitive tools: No more walls (Vol. 2).* Mahwah, NJ: Lawrence Erlbaum Associates.

Lajoie, S. P., & Azevedo, R. (2000). Cognitive tools for medical informatics. In S. P. Lajoie (Ed.), *Computer as cognitive tools, Volume Two: No more walls* (pp. 247–271). Mahwah, NJ: Lawrence Erlbaum Associates.

Lajoie, S. P., & Azevedo, R. (2006). Teaching and learning in technology-rich environments. In P. A. Alexander & P. H. Winne (Eds.), *Handbook of educational psychology* (2nd ed., pp. 803–821). Mahwah, NJ: Lawrence Erlbaum Associates.

Land, S. M. (2000). Cognitive requirements for learning with open-ended learning environments. *Educational Technology Research and Development, 48*(3), 61–78.

Land, S. M., & Hannafin, M. J. (2000). Student-centered learning environments. In D. Jonassen & S. Land (Eds.), *Theoretical foundations of learning environments* (pp. 1–23). Mahwah, NJ: Lawrence Erlbaum Associates.

Lin, X. (2001). Designing metacognitive activities. *Educational Technology Research and Development, 49*(2), 23–40.

Lin, X., & Lehman, J. D. (1999). Supporting learning of variable control in a computer-based biology environment: Effects of prompting college students to reflect on their own thinking. *Journal of Research in Science Teaching, 3*(7), 837–858.

Linn, M. C., Bell, P., & Hsi, S. (1998). Using the Internet to enhance student understanding of science: The Knowledge Integration Environment. *Interactive Learning Environments, 6*(1/2), 4–38.

Lynch, C., Ashley, K., Pinkwart, N., & Aleven, V. (2009). Concepts, structures, and goals: Redefining ill-definedness. *International Journal of Artificial Intelligence in Education, 19*(3), 253–266.

Palincsar, A. S., & Brown, A. L. (1984). Reciprocal teaching of comprehension-fostering and comprehension-monitoring activities. *Cognition and Instruction, 2*, 117–175.

Pea, R. (1985). Beyond amplification: Using computer to reorganize mental functioning. *Educational Psychologist, 20*(4), 167–182.

Piaget, J. (1985). *The equilibrium of cognitive structures: The central problem of intellectual development* (T. Brown & K. J. Thampy, Trans.). Chicago: University of Chicago Press.

Pintrich, P. R. (2000). The role of goal orientation in self-regulated learning. In M. Boekaerts, P. R. Pintrich, &

M. Zeidner (Eds.), *Handbook of self-regulated learning* (pp. 451–502). San Diego, CA: Academic.

Pressley, M., & McCormick, C. B. (1987). *Advanced educational psychology for educators, researchers, and policy makers*. New York, NY: HarperCollins.

Rosenshine, B., Meister, C., & Chapman, S. (1996). Teaching students to generate questions: A review of the intervention studies. *Review of Educational Research, 66*(2), 181–221.

Salomon, G. (1993). On the nature of pedagogic computer tools: The case of the writing partner. In S. P. Lajoie & S. J. Derry (Eds.), *Computers as cognitive tools* (pp. 179–196). Hillsdale, NJ: Lawrence Erlbaum Associates.

Salomon, G., Globerson, T., & Guterman, E. (1989). The computer as a zone of proximal development: Internalizing reading-related metacognitions from a reading partner. *Journal of Educational Psychology, 81*(4), 620–627.

Scardamalia, M., & Bereiter, C. (1985). Fostering the development of self-regulation in children's knowledge processing. In S. F. Chipman, J. W. Segal, & R. Glaser (Eds.), *Thinking and learning skills: Vol.2. Research and open questions* (pp. 563–577). Hillsdale, NJ: Lawrence Erlbaum.

Scardamalia, M., Bereiter, C., & Steinbach, R. (1984). Teachability of reflective processes in written composition. *Cognitive Science, 8*, 173–190.

Scardamalia, M., & Bertiter, C. (1989). Computer-supported intentional learning environments. *Journal of Educational Computing Research, 5*(1), 51–68.

Sinnott, J. D. (1989). A model for solution of ill-structured problems: Implications for everyday and abstract problem solving. In J. D. Sinnott (Ed.), *Everyday problem solving: Theory and application* (pp. 72–99). New York, NY: Praeger.

Voss, J. F., & Post, T. A. (1988). On the solving of ill-structured problems. In M. H. Chi, R. Glaser, & M. J. Farr (Eds.), *The nature of expertise* (pp. 261–285). Hillsdale, NJ: Lawrence Erlbaum Associates.

Voss, J. F., Wolfe, C. R., Lawrence, J. A., & Engle, R. A. (1991). From representation to decision: An analysis of problem solving in international relations. In R. J. Sternberg & P. A. Frensch (Eds.), *Complex problem solving: Principles and mechanisms*. Hillsdale, NJ: Lawrence Erlbaum Associates.

Vygotsky, L. S. (1978). *Mind in society*. Cambridge, MA: Harvard University Press.

Wineburg, S. S. (1998). Reading Abraham Lincoln: An expert-expert study in the interpretation of historical texts. *Cognitive Science, 22*, 319–346.

Zimmerman, B. J., & Campillo, M. (2003). Motivating self-regulated problem solvers. In J. E. Davidson & R. J. Sternberg (Eds.), *The psychology of problem solving* (pp. 233–262). New York NY: Cambridge University Press.

16 Technology-Rich Tools to Support Self-Regulated Learning and Performance in Medicine

Susanne P. Lajoie, Laura Naismith, Eric Poitras, Yuan-Jin Hong, Ilian Cruz-Panesso, John Ranellucci, Samuel Mamane, and Jeffrey Wiseman

Abstract

Medical students' metacognitive and self-regulatory behaviors are examined as they diagnose patient cases using BioWorld, a technology rich learning environment. BioWorld offers an authentic problem-based environment where students solve clinical cases and receive expert feedback. We evaluate the effectiveness of key features in BioWorld (the evidence table and visualization maps) to see whether they promote metacognitive monitoring and evaluation. Learning outcomes were assessed through novice/expert comparisons in relation to diagnostic accuracy, confidence, and case summaries. More specifically we examined how diagnostic processes and learning outcomes were refined or improved through practice at solving a series of patient cases. The results suggest that, with practice, medical students became more expert-like in the processes involved in making crucial clinical decisions. The implications of these findings for the design of features embedded within BioWorld that foster key metacognitive and self-regulatory processes are discussed.

This chapter explores how metacognition and self-regulated learning (SRL) are supported in the context of BioWorld (Lajoie, 2009), a technology-rich learning environment for promoting clinical reasoning in medical students. BioWorld was designed using a cognitive apprenticeship framework (Collins, Brown, & Newman, 1987), whereby instruction is based on modeling expert knowledge, coaching skills in the context of practice, and fading assistance when no longer needed. The first section of the chapter presents the theoretical perspectives, followed by a description that drives the design of BioWorld features that support metacognition and SRL. We then describe these specific features followed by a series of empirical studies that support the claim that BioWorld supports medical students to

S.P. Lajoie (✉) • L. Naismith • E. Poitras • Y.-J. Hong • I. Cruz-Panesso • J. Ranellucci
Advanced Technologies for Learning in Authentic Settings (ATLAS), Department of Educational and Counselling Psychology, McGill University, Montreal, Canada
e-mail: susanne.lajoie@mcgill.ca

S. Mamane • J. Wiseman
Advanced Technologies for Learning in Authentic Settings (ATLAS), Faculty of Medicine, McGill University, Montreal, Canada

R. Azevedo and V. Aleven (eds.), *International Handbook of Metacognition and Learning Technologies*, Springer International Handbooks of Education 26, DOI 10.1007/978-1-4419-5546-3_16,

self-regulate their cognition, motivation, and behavior. More specifically, we look at how metacognitive monitoring and evaluation of knowledge is supported in BioWorld as students use the evidence table and visualization maps.

Theoretical Framework

The term metacognition originates from Flavell (1979) who described the concept from a developmental perspective as thinking about one's own thinking (Lajoie, 2008). According to Flavell, one's metacognitive skills include establishing goals to attain understanding, the employment of strategies to achieve such goals, and the assessment of one's progress in accomplishing them. In a general sense, the basis of metacognition rests within the individual, as it deals with the individual's ability to reflect on new or existing cognitive structures (Dinsmore et al., 2008). One must also consider the interaction between the person, behavior, and environment where one component influences the other. Bandura stresses this reciprocal determinism in describing the relationship between behavioral, emotional, and cognitive regulation (Bandura, 1986). He emphasized that an individual's will to learn, or motivation to learn, was key to maintaining effortful learning (Bandura, 1997).

Self-regulated learning (SRL) was seen at the outset as an integrated theory of learning (Corno & Mandinach, 1983) that examined the interaction of cognitive, motivational, and contextual factors. Whereas metacognition stresses the development of the learner's ability, knowledge, and accomplishments, self-regulation stresses the reciprocal determinism of the environment on the individual, mediated through behavior. Dinsmore et al. (2008) distinguish between those studying SRL and metacognition, suggesting that the former focus on how the environment stimulates the individual's awareness and regulatory response, whereas the latter researchers emphasize that the mind of the individual is the trigger for subsequent judgments.

Models of SRL

Various SRL models exist (e.g., Azevedo, Moos, Greene, Winters, & Cromley, 2008; Boekaerts, 1997; Corno & Mandinach, 1983; Pintrich, 2000; Winne, 2001; Winne & Hadwin, 1998; Zimmerman, 2000) that describe the relationship between various components and elements of learning. Most models integrate elements of both metacognition and self-regulation, though each emphasizes a different aspect of the complex interrelationship between the individual and contextual characteristics of self-regulatory skills (Pintrich & De Groot, 1990; Winne, 2001; Zimmerman, 2000). Corno and Mandinach, for instance, stress the volitional aspects of SRL, while Winne and Hadwin focus on its cognitive dimension, and McCaslin and Hickey (2001) stress the sociocultural aspects of SRL. Azevedo and colleagues examine SRL as an event, capturing the deployment of SRL processes at different levels of granularity (e.g., macro- and microlevel) and distinguishing between their positive and negative valence (e.g., appropriate vs. inappropriate) as they occur through time (Azevedo, 2009; Azevedo, Moos, Witherspoon, & Chauncey, 2010; Greene & Azevedo, 2010). Alternatively, Winne and colleagues (Butler & Winne, 1995; Winne, 2001; Winne & Hadwin, 1998; Winne & Perry, 2000) describe how self-regulated learning pivots on metacognitive monitoring and metacognitive control and emphasize that SRL is progressive.

Despite these differences, SRL researchers share Pintrich's (2000) four basic assumptions: that learners actively construct their own meanings, goals, and strategies from the information available in the *external* environment along with information in their own minds (the *internal* environment); that learners can monitor, control, and regulate specific aspects of their own cognition, motivation, and behavior along with certain environmental features; that there is a standard with which comparisons are made to reach, monitor their progress, and then adapt and regulate their cognition, motivation, and behavior to attain these goals; and that SRL activities mediate between personal and contextual traits and actual achievement or performance.

Furthermore, Pintrich et al. (Pintrich, 2000; Pintrich & De Groot, 1990; Pintrich, Wolters, & Baxter, 2000) describe four phases and areas of regulation. Significantly, the planning, monitoring, control, and reflection phases can be applied to four areas of regulation: cognition, motivation, behavior, and context. It follows that context, which encompasses physical environment, social interactions, and task characteristics, can either facilitate or hinder students' ability to self-regulate.

SRL skills such as self-monitoring follow a developmental trajectory, from novice to expert (Chi, Glaser, & Farr, 1988; Lajoie, 2003). Fundamentally, experts are able to identify relevant information, monitor and select appropriate problem-solving strategies, recognize what they understand, and identify when they have made mistakes. In contrast, there is an absence of self-monitoring skills among novices (Zimmerman & Schunk, 2001). We investigate the SRL trajectory in medicine by exploring how BioWorld supports the development of professional proficiency in diagnostic reasoning (Lajoie, 2009). Although BioWorld was not designed exclusively for the purpose of fostering metacognition and SRL, decisions were taken to support metacognition and SRL in the context of developing expertise in diagnostic reasoning. We describe these decisions below and define metacognition and SRL pertaining to diagnostic reasoning in the context of the BioWorld experience.

Metacognition and Self-Regulated Learning in Medical Problem Solving with BioWorld

The Context

Problem-based learning approaches that are incorporated early on in the medical curriculum provide students with opportunities to apply their basic science knowledge to clinical practice problems. Experiential learning through clinical clerkships is accepted as an effective way of gaining clinical reasoning skills and integrating newly acquired competencies into managing cases (Maudsley & Strivens, 2000). However, it tends to be inefficient when students only see a few clinical problems. Furthermore the effectiveness of this approach depends on the availability of experienced medical supervisors who are available to provide effective teaching and feedback during clinical practice.

Computer-based learning environments afford the opportunity for medical students to gain additional experiential-style learning opportunities in a condensed time frame in a supported environment. BioWorld was designed with specific cognitive tools to support learning through practicing and refining skills in relation to medical diagnosis (Lajoie, 2009). Here we explore the effectiveness of specific tools designed to support metacognition and self-regulated learning within BioWorld, in particular the intersection between how the environment can stimulate individual awareness and how the mind serves as an initiator for judgments and evaluations.

Figure 16.1 provides an overview of the BioWorld interface. Each problem starts with a patient case history where students formulate their differential diagnoses. Once students select their primary diagnosis, they report their confidence in this hypothesis by using the *belief meter* (%certainty). Students gather evidence from the case history in support of a particular hypothesis using the *evidence table* that remains visible throughout the problem-solving activity. There is an online *library* where students access declarative knowledge about the disease they are researching. Information in the library represents the symptoms, diagnostic tests, and transmission routes of a specific disease, as well as a glossary of medical terminology. In order to solve problems, students must conduct diagnostic tests to confirm or disconfirm their diagnoses. They do so by ordering tests on the *patient chart*, where the outcomes of their tests are recorded. This chart is a procedural knowledge tool since it provides a way for actions to be conducted in the context of problem solving. A simulated *consultation tool* is present and learners can obtain feedback during the data collection process as

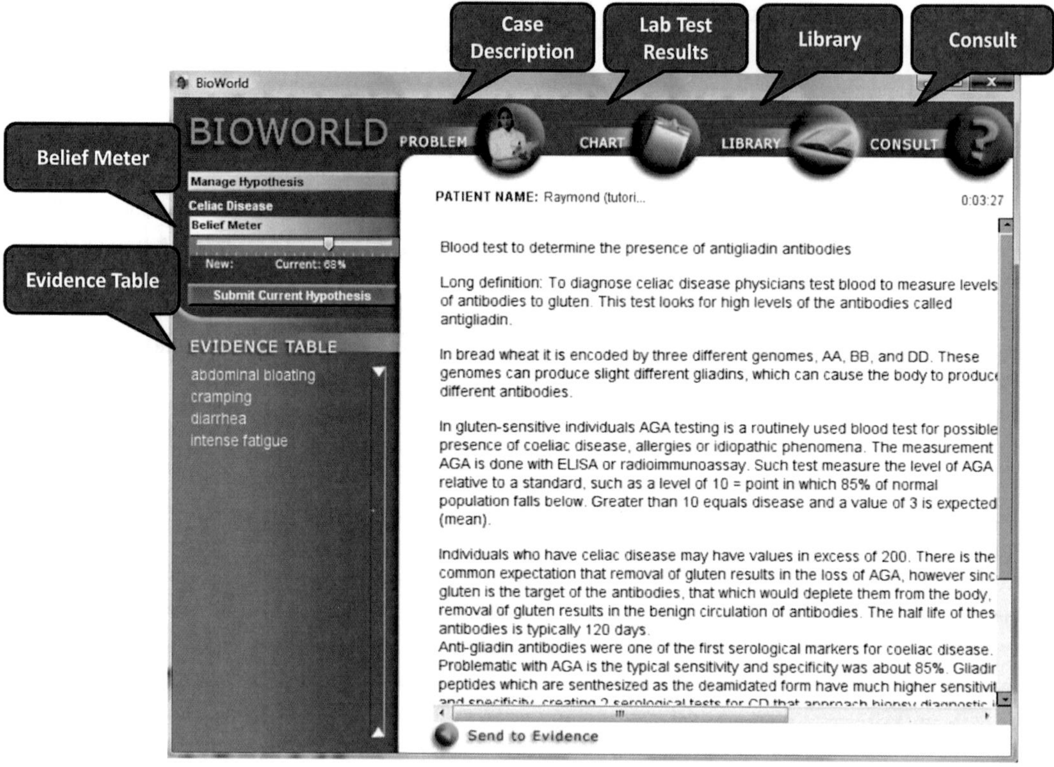

Fig. 16.1 Overview of BioWorld

well as from the *expert summary* provided after they post their final diagnosis.

BioWorld includes several features that serve as metacognitive tools (Lajoie & Azevedo, 2006) that promote metacognitive monitoring and control strategies critical to medical diagnostic reasoning. Below, we describe the role that the evidence table, the expert summaries, and the expert solution visualization maps play in fostering metacognition both during problem solving and after reaching a final diagnosis for a particular case. These features are described below.

Evidence Table

As students solve cases, they select and post the evidence they see as relevant to solving the case using the evidence table (see Fig. 16.1). Once the evidence is posted to the table, it remains visible throughout the problem-solving activity. In doing so, the evidence table serves as an external reminder to students of the data they considered relevant to the case. Students are encouraged to engage in metacognitive control processes through assessing the relevance and implications of the evidence they gather – from the case description and lab tests – in relation to their diagnosis. In doing so, students decide whether the test they ordered helped verify or eliminate a diagnosis and whether they need to order a new test, reconsult the case description, or revise/submit their hypothesis.

Visualization Map

Students' retrospective reflection about their diagnostic reasoning processes after each case is solved is supported in two ways: first as a simple comparison with the evidence that an expert used to solve the problem and, second, through a visualization map that documents expert diagnostic reasoning processes. The visualization maps represent expert physicians' solution processes and explanations (Gauthier, 2009; Gauthier, Naismith, Lajoie, & Wiseman, 2008). These maps are constructed by capturing expert physicians' problem-solving processes through the use of a concurrent think aloud protocol (Ericsson & Simon, 1993) augmented with the screen capture and log file data recorded while using BioWorld. The expert physicians' solution paths for each case were merged together to provide evidence of commonalities and differences in their diagnostic reasoning towards a particular case. The visual representations help pinpoint such differences with regard to the sequence of events that characterize the medical diagnostic process.

These expert models can be used as scaffolds where learners can compare their own processing actions with proficient problem solvers. It allows medical students to reflect on their own reasoning by comparing when and how their solution paths differed from expert physicians' as well as consider different reasoning paths that lead to the same diagnosis. Schoenfeld (1983) referred to this type of activity as an abstracted replay where students can replay or rethink their own actions by focusing students' attention on the critical decisions or actions taken by experts. In the case of BioWorld, the student had to chose, or control, these metacognitive skills to compare their diagnostic reasoning strategies with that of an expert's. Simply demonstrating a model does not mean that learners are actively engaged with it.

Overview of Empirical Evidence of BioWorld's Role in Fostering Metacognition

In this section, we describe three empirical studies that examine the role of BioWorld in fostering metacognitive processes that are crucial in performing medical diagnoses. First, we investigate the impact of the expert solution visualization maps on students' medical diagnostic process (Gauthier et al., 2008). Second, we investigate the effects of the evidence table on students' ability to monitor and assess the medical diagnostic process (McCurdy et al., 2010). Third, we replicate the findings obtained from the second study and expand this design to determine whether the evidence table assists students in writing case summaries (Lajoie et al., in prep.). In the following sections, we provide an overview of each study in terms of its research question, methods, experimental design, results, and conclusions. We then discuss the implications of our findings for learning about medical diagnosis in BioWorld.

Study 1: Do Visual Representations of Experts' Solutions Scaffold Self-Regulation?

In this study, we investigate the effects of providing expert solution visualization maps to medical students after they submit their final diagnoses in BioWorld (Gauthier et al., 2008). We expected that the expert solution visualization maps would serve as a metacognitive tool (Lajoie & Azevedo, 2006) in terms of assisting medical students to reflect on the diagnostic process, thereby improving their accuracy and confidence in performing medical diagnoses.

Methods

Eighteen second-year medical students participated in this study. Students were randomly assigned to either the treatment or control condition. The eight participants assigned to the treatment condition were shown the visualization map after they solved each case using BioWorld, while the ten participants assigned to the control condition used BioWorld without the visualization maps. The study took place over a 2-day period in a computer laboratory. On day 1, students were given a guided tour of how to use BioWorld and then solved the first case. On day 2, students solved the remaining 2 cases.

Experimental Design

Students were examined as they learned to solve patient cases using BioWorld. The study follows a mixed factorial design with group as a between-subjects factor (treatment and control groups), case as a within-subjects factor (pheochromocytoma,

Table 16.1 Proportion of frequencies for accuracy and average confidence ratings for final diagnoses

	Accuracy of final diagnoses			
	Control		Treatment	
Cases	Correct	Incorrect	Correct	Incorrect
Case 1 (pheochromocytoma)	0.20	0.80	0.50	0.50
Case 2 (type 1 diabetes)	0.90	0.10	1.00	0.00
Case 3 (hyperthyroidism)	0.70	0.30	0.87	0.13
	Confidence in final diagnoses			
	Control		Treatment	
Cases	Correct	Incorrect	Correct	Incorrect
Case 1 (pheochromocytoma)	57.50	73.63	62.00	67.50
Case 2 (type 1 diabetes)	91.44	75.00	86.75	–
Case 3 (hyperthyroidism)	85.00	71.67	90.57	40.00

type 1 diabetes, and hyperthyroidism), and the accuracy of the final diagnosis and self-reported confidence levels as the dependent variables.

Results

There was no significant difference in average diagnostic accuracy of medical students across conditions, $t(16)=-1.43$, $p>0.05$. The medical students who had the benefit of the expert solution visualization maps were only slightly more accurate, on average, than those who did not have the maps ($M=0.79$, $SD=0.25$, vs. $M=0.60$, $SD=0.31$). Likewise there was no significant difference in average diagnostic confidence for the two groups ($t(16)=0.30$, $p>0.05$). The medical students who saw the expert solution visualization maps were on average as confident as those who did not ($M=78.58$, $SD=13.35$, vs. $M=80.40$, $SD=12.33$).

Accuracy and confidence levels seemed to vary based on the type of case. For example, diagnosing pheochromocytoma was more difficult than the other cases as indicated by incorrect diagnosis (see Table 16.1). Students in the control condition who made an incorrect diagnosis of the pheochromocytoma case were more confident at the time they submitted their final diagnosis ($M=73.63$) than those who had the correct diagnosis ($M=57.50$). A similar pattern emerged for students assigned to the treatment condition, although the difference between the means was less pronounced ($M=67.50$ vs. $M=62.00$). In contrast to these findings, diagnosing cases of type 1 diabetes and hyperthyroidism were less difficult. Furthermore, those who obtained a correct diagnosis were more confident in their final diagnosis (range=85.00–91.44).

Conclusion

Our hypothesis was that the expert solution visualization maps would foster self-reflection in relation to the diagnostic process and that, consequently, medical students would be more accurate and confident in reaching their final diagnoses. Our findings suggest that both groups who used BioWorld improved with respect to their accuracy and self-confidence in solving cases and that the effects of the visualization maps were small. More research on the effectiveness of these maps as scaffolds are needed. Students may need more guidance interpreting the expert visualization maps. For example, they may need a debriefing with a human tutor to point out how and why an expert selected strategies different from their own. It is also possible that self-regulation during problem solving is more effective than reflection tasks after problem solving. In the next section, we use a mixed methods approach to delve more deeply into this data to establish how the evidence table assists medical students to monitor and assess the evidence they collect.

Study 2: The Effect of the Evidence Table on the Medical Diagnosis Process

In this study, we compare how medical students and expert physicians use the evidence table to regulate the medical diagnostic process during learning with BioWorld (McCurdy et al., 2010). The research questions explored are the following: do expert physicians differ from medical students in the use of the evidence table while making medical diagnoses in BioWorld, and do they benefit differently from the evidence table? We expected that all participants would use the evidence table as a metacognitive tool (Lajoie & Azevedo, 2006) to monitor and assess their own medical diagnostic processing, through the posting and review of their own evidence selection pertaining to their final diagnosis. We anticipated that experts would benefit more than novices since they have more established metacognitive resources.

Methods

The data used to answer this set of questions were gathered from past studies with medical students (see study 1, Gauthier et al., 2008) and expert physicians (see Gauthier, 2009) diagnosing the same three cases using BioWorld. Data from a total of 18 second-year medical students and 5 physicians from the same university system were examined. We focused our investigation on how medical students and expert physicians selected specific evidence items that supported their final diagnosis for each case. We examined the proportion of the total number of evidence items entered into the evidence table that was prioritized as being relevant to their medical diagnoses (i.e., # evidence items prioritized/# evidence items selected). We also examined the proportion of evidence items that medical students prioritized that matched with the expert physician's prioritized list (i.e., # expert-like evidence items prioritized/# total evidence items selected by students). For example, a student that had six expert-like evidence items prioritized out of a total number of 8 item selections would have more relevant expert-like moves than a student that had six expert-like evidence items prioritized over 16 item selections. This metric identifies those students who are more or less focused on the key elements needed to make an accurate diagnosis.

Experimental Design

The study follows a mixed factorial design with group as a between-subjects factor (student and physician groups), case as a within-subjects factor (pheochromocytoma, type 1 diabetes, and hyperthyroidism), and three dependent variables (the proportion of the total amount of evidence items that were prioritized as relevant to making the final diagnosis, the proportion of evidence that was taken from the problem statement, and the proportion of evidence taken from the diagnostic tests).

Results

The results of the repeated measures ANOVA show that the proportion of the total amount of evidence items that were prioritized differs across cases and groups, $F(2, 32)=7.54$, $p<0.05$, and $F(1, 16)=7.96$, $p<0.05$, respectively. More evidence was prioritized for the hyperthyroidism case, followed by type 1 diabetes and the pheochromocytoma. In other words, both novices and experts were more selective in relation to the evidence that they prioritized to reach a diagnosis of pheochromocytoma ($M=0.65$, $SD=0.32$) as opposed to type 1 diabetes and hyperthyroidism ($M=0.79$, $SD=0.23$, and $M=0.84$, $SD=0.23$). However, experts were more selective in prioritizing their evidence across all of the cases, since they selected less evidence to support their final arguments ($M=0.52$, $SD=0.20$), respectively, than medical students ($M=0.83$, $SD=0.25$). The interaction between group and case was not statistically significant ($F(2, 32)=1.38$, $p>0.05$).

In regard to differences in prioritization of problem statement items, there was a between-group difference ($F(1, 16)=5.91$, $p<0.05$) but no case effect ($F(2, 32)=1.33$, $p>0.05$) and no interaction between cases and groups ($F(2, 32)=1.25$, $p>0.05$). Experts were more selective ($M=0.59$, $SD=0.17$) than novices ($M=0.83$, $SD=0.28$) in their prioritization of evidence found in the problem statement. The proportion of diagnostic tests prioritized did not differ across cases ($F(2, 32)=2.03$, $p>0.05$) nor across groups ($F(1,16)=0.99$, $p>0.05$). However, there was an interaction between group and cases ($F(2, 32)=6.82$, $p<0.05$). The novices were less

Table 16.2 ANOVAs performed on the proportion of expert-like total amount of evidence items, problem statement items, and diagnostic test items

Variables	Source	*df*	*MS*	*F*	*p*
Expert-like proportion of total evidence items	Cases	2	0.77	21.34	0.001*
	Error	26	0.04		
Expert-like proportion of problem statement items	Cases	2	0.69	14.24	0.001*
	Error	26	0.05		
Expert-like proportion of diagnostic tests	Cases	2	0.70	10.67	0.001*
	Error	26	0.07		

*$p<0.001$

Table 16.3 Fisher's least significant difference multiple comparison tests on the proportion of expert-like total amount of evidence items, problem statement items, and diagnostic test items

Variables	Case 1 pheochromocytoma	Case 2 type 1 diabetes	Case 3 hyperthyroidism
Expert-like proportion of total evidence items	0.19	0.59	0.60
Expert-like proportion of problem statement items	0.36	0.80	0.63
Expert-like proportion of diagnostic tests	0.16	0.47	0.60

Note: all pairwise comparisons significant at $p<0.05$

selective in regard to the evidence selected for the type 1 diabetes case ($M=0.91$, $SD=0.21$) as opposed to the pheochromocytoma and hyperthyroidism cases ($M=0.65$, $SD=0.39$, and $M=0.84$, $SD=0.36$, respectively). In contrast, the experts were more selective in regard to the evidence selected for the type 1 diabetes case ($M=0.37$, $SD=0.28$) as opposed to the pheochromocytoma and hyperthyroidism cases ($M=0.79$, $SD=0.25$, and $M=0.82$, $SD=0.27$, respectively).

Given the group and case differences, a more detailed analysis was conducted to compare medical students with experts. Table 16.2 presents the repeated measures ANOVA on the proportion of expert-like matches for total evidence selected as well as specific evidence matches with expert-like problem statement items and diagnostic tests. Case effects were found for all three variables. Fisher's least significant difference multiple comparisons test was conducted to determine which cases were solved in a manner that matched the expert physician's solution (see Table 16.3). Medical students differed most from the experts when diagnosing pheochromocytoma. In diagnosing pheochromocytoma, only a small proportion of medical students' evidence items matched with the ones the expert prioritized, as opposed to diagnosing type 1 diabetes and hyperthyroidism ($M=0.19$ vs. $M=0.59$ and $M=0.60$). We further analyzed the type of evidence prioritized, in terms of diagnostic tests and items found in the problem statement. Group differences across cases were found in regard to the proportion of expert-like diagnostic tests that were prioritized by medical students, $F(2, 26)=10.67$, $p<0.001$. Once again case differences were examined using LSD comparisons test, which showed that there was a smaller proportion of matches between medical students and experts on the diagnostic tests ordered and prioritized while diagnosing pheochromocytoma ($M=0.16$). The proportion of problem statement items that were prioritized and that matched the experts solution was also found to differ across cases, $F(2, 26)=14.24$, $p<0.001$. The Fisher's LSD results show that all of the pairwise comparisons were significant. Students differed most from the experts when diagnosing pheochromocytoma ($M=0.36$); however closer matches were found for hyperthyroidism ($M=0.63$) and type 1 diabetes ($M=0.80$).

Conclusion

We compared the evidence that was prioritized by the medical students and expert physicians based on the assumption that overlapping patterns of behaviors are indicative of better diagnostic reasoning processes by the students. The results suggest that expert physicians engage in more metacognitive processes than novice medical students while using the evidence table to reach a final diagnosis. In contrast to novices, experts prioritize less evidence from the problem statement and clinical tests. Expert physicians are also relatively selective and consistent in regard to the evidence items that they prioritize. In contrast, novices were less selective in regard to the evidence that they prioritize. However, novices become more expert-like in the manner in which they solved the cases with experience using BioWorld. This finding supports the belief that there is a developmental trajectory for self-regulated monitoring and control processes. Case analyses revealed that the greatest expert-novice differences were for the pheochromocytoma case, with less overlap between experts and novices on this case in terms of how evidence was selected and prioritized. Given this was the most difficult case, some discrepancy is to be expected.

These findings show promise, but further research was needed to verify whether the positive impact of solving cases with BioWorld can be attributed to case complexity or to practicing and refining skills in relation to diagnostic reasoning with BioWorld. The evaluation of the effectiveness of the evidence table as a metacognitive tool must take into account the skill level of the participant, the order of the cases, as well as the level of complexity of the cases. These factors impact students' ability to monitor and assess their efforts to prioritize the evidence and solve the cases. Novices may need more scaffolding in terms of using the evidence table more efficiently. In the next section, we present a follow-up study which replicated and elaborated these findings with a different sample. The order and complexity of the cases were further examined.

Study 3: The Effects of the Evidence Table on Prioritizing Evidence and Writing Case Summaries

We build on the McCurdy et al. (2010) study with regard to the influence of the evidence table on the diagnostic reasoning processes in BioWorld (Lajoie et al., in prep.). In this study, we used a pre- and posttest evaluation of learning outcomes as well as a medical student/physician comparison in terms of the evidence that was prioritized and summarized. The primary research questions addressed in this study are the following: does having the benefit of the evidence table assist medical students in performing medical diagnoses in BioWorld, and does the evidence table assist participants while writing case summaries? We compare how medical students and physicians use the evidence table to regulate the medical diagnostic process and write case summaries.

Given that the evidence table provides a means to monitor and assess one's thinking with respect to the diagnostic process, we anticipated that it would serve as a metacognitive tool that would also help learners when they were writing their case summaries where they document how and why they reached a particular diagnosis. We anticipated that the evidence that was prioritized and summarized by the medical students would become more expert-like (overlapping more with physician responses) as they used BioWorld. We also expected that accuracy and confidence in their final diagnoses should increase after practicing and refining their skills using BioWorld.

Methods

Twelve second-year medical students participated in the study. The study took place over a 2-day period in a computer laboratory. The methodology used in this study was similar to the one used in study 2 above (McCurdy et al., 2010), with several exceptions. First, we added a pre- and posttest evaluation of learning outcomes, each one consisting of a case that had to be solved by the students in BioWorld. Second, we compared the medical students' prioritized evidence and case summaries to the expert physicians' solutions by counting the number of matching idea units (see Lajoie et al., in prep.). Third, we included two questionnaires that were administered during the posttest. The first questionnaire, based on the On-line Motivation Questionnaire (OLM) (Boekaerts, 2002), measures students' perception of the usefulness of BioWorld as well as their motivation to solve cases. The second measure assessed students' perceived difficulty of each case. On day 1 students were given a guided tour of the software and administered questionnaires. They then solved the type 1 diabetes case. The more difficult cases, hyperthyroidism and pheochromocytoma, were presented in random order on day 2 to rule out the effects of case complexity (one case being more difficult than another) in evaluating practice effects with BioWorld.

Table 16.4 Means and standard deviations of accuracy and confidence in regard to the final diagnosis at pre- and posttest

	Means (standard deviations)	
Variables	Pretest	Posttest
Accuracy	0.75 (0.45)	0.92 (0.29)
Confidence	0.79 (0.11)	0.95 (0.06)

On the post-questionnaire, students were asked to rate the helpfulness of BioWorld on a five-point Likert scale (1 = not helpful; 5 = very helpful). The mean response was 3.83 (SD=0.72), suggesting that students perceived BioWorld to be a useful learning tool. From the OLM, students also reported that they put in a lot of effort in solving each patient case (M=2.97, SD=0.51)

Experimental Design

The study follows a mixed factorial design with cases as a within-subjects factor (pretest case, pheochromocytoma, type 1 diabetes, hyperthyroidism, and posttest case), and the dependent variables were the proportion of expert-like evidence items that were prioritized and summarized, the accuracy of the final diagnosis, self-reported confidence levels, as well as their reactions and motivation towards using BioWorld. A repeated measures analysis was performed in which the data from all participants was compared to those of the expert physicians, in accordance to the methodology followed by McCurdy et al. (2010).

Results

The results obtained from the repeated measures analysis of variance show a statistically significant difference between cases in terms of the proportion of expert-like evidence items that were prioritized, $F(2, 20)=7.40$, $p<0.01$. We examined this case effect further by performing post hoc comparisons using the Fisher's LSD that indicated a higher overlap between medical students and experts on prioritizing evidence items on cases provided on day 2. The proportion of expert-like prioritized evidence was significantly lower on day 1 (type 1 diabetes case) than for the hyperthyroidism and pheochromocytoma cases solved on day 2 (M=0.62 vs. M=0.82, and M=0.72). However, the results of the RM-ANOVA showed no significant differences between the cases in terms of the proportion of evidence items that were expert-like that appear in the case summaries, $F(2, 12)=0.76$, $p=0.49$. We calculated the proportion of expert-like idea units in the students' case summaries by dividing the number of idea units that matched an idea unit mentioned in an expert case summary by the total number of idea units mentioned. We compared across cases, excluding the five students who did not write a summary for each case. The observed power for this analysis, calculated at $\alpha=0.05$, was low (0.15) due to the missing data.

To assess students' overall performance in BioWorld, we examined the accuracy of their final diagnoses, anticipating an increase in accuracy from pre- to posttest. Accuracy was measured with a value of 1 indicating correct and 0 indicating incorrect. Given the small sample size (N=12), we used the Wilcoxon's Matched-Pairs Signed-Ranks Test to assess the significance of these differences. Though students increased in accuracy from pretest to posttest, this difference was not significant, $Z=-1.00$, $p=0.32$. We also looked at whether students' confidence in their final diagnoses increased from pre- to posttest, again using a Wilcoxon's Matched-Pairs Signed-Ranks Test. Confidence was interpreted as the belief meter value at the time a student submitted his or her final diagnosis. We expected a statistically significant increase in confidence levels from pre- to posttest, and this hypothesis was supported, $Z=-2.98$, $p<0.01$. Table 16.4 displays the means and standard deviations for the two overall performance variables.

Conclusion

We evaluated the effectiveness of the evidence table in terms of assisting medical students to monitor and assess the medical diagnosis process and write case summaries. We compared the evidence that was prioritized and summarized by the medical students and expert physicians based on the assumption that overlapping patterns of behaviors are indicative of better performance on the part of the students. Overall, medical students obtained an average of 60–80% overlap in the amount of evidence that was prioritized and summarized by the expert physicians. The results demonstrate that practicing medical diagnosis with BioWorld had a positive effect on students in that they increased from day 1 to day 2 in the proportion of expert-like evidence that was prioritized. Given that students were given the most complex and challenging cases on day 2 makes this practice effect more important. However, there was no increase in the amount of expert evidence reported in case summaries over time. This finding may be due to the fact that students were not experienced with writing case summaries and that fewer students completed the case summaries.

We expected that medical students would become more confident in their medical diagnoses after practicing with BioWorld. Accordingly, the confidence in performing medical diagnoses increased from pre- to posttest cases. On the one hand, this provides preliminary evidence in favor of the benefit of practicing medical diagnosis with BioWorld. On the other hand, the increase in levels of accuracy showed more variability across students and was not statistically significant, which suggests that medical students may sometimes be overconfident in submitting their final diagnoses.

Finally, the pre-/post-questionnaire data revealed that learners put in a lot of effort solving cases and found BioWorld to be a useful learning tool.

Discussion

The competitive entry requirements for medical school generally result in cohorts of students that are of high ability and motivated to succeed. Such students are likely to be receptive to the introduction of computer-based tools that provide practice problems and insight into expert clinical reasoning. In fact, we found this to be true in study 3 where we used a modified version of Boekaert's (2002) motivation questionnaire as a premeasure that demonstrated that students were motivated to use BioWorld. BioWorld provides an authentic experience of clinical reasoning, complementing the time-constrained learning within a hospital setting.

For students to benefit from the learning opportunities provided, they must develop appropriate domain-specific self-regulated learning skills. BioWorld is designed to make learners' medical diagnostic processes more visible, thus fostering metacognitive skills that are critical to reaching a final diagnosis. In the following section, we summarize the ways in which BioWorld served as an external regulator of medical students' diagnostic reasoning and how the BioWorld context played an important role in stimulating engagement and motivation to learn.

Empirical Support for SRL with BioWorld

In the first study, expert solution visualization maps were presented to medical students after they submitted their final diagnosis for each case. Our assumption was that the maps would promote metacognitive processes in that students would reflect on their diagnostic reasoning skills by monitoring and comparing their own learning processes with that of an expert. We examined whether students who had the benefit of such maps would outperform students in terms of diagnostic accuracy and also achieve higher levels of confidence. Group differences were nonsignificant in that both groups improved their performance accuracy and confidence levels as a function of working with BioWorld cases. The effects of the maps appear to be small. Further analyses will be conducted on the think aloud protocol data in order to determine whether students pinpoint discrepancies between their own performance and that of experts. Future directions may include more directed animations of how individuals differed from the experts or incorporating human instructors in abstracted replay sessions that debrief the diagnostic reasoning process.

Our assumption was that the evidence table would foster self-regulatory processes that are critical to diagnostic reasoning. In particular, the table should help learners monitor their reasoning and help them be more aware of the implications of their evidence in relation to the accuracy of their diagnosis. If using the table correctly, learners should engage in remedial strategies, i.e., readjusting their hypotheses when diagnostic test results did not confirm their diagnosis. These self-regulatory processes should result in medical students eventually prioritizing their evidence in a more expert-like manner. As such, we examined both medical students and physicians to see whether they collected and used evidence differently. Not surprisingly, our findings support the expertise literature (Chi et al., 1988), in that the physicians (experts) engaged in more metacognitive processing than medical students (relative novices). The experts in this study were relatively selective in the type of evidence they used and prioritized as compared to the novices. Case difficulty was considered a possible confounding effect in the learning process, and hence, study 2 counterbalanced this variable and found a developmental trajectory in that students became more expert-like as they practiced medical diagnosis with BioWorld.

Study 3 expanded on the results from study 2 in that we explored the relationship between the evidence medical students collected and prioritized and used in their case summaries. Once again, we anticipated improved performance as a result of practice with BioWorld, as shown in an increase in the amount of expert-like evidence items over time. The results confirmed this training effect since there was a significant increase from the first to the second day in the overlap between medical students and experts in terms of proportion of evidence prioritized. This finding provides support to our hypothesis that the evidence table served effectively as a metacognitive tool. Students were more likely to exhibit SRL monitoring and control behaviors for the later cases, suggesting that BioWorld stimulated metacognitive awareness in a progressive or developmental manner, which supports Winne and colleagues' model of SRL following a developmental trajectory. A similar trend is suggested by the case summary data, but we were unable to detect statistically significant relationships, likely due to missing data and the resulting low power of the analysis. Future studies will need to consider longer treatments to promote stronger effects. Furthermore, we will need to overcome the small sample size issues. We may need to find alternative method of recruiting participants in this specialized area who already have a full medical curriculum that competes for their time.

The third study also revealed that students put in a great deal of effort solving cases in BioWorld and that BioWorld successfully engaged student interest and motivation to learn. Students reported that BioWorld met their initial expectations, suggesting that they are able to employ metacognitive judgment in terms of assessing the prospective helpfulness of learning tools. These findings support Bandura's notion that an individual's will to learn is necessary to maintain effortful learning and suggests that BioWorld is effective in providing a context that facilitates students' ability to self-regulate (Pintrich, 2000).

Overall, the three studies reveal that medical students generally increased from pre- to post-test, in terms of accuracy of their final diagnosis, although not significantly. The sample of students demonstrated relatively high ability in solving cases. In analyzing the accuracy differences, we noted that it was possible for students to obtain the correct diagnosis, but they miss important aspects of the case, i.e., a possible life-threatening complication. Evaluating accuracy as an isolated variable may thus be an inappropriate measure of students' clinical reasoning ability. Measures such as the proportion of prioritized evidence items that were expert-like provide a more nuanced measurement of students' ability to discriminate between expert-like and non-expert-like evidence.

Students who used BioWorld demonstrated a statistically significant increase in confidence level from pre- to posttest. We anticipated that confidence would increase with better problem-solving ability. However, we also observed incidents of overconfidence, in which students selected a high value for the belief meter, but did not document appropriate evidence to support their diagnoses. The literature suggests that novice physicians find it particularly difficult to accurately assess their level of competence when they are "unskilled and unaware of it" (Hodges, Regehr, & Martin, 2001). To address this situation, it may be necessary for BioWorld to incorporate additional metacognitive scaffolds to prompt students to reflect on how they arrived at a particular diagnosis and how often they have encountered such a disease in their previous studies and clinical experience.

Implications and Future Research

We have provided evidence that advanced learning technologies can be designed to support self-regulated learning. Our goal in designing BioWorld was to help novice medical students become more expert-like in the processes they take to make clinical decisions. The expertise literature demonstrates that one dimension of expertise is higher metacognitive skills. Tools in BioWorld such as the evidence table support participants in their metacognitive monitoring of the choices they make while trying to solve a patient case as well as support for decisions and control of what they see as relevant or irrelevant to the overall decision-making process. In this regard, the evidence table was found to be effective in promoting more expert-like behavior, as a function of supporting metacognitive skills. However, the expert solution visualization maps were also designed to support self-regulation by providing a post-reflection tool to compare one's own decisions with that of an expert. However, we did not find support that this feature was used appropriately. Future research is needed to determine if further scaffolding is needed in how to use these maps. Future studies are needed that are of longer duration, with more patient cases to solve and with more students to validate the current research.

References

Azevedo, R. (2009). Theoretical, methodological, and analytical challenges in the research on metacognition and self-regulation: A commentary. *Metacognition & Learning, 4*(1), 87–95.

Azevedo, R., Moos, D. C., Greene, J. A., Winters, F. I., & Cromley, J. G. (2008). Why is externally-facilitated regulated learning more effective than self-regulated learning with hypermedia? *Educational Technology Research and Development, 56*, 45–72.

Azevedo, R., Moos, D. C., Witherspoon, A. M., & Chauncey, A. D. (2010). Measuring cognitive and metacognitive regulatory processes used during hypermedia learning: Theoretical, conceptual, and methodological issues. *Educational Psychologist, 45*(4), 1–14.

Bandura, A. (1986). *Social foundations of thought and action: A social cognitive theory*. Englewood Cliffs, NJ: Prentice-Hall.

Bandura, A. (1997). *Self-efficacy: The exercise of control*. New York: Freeman.

Boekaerts, M. (1997). Self-regulated learning: A new concept embraced by researchers, policy makers, educators, teachers, and students. *Learning and Instruction, 7*(2), 161–186.

Boekaerts, M. (2002). The on-line motivation questionnaire: A self-report instrument to assess students' context sensitivity. In P. Pintrich & M. Maehr (Eds.), *New directions in measures and methods* (pp. 77–120). Oxford, UK: Elsevier.

Butler, D. L., & Winne, P. H. (1995). Feedback and self-regulated learning: A theoretical synthesis. *Review of Educational Research, 65*(3), 245–281.

Chi, M. T. H., Glaser, R., & Farr, M. J. (Eds.). (1988). *The nature of expertise*. Hillsdale, NJ: Erlbaum.

Collins, A., Brown, J. S., & Newman, S. E. (1987). Cognitive apprenticeship: Teaching the craft of reading, writing, and mathematics. In L. B. Resnick (Ed.), *Knowing, learning, and instruction: Essays in honor of Robert Glaser* (Vol. 5, pp. 453–494). Hillsdale, NJ: Erlbaum.

Corno, L., & Mandinach, E. B. (1983). The role of cognitive engagement in classroom learning and motivation. *Educational Psychologist, 18*, 88–108.

Dinsmore, D. L., Alexander, P. A., & Loughlin, S. M. (2008). Focusing the conceptual lens on metacognition, self-regulation, and self-regulated learning. *Educational Psychology Review, 20*, 391–409.

Ericsson, K. A., & Simon, H. A. (1993). *Protocol analysis; Verbal reports as data (revised edition)*. Cambridge, MA: Bradfordbooks/MIT.

Flavell, J. H. (1979). Metacognition and cognitive monitoring: A new area of cognitive-developmental inquiry. *American Psychologist, 34*, 906–911.

Gauthier, G. (2009). *Capturing and representing the reasoning processes of expert clinical teachers for case-based teaching*. Unpublished doctoral dissertation. McGill University, Montreal, Canada.

Gauthier, G., Naismith, L., Lajoie, S. P., & Wiseman, J. (2008). Using expert decision maps to promote reflection and self-assessment in medical case-based instruction. In V. Aleven, K. Ashley, C. Lynch, & N. Pinkwart (Chairs), *Intelligent tutoring systems for ill-defined domains* (pp. 68–80). Workshop conducted at the 9th International Conference on Intelligent Tutoring Systems, Montreal, Canada.

Greene, J. A., & Azevedo, R. (2010). The measurement of learners' self-regulated cognitive and metacognitive processes while using computer-based learning environments. *Educational Psychologist, 45*(4), 203–209.

Hodges, B., Regehr, G., & Martin, D. (2001). Difficulties in recognizing one's own incompetence: Novice physicians who are unskilled and unaware of it. *Academic Medicine, 76*(10), S87–S89.

Lajoie, S. P. (2003). Transitions and trajectories for studies of expertise. *Educational Researcher, 32*(8), 21–25.

Lajoie, S. P. (2008). Metacognition, self regulation, and self-regulated learning: A rose by any other name? *Educational Psychology Review, 20*, 469–475.

Lajoie, S. P. (2009). Developing professional expertise with a cognitive apprenticeship model: Examples from Avionics and Medicine. In K. A. Ericsson (Ed.), *Development of professional expertise: Toward measurement of expert performance and design of optimal learning environments* (pp. 61–83).: Cambridge University Press.

Lajoie, S. P., & Azevedo, R. (2006). Teaching and learning in technology-rich environments. In P. Alexander & P. Winne (Eds.), *Handbook of educational psychology*. Mahwah, NJ: Erlbaum.

Lajoie, S. P., Naismith, L., Poitras, E., Hong, Y. J., Panesso-Cruz, I., Ranellucci, J., & Wiseman, J. (in prep.) BioWorld: An advanced learning technology for authentic inquiry in medical reasoning.

Maudsley, G., & Strivens, J. (2000). Promoting professional knowledge, experiential learning and critical thinking for medical students. *Medical Education, 34*, 535–544.

McCaslin, M., & Hickey, D. T. (2001). Educational psychology, social constructivism, and educational practice: A case of emergent identity. *Educational Psychologist, 36*(2), 133–140.

McCurdy, N., Naismith, L., & Lajoie, S. P. (2010). Using metacognitive tools to scaffold medical students developing clinical reasoning skills. In *Cognitive and metacognitive educational systems* (Tech. Rep. FS-10-01, pp. 52–56). Menlo Park, CA: AAAI.

Pintrich, P. R. (2000). The role of goal orientation in self-regulated learning. In M. Boekaerts, P. R. Pintrich, & M. Zeidner (Eds.), *Handbook of self-regulation* (pp. 451–502). San Diego, CA: Academic.

Pintrich, P. R., & De Groot, E. V. (1990). Motivational and self-regulated learning components of classroom academic performance. *Journal of Educational Psychology, 82*(1), 33–40.

Pintrich, P. R., Wolters, C., & Baxter, G. (2000). Assessing metacognition and self-regulated learning. In G. Schraw & J. Impara (Eds.), *Issues in the measurement of metacognition* (pp. 43–97). Lincoln, NE: Buros Institute of Mental Measurements.

Schoenfeld, A. H. (1983). *Mathematical problem solving*. Orlando, FL: Academic.

Winne, P. H. (2001). Self-regulated learning viewed from models of information processing. In B. J. Zimmerman & D. H. Schunk (Eds.), *Self-regulated learning and academic achievement: Theoretical perspectives* (2nd ed., pp. 153–189). Hillsdale, NJ: Erlbaum.

Winne, P. H., & Hadwin, A. F. (1998). Studying as self-regulated learning. In D. J. Hacker, J. Dunlosky, & A. C. Graesser (Eds.), *Metacognition in educational theory and practice* (pp. 277–304). Mahwah, NJ: Erlbaum.

Winne, P. H., & Perry, N. E. (2000). Measuring self-regulated learning. In M. Boekaerts, P. R. Pintrich, & M. Zeidner (Eds.), *Handbook of self-regulation* (pp. 531–566). San Diego, CA: Academic.

Zimmerman, B. J. (2000). Attaining self-regulation: A social cognitive perspective. In M. Boekaerts, P. R. Pintrich, & M. Zeidner (Eds.), *Handbook of self-regulation* (pp. 13–39). San Diego, CA: Academic.

Zimmerman, B. J., & Schunk, D. H. (Eds.). (2001). *Self-regulated learning and academic achievement: theoretical perspectives* (2nd ed.). Mahwah, NJ: Erlbaum.

17 Challenges of Investigating Metacognitive Tool Use and Effects in (Rich) Web-Based Learning Environments

Susanne Narciss, Hermann Koerndle, and Antje Proske

Abstract

This chapter summarizes the rationale and findings of several studies using rich open-ended web-based learning environments (Web-LEs) as learning technology in higher education. The purpose of the studies was to examine self-regulated learning activities by tracing university students' learning activities within a rich open-ended Web-LE by log file data. Hence, the Web-LEs used in these studies provided non-embedded as well as embedded tools supporting cognitive as well as metacognitive learning activities. Students in all studies were free to decide when and how to use these tools. To use them, they had to activate the selected tool explicitly by clicking on the respective button on the Web-LEs' interface. The rationale for the design of the Web-LEs and for analyzing and interpreting the log file data was derived from psychological task analyses which were based on a multidimensional view of self-regulated learning within Web-LEs (e.g., Narciss et al., 2007; Winter, 2008). This chapter outlines this rationale, describes the resources and tools of the rich Web-LE called *Study Desk*, and summarizes several studies investigating how students used the tools of the *Study Desks*. Finally, limitations, challenges and implications of using log file data for investigating self-regulated learning with rich Web-LEs are discussed.

S. Narciss (✉) • H. Koerndle • A. Proske
Psychology of Learning and Instruction, Technische Universität Dresden, Dresden, Germany
e-mail: susanne.narciss@tu-dresden.de

R. Azevedo and V. Aleven (eds.), *International Handbook of Metacognition and Learning Technologies*, Springer International Handbooks of Education 26, DOI 10.1007/978-1-4419-5546-3_17,

Web-Based Learning in Higher Education

Web-based learning environments are increasingly used as components of learning scenarios in higher education. *Web-based learning environments* (Web-LEs) are characterized as (e.g., Narciss, Proske, & Körndle, 2007) (a) providing nonlinear access to multiple information resources (e.g., electronic textbooks, online-libraries, databases, electronic archives, electronic encyclopedias), (b) coding and storing various content in multiple representations (e.g., text, figures, symbolic notations, audiovisual formats, simulations), (c) presenting information for auditive, visual, or audiovisual information processing (e.g., written or spoken text, static or animated figures, simulations or animations), and (d) providing different types of interactivity (e.g., technical manipulation of resources, social interaction and mental engagement).

With the rapid progression of the capacities of modern information technologies, a large variety of Web-LEs has been developed and implemented in different types of instructional scenarios in higher education (e.g., Azevedo & Jacobson, 2008). Web-LEs used in higher education span from Web-LEs which merely deliver course material the like texts, lecture slides, and lists of helpful references, to more sophisticated rich Web-LEs. Rich Web-LEs do not only provide access to course-related materials, media, and resources, but they also provide tools and resources for supporting students in self-regulating their learning processes. Furthermore, due to the diversity and richness of the information materials, resources and tools accessible through a rich Web-LE are to a certain degree open-ended (Hannafin, Land, & Oliver, 1999).

This chapter summarizes the rationale and findings of several studies using rich open-ended Web-LEs as learning technology for supporting undergraduate psychology and teacher education students in acquiring and deepening their knowledge of psychological learning theories (e.g., classical conditioning, operant conditioning, social-cognitive theory of learning). These Web-LEs on learning theories have been developed to complement lectures and seminars in Educational Psychology and General Psychology.

The main purpose of the studies was to gain insights in *self-initiated* self-regulated learning activities by tracing students' learning activities within a rich open-ended Web-LE by log file data. Hence, the Web-LEs used in these studies provided non-embedded as well as embedded tools (Clarebout & Elen, 2006, 2008), which could be used as a support for self-regulated learning activities such as: (a) orientation by getting an overview on the material, resources, structure and size of the Web-LE, (b) active, elaborative processing tactics (e.g., highlighting important concepts; making notes; summarizing) or strategies (i.e., using configurations of tactics in a purposeful way, Wade, Trathen, & Schraw, 1990), (c) monitoring and evaluating understanding, and (d) monitoring learning progress as well as outcomes. To render students' self-initiated access to the non-embedded tools visible in the log file data, students in all studies were free to decide when and how to use the tools. If they decided to use them, they had to activate the selected tool explicitly by clicking on the respective button on the Web-LEs' interface (see Sect. "*Study Desk*: A Rich Web-LE with Metacognitive Tools" for more details).

The rationale for analyzing and interpreting the log file data, traced based on students' use of the resources and tools of these Web-LEs, was derived from cognitive and metacognitive task analyses which were based on a multidimensional view of self-regulated learning activities within Web-LEs (e.g., Narciss et al., 2007; Winters, Greene, & Costich, 2008). In the following sections we first outline this rationale, before we present in more detail the resources and tools of a Web-LE called *Study Desk*. Then we summarize several studies conducted with several rich open-ended *Study Desks*. Finally, limitations, challenges, and implications of using log file data for investigating self-regulated learning with rich Web-LEs are discussed.

Self-Regulation and Metacognition in Web-Based Learning

When studying with a rich open-ended Web-LE students have to cope with (a) technical and operational challenges (i.e., accessing electronic resources; handling technical tools), (b) cognitive challenges (i.e., decoding, comprehending and integrating information represented in various codes and presented through various modalities), and (c) metacognitive or self-regulated learning challenges (i.e., planning, monitoring, regulating, evaluating the process and products of learning, see for example Azevedo, 2007; Zimmerman, 2000).

Recent reviews reveal that the concepts of *self-regulation*, *self-regulated learning*, and *metacognition* have been conceptualized and used in various ways (Alexander, 2008; Dinsmore, Alexander, & Loughlin, 2008; Kaplan, 2008). Some researchers view the concepts of self-regulation, self-regulated learning, and metacognition as distinct constructs, others as constructs which share core assumptions and are nested within each other (e.g., Azevedo, 2005, 2007). Our work is based on the latter conceptualization: More specifically, we adopted a multidimensional view on self-regulated learning (SRL) which integrates common assumptions of SRL-models (e.g., Boekaerts, 1997; Butler & Winne, 1995; Zimmerman, 2000) and metacognition frameworks (e.g., Flavell, 1979, 1985; Winne, 2001; Winne & Hadwin, 1998).

The basic assumption of this multidimensional view is that SRL-activities serve to adapt students' goal-directed learning activities to the individual and situational conditions and challenges of the learning process. Inspired by metacognition frameworks (Flavell, 1979; Winne & Hadwin, 1998) we distinguish between several "objects" which might be addressed by SRL-activities, including (a) the learning person, (b) the learning task, or more generally spoken the conditions of the learning environment, (c) the learning behavior, namely, study tactics or strategies, as well as (d) the learning outcomes or products. Figure 17.1 provides an overview on the large variety of aspects which might be addressed by SRL-activities when studying with a Web-LE.

Drawing from information processing models of SRL and metacognition (i.e., Pressley, Borkwski, & Schneider, 1989; Winne & Hadwin, 1998, 2008), we assume that SRL-activities may occur in various stages or phases of learning and along various levels of regulation (see also Azevedo, 2007). In line with Winne and Hadwin's (1998) COPES framework we assume that the learning process starts with an orientation or task analysis phase in which students analyze the individual and situational conditions of the task and learning environment at hand. In doing so they may generate a subjective representation of these conditions. This subjective representation serves as a basis for the second phase, the planning phase. In the planning phase learners have to select and specify goals and subgoals, conduct means-end analysis in order to select study tactics and strategies they might apply to achieve these goals, outline a learning plan; that is make decisions when, why and how to use which study tactics and strategies. In a third stage, the processing phase (referred to as performance by Zimmerman, 2000), students have to activate and control the selected study tactics and strategies. Furthermore, they have to monitor and if necessary adapt, adjust or even alter either their tactics and strategies, or their plans and goals, or even their subjective representation of the conditions of the learning tasks and environment. In studying with a rich open-ended Web-LE this means that students may for example apply the activity of monitoring with regard to (a) a concrete local cognitive learning activity the like decoding the meaning of data in a graphic, or (b) metacognitive activities the like assessing progress towards goal achievement. In the final phase, the evaluation or reflection phase, students have to assess the products and outcomes of learning as well as the process of learning. This includes evaluating (a) the artifacts produced during studying, and (b) the final state of knowledge and skills in comparison to the learning goals set in the planning phase.

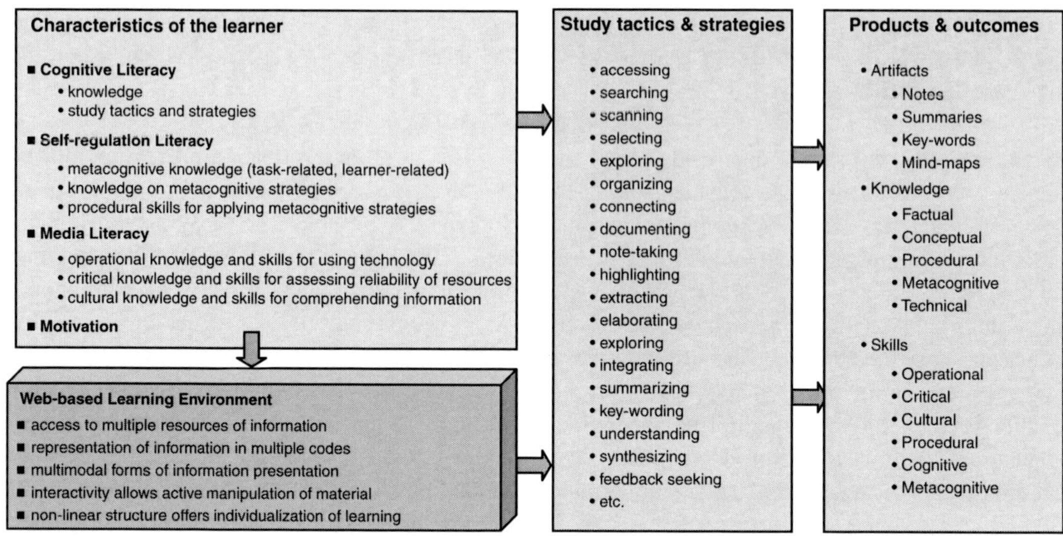

Fig. 17.1 Learner-related, task-related, behavior-related, and outcome-related aspects of studying with Web-LEs which might be addressed through self-regulatory activities

Table 17.1 provides an overview on the variety of SRL-activities which may occur in the four phases of self-regulated learning with a Web-LE.

Study Desk: A Rich Web-LE with Metacognitive Tools

The Web-LEs we used for the investigation of students self-regulated learning activities consist of (a) various electronic resources (i.e., textbook-like web-site chapters, learning tasks, elaboration resources such as www-links, slides, references, and glossaries), (b) learning or processing tools such as a highlighting tool, a note-taking tool, as well as an integrator tool, and (c) tools providing support for metacognitive activities (hereafter referred to as *metacognitive tools*), including an overview on all available resources, materials, and tools (material table), as well as a progress report providing access to a learning activity protocol and a learning task protocol (for more details see Narciss et al., 2007, http://studierplatz2000.tu-dresden.de).

For the integration of all materials we used the *s2w-compiler* (Study-to-Web Compiler), a generic authoring tool which supports instructors in combining and integrating multiple learning materials and media into an integrated interface (http://studierplatz2000.tu-dresden.de/s2w). We call a Web-based learning environment designed with the *s2w-compiler Studierplatz* (in English: *Study Desk*), that is, a working space for learning and studying.

The textbook-like Web-site chapters, their subchapters and all other learning materials related to these chapters are organized in a hierarchical content structure. All the textbook chapters and resources of the *Study Desks* used for the present studies were developed and/or selected on the basis of several comparative analyses of traditional and online instructional resources (e.g., textbooks, Web-Sites; electronic media archives). They addressed historical aspects of psychological learning theories, basic and applied concepts, experimental methods and applications of empirical findings, as well as a discussion of the potential and limitations of these learning theories and their empirical findings. Table 17.2 presents an overview about the topics, text pages, and resources that have been integrated into the *Study Desks* used for the present studies.

Study Desk-Interface

As illustrated in Table 17.2, a *Study Desk* offers access to a large variety of electronic resources

Table 17.1 Overview on self-regulated learning activities when studying with a Web-LE

	"Object" of metacognition and regulation		
Phase of learning	Person—Student	Task—Study with Web-LE	Behavior—Learning activities
Orientation	Analyze individual prerequisites, i.e. • Knowledge • Skills • Motivation	Analyze conditions of Web-LE, i.e., • Amount of resources • Type of resources • Content structure	Analyze technical and operational conditions, i.e., • Availability of tools • Accessibility of resources
Planning		Select and specify goals and subgoals Conduct means-end analyses for selecting study tactics or strategies Decide when, how, why to apply the selected study tactics and strategies Outline a schedule documenting these decisions	
Processing	Monitor understanding Monitor individual progress	Activate and control the selected study tactics or strategies Monitor relevancy and reliability of resources	Monitor study tactics Monitor study strategies
	Adapt, adjust or alter individual goals	Adapt, adjust or alter subjective representation of Web-LE	Adapt, adjust or alter • Study tactics • Study strategies
Evaluating	Assess achieved level of • Knowledge • Skills • Motivation	Assess utility and value of • Resources • Content • Tools	Assess adequacy of selected • Study tactics • Study strategies • Technical operations

Table 17.2 Number of textbook chapters and related multimedia materials of several *Study Desks*

Topic of the *Study Desk*	Main chapters	Text pages	Learning tasks	Elaboration resources
Introduction to learning theories	3	17	21	61
Classical conditioning	5	28	42	30
Operant conditioning	9	136	75	128
Purposive behaviorism	4	26	16	9
Socio-cognitive theory of learning	4	15	26	27
Behaviorist learning theories	4	118	146	175

and tools. To support students in their cognitive and metacognitive activities, all resources and tools of a *Study Desk,* its content-related structure, as well as the history of learner activities are elicited through the *Study Desk*-interface. To this end, the *Study Desk*-interface is subdivided in several frames. More specifically, the *Study Desk*-interface offers the following information (see Fig. 17.2):

1. Information on the content structure is offered by a hierarchically structured table of contents. As scientific topics tend to be complex, this table of contents is presented in such a way that at first only the main chapters are indicated, thus offering a general overview. A mouse click on one of the entries gives a detailed view of its respective subchapters.
2. Running-titles in the top frame provide information on the current (sub-)chapter.
3. Labeled user buttons in the bottom frame of the screen provide information on the availability of multiple multimedia resources (e.g., references, links to relevant Web-pages, videos, learning tasks and exercises). The button is blue if a resource is available in the current chapter and grey if unavailable.
4. The availability of learning or processing tools (i.e., highlighting, note-taking, and integrator) is flagged through the green buttons in the bottom frame.
5. The activity history is signalized through changing colors of the symbols in the table of contents. If a chapter has been accessed the color of the symbol changes from blue to turquoise.
6. The availability of monitoring tools (i.e., progress report; learning task report; glossary; material overview) is indicated through a list in the bottom part of the content-structure frame.

Learning or Processing Tools

A *Study Desk* provides tools for the active processing of the learning material. These tools enable learners to highlight certain sections, make notes and integrate material they consider of interest or importance into an individual dossier (the integrator). These tools permit the application of widely-used conventional study methods with which the students are familiar. If students want to use these tools, they have to activate them by clicking on the related buttons in the bottom frame of the screen. For example, to highlight interesting or important words, sentences, paragraphs or pictures, the learner activates the marking tool, chooses a color, clicks on the first word or element of interest, and then clicks on its last word or element. Consequently, the space between these words or elements is highlighted in the selected color. When taking notes, the learner activates the note-taking tool, clicks on the word or element of the working space referring to the intended note and writes the note into the note-taking window. These notes are saved and flagged in the working window by a small yellow tag (see Fig. 17.2). By clicking on this tag, the content of the note appears like a tooltip. To document and organize material, learners activate the integrator tool and save all materials they consider important (e.g., slides, web sites, pictures, etc.) with their individual notes to an individual dossier. It allows that the collected material can be played in a slide-show.

Elaboration Resources

A *Study Desk* provides access to various elaboration resources, which offer students the

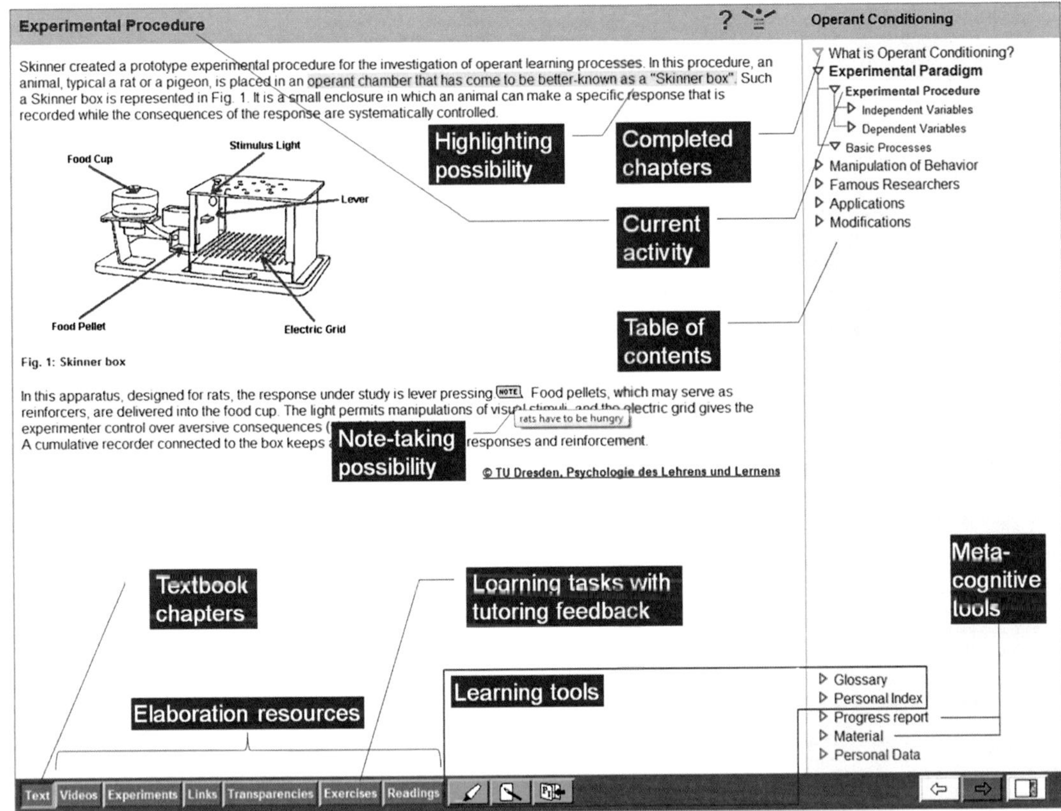

Fig. 17.2 Interface of the Web-LE "*Study Desk*"

opportunity of processing the content from various perspectives. For the present studies students had access to lecture slides, videos, simulations of experiments, a list of various commented Internet resources as well as references, suggested readings and original research papers. Furthermore, the learning tasks integrated into the *Study Desk* may serve as a resource for elaborating the knowledge acquired through studying the various materials.

Metacognitive Tools

As detailed in Sect. "Self-Regulation and Metacognition in Web-Based Learning", orientation, planning, monitoring and evaluating are core metacognitive activities within self-regulated learning. Thus, the *Study Desk* offers access to several metacognitive tools, including tools supporting (a) orientation and monitoring progress, and (b) monitoring understanding.

Orientation and progress monitoring tools. Students can for example access a material table providing an overview on the amount, structure and types of resources and materials which can be accessed in this *Study Desk*. They can furthermore access the protocol of all learning activities, including a progress and task report. Accessing these reports, learners may check which chapters they have already completed, the amount of material and media still at their disposal as well as the number of accomplished and unaccomplished learning tasks.

Interactive learning tasks as tools supporting the monitoring of understanding. In order to monitor not only progress towards learning goals but also understanding, students can also access and work on the learning tasks integrated into the *Study*

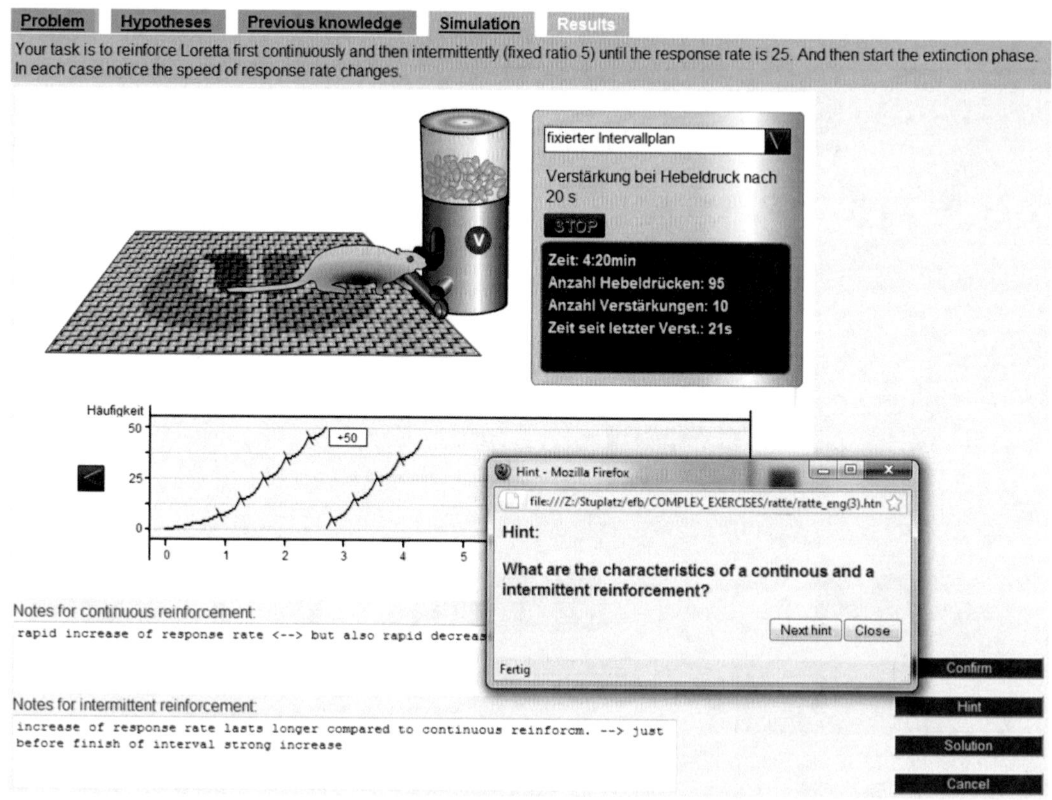

Fig. 17.3 Sample of an interactive learning task on the topic of operant conditioning

Desk. These learning tasks permit multiple-try solution possibilities and include informative tutoring feedback enabling learners to correct mistakes, to evaluate their learning progress, and to decide how they will proceed further in their learning process. The learning tasks were developed and designed on the basis of our interactive learning tasks approach (Körndle, Narciss, & Proske, 2004; Narciss, Proske, & Körndle, 2004). For the technical implementation of these tasks the EF-Editor was used (Proske, Körndle, & Narciss, 2004a, 2004b, 2005). The development of the interface for the EF-learning tasks is, on the one hand, based on the psychological knowledge on systematic task construction (Anderson & Krathwohl, 2001; Jonassen, Tessmer, & Hannum, 1999; Klauer, 1987). On the other hand, it is based on Narciss's conceptual framework for the design of informative tutoring feedback (Narciss, 2006, 2008; Narciss & Huth, 2004). Figure 17.3 illustrates an interactive learning task on operant conditioning.

The interface of an EF-learning task contains (a) the item stem in the top frame, (b) response fields in the working frame, (c) multiple-try solution possibilities including informative tutoring feedback messages, and (d) buttons providing access to hints and/or to the correct solution. For example, by clicking on the Hint-button general tutoring information is given to the learner in a first step (see Fig. 17.3). For complex learning tasks several increasingly specific hints can be delivered successively. These hints are presented so as to tutor students in detecting errors, overcoming obstacles and applying more efficient strategies towards solving learning tasks. After learners fail on the first response, the program delivers immediate feedback indicating a mistake has been made. They then receive a prompt to use available hint information (program control). To receive this information, the learners have to take action, that is, they click on the "Hint" button. After the next incorrect attempt the system (a) gives an evaluation of the overall performance (e.g., your response is 80% correct) and (b) marks correctly answered parts of the question green, while incorrectly answered question parts are labeled red. Again, the learner is prompted to use the hint information. Hence, working on interactive learning tasks should support students in monitoring their understanding within the Web-LE.

Studying Overt Cognitive and Metacognitive Activities and Their Relationships to Performance with *Study Desks*

The *Study Desks* on learning theories were used in several studies aiming at investigating overt cognitive and metacognitive learner activities through tracing students' access and use of tools and resources. In a first study, the tool-use study, the type and frequency of metacognitive tool use was investigated (Narciss et al., 2007). A second study, the learning-activity study, studied the influence of tool use on subsequent performance (Proske, Narciss, & Körndle, 2007). While in these two studies a quasi-experimental design in a blended learning situation at the university was employed, the third study examined learners' activities and performance in a controlled laboratory setting. In the latter setting students worked two sessions of 90 min each with a *Study Desk*. This third study aimed also at investigating relationships among students' activities, self-evaluated competencies and performance (Narciss, Peters, Körndle, Dupeyrat, & Huet, 2009; Peters, 2010). These studies report on the use of metacognitive tools and resources in rich open-ended Web-LEs, with non-embedded support devices. In each case, learners were free to decide when to use the embedded tools. The methods and results of these studies are summarized in the following sections.

Study 1: How Do Students Access and Use the *Study Desk* Resources and Tools in a Natural University Setting?

The tool-use study focuses on the question whether university students use the *Study Desks*, and if so, whether they use the resources and tools provided by a *Study Desk* in a natural university setting (Narciss et al., 2007). Research shows that providing tools is a necessary, but not a sufficient condition for efficient self-regulated learning with open-ended learning environments (Clarebout & Elen, 2006, 2008). Thus, the main purpose of this study was to investigate to what extent the interface of a *Study Desk* initiates task and content-related learning activities (marking, note-taking and elaboration), as well as metacognitive activities (monitoring and evaluating the learning process and outcomes).

Design and participants. Seventy-two university students of an introductory lecture to general psychology participated in the study (48 women, 24 men; M age = 22.0). Most students were in the second year of their studies. Over a university semester (3 months) students could access five *Study Desks* which complemented the learning theories curriculum of the introductory lecture to general psychology. While one *Study Desk* provided an introduction to psychological learning theories, the other *Study Desks* each addressed a particular learning theory: (a) Classical Conditioning, (b) Operant Conditioning, (c) Purposive Behaviorism, and (d) Socio-cognitive theory of learning (see also Table 17.2). The successful completion of the lecture required students to pass a test at the end of the semester. Students were free to work on the five *Study Desks* as many times and as long as desired. Furthermore, there were no restrictions regarding learning objectives and topics.

Measures. All students' activities were recorded in log-files in which frequency and time of each learning activity were automatically recorded and summarized. The measure of *total working time* represents the sum of time on all learning activities. Yet, there was a high variability in the amount of available material in the five *Study Desks*, the number of selected *Study Desks* and the time spent on the selected *Study Desks* (see Narciss et al., 2007). In order to account for this variability, the measure of *time on a particular learning activity* was standardized using percentages. As such, the time on a particular learning tool, elaboration resource or monitoring tool was expressed as percentage of total working time. The same was true for the learning tasks. As the interactive learning tasks of the *Study Desks* offer students the possibility to complete tasks in several attempts and provide them with informative tutoring feedback (Narciss, 2006, 2008), the percentage of correctly solved learning tasks in a first attempt was used to assess students' *online performance* during working with the five *Study Desks*. Again, this measure was standardized, i.e., it represented the number of correctly solved learning tasks related to the number of learning tasks students had at their disposal within their selected *Study Desks*.

Statistical analyses. An exploratory analysis of total working time revealed a huge variability in the time students spent with the *Study Desks* (M=194.5 min, SD=229.9). Due to this, the sample was divided into three percentiles by means of total working time for analysis of students' learning activities: (a) <40 group: students working less than 40 min, (b) 40–180 group: students working between 40 and 180 min, and (c) >180 group: students working more than 180 min. Nonparametric methods (e.g., Kruskal–Wallis test) were used for further statistical analyses.

Selected results and conclusions. Students of all groups spent more than two thirds of their total working time processing texts (65.3–72.4%). Relative time on learning tasks ranged from 7.2 to 15.1% of total working time. The learning tools were used during 6.1–10% of total working time. The percentage of time on elaboration resources ranged from 2.7 to 5.8%, whereas the monitoring tools were hardly used (0.3–1.7%, for detailed information see Narciss et al., 2007). Furthermore, it was found that the >180 group worked on 25% of the learning tasks, whereas the students of the other groups only processed ca. 5% of the available tasks. In addition, the online performance of the >180 group was statistically significant better than the online performance of the other two groups.

The results of the tool-use study show that there is a huge variability in total working time. Whereas some students studied for only a few minutes, others spent more than 7 h with the *Study Desks*. Furthermore, the results indicate that students employ relatively the same study tactics in web-based learning environments as they do with printed textbooks. Students spent most of their total working time studying texts, whereas substantially less time was invested in processing learning tasks and using the learning and elaboration tools. Moreover, only a very small number of students used the monitoring tools. It was also found that students who worked longer with the *Study Desks* (>180 group) also used more learning tasks and solved more of them correctly without informative tutoring feedback. This is worth noting, because one might expect that working on more tasks makes it more likely to make errors.

Study 2: How Are Learner Activities Related to Performance in a Natural Setting?

The tool-use study revealed a large variability in frequencies and durations of the various study activities traced through the log files. Furthermore, it revealed that students who worked for at least 3 h with the *Study Desks* accessed and processed more learning tasks and achieved a higher level of performance in answering these tasks. Due to organizational constraints of this study it was however not possible to examine the relationships among study activities and performance measured in a controlled posttest. Thus, the purpose of the learning-activity study was to investigate the relationship between learning activities, online performance, and posttest performance (Proske et al., 2007).

Design and participants. As the tool-use study, the learning-activity study took place in a blended learning setting in higher education. The participants were 105 students (73 women, 32 men, M age=23 years) attending a Psychology lecture, "Introduction to Psychology", at TU Dresden, Germany. Most participants were in the second year of study, with Psychology as a minor field of study. Students were provided with the same five

Study Desks as in the tool-use study over a period of 3 months. There were no restrictions regarding the learning objectives and selected topics. Out of the 105 students attending the lecture, a total of 84 students used at least one of the *Study Desks*. At the end of the term students had the possibility to complete an electronic posttest to receive certification for the lecture. This test was made available online over a period of 1 month. Seventy-seven students participated in it. Most (n=50) had worked with the provided *Study Desks* beforehand, whereas 27 students wrote the test without having used them (for detailed information see Proske et al., 2007).

Measures and statistical analyses. The measures of total working time, time on a particular learning activity, as well as online performance were equal to the tool-use study. In addition to these time measures, the *quantity of processed texts and learning tasks* was recorded. These raw data were transformed into individualized percentage measures. They represent the conditional percentage of processed texts and learning tasks given the amount of material students had at their disposal within the number of *Study Desks* they had selected.

The posttest was passed if at least 70% of the exercises from each topic had been correctly solved in no more than two attempts. After a student failed on his first solution attempt, he received immediate feedback indicating a mistake had been made. Therefore, *posttest performance* was represented by the percentage of correctly answered test exercises in the first solution attempt. Due to high standard deviations in the distributions of learning activity variables and achievement measures, we used nonparametric methods (e.g., Chi-Square Test; Spearman's Rho Correlational Coefficient).

Selected results and conclusions. The results regarding learning activities were similar to the results of the tool-use study. With respect to posttest performance it was found that students who had worked with a Study Desk achieved a significantly higher level of posttest performance than students who did not work with a Study Desk (for detailed information see Proske et al., 2007).

Spearman's Rho Correlations Coefficients were computed to examine relations between learning activities, online performance, and posttest performance. The results showed that the longer a student worked with the *Study Desks*, the more the tools were used and the better the online and posttest performance. The correlational analysis showed further that the better the online performance the longer students used the monitoring tools. Longer text reading was associated to lower online performance. Posttest performance was positively associated to amount of processed learning texts, learning tasks, and total working time. Furthermore, it was found that the more texts and learning tasks were processed within the *Study Desks*, the better the posttest performance. Apart from the learning tools no relationship was found between time-on-tools and posttest performance.

Students' access and use of the *Study Desk* resources and tools, especially interactive learning tasks and the learning tools for marking and note-taking was not only significantly correlated with online performance, but also with posttest performance. These findings are in line with Wagner (1997), who regards interactivity in web-based learning environments as a means of performance improvement. Time-on-text was significantly negatively correlated with online performance. This implies that overuse of the learning medium text may be considered an ineffective study strategy (Berge, 1999). However, this study confirmed the results of the tool-use study. Whereas 85% of the students used the interactive learning tasks, much less used the learning tools, elaboration resources and monitoring tools. This finding is in line with prior studies, which have found that learners do not always use resources and tools of a Web-LE efficiently (Chen & Rada, 1996; Scheiter & Gerjets, 2007). In addition, following Kaplan's reflections on the variety of students' individual study objectives (Kaplan, 2008), one has to consider that accessing and using the resources of a rich Web-LE may depend also on the students' aims when working with the *Study Desks* (see also Niederhauser, 2008). Finally, students in this university setting also had the possibility to prepare themselves for the electronic posttest with traditional learning materials.

Study 3: How Do Self-Evaluations Relate to Learner Activities and Performance?

Analyzing the data from the first two studies was very difficult because of the huge variability in frequency and time of students' access and use of the *Study Desks* and their resources and tools. Thus, the purpose of the third study was to investigate overt cognitive and metacognitive student activities in a controlled setting. Furthermore, this study aimed at investigating the role of self-evaluations of competences in self-regulated learning with a rich Web-LE.

Participants and Design. Participants were 190 teacher education students attending a lecture on "Introduction to Psychology" at the TU Dresden, Germany (147 women, 43 men, M age = 22 years). Participants had to study two sessions of about 90 min (study sessions) each with one Web-LE *Study Desk – Behaviorist Learning Theories* (see Table 17.2). Within these sessions they were free to study on their own pace and with the material and tools they considered relevant. Hence, they had to self-regulate their activities. All learners' activities were tracked by log files. One week before and after these study sessions, students had to complete a test assessing their level of knowledge and to answer several questionnaires, including items addressing self-evaluation of competences regarding their media literacy skills, their SRL-skills, and their cognitive capabilities in acquiring knowledge on learning theories (pretest and posttest sessions). Furthermore, at the beginning and the end of each study session the self-evaluation measures addressing cognitive and media literacy skills were collected.

Measures and statistical analyses. As in the previous studies, all learning activities were tracked by log files. As in the previous studies, each individual log file recorded the frequency and the amount of time spent with (a) accessing and studying textbook chapters, (b) accessing and working on learning tasks, (c) accessing elaboration resources (i.e., slides, www-links, videos, glossary), (d) activating and using active learning tools (i.e., highlighting tool, note taking tool, integrator tool), and (e) accessing and attending to metacognitive resources (i.e., progress and task report, material table).

Pretest and posttest performance was assessed 1 week before and after the study sessions. Participants completed a test assessing their knowledge. This test consisted of 22 computer-based items which were constructed with the EF-editor and provided through the *Study Desk*-interface. These items addressed core concepts of behaviorist learning theories and their application. As in the previous studies, *online performance* was measured by the percentage of correctly solved learning tasks during the study sessions.

Self-evaluation measures. At the beginning of the pretest and posttest sessions, participants answered several questionnaires addressing various measures of self-evaluation of competences. These questionnaires included items addressing self-evaluation of competences regarding students' media literacy skills, their SRL-skills, and their cognitive capabilities in acquiring knowledge on learning theories. As mentioned above, the self-evaluation measures addressing cognitive and media literacy skills were also collected at the beginning and the end of each study session.

Selected results and conclusions. The log file analyses of frequencies and time-on-learning activities revealed that on average students spent 58% of their total working time with the textbook chapters, 24% with the interactive learning tasks, 11% with the elaboration resources, 6% with the learning or processing tools and 0.4% with the metacognitive tools. Yet, as in the previous studies there was a huge variability in these measures. Some students spent almost all their time during the study sessions with studying textbook chapters, whereas others spent their time with a variety of learning activities. Furthermore, despite the controlled time-frame (90 min for one session including responding online to self-evaluation questionnaires at the beginning and the end of the session, as well as studying instructions) students' total working time over two sessions ranged from 90 min to 162 min (mean 124 min.; SD 9 min,).

Comparing students' activities during the two sessions elicited several statistically significant differences. Students' total working time was significantly higher (63.5 min.) in the second than in the first sessions (60.5 min.). Mean time spent on textbook chapters was significantly higher in the first (62.5% of total working time) than in the second session (52.7% of total working time). The same is true for time spent with elaboration resources (13.6% vs. 7.7%) and learning tools (8.9% vs. 4.2%), whereas mean time spent on learning tasks was significantly higher in the second (31.7%) than in the first session (15.6%). These differences indicate that during the first session students spent more time with mere information processing, whereas during the second session they spent more time with learning task processing. This learning task processing may have served to some extent to monitor or evaluate the progress in knowledge acquisition.

Furthermore, analyses of changes in performance and self-evaluation measures revealed that performance and self-evaluation accuracy increased over the four sessions of this study. It is worth emphasizing here that self-evaluation strength did not increase from pretest to posttest, whereas there was an increase in self-evaluation accuracy from pretest to posttest. Hence, further research on the role of self-evaluations in self-regulated Web-based learning should include not only measures of self-evaluation strength but also measures of self-evaluation accuracy.

Finally, we found that self-evaluation accuracy was significantly correlated to several learning activities. Most importantly, to the time spent on studying textbook chapters vs. the time spent on working with the learning tasks of the Web-LE. The higher self-evaluation accuracy the less time students spent with the textbook chapters, but the more time they spent with the learning tasks in both study sessions. This result confirms assumptions about the role of learning tasks in self-regulated learning contexts. A core function of learning tasks is to provide students with occasions for applying and self-evaluating their acquired knowledge (Körndle et al., 2004; Narciss, Proske, & Körndle, 2004).

Furthermore, small but significant positive correlations among self-evaluation accuracy and the time spent on attending to metacognitive support of the Web-LE are worth noting. The higher self-evaluation accuracy, the more time students spent with attending to the overview of the Web-LE and the progress reports on study and task activities. Yet, this result has to be considered with caution, first because the correlations are rather small, second because several students did not attend to the metacognitive tools at all.

Comparative Summary of Methods and Results

In summary, the presented studies are methodologically equivalent regarding the following aspects: In all studies *Study Desks,* i.e., rich open-ended Web-LEs with embedded and non-embedded resources and tools, were provided to university students as a complement to main lectures and seminars. Furthermore, in all studies students' activities were recorded in log files and these log files were used to analyze frequencies and durations of accessing and/or using the resources and tools of the *Study Desks.* Moreover, in all studies the focus of interest was on investigating *self-initiated* study activities. Thus, in the first two studies data were collected in a natural context over 3 months. Within these natural contexts the *Study Desks* were provided as complements to main lectures in Educational and General Psychology. More specifically, during one university semester (3 months) students could (a) attend to a weekly lecture session (90 min), and (b) study on their own with the *Study Desks* and/or other study materials (e.g., textbooks, scripts). The availability of the *Study Desks* was regularly prompted by the lecturers. However, students were free to access and work with the *Study Desks* whenever they decided to do so. In the third study data were gathered in a more controlled context with pretest and posttest sessions as well as two treatment sessions. Yet, in order to keep the setting as natural as possible, there were no restrictions regarding when and how students accessed and worked with the resources and tools of the *Study Desk* within the two treatment sessions.

Given these methodological similarities of the three studies it may be no surprise that their results are also rather similar: The field studies revealed a high variability in total working time. This variability in total working time was reduced in the third study, yet, it was still apparent. All studies elicited similar patterns of study activities: Students accessed the text-book like Web-pages of the *Study Desks* most frequently and spent most of their total working time on these pages. Accessing and processing learning tasks was the second most frequently observed study activity. The elaboration resources and the learning tools were significantly less used than the learning tasks. Finally, metacognitive tools were only hardly used.

Regarding relationships among study activities and performance measures all studies revealed that total working time in Web-LEs is positively related to better achievement during learning. Furthermore, learners' posttest performance was positively related to the amount of tool use, in particular to the use of learning tasks. Finally, frequency of learning task use was positively related to an increase in learning outcomes (Peters, 2010; Proske et al., 2007).

Methodological and Analytical Challenges

As revealed by our studies with the *Study Desks*, researchers investigating overt cognitive and metacognitive student activities in self-regulated learning with a rich Web-LE have to face several methodological and analytical challenges in analyzing the log file data traced through the learning process. These challenges include the variability of learner activities when studying with a rich Web-LE as well as the problem of identifying and interpreting events and activities in the log file data, by relating them to concrete SRL-activities.

Variability of Learner Activities in Rich Web-LE

Researchers in the field of self-regulated learning are confronted with the trade-off between controlling conditions of data collection and keeping the instructional setting as natural as possible in order to allow SRL-activities. In many studies on self-regulated learning with a variety of computer-based learning environments, the researcher decided in favor of controlling conditions of data collection, and thus used closed learning environments. As a consequence, it is questionable if the data gathered in these studies really reflect *self-initiated* SRL-activities (Winters, Greene, & Costich, 2008). As we wanted to capture and investigate *self-initiated* cognitive and metacognitive study activities we used a rich open-ended Web-LE and gathered data in natural university settings. This resulted in a tremendous variability of the frequencies and durations students worked with the Web-LE. In the more controlled experimental setting of the third study, this variability was reduced but still apparent. To account—at least partly for this variability—we used several strategies. For example, in the tool-use study we assigned post hoc the students to user subgroups defined by differences in their total working time. Moreover, in all studies we used relative measures of *time on a particular learning activity* by computing percentages of total working time for each study activity traced in the log files.

Analyze and Interpret Log File Data

Using log file data to determine access frequencies and times in Web-LEs accessible through standard browser is not a trivial task, because for example standard browsers offer back and forward buttons which allow movements between already visited pages. In general, these back and forward moves are not traced in the log files because the already visited pages are retrieved from the local browser cache. Yet, the back and forward buttons are one of the most frequently tools used (Scheuer, Mühlenbrock, & Melis, 2007).

The *Study Desk*-interface does not offer back and forward buttons which allow movements between already visited pages. In contrast, students have to access next pages of a chapter, or other resources and tools explicitly by clicking on the respective chapter title in the table of contents or on the resource or tool button displayed in the bottom or the navigation frame. Thus, the log files produced with a *Study Desk* may be more reliable as log files from standard browsers with back and forward buttons.

Despite this advantage of a *Study Desk* analyzing and interpreting the log file data with regard to cognitive or metacognitive activities is challenging, because several resources and tools of a *Study Desk*—and of many other Web-LEs—are multifunctional. Consequently, they can be accessed and used for task-related cognitive activities or for metacognitive activities. For example, the glossary can be accessed whether a student wants to look up the meaning of an unfamiliar concept or if she wants to monitor the accuracy of her understanding of the concept. The access and processing of learning tasks may also occur for various purposes: Students may for example access and process learning tasks (a) before accessing other course material, in order to assess their prior level of knowledge and skills, (b) during Web-based learning, for example after having studied a chapter, in order to monitor their understanding or progress toward learning goals, as well as in order to elaborate the acquired knowledge, and (c) in the evaluation stage of Web-based learning in order to assess their final level of knowledge and skills. Given this multifunctionality of resources and tools, tracing frequencies and durations of their access and use without taking into account the context or action history, may be not enough for identifying when and how students are involved in cognitive or metacognitive activities.

Implications for Future Research

Methodological and Analytical Implications

To interpret students' behavior from log file data meaningfully, it seems to be necessary to analyze in meaningful patterns or sequences of activities the students perform during Web-based learning. A promising tool, the Weblog Analysis Tool, in this direction has been for example presented by Ceddia, Sheard, and Tibbey (2007). Based on the present data and experiences from explorative studies (e.g., Kapp, Narciss, Körndle, & Proske, 2011; Narciss, Körndle, Reimann, & Muller, 2004) it seems to be particularly fruitful to investigate in more detail when and how students access the interactive learning tasks. In doing so researchers should apply an event-related methodology of analyzing the log file data (see for example Mühlenbrock, 2005; Scheuer et al., 2007). More specifically, future studies should aim at identifying events that precede and follow successful or unsuccessful steps in the process of task completion. Preceding events may be for example the end of another activity (i.e., reading a text, watching a video, exploring a simulation). Subsequent events may be the return to the resource or tool used before learning task processing, the access to learning protocols, or the access to other instructional resources, which in case of unsuccessful task completion may provide assistance (e.g., a glossary). Using such an event-related methodology would contribute at least partly to overcome the problem of misinterpreting the access to multifunctional resources and tools. Furthermore, it could be used to investigate how patterns or sequences of activities relate to performance, in order to gain insights in their effectiveness.

Additionally, mixed-method approaches combining analyses of log file data with think-aloud protocols, eye-tracking data, or video-monitoring of student activities are recommended for further studies. Yet, including these methods is only possible in laboratory settings and more intrusive than mere activity tracing through log files (see for example Azevedo, Moos, Johnson, & Chauncey, 2010; Bannert & Mengelkamp, 2008; Greene & Azevedo, 2010; Winne, 2010).

Implications for Tool Design

Many Web-LEs provide students with embedded and non-embedded tools, in order to support students in a variety of ways during their study activities. Yet, for research purposes this combination of embedded and non-embedded tools may be critical, because study activities such as for example monitoring by using an embedded tool which is always visible cannot be traced in the log files. Our findings indicate that students hardly accessed the non-embedded monitoring tools (i.e., progress reports, and material overview), might be to some extent explained by this problem. To monitor progress when studying with a *Study Desk* students need not access the monitoring tools, because their content-related activities are traced and visualized through changing colors in the table of contents. Thus, for future studies, the Web-LE should be designed in such a way that covert student activities (i.e., monitoring progress through changes in the tables of contents) are transformed into overt student activities. This involves rendering embedded tools if possible into non-embedded resources and tools.

References

Alexander, P. A. (2008). Why this and why now? Introduction to the special issue on metacognition, self-regulation, and self-regulated learning. *Educational Psychology Review, 20*(4), 369–372.

Anderson, L. W., & Krathwohl, D. R., (Eds.) (2001). *A Taxonomy for Learning, Teaching, and Assessing: A Revision of Bloom's Taxonomy of Educational Objectives*. New York: London Longman.

Azevedo, R. (2005). Computer environments as metacognitive tools for enhancing learning. *Educational Psychologist, 40*(4), 193–197.

Azevedo, R. (2007). Understanding the complex nature of self-regulatory processes in learning with computer-based learning environments: An introduction. *Metacognition and Learning, 2*(2), 57–65.

Azevedo, R., & Jacobson, M. (2008). Advances in scaffolding learning with hypertext and hypermedia: A summary and critical analysis. *Educational Technology Research & Development, 56*(1), 93–100.

Azevedo, R., Moos, D. C., Johnson, A. M., & Chauncey, A. D. (2010). Measuring cognitive and metacognitive regulatory processes during hypermedia learning: Issues and challenges. *Educational Psychologist, 45*(4), 210–223.

Bannert, M., & Mengelkamp, C. (2008). Assessment of metacognitive skills by means of instruction to think aloud and reflect when prompted. Does the verbalisation method affect learning? *Metacognition and Learning, 3*(1), 39–58.

Berge, Z. L. (1999). Interaction in post-secondary web-based learning. *Educational Technology, 41*(1), 5–11.

Boekaerts, M. (1997). Self-regulated learning: A new concept embraced by researchers, policy makers, educators, teachers, and students. *Learning and Instruction, 7*(2), 161–186.

Butler, D. L., & Winne, P. H. (1995). Feedback and self-regulated learning: A theoretical synthesis. *Review of Educational Research, 65*(3), 245–281.

Ceddia, J., Sheard, J., & Tibbey, G. (2007). WAT: A tool for classifying learning activities from a log file. In S. Mann & A. Simon (Eds.), *Proceedings of the ninth Australasian conference on computing education* (Vol. 66, pp. 11–17). Australian Computer Society: Ballarat, Australia.

Chen, C., & Rada, R. (1996). Interacting with hypertext: A meta-analysis of experimental studies. *Human-Computer Interaction, 11*(2), 125–156.

Clarebout, G., & Elen, J. (2006). Tool use in computer-based learning environments: Towards a research framework. *Computers in Human Behavior, 22*(3), 389–411.

Clarebout, G., & Elen, J. (2008). Tool use in open learning environments: In search of learner-related determinants. *Learning Environments Research, 11*(2), 163–178.

Dinsmore, D. L., Alexander, P. A., & Loughlin, S. M. (2008). Focusing the conceptual lens on metacognition, self-regulation, and self-regulated learning. *Educational Psychology Review, 20*(4), 391–409.

Flavell, J. H. (1979). Metacognition and cognitive monitoring: A new area of cognitive-developmental inquiry. *American Psychologist, 34*(10), 906–911.

Flavell, J. H. (1985). *Cognitive development* (2nd ed.). Englewood Cliffs, NJ: Prentice Hall.

Greene, J. A., & Azevedo, R. (2010). The measurement of learners' self-regulated cognitive and metacognitive processes while using computer-based learning environments. *Educational Psychologist, 45*(4), 203–209.

Hannafin, M., Land, S., & Oliver, K. (1999). Open learning environments: Foundation, methods, and models. In C. M. Reigeluth (Ed.), *Instructional-design theories and models: A new paradigm of instructional theory* (Vol. II, pp. 115–140). Mahwah, NJ, USA: Lawrence Erlbaum.

Jonassen, D. H., Tessmer, M., & Hannum, W. H. (1999). *Task analysis methods for instructional design*. Mahwah, NJ: Lawrence Erlbaum.

Kaplan, A. (2008). Clarifying metacognition, self-regulation, and self-regulated learning: What's the purpose? *Educational Psychology Review, 20*(4), 477–484.

Kapp, F., Narciss, S., Körndle, H., & Proske, A. (2011). Interaktive Lernaufgaben als Erfolgsfaktor für E-Learning (Interactive learning tasks as a success factor for e-learning). *Zeitschrift für E-Learning, 6*, 21–32.

Klauer, K. J. (1987). *Kriteriumsorientierte Tests [Criteria-oriented tests]*. Göttingen, Germany: Hogrefe.

Körndle, H., Narciss, S., & Proske, A. (2004). Konstruktion interaktiver Lernaufgaben für die universitäre Lehre [Construction of interactive learning tasks for university instruction]. In D. Carstensen & B. Barrios (Eds.), *Campus 2004. Kommen die digitalen Medien an den Hochschulen in die Jahre?* (pp. 57–67). Münster, Germany: Waxmann.

Mühlenbrock, M. (2005). Automatic action analysis in an interactive learning environment. In C. Choquet, V. Luengo, & K. Yacef (Eds.), *Proceedings of the workshop on usage analysis in learning systems at the 12th international conference on artificial intelligence in education AIED-2005* (pp. 73–80). The Netherlands: Amsterdam.

Narciss, S. (2006). *Informatives tutorielles Feedback. Entwicklungs- und Evaluationsprinzipien auf der Basis instruktionspsychologischer Erkenntnisse [Informative tutoring feedback. Design and evaluation principles on the basis of instructional psychology]*. Münster: Waxmann.

Narciss, S. (2008). Feedback strategies for interactive learning tasks. In J. M. Spector, M. D. Merrill, J. J. G. van Merriënboer, & M. P. Driscoll (Eds.), *Handbook of research on educational communications and technology* (3rd ed., pp. 125–144). Mahwah, NJ: Lawrence Erlbaum.

Narciss, S., & Huth, K. (2004). How to design informative tutoring feedback for multi-media learning. In H. M. Niegemann, D. Leutner, & R. Brünken (Eds.), *Instructional design for multimedia learning* (pp. 181–195). Münster: Waxmann.

Narciss, S., Körndle, H., Reimann, G., & Müller, C. (2004). Feedback-seeking and feedback efficiency in web-based learning – How do they relate to task and learner characteristics? In P. Gerjets, P. A. Kirschner, J. Elen, & R. Joiner (Eds.), *Instructional design for effective and enjoyable computer-supported learning. Proceedings of the first joint meeting of the EARLI SIGs Instructional Design and Learning and Instruction with Computers [CD-ROM]* (pp. 377–388). Tübingen: Knowledge Media Research Center.

Narciss, S., Peters, S., Körndle, H., Dupeyrat, C., & Huet, N. (2009). *Self-evaluation accuracy? How does it relate to learners' activities and performance in self-regulated web-based learning?* Paper presented at the 13th biennal conference of the European Association for Research on Learning and Instruction (EARLI).

Narciss, S., Proske, A., & Körndle, H. (2004). Interaktive Aufgaben für das computergestützte Lernen. Vom ersten Entwurf bis zur technischen Realisierung [Interactive learning tasks for computer-supported learning. From first draft to technical realisation]. In U. Schmitz (Ed.), *Linguistik lernen im Internet*. Tübingen, Germany: Gunter Narr.

Narciss, S., Proske, A., & Körndle, H. (2007). Promoting self-regulated learning in web-based learning environments. *Computers in Human Behavior, 23*(3), 1126–1144.

Niederhauser, D. (2008). Educational hypertext research. In J. M. Spector, M. D. Merrill, J. J. G. van Merriënboer, & M. P. Driscoll (Eds.), *Handbook of research on educational communications and technology* (3rd ed., pp. 199–210). Mahwah, NJ: Lawrence Erlbaum.

Peters, S. (2010). *Fähigkeitskonzepte beim selbstregulierten Lernen mit Multimedia [The role of task-specific self-concepts in self-regulated multimedia learning]*. Hamburg: Dr. Kova .

Pressley, M., Borkwski, J. G., & Schneider, W. (1989). Good information processing: What it is and how education can promote it. *International Journal of Educational Research, 13*(8), 857–867.

Proske, A., Körndle, H., & Narciss, S. (2004a). The Exercise Format Editor: A multimedia tool for the design of multiple learning tasks. In H. M. Niegemann, D. Leutner, & R. Brünken (Eds.), *Instructional design for multimedia learning* (pp. 149–164). Münster, Germany: Waxmann.

Proske, A., Körndle, H., & Narciss, S. (2004b). How the Exercise Format-Editor supports the design of interactive learning tasks. In G. Richards (Ed.), *Proceedings of the world conference on e-learning in corporate, government, healthcare, and higher education 2004* (pp. 2881–2887). Washington, DC, USA: AACE.

Proske, A., Körndle, H., & Narciss, S. (2005). The exercise format editor – Supporting the systematic construction of interactive learning tasks. In K. P. Jantke, K. P. Fähnrich, & W. S. Wittig (Eds.), *Marktplatz Internet: Von e-Learning bis e-Payment: Tagungsband der 13 Leipziger Informatik-Tage* (pp. 429–435). Bonn, Germany: Gesellschaft für Informatik.

Proske, A., Narciss, S., & Körndle, H. (2007). Interactivity and learners' achievement in web-based learning. *Journal of Interactive Learning Research, 18*(4), 511–531.

Scheiter, K., & Gerjets, P. (2007). Learner control in hypermedia environments. *Educational Psychology Review, 19*(3), 285–307.

Scheuer, O., Mühlenbrock, M., & Melis, E. (2007). Results from action analysis in an interactive learning environment. *Journal of Interactive Learning Research, 18*(2), 185–205.

Wade, S. E., Trathen, W., & Schraw, G. (1990). An analysis of spontaneous study strategies. *Reading Research Quarterly, 25*(2), 147–166.

Wagner, E. D. (1997). Interactivity: From agents to outcomes. *New Directions for Teaching and Learning, 71*, 19–26.

Winne, P. H. (2001). Self-regulated learning viewed from models of information processing. In B. J. Zimmerman & D. H. Schunk (Eds.), *Self-regulated learning and academic achievement: Theoretical perspectives* (2nd ed., pp. 153–189). Mahwah, NJ, USA: Lawrence Erlbaum.

Winne, P. H. (2010). Improving measurements of self-reglated learning. *Educational Psychologist, 45*(4), 267–276.

Winne, P. H., & Hadwin, A. F. (1998). Studying as self-regulated learning. In D. J. Hacker, J. Dunlosky, & A. C. Graesser (Eds.), *Metacognition in educational theory and practice* (pp. 277–304). Mahwah, NJ, USA: Lawrence Erlbaum.

Winne, P. H., & Hadwin, A. F. (2008). The weave of motivation and self-regulated learning. In D. H. Schunk & B. J. Zimmerman (Eds.), *Motivation and self-regulated learning: Theory, research, and applications* (pp. 297–314). Mahwah, NJ, USA: Lawrence Erlbaum.

Winters, F., Greene, J., & Costich, C. (2008). Self-regulation of learning within computer-based learning environments: A critical analysis. *Educational Psychology Review, 20*(4), 429–444.

Zimmerman, B. J. (2000). Attaining self-regulation: A social cognitive perspective. In M. Boekaerts, P. R. Pintrich, & M. Zeidner (Eds.), *Handbook of self-regulation* (pp. 13–39). San Diego, CA: Academic.

Analyzing Navigation Patterns to Scaffold Metacognition in Hypertext Systems

18

Sadhana Puntambekar, Sarah A. Sullivan, and Roland Hübscher

Abstract

One of the affordances of hypertext environments is the freedom to choose the order of information presentation. However, learners may have difficulty self-regulating their learning in order to make navigation decisions that align with their goals. This chapter presents our work in helping students learn from hypertext using the CoMPASS hypertext system in middle school science classes. The CoMPASS system design includes navigable concept maps that reflect connections among concepts in the domain of physics and are used to help students understand the relationships between science ideas. In CoMPASS, students' self-regulated behavior is detected through the use of computer-generated log files that allow us analyze student navigation behavior post hoc and create clusters of navigation patterns. We are then able to examine these clusters of navigation patterns to determine differences in students' SRL processes and the types of scaffolding that they may need. This chapter presents five different navigation pattern clusters that have been identified as typical of students' navigation behavior in CoMPASS. We further discuss how these clusters will be matched to the navigation behaviors of future students and used to inform an algorithm that will provide adaptive real-time navigation prompts in order to scaffold metacognition and self-regulated learning.

S. Puntambekar (✉) • S.A. Sullivan, Ph.D.
Learning Sciences Program, Educational Psychology Department, University of Wisconsin, Madison, WI, USA
e-mail: puntambekar@education.wisc.edu

R. Hübscher, Ph.D.
Information Design, Bentley University, Waltham, MA, USA

R. Azevedo and V. Aleven (eds.), *International Handbook of Metacognition and Learning Technologies*, Springer International Handbooks of Education 26, DOI 10.1007/978-1-4419-5546-3_18,

Introduction

As the use of hypertexts and other digital media environments is becoming increasingly ubiquitous in education, a new form of literacy will become more important. Digital technology changes the way in which we write and think about writing (Bolter, 2001). In traditional text, there is a clear sequencing of ideas into sections and subsections, although expert readers are known to traverse the text in a nonlinear way. In a printed text, associative relationships define organization that lies beneath the order of the pages and chapters, as in an index (Bolter, 1991). But writers of hypertext often connect the associative and semantic links in multiple ways. Therefore, the navigational choices that readers make when using hypertext lead to multiple ways in which meaning from the text may be structured (Bolter, 1998). Hypertext connects sections (i.e., nodes) of text in a nonlinear way through semantic links (Rouet, 2006). These nodes can vary in size and complexity and can potentially be created from a range of different representations, such as a paragraph of text, an entire web page, or graphics (Bolter, 2001). Hypertext and hypermedia environments, because of their nonlinearity, lend themselves well to helping students understand how science ideas and principles are interconnected and can make *unseen* connections visible. The real strength of educational hypertext systems lies in the presentation of conceptual content in ways that *show the numerous and multiple interrelationships* between and among concepts, even across (what are typically taught as) disparate subject areas.

In a printed text, associative relationships define the organization that underlies the order of pages and chapters (Bolter, 1991), yet making explicit these associative lines of thought is difficult in linear text. In contrast to linear text, hypertext allows the author to use more explicit visual cues, such as hyperlinks or interactive graphical representations, to provide guidance to the reader as to the relationships among units of information. However, this means that the reader must decide how to navigate through the text and devote cognitive resources to understanding these relationships (Bolter, 2001; Sharples, 1999). Readers must develop an understanding of connections between closely related nodes of information, or intertextual relations, and must also understand where a unit of information fits with respect to multiple other information nodes in the global structure of the system (Bolter, 2001; Puntambekar & Stylianou, 2005; Rouet, 2006).

Although one of the affordances of hypertext is the freedom to choose the order of information presentation, the ability to choose one's own navigational path may cause confusion for readers who are trying to establish the global structure of the text (Rouet, 2006). Especially for adolescent learners, the employment of adaptive self-regulation strategies to take advantage of the flexible access to information in hypertext and hypermedia environments has often been found to be lacking (e.g., Azevedo, Moos, Greene, Winters, & Cromley, 2008). Therefore, the ways in which learners actively engage with multiple nodes of information in a hypertext environment are an important component of study to understand learning from hypertext. Other individual learner characteristics have also been identified as important factors that influence navigation in hypertext environments, including prior knowledge (e.g., Alexander, Kulikowich, & Jetton, 1994), system structure (e.g., Puntambekar, Stylianou, & Hübscher, 2003), and beliefs about learning and the task (Braten, Britt, Stromso, & Rouet, 2011; Rouet & Coutelet, 2008). However, learners' metacognitive abilities, which are fundamental to self-regulated learning (SRL), have also been shown to significantly impact navigation behaviors (Schwartz, Anderson, Hong, Howard, & McGee, 2004).

Self-regulated learners are metacognitively and motivationally engaged in the processes of their learning (Green & Azevedo, 2007). Metacognition can be thought of as being aware of one's processes of working toward a learning goal, monitoring progress toward the goal, and detecting and correcting errors (Azevedo, 2005a). The ability to self-regulate one's learning processes is an essential component of successful metacognition (e.g., Azevedo, 2005a;

Azevedo, Guthrie, & Seibert, 2004). Engaging in self-regulation is an active, constructive process in which learners set goals for their learning and then monitor and regulate their cognition and behavior to reach those goals (Azevedo et al., 2004). This may include things, such as using fix-up strategies when there is a breakdown in comprehension or evaluation of whether navigation choices are helpful to reach the learning goal (Coiro & Dobler, 2007). To regulate their learning, students must adapt their processing operations based on their success with the learning task. However, research indicates that students often have difficulty with self-regulating their learning, particularly in conceptually rich domains, such as science (Azevedo, 2005b). This chapter presents our work in helping students learn from hypertext using the CoMPASS hypertext system (Puntambekar et al., 2003; Puntambekar, Stylianou, & Goldstein, 2007) in middle school science classes.

Our main research questions were the following: (1) What are the navigation patterns that students typically follow? (2) How can students' navigation patterns be grouped into a few clusters to provide adaptive support for navigation and learning?

Background and Context

Understanding Connections in Science

A key aspect of science understanding is the integration of knowledge (Linn, 2006) into a framework consisting of relationships among concepts and principles (Hiebert & Carpenter, 1992; Newton & Newton, 2000; Ruiz-Primo & Shavelson, 1996). Glynn, Yeany, and Britton (1991) state that "without the construction of relations, students have no foundation and framework on which to build meaningful conceptual networks" (p. 6). Research on experts and novices indicates that experts represent their knowledge differently (Chi, Hutchinson, & Robin, 1989; Chi & Koeske, 1983). Specifically, expert learners' knowledge is represented in ways that show richer organization, often organized around the central principles of the domain that can be generalized (Cheng, 1999; Hmelo-Silver, Marathe, & Liu, 2007; Kozma, 2000; Pearsall, Skipper, & Mintzes, 1997). Studies examining science learning have emphasized a need for students to learn science as a connected body of knowledge rather than a set of discrete facts (e.g., Hmelo-Silver et al., 2007; Kozma, 2000; Ruiz-Primo & Shavelson, 1996). One way for students to develop a rich conceptual understanding of a domain is to engage in activities that require them to actively organize and synthesize information from many sources (Rouet, 2006; Spitulnik, Zembal-Saul, & Krajcik, 1998).

The use of hypertext environments to present information has been proposed as a means to get learners more actively engaged in thinking about connections among concepts (Shapiro & Niederhauser, 2004). Hypertext and hypermedia environments composed of multiple linked documents offer a unique opportunity to help students understand the connections between science ideas that are often covered as disparate topics in traditional science texts and curricula. As described by Sasot and Suau (2000), one of the most interesting aspects of hypertext systems is that they can express, in a particularly forceful way, the often implicit relationships that exist between science concepts. Furthermore, multiple passes through the same material can build richer knowledge representations (Spiro, Feltovich, Jacobson, & Coulson, 1991). Hypertext has been described as multilinear because each reading could constitute a different path through the material, and as a result, different concepts and connections will be emphasized in each reading (Bolter, 1998, 2001). Active readers of hypertext may form an understanding of connections and conceptual relationships as they make their own decisions about how to proceed through the text.

Representing Connections in CoMPASS Using Concept Maps

In the CoMPASS system, concept maps that reflect the connections in the domain are used to help students understand the relationships between science ideas. The system is designed to help students learn physics in middle schools, and the two major topics in the system are *work and energy* and *forces and motion*. Students use the system as they engage in design-based curricula that span 6–8 weeks of science content. As they engage in science investigations related to their design challenge, students use the CoMPASS system to find out more information about the science topics they need to plan their investigations, make sense of their data, and complete their designs. Visual representations (Glinert, 1990), such as concept maps, accentuate relevant characteristics of a representation (Hübscher, 1997; Narayanan & Hübscher, 1998) and make higher-order relations more accessible (Tufte, 1990). Concept maps can represent meaningful relationships between concepts and structure or organize knowledge in an integrated manner (Edmondson, 2000; Novak & Gowin, 1984). Ideas in a concept map are presented in the form of nodes connected with labeled links. Novak and Gowin (1984) hold that these representations are visual maps of pathways that connect concepts with their meanings and can offer *a schematic summary* of ideas.

Since their emergence in education research, concept maps have been used to facilitate student learning and engagement (Novak & Cañas, 2004). Of particular interest is their application in scaffolding student learning from text and in shaping student comfort with writing. Nesbit and Adesope (2006) have argued that because concept maps eliminate redundant information and colocate similar concepts, their use in the classroom can facilitate student understanding of text. They noted that students who learn to create and read concept maps appear more capable of extracting meaning and identifying concepts and their relations both within a text and within other sources of information. These authors also reviewed several research studies that suggested students with lower verbal ability might better comprehend concept maps. Map syntax is comparatively standard and less complicated than the often dense language in textbooks or scholarly texts. In addition, concept maps can also serve as useful metacognitive aids and scaffolds for integrating and fostering student learning more broadly (Novak & Cañas, 2008; Trowbridge & Wandersee, 1998).

Bransford, Brown, and Cocking (2000) emphasized that for meaningful learning to occur, students must concentrate on central ideas and conceptual relationships. Such elements reflect the domain structure or expert understanding of the discipline and foster the development of background knowledge. Current research by Novak and Cañas (2008) focuses on the use of *expert skeleton* maps as guides or scaffolds to facilitate learning, especially when students have difficulty or are unfamiliar with the domain of study. They posit that maps constructed by an expert in the field can provide a strong base from which students can construct meaning. Tergan, Engelmann, and Hesse (2008) compared the effectiveness of digital concept maps with digital concept lists on search time, number of correct decisions, and reported cognitive load of participants in an information search task. They found that participants using concept maps generally outperformed those using concept lists in learning and assessment of functional relationships between topics. (For category relationships alone, no significant differences were found.) Concept maps also have potential as information search tools that make visible the functional semantic links and structural links that explicitly indicate the relevance of topics to the search task (Tergan et al., 2008).

Supporting Navigation and Learning

Each page in CoMPASS is a description of a science concept within a topic. When students choose a concept, CoMPASS presents them with a description of that concept along with a navigable map that shows them the related concepts. For example, in the *work and energy* unit, students may navigate to the concept of *work* within the topic of *pulley*, which has related concepts, such as *force* and *distance*. A concept map of the science concept the learner is focused on and the related concepts takes up the left half of the CoMPASS screen, and a textual description takes up the right half (see Fig. 18.1). The maps are *dynamically constructed* and displayed with the

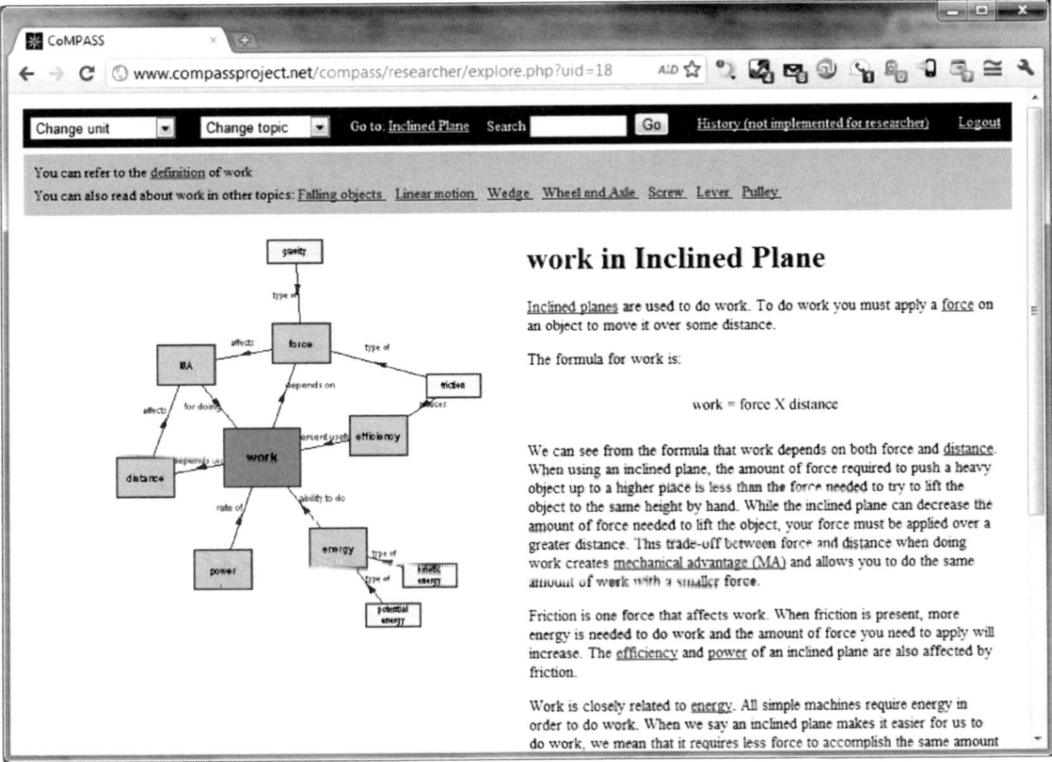

Fig. 18.1 Screen shot from CoMPASS

fisheye technique (Bedersen & Hollan, 1995; Furnas, 1986) every time the student selects a concept. The selected (focal) concept is at the center of the map, with the most closely related concepts at the first level of magnification and those less closely related at the outer level of the map. The fisheye view is organized such that the concepts that are *most related conceptually* to the focal concept are displayed close to each other *spatially*. The maps were designed in consultation with physics experts to represent relationships using conceptual *relationship strength*, which determines the spatial proximity of the concepts. Further, the connections on the map are labeled with arrows and a description to help students identify the direction and type of relationships among concepts. The maps in CoMPASS mirror the structure of the domain to aid deep learning and *are designed to help students make connections*, giving students alternative paths to pursue for any particular activity, so that they can see how different phenomena are related to each other. The dynamic changes in the concept maps based on the concepts selected by students, together with the text in the CoMPASS system, help students to see these relationships.

In CoMPASS, students can easily switch views using a navigation bar at the top of the screen to go to a topic related to the one they are currently learning about (see Fig. 18.2). This provides global coherence because students can see what other related topics they can go to. In addition, they can also view a particular concept from multiple perspectives as described below.

CoMPASS also supports alternative views of concepts. For example, a student might be interested in learning about *force* in the context of a lever. She can change *views* anytime (top right of screen in Fig. 18.2) so that she can study the same phenomenon (force) in other contexts, such as inclined planes or pulleys. Science tends to be a complex domain in which learning involves understanding multiple relationships among important concepts and topics, which can be

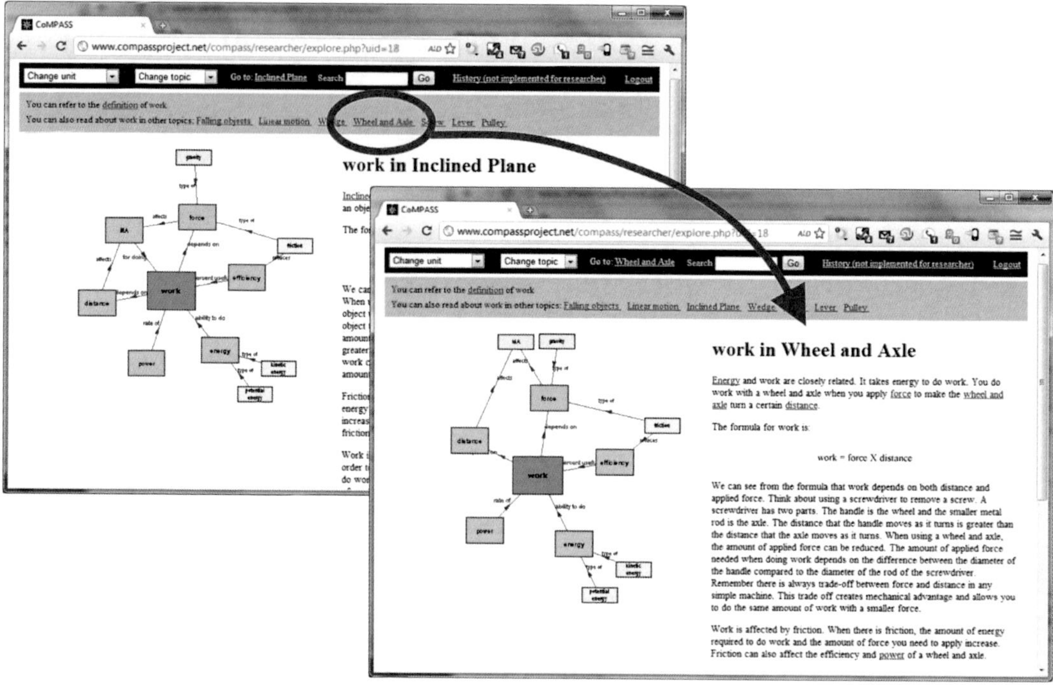

Fig. 18.2 Changing topic for the same concept *work*

represented by a web or a network. As described by Spiro et al. (1991) in the cognitive flexibility theory, revisiting the same material at different times, in rearranged contexts, for different purposes, and from different conceptual perspectives is essential for attaining the goals of advanced knowledge acquisition. The alternative views that CoMPASS offers can help students to study science concepts and phenomena in depth by visiting them in multiple contexts.

The CoMPASS hypertext system both supports and is able to detect SRL. The expert-designed concept maps make explicit the semantic relationships among concepts and provide students with a *visual scaffold* that they can use to select concepts appropriate to their goals, aiding them in making navigation decisions and regulating their learning. Students' navigation choices are saved in the database, and a history of navigation choices is presented to students so that they see what concepts they visited. Later in this chapter, we discuss how the information in the database is being used to provide adaptive support to students.

CoMPASS in Science Classes

The CoMPASS hypertext is used in conjunction with design challenges that provide students with a context for their science investigations. The challenges were developed specifically as experiences that enable the students to see the interconnections between concepts. For example, in the work and energy unit, students design the best pulley system to lift a bottle of water. Hands-on activities provide concrete experience collecting data to look for patterns that highlight relationships among concepts. As students try out different pulleys (double, triple) and put them together, they learn about science content, such as force, work, distance, and mechanical advantage. Information about conceptual relationships that students learn from CoMPASS can help them connect their experiential activities to broader scientific patterns and relationships.

In the study described here, 74 sixth-grade students used the Simple Machines module in CoMPASS as a resource in a design-based curriculum that we developed in collaboration with the teachers. Elsewhere, we have reported that students who used CoMPASS did significantly better in posttest measures of factual knowledge as well as in a concept mapping test (e.g., Puntambekar et al., 2003). In this chapter, we focus on an analysis of students' navigation paths based on the pathfinder algorithm and the k-means clustering algorithm (explained in the next section) and how we are using what we learned through this analysis to build adaptive, scaffolded navigation.

Students were presented with the problem of building a device using pulleys that got the most work done with the least effort in lifting a 16-oz can. The task was fairly complex and open-ended, and students used CoMPASS on two consecutive days to help gather information to solve the problem. Students used CoMPASS for a total of 30 min on each of the 2 days, and log files were collected for each session.

Navigation and Log Files

Researchers have used analyses of log file data to distinguish patterns in problem solving (Barab, Fagan, Kulikowich, & Young, 1996), to identify differences in students' navigational styles by clustering them into groups (Lawless & Kulikowich, 1996; Puntambekar et al., 2003), and to investigate meaningful navigation paths chosen by students (Rowe, Cooke, Hall, & Halgren, 1996). Learning in a hypermedia environment involves the cognitive reconstruction of a domain space through repeated traversals of that space (Jacobson & Spiro, 1995). Further, to fully understand information presented in a hypertext environment, a reader needs to comprehend the text in the individual nodes as well as the relationships presented in the overall structure of the hypertext. Therefore, the paths that users choose have a powerful influence on learning outcomes. A comprehensive analysis of navigational patterns can provide useful insights into how students process the information and can be used to provide support for SRL in nonlinear learning environments (Niegemann, 2001).

In CoMPASS, students' self-regulated behavior is detected through the use of computer-generated log files that allow us to record the nodes of information students went to, the order that they visited them, and the amount of time spent on each. Log file data allows us to analyze student navigation behavior post hoc and create clusters of navigation patterns. We can then examine these clusters of navigation patterns to determine differences in students' SRL processes and the types of scaffolding that they may need.

Identification of Navigation Patterns

We have used the pathfinder algorithm to study students' navigational paths based on log files of navigation behavior, which are often used to assess student learning in computer-based environments. Pathfinder, a graph theoretic technique, allows one to represent and compare *dynamic* properties of navigational paths (Schvaneveldt, 1990). Pathfinder yields a network representation of navigation patterns that consists of nodes and links. The pathfinder analysis will enable us to look into the ways in which representations change as students use CoMPASS and to analyze the richness of students' navigational paths (based on the concepts visited and the relationships between them).

The pathfinder algorithm attempts to remove extraneous navigation paths to reveal the underlying structure of the navigation behavior. The original pathfinder procedure is applied to graphs with proximity data. It was adapted to work with link weights representing the number of traversals between two nodes and runs in $O(n^3)$ where n is the number of nodes (Quirin, Cordón, Santamaría, Vargas-Quesada, & Moya-Anegón, 2008). As a result, the links which had a more frequently traveled path available between the two end nodes were removed.

The pathfinder networks were then clustered using the k-means algorithm, which assigns each network repeatedly to the *closest* cluster until no further reassignments are necessary. The distance measure used captures the structural similarity of

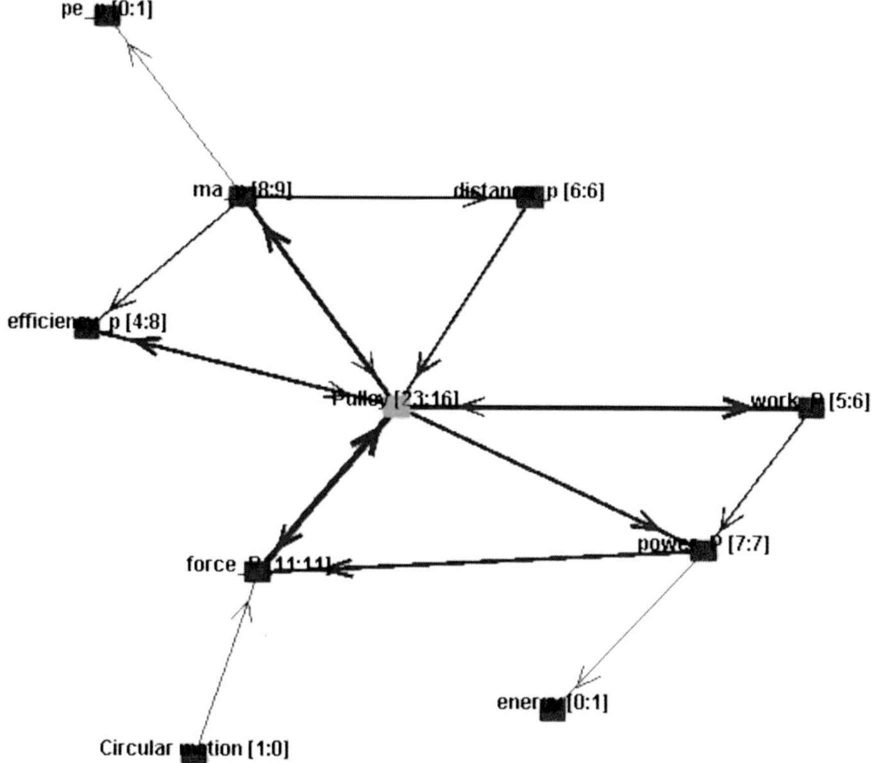

Fig. 18.3 Cluster 1 with rich within topic but sparse global level navigation

graphs and is based on how many links each node has in common between the two graphs to be compared (Hübscher & Puntambekar, 2004). Although this algorithm does not necessarily return an optimal result, it has enabled us in finding a set of characterizing navigation patterns representative of most students.

Identification of Clusters

The analysis revealed five different clusters based on the similarity of navigation patterns. The patterns are distinguished based on the richness of navigation within a topic, across topics, and across multiple views for a concept. The clusters do not suggest the desirable ways to navigate; they helped us understand the different ways in which students navigated, and we used a bottom-up approach to examine the clusters and provide support so that students could expand their navigation choices while at the same time working within the parameters of their goals. The clusters of navigation patterns show the number of times students *navigated to* a concept and the number of times students *navigated from* a concept and from which concepts students navigated to others. For example, [3:2] means that students *went to* a concept three times and *went from* that concept to another concept two times. Further, the label of each node also indicates in which topic students were reading about a concept. For example, "force_p" means that students navigated to the concept of force within the topic of pulleys and "force_ip" means that they navigated to this concept within the topic of inclined planes.

Cluster 1 (Fig. 18.3) shows that students visited all of the relevant concepts within a topic. The topic overview (pulley) is the hub from where most of the transitions started. Although the topic overview is the center, there are many transitions between related concepts. For instance, there are transitions

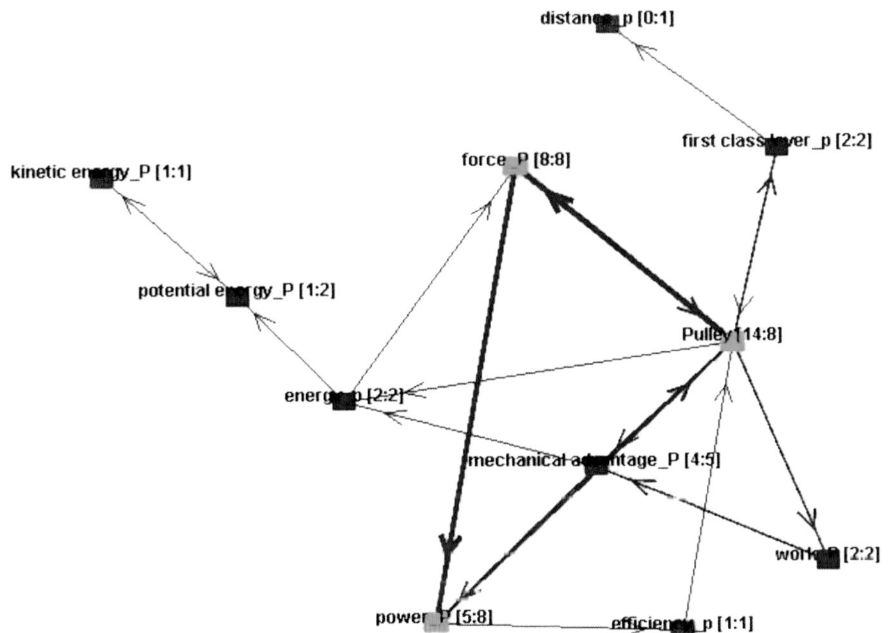

Fig. 18.4 Cluster 2 with sparse local level but rich global level navigation

between power and force, work and power, mechanical advantage (ma) and distance. This indicates that students used the maps for navigation and used the related concepts shown in the maps as a way to guide their navigation. Not only were these concepts related to one another, but they were also goal relevant and would help students with completing their design challenges. This cluster illustrates multiple *circular paths* that students followed, i.e., pulley → ma → distance → pulley, pulley → power → force → pulley. It also shows several double-sided arrows indicating that students were not linear in their navigation. However, students in this cluster stayed predominantly in one topic (pulleys) and failed to navigate to the related topic of levers, which was a closely related topic. Students whose navigation paths belong to this cluster also failed to visit concepts in alternative views, i.e., ma in levers as compared to ma in pulleys. At a local level, i.e., within a topic, cluster 1 is indicative of navigation that is rich in terms of the visits to related concepts within a particular topic. However, students did not really explore the relationship of this topic with other topics, so the navigation was sparse at the global (topical) level.

Cluster 2 (Fig. 18.4) also has the topic overview as the center, but the navigation pattern is very different. There is a single circular path with the most frequent transitions, showing that students visited three concepts—ma, power, and force—more often than other concepts. The network also shows that students sought additional details about the concept *energy* by visiting the forms of energy, while students in cluster 1 stayed mostly at the first level of detail and did not go deeper into the links that further described the types of energy. Another interesting feature of cluster 2 is that students also navigated to a related topic, i.e., levers. Classroom observations support this in that students who visited related topics (at the global level) also asked the teacher questions about the similarities between the pulley and the lever. The navigation pattern in cluster 2 better indicates navigation at the global level, i.e., navigation to other related topics and concepts, than cluster 1, but is not as rich in terms of navigation at the local level.

Clusters 3 and 4 (Figs. 18.5 and 18.6) show navigation patterns that are completely different from clusters 1 and 2. These clusters do not have a clear

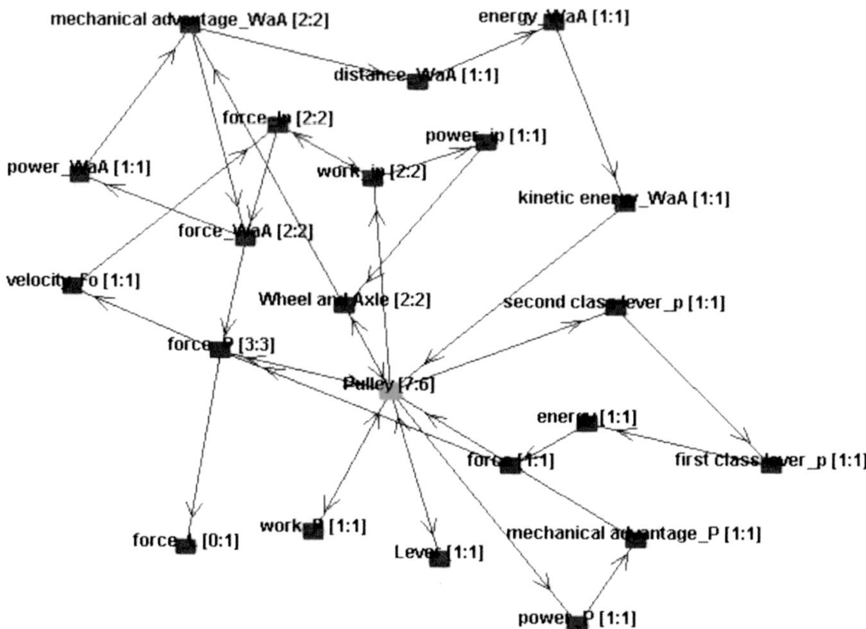

Fig. 18.5 Cluster 3 with rich *views* level but sparse local and global level navigation

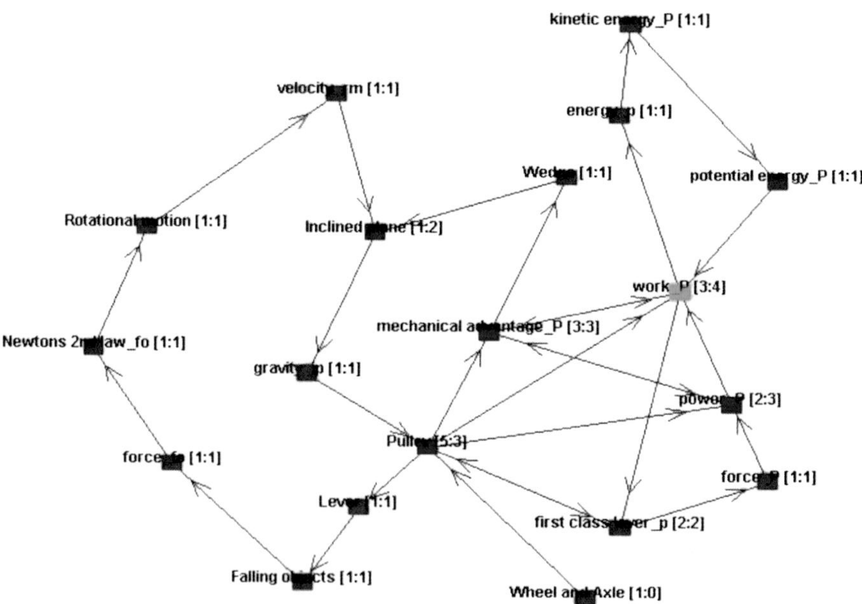

Fig. 18.6 Cluster 4 with primarily random navigation

center, and students have visited numerous concepts within the topic of pulley and in other topics. Cluster 3 shows that students visited numerous concepts, in many of the topics, making an extensive use of the alternative views (e.g., force_WaA, force_p, force_ip, as indicated in Fig. 18.5) presented in CoMPASS, making this pattern rich at the *views* level. However, this cluster is pretty

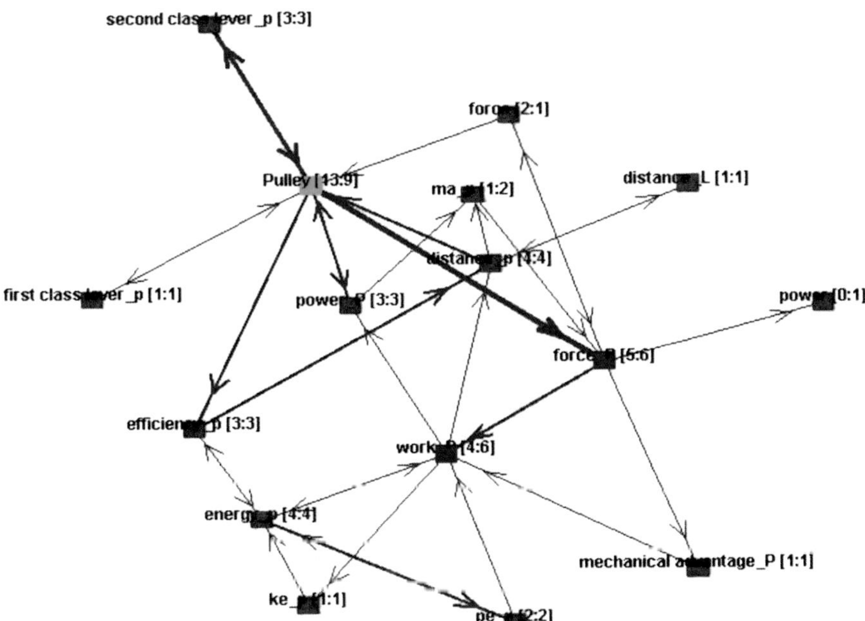

Fig. 18.7 Cluster 5 with focused within topic navigation

sparse at both the local and the global levels because students did not have many transitions between the related concepts in any of the topics. Cluster 4 shows a more or less random pattern in which students visited topics as well as concepts that were not related to their goal. Students in this cluster visited several topics that were unrelated, such as rotational motion. Clearly, these students needed more support to understand the structure of the system for them to navigate and learn more effectively.

Cluster 5 (Fig. 18.7) has navigation patterns that can be described as being between clusters 1 and 3 because the students in this cluster show breadth in navigation in that they visited many concepts. Students visited several concepts within the topic of pulley, but they primarily focused on two nodes of information: pulley and force.

Using Clusters as Basis for Scaffolding

In previous studies, we found that students could be supported on the basis of their navigation patterns. We used their navigation to provide prompts in a paper-and-pencil format, mainly designed to help students regulate their navigation (e.g., the maps show related concepts; be sure to check what concepts are related to your current node before clicking on the next concept). We found that students who received support performed significantly better in their physics knowledge tests than those who did not (e.g., Puntambekar & Stylianou, 2005). In our current work, we are building scaffolding in the CoMPASS system to make it more adaptive to students with a range of navigation and learning needs. All the navigation behaviors have been assigned to one of five typical navigation patterns as found in the cluster analysis. This suggests that it is sensible to associate a new navigation behavior with one or more of these five patterns. This allows us to classify the learners based on their use of CoMPASS and scaffold them with adaptive prompts based on this classification. We approach this with a simple three-phase approach based on heuristic classification scheme (Clancey, 1985; Hübscher & Puntambekar, 2008) as follows.

This heuristic classification scheme describes a process that the scaffolding algorithm of CoMPASS goes through each time it computes what kind of text prompt should be shown to the learner. This process consists of an abstraction phase, a heuristic match, and a refinement phase. In the abstraction phase, the learner's real-time navigation behavior is associated, to some degree, with the various characteristic patterns found in the cluster analysis. This is based on our observation that most students can be assigned reasonably well to one or more of the clusters that we have found earlier (Puntambekar et al., 2003), even if relatively little real-time navigation data is available. Then, the heuristic match suggests an appropriate type of text prompt based on this categorization and other information about the learner like reading skills, satisfied prerequisites, or age. Finally, in the refinement phase, a specific prompt is selected which is not just dependent on the heuristic match phase but may also take into consideration what type of prompts has been shown to the students earlier in the same session.

The three phases are implemented in Jess (Friedman-Hill, 2003) using forward chaining rules and certainty factors. This enables a clear and explicit representation of the different types of knowledge we are using, including navigation classification, pedagogical, and linguistic knowledge. Certainty factors allow us to associate the learners to more than one typical pattern and to suggest more than one appropriate prompt. Whichever prompt will have the most support based on all three reasoning phases will be selected. The following is a simple example for classifying navigation behavior for a pattern where the navigation stays within the goal topic without moving to a related topic. In the example rules below, symbols starting with a "?" are variables.

```
RULE student-within-goal-topic
  IF current-phase (categoriza-
tion) AND
      navigate-to (?topic,
    ?concept) AND
      is-goal-topic(?topic)
  THEN
      ASSERT cluster(within-
goal-topic,+0.8)
```

Rule student-within-goal-topic can be read as follows: If the current phase is categorization and there is a navigation move to a concept ?concept in topic ?topic, and topic ?topic is the goal topic, then we have found some evidence that the navigation behavior is indeed within-goal-topic. The ASSERT statement states that the certainty factor for the conclusion is +0.8. Certainty factors range from +1.0 (total belief) to −1.0 (total disbelief) and are useful to capture uncertain knowledge, yet not without fault.

Based on the clusters, we have a set of rules to provide prompts to help students with their navigation. For example, below are two conditions for the basis of prompts. The scaffolding mechanism uses three levels of prompts from less directive to most directive as illustrated in the following rules. Note that more directive prompts are asserted with lower certainty factors and thus will be used after less directive ones have been used assuming we add a rule stating not to say the same sentence twice.

```
RULE few-topics-in-goal-topic
  IF current-phase(find-treatment-
type) AND
   cluster(within-goal-topic,?cf)
   THEN
 ASSERT treatment-type
 (encourage-goal-related-
concepts,?cf)
 RULE goal-related-topics
  IF current-phase(refinement)
AND
 treatment-type(encourage-goal-
related-concepts,?cf)
   concepts(?topic,?concepts)
   THEN
      ASSERT prompt("Can you
think of some concepts that are
related to the one you are
reading?", 1.0 * ?cf)
      ASSERT prompt("What are
some concepts relevant to your
goal for today?", 0.8 * ?cf)
         ASSERT prompt("Read
 concepts ?concepts.", 0.5 * ?cf)
```

The goal of these rules, and thus, the prompts, is not to direct the learners toward some optimal behavior. Clusters are categorized as effective or ineffective. Being in a certain cluster may imply certain deficiencies that will then be addressed by a prompt. For instance, a learner who focuses on just one concept may have too narrow a perspective, and the goal of a prompt may be to broaden the student's exploration. As a result, a student may be associated with different clusters which may be simply a result of a prompt but also other contextual factors, like the domain of the problem or the kind of task to solve.

Conclusion

Although useful, using clusters representing typical navigation patterns does have some limitations. By addressing these limitations, we may find even more suitable ways of characterizing the students' typical navigation behavior. One limitation is the preprocessing of the log file data. For instance, we ignore visits of less than 10 s since we assume that students are not able to do any reasonable processing of a page in such short time. By doing this, we get rid of some *noise* in navigation in which students do not spend enough time in a topic or concept to actually read anything about it. Nevertheless, we also may be eliminating intermediate components of navigation behavior that help students to maintain orientation but are now not showing up in their navigation patterns. We also ignore the temporal character of the navigation behavior and only analyze the number of link traversals independent of their order. In future iterations, we plan on taking into account temporal characteristics of students' navigation patterns by using navigation across multiple sessions and changes therein. Finally, the students get to see only a part of the concept map limited to the current focus and concepts no further than two links away. So, only concepts that are reasonably closely related to the current focus are displayed, thus limiting the possible paths that students can take. Of course, this *limitation* is by design to keep students from wandering off too far.

The work described in this chapter is a first step toward supporting SRL in hypertext environments. We have strived to achieve a balance between providing support and allowing students to explore the hypertext systems, which is a key strength of hypertext and hypermedia environments.

References

Alexander, P. A., Kulikowich, J., & Jetton, T. (1994). The role of subject-matter knowledge and interest in the processing of linear and nonlinear texts. *Review of Educational Research, 64*, 201–252.

Azevedo, R. (2005a). Computers as metacognitive tools for enhancing learning. *Educational Psychologist, 40*(4), 193–197.

Azevedo, R. (2005b). Using hypermedia as a metacognitive tool for enhancing student learning? The role of self-regulated learning. *Educational Psychologist, 40*(4), 199–209.

Azevedo, R., Guthrie, J. T., & Seibert, D. (2004). The role of self-regulated learning in fostering students' conceptual understanding of complex systems with hypermedia. *Journal of Educational Computing Research, 30*(1 and 2), 87–111.

Azevedo, R., Moos, D. C., Greene, J. A., Winters, F. I., & Cromley, J. G. (2008). Why is externally-facilitated regulated learning more effective than self-regulated learning with hypermedia? *Educational Technology Research and Development, 56*, 45–72.

Barab, S. A., Fagan, B. R., Kulikowich, J. M., & Young, M. F. (1996). Assessing hypermedia navigation through pathfinder: Prospects and limitations. *Journal of Educational Computing Research, 15*(3), 185–205.

Bedersen, B. B., & Hollan, J. (1995). Pad++: A zooming graphical interface for exploring alternate interface physics. In P. Szekely (Ed.), *Proceedings of the Seventh Annual ACM Symposium on User Interface Software and Technology* (pp. 17–26). New York: ACM Press.

Bolter, J. D. (1991). *Writing space: The computer, hypertext, and the history of writing*. Hillsdale, NJ: Erlbaum.

Bolter, J. D. (1998). Hypertext and the question of visual literacy. In D. Reinking, M. McKenna, L. Labbo, & R. Kiefer (Eds.), *Handbook of literacy and technology*. Mahwah, NJ: Lawrence Erlbaum.

Bolter, J. D. (2001). *Writing space: Computers, hypertext and the remediation of print*. Mahwah, NJ: Lawrence Erlbaum.

Bransford, J. D., Brown, A., & Cocking, R. (Eds.). (2000). *How people learn*. Washington, DC: National Academy Press.

Braten, I., Britt, M. A., Stromso, H. I., & Rouet, J.-F. (2011). The role of epistemic beliefs in the comprehension of multiple expository texts: Toward an integrated model. *Educational Psychologist, 46*(1), 48–70.

Cheng, P. C.-H. (1999). Unlocking conceptual learning in mathematics and science with effective representational systems. *Computers in Education, 33*, 109–130.

Chi, M. T. H., Hutchinson, J., & Robin, A. F. (1989). How inferences about novel domain-related concepts can be constrained by structured knowledge. *Merrill-Palmer Quarterly, 35*, 27–62.

Chi, M. T. H., & Koeske, R. (1983). Network representation of a child's dinosaur knowledge. *Developmental Psychology, 19*, 29–39.

Clancey, W. J. (1985). Heuristic classification. *Artificial Intelligence, 27*, 289–350.

Coiro, J., & Dobler, E. (2007). Exploring the online reading comprehension strategies used by sixth-grade skilled readers to search for and locate information on the Internet. *Reading Research Quarterly, 42*(2), 214–257.

Edmondson, K. M. (2000). Assessing science understanding through concept maps. In J. J. Mintzes, J. H. Wandersee, & J. D. Novak (Eds.), *Assessing science understanding: A human constructivist view* (pp. 19–40). San Diego, CA: Academic.

Friedman-Hill, E. (2003). *Jess in action: Java rule-based systems.* Greenwich, CT: Manning Publications Company. Web site http://herzberg.ca.sandia.gov/jess/.

Furnas, G. W. (1986). Generalized fisheye views. In *Proceedings of the SIGCHI Conference on Human Factors in Computing Systems* (pp. 16–23). New York: ACM Press.

Glinert, E. P. (1990). *Visual programming environments: Paradigms and systems*. Los Alamitos, CA: IEEE Computer Society Press.

Glynn, S. M., Yeany, R. H., & Britton, B. K. (1991). *The psychology of learning science*. Hillsdale, NJ: Erlbaum.

Green, J. A., & Azevedo, R. (2007). A theoretical view of Winne & Hadwin's model of self-regulated learning: New perspectives and directions. *Review of Educational Research, 77*(3), 334–372.

Hiebert, J., & Carpenter, T. (1992). Learning and teaching with understanding. In D. Grouws (Ed.), *Handbook of research on mathematics research and teaching* (pp. 65–100). New York: Macmillan.

Hmelo-Silver, C. E., Marathe, S., & Liu, L. (2007). Fish swim, rocks sit, and lungs breathe: Expert-novice understanding of complex systems. *The Journal of the Learning Sciences, 16*, 307–331.

Hübscher, R. (1997). Visual constraint rules. *Journal of Visual Languages and Computing, 8*, 425–451.

Hübscher, R., & Puntambekar, S. (2004). Modeling learners as individuals and as groups. In P. De Bra & W. Nejdl (Eds.), *Adaptive hypermedia and adaptive web-based systems* (Vol. LNCS 3137, pp. 300–303). Berlin: Springer.

Hübscher, R., & Puntambekar, S. (2008). Integrating knowledge gained from data mining with pedagogical knowledge. In R. S. J. d. Baker, T. Barnes & J. E. Beck (Eds.),*Educational Data Mining 2008: 1st International Conference on Educational Data Mining, Proceedings*. Montreal, Quebec, Canada.

Jacobson, M. J., & Spiro, R. J. (1995). Hypertext learning environments, cognitive flexibility, and the transfer of complex knowledge: An empirical investigation. *Journal of Educational Computing Research, 12*(5), 301–333.

Kozma, R. (2000). The use of multiple representations and the social construction of understanding in chemistry. In M. Jacobson & R. Kozma (Eds.), *Innovations in science and mathematics education: Advanced designs for technologies of learning* (pp. 11–46). Mahwah, NJ: Erlbaum.

Lawless, K. A., & Kulikowich, J. M. (1996). Understanding hypertext navigation through cluster analysis. *Journal of Educational Computing Research, 14*(4), 385–399.

Linn, M. C. (2006). The knowledge integration perspective on learning and instruction. In R. K. Sawyer (Ed.), *Cambridge handbook for the learning sciences* (pp. 243–264). New York: Cambridge University Press.

Narayanan, N. H., & Hübscher, R. (1998). Visual language theory: Towards a human-computer interaction perspective. In B. Meyer & K. Marriott (Eds.), *Visual language theory* (pp. 85–127). New York: Springer.

Nesbit, J. C., & Adesope, O. O. (2006). Learning with concept and knowledge maps: A meta-analysis. *Review of Educational Research, 76*(3), 413–448.

Newton, D. P., & Newton, L. D. (2000). Do teachers support causal understanding through their discourse when teaching primary science? *British Educational Research Journal, 26*(5), 599–613.

Niegemann, H. M. (2001). *Analyzing navigation patterns of learning in hypermedia learning environments.* Paper presented at the annual meeting of the American Educational Research Association (AERA), Seattle, WA.

Novak, J. D., & Cañas, A. J. (2004). Building on constructivist ideas and CmapTools to create a new model for education. In A. J. Cañas, J. D. Novak, & F. M. González (Eds.), *Concept maps: Theory, methodology, technology, proceedings of the 1st international conference on concept mapping*. Pamplona, Spain: Universidad Pública de Navarra.

Novak, J. D., & Cañas, A. J. (2008). *The theory underlying concept maps and how to construct and use them.* Technical Report IHMC CmapTools 2006–01 Rev 01–2008. Florida Institute for Human and Machine Cognition. Retrieved from http://cmap.ihmc.us/Publications.

Novak, J. D., & Gowin, D. B. (1984). *Learning how to learn*. Cambridge, UK: Cambridge University Press.

Pearsall, N. R., Skipper, J. E. J., & Mintzes, J. J. (1997). Knowledge restructuring in the life sciences: A longitudinal study of conceptual change in biology. *Science Education, 81*(2), 193–215.

Puntambekar, S., & Stylianou, A. (2005). Designing navigation support in hypertext systems based on navigation patterns. *Instructional Science, 33*(5), 451–481.

Puntambekar, S., Stylianou, A., & Goldstein, J. (2007). Comparing classroom enactments of an inquiry curriculum: Lessons learned from two teachers. *The Journal of the Learning Sciences, 16*(1), 81–130.

Puntambekar, S., Stylianou, A., & Hübscher, R. (2003). Improving navigation and learning in hypertext environments with navigable concept maps. *Human Computer Interaction, 18*(4), 395–428.

Quirin, A., Cordón, O., Santamaría, J., Vargas-Quesada, B., & Moya-Anegón, F. (2008). A new variant of the Pathfinder algorithm to generate large visual science maps in cubic time. *Information Processing and Management, 44*, 1611–1623.

Rouet, J.-F. (2006). Using hypertext systems. In J.-F. Rouet (Ed.), *The skills of document use: From text comprehension to web-based learning* (pp. 122–138). Mahwah, NJ: Lawrence Erlbaum Associates.

Rouet, J.-F., & Coutelet, B. (2008). The acquisition of document search strategies in grade school students. *Applied Cognitive Psychology, 22*, 389–406.

Rowe, A. L., Cooke, N. J., Hall, E. P., & Halgren, T. L. (1996). Toward an on-line knowledge assessment methodology: Building on the relationship between knowing and doing. *Journal of Experimental Psychology, 2*(1), 31–47.

Ruiz-Primo, M. A., & Shavelson, R. J. (1996). Problems and issues in the use of concept maps in science assessment. *Journal of Research in Science Teaching, 33*(6), 569–600.

Sasot, A., & Suau, J. (2000). Improving teaching materials: The structuring of learning, the interrelationship of information and the search for higher levels of interactivity. *Interactive Educational Multimedia, 1*, 35–46.

Schvaneveldt, R. W. (1990). *Pathfinder associative networks: Studies in knowledge organization*. Norwood, NJ: Ablex.

Schwartz, N., Anderson, C., Hong, N., Howard, B., & McGee, S. (2004). The influence of metacognitive skills on learners' memory of information in a hypermedia environment. *Journal of Educational Computing Research, 31*, 77–93.

Shapiro, A. M., & Niederhauser, D. (2004). Learning from hypertext: Research issues and findings. In D. H. Jonassen (Ed.), *Handbook of research on educational communications and technology* (2nd ed., pp. 605–620). Mahwah, NJ: Erlbaum.

Sharples, M. (1999). *How we write: Writing as creative design*. New York: Routledge.

Spiro, R. J., Feltovich, P. J., Jacobson, M. J., & Coulson, R. J. (1991). Cognitive flexibility constructivism and hypertext: Random access instruction for advanced knowledge acquisition in ill-structured domains. *Educational Technology, 31*(5), 24–33.

Spitulnik, M. W., Zembal-Saul, C., & Krajcik, J. S. (1998). Using hypermedia to represent emerging student understanding: Science learners and preservice teachers. In J. J. Mintzes, J. H. Wandersee, & J. D. Novak (Eds.), *Teaching science for understanding: A human constructivist view* (pp. 229–259). San Diego, CA: Academic.

Tergan, S.-O., Engelmann, T., & Hesse, F. W. (2008). Digital concept maps as powerful interfaces for enhancing information search: An experimental study of the effects of semantic cueing. In A. J. Cañas, P. Reiska, M. Åhlberg, & J. D. Novak (Eds.), *Concept mapping: Connecting educators. Proceedings of the third international conference on concept mapping*. Tallinn, Finland: Estonia and Helsinki.

Trowbridge, J. E., & Wandersee, J. H. (1998). Theory-driven graphic organizers. In J. J. Mintzes, J. H. Wandersee, & J. D. Novak (Eds.), *Teaching science for understanding: A human constructivist view* (pp. 95–131). San Diego, CA: Academic.

Tufte, E. R. (1990). *Envisioning information*. Cheshire, CT: Graphics.

19 Development of Task Understanding and Monitoring in Information Retrieval Environments: Demystifying Metacognitive and Self-Regulatory Mechanisms in Graduate Learners Using Topic Maps Indexing Technologies to Improve Essay-Writing Skills

Vivek Venkatesh, Kamran Shaikh, Amna Zuberi, Kathryn Urbaniak, Timothy Gallant, and Arun Lakhana

Abstract

The empirical research reported in this chapter explores learner metacognition and self-regulation in information retrieval environments equipped with a powerful indexing technology called Topic Maps. The theoretical foundation for our work lies in the nexus of theories of self-regulation and those of cognitive information retrieval. Through a series of mixed-method studies conducted at the Topic Maps laboratory at Concordia University, we describe academic self-regulatory processes associated with graduate learners' understandings of ill-structured academic writing tasks and attempt to relate them to learners' metacognitive ability to judge their own performance on iterations of these writing tasks. The thirty-eight participants in the studies described in this chapter used the Topic Maps technology throughout a semester to navigate a repository of instructor-annotated essays. The repository was designed not only to help learners complete their own writing assignments, but also to improve their task understanding and better calibrate their performance from one instantiation of the writing assignment to the next. Results are discussed in light of the novel intra-sample statistical analyses used to uncover relationships between academic performance, metacognition and task understanding.

V. Venkatesh (✉) • K. Shaikh • A. Zuberi
• K. Urbaniak • T. Gallant • A. Lakhana
Topic Maps Laboratory—Learning for Life Centre,
Department of Education, Concordia University,
Montréal, QC, Canada
e-mail: vivek.venkatesh@education.concordia.ca

R. Azevedo and V. Aleven (eds.), *International Handbook of Metacognition and Learning Technologies*, Springer International Handbooks of Education 26, DOI 10.1007/978-1-4419-5546-3_19,

Introduction

This chapter provides a theoretical overview and empirical review of research conducted at Topic Maps laboratory at the Learning for Life Centre at Concordia University. The research reported herein uncovers a heretofore unexplored intersection between theories of self-regulation and those of cognitive information retrieval (CIR). Through a series of mixed-method studies, we describe academic self-regulatory processes associated with graduate learners' understandings of ill-structured academic writing tasks and attempt to relate them to learners' metacognitive ability to judge their own performance on iterations of these writing tasks. Our work explores learner metacognition and self-regulation in information retrieval environments equipped with a powerful indexing technology called Topic Maps (International Organization for Standardization [ISO] 13250, 2002). Participants in the studies described in this chapter used topic maps technology throughout a semester to navigate a repository of instructor-annotated essays. The repository was designed not only to help learners complete their own writing assignments but also to improve their task understanding and better calibrate their performance from one instantiation of the writing assignment to the next. Topic Maps and its related components have been developed by a group of computer scientists, educational technologists and indexing specialists into an international industry standard, ISO 13250, through collaboration in the ISO Joint Technical Committee 1/ Subcommittee 34/Working Group 3—Document Description and Processing Languages—Information Association. Venkatesh, the research team leader and creator of Topic Maps laboratory at Concordia University, has represented the Canadian delegation in the development of ISO13250 since 2004.

Overview of Technological Framework

The creation and deployment of indexes to aid search-and-retrieval operations in online learning environments has been well researched in the past decade (e.g. see Bourdeau, Mizoguchi, Hayashi, Psyche, & Nkambou, 2007; and Gasevic & Hatala, 2006 for examples of indexing mechanisms in web-based learning contexts). While seen as a worthwhile successor to keyword-based searches, we are only beginning to scratch the surface on how to implement a variety of indexes in online learning environments to better exploit their ability to represent the semantic relationships within a content domain (e.g. see research reported in Aleven, 2006; Baeza-Yates, 2003; Crampes & Bourdeau, 2004; Henri et al., 2006; Magnan & Paquette, 2006). Research by members of our team using Topic Maps indexing technologies has begun to provide empirical evidence of how the manual design of indexes can influence learners' cognitions and academic performance during an online or blended learning experience (Shaikh, Zuberi, & Venkatesh, in press; Venkatesh et al., 2007; Venkatesh, 2008; Venkatesh & Shaikh, 2008, 2011; Venkatesh, Shaikh, & Zuberi, 2010).

Topic Maps

Topic Maps are a form of indexing that describe an ontology, i.e. the relationships between concepts within a domain of knowledge and link elements of this ontology to descriptive resources. Topic Maps are malleable—the concept and relationship creation process is dynamic and user-driven. In addition, Topic Maps are scalable and can hence be conjoined and merged. Perhaps, most impressively, Topic Maps provide a distinct separation between resources and concepts,[1]

[1] In the interest of avoiding confusion with nomenclatures, we would like to point out the difference between concept maps and Topic Maps. Concept maps refer to the organization of information using a visual language through the definition of concepts, the linking of two or more concepts and the labeling of these aforementioned links. Topic Maps are an indexing technology that allows the subjects in a specified domain to be identified and related using strict ontological procedures while subsequently being linked to resources that help describe them. Concept maps are rooted in educational methods and related instructional interventions; Topic Maps were born from the notion of ontologies and related knowledge engineering procedures. Hence, in this chapter we do not explicitly discuss the use of concept maps in relation to Topic Maps.

thereby facilitating migration of the data models therein. Topic Maps separate the interrelated topics in a given body of knowledge from the actual resources that describe these topics. They provide context-based searches that can match context-specific search criteria entered by users (Garshol, 2004; Pepper, 2002).

As a search-and-retrieval technology, Topic Maps provide a method to code content in terms of topics, the relationships between these topics and any additional informational resources associated with the target subject matter. This allows for greater flexibility in searching because users not only gain access to information directly associated to a topic but also retrieve information regarding related topics. Users' queries may be expressed as keywords, which will trigger a search in Topic Maps for matching terms. Results are returned not by keyword "hits" but rather by the concepts or ideas present in a corpus. A search will return fewer, more relevant "hits" matching the keyword with the appropriate semantic context. Given their advanced capability of representing information, Topic Maps can support learning within an online learning environment in that content across functions can be integrated through search functionality triggered by a learner's query. Topic Maps can help to provide learners with a uniquely individualised tool that customises how content is accessed and potentially organised.

Topic Maps technologies are extensively employed to navigate databases of information in the fields of medicine, military and corporations. Many of these proprietary Topic Maps are machine-generated through the use of context-specific algorithms which read a corpus of text and automatically produce a set of topics along with the relationships among them. However, as Venkatesh et al. (2010) note, apart from the empirical work produced in Topic Maps laboratory at Concordia University, there has been little, if any, research on how to use cognitive notions of mental models, knowledge representation and decision-making processes employed in problem-solving situations as a basis for the design of ontologies for Topic Maps.

Overview of Educational Context

Navigation of Information in Online Learning Environments

Research on educational applications of indexes such as Topic Maps has come into focus as a result of the ubiquitous adoption of course management systems like WebCT® and Moodle® across postsecondary educational institutions, both in North America and in Europe. The adoption of these systems within the framework of higher education has not been complemented by a theoretically sound design of the instructional experiences therein (McGee, Carmean, & Jafari, 2005; Shaw & Venkatesh, 2005). In fact, it has become rather clear that one of the pitfalls in these course management systems is their pitiful and often nonexistent approach to the navigation of the complex webs of information posted therein. Students are therefore at a distinct disadvantage when it comes to completing their academic assignments if they involve having to conduct search-and-retrieval operations.

Development of Writing Skills in Graduate Learners

Essay writing is considered to be the "default genre" for measurement of understanding and, dare we say, higher-order cognitive processing in higher education in developed nations (Andrews, 2003). It would be to our distinct advantage to continue to develop higher-order cognitive skills in postsecondary learners, given that the Canadian Council on Learning (2007) has advocated that our graduates not only learn to adapt to the shifting landscape of the job market in an increasingly international context but also to innovate, create and transfer knowledge on their jobs. Such a tall order would necessitate that our future workforce learn to be creative as well as self-regulated and thereby transfer their postsecondary skills to their jobs (Simard et al., 2007). Ill-structured essay writing has been empirically demonstrated as an activity that stimulates advanced cognitive processing (Andrews, 2003; Lindblom-Ylänne & Pihlajamäki, 2003) and self-regulation (Tynjälä, 2001; Venkatesh & Shaikh, 2008, 2011) in post-secondary learners. It follows, then, that web-based instructional systems implemented in our universities should provide learners with appropriate software tools to manipulate materials while engaging in ill-structured tasks.

The research evidence presented in this chapter demonstrates how a new generation of indexes might improve the manner in which learners traverse content in a repository, thereby positively affecting both their academic performance and individual self-regulatory abilities. Our research explores how to improve the design of online indexes for repositories used to improve ill-structured essay writing, thereby creating graduates who better meet organizations' human resource needs for the "knowledge worker".

Choice of Domain for Implementation of Topic Maps

In an initial experiment, Venkatesh et al. (2007) studied the difference between the undergraduate learners' use of Topic Maps ($n = 18$) versus the use of search engines ($n = 16$) in retrieving information from an online learning repository. Topic Maps were represented by a manually created ontology of how an expert would organize and browse the information contained in six articles contained within the repository. The articles addressed operational issues surrounding the development of course management systems and were targeted at graduate learners. Learners were required to browse the repository, for a maximum of 30 min (so as to replicate an examination setting) to answer two ill-structured questions related to the content of these six articles. The first question addressed the role of information technology in the selection and purchase of a learning content management system. The second question addressed the importance of the concept of interoperability in selecting and purchasing a learning content management system. One of the subject matter experts recruited for the study proposed model answers to the two questions, each consisting of four themes. Themes were derived from statements made across the six articles and required participants to synthesise and relate material contained in multiple sources (i.e. articles). After controlling for prior knowledge, it was found that participants who used Topic Maps had a significantly larger number of correct themes for their answers to both questions (effect sizes calculated by Cohen's d were 1.17 for question 1 and 2.44 for question 2). Exit interviews conducted with the learners in both Topic Maps and search engine conditions indicated that the usage of an index which represented how an expert might organize the myriad topics helped those who were using Topic Maps to locate themes and prepare answers with far more confidence than those who used the search engine. In addition, learners in Topic Maps condition also reported lesser misalignment with the criteria for the assessment of the two ill-structured questions that they were supposed to answer. Specifically, participants mentioned the ease with which Topic Maps allowed them to look for relational elements across multiple sources of information.

To further explore the relationships between academic performance, metacognitive and self-regulatory processes in postsecondary learners navigating information in online environments, Venkatesh (2008) built a customized repository indexes through Topic Maps for a "theories of e-learning" course he offers in the Department of Education at Concordia University. This setting serves as the context for the empirical work carried out thus far by members of the Topic Maps laboratory. When described in technical terms, the repository consists of a web-based, specialized (i.e. context-specific), learner neo-corpus (i.e. a collection of artefacts created by learners themselves) which employs Topic Maps technology as a front-end navigational and information retrieval tool. The artefacts used for the repository are 132 essays written by 33 learners who have taken the "theories of e-learning" course, along with Venkatesh's comments on the essays. The ontologies used to create Topic Maps are grounded in (a) the knowledge representations of instructor and/or learner, (b) the assessment criteria being applied in grading the essay, namely, Biggs' and

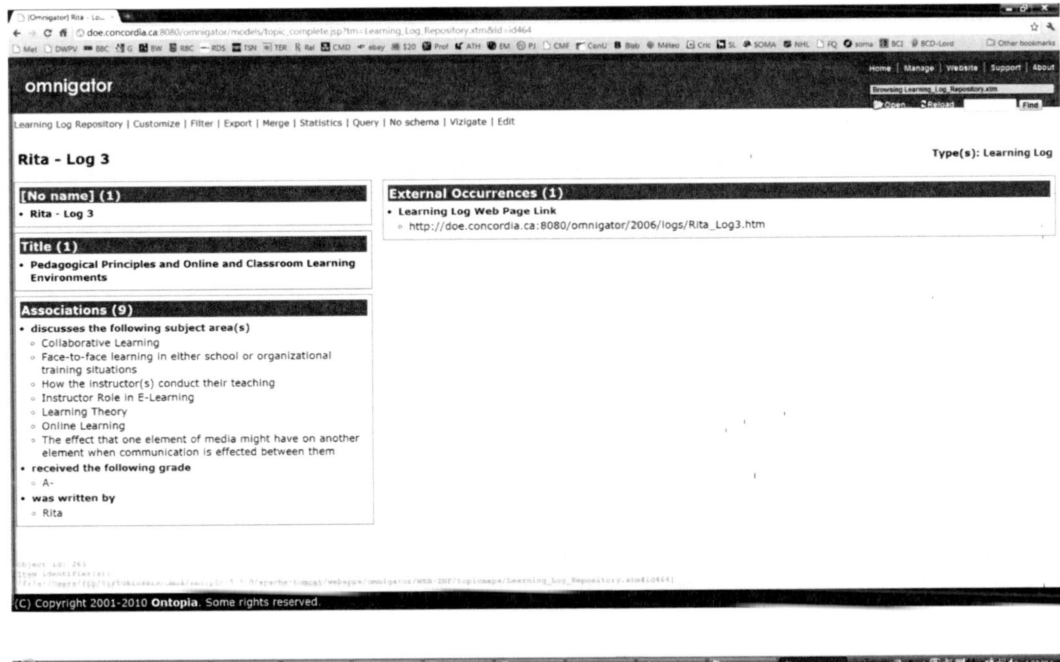

Fig. 19.1 Screenshot of Topic Maps page describing content of essay in repository

Collis' (1982) and Biggs' (1991, 1996) Structure of Observed Learning Outcome (SOLO) taxonomy and (c) the content of the essays. The SOLO taxonomy describes how learners analyse, synthesise and represent subject matter in a given domain and refers to five levels (in order of increasing complexity): prestructural, unistructural, multistructural, relational and extended abstract (detailed definitions of these levels are available in Biggs & Collis, 1982) Topic Maps enables access to specific portions of the essays to view instructor annotations on how a particular student's writing conforms to or digresses from the SOLO assessment criteria. In developing the indexes for our Topic Maps, we adopted a combination of Hersh, Pentecost and Wickam's (1996) approach to task-based information retrieval indexes and Kabel, de Hoog, Wielinga and Anjewierden's (2004) procedure of developing task-based ontologies. By focusing on the assessment criteria for the essay-writing task, we allowed for the explicit representation of the various facets of the SOLO taxonomy assessment criteria for the writing task as well as its relationship to other indexes such as author of essays, grade received and content covered in the essays. In order to represent the resultant ontology through the use of Topic Maps, we created a set of topics, associations (i.e. relationships between topics) and occurrences (i.e. resources to describe topics) as per Pepper's (2002) and Garshol's (2004) guidelines (see Fig. 19.1 for a screenshot of a page describing content of essays in Topic Maps).

Software Used and Modifications to Configuration

In keeping with the spirit of developing and sharing Topic Maps standards by the ISO committee to which Venkatesh belongs, we decided to use Ontopia Knowledge Suite (OKS, www.ontopia.net) open-source software to build and display the online repository of annotated student essays for the "theories of e-learning course". OKS includes three applications: Ontopoly, Omnigator and Apache Tomcat.

Ontopoly, Topic Maps editor, effectively allows Topic Maps architect to define and populate subject areas, relationships between subject areas and links to artefacts that are related to those subject areas. Omnigator, Topic Maps browser, is a rudimentary application that allows end users to view and navigate Topic Maps. Finally, Apache Tomcat is a configurable webserver that enables Internet access to the editing and browsing applications. In order to trace how users navigated our repository, we configured the webserver to enable both account authentication (so that users must log in to the application before browsing) and access logging (to keep track of which parts of the repository were accessed by each user). To summarize the trace data for each user's account, we wrote a Perl script that parses the webserver access logs.

Incorporating Theoretical Frameworks of Self-Regulation and Cognitive Information Retrieval in Ontology Construction for Topic Maps

We subscribe to the notion that cognitive information processing and its related theories should be instrumental in providing a framework for the design of ontologies that describe Topic Maps for efficient navigation of online learning material. We contend, however, that ontology construction for indexes should also take into account how learners regulate cognitions and metacognitions with respect to academic tasks, as well as how information retrieval is closely tied to elements of academic self-regulation (Venkatesh, 2008; Venkatesh et al., 2010).

Self-regulated learners apply both cognitive and metacognitive strategies to complete academic tasks, taking into account contextual and task-specific conditions. While much is known about how to build self-regulatory competencies using sound instructional design principles, educational psychologists still struggle to understand and describe the interactions between the individual components of self-regulated learning. Perhaps this is an artefact of classic conceptions of self-regulated learning as a complex, process-oriented theoretical construct. This epistemological assumption makes it difficult to tease apart how learners view the rationale for completing an academic task and how well they monitor their performance in terms of the instructor's assessment criteria.

Defining Task Understanding for Information Retrieval Environments

Task understanding, a critical phase in SRL when viewed from an educational psychology perspective, draws on two distinct but interacting elements, namely, individuals' perceptions of the academic task and of themselves as learners within a particular academic context. Learners' perceptions of the academic task include both the nature of the task and the associated assessment criteria. Learners recursively refine and reflect on their perceptions of the nature of the task, including (a) the rationale for performing the task (e.g. mastery/performance orientation and intrinsic/extrinsic motivation for undertaking the task), (b) the procedures to be undertaken to perform the task and the required outputs, (c) the materials that are available to perform the task and (d) the conditions under which the task must be performed (Venkatesh & Shaikh, 2011). Learners also need to grapple with the assessment criteria that the instructor uses to judge their task performance. It therefore appears that task understanding involves a close interaction between learners' and the instructor's perceptions of the academic task. In addition to task-associated elements, task understanding is influenced by the learners' knowledge of self-as-learner, including preferred learning styles and learning needs, prior content and task-specific knowledge and context-specific motivational and emotional anxiety and efficacy.

Ingwersen's (2000) theory of CIR provides some interesting overlaps with the concept of task understanding as a self-regulatory process. CIR theory describes how learners' cognitions adapt to the task-specific and contextual conditions encountered in information retrieval environments. A typical information retrieval task would include searching a repository using keywords, collating information across different sources or populating repositories with validated information. Essentially, CIR acknowledges that information-seeking behaviours affect the way individuals perceive how knowledge can be organized. From a social constructivist standpoint, the collective cognitive structures that are represented in an information retrieval system are a result of the social interactions that lead to knowledge creation, the information represented within the subject domains, as well as science and learning paradigms that underlie the design of the information retrieval environment.

Two factors in Ingwersen's model, namely, the *users' cognitive space* and the *contextual environment* surrounding the task, are very important subcomponents of the task-understanding component of SRL and the instructional design perspectives that stem thereof. According to CIR theory, the task and the user's perception of it are considered just as valuable as the information need. In fact, Ingwersen also points out that the perception of the work task (e.g. creating an entry for an online encyclopaedia) leads to perceived information need (e.g. looking for synonyms for a scientific term, comparing definitions of a scientific term across different contexts). In a cognitive sense, user perception of a work task is more likely to be stable over the information retrieval session than the corresponding dynamic information need. However, from a cognitive psychology standpoint, research has demonstrated that perceptions of the work task have been empirically shown to evolve continuously as learners tackle academic tasks (e.g. Shaikh et al., in press; Venkatesh, 2008; Venkatesh & Shaikh, 2008, 2011; Winne & Hadwin, 1998). Given these diverging perspectives, there is sufficient reason to refine conceptions of task understanding by taking into account empirical evidence from the fields of both information retrieval and cognitive psychology. This interdisciplinary lens on task understanding might illuminate how instructional designers can achieve the often conflicting objectives of satisfying online learners' information needs and improving their performance on a given academic task. When information need is misconstrued, performance on a dependent task is more liable to deteriorate. Logically, therefore, the design of indexes for online repositories that purport to improve self-regulatory processes, such as Topic Maps environment described in this chapter, should be informed not only by well-known principles for instructional design but also by guidelines emanating from Ingwersen's theory of CIR.

Metacognitive Monitoring of Performance During Writing Activities

Another critical component of academic self-regulation being explored in our programme of research is metacognitive monitoring or learners' abilities to evaluate their performance and learning while engaging in an academic task (Winne, 2004). While monitoring has been described as an eccentric phenomenon, with variations from one individual to the next (Nietfeld, Enders, & Schraw, 2006; Schraw, Dunkle, Bendixen, & Roedel, 1995), research on monitoring or calibration proficiencies in college students taking multiple-choice tests has revealed both domain-specific and domain-general-monitoring abilities in students (Nietfeld, Cao, & Osborne, 2006; Schraw & Nietfeld, 1998). There is, however, a paucity of research on the development of monitoring skills in graduate learners in the context of writing tasks requiring higher-order thinking, as well as whether adults use their monitoring skills in similar ways when tackling different types of academic activities (Nietfeld, Cao, & Osborne, 2005; Nietfeld & Schraw, 2002).

There is a paucity of empirical evidence describing the relationship between learners' accuracy in monitoring and their performance; studies supporting the relationships between prediction (monitoring) accuracy and performance are few and far between (Nietfeld et al., 2005, Nietfeld, Cao et al., 2006, Nietfeld, Enders et al., 2006; Pressley & Schneider, 1997). In fact, there are instances of studies that point out the contrary, i.e. that improved performance in test-taking situations is related to less accurate monitoring (e.g. Begg, Martin, & Needham, 1992) or that improved performance cannot be attributed to improved monitoring (e.g. Dunlosky & Connor, 1997). While purely experimental designs (as suggested by Thiede, Dunlosky, Griffin, & Wiley, 2005) allow researchers to compare performances among students with variable monitoring proficiencies in well-structured tasks, the question still remains as to how one can better design instructional tools to help learners, both at secondary and postsecondary levels, regulate their performance on more complex and consequential academic tasks (see Mevarech & Fridkin, 2006; White & Frederiksen, 1998; and Zimmerman & Moylan, 2009, for examples of instructional interventions focused on improvement of metacognitive processes). In the context of our programme of research, preparing graduate learners for the educational technology-related workforces includes helping these knowledge workers to become better judges of their own performance on ill-structured written tasks, thereby increasing the efficiency with which such tasks can be accomplished. Through the sustained implementation and use of a Topic Maps indexing tool, we present empirical evidence of how learners' monitoring, task understanding and academic performance influence one another and help describe, in more complete terms, how self-regulatory processes unfold as learners engage in online information retrieval activities.

Empirical Findings on Task Understanding, Monitoring and Academic Performance

Educational Context

Thirty-eight volunteers, 15 of whom were male, were recruited from a total of four sessions of a graduate, classroom- and laboratory-based "theories of e-learning" course given by Venkatesh. Pretests of content knowledge and essay-writing ability were conducted during the first class of each session. A total of six essays were written by each of the 38 participants over the duration of the course. As mentioned earlier in the chapter in the section "Overview of Educational Context", assessment criteria used to grade the essays were developed using Biggs' and Collis' (1982) and Biggs' (1991, 1996) SOLO taxonomy; criteria were made explicit to all learners before the writing of the first essay. This writing assignment was classified as ill-structured because (a) the goals of the essay were not well defined, (b) the constraints imposed by contextual factors were not readily apparent, (c) the solution to the essay-writing problem was not easily known and (d) there were multiple perspectives on both the solution and the solution path. Each essay was accompanied by a self-assessment tool, the Task Analyzer and Performance Evaluator (TAPE, Venkatesh, 2008; Venkatesh & Shaikh, 2011), designed to help learners articulate their justifications for meeting the assessment criteria. The TAPE self-assessment enabled learners to predict their performance and state their confidence in their predictions. In addition the TAPE asked learners to justify how they felt they had met the assessment criteria for their writing assignment. Students were asked to ensure that the topic of their essay was related to the course content on development of theories for e-learning; students chose to write essays on subjects as diverse as "practitioner-oriented knowledge management principles for e-learning assignments" and "healthcare industry and e-learning courses" to "development of learner motivation in online learning environments". Essays were submitted and graded online, feedback from the instructor was embedded and the assignments were returned to the learner within 72 hours of submission along with comments on the portion of the TAPE that dealt with learners' justifications of having met the criteria. All 38 learners had access to the repository of 132 instructor-annotated essays which was indexed by a Topic Maps. Students were free to use these annotated essays as sources for their own writing assignments or as examples of how the instructor would be grading their essays.

Due to scheduling-related constraints, 15 learners enrolled in the regular, 13-week long fall and winter semester courses were given access to the repository 4 weeks into the term (after having written three essays), whereas 23 others who were registered for intensive 6-week long summer courses received access to the repository after writing their first essay. Semi-structured timeline interviews (Schamber, 2000) were conducted with each of the 38 learners, at least once, to discuss their use of Topic Maps. Consent forms were signed and all data were collected in accordance with principles outlined by the American Psychological Association; ethical approval was obtained from Concordia University's Human Research Ethics Committee. While all participants were aware of Venkatesh's research programme, consent forms were only made available to the research team after final grades for the courses were submitted to the university.

Data Collection

Data were collected longitudinally over the course of multiple semesters and included the following:

- Demographic information and pretests of knowledge and essay-writing experience.
- Written essays.
- Written responses to the TAPE self-assessment for each essay.
- Performance predictions and confidence in performance predictions for each essay via the TAPE self-assessment.
- Instructor's performance assessment for each essay (grades and written feedback).
- Instructor's feedback regarding TAPE self-assessment questions related to assessment criteria.
- Semi-structured interviews with learners related to perceptions of task understanding, monitoring capabilities and academic performance.
- Computer-generated trace files related to use of the repository indexed by a Topic Maps; data collected included information time stamps and locations within Topic Maps that students browsed.
- Timeline interviews with learners related to decisions taken while browsing the repository.

Salient Quantitative Findings

In an initial quantitative exploration, Venkatesh and Shaikh (2011) used a novel approach called intra-sample statistical analysis (ISSA) (Shaffer & Serlin, 2004) to reveal the complex relationships between task understanding, metacognitive monitoring and academic performance. Shifting from learner to work task as unit of analysis provides a unique lens to describe how learners strategically adapt their self-regulatory processes while navigating the repository using Topic Maps. Furthermore, the analyses in Venkatesh and Shaikh (2011) propose the re-theorization of classic monitoring measures such as discrimination (i.e. learner's ability to assign an appropriate level of confidence to a performance prediction) and bias (i.e. degree to which learners are over- or under-confident in their predictions) in light of learners' performance prediction capabilities.

When considering essays as unit of analysis, a multiple-regression procedure reveals that essay-specific performance can be significantly predicted by a positive relationship with four combined measures of task understanding and monitoring (the variance accounted for by the four measures was 39%). The four measures included feedback on self-assessment, absolute accuracy in prediction, discrimination, and performance prediction. This relationship holds true even in the face of using individual learners and time as fixed factors; in fact, these fixed factors accounted for no more than 12% of the variance in performance. In addition, the models resulting from the follow-up non-parametric regressions reveal precisely how the measures of task understanding and monitoring engage in a complex battle to influence how essay-specific performance might fluctuate in the context of the ill-structured writing assignment assigned for the four sections of the "theories of e-learning" course described. Specifically, the models proposed by the multinomial regression procedures indicate that, over time, increased confidence and inaccurate predictions reduce the likelihood of improved performance. However, an increase in essay-specific bias (as defined by the ISSA procedure) and the ability to improve task understanding influence performance positively. In light of these results, it seems necessary to reconceptualise the seemingly conflicting directions that seem to pull apart the self-regulatory mechanisms that guide how learners perceive their comprehensions of tasks and how they calibrate their performance. On the one hand, patterns in certain monitoring proficiencies, such as accuracy and confidence, tend to reduce the probability of performing well on the writing task, whereas other monitoring measures such as bias (in combination with task understanding) lead to improved performance. These results led to Venkatesh and Shaikh (2008) conducting qualitatively oriented inductive content analysis on the interview and trace data collected to uncover how learners' task understanding and monitoring might influence performance on the essay-writing task.

Salient Qualitative Findings

Venkatesh and Shaikh (2008) show how learners' metacognitive monitoring abilities are dependent on specific navigation experiences in the repository. Of the 38 participants, 12 were selected as a theoretical sample based upon iterations required for performance improvement. Learners were first selected based on their performance being in a B range or lower (i.e. B+, B, B– and C) for their first essay. Subsequently, these learners were placed within two categories—improving to an A range grade after two versus three or more attempts at the essay-writing task. This categorization placed seven individuals, three of whom were females, in the two-essay improvement group (2IG) and five females in the three-essay improvement group (3IG). Our sampling strategy allows us to observe how task understanding might have fluctuated across a number of its psychological dimensions, as well as the role that time on task might have played in the relationship between performance improvement and task understanding.

We compared learners from the 2IG and 3IG groups on their perceptions of the assessment criteria, knowledge of self-as-learner (as determined in learners' responses to their TAPE self-assessments as well as in their interviews), perceptions of the instructor as well as their information need. Learners cycled through various stages of development of their perceptions of the assessment criteria, as was evidenced in their TAPE self-assessment responses as well as in the interviews. In accordance with Ingwersen's theory of CIR, perceptions of the assessment criteria and rationale did, in fact, stabilise over time, regardless of learners' information need.

It became clear, at the outset of the analysis, that knowledge of self-as-learner played the most crucial role in instigating navigation strategies in the repository. In fact, some clear distinctions were seen in the two groups of theoretically sampled learners. Learners from the 3IG preferred to use class discussions (an operationalization of knowledge of self-as-learner) in choosing subjects to search for while navigating Topic Maps-enabled repository, whereas those in the 2IG overwhelmingly initiated search activities based on perceptions of the instructor and instructor feedback on their own essays. Eventually, learners in the 3IG did shift their search strategies to better reflect the need to align with assessment criteria.

Learners' perceptions of their instructor as well as of the feedback provided by the instructor were instrumental to the development of their task understanding, in all of the 12 cases across the two groups. Learners repeatedly emphasized the importance of having open and accessible instructor feedback on the essays of their peers. Most learners had specific information needs while exploring the repository. In stark contrast to Ingwersen's (2000) hypothesis, but in concordance with conjectures made in Venkatesh (2008), learners' information needs fluctuated (e.g. from searching using the grade index to subject index to author index, not necessarily in that order) as their task understanding improved.

Methodological Implications and Their Influence on Self-Regulation Theory Building Exercises

Work Task as Unit of Analysis

In an attempt to better explicate the relationship between a single facet of task understanding, namely, learners' perceptions of the ill-structured writing assignment's assessment criteria and their variable monitoring proficiencies, Venkatesh and Shaikh (2011) propose that the work task be treated as a unit of analysis as opposed to the individual learner. The theoretical basis for conducting this procedure is detailed in Shaffer and Serlin's (2004) landmark piece on ISSA. When confronted with data organized and analysed by learner as unit of analysis, it is not uncommon to notice that the lack of a large sample combined with the repeated measure procedures leaves very little room for powerful statistical results. Treating the work task, or in our case, the essay, as unit of analysis enables us to employ powerful, multivariate statistical procedures, with a relatively larger sample, so as to confirm some of the qualitative observations made in Venkatesh and Shaikh (2008) and provide fodder for future theoretical and research considerations in the area of exploring the development of monitoring proficiencies.

Two major issues taken into consideration before commencing the essay-based analyses in Venkatesh and Shaikh (2011) were those of generalizability and exchangeability/interchangeability (Shaffer & Serlin, 2004). All essay-based analyses are generalized to all essays that could possibly have been written by the set of 38 learners registered in the four session of the "theories of e-learning" course. In addition, while treating an individual essay as unit of analysis, after taking into account all possible measured factors, including the writer of the essay, session in which it was written, and the numerical sequence in which the essay was written, essays can be considered exchangeable or interchangeable with one another. The notion of exchangeability demands that one treats individual learners as fixed effects in any multivariate model so as to contextualize the results to the sample of individuals from which the essays were drawn.

Factoring Performance Predictions in Calculating Monitoring Proficiencies

An important aspect of our programme of research is introducing the concept of performance prediction capability and its relation to the performance assessments and students' prediction confidence scores. Prior statistical investigations of monitoring (e.g. Nietfeld et al., 2005, Nietfeld, Cao et al., 2006, Nietfeld, Enders et al., 2006; Schraw et al., 1995; Schraw & Nietfeld, 1998) do not deal with the notion of students' performance prediction capabilities and how these predictions might be related to their actual performance and confidence. Schraw and his colleagues investigated monitoring in the context of multiple-choice questions, and hence, students did not predict *how* correct their responses were; rather, they stated their confidence that their answers were correct. In fact, in most prior studies reviewed, students implicitly predicted perfect performance. To further exacerbate the problem, monitoring proficiencies have traditionally been calculated using performance and confidence scores alone. Venkatesh and Shaikh (2011) propose that the concept of performance prediction capabilities adds a new dimension to measuring monitoring proficiencies. Measures of monitoring proficiencies like discrimination and bias should take into account performance predictions, performance assessments and prediction confidence when being derived. When performance is not gauged simply in terms of "right" and "wrong" answers but is instead mostly graded on a scale, then students' monitoring abilities need to account for any over- or underestimation of performance before considering the effect of their prediction confidence.

Selection of Theoretical Samples for Qualitative Analyses

Our research has found that learners' task understanding with respect to ill-structured writing assignments is dependent on myriad factors, especially when these learners are confronted with the overhead of an information retrieval activity. These include the usual suspects, namely, the traditional cognitive psychology-related constructs of perceptions about the rationale for completing the task as well as its assessment criteria and knowledge of self-as-learner (Venkatesh, 2008; Venkatesh &

Shaikh, 2008, 2011). When describing how people think in information retrieval contexts, Ingwersen (2000) contends that when learners navigate a search-and-retrieval system, their cognitive notion of task understanding remains more stable than their perceptions of information need. On the other hand, while learners' navigation strategies (which are dependent on their information need) should ideally be grounded in their task understanding, it is generally accepted that this understanding evolves, for better or for worse, as they attempt completion of an academic task. In addition, Shaikh et al. (2012) illustrate the temporal effects of instructor feedback on learners' self-regulation while engaging in an academic task. Essentially, Shaikh et al. (2012) contend that learners prioritise a triad of perceptions in a hierarchical scheme, namely, the instructor, self-as-learner and task. Over time and experience in a learning environment, learners choose which of these three perceptions take precedence, thereby influencing to varying degrees, how cognitions are employed to successfully meet the criteria for completion of a task. The divergence of opinions and findings in the literature raises the question as to whether the CIR model, as conceived by Ingwersen, is incompatible with theoretical constructs associated with self-regulatory processes. If this is the case, could some of these differences be partially explained by the shifting hierarchy of perceptions outlined in Shaikh et al. (2012)? Our rationale for conducting qualitative content analyses on trace data and timeline interviews is rooted in this conundrum.

In treating the group of learners as a whole unit in a case study (e.g. Venkatesh, 2008; Venkatesh & Shaikh, 2011), we are unable to tease apart the facets of task understanding that might influence learners' performance improvement, information needs and navigation strategies over time. By shifting the unit of analysis to a theoretically sampled group of learners, we respond to both Shaikh et al. (2012) and Venkatesh and Shaikh's (2011) calls to better illuminate which aspects of task understanding might be affected by, and in turn, influence performance. In addition, we might also be better able to unravel the enigma behind whether task understanding remains stable across an information retrieval task or whether it responds to higher-level self-regulatory mechanisms and is continuously refined and, hence, unstable.

Significance for Design Promoting Metacognition and Self-Regulation

Results from our Topic Maps laboratory's empirical studies carry implications for instructional design to promote self-regulation. While it has been established in cognitive psychological terms that learner task understanding is a crucial component of academic self-regulation, the data and analyses we report offer specific suggestions as to how individual components of task understanding can be ameliorated when learners are tackling ill-structured writing tasks using online information repositories. For example, learners adjusted their perceptions of the rationale for completing the essay task and the assessment criteria using various resources, including the instructor's feedback on their essays, class discussions, the course outline and the instructor's annotations to other learners' writings. In the case of graduate learners accessing information online, there seems to be an academic self-regulatory mechanism that enables learners to employ distinct strategies to ensure that they have understood the criteria in the same ways as the instructor. In short, we recommend providing opportunities for learners to view assessment criteria through multiple perspectives and various interactions (e.g. learner–learner, learner–instructor, learner–content; see Cho, Chung, King, & Schunn, 2008 for examples of peer assessment in essay writing).

Our results also point to the singular facet of knowledge of self-as-learner as a fundamental theoretical construct that influenced how the graduate learners in our studies chose to navigate the repository. It would not be too much of a stretch to suggest that learners should be allowed to control their navigation through such online repositories by harnessing the associative powers of indexing technologies like Topic Maps. Individual preferences, such as browsing by subject, author, essay or grade, could be better facilitated to allow users to create their own topic-centric associations, thereby personalizing their route through the complex webs of information in online repositories. Note, however, that Venkatesh et al. (2007) as well as Shaw and Venkatesh (2005) warn that user-generated indexes should undergo strict content validation, without which the domains represented by technologies such as Topic Maps are rendered useless due to specious content.

A pressing question that arises from the results of our research is to what extent is information need, as experienced by graduate learners attempting to improve their performance on an ill-structured essay-writing task, context- and/or learner-dependent? We can partially answer this question by taking the easy route and pointing to individual differences and preferences. However, that would belie the complex dance that task understanding and information need engage in when learners employ cognition to retrieve online information. While we are aware that information needs morph as learners attempt to improve their task understanding, our results indicate the need to explore specific conditions that might govern how, when and why changes in learner cognition would influence these needs.

Designing Indexes for Online Information Retrieval

Our research shows that Topic Maps build enriched representations of academic work tasks, which can be viewed both from the perspective of the content covered in the task as well as from the perspective of the criteria used by the instructor in grading the academic task. While the context for the research reported limits the scope of our work to graduate learners engaged in writing assignments, our laboratory is preparing to roll out two environments indexed by Topic Maps. In the first instance, we have built a Topic Maps-enabled system to help undergraduate pre-service teachers navigate science-related concept maps, and second, we have designed a website indexed by Topic Maps to help international students learn rhetorical strategies for tackling writing assignments in the subject area of English as a second language. In the foreseeable future, our research in these two contexts will help us to paint a more complete portrait of the effect of using Topic Maps indexes in online learning environments.

In conclusion, convincing designers of online learning to adopt Topic Maps as an indexing scheme is not an easy task, but we reproduce the following arguments, offered by an anonymous Topic Maps expert on a draft of the Venkatesh (2008) paper, that might help tilt the scale in favour of designing the next generation of digital repositories with the help of Topic Maps:

1. The subject-centric nature of Topic Maps (topics as the core building block, constituting points of collocation) both helps learners to identify the core concepts within some new piece of knowledge that they are seeking to acquire and substantially aids "findability"/"searchability", thus reducing the time spent searching and increasing the time available for knowledge acquisition.
2. The associative nature of Topic Maps (associations as the device that links topics into a meaningful structure) provides for ease of navigation and even more importantly, perhaps, reflects the way in which learners acquire new knowledge, i.e. by associatively fitting it into pre-existing knowledge structures that have already been acquired. The notion of schema reconstruction, popular within both the CIR and information processing theories, would easily explain this powerful feature of Topic Maps-based indexes.
3. The classificatory nature of Topic Maps (i.e. the way in which Topic Maps encourage the classification of topics and associations into types) might conceivably help learners to acquire an overall understanding of the key concepts within a domain before having to bother about the details of the individuals, thus providing a more step-by-step approach to acquiring knowledge.

Acknowledgements The work reported herein is made possible through grants received by the government of Québec's *fonds québecois de recherché sur la société et la culture* as well as from faculty of Arts and Sciences at Concordia University. The authors would like to thank Stef Rucco, Technical Manager of the Department of Education at Concordia University, for his help in setting up, upgrading and securing the Ontopia Knowledge Suite on the department servers.

References

Aleven, V. (2006). An intelligent learning environment for case-based argumentation. *Technology, Instruction, Cognition and Learning, 4*(2), 191–241.

Andrews, R. (2003). The end of the essay? *Teaching in Higher Education, 8*(1), 117–128.

Baeza-Yates, R. (2003). Information retrieval in the web: Beyond current search engines. *International Journal of Approximate Reasoning, 34*(2–3), 97–104.

Begg, I. M., Martin, L. A., & Needham, D. R. (1992). Memory monitoring: How useful is self-knowledge about memory? *European Journal of Cognitive Psychology, 4*, 195–218.

Biggs, J. B. (1991). Student learning in the context of school. In J. B. Biggs (Ed.), *Teaching for learning: The view from cognitive psychology* (pp. 7–29). Hawthorn, VA: The Australian Council for Educational Research Ltd.

Biggs, J. B. (1996). Enhancing teaching through constructive alignment. *Higher Education, 32*, 347–364.

Biggs, J. B., & Collis, K. (1982). *Evaluating the quality of learning: The SOLO taxonomy*. New York: Academic.

Bourdeau, J., Mizoguchi, R., Hayashi, Y., Psyche, V., & Nkambou, R. (2007). When the domain of the ontology is education. *Proceedings of LORNET 2007, User Centered Knowledge Environments: From Theory to Practice, the Fourth Annual LORNET Conference I2LOR 2007 of the LORNET Research Network*. Montreal, QC: Lornet.

Canadian Council on Learning [CCL] (2007). *Post-secondary education in Canada: Strategies for success*. Retrieved November 30, 2010, from http://www.ccl-cca.ca/CCL/Reports/PostSecondaryEducation?Language=EN.

Cho, K., Chung, T. R., King, W. R., & Schunn, C. D. (2008). Peer-based computer-supported knowledge refinement: An empirical investigation. *Communications of the ACM, 51*(3), 83–88.

Crampes, M., & Bourdeau, J. (2004). Editorial du numéro spécial, Ontologies pour les EIAH, *Revue Sciences et Technologies de l'Information et de la Communication pour l'Education et la Formation, 11*, 223–230. Retrieved November 30, 2010, from http://sticef.univ-lemans.fr/num/vol2004/sticef_2004_edito_special.htm.

Dunlosky, J., & Connor, L. T. (1997). Age differences in the allocation of study time account for age differences in memory performance. *Memory & Cognition, 25*, 691–700.

Garshol, L. M. (2004). Metadata? Thesauri? Taxonomies? Topic Maps! Making sense of it all. *Journal of Information Science, 30*(4), 378–391.

Gasevic, D., & Hatala, M. (2006). Ontology mappings to improve learning resource search. *British Journal of Educational Technology, 37*(3), 375–389.

Henri, F., Gagné, P., Maina, M., Gargouri, Y., Bourdeau, J., & Paquette, G. (2006). Development of a knowledge base as a tool for contextualized learning. *AI and Society, 20*, 271–287.

Hersh, W., Pentecost, J., & Wickam, D. (1996). A task-oriented approach to information retrieval evaluation. *Journal of the American Society for Information Science, 47*(1), 50–56.

Ingwersen, P. (2000). Cognitive information retrieval. *Annual Review of Information Science and Technology, 34*, 3–52.

International Organization for Standardisation [ISO] (2002). *Topic maps*. Retrieved November 30, 2010, from http://www.y12.doe.gov/sgml/sc34/document/0129.pdf.

Kabel, S., de Hoog, R., Wielinga, R., & Anjewierden, A. (2004). The added value of task and ontology-based markup for information retrieval. *Journal of the American Society for Information Science and Technology, 55*(4), 348–382.

Lindblom-Ylänne, A., & Pihlajamäki, H. (2003). Can a collaborative network environment enhance essay-writing processes? *British Journal of Educational Technology, 34*(1), 17–30.

Magnan, F., & Paquette, G. (2006). Telos: An ontology-driven e-learning OS. In S. Weibelzahl & A. Cristea (Eds.) *Proceedings of Workshops held at the Fourth International Conference on Adaptive Hypermedia and Adaptive Web-Based Systems* (AH2006). Lecture Notes in Learning and Teaching. Dublin: National College of Ireland.

McGee, P., Carmean, C., & Jafari, A. (2005). *Course management systems for learning: Beyond accidental pedagogy*. Hershey, PA: Idea Group.

Mevarech, Z., & Fridkin, S. (2006). The effects of IMPROVE on mathematical knowledge, mathematical reasoning and meta-cognition. *Metacognition and Learning, 1*(1), 85–97.

Nietfeld, J. L., Cao, L., & Osborne, J. W. (2005). Metacognitive monitoring accuracy and student performance in the postsecondary classroom. *The Journal of Experimental Education, 74*(1), 7–28.

Nietfeld, J. L., Cao, L., & Osborne, J. W. (2006). The effect of distributed monitoring exercises and feedback on performance, monitoring accuracy and self-efficacy. *Metacognition and Learning, 1*, 159–179.

Nietfeld, J. L., Enders, C. K., & Schraw, G. (2006). A Monte Carlo comparison of measures of relative and absolute monitoring accuracy. *Educational and Psychological Measurement, 66*, 258–271.

Nietfeld, J. L., & Schraw, G. (2002). The effect of knowledge and strategy training on monitoring accuracy. *The Journal of Educational Research, 95*(3), 131–142.

Pepper, S. (2002). *The TAO of Topic Maps*. Retrieved November 30, 2010, from http://www.ontopia.net/topicmaps/materials/tao.html.

Pressley, M., & Schneider, W. (1997). *Introduction to memory development during childhood and adolescence*. Mahwah, NJ: Erlbaum.

Schamber, L. (2000). Time-line interviews and inductive content analysis: Their effectiveness for exploring cognitive behaviors. *Journal of the American Society for Information Science, 51*(8), 734–744.

Schraw, G., Dunkle, M. E., Bendixen, L. D., & Roedel, T. D. (1995). Does a general monitoring skill exist? *Journal of Educational Psychology, 87*, 433–444.

Schraw, G., & Nietfeld, J. (1998). A further test of the general monitoring skill. *Journal of Educational Psychology, 90*, 236–248.

Shaffer, D. W., & Serlin, R. C. (2004). What good are statistics that don't generalize? *Educational Researcher, 33*, 14–25.

Shaikh, K., Zuberi, A., & Venkatesh, V. (2012) Exploring counter theoretical instances of graduate learners' self-regulatory processes when using online repositories. *International Journal of Technologies in Higher Education, 9*, 6–19.

Shaw, S., & Venkatesh, V. (2005). The missing link to enhanced course management systems: Adopting learning content management systems in the educational sphere. In P. McGee, C. Carmean, & A. Jafari (Eds.), *Course management systems for learning: Beyond accidental pedagogy* (pp. 206–231). Hershey, PA: Idea Group.

Simard, A., Broome, J., Drury, M., Haddon, B., O'Neil, B., & Pasho, D. (2007). *Understanding knowledge services at Natural Resources Canada*. Retrieved November 30, 2010, from http://dsp-psd.pwgsc.gc.ca/collection_2007/nrcan-rncan/M4-45-2006E.pdf.

Thiede, K. W., Dunlosky, J., Griffin, T. D., & Wiley, J. (2005). Understanding the delayed-keyword effect on metacomprehension accuracy. *Journal of Experimental Psychology: Learning, Memory, and Cognition, 31*(6), 1267–1280.

Tynjälä, P. (2001). Writing, learning and the development of expertise in higher education. In P. Tynjälä et al. (Eds.), *Writing as a learning tool: Integrating theory and practice* (pp. 37–56). Amsterdam, Netherlands: Kluwer Academic.

Venkatesh, V. (2008). Topic maps as indexing tools in e-learning: Bridging theoretical and practical gaps between information retrieval and educational psychology. *International Journal of Advanced Media and Communication, 2*(3), 221–235.

Venkatesh, V., & Shaikh, K. (2008). Investigating task understanding in online repositories equipped with Topic Map indexes: Implications for improving self-regulatory processes in graduate learners. *International Journal of Technologies in Higher Education, 5*(3), 22–35.

Venkatesh, V., & Shaikh, K. (2011). Uncovering relationships between task understanding and monitoring proficiencies in post-secondary learners: Comparing work task and learner as statistical units of analyses. *Education Research International*, 2011, Article ID 735643, 11 pages. Retrieved June 20, 2011 from: http://downloads.hindawi.com/journals/edu/2011/735643.pdf.

Venkatesh, V., Shaikh, K., & Zuberi, A. (2010). Topic maps as indexing tools in the educational sphere: Theoretical foundations, review of empirical research and future challenges. In K. Perusich (Ed.), *Cognitive maps* (pp. 1–12). Vienna, Austria: In-Tech.

Venkatesh, V., Shaw, S., Dicks, D., Lowerison, G., Zhang, D., & Sanjakdar, R. (2007). Topic maps: Adopting user-centred indexing technologies in course management systems. *Journal of Interactive Learning Research, 18*(3), 429–450.

White, B. Y., & Frederiksen, J. R. (1998). Inquiry, modeling, and metacognition: Making science accessible to all students. *Cognition and Instruction, 16*(1), 3–118.

Winne, P. H. (2004). Students' calibration of knowledge and learning processes: Implications for designing powerful software learning environments. *International Journal of Educational Research, 41*, 466–488.

Winne, P. H., & Hadwin, A. F. (1998). Studying as self-regulated learning. In D. J. Hacker, J. Dunlosky, & A. C. Graesser (Eds.), *Metacognition in educational theory and practice* (pp. 277–304). Mahwah, NJ: Erlbaum.

Zimmerman, B. J., & Moylan, A. R. (2009). Self-regulation: Where metacognition and motivation intersect. In D. J. Hacker, J. Dunlosky, & A. C. Graesser (Eds.), *Handbook of metacognition and education* (pp. 299–315). New York: Routledge.

nStudy: Tracing and Supporting Self-Regulated Learning in the Internet

20

Philip H. Winne and Allyson F. Hadwin

Abstract

We set the stage for this chapter by recapitulating Winne and Hadwin's (1998) model of self-regulated learning and identifying three obstacles learners face when they strive to effectively self-regulate learning autonomously. In this context, we provide an overview of the nStudy software system, a web application that offers learners a wide array of tools for identifying and operating on information they study. We designed nStudy to be a laboratory for learners and researchers alike to explore learning skills, metacognition and self-regulated learning. As learners use nStudy's tools to study information in the Internet or researchers' specially prepared HTML material, nStudy logs fine-grained, time-stamped trace data that reflect the cognitive and metacognitive events in self-regulated learning. Next steps in work on the nStudy system are to add tools learners that provide feedback they can use to advance personal programs of research on improving learning skills and gainfully self-regulating learning.

Context

Today's learners are making extensive use of information resources in the Internet to do homework assignments, mine information for term papers, and pursue curiosity-driven investigations. Easy and inexpensive means for online self-publication—e.g., blogs and free server space—coupled with the exploding popularity of ebooks and ebook readers leads us to conjecture that the Internet is quickly becoming learners' chief information resource.

The Internet's extensive scope, accessibility, and openness has drawbacks. In our experience, very few online authors, Web site designers, and other information providers configure online information in ways that promote or, at least, don't interfere with learning processes. (see Mayer, 2005, for a compendium of these principles.) Our informal survey of Internet

P.H. Winne (✉)
Simon Fraser University, Burnaby, BC, Canada V5A 1S6
e-mail: winne@sfu.ca

A.F. Hadwin
University of Victoria, Victoria, BC, Canada V8W 3N4
e-mail: hadwin@uvic.ca

R. Azevedo and V. Aleven (eds.), *International Handbook of Metacognition and Learning Technologies*, Springer International Handbooks of Education 26, DOI 10.1007/978-1-4419-5546-3_20,

information sources shows that the accuracy and reliability of information varies wildly, and that empirically validated guidelines for promoting learning are rarely evident with respect to the organization and layout of information, adjuncts (summaries, tables, figures, etc.), cues (e.g., font styles), and other widely researched features of instructional design. Compounding these flaws, some information sources overuse features that spike superficial appeal at likely cost to promoting deep understanding. As well, the sheer scope of information and its unsystematic cataloguing substantially increases the challenge learners face to select, coordinate, and synthesize information from hundreds of thousands of potential sources. In this context, learners face an intimidating task. They must simultaneously be skilled librarians, content appraisers, curriculum organizers, self-teachers, and learning skills specialists. Skills they need to succeed are underdeveloped (Nist & Holschuh, 2000; Pressley, Yokoi, van Meter, Van Etten, & Freebern, 1997). Thus, in an already cognitively demanding situation, learners also should work on improving learning skills. In short, learners seeking to learn from information resources in the Internet *must* excel at productively self-regulating learning.

Unfortunately, learners have a high probability of failing at this task. Tens of thousands of experiments over more than a century of research in educational psychology validate at least one clear, generalizable, and powerful finding: Learners who participate in unstructured control groups or "business as usual" comparison groups studying information sources that are not carefully instructionally designed and who have only accumulated experience to guide learning fare poorly compared to learners who participate in treatments designed by researchers. This disadvantage for "learning as usual" is particularly disconcerting because most of these less successful participants in research have been undergraduates with the "benefit" of 12–16 years of formal education!

We foresee two fundamentally different ways to address this challenge for learners foraging for knowledge in the Internet. One is to develop software technologies that can intelligently intervene to help learners compensate for deficits in the instructional design of information they locate and in underdeveloped skills for learning. Other chapters in this Handbook report advances on this front. A second approach is to provide learners with tools they can use to carry out a progressive program of personal research that helps them productively self-regulate learning so they become more effective at learning. To set the stage for this second approach, we first sketch a model of self-regulated learning (SRL) and its empirical support for self-improving learning.

Theory

SRL is a cognitively and motivationally active approach to learning. We posit learners engage in four weakly sequenced and recursive phases of cognitive and behavioral activity (Winne, 2011; Winne & Hadwin, 1998; see Fig. 20.1).

In phase 1, a learner surveys features of an assigned (or self-chosen) task as well as the environment surrounding it. The environment includes external conditions—e.g., standards a teacher will use to grade a project, resources such as lexicons and search engines—and internal conditions—e.g., interest in the topic, self-efficacy, and tactics the learner for studying information. The result of this survey is raw materials from which the learner constructs an understanding of the task as it is first presented and a string of updated states of that task as work progresses. Without accurate perceptions of tasks, academic performance suffers (Miller & Hadwin, 2010).

In phase 2, the learner sets goals and, conditional on them, selects and organizes learning tactics to forge a provisional plan for reaching goals. Setting goals with enough specificity to guide frequent metacognitive monitoring and control is a challenging task. It requires learners to have accurate perceptions about a task's features plus skill to break distal goals into specific, measurable, achieivable, proximial and action-oriented standards that can be monitored and potentially revised on an ongoing basis (Webster, Helm, Hadwin, Gendron, & Miller, 2010).

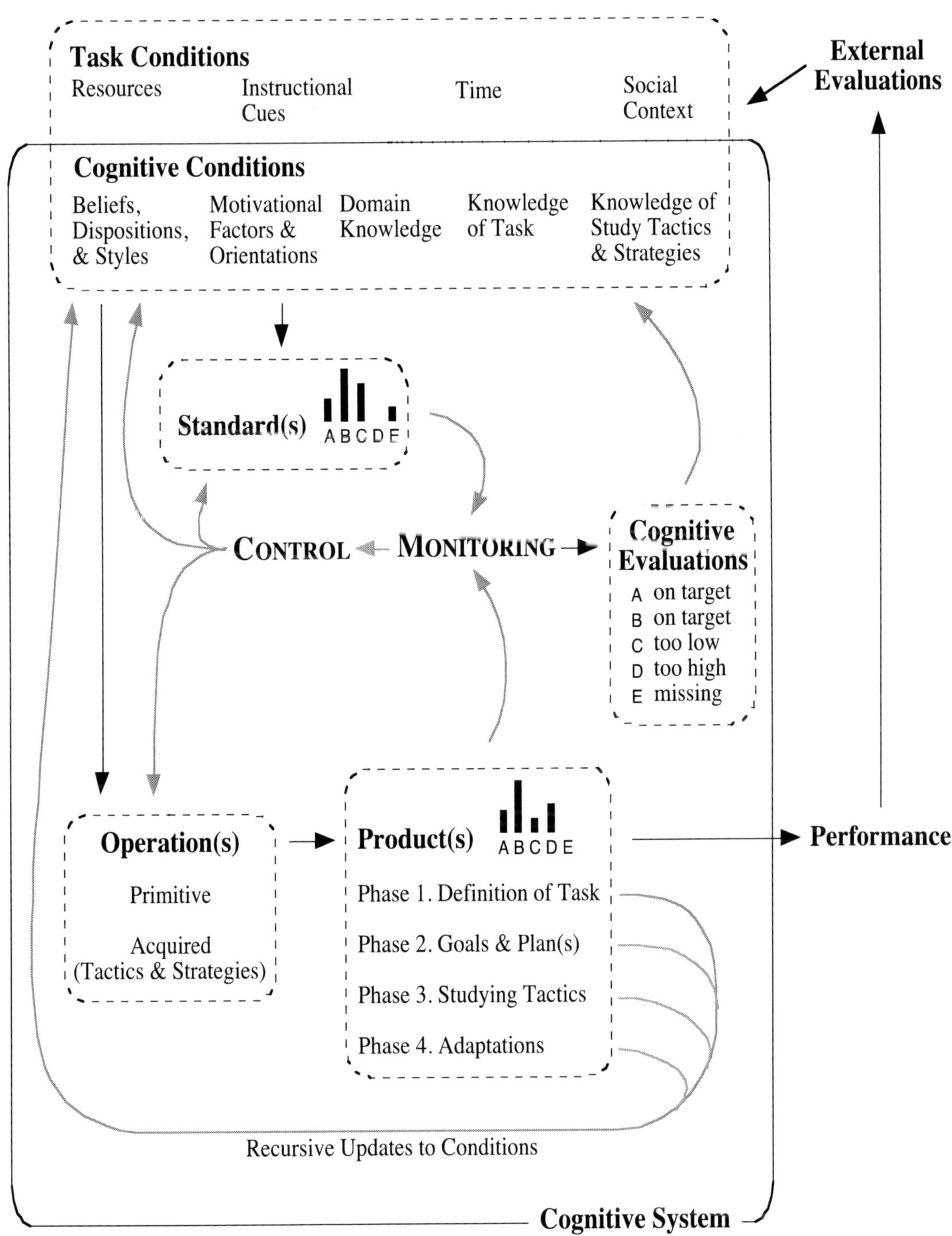

Fig. 20.1 Winne and Hadwin's 4-phase model of self-regulated learning. Reprinted with permission from Winne, P. H., & Hadwin, A. F. (1998). Studying as self-regulated learning. In D. J. Hacker, J. Dunlosky, & A. C. Graesser (Ed.), *Metacognition in educational theory and practice* (pp. 277–304). Mahwah, NJ: Lawrence Erlbaum Associates

Choosing how to approach goals is cognitively demanding. Theoretically, it involves (a) forecasting products that tactics can create (outcome expectations), (b) estimating the value of each outcome (its incentive), (c) assessing efficacy for carrying out each tactic and the overall plan (self-efficacy), (d) considering attributions for results and the affect(s) linked to attributions (e.g., attributing success to ability is rewarding but attributing failure to ability is punishing), and (e) judging the marginal utility of choosing one versus another plan (see Winne, 1997; Winne & Marx, 1989).

In phase 3, the learner initiates work on the task. As work unfolds, the learner metacognitively monitors progress relative to (a) subgoals and (b) the plan generated in phase 2. Metacognitive control may be exercised to make minor adjustments on the fly. Learners are not particularly adept at choosing and adapting tactics to adress specific challenges they encounter (Hadwin, Webster, Helm, McCardle, & Gendron, 2010; McCardle et al., 2010).

In phase 4, the learner takes a wide view of phases 1 through 3 to consider large-scale changes in the definition of the task, the goals and plans for reaching them, and the nature of interactions with resources to get the task done. This is perhaps the most challenging phase in the self-regulatory cycle. It requires synthesizing information within as well as across studying events, then systematically investigating the root source of learning problems. Students are challenged to systematically analyze their learning even within one academic task that spans multiple studying events (Hadwin, 2000). Furthermore, when learners neglect to recognize patterns in the match of tactics to challenges in studying, maladaptive regulation patterns can emerge and motivation may be undermined (Hadwin, Webster et al., 2010).

Throughout each phase and not just in phase 3, the active learner metacognitively monitors processes and results, and may exercise metacognitive control to make changes. Because the learner can "jump" to any phase from any other phase, or choose to revise the same phase, we theorize that work on a task need not unfold serially—phases of SRL are weakly sequenced and can generate information for any other phase. SRL is recursive.

Research on the Model of SRL

Work on SRL in academic contexts emerged in the 1980s growing mainly from studies investigating learning strategies. Two important findings were established in that seminal research. First, learners could be taught learning tactics[1]—methods that built comprehension of text, self-questioning techniques, and so forth—and, as a result, they learned more than peers not taught these cognitive tools (cf. Hadwin & Winne, 1996; Hattie, Biggs, & Purdie, 1996). Second, after learners had acquired tactics and experienced success using those tactics, they infrequently transferred or generalized use beyond the training context or when encouragements to use the tactics were withdrawn (see Zimmerman, 2008). This invited theorizing to explain why learners did not persist in using tactics they could use and had personally experienced to benefit learning.

The second of these findings makes clear an obvious but previously slippery fact: learners are agents. They choose how they will learn. Beyond recognizing agency, however, the question of how and why learners choose tactics for learning—how they self-regulate learning—became a critical issue.

Greene and Azevedo (2007) examined a broad sample of empirical work in an incisive theoretical review of research related to our 4-phase model of SRL. Their analysis provides warrants for our model overall as well as many of its specifics. Greene and Azevedo also identified a few key points where more research is needed to clarify and test our model.

Three Obstacles to Improving Learningon One's Own

For reasons not yet clear, learners are unreliable observers of (a) features of tasks that

[1] Researchers far more commonly use the term strategies in this regard but we perceive these cognitive scripts typically provide meager opportunity for strategic judgment; see Winne (2011). Hence, we use a term that reflects a more straightforward IF–THEN architecture with less complexity, namely, tactics.

should guide planning about how to accomplish tasks (Hadwin, Oshige, Miller, & Wild, 2009; Miller, 2009; Oshige, 2009) and (b) tactics they use in learning (see Winne & Jamieson-Noel, 2002; Winne, Jamieson-Noel, & Muis, 2002; Winne & Perry, 2000). Except in social settings where a peer or teacher can supplement data that learners themselves collect, having unreliable data inhibits productive SRL because decisions about how to adapt learning are based on inaccurate output from metacognitive monitoring.

Second, when learners try to use learning tactics that were only recently introduced or tactics they have not practiced extensively—that is, when tactics are not automated—learners are likely to experience a utilization deficiency (Bjorklund, Miller, Coyle, & Slawinski, 1997). A utilization deficiency is a situation where a learning tactic would be effective if the learner chose to use it under appropriate conditions and applied it skillfully. But, when conditions are not appropriate or the learner's skill with the tactic is not well developed, achievement suffers and learners understandably are less motivated to continue using the tactic. As a result, they may abandon a tactic that, under less demanding circumstances or with practice, could become an effective tool for learning.

Third, earlier studies in which learners (a) were taught learning tactics and (b) had opportunity to observe that the tactics improved their achievement also document that learners faltered in transferring tactics (see Zimmerman, 2008). Perhaps learners perceived insufficient incentive to apply the extra effort to use these tactics outside the focused context of research. Perhaps they judged the tactics were too complicated or they were unsure whether tactics were appropriate in new situations that differed from the context in which they were learned and practiced. Or, perhaps learners were able to use the tactics in the research context mainly because, unlike the unrestrained Internet, researchers carefully structured materials and managed other factors in the external environment so extraneous cognitive load was limited because this enhances the experiment's sensitivity to detect what the researchers were investigating.

Implications of the Model and Related Research

In each phase of SRL, learners seek out and process data that are input to metacognitive monitoring. Topics monitored are factors they believe affect learning—e.g., effort applied, complexity of the task, familiarity with content, perceptions of ability, etc. (e.g., see Koriat, Ma'ayan, & Nussinson, 2006)—along with attributes they perceive about the state of their work—degree of completion, quality of products, consequences likely to be experienced, etc. In phase 1, data that describe conditions in the external environment and data each learner perceives about her or his internal cognitive, motivational and affective factors are raw materials for developing an understanding of tasks at hand. In the other phases of SRL, learners gather data about qualities of processes and products that metacognitive monitoring compares to goals for processes and products. In cases where a learner's current toolkit of learning tactics is not sufficient, the learner may seek out information about new tactics that might help to make minor adjustments on-the-fly in phase 3 of SRL or, if necessary, to reformulate how they approach learning in a major way in phase 4.

In short, without reliable, revealing and relevant data that support making valid inferences about all four phases of SRL, learners will be handicapped. But data can be hard to come by. Fine-grained records that describe how learning unfolds are not a natural byproduct of "getting the work done." Moreover, learners often overlook data. They are not clear that data are available. For example, we have never encountered a student who explicitly kept track of whether information they highlighted as they studied was more memorable than material they did not highlight. While some recognized the possibility to record and analyze these data, effort estimated to carry out this "personal research project" (Winne, 2010b) was too great.

In this context, we suggest learners could profit if software tools helped them identify, access and process data about the environment and how a learning task is situated within it, their goals, how they study, and what happens when they make minor or occasionally major adjustments to learning tactics. Next we describe a software environment, nStudy, that we and colleagues designed and implemented to help learners at the same time it gathers extensive data that researchers want for their work on learning and SRL.

nStudy

nStudy (Winne, Hadwin, & Beaudoin, 2010) is a Web application that runs in the Firefox Web browser. It was designed primarily as a tool for gathering fine-grained, time-stamped data about operations learners apply to information as they study online materials. Several features of nStudy's toolkit also were designed to leverage well-established principles that research shows can improve learning.

The Browser and Linking Tools

nStudy displays HTML content that an instructor or researcher designs, or that is available in the Internet. Once learners access a Web page using its universal resource locator (URL), they can operate on information they find there. Each operation builds a link between specific information a learner selects on the Web page and other nStudy tools. As the learner constructs links, nStudy accumulates titles for each linked tool in a table that is organized by the kind of tool to which each information selection is linked.

Tags

To tag information in a Web page, the learner selects target text, mod-clicks[2] to expose a contextual popup menu and chooses a tagging option. In Fig. 20.2, in addition to a universally available generic tag titled *Highlight*, the contextual menu shows the five tags the learner has most recently used. In Fig. 20.2, these are as follows: Can do, Can't do, Fallacy, funny, and is this a learning objective. A *Tags...* option allows the learner to review all tags that have been constructed before assigning a particular tag, and to create new tags. Tagging the selected text formats it to have a colored background, per the learner's preferences, and posts the selection, called a quote, to a panel at left. The panel shows quotes for all the kinds of links the learner has forged to (a) quotes in this Web page or to (b) the bookmark that addresses the Web page as a whole, as well as terms appearing in the window (discussed later). Double clicking on an item in the panel opens the window containing its information.

Notes and Terms

Learners can annotate quotes and bookmarks to Web pages by creating notes and terms. Figure 20.3 shows a note. nStudy assigns new notes a default title of *untitled*, which invites learners to change it to a meaningful description. Characterizing information by classifying it is a form of generative processing that promotes learning (Wittrock, 2010).

For every note, nStudy automatically records the quote the learner selected in the browser, if there is one, and provides a link to the source using the bookmark's title. On making a new note, the learner chooses a schema for organizing information in the annotation by selecting an option from the dropdown *Select Form*. A basic note form is provided with a single text field: *Description*. As Fig. 20.4 shows, researchers and learners can customize any note's form to adapt a schema for an annotation that satisfies particular standards. Forms can be a one off for use in only one particular note or saved for future use. A variety of fields are available to create forms using a drag-and-drop operation. In the properties tab (not shown), properties of the field can be defined such as end points for a slider and text describing options in a combobox.

The researcher or learner can create terms to build a lexicon of foundational concepts in the domain of study. Terms use a single form including three fields: title, quotes, and description (see Fig. 20.5).

[2] A mod-click is a right-click in the Windows operating systems and a control-click in the Apple operating system.

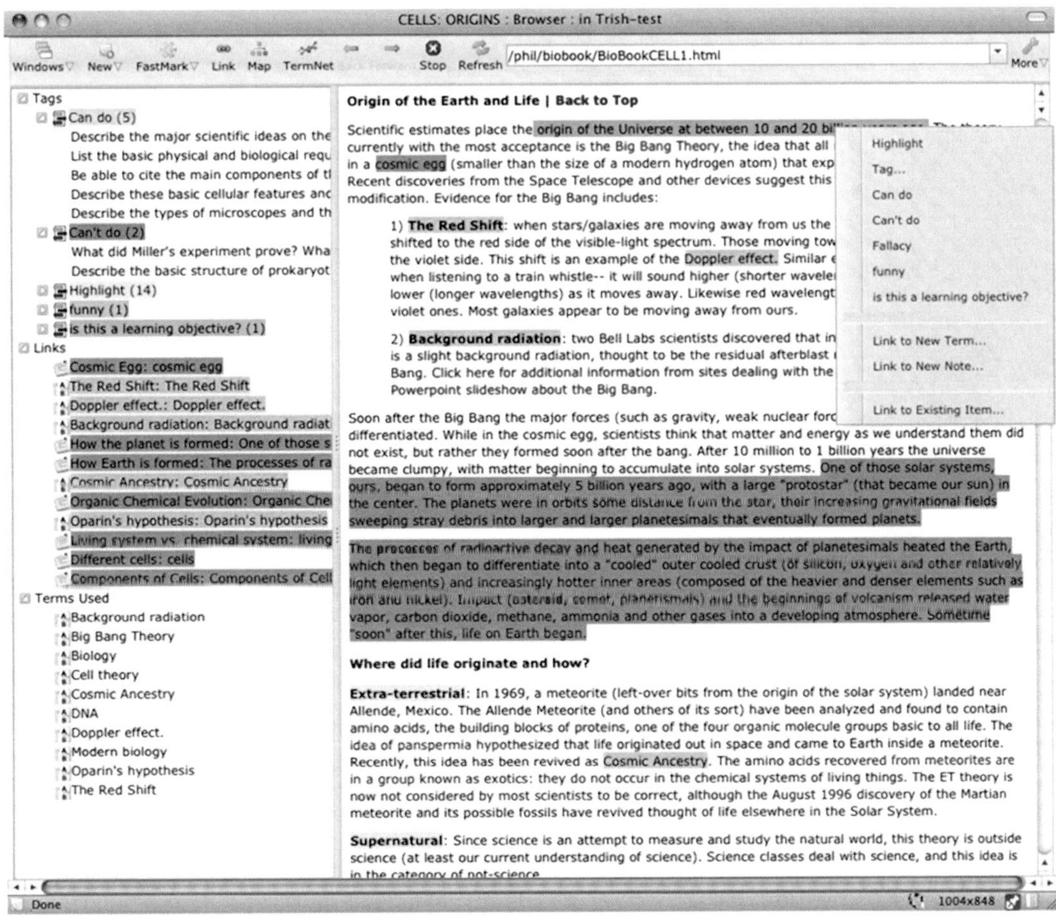

Fig. 20.2 nStudy browser, table of quotes, and linking tools

Terms and Termnet

Whenever the learner opens a browser, note, or term window, nStudy surveys its contents to identify terms appearing in any field and lists each term in the left panel under *Terms Used*. This list displays the subset of all key concepts in the larger domain of study that appear in the window in which the learner is currently working.

Learners often work nearly simultaneously with several windows. To help conceptualize how key concepts form bundles of information, any term that appears in any window the learner has open is shown in the Termnet window (see Fig. 20.6). The Termnet structures its node-link display using a simple semantic relation: if the description of one term used another term, a link is built between two terms. Literally, the link represents an "in terms of …" relation. For example, suppose "working memory" is a term. If another term titled "cognitive load" is described as "the degree to which working memory is challenged by factors that are intrinsic, germane and extraneous to mastering a learning task" nStudy will link the term "cognitive load" to the term "working memory."

Other nStudy Tools

Each learner has a private workspace. Several learners can collaborate in a shared workspace where each has full privileges to introduce, link, edit and delete information. Information items can be easily exchanged across workspaces if learners have a peer's user name. This creates

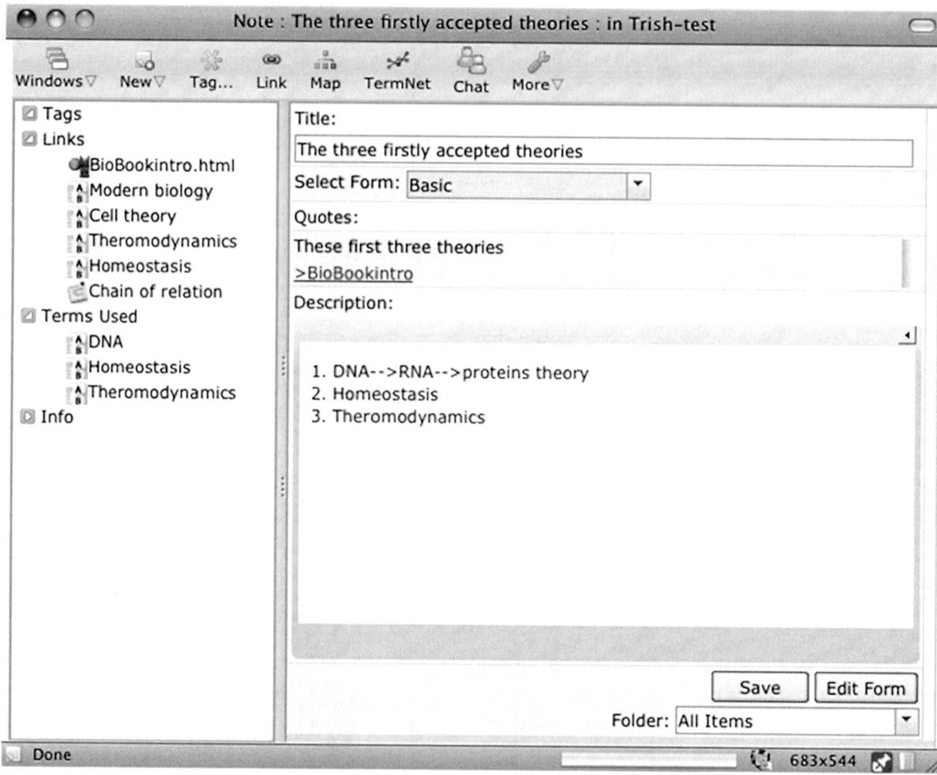

Fig. 20.3 A basic note in nStudy

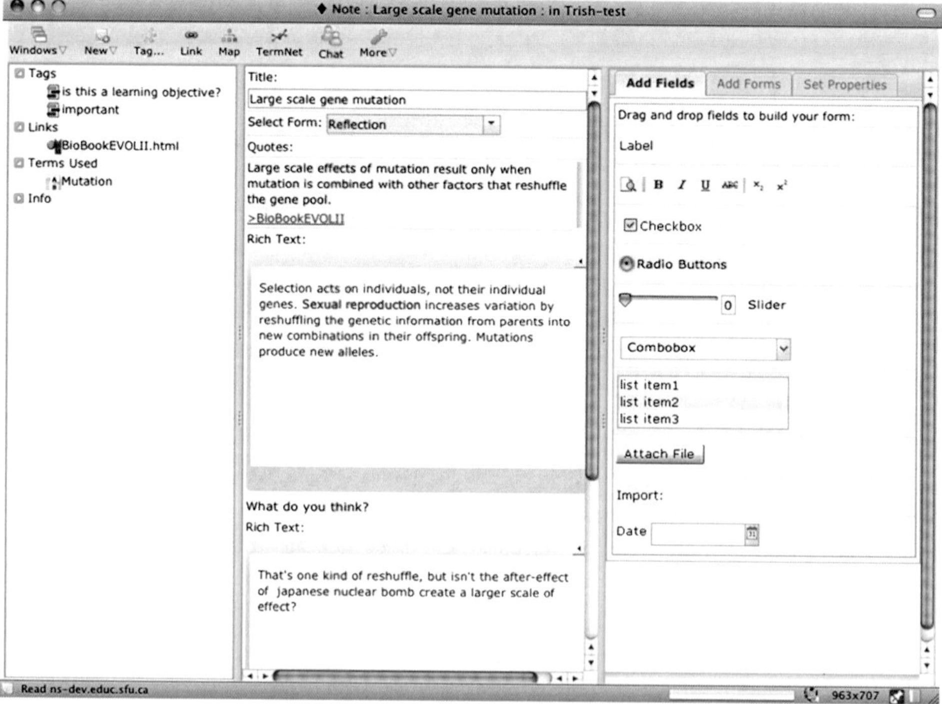

Fig. 20.4 An nStudy note showing a form and the editor for modifying and creating new forms that operationalize new schemas for notes

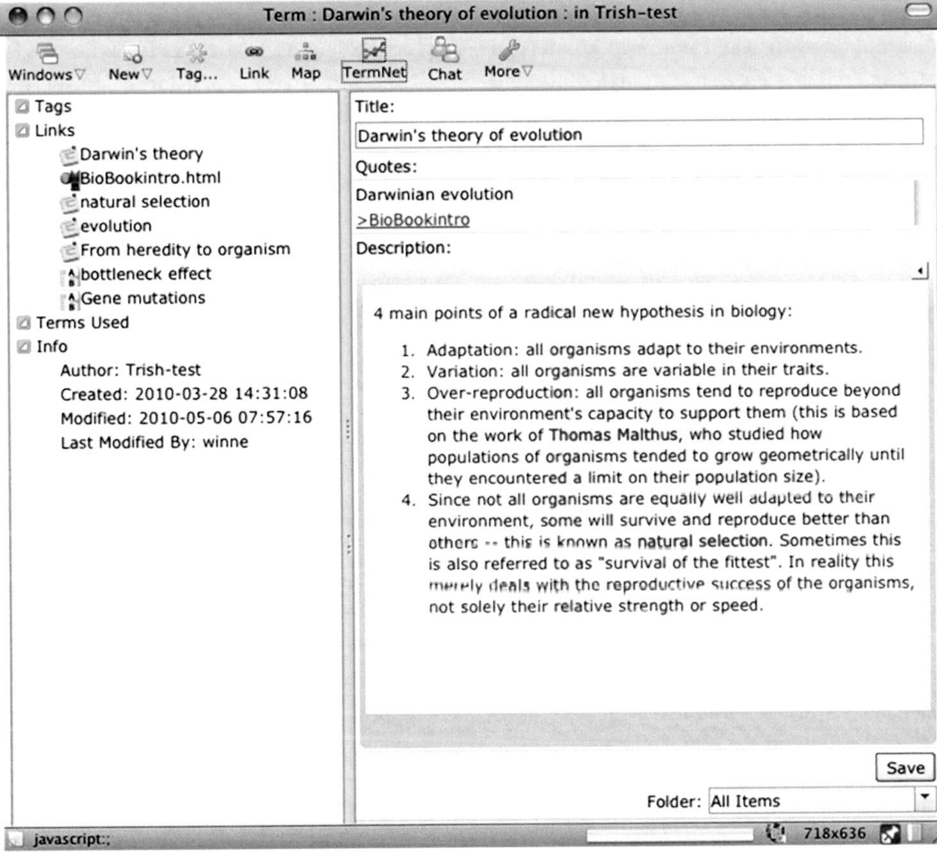

Fig. 20.5 An nStudy term

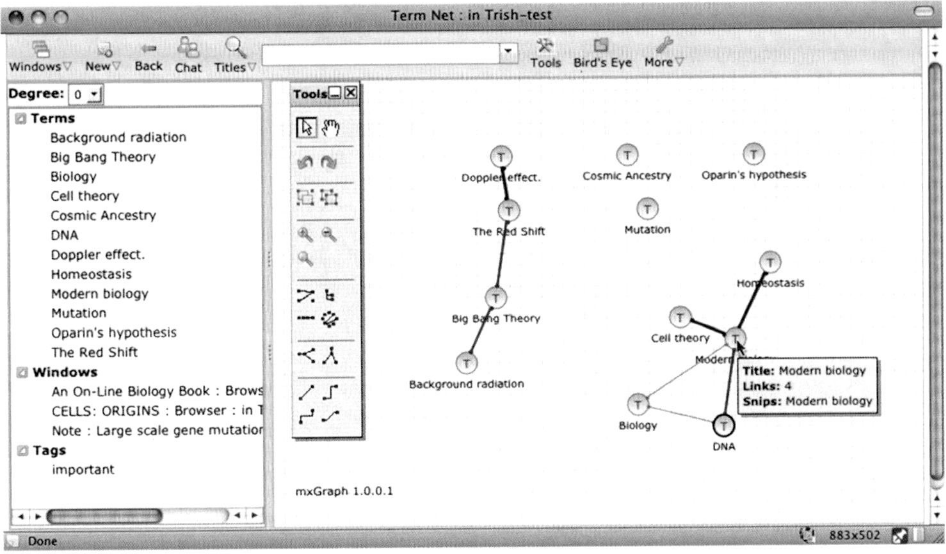

Fig. 20.6 An nStudy Termnet showing terms used in all windows currently open

opportunities for three forms of computer-supported collaborative learning: (a) sequential collaboration where work is circulated to and augmented by team members; (b) convergent collaboration where each members' work is exported from individual workspaces into a shared workspace where it is compiled and organized by the team; and (c) emergent collaboration in a shared workspace where all collaborative planning and work occurs.

A Chat tool allows learners to discuss content synchronously online. It affords opportunities for collaborators (and researchers) to experiment with varying architectures for synchronous collaboration by providing two dropdown lists configured by a researcher or instructor where learners can choose (a) a role and (b) view and enter into the chat any of several prompts that align to each role. For example, a learner may choose among a set of cogntive roles (e.g., forecaster, summarizer), a set of metacognitive roles (e.g., monitor, planner, evaluator), or a set of functional roles (e.g., recorder, leader). Corresponding prompts help collaborators take on a role in the chat. For example, a planner might have prompts, such as: What steps should we follow? What is our goal for this part? Roles and prompts can alert students to co-regulate one another ("Do you have a plan?" "I think you might be a little off track.") or jointly share regulation ("What is our main goal?" "Are we meeting our goal?") Chats are saved and can be annotated like a Web page. Thus, they become recoverable information resources for future tasks, including serving as models for collaboration upon which to improve.

Shared workspaces, the ability to exchange objects across workspaces and chats that can be structured by roles and prompts create opportunities for students to self-regulate, to co-regulate each other's work, and to share regulation (Hadwin, Oshige, Gress, & Winne, 2010). nStudy does not dictate features of regulation but supports and implicitly guides those events. Trace data about learners' activities advance research on collaboration and regulation by revealing: (a) products created by solo and collaborative work that are metacognitively monitored, (b) standards used in metacognitive monitoring, (c) operations controlled or regulated and (d) conditions under which regulation occurs (see Winne, Hadwin, & Perry, 2013).

In nStudy's Concept Map window, learners can build maps from scratch by creating notes, terms, bookmarks and other nStudy items, then linking, grouping and spatially arranging them. From within any of nStudy's information items, e.g., a note, a concept map of that item and other items linked to it can be constructed by clicking a button in the toolbar, *Map*.

In nStudy's Document window, learners can compose essays, poetry, lab reports and other text documents using rich text (HTML) formatting tools. Selections within a document can be annotated like a browser. Also, a basic difference tool is available to track changes across versions of a document.

The Library is a table that lists every information item within a workspace (see Fig. 20.7). The table can be filtered by (a) type of information item, (b) folders into which items are organized, (c) tags applied to items, as well as various metadata, such as: creator, last editor, date modified, and so on. A search tool is available to identify items that have particular information in titles, content, or both. The learner can operate on one or a set of several items by selecting, mod-clicking to expose a contextual menu and choosing a desired operator.

Data Logs

As the learner operates on information using nStudy's tools, the software unobtrusively logs fine-grained data: which window has focus (is active), what its title is, what information was selected, when the contextual menu was exposed, which operator is selected from the menu, and so forth. Each low-level entry in the log is time stamped to the millisecond (as accurately as the computer chip's cycle permits) to represent every observable operation the learner applied to information in a study session plus the information on which each operation was applied. In nStudy's data analysis module, patterns of these very low level events are organized into "human-level" events like: make new note, review term, modify concept map and so forth. In effect, these organized data instantiate a time-sequenced script that describes which tactics a

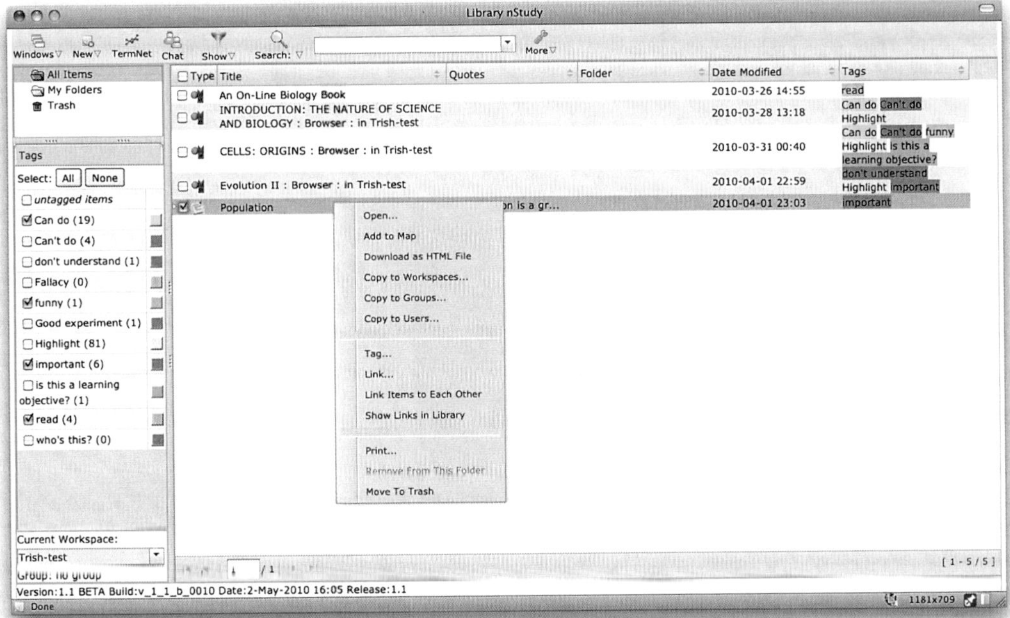

Fig. 20.7 nStudy's Library and Operators

learner applied to which information and, by looking backward along the timeline for a chosen number of events, the context for any particular event.

Measurements

Trace data are performance-based data learners generate unobtrusively as they apply cognitive and metacognitive operations to information a learner selects (Winne, 1982; Winne, 2010a). nStudy was designed to record extensive, fine-grained, time-stamped traces without intruding on learners' tasks other than by affording them choices among nStudy's tools. In contrast to think aloud and self-report data, trace data are not degraded by learners' unknown sampling of experience, biases in their verbal expression, temporal distance from actual events and other factors that may degrade the accuracy and completeness of learners' recall, perceptions and interpretations about how they learn.

Trace data can be analyzed in multiple ways and articulated with other data to paint a fuller picture of how learners study and learn (see Winne, Zhou, & Egan, 2010). For example, nStudy notes that offer learners a form for describing goals and a slider for recording an estimate of success can record whether learners explicitly set goals and what goals they set. A simple count of goal notes can index a learner's propensity to set goals. Because a trace log is a full record of a learner's observable tool-supported interactions with content, it can be analyzed to identify contexts that (a) precede a learner's creation of goals and (b) prompt the learner to revisit goals to adjust estimate of success.

Trace data also afford opportunities to measure the presence and qualities of learning strategies by constructing a transition matrix across traces and then a graph of transitions (see Fig. 20.8). Briefly, the transition matrix records tallies that signify a row event is followed by a column event (e.g., A is followed by B) and, after recording a tally, B is the event to be followed by another event (e.g., B is followed by D). Patterns of traces can then be quantified for properties, such as degree of regularity of the pattern, the congruence of one pattern to another, and whether specific neighborhoods of the graph play the same role relative to the graph as a whole (see Winne et al., 2002). This approach

Sequence of traces: A B D B C E D B C E D A C E D A B C F ...

Transition Matrix

	A	B	C	D	E	F
A		//	/			
B			///	/		
C					///	/
D	//	//				
E				///		
F						

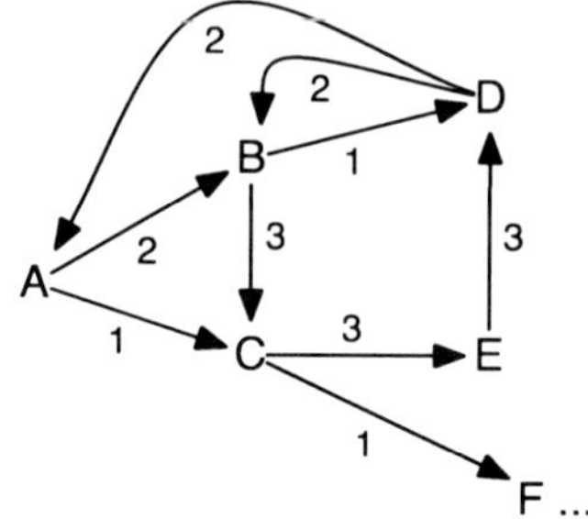

Fig. 20.8 A trace sequence, its transition matrix, and a graph of the pattern of traces

to analyzing trace data allows researchers to characterize qualities of a learner's activity in terms such as the "shape" of learning strategies (linear, cyclical, branching, etc.), levels of activity, and novelty or repetitiveness of responses to interventions or unexpected events. Hadwin, Nesbit, Jamieson-Noel, Code, and Winne (2007) applied this form of analysis to describe learners' levels and forms of cognitive and metacognitive activity in studying, such as the variability in a learner's use of tactics and the emphasis a learner placed on metacognitive monitoring.

Interventions

nStudy's browser, terms, notes, and documents are a vehicles for instructional designers and researchers to provide learners with HTML and rich text content that operationalize various kinds of interventions. For example, hyperlinks in HTML Web pages can define a structure of navigation. Forms designed for notes can provide learners with schemas for arguments or self-generated explanations. Semantic and syntactic properties can be varied in descriptions for provided terms. Questions, designs for headings, advance organizers and typography (e.g., bullet versus number lists; bolding) can be implemented in several of nStudy's tools.

On the horizon are tools that will extend nStudy into the arenas of (a) learner-driven interactions that directly express SRL and (b) adaptive tutoring.

SRL as a Program of Personal Research

When learners exercise metacognitive control, theory specifies they choose a particular tactic because, in part, they predict it will generate a particular result. For example, learners may believe that highlighting is a form of rehearsal that increases recall of material they highlight. These expectations are hypotheses about relations between learning events and outcomes. Each instantiation of metacognitive control to highlight information generates data to test the hypothesis. Over the span of a school term or an undergraduate course, learners could generate expansive data in a longitudinal field trial to discover "What works?"

We conjecture that SRL is often less productive than it might be because learners are neither trained to research their learning nor do they have easy access to data and tools for analyzing data. Learners could profit from tools that support a program of personal research on learning. For example, suppose a learner is interested to research whether learning is better supported by taking basic notes or notes that use forms for recording information according to particular schemas. Suppose in a review exercise, the learner links each test item to all the notes relevant to that item. Coupled with the log of studying events, it would be possible to analyze achievement as a function of annotations made using the basic form versus tailored forms. While this is a very simple example, the principle has broad scope. Supplemented with tools for analyzing trace data that nStudy records, a learner could examine the complete population of learning activities bearing on how learning events relate to achievement, as well as other dimensions, such as efficiency, interest in content, and so forth.

Just-in-Time Interventions

Suppose the learner has already investigated several research questions about how different study tactics affect learning. Each expression of kinds of traces that the learner researches can be transformed into a rule to identify those traces in future. When the learner records the results of self-focused research on learning—e.g., using notes with forms tailored to tasks promotes learning more than using basic notes—nStudy could be extended to monitor how the student uses basic notes and notes with tailored forms. Should the learner study using only basic notes that exceed some count (e.g., four successive basic notes), nStudy could offer a hint about studying: "Would it be appropriate to develop a note form for this content?" Such just-in-time hints are a subtle form of feedback about how the learner is studying that may elevate and focus metacognitive monitoring, as well as remind the learner of tactics for learning that, in the learner's personal history, may have a better chance to help reach goals. Importantly, these hints create opportunities for learners to regulate their learning by deciding whether (and how) to adapt learning after the co-regulatory prompt. Leaving decisions in the hands of learners is essential for learning to be self-regulated or co-regulated where learners productively exchange information about adapting their reciprocal and interdependent activities in collaborative tasks (Winne et al., 2013).

Challenges

Our design goal for nStudy was, on the one hand, to collect extensive, fine-grained, time-stamped data that trace cognitive, metacognitive, and motivated actions learners apply to specific information as they study; and, on the other hand, to afford learners a wide range of choices for expressing these learning-related events by offering tools they might want to use and that did not require extensive instruction or necessitate major changes in common studying activities. As one example, consider highlighting. A highlight is a nonspecific tag that is nearly ubiquitous among learners. nStudy extended this affordance by providing a tool with which learners could create and apply any number of specific tags. We reasoned that applying more specific tags traces metacognitive engagement in the form of using multiple standards—the tags—to monitor information's meaning (e.g., "general law" or "main point") and possible uses (e.g., "review for test" or "evidence for hypothesis"). As well, when learners create new tags, this is strong evidence for metacognitive monitoring that a current set of tags is insufficient to achieve goals. Moreover, because learners do not naturally highlight very effectively (e.g., Bell & Limber, 2010) and, as might occur in a workspace shared among group members, preexisting highlighting can impair metacognition (Gier, Kreiner, & Natz-Gonzalez, 2009). Thus, nStudy's design amplifies opportunities for learners to engage in SRL by providing a desirable difficulty that potentially enriches encoding (Thomas & McDaniel, 2007).

A challenge in this regard arises because desirable difficulties require more effort of learners and, in a rational sense, learners strive to balance effort against returns—as we described earlier, we hypothesize they seek to optimize utility. Thus, nStudy affords opportunities for learners to explore the relative utilities of a wide variety of study tactics. But we conjecture we conjecture affordance alone is insufficient. This challenge leads to a major focus for future work, which we describe next.

Early usability testing revealed that learners commonly avoided these cognitively effortful judgments about tags—they just wanted to highlight. For some, marking/highlighting was a first step in a more complex strategy in which they would later return to highlighted material and engage more generative processing. Other learners perceived the effort of classifying marked text outweighed its potential utility. As designers we were confronted with a challenge. If we created the opportunity to simply mark text, we might not see the list of potential ways to classify information they were highlighting; but, if we forced them to classify, they might abandon the tool because it was effortful or ill-matched to their strategic plan. We settled on a middle ground, where learners could simply select "highlight" from the top of a list of recent tags and repeat that "fast mark" throughout their studying. In this way, students were invited to review the list of possible ways of tagging their selections but not forced to do that.

Future

Space constraints prevent fully addressing how nStudy and research can evolve. Here, we highlight a particular issue arising from the preceding section and briefly introduce several avenues for future work.

Feedback About Operations That Generate Achievements

Feedback is a powerful influence on learning (Butler & Winne, 1995; Hattie & Timperley, 2007). Many of today's state-of-the-art software systems provide feedback about achievements in the domain learners study, such as physics or ecology. However, to our knowledge, no software learning system offer learners feedback about *how* they learn using any of the formats for knowledge that can represent study tactics and learning strategies: conditional, declarative and procedural (Winne, 2010b). nStudy is poised to accomplish this using the extensive, fine-grained, time-stamped traces it logs about how a learner operates on information in nStudy's environment.

We are planning supplements to nStudy's tools that would allow learners to use a controlled vocabulary to ask and receive answers to questions, such as: "How did I study differently for concepts A, B, and C that I know well compared to concepts D, E, and F that I know less well?" nStudy's response might be a graphical display of traces like that displayed in Fig. 20.8 that shows not merely the unconditional frequency of various operations but conditional (contextual) relations among binary pairs of operations, as well as an overall "strategy." This sort of question could be elaborated include a time dimension—"... and how did I change my strategy in November compared to September?" A response would show different graphs that depict strategy in a visual way plus an index, ranging from 0 to 1, that quantifies the degree of change. We believe this kind of process feedback is a key to scaffolding productive SRL.

A Grander Vision: The Research Co-Op

nStudy is a shell—any content that can be represented in an HTML format is content that learners can use nStudy to study. All learners need to use nStudy is the Firefox Web browser and an account on nStudy's server. The data that nStudy gathers about how learners study, regardless of the subject they study or their age, is in a single format. These features afford the research community expansive latitude to pursue research across disciplines and many levels of education yet meld their research in ways not heretofore possible. We echo Winne's (2006) argument that widespread adoption of systems like nStudy could significantly accelerate research's production of authentic, useful results. A simple and proven model might be to form a "research co-op" bearing modest resemblance to retail co-op enterprises. Users and researchers, for modest fees that support infrastructure, could avail themselves of massive data warehouses that would support data mining for principles about how to promote learning. Modifications to nStudy that might be suggested from this work can be distributed by upgrading the nStudy software once, on the server, which makes them immediately available at no additional cost.

Supplementing nStudy's data warehouse with other forms of data, such as measures of achievement and measures of what learners describe about themselves and their approaches to learning (self-reports of motivational constructs, self-reports about studying temporally removed from actual studying, surveys and inventories, and self-reports gathered as studying unfolds as punctuated narrative, i.e., think aloud) would create a resource that we predict would immediately and importantly accelerate harvesting fruit of research on learning.

Acknowledgments Support for this research was provided by grants to Philip H. Winne from the Social Sciences and Humanities Research Council of Canada (410-2007-1159 and 512-2003-1012), the Canada Research Chair Program and Simon Fraser University; and to Allyson F. Hadwin and Philip H. Winne from the Social Sciences and Humanities Research Council of Canada (410-2008-0700).

References

Bell, K. E., & Limber, J. E. (2010). Reading skill, textbook marking, and course performance. *Literacy Research and Instruction, 49*, 56–67.

Bjorklund, D. F., Miller, P. H., Coyle, T. R., & Slawinski, J. L. (1997). Instructing children to use memory strategies: Evidence of utilization deficiencies in memory training studies. *Developmental Review, 17*, 411–442.

Butler, D. L., & Winne, P. H. (1995). Feedback and self-regulated learning: A theoretical synthesis. *Review of Educational Research, 65*, 245–281.

Gier, V. S., Kreiner, D. S., & Natz-Gonzalez, A. (2009). Harmful effects of preexisting inappropriate highlighting on reading comprehension and metacognitive accuracy. *The Journal of General Psychology, 136*, 287–300.

Greene, J. A., & Azevedo, R. (2007). A theoretical review of Winne and Hadwin's model of self-regulated learning: new perspectives and directions. *Review of Educational Research, 77*, 334–372.

Hadwin, A. F. (2000). *Building a case for self-regulating as a socially constructed phenomenon*. Unpublished doctoral dissertation, Simon Fraser University, Burnaby, British Columbia, Canada.

Hadwin, A. F., Nesbit, J. C., Code, J., Jamieson-Noel, D. L., & Winne, P. H. (2007). Examining trace data to explore self-regulated learning. *Metacognition and Learning, 2*, 107–124.

Hadwin, A. F., Oshige, M., Gress, C. L. Z., & Winne, P. H. (2010). Innovative ways for using gStudy to orchestrate and research social aspects of self-regulated learning. *Computers in Human Behavoir, 26*, 794–805.

Hadwin, A. F., Oshige, M., Miller, M., & Wild, P. (2009). *Examining student and instructor task perceptions in a complex engineering design task: Paper proceedings presented for the 6th International Conference on Innovation and Practices in Engineering Design and Engineering Education (CDEN/C2E2)*, Hamilton, ON, Canada: McMaster University.

Hadwin, A. F., Webster, E., Helm, S., McCardle, L., & Gendron, A. (2010). *Toward the study of intra-individual differences in goal setting and motivation regulation*. Paper presented at the Annual meeting of the American Educational Research Association, Denver, CO.

Hadwin, A. F., & Winne, P. H. (1996). Study skills have meager support: A review of recent research on study skills in higher education. *Journal of Higher Education, 67*, 692–715.

Hattie, J., Biggs, J., & Purdie, N. (1996). Effects of learning skills interventions on student learning: A meta-analysis. *Review of Educational Research, 66*, 99–136.

Hattie, J., & Timperley, H. (2007). The power of feedback. *Review of Educational Research, 77*, 81–113.

Koriat, A., Ma'ayan, H., & Nussinson, R. (2006). The intricate relationships between monitoring and control in metacognition: Lessons for the cause-and-effect relation between subjective experience and behavior. *Journal of Experimental Psychology. General, 135*, 36–69.

Mayer, R. E. (Ed.). (2005). *The Cambridge handbook of multimedia learning*. New York: Cambridge University Press.

McCardle, L., Miller, M., Gendron, A., Helm, S., Hadwin, A., & Webster, E. (2010). *Regulation of motivation: Exploring the link between students' goals for motivational state and strategy choice in university tasks*. Paper presented at the annual meeting of the Canadian Society for the Study of Education. Montreal, QC.

Miller, M. F. W. (2009). *Predicting university students' performance on a complex task: Does task understanding moderate the influence of self-efficacy?* Unpublished Master's thesis. University of Victoria, Victoria, BC, Canada.

Miller, M. F. W., & Hadwin, A. F. (2010). *Supporting university success: Examining the influence of explicit and implicit task understanding and self-efficacy on academic performance*. Paper presented at the Annual meeting of the Canadian Society for the Study of Education, Montreal, QC.

Nist, S., & Holschuh, J. (2000). Comprehension strategies at the college level. In R. F. Flippo & D. C. Caverly (Eds.), *Handbook of college reading and study strategy research* (pp. 75–104). Mahwah, NJ: Lawrence Erlbaum Associates.

Oshige, M. (2009). *Exploring task understanding in self-regulated learning: Task understanding as a predictor of academic success in undergraduate students*. Unpublished Master's thesis. University of Victoria, Victoria, BC, Canada.

Pressley, M., Yokoi, L., van Meter, P., Van Etten, S., & Freebern, G. (1997). Some of the reasons preparing for exams is so hard: What can be done to make it easier? *Educational Psychology Review, 9*, 1–38.

Thomas, A. K., & McDaniel, M. A. (2007). Metacomprehension for educationally relevant materials: Dramatic effects of encoding-retrieval interactions. *Psychonomic Bulletin & Review, 14*, 212–218.

Webster, E., Helm, S., Hadwin, A. F., Gendron, A., & Miller, M. (2010). *Academic goals and self-regulated learning: An analysis of changes in goal quality, goal efficacy, and goal attainment over time.* Poster presented at the Annual Meeting of the American Educational Research Association, Denver, CO.

Winne, P. H. (1982). Minimizing the black box problem to enhance the validity of theories about instructional effects. *Instructional Science, 11*, 13–28.

Winne, P. H. (1997). Experimenting to bootstrap self-regulated learning. *Journal of Educational Psychology, 89*, 397–410.

Winne, P. H. (2006). How software technologies can improve research on learning and bolster school reform. *Educational Psychologist, 41*, 5–17.

Winne, P. H. (2010a). Improving measurements of self-regulated learning. *Educational Psychologist, 45*, 267–276.

Winne, P. H. (2010b). Bootstrapping learner's self-regulated learning. *Psychological Test and Assessment Modeling, 52*, 472–490.

Winne, P. H. (2011). A cognitive and metacognitive analysis of self-regulated learning. In B. J. Zimmerman & D. H. Schunk (Eds.), *Handbook of self-regulation of learning and performance* (pp. 15–32). New York: Routledge.

Winne, P. H., & Hadwin, A. F. (1998). Studying as self-regulated learning. In D. J. Hacker, J. Dunlosky, & A. C. Graesser (Eds.), *Metacognition in educational theory and practice* (pp. 277–304). Mahwah, NJ: Lawrence Erlbaum Associates.

Winne, P. H., Hadwin, A. F., & Beaudoin, L. P. (2010). *nStudy: A web application for researching and promoting self-regulated learning (version 2.0) [computer program]*. Burnaby, BC, Canada: Simon Fraser University.

Winne, P. H., Hadwin, A. F., & Perry, N. E. (2013). Metacognition and computer-supported collaborative learning. In C. Hmelo-Silver, A. O'Donnell, C. Chan & C. Chinn (Eds.), *International handbook of collaborative learning* (pp. 462–479). New York: Taylor & Francis.

Winne, P. H., & Jamieson-Noel, D. L. (2002). Exploring students' calibration of self-reports about study tactics and achievement. *Contemporary Educational Psychology, 27*, 551–572.

Winne, P. H., Jamieson-Noel, D. L., & Muis, K. (2002). Methodological issues and advances in researching tactics, strategies, and self-regulated learning. In P. R. Pintrich & M. L. Maehr (Eds.), *Advances in motivation and achievement: New directions in measures and methods* (Vol. 12, pp. 121–155). Greenwich, CT: JAI Press.

Winne, P. H., & Marx, R. W. (1989). A cognitive processing analysis of motivation within classroom tasks. In C. Ames & R. Ames (Eds.), *Research on motivation in education* (Vol. 3, pp. 223–257). Orlando, FL: Academic.

Winne, P. H., & Perry, N. E. (2000). Measuring self-regulated learning. In M. Boekaerts, P. Pintrich, & M. Zeidner (Eds.), *Handbook of self-regulation* (pp. 531–566). Orlando, FL: Academic.

Winne, P. H., Zhou, M., & Egan, R. (2010). Assessing self-regulated learning skills. In G. Schraw (Ed.), *Assessment of higher-order thinking skills*. New York: Routledge.

Wittrock, M. C. (2010). Learning as a generative process. *Educational Psychologist, 45*, 40–45.

Zimmerman, B. J. (2008). Investigating self-regulation and motivation: Historical background, methodological developments, and future prospects. *American Educational Research Journal, 45*, 166–183.

Part IV

Intelligent Tutoring Systems and Tutorial Dialogues Systems

21 Help Seeking and Intelligent Tutoring Systems: Theoretical Perspectives and a Step Towards Theoretical Integration

Vincent Aleven

Abstract

Help seeking is a strategy highlighted in a number of theories of self-regulated learning (SRL). We focus on the help-seeking behavior of students during tutored problem solving with an intelligent tutoring system (ITS), specifically, the Geometry Cognitive Tutor. ITSs are an advanced type of computer-based learning environment (CBLE) and are in widespread use. These systems typically provide step-by-step guidance with complex problems, including on-demand help. A number of theories shed light on how on-demand help focused on problem-solving principles can help students acquire robust knowledge (i.e., knowledge that transfers to novel situations, lasts over time, and may facilitate future learning), but they also highlight challenges students face in doing so. These theories include the ACTR theory of cognition and learning, the Knowledge-Learning-Instruction theoretical framework focused on learning from instruction, SRL theories, and educational psychology theories of help seeking. Given the variety of perspectives, we see a strong need for theoretical integration. As a modest first step, we review our own work on rule-based modeling of help seeking, which integrates cognitive and metacognitive aspects within a single modeling framework.

Help seeking is a key self-regulatory skill, highlighted in a number of theoretical models of self-regulated learning (e.g., Pintrich, 2004; Zimmerman, 2011). In the educational psychology literature, help seeking is often viewed as an important strategy that helps learners progress on their path to independent competence in a domain (e.g., Karabenick & Newman, 2006; Newman, 2008; Zusho, Karabenick, Bonney, & Sims, 2007). In this chapter, we focus on help seeking with a particular type of advanced learning technologies, namely, intelligent tutoring systems (ITSs) (Nkambou, Bourdeau, & Mizoguchi, 2010; VanLehn, 2006; Woolf, 2009). These systems are starting to be widely used in the US, especially, Cognitive Tutors, a type of ITS grounded in cognitive theory and cognitive modeling (e.g., Aleven,

V. Aleven (✉)
Human-Computer Interaction Institute,
Carnegie Mellon University, 5000 Forbes Avenue,
Pittsburgh, PA 15213, USA
e-mail: aleven@cs.cmu.edu

R. Azevedo and V. Aleven (eds.), *International Handbook of Metacognition and Learning Technologies*,
Springer International Handbooks of Education 26, DOI 10.1007/978-1-4419-5546-3_21,

2010; Anderson, Corbett, Koedinger, & Pelletier, 1995; Corbett, Kauffman, MacLaren, Wagner, & Jones, 2010; Koedinger & Aleven, 2007; Koedinger & Corbett, 2006; Ritter, Kulikowich, Lei, McGuire, & Morgan, 2007). They support learners in acquiring complex cognitive skills and understanding. Typically, ITSs provide step-by-step help and feedback during problem-solving practice. Our focus is on learner's use of *on-demand help* offered by these systems, explanatory help messages provided at the learner's request. These messages state how to proceed with the problem at hand and typically explain that advice with reference to key problem-solving principles of the domain (e.g., geometry theorems). There is evidence that this form of help can be an important influence on learning from tutored problem solving, but there is also substantial evidence that this promise is often not met (e.g., Aleven, Stahl, Schworm, Fischer, & Wallace, 2003). In particular, using on-demand help effectively is challenging for low prior knowledge students (i.e., those who, objectively speaking, would appear to need help the most) (Wood & Wood, 1999).

We define help seeking as episodes in which a learner, in the context of a specific learning activity (e.g., studying a worked example, solving a problem, or learning a complex concept in a hypermedia environment) takes the initiative to seek assistance from a source within or outside of the learning environment, as opposed to persisting at trying to make progress independently. The external source may be a human being (e.g., a peer learner, teacher, or tutor), it may be a source on a computer or on the Internet, or it may be a book, manual, or reference work. For example, a student may request a context-specific help message from an ITS or pedagogical agent, may use Google or Wikipedia to gather information they need to learn, or may post a question or request for help to an online forum, web-based group, or web-based tutoring service. Our notion of help seeking includes searching online for instructional explanations or instructional materials (e.g., short instructional videos such as those found on YouTube or the Khan Academy website[1]). As discussed further below, help seeking, when done judiciously, can be an adaptive strategy. Not only can it help learners in completing a learning task, more importantly, it can also help them learn more from a task than would they have without help. Not all forms of seeking help are adaptive, however. For instance, seeking help aimed too strongly at getting through problems without regard for understanding, often dubbed "executive" help seeking (e.g., Nelson-Le Gall, 1985), can be detrimental to learning. Below we discuss different forms of maladaptive help seeking, for which we prefer to use the term help abuse (Aleven, McLaren, Roll, & Koedinger, 2006). Not seeking help can be maladaptive as well under certain circumstances (help avoidance).

Often, the impetus to seek help is that the learner realizes that they are not succeeding in or not likely to succeed in a given learning task or in specific aspects of a given learning task (e.g., a particular step within a practice problem they are attempting to solve). This realization may be the result of the learner's monitoring of whether they have the requisite knowledge or skills, either as they size up task demands at the beginning of the task or as they progress through the task. The impetus can also be feedback from the learning environment. For example, an ITS may give feedback that the learner's attempt at solving a step in a problem is not correct. As a result, the learner may be aware that she does not have the requisite understanding to successfully complete the step, especially if they have repeatedly attempted it and not been able to get it right. Additionally, some help-seeking episodes are preplanned, such as planning to make a certain amount of progress on a homework assignment and then go to an instructor's office hours. Even though these episodes are preplanned, the specific content targeted in these preplanned help-seeking episodes can be based on self-monitoring (e.g., if the learner kept a list of questions to ask).

Help seeking involves metacognition for a number of reasons. It involves both metacognitive monitoring and control, key components of metacognition (e.g., Brown, 1987; Flavell, 1979). First, as discussed, help-seeking episodes are often (though not always) triggered by metacognitive monitoring. Learners often seek help because they realize they lack the knowledge to

[1] http://www.khanacademy.org/

succeed on their own. As they size up the task demands prior to actually executing a learning task, they may realize that the task is unfamiliar or that they do not know how to solve it. In addition, they may monitor their cognitive activity in the process of solving the task and realize that they are not on track or may not have the knowledge to succeed. The metacognitive judgment that triggers help seeking may or may not be accurate—a student may underestimate her ability to solve the task independently and seek help even though—objectively—the help is unnecessary (see e.g., Nelson-Le Gall, Kratzer, Jones, & DeCooke, 1990). Conversely, a student may underestimate their need for help. Second, when the decision to seek help is based on metacognitive judgment, we view the act of seeking help as an exercise of metacognitive control: The learner changes course within a learning task (e.g., switches from solving a problem to reading relevant background material or hints), in order to increase its effectiveness or efficiency. A third reason is that learners, as they process the help received, need to make further metacognitive judgments. Depending on their goals, they need to decide whether the help received fills their perceived knowledge gap or helps them become "unstuck" in the learning activity. This judgment is often a judgment of learning (JOL) (e.g., Dunlosky & Metcalfe, 2008), as the learner judges her understanding of new information. One way in which they may do so is by self-explaining the help received (Aleven & Koedinger, 2002; Chi, 2000; McNamara & Magliano, 2009). When used to monitor one's understanding, self-explanation is often viewed as metacognitive in nature (Renkl, Berthold, Grosse, & Schwonke, 2013).

ITSs are an attractive platform to study relations between help seeking and learning and more generally between metacognition and learning (e.g., Aleven & Koedinger, 2000; Wood & Wood, 1999). First, understanding how help and help seeking influence learning with ITSs is of substantial practical importance, because these types of systems are used widely. For example, at the time of this writing, Cognitive Tutors (Anderson et al., 1995; Koedinger & Aleven, 2007; Koedinger & Corbett, 2006) are being used in approximately 2,750 US schools as part of mathematics curricula. A welcome "side effect" of this widespread use is that research in this area can often be carried out in real educational settings, as part of the regular instruction. Second, ITSs support a common kind of learning activity (problem solving) and provide a common kind of help, namely, principle-based hints, a form of instructional explanations (Wittwer & Renkl, 2008). Thus, help seeking with ITSs is representative of a wide class of learning behaviors, even if it has some unique properties. For example, in ITSs, the help content is tailored to the specific problem step and problem-solving strategy taken so far, which is not so for many forms of help (e.g., Wikipedia). Further, the process of seeking and receiving help from an ITS is characterized by an intermediate level of interactivity, compared to alternatives (e.g., less back-and-forth between the help giver and the help receiver than in human face-to-face dialogue but as much or more back-and-forth than when posing questions in an online forum or looking up information in reference works such as Wikipedia). A third reason that ITSs are an appropriate platform for investigating help seeking and SRL more generally is that while ITSs are designed to make learning as efficient and effective as possible and provide a considerable amount of external regulation, they leave important self-regulatory choices to learners. Evidence is mounting that the way learners regulate their learning activities with these systems strongly influences the learning outcomes they attain, including the way they use a system's help facilities (e.g., Koedinger, Aleven, Roll, & Baker, 2009). In other words, it is becoming increasingly clear that self-regulation, including help seeking, is an important influence on students' learning results with these systems. Fourth, a methodological advantage of using ITSs is that they produce log data, detailing the interactions that learners have with these systems. These data can be mined to yield insight into the effective and ineffective help-seeking behaviors that learners exhibit, as well as their relation with learning. We use an open access facility called *DataShop* (Koedinger et al., 2011; Koedinger, Cunningham, Skogsholm, & Leber, 2008; Stamper, Koedinger, et al., 2011) that greatly facilitates this kind of analysis. Use of log data has long been a staple of both ITSs research (e.g., Anderson, Conrad, & Corbett, 1989) and SRL research (Hadwin, Nesbit, Jamieson-Noel, Code, & Winne, 2007; Winne, 2010; Zimmerman, 2008) and is compatible with recent emphasis on event-based approaches to studying SRL (e.g., Azevedo, Moos, Johnson, & Chauncey, 2010). For instance, Aleven and Koedinger (2000) and Shih, Koedinger, and Scheines (2008) conducted analyses of students' help-seeking behavior based on log data from an ITS.

The line of work discussed in this chapter differs from most other work on metacognition in computer-based learning environments (CBLEs) with respect both to the type of learning activities and the nature of the support that the learning environment provides. In ITSs, the main student activity is problem-solving practice. Much other work focuses on conceptual learning in ill-structured domains with open-ended CBLEs such as multimedia, hypertext, hypermedia, or textual materials. Further, in ITSs, the tutor provides step-by-step guidance, such as detailed feedback and, upon the student's request, advice on what to do next. In most hypermedia systems (e.g., Azevedo & Jacobson, 2008; Chen, 2002; Jacobson, 2008; Jacobson & Archodidou, 2000), by contrast, there is no tutor that provides guidance and there is no feedback on learning activities. It may be that hypermedia environments provide greater scope for student self-regulation to occur and influence learning than ITSs do and may involve many metacognitive monitoring and control strategies that are not prevalent in learning with ITSs (e.g., Azevedo & Witherspoon, 2009). However, even in ITSs, there is significant scope for self-regulation to impact students' robust learning outcomes (i.e., knowledge that transfers to novel situations, lasts over time, and may facilitate future learning; Koedinger, Corbett, & Perfetti, 2012). Help seeking is one way. Interestingly, recent work on adding tutoring to hypermedia environments (Azevedo et al., 2013; Azevedo, Johnson, Chauncey, & Graesser, 2011) aims to combine the strengths of the two types of learning environments.

In this chapter, we focus on theory. Research on help seeking with ITSs is grounded in a number of different theoretical frameworks. First, from their earliest beginnings, Cognitive Tutors have been grounded in the ACT-R theory of cognition and learning (Anderson, 1993; Anderson & Lebière, 1998). Anderson (1993) discussed help seeking from the perspective of ACT-R. Second, we look at help seeking from the perspective of the KLI framework (knowledge, learning, instruction), a recent theoretical framework focused on how instruction in academic domains can bring about robust learning (Koedinger et al., 2012). While ACT-R and KLI are primarily cognitive theories, it is important also to look at help seeking from the perspective of metacognition and SRL theoretical frameworks (e.g., Pintrich, 2004; Zimmerman, 2000); these cyclical frameworks tend to view help seeking as one of a large set of strategies learners use to regulate their own learning. Third, researchers in developmental and educational psychology have looked at the role of help seeking in child development and academic learning (e.g., Nelson-Le Gall, 1985; Karabenick & Newman, 2006). These three theoretical perspectives on help seeking each have complementary strengths but have largely been separate. One of our key points in this chapter is that this separation is an undesirable state of affairs and that much is to be won by greater theoretical integration.

We start the chapter with a very brief overview of ITSs, illustrating the kind of principle-based on-demand help they provide to learners, as well as the other ways in which they guide learners during complex problem solving. Next, we look at help seeking within ITSs from the perspective of the three research traditions mentioned above, cognitive, SRL, and educational psychology. We discuss how these theories provide complementary perspectives on the use of principle-based help during problem solving. We believe much would be won by moving towards theoretical integration and briefly discuss advantages of doing so. Finally, we present a modest first step towards integration of the theoretical frameworks:

We look at our own work in modeling help seeking using a production rule formalism from the viewpoint of theoretical integration.

Intelligent Tutoring Systems and Help Seeking

ITSs are systems that support learners as they learn a complex cognitive skill through problem-solving practice. ITSs have effectively supported learners in a variety of domains such as mathematics (Aleven & Koedinger, 2002; Anderson et al., 1995; Beal, Walles, Arroyo, & Woolf, 2007), chemistry (McLaren, DeLeeuw, & Mayer, 2011), physics (VanLehn et al., 2005), basic computer programming (Anderson et al., 1989; Mitrovic, Martin, & Mayo, 2002), and logic (Scheines & Sieg, 1994; Stamper, Barnes, & Croy, 2012; Stamper, Eagle, Barnes, & Croy, 2011). ITSs started out in research labs but have successfully made the transition into regular, real-world use (Koedinger, Anderson, Hadley, & Mark, 1997; Mitrovic, Martin, & Mayo, 2002). A wide range of evaluation studies indicate that curricula that include ITSs enhance student learning, compared to more typical forms of school instruction (e.g., Koedinger & Aleven, 2007; Koedinger et al., 1997; Ritter et al., 2007; VanLehn, 2011; but see Campuzano, Dynarski, Agodini, & Rall, 2009).

Typically, ITSs provide a user interface in which the problem is broken down into steps and provide guidance with respect to these steps, not just with respect to final problem solutions (e.g., VanLehn, 2006). This step-by-step guidance includes feedback on whether each step is correct as well as on-demand hints. The step-by-step nature of the guidance is a key reason for the effectiveness of ITSs, compared to simpler systems (often called CAI or CBT systems) that provide guidance only at the end of problems, but do not provide guidance with respect to solution steps. VanLehn's (2011) meta-review indicates that the effectiveness of ITSs (defined as systems that provide guidance at the step level) over classroom instruction is greater than that of systems that provide guidance at the end of each problem only (effect size of $d=0.76$ and $d=0.3$, respectively, in VanLehn's analysis). Step-level feedback, a key aspect of the step-by-step guidance that ITSs offer, has been shown to be very effective (e.g., Corbett & Anderson, 2001), but may not—by itself—fully account for the effectiveness of ITSs. In VanLehn's (2006) words, "A tutoring system that gives minimal feedback [i.e., feedback on the correctness of steps, without further explanation] should also have the ability to hint next steps. … With minimal feedback but no next-step hints, students often guess repeatedly then give up in frustration."

We focus on Cognitive Tutors, a particular type of ITSs illustrated in Fig. 21.1. In the unit illustrated in Fig. 21.1, the student learns to employ various theorems related to triangles to solve geometry problems. Given a diagram, her task is to find an unknown angle measure in the diagram, which often requires multiple steps, each involving application of one or more theorems. As the student works through the problem step-by-step, the tutor provides guidance in the form of feedback and hints.

Cognitive Tutors share all the characteristics of ITSs described above and are characterized additionally by a strong grounding in cognitive theory, cognitive task analysis, and cognitive modeling. Cognitive Tutors interpret student problem-solving behavior with respect to a rule-based cognitive model that captures the targeted cognitive skill. In essence, the model is capable of solving the tasks in the various ways that it would be reasonable for students to solve them. Further, Cognitive Tutors track individual learners' knowledge growth over time, using a Bayesian knowledge-tracing algorithm to calculate probabilities that each individual learner masters each of the targeted skills captured in the cognitive model (Corbett & Anderson, 1995). Based on this assessment of a learner's skill, they select problems that address each learner's specific difficulties. This method for individual problem selection has been shown to have a substantial positive influence on student learning, compared to fixed problem sets (e.g., Corbett, McLaughlin, & Scarpinatto, 2000).

In this chapter, we focus on one form of step-level guidance that many ITSs offer, namely,

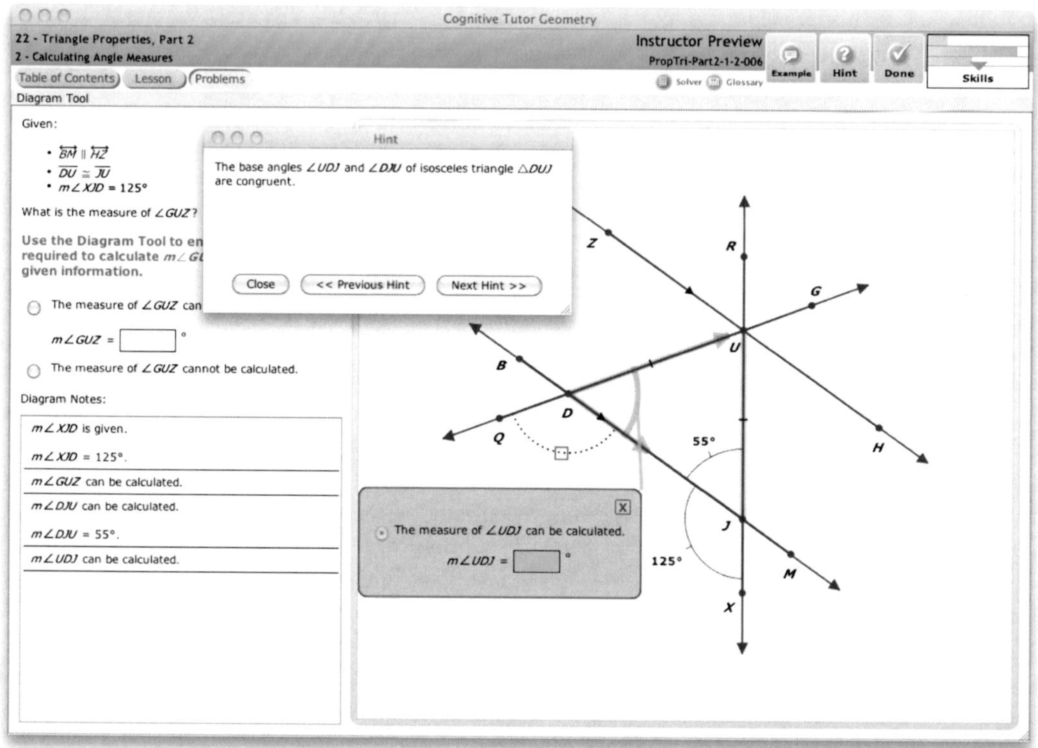

Fig. 21.1 The Geometry Cognitive Tutor served as platform for our research on help seeking in ITSs (e.g., Aleven & Koedinger, 2000). This figure shows the current version

on-demand, context-sensitive hints. As mentioned, ITSs provide a substantial amount of external regulation, but on-demand help is one area in which they leave substantial room for self-regulation. Students can typically request hints at any time as they are working through a problem. Therefore, as they work with the tutor, they continuously face the (metacognitive) decision whether to seek help from the tutor or whether to continue to try to solve the problem independently. In the Geometry Cognitive Tutor, for example, they can click the button marked "Hint" at the top right (see Fig. 21.1). The tutor's hints provide advice with respect to the next step, in a manner that is sensitive to the particular solution path taken so far by the student. Typically, multiple hint levels are available, with more general hints preceding more specific ones. In the Geometry Cognitive Tutor, hints may provide advice as to what angle to work on next. For example, the hints for the next angle to work on in Fig. 21.1 are:

1. Given the information you currently have, which angle should you select next?
2. You know $m\angle DJU$. Which angle does that help you calculate?
3. Given that you know $m\angle DJU$, you can calculate $\angle UDJ$ due to **Isosceles Triangle Base Angles**. Select $\angle UDJ$.

Once the student has selected an angle to work on, the tutor (upon the student's request) gives hints for calculating the measure of the selected angle, for example (for the angle worked on in Fig. 21.1):

1. Enter the measure of $\angle UDJ$.
2. The base angles $\angle UDJ$ and $\angle DJU$ of isosceles triangle ΔDUJ are congruent.
3. Enter 55.

As illustrated in these hint sequences, hints often justify the next step in terms of one or more domain-specific problem-solving principles (e.g., geometry theorems). In doing so, they may map the principle to the step (i.e., explain *how* it applies).

The last hint, often referred to as the "bottom-out hint," often gives the solution to the step. In many ITSs, the student has full control over which hint levels they see, although there are some notable exceptions (e.g., Wood & Wood, 1999).

We emphasize that our conception of next-step hints pertains exclusively to messages about what is to be done next and does not encompass feedback on what the student has done so far. Further, we focus on hints requested by the student, not on hints volunteered by the system. Thus, from a metacognitive perspective, we focus on situations where students are likely to exercise metacognitive monitoring and metacognitive control as they are aided by an ITS. Where we go outside of this focus, we say so explicitly.

Empirical Research on Help Seeking with ITSs

Researchers in the field of ITS have studied relations between students' help-seeking behavior and their learning outcomes. Overall, this literature paints a complicated picture. It indicates that deliberate use of on-demand help tends to be associated with better learning outcomes, but much depends on how students use hints, and students often do not use hints effectively. Some recent educational data mining studies even suggest that students are generally better off trying to solve the steps in tutor problems rather than asking for help. (This finding is likely to be specific to problem-solving activities with immediate feedback.) Although a number of experimental studies showed or suggested that on-demand help can have a positive effect on student learning, a rigorous, definitive demonstration that on-demand principle-based hints offered by an ITS help students learn better is still lacking. Overall, a fair interpretation of this literature is that on-demand principle-based help, when used properly, does help students obtain better learning outcomes, but learning from principle-based explanations is harder for students than commonly thought (see also Wittwer & Renkl, 2008). The literature suggests further that providing answers in bottom-out hints, as many Cognitive Tutors and other ITSs do, may not just help students get through problems without being stuck for prolonged periods of time but may also help them learn, as the bottom-out hints essentially turn the open problem step into a worked example for the student to study and, ideally, to self-explain.

To expand slightly on this brief summary, a number of studies have established positive correlations between students' use of help and their learning outcomes. In what was likely the earliest reported study on help seeking and tutoring systems, Wood and Wood (1999), found a positive correlation between students' tendency to seek help (frequency of help use, relative to the number of errors they make) and their learning outcomes. This correlation was significant for students with lower prior knowledge, suggesting that help seeking is especially important for those coming in with low prior knowledge. Beck, Chang, Mostow, and Corbett (2008), using a variety of educational data mining techniques, also found positive relations between help seeking and learning with an ITS for reading for elementary school students, although these relations were significant for only one of three methods used. The help provided by their ITS pertained to the pronunciation of written words and was therefore different from the principle-based help that many ITSs provide. Luckin and Hammerton (2002) conducted a study with an ITS based on Vygotskian principles and found that students with above-average learning gains tended to seek more and deeper help than students with below-average learning gains. As discussed further below, in our own work with the Geometry Cognitive Tutor (e.g., Aleven, McLaren, & Koedinger, 2006), we found negative correlations between the *raw* frequency of help use and students' learning gains, but we found positive relations when we used a model of effective help seeking to distinguish between forms of help seeking expected to be productive versus not productive.

This latter result suggests that much depends on how students use the on-demand help facilities of an ITS. Other studies have had similar findings. Recent educational data mining research with tutor log data from the Geometry Cognitive Tutor found that the amount of time students spend with bottom-out hints (as mentioned, the bottom-out hint is the last hint level in the sequence for any given step and basically gives the answer) is associated with greater learning gains (Shih, Koedinger, & Scheines, 2008). One interpretation of this finding is that some students spontaneously self-explain bottom-out hints as if they were a step in a worked-out example problem, and those who do come away with better learning results. The Shih et al. study leaves unaddressed the question of whether self-explaining earlier hint levels, which as mentioned provide principle-based explanations of problem steps, can be effective over and above self-explaining bottom-out hints. Other recent research with the Geometry Cognitive Tutor found that deliberate hint use may mediate the effect on learning of an intervention aimed at supporting periodic self-assessment of problem-solving skill, especially for lower prior knowledge students (Long & Aleven, 2012). In this study, students who periodically filled out off-line paper "skill diaries" used the tutor's hints more deliberately and had better learning results. The more deliberate hint use was manifested in fewer hint requests, but more time per hint, suggesting that students got more out of the hints that they studied, perhaps due to more deliberate use. More generally, these studies demonstrate an association between how students use hints and their learning outcomes, suggesting that self-regulation influences how students learn with ITSs. Perhaps the deliberateness of student help seeking will emerge as an interesting behavioral indicator of student self-regulation with ITSs.

On the other hand, our research with the Geometry Cognitive Tutor has found that students' help use is often less than ideal. Students often "abuse" hints to find answers without understanding and at other times, avoid requesting help even after they have made multiple errors on a step (Aleven & Koedinger, 2000; Aleven et al., 2006; see also Aleven et al., 2003). Perhaps it should come as no surprise then that some studies are finding that trying steps (with feedback from the ITS) may help students' learn more than providing hints (e.g., Roll, Baker, Aleven, & Koedinger, under review; Shih, Koedinger, & Scheines, 2010), suggesting that students need better support in learning from hints.

We know of no study that rigorously established that the provision of principle-based on-demand hints *causes* students working with an ITS to learn better. Establishing such a conclusion would require an experimental study comparing two (or more) versions of an ITS, one with principle-based on-demand hints and one without, in which the condition with hints had more robust learning outcomes (or greater learning efficiency). A few studies came very close to providing such a demonstration. First, a study by Anderson, Conrad, and Corbett (1989) with the Lisp Cognitive Tutor demonstrated that explanatory messages from an ITS, both hints and feedback, can lead to more efficient learning compared to "minimal messages." However, the study falls short of definitively establishing a causal connection between *on-demand* principle-based hints and learning because, between the two conditions, the study varied not only the hint content but also the content of system-initiated feedback messages. Thus, it is possible that the greater learning efficiency is due solely to the system's feedback messages; system-initiated feedback messages however may involve different metacognitive monitoring and control strategies than the use on-demand help. Second, a study by Stamper et al. (2011) with an ITS for logic proof found that when on-demand hints were available, students attempted and completed more problems and had improved learning outcomes than when on-demand hints were not available (and the system provided correctness feedback only). Thus, the study suggests a causal relation between the availability of hints and learning, but it falls short of being a definitive confirmation, as it was not a true experimental study.

Overall, the empirical record provides some tantalizing evidence to suggest that the provision of help on demand, and students' help seeking, can influence learning in a positive way but also underlines that learning from on-demand, principle-based help, as currently supported in ITSs, is challenging for students. With that background, let us now turn to theoretical perspectives.

Theoretical Perspectives on Help Seeking

As mentioned, research on help seeking in ITSs relates to a number of theoretical perspectives, so many in fact that it is difficult to review all of them in sufficient depth in a single chapter. We look at three relevant strands of theory: cognitive theories, theories of self-regulated learning (SRL), and models of help seeking put forward by educational psychology researchers. In the current section, we highlight the complementary perspectives that these theories provide.

Cognitive Perspective

We start with a cognitive perspective, by reviewing the ACT-R perspective on the role of next-step hints in the context of tutored problem solving (e.g., Anderson, 1993). As we will see, this theory addresses cognitive aspects without much (if any) reference to metacognition. The ACT-R theory of cognition and learning has long been a theoretical foundation for Cognitive Tutors, which as mentioned are a widely used type of ITS. We believe, however, that the same theoretical underpinnings also pertain to other types of ITSs. ACT-R stipulates that expertise within a particular task domain requires the acquisition of two different types of interrelated knowledge, with different psychological properties, namely, declarative and procedural knowledge. Under ACT-R, declarative knowledge is knowing *that* and procedural knowledge is knowing *how*. Declarative knowledge can be encoded "more or less directly" from instruction (Anderson et al., 1995). It is verbalizable (typically) and is flexible: A given declarative knowledge "chunk" can be applied in different ways towards specific goals (e.g., goals or subgoals in problem-solving tasks), provided that appropriate interpretive procedures are available. In many domains (e.g., geometry), a key form of declarative knowledge is knowledge of the relevant problem-solving principles. This kind of knowledge enables a learner to state a given principle and to consciously reason about various aspects of it, such as its rationale, whether it applies in a given problem situation, what additional information may need to be calculated first in order for it to be applicable, and so on.

Procedural knowledge, by contrast, is efficient and goal specific. This kind of knowledge is evident in the fluent execution of a well-practiced skill. For example, in the domain of geometry, procedural knowledge enables experts to quickly recognize how to solve the next step in a geometry problem, without having to search through their declarative knowledge of problem-solving principles. Procedural knowledge is not verbalizable[2] and not open to conscious introspection. It is acquired through practice.

Prior theory about ITSs based on ACT-R has emphasized procedural learning through problem-solving practice. Under ACT-R, procedural knowledge is viewed as being composed of small units called production rules. The (many) production rules that make up a complex cognitive skill can be learned independently and strengthened through practice. Steps in Cognitive Tutor problems are viewed as opportunities to acquire or strengthen specific production rules. Using its cognitive model, a Cognitive Tutor interprets students' performance and tracks each individual student's knowledge growth in terms of production rules. The production rules in the model are presumed to be an accurate representation of the knowledge acquired by students. That is, the model is assumed to have psychological fidelity (e.g., Aleven, 2010).

Despite the emphasis on procedural knowledge, it is important not to lose sight of the role of

[2] If procedural knowledge cannot be verbalized, how it is that people can explain procedures? When people explain a procedure, they either draw on declarative knowledge of the procedure rather than the actual procedural knowledge itself, or, if they explain the procedure while actually carrying it out, they may be verbalizing the *products* of the procedure (i.e., goals and intermediate results produced in working memory) rather than their procedural knowledge. If in the latter context they explicate the conditions under which specific steps in the procedure are appropriate, it is likely that they are reconstructing these conditions on the fly, for example, by generalizing from the task that they are demonstrating.

declarative knowledge in expertise and skill acquisition. First, acquiring declarative knowledge is often an important instructional goal in itself. The most flexible forms of expertise in a given domain usually consist of a mix of procedural and declarative knowledge, given the complementary strengths of each type of knowledge (e.g., Aleven & Koedinger, 2002; Anderson et al., 1995; Bransford, Brown, & Cocking, 2000; Hatano & Inagaki, 1986; Kilpatrick, Swafford, & Findell, 2001; Ma, 1999). Second, under ACT-R, declarative knowledge can help in the development of robust procedural knowledge. Procedural knowledge components are sometimes (but by no means exclusively) derived from application, to specific problem-solving goals, of declarative knowledge, such as declarative encodings of examples or instructional explanations of problem-solving principles. For example, in the absence of specific procedural knowledge related to a particular problem-solving (sub)goal, declaratively encoded examples may be applied in an analogical manner during problem solving.

Help seeking and metacognition are not addressed in ACT-R proper, but (to a degree) help seeking is addressed in a set of eight "Cognitive Tutor principles" that have been distilled from the experience of applying ACT-R to the design of ITSs (Anderson et al., 1995; Koedinger & Corbett, 2006). These principles provide practical guidelines for the design of ITSs, compatible with ACT-R. The principle most relevant to help seeking is principle #4: *Promote an abstract understanding of the problem-solving knowledge.* Anderson et al. (1995, p. 180) note that students often encode problem-solving examples in an overly specific manner, without suitably abstracting them, leading to the acquisition of overly specific procedural knowledge (and failure to achieve even near transfer). They suggest that the use of (suitably) abstract language in hint and error messages can aid in the acquisition of appropriately contextualized procedural knowledge (i.e., procedural knowledge that is appropriately general but not overgeneral), although they do not provide further information about how to construct effective help messages.

Under ACT-R, then, the main function of principle-based hints in ITSs is to help students acquire relevant declarative knowledge, both because this knowledge is a useful component of expertise in the given domain and because it can guide the acquisition of robust (appropriately contextualized) procedural knowledge. In particular, it may help avoid acquisition of overly narrow/specific procedural knowledge. We do not mean to imply that declarative knowledge should always be acquired first (e.g., Rittle-Johnson, Siegler, & Alibali, 2001), nor that it is always necessary. A further role for hints is to reduce floundering during problem solving (i.e., searching for a solution step without having sufficient knowledge to find it). ACT-R predicts no advantage for searching unsuccessfully for problem steps (Anderson, 1993). Avoiding floundering may make learning more efficient, and it may help to prevent frustration on the part of students (cf. VanLehn, 2006, quoted above).[3]

A second theoretical framework, the knowledge-learning-instruction (KLI) framework (Koedinger et al., 2012), highlights an aspect of learning from tutor hints that has not received much attention in theorizing about ITSs based on ACT-R. Under KLI, it becomes clear that understanding problem-solving principles, conveyed through instructional explanations or tutor hints, requires sense-making processes (defined below) that pose a significant challenge to students.

The KLI framework, like ACT-R, is primarily cognitive in nature and does not (currently) address metacognition explicitly. It addresses robust learning in academic domains but, unlike ACT-R proper, is concerned with how *instruction* can support robust learning. As mentioned, in the KLI framework, robust learning is defined as

[3] From a metacognitive perspective, this stance may be too extreme. Allowing students to explore *some* suboptimal solution paths to limited depth may help them develop metacognitive awareness and skill, such as skill at answer checking, error detection, and error correction (e.g., Koedinger et al., 2009; Mathan & Koedinger, 2005). However, the conditions under which allowing such limited exploration is more productive than providing immediate feedback are very poorly understood. This issue is beyond the scope of this chapter.

learning that lasts, transfers to new situations, and facilitates future learning, typical desired outcomes of instruction. In addition, KLI makes a distinction between verbal and nonverbal knowledge, somewhat akin to ACT-R's distinction between declarative and procedural knowledge. KLI recognizes three main categories of learning mechanisms:

1. *Sense making* (verbal processes in which students reason, make inferences, construct explanations and arguments, and so on)
2. *Induction and refinement* (nonverbal processes in which students refine the applicability conditions of knowledge; KLI assumes a wide variety of induction/refinement mechanisms, many of them well known from the cognitive science literature, such as perceptual chunking, rule or schema induction, and analogy)
3. *Fluency and memory building* (nonverbal processes such as memory strengthening and knowledge compilation, by which knowledge, as it is used repeatedly, is proceduralized and its execution becomes fast and effortless)

The KLI framers stipulate that a single mechanism by itself will rarely support fully robust learning in a domain (such as geometry) with complex knowledge components. KLI also provides a taxonomy of instructional principles that links principles and the three categories of learning mechanisms presented above. This set is much broader than the set of Cognitive Tutor principles grounded in ACT-R, and discussed above (Anderson et al., 1995) and is not focused on ITSs per se. It does not currently include any principles related specifically to help seeking however, so let us now consider how the KLI framework helps us understand the use of on-demand help in the context of tutored problem solving.

In the KLI framework, problem-solving practice (such as that supported by ITSs) primarily involves two of the three KLI learning mechanisms: refinement/induction of nonverbal knowledge as well as fluency and memory-building processes. During the initial phase of practice in a novel domain, a student is likely to make errors, forcing him or her to refine/induce the applicability conditions of the relevant nonverbal knowledge components (the KLI definition of induction/refinement). Through the use of these mechanisms, the learner may eventually reach a phase in which her performance is highly accurate, and the main effect of further practice is faster, more accurate performance (the KLI definition of fluency building). Under KLI, refinement/induction processes and fluency-building processes primarily affect nonverbal (procedural) knowledge and have little or no influence on the acquisition of verbal knowledge. In many domains, however, learners also need to acquire verbal conceptual knowledge of key problem-solving principles. This type of knowledge has two key roles: It is an important component of expertise in its own right in many domains (e.g., those in which learners are required to state principles such as Newton's laws and explain solutions), and it facilitates the creation and refinement of nonverbal knowledge through induction, refinement, and fluency-building processes. That is, verbal knowledge may help ensure a properly abstracted encoding of (nonverbal) problem-solving knowledge. Acquiring such knowledge may best be done through the third class of KLI learning mechanisms, namely, sense making.

On-demand hints provide some grist for sense-making processes and perhaps implicitly prompt students to engage in such processes, just by the fact that they are being presented in the tutor interface. When studying hints, a student may try, verbally, to understand or reason about the information that is provided (the KLI definition of sense making). A key mechanism for doing so is self-explanation (Aleven & Koedinger, 2002; Chi, 2000; Chi, Bassok, Lewis, Reimann, & Glaser, 1989; Hausmann & VanLehn, 2007; see also Koedinger et al., 2012, pp. 783–784). For example, as they interpret tutor hints, students may explain to themselves how key conditions of the problem-solving principles relate to concepts they have learned or to other principles. Alternatively, a student may explain how the principle maps onto the problem at hand (e.g., Butcher & Aleven, 2010; in press). Students may even reason about why the principle holds in general or about the fundamental role that principles play in problem solving in the domain they are studying. These self-explanations may lead to an enhanced understanding of the principles and their relations with other domain-specific knowledge and thus to more robust, integrated knowledge. Whether effective sense-making processes occur, however, depends largely on the learner, in particular, on whether learners will decide to self-explain tutor hints and if they do, whether they will generate useful self-explanations. This issue is not addressed in KLI, as discussed further below.

In sum, both ACT-R and KLI stipulate that in many domains, including mathematics and science, robust learning requires that learners acquire both declarative, verbal knowledge and procedural, nonverbal knowledge. The verbal knowledge may help learners reason about principles in various important ways and may guide induction/refinement and fluency-building processes. Principle-based hints such as those offered by ITSs are one way of accomplishing these goals, although ideally not the only way. The KLI account enriches the ACT-R account by highlighting the sense-making processes that must occur if such hints are to contribute to robust learning. It may be clear, however, that ACT-R and KLI provide a *cognitive* perspective on help seeking and that neither of these theories addresses metacognitive aspects of learning from tutor hints.

Implicit Connections Between Cognitive Perspective and Metacognition

As mentioned, viewed from a metacognitive perspective (e.g., Brown, 1987; Flavell, 1979), help seeking involves metacognitive monitoring and control. Although ACT-R and KLI have not made explicit connections to metacognitive theory, they do touch on issues of metacognitive monitoring and control as they relate to learners seeking help with problem-solving activities. First, as mentioned, Cognitive Tutors and other types of ITSs typically make hints available *at the student's request*, as opposed to having the system decide when hints are likely to be beneficial. However, nothing in ACT-R or KLI compels us to create systems that hold back hints until students request them. It would not be difficult to create systems that, for example, volunteer hints at appropriate times, in addition to providing them at the student's request. (Indeed, simple strategies for doing so have been pursued in Cognitive Tutors.) Anderson et al.'s (1995, p. 199) rationale for giving hints at the student's request is that learners have better memory for materials that they generate themselves, compared to materials presented to them. The optimistic vision is that students will request hint levels exactly insofar as these hint levels communicate (or help them construct) knowledge that they could not generate for themselves. Anderson (1993) argues further that students know better than ITSs when they need help. For example, they may be better able to judge than the ITS when an error is a result of a fundamental lack of understanding versus a slip that is easily spotted and can be fixed without further help. An implicit assumption in this theorizing is that students are capable of assessing their own knowledge in relation to the problem at hand, a form of metacognitive monitoring. However, as research on metacognition has shown, this assumption is not necessarily accurate, as people tend to be poor in assessing their own knowledge and understanding (Boekaerts & Rozendaal, 2010; Dunlosky & Lipko, 2007; Feyzi-Behnagh, Khezri, & Azevedo, 2011; Glenberg & Epstein, 1985; Koriat & Bjork, 2005; Nelson, 1996; Simons & Chabris, 2011; Tousignant & DesMarchais, 2002; Winne, 1995), potentially reducing the effectiveness of on-demand help.

A second implicit connection between cognitive and metacognitive theory is that some of the sense-making processes in the KLI framework can be viewed as metacognitive in nature, even if the KLI framers do not explicitly describe them as such. For instance, self-explanation (a key sense-making strategy in KLI) is often viewed as a metacognitive monitoring strategy, especially when it is used for purposes of assessing one's knowledge (e.g., Aleven & Koedinger, 2002; McNamara & Magliano, 2009; Renkl et al., 2013). Self-explanation can help not only in monitoring but also in repairing knowledge gaps (Chi, 2000; VanLehn, Jones, & Chi, 1992). However, not all learners spontaneously self-explain instructional materials, and when they do, not all generate accurate self-explanations (Renkl, 1997), which may limit the effectiveness of on-demand hints. Prompts for self-explanation have been shown to be helpful in a variety of domains and with a variety of different learning materials (Aleven & Koedinger, 2002; Chi, de Leeuw, Chiu, & LaVancher, 1994; Renkl, Stark, Gruber, & Mandl, 1998). One of the KLI instructional principles ("Prompted self-explanation") therefore recommends including such prompts in instructional materials. We know of no ITS, however, in which on-demand hints are accompanied by prompts to self-explain the hints. A number of ITSs incorporate self-explanation prompts, but they ask students to explain steps in worked examples or problems, not hints (e.g., Aleven & Koedinger, 2002; Conati, 2013; Conati & VanLehn, 2000; Otieno, Schwonke, Renkl, Aleven, & Salden, 2011; Salden, Aleven, Schwonke, & Renkl, 2010).

In short, accounts of help seeking and help use in terms of cognitive theories have touched on concerns relevant to metacognitive theory but have not made explicit connections. In addition, they do not provide a perspective on how help seeking is part of a broader set of self-regulation strategies that students use as they approach a complex learning task with varying goals and ambitions.

Self-Regulated Learning Perspective

These issues bring us to theories of self-regulated learning (e.g., Pintrich, 2004; Winne & Hadwin, 1998; Zimmerman, 2008). Such theories often take a comprehensive view of the ways in which learners, faced with a challenging learning task (e.g., learning a complex procedure or learning about a complex set of interrelated concepts), regulate their learning in a cyclical manner, potentially calling upon many different learning strategies. After deciding on a learning task, learners size up task demands, select standards by which they will judge their progress, plan learning strategies to tackle the task, execute their plan, monitor progress against the selected standards, and adjust their learning strategies and/or the standards. They may also reflect on the experience, possibly updating metacognitive or motivational beliefs and attributions. They do so in an opportunistic, iterative, cyclical fashion. Different theories distinguish different task phases, realms, and strategies, but cyclical monitoring and adjusting the plan of action and learning strategies is characteristic of many theoretical models.

Help seeking fits this cyclical framework very well. The decision to seek help typically represents a change of learning strategy, namely, from trying to complete the given learning task independently to seeking our and utilizing additional resources. Often the strategy change is triggered by the learner's monitoring of her task progress in light of the active standards. At other times, it is informed by feedback from the learning environment, and occasionally, it is preplanned. Often, the decision to seek help is an adaptive, opportunistic response for when things do not go according to plan. Many theories of self-regulated learning regard help seeking as one of many strategies that students use to attain their academic goals. For example, help seeking is a key behavioral strategy (among many) in Pintrich's (2004) model of self-regulated learning. According to this model, good students actively monitor their need for help and know when, why, and from whom to seek help. Likewise, Zimmerman (2011) views help seeking in individual and social as a key behavioral manifestation of self-regulation. In Zimmerman's (2000, 2008) social-cognitive three-phase cyclical model of self-regulated learning, help seeking is a self-control mechanism that can be operative in the performance phase of the SRL cycle (the second of three phases in his cycle), in which the learner acts, in an adaptive manner, based on a plan made during the earlier forethought phase of the cycle.

Early empirical research based on these theoretical frameworks produced mixed findings about the relation between students' use of help-seeking strategies and learning. An interview study by Zimmerman and Martinez-Pons (1986) with 80 high-school sophomores found that higher-achieving students, compared to their lower-achieving peers, reported that they sought help more frequently from peers, teachers, and parents. They also reported higher overall use of self-regulation strategies than the lower-achieving group. By contrast, a study with 380 college students by Pintrich, Smith, Garcia, and McKeachie

(1993) found no significant correlation between seeking help from instructors or peers and course grades. (It also did not find a relation between peer learning and course grades.) This study employed the Motivated Strategies for Learning Questionnaire (MSLQ), which includes, in a section entitled "Resource Management," items addressing help seeking together with behaviors such as managing time and study environment, effort management, and peer learning. Thus, these studies provide only mixed support for the importance of help seeking as a self-regulatory strategy. A limitation of this early work is that it is based on self-report rather than behavioral measures of help seeking.

In more recent work on SRL with hypermedia by Azevedo and colleagues (Azevedo, Cromley, & Seibert, 2004; Azevedo, Cromley, Winters, Moos, & Greene, 2005), help seeking is viewed as a way in which a student adapts to task difficulty. SRL processes were analyzed based on extensive coding of think-aloud protocols, thus providing a behavioral measure of help seeking (and avoiding the limitation of the work mentioned above). In two studies, help seeking was one of many SRL processes that correlated with learning gains. Further, students working with a hypermedia system sought help more frequently when a human tutor provided adaptive scaffolding of SRL processes, a condition that also had the highest learning gains. (In the control condition, no human tutor was available.) Although this type of help seeking is somewhat different from on-demand next-step help provided by ITSs—the participants in the Azevedo et al. studies typically sought feedback on what they had just done, whereas in ITSs we have focused on next-step help—these results provide further evidence that help seeking can be a useful SRL strategy.

Not all theories of SRL include help seeking. For instance, Winne and Hadwin (1998, 2008) do not mention help seeking as a component of their COPES model of self-regulated learning. Nonetheless, it seems that help-seeking strategies could readily be accounted for in this model, for instance as a way in which learners enact a metacognitive control action (strategy change) when their monitoring indicates that the products of the current strategy do not meet current standards. Similarly, help seeking is not included in Boekaert's (2007) model, but it would be a surprise if affective dimensions of help seeking were somehow found to be incompatible with this model.

Given the comprehensive perspective on student learning that many SRL theories take, one would expect them not just to indicate in which broad phases of the SRL cycle particular strategies are effective but also to specify in detail the specific context and circumstances in which each strategy (e.g., help seeking) is likely to be more effective than other possible strategy choices. To the best of our knowledge, however, SRL theories have not, with considerable specificity, identified and described the *conditions* under which particular strategies, such as help seeking, should be chosen, nor do these theories relate help seeking to specific metacognitive monitoring processes, such as Feeling of Knowing (FOK) and Judgments of Learning (JOL) (e.g., Azevedo et al., 2004; Dunlosky & Metcalfe, 2008), which presumably inform the decision to seek help from an external source. (In this chapter, we use the terms self-assessment and self-monitoring interchangeably.) For example, persistence in the face of a problem-solving impasse (i.e., trying to solve the step independently, as opposed to seeking help) should be viewed as an adaptive response when the learner, according to his or her own self-assessment or metacognitive monitoring, has sufficient knowledge to recover from the impasse and learn from doing so. In other instances, however, such persistence may best be viewed as maladaptive, for instance, as help avoidance. A further limitation is that SRL theories do not typically refer to cognitive mechanisms or learning mechanism identified by cognitive theories. Ultimately, one expects that learners' self-regulated strategy choices marshal learning mechanisms (in the KLI or ACT-R sense) that produce desirable learning outcomes. However, connections between SRL strategies and cognitive learning mechanisms have received little attention from SRL theorists, although notable exceptions exist (e.g., Rawson & Dunlosky, 2013; Thiede, Griffin, Wiley, & Redford, 2009).

Educational Psychology Perspective

As our third theoretical perspective, we briefly look at a substantial line of work in educational psychology focused on help seeking. This research area also attracted developmental and social psychologists. This work did not examine help seeking in the context of larger theories of SRL but typically has looked at help seeking in greater detail than the SRL work reviewed previously. The work also did not tend to study help-seeking in the context of CBLEs, which is one reason we only treat it briefly here. While the work highlights many social factors affecting people's willingness or reluctance to seek help (e.g., Newman & Goldin, 1990), we focus on work that highlights the central role of self-assessment in help seeking, such as a model of help seeking originally presented by Nelson-Le Gall (1981) and later elaborated by Newman (1994; see also Ryan, Pintrich, & Midgley, 2001). According to this model, self-assessment is a crucial first step of any help-seeking episode, in which one becomes aware of one's need for help. The ability to assess task difficulty, monitor task progress, and evaluate one's own comprehension and knowledge are major metacognitive functions (Nelson-Le Gall, 1981; Newman, 1998; Winne & Jamieson-Noel, 2002). There is evidence that individuals who are better at detecting gaps in their understanding or are better at self-assessment have better learning results (Chi et al., 1989; Paris & Paris, 2001; White & Frederiksen, 1998), although there is also much evidence that humans are quite poor at making accurate metacognitive judgments, as discussed above. The relation between self-assessment and help seeking was highlighted by a study by Nelson-Le Gall et al. (1990), who found that help seeking is related more strongly to children's subjective assessment of their performance than to objective measures of correctness.

To sum up, it may have become clear that not all aspects of on-demand help in ITSs have a strong grounding in theory, although this situation may be rather typical of instructional design, generally. From a theoretical perspective, on-demand hints are an imperfect, although perhaps hard to improve-upon, partial solution to a difficult instructional design problem, namely, to help students acquire appropriately contextualized problem-solving knowledge.

This section highlights the richness of theoretical perspectives on help seeking but also highlights a lack of integration of prior theorizing. Accounts of help seeking in terms of cognitive theories have touched on concerns relevant to metacognitive theory but left them implicit and did not discuss implications of a metacognitive view on help seeking. On the other hand, SRL theories have identified help seeking as an important strategy but have not discussed specific relations to other strategies, or contexts in which help seeking is appropriate, or the cognitive learning mechanisms marshaled through help seeking. It seems, therefore, that there is much to be gained from efforts aimed at unifying cognitive and SRL theoretical perspectives on help seeking. The same can be said of cognitive theory and SRL theory more generally. Without taking into account SRL theories, cognitive perspectives may have a difficult time accounting for variability among learners. Conversely, without a cognitive perspective, it is likely that SRL theories will have a difficult time accounting for how different strategy choices lead to different learning outcomes. Perhaps pointing out the "connects and disconnects" between cognitive theories and theories of self-regulated learning, as we have started to do in this chapter, is a useful first (albeit modest) step towards theory integration.

A Model of Help Seeking as Facilitating Theoretical Integration

In this section, we look at an approach we have taken in our own prior work on help seeking that, we believe, represents a first step towards theoretical integration. Specifically, we have used rule-based modeling as a tool to study metacognition by creating a model of help seeking during tutored problem solving (e.g., Aleven & Koedinger, 2000; Aleven et al., 2006; Aleven, Roll, McLaren, & Koedinger, 2010). The use of production rules to model aspects of SRL had previously been advocated by Winne and colleagues (Winne, 2010; 2011; Winne & Hadwin, 1998; Winne, Zhou, & Egan, 2011), but our work takes a critical next step by explicating a model that details the conditions under which metacognitive strategy choices are appropriate. The model is executable on a computer and can be run against data of student-tutor interactions in order to assess students' help-seeking behavior. In the current section, we give a brief overview of the model. In the next section, we discuss this work from the perspective of theoretical integration: The model unites cognitive and metacognitive aspects into the same modeling frame.

The model captures a recurrent metacognitive cycle in tutored problem solving in which a learner, faced with a step in a tutor problem, must decide between trying the step or seeking help. As mentioned, this strategy choice is a key way in which a learner engaged in problem-solving practice exercises metacognitive control. The model is based on theoretical and empirical cognitive task analysis (Aleven et al., 2006). Further, it is meant to be compatible both with models of SRL (i.e., an observed SRL event) and the models of help seeking put forward in the educational psychology literature (i.e., a strategic response to self-assessment). We do not mean to claim that the model comprehensively covers all SRL processes used during tutored problem solving, only that it captures some important processes. Other SRL models are more comprehensive, but the current model is more specific. It is implemented as a set of production rules that capture, in IF-THEN format, the conditions under which a learner working with an ITS does well to independently attempt a problem step versus requesting a context-sensitive hint from the system. Ideally, a student seeks help (i.e., requests a hint from the system) when not having sufficient knowledge to understand the step or learn much from the step and attempts the step otherwise. Self-assessment is therefore a key element of the model; including self-assessment is one way in which the model integrates cognitive and metacognitive aspects. The model is summarized in Tables 21.1 and 21.2. These tables present a more concise and accessible overview than the production rules themselves would, although we do give examples of production rules below.

As indicated in the tables, the model specifies, for each of the two main strategy choices (seek help or attempt the step) the conditions under which that

Table 21.1 Conditions for seeking help specified by the production rule model of help seeking

Requesting help is *preferred* when:
- The step is unfamiliar to the student (as indicated by self-assessment)
- Or when the student made an error (as indicated by feedback from the geometry tutor) and it is not clear how to fix the error (as indicated by self-assessment)
- Or the student just read a hint and it was found not to be helpful (as indicated by self-assessment)
- Provided that the student has not yet seen all hint levels for the given step and the hint request is deliberate (i.e., the student spent a reasonable amount of time before the request)

Requesting help is *acceptable* when:
- The step is familiar, but the student does not have a clear sense of what to do (as indicated by self-assessment)
- Or the previous action was also a hint request (in other words, requesting the next hint level is always acceptable)
- Provided that the hint request is deliberate (meaning adequate time was spent)

Requesting help is *not acceptable:*
- In all other situations (e.g., when on a familiar step, the student requests a hint right away, without first trying the step, or when the student did not spend an adequate amount of time reading or rereading a hint level before requesting the next hint level)

Table 21.2 Conditions for trying a step specified by the production rule model of help seeking

Trying a step is *preferred* when:
- The step is familiar to the student (as indicated by self-assessment), and the student did not just make an error on the step that he or she does not know how to fix (as indicated by self-assessment)
- Or the student has just read a hint that was helpful (as indicated by self-assessment)
- Or if the student has seen all the hints for the step, unless they have also made an error that they do not know how to fix (in which case asking the teacher is preferred)
- Provided that the attempt was deliberate (meaning adequate time was spent)

Trying a step is *acceptable* when:
- The attempt is correct (even if according to other criteria, the student should have sought help, or the step was not done in deliberate fashion—i.e., was hasty)

Trying a step is *not acceptable*:
- In all other situations (e.g., when the student has read a hint and it is not helpful)

choice is preferred, acceptable, or deemed not a good choice.[4] At the outset of working on a step in a tutor problem, the decision to seek help or attempt the step will be based on the student's assessment of the familiarity of the step, essentially, a FOK judgment (Azevedo et al., 2004; Dunlosky & Metcalfe, 2008), that is, a judgment learners make with respect to their own knowledge based on prior exposure or practice (or lack thereof). If the step is unfamiliar, seeking help is the preferred strategy. Attempting an unfamiliar step is the preferred strategy only after a sufficient number of hints have been read so that the student has a sense of what to do. Attempting a step without requesting help is acceptable if the student has a sense of what to do, a higher bar than mere familiarity. After an initial unsuccessful attempt at solving the step, the decision whether to seek help or not is informed by tutor feedback, but tutor feedback does not do away with the need for metacognitive monitoring. The preferred approach is for the student to (deliberately) try to make sense of the error and reattempt the step only when it is clear how to fix the error. As before, the key judgment to be made is whether or not the student has a clear sense of what to do. Finally, after requesting a hint level, the student must make a judgment as to whether they have understood the hint sufficiently well in order to succeed with the step at hand, arguably, a judgment of learning (JOL). JOLs are judgments by learners of their own understanding of materials just studied (Azevedo et al., 2004; Dunlosky & Metcalfe, 2008). The model thus explicates how help seeking depends on self-assessment processes such as FOK and JOL and how it relates to learning by problem solving.

To illustrate how production rules are used to capture the basic metacognitive cycle described above and model the detailed conditions under which a strategy choice is preferred, acceptable, or not acceptable, we show three rules that model the situation where the student has requested a hint, evaluates whether it is helpful through careful reading, and upon deciding that it is not, requests to see the next hint level:

IF
  There is a subgoal to evaluate a hint (meaning that the student's previous action was to request a hint, and the system presented a hint)
THEN
  Set a subgoal to deliberately read and think about the hint
  And set a subgoal to decide whether to request the next hint,
  And remove the subgoal to evaluate the hint

IF
  There is a subgoal to deliberately read and think about a hint
  And the current hint level is a new hint level (as opposed to rereading a hint level seen before)
THEN
  Spend a reasonable amount of time processing the new hint
  And remove the subgoal

IF
  There is a subgoal to decide whether to request the next hint
  And the current hint is not helpful
  And the student has not yet seen all the hints for the current step
THEN
  Request the next hint
  And set a subgoal to evaluate the hint

To illustrate how the production rules capture alternative choices under different conditions, the following rule captures a different strategy choice when in the same situation as above, the student's assessment of a hint's helpfulness is different:

IF
  There is a subgoal to decide whether to request the next hint
  And the current hint has been evaluated as being helpful

[4] These categories stem from the use of the model in the context of automated tutoring. A tutor will recommend and accept steps that are preferred, accept steps that are acceptable (but not recommend them if they are not also preferred), and reject steps that are neither (i.e., are not acceptable). In off-line analyses of students' help-seeking behavior, we distinguished between acceptable and not acceptable steps, without further subdividing acceptable steps into preferred and non-preferred steps.

THEN
Try the step
And set a subgoal to evaluate the result of trying the step

More than half of the rules in the model capture help-seeking errors, the various ways in which students' strategy choices can fall in the "not acceptable" category of Tables 21.1 and 21.2. We grouped them and organized them in hierarchical fashion to create what we call a metacognitive error taxonomy (Aleven et al., 2006). The taxonomy includes major categories such as help avoidance, help abuse, and try-step abuse, subdivided into finer-grained categories. The model therefore provides much finer grain in capturing maladaptive help-seeking behaviors than prior work in educational or developmental psychology, which has focused on broad categories such as instrumental versus executive help seeking (e.g., Nelson-Le Gall, 1985). Executive help seeking has been defined as focused on supporting performance or completing a task, whereas instrumental help-seeking episodes are defined by their aim to support the acquisition of new skills or knowledge.

In implementing the model, we were forced to be specific about what it means to "spend a reasonable amount of time" processing one of the tutor's hint messages and what it means for a hint to be "helpful." In other rules, we needed to give a precise specification of what it means for a step to be "familiar" and what it means for a student to have "a sense of what to do." As can be seen in Tables 21.1 and 21.2, as well as the rule examples given above, these notions are part of the conditions under which the different strategies are appropriate. To define what it means for a step to be familiar or for a student to have a sense of what to do on a step (essentially, outcomes of students' self-assessment of their mastery of the domain-specific knowledge components involved in each problem step), we made use of the probabilities of skill mastery computed by the Geometry Cognitive Tutor. As mentioned, the tutor computes these probabilities in the course of its regular operation using its Bayesian knowledge-tracing algorithm, based on students' performance on the tutored problems. Specifically, we defined context-sensitive thresholds on the probability of knowing or not knowing skills targeted in the instruction. The thresholds were based on educational data mining of log data from the Geometry Cognitive Tutor (Aleven et al., 2006). We define familiar steps as steps for which the skill mastery probability is above 0.4 but below 0.6 (meaning that the probability that the student has fully learned the requisite domain-specific knowledge components is between 0.4 and 0.6, according to the Geometry Cognitive Tutor's determination). We define steps for which the student has a sense of what to do as steps for which the estimated probability of skill mastery is 0.6 or higher. By contrast, for a skill to be deemed *mastered* by the tutoring software, the probability of mastery needs to be 0.95 or higher (Corbett & Anderson, 1995). To define the notion of "working deliberately" in a context-sensitive manner, we set context-sensitive thresholds for the minimum amount of time spent when starting to work on a step, when reading hints, or when following up on an incorrect attempt at solving a step. In doing so, we assumed that a student reading the tutor's hints will not exceed 600 words/min, a level that is well above average reading rates reported in the literature (e.g., Card, Moran, & Newell, 1983).

The model has been used for two main purposes: It has been used for off-line analysis of students' help-seeking behavior (Aleven et al., 2006), and it has been used as the "smarts" in a tutor agent that provides feedback on students' help-seeking behavior (Aleven et al., 2010; Roll, Aleven, McLaren, & Koedinger, 2011). In the first line of work, we started out by distilling from tutor log data, simple frequency measures of students' help-seeking behavior (e.g., on what percentage of steps in tutor problems they requested tutor hints). We then computed correlations between these aspects of students' help-seeking behavior and students' learning gains, measured by a paper geometry pre- and posttest. Our analyses yielded negative correlations between the frequency of help use and learning gains from pretest to posttest (Aleven et al., 2006). Students who requested help from the tutor more often had lower learning gains than students who used help less often. However, this analysis has a number of limitations that make it difficult to interpret these correlations. First, this analysis assumes that seeking help more often is better (i.e., leads to more robust learning). However, there is no reason to assume that seeking help more frequently (i.e., a larger number of help request per problem step) should lead to higher learning gains. In particular, when hints are used to obtain answers without trying to understand the reason why the answer is correct, students may not learn much from the hints. Further, sometimes *not* seeking help is more appropriate; seeking help in such situations may be detrimental to learning. Such differences are hidden in frequency counts. A second fundamental limitation is that the analysis is subject to selection effects. That is, the students who needed help more often were likely to be the less-prepared students or lower-aptitude students. The negative correlation might indicate simply that students who are in trouble more often during the learning process tend to have lower learning gains. This selection effect may obscure any possible positive influence that help use may have on student learning (but see Goldin, Koedinger, & Aleven, 2012).

Off-line use of the model enabled us to address the first limitation. That is, by running the model against log data, we were to classify students' actions captured in the log data into effective and ineffective help-seeking behaviors, corresponding to the categories of acceptable and non-acceptable behaviors defined in Tables 21.1 and 21.2. We further divided the ineffective help-seeking behaviors according to the taxonomy of ineffective help seeking described above. With this subdivision, a more nuanced picture of the relations between help seeking and learning emerged (Aleven et al., 2006). Ineffective help-seeking behaviors (in particular help abuse) were frequent and correlated negatively with learning ($r=-0.66$). Effective help use therefore correlated positively with learning. Some of the less frequent ineffective help-seeking behaviors did not strongly correlate with learning, namely, those we called "try-step abuse," which included frequent guesses at answers. Further, help avoidance correlated negatively with learning in some analyses but not others, suggesting that this form of ineffective help seeking may not be detrimental to learning in an environment with immediate feedback on problem solving.

In the second line of work, the model was used to provide feedback on students' help-seeking behavior in the context of geometry learning. This line of work helped us address the second limitation of the correlational analysis described above, namely, that selection effects obscure the relation between help seeking and learning. We conducted an experimental study to investigate whether improved help seeking (due to feedback on help seeking) leads to improved learning, so as to test a causal relation between help seeking and learning during tutored problem solving. Specifically, we created a tutor agent based on the help-seeking model. We integrated this tutor agent within the Geometry Cognitive Tutor, enabling this tutor to provide tutoring on help seeking in addition to tutoring with respect to geometry.[5] This tutor agent assessed students' help-seeking behavior online, as students were using the Geometry Cognitive Tutor to solve geometry problems, by comparing the student's actual actions against those deemed acceptable by the model (see Tables 21.1 and 21.2). The model's fine-grained error taxonomy for help-seeking errors was again helpful, because it allowed the tutor agent to provide specific feedback on instances of maladaptive help-seeking behavior.

In an extensive classroom study (Aleven et al., 2010; Roll et al., 2011), we found that feedback on help seeking, in the context of tutored problem solving, led to a lasting improvement in students' help-seeking behavior. Students who had received feedback from the help-seeking tutor agent used help more deliberately even after the intervention. When they used help, they spent more time per hint level accessed and progressed less deeply into each hint sequence (i.e., accessed fewer levels). These findings suggest that they got more out of the hint levels that they did access, due to more deliberate processing. The greater reliance on earlier hint levels that was found would seem

[5] The work relates to recent work on integrating metacognitive tutoring into hypermedia environments (Azevedo et al., 2011; Azevedo et al., 2013) or environments with teachable agents (Leelawong & Biswas, 2008).

to be beneficial to students especially given that the earlier hints are more conceptual (i.e., discuss which problem-solving principle applies and how). Unfortunately, the hypothesis that students' domain-level learning (as measured by learning gains from pretest to posttest) would improve as a result of improved help seeking was not confirmed. One way of interpreting these results is that even with more deliberate help requests and more deliberate processing of help messages, the sense-making processes needed for learning from principle-based explanations (discussed in detail in the section on the KLI framework) remain challenging for students. A more complete help-seeking tutor may need to support these processes more explicitly, or ideally, help students learn to support them for themselves. It is possible also that the pretest and posttest used were not sensitive enough to measure improvement in students' conceptual knowledge, due to help seeking.

Discussion

Although the production rule model of help seeking is far from a comprehensive model of self-regulation during tutored problem solving, it does relate help seeking and learning from principle-based help messages to other learning strategies (problem solving) and metacognitive processes (self-assessment processes, deliberate work habits). A further advance is that it articulates specific conditions under which seeking help is deemed the better choice, compared to an alternative strategy choice, namely, to persist in problem-solving attempts. Detailing conditions of strategy choice is a key challenge for SRL theories and is of critical importance for furthering the research agenda that views SRL as a process (or event). (This research agenda has in recent years been embraced by a considerable number of SRL researchers.) Normative models that specify when strategies are appropriate make it possible to distinguish effects of effective and ineffective use of strategies. They also make it possible to do intervention studies that test causal relations between SRL strategies and learning, as illustrated above. The model of help seeking is not without limitations. As mentioned, it is not as comprehensive as other models of self-regulated learning. For instance, it does not capture any influence of aspects of student motivation, nor does it capture all phases of self-regulation or all strategies that students are likely to bring to bear in the context of tutored problem solving. An interesting research agenda is to expand this model with additional aspects of self-regulation (e.g., planning, reviewing the problem statement, spontaneous self-explanation without being prompted by the software, spontaneous, unprompted end-of-problem reflection, whether to be on-task or engage in off-task behavior). Each of these choices may influence student learning, at minimum for certain subsets of students.

We believe the model of help seeking represents a step towards theoretical integration. As argued above, it brings together both cognitive and metacognitive aspects in a more detailed and specific way than SRL theories typically do. By capturing both cognitive and metacognitive strategies in a shared format, namely, IF-THEN rules, it highlights a fundamental similarity between cognition and metacognition. In the parlance of the KLI theoretical framework (Koedinger et al., 2012), the model's production rules are examples of *metacognitive knowledge components*. Under KLI, a complex cognitive skill is assumed to be made up of small, interrelated knowledge components, expressed in IF-THEN format, similar to production rules in ACT-R. An essential distinction between cognitive and metacognitive knowledge components may be that metacognitive knowledge components have, in their IF-part, conditions that involve the learner's assessment of their own knowledge or skills relative to the task at hand. As a specific type of knowledge components, metacognitive knowledge components should be subject to the same constraints as knowledge components more generally, such as constraints on their acquisition. Fundamentally, all metacognition is *also* cognition. A shared modeling formalism helps highlight properties and constraints that are shared, and will facilitate further empirical work, for example, on the acquisition of metacognitive skill, a topic not addressed in the current chapter.

Much is left to be done. Greater theoretical integration looms as an interesting grand challenge for researchers working in the intersection of cognitive theories, self-regulated learning, and computer-based learning environments.

Acknowledgements The writing of this chapter was supported by the Pittsburgh Science of Learning Center, which is funded by the National Science Foundation (# SBE 0836012). Roger Azevedo, Matt Bernacki, Albert Corbett, Yanjin Long, Timothy Nokes, and Charles Perfetti gave very helpful comments on earlier versions of the chapter. We gratefully acknowledge their contributions.

The writing of this chapter was sponsored by National Science Foundation award SBE0354420 to the Pittsburgh Science of Learning Center.

References

Aleven, V. (2010). Rule-based cognitive modeling for intelligent tutoring systems. In R. Nkambou, J. Bourdeau, & R. Mizoguchi (Eds.), *Advances in intelligent tutoring systems* (pp. 33–62). Berlin: Springer.

Aleven, V., & Koedinger, K. R. (2000). Limitations of student control: Do students know when they need help? In G. Gauthier, C. Frasson, & K. VanLehn (Eds.), *Proceedings of the 5th International Conference on Intelligent Tutoring Systems, ITS 2000* (pp. 292–303). Berlin: Springer.

Aleven, V., & Koedinger, K. R. (2002). An effective metacognitive strategy: learning by doing and explaining with a computer-based Cognitive Tutor. *Cognitive Science, 26*(2), 147–179.

Aleven, V., McLaren, B. M., & Koedinger, K. R. (2006). Towards computer-based tutoring of help-seeking skills. In S. Karabenick & R. Newman (Eds.), *Help seeking in academic settings: Goals, groups, and contexts* (pp. 259–296). Mahwah, NJ: Erlbaum.

Aleven, V., McLaren, B., Roll, I., & Koedinger, K. (2006). Toward meta-cognitive tutoring: A model of help seeking with a Cognitive Tutor. *International Journal of Artificial Intelligence in Education, 16*, 101–128.

Aleven, V., Roll, I., McLaren, B. M., & Koedinger, K. R. (2010). Automated, unobtrusive, action-by-action assessment of self-regulation during learning with an intelligent tutoring system. *Educational Psychologist, 45*(4), 224–233.

Aleven, V., Stahl, E., Schworm, S., Fischer, F., & Wallace, R. M. (2003). Help seeking and help design in interactive learning environments. *Review of Educational Research, 73*(3), 277–320.

Anderson, J. R. (1993). *Rules of the mind*. Hillsdale, NJ: Erlbaum.

Anderson, J. R., Conrad, F. G., & Corbett, A. T. (1989). Skill acquisition and the Lisp Tutor. *Cognitive Science, 13*, 467–505.

Anderson, J. R., Corbett, A. T., Koedinger, K. R., & Pelletier, R. (1995). Cognitive tutors: Lessons learned. *The Journal of the Learning Sciences, 4*(2), 167–207.

Anderson, J. R., & Lebière, C. (1998). *The atomic components of thought*. Mahwah, NJ: Erlbaum.

Azevedo, R., Cromley, J. G., & Seibert, D. (2004). Does adaptive scaffolding facilitate students' ability to regulate their learning with hypermedia? *Contemporary Educational Psychology, 29*, 344–370.

Azevedo, R., Cromley, J. G., Winters, F. I., Moos, D. C., & Greene, J. A. (2005). Adaptive human scaffolding facilitates adolescents' self-regulated learning with hypermedia. *Instructional Science, 33*, 381–412. doi:10.1007/s11251-005-1273-8.

Azevedo, R., Harley, J., Trevors, G., Feyzi-Behnagh, R., Duffy, M., & Bouchet, F. (2013). Using trace data to examine the complex roles of cognitive, metacognitive, and emotional self-regulatory processes during learning with multi-agent systems. In R. Azevedo & V. Aleven (Eds.), *International Handbook of Metacognition and Learning Technologies* (pp.). Springer International Handbooks of Education 26 New York: Springer. DOI: 10.1007/978-1-4419-5546-3_21.

Azevedo, R., & Jacobson, M. J. (2008). Advances in scaffolding learning with hypertext and hypermedia: A summary and critical analysis. *Educational Technology Research and Development, 56*(1), 93–100.

Azevedo, R., Johnson, A. M., Chauncey, A., & Graesser, A. (2011). Use of hypermedia to assess and convey self-regulated learning. In B. Zimmerman & D. Schunk (Eds.), *Handbook of self-regulation of learning and performance* (pp. 102–121). New York: Routledge.

Azevedo, R., Moos, D. C., Johnson, A. M., & Chauncey, A. D. (2010). Measuring cognitive and metacognitive regulatory processes during hypermedia learning: Issues and challenges. *Educational Psychologist, 45*(4), 210–223. doi:10.1080/00461520.2010.515934.

Azevedo, R., & Witherspoon, A. M. (2009). Self-regulated learning with hypermedia. In D. J. Hacker, J. Dunlosky, & A. C. Graesser (Eds.), *Handbook of metacognition in education* (pp. 319–339). Mahwah, NJ: Routledge.

Beal, C. R., Walles, R., Arroyo, I., & Woolf, B. P. (2007). Online tutoring for math achievement: A controlled evaluation. *Journal of Interactive Online Learning, 6*, 43–55.

Beck, J. E., Chang, K., Mostow, J., & Corbett, A. T. (2008). Does help help? Introducing the bayesian evaluation and assessment methodology. In B. Woolf, E. Aimeur, R. Nkambou, & S. Lajoie (Eds.), *Proceedings of the 9th International Conference on Intelligent Tutoring Systems* (pp. 383–394). Berlin: Springer.

Boekaerts, M. (2007). Understanding Students' affective processes in the classroom. In P. Schutz, R. Pekrun, & G. Phye (Eds.), *Emotion in education* (pp. 37–56). San Diego, CA: Academic Press.

Boekaerts, M., & Rozendaal, J. S. (2010). Using multiple calibration indices in order to capture the complex picture of what affects students' accuracy of feeling of confidence. *Leaning and Instruction, 20*, 372–382.

Bransford, J. D., Brown, A. L., & Cocking, R. R. (2000). *How people learn: Brain, mind, experience, and school*. Washington: National Academic Press.

Brown, A. (1987). Metacognition, executive control, self-regulation, and other mysterious mechanisms. In F. E. Weinert & R. H. Kluwe (Eds.), *Metacognition, motivation, and understanding* (pp. 65–116). Hillsdale, NJ: Erlbaum.

Butcher, K. R., & Aleven, V. (2010). Learning during intelligent tutoring: When do integrated visual-verbal representations improve student outcomes? In S. Ohlsson & R. Catrambone (Eds.), *Proceedings of the 32nd Annual Meeting of the Cognitive Science Society* (pp. 2888–2893). Austin, TX: Cognitive Science Society.

Butcher, K., & Aleven, V. (in press). Using student interactions to foster rule-diagram mapping during problem solving in an intelligent tutoring system. *Journal of Educational Psychology*.

Campuzano, L., Dynarski, M., Agodini, R., & Rall, K. (2009). *Effectiveness of reading and mathematics software products: Findings from two student cohorts*. Washington, DC: U.S. Department of Education, Institute of Education Sciences.

Card, S., Moran, T., & Newell, A. (1983). *The psychology of human-computer interaction*. Mahwah, NJ: Erlbaum.

Chen, S. (2002). A cognitive model for non-linear learning in hypermedia programmes. *British Journal of Educational Technology, 33*(4), 449–460.

Chi, M. T. H. (2000). Self-explaining expository texts: The dual processes of generating inferences and repairing mental models. In R. Glaser (Ed.), *Advances in instructional psychology* (pp. 161–237). Mahwah, NJ: Erlbaum.

Chi, M. T. H., Bassok, M., Lewis, M. W., Reimann, P., & Glaser, R. (1989). Self-explanations: How students study and use examples in learning to solve problems. *Cognitive Science, 13*, 145–182.

Chi, M. T. H., de Leeuw, N., Chiu, M., & LaVancher, C. (1994). Eliciting self-explanations improves understanding. *Cognitive Science, 18*, 439–477.

Conati, C. (2013). Modeling and scaffolding self-explanation across domains and activities. In R. Azevedo & V. Aleven (Eds.), *International Handbook of Metacognition and Learning Technologies* (pp.). Springer International Handbooks of Education 26 New York: Springer. DOI: 10.1007/978-1-4419-5546-3_21.

Conati, C., & Vanlehn, K. (2000). Toward computer-based support of meta-cognitive skills: A computational framework to coach self-explanation. *International Journal of Artificial Intelligence in Education, 11*(4), 389–415.

Corbett, A. T., & Anderson, J. R. (1995). Knowledge tracing: Modeling the acquisition of procedural knowledge. *User Modeling and User-Adapted Interaction, 4*, 253–278.

Corbett, A. T., & Anderson, J. R. (2001). Locus of feedback control in computer-based tutoring: Impact on learning rate, achievement and attitudes. In J. Jacko, A. Sears, M. Beaudouin-Lafon, & R. Jacob (Eds.), *Proceedings of ACM CHI'2001 Conference on Human Factors in Computing Systems* (pp. 245–252). New York: ACM Press.

Corbett, A., Kauffman, L., MacLaren, B., Wagner, A., & Jones, E. (2010). A Cognitive Tutor for genetics problem solving: Learning gains and student modeling. *Journal of Educational Computing Research, 42*(2), 219–239.

Corbett, A., McLaughlin, M., & Scarpinatto, K. C. (2000). Modeling student knowledge: Cognitive Tutors in high school and college. *User Modeling and User-Adapted Interaction, 10*, 81–108.

Dunlosky, J., & Lipko, A. (2007). Metacomprehension: A brief history and how to improve its accuracy. *Current Directions in Psychological Science, 16*, 228–232.

Dunlosky, J., & Metcalfe, J. (2008). *Metacognition*. Thousand Oaks, CA: Sage.

Feyzi-Behnagh, R., Khezri, Z., & Azevedo, R. (2011). An investigation of accuracy of metacognitive judgments during learning with an intelligent multi-agent hypermedia environment. In L. Carlson, C. Hölscher, & T. Shipley (Eds.), *Proceedings of the 33rd Annual Conference of the Cognitive Science Society* (pp. 96–101). Austin, TX: Cognitive Science Society.

Flavell, J. (1979). Metacognition and cognitive monitoring. A new area of cognitive development inquiry. *American Psychologist, 34*, 906–911.

Glenberg, A. M., & Epstein, W. (1985). Calibration of comprehension. *Journal of Experimental Psychology: Learning, Memory, and Cognition, 11*, 702–718.

Goldin, I., Koedinger, K. R., & Aleven, V. (2012). Learner differences in hint processing. In K. Yacef, O. Zaïane, A. Hershkovitz, M. Yudelson, & J. Stamper (Eds.), *Proceedings of the 5th International Conference on Educational Data Mining (EDM 2012)* (pp. 73–80). Worcester, MA: International Educational Data Mining Society.

Hadwin, A. F., Nesbit, J. C., Jamieson-Noel, D., Code, J., & Winne, P. H. (2007). Examining trace data to explore self-regulated learning. *Metacognition and Learning, 2*, 107–124. doi:10.1007/s11409-007-9016-7.

Hatano, G., & Inagaki, I. (1986). Two courses of expertise. In H. A. H. Stevenson & K. Hakuta (Eds.), *Child development and education in Japan* (pp. 262–272). New York: Freeman.

Hausmann, R. G. M., & VanLehn, K. (2007). Explaining self-explaining: A contrast between content and generation. In R. Luckin, K. R. Koedinger, & J. Greer (Eds.), *Proceedings of the 13th International Conference on Artificial Intelligence in Education* (pp. 417–424). Amsterdam: IOS Press.

Jacobson, M. J. (2008). Hypermedia systems for problem-based learning: Theory, research, and learning emerging scientific conceptual perspectives. *Educational Technology, Research, and Development, 56*, 5–28.

Jacobson, M. J., & Archodidou, A. (2000). The design of hypermedia tools for learning: Fostering conceptual change and transfer of complex scientific knowledge. *The Journal of the Learning Sciences, 9*(2), 145–199.

Karabenick, S., & Newman, R. (Eds.). (2006). *Help seeking in academic settings: Goals, groups, and contexts*. Mahwah, NJ: Erlbaum.

Kilpatrick, J., Swafford, J., & Findell, B. (Eds.). (2001). *Adding it up: Helping children learn mathematics. Mathematics Learning Study Committee, Center for Education, Division of Behavioral and Social Sciences and Education*. Washington, DC: Academy Press.

Koedinger, K. R., & Aleven, V. (2007). Exploring the assistance dilemma in experiments with Cognitive Tutors. *Educational Psychology Review, 19*(3), 239–264.

Koedinger, K. R., Aleven, V., Roll, I., & Baker, R. (2009). In vivo experiments on whether supporting metacognition in intelligent tutoring systems yields robust learning. In D. J. Hacker, J. Dunlosky, & A. C. Graesser (Eds.), *Handbook of metacognition in education* (pp. 897–964). The Educational Psychology Series. New York: Routledge.

Koedinger, K. R., Anderson, J. R., Hadley, W. H., & Mark, M. A. (1997). Intelligent tutoring goes to school in the big city. *International Journal of Artificial Intelligence in Education, 8*, 30–43

Koedinger, K. R., Baker, R., Cunningham, K., Skogsholm, A., Leber, B., & Stamper, J. (2011). A data repository for the EDM community: The PSLC DataShop. In C. Romero, S. Ventura, M. Pechenizkiy, & R. S. J. D. Baker (Eds.), *Handbook of educational data mining* (pp. 43–55). Boca Raton, FL: CRC Press.

Koedinger, K. R., & Corbett, A. T. (2006). Cognitive tutors: Technology bringing learning sciences to the classroom. In R. K. Sawyer (Ed.), *The Cambridge handbook of the learning sciences* (pp. 61–78). New York: Cambridge University Press.

Koedinger, K. R., Corbett, A. C., & Perfetti, C. (2012). The Knowledge-Learning-Instruction (KLI) framework: Bridging the science-practice chasm to enhance robust student learning. *Cognitive Science, 36*(5), 757–798. doi:10.1111/j.1551-6709.2012.01245.x.

Koedinger, K., Cunningham, K., Skogsholm, A., & Leber, B. (2008). An open repository and analysis tools for fine-grained, longitudinal learner data. In R. S. J. D. Baker, T. Barnes, & J. E. Beck (Eds.), *Proceedings of the 1st International Conference on Educational Data Mining, EDM 2008* (pp. 157–166). Worcester, MA: International Educational Data Mining Society.

Koriat, A., & Bjork, R. A. (2005). Illusions of competence in monitoring one's knowledge during study. *Journal of Experimental Psychology: Learning, Memory, and Cognition, 31*, 187–194.

Leelawong, K., & Biswas, G. (2008). Designing learning by teaching agents: The Betty's Brain system. *International Journal of Artificial Intelligence in Education, 18*(3), 181–208.

Long, Y., & Aleven, V. (2012). Skill diaries: Can periodic self-assessment improve students' learning with an intelligent tutoring system? In S. A. Cerri, W. J. Clancey, G. Papadourakis, & K. Panourgia (Eds.), *Proceedings of the 11th International Conference on Intelligent Tutoring Systems, ITS 2012* (pp. 673–674). Berlin: Springer.

Luckin, R., & Hammerton, L. (2002). Getting to know me: Helping learners understand their own learning needs through metacognitive scaffolding. In S. Cerri, G. Gouardères, & F. Paraguaçu (Eds.), *Proceedings of the 6th International Conference on Intelligent Tutoring Systems, ITS 2002* (pp. 759–771). Berlin: Springer. doi: 10.1007/3-540-47987-2_76.

Ma, L. (1999). *Knowing and teaching elementary mathematics: Teachers' understanding of fundamental mathematics in China and the United States*. Mahwah, NJ: Erlbaum.

Mathan, S. A., & Koedinger, K. R. (2005). Fostering the intelligent novice: Learning from errors with metacognitive tutoring. *Educational Psychologist, 40*(4), 257–265.

McLaren, B. M., DeLeeuw, K. E., & Mayer, R. E. (2011). Polite web-based intelligent tutors: Can they improve learning in classrooms? *Computers & Education, 56*(3), 574–584. doi:10.1016/j.compedu.2010.09.019.

McNamara, D. S., & Magliano, J. P. (2009). Self-explanation and metacognition: The dynamics of reading. In D. J. Hacker, J. Dunlosky, & A. Graesser (Eds.), *Handbook of metacognition in education* (pp. 60–81). New York: Routledge/Taylor & Francis.

Mitrovic, A., Martin, B., & Mayo, M. (2002). Using evaluation to shape ITS design: Results and experiences with SQL-Tutor. *International Journal of User Modeling and User-Adapted Interaction, 12*(2–3), 243–279.

Nelson, T. O. (1996). Consciousness and metacognition. *American Psychologist, 51*, 102–116.

Nelson-Le Gall, S. (1981). Help-seeking: An understudied problem-solving skill in children. *Developmental Review, 1*, 224–246.

Nelson-Le Gall, S. (1985). Help-seeking behavior in learning. *Review of Research in Education, 12*, 55–90.

Nelson-Le Gall, S., Kratzer, L., Jones, E., & DeCooke, P. (1990). Children's self-assessment of performance and task-related help-seeking. *Journal of Experimental Child Psychology, 49*, 245–263.

Newman, R. S. (1994). Adaptive help seeking: A strategy of self-regulated learning. In D. H. Schunk & B. J. Zimmerman (Eds.), *Self-regulation of learning and performance: Issues and educational applications* (pp. 283–301). Hillsdale, NJ: Erlbaum.

Newman, R. S. (1998). Adaptive help seeking: A role of social interaction in self-regulated learning. In S. A. Karabenick (Ed.), *Strategic help seeking. Implications for learning and teaching* (pp. 13–37). Mahwah: Erlbaum.

Newman, R. S. (2008). The motivational role of adaptive help seeking in self-regulated learning. In D. H. Schunk & B. J. Zimmerman (Eds.), *Motivation and self-regulated learning: Theory, research, and applications* (pp. 315–37). New York: Erlbaum.

Newman, R. S., & Goldin, L. (1990). Children's reluctance to seek help with schoolwork. *Journal of Educational Psychology, 82*, 92–100.

Nkambou, R., Bourdeau, J., & Mizoguchi, R. (Eds.). (2010). *Advances in intelligent tutoring systems*. Berlin: Springer.

Otieno, C., Schwonke, R., Renkl, A., Aleven, V., & Salden, R. (2011). Measuring learning progress via self-explanations versus problem solving - a suggestion for optimizing adaptation in intelligent tutoring systems. In L. Carlson, C. Hölscher, & T. Shipley (Eds.), *Proceedings of the 33rd Annual Conference of the Cognitive Science Society* (pp. 84–89). Austin, TX: Cognitive Science Society.

Paris, S. G., & Paris, A. H. (2001). Classroom applications of research on self-regulated learning. *Educational Psychologist, 36*(2), 89–101.

Pintrich, P. R. (2004). A conceptual framework for assessing motivation and self-regulated learning in college students. *Educational Psychology Review, 16*(4), 385–407.

Pintrich, P. R., Smith, D. A. F., Garcia, T., & McKeachie, W. J. (1993). Reliability and predictive validity of the motivated strategies for learning questionnaire (MLSQ). *Educational and Psychological Measurement, 53*, 801–813.

Rawson, K. A., & Dunlosky, J. (2013). Retrieval-Monitoring-Feedback (RMF) technique for producing efficient and durable student learning. In R. Azevedo & V. Aleven (Eds.), *International Handbook of Metacognition and Learning Technologies* (pp.). Springer International Handbooks of Education 26 New York: Springer. doi: 10.1007/978-1-4419-5546-3_21.

Renkl, A. (1997). Learning from worked-out examples: a study on individual differences. *Cognitive Science, 21*, 1–29.

Renkl, A., Berthold, K., Grosse, C. S., & Schwonke, R. (2013). Making better use of multiple representations: How fostering metacognition can help. In R. Azevedo & V. Aleven (Eds.), *International Handbook of Metacognition and Learning Technologies* (pp.). Springer International Handbooks of Education 26 New York: Springer. DOI 10.1007/978-1-4419-5546-3_21.

Renkl, A., Stark, R., Gruber, H., & Mandl, H. (1998). Learning from worked-out examples: The effects of example variability and elicited self-explanations. *Contemporary Educational Psychology, 23*, 90–108.

Ritter, S., Kulikowich, J., Lei, P., McGuire, C., & Morgan, P. (2007). What evidence matters? A randomized field trial of Cognitive Tutor® Algebra I. In T. Hirashima, H. U. Hoppe, & S. Shwu-Ching Young (Eds.), *Supporting learning flow through integrative technologies* (pp. 13–20). The Netherlands: IOS Press.

Rittle-Johnson, B., Siegler, R. S., & Alibali, M. W. (2001). Developing conceptual understanding and procedural skill in mathematics: An iterative process. *Journal of Educational Psychology, 93*(2), 346–362.

Roll, I., Aleven, V., McLaren, B. M., & Koedinger, K. R. (2011). Improving students' help-seeking skills using metacognitive feedback in an intelligent tutoring system. *Learning and Instruction, 21*(2), 267–280.

Roll, I., Baker, R. S. J. d., Aleven, V., & Koedinger, K. R. (under review). The effect of overuse and underuse of help resources in intelligent tutoring systems. Manuscript submitted for publication.

Ryan, A. M., Pintrich, P. R., & Midgley, C. (2001). Avoiding seeking help in the classroom: Who and why? *Educational Psychology Review, 13*(2), 93–114.

Salden, R., Aleven, V., Schwonke, R., & Renkl, A. (2010). The expertise reversal effect and worked examples in tutored problem solving: Benefits of adaptive instruction. *Instructional Science, 38*(3), 289–307. doi:10.1007/s11251-009-9107-8.

Scheines, R., & Sieg, W. (1994). Computer environments for proof construction. *Interactive Learning Environments, 4*(2), 159–169.

Shih, B., Koedinger, K. R., & Scheines, R. (2008). A response time model for bottom-out hints as worked examples. In R. S. J. D. Baker, T. Barnes, & J. Beck (Eds.), *Proceedings of the 1st International Conference on Educational Data Mining, EDM 2008* (pp. 117–26). Worcester, MA: International Educational Data Mining Society.

Shih, B., Koedinger, K. R., & Scheines, R. (2010). Unsupervised discovery of student learning tactics. In R. S. J. D. Baker, A. Merceron, & P. I. Pavlik Jr. (Eds.), *Proceedings of the 3rd International Conference on Educational Data Mining, EDM 2010* (pp. 201–210). Worcester, MA: International Educational Data Mining Society.

Simons, D. J., & Chabris, C. F. (2011). What people believe about how memory works: A representative survey of the U.S. population. *PLoS One, 6*(8), e22757. doi:10.1371/journal.pone.0022757.

Stamper, J., Barnes, T., & Croy, M. (2012). Enhancing the automatic generation of hints with expert seeding. *International Journal of Artificial Intelligence in Education, 21*(2), 153–167.

Stamper, J., Eagle, M., Barnes, T., & Croy, M. (2011). Experimental evaluation of automatic hint generation for a logic tutor. In J. Kay, S. Bull, & G. Biswas (Eds.), *Proceeding of the 15th International Conference on Artificial Intelligence in Education (AIED2011)* (pp. 345–352). Berlin: Springer.

Stamper, J., Koedinger, K. R., Baker, R., Skogsholm, A., Leber, B., Demi, S., et al. (2011). Managing the educational dataset lifecycle with DataShop. In J. Kay, S. Bull, G. Biswas, & T. Mitrovic (Eds.), *Proceeding of the 15th International Conference on Artificial Intelligence in Education (AIED2011)* (pp. 557–559). Berlin: Springer.

Thiede, K. W., Griffin, T. D., Wiley, J., & Redford, J. (2009). Metacognitive monitoring during and after reading. In D. J. Hacker, J. Dunlosky, & A. C. Graesser (Eds.), *Handbook of metacognition in education* (pp. 85–106). The Educational Psychology Series. New York: Routledge.

Tousignant, M., & DesMarchais, J. E. (2002). Accuracy of student self-assessment ability compared to their own performance in a problem-based learning medical program: a correlation study. *Advances in Health Sciences Education, 7*, 19–27.

VanLehn, K. (2006). The behavior of tutoring systems. *International Journal of Artificial Intelligence in Education, 16*(3), 227–265.

VanLehn, K. (2011). The relative effectiveness of human tutoring, intelligent tutoring systems, and other tutoring systems. *Educational Psychologist, 46*(4), 197–221.

VanLehn, K., Jones, R. M., & Chi, M. T. H. (1992). A model of the self-explanation effect. *Journal of the Learning Sciences, 2*(1), 1–60.

VanLehn, K., Lynch, C., Schultz, K., Shapiro, J. A., Shelby, R. H., Taylor, L., et al. (2005). The Andes physics tutoring system: Lessons learned. *International Journal of Artificial Intelligence in Education, 15*(3), 147–204.

White, B., & Frederiksen, J. (1998). Inquiry, modeling, and metacognition: Making science accessible to all students. *Cognition and Instruction, 16*(1), 3–117.

Winne, P. H. (1995). Inherent details in self-regulated learning. *Educational Psychologist, 30*, 173–187.

Winne, P. H. (2010). Improving measurements of self-regulated learning. *Educational Psychologist, 45*(4), 267–276. doi:10.1080/00461520.2010.517150.

Winne, P. H. (2011). A cognitive and metacognitive analysis of self-regulated learning. In B. J. Zimmerman & D. H. Schunk (Eds.), *Handbook of self-regulation of learning and performance* (pp. 15–32). New York: Routledge.

Winne, P. H., & Hadwin, A. F. (1998). Studying as self-regulated learning. In D. J. Hacker, J. Dunlosky, & A. C. Graesser (Eds.), *Metacognition in educational theory and practice* (pp. 279–306). Hillsdale, NJ: Erlbaum.

Winne, P. H., & Hadwin, A. F. (2008). The weave of motivation and self-regulated learning. In D. H. Schunk & B. J. Zimmerman (Eds.), *Motivation and self-regulated learning: Theory, research, and applications* (pp. 297–314). Mahwah, NJ: Lawrence Erlbaum.

Winne, P. H., & Jamieson-Noel, D. (2002). Exploring students' calibration of self reports about study tactics and achievement. *Contemporary Educational Psychology, 27*, 551–572.

Winne, P. H., Zhou, M., & Egan, R. (2011). Designing assessments of self-regulated learning. In G. Schraw & D. H. Robinson (Eds.), *Assessment of higher-order thinking skills* (pp. 89–118). Charlotte, NC: Information Age.

Wittwer, J., & Renkl, A. (2008). Why instructional explanations often do not work: A framework for understanding the effectiveness of instructional explanations. *Educational Psychologist, 43*(1), 49–64.

Wood, H., & Wood, D. (1999). Help seeking, learning and contingent tutoring. *Computers & Education, 33*(2/3), 153–169.

Woolf, B. P. (2009). *Building intelligent interactive tutors: Student-centered strategies for revolutionizing e-learning*. Burlington, MA: Morgan Kaufmann.

Zimmerman, B. J. (2000). Attaining self-regulation: A social cognitive perspective. In M. Boekaerts, P. R. Pintrich, & M. Zeidner (Eds.), *Handbook of self-regulation* (pp. 13–39). San Diego, CA: Academic Press.

Zimmerman, B. J. (2008). Investigating self-regulation and motivation: Historical background, methodological developments, and future prospects. *American Educational Research Journal, 45*(1), 166–183.

Zimmerman, B. J. (2011). Motivational sources and outcomes of self-regulated learning and performance. In B. J. Zimmerman & D. H. Schunk (Eds.), *Handbook of self-regulation of learning and performance* (pp. 49–64). New York: Routledge.

Zimmerman, B. J., & Martinez-Pons, M. (1986). Development of a structured interview for assessing students' use of self-regulated learning strategies. *American Educational Research Journal, 23*, 614–628.

Zusho, A., Karabenick, S. A., Bonney, C. R., & Sims, B. C. (2007). Contextual determinants of motivation and help seeking in the college classroom. In R. P. Perry & J. C. Smart (Eds.), *The scholarship of teaching and learning in higher education: An evidence-based perspective* (pp. 611–59). Dordrecht, The Netherlands: Springer.

22 AnimalWatch: An Intelligent Tutoring System for Algebra Readiness

Carole R. Beal

Abstract

The AnimalWatch tutoring system provides students with instruction in algebra readiness problem solving, including basic computation, fractions, variables and expressions, basic statistics and simple geometry. Students solve word problems that include authentic environmental science content, and can access a range of multimedia resources that provide instructional scaffolding, such as video lessons and worked examples. Because providing learners with choices is associated with enhanced motivation, AnimalWatch is designed to allow students to decide what science topic they would like to learn about, and when they would like to navigate between different modules in the system. Several evaluation studies in classroom settings have found positive effects of AnimalWatch on study-specific measures of problem solving. Benefits have been strongest for students who are struggling in math, suggesting that technology-based learning can be especially effective for this population.

AnimalWatch is an intelligent tutoring system (ITS) that provides middle school students with adaptive instruction in math word problem solving. The ability to solve word problems is considered to be a critically important component of mathematics proficiency (Kintsch & Greeno, 1985; National Council of Teachers of Mathematics, 2000). Solving such problems goes beyond the direct application of a procedure to a set of provided numbers; rather, to solve a word problem, students must find and relate the relevant information while overlooking other information, and identify what the problem is actually asking (Koedinger & Nathan, 2004). In general, word problems are thought to be more challenging than de-contextualized problems, due to the need to "translate" the story information into a numerical representation (LeBlanc & Weber-Russell, 1996; Nathan & Koedinger, 2000). AnimalWatch addresses the need for instructional resources that target word problem solving through interactive online resources that provide students with guidance about the appropriate solution strategies.

The word problems in the AnimalWatch ITS have a unique focus on environmental science.

C.R. Beal (✉)
School of Information Science, University of Arizona,
P.O. Box 210077, Tucson, AZ 85721, USA
e-mail: crbeal@email.arizona.edu

R. Azevedo and V. Aleven (eds.), *International Handbook of Metacognition and Learning Technologies*, Springer International Handbooks of Education 26, DOI 10.1007/978-1-4419-5546-3_22,

The problems involve authentic science content and numerical information about various endangered species, including the Snow Leopard, the North Atlantic Right Whale, the Mongolian Takhi Wild Horse, the Giant Panda, and others. The unit about a particular species might include problems about its characteristics, habitat, current threats due to environmental issues (e.g., habitat loss) and history. Much of the science content in the word problems comes from partnerships with science education organizations and research units such as the San Diego Zoo Conservation Research Center, the New England Aquarium, and others (Beal & Arroyo, 2002).

Each word problem in the AnimalWatch ITS includes a graphic, such as an image of the endangered species or its habitat. In addition, each word problem includes a set of help resources designed to assist the student with the math operation required for the problem. There are several types of help resources, including worked examples showing the steps involved in a similar problem (e.g., same operation but with slightly different numbers), interactive examples (e.g., the student enters numbers and is guided through the solution), virtual manipulatives (e.g., the student divides a bar into sections as part of a fractions problem), and video lessons (e.g., short video clip of a teacher working through a problem at a whiteboard with narration). All of the word problems include at least one help resource, and most of the problems include multiple resources.

The AnimalWatch word problems involve algebra readiness math topics that are aligned with the California Mathematics Content Standards for Grade 6, including the following:

- Number sense: basic computation operations, and fraction problems with like and unlike denominators.
- Algebra and Functions: Students learn to solve one variable equations, as well as problems involving unit conversion, interest calculations, and rates.
- Statistics and Probability: Students learn about measures of average (mean, median, mode).
- Geometry and Measurement: Students learn about geometric shapes, figures, and angles.

Although the primary target user group is Grade 6 students, AnimalWatch has also been used by older students who need to review this algebra readiness material. As one discouraged high school math teacher commented when she asked if her failing Grade 9 students could use AnimalWatch to review basic math facts, "If you can't do division, you aren't going to pass Algebra 1."

AnimalWatch was initially developed as a standalone application that had to be installed on students' computers. As powerful Web technologies emerged that could support interactive instruction, AnimalWatch was subsequently re-implemented as a Web-based system. Students now log in to the AnimalWatch application from the project Web site (http://www.animalwatch.org). As they solve the AnimalWatch math problems, their actions are automatically recorded by the server computer running the AnimalWatch software. The data sets include records of students' solutions to the word problems, including the number of incorrect answer attempts per problem, latencies, and whether students viewed any of the multimedia resources on each problem, such as videos and worked examples. These data can be extracted for analysis of students' performance and estimates of their learning strategies (Cohen & Beal, 2009).

Theoretical Framework

The design of the AnimalWatch ITS reflects the theoretical framework that has guided most intelligent tutoring systems, that is, that students will learn best when provided with moderately challenging problems that are accompanied by "scaffolding" meaning hints, worked examples, and integrated instruction that will help the student find the solution (Brown, Ellery, & Campione, 1998; Murray & Arroyo, 2002; Woolf, 2009). Intelligent tutoring systems are designed with the goal of matching the instruction provided by human tutors, generally considered to be the "gold standard" for instructional effectiveness (Bloom, 1984). Studies of experienced human math tutors reveal that they use a range of strategies to support students' learning while sustaining motivation (Lepper,

Woolverton, Mumme, & Gurtner, 1993). Tutors often alternate between choosing problems that the student can solve with some guidance, and selecting problems that the student can solve easily on his or her own. The balance of challenge and success is especially encouraging for students with low math self-efficacy (Beal, Qu, & Lee, 2008).

The instructional behavior of the AnimalWatch ITS is determined by the interaction between the pedagogical model and the student model (Beck, Woolf, & Beal, 2000). The pedagogical model includes the curriculum of math topics included in the ITS, along with a network linking the topics in prerequisite relationships. For example, students will work on basic arithmetic topics before moving on to fractions; within fractions, students will work on operations with like denominators before operations with unlike denominator fractions. Each word problem in the AnimalWatch database is indexed by math topic and difficulty within the topic (e.g., problems involving single digits are assumed to be easier than those involving multiple digits).

In addition to the pedagogical model, AnimalWatch maintains a model of the student's estimated proficiency with the target math topics (Beck et al., 2000). The proficiency estimate is continually revised as the student works on problems involving that topic. The pedagogical model utilizes an adaptive problem selector to search through the database of word problems to select an appropriate problem for presentation to the student. If the student makes several errors on a problem, the problem selector will attempt to locate another similar problem. For example, if the student makes errors on two word problems involving multi-digit division, the proficiency estimate will be relatively low, but if the student solves the next two division problems correctly, the proficiency estimate will be increased. As the student demonstrates success with problems involving one topic, the pedagogical model will move on to the next topic in the math curriculum. The problem selector will also periodically choose a problem involving an easier skill, to verify that the student has retained mastery of those earlier skills.

Learner Choice

The self-regulation theoretical framework holds that learners need to identify good strategies and to figure out how to allocate their time and attention to accomplish their goals (Azevedo & Cromley, 2004; Boekaerts & Corno, 2005; Zimmerman, 1990; Zimmerman & Schunk, 2011). This view is supported by research indicating that learners' motivation in technology-based learning environments is enhanced by opportunities to make choices (Cordova & Lepper, 1996). However, students in classroom situations typically have very little choice about what to learn about or how to go about learning the information. Similarly, traditional tutoring systems do not provide students with many opportunities to choose what they want to learn and how to proceed. For example, in AnimalWatch, the problem selector chooses the sequence of problems that the student will see; he or she does not get to decide on the problems that he or she would like to solve. Therefore, as AnimalWatch was being designed, we explicitly searched for ways to balance the directive aspects of the pedagogical model with opportunities for students to make decisions about their own learning. This approach led to the inclusion of several features.

Options for Choosing Content

One student choice offered in AnimalWatch involves the science content that the student would like to learn about. More specifically, students are provided with a choice of several endangered species themes, with sets of word problems organized into "adventures" or virtual narratives. Students can start with the Giant Panda and then move to problems about the Takhi Wild Horse whenever they want, or choose the White Shark and then switch to the California Condor unit. When students move from one endangered species topic to another, the student model maintains its estimate of their proficiency and their current point in the curriculum, and selects similar problems about the new species.

One challenge faced in the project was how to ensure that all students make similar progress through the narrative when they do not all make equivalent progress through the math curriculum. When students choose a particular endangered species, they work through several (usually four) distinct modules with problems that form a coherent story line. For example, the student who selects the Takhi Wild Horse first completes a level with problems about the wild horse, its evolutionary history, and how it differs from domestic horses. Then, the student moves on to a level with content about Mongolia and its deserts, representing the native habitat of the wild horse. We adopted the structured narrative format early in the system's design, because students indicated that facing a seemingly unending sequence of math problems was daunting, and that they needed some indication that they were making progress as the result of their problem solving.

The interface was updated to show the levels available for each endangered species adventure, with those currently available in full color whereas those that the student had not yet achieved shown in a faded mode. This is quite similar to the concept of levels in a computer game design. However, in a game design, the student would have to achieve some criterion level of performance in math to "unlock" the subsequent level. The challenge is that students vary in math proficiency and it is not necessarily possible to ensure that everyone can achieve the required criterion within a classroom context. We cannot assume that a student user can simply try again to perform to criterion within a level; there may not be more time available (e.g., if the class has one session in the computer lab that week). At the same time, we want students to feel successful—if they do not succeed in a context where many of their peers are doing well, motivation is likely to decline. This is particularly important for special education students—perhaps a student works more slowly than his or her classmates and would not be expected to complete as many problems in a class period. Even so, the student should still have a feeling of success through having a fair opportunity to "pass" a level. This philosophy is directly linked to the theoretical framework of ITS research—students should be challenged but also be able to succeed—with "success" being defined for the individual.

The initial solution adopted in the AnimalWatch project was to ensure that all the ITS topics were available for all levels. Thus, a student who wanted to work on the Giant Panda adventure could make progress through four segments of the adventure narrative even if the problem selector estimated that the student still needed to work on computation. Other students could make progress through the Panda adventure while working on fractions and other more challenging material. It required a significant development effort to generate sufficient content for all endangered species and all math topics but the investment in content development was determined to be warranted based on the theoretical principle that students needed to be challenged but also to experience success and a sense of progress.

Upon reflection, the strategy made sense from the pedagogical perspective but presented considerable challenges from the development point of view. More specifically, considerable content was created but not all of it was utilized—a challenge faced by other leveled application such as computer games, where much of the cost goes to creating levels that relatively few players access (Beal & Beck, 2002). In addition, a post-hoc analysis indicated that there were unintended effects on the pedagogical behavior of the problem selector, which was set to move on to the next level of difficulty or the next curriculum topic at the point where no qualified problems could be located (Arroyo, Murray, Beck, Woolf, & Beal, 2003). For example, if the student made errors on three double-digit multiplication problems about the Right Whale in sequence and then solved the next one correctly without errors, one would ideally want to present another similar problem to check that the student really understood the solution procedure. However, when no such problem was available, the problem selector would fall back on easier problems. In effect, the problem selective was constrained by the inability to find enough qualifying problems to sustain the pedagogical strategy, even though AnimalWatch had over 800 word problems available. The lesson learned was that content was the bottleneck when it came to providing students with choice, which was important in the self-regulation framework, and also a sense of progress, which was important to sustain their engagement.

Problem Solving Options

In addition to providing students with a choice of science content, AnimalWatch was also designed so that students would have choices about their strategies for approaching a problem. In the word problem solving modules, the student has several options when he or she is working on a problem. One option is to try to answer the problem. In the current design, the student has up to three tries to solve each problem. In early studies with prototype versions of AnimalWatch, data indicated that students could self-correct about 40% of their own errors, suggesting that many errors reflected minor computation problems or misunderstanding of what the problem was asking (Arroyo et al., 2003). Allowing students the opportunity to review and diagnose where they might have gone wrong on their own was determined to be more consistent with self-regulation theories than forcing them to follow a prescribed solution path.

AnimalWatch is also designed to provide students with some form of scaffolding to help them solve the problem, without providing the solution directly. When the student enters an incorrect answer, he or she receives feedback in the form of a simple text message. A second incorrect answer elicits a different feedback message. About two-thirds of the feedbacks are specific to the problem, for example, "Convert both fractions so that they have a common denominator," followed by "Did you express both fractions with a denominator of 12?" Other feedback messages are more generic, including suggesting that the student view one of the help resources (e.g., watch the video about how to find a common denominator), read the problem again or ask the teacher for help.

Notice that AnimalWatch is designed to allow the student to decide when to utilize the help resources; the system does not force the student into the help area. This is in contrast to the "model tracing" design in ITS research in which the student is explicitly guided to perform the steps required to solve the problem in the appropriate sequence. Model tracing has many advantages in terms of ensuring that the student learns the solution path and providing diagnostic information about possible misconceptions. However, model tracing can be overly prescriptive; students may not have the opportunity to reflect on where they went wrong and to correct their own errors. Therefore, AnimalWatch allows students to decide whether or not to activate the help resources; they are not required to do so. Students are also offered a choice about different formats, including worked examples that are much like PowerPoint presentations, interactive widgets that illustrate a specific concept or procedure, and brief video lessons.

Students also have the option to indicate that a particular word problem is too hard for him or her at that point. When the student clicks the "too hard" icon, he or she is asked to confirm the choice, and has the option to return to the problem at that point or to move on to the next problem. Students who are skilled self-regulated learners continually assess how well they are doing and make choices about the most effective use of their study time. If a particular problem is simply too hard or confusing, even with the resources available, it makes strategic sense to move on to another problem. Interestingly, although "help abuse" (behaviors in which the student deliberately walks through the help resources to find the correct answer) can be a concern with traditional model-tracing tutors, abuse of the "too hard" option has been relatively rare in AnimalWatch.

Alternate Activities

To provide students with additional opportunities to direct their own learning, we added multiple modules to AnimalWatch, and allowed students to decide how to allocate their time between different modules. Thus, in addition to the core word problem solving modules about endangered species,

AnimalWatch now includes "SkillBuilder" units that are designed to build proficiency with basic math facts. The SkillBuilders are based on research by Royer and his colleagues who found a relation between students' knowledge of basic math facts and their performance on tests of math problem solving (Royer, Tronsky, Chan, Jackson, & Merchant 1999). If the student's limited cognitive resources are absorbed by the need to perform minor computations then the student will have less cognitive capacity to form the appropriate problem representation, identify the necessary operation, and track progress to the solution. Royer and colleagues have shown that when students practice basic math facts their performance on test-type math problems improves (Arroyo, Woolf, Royer, Tai, & English, 2010; Royer et al., 1999).

Based on this research, the SkillBuilders in the AnimalWatch ITS include ten true–false trials involving simple math facts in which the student's goal is to respond as accurately and as quickly as possible. For example, one SkillBuilder presents the student with trials in which he or she must determine if a fraction and a percent are equivalent, such as "1/4 = 25%" (true) or "1/2 = 75%" (false). Difficulty is intentionally set to be relatively low so that students can do well with practice, which encourages repetition and builds fluency with the target facts and operations.

Each word problem solving module in AnimalWatch now includes one or more SkillBuilders that target math facts and vocabulary items that will support the math topics in the module. Many students appear to enjoy the fast pace as an alternative to the more demanding word problem modules. Students also appear motivated by the fact that with practice they can achieve high scores on a SkillBuilder. We have even observed students pair up and start the same SkillBuilder together in a competition to see who can get the fastest time and a perfect score. Of course, providing students with choices about where to allocate their studying time leaves open the possibility that students may not make good decisions. In some cases, students spend most of their time on SkillBuilders and will attempt to avoid the word problem module unless their teacher directs them to work on word problems. We are currently investigating the relation between student characteristics, such as gender, prior math achievement, mathematics motivation, and status as an English Learner or English Primary student, and the proportion of time that the student spends in the SkilllBuilders relative to the core word problem solving modules.

Summary of Empirical Findings

The AnimalWatch ITS has gone through several "waves" of evaluations. In the early days of the project, the primary focus was on supporting students' feelings of self-efficacy as they solved challenging math problems. The hypothesis was that when students receive instruction that blends challenge with scaffolding to ensure problem solving success, their confidence should be sustained. We evaluated the impact of AnimalWatch on students' self-concept in mathematics, as indicated by self-report survey responses, yielding positive results (Arroyo et al., 2003; Beck, Arroyo, Woolf, & Beal, 1999).

In subsequent work, the initial evaluation was extended include a consideration of how students' math problem solving evolved as they worked with AnimalWatch. More specifically, we compared students' error rates for word problems presented early in a problem sequence (e.g., a series of five multi-digit division problems) with error rates on subsequent problems in the sequence. Results indicated that students were less likely to make errors on problems presented later in the sequence, suggesting that students were learning from the ITS (Arroyo, 2003; Arroyo et al., 2003).

As the AnimalWatch ITS was expanded to include a broader range of math topics and additional help resources, the focus of the research effort shifted more towards evaluation of its impact on students' math proficiency using pre–post test designs with comparison groups. In one study, the impact of AnimalWatch was compared to the impact of working with a human math tutor in a small group setting (Beal, Shaw, & Birch, 2007). The participants attended a 6 week academic summer program in which they spent 2 h per week on literacy activities, and 2 h per week on math. One group of participants was assigned to work for 1 h per week with AnimalWatch and the additional hour with a math tutor. The second group worked for 2 h per week with a math tutor. The summer program math tutors were experienced math teachers who worked with groups of 4–6 students. Students completed a pre test of math problem solving at the start of the program, and a post test at the program's conclusion. There was no difference in performance between the two groups at the beginning; both groups showed significant improvement by the end of the program. This result indicates that students who worked with AnimalWatch for half of their instructional time showed as much improvement as those who received all their math instruction from a human tutor.

Results in another study demonstrated that students who had more sessions with AnimalWatch improved more than those with less access to the software (Beal, Adams, & Cohen, 2010). Although the original intention was to have all the study participants complete at least six sessions with the ITS, the realities of research in urban schools impeded the original design. The research schedule was frequently interrupted by unexpected teacher transfers, technical issues (e.g., laptop carts not charged overnight as planned), and classroom lockdowns due to police activity. In addition, there was a high level of student turnover, with absences, transfers and new enrollments occurring on a daily basis. In effect, the design evolved in a comparison of students who had the chance to work with the ITS for more versus fewer sessions.

Results indicated that although there was overall improvement from pre to post-test, the improvement was stronger for students who had multiple sessions with AnimalWatch. Although not particularly surprising, this finding provided some support for the interpretation that students' improved performance from pre to post test was not due to the novelty of learning math with a computer. Additionally, improvement was greater for students whose pre test scores were relatively low and these students were most likely to use the multimedia help resources that are integrated into AnimalWatch. Thus, this study linked pre to post test change with opportunity to use the ITS, and with students' actual use of the help resources in the system.

In another study, we compared pre to post test change for students who worked with AnimalWatch for three class sessions, and those who continued with class instruction (Beal, Arroyo, Cohen, & Woolf 2010). The results showed no overall improvement for either comparison group students or AnimalWatch users, perhaps due to the relatively limited number of sessions with the ITS. However, an exploratory analysis focusing on scores for low achieving students in the AnimalWatch group showed that they did improve from pre to post test, whereas low achieving comparison group students did not improve. In addition, we found a significant relation between using the multimedia help resources in AnimalWatch and significant improvement from pre to post test. After the post test had been administered, the students in the control group had the opportunity to use the ITS. The results indicated that the original control group students who had performed poorly on the pre test were most likely to use the help resources in the ITS.

Additional research has focused on the impact of AnimalWatch on math problem solving for students with different levels of proficiency with English. The student population in the USA is increasingly diverse, but the language of instruction in all states is English (August & Shanahan, 2006). Because AnimalWatch focuses directly on word problem solving, it is reasonable to predict that students' proficiency with English might affect their ability to comprehend a math word problem, identify the appropriate math operation, and evaluate whether the answer makes sense in the context of the problem. Interestingly, the research base on the potential impact of reading proficiency on math word problem solving is surprisingly limited. Some studies indicate that English Learners perform worse than English Primary students on math test items that involve unfamiliar vocabulary (Martiniello, 2008).

However, other studies show no real benefits from accommodations such as simplified English or extra time on tests, which presumably would help if the student needed more time to read the English text (for a review see ref. Kieffer, Lesaux, Rivera, & Francis, 2009).

In one study of English Learners and English Primary students who worked with AnimalWatch, results showed that the English Learners performed less well on the pre test and post test, but that both groups showed significant improvement after working with the ITS (Beal, Adams, & Cohen, 2010). Data regarding the English Learners' proficiency with English was obtained, including measures of listening comprehension, conversational proficiency, and reading proficiency. Only reading proficiency was related to math problem solving in AnimalWatch.

In a subsequent analysis, we investigated students' problem solving on math problems varying in the readability of the English text. AnimalWatch problems involve a good deal of scientific content, and may also contain unusual vocabulary related to the environmental science content and themes of the virtual adventures, which might presumably impede the problem solving of English Learners. The word problems were processed by the REAP algorithm developed by the Language Technologies Institute at Carnegie Mellon University, which assigns a grade level readability metric for each problem. REAP considers both vocabulary frequency and grammatical structure and has been validated with relatively short texts (such as math word problems), in contrast to other algorithms for assessing text readability (Heilman, Collins-Thompson, Callan, & Eskenazi 2007).

After obtaining a readability metric for each word problem, we then searched through the AnimalWatch student record database to locate records for word problems that had been solved by at least 20 English Learners and 20 English Primary students. These records consisted of time-stamped flat files representing the sequence of actions on each problem (e.g., problem is presented, student enters answer after some latency, answer is evaluated as correct or incorrect, student clicks "help" icon, answer is entered, answer is evaluated as correct, student clicks "next problem" icon, etc.). The primary metrics of problem solving for the present analyses were the total time on each problem (number of seconds), the number of incorrect answer attempts on the problem, if the correct answer was ever entered, and whether the multimedia hints were accessed during the problem.

Initial comparisons indicated that the English Primary students performed better overall than the English Learners, who took longer on each problem, made more incorrect answer attempts on the problems, and were less likely to enter the correct answer than English Primary students (Cirett & Beal, 2010). One might assume that students who had trouble reading the word problem text would simply give up but if anything, several aspects of the data suggested that the English Learners tried harder. For one thing, the English Learners were more likely than the English Primary students to activate the multimedia help resources, which included video lessons that might have been especially accessible. In addition, an estimate of "gaming" behavior (e.g., the student rapidly enters wrong answers until the correct answer is shown) indicated that although gaming levels were low overall, this behavior was more likely to be observed for English Primary students. Finally, analyses now being conducted appear to suggest that the English Learners allocate more of their instructional time to the SkillBuilders than is the case for the English Primary students, who do not have the same challenges in reading the problems in the word problem module. From the perspective of self-regulated learning theory, the English Learners appeared to be behaving quite strategically given the constraints presented by the difficulty that they experience with reading the word problems.

Current Challenges

Efficacy

One challenge is to learn if AnimalWatch instruction can help students improve standardized math test scores. Although results with study-specific tests have been encouraging, transfer to test performance is often quite difficult to demonstrate, and the qualities that make AnimalWatch appealing to students, such as the contextualized problems, availability of learner choice and narrative organization of problem sequences, may actually undermine transfer to more traditional math problems. An efficacy evaluation of AnimalWatch is now being conducted by an independent research institute.

Personalized Feedback

A second challenge is to establish the optimal level of customized and individualized feedback provided to students about their problem solving performance while also preserving students' sense of autonomy and agency while using AnimalWatch. In research with another math tutoring system for geometry (Wayang Outpost), we found that students found that individualized messages about their performance were believable and accurate (e.g., diagnosing guessing behavior) but at the same time, students expressed dislike for the notion that the computer was "tracking" and analyzing their behavior (Beal & Lee, 2005). Also, increasing the level of customized feedback provided when students enter the wrong answer would require diagnosing the errors, which currently is not done by AnimalWatch (i.e., the ITS recognizes that the answer is not correct but does not relate the error to possible misconceptions). We are now investigating how students can be provided with increased individualized feedback in AnimalWatch while still allowing them to feel that they have control over their own learning while using the ITS. One option is to allow teachers to enter problem specific suggestions for individual students, based on teachers' knowledge of the types of errors that the student is likely to make.

Accessibility

A third challenge is to ensure that the AnimalWatch tutoring system is fully accessible to all students, including those with special needs. In particular, the AnimalWatch interface relies on graphical icons for navigation, and is not accessible to students with visual impairments. With the growth of interest in Universal Design for Learning, it is becoming increasingly important to provide students with alternate ways to access instruction in technology-based learning systems (CAST, 2007). In the AnimalWatch project, we have investigated the potential of text-to-speech technology to make the word problems and instruction available to students who are educationally blind, meaning that they have no usable vision. The "AnimalWatch-VI" prototype for blind students includes word problems in audio format. The audio problems are generated with text-to-speech software and stored in the AnimalWatch database. The student accesses and navigates the system using simple keyboard commands (e.g., "Press p to listen to the problem") learned in a brief tutorial.

We conducted one field study with 14 blind students in California who solved up to 32 word problems in the AnimalWatch-VI prototype (Beal & Shaw, 2009). The results indicated that the blind students could use the system successfully. However, relative to typically sighted students who had solved the same word problems, the blind students made more incorrect answer attempts per problem and had to listen to the problems multiple times because the prototype did not include any scaffolding to help students solve the problem. Therefore, in a subsequent version of the prototype, we added two audio hints for each word problem. The first hint indicated the math operation needed for the problem (e.g., "This is a division problem") and the second hint provided more specific guidance about what to do (e.g., "Divide 54 by 9"). A second field test with 12 blind students in Arizona indicated that the availability of hints reduced the number of times that students had to listen to the problem. There was also a relation between students' math proficiency (based on reports provided by their teacher of students with visual impairments) and their use of hints, with students who were struggling in math being most likely to listen to the hints during problem solving.

Although blind students' reactions to the AnimalWatch-VI program were not formally assessed in the field studies, their spontaneous remarks and comments were highly enthusiastic. In particular, students indicated that they appreciated the fact that they could control their interaction with the software without having to rely on their TVI. Giving blind students responsibility for their own learning is consistent with the principles of self-determination, which have been identified as important for students with visual impairments. Although there has not yet been an explicit connection between self-determination principles and theories of self-regulated learning, it is not a major leap to suggest that designing software that can allow students with disabilities the opportunity to work independently would be consistent with the vision of the self-regulated learner as one who sets his or her own goals, chooses learning strategies, and monitors his or her own progress. The AnimalWatch-VI system is still quite limited; in particular, it does not yet provide any support for students with low vision (who make up 90% of students with visual impairments). However, the project illustrates the challenges and the potential rewards of ensuring that technology-based systems are fully accessible to students who need alternate forms of access to instruction.

Conclusions

The AnimalWatch project has been in progress for more than a decade, and its design has evolved considerably during that time. The changes have resulted from the emergence of new technologies, including opportunities to include multimedia and other interactive materials, as well as technologies for capturing and analyzing students' problem solving data in real time. In addition, the design of AnimalWatch has been adjusted over the years in response to evaluations conducted in authentic classroom contexts in which students have used the ITS as part of their math instruction. Although moving from the research lab into the classroom is not without challenges, the feedback provided by students and the opportunity to observe how students interact with instructional technology is invaluable for shaping ITS design. More specifically, AnimalWatch began as a fairly traditional intelligent tutoring system with a problem selector that directed what the student should learn and determined the instructional sequence. In its current form, the AnimalWatch system reflects a design philosophy that allows students to make decisions about what they want to work on and the strategies that they want to adopt. The evolution of the system reflects research from the framework of self-regulated learning and the vision of the self-regulated learner as one that sets his or her own goals, chooses appropriate strategies, and evaluates his or her own progress. Consistent with this framework, there are indications in some of our research that technology-based learning environments may actually be most helpful for students who are not doing well in the traditional classroom: Students who start out doing poorly or who face additional challenges related to English proficiency or visual impairments tend to show significant improvement after working with the ITS. In the context of educational research, this is an unusual finding; most often, educational interventions have the greatest benefit for those students who were doing well to begin with (Ceci & Papierno, 2005). Technology-based environments may be especially effective in helping struggling students make the connection between their learning behaviors and their performance outcomes, and demonstrating to them that they can succeed by using appropriate strategies, such as using the help resources that are readily available in the ITS to master new skills.

Acknowledgments Over the years, the AnimalWatch project has benefitted from the contributions of many talented people, including Ivon Arroyo, Beverly P. Woolf, Joseph Beck, David Marshall, David Hart, Rachel Wing, and Mary Anne Ramirez at the University of Massachusetts Amherst; Erin Shaw, Jean-Philippe Steinmetz, Mike Birch, and Teresa Dey at the University of Southern California; Thomas Hicks, William Mitchell, Jane Strohm, Timothy Brown, and Wesley Kerr at the University of Arizona; and Niall Adams at Imperial College London. The AnimalWatch project has been supported by grants from the National Science Foundation (HRD 9555737,

9714757) and the Institute of Education Sciences (R305K0500086, R305K090197). The views expressed in this chapter are not necessarily those of the sponsoring agencies.

References

Arroyo I. (2003). *Quantitative evaluation of gender differences, cognitive development differences and software effectiveness for an elementary mathematics intelligent tutoring system.* Unpublished doctoral dissertation, School of Education, University of Massachusetts, Amherst.

Arroyo, I., Murray, T., Beck, J. E., Woolf, B. P., & Beal, C. R. (2003). A formative evaluation of AnimalWatch. In *Proceedings of the 11th International Conference on Artificial Intelligence in Education* (pp. 371–373). Amsterdam: IOS.

Arroyo, I., Woolf, B. P., Royer, J. M., Tai, M., & English, S. (2010). Improving math learning through intelligent tutoring and basic skills training. *Proceedings of Intelligent Tutoring Systems: Lecture Notes in Computer Science, 6094* (pp. 423–432). Berlin: Springer.

August, D. L., & Shanahan, T. (2006). *Developing literacy in second language learners: Report of the National Literacy Panel on Language Minority Youth.* Hillsdale: Erlbaum.

Azevedo, R., & Cromley, J. G. (2004). Does training on self-regulated learning facilitate students' learning with hypermedia? *Journal of Educational Psychology, 96*, 523–535.

Beal, C. R., Adams, N. M., & Cohen, P. R. (2010). Reading proficiency and mathematics problem solving by high school English language learners. *Urban Education, 45*, 58–74.

Beal, C. R., & Arroyo, I. (2002). The AnimalWatch project: Creating an intelligent computer math tutor. In S. Calvert, A. Jordan, & R. Cocking (Eds.), *Children in the digital age* (pp. 183–198). Westport: Greenwood.

Beal, C. R., Arroyo, I., Cohen, P. R., & Woolf, B. P. (2010). Evaluation of AnimalWatch: An intelligent tutoring system for arithmetic and fractions. *Journal of Interactive Online Learning, 9*, 65–77.

Beal, C. R., & Beck, J. E. (2002). Intelligent user modeling and interactive entertainment. *Proceedings of the American Association of Artificial Intelligence Spring Symposium*. Menlo Park, CA: AAAI Press.

Beal, C. R., & Lee, H. (2005). Creating a pedagogical model that uses student self reports of motivation and mood to adapt ITS instruction. *Proceedings of the Workshop on Emotion and Motivation in Educational Software (EMES)*. Amsterdam: IOS Press.

Beal, C. R., Qu, L., & Lee, H. (2008). Mathematics motivation and achievement as predictors of high school students' guessing and help seeking with instructional software. *Journal of Computer Assisted Learning, 24*, 507–514.

Beal, C. R., & Shaw, E. (2009). An online math problem solving system for middle school students who are blind. *Journal of Online Learning and Teaching, 5*, 630–638.

Beal, C. R., Shaw, E., & Birch, M. (2007). Intelligent tutoring and human tutoring in small groups: An empirical comparison. In R. Luckin, K. R. Koedinger, & J. Greer (Eds.), *Artificial intelligence in education: Building technology rich learning contexts that work* (pp. 536–538). Amsterdam: IOS.

Beck, J. E., Arroyo, I., Woolf, B. P., & Beal, C. R. (1999). An ablative evaluation. In *Proceedings of the Ninth International Conference on Artificial Intelligence in Education* (pp. 611–613). Amsterdam: IOS Press.

Beck, J. E., Woolf, B. P., & Beal, C. R. (2000). Learning to teach: A machine learning architecture for intelligent tutor construction. In *Proceedings of the Seventeenth National Conference on Artificial Intelligence* (pp. 552–557). Austin, TX: AAAI Press.

Bloom, B. S. (1984). The 2 sigma problem: The search for methods of group instruction as effective as one-to-one tutoring. *Educational Researcher, 13*, 4–16.

Boekaerts, M., & Corno, L. (2005). Self regulation in the classroom: A perspective on assessment and intervention. *Applied Psychology: An International Review, 54*, 199–231.

Brown, A. L., Ellery, S., & Campione, J. (1998). Creating zones of proximal development electronically. In J. Greeno & S. Goldman (Eds.), *Thinking practices: A symposium in mathematics and science education* (pp. 341–368). Hillsdale: Erlbaum.

Ceci, S. J., & Papierno, P. B. (2005). The rhetoric and reality of gap closing: When the "have-nots" gain but the "haves" gain even more. *American Psychologist, 60*, 149–160.

Center for Applied Special Technology (CAST). (2007). *Summary of 2007 national summit on universal design for learning working groups*. Wakefield: CAST.

Cirett, F. G., & Beal, C. R. (2010). Problem solving by English learners and English primary students in an algebra readiness ITS. *Proceedings of the 23rd International FLAIRS Conference*. Menlo Park CA: AAAI Press. Retrieved from http://www.aaai.org/ocs/index.php/FLAIRS/2010/paper/view/1250.

Cohen, P. R., & Beal, C. R. (2009). Temporal dating mining for educational applications. *International Journal of Software and Informatics, 3*, 29–44.

Cordova, D., & Lepper, M. (1996). Intrinsic motivation and the process of learning: Beneficial effects of contextualization, personalization, and choice. *Journal of Educational Psychology, 88*, 715–730.

Heilman, M., Collins-Thompson, K., Callan, J., & Eskenazi, M. (2007). Combining lexical and grammatical features to improve readability measures for first and second language texts. *Proceedings of the Human Language Technology Conference*. Rochester, NY.

Kieffer, M. M., Lesaux, N. K., Rivera, M., & Francis, D. J. (2009). Accommodations for English language learners taking large-scale assessments: Meta-analysis on effectiveness and validity. *Review of Educational Research, 79*, 1168–1201.

Kintsch, W., & Greeno, J. G. (1985). Understanding and solving word arithmetic problems. *Psychological Review, 92*, 109–129.

Koedinger, K. R., & Nathan, M. J. (2004). The real story behind story problems: Effects of representations on quantitative reasoning. *The Journal of the Learning Sciences, 13*, 129–164.

LeBlanc, M. D., & Weber-Russell, S. (1996). Text integration and mathematics connections: A computer model of arithmetic word problem-solving. *Cognitive Science, 20*, 357–407.

Lepper, M. R., Woolverton, M., Mumme, D., & Gurtner, J. (1993). Motivational techniques of expert human tutors: Lessons for the design of computer-based tutors. In S. P. Lajoie & S. J. Derry (Eds.), *Computers as cognitive tools* (pp. 75–105). Hillsdale: Erlbaum.

Martiniello, M. (2008). Language and the performance of English language learners in math word problems. *Harvard Educational Review, 78*, 333–368.

Murray, T., & Arroyo, I. (2002). Toward measuring and maintaining the zone of proximal development in adaptive instructional systems. Proceedings of the 6th International Conference on Intelligent Tutoring Systems. In S. A. Cerri, G. Gouardères & F. Paraguaçu (Eds.), *Lecture notes in computer science 2363* (pp. 133–145). Berlin: Springer.

Nathan, M. J., & Koedinger, K. R. (2000). Teachers' and researchers' beliefs of early algebra development. *Journal of Mathematics Education Research, 31*, 168–190.

National Council of Teachers of Mathematics. (2000). *Principles and standards for school mathematics*. Reston: National Council of Teachers of Mathematics.

Royer, J. M., Tronsky, L. N., Chan, Y., Jackson, S. J., & Merchant, H. (1999). Math fact retrieval as the cognitive mechanism underlying gender differences in math test performance. *Contemporary Educational Psychology, 24*, 181–266.

Woolf, B. P. (2009). *Building intelligent interactive tutors: Student-centered strategies for revolutionizing e-learning*. Burlington: Morgan Kaufman.

Zimmerman, B. J. (1990). Self-regulated learning and academic achievement: An overview. *Educational Psychologist, 25*, 3–17.

Zimmerman, B. J., & Schunk, D. (2011). *Handbook of self-regulation of learning and performance*. London: Routledge.

Open Learner Models as Drivers for Metacognitive Processes

23

Susan Bull and Judy Kay

Abstract

Maintaining a model of the learner's understanding as they interact with an e-learning environment allows adaptation to the learner's educational needs. An Open Learner Model makes this machine's representation of the learner available to them. Typically, the state of the learner's knowledge is presented in some form, ranging from a simple overall mastery score, to a detailed display of how much and what the learner appears to know, their misconceptions and their progress through a course. This means that an Open Learner Model provides a suitable interface onto the learner model for use by the learner, and in some cases for others who support their learning, including peers, parents and teachers. This chapter considers some of the similarities between the goals of supporting and encouraging metacognition in intelligent tutoring systems and learning in general, and the benefits of opening the learner model to the user. We provide examples of two important classes of open learner models: those within a particular teaching system and those that are first-class citizens with value independently of a teaching system. The chapter provides a foundation for understanding the range of ways that Open Learner Models have already been used to support learning as well as directions yet to be explored, with reference to encouraging metacognitive activity and self-directed learning.

S. Bull (✉)
Electronic, Electrical and Computer Engineering, University of Birmingham, Birmingham, UK
e-mail: s.bull@bham.ac.uk

J. Kay
School of Information Technologies, University of Sydney, Sydney, NSW, Australia
e-mail: judy.kay@sydney.edu.au

R. Azevedo and V. Aleven (eds.), *International Handbook of Metacognition and Learning Technologies*, Springer International Handbooks of Education 26, DOI 10.1007/978-1-4419-5546-3_23,

Introduction

The type of learning technology addressed in this chapter is adaptive learning environments, or intelligent tutoring systems (ITS). This technology typically has three main components: a model of the domain or subject of study (e.g. a model of topics, concepts and interrelationships between concepts); a learner model, capturing the individual user's understanding of the domain, as inferred during their interaction (e.g. from navigation choices, answers to questions, problem-solving attempts, time on task); and a pedagogical model to allow personalisation of the teaching or guidance, for the learner. In this chapter we focus on the learner model and promoting metacognitive activity by providing the learner with access to the model of their knowledge.

Metacognition has been defined in many ways, but it is generally considered to involve higher-order thinking *about* cognition, for example, involving knowledge about cognition. Importantly, it relates to regulation or monitoring of cognition, with the associated aspects of learner control over their own learning processes. (See, e.g. Georghiades, 2004; Schraw, 1998; Veenman, Van Hout-Wolters, & Afferbach, 2006.) Much of the work refers back to Flavell's introduction of "metacognition and cognitive monitoring", presented through discussion of metacognitive knowledge (comprising knowledge of person, task and strategy variables) and metacognitive experiences (Flavell, 1979). The importance of enhancing metacognitive awareness in learners has often been argued (e.g. Schoenfeld, 1987; Schraw, 1998), including the use of computer-based metacognitive support, such as for training general learning ability (Derry & Murphy, 1986); tutoring help-seeking strategies (Roll, Aleven, McLaren, & Koedinger, 2007); developing self-awareness through learning by teaching (Wagster, Tan, Biswas, & Schwartz, 2007); a reflection assistant for problem-solving (Gama, 2004); and encouraging learners to develop greater awareness of cognitive and metacognitive learning strategies (Bull, 1997).

Although metacognition is often described as requiring conscious processing and application, it has also been suggested that some lower levels of consciousness in processing may still be metacognitive, for example, through habitual regulatory behaviour (Veenman et al., 2006). It is this latter view that we adopt in this chapter: we acknowledge both the benefits of explicit metacognitive instruction or support and the potential to support metacognitive activity in a less explicit manner. We discuss these issues with reference to open learner models.

As stated above, modelling a learner's understanding (e.g. from questioning, tasks, help or hints requested) allows an ITS to adapt the interaction to suit the student. Open learner models (OLM) are learner models that are accessible, or "open" to the learner they represent. (See Bull & Kay, 2007; Dimitrova, McCalla, & Bull, 2007 for recent overviews of open learner modelling.) There are many reasons for making a learner model open to the learner, and we discuss these in the next section, noting the links and the relevance of many of these goals for metacognition. In the following section, we explore metacognition in relation to two types of open learner model: those embedded in a tutoring system and those used independently of the larger tutoring environment. We explain these ideas with carefully chosen examples which illustrate some of the breadth of possibilities explored in research into open learner modelling. We conclude with a discussion of the links between learner control of their learning and open learner modelling and the essential role that OLMs can play in supporting metacognition and metacognitive development.

Metacognition in Open Learner Modelling

The SMILI:) (Student Models that Invite the Learner In) Open Learner Modelling Framework (Bull & Kay, 2007) provides a method of describing and analysing existing

OLMs, and it offers a set of guidelines for the designer of an OLM to consider. The framework aims to improve understanding of the nature of OLMs and their potential roles. Its elements can facilitate comparisons between OLMs and systems that use OLMs.

SMILI:) identifies various purposes for opening the model. We now summarise these, italicising those that are particularly relevant for metacognition:

- Improving learner model accuracy by allowing the learner to make contributions to their learner model
- *Promoting learner reflection through confronting students with representations of their understanding*
- *Facilitating planning and/or monitoring of learning*
- *Facilitating collaboration amongst learners*
- Facilitating competition amongst learners
- Supporting navigation
- The right of access to information stored about oneself
- *Learner control over and responsibility for their learning*
- Trust in the learner model content
- *Formative assessment*
- Summative assessment

While some of the above points have not been specifically identified as means to support metacognition, it is clear that this might also apply in such cases. For example, allowing learners to provide information directly for their learner model, to help increase its accuracy, can have the effect of prompting learners to think about their knowledge and understanding more precisely. Similarly, an OLM that facilitates navigation to other parts of a system through some kind of highlighting of links may also help learners to more deeply consider the structure and prerequisites within a domain.

Most OLMs are embedded in an ITS, and so designing the open learner model involves design decisions and compromises. It is necessary to ensure that the OLM does not compromise the effectiveness of the main teaching interface. So, design for externalisation of the learner model requires decisions about integrating viewing of the model into the larger interaction. We provide examples of OLMs in ITSs in Sect. 2.1, with a focus on how the OLMs aim to support metacognition.

Independent OLMs exist independently of any single system or ITS (Bull et al., 2008). Learner modelling occurs in the usual manner, but the primary purpose of the independent OLM is to help learners to recognise any problematic issues themselves, through inspection of their learner model, and then independently carry out appropriate work to overcome difficulties identified. This approach has links with the goals of enhancing metacognitive behaviours, with a focus on encouraging learner independence. We consider independent OLMs in Sect. 2.2.

Supporting Metacognition with Open Learner Models in Intelligent Tutoring Systems

Learner models are the core drivers of personalisation in an ITS. They may well be the defining component of an ITS, since there is such diversity in the other elements that may be needed for any particular tutoring system. Learner models can take many forms. The most appropriate depends on many factors, including pragmatics, such as the system's knowledge representation and reasoning approach for the domain knowledge and the teaching expertise. Others relate to the needs of the particular user, for example, their age and goals.

The dominant form of learner model reported in the ITS literature appears to be an overlay of the domain expertise. This means that the ease with which a model may be made available and understandable to a learner depends upon the representation of the domain. When that domain expertise is large or complex, it may be very difficult to make it usefully open to the learner. A natural approach to this problem is to define a part of the learner model that summarises the key elements that are meaningful and helpful for a learner.

One excellent example of this is in the SQL-Tutor (Mitrovic & Martin, 2002). This is a constraint-based tutor which makes use of a hundreds of constraints. It would be quite difficult to create a meaningful interface onto these. Instead, it

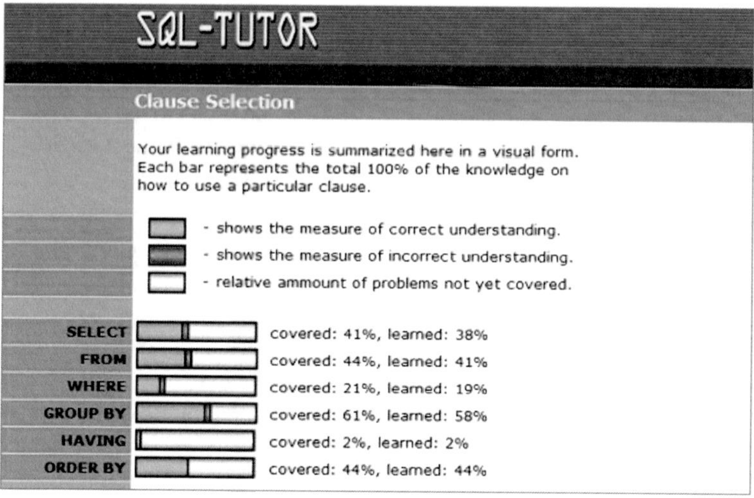

Fig. 23.1 Skill metres of the SQL-Tutor (Mitrovic & Martin, 2007)

presents a summary of the aspects that make sense from a student's perspective as illustrated in Fig. 23.1. It shows just six aspects of the learning domain, each a key element of SQL. For each of these, the learner can see their progress in terms of the demonstrated correct understanding (the left-most green part of each bar), incorrect understanding (the central red part) and the remaining white part indicating course content the student has yet to cover. In the figure, we can see that this student is only about halfway through the content but has mainly demonstrated correct understanding so far. A comprehensive evaluation of this approach showed significant learning benefits, especially for weaker students, and positive attitudes to this high-level progress indicator (Mitrovic & Martin, 2007). Notably, the open learner model assisted students in making better choices about problems they should tackle, a metacognitive skill for managing their learning. This form of open learner model has also been used in cognitive tutors (Corbett & Anderson, 1994) which also have a large complex underlying learner model but present the learner with a simple interface that has a readily understood skill metre.

A similar role for an OLM, as a starting point for the student to decide what to learn next, is found in the QuizGuide (Brusilovsky & Sosnovsky, 2005) adaptive educational hypermedia system (illustrated in Fig. 23.2 by the targets and arrows). Although this is for the same broad domain (SQL), the underlying system representation is quite different, being based on a coding of each available task with the concepts or learning objectives. In both cases, the key issue is that the information made available to learners facilitates their ability to determine how well they are progressing in different aspects of the domain, providing a support for reflection (e.g. encouraging them to think about their understanding, skills or level and think about their learning process). From this, the OLM facilitates learners' control of their learning as it helps them decide what to learn and how to plan their learning, important metacognitive skills. Indeed, these interfaces also help learners monitor their progress, because they can monitor the effectiveness of their plan, in terms of the changes in the open learner model.

A rather different approach to open learner modelling is illustrated in Simprac (Chesher, 2005; Chesher, Kay, & King, 2005), a tutor for medical students learning about the long-term management of chronic illness (Fig. 23.3). At the top left is one of the consultation interfaces; in this example, the interface enables the learner to examine parts of the simulated patient. The middle-right screen is presented to the learner at the end of each consultation with the simulated patient. It shows the learner each of their actions in the last consultation, and they are asked to

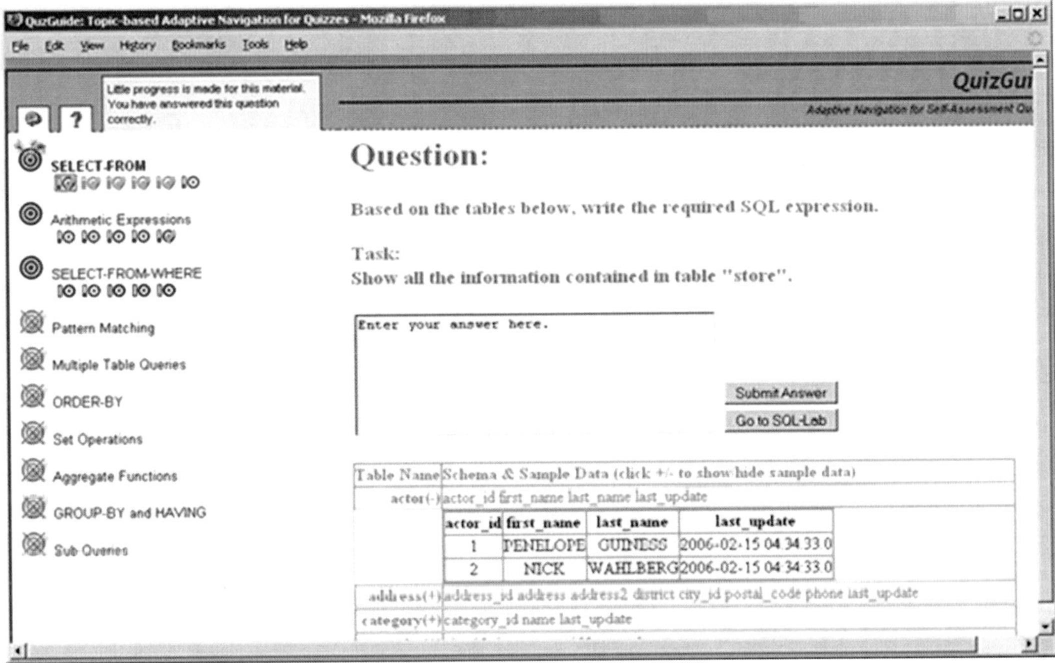

Fig. 23.2 Arrows in targets in QuizGuide (Brusilovsky & Sosnovsky, 2005)

reflect on these by assessing the importance of each question they asked the patient, as well as each aspect of the examination and tests ordered. The lower histogram shows the learner's performance in terms of the issues they explored, compared against their cohort.

One of the challenges of this domain is that learners can easily become entrenched in one perspective of the problem and its management: in spite of evidence that a management plan is ineffective, doctors may fail to recognise that this is the case. Accordingly, this tutor was created with a *reflective layer*, a set of interface elements that were designed to encourage the learner to reflect on their actions in the last consultation. To do this, the interface calls on the learner to reflect on *all* elements of the series of simulated consultations with patients. Following Schön (1987), the tutor supports reflection at two levels. First, it supports *reflection-on-action* meaning that the learner pauses at the end of a consultation to reflect on the step in that consultation. It also supports *reflection-on-reflection*, as the learner is encouraged to reflect on the way that they did the reflection phase. These are all metacognitive actions. For the core goals of supporting metacognition, an important aspect of the design of this OLM is that it shows learners their own performance in relative terms at two levels. First, it shows their performance compared with the expectations of the author of the tutor, an approach that can ensure that the tutor fits in with the teaching approach of a course and programme. Second, it shows their skill compared with a relevant, matched group of learners. In Simprac, there are three groups: medical students, general practitioners and experts in the particular domain of the tutorial. This tutor deals with a very different class of task from the SQL of the systems above: notably, there is some disagreement between experts about the best practice. It may be unrealistic and discouraging to show a medical student their performance against an expert, especially as an expert may be able to use quite different strategies from those that are best for a medical student. There are open questions about how to design and present a learner model that can best support reflection and particularly how to do it in ways that facilitate learning of the domain and of metacognitive skills. However, one important

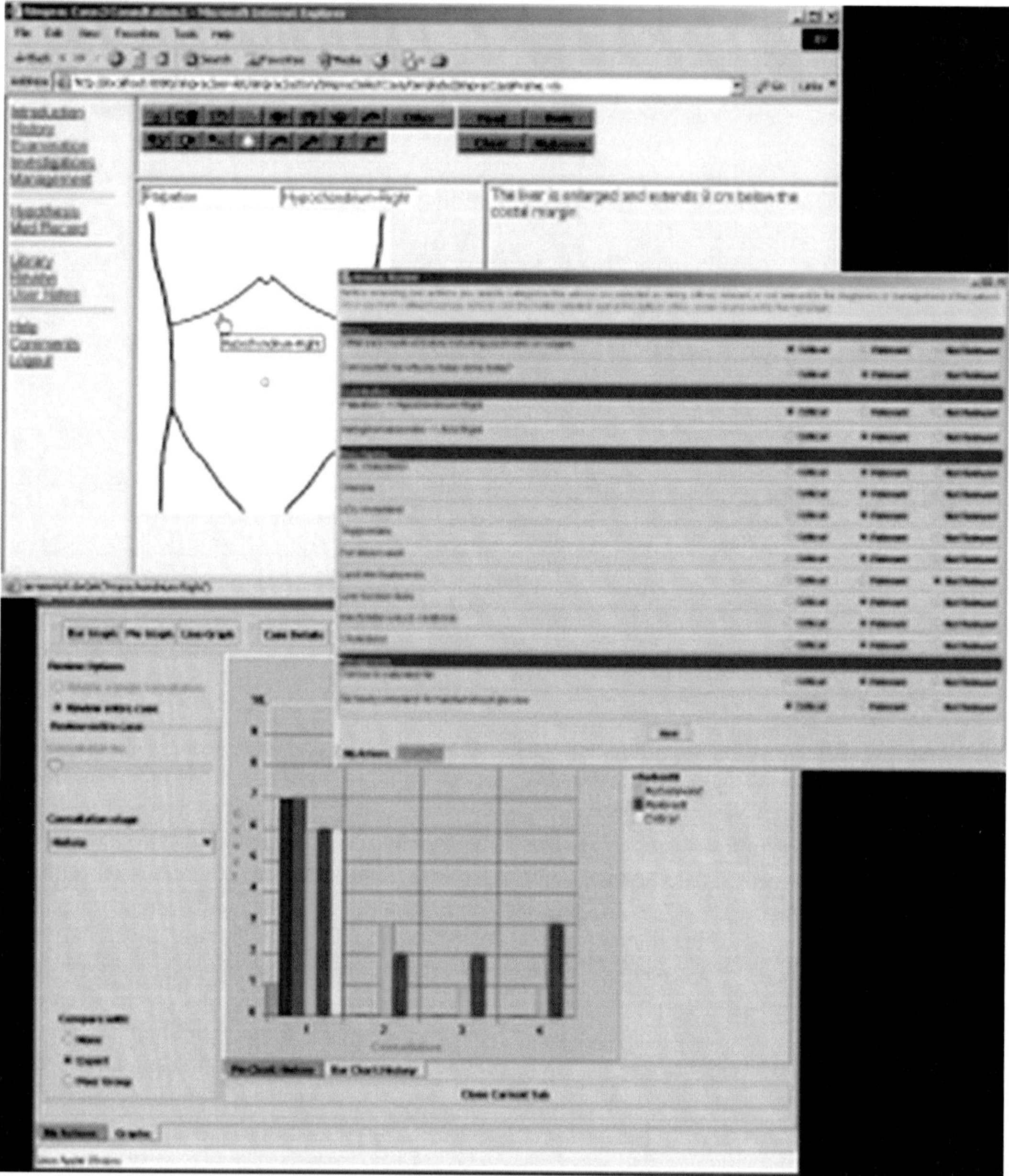

Fig. 23.3 Simprac OLM (Chesher, 2005; Chesher et al., 2005)

issue involves ensuring that the learner can compare their own progress and performance against meaningful standards that fit into any broader learning context.

While the above examples make available a quite small (part of a) model, there may be cases where there is value in enabling a learner to gain an overview of a large model. This issue has been explored in SIV (Kay & Lum, 2005). The SIV visualisation enables a learner to see their progress over the hundreds of elements in a course in user interface design. The left part of the screen in Fig. 23.4 shows the learner's knowledge of concepts by the size, colour and positioning of the concept labels. The ontology underlying SIV was critical for enabling learners to move up and

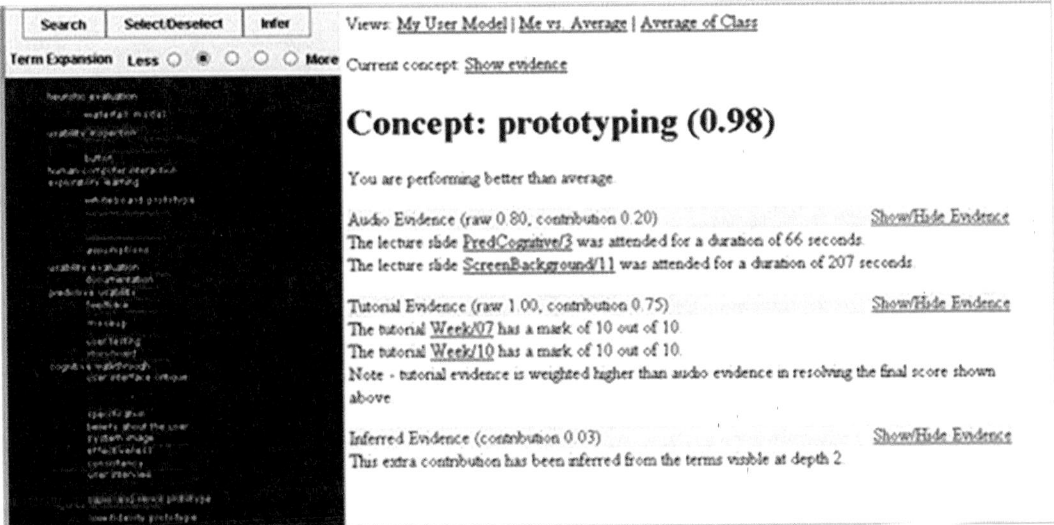

Fig. 23.4 The SIV overview (Kay & Lum, 2005)

down granularity levels, and it also enables learners to focus on sets of related concepts within the domain. Students use this to plan their study for final examinations, with the OLM showing areas where they have weakness. Notably, the evidence available for this OLM comes from sources of varying reliability (shown to the user as illustrated in the right of the screen in Fig. 23.4), and different learners interpreted that evidence differently, some valuing one source highly while other students did not. This raises the question of providing learners with control over the system's interpretation of evidence that informs their learner model: without this, the individual learner will find the OLM less useful. This raises some additional issues for metacognition and learner control, particularly whether the learner is entitled to decide how to value the different sources of learner modelling evidence.

SIV also provides a summary view of learning progress of the class, which is also invaluable for the teacher. To this point, we have focused on metacognition in relation to the learner. However, any ITS, learning management system (LMS) or similar tool that is used in the context of a course, with lectures, labs and other activities, has the potential to support metacognitive skills of the *teacher*. A suitable OLM can enable the teacher to assess the effectiveness of their own teaching or a particular innovation: the OLM can show the progress of the class and potentially this class compared with other relevant cohorts. Essentially, the teacher is a learner who is continuously learning how to teach. This metacognitive role for the OLM has broad significance. It has been shown to be effective in the context of a Logic Tutor (Merceron & Yacef, 2003) and has been explored in the context of a widely used LMS: CourseVis showed a high-level representation of a class activity on the LMS (Mazza & Dimitrova, 2004). While the classroom teacher has a different relationship to an ITS than that of a student, there is potential for important learning gains if the teacher's metacognition is scaffolded by an OLM.

Independent Open Learner Models to Facilitate Metacognitive Activity

Unlike the examples in the previous section, we here consider OLMs as first-class citizens that have value on their own, independently of any particular teaching system and potentially making use of learning data from multiple teaching systems. We consider this class of OLM likely to become of increasing importance, as there are growing numbers of electronic learning support

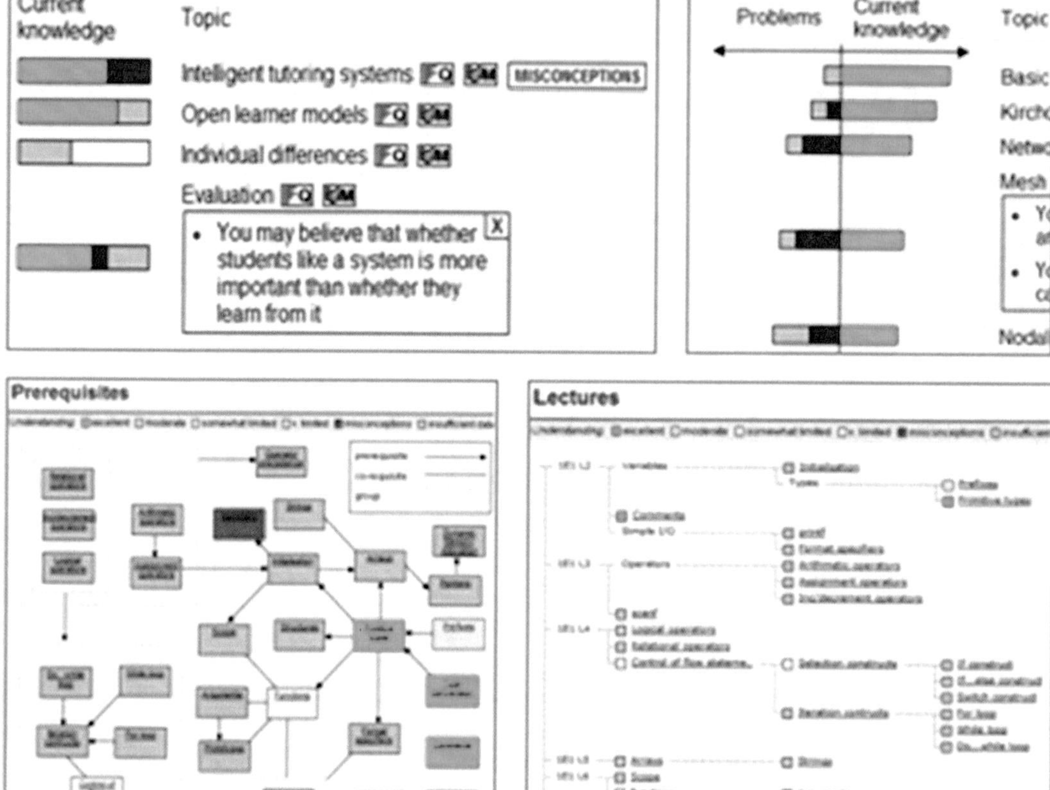

Fig. 23.5 Independent OLMs with simple displays (*top* OLMlets Bull et al., 2006) and structured displays (*lower* Flexi-OLM Mabbott & Bull, 2006)

tools of various sort, including the ubiquitous LMS, conventional software tools that are used as part of the learning as well as the many online e-learning tools and ITSs.

These independent OLMs are designed for use independently of individualised teaching or guidance as is typically provided by an ITS. Such independent OLMs usually have, as their primary aim, the promotion of metacognitive activities, such as self-assessment, self-monitoring, reflection and planning (as in some of the above examples), but within an overall context of encouraging autonomous or independent learning outside the system. Students can use these OLMs to help them identify their knowledge and difficulties and plan where they need to invest effort to overcome any problems. The responsibility for determining and undertaking appropriate activities lies with the learner. Therefore, an independent OLM may or may not have a domain model: the domain may be as simple as an unstructured list of topics (we would not consider this to be a "model") or may comprise complex relationships of some kind to support diagnosis for the learner model contents. Either way, the role of the independent OLM is *not* to teach domain content, rather to promote and support independent learning and decisions by the user.

Two independent OLMs displaying learner models at different levels of detail/structure have demonstrated the possibility to support students alongside lecture courses—that is, in real-use settings (Bull et al., 2008). Figure 23.5 illustrates the simple skill metre and a similar graphical overview of knowledge level in OLMlets (Bull, Quigley, & Mabbott, 2006), and the structure of map and tree views of the Flexi-OLM learner model (Mabbott & Bull, 2006). In each case, colour is used to represent the level of knowledge of a topic or concept, and short text statements of misconceptions can be viewed, designed to prompt learners into investigating their specific problems. For example, from OLMlets used in an adaptive learning environments course: "You may believe that whether students like a system is more important than whether they learn from it"; "You may believe that a system does not have to understand the learner model." From an introductory mathematics course: "You may believe that denominators are added when adding fractions"; "You may believe that, when adding matrices, the individual terms within a matrix are added together."

OLMlets was designed specifically to promote formative assessment (i.e. assessment designed to provide feedback to support the learning process—rather than summative assessment that produces a grade or mark) and learner autonomy for independent use alongside a range of courses (Bull et al., 2006). Learners answer questions relating to the key concepts of a course and view a simple overview of their knowledge levels and statements of their misconceptions (top of Fig. 23.5), as a starting point for their independent work. The simplicity of the model presentation reflects the simplicity of the underlying learner model, as it is intended for easy introduction by instructors, into a variety of courses. Deployment of OLMlets throughout several university electronic, electrical and computer engineering modules showed that students will use an OLM such as this to support their learning and are able to do so in a manner that suits their learning preferences, and the structured tree and map views of Flexi-OLM (bottom of Fig. 23.5) were also used by many students taking the Cprogramming module for which it was designed (Bull et al., 2008). As no additional computer tutoring or metacognitive support was provided in either case, any usage of the OLMs suggests that learners were gaining some benefit simply from the availability of an independent OLM. Thus, although we do not have specific information about how students were using these OLMs (e.g. to recognise their knowledge state, to plan their learning, to reflect on their difficulties), the fact that they were using them suggests that some kind of metacognitive activity was taking place that students perceived as helpful.

A clear example of an independent OLM to prompt metacognition is the Notice OLM (Shahrour & Bull, 2008). Notice is based on the second-language acquisition literature on awareness and "noticing" language features in language learning (Rutherford & Sharwood Smith, 1985; Schmidt, 1990) and "noticing the gap" between one's own language rules and the (correct) target language forms (Schmidt & Frota, 1986): issues that have much in common with the general metacognition literature. Notice uses salience/highlighting techniques [recommended for computer-assisted language learning (e.g. Chapelle, 1998)], to draw the learner's attention to grammatical elements. Figure 23.6 shows the "comparison view". coloured highlighting in the learner model (left) indicates the correctness of the student's use of irregular plural nouns based on the learner model representations, next to native speaker or expert use (the system model: right). This is one method of encouraging learners to "notice the gap" between their language and the language to which they have been exposed (Schmidt & Frota, 1986), as mentioned above.

Notice was found to facilitate immediate noticing of language elements (irregular plural nouns and irregular simple past verbs) by adult second-language learners, and much of this knowledge was retained at a significant level, as demonstrated in a delayed post-test 1 week after the experimental session (where no teaching of the target features had taken place in the meantime) (Shahrour & Bull, 2008). While we do not know whether learners remembered the forms based on their interaction with the OLM or whether they subsequently actively tried to notice or find out about the forms (as is one of the key aims of an independent OLM), it does appear that this kind of approach can be useful to prompt noticing in language learning. It will be interesting to explore the extent to which this may also apply in other subjects.

Negotiated learner models are interactive OLMs that allow the student to negotiate the learner model contents with the system (Bull & Pain, 1995; Dimitrova, 2003; Kerly & Bull, 2008).

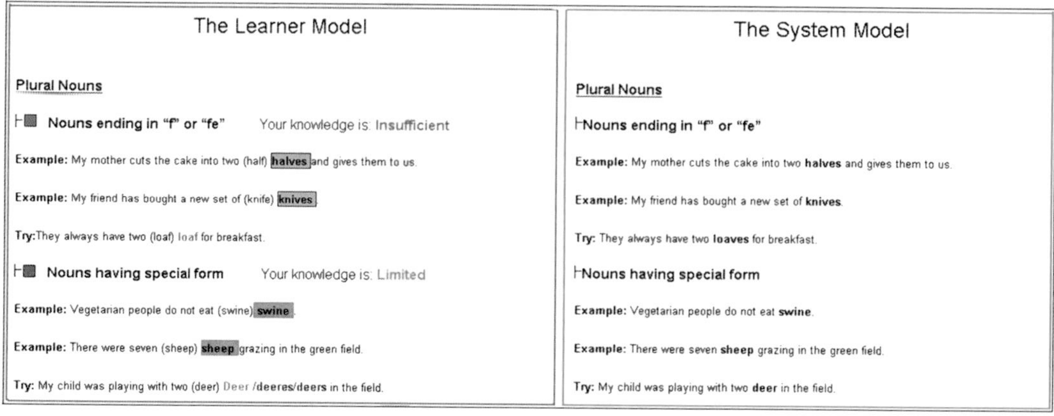

Fig. 23.6 The Notice OLM for language learning (Shahrour & Bull, 2008)

The pronoun is:	**YOUR CONFIDENCE**	**SYSTEM CONFIDENCE**
Pre-verbal in negatives *Não os compra*	unsure	very sure
Post-verbal in positive main clauses *Compra-os*	almost sure	unsure

system: The system's confidence in *your use* of the rule for positive main clauses is currently: unsure. What do you believe the system's confidence should be?

▪ very sure ▪ almost sure ▪ very unsure ▪ (cancel)

student (selects): very sure.

system: Your choice of 'very sure' is different from the system's assessment. What do you wish to do?

▪ accept system's decision ▪ system justify itself ▪ view student model ▪ accept compromise ▪ justify myself

student (selects): system justify itself.

system: You are trying to change the system's confidence from 'unsure' to 'very sure'. This confidence value is too high. Your last five attempts to place the pronoun in positive main clause statements were:

*O Manuel a mostrou no mapa. O Manuel mostrou-a no mapa. *O homem o comeu rapidamente.
*O Manuel mostrou a no mapa. O homem comeu-o rapidamente.

You have probable transfer from Spanish for pronoun placement twice.

Fig. 23.7 Negotiating the learner model in Mr. Collins (Bull & Pain, 1995)

If the student disagrees with any of the system-inferred learner model data, they can challenge the system in an attempt to change the model, with each party required to justify their beliefs about the student's knowledge, through discussion. For example, the system may offer the learner the opportunity to compromise (i.e. agree on an intermediate representation of knowledge, if the system's and the student's confidence in the learner's knowledge are sufficiently close to allow a compromise to be a reasonable action); the student may provide the information that they have forgotten certain concepts since their last interaction, indicating that the learner model has "slipped backwards" or that their understanding has increased due to a lecture or from reading undertaken between sessions with the system; and the system may require the student to convince it to change its model by taking a short test to demonstrate their knowledge (or lack of knowledge). The top of Fig. 23.7 shows an excerpt of the display of learner confidence in their knowledge placed alongside the system's confidence in their knowledge, in order to highlight any differences to the learner; below is an excerpt from a student attempt to challenge the learner model in menu-based model negotiation in Mr. Collins (Bull & Pain, 1995). Such negotiation of the learner model is designed (1) to help improve the accuracy of the model by allowing the student to contribute infor-

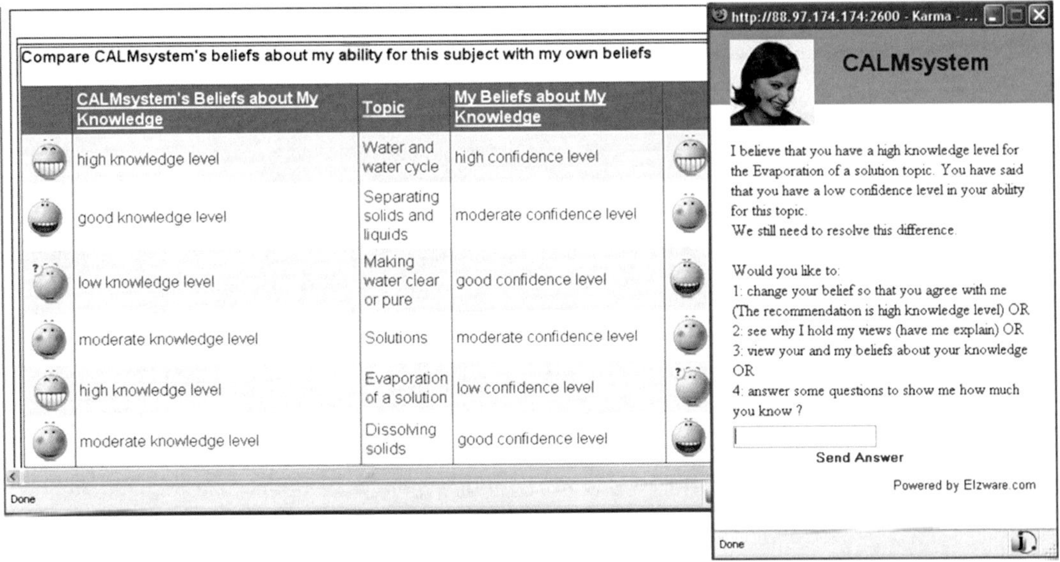

Fig. 23.8 Negotiating the learner model in CALMsystem (Kerly & Bull, 2008)

mation for consideration in the modelling process and (2) through the process of discussion of the learner's knowledge, to prompt learners to reflect on their understanding and develop a greater awareness of their learning needs. This also places some of the responsibility for the learning interaction, with the learner. The latter point is particularly relevant for promoting metacognition.

In CALMsystem (Kerly & Bull, 2008), the learner's level of knowledge of topics is displayed for comparison to the system's inferences about their knowledge (left of Fig. 23.8). However, the model negotiation process is more flexible than in Mr. Collins, using natural language in discussion with a chatbot (right of Fig. 23.8). Statements such as the following to the chatbot (by 10–11-year-olds) are indicative of self-monitoring: "but I need more work on it", "I am getting better", "I have changed my mind about my beliefs", and "can I change a belief [in the model] about separating solids and liquids please". A study over two sessions with children aged 10–11 in a science class demonstrated significant improvements in self-assessment accuracy both in an inspectable-only condition (left of Fig. 23.8) and a full negotiated learner modelling approach (both parts of Fig. 23.8) and with significant improvements in the negotiated condition over the inspectable condition (Kerly & Bull, 2008). It appears, therefore, that use of a simple inspectable model for this age group can help learners, but the process of discussion of their knowledge can bring further benefits and so could be recommended where such an approach would integrate well with the aims and interactions with a system.

As with Simprac (Chesher, 2005; Chesher et al., 2005) in the previous ITS section and Notice (Shahrour & Bull, 2008) in this independent OLMs section, OLMlets (top of Fig. 23.5) allows students to compare their knowledge against a standard. Here instructors input the expected level of knowledge for each stage of the course (defined by week, day or lecture number, as appropriate), and students can view their own skill metres (or other representations) alongside the expected knowledge for the current stage of the course, displayed in the same form, to support their self-evaluations and planning in the context of present expectations (Bull et al., 2006). This allows students to, for example, note that although their current level of understanding of a concept may be quite low, it is nevertheless in line with expectations for that stage of the course. OLMlets also allows students to release their model data to their instructors, thus offering the benefits to teachers suggested above in ITS contexts, in the use of independent OLMs, and has been shown able to promote spontaneous (face-to-face) peer discussion and help-seeking amongst students when they choose to release their learner models to each other (Bull & Britland, 2007). This is therefore another common goal of metacognition researchers and open learner modelling researchers. Furthermore, an OLM designed to help parents help their children with fractions was found also to highlight to parents misconceptions that they themselves held about calculating fractions (Lee & Bull, 2008).

This section suggests that independent OLMs can in themselves enhance metacognitive behaviours related to the identification of knowledge, regulation of learning or planning of learning activities, and they can be used to prompt actions to facilitate learner independence.

Long-Term Open Learner Models

The examples above have all been associated with a rather limited context. In the life of the learner, we might build a quite comprehensive learner model that draws on the full range of evidence about the learner's progress. This learner model could then support reflection on long-term learning, such as reading progress over the whole of primary school education or mathematics progress through the whole of school. A key value of such a model would be as an OLM for reflection by learners, perhaps in conjunction with their teachers and parents, to monitor progress; identify serious, long-term problems; and plan learning.

In Fig. 23.4, at the left of the SIV display, the user model visualisation tool is a generic learner model display for large user models (Apted, Kay, Lum, & Uther, 2003). We have used it in several contexts. For example, it was initially designed for use in a Graduate Medical Programme where it aimed to show students their progress on around 600 learning topics that span 2 years of study. In this case, the evidence for learning came from a system that students could use to do multiple-choice self-tests. Even the example of Fig. 23.4 involved a semester long course with two main sources of evidence about learning:

- Student grades, extracted from an LMS, where this provided marks from the weekly lab sessions and the marks on each of the questions of the final exam
- Evidence based on interaction with an online lecture delivery system where students listened to online audio that was associated with "slides" with the amount of time students spent on each slide matched against the known audio length, to infer which lecture slides the student appeared to have "attended"

This is an interesting example since it involves multiple sources of evidence and each is of quite different grain size (Kay & Lum, 2005). Importantly, the visualisation display can be used independently of any application, taking an arbitrary learner model in the required format and making it available to the learner for reflection on their progress. It enables a learner to identify areas that the learner model indicates they are weakest in. The display can be configured to allow the learner to define their own standard; for example, one learner may only want concepts treated as known if they have a current knowledge level of at least 80% while another learner may set this threshold at 60%.

Another example of a long-term learner model is shown in Fig. 23.9. This is one of several OLM created for use in conjunction with a project management tool used for educational purposes (Kay, Maisonneuve, Yacef, & Reimann, 2006; Reimann & Kay, 2010). It was used over a semester in a software engineering capstone project subject where students worked in teams to create software. The project management tool is widely used by programmers. One of the goals of this subject is that students develop their group work skills and this learner model assists them and their facilitators to see aspects of the team operation. The display in the figure shows the interaction between team members on the wiki, where an interaction was judged to occur when two people edited the same wiki page. The heavier the line, the more the interaction. In the actual inter-

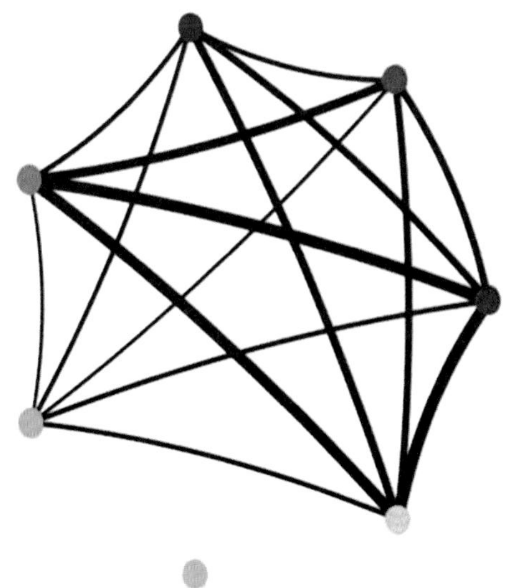

Fig. 23.9 Example of an interaction diagram

face, each coloured dot is labelled with the learner's login ID (removed here to anonymise the display).

We can easily see that all team members are interacting with the exception of the person represented by the (green) dot near 6 o'clock. We can also see that some people interact more than others. We include this example to illustrate important possibilities offered by OLMs to support long-term learning:

- They can display some of the many sources of long-term data that is available as digital traces of activity.
- They can be integrated into arbitrary online tools, including those that were *not* explicitly designed for learning.
- The addition of an OLM creates new possibilities for people to learn, based upon reflecting on the OLM, potentially realising that they have strengths and weaknesses they were not previously aware of.
- It can support the learner in monitoring their progress as they aim to change those behaviours.
- It is particularly valuable when the individual learner can see themselves in relation to relevant peer groups so that they can assess the significance of their personal performance.

While this representation does not show the quality of contributions, it does provide other important information that may prompt metacognitive behaviours. Returning to the OLMlets independent OLM (top of Fig. 23.5), based on use across courses in a degree, students can follow their progress towards the range of more general learning outcomes required for a professional-accredited engineering degree (Bull & Gardner, 2010). Each learning outcome is listed with the courses contributing to this learning outcome included and level of understanding indicated by colour (two learning outcomes are given as examples in Fig. 23.10). Each course may contribute to several or many learning outcomes. The aim is to help students identify the general engineering skills required of a professional engineer and how their courses combine to help them achieve these skills, and their own progress is indicated as a focus for their attention.

OLMs have the potential to support such metacognitive, long-term learning outcomes as they can be readily applied to arbitrary data collections by the learner as part of their long-term lifelong learning. Within more formal learning contexts, we need to make it easy for teachers to integrate arbitrary data sources into OLMs for use by their students, making use of suitable information that enables the individual to better assess their own achievements in relation to the standards that are relevant for their context.

Discussion: Links Between Research Directions in Metacognition and Open Learner Modelling

We have described a range of approaches to open learning modelling, in terms of the relationship to an ITS and some of the forms that OLMs have taken. We have also identified several issues that are important for an OLM to provide effective support for metacognitive activities of reflection, self-monitoring as well as planning and control of learning processes. If metacognitive skills were explicitly modelled by an ITS, an interactive OLM for these, too, could be the basis for a metacognitive

B20 Workshop and laboratory skills.

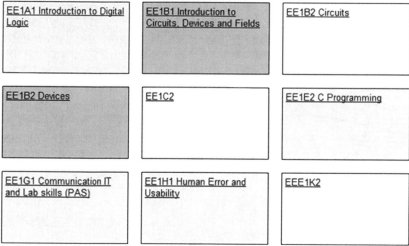

EE1A1 Introduction to Digital Logic
EE1B1 Introduction to Circuits, Devices and Fields
EE1B2 Circuits
EE1B2 Devices
EE1C2
EE1E2 C Programming
EE1G1 Communication IT and Lab skills (PAS)
EE1H1 Human Error and Usability
EEE1K2

B21 Understanding of contexts in which engineering knowledge can be applied (e.g. operations and management, technology development, etc).

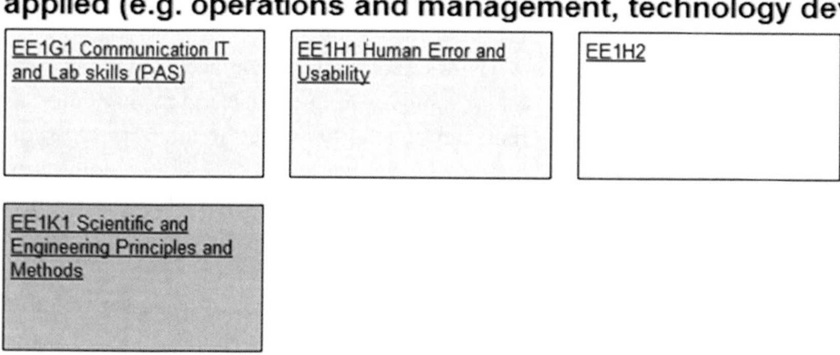

Fig. 23.10 An example of an independent OLM linking elements across a degree

activity and could provide an additional source of evidence about these skills in the learner's self-perceptions. An interactive OLM, which allows the learner to provide evidence about their knowledge directly to the OLM, is in line with a philosophy that encourages the learner to take *control* over and *responsibility* for their learning.

There are many issues that we have touched on and which are important for future roles for OLMs to support metacognition. One of these relates to *capturing, recording or extracting metacognitive aspects of students' learning processes*. The log of student actions and interactions with their OLM could provide a key source of evidence about metacognition. This suggests a role for OLMs that show these inferred models of metacognition. This may help learners become more aware of their own metacognitive processes. This leads to the issue of *evaluating the effect of metacognitive feedback and interventions* and poses a rather interesting new interface challenge for OLMs since it seems likely that a learner (and their human supporters, such as parents and teachers) may need new forms of interface that make it easy to see changes in the learner model in terms of such interventions. Designing tasks for metacognitive assessment is a potential role for OLMs. For example, a student can be asked to rate their own expertise and then be provided with the system's corresponding assessment in the OLM.

Another key aspect relates to *interpreting and assessing metacognitive behaviour*, which is precisely what a teacher or facilitator does when discussing an OLM with students. There is potential for exploring support for explicit recording of these processes so that they can be revisited as part of long-term reflection on progress. The automation of this process is becoming increasingly feasible by exploiting educational data mining techniques (EDM).

Another important potential use for OLMs could be supported by better understanding how to design tasks for metacognitive assessment. This is completely congruous with OLM since the learner's interaction with their OLM is often just such a task. Although there has not been much work on the explicit use of OLMs for displaying the parts of the learner model that represent metacognitive skills, this seems a promising direction to explore. It should lead to more generic OLM interfaces that might be available as an additional layer of support for reflection, beyond the domain-specific aspects that each demand different interfaces. We can even envisage that learners may expect every tool to provide them with such a metacognitive OLM interface or that data for it is stored in a way that enables the learner to explore it independently. We can envisage that this will support new OLMs and associated techniques for measuring and displaying metacognition over time or in changing contexts. Such generic tools create new possibilities for assessing metacognition in educational technologies compared to the classroom or the lab.

There is considerable potential for exploiting research on metacognition to inform work on OLMs as well as in the improved understanding of the ways that OLMs can support metacognitive processes and help develop metacognitive skills. We have distinguished two contexts for OLMs. When they are *within* an ITS, there is potential for careful design of the ITS and OLM, in terms of the interface and the underlying learning experiences so that there are immediate links between learning activities and the OLM. We have much to learn about the best ways to do this and how it may interact with many aspects, such as trust, gaming, exploration and toying with the ITS. We have also indicated some of the different possibilities and issues for a learner model that exists *outside* a particular ITS and the ways that its OLM interfaces might support and encourage metacognitive activities. In both of these roles, OLMs can serve several purposes, most being strongly linked to metacognitive activities of reflection, monitoring progress, planning both in the short and long term and aiding the learner in taking responsibility and control of their own learning and progress.

Acknowledgements We thank Peter Brusilovsky, Douglas Chesher, Alice Kerly, Andrew Mabbott, Tanja Mitrovic and Gheida Shahrour for their screen shots and contributions to this chapter. This chapter is an extended version of a paper presented at the Metacognition Workshop at the 2008 Intelligent Tutoring Systems conference.

References

Apted, T., Kay, J., Lum, A., & Uther, J. (2003). Visualisation of ontological inferences for user control of personal web agents. In E. Banissi, K. Borner, C. Chen, G. Clapworthy, C. Maple, A. Lobben, C. Moore, J. Roberts, A. Ursyn, & J. Zhang (Eds.), *Proceedings of IV03-VSW, Information Visualisation—Semantic Web Visualisation*, IEEE, pp. 306–311.

Brusilovsky, P. & Sosnovsky, S. (2005). Engaging students to work with self-assessment questions: A study of two approaches, *Proceedings of 10th Annual Conference on Innovation and Technology in Computer Science Education* (pp. 251–255). New York: ACM Press.

Bull, S. (1997). Promoting effective learning strategy use in CALL. *Computer Assisted Language Learning Journal, 10*(1), 3–39.

Bull, S., & Britland, M. (2007). Group interaction prompted by a simple assessed open learner model that can be optionally released to peers. In P. Brusilovsky, K. Papanikolaou, & M. Grigoriadou (Eds.), *Proceedings of Workshop on Personalisation in E-Learning Environments at Individual and Group Level (PING)*, User Modeling.

Bull, S., & Gardner, P. (2010). Raising learner awareness of progress towards UK-SPEC learning outcomes. *Engineering Education: Journal of the Higher Education Academy Engineering Subject Centre, 5*(1), 11–22.

Bull, S., & Kay, J. (2007). Student models that invite the learner in: The SMILI:) open learner modelling framework. *International Journal of Artificial Intelligence in Education, 17*(2), 89–120.

Bull, S., Mabbott, A., Gardner, P., Jackson, T., Lancaster, M. J., Quigley, S., et al. (2008). Supporting interaction preferences and recognition of misconceptions with independent open learner models. In W. Neijdl, J. Kay, P. Pu, & E. Herder (Eds.), *Adaptive hypermedia and adaptive web-based systems* (pp. 62–72). Berlin, Heidelberg: Springer.

Bull, S., & Pain, H. (1995). "Did I say what I think I said, and do you agree with me?": Inspecting and questioning the student model. In J. Greer (Ed.), *Artificial Intelligence in Education 1995* (pp. 501–508). Charlottesville, VA: Association for the Advancement of Computing in Education.

Bull, S., Quigley, S., & Mabbott, A. (2006). Computer-based formative assessment to promote reflection and learner autonomy. *Engineering Education: Journal of the Higher Education Academy Subject Centre, 1*(1), 8–18.

Chapelle, C. A. (1998). Multimedia CALL: Lessons to be learned from research on instructed SLA. *Language Learning and Technology, 2*(1), 22–34.

Chesher, D. (2005). *Exploring the use of web-based virtual patient to support learning through reflection*, Ph.D. Thesis, University of Sydney.

Chesher, D., Kay, J., & King, N. J. (2005). SIMPRAC: Supporting reflective learning within a new computer-based virtual patient simulator. *Online Proceedings of the AIED (Artificial Intelligence in Education) 2005 Workshop on Learner Modelling for Reflection, to Support Learner Control, Metacognition and Improved Communication between Teachers and Learners (LeMoRe05)*, pp. 72–80.

Corbett, A., & Anderson, J. (1994). Knowledge tracing: Modeling the acquisition of procedural knowledge. *User Modeling and User-Adapted Interaction, 4*(4), 253–278.

Derry, S., & Murphy, D. A. (1986). Designing systems that train learning ability: From theory to practice. *Review of Educational Research, 56*(1), 1–39.

Dimitrova, V. (2003). STyLE-OLM: Interactive open learner modelling. *International Journal of Artificial Intelligence in Education, 13*, 35–78.

Dimitrova, V., McCalla, G., & Bull, S. (2007). Open learner models: future research directions. *International Journal of Artificial Intelligence in Education, 17*(3), 217–226.

Flavell, J. H. (1979). Metacognition and cognitive monitoring: A new area of cognitive-developmental enquiry. *American Psychologist, 34*(10), 906–911.

Gama, C. (2004). Metacognition in interactive learning environments: The reflection assistant model. In J. C. Lester, R. M. Vicari, & F. Paraguacu (Eds.), *Intelligent Tutoring Systems: 7th International Conference* (pp. 668–677). Berlin, Heidelberg: Springer.

Georghiades, P. (2004). From the general to the situated: Three decades of metacognition. *International Journal of Science Education, 26*(3), 365–383.

Kay, J., & Lum, A. (2005). Exploiting readily available web data for scrutable student models, *12th International Conference on Artificial Intelligence in Education* (pp. 338–345). Amsterdam: IOS Press.

Kay, J., Maisonneuve, N., Yacef, K., & Reimann, P. (2006). The big five and visualisations of team work activity. In M. Ikeda, K. D. Ashley, & T. Chan (Eds.), *Intelligent Tutoring Systems: Proceedings 8th International Conference, ITS 2006* (pp. 197–206). Jhongli, Taiwan: Springer

Kerly, A., & Bull, S. (2008). Children's interactions with inspectable and negotiated learner models. In B. P. Woolf, E. Aimeur, R. Nkambou, & S. Lajoie (Eds.), *Intelligent Tutoring Systems: 9th International Conference* (pp. 132–141). Berlin, Heidelberg: Springer.

Lee, S. J. H., & Bull, S. (2008). An open learner model to help parents help their children. *Technology, Instruction Cognition and Learning, 6*(1), 29–51.

Mabbott, A., & Bull, S. (2006). Student preferences for editing, persuading and negotiating the open learner model. *Intelligent tutoring systems* (pp. 481–490). Berlin, Heidelberg: Springer.

Mazza, R., & Dimitrova, V. (2004). Visualising student tracking data to support instructors in web-based distance education, *13th International World Wide Web Conference—Alternate Educational Track*, pp. 154–161.

Merceron, A., & Yacef, K. (2003). A web-based tutoring tool with mining facilities to improve learning and teaching. In F. Verdejo, & U. Hoppe (Eds.), *Proceedings of 11th International Conference on Artificial Intelligence in Education (AIED03)* (pp. 201–208). Amsterdam: IOS Press.

Mitrovic, A., & Martin, B. (2002). Evaluating the effects of open student models on learning. In P. de Bra, P. Brusilovsky, & R. Conejo (Eds.), *Proceedings of 2nd International Conference on Adaptive Hypermedia and Adaptive Web-based Systems* (pp. 296–305). Berlin, Heidelberg: Springer.

Mitrovic, A., & Martin, B. (2007). Evaluating the effect of open student models on self-assessment. *International Journal of Artificial Intelligence in Education, 17*(2), 121–144.

Reimann, P., & Kay, J. (2010). Learning to learn and work in net-based teams: Supporting emergent collaboration with visualization tools. *Designs for learning environments of the future* (pp. 143–188). New York: Springer

Roll, I., Aleven, V., McLaren, B. M., & Koedinger, K. (2007). Designing for metacognition—applying cognitive tutor principles to the tutoring of help seeking. *Metacognition and Learning, 2*, 125–140.

Rutherford, W. E., & Sharwood Smith, M. (1985). Consciousness-raising and universal grammar. *Applied Linguistics, 6*(3), 274–282.

Schmidt, R. (1990). The role of consciousness in second language learning. *Applied Linguistics, 11*(2), 129–158.

Schmidt, R., & Frota, S. (1986). Developing basic conversational ability in a second language, a case study of an adult learner of portuguese. In R. Day (Ed.), *Talking to learn: Conversation in second lan-*

guage acquisition (pp. 237–326). Rowley, MA: Newbury House.

Schoenfeld, A. H. (1987). What's all the fuss about metacognition? In A. H. Schoenfeld (Ed.), *Cognitive science and mathematics education* (pp. 189–215). Hillsdale, NJ: Lawrence Erlbaum Associates.

Schön, D. A. (1987). *Educating the reflective practitioner, toward a new design for teaching and learning in the professions*. San Francisco: Jossey-Bass.

Schraw, G. (1998). Promoting general metacognitive awareness. *Instructional Science, 26*, 113–125.

Shahrour, G., & Bull, S. (2008). Does "Notice" prompt noticing? Raising awareness in language learning with an open learner model. In W. Neijdl, J. Kay, P. Pu, & E. Herder (Eds.), *Adaptive hypermedia and adaptive web-based systems* (pp. 173–182). Berlin, Heidelberg: Springer.

Veenman, M. V. J., Van Hout-Wolters, B. H. A. M., & Afferbach, P. (2006). Metacognition and learning: Conceptual and methodological considerations. *Metacognition and Learning, 1*(1), 3–14.

Wagster, J., Tan, J., Biswas, G., & Schwartz, D. (2007). How metacognitive feedback affects behavior in learning and transfer, *Workshop on Metacognition and Self-Regulated Learning*, International Conference on Artificial Intelligence in Education.

Modeling and Scaffolding Self-Explanation Across Domains and Activities

24

Cristina Conati

Abstract

In this chapter, we describe our research on providing computer-based support for the meta cognitive skill of self-explanation. The distinguishing element of our work is that we aim at providing support for self-explanation that is student-adaptive, i.e., tailored to the specific needs and traits of each individual, e.g., relevant knowledge and tendency to self-explain spontaneously. Adapting to these elements requires building models that can measure them in real-time during interaction. In this chapter, we illustrate how we built such models for two different intelligent learning environments (ILEs): one that helps college students self-explain worked-out solutions of physics problems, and one that supports self-explanation during interaction with an interactive simulation for mathematical functions.

Introduction

In this chapter, we provide an overview of research we have conducted over the years to devise computer-based intelligent support to the meta-cognitive skill known as self-explanation. Extensive cognitive science research has shown that self-explanation is a meta-cognitive skill that plays a major role in students' ability to self-regulate their learning, by allowing the student to both monitor her understanding during the learning activity, and to improve it by initiating targeted reasoning (Chi, 2000). A large part of the existing results from cognitive science relate to self-explanation during problem solving or example studying in procedural domains, although there has also been work on how self-explanation affects the learning of complex concepts from explanatory text. In the first part of the chapter, we describe the work we have done, based on these results, to devise an ILE (the SE-Coach) that can help college students self-explain worked-out solutions of physics problems.

Our main research assumption is that support to self-explanation should be *user-adaptive*, i.e., tailored to take into account individual differences both at the cognitive and meta-cognitive level. Thus, we briefly describe the student modeling techniques that we have devised in the SE-Coach

C. Conati, M.Sc., Ph.D. (✉)
Department of Computer Science, University of British Columbia, 2366 Main Mall, Vancouver, BC V6G3C1, Canada
e-mail: conati@cs.ubc.ca

R. Azevedo and V. Aleven (eds.), *International Handbook of Metacognition and Learning Technologies*, Springer International Handbooks of Education 26, DOI 10.1007/978-1-4419-5546-3_24,

project, the user-adaptive interventions we have built based on the model, and a formal evaluation of their effectiveness. The evaluation is a controlled study that compares the pedagogical effectiveness of the SE-Coach with that of a non-adaptive version, measured in terms of improvement in student problem solving performance.

In the second part of the chapter, we illustrate how we have progressed toward modeling and supporting self-explanation during a radically different learning activity: learning via exploration of an interactive simulation for mathematical functions. We describe the adaptive interventions that we have been designing for this activity, as well as the student modeling techniques that support them, including the addition of eye-tracking data to improve the model's ability to capture student's behaviors related to self-explanation. Finally, we report results on a formal evaluation of the student model's accuracy in assessing student self-explanation and related learning.

Related Work

Recent years have seen an increasing interest in designing ILEs that can explicitly support student meta-cognitive development. The majority of the work has targeted self-explanation in a variety of instructional activities, including studying textual example solutions (e.g., Conati & Vanlehn, 2000; Crippen & Boyd, 2007), viewing examples as Flash videos, (McLaren, Lim, & Koedinger, 2008), engaging in pure problem solving (e.g., Aleven & Koedinger, 2002; Mitrovic, 2003), and problem solving with multiple representations (Rau, Aleven, & Rummel, 2009).

Researchers have also started investigating support for other meta-cognitive skills, ranging from the ability to seek help effectively (Roll, Aleven, McLaren, & Koedinger, 2007), using examples during analogical problem solving (Muldner & Conati, 2007) and successfully engaging in self-regulated learning (SRL), a comprehensive process by which students set their own learning goals, plan actions to achieve them and then self-monitor their progress towards these goals as they engage in the target activities (Azevedo, Witherspoon, Chauncey, Burkett, & Fike, 2009; Tan, Biswas, & Schwartz, 2006).

One component of devising environments that can support meta-cognition is to design interface affordances that can scaffold the desired meta-cognitive processes (e.g., Azevedo et al., 2009; Chi & VanLehn, 2007; Luckin & Hammerton, 2002; van Joolingen, 2000). A second, equally important element is providing proactive support during interaction to complement interface scaffolding for those students who need more meta-cognitive guidance. Since providing proactive support is the focus of our research on self-explanation, here we discuss in more detail a few examples of other work that has targeted this type of intervention. Normit-SE (Mitrovic 2003), an ITS that provides scaffolding for self-explanation during problem solving on database data normalization, asks students to explain every new or incorrect problem solving step they generate. The Geometry tutor is an ITS designed to support self-explanation during geometry problem solving by allowing students to type free-form self-explanations and providing feedback on their correctness. Roll et al. (2007) have devised a model that enables an ITS to track and scaffold a student's tendency to effectively use the available help facilities. Tan et al., Betty's Brain is an environment that uses teachable agents to help students learn both domain and self-regulatory skills. To support the latter, the environment can recognize a number of interaction patters indicating poor SRL (e.g., teaching the agent new concepts but no relationships between them), and provides feedback accordingly. In our work, we focus on providing both interface scaffolding and adaptive feedback for self-explanation during example studying and exploration of interactive simulation. However, the distinguishing feature of our research on self-explanation during example studying is that we investigate how to provide adaptive support only to those students who do not self-explain spontaneously, as opposed to asking students to self-explain every time they look at a relevant piece of instructional material (as done, for instance in Crippen & Boyd, 2007; McLaren et al., 2008; Rau et al., 2009). Our research on supporting exploratory learning with interactive simulations is the first attempt to look at self-explanation in the context of this educational activity.

SE-Coach: Adaptive Scaffolding for Self-Explanation During Example Studying

The SE-Coach is an Intelligent Learning Environment (ILE from now on), designed to help students self-explain worked-out example solutions in introductory physics. The rationale underlying the design of the SE-Coach is founded in Cognitive Science findings showing that students can greatly benefit from studying examples after receiving theoretical instruction on a domain and before starting to solve problems in that domain. The effectiveness of this example-studying activity, however, is mediated by how well students process the available example solutions. Students who consistently engage in self-explanation to better understand the examples show the greatest benefit during problem solving, while students who study the examples more superficially don't necessarily learn from this activity. Cognitive science studies have further shown that prompting for self-explanation can help those students who tend to not self-explain spontaneously (see Chi, 2000 for an overview). The goal of the SE-Coach is to automate the provision of this prompting by monitoring students as they study examples, and by providing adaptive interventions to help students self-explain when they don't do so spontaneously. The notion that the SE-Coach's prompts should be tailored to those students who do not otherwise self-explain is one of the key points of this research. Other researchers have investigated prompting for self-explanation in a less individualized fashion (see previous section).

We argue, however, that having tailored prompts is important to reduce intrusiveness and increase efficacy. If a student is asked to self-explain when s/he has already done it on her own, or when she does not need the extra information processing, the system may lose credibility and the student may end up ignoring prompts when they are justified. Generating tailored prompts is especially important in the presence of complex examples, like the physics example shown in Fig. 24.1 (left), because in this context there are many pieces of self-explanation that can be generated (several for each element of the worked-out solution) and prompting for all of them indiscriminately would greatly disrupt the student's study process. To facilitate self-explanation for those students who need guidance, the SE-Coach provides a menu-based interface that support the generation of self-explanation relevant to understand physics problem solutions. To determine when to intervene in the student's example study process with more proactive prompts, the SE-Coach relies on a *probabilistic student model*. A student model is a representation of a set of relevant student traits that is updated automatically during interaction with the target educational software based on related student's behaviors. The SE-Coach student model uses a formalism for reasoning under uncertainty known as Bayesian networks to assess how well students understand the instructional material by capturing self-explanations that the students generate via the interface (*explicit self-explanations* from now on), as well as self-explanations that students generate in their head (*implicit self-explanation*). Having a probabilistic student model is important because, as we see in a later section, there is a high degree of uncertainty in capturing student self-explanation and related learning from observable student behaviors. In the next two subsections, we first briefly describe the SE-Coach interface to support self-explanation, and then we illustrate the SE-Coach student model as well as the mechanisms that allow it to assess the student's self-explanation behavior.

SE Interface to Support Self-Explanation

The SE-Coach's interface allows students to read and self-explain example solutions like the one in Fig. 24.1 under the coach's supervision. To monitor these tasks, the SE-Coach interface includes two mechanisms: a masking interface to track

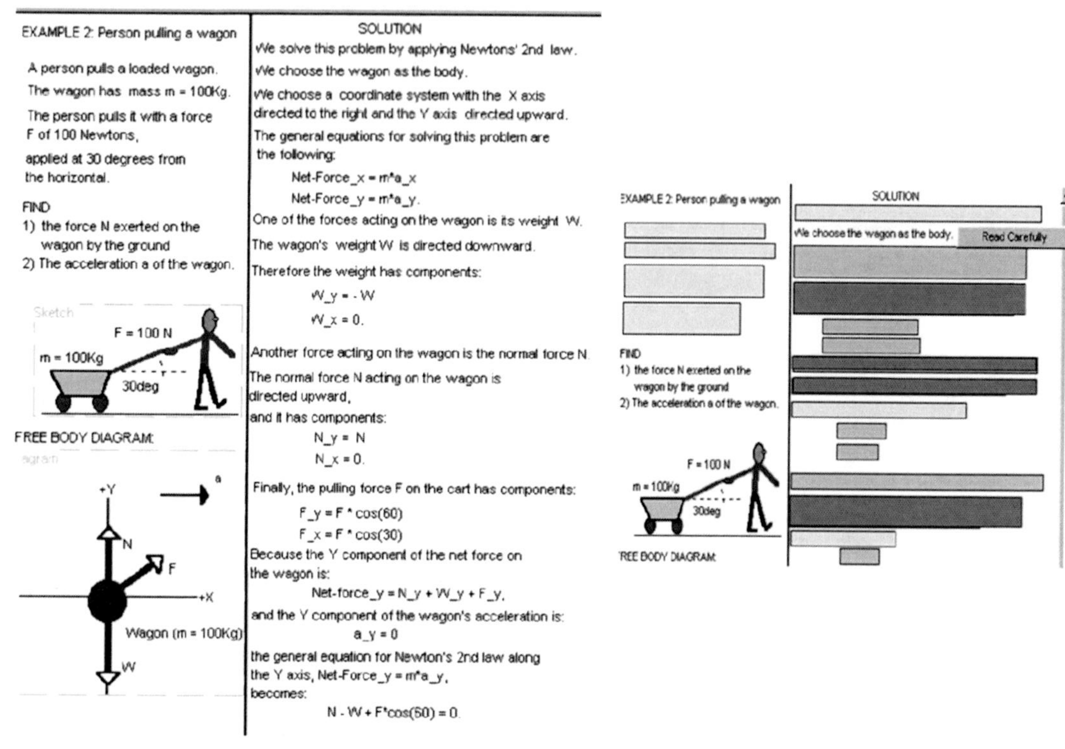

Fig. 24.1 Sample physics example solution (partial, *left*) and masking interfaces (*right*)

students' attention and a set of menu based tools that allow students to constructively generate self-explanations.

Figure 24.1 (right) shows how the Newtonian physics example in Fig. 24.1 (left) is presented with the masking interface. Relevant example parts (e.g., sentences in the problem statement, the problem's free body diagram and individual steps in the worked-out solution) are covered by masking boxes. To view an example part, the student needs to move the mouse over the box that covers it. When the student uncovers an example part, a "self-explain" button appears next to it, as a reminder to self-explain. Clicking on this button activates more specific prompts that suggest two kinds of self-explanations known to be highly effective for learning. These are as follows: (1) explain an example solution step in terms of domain principles (*step correctness*); (2) explain the role of a solution step in the underlying solution plan (*step utility*). The interface provides tools to help students generate these two kinds of explanations. For instance, to explain *step correctness*, the student can browse a hierarchy of physics rules (known as the Rule Browser, see Fig. 24.2), select one that she thinks justifies the current solution step, and fill-out a partial definition of the rule by selecting relevant options in a pull-down menu (Rule template in Fig. 24.2, right).

The SE-Coach provides feedback on the correctness of the student selection, based on its internal representation of how each problem solution derives from physics principles. A similar mechanism, based on a menu-based tool known as the Plan Browser, is available to explain *step utility*. It should be noted that a student can terminate a self-explanation attempt at any point, even if the correct explanation has not been generated.

The student's reading and self-explanation actions are used to dynamically update the student model Bayesian network that, at any time during interaction, assesses the student's understanding of the different example parts. If a student tries to close the example when the student model indicates that there are still some parts that are prob-

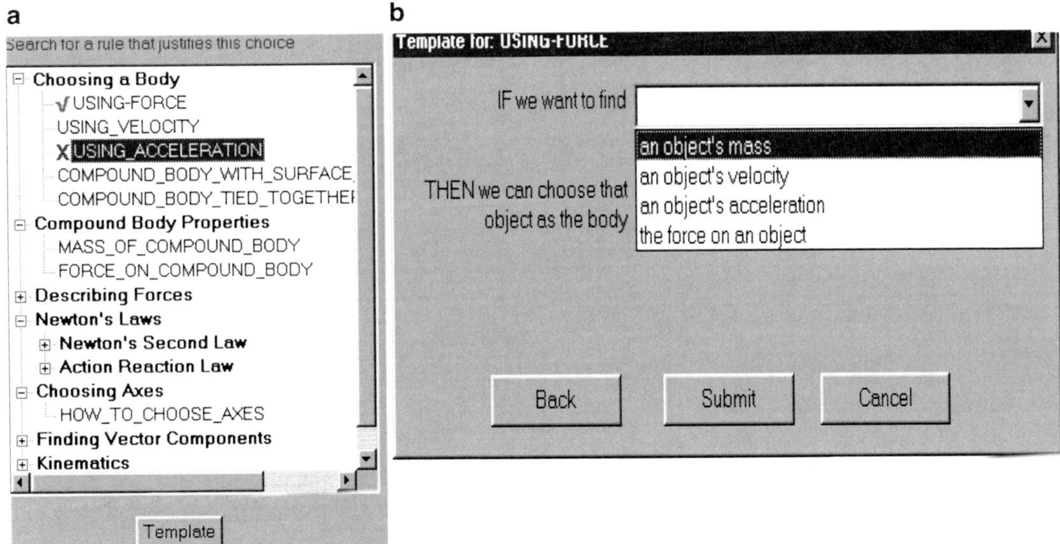

Fig. 24.2 Rule browser and a sample rule template (*left*)

lematic for him, the interface generates a warning and highlights the corresponding masking boxes. It also changes the "self-explain" button for each highlighted line, to indicate what the student should do to better self-explain the line. The revised prompt for a step will include "use the Rule Browser" and/or "use the Plan Browser" items if the student model indicates that the student has problems using the related physics and planning rule to explain it; it will say "read more carefully" (as in Fig. 24.1, right), if the student model indicates that the student understands the relevant rules but is not giving enough attention to the step. As the student performs new reading and self-explanation actions to follow the SE-Coach's suggestions, the boxes' color and the related prompts change dynamically to reflect the updates in the student model probabilities, as we describe later.

The SE-Coach's Student Model to Capture Self-Explanation

As we mentioned at the beginning of this section, one of the key principles underlying the SE-Coach design is that self-explanation support should be given only to those students who need it; the SE-Coach should not ask spontaneous self-explainers to always make their self-explanations explicit through the SE-Coach interface tools. Thus, the student model must be able to recognize *implicit self-explanation*, i.e., when a student self-explains spontaneously without using the SE-tools. The only information available to the model to assess implicit self-explanation is latency data on student's attention and estimates of student's domain knowledge. This adds uncertainty to the assessment, because both student's attention and student's knowledge cannot be unambiguously determined. Additional uncertainty comes from the fact that little research exists on how people learn from explanations generated via menu selections and template filling. Thus, even when students generate correct self-explanations through the interface tools described in the previous section, there is uncertainty about how these self-explanations reflect learning and understanding. The SE-Coach's student model formally handles this uncertainty by using Bayesian networks. Following the approach proposed in (Conati, Gertner, & VanLehn, 2002), the student model Bayesian network is built automatically for each example, as illustrated in the next section.

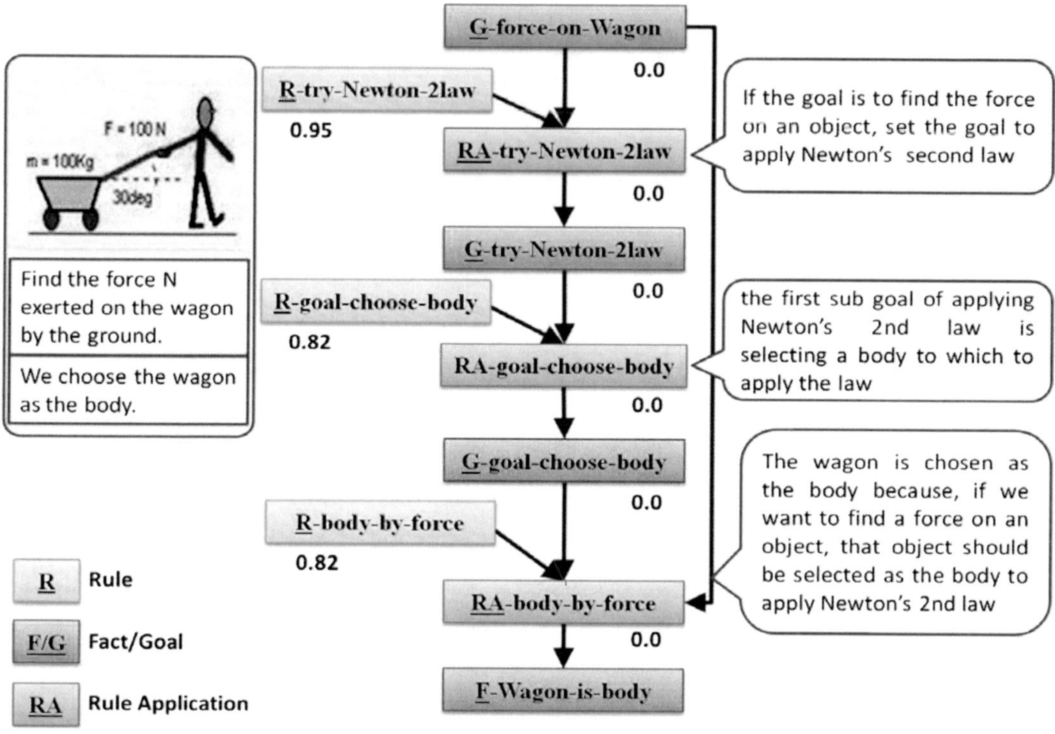

Fig. 24.3 Segment of the student model for the example in Fig. 24.1. The *bubbles to the right* represent the self-explanations corresponding to the related RA nodes in the graph

The SE-Coach Model of Correct Self-Explanation

For each example available in the SE-Coach, an automatic problem solver builds a model of correct self-explanation (SE model), starting from a knowledge base of rules describing physics principles and abstract planning steps. The resulting SE model (see Fig. 24.3) is a dependency network that encodes how the intermediate facts and goals in a solution (F- and G- nodes in Fig. 24.3) derive from domain rules (R- nodes in Fig. 24.3) and from facts and goals matching the rules' preconditions. These derivations are explicitly represented in the SE model by rule-application nodes (RA- nodes in Fig. 24.3) and correspond exactly to the self-explanations for *step correctness* and *step utility* that the SE-Coach targets. The self-explanations specific to the RA nodes in Fig. 24.3 are listed in the corresponding bubbles to the right of the figure. For instance, the node *RA-body-by-force* in, encodes the explanation that the Wagon in the example is chosen as the body because a physics rule (represented by the rule node *R-body-by force* in Fig. 24.3) says that if we want to find a force on an object, that object should be selected as the body to which to apply Newton's 2nd law. The node *RA-goal-choose-body* encodes the explanation that choosing the wagon as the body fulfils the first subgoal of applying Newton's 2nd law, i.e., selecting a body to which to apply the law (represented by the rule node *R-goal-chose-body* in Fig. 24.3).

When a student opens an example, the actual student model Bayesian network for the current session is automatically created from the SE model for that example and from a student's long term model. The structure of the Bayesian network derives directly from the SE model. All nodes in the initial network have binary values representing the probability that the student knows rules, goals and facts in the example solution and that she has explained the related derivations. As a student performs reading and self-explanation (SE) actions, the initial Bayesian network is dynamically updated with nodes representing these actions (see Fig. 24.3).

Modeling Implicit and Explicit Self-Explanation

Read nodes (nodes with prefix Read in, Fig. 24.3) represent viewing items in the masking interface. The values of read nodes reflect the duration of viewing time and can be LOW (time insufficient for reading), OK (time sufficient for reading only) or LONG (time sufficient for self-explanation).[1] Each read node connects to the SE model node reflecting the semantic content of the viewed item. For instance, the links from Read nodes to F_ and G_ nodes represent the student's reading the lines "Find the force N exerted on the wagon by the ground" and "We choose the wagon as the body," respectively. These links indicate that viewing time influences the probability of knowing the related content.

The fact that the student viewed an example item does not necessarily mean that the student self-explained it. However, the longer the student viewed an example item, the higher the probability that he self-explained it. This relationship between viewing time and self-explanation is encoded in the student model by linking a read node that represents viewing an example item with the rule-application nodes that represent self-explanation for correctness and utility for that item (see, for instance, links from Read_ nodes to RA_ nodes in Fig. 24.3). The conditional probability tables (CPT) that encode the probabilistic dependencies between these rule-application nodes and its parents is defined to represent the following relationships: a student cannot self-explain a derivation correctly if he does not have the necessary knowledge (i.e., the rule and its preconditions), no matter for how long the student attended to the derivation. If the student has all the necessary knowledge, the probability that proper self-explanation occurred increases with viewing time.

Nodes representing the student's explicit self-explanation actions (SE nodes) are dynamically added to the Bayesian network as these actions occur. The CPT modeling the influence of a correct SE action on the probability that a student understands the corresponding rule is mediated by the current student knowledge of that rules and by how many incorrect attempts the student generates before reaching the correct self-explanation.

Assessment

At any time during the student's interaction with the SE-Coach, the probabilities in the Bayesian network assess how the student's domain knowledge and example understanding change with the student's interface actions. In particular, the probabilities associated with rule-application nodes represent the probability that the student self-explained the corresponding derivations. Rule-application nodes with probability below a given threshold become the target of the SE-Coach interventions.

Shows the probabilities in the student model after a student viewed the line "Find the force N exerted on the wagon by the ground" long enough for reading it, viewed the line "We choose the wagon as the body" quite longer and self-explained the planning rule behind this line. After these actions are processed by the model, there is only one Rule-Application node that still has a low probability, the non-shaded node *RA-body-by-force*. From this node's descendant, *F-wagon-is-the-body*, the SE-Coach infers that the missing explanation relates to the first line in the example solution. From the fact that the only input node with low probability for *RA-body-by-force* is the rule *R-body-by-force*, the SE Coach detects that the missing explanation relates to this rule. Hence, it adds the first solution line among the lines to highlight in the masking interface and modifies its self-explain button to suggest self-explaining the physics rule related to this line. When low probability of a rule-application node is caused only by too short reading time, the "self-explain" button for the related

[1] The values are based on thresholds that assume a reading speed of 3.4 words per second, i.e., an average-speed reader (see Conati et al., 2002 for more details).

solution line is turned into a hint suggesting to read more carefully.

The student is not obligated to follow the SE-Coach's suggestions. When the student decides to close an example, the student model Bayesian network is discarded, but the new rule nodes' probabilities are saved in the so-called long-term student model. They will become the new priors in the student model for the next example study task and will influence the system's interventions accordingly.

Evaluation of the SE-Coach

The SE-Coach was evaluated in a controlled study with 56 college students who had been studying Newton's Laws as part of an introductory physics course. The students came from four different colleges. During the one-session study, students first took a pretest on Newton's Laws, then studied related examples with the SE-Coach and finally took a posttest equivalent to the pretest. The study had two conditions. In the *experimental* (*SE*) condition, 29 students studied examples with the complete SE-Coach. In the *control* condition, 27 students studied examples with the masking interface including the *self-explain* prompts that appear when a line is uncovered. However, these students had no access to the subsequent levels of scaffolding (i.e., the browsers and templates described in Sect. 3.1), nor to the adaptive coaching described in Sect. 3.2.3. The purpose of these two conditions is to compare the effectiveness of complex, user-adaptive scaffolding for self-explanation against simple, nonadaptive prompts that simply remind students to self-explain at every example line that they uncover.

As we reported in (Conati & VanLehn, 2000), the analysis of the students' learning gains show that the SE-Coach's multiple and adaptive levels of scaffolding for self-explanation improve students' problem solving when students are in the early stage of cognitive skill acquisition. In particular, students who had just started covering Newton's laws (*late-start* students from now on) learned significantly better with the adaptive version of the tutor than with the control version, while there was no difference between the two conditions for students who had started covering Newton's laws earlier in the term (*early-start* students). These students didn't know more physics than the late-start student (as shown by the two groups' similar performance in the pretest). However, their different exposure to the example topics did seem to impact how they interacted with examples. For instance, we have indications that the milder form of scaffolding provided by the SE-Coach in the control condition (i.e., the masking interface and untailored reminders) was sufficient to trigger effective self-explanation in early start students, but not in late-start students. In the experimental condition, although there was no difference in how frequently late and early-start students accessed the SE tools, early-start students engaged in significantly fewer attempts to correct self-explanations that had been flagged as incorrect by the SE-Coach. We take this difference as an indication that, in the experimental condition, early-start students put less effort in learning from the SE-Coach tools than late-start students, perhaps because they overestimated their understanding of the subject matter, and thus they learned less.

In summary, our results provide encouraging evidence that it is possible and useful, if done at the right time, to provide students with individualized guidance to studying examples before moving to problem solving. This guidance, delivered through adaptive prompts and a set of menu-based tools designed to scaffold the self-explanation process, seems to be beneficial for students who have just started learning a topic. Simpler scaffolding based on untailored reminders to self-explain appears to be more effective for students who have already had substantial exposure to the topic.

Discussion

In this section, we have illustrated how the SE-Coach includes an interface and a student model that allow it to monitor a student reading and self-explanation behavior while they study physics examples. This monitoring allows The

SE-Coach to prompt students to explicitly generate self-explanations using its ad-hoc interface tools *only* when the student model assesses that this can be beneficial for the student. In particular, the interface helps those students who do not self-explain by drawing the students' attention to example parts that may be problematic for them and by providing specific scaffolding on what knowledge these explanations should tap. Asking students to always make their explanations explicit through the interface tools would of course enable more accurate assessment of their understanding, but would also burden the students who are natural self-explainers with unnecessary work, possibly compromising the constructive, spontaneous nature of their self-explanations and their motivation to use the system.

It should be noted that the SE-Coach model represents self explanation operationally, but not explicitly. That is, model structure allows the SE-Coach to generate probabilistic predictions of if and how a student self-explains based on the semantics of rule application nodes. There are, however, no variables in the model that *directly* represent implicit self-explanation behavior. This choice makes the model hard to extend with new sources of information to detect implicit self-explanation, such as more precise ways to track student's attention, speech etc. It also makes it hard to give the system the ability to *explain* its assessment to the student, because the system does not have access to the semantic information that identifies self-explanation in the current structure. In the next part of the chapter, we describe a research project that addresses this limitation of the SE-Coach in the context of scaffolding self-explanation during a different study activity: learning via exploration interactive simulations

ACE: Adaptive Scaffolding of Self-Explanation During Exploration-Based Learning

The Adaptive Coach for Exploration (ACE) project investigates how to provide individualized support to students as they learn from free exploration of interactive simulations (Bunt, Conati, Hugget, & Muldner, 2001). The need for support is justified by studies showing that free exploration is a very effective way of learning for students with the adequate abilities (e.g., adequate background knowledge and self-regulatory skills), but it may not work as well for students who need more structure and guidance (e.g., Shute & Glaser, 1990); The goal of the ACE project is to find ways to capture students' ineffective exploratory behaviors, and provide adaptive scaffolding to improve them. Modeling exploratory behaviors is hard because what constitutes effective exploration is not as well defined as, for instance, what constitutes effective problem solving. There is no clear definition of correctness; *how* or *how much* a student needs to explore in order to grasp the target concepts depends on a variety of factors including the student background knowledge and how the student uses this knowledge to make sense of the outcome of her exploration. The latter is a form of self-explanation, which distinguishes students who may be performing many exploratory actions but don't learn because they fail to reason about their outcomes, from students who try to explain what they observe in terms of the target domain.

One of the main challenges of the ACE project has been to define a student model that captures at least some of the elements that define effective exploration, i.e., exploration that helps students understand the target domain. We have addressed the challenge by using, once again, a probabilistic approach that combines in a Bayesian network information on what is relevant to explore in the target domain, what the student already knows about it and if/how the student self-explain during exploration.

While the general approach is conceptually similar to the one we used for the SE-Coach, there are two main differences. First, the ACE student model has a much more explicit representation of self-explanation. Second, ACE uses eye-tracking to get more precise information on student's behaviors related to self-explanation.

As a testbed for this research, we have devised an exploratory learning environment that targets the understanding of mathematical functions. In the next subsections, we first describe the

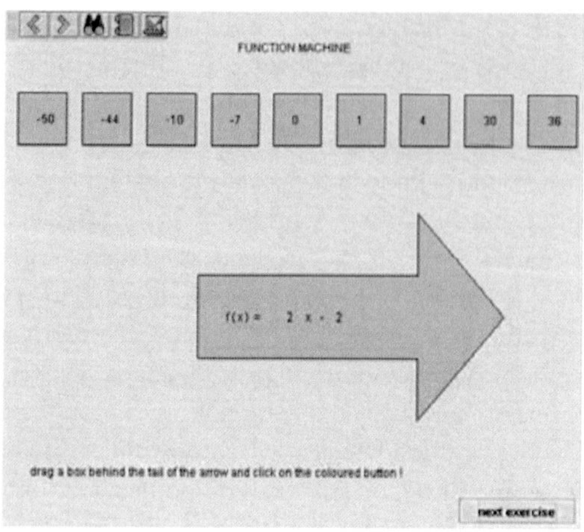

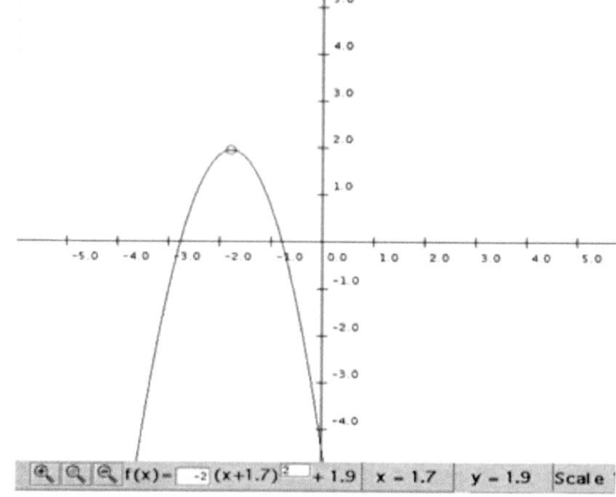

Fig. 24.4 ACE's machine and Plot Unit

environment and then we illustrate the student model we have implemented to track and support student exploration, self-explanation and learning in the environment.

The ACE Exploratory Environment

The ACE environment provides a series of activities to help students understand function-related concepts through exploration. These activities are divided into units and exercises. Units are collections of exercises whose material is presented with a common theme and mode of interaction. Exercises within the units differ in function type and equation. Figure 24.2 shows the main interaction window for two of ACE's units: the *Machine Unit* and the *Plot Unit*. ACE also has a third unit, the *Arrow Unit*, not displayed for brevity.

The Machine and the Arrow Unit each provide a different activity designed to allow a learner to explore the relationship between input and output of a given function. In the Machine Unit, the learner can drag any of the inputs displayed at the top of the screen to the tail of the "machine" (the large arrow shown in Fig. 24.4, left), which then computes the corresponding output. The Arrow Unit allows the learner to map, given a function, a selection of function's inputs to a selection of given outputs, and is the only unit within ACE that has a clear definition of correct behavior (i.e., the student must map the chosen input values to the correct output values). The Plot Unit (Fig. 24.4, right) allows the learner to explore the relationship between a function's graph and its equation by manipulating either one of the entities, and then observing the corresponding changes in the other.

While performing a variety of exploratory actions is a fundamental component of effective exploration, the reasoning that goes with these actions is crucial to define the outcome of the exploration process. Ideally, the student should engage in a form of discovery process by which the target domain is explored in search of possible regularities, hypotheses on these regularities are formulated, and further domain exploration is used for hypothesis testing (e.g., Shute & Glaser, 1990). We currently do not explicitly support this discovery process in ACE, but we support one of its building blocks, self-explanation of exploratory actions. To understand how self-explanation plays a key role in effective exploration, consider a learner who, in the ACE Plot Unit, moves a function graph around the screen, and rarely stops to consider how the movements change the function equation. Although this learner is performing many exploratory actions, she can hardly learn from them because she is not reflecting on (self-explaining) their outcomes. We observed this phenomenon in several learners during pre-

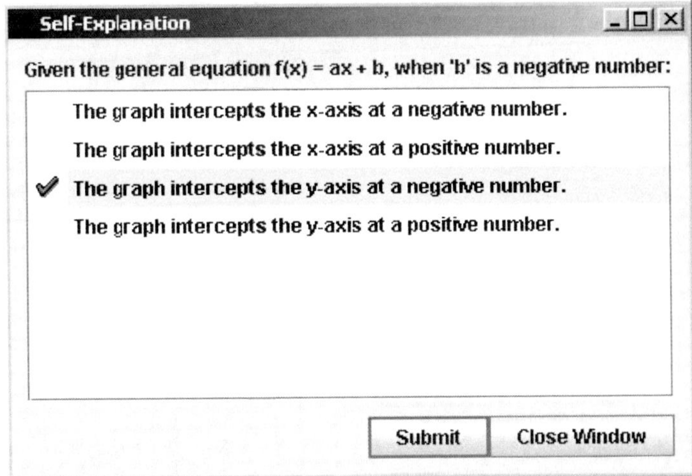

Fig. 24.5 Example of ACE self-explanation tools

liminary evaluations of ACE, and thus decided to add to the environment tools to scaffold the self-explanation process, similar to the tools available with the SE-Coach (Bunt, Conati, & Muldner, 2004). These tools include menu-based dialogue boxes that allow students to define various principles that can be discovered by playing with the ACE simulations. Figure 24.5, for instance, shows the dialogue box that allows the student to explain the relation between the negative coefficient of a line function and its intercept. The student can access these dialogue boxes at will during interaction, but they can also be suggested to the student by the ACE's Coach.

The Coach is a component designed to support the exploration process by providing the student with tailored hints when ACE's student model predicts that a student has difficulties exploring effectively. If the learner tries to move on to a new exercise before the student model assesses that the learner has explored the current exercise sufficiently, the Coach will generate a warning, suggesting that the learner stay with the current exercise a bit longer. These warnings also remind the learner of the availability of more specific hints, accessible by clicking on a *Get Hint* button (not shown). Hints are supplied to the learner at increasing levels of detail, ranging from a generic suggestion to explore the current exercise more thoroughly, to exactly what things to explore (e.g., "You should see what the line function graph looks like when its equation has a negative *b* coefficient").

The Coach uses the Student Model's assessment to decide which concept the hint should target. The student model also allows the Coach to identify students who likely are not self-explaining during exploration. As soon as the Coach detects lack of self-explanation, it generates a prompt to trigger the process. The prompt can be, as in the case of the hints, a generic reminder to self-explain (see Fig. 24.6) or a more direct suggestion that the Coach implements by opening for the student the menu-based SE tool relevant to generate the target self-explanation. Since the system is designed to maintain as much as possible the learner's freedom and control in the exploratory process, it is up to the learner to decide which of the Coach's suggestions to follow and which to disregard.

ACE Student Model

Modeling Domain Exploration

ACE student's model is the result of an iterative design-and-evaluation process that helped us define what constitutes effective exploration of the interactive simulations provided by the ACE interface. The model uses Bayesian networks to capture the probabilistic dependencies between the various exploration levels available in ACE,

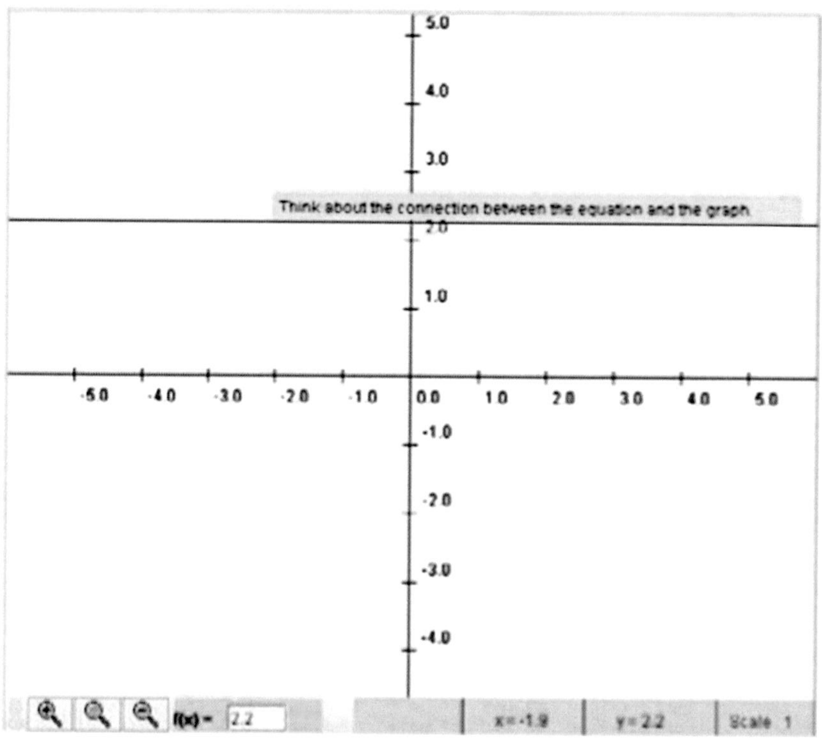

Fig. 24.6 Initial prompt to self-explain in ACE

and how student exploration and learning changes overtime during interaction. To model exploration at the various levels of granularity afforded by the interface, the SE-Coach includes the following types of nodes: *Relevant Exploration Cases*, representing exploration of individual exploration cases in an exercise (e.g., changing the slope of a line to three, a positive number, in the Plot Unit); *Exploration of Exercises* and *Exploration of Units,* representing adequate exploration for the various ACE exercises and units, respectively; and *Exploration of Categories,* representing the exploration of groups of relevant exploration cases that appear across multiple exercises (e.g., all of the exploration cases involving a positive slope in the Plot Unit). The links among the different types of exploration nodes represent how they interact to define effective exploration. Exploration nodes have binary values representing the probability that the learner has sufficiently explored the associated items. Figure 24.7 (left) shows a high-level representation of the various types of exploration nodes and their relationships; Fig. 24.7 (right) shows a snapshot of the actual nodes in the model after the student opens an exercise in the Plot Unit (node e_0 in the figure) and changes the intercept parameters of the corresponding function first to a positive and then to a negative number (nodes e_0 $case_0$ and e_0 $case_1$ in the figure). The links here reflect how exploration of a specific exercise (e_0 in Fig. 24.7) is influenced by specific simulation cases explored within that exercise (nodes e_0 $case_0$ and e_0 $case_1$ in the figure). These cases also influence exploration of relevant categories (represented by nodes *Negative Intercept* and *Positive Intercept* in Fig. 24.7, right), while exercise exploration in turns influences exploration of the corresponding using (represented by the *Plot Unit* node in this case). The student model also includes binary nodes representing the probability that the learner understands the relevant pieces of knowledge. The links between knowledge and exploration nodes represent the fact that the

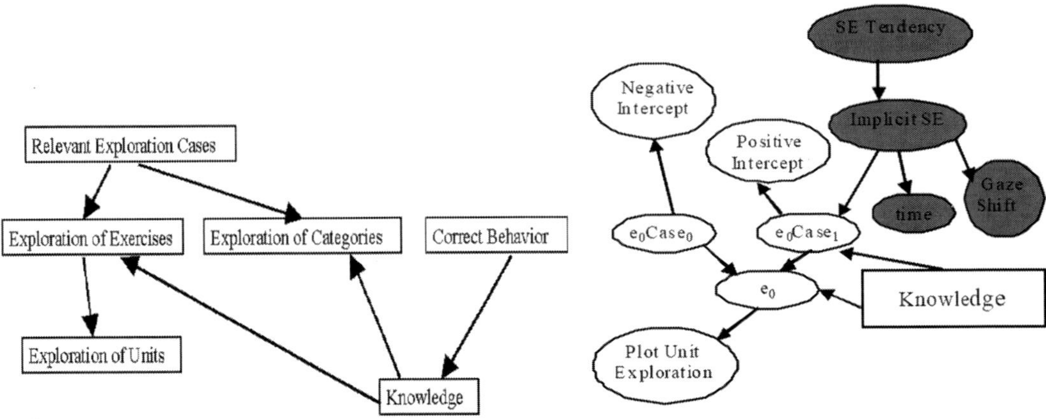

Fig. 24.7 ACE model. Different exploration levels (*left*); Snapshot of model details (*right*)

degree of exploration needed to understand a concept depends on how much knowledge a learner already has. Knowledge nodes are updated only through actions for which there is a clear definition of correctness. Thus, these nodes are never updated within the Machine and Plot Unit, since they consist of purely exploratory activities.

While existing knowledge plays an important role in assessing how well a student is exploring, as we discussed in the previous section another key element is whether the student self-explains her exploratory actions. Thus the ACE's student model also includes nodes and links that allow it to model the student self-explanation behavior. As for the SE-Coach, this self-explanation behavior includes both self-explanations built via the ACE's tools (*explicit* self-explanation) as well as self-explanations that a student generates spontaneously in her head (*implicit* self-explanation). In this section we focus on the latter because it is the most interesting from a modeling perspective. In particular, we illustrate the improvements we made to the approach used in the SE-Coach to make tracking of student self-explanation more thorough and accurate.

Modeling Self-Explanation During Exploration

The reader should recall from Sect. 3.2 that, in the SE-Coach student model, assessment of self-explanation is based solely on latency of student attention on a given example line and student knowledge of the relevant domain principles. However, there are at least two other factors that can provide an indirect indication of a student's self-explanation behavior in ACE: whether or not the learner is observing the results of her exploration actions, and the learner's known tendency to spontaneously self-explain. Consider, for instance, the case of the learner who is continually altering a graph in the Plot Unit. ACE's student model could be more confident that this is a sign of good exploration if the learner looks at both the graph and the equation as they change. Knowing a priori that the learner has a tendency to self-explain could further increase the model's confidence that the learner is engaging in the relevant reasoning as she is experimenting with the simulation.

The ACE's student model takes all these factors into account by using the structure in Fig. 24.7, right. The probability that a learner's action reflects effective exploration of a given case depends on both the probability that the student self-explained the action and the probability that she knows the corresponding concept. Factors influencing the probability that implicit self-explanation occurred include: (1) the *tendency* that the learner has to self-explain (SE tendency node in the figure); (2) the *time* spent on the case (i.e., between performing the related exploratory action and a subsequent action); (3) whether the student actually looked at the changes her action generated (*gaze shift* node in the figure). The directions of the links between the *implicit SE* node and these factors show how this model enforces a clear separation between the causes of implicit self-explanation (e.g., student SE tendency) and its observable effects, (e.g., gaze shifts and time on action). These effects are encoded as independent predictors, as in a naïve Bayesian classifier.

The main advantage of this approach is that it is highly modular, facilitating the addition of new factors as causes of implicit self-explain (e.g., ACE's self-explanation prompts) or additional observable effects (e.g., student speech) become available. Adding additional effects is especially straightforward, because it only requires defining the probabilistic relation between implicit self-explanation and each new effect.

For the version of the model in Fig. 24.7, all relevant probabilities related to the Implicit SE node were learned from data from an ad-hoc user study. This data currently focus on interaction with the Plot Unit. In this study, 36 participants had their gaze monitored via an eye-tracker while interacting with ACE (Conati & Merten, 2007). The students were asked to verbalize all of their thoughts during interaction, and their interface actions were logged and synchronized with data from the eye tracker. This data captured gaze shifts between the plot and equation area after a plot move or equation change in the Plot Unit. While other attention patterns may be relevant, we decided to focus on this particular attention pattern as a proof-of-concept to show the value of attention data to detect self-explanation because it provides intuitive evidence that the student is at least attending to the effect of a specific action in the Plot Unit. During the study, participants also took a pretest and a posttest on mathematical functions.

Two researchers (to assure coding reliability) categorized student verbalizations after equation and plot changes as instances of self-explanation versus speech not conducive to learning. Then, they mapped these verbalizations onto presence/absence of gaze shifts and latency until the next action, to obtain frequency data that we used to set the conditional probability of gaze shift and time of action given implicit self-explanation. Data from the study was also used to define the CPT for implicit self-explanation given tendency to self-explain. Study participants were divided into *self-explainers*—those who self-explained at least 20% of the time—and *non-self-explainers*—those who did not. We found that self-explainers and non-self-explainers generated implicit self-explanations on average 79.8% and 13.3% of the time, respectively. These frequencies were then used to set the conditional probability for the Implicit SE node given tendency to self-explain. Incidentally, we found that the group of students that were categorized as self-explainers obtained a mean 24% learning gain, significantly higher (at the 0.05 level) than the 5.7% gain achieved by non-self-explainers, confirming that self-explanation has a significant effect on overall learning during exploration of an interactive simulation.

In the next section, we describe an evaluation of the ACE student model showing that it effectively tracks not only self-explanation, but also consequent learning, thanks especially to the input from eye-tracking data.

Evaluations of ACE

The Coach's prompts to continue exploring an exercise, and the corresponding hints were evaluated with a version of the student model that did not capture self-explanation (Bunt et al., 2001). The study showed these prompts to be effective in directing student exploration when they appeared, although that version of the ACE model underestimated student exploration and thus some learners did not receive as many prompts as they could have used.

The full version of ACE including the student model described in the previous section and hints for both exploration and self-explanation has yet to be evaluated. We have, however, evaluated the complete student model using the data from the study described in the previous section. We compared the complete model against (1) a model using only time as predictor of self-explanation and (2) an earlier version of the model that ignores self-explanation and uses only the number of interface actions as a predictor of effective exploration. We ran a leave-one-out cross-validation over the 36 study participants (see Conati &

Merten, 2007 for additional data analysis). This procedure involved isolating each of the 36 participants in turn, setting model parameters using the data from all remaining 35 participants, and then using the resulting model to assess self-explanation and learning for the test participants. Model performance on assessing self-explanation was evaluated against the self-explanation labels generated by the human judges as part of the study. Performance on assessing learning was evaluated by comparing the posterior probabilities of nodes representing successful exploration of specific concepts and student performance on posttest questions targeting these concepts. We report the average accuracy over all 36 participants, as the average of the model's sensitivity (or true positive rate) and specificity (or true negative rate). We found the following:

- The model including both gaze and time data reached an accuracy of 76.4% and provides better assessment of student self-explanation than the model using only time (67.2%). The difference is statistically significant ($p<0.05$).
- Assessing self-explanation improves the assessment of student exploratory behavior, and the accuracy of the latter increases with increased accuracy of self-explanation assessment. Thus, the complete model reaches the highest accuracy on learning (77.5%), followed by the model based on time only (70.4%). All improvements are statistically significant.

Discussion

The results presented in the previous sections show that capturing implicit student self-explanation during interaction with ACE is possible and important not only to enable tailored support to this meta-cognitive skill, but also to improve model's ability to assess and support effectiveness of student exploratory behavior. The next step of this research is to evaluate adaptive interventions based on the model we presented in the previous section, especially the prompts to scaffold self-explanation. These prompts currently appear near the area of the Plot Unit that requires self-explanation (e.g., the plot of a line function in Fig. 24.6), as soon as the student model assesses that the student is not self-explaining. We have chosen this approach, rather than waiting until the student tries to close the current exercise as ACE does for exploration prompts, because it is important that self-explanation of each action happens in context. Given the open-ended nature of the interaction with the SE-Coach, it would be hard to recreate the relevant context if students were asked to self-explain individual actions at the end of an exercise's exploration. Presenting the prompts in the middle of the exploration process, however, runs the danger of being intrusive, especially if the prompts are not justified. An alternative is to make the prompts appear on the side of the main interaction window, so that the student can more easily ignore them if they are not useful. We are planning to evaluate these two alternative designs to investigate how to strike the right balance between prompt unobtrusiveness and efficacy. We also want to extend the student model to cover the other ACE units, after collecting the necessary self-explanation data.

Conclusions

In this chapter, we discussed our research on providing student-adaptive support for the meta-cognitive skill of self-explanation. One contribution of our research is the design and development of student models that assess a student's self-explanation behavior, so that adaptive support can be tailored to it. Other researchers have investigated generating prompts for self-explanation. However, these prompts are either not tailored (e.g., the student is asked to self-explain every piece of relevant instructional material or each of her problem solving actions) or are tailored to more indirect evidence of need for self-explanation (e.g., whether a problem solving action has been taken for the first time or is incorrect). While some of these non-tailored approaches have generated encouraging results (e.g., Aleven & Koedinger, 2002; Crippen & Boyd, 2007; McLaren et al., 2008) there is still large room for improvement. We argue that prompts more adaptive to the students' actual self-explanation needs may be more salient, less intrusive and thus more effective to improve student learning and long-term self-explanation ability. In the first part of this chapter, we showed support for this claim in relation to the SE-Coach, an ILE that generates adaptive support for self-explanation while students study physics examples. In particular, we showed that the adaptive support makes a difference for students who have just started learning the examples' topic, while untailored prompts worked as well as the adaptive support for more advanced students.

Assessing student self-explanation behavior unobtrusively requires recognizing when students self-explain spontaneously in their head. This requirement is hard to fulfill for a software system that has no direct access to students' thoughts or verbalizations. In the second part of the chapter, we described our investigation of eye-tracking information on student attention as a way to improve recognition of student spontaneous self-explanation in the context of learning by exploration of interactive simulations. The contributions of this work are twofold: first, we showed the relevance of self-explanation in exploration-based learning, an activity in which this meta-cognitive skill was yet to be studied. Second, we showed that information on user attention patterns collected via an eye-tracking significantly increases a model's ability to capture self-explanation, compared to a lower-level time-based predictor.

Based on latency on interface actions, we now need to demonstrate that having this more sophisticated model improves support for self-explanation during exploration-based learning, compared to nonadaptive forms of scaffolding. We also need to show that our adaptive scaffolding improves not only learning of the target domain/skills but also the student's long-term self-explanation ability. Finally, we want to generalize this research to computer-based educational games. Edu-games are another educational activity that, like interactive simulations, relies on unstructured, open interaction with a rich but possibly distracting or confusing environment and thus may benefit from interventions that trigger student deep reasoning via self-explanation at the appropriate times.

References

Aleven, V., & Koedinger, K. R. (2002). An effective meta-cognitive strategy: Learning by doing and explaining with a computer-based Cognitive Tutor. *Cognitive Science, 26*(2), 147–179.

Azevedo, R., Witherspoon, A., Chauncey, A., Burkett, C., & Fike, A. (2009). Meta-tutor: A meta-cognitive tutor for enhancing self-regulated learning. *AAAI Fall Symposium on Cognitive and Meta-Cognitive Educational Systems* (pp. 14–19).

Bunt, A., Conati, C., Hugget, M., & Muldner, K. (2001). On improving the effectiveness of open learning environments through tailored support for exploration. *AIED 2001, 10th World Conference of Artificial Intelligence and Education.*

Bunt, A., Conati, C., & Muldner, K. (2004). Scaffolding self-explanation to improve learning in exploratory learning environments. *Proceedings of ITS 2004, 7th International Conference on Intelligent Tutoring Systems*, Lecture Notes in Computer Science, Vol. 3220/2004 (pp. 656–667), Berlin/Heidelberg: Springer.

Chi, M. T. (2000). Self-explaining expository texts: The dual processes of generating inferences and repairing mental models. In R. Glaser (Ed.), *Advances in instructional psychology* (pp. 161–238). Mahwah: Lawrence Erlbaum Associates.

Chi, M., & VanLehn, K. (2007). The impact of explicit strategy instruction on problem solving behaviors across intelligent tutoring systems. *29th Annual Conference of the Cognitive Science Society.*

Conati, C., Gertner, A., & VanLehn, K. (2002). Using bayesian networks to manage uncertainty in student modeling. *Journal of User Modeling and User-Adapted Interaction, 12*(4), 371–417.

Conati, C., & Merten, C. (2007). Eye-tracking for user modeling in exploratory learning environments: An empirical evaluation. *Knowledge Based Systems, 20*(6), 557–574.

Conati, C., & Vanlehn, K. (2000). Toward computer-based support of meta-cognitive skills: A computational framework to coach self-explanation. *International Journal of Artificial Intelligence in Education, 11*, 389–415.

Crippen, K., & Boyd, L. (2007). The impact of web-based worked examples and self-explanation on performance, problem solving, and self-efficacy. *Computers in Education, 49*(3), 809–821.

Luckin, R., & Hammerton, L. (2002). Getting to know me: Helping learners understand their own learning needs through metacognitive scaffolding. In: *Intelligent Tutoring Systems: 6th International Conference on Intelligent Tutoring Systems, ITS 2002.* Springer.

McLaren, B., Lim, S., & Koedinger, K. (2008). When and how often should worked examples be given to students? New results and a summary of the current state of research. *30th Annual Conference of the Cognitive*

Science Society (pp. 2176–2181). Austin, TX: Cognitive Science Society.

Mitrovic, A. (2003). Supporting self-explanation in a data normalization tutor. *Supplementary proceedings, AIED 2003* (pp. 565–577).

Muldner, K., & Conati, C. (2007). Evaluating a decision-theoretic approach to tailored example selection. *IJCAI 2007, 20th International Joint Conference in Artificial Intelligence* (pp. 483–488).

Rau, M., Aleven, V., & Rummel, N. (2009). Intelligent tutoring systems with multiple representations and self-explanation prompts support learning of fractions. *14th International Conference on Artificial Intelligence in Education, AIED 2009* (pp. 441–449). Amsterdam: IOS Press.

Roll, I., Aleven, V., McLaren, B. M., & Koedinger, K. R. (2007). Can help seeking be tutored? Searching for the secret sauce of metacongitive tutoring. *International Conference on Artificial Intelligence in Education 2007*.

Shute, V. J., & Glaser, R. (1990). A large-scale evaluation of an intelligent discovery world: Smithtown. *Interactive Learning Environments, 1*(1), 1–77.

Tan, J., Biswas, G., & Schwartz, D. (2006). Feedback for metacognitive support in learning by teaching environments. *Meeting of the Cognitive Science Society* (pp. 828–833). Vancouver.

van Joolingen, W. (2000). Designing for collaborative discovery learning. *5th International Conference on Intelligent Tutoring Systems* (pp. 202–211).

25 Towards Improving (Meta)cognition by Adapting to Student Uncertainty in Tutorial Dialogue

Diane Litman and Kate Forbes-Riley

Abstract

We hypothesize that enhancing computer tutors to respond to student uncertainty over and above correctness is one method for increasing both student learning and self-monitoring abilities. We test this hypothesis using spoken data from both wizarded and fully-automated versions of a spoken tutorial dialogue system, where tutor responses to uncertain and/or incorrect student answers were manipulated. Although we find no significant improvement in metacognitive metrics (computed using speech and language information) when responding to uncertainty and incorrectness as compared to when responding only to incorrectness, we find that some metacognitive metrics significantly correlate with student learning. Our results suggest that monitoring and responding to student uncertainty has the potential to improve both cognitive and metacognitive student abilities.

Introduction

Speech and language researchers have shown that speaker uncertainty is associated with linguistic signals (Dijkstra, Krahmer, & Swerts, 2006, Liscombe, Venditti, & Hirschberg, 2005, Nicholas, Rotaru, & Litman, 2006, Pon-Barry, 2008), while tutoring researchers have hypothesized that tutors use such signals to detect and address student uncertainty in order to improve performance metrics including student learning, persistence, and system usability (Aist, Kort, Reilly, Mostow, & Picard, 2002, Litman, Moore, Dzikovska, & Farrow, 2009, Tsukahara & Ward, 2001). For example, VanLehn et al. (2003) propose that both student uncertainty and incorrectness signal "learning impasses," i.e., student learning opportunities. While correlational studies have shown a link between learning and student uncertainty as well as the related notion of confusion in tutorial dialogue (Craig, Graesser, Sullins, & Gholson, 2004, Forbes-Riley, Rotaru, & Litman, 2008b), few controlled experiments have investigated whether responding to student impasses involving uncertainty improves learning, and those that did yielded overall null results (e.g., (Pon-Barry et al., 2006)). To date, most computer dialogue tutors respond based only on student correctness.

D. Litman (✉) • K. Forbes-Riley
Learning Research and Development Center,
University of Pittsburgh, Pittsburgh, PA 15260, USA
e-mail: litman@cs.pitt.edu

R. Azevedo and V. Aleven (eds.), *International Handbook of Metacognition and Learning Technologies*, Springer International Handbooks of Education 26, DOI 10.1007/978-1-4419-5546-3_25,

In prior work, we experimentally compared learning gains across versions of a spoken tutorial dialogue system that differed in whether and how they adapted to student uncertainty. In our experimental conditions, the system provided additional knowledge at places of uncertainty; in the control conditions, the system either did not provide this knowledge, or provided such knowledge randomly. In a first experiment we used a wizarded form of our system, where uncertainty and correctness were manually annotated in real time by a human "wizard" (Forbes-Riley & Litman, 2009a, 2011b). Our results demonstrated that responding to student uncertainty, over and above correctness, did indeed lead to performance improvements along cognitive dimensions. In a subsequent experiment we used a fully automated version of our system, where uncertainty in each student turn was (noisily) detected using acoustic-prosodic and lexical features extracted from the speech signal, as well as dialogue features. Our results were again that enhancing our system to respond to uncertainty yielded higher student learning gains than non-adaptive control systems, but here the difference was only significant for a subset of students after we controlled for the proportion of additional tutoring content received during the tutoring interaction. In particular, students who received the adaptation learned significantly more than students in a control condition who randomly received an equal proportion of additional tutoring content. Based on system error analyses we concluded that the uncertainty adaptation had only a small effect on learning in the fully automated system because the system did not automatically recognize student uncertainty often enough and thus did not give the adaptation often enough (see Forbes-Riley & Litman (2011a) for further details).

In this chapter we turn our attention to student metacognition. First, we show how to construct measures of student metacognitive performance (e.g., monitoring accuracy, bias, discrimination) using the manually and automatically created tutor annotations of student uncertainty and correctness available from our prior wizarded and fully automated experiments, respectively. Next, we examine whether our prior tutor adaptations to student uncertainty—which have already been shown to improve cognition—can also improve metacognition. Finally, we examine whether our measures of metacognitive performance are correlated with our measures of cognitive performance (i.e., learning gain), and whether such correlations are robust to the noise introduced by speech and language processing techniques. Analyses of the data from both our wizarded and fully automated experiments demonstrate that by responding to student uncertainty in new ways, tutorial dialogue systems have the potential to further improve both cognitive and metacognitive performance.

Systems and Data

This research uses corpora of dialogues (see Figs. 25.2–25.3 for examples) between students and both ITSPOKE-WOZ and ITSPOKE-AUTO, wizarded and fully automated versions of ITSPOKE (**I**ntelligent **T**utoring **SPOKE**n dialogue system), respectively. ITSPOKE in turn is a speech-enabled version of the Why2-Atlas qualitative physics tutor (VanLehn et al., 2002), which asks "why-type" questions relating to Newtonian physics.[1] The corpora were collected in our prior experiments evaluating the utility of enhancing ITSPOKE to respond to impasses involving student uncertainty over and above correctness, in wizarded (Forbes-Riley & Litman, 2009a, 2011b) and fully automated (Forbes-Riley & Litman, 2011a) conditions. The target audience for ITSPOKE are novices, i.e., college students who have never taken college-level physics.

The conceptual framework of our work is based on the theory of learning impasses. Motivated by research that views uncertainty as well as

[1] The version of ITSPOKE used here differs from the original ITSPOKE and Why2-Atlas in that the system has been reimplemented using the TuTalk tools for authoring tutorial dialogue systems (Jordan, Hall, Ringenberg, Cui, & Rosé, 2007) and does not include the essay writing component of Why2-Atlas. As will be discussed, several versions of ITSPOKE used in the experiments reported here (in particular, in the experimental but not in the control conditions) have in addition been enhanced to detect and adapt to student uncertainty.

Fig. 25.1 Different Impasse State Severities

Nominal State:	InonU	IU	CU	CnonU
Scalar State:	3	2	1	0
Severity Rank:	most	less	least	none

incorrectness as signals of "learning impasses" (VanLehn et al., 2003), i.e., opportunities for the student to learn the material that he/she is incorrect or uncertain about, the original version of ITSPOKE was modified to associate one of four impasse states with every student answer. The four impasse states correspond to all possible combinations of binary student *uncertainty* (uncertain (**U**), nonuncertain (**nonU**)[2]) and *correctness* (incorrect (**I**), correct (**C**)), as shown in Fig. 25.1.[3]

The incorrectness component of each state reflects the actual accuracy of the student's answer, while the uncertainty component reflects the tutor's perception of the student's awareness of this accuracy. The scalar ranking of impasse states in terms of severity combines these two components and will be discussed below. While the original ITSPOKE only remediated incorrectness impasses (InonU and IU states), our uncertainty-adaptive ITSPOKE also remediates all uncertainty impasses (CU states – note that IU impasses were already remediated in the original non-adaptive system). Impasse theory is similar to cognitive disequilibrium theory (Craig, Graesser, Sullins, & Gholson, 2004), which predicts that confusion is likely to occur during cognitive disequilibrium, and that trying to restore equilibrium will lead to learning gains.

ITSPOKE-WOZ

The ITSPOKE-WOZ corpus consists of 405 dialogues between 81 students and ITSPOKE-WOZ, a semi-automatic version of ITSPOKE where a human "wizard" performed speech recognition as well as correctness and uncertainty annotation. That is, each student turn was annotated in real time by the wizard during the experiment, producing the binary student uncertainty and correctness tags.[4] Using a wizard allowed us to examine the impact of adapting to uncertainty impasses in upper-bound tutorial dialogue conditions, that is, without the errors introduced by using automated speech and language processing components. In both human and automatic detection of uncertainty, common indicators of student uncertainty include lexical hedges (e.g.,"I think"), pitch features (e.g., rising intonation), temporal features (e.g., pausing), and energy features (e.g,. soft-spokeness). Such features have been validated both through interannotator agreement studies and automatic detection studies (c.f., Forbes-Riley & Litman 2011a).

The experimental procedure for collecting the corpus was as follows: subjects who had never taken college physics read a short physics text, took a multiple-choice pretest, worked five problems[5] (i.e., engaged in five dialogues) with ITSPOKE, took a survey[6], and took an isomorphic posttest.

The experiment had two control and two experimental conditions. Complete details about these conditions are provided elsewhere (Forbes-Riley & Litman, 2011b); here we briefly outline the differences between them.

[2]A 'nonuncertain' answer may be certain or neutral.

[3]For example, the 6,561 student turns in the ITSPOKE-WOZ corpus are distributed among these states as follows: 650 InonU (10%), 764 IU (12%), 727 CU (11%), and 4,420 CnonU (67%).

[4]This wizard displayed interannotator agreement of 0.85 and 0.62 Kappa on post-experimental labeling of correctness and uncertainty, respectively, in prior studies (Forbes-Riley & Litman, 2008).

[5]For example, the problem referred to in the dialogue excerpts in Figs. 25.2–25.3 is: "Suppose a man is running in a horizontal line at a constant velocity. He tosses a pumpkin vertically up while he is running. Where will the pumpkin land relative to the man? Assume that air resistance is negligible."

[6]The survey is not used in this paper; see (Forbes-Riley & Litman, 2009a) for the survey usage.

ITSPOKE1: If the force of the man weren't greater than the force of gravity, the pumpkin wouldn't be tossed up into the air. But we know that it is. So the direction of the net force must be upwards. Does the pumpkin accelerate while the man is tossing it? If yes, please specify the direction of the acceleration.

STUDENT1: um... up. *[CU]*

ITSPOKE2: Fine. *[FEEDBACK]*

Fig. 25.2 Example of *nonAdapt* ITSPOKE Response to **CU** Answers

ITSPOKE1: If the force of the man weren't greater than the force of gravity, the pumpkin wouldn't be tossed up into the air. But we know that it is. So the direction of the net force must be upwards. Does the pumpkin accelerate while the man is tossing it? If yes, please specify the direction of the acceleration.

STUDENT1: Yes, uh vertically ... up, well, yeah, vertically up. *[CU]*

ITSPOKE2: Right. *[FEEDBACK]* To analyze the pumpkin's acceleration we will use Newton's Second law. What's the definition of this law? *[REMEDIATION SUBDIALOGUE]*

Fig. 25.3 Example of *Simple* Uncertainty Adaptation (for **CU** Answers only)

The *nonAdapt* control condition remediated only incorrectness impasses (**InonU, IU**), as in the original ITSPOKE. An example dialogue excerpt from this condition is shown in Fig. 25.2 . As shown, **ITSPOKE2** provides feedback indicating the correctness of the **CU** answer and ignores the uncertainty.

In contrast, the two experimental conditions remediated both uncertainty and incorrectness impasses (**InonU, IU, CU**), but each used a different approach. The *Simple* experimental condition used the same remediation for all impasse types, with only feedback phrases varying based on answer correctness (e.g., "That's right" versus "That's wrong"). An example dialogue excerpt is shown in Fig. 25.3 . As shown, **ITSPOKE2** provides feedback indicating the correctness of the **CU** answer and then responds to the uncertainty by providing the same remediation subdialogue (i.e., a series of additional questions) that would have been provided if the student answer were incorrect. Only the first question in this remediation subdialogue is shown. Note that **IU and InonU** answers already receive this remediation subdialogue (because they are incorrect). Therefore, the *Simple* uncertainty adaptation impacts only **CU** answers.

In contrast to the *Simple* experimental condition, the *Complex* experimental condition used different dialogue act presentations of the incorrect answer content (e.g., remediation subdialogue questions versus "bottom out" statements) *and* different feedback phrases (e.g., "That's exactly right, but you seem unsure" for **CU** versus "Great try, but I think you know there is a mistake in your answer" for **IU**) to respond to each impasse type (**CU, IU, InonU**). Example dialogue excerpts for each impasse type are shown in Fig. 25.4 . As shown, in each case, **ITSPOKE2** provides feedback responding to the specific impasse type of the answer and then provides the same additional content responding to the impasse, but the dialogue act used to present

ITSPOKE1: If the force of the man weren't greater than the force of gravity, the pumpkin wouldn't be tossed up into the air. But we know that it is. So the direction of the net force must be upwards. Does the pumpkin accelerate while the man is tossing it? If yes, please specify the direction of the acceleration.

STUDENT1: It accelerates upwards?? *[CU]*

ITSPOKE2: Great answer, but you don't sound very certain so let's go over it. *[FEEDBACK]* The pumpkin does have an acceleration and it points vertically up. We would use Newton's Second law to prove this (Net Force = Mass * Acceleration). Since the net force on the pumpkin is non-zero and points up, this law tells us its acceleration must also be non-zero and point up. *[NEW BOTTOM OUT]*

STUDENT1: Vertically?? *[IU]*

ITSPOKE2: I'm sorry. It sounds like you already know there's an error. Let's work it out. *[FEEDBACK]* The pumpkin does have an acceleration and it points vertically up. Let's work through the proof of this step by step.*[NEW BOTTOM OUT]* To analyze the pumpkin's acceleration we will use Newton's Second law. What's the definition of this law? *[REMEDIATION SUBDIALOGUE]*

STUDENT1: Yes, negative 9.8 meters per second squared. *[InonU]*

ITSPOKE2: Good try, but there's a mistake in your answer that we need to work through. *[FEEDBACK]* To analyze the pumpkin's acceleration we will use Newton's Second law. What's the definition of this law? *[REMEDIATION SUBDIALOGUE]*

Fig. 25.4 Example of *Complex* Uncertainty Adaptation for **CU, IU, and InonU** Answers

this additional content depends on the specific impasse type of the answer.[7]

Finally, the *Random* control condition treated a percentage of random correct answers as incorrect, to control for the additional content in the experimental conditions. The motivation for and further details of each experimental condition are discussed in detail elsewhere (Forbes-Riley & Litman, 2009a, 2011b).

[7]The dialogue act variations were developed based on analysis of human tutor responses to uncertainty in a human tutoring corpus (see (Forbes-Riley & Litman, 2009a) for further details).

ITSPOKE-AUTO

The ITSPOKE-AUTO corpus consists of 360 dialogues between 72 students and ITSPOKE-AUTO, a fully automated version of ITSPOKE in which speech recognition as well as correctness and uncertainty annotation were automatically performed by speech and language processing components. Student speech was digitized from microphone input and sent to the Sphinx2 speech recognizer (Huang et al., 1993), whose stochastic language models were trained on the ITSPOKE-WOZ corpus and prior ITSPOKE corpora. Correctness was automatically labeled on the speech recognition output using the TuTalk semantic analyzer (Jordan et al., 2007), which was trained on the ITSPOKE-WOZ corpus. Uncertainty was automatically labeled on the speech recognition output using an uncertainty model built with WEKA software (Witten & Frank, 1999) from features of the student speech and dialogue context, including lexical, pitch, temporal, and energy features as well as tutor question and gender. The uncertainty model is a logistic regression equation that was trained on the ITSPOKE-WOZ corpus, where the wizard's labels were the ground truth labels. The most important predictors of student uncertainty in the model were pitch and lexical features of the student's current turn, as well as the type of tutor question in the preceding turn.

The ITSPOKE-AUTO corpus was collected using the procedure from the ITSPOKE-WOZ experiment, although the experimental conditions were changed in two ways. First, the *Complex* experimental condition was removed. We removed this condition as only *Simple* yielded learning improvements for ITSPOKE-WOZ (Forbes-Riley & Litman, 2009a, 2011b). Second, *Random* was changed so that ITSPOKE-AUTO randomly remediated after only CnonU answers (non-impasse states). We changed this condition because in ITSPOKE-WOZ neither wizarded experimental condition outperformed *Random* (Forbes-Riley & Litman, 2009a, 2011b); we hypothesized this was because CU impasses were sometimes adapted to in *Random*. Full details of the ITSPOKE-AUTO system, including a performance analysis of the speech and language processing components and their impact on the learning results, are presented elsewhere (Forbes-Riley & Litman, 2010, 2011a).

Metacognitive Measures

In this section we introduce several ways of combining the corpus uncertainty and correctness annotations into single quantitative performance measures. Note that all measures are computed on a per student basis (over all five dialogues).

Our first measure is based on a ranking of impasses by severity. In particular, we first associate a scalar **impasse severity** value with each student answer in our corpus, based on either our wizard's or automatically computed correctness and uncertainty annotations. We then compute an average impasse severity per student, according to whether the impasses were due to uncertainty, incorrectness, or both. Our severity values were proposed in our earlier work (Forbes-Riley, Litman, & Rotaru, 2008a) and are shown in Fig. 25.1. According to our ranking, the most severe type of impasse (severity 3) occurs when a student is incorrect but not aware of it. States of severity 2 and 1 are of increasingly lesser severity: the student is incorrect but aware that he/she might be, and the student is correct but uncertain about it, respectively. Finally, no impasse exists when a student is correct and not uncertain about it (severity 0). These severity rankings reflect our belief that to resolve an impasse, a student must first perceive that it exists. Incorrectness simply indicates that the student has reached an impasse, while uncertainty—in a correct or incorrect answer—indicates that the student perceives he/she has reached an impasse.

From the standpoint of measuring metacognition, average impasse severity represents the simplest of our measures. Each impasse state reflects a current state of "self-monitoring": states 1 and 3 are currently inaccurate self-monitoring, while states 0/2 are currently perfect self-monitoring. However, the ranking of states adds a further cognitive component to the metric, by indicating how far the current self-monitoring state is from objective correctness.

The rest of our measures are taken from the metacognitive performance literature. The knowledge monitoring accuracy measure that we use is the Hamann coefficient **(HC)** (Nietfeld, Enders, & Schraw, 2006).[8] This measure has previously been used to measure the monitoring accuracy of one's own knowledge ("feeling of knowing" (FOK)), which is closely related to uncertainty. Psycholinguistics research has shown that speakers

[8] While the Gamma measure is often also used, there is a lack of consensus regarding the relative benefits of Gamma versus HC (Nietfeld et al., 2006), and we have found HC to be more predictive for our corpus (Litman & Forbes-Riley, 2009b).

	Correct	Incorrect
Nonuncertain	CnonU	InonU
Uncertain	CU	IU

Fig. 25.5 Measuring Student Metacognitive Performance

display FOK in conversation using linguistic cues (Smith & Clark, 1993) and that listeners can use the same cues to monitor the FOK of someone else ("feeling of another's knowing" (FOAK)) (Brennan & Williams, 1995). High and low FOK/FOAK judgments have also been associated with speaker certainty and uncertainty, respectively (Dijkstra et al., 2006).

HC measures absolute knowledge monitoring accuracy, or the accuracy with which certainty reflects correctness. HC ranges in value from -1 (no knowledge monitoring accuracy) to 1 (perfect accuracy). We compute HC from our correctness and uncertainty annotations as shown below; the numerator subtracts cases where (un)certainty is at odds with (in)correctness from cases where they correspond, while the denominator sums over all cases.

$$\mathrm{HC} = \frac{(\mathrm{CnonU} + \mathrm{IU}) - (\mathrm{InonU} + \mathrm{CU})}{(\mathrm{CnonU} + \mathrm{IU}) + (\mathrm{InonU} + \mathrm{CU})}$$

To illustrate the reasoning behind HC and the other metacognitive performance measures used in this paper, consider an FOK-type experimental paradigm (Smith & Clark, 1993), where subjects (1) respond to a set of general knowledge questions, (2) take a survey, judging whether or not[9] they think they would be uncertain about the answer to each question in a multiple choice test, and (3) take such a multiple-choice test. In FOAK-type paradigms such as ours, the *tutor* annotates the correctness and uncertainty for each student answer. As shown in Fig. 25.5 , such FOK or FOAK data can be summarized in an array where each cell represents a mutually exclusive option: the row labels represent the possible uncertainty judgments (nonuncertain or uncertain), while the columns represent the possible correctness results of the multiple-choice test (correct or incorrect). Given such an array, various relationships between the correctness of answers, and the judged uncertainty of the answers, can then be computed.

Following Saadawi et al. (2009), who investigate the role of immediate feedback and other metacognitive scaffolds in a medical tutoring system, we additionally measure metacognitive performance in terms of **bias** and **discrimination** (Kelemen, Frost, & Weaver, 2000). As with HC, we compute these measures using our tutor's correctness and uncertainty annotations.

Bias measures the overall degree to which confidence matches correctness. Bias scores greater than and less than zero indicate overconfidence and underconfidence, respectively, with zero indicating best metacognitive performance. We compute bias as shown below. The first term represents the relative proportion of confident answers (certain cases/all cases); the second represents the relative proportion of correct answers.

$$\mathrm{bias} = \frac{\mathrm{CnonU} + \mathrm{InonU}}{\mathrm{CnonU} + \mathrm{InonU} + \mathrm{CU} + \mathrm{IU}} - \frac{\mathrm{CnonU} + \mathrm{CU}}{\mathrm{CnonU} + \mathrm{InonU} + \mathrm{CU} + \mathrm{IU}}$$

Discrimination measures the ability to discriminate performance in terms of (in)correctness. Discrimination scores greater than zero indicate higher metacognitive performance. As shown below, the first term represents the proportion of correct answers judged as certain, and the second term represents the proportion of incorrect answers judged as certain.

$$\mathrm{discrimination} = \frac{\mathrm{CnonU}}{\mathrm{CnonU} + \mathrm{CU}} - \frac{\mathrm{InonU}}{\mathrm{InonU} + \mathrm{IU}}$$

To illustrate the computation of our metacognitive performance metrics, suppose the annotated dialogue excerpt in Fig. 25.4 represented our entire dataset (from a single student). Then we would have the following values for our metrics for that student:

[9] Likert scale rating schemes are also possible.

Table 25.1 Means across ITSPOKE-WOZ experimental conditions and partial Correlations with posttest, for impasse severity, monitoring accuracy, bias, and discrimination

Measure	Means nonAdapt	Random	Simple	Complex	Correlation R	p
	(n=21)	(n=20)	(n=20)	(n=20)	(n=81)	
Impasse severity	0.73	0.60	0.59	0.59	−0.56	0.00
Monitoring accuracy	0.52	0.62	0.62	0.58	0.42	0.00
Bias	−0.02	−0.01	−0.03	−0.01	−0.21	0.06
Discrimination	0.41	0.48	0.46	0.34	0.32	0.00

$$\text{impasse severity} = \frac{(1+2+3)}{3} = 2$$

$$\text{HC} = \frac{(0+1)-(1+1)}{(0+1)+(1+1)} = -\frac{1}{3}$$

$$\text{bias} = \frac{0+1}{0+1+1+1} - \frac{0+1}{0+1+1+1} = \frac{1}{3} - \frac{1}{3} = 0$$

$$\text{discrimination} = \frac{0}{0+1} - \frac{1}{1+1} = \frac{0}{1} - \frac{1}{2} = -\frac{1}{2}$$

Results

In this section we investigate whether the measures introduced in the previous section differ across our experimental conditions, and/or predict student learning gains, using the corpora from both the ITSPOKE-WOZ and ITSPOKE-AUTO experiments. We first run a one-way ANOVA with condition as the between-subject factor, along with a planned comparison for each pair of conditions, hypothesizing the following performance ranking: *Complex* > *Simple* > *Random* > *nonAdapt*. Even though our experiment was designed to only impact learning gain, we hypothesized that the experimental conditions might still reduce impasse severity: by responding contingently to uncertainty the tutor responded to, and thus perhaps resolved, more impasse types. For similar reasons, we hypothesized that the experimental conditions might also improve student accuracy in monitoring their own uncertainty (i.e., FOK), particularly in *Complex* where the tutor's feeling of the student's uncertainty (i.e., FOAK) was explicitly stated. Our HC metric measures inferred (rather than actual) student self-monitoring accuracy (because it was derived from our tutor's uncertainty labels, rather than student judgments of their own uncertainty). We had similar hypotheses for bias and discrimination.

Second, we compute a partial Pearson's correlation over all students between each metacognitive measure and posttest score, controlled for pretest score to measure learning gain. We hypothesized that even if we did not find any metacognitive differences between conditions, lower impasse severities, higher self-monitoring accuracies, less bias, and better discrimination would still be better for students overall, from a cognitive perspective. Our rational for this hypothesis was, simply put, that students who are more accurate in their self-monitoring know when their answers are incorrect, and thus know when to take steps to correct their errors after the system provides the correct answer and the reasoning behind it.

ITSPOKE-WOZ

The "Means" columns in Table 25.1 show the means per condition in the ITSPOKE-WOZ experiment, where each metacognitive measure was computed using the wizard's uncertainty and correctness annotations. As predicted, both experimental conditions had lower average impasse severity than *Random*, and *Random* was lower than *nonAdapt*. While a one-way ANOVA with post hoc Tukey showed no statistically significant differences or trends among these means (p = 0.19), paired contrasts showed trends for individual differences between *Random* and *nonAdapt* (p = 0.10), *Simple* and *nonAdapt* (p = 0.06), and between *Complex* and *nonAdapt* (p = 0.08). With respect to both inferred self-monitoring accuracy (HC) and bias, the ANOVAs showed no

Table 25.2 Means across ITSPOKE-AUTO experimental conditions, and partial correlations with posttest, for impasse severity, monitoring accuracy, bias, and discrimination

Measure	Means nonAdapt	Random	Simple	Correlation *R*	*p*
	(n=25)	(n=23)	(n=24)	(n=72)	
Impasse severity	0.94	0.98	0.98	−0.40	0.001
Monitoring accuracy	0.44	0.41	0.42	0.35	0.003
Bias	0.21	0.20	0.22	−0.36	0.002
Discrimination	0.19	0.20	0.19	−0.04	0.768

statistically significant differences or trends across conditions. However, for HC, the paired contrasts showed a trend for differences between *Simple* and *nonAdapt* (p = 0.06), and *Random* and *nonAdapt* (p = 0.06) in the predicted directions. With respect to discrimination, the ANOVA indicated a trend for a difference among the means (p = 0.09), with paired contrasts showing significant differences between *Simple* and *Complex* (p = 0.04), and between *Random* and *Complex* (p = 0.02); note, however, that contrary to our predictions, discrimination was lowest in *Complex*.

Although we only find weak support for differences in metacognitive performance between conditions, we still hypothesize that better metacognitive performance is better for students from a learning perspective. The last two columns in Table 25.1 show the Pearson's Correlation Coefficient (R) between each metacognitive measure and posttest after controlling for pretest, and the significance of the correlation (p), over all 81 students. As predicted, average impasse severity is significantly negatively correlated with learning,[10] while inferred self-monitoring accuracy (HC) and discrimination are significantly positively correlated with learning. There is also a trend for bias to be negatively correlated with learning, suggesting that underconfidence is better than overconfidence.

ITSPOKE-AUTO

The "Means" columns in Table 25.2 show the means per condition in the ITSPOKE-AUTO experiment, where each metacognitive measure was computed using the automatic uncertainty and correctness annotations. The table shows that the differences were typically not in the predicted directions, although nothing was statistically significant.[11] These results thus suggest that once noise is introduced after automating speech and language processing, we no longer see even weak support for improvements in metacognitive performance for our experimental condition.

Nonetheless, we still hypothesize that even under noisy conditions, lower impasse severities, higher self-monitoring accuracies, less bias, and better discrimination will be predictive of better cognitive performance. Thus we again computed partial correlations with posttest over all students, as originally reported in Forbes-Riley and Litman (2010). With the exception of discrimination, the ITSPOKE-AUTO correlations shown in the last two columns of Table 25.2 replicate the ITSPOKE-WOZ correlations of Table 25.1. Other comparisons between our wizarded and automated results (e.g., learning correlations with additional independent measures and regressions with multiple independent measures) can be found in Forbes-Riley and Litman (2010).

[10] In contrast, a measure of impasse *resolution* might positively correlate with learning, as resolving an impasse could reduce the severity of future impasse opportunities. In a prior ITSPOKE experiment, we in fact improved student learning by detecting and re-remediating one particular type of unresolved incorrectness impasse (Rotaru & Litman, 2009).

[11] The p-values for the 4 ANOVAs comparing the metacognitive metrics were respectively 0.83, 0.75, 0.72, 0.91. Due to both these extremely high p-values, and the fact that the means were not as predicted, we did not run the paired comparisons.

Discussion

We presented an analysis of student metacognitive performance using data from both wizarded and fully automated dialogue tutors that adapt to student uncertainty. The performance measures examined include several measures of metacognitive performance taken from various literatures but have been adapted for our tutorial dialogue context by computing them from tutor annotations of student uncertainty and correctness. We also introduce a new learning impasse severity measure derived from a theory of uncertainty and incorrectness as learning impasses. While in prior work we demonstrated that remediating after uncertainty impasses improves learning in both wizarded and fully automated conditions (Forbes-Riley & Litman 2011a, 2011b), our results here suggest that further investigation into better ways of remediating student uncertainty holds promise for further improving student cognitive as well as metacognitive performance.

With respect to improving cognitive performance, our correlation results suggest that if we can enhance our tutor to improve metacognitive performance, we may also further improve cognitive performance. Our correlations show that (tutor perception of) **impasse severity**, **self-monitoring accuracy**, and **bias** significantly or as a trend predict student learning (negatively, positively, and negatively, respectively) in both our wizarded and fully automated corpora. Although correlation does not imply causality, our findings motivate future modifications of our system to increase student learning. For example, we plan to develop remediations that are better optimized for each impasse type, particularly for impasses with the highest severity. We also plan to enhance our tutor to not only remediate domain content after impasses (as in the current experiment), but to also remediate inferred student knowledge monitoring abilities.

With respect to improving metacognition, our ANOVA results suggest that under upper-bound wizarded conditions, remediating student uncertainty holds promise for improving student metacognitive abilities (in our study, impasse severity and self-monitoring accuracy). However, the results with ITSPOKE-AUTO suggest that achieving this potential will require very high performing speech and language components.

In particular, while our ANOVAs for ITSPOKE-WOZ show that **impasse severity** doesn't differ significantly across conditions, the means are consistent with our predictions, and there are statistical pairwise trends suggesting improvement between all conditions and *non-Adapt* (the original system). We also see similar results for *Simple* and *Random* compared to *non-Adapt* with respect to inferred self-monitoring accuracy (**HC**). These are promising findings, as our current interventions were designed to improve only student correctness on the posttest, not to reduce impasse severity or increase monitoring accuracy. In the future we would like to enhance our interventions to directly target student knowledge monitoring, and to better measure such improvements by incorporating FOK ratings into our testing. There is increasing interest in using intelligent tutoring systems to teach metacognition and we plan to build on this literature (e.g., Aleven & Roll 2007, Roll & Aleven 2008, Saadawi et al. 2009).

We found it surprising that neither experimental condition outperformed *Random*, even after we changed *Random* in ITSPOKE-AUTO to only adapt after CnonU answers (non-impasse states). Since a "nonuncertain" (nonU) answer may actually be certain or neutral, we hypothesize that adapting to CnonUs might still be effective at increasing certainty.

Finally, we recently found interactions between learning and user classes based on user domain expertise and gender in the wizarded corpus (Forbes-Riley & Litman, 2009b); we will investigate whether the interactions with these classes extend to the student metacognitive metrics discussed in this paper.

In conclusion, our work shows that the student speech signal holds important information about metacognition that most intelligent tutoring systems researchers have not yet mined. In particular, uncertainty is conveyed at least partially and sometimes most strongly through speech and tells us something about the student's accuracy of self-monitoring, which itself relates to learning. Although we have not yet attempted to dynamically adapt to metacognitive performance in our dialogue tutor to help students learn better at the cognitive level, or even improve metacognitive abilities, our results suggest that this is a plausible approach for future directions.

Acknowledgements This work is supported by NSF Award 0631930. A preliminary version of the wizarded results was presented at the AAAI Symposium on Cognitive and Metacognitive Educational Systems (Litman & Forbes-Riley, 2009a), while a subset of our automated results (the correlations) were previously published at ITS 2010 (Forbes-Riley & Litman, 2010).

References

Aist, G., Kort, B., Reilly, R., Mostow, J., & Picard, R. (2002). Experimentally augmenting an intelligent tutoring system with human-supplied capabilities: Adding human-provided emotional scaffolding to an automated reading tutor that listens. In *Proceedings of Intelligent Tutoring Systems Workshop on Empirical Methods for Tutorial Dialogue Systems* (pp. 483–490), San Sebastian, Spain.

Aleven, V., & Roll, I. (Eds.) (2007). *AIED workshop on metacognition and self-regulated learning in intelligent tutoring systems.*

Brennan, S.E., & Williams, M. (1995). The feeling of another's knowing: Prosody and filled pauses as cues to listeners about the metacognitive states of speakers. *Journal of Memory and Language,34*, 383–398.

Craig, S., Graesser, A., Sullins, J., & Gholson, B. (2004). Affect and learning: An exploratory look into the role of affect in learning with AutoTutor. *Journal of Educational Media,29*(3), 241–250.

Dijkstra, C., Krahmer, E. J., & Swerts, M. (2006). Manipulating uncertainty: The contribution of different audiovisual prosodic cues to the perception of confidence. In R. Hoffmann & H. Mixdorff (Eds.), *Proceedings of Speech Prosody 2006*, Dresden: TUDpress.

Forbes-Riley, K., & Litman, D. J. (2008). Analyzing dependencies between student certainness states and tutor responses in a spoken dialogue corpus. In L. Dybkjaer & W. Minker (Eds.), *Recent Trends in Discourse and Dialogue*. Berlin: Springer.

Forbes-Riley, K., & Litman, D. (2009a). Adapting to student uncertainty improves tutoring dialogues. In *Proceedings of the 14th International Conference on Artificial Intelligence in Education,* AIED 2009, July 6–10, 2009, Brighton, UK. Frontiers in Artificial Intelligence and Applications 200 IOS Press 2009, ISBN 978-1-60750-028-5.

Forbes-Riley, K., & Litman, D. (2009b). A user modeling-based performance analysis of a wizarded uncertainty-adaptive dialogue system corpus. In *Proceedings of the 10th Annual Conference of the International Speech Communication Association*, Brighton, UK.

Forbes-Riley, K., & Litman, D. (2010). Metacognition and learning in spoken dialogue computer tutoring. In *Proceedings of the 10th International Conference on Intelligent Tutoring Systems (ITS)*, Pittsburgh, PA.

Forbes-Riley, K., & Litman, D. (2011a). Benefits and challenges of real-time uncertainty detection and adaptation in a spoken dialogue computer tutor. *Speech Communication, 53*(9–10), 1115–1136.

Forbes-Riley, K., & Litman, D. (2011b). Designing and evaluating a wizarded uncertainty-adaptive spoken dialogue tutoring system. *Computer Speech and Language, 25*(1), 105–126.

Forbes-Riley, K., Litman, D., & Rotaru, M. (2008a). Responding to student uncertainty during computer tutoring: A preliminary evaluation. In *Proceedings of the 9th International Conference on Intelligent Tutoring Systems (ITS),* Montreal, Canada, June.

Forbes-Riley, K., Rotaru, M., & Litman, D. (2008b). The relative impact of student affect on performance models in a spoken dialogue tutoring system. *User Modeling and User-Adapted Interaction,18*(1–2), 11–43

Huang, X. D., Alleva, F., Hon, H. W., Hwang, M. Y., Lee, K. F.,& Rosenfeld, R. (1993). The SPHINX-II speech recognition system: An overview. *Computer Speech and Language,2*, 137–148.

Jordan, P., Hall, B., Ringenberg, M., Cui, Y., and Rosé, C. (2007). Tools for authoring a dialogue agent that participates in learning studies. In *Artificial Intelligence in Education (AIED)*, pp. 43–50.

Kelemen, W. L., Frost, P. J., & Weaver, C. A. (2000). Individual differences in metacognition: Evidence against a general metacognitive ability. *Memory and Cognition,28*, 92–107.

Liscombe, J., Venditti, J., & Hirschberg, J. (2005, September). Detecting certainness in spoken tutorial dialogues. In *Proceedings of Interspeech/Eurospeech Conference on Speech Communication and Technology*, Lisbon, Portugal.

Litman, D., & Forbes-Riley, K. (2009a). Improving (meta) cognitive tutoring by detecting and responding to uncertainty. Technical Report FS-09-0:Cognitive and Metacognitive Educational Systems: Papers from the AAAI Symposium, AAAI Arlington, VA, November.

Litman, D., & Forbes-Riley, K. (2009b). Spoken tutorial dialogue and the feeling of another's knowing. In *Proceedings of the 10th Annual Meeting of the Special Interest Group on Discourse and Dialogue (SIGDIAL)*, London.

Litman, D., Moore, J., Dzikovska, M., & Farrow, E. (2009, July). Using natural language processing to analyze tutorial dialogue corpora across domains and modalities. In *Proceedings of the 14th International Conference on Artificial Intelligence in Education,* AIED 2009, Brighton, UK. Frontiers in Artificial Intelligence and Applications 200 IOS Press 2009, ISBN 978-1-60750-028-5.

Nicholas, G., Rotaru, M., & Litman, D. J. (2006). Exploiting word-level features for emotion prediction. In *Proceedings of IEEE/ACL Workshop on Spoken Language Technology*, Aruba.

Nietfeld, J. L., Enders, C. K., & Schraw, G. (2006). A Monte Carlo comparison of measures of relative and absolute monitoring accuracy. *Educational and Psychological Measurement,66*, 258–271.

Pon-Barry, H. (2008). Prosodic manifestations of confidence and uncertainty in spoken language. In *Proceedings of the 9th Annual Conference of the International Speech Communication Association,* September 2008 (pp. 74–77). Brisbane, Australia.

Pon-Barry, H., Schultz, K., Bratt, E. O., Clark, B., & Peters, S. (2006). Responding to student uncertainty in spoken tutorial dialogue systems. *International Journal of Artificial Intelligence in Education,16*, 171–194.

Roll, I., & Aleven, V., (Eds.) (2008). *ITS Workshop on meta-cognition and self-regulated rearning in educational technologies.*

Rotaru, M., & Litman, D. J. (2009). Discourse structure and performance analysis: Beyond the correlation. In *Proceedings of the 10th Annual Meeting of the Special Interest Group on Discourse and Dialogue (SIGDIAL)*, London.

Saadawi, G. M. E., Azevedo, R., Castine, M., Payne, V., Medvedeva, O., Tseytlin, E., Legowski, E., azen Jukic, D., & Crowley, R. S. (2009). Factors affecting feeling-of-knowing in a medical intelligent tutoring system: The role of immediate feedback as a metacognitive scaffold. *Advances in Health Sciences Education,15*, 9–30.

Smith, V. L. and Clark, H. H. (1993). On the course of answering questions. *Journal of Memory and Language,32*, 25–38.

Tsukahara, W., & Ward, N. (2001). Responding to subtle, fleeting changes in the user's internal state. In *Proceedings of SIG-CHI on Human Factors in Computing Systems* (pp.77–84).

VanLehn, K., Jordan, P. W., Rosé, C., Bhembe, D., Böttner, M., Gaydos, A., Makatchev, M., Pappuswamy, U., Ringenberg, M., Roque, A., Siler, S., Srivastava, R., & Wilson, R. (2002). The architecture of Why2-Atlas: A coach for qualitative physics essay writing. In *Proceedings of the International Conference on Intelligent Tutoring Systems* (pp.158–167).

VanLehn, K., Siler, S., & Murray, C. (2003). Why do only some events cause learning during human tutoring? *Cognition and Instruction,21*(3), 209–249.

Witten, I. H., & Frank, E. (1999). Data Mining: Practical Machine Learning Tools and Techniques, I. H. Witten & E. Frank and Mark Hall, January 2011, Morgan Kaufmann Publishers (ISBN: 978-0-12-374856-0).

Making Better Use of Multiple Representations: How Fostering Metacognition Can Help

26

Alexander Renkl, Kirsten Berthold, Cornelia S. Grosse, and Rolf Schwonke

Abstract

Modern learning technology (e.g., hypermedia systems) usually provides information in various forms such as text, "realistic" pictures, formal graphs, or algebraic equations in order to foster learning. However, it is well known that learners usually make sub-optimal use of such multiple external representations. In this chapter, we present a series of experiments with older students (senior high-school and up) that analyzed the effects of two metacognitive intervention procedures: self-explanation prompts and "instruction for use" (information on how to use multiple representations). Basically, both interventions foster conceptual understanding and procedural skills. However, there are important boundary conditions. For example, if learners have little prior knowledge they cannot react productively to self-explanation prompts.

Modern learning technology (e.g., hypermedia systems, intelligent tutoring systems, microworlds) usually provides information in various forms such as text, "realistic" pictures, formal graphs, or algebraic equations. In other words, information is presented by multiple external representations (MER). Although these MER can support learning processes in various ways, the integration function is most important (see Ainsworth, 2006). This function refers to the fact that internally representing and integrating different external representations on an abstract level can lead to deeper understanding. Actually, it is typical of experts to have multiple internal representations (de Jong et al., 1998). Consider the example of linear regression: In order to approach expert-like understanding, a learner has to encode and integrate verbal-conceptual information about the meaning and interpretation of regression analyses, the corresponding equation (e.g., $y=a+bx$), and typical scatter plots with regression lines.

An instructional problem arises from the fact that students very often do not spontaneously integrate different MER and they may not be successful even when trying to do so (e.g., Ainsworth, 2006). As a consequence, although MER presented by learning technology are

A. Renkl (✉) • K. Berthold • C.S. Grosse • R. Schwonke
Department of Psychology, University of Freiburg, Engelbergerstraße 41, D-79085 Freiburg, Germany
e-mail: renkl@psychologie.uni-freiburg.de

R. Azevedo and V. Aleven (eds.), *International Handbook of Metacognition and Learning Technologies*, Springer International Handbooks of Education 26, DOI 10.1007/978-1-4419-5546-3_26,

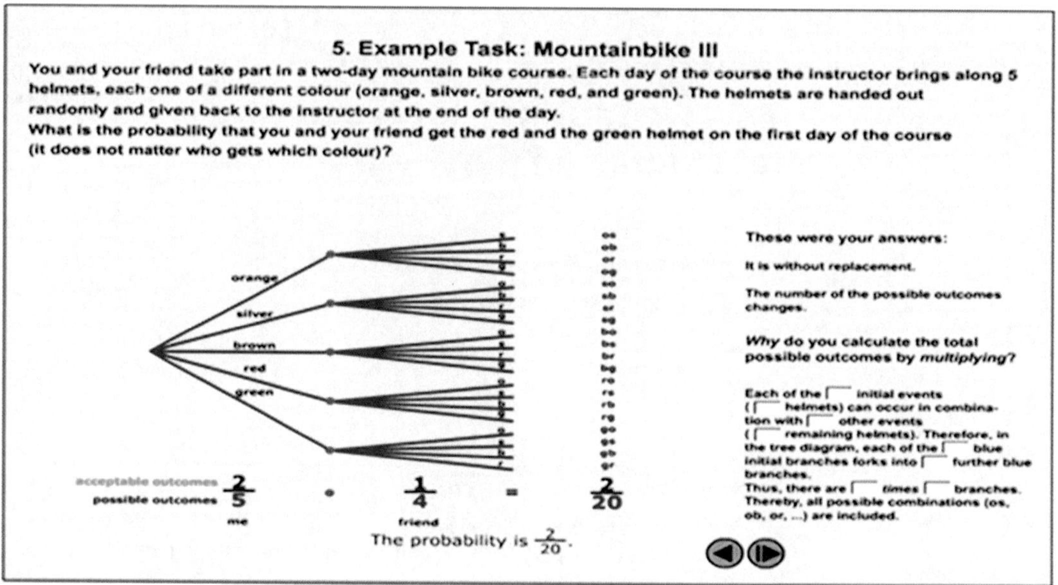

Fig. 26.1 Screenshot from a learning environment with worked examples from the domain of probability

expected to foster learning, they frequently do not enhance and sometimes even impede learning (e.g., Ainsworth, Bibby, & Wood, 2002). Against this background, learners must be supported to productively use MER.

Typical instructional procedures to support the integration of MER include measures that make the particular elements in one representation that correspond to particular elements in another representation salient. For example, text and pictures are often presented in an integrated format, meaning that both information sources are not provided in separate information boxes; instead the text parts are located in close proximity to the corresponding parts of the picture (e.g., Chandler & Sweller, 1991). Another possibility is color coding (e.g., Kalyuga, Chandler, & Sweller, 1999) in which the same colors are used for corresponding information elements in different presentations. Although such instructional procedures can foster learning, they have the disadvantage of just supporting the mapping of different presentations on the surface level (e.g., Berthold & Renkl, 2009; Seufert & Brünken, 2006). They do not directly support the integration of different representations at an abstracted and deep (i.e., semantic) level. For example, Fig. 26.1 provides a multi-representational worked example. By integrating the tree diagram and the equation, it becomes clear why the fractions have to be multiplied. Ideally, the learners would integrate the multiplication sign of the equation and the "points of branching" in the tree diagram. This is done in order to understand the underlying structure, that is, that the multiplication sign stands for the inclusion of all possible combinations represented by the 20 branches in the pictorial tree diagram. The employed color coding, however, just hints at "which belongs to what" but it does not convey conceptual information; the latter has to be inferred by integrating the MER on an abstract, semantic level.

In a series of studies, we investigated two measures tightly related to metacognition in order to foster the integration of MER provided in computer-based learning environments at the semantic level: (a) self-explanation prompts and (b) informing the learners about the function of MER. We employed learning environments about mathematics, typically but not exclusively about probability (see Fig. 26.1). The learners could gain conceptual understanding of the domain as well as domain-specific problem-solving skills (i.e., procedural knowledge). The participating learners were typically senior high-school students or university freshmen.

Self-Explanation Prompts

The Self-Explanation Effect

Chi, Bassok, Lewis, Reimann, and Glaser (1989) introduced the "self-explanation effect" by showing that students who engage in actively explaining the solution procedures of worked examples to themselves achieve better learning outcomes; the *self* in self-explanation, thus, refers both to the agent who provides the explanation and, even more importantly, to the addressee of the explanation. Different concrete learning activities are subsumed under the umbrella of self-explanation depending on the specific authors and, in part, on the specific study (for a recent overview, see Fonseca & Chi, 2011). In any case, self-explanations go beyond the information given. Four very typical types of self-explanations are principle-based self-explanations (i.e., relating solution or problem features to underlying domain principles), goal-operator elaborations (i.e., the subgoals that were achieved by certain operators are explicated), elaborations on preconditions to apply certain operators, and identifying communalities and differences between examples or problems (see Chi et al., 1989; Reimann & Neubert, 2000; Renkl, 1997, 2011).

Meanwhile, it has been shown that self-explanations foster knowledge acquisition in a variety of learning methods such as text learning (Chi, de Leeuw, Chiu, & LaVancher, 1994; Ozuru, Briner, Best, & McNamara, 2010) or problem solving (e.g., Aleven & Koedinger, 2002). Roy and Chi (2005) also argued that self-explanations are especially helpful when learning from MER (called multimedia in their chapter); however, they mainly relied on indirect evidence.

An instructional problem is that many learners do not spontaneously engage in effective self-explanation activities (Renkl, 1997). A well-established approach of assistance is the use of self-explanation prompts (see Koedinger & Aleven, 2007). Prompts are questions or hints that induce productive learning processes. They are designed to overcome passive or superficial processing by inducing activities that the learners are, in principle, capable of but do not spontaneously demonstrate or demonstrate to an unsatisfactory degree (production deficiency; e.g., Pressley et al., 1992). For example, Atkinson, Renkl, and Merrill (2003) showed that prompting principle-based self-explanations in a computer-based learning environment that provided worked examples on probability led to favorable learning outcomes (for similar findings on self-explanation prompts in computer-based learning environments see, e.g., Aleven & Koedinger, 2002; Conati & VanLehn, 2000; Schworm & Renkl, 2007).

Is Self-Explanation Metacognition?

Self-explanation is often considered to be a metacognitive learning strategy (e.g., Aleven & Koedinger, 2002; Conati & VanLehn, 2000). Against the background of the classical notion of metacognition as "cognition about cognition" (e.g., Efklides, 2008; Flavell, 1979; Nelson, 1996), one might argue that self-explanation is "just" a cognitive learning strategy because activities such as justifying solution steps by underlying principles or subgoals to be achieved are not related to cognition but to the learning domain. So, is self-explanation really a metacognitive activity? The answer provided in this chapter is very clear: yes and no. How can such an answer be clear?

Recently, Renkl (2008, 2009) has argued that categorizing certain learning activities into the usual strategy categories is rarely convincing. For example, Weinstein and Mayer's (1986) classic taxonomy "generating an example" would be classified as a cognitive strategy or, more specifically, as an elaboration (i.e., relating new contents to prior knowledge or experiences), but not as a metacognitive strategy. However, learning activities such as "generating an example" can, of course, fulfill several functions. The effort of "generating an own example" has not only an elaborative function but also it can tell the learners whether or not they have understood a concept or principle (i.e., usually it requires understanding to generate an own example). Against the background that certain learning activities can very often fulfill different functions, Renkl (2008, 2009) argues that the analysis of learning activities should mainly consider the function of activities, being aware (a) that "superficially" different learning activities can fulfill the same function (e.g., generating an example and self-questioning can both have the function of comprehension monitoring) and (b) that one activity can fulfill different functions (e.g., generating an example can have both the functions of comprehension monitoring and of elaboration).

Under such a functional perspective, a "clear answer" might be to say yes and no when considering self-explanation as metacognition. The typical self-explanation activity of principle-based explanation (i.e., relating a solution or problems feature to a domain principle) elaborates on the learning contents on the one hand. On the other hand, it can lead to metacognitive knowledge about task types and solution strategies (Flavell, 1979). In particular, self-explanations should lead to conditional knowledge (Paris, Lipson, & Wixson, 1983; Schraw, 1998), that is, knowledge about the "when and why" of knowledge, in particular about solution strategies.

Experiments on Prompting Self-Explanation for Processing Multiple Representations

In three experiments, we employed learning environments in the domains of combinatorics and probability. When teaching these closely related domains, it is common to use multiple representations. In addition to text (e.g., problem formulations), there are two types of typical solution methods: arithmetic solution (relying on an equation) and pictorial solution (relying on a tree diagram). In all experiments, we tested self-explanation prompts as an instructional support procedure. As the main dependent variables, we assessed conceptual understanding and problem-solving performance (procedural knowledge).

Grosse and Renkl (2006, Exp. 1) analyzed the effects of self-explanation prompts in comparison to instructional explanations or no such support when students learned combinatorics from worked examples with multi-representational solutions (i.e., arithmetic equation *and* pictorial tree diagram). We tested 170 student teachers of an educational university (mean age approximately 22 years) in a 2×3-factorial experiment: (a) type of solutions (multi-representational solutions vs. mono-representational solutions) and (b) instructional support (self-explanation prompts vs. instructional explanations vs. no support).

The learning materials included two pairs of examples (four examples in total). Each example could be solved by two different methods (arithmetic equation or pictorial tree diagram). Each pair contained two structurally identical problems that also shared a number of surface features in order to make the correspondence salient to the learners. The first factor, *solutions*, referred to the number of different presented solutions (multi-representational solutions vs. mono-representational solutions). In the "multi-representational solution" conditions, the two almost identical examples of a pair were solved using different solution methods (i.e., a pictorial tree diagram in one example and an arithmetic equation in the other example). Thus, the participants could learn that more or less the same problem can be solved by two different solutions procedures. In the "mono-representational solution" conditions, both examples of a pair were solved with the same solution method; the two examples of one pair included a pictorial tree diagram, and the two examples of the other pair included an arithmetic equation. Thus, two different solution methods were demonstrated in the "mono-representational" conditions as well. However, they were not presented as being interchangeable. The second factor, *instructional support*, referred to the help the learners received: open self-explanation prompts vs. instructional explanations vs. no support. For the multi-representational solutions conditions, self-explanation prompts and instructional explanations concentrated on commonalities between the pictorial and arithmetic solutions and on advantages and disadvantages of these methods dependent on the given problem type. The learners in the "self-explanation prompts" condition were asked to answer in written form, for example, the following question for an example pair: "Where do you see commonalities and differences between the two solution methods?" The instructional explanations could be regarded as the answers to the self-explanation prompts. The self-explanation prompts and instructional explanations for the "mono-representational solution" conditions focused on a single solution but were roughly equivalent to those used for the multi-representational solution groups with respect to the number of covered aspects and time necessary to process them (as determined by pilot studies).

We found that multi-representational solutions fostered conceptual knowledge and procedural knowledge. However, no positive effect was found for instructional support in the form of self-explanation prompts or instructional explanations. Self-explanation prompts actually even led to inferior conceptual understanding when learning with MER compared to having no support at all (no negative prompt effect when learning with mono-representational solutions). This finding confirmed recent assumptions that the demand to self-explain complex material (i.e., including MER) may take cognitive load over the limits (Kalyuga, 2010; Sweller, 2006). Thus, even when self-explanations are prompted, they can be ineffective or can even have a detrimental effect with respect to conceptual understanding.

In line with this conclusion, we also found in a pilot study in the domain of probability that learners have difficulties with self-explanation prompts added to complex multi-representational materials (see Berthold, Eysink, & Renkl, 2009). When we used open self-explanation prompts (i.e., open questions inducing self-explanations such as "Why do you calculate the total acceptable outcomes by multiplying?"), the learners had severe difficulties in adequately answering such prompts. Often the learners could not provide the correct explanation. Thus, we assumed that the learners might benefit from stronger instructional support than open self-explanation prompts (cf. Roy & Chi, 2005). We chose to also include a condition with some form of instructional assistance (Koedinger & Aleven, 2007). Hence, in the main study of Berthold et al. (2009), we tested the effects of three conditions: "assisting self-explanation prompts" that directed the learners to integrate the MER on a conceptual level, open self-explanation prompts, and no self-explanation prompts. We presented eight worked examples with multi-representational solutions from the domain of probability in a computer-based learning environment. Participants were 62 psychology students with a mean age of about 25 years. In all conditions, a relating aid consisting of color coding and flashing was included to help learners see which elements in different representations corresponded to each other on a surface level (see Fig. 26.1). By supporting the learners in finding the corresponding parts in different representations, cognitive capacity for self-explanation and learning should have been increased.

The experimental variation was realized as follows. Participants in the condition assisting self-explanation prompts received six questions such as "Why do you calculate the total acceptable outcomes by multiplying?" in each worked-out example. In the first worked-out example of each pair of isomorphic examples, the answers were supported in the form of fill-in-the-blank self-explanations (e.g., "There are ___ times ___ branches. Thereby, all possible combinations are included," see Fig. 26.1). In the isomorphic examples that followed, this support was faded out, and the participants received six open self-explanation prompts. The answers had to be typed into corresponding text boxes. In the condition open self-explanation prompts, the learners were provided with six open self-explanation prompts only (e.g., open answer to "Why do you calculate the total acceptable outcomes by multiplying?") in each worked-out example. The assisting self-explanation prompts and the open prompts put an emphasis on integrating the pictorial and arithmetic representations to each other on a structural level. For example, the prompt, "Why is there a 4 in the denominator of the second single experiment, even though there are

20 branches in the tree diagram?" referred to the arithmetic representations ("the 4 in the denominator") *and* to the pictorial representations ("20 branches in the tree diagram"). To answer this question, the learners had to relate the denominator of the arithmetic equation to the corresponding branches of the pictorial tree diagram. Thereby, they could understand that the 4 stands for the number of remaining events of one initial branch. Due to the fact that there are five initial branches in the first single experiment, five times four branches, that is, 20, are included.

In the condition without self-explanation prompts (control condition), the learners studied the same worked examples as presented in the other two conditions. The only difference was that the learners of the condition without self-explanation prompts were merely provided with a text box in order to take notes. They did not receive any prompts.

Both types of self-explanation prompts fostered conceptual knowledge. Furthermore, assisting self-explanation prompts had additional effects on conceptual understanding in comparison to open self-explanation prompts. The effect on conceptual understanding was mediated by self-explanations that not only relate a solution step to an underlying principle but also explicate the rationale of the principle (e.g., "For the denominator, there are five *times* four branches. Thus, each of the five first branches of the tree diagram forks out in four further branches as each of the five first events can occur in combination with one of the four remaining events," Berthold & Renkl, 2009). With respect to procedural knowledge, the pattern of results shows that either type of prompts was effective; the two prompt types did not differ.

To conclude, both prompt types fostered procedural knowledge. For conceptual knowledge assisting self-explanation prompts, interleaved with open self-explanation prompts, worked best because they supported the learners in generating self-explanations about the rationale of a principle. The overall pattern of performance indicated that assisting self-explanation prompts best fostered the integration of MER. In particular for enhancing high-quality self-explanations and conceptual understanding, assisting self-explanation prompts should be provided.

In a further experiment, Berthold and Renkl (2009) took up the findings on the effects of self-explanation prompts. We used a relating aid and assisting self-explanation prompts that were more or less identical to the ones used in Berthold et al. (2009). In a computer-based learning environment which was also almost identical to Berthold et al., 170 high-school students (mean age approx. 16 years) learned about probability theory. We varied the type and number of representations (multi-representational solutions vs. mono-representational solutions) and the availability of two support procedures: (a) a relating aid and (b) assisting self-explanation prompts (for details of the complex experimental design of this study, see Berthold & Renkl). In the multi-representational conditions, the solution steps were provided in the form of both a pictorial tree diagram and an arithmetic equation in each example. In the mono-representational conditions, which we included to have a baseline for evaluating the effects of multiple solutions, the solution steps were presented in the form of a pictorial tree diagram *or* an arithmetic equation.

We found that MER per se did not foster conceptual understanding. In contrast, both support instructional procedures enhanced it: The relating aid and assisting self-explanation prompts had additive effects on conceptual understanding. Similar to Berthold et al. (2009), the effects of self-explanation prompts on conceptual knowledge were mediated by self-explanations that not only relate a solution step to an underlying principle but also explicate the rationale of the principle.

Interestingly, there was a relatively small but statistically significant negative effect of self-explanation prompts on procedural knowledge. This detrimental effect was mediated by prompt-induced incorrect self-explanations in terms of mixing up different probability principles. Hence, the assisting prompts had double-edged effects: positive effects on conceptual knowledge, via the elicitation of productive self-explanations, and simultaneously negative effects on procedural knowledge, via the elicitation of incorrect self-explanations (for analogous double-edged effects of self-explanation prompts, see also Berthold, Röder, Knörzer, Kessler, & Renkl, 2011). Note, however, that Berthold et al. (2009) found positive effects for the same type of prompts and the same learning contents on both conceptual and procedural knowledge. The main difference between these experiments was how advanced the participating learners were. Whereas generally positive effects were found for university students in a (selective) psychology program, the double-edged effects were found for high-school students. For the latter learners, the learning materials were more complex in relation to their prior knowledge. Hence, a tentative conclusion is that prompts lose their general effectiveness if learners are heavily loaded by the complexity of the learning materials (Kalyuga, 2010; Sweller, 2006). Prompts added to the learning material may overload them or "enforce" that they concentrate on selected aspects (i.e., conceptual aspects) in order to prevent overload.

In summary, prompting self-explanation can help learning from MER. However, there are boundary conditions to be considered. Prompts can lead to negative effects if the learners are confronted with learning materials that are very complex in relation to their prior knowledge. In addition, it may depend on the desired learning outcomes whether prompts are effective and whether it is sensible to employ assisting prompts. Assisting prompts are particularly helpful when conceptual understanding should be fostered.

"Instructions for Use" of Multiple Representations

The rationale of employing prompts is to more or less directly activate self-explanations. As previously shown, such an "intrusive" method can have detrimental side effects, presumably by posing overwhelming demands to the learners. Another, more indirect option to induce effective processing of MER might be to inform the learners about what to do with MER. Note, however, that such an intervention also presupposes that the learners just have a production deficiency, that is, they can "produce" the appropriate strategy if they are first informed how to use the MER.

Metacognitive Knowledge on How to Use the Affordances of Learning Environments

A typical metacognitive instructional procedure is to inform learners about "what to do with strategies." In other words, the learners are provided with conditional knowledge about when and why to use certain knowledge such as strategies (Paris, Lipson, & Wixson, 1983). In recent studies, we expanded this idea and informed learners about "what to do" with the instructional affordances of a learning environment (e.g., multiple representations). Although this knowledge is not about strategies or about tasks (i.e., the learning tasks; see Flavell, 1979), it can be considered metacognitive knowledge about the instructional context, that is, about how to use the instructional features of a learning environment.

When instructional designers include certain elements into learning environments, they may rely on certain models, empirical findings, and—in many cases—on their intuitive knowledge about what can help learning. For example, when they present information in MER, they have some ideas on how these instructional features should be used. In the case of MER, it is typically expected that the learners relate the different representations to each other in order to gain deeper understanding (e.g., Ainsworth, 2006; Berthold et al., 2009). Often, however, the learners ignore some representations and concentrate on only one type of representation that seems to be most useful to them (Ainsworth, 2006). Such behavior can be seen as a strategy deficit on the learner's side (e.g., a production deficiency); accordingly prompts that activate effective strategies seem to be a sensible remedy (see Berthold et al., 2009; Berthold & Renkl, 2009). However, one can also ask: How should learners know what the ideas of the instructional designer on how to use the learning environment were? Maybe the deficit of suboptimal use of instructional affordances such as MER is, at least in part, a "deficit" of the instructional designer who has not provided "instructions for use." Actually, Schwonke, Berthold, and Renkl (2009) found that learners are hardly aware of any helpful function that MER can have.

Experiments on "Instructions for Use"

Schwonke, Renkl et al., (2009) used a slightly modified version of the learning environment of Berthold and Renkl (2009; version without relating aid and prompts). We tested the effects of informing learners about how to use MER on learning outcomes. More specifically, we briefly explained to the learners that there are two solutions procedures—tree diagram and arithmetic equation—and that the tree diagram should be used to gain an understanding on how the arithmetic equation is related to the problem formulation. For this purpose, we used the metaphor of a bridge ("... the tree diagrams 'build' a bridge between the problem texts and the equations..."). This instruction consisted just of an enrichment of one introductory screen that oriented the learners about the upcoming type of learning tasks in the form of worked examples. In addition, a line drawing of a bridge shortly popped up between the single worked examples as a reminder.

In this experiment, 30 students of psychology were randomly assigned to the "informed" condition and a control condition (introductory screen without instructions for the use of MER and without "reminding" line drawings). In addition, we collected eye-tracking data in order to gain some insight into learning processes.

The instructions for use led to higher learning outcomes (as assessed by a posttest that included problems tapping conceptual and procedural knowledge) without leading to increased learning time. In addition, this effect was mediated by altering the patterns of attention of students with different levels of prior knowledge, as assessed by eye-tracking (e.g., preventing learners with high prior knowledge to neglect the tree diagrams and leading the low-prior-knowledge learners to study the presented examples more efficiently; for details see Schwonke, Renkl et al., 2009).

In a nutshell, a lean intervention that provides metacognitive knowledge about the use of MER can lead to substantial learning gains. A restriction of this study might be seen in the fact that our instructions for use concentrated on just one aspect of certain MER. However, complex learning environments pose many problems to the learners when they try to optimally use its multiple information sources and representations. In other words, when learning environments are suboptimally constructed in the sense that they require manifold integration demands, "instruction for use" as employed by Schwonke, Renkl et al., (2009) might not work.

Schwonke, Ertelt, Otieno, Renkl, Aleven, & Salden (2013) employed a rather complex learning environment that is widely used in the field: Cognitive Tutor (Koedinger & Aleven, 2007; Koedinger & Corbett, 2006; see also Carnegielearning.com, 2011). This learning environment is an intelligent tutor system, primarily for mathematics learning. We used a Cognitive Tutor lesson on geometry that included worked solution steps that were gradually faded and replaced by steps to be solved by the learners; this version proved to be particularly effective in prior studies (e.g., Schwonke, Renkl et al., 2009). Nevertheless, informal observations showed that many learners had difficulties in handling this in the generally effective environment. These difficulties are not really surprising given that the geometry lesson involved MER (e.g., problem text, diagrams, and computations) and a number of support facilities such as hints for performance demands, a glossary including the relevant geometry principles, and areas providing an overview of the single subgoals to be achieved when solving the geometry problems at hand; these help devices also included multiple representations. We tested the effects of a cue card providing metacognitive knowledge about what to do with all these elements (Fig. 26.2). The design of the cue card was partly inspired by a help-seeking model developed by Aleven and Koedinger (2000).

In this experiment, 60 high-school students with a mean age of about 14 years were randomly assigned to one of two conditions. Half of the participants worked on a Cognitive Tutor geometry

1. How do I solve the problem?

   a. Which are the known values in the problem text? Can you locate the known values in the line drawing?

   b. Which are the unknown values in the problem text? Can you locate the unknown values in the line drawing?

   c. How are the known values and unknown values related mathematically?

2. What can I do when I get stuck?

   a. If you want to find out which value to calculate next then take a look at the overview tool.

   b. If you want to find out about the relevant mathematical principle then take a look at the glossary tool.

   c. If you want to find out how to proceed in the present problem then take a look at the hints tool.

Fig. 26.2 Cue card providing metacognitive knowledge about the use of different elements of a Cognitive Tutor lesson (translated from German)

lesson while having metacognitive support in the form of the cue card available; the other half of the participants worked without a cue card. The length of the lesson was about 1 h. As learning outcomes, we used measures of conceptual and procedural knowledge. Again, eye-tracking should help to get insight into learning processes.

We found that the provision of the cue card reduced learning time by about 20% in comparison to the control condition. With respect to conceptual knowledge, learners with low prior knowledge profited from the cue card; no such positive effect was found for learners with high prior knowledge. With respect to procedural knowledge, we also found that the learners with clearly below-average prior knowledge (lower third) profited from the cue card. Mediation analyses with the eye-tracking data suggested that the cue card effects on conceptual knowledge were in particular due to a more focused use of the Cognitive Tutor's different elements. Low-prior-knowledge students spend less time on inspecting available help facilities, while they simultaneously achieved better learning outcomes. Obviously, unfocussed and overextended use of the help facilities was prevented by the cue card. In a nutshell, the cue card had positive effects for all learners in terms of reducing learning time. However, only learners with low prior knowledge also gained more knowledge within this reduced learning time.

In summary, the studies by Schwonke, Berthold et al. (2009) and Schwonke et al. (2013) showed that providing learners with metacognitive knowledge about the affordances of the learning environments can be sensible. It is important to note that these interventions were very parsimonious. Such interventions did not increase learning time in Schwonke, Berthold et al. (2009) and even saved time in Schwonke et al. (2013). Nevertheless, we have to admit that the positive effects were different in both studies: Schwonke, Berthold et al. (2009) found "generally" enhanced learning outcomes, whereas Schwonke et al. (2013) found "generally" reduced learning times and enhanced outcomes for low-prior-knowledge learners. In addition, the cue card of Schwonke et al. (2013) included a number of elements that were not related to MER. Hence, it might be that other aspects and not primarily the information about MER were effective. Substantial further research is needed in order to determine the *specific* effects and their particular boundary conditions (e.g., prior knowledge level of the learners) that the *different* metacognitive information about learning environments' affordances has.

Conclusions and Outlook

In this final section, we outline the most important points that we have learned from our studies and the issues that have to be addressed in further studies. In doing so, we touch on theoretical, methodological, and instructional issues.

(a) One important issue relates to the *generalizability* of our findings. We have gained some knowledge about how to foster mathematics learning of senior high-school students and university students by self-explanation prompts and by "instruction for use." Obviously, it is not straightforward to generalize our finding to other learning domains and to younger learners. With respect to the generalizability to other age groups, it is important to note that we found striking differences even between university students (Berthold et al., 2009) and senior high-school students (Berthold & Renkl, 2009). Although this difference in educational level does not seem to be so large at a first glance, it seems all the more implausible that the present findings can be generalized to younger learners. Also developmental research on metacognition and strategies (for an overview, see Schneider & Bjorklund, 1998) shows that substantial development can be found up until the age of 16 (i.e., the average age of the participants in Berthold & Renkl). Hence, younger students might have not only production deficiencies that can be remedied by prompts or "instructions for use" but also more profound deficits (e.g., mediation deficiencies, meaning that the learners are not able to execute the relevant strategies appropriately). Successful interventions with younger students might need additional instructional components by which strategies are explicitly taught (e.g., via modeling or worked examples; see Hübner, Nückles, & Renkl, 2010).

(b) Although we have shown that self-explanation prompts can be helpful when learning from multiple representations, the pattern of results clearly shows that there are boundary conditions, even for a given educational level. If these conditions are not met, even negative effects can result. As discussed, one important boundary condition seems to be the complexity of the learning materials in relation to the learners' prior knowledge. Prompts can be useless or even detrimental when necessary prior knowledge prerequisites are missing. A theoretical as well as instructional problem is that we presently lack ways to specify, a priori and in a precise manner, what prior knowledge is "necessary." It might not be too difficult to determine whether a learner just has a production deficiency so that s/he is actually able to provide adequate self-explanations when prompted. However, it might be much more difficult to determine when a learner gets overloaded by prompts. Perhaps recent developments in online measures of cognitive load (Park & Brünken, 2010: deviations in foot tapping rhythm; Walter, Cierniak, Bogdan, Rosenstiel, & Gerjets, 2010: EEG measures) can help to solve this challenge in the future, at least for research purposes (such measures are still too intrusive for practical use in the field). Prompts can be automatically omitted if learners show (too) high cognitive load. Nevertheless, it would be desirable to first refine our theoretical models of self-explanation so that precise assumptions can be made about prior knowledge prerequisites necessary for prompts to be effective.

(c) The idea to provide instructions for use with respect to the central affordances of learning environments is relatively new (for similar approaches see Roll, Aleven, McLaren, & Koedinger, 2007, 2011). This instructional procedure seems to be promising because it is parsimonious and can even save learning time (i.e., greater learning efficiency). It has to be noted, however, that so far, all we have are initial promising studies, and these studies used instructions for use that were rather specific to the respective learning environments. What is presently missing is a general rationale or a set of principles to guide the construction of instructions for use that fit other learning environments. A sound basis for the construction of instructions for use might come from usability studies (Nielsen, 1994) or learning process data (e.g., thinking aloud protocols) showing suboptimal use of the learning environment. Such evidence might reveal that learners lack specific knowledge about how to best use the affordances of a given learning environment. However, in practical settings such data are often not available, rather informal observations and "intuition" have to be used in order to determine what information might best help the learners to work in a learning environment. On the other hand, we assume that future learning technologies will more easily produce usable log data of student activities so that information about how learners use these environments will be increasingly available.

In addition, it is also open as to when it is best to provide instructions for use: in advance (Schwonke, Berthold et al., 2009) or concurrently with the learning environment (Schwonke et al., 2013)? Both options have advantages and disadvantages. For example, providing a "concurrent" cue card as in Schwonke et al. (2013) might be suboptimal because it creates a type of split-attention problem (i.e., problems in relating the contents of the cue card with the learning environment and distraction from the learning contents). On the other hand, instructions for use provided in advance might be forgotten when working in the learning environments. Further research has to compare different options to present such instructions.

References

Ainsworth, S. E. (2006). DeFT: A conceptual framework for considering learning with multiple representations. *Learning and Instruction, 16*, 183–198.

Ainsworth, S. E., Bibby, P. A., & Wood, D. J. (2002). Examining the effects of different multiple representational systems in learning primary mathematics. *The Journal of the Learning Sciences, 11*, 25–61.

Aleven, V., & Koedinger, K. (2000). Limitations of student control: Do students know when they need help? In G. Gauthier, C. Frasson, & K. VanLehn (Eds.), *Proceedings of the 5th International Conference on Intelligent Tutoring Systems* (pp. 292–303). Berlin: Springer.

Aleven, V., & Koedinger, K. R. (2002). An effective metacognitive strategy: Learning by doing and explaining with a computer-based Cognitive Tutor. *Cognitive Science, 26*, 147–179.

Atkinson, R. K., Renkl, A., & Merrill, M. M. (2003). Transitioning from studying examples to solving problems: Combining fading with prompting fosters learning. *Journal of Educational Psychology, 95*, 774–783.

Berthold, K., Eysink, T. H., & Renkl, A. (2009). Assisting self-explanation prompts are more effective than open prompts when learning with multiple representations. *Instructional Science, 37*, 345–363.

Berthold, K., & Renkl, A. (2009). Instructional aids to support a conceptual understanding of multiple representations. *Journal of Educational Psychology, 101*, 70–87.

Berthold, K., Röder, H., Knörzer, D., Kessler, W., & Renkl, A. (2011). The double-edged effects of explanation prompts. *Computers in Human Behavior, 27*, 69–75.

Carnegielearning.com (2011). *The Carnegie learning web sites* (retrieved 01/05/2011).

Chandler, P., & Sweller, J. (1991). Cognitive load theory and the format of instruction. *Cognition and Instruction, 8*, 293–332.

Chi, M. T. H., Bassok, M., Lewis, M. W., Reimann, P., & Glaser, R. (1989). Self-explanations: How students study and use examples in learning to solve problems. *Cognitive Science, 13*, 145–182.

Chi, M. T. H., de Leeuw, N., Chiu, M. H., & LaVancher, C. (1994). Eliciting self-explanations improves understanding. *Cognitive Science, 18*, 439–477.

Conati, C., & VanLehn, K. (2000). Toward computer-based support of meta-cognitive skills: A computational framework to coach self-explanation. *International Journal of Artificial Intelligence in Education, 11*, 398–415.

de Jong, T., Ainsworth, S., Dobson, M., van der Hulst, A., Levonen, J., Reimann, P., Sime, J.-A., van Someren, M. W., Spada, H., & Swaak, J. (1998). Acquiring knowledge in science and mathematics: The use of multiple representations in technology-based learning environments. In M. van Someren, P. Reimann, H. P. A. Boshuizen, & T. de Jong (Eds.), *Learning with multiple representations* (pp. 9–40). Amsterdam: Pergamon.

Efklides, A. (2008). Metacognition: Defining its facets and levels of functioning in relation to self-regulation and co-regulation. *European Psychologist, 13*, 277–287.

Flavell, J. H. (1979). Metacognition and cognitive monitoring: A new area of cognitive developmental inquiry. *American Psychologist, 34*, 906–911.

Fonseca, B. A., & Chi, M. T. H. (2011). Instruction based on self-explanation. In R. E. Mayer & P. A. Alexander (Eds.), *Handbook of research on learning and instruction* (pp. 296–321). New York, NY: Routledge.

Grosse, C. S., & Renkl, A. (2006). Effects of multiple solution methods in mathematics learning. *Learning and Instruction, 16*, 122–138.

Hübner, S., Nückles, M., & Renkl, A. (2010). Writing learning journals: Instructional support to overcome learning-strategy deficits. *Learning and Instruction, 20*, 18–29.

Kalyuga, S. (2010). Schema acquisition and sources of cognitive load. In J. Plass, R. Moreno, & R. Brünken (Eds.), *Cognitive load theory and research in educational psychology* (pp. 48–64). New York, NY: Cambridge University Press.

Kalyuga, S., Chandler, P., & Sweller, J. (1999). Managing split-attention and redundancy in multimedia instruction. *Applied Cognitive Psychology, 13*, 351–371.

Koedinger, K. R., & Aleven, V. (2007). Exploring the assistance dilemma in experiments with Cognitive Tutors. *Educational Psychology Review, 19*, 239–264.

Koedinger, K. R., & Corbett, A. T. (2006). Cognitive tutors: Technology bringing learning sciences to the classroom. In R. K. Sawyer (Ed.), *The Cambridge handbook of the learning sciences*. New York, NY: Cambridge University Press.

Nelson, T. O. (1996). Consciousness and metacognition. *American Psychologist, 51*, 102–116.

Nielsen, J. (1994). *Usability engineering*. Boston, MA: Academic.

Ozuru, Y., Briner, S., Best, R., & McNamara, D. S. (2010). Contributions of self-explanation to comprehension of high and low cohesion texts. *Discourse Processes, 47*, 641–667.

Paris, S. G., Lipson, M. Y., & Wixson, K. K. (1983). Becoming a strategic reader. *Contemporary Educational Psychology, 8*, 293–316.

Park, B., & Brünken, R. (2010). *How to measure cognitive load in working memory while learning? An experimental dual-task study of continuous secondary tasks with internalized cues*. Paper presented at the "4th International Cognitive Load Theory Conference 2010", Hong Kong and Macau (China).

Pressley, M., Wood, E., Woloshyn, V. E., Martin, V., King, A., & Menke, D. (1992). Encouraging mindful use of prior knowledge: Attempting to construct explanatory answers facilitates learning. *Educational Psychologist, 27*, 91–109.

Reimann, P., & Neubert, C. (2000). The role of self-explanation in learning to use a spreadsheet through examples. *Journal of Computer Assisted Learning, 16*, 316–325.

Renkl, A. (1997). Learning from worked-out examples: A study on individual differences. *Cognitive Science, 21*, 1–29.

Renkl, A. (2008). Lehren und Lernen im Kontext der Schule [Teaching and learning in schools]. In A. Renkl (Ed.), *Lehrbuch Pädagogische Psychologie* (pp. 109–153). Bern: Huber.

Renkl, A. (2009). Wissenserwerb [Knowledge acquisition]. In E. Wild & J. Möller (Eds.), *Pädagogische Psychologie* (pp. 3–26). Berlin: Springer.

Renkl, A. (2011). Instruction based on examples. In R. E. Mayer & P. A. Alexander (Eds.), *Handbook of research on learning and instruction* (pp. 272–295). New York, NY: Routledge.

Roll, I., Aleven, V., McLaren, B., & Koedinger, K. (2007). Designing for metacognition—applying Cognitive Tutor principles to metacognitive tutoring. *Metacognition and Learning, 2*, 125–140.

Roll, I., Aleven, V., McLaren, B. M., & Koedinger, K. R. (2011). Improving students' help-seeking skills using metacognitive feedback in an intelligent tutoring system. *Learning and Instruction, 21*, 267–280.

Roy, M., & Chi, M. T. H. (2005). The self-explanation principle in multimedia learning. In R. E. Mayer (Ed.), *Cambridge handbook of multimedia learning* (pp. 271–286). New York, NY: Cambridge University Press.

Schneider, W., & Bjorklund, D. F. (1998). Memory. In W. Damon, D. Kuhn, & R. S. Siegler (Eds.), *Handbook of child psychology* (Cognition, perception, and language, Vol. 2, pp. 467–521). New York: Wiley.

Schraw, G. (1998). Promoting general metacognitive awareness. *Instructional Science, 26*, 113–125.

Schwonke, R., Berthold, K., & Renkl, A. (2009). How multiple external representations are used and how they can be made more useful. *Applied Cognitive Psychology, 23*, 1227–1243.

Schwonke, R., Ertelt, A., Otieno, C., Renkl, A., Aleven, V., & Salden, R (2013). Metacognitive support promotes an effective use of instructional resources in intelligent tutoring. *Learning & Instruction, 23*, 136–150.

Schwonke, R., Renkl, A., Krieg, K., Wittwer, J., Aleven, V., & Salden, R. (2009). The worked-example effect: Not an artefact of lousy control conditions. *Computers in Human Behavior, 25*, 258–266.

Schworm, S., & Renkl, A. (2007). Learning argumentation skills through the use of prompts for self-explaining examples. *Journal of Educational Psychology, 99*, 285–296.

Seufert, T., & Brünken, R. (2006). Cognitive load and the format of instructional aids for coherence formation. *Applied Cognitive Psychology, 20*, 321–331.

Sweller, J. (2006). The worked example effect and human cognition. *Learning and Instruction, 16*, 165–169.

Walter, C., Cierniak, G., Bogdan, M., Rosenstiel, W., & Gerjets, P. (2010). *Load adaptive tutor systems based on brain-computer interfaces*. Paper presented at the "4th International Cognitive Load Theory Conference 2010", Hong Kong and Macau (China).

Weinstein, C. E., & Mayer, R. E. (1986). The teaching of learning strategies. In C. M. Wittrock (Ed.), *Handbook of research in teaching* (pp. 315–327). New York: Macmillan.

27 Assessing Students' Problem Solving Ability and Cognitive Regulation with Learning Trajectories

Ron Stevens, Carole R. Beal, and Marcia Sprang

Abstract

Learning trajectories have been developed for 1650 students who solved a series of online chemistry problem solving simulations using quantitative measures of the efficiency and the effectiveness of their problem solving approaches. These analyses showed that the poorer problem solvers, as determined by item response theory analysis, were modifying their strategic efficiency as rapidly as the better students, but did not converge on effective outcomes. This trend was also observed at the classroom level with the more successful classes simultaneously improving both their problem solving efficiency and effectiveness. A strong teacher effect was observed, with multiple classes of the same teacher showing consistently high or low problem solving performance.

The analytic approach was then used to better understand how interventions designed to improve problem solving exerted their effects. Placing students in collaborative groups increased both the efficiency and effectiveness of the problem solving process, while providing pedagogical text messages increased problem solving effectiveness, but at the expense of problem solving efficiency.

Context

We have been developing reporting systems for problem solving which are helping to measure how strategically students are thinking about scientific problems and whether interventions to improve this learning are having the desired effect. The system is termed IMMEX (Interactive MultiMedia Exercises), and is an online library of problem solving science simulations coupled with layers of probabilistic tools for assessing

R. Stevens (✉)
UCLA IMMEX Project, Brain Research Institute,
UCLA School of Medicine, 5601 W. Slauson Ave. #272,
Culver City, CA 90230, USA
e-mail: immex_ron@hotmail.com

C.R. Beal
School of Information Science, University of Arizona,
P.O. Box 210077, Tucson, AZ 85721, USA

M. Sprang
Placentia-Yorba Linda Unified School District,
1830 N. Kellogg Drive, Anaheim, CA 92807, USA

R. Azevedo and V. Aleven (eds.), *International Handbook of Metacognition and Learning Technologies*, Springer International Handbooks of Education 26, DOI 10.1007/978-1-4419-5546-3_27,

students' problem solving performance, progress, and retention (Soller & Stevens, 2007; Stevens & Palacio-Cayetano, 2003; Stevens, Soller, Cooper, & Sprang, 2004; Stevens, Wang, & Lopo, 1996; Cooper, Cox, Nammouz, Case, & Stevens, 2008; Thadani, Stevens, & Tao, 2009).

IMMEX problems are what Frederiksen (1984) referred to as "structured problems requiring productive thinking," meaning they can be solved through multiple approaches, and students cannot rely on known algorithms to decide which resources are relevant and how the resources should be used. IMMEX problems are rich in cognitive experiences with over 90% of the utterances of students when solving a series of cases being cognitive or metacognitive in nature (Chung et al., 2002), and is an environment where instruction can be varied and the effects of different interventions tested.

IMMEX supports detailed assessments of students' overall problem solving effectiveness and efficiency by combining solution frequencies (or IRT estimates) which are outcome measures and artificial neural network (ANN) and hidden Markov modeling (HMM) performance classifications which provide a strategic dimension (Stevens, 2007; Stevens & Thadani, 2007; Stevens & Casillas, 2006) To simplify reporting and to make the models more accessible for teachers, these layers of data can be combined into an economics-derived approach which considers students' problem solving decisions in terms of the resources available (what information can be gained) and the costs of obtaining the information.

Extensive prior research has shown that students vary widely in how systematically and effectively they approach IMMEX problems (Stevens et al., 2004; Soller & Stevens, 2007). Some students carefully and systematically look for information sources that are appropriate for the current case, keep track of the information that they are accessing, and answer when the information they have reviewed is sufficient to support the answer, whereas other students are less systematic, often reinspecting information they have already viewed (Stevens & Thadani, 2007; Soller & Stevens, 2007). In this regard, IMMEX performances are reflections of students' ability (i.e., effectiveness) as well as their regulation of cognition (i.e., efficiency).

Students who review all available problem resources are not being very efficient, although they might eventually find enough information to arrive at the right answer. Other students might not look at enough resources to find the information required to solve the problem, i.e., they are being efficient but at the cost of being ineffective. Students demonstrating high strategic efficiency should make the most effective problem solving decisions using the fewest number of the resources available. As problem solving skills are gained this should be reflected as a process of resource reduction (i.e., higher efficiency) and improved outcomes (greater effectiveness) (Haider & Frensch, 1996).

Dissecting problem solving along these two dimensions provides an opportunity to detail how classroom practices like collaborative learning or the provision of pedagogical or metacognitive prompts can influence problem solving outcomes. Do they equally affect the efficiency and effectiveness of the problem solving process or are there differential effects? This is the framing question for this study.

Theoretical Background

Most theoretical frameworks for metacognition identify two major components: knowledge of cognition (declarative and procedural knowledge) and regulation of cognition (or executive component) (Schraw, 2001; Schraw, Brooks, & Crippen, 2005; Schraw, Crippen, & Hartley, 2006). The former is often understood as metacognitive awareness and has received considerably more attention than the regulation of cognition, which comprises the repertoire of actions in which an individual engages while performing a task. Consistent with this framework, metacognition occurs when individuals plan, monitor, and evaluate their own cognitive behavior in a learning environment or problem space (Ayersman, 1995).

Despite its importance, the study of metacognition has been slowed by the lack of simple, rapid, and automated assessment tools. Technology-based learning environments provide the foundation for a new era of integrated, learning-centered assessment systems (Quellmalz & Pellegrino, 2009). It is now becoming possible to rapidly

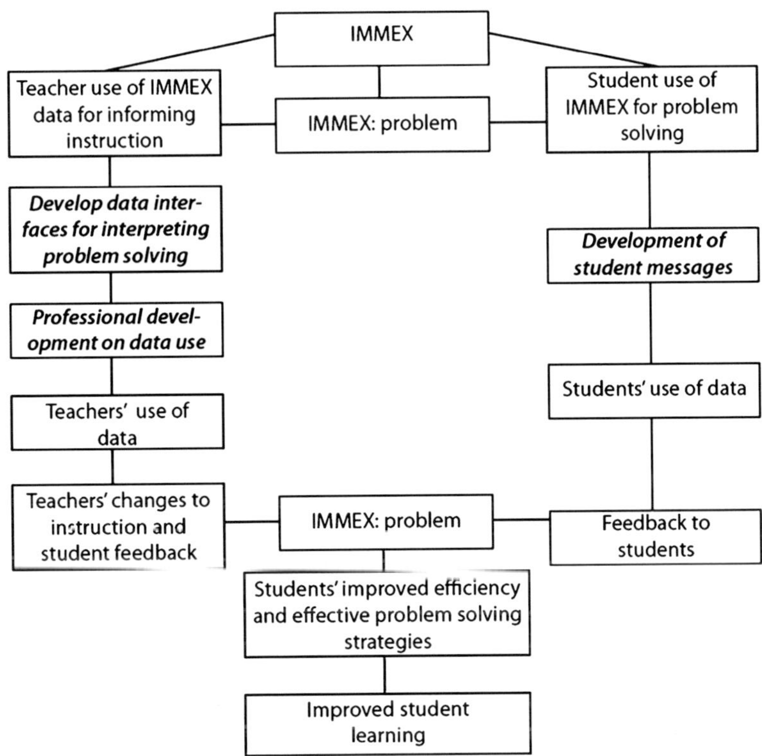

Fig. 27.1 Proposed approaches for improving student's problem solving skills

acquire data about students' changing knowledge, skill and understanding as they engage in real-world complex problem solving, and to create predictive models of their performance both within problems (Murray & VanLehn, 2000) as well as across problems and domains (Stevens et al., 2004). A range of analytic tools are being applied in these analyses including Bayesian Nets (Mislevy, Almond, Yan, & Steinberg, 1999), computer adaptive testing based on item response theory (IRT) (Linacre, 2004), and regression models and artificial neural networks (ANN) (Beal, Mitra, & Cohen, 2007; Soller & Stevens, 2007), each of which possesses particular strengths and limitations (Williamson, Mislevy, & Bejar, 2006).

How can this data be best put to use? A proposed model for improving problem solving approaches is shown in Fig. 27.1 and is based along two dimensions: (1) Teacher professional development and classroom practice and (2) direct student feedback.

Recent analyses of traditional assessment approaches and professional development models indicate that interventions often fail because teachers either do not fully understand how to implement them, or are not adequately supported in their efforts to implement them (Desimone, 2002; Lawless & Pellegrino, 2007; Spillane, Reiser, & Reimer, 2002). Simply increasing teachers' access to assessment data, however, may only exacerbate the challenges that they face in crowded classrooms when adapting instruction. Thus, new approaches are needed to provide teachers with accurate, predictive, and useful data about their students' learning in ways that are easily and rapidly understood. Data available in real time that speak to process as well as outcomes and that are intuitively easy to understand would seem to be minimum requirements.

Finding the optimum granular and temporal resolutions for reporting this assessment data will be a fundamental challenge for making the data accessible, understandable and useful for a diverse audience (e.g., teachers, policy makers and students) as each may have different needs across these dimensions (Alberts, 2009; Loehle, 2009). If the model resolution is general and/or delayed then important dynamics of learning may be lost or disguised for teachers. If the resolution is too complex or the reporting too frequent the analysis will become intrusive and cumbersome.

Teachers however are only one side of the learning equation; we need to consider students as well. Overall, prior research suggests that students' undirected problem solving in science domains tends to be relatively unsystematic, and that students are often unselective with regard to the evidence that is collected and considered. Students' difficulties with problem solving can be especially evident in technology-based learning environments, which often require careful planning and progress monitoring to use effectively (Schauble, 1990; Stark, Mandl, Gruber, & Renkl, 1999). When students can readily explore multiple sources of information and experiment with different combinations of factors, they can easily become distracted from the primary objective of using the information to solve the problem.

One approach to improving students' problem solving is to link the technology-based activity with classroom activities designed to help students adopt good problem solving strategies and help monitor their progress. Such activities would remind students to make sure that the goal of the problem is clearly understood, identify the information that will be most helpful in solving the problem, and monitor their progress towards the solution. Adapting this approach, Schwarz and White (2005) found that students improved in their understanding of the role of models in scientific problem solving when the computer-based activity of designing models was enhanced with a classroom-based curriculum. Although the results were encouraging, one limitation was that the program was quite intensive, involving 10 weeks of classroom activities and support from university researchers. Thus, the curriculum-embedded approach might be difficult for many science teachers to implement on their own, given limited resources and constraints on classroom science activities.

Task and Analytic Approaches

The architecture of IMMEX contains a series of tasks, a student management and organization system, a data warehouse and an analytic modeling and reporting module. One IMMEX task is called *Hazmat*, which provides evidence of a student's ability to conduct qualitative chemical analyses. The problem begins with a multimedia presentation, explaining that an earthquake caused a chemical spill in the stockroom and the student's challenge is to identify the chemical. The problem space contains 22 menu items for accessing a Library of terms, the Stockroom Inventory, or for performing Physical or Chemical Testing. When the student selects a menu item, she verifies the test requested and is then shown a presentation of the test results (e.g., a precipitate forms in the liquid). Students continue to gather the information they need to identify the unknown chemical so they can solve the problem (Fig. 27.2).

Hazmat contains 38 problem cases which involve the same basic scenario but vary in difficulty due to the properties of the different unknown compounds being studied. These multiple instances provide many opportunities for students to practice their problem solving and also provide data for Item Response Theory (IRT) estimates of problem solving ability which can be useful for comparing outcomes with more traditional ability measures such as grades.

IMMEX also supports detailed analyses of students' overall problem solving effectiveness and efficiency by combining outcome measures like IRT (as a measure of overall problem solving ability), and ANN (as a measure of problem solving strategy) and hidden Markov modeling (HMM) classifications (which provide a predictive measure of problem solving progress). Sample visualizations of these formats are shown in Fig. 27.3. This layered analytical approach has been very useful from a research perspective for distinguishing gender differences in problem solving approaches (Soller & Stevens, 2007) and documenting the effects of collaborative groups during problem solving (Cooper et al., 2008).

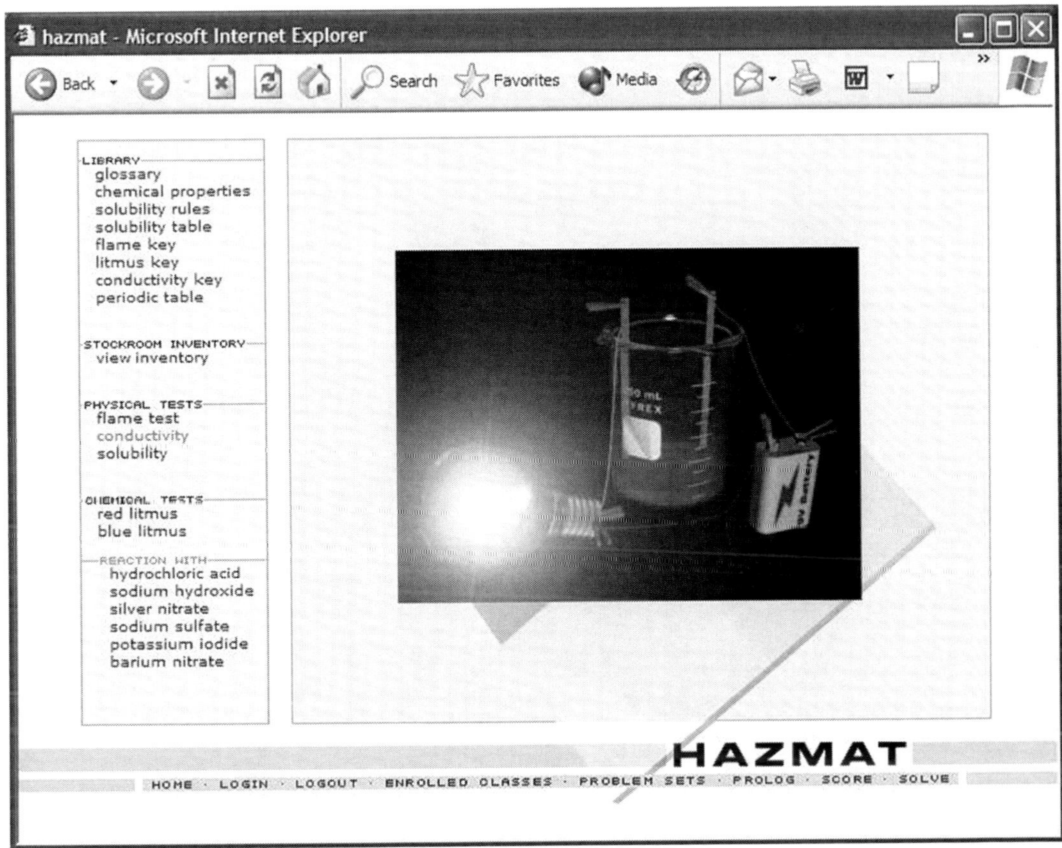

Fig. 27.2 *HAZMAT.* This screen shot of *Hazmat* shows the test items available (Library, Physical Tests, Chemical Tests) on the *left side* of the screen and a sample test result of a conductivity reaction in the *center*

We have combined the measures shown in Fig. 27.3 to simplify reporting using an economics-inspired approach which considers students' problem solving decisions in terms of the resources available (what information can be gained) and the costs of obtaining the information (Stevens & Thadani, 2007).

The strategy used (or the efficiency of the approach) is described by artificial neural network analysis which is a classification system. In this system, the artificial neural network's observation (input) vectors describe sequences of individual student actions during problem solving (e.g., Run_Red_Litmus_Test, Study_Periodic_Table, Reaction_with_Silver_Nitrate). The neural network then orders its nodes according to the structure of the data. The distance between the nodes after the reordering describes the degree of similarity between students' problem solving strategies. For example, the neural networks identified situations in which students applied ineffective strategies, such as running a large number of chemical and physical tests, or not consulting the glossaries and background information.

The neural networks also identified effective problem solving strategies such as selecting a variety of applicable tests while also consulting background information. This method is able to identify other domain-specific problem-specific strategies such as repeatedly selecting specific tests (e.g., flame or litmus tests) when presented with compounds involving hydroxides (Stevens

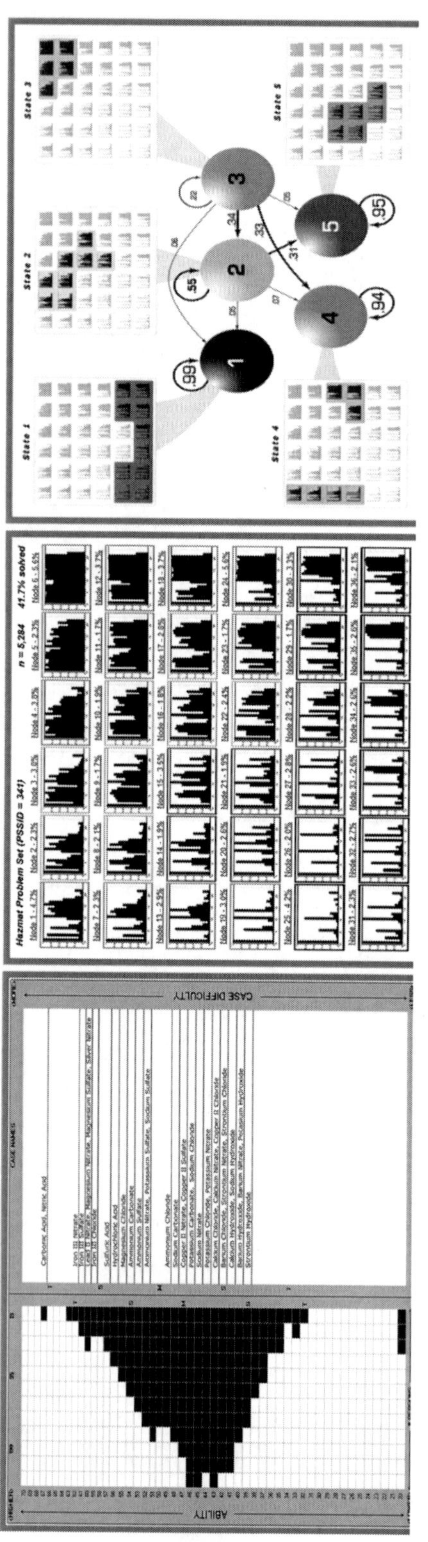

Fig. 27.3 Sample representations of item response theory ability estimates (*left*), Artificial neural network performance classifications (*middle*), and Hidden Markov modeling prediction models (*right*)

et al., 2004). Figure 27.4 (left) shows one ANN node in a 36-node network that was constructed from 5,284 performances of university and high school chemistry students. Figure 27.4 (right) shows the entire 36-node network representing the 36 different problem solving strategies used by the students. Each node of the network is represented by a histogram showing the frequency of items selected by students. For example, there were 22 tests related to Background Information (items 2–9), Flame Tests, Solubility and Conductivity (items 9–13), Litmus tests (items 14, 15), Acid and Base Reactivity (items 16, 17), and Precipitation Reactions (items 18–22).

Student performances that were grouped together at a particular node represented problem solving strategies adopted by students who always selected the same tests (i.e., those with a frequency of 1). For instance, all Node 15 performances shown in the left-hand side of Fig. 27.5 contain the items 1 (Prologue) and 11 (Flame Test). Items 5, 6, 10, 13, 14, 15, and 18 have a selection frequency of 60–80%, meaning that any individual student performance that falls within that node would most likely contain some of those items. Items with a selection frequency of 10–30% were regarded more as background noise than significant contributors to the strategy represented by that node.

The topology of the trained neural network provides information about the variety of different strategic approaches that students apply in solving IMMEX problems. First, it is not surprising that a topology is developed based on the quantity of items that students select. The upper right hand of the map (nodes 6, 12) represents strategies where a large number of tests are being ordered, whereas the lower left contains clusters of strategies where few tests are being ordered. There are also differences that reveal the quality of information that students use to solve the problems. Nodes situated in the lower right hand corner of Fig. 27.4 (nodes 29, 30, 34, 35, 36) represent strategies in which students selected a large number of items, but no longer needed to reference the Background Information (items 2–9). The classifications developed by ANN therefore reflect how students perceive the problem space, and are regulating their test selections in response to these perceptions.

While ANN nodal classifications provide a snapshot of what a student did on a particular performance, it would be instructionally more helpful if it were possible to automatically track and report changes in strategy over time. In order to generate a time series that could potentially be predictive of future work, a series of these performances must be grouped together and classified by another type a classifier, in our case, a hidden Markov modeling technique. Similar to the training of the artificial neural network classifier a training set of hundreds/thousands of sequences of student performances are used for training where students performed 4–10 *Hazmat* cases. This training results in HMM model classifiers which can categorize future sequences of performances.

Figure 27.5 shows the results of such training and illustrates a fundamental component of IMMEX problem solving: individuals who perform a series of these simulations stabilize with preferred strategies after 2–4 problem instances. This data shows hidden Markov models of the problem solving strategies of 1,790 students who performed seven of the *Hazmat* simulations. Many students began their problem solving with a limited (these are termed State 1 strategies) or extensive search (State 3) of the problem space. These designations arise from the association of certain ANN nodal classifications with different HMM States. With practice, these strategies decreased and they became more efficient and effective (States 4 and 5).

These characterizations help in determining which students may be guessing, failing to evaluate their processes, or randomly selecting items, i.e., issues with metacognition. Several advantages of this concurrent assessment include high automation and time efficiency, minimal susceptibility to researcher's bias, and a more naturalistic problem solving setting. As described below, this type of analysis can be further collapsed into three descriptors to identify metacognitive levels: high, intermediate, and low metacognition use for comparisons with other metacognitive metrics (Cooper et al., 2008).

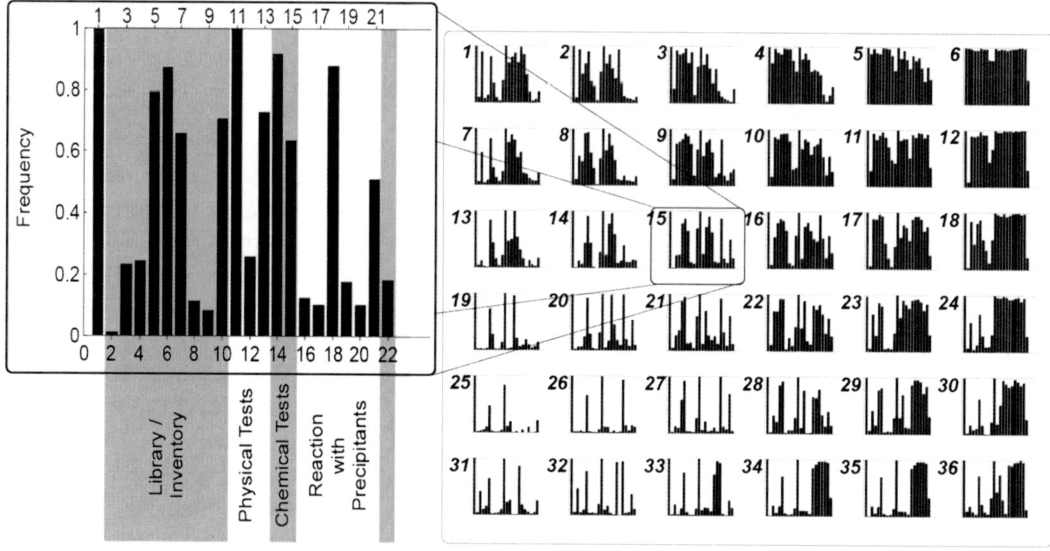

Fig. 27.4 Neural network performance patterns. The 36 Neural network nodes are represented by a 6×6 grid of 36 graphs. The nodes are numbered 1 through 36 left-to-right and top-to-bottom; for example, *the top row* is comprised of nodes 1 through 6. As the neural network is iteratively trained, the performances are automatically grouped into these 36 nodes so that each node represents a different generalized problem solving strategy. These 36 classifications are observable descriptive classes that can serve as input to a test-level scoring process or linked to other measures of student achievement or cognition. They may also be used to construct immediate or delayed feedback to the student

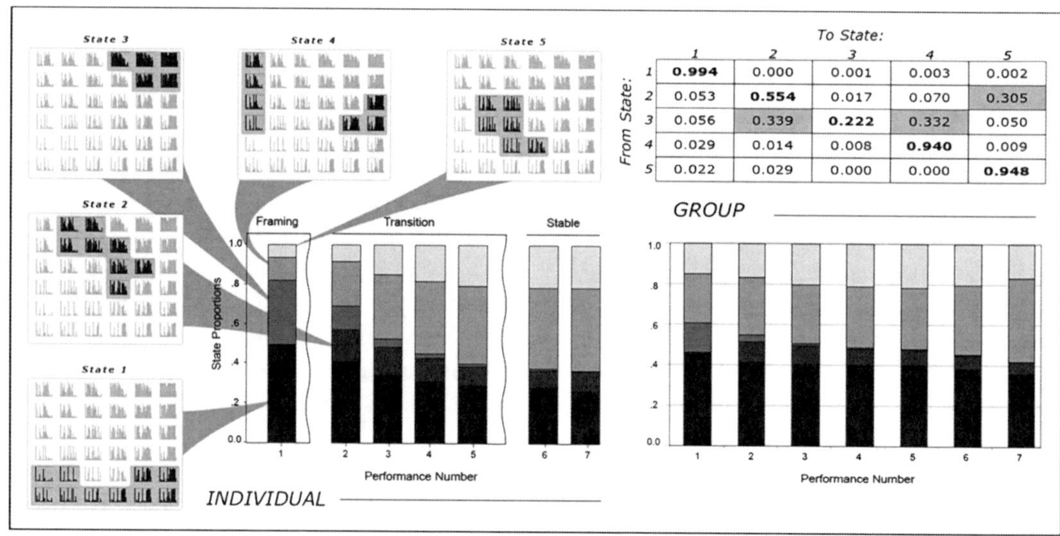

Fig. 27.5 Modeling individual and group learning trajectories. This figure illustrates the strategic changes as individual students or groups of students gain experience in *Hazmat* problem solving. Each *stacked bar* shows the distribution of HMM states for the students (N= 1,790) after a series (1–7) of performances. These states are also mapped back to the 6×6 matrices which represent 36 different strategy groups identified by self-organizing ANN. The *highlighted boxes* in each neural network map indicate which strategies are most frequently associated with each State. From the values showing high cyclic probabilities along the diagonal of the HMM transition matrix (*upper right*), States 1, 4, and 5 appear stable, suggesting once adopted, they are continually used. In contrast, students adopting State 2 and 3 strategies are more likely to adopt other strategies (*gray boxes*)

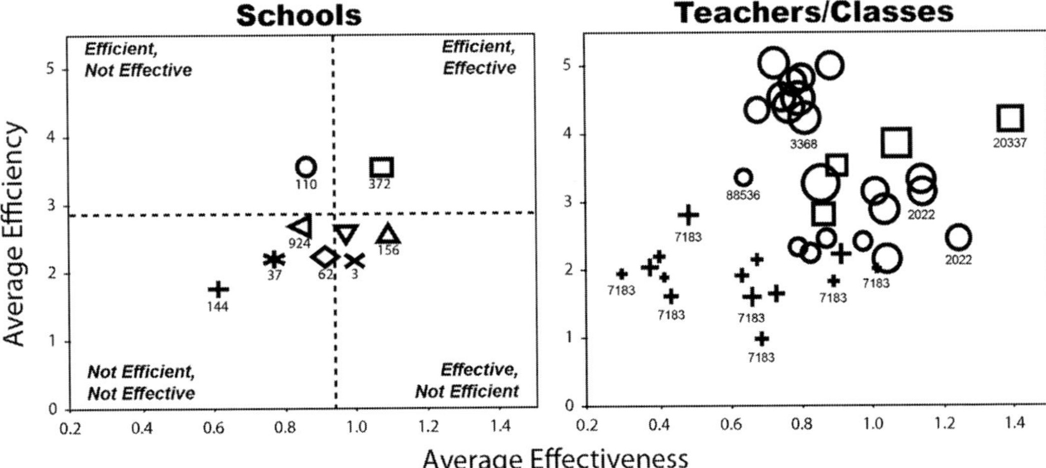

Fig. 27.6 Aggregated efficiency and effectiveness measures of schools and classrooms that performed *Hazmat*. The dataset was aggregated by schools (*left*) and then by teachers (*symbols and text*) and classrooms (*right*) and the efficiency (on a scale of 0–6) and effectiveness (on a scale of 0–2) measures calculated as described earlier. The symbol sizes are proportional to the number of performances. Each axis in (**a**) is bisected by *dotted lines* indicating the average efficiency and effectiveness measures of the dataset creating quadrant combinations of high and low efficiency and effectiveness

Figure 27.5 also illustrates how modifications to instruction can shift the dynamics of repetitive problem solving. The series of histograms in the right of this figure show that students in collaborative groups stabilize their strategies more rapidly than individuals and there are fewer performances where extensive searching occurs (i.e., State 3 strategies).

Learning Trajectories and Effects of Metacognition-Linked Interventions

The data gathered as students work with IMMEX provide rich, real-time assessment information along the efficiency and effectiveness dimensions. Figure 27.6 shows a modeling across schools and teachers/classrooms (66 classrooms, 62,774 performances) where an index of strategic efficiency is plotted against an effectiveness (i.e., solution frequency) rate. The quadrants generated by intersections of the averages of these measures reflect (1) mostly guessing (upper left corner), (2) performances where students view many resources, but miss the solution (lower left), (3) performances where many resources are being viewed and the problem is being solved (lower right) and (4) the performances where few resources are used and the problem is solved (upper right). As expected by the visualization format, schools are distributed across the quadrants (Fig. 27.6, left). A second level of analysis showing problem solving performance across five teachers as well as their classrooms where the different classes of the same teacher are shown by the symbols, and the different teachers identified by numbers (Fig. 27.6, right). The clustering of the different classrooms of the teachers (for instance, the +'s in the lover left hand corner and the squares in the upper right corner), illustrates a significant teacher effect perhaps reflecting different instructional methods (Zimmerman, 2007). Follow-up classroom observation studies by Thadani et al., (2009) suggest that the teacher's mental model of the problem space, and approach for solving the problem, can have a major effect on the approach adopted by the students.

Tracking problem solving efficiency and effectiveness as multiple *Hazmat* problems are performed creates a learning trajectory (Fig. 27.7) which is an important formative assessment tool

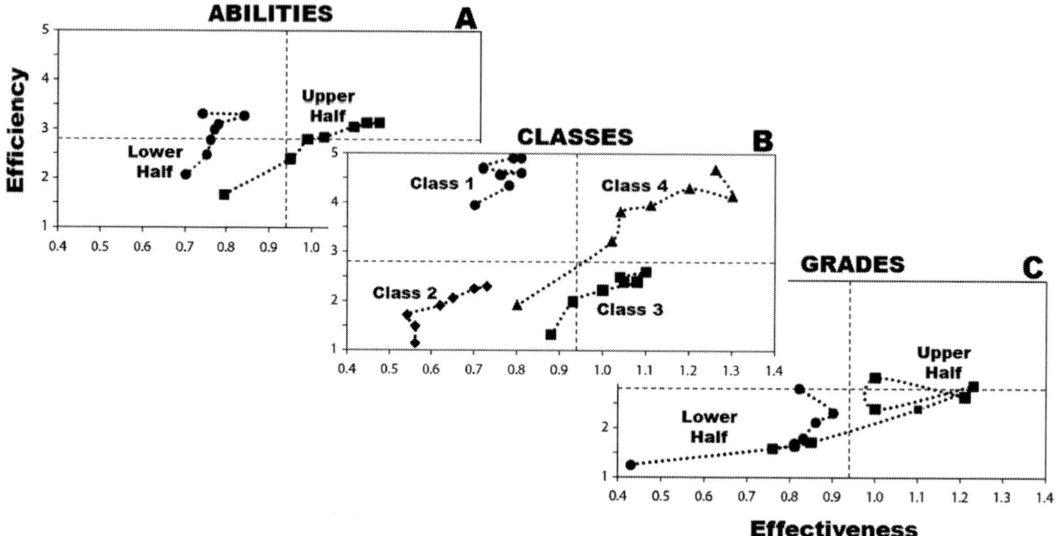

Fig. 27.7 Learning trajectories of classes and students of different abilities. (**a**) The dataset ($n=62{,}774$) was divided into lower (IRT scores=3.4–49.3) and higher (IRT scores=49.4–60.3) *Hazmat* problem solving ability students and the learning trajectories plotted. (**b**) The Efficiency/Effectiveness measures are stepwise plotted for seven *Hazmat* performances for four representative classes. (**c**) A dataset (82 students, 780 *Hazmat* performances) for three Advanced Placement Chemistry classes was divided into high and low categories based on the final course grade and the learning trajectories calculated

showing how students improve with practice (Lajoie, 2003). Learning trajectories show that the poorer problem solvers, as determined by IRT analysis, are modifying their strategic efficiency as rapidly as the better students, as shown by the position changes along the Efficiency axis, but they are not converging on effective outcomes (Fig. 27.7a). Figure 27.7b shows that this trend can be observed in classrooms as well, (e.g., Class 1). While the more successful classes (e.g., Class 4) simultaneously improved both their problem solving efficiency and effectiveness, the lower performing classes showed gains only in efficiency The learning trajectories are also important as changes in problem solving progress can be detected after as few as two to four student performances providing an opportunity for intervention before poor approaches have been learned. For instance, a teacher could initiate an intervention with a smaller group of students and after they have performed part of their assignment the teacher can observe online whether this was having a positive, negative or neutral effect and either continue or modify the intervention.

A similar analysis was conducted for 80 students in three Advanced Placement Chemistry classes who were separated into the upper and lower halves based on their final course grades. Again, the learning trajectories of the lower half of the students showed similar increases in strategic efficiency as the upper half of the students, but remained lower in effectiveness. (The correlations between the final grades and the efficiency index, ability estimates by IRT, and the solved rates (i.e., effectiveness) were $R2=0.06, p=0.02$, $R2=0.006, p=0.49$, $R2=0.02, p=0.23$).

Thus from the perspectives of problem solving abilities, course grades, and perhaps the instructional environment it would appear that some students are differentially struggling with the efficiency versus effectiveness aspects of problem solving a that interventions designed to improve these skills may be useful; the question is, which intervention will work with which efficiency/effectiveness dimension? From a formative assessment perspective learning trajectories can provide evidence as to whether interventions adopted to improve learning are working.

One such approach is to integrate guidance about problem solving directly into the technology-based learning environment. Such guidance may include the types of suggestions and prompts about the metacognitive aspects of good problem solving that have been associated with effective teacher implementation and skilled instruction from expert human tutors. More specifically, good problem solvers do more than apply known procedures to familiar problems. Rather, they consider carefully the nature of the problem before starting to work, plan an appropriate approach, implement the plan, and continually evaluate progress towards the solution (Cooper & Sandi-Urena, 2009; Swanson, 1990). Good problem solvers also recognize that difficult problems may require time and effort to solve, and that some "moments in the dark" are to be expected during the problem solving process. If the kinds of metacognitive guidance provided by skilled teachers could be integrated directly into simulation learning environments, then we might expect to find students adopting better strategies.

The benefits of individualized instruction have been well documented in studies of expert human tutors, in terms of enhanced learning outcomes for novices (Lepper, Woolverton, Mumme, & Gurtner, 1993). The benefits of individualized instruction have also been documented in the context of Intelligent Tutoring Systems (ITS) software for mathematics instruction (Anderson, Carter, & Koedinger, 2000; Heffernan & Koedinger, 2002; Koedinger, Corbett, Ritter, & Shapiro, 2000). Moreno and Duran (2004) found that students who received guidance while working in a discovery-based simulation showed stronger posttest performance and higher transfer rates than students who did not receive guidance. Studies of ITS have also indicated that students who seek out and use multimedia resources show stronger learning outcomes than students who do not use the instructional resources (Walles, Beal, Arroyo, & Woolf, 2005). While in the past ITS have primarily targeted the cognitive aspects of the student, they are increasingly being expanded to contribute to the learners' intrinsic motivation (Conati & Zhao, 2004). Within the development and study of student feedback, we wanted to find empirical evidence of how students use direct feedback from IMMEX to help them improve the way they problem solve.

The opposite pole to individual learning is collaborative learning. As tasks have become more complex and distributed, organizations have increasingly turned to the use of teams to share the effort and most have largely become team based. It is not surprising therefore that mastering teamwork is regarded as a cornerstone of twenty-first century learning and finding ways to improve communication and collaboration is an important area of research (Partnership for 21st Century Skills, 2013). Researchers have collected evidence of metacognition development during collaborative work and through the practice of collective metacognitive activities (Case, Gunstone, & Lewis, 2001; Georghiades, 2006). Hausmann, Chi, and Roy (2004) have extensively studied the benefits that are associated with collaboration. Learning in dyads therefore would also seem like a useful potential intervention for measuring its' effects on problem solving efficiency and effectiveness.

The learning trajectory for students ($N = 50{,}062$ performances, dotted line with open circle) who improved at their own pace is characterized by progressive improvement across both the efficiency and effectiveness dimensions which begins to plateau after around four performances (Fig. 27.8). This plateau mirrors the stabilization of strategies and abilities we have previously documented using HMM and IRT (Stevens & Casillas, 2006; Stevens & Thadani, 2007).

A second learning trajectory is from students who received text messages that were integrated into the prologue of each problem, i.e., before the student began actually working on the problem. (n = 11,497 performances, dotted line with open square). They were specifically designed to encourage students to reflect on their problem solving. The messages appeared during the Prologue of each *Hazmat* problem (i.e., during problem framing) and were randomly selected for each case from the message bank, with the restriction that a particular message would only

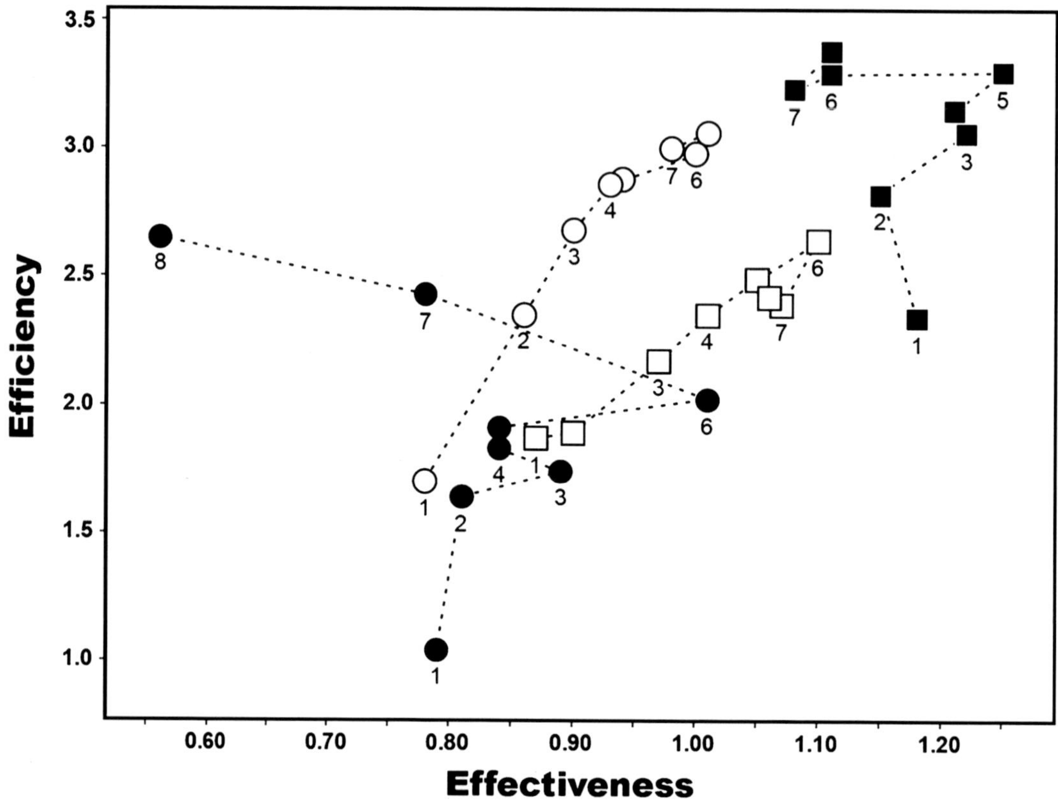

Fig. 27.8 *Hazmat* learning trajectories. The vertices of effectiveness and efficiency were calculated for students in different intervention groups after each of eight (*sequentially numbered*) *Hazmat* problem performances

be shown once to an individual student. The messages suggested for example are as follows: "When you read the IMMEX problem, don't let yourself rush into trying different things. Stop and think for a minute first." What have you learned in science class that could help you identify the right place to start?

It is important to note that the scaffolding messages did not provide information about the science content that would help the student solve the problem. In fact, all the relevant science content information is already available in the case; the student's task is to think about which information might be most useful, that is, to be focused and selective. The scaffolding messages were designed to address problem solving as a process and to encourage students to focus on their actions and the goal of solving the problem (i.e., regulation), rather than to explore the simulation. Students who received the metacognitive—directed hints became less efficient, meaning that they looked at more problem materials, but they also became more effective problem solvers.

A control group of students ($n = 1{,}215$ performances, dotted line with filled circle) also received messages during the Prologue, but here the messages were designed to be generic academic advice (e.g., "It's a good idea to keep up with the reading for your science class."). These students became less efficient as well as less effective. Thus, the message content was critical to improving students' problem solving; the presence of text messages alone was not helpful. Finally, grouping students into pairs ($n = 5{,}577$ performances, dotted line with filled square), improved both the efficiency as well as the effectiveness of the problem solving strategies.

Discussion

The studies described have traced the changes in students' problem solving ability (i.e., effectiveness) as well as their regulation of their cognition (i.e., efficiency) as they gained problem solving experience. They also showed the differential effects of interventions targeted to groups or individuals on these two problem solving dimensions. The greatest positive effect on both efficiency and effectiveness was gained by having students perform simulations in groups. In a separate study, Case et al. (2007) have shown that these positive benefits persisted when students were subsequently asked to solve additional problems on their own.

More recently Sandi-Urena et al. (2010) have shown that a non-related form of collaborative learning was sufficient to promote improved problem solving ability. Their intervention used a pretest/posttest experimental design. The intervention was a three phase "problem solving" activity that involved neither a chemistry problem nor was it directly associated with the IMMEX assessment system or problem solving activities. The intervention took place over 3 weeks. Phase one involved a small group collaborative problem solving activity and was designed to promote metacognition by the use of prompts and social interaction. The problems required students to sort through extraneous information and could not be solved by rote methods or without monitoring and evaluating their progress (core components of metacognitive skillfulness). Phase two, where students solved another problem for homework, was designed to promote individual reflection, and phase three provided students with feedback and summaries of their activities. Students were asked to reflect on what they had learned during the process and what it meant for their approach to future problem solving activities.

A comparison of student performances before and after this intervention indicated that they used more efficient strategies, and had higher problem solving ability after the intervention. Even thought there was no explicit link between the metacognitive intervention and the IMMEX problems, the intervention made students more likely to monitor and evaluate their progress though the problem, leading to increased problem solving ability.

The interventions targeted to individuals also shifted the shapes of learning trajectories. The inclusion of pedagogical messages or hints while the students were framing the problem showed different effects depending on the content of the messages. The messages that were designed with metacognition in mind improved the ability of the student to solve problems, but decreased the efficiency of the process, e.g., they seemed to make the students more reflective or cautious. This was, in fact the goal of these messages, to foster improved cognitive regulation. The messages that were general study aids also had an effect on the students' problem solving in that they decreased both the efficiency and the effectiveness of the problem solving, i.e., they were deleterious along both dimensions. While the possibility exists that they may have been a problem solving distraction for the students, given the magnitude of the effects we chose not include such messages in subsequent studies.

Recently these studies have been extended to middle school classrooms using an IMMEX problem set called *Duck Run* (Beal & Stevens, 2011). This is also a chemistry problem set where the prologue describes that an unknown substance has been illegally dumped into a local duck pond, possibly putting the local wildlife at risk. The student's task is to identify the substance so that it can be properly removed. Students who worked with the message-enhanced version were more likely to solve the problems and to use more effective problem solving strategies than students who worked with the original version. Benefits of the messages were observed for students with relatively poor problem solving skills, and for students who used exhaustive strategies. It would seem therefore that the beneficial effects of well-constructed messages immediately prior to problem solving are generalizable to multiple grade levels.

Combined these studies show that technology can provide dynamic models of what students are doing as they learn problem solving without creating a burden on educational systems. While illustrated for chemistry, such models are applicable to other problem solving systems where learning progress is tracked longitudinally. When shared with teachers and students in real time they can provide a roadmap for better instruction by highlighting problem solving processes and progress and documenting the effects of classroom interventions and instructional modifications. The differences observed across schools, teachers, and student abilities shifts the focus to the classroom and may provide a means for matching students and instruction or matching teachers with professional development activities.

Acknowledgments Supported in part by National Science Foundation Grants DUE 0512203 and ROLE 0528840 and by a grant from the US Department of Education's Institute of Education Sciences (R305H050052).

References

Alberts, B. (2009). Redefining science education. *Science, 323*(5913), 437.

Anderson, J. R., Carter, C., & Koedinger, K. R. (2000). Tracking the course of mathematics problems. National Science Foundation, ROLE Award, Carnegie Mellon University.

Ayersman, D. J. (1995). Effects of knowledge representation format and hypermedia instruction on metacognitive accuracy. *Computers in Human Behavior, 11*(3–4), 533–555.

Beal, C. R., Mitra, S., & Cohen, P. R. (2007). Modeling learning patterns of students with a tutoring system using Hidden Markov Models. *Proceedings of the13th International Conference on Artificial Intelligence in Education*. Amsterdam: IOS press.

Beal, C.R., & Stevens, R. (2011). Improving students' problem solving in a web-based chemistry simulation through embedded metacognitive messages. *Technology Instruction, Cognition and Learning, 8*(3–4) 255–271.

Case, J., Gunstone, R., & Lewis, A. (2001). Students' metacognitive development in an innovative second year chemical engineering course. *Research in Science Education, 31*, 313–335.

Case, E., Stevens, R., & Cooper, M. M. (2007). Is collaborative grouping an effective instructional strategy? Using IMMEX to find new answers to an old question. *Journal of College Science Teaching, 36*(6), 42.

Chung, G. K. W. K., deVries, L. F., Cheak, A. M., Stevens, R. H., & Bewley, W. L. (2002). Cognitive process validation of an online problem solving assessment. *Computers and Human Behavior, 18*(6), 669–684.

Conati, C., & Zhao, X. (2004). Building and evaluating an intelligent pedagogical agent to improve the effectiveness of an educational game. *Proceedings of the 9th International Conference on Intelligent user Interfaces* (pp. 6–13). Funchal, Madeira, Portugal.

Cooper, M. M., Cox, C. T., Jr., Nammouz, M., Case, E., & Stevens, R. H. (2008). An assessment of the effect of collaborative groups on students' problem solving strategies and abilities. *Journal of Chemical Education, 85*(6), 866–872.

Cooper, M. M., & Sandi-Urena, S. (2009). Design and validation of an instrument to assess metacognitive skillfulness in chemistry problem solving. *Journal of Chemical Education, 86*(2), 240–245.

Desimone, L. (2002). How can comprehensive school reform models be successfully implemented? *Review of Educational Research, 72*(3), 433–479.

Frederiksen, N. (1984). Implications of cognitive theory for instruction in problem solving. *Review of Educational Research, 54*(3), 363–407.

Georghiades, P. (2006). The role of metacognitive activities in the contextual use of primary pupils' conceptions of science. *Research in Science Education, 36*, 29–49. doi:10.1007/s11165-004-3954-8.

Haider, H., & Frensch, P. A. (1996). The role of information reduction in skill acquisition. *Cognitive Psychology, 30*(3), 304–337.

Hausmann, R. G., Chi, M. T. H., & Roy, M. (2004). Learning from collaborative problem solving: An analysis of three hypothesized mechanisms. *26th Annual Conference of the Cognitive Science Society* (pp. 547–552). Chicago, IL.

Heffernan, N. T., & Koedinger, K. R. (2002). An intelligent tutoring system incorporating a model of an experienced human tutor. *Proceedings of the Sixth International Conference on Intelligent Tutoring Systems,* Biarritz, France.

Koedinger, K. R., Corbett, A. T., Ritter, S., & Shapiro, L. J. (2000). *Carnegie learning's cognitive tutor: Summary research results. White paper*. Pittsburgh: Carnegie Learning.

Lajoie, S. P. (2003). Transitions and trajectories for studies of expertise. *Educational Researcher, 32*(8), 21–25.

Lawless, K. A., & Pellegrino, J. W. (2007). Professional development in integrating technology into teaching and learning: knowns, unknowns, and ways to pursue better questions and answers. *AERA Review of Educational Research, 77*(4), 575–614.

Lepper, M. R., Woolverton, M., Mumme, D., & Gurtner, J. (1993). Motivational techniques of expert human tutors: Lessons for the design of computer-based tutors. In S. P. Lajoie & S. J. Derry (Eds.), *Computers as cognitive tools* (pp. 75–105). Hillsdale: Erlbaum.

Linacre, J. M. (2004). *WINSTEPS Rasch measurement computer program*. Chicago: Winsteps.com.

Loehle, C. (2009). A guide to increased creativity in research—Inspiration or perspiration. *Bioscience, 40*, 123–129.

Mislevy, R. J., Almond, R. G., Yan, D., & Steinberg, L. S. (1999). Bayes nets in educational assessment: Where do the numbers come from? In K. B. Laskey & H. Prade (Eds.), *Proceedings of the fifteenth conference on uncertainty in artificial intelligence* (pp. 437–446). San Francisco: Morgan Kaufmann.

Moreno, R., & Duran, R. (2004). Do multiple representations need explanations? The role of verbal guidance and individual differences in multimedia mathematics learning. *Journal of Educational Psychology, 96*, 492–503.

Murray, R. C. & VanLehn, K. (2000). A decision-theoretic, dynamic approach for optimal selection of tutorial actions. In G. Gauthier, C. Frasson, & K. VanLehn (Eds.), *Intelligent Tutoring Systems, Fifth International Conference, ITS 2000, Montreal, Canada* (pp. 153–162). New York: Springer.

Partnership for 21st Century Skills. Retrieved February 8, 2013, http://www.p21.org.

Quellmalz, E. S., & Pellegrino, J. W. (2009). Technology and testing. *Science, 323*(5910), 75–79.

Sandi-Urena, S., Cooper, M. M., & Stevens, R. H. (2010). Enhancement of metacognition use and awareness by means of a collaborative intervention. *International Journal of Science Education*. doi:10.1080/09500690903452922. Retrieved from. http://dx.doi.org/10.1080/09500690903452922. First published on: 2 February 2010 (iFirst).

Schauble, L. (1990). Belief revision in children. *Journal of Experimental Child Psychology, 49*, 31–57.

Schraw, G. (2001). Promoting general metacognitive awareness. In H. J. Hartman (Ed.), *Metacognition in learning and instruction* (pp. 3–16). Dordrecht: Kluwer.

Schraw, G., Brooks, D. W., & Crippen, K. J. (2005). Using an interactive, compensatory model of learning to improve chemistry teaching. *Journal of Chemical Education, 82*(4), 637–640.

Schraw, G., Crippen, K. J., & Hartley, K. (2006). Promoting self-regulation in science education: Metacognition as part of a broader perspective on learning. *Research in Science Education, 36*, 111–139.

Schwarz, C. V., & White, B. Y. (2005). Metamodeling knowledge: Developing students' understanding of scientific modeling. *Cognition and Instruction, 23*(2), 165–205.

Soller, A., & Stevens, R. H. (2007). Applications of stochastic analyses for collaborative learning and cognitive assessment. In G. Hancock & K. Samuelson (Eds.), *Advances in latent variable mixture models*. Charlotte: Information Age Publishing.

Spillane, J. P., Reiser, B. J., & Reimer, T. (2002). Policy implementation and cognition: Reframing and refocusing implementation research. *Review of Educational Research, 72*(3), 387–431.

Stark, R., Mandl, H., Gruber, H., & Renkl, A. (1999). Instructional means to overcome transfer problems in the domain of economics: Empirical studies. *International Journal of Educational Research, 31*, 591–609.

Stevens, R. H., & Palacio-Cayetano, J. (2003). Design and performance frameworks for constructing problem-solving simulations. *Cell Biology Education, 2*(3), 162–179.

Stevens, R. H., Soller, A., Cooper, M., & Sprang, M. (2004). Modeling the development of problem solving skills in chemistry with a web-based tutor. In J. C. Lester, R. M. Vicari, & F. Paraguaca (Eds.), *Intelligent Tutoring Systems, 7th International Conference Proceedings* (pp. 580–591). Berlin: Springer.

Stevens, R. H., Wang, P., & Lopo, A. (1996). Artificial neural networks can distinguish novice and expert strategies during complex problem solving. *Journal of the American Medical Informatics Association, 3*(2), 131–138.

Stevens, R. H. (2007). A value-based approach for quantifying student's scientific problem solving efficiency and effectiveness within and across educational systems. In R. W. Lissitz (Ed.), *Assessing and modeling cognitive development in school* (pp. 217–240). Maple Grove: JAM.

Stevens, R. H., & Thadani, V. (2007). Quantifying student's scientific problem solving efficiency and effectiveness. *Technology, Instruction, Cognition and Learning, 5*(2–3–4), 325–337.

Stevens, R. H., & Casillas, A. (2006). Artificial neural networks. In R. E. Mislevy, D. M. Williamson, & I. Bejar (Eds.), *Automated scoring of complex tasks in computer based testing: An introduction* (pp. 259–312). Mahwah: Lawrence Erlbaum.

Swanson, H. L. (1990). Influence of metacognitive knowledge and aptitude on problem solving. *Journal of Educational Psychology, 82*(2), 306–314.

Thadani, V., Stevens, R. H., & Tao, A. (2009). Measuring complex features of science instruction: developing tools to investigate the link between teaching and learning. *Journal of the Learning Sciences, 18*(2), 285–322.

Walles, R., Beal, C. R., Arroyo, I., & Woolf, B. P. (2005, April). Cognitive predictors of response to web-based tutoring. Accepted for presentation at the biennial meeting of the Society for Research in Child Development, Atlanta, GA.

Williamson, D. M., Mislevy, R. J., & Bejar, I. I. (Eds.). (2006). *Automated scoring of complex tasks in computer based testing*. Mahwah: Erlbaum Associates.

Zimmerman, C. (2007). The development of scientific thinking skills in elementary and middle school. *Developmental Review, 27*(2), 172–223.

Part V

Multi-agent Systems to Measure and Foster Metacognition and Self-Regulated Learning

Using Trace Data to Examine the Complex Roles of Cognitive, Metacognitive, and Emotional Self-Regulatory Processes During Learning with Multi-agent Systems

28

Roger Azevedo, Jason Harley, Gregory Trevors, Melissa Duffy, Reza Feyzi-Behnagh, François Bouchet, and Ronald Landis

Abstract

This chapter emphasizes the importance of using multi-channel trace data to examine the complex roles of cognitive, affective, and metacognitive (CAM) self-regulatory processes deployed by students during learning with multi-agent systems. We argue that tracing these processes as they unfold in real-time is key to understanding how they contribute both individually and together to learning and problem solving. In this chapter we describe MetaTutor (a multi-agent, intelligent hypermedia system) and how it can be used to facilitate learning of complex biological topics and as a research tool to examine the role of CAM processes used by learners. Following a description of the theoretical perspective and underlying assumptions of self-regulated learning (SRL) as an event, we provide empirical evidence from five different trace data, including concurrent think-alouds, eye-tracking, note taking and drawing, log-files, and facial recognition, to exemplify how these diverse sources of data help understand the complexity of CAM processes and their relation to learning. Lastly, we provide implications for future research of advanced leaning technologies (ALTs) that focus on examining the role of CAM processes during SRL with these powerful, yet challenging, technological environments.

The widespread use of advanced learning technologies (ALTs) poses numerous challenges for learners of all ages. Learning with these non-linear, multi-representational, open-ended learning environments typically involves the use of numerous self-regulatory processes, such as planning, cognitive strategies, metacognitive monitoring and regulation, emotions, and motivation. Unfortunately, learners do not always monitor and regulate these processes during learning

R. Azevedo, Ph.D. (✉) • J. Harley • G. Trevors • M. Duffy • R. Feyzi-Behnagh • F. Bouchet
Laboratory for the Study of Metacognition and Advanced Learning Technologies, Department of Educational and Counselling Psychology, McGill University, 3700 McTavish Street, Montreal, QC, Canada H3A 1Y2
e-mail: roger.azevedo@mcgill.ca

R. Landis
Illinois Institute of Technology, College of Psychology, 3105 S. Dearborn St., Life Sciences #252, Chicago, IL 60616, USA
e-mail: rlandis@iit.edu

R. Azevedo and V. Aleven (eds.), *International Handbook of Metacognition and Learning Technologies*, Springer International Handbooks of Education 26, DOI 10.1007/978-1-4419-5546-3_28,

with ALTs, which limits their effectiveness as educational tools for enhancing learning about complex and challenging topics. Metacognition and self-regulation comprise a set of key processes that are critical for learning about conceptually rich domains with ALTs, such as hypermedia, intelligent tutoring systems, simulations, multi-agent tutoring systems, serious games, and other hybrid systems. We argue that learning with ALTs involves a complex set of interactions between cognitive, affective, metacognitive, and motivational processes. Although we acknowledge the importance of motivation in learning, it is not a process that we will be discussing in this chapter given our current measurement of it, and we will therefore focus on cognitive, affective, and metacognitive (CAM) processes.

Recent interdisciplinary research provides evidence that learners of all ages struggle when learning about conceptually rich domains with ALTs (Aleven, Roll, McLaren, & Koedinger, 2010; Azevedo, Johnson, Chauncey, & Graesser, 2011; Biswas, Jeong, Kinnebrew, Sulcer, & Roscoe, 2010; Greene, Moos, & Azevedo, 2011). In brief, this research indicates that learning about conceptually rich domains with ALTs is particularly difficult because it requires students to continuously monitor and regulate several key aspects of their learning. For example, regulating one's learning involves the following: analyzing the learning context, setting and managing meaningful learning subgoals, determining which learning and problem-solving strategies to use, assessing whether selected learning strategies are effective in meeting the learning subgoals, monitoring and making accurate judgments regarding one's emerging understanding of the topic and contextual factors, and determining whether there are aspects of the learning context that could be used to facilitate learning. During self-regulated learning (SRL), students need to deploy several metacognitive processes to determine whether they understand the material. Students must also consider whether it is necessary for them to modify their plans, goals, strategies, and efforts in relation to dynamically changing contextual conditions. Further, students must monitor, modify, and adapt to fluctuations in their motivational and affective states, and determine how much social support (if any) they may need to perform a task. Depending on the learning context, instructional goals, perceived task performance, and progress made toward achieving the learning goal(s), students may also need to modify certain aspects of their cognition, affect, metacognition, and motivation. As such, we argue that self-regulation plays a critical role in learning with ALTs.

In this chapter, we provide an overview of the theoretical SRL model that serves as the foundation of our research and fundamental assumptions. We then describe how features of a multi-agent, intelligent hypermedia system (i.e., MetaTutor) support learners in regulating several aspects of their learning. We also provide specific examples of key monitoring and regulatory processes used prior to, during, and following learning with MetaTutor. In addition, we provide extensive evidence from five different types of trace data (i.e., concurrent think-alouds, eye-tracking, note-taking and drawing, log files, and facial recognition) and indicate how they contribute to our understanding of SRL. Finally, we present several implications for future research of ALTs that focus on metacognition and SRL.

Self-Regulated Learning as an Event: Theoretical Framework

SRL frameworks, models, and theories attempt to explain how cognitive, affective, metacognitive, and motivational processes and contextual factors influence the learning process (Boekaerts, 2011; Pintrich, 2000; Winne, 2001; Winne & Hadwin, 1998, 2008; Zimmerman, 2000, 2008; Zimmerman & Schunk, 2011). Although there are important differences between various theoretical definitions, self-regulated learners are generally characterized as active and efficient at managing their own learning through monitoring and strategy use (Boekaerts, Pintrich, & Zeidner, 2000; Butler & Winne, 1995; Efklides, 2011; Greene & Azevedo, 2007, 2009; Pintrich, 2000; Winne, 2001; Winne & Hadwin, 1998, 2008; Zimmerman & Schunk, 2001, 2011). Students are self-regulated to the degree that they are metacognitively, motivationally, and behaviorally active participants in their learning (Zimmerman, 1989). The goal of this section is to briefly describe the theoretical basis underlying our research on MetaTutor to understand the temporal dynamics of SRL processes deployed during learning with the system.

SRL involves actively constructing an understanding of a topic or domain, such as human biology (e.g., body systems), by creating subgoals; using learning strategies; monitoring and regulating certain aspects of cognition, behavior, emotions, and motivation; and modifying behavior to achieve the desired goal(s) (see Boekaerts et al., 2000; Pintrich, 2000; Zimmerman & Schunk, 2001). Though this is a common definition of SRL, the literature includes multiple theoretical perspectives that make different assumptions and focus on different constructs, processes, and phases (see Azevedo et al., 2010; Dunlosky & Lipko, 2007; Metcalfe & Dunlosky, 2008; Pintrich, 2000; Schunk, 2008; Winne & Hadwin, 2008; Zimmerman & Schunk, 2011). For present purposes, we further specify SRL as a concept superordinate to metacognition that incorporates both metacognitive monitoring (i.e., knowledge of cognition or metacognitive knowledge) and metacognitive control (i.e., involving the skills associated with the regulation of metacognition), as well as processes related to manipulating contextual conditions and planning for future activities within a learning episode. Ultimately, SRL is based on the assumption that learners exercise agency by consciously monitoring and intervening in their learning.

Our research is theoretically influenced by contemporary models of SRL that emphasize the temporal deployment of these processes during learning (Azevedo, Moos et al., 2010). As such, multiple measures must be used to detect, track, and model learners' use of cognitive, affective, and metacognitive (CAM) processes during learning. Underlying our approach is Winne and Hadwin's SRL model (1998, 2008), which proposes that learning occurs in four basic phases: (1) task definition, (2) goal setting and planning, (3) studying tactics, and (4) adaptations to metacognition. The Winne and Hadwin model emphasizes the role of metacognitive monitoring and control as the central aspects of learners' ability to acquire complex material across different instructional contexts (e.g., using a multi-agent system to track and foster SRL) in that information is processed and analyzed within each phase of the model. Recently, Azevedo and colleagues (Azevedo, Feyzi-Behnagh, Duffy, Harley, & Trevors, 2012a, Azevedo, Landis et al., 2012b, Azevedo, Bouchet et al., 2012c; Azevedo & Feyzi-Behnagh, 2011; Azevedo, Cromley, Moos, Greene, & Winters, 2011; Azevedo & Witherspoon, 2009) extended this model and provided extensive evidence regarding the role and function of several dozen CAM processes during learning with ALTs (e.g., using an intelligent, hypermedia multi-agent system).

In brief, the following assumptions are associated with the current model. First, successful learning involves individuals monitoring and controlling (i.e., regulating) key CAM processes. Second, SRL is context-specific and successful learning may require a learner to increase/decrease the use of certain key SRL processes at different points in time. Third, a learner's ability to monitor and control both internal (e.g., prior knowledge) and external factors (e.g., changing dynamics of the learning environment, relative utility of an agent's prompt) is crucial. Fourth, a learner's ability to make adaptive, real-time adjustments to internal and external conditions, based on accurate judgments of their use of CAM processes, is fundamental to successful learning. Finally, certain CAM processes (e.g., interest, self-efficacy, task value) are necessary to motivate a learner to engage and deploy appropriate CAM processes during learning and problem solving.

An important strength of this model is that it deals specifically with the person-in-context perspective and postulates that CAM processes occur throughout learning with a multi-agent system, which is useful in examining when and how learners regulate learning. The focal macro-level processes discussed in this chapter are reading, metacognitive monitoring, and learning strategies. Reading behavior is critical since it is the most important activity related to acquiring, comprehending, and using content knowledge related to a particular topic. During reading, learners need to monitor and regulate several key processes, such as the following: (1) selecting relevant content (i.e., text and diagrams) based on their current subgoal; (2) spending appropriate amounts of time on each page, depending on their relevance regarding their current subgoal; (3) deciding when to switch or create a new subgoal; (4) making accurate assessments of their emerging understanding; (5) conceptually connecting content with prior knowledge; (6) adaptively selecting, using, and assessing the effectiveness of several learning strategies (e.g., rereading, coordinating informational sources, summarizing, making inferences); and (7) making adaptive changes to behavior based on a variety of external (e.g., quiz scores, quality and timing of agents' prompts and feedback) and internal sources (e.g., affective experiences, including both positive and negative emotions, perception of task difficulty). In sum, SRL involves the continuous monitoring and regulation of CAM processes during learning with multi-agent, intelligent hypermedia systems (e.g., MetaTutor).

MetaTutor: An Adaptive, Multi-agent Hypermedia Learning System for Biology

MetaTutor is a multi-agent, adaptive hypermedia learning environment, which presents challenging human biology science content. The primary goal underlying this environment is to investigate how ALTs can adaptively scaffold SRL and metacognition within the context of learning about complex biological content (Azevedo, Feyzi-Behnagh et al., 2012). MetaTutor is grounded in a theory of SRL that views learning as an active, constructive process whereby learners set goals for their learning and then attempt to monitor, regulate, and control their cognitive and metacognitive processes in the service of those goals (Winne & Hadwin, 2008). More specifically, MetaTutor is based on several theoretical assumptions of SRL that emphasize the role of cognitive, metacognitive (where metacognition is conceptualized as being subsumed under SRL), motivational, and affective processes (Pekrun, 2006; Pintrich, 2000; Winne & Hadwin, 2008; Zimmerman & Schunk, 2011). Moreover, learners must regulate their cognitive and metacognitive processes in order to integrate multiple informational representations available from the system. Although all students have the potential to regulate, few students do so effectively, possibly due to inefficient or insufficient cognitive or metacognitive strategies, knowledge, or control.

MetaTutor is both (1) a learning tool designed to teach and train students to self-regulate (e.g., by modeling and scaffolding metacognitive monitoring, facilitating the use of effective learning strategies, and setting and coordinating relevant learning goals), and (2) a research tool used to collect trace data on students' CAM processes deployed during learning.

As a learning tool, MetaTutor has a host of features that embody and foster SRL (see Fig. 28.1). These include four pedagogical agents (PAs), which guide students through the learning session and prompt students to engage in planning, monitoring, and strategic learning behaviors. In addition, the agents can provide feedback and engage in a tutorial dialogue in order to scaffold students' selection of appropriate subgoals, accuracy of metacognitive judgments, and use of particular learning strategies. The system also offers the possibility for the learners to express metacognitive monitoring and control processes through the use of a palette of actions (see in Fig. 28.1). For example, learners can click on a button to indicate that they want to make a statement about their understanding of a page and then indicate on a scale that their understanding is poor. They can also indicate that they want to summarize the content of that page and then type freely their summary in a text box.

Additionally, MetaTutor collects information from user interactions to provide adaptive feedback on the deployment of students' SRL behaviors. For example, students can be prompted to self-assess their understanding (i.e., system-initiated judgment of learning [JOL]) and are then administered a brief quiz. Results from the self-assessment and quiz allow PAs to provide adaptive feedback according to the calibration between

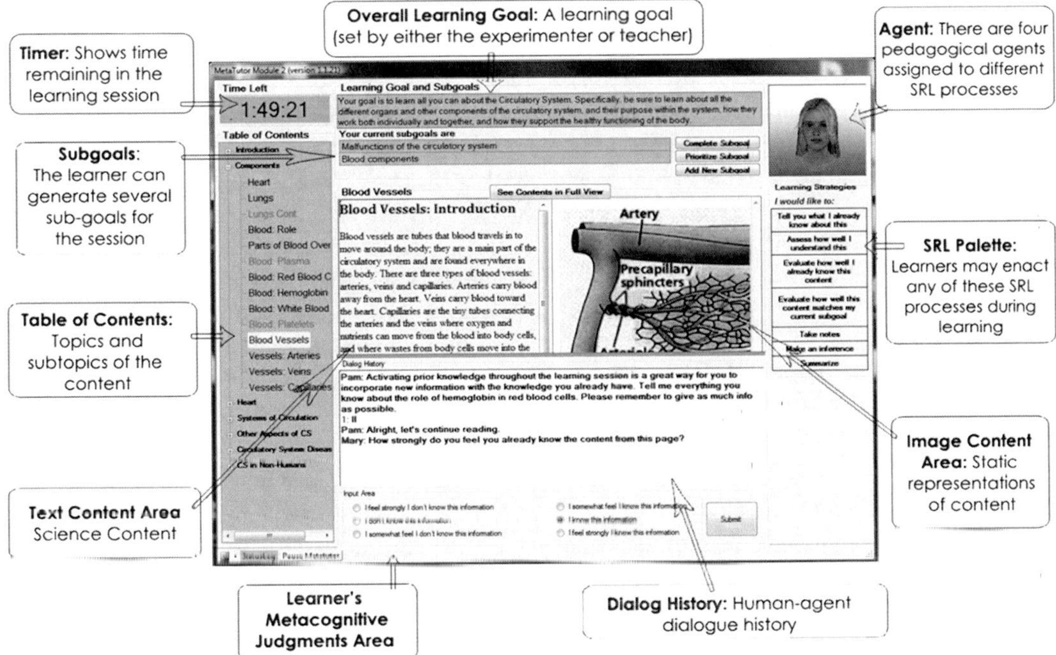

Fig. 28.1 Annotated screenshot of the MetaTutor interface

students' confidence of comprehension and their actual quiz performance.

The system's interface layout also supports SRL processes. As depicted in Fig. 28.1, an embedded palette provides students with the opportunity for initiating an interaction with the system according to the SRL process selected (e.g., take notes). Overall, in line with its theoretical foundations, MetaTutor supports and fosters a variety of SRL behaviors, including prior knowledge activation, goal setting, evaluation of learning strategies, integrating information across representations, content evaluation, summarization, note-taking, and drawing. Importantly, it also scaffolds specific metacognitive processes, such as judgments of learning, feelings of knowing, and monitoring progress toward goals (Feyzi-Behnagh, Khezri, & Azevedo, 2011).

There are some aspects of the espoused theoretical models of SRL yet to be implemented. Initially, the theoretical and empirical foci have been on cognitive, metacognitive, and behavioral learning processes. Thus, this ALT does not extensively incorporate the motivational and affective dimensions of SRL into its design. Affective-related elements are currently collected by the system and analyzed following learners' interaction with MetaTutor. Moving forward, the varieties and regulation of learners' affective processes, the affective qualities of human-agent interaction, and how the system and learners' self-regulation influence the activation, awareness, and motivation will be areas of interest with important implications for SRL theory and instructional design.

Self-Regulated Learning with MetaTutor: Understanding the Nature of CAM Processes Prior to, During, and Following Learning

When interacting with the current version of MetaTutor, during a 2-h session, a student is asked to learn about the human circulatory system. The environment contains 41 static diagrams and hundreds of paragraphs containing 7,545 words. Each of these representations of information is organized similarly to sections and subsections of book chapters, thus allowing students to navigate freely throughout the environment (see table of contents on the left of Fig. 28.1). In addition to CAM processes, motivational and emotional processes may also be assessed during the MetaTutor session. In this section, we describe the nature and role of CAM processes experienced by learners prior to, during, and following their learning session with MetaTutor.

CAM Processes Prior to Using MetaTutor

Once a student is given the overall learning goal for the session and prior to using MetaTutor, she or he analyzes the learning situation, sets meaningful learning goals, and determines which strategies to use based on the task conditions. The student may also generate motivational goals and beliefs based on prior experience with the topic and learning environment, success with similar tasks, contextual constraints (e.g., perception of scaffolding and feedback provided by a PA), and contextual demands (e.g., a time limit for completion of the task).

For example, a student may espouse different achievement goals and beliefs about knowledge prior to engaging with the learning environment. According to achievement goal theory (see Ames, 1992; Ames & Archer, 1988; Hulleman, Schrager, Bodmann, & Harackiewicz, 2010), some students may espouse a more dominant mastery goal for learning if their prior experiences in classroom environments encouraged them to increase competencies by focusing on personal progress. In contrast, other students may enter the learning environment with a tendency to strive for competition and outperform other students, particularly if their learning experiences typically emphasized the importance of performance through peer comparisons.

Further, students' beliefs about the nature of knowledge and what it means to know—their epistemic beliefs—are another active component during the task definition phase (Muis, 2007). Students adapt their cognitive processing during the preparatory planning phases of learning in response to task complexity, a relationship that is mediated by their epistemic beliefs. That is, students who espouse beliefs in unstructured and variable knowledge report using a greater proportion of deep cognitive processing across all tasks (Bromme, Pieschl, & Stahl, 2010). These constructivist beliefs about knowledge and knowing allow for a greater perception of task complexity and flexibility in selecting strategies best suited to accomplish the task. Such beliefs and motivational approaches can be shaped by previous academic experiences, perceptions, and attitudes, as well as by the instructions provided at the beginning of the MetaTutor learning session. Importantly, differences in goal orientations and epistemic beliefs will likely influence the strategies deployed during learning, as well as the criteria learners use to evaluate success or failure.

Additionally, students may have particular emotional responses prior to interacting with MetaTutor. These may be based on either an existing trait emotion (e.g., more habitual, reoccurring emotions, such as trait test anxiety) that would be aroused by the learning environment or prospective emotional responses that relate to potential outcomes of the particular academic achievement activity (e.g., hope to learn as much as possible about the circulatory system) (Pekrun, 2006).

CAM Processes Deployed During Learning with MetaTutor

During the course of learning, a student may assess whether particular strategies are effective in meeting learning subgoals, evaluate their emerging understanding of the topic, and make the necessary adjustments regarding knowledge, behavior, effort, and other aspects of the learning context. Ideally, the self-regulated learner will make adaptive adjustments, based on continuous metacognitive monitoring and control related to the standards of the particular learning task and that these adjustments will facilitate decisions regarding when, how, and what to regulate (Pintrich, 2000; Schunk, 2001; Winne, 2005;

Winne & Hadwin, 1998, 2008; Winne & Nesbit, 2009; Zimmerman, 2008; Zimmerman & Schunk, 2011). These monitoring and control processes may interact with motivational facets of learning, such as self-efficacy and epistemic beliefs. Self-efficacy represents an individual's perceived capacity to successfully complete a learning task (Schunk & Usher, 2011), such as completing a subgoal created within MetaTutor. During the learning session, a student's confidence about his or her capability to master a certain concept or complete a subgoal may influence his or her decisions about which pages to read in MetaTutor, how long to persist on challenging material, and resilience to adverse outcomes, such as poor performance on quizzes.

Another factor that influences online metacognitive behaviors is students' epistemic beliefs, which are related to the standards that are set for subsequent learning (Muis, 2007). Standards for learning are used to compare an emerging learning product (e.g., comprehension of a text) with the initial goal that was set (e.g., studying in order to be prepared for the posttest). If, for example, a student holds a belief in simple knowledge, he or she may judge that memorization of key terms is an adequate standard for learning, without being motivated to consider their interconnectedness across multiple representations and pages in MetaTutor (Dahl, Bals, & Turi, 2005; Schommer, 1998). In contrast, a belief in complex knowledge motivates a greater effort at understanding its interconnectedness (Muis, 2007; Muis & Franco, 2009). Both self-efficacy and epistemic beliefs can potentially change during learning depending on a host of variables, such as performance on quizzes, self-evaluations about the effectiveness of learning strategies deployed, and emotions experienced during the learning process (e.g., learning-centered emotions).

Activity emotions are also subject to change based on learners' evolving appraisals, such as control and task value, regarding progress toward achieving learning goals (Pekrun, 2006). These emotions are also influenced by learners' ability to adaptively regulate their emotions (Gross, Sheppes, & Urry, 2011). Therefore, a learner may approach MetaTutor feeling hopeful (prospective emotion) that he or she will be able to learn about a particular topic of importance (i.e., an appraisal of positive value and medium control), such as the relationship between the circulatory and nervous system, but become frustrated (activity emotion) after learning that this goal cannot be set because MetaTutor does not cover the nervous system (i.e., appraisal of low control). The learner may then question whether the learning session will hold anything of interest (i.e., an appraisal of negative value). The learner, however, may be effective in dampening their frustration and rather than giving up and disengaging with the task (i.e., becoming bored), instead be able to set a subgoal more focused on the circulatory system that is still of personal interest. After having proposed a new subgoal (e.g., to learn about malfunctions of the circulatory system), the learner may then experience enjoyment. In this type of positively valenced emotional state, the learner is better poised to approach and succeed in the achievement task (Pekrun, 2006; Pekrun, Goetz, Frenzel, Petra, & Perry, 2011).

CAM Processes Following Learning with MetaTutor

Following the learning session with MetaTutor, the learner may make several cognitive, motivational, and behavioral attributions that affect subsequent learning (Pintrich, 2000; Schunk, 2001). Learners' retrospective emotions may be aroused based on their success or failure regarding goal achievement, as well as motivational factors, such as appraisals of control and value (Pekrun, 2006; Weiner, 1985). For example, if learners were successful in achieving their goal, the control-value theory of achievement emotions predicts that they would experience pride if they cared about the goal (positive value) and felt that they were responsible for their success. Conversely, they would be expected to experience shame if they were unsuccessful, cared about the goal, and felt responsible for their failure. The experience of pride or shame may have motivational consequences. That is, learners may either be more eager to learn about content and do so using the intelligent tutoring system or become less interested in learning and/or interacting with intelligent PAs. In other words, a combination of emotions, perceived task value, and personal explanations for success or failure may influence students' response to the learning environment, feelings about performance, and attitudes toward similar learning situations.

The preceding scenarios represent an idealistic approach to self-regulating one's learning with an ALT, such as MetaTutor. Unfortunately, the typical learner does not engage in all of these adaptive CAM processes during learning with ALTs (see Azevedo & Witherspoon, 2009; Biswas et al., 2010).

Multi-level Processes of SRL During Learning with MetaTutor: Converging Evidence

As a research tool, MetaTutor is capable of measuring the deployment of self-regulatory processes through the collection of rich, multi-stream data, including self-report measures of SRL, online measures of cognitive and metacognitive processes (e.g., concurrent think-alouds), dialogue of agent-student interactions, physiological measures of motivation and emotions, emerging patterns of effective problem-solving behaviors and strategies, facial data on both basic (e.g., anger) and learning-centered emotions (e.g., boredom), and eye-tracking data regarding the selection, organization, and integration of multiple representations of information (e.g., text, diagrams). The collection of these various data streams is critical to enhancing our understanding of when, how, and why students regulate or not their learning and adapt their regulatory behaviors. These data are then used to develop computational models designed to detect, track, model, and foster students' SRL processes during learning (for a review see Azevedo, Moos et al., 2010). In this section, we present data from five different sources that exemplify the complex nature of trace data in terms of frequency of use, level of granularity, temporal sequencing, ease of inference making regarding specific macro-level SRL processes, and the role of context needed, in order to understand how the trace data can augment understanding of conceptual, measurement, and analytical issues. As such, we present data associated with concurrent think-alouds, eye-tracking, note-taking and drawing, log files, and facial detection of emotions.

Concurrent Think-Aloud Protocols: SRL Events Based on Microlevel Processes

Azevedo and colleagues have provided detailed analyses of the dozens of cognitive and metacognitive processes used by learners of all ages (e.g., middle-school, high-school, and college students) when using several ALTs (see Azevedo, 2007; Azevedo, Cromley, Winters, Moos, & Greene, 2005, Azevedo, Moos, Greene, Winters, & Cromley, 2008, Azevedo, Moos et al., 2010; Azevedo et al., 2012a; Azevedo & Witherspoon, 2009; Greene & Azevedo, 2007, 2009). Their analyses of SRL processes during learning with ALTs are of particular relevance since SRL is treated as an event. Their analyses of hundreds of concurrent think-aloud protocols and other process data (e.g., log-file and video analyses) provide detailed evidence of the macro-level (e.g., metacognitive monitoring) and microlevel processes (e.g., JOL) and valence that augments Winne and Hadwin's (1998, 2008) model. In general, these processes include planning, monitoring, strategy use, and handling of task difficulty and demands (see Azevedo, Moos et al., 2010 for details). The conceptual, theoretical, methodological, and analytical assumptions and issues regarding the use of concurrent think-alouds to examine SRL processes are well documented by Azevedo and colleagues (see Azevedo et al., 2005, 2007, 2010; Azevedo & Witherspoon, 2009; Greene & Azevedo, 2007, 2010 for details). In this section, we contextualize our definitions with examples of metacognitive processes typically used with MetaTutor and then present how learners' monitoring processes and corresponding judgments are addressed by regulatory processes.

Monitoring Processes During Learning with MetaTutor

As previously mentioned, Winne and colleagues' model provides a macro-level framework for the cyclical and iterative phases of SRL. The data presented in this section exemplify the microlevel processes that can augment Winne's model. In particular, we present six metacognitive monitoring processes we have identified as essential to promoting students' SRL with MetaTutor. Some of these monitoring processes include valence, positive (+) or negative (−), which indicates the learners' evaluation of the content, their understanding, progress, or familiarity with the material. For example, a learner might state that the current content is either appropriate (positive content evaluation) or inappropriate (negative content evaluation) given their current learning subgoal and valence associated with the evaluation (and accuracy of the metacognitive judgment). They may also make choices about how and which metacognitive regulatory process to choose in order to address the result of the metacognitive judgment (e.g., set a new subgoal, summarize content).

JOL is when a learner becomes aware that he or she does (+) or does not (−) know or understand something just read or inspected (e.g., diagram). Feeling of knowing (FOK) is when the learner is aware of having (+) or having not (−) read, heard, or inspected something in the past (e.g., prior to the learning session) and having (+) or not having (−) some familiarity with the material (e.g., never presented in a previous biology class). Self-test (ST) is when a learner poses a question to himself or herself to assess understanding of the content and determine whether to proceed with additional content or to readjust strategy use. In monitoring progress toward goals (MPTG), learners assess whether previously set goals have been met (+) or not met (−) given particular time constraints. This monitoring process includes a learner comparing the goals set for the learning task (i.e., set during the subgoal phase) with those already accomplished and those that still need to be addressed. A related metacognitive process, time monitoring (TM), involves the learner becoming aware of the remaining time allotted for the learning task. Content evaluation (CE) occurs when a learner monitors the appropriateness (+) or inappropriateness (−) of the current learning content (e.g., text, diagram, or other type of static and dynamic external representation of information) given the overall learning goal and subgoals. In sum, these are just a few of the relevant metacognitive monitoring processes used by students during learning with MetaTutor. Based on our previous discussions of SRL models, these processes play important roles in facilitating and supporting students' SRL with ALTs.

Self-Regulation of Learning Based on Metacognitive Monitoring Processes

In this section, we describe the learner's application of these six monitoring processes within the context of self-regulation with MetaTutor. The processes described in this section are based on empirical findings (e.g., Azevedo et al., 2010, 2012a; Johnson, Azevedo, & D'Mello, 2011). For each monitoring process, we provide the aspects of the learning environment (i.e., MetaTutor) that are evaluated by learners and illustrate them using examples of task and cognitive conditions.

FOK is used when the learner is monitoring the correspondence between his or her own preexisting domain knowledge and the current content. The learner's domain knowledge and the learning resources are the aspects of the learning situation being monitored when a learner engages in FOK. If a learner recognizes a mismatch between preexisting domain knowledge and learning resources (negative valence), more effort should be expended in order to align the knowledge and resources. Following more effortful use of the learning material, a learner is more likely to experience more positive FOKs. However, if a learner experiences familiarity with some piece of material (positive valence), a good self-regulator will attempt to integrate the new information with existing knowledge by summarizing or taking notes. Often, a learner will erroneously make a positive FOK toward material and quickly move on to other material with several misconceptions still intact. These occurrences can be prevented through feedback from the agent based on the results of the quiz administered after FOK (and JOL) to check content understanding.

In contrast to FOK, JOL is used when a learner is monitoring the correspondence between his or her own emerging understanding of the domain and the learning resources. Similar to feelings of knowing, when engaging in JOL, a learner is monitoring domain knowledge and learning resources. If a learner recognizes that his or her emerging understanding of the material is not congruent with the material (i.e., the learner is confused), more effort should be applied to understanding the material. A common strategy employed after a negative JOL is rereading previously encountered material. In order to capitalize on rereading, a good self-regulator should pay particular attention to confusing elements in a textual passage or diagram. When a learner expresses a positive JOL, he or she might self-test to confirm that the knowledge is as accurate as the evaluation suggests. As with FOK, learners often overestimate their emerging understanding and progress too quickly to other material.

Learners apply self-testing (ST) as a way to monitor their emerging understanding of content. When tackling difficult material, learners should occasionally assess their level of understanding of the material by engaging in ST. If the results of this self-test are positive, the learner can progress to new material. If, however, the learner recognizes that emergent understanding is not congruent with what is stated in the material, he or she should revisit the content. Learners can engage in FOK, JOL, and ST using a palette of self-regulating processes available in MetaTutor. When doing so, a learner is provided with a 6-point Likert scale to evaluate knowledge (FOK) or learning (JOL) about the material just read on the current page. Such assessment is then systematically followed by a quiz (ST). The feedback provided by the agent can, therefore, not only be associated with a learner's actual knowledge but also related to the validity of the individual's self-monitoring. Specifically, the agent can indicate situations in which an individual expressed confidence with the material, yet obtained a poor quiz score.

When monitoring progress toward goals (MPTG), a learner is monitoring the fit between learning results and previously set learning goals for the session. Aspects of the learning situation monitored during MPTG are the learner's domain knowledge, expectations of results, and the learning goals. Closely related to time monitoring, MPTG is an essential monitoring activity that learners should use to stay "on track" for the completion of the learning task. A learner may be able to generate several critical subgoals, but if he or she does not monitor their completion or incompletion, the subgoal generation SRL strategy will be inadequate. When a learner monitors goal progress and realizes that only one of three has been accomplished in 75% of the time devoted to the learning task, a good self-regulator will revisit the remaining subgoals and decide which is most important to pursue next. In time monitoring (TM), a learner is monitoring the available time with respect to learning goals. These learning goals can be either the global learning goal defined before engaging in the learning task or subgoals created by the learner during the learning episode. If the learner recognizes that very little time remains and few of the learning goals have been accomplished, adaptations should be made. For example, if a learner has been reading a very long passage for several minutes and realizes that learning goals have not been accomplished, a good self-regulator will begin scanning remaining material for information related to the goals not yet reached. In MetaTutor, learners can use the system interface to prioritize subgoals (e.g., to revisit a current subgoal if there is still time left) or confirm that they have finished learning about a particular subgoal (see Fig. 28.1 for the list of self-set subgoals that are always present). In the latter case, the learner is prompted with a long quiz to help them self-test their understanding of all the materials related to this subgoal. The learner can also monitor progress by referring to a progress bar that indicates the percentage of relevant material reviewed for the current subgoal. Moreover, pages already visited are marked in the table of contents, which can facilitate the scanning strategy if they want to apply it.

When learners engage in content evaluation (CE), they are monitoring the appropriateness of the learning material they are currently reading or viewing with regard to their current subgoal(s). In contrast to CE, evaluation of adequacy of content relates to the learner's assessment of the appropriateness of available learning content, rather than content currently being inspected. The aspects of the learning situations monitored in both of these processes are the learning resources and the learning goals. The learner should remain aware of whether learning goals and learning resources are complementary. If a learner evaluates a particular piece of material as particularly appropriate given their learning goal (positive valence), more cognitive resources should be directed toward this material. Conversely, if particular content is evaluated as inappropriate with respect to a learning goal, a good self-regulator will navigate away from (or simply avoid) this content to seek more appropriate material. A learner can perform CE using the SRL palette, in which case he or she has to state if a particular page and/or image is relevant to the current subgoal. The agent can provide feedback related to the accuracy of this assessment.

In sum, these monitoring processes and corresponding regulatory processes are based on studies examining the role of self-regulatory processes deployed by learners during learning with open-ended hypermedia learning environments. They also play a critical role during learning with other ALTs described in the next section.

Using Eye-Tracking Data to Trace and Infer Self-Regulatory Processes

Eye-tracking has been used extensively in reading research (see Just & Carpenter, 1980; Rayner, 1998), and its use has extended to ALTs, such as multi-agent systems (e.g., Conati & Merten, 2007). Eye-tracking provides fine-grain information about the allocation of a learner's visual attention in terms of what, for how long, and in what order an object is attended to (Scheiter & Van Gog, 2009). The information obtained from this channel is important since the objects, text, or images being fixated on by the eyes indicate that they are being processed in the mind (eye-mind assumption; Just & Carpenter, 1980). Eye-tracking provides us with data that is time-stamped to the millisecond and includes the location and duration of gaze fixation, saccades, pupil diameter, blinks, and gaze behavior patterns. Within MetaTutor, we use the time-stamped data stream and align it with other data sources and channels, including concurrent think-alouds, video footage of a learner's face, and reading behavior. Aligning these data channels allows us to understand how learners perceptually attend and process multimedia materials (e.g., text, diagrams, images, and videos) presented and accessible both linearly and nonlinearly in MetaTutor.

In MetaTutor, where learning material about the human circulatory system is presented in text and diagram format, data from eye-tracking provides valuable information about how learners navigate between the text and diagram(s) (i.e., coordinate informational sources, COIS), how long and how many times they fixate on relevant and irrelevant parts of the text and diagram (e.g., relevant and irrelevant Areas of Interest, AOIs), and how they integrate information presented in multiple representations. These data are critical because they reveal processes often not verbalized by learners in think-aloud protocols (Azevedo, Moos et al., 2010). For example, repeat and prolonged fixations on irrelevant AOIs (e.g., septum) may indicate that the learner does not recognize or understand that the specific part of the diagram is irrelevant. Ideally, PAs in the learning environment should scaffold learners by guiding their attention to relevant material or parts of the interface, which are conducive to the successful completion of the learners' current subgoal. In another example, prolonged fixation on a specific portion of text for which a negative JOL had been made may indicate that the learner is spending time rereading that section to gain a better understanding of the text on that page. This inference needs to be corroborated by examining subsequent behaviors (e.g., clicking the SRL palette to indicate that they understand the textual content or verbalizing a positive JOL). In a similar way, a prolonged fixation after a negative FOK may indicate that the learner has recognized that the material is unfamiliar to them and is spending time to read and learn it more carefully. These metacognitive judgments can be made by learners either by verbalizing in their think-aloud protocol or by clicking on a button in the SRL palette embedded in MetaTutor's interface to indicate that they want to make a judgment. When several channels of data are collected (e.g., think-aloud protocol and eye-tracking) in an experiment, eye-movement traces can be triangulated with think-aloud protocols to investigate different planning, monitoring (e.g., metacognitive judgments), and strategy deployment processes (e.g., rereading, COIS). Analysis of fixation location and duration on different parts of a learning environment's interface can assist in improving the design of the interface and the presentation of the learning material in order to further scaffold learners' SRL.

One of the important channels of data obtained from eye-tracking is pupil diameter. The pupillary response has been associated with increased mental processing activity and task difficulty. Many studies have provided evidence that cognitive processing load is associated with pupil dilation (see reviews by Beatty, 1982, 1988; Hyönä, 1995). According to the working memory model by Just and Carpenter (1992), there is a trade-off between processing demands and cognitive resources, such that when more resources are allocated to one process, less remains for the other. In other words, when processing difficult and complex learning material, there will be a higher processing load on the working memory, which will allow only limited resources to be free for attending to higher-order processes like metacognition. Investigating pupil dilation data obtained from eye-tracking can be helpful in identifying the instances during the learning task requiring high cognitive processing, which will assist in developing metacognitive scaffolds that can help learners manage their available cognitive resources, direct their actions (e.g., rereading difficult or misunderstood material), and off-load their working memory by using effective learning strategies (e.g., taking notes).

Note-Taking and Drawing: Integrating Knowledge During Learning

Although there are many SRL processes that students may deploy to facilitate learning, note-taking and drawing provide important opportunities for learners to synthesize information and build coherent mental representations of the material. Within an SRL framework, note-taking and drawing represent instantiations of SRL strategies that may vary in quantity (e.g., frequency and duration) and quality (e.g., depth of cognitive processing). As such, not all learners engage in these processes in the same way. For instance, different note-taking patterns or drawing behaviors may emerge according to the degree of metacognitive monitoring, instructional support, and learners' level of prior knowledge (Moos & Azevedo, 2008). To better understand the relations between these types of strategies and learning outcomes within MetaTutor, note-taking and drawing events are collected as trace data while students interact with the learning environment. The following section describes how these data are collected within MetaTutor, the analytical approaches employed by our research team, and the potential of these data sources to improve scaffolding and advance our understanding of SRL within ALTs.

An instructional video is displayed at the beginning of the learning session with MetaTutor to advise students about the note-taking and drawing features available throughout the session. Learners can take notes in two ways: (1) by selecting the note-taking feature from the SRL palette embedded within MetaTutor and (2) by pen and paper using a digital notepad located on the desk beside the computer. Learners can also use this notepad to draw diagrams. Each time the learner selects the take notes (TN) button on the palette, a new window appears for learners to type notes. There are three tabs associated with this feature. The tab that automatically displays is page notes. Notes under this tab are associated with the page the learner is currently viewing. Under the page note overview tab, learners can view a list of pages associated with their notes. There is also a general notes tab available for learners to take notes that are not directly associated with a particular page. Learners can select save and close to exit this window and return to it at a later time.

The note-taking feature is entirely learner-initiated (i.e., agents do not prompt activation of this learning strategy). In contrast, learners receive prompts from a PA to draw at various points throughout the session. Specifically, when a learner has viewed a relevant page, but has not opened the image associated with the page, he or she is prompted within 45 s to draw. Students are also prompted to draw after they have had an image open for 96 s. These prompts are referred to as coordinating informational sources as they encourage students to integrate multiple sources of information, such as text and images, by drawing visual representations.

Time-stamped log files capture learners' note-taking and drawing events for subsequent analyses. For example, if a learner draws a diagram on the notepad, a record is created in the log file to indicate the time of occurrence and duration of the event. Thus, the frequency and duration can be captured to provide process data in relation to other SRL events and materials that the learner viewed before and after the drawing was created. Furthermore, the hard copy of a learner's diagram can be analyzed for quality and potential misconceptions related to the topic. Similarly, notes typed in the note-taking viewer are also time-stamped and stored in the log files. These types of data can also be analyzed in relation to other SRL process and learning outcomes, including posttest scores.

There are several approaches to analyzing note-taking and drawing within an SRL framework. In previous research (e.g., Trevors, Duffy, & Azevedo, 2011), we have extracted log-file data to obtain frequencies of note-taking episodes (measured by the number of times participants selected TN from the SRL palette), as well as experimental conditions, learning efficiency scores, prior knowledge, and note-taking text. Notes can be segmented into idea units or naturalist segments (Chi, 1997) and subsequently coded for quality using theoretically grounded coding schemes. For example, we have used depth of cognitive processing frameworks (see Entwistle & Peterson, 2004) to determine whether a segment of notes represents either content reproduction (i.e., verbatim copying of the text) or elaboration (i.e., text-based or prior knowledge-based inferences). Video and screen recordings can also be used during coding to determine whether notes represent a deep or shallow level of strategy use. For example, while evaluating a participant's notes, these recordings can be played to determine which section of text the participant viewed and what types of verbalizations were made during note-taking. This allows coders to verify whether the participant integrated ideas from multiple sections or copied the text verbatim. Based on these analyses, we have found that students frequently engage in content reproduction (i.e., shallow processing), which is negatively related to achievement. Furthermore, although the presence of agents resulted in decreased note-taking behaviors among low prior knowledge learners, the agents did not effectively promote more adaptive note-taking strategies, such as elaboration. As a result, we have modified the architecture of MetaTutor to scaffold deeper level note-taking strategies through modeling and prompts from PAs. Moving forward with this research, future analyses may also involve examining learners' drawing behaviors in relation to note-taking strategies and learning outcomes. Moreover, triangulating these events with eye-tracking and think-aloud data could help to provide a more detailed analysis of the role of note-taking and drawing for SRL. For instance, eye-tracking data would allow us to systematically analyze exactly which sentences or images were viewed before, during, and after note-taking and drawing. Additionally, analyses of think-aloud data may allow us to determine whether there were specific types of metacognitive processes that prompted these learning strategies.

Log Files: Event-Based Traces During System Interaction

Within ALTs, log files provide a time-stamped record of every key stroke and mouse click on system features made by the learner. From this unobtrusive source of data, a great many inferences can be made into learners' real-time cognitive and metacognitive processes (e.g., Aleven et al., 2010; Malmberg, Jarvenoja, & Jarvela, 2010; Schoor & Bannert, 2012). MetaTutor log files collect hundreds of user- and system-initiated actions every millisecond during a learning session. Computerized log files provide an automatic record of learners' interactions with the system, which includes, but is not limited to, natural language input by the learner, questionnaire, quiz, and test responses; mouse clicks on any system feature (e.g., concept maps); the frequency and duration of all seven of MetaTutor's interface layouts viewed by the learner; metacognitive judgments; time spent on individual content pages; time spent with individual diagrams visible; and the use of any external equipment connected to the system (e.g., digital writing pad). Additionally, log files also record all events performed by the system. In MetaTutor, this includes learner-agent dialogue moves, text of verbal instructions, feedback, and scaffolding by the four PAs or any system-initiated event, such as the onset of testing, summarizing, or comprehension monitoring activities. In addition, the exact learner- and system-initiated rules triggered by several conditions (e.g., time thresholds) are also logged in the file.

Given the broad scope of information contained in log files, researchers are able to know, for example, how long a learner spent viewing an instructional text, how often he or she went back and forth between the text and related diagram or video, and the frequency and content of summarizations (or other learning products). Furthermore, log files provide a transcription of a PA's instructions to the learner to evaluate understanding of the current content, the administration and results of a quiz, and the feedback based on the accuracy of the learner's subjective self-evaluations of comprehension vis-à-vis objective quiz results.

Careful tailoring of system design and features, as described in the example above, can provide evidence of learners' cognitive and metacognitive processes while minimizing inferences made by researchers. At the cognitive level, the duration of viewing instructional text can be inferred as time spent reading. Likewise, all things being equal, a longer reading time is evidence of increased cognitive processing of textual content (Lorch & van den Brock, 1997; O'Brien, 1995; Zwann & Singer, 2003). Reading times can be affected by the inclusion of multiple representations of information (van Someren, Reimann, Boshuizen, & de Jong, 1998) or conflicting information (Albrecht & O'Brien, 1993; Cook, Halleran, & O'Brien, 1998). Navigating to and viewing related multimedia can be considered as an attempt to integrate multiple representations of informational sources. At the metacognitive level, features or sequences of events can be designed to promote and record self-monitoring and self-regulation of cognition. For example, Table 28.1 depicts the interactions between a learner and MetaTutor during a sequence of scaffolded monitoring. In this table, the first and second columns represent numbered events with associated time stamps during the session (in milliseconds), respectively. The third and fourth columns depict the layout number and title (e.g., Student Input). Lastly (or finally), the fourth and fifth columns are a record of activities as well as the student input and agent output. In this example, a PA prompts the learner to reflect on his or her comprehension of the current content after navigating away from the page too quickly to read (e.g., < 7 s). At entry 619, the learner rates her understanding as 5 (on the 6-point Likert scale described earlier) or higher. She obtains a high quiz score, for which he or she receives positive feedback and encouragement from the agent to move onto new content at entry 632. For researchers, this episode is evidence of a calibrated metacognitive judgment, onto which various analytical procedures can be applied.

Specifically, educational data mining techniques provide new opportunities for researchers to represent internal cognitive and metacognitive states and their interactions. Biswas et al. (2010) describe hidden Markov modeling (HMM) as an analytical method to discern mental states and probabilistic transitions between these states, such as transitioning from the creation of a learning product to a monitoring state. Although these states cannot be directly recorded in log files, they are ascertained on the basis of learner's

Table 28.1 A 1-min excerpt of a log file depicting a learner's judgment of learning, quiz results, and positive feedback from a pedagogical agent, Mary

614	5310156	2	0	AdaptiveRules	[JOL] (rule: Prompt JOL when page is changing sooner than enough) Starting action: MonitoringFlow (JOLHowWell)
615	5310171	3	Mary	MaryJOLRating	How well do you feel that you understand the content you have read on this page?
616	5310187	8	Mary	MaryJOLRating	Start
617	5310203	7	Input with content	907	
618	5316031	8	Mary	MaryJOLRating	Stop
619	5317453	3	StudentInput	NA	5
620	5317468	2	0	MonitoringFlow	Begin quiz for page 11
621	5317468	7	InputEnlarged	172	
622	5317484	3	Mary	QuizStarted	Let's take a short quiz on this content to see how well you understood
623	5317484	8	Mary	QuizStarted	Start
624	5322031	8	Mary	QuizStarted	Stop
625	5335843	3	StudentInput	NA	1
626	5335859	4	Page12_5	NearMiss	Inference—no
627	5344734	3	StudentInput	NA	3
628	5344750	4	Page12_6	Target	Inference—yes
629	5351546	3	StudentInput	NA	3
630	5351546	4	Page12_2	Target	Text-based—yes
631	5351562	7	InputWith Content	266	
632	5351562	3	Mary	MaryJOLHighCorrect ConfidenceFeedback	Very good. You got a high score on the quiz. Since you seem to understand this stuff pretty well, should we move on to another page?
633	5351593	8	Mary	MaryJOLHighCorrect ConfidenceFeedback	Start
634	5360031	8	Mary	MaryJOLHighCorrect ConfidenceFeedback	Stop

recordable interactions within ALTs; multiple monitoring activities, such as the JOL in Table 28.1, can be grouped together to form the basis for one state, thus providing a higher-level perspective on log-file data (Biswas et al., 2010). Similarly, cluster analysis can group learners across a large number of variables (i.e., multivariate differences), discerning what similar patterns of learner interactions are more and less effective within MetaTutor (Bouchet, Harley, Trevors, & Azevedo, 2012; Bouchet, Kinnebrew, Biswas, & Azevedo, 2012). Latent profile analysis (LPA), latent class analysis (LCA), and latent growth modeling (LGM) are additional analytic techniques that hold great promise for using log-file data to model intraindividual changes during the learning session. These techniques permit the identification of individual growth curves (trajectories) with the opportunity of identifying particular groups/classes of similar curves. Employing these analytical techniques with log-file data provides insight into dynamic cognitive and metacognitive processes not gained with traditional analysis, such as simple frequency counts or pre-post scores alone.

The use of any single data source to understand phenomena as complex as learning has inherent limitations. First, the strength of log-file data rests on the degree to which the system's features and analytic techniques are grounded in a theory of learning. Data from Table 28.1 are meaningful because an explicit decision was made to design a system feature to measure calibration of metacognitive judgment, which can then be analyzed with other monitoring behavior as a reflection of an underlying mental state. Weaker empirical conclusions result from a lack of theoretical explicitness in system design and data analysis. Second, log files are only one limited perspective of the events that occur in a learning session. What information was the learner attending to when making an initial JOL? What influence, if any, would positive or negative feedback have on the learner's subsequent cognitive, metacognitive, affective, or motivational processes? To answer these relevant questions, researchers need greater context than log files can provide. These issues speak to the need to integrate multiple streams of data to generate defensible inferences about relevant learning processes. In sum, we address these issues by triangulating multiple streams of data (i.e., concurrent think-alouds, eye-tracking, note-taking behavior) during learning with MetaTutor.

Emotional Attribution Through Facial Expression Analyses

In addition to the emerging use and convergence of data streams to understand and measure cognitive and metacognitive processes, we have also begun to collect and examine video data of students' facial expressions during learning with MetaTutor. This data stream is vital, in that it provides a new data source necessary to understand the fluctuations in students' emotions during learning. Facial expressions are configurations of different micro-motor (small muscle) movements in the face, which are used to infer a person's discrete emotional state. Facial expressions have been a popular and well-researched method for analyzing participants' emotional states for decades (Ekman & Friesen, 1978, 2003), and to this day they remain one of the most widely used, as well as one of the most theoretically and empirically grounded emotional measurement channels (Arroyo et al., 2009; Calvo & D'Mello, 2010, 2011; D'Mello & Graesser, 2010; Ekman, 1992; Zeng, Pantic, Roisman, & Huang, 2009). Accordingly, facial expression analysis has been the primary method through which we have detected and traced learners' experience of emotions throughout their learning session with MetaTutor (Azevedo & Chauncey Strain, 2011; Harley, Bouchet, & Azevedo, 2011; Harley, Bouchet, & Azevedo, 2011, 2012a, 2012b).

Our work analyzing emotions has utilized Noldus FaceReader™ 3.0 and 4.0, a software program that analyzes learners' facial expressions and provides a classification of their emotional states. The program uses an active appearance model to match and track learners' faces and then relies on an artificial neural network trained on a database of high-quality facial images from 70 individuals (Lundqvist, Flykt, & Öhman, 1998) acting out Ekman and Friesen's six basic emotions (Ekman, 1992) in addition to a neutral emotion. FaceReader has been validated through comparison with human coders' ratings of basic emotions (Terzis, Moridis, & Economides, 2010) and specified acted emotions (Van Kuilenburg, Wiering, & Den Uyl 2005).

Additionally, using an automatic facial recognition software program confers us the advantage of analyzing learners' facial expressions much faster than if we were to use Ekman and Friesen's Facial Action Coding System (FACS; Ekman & Friesen, 1978, 2003), which is highly human-resource intensive to use, train, and certify coders. In short, FaceReader is able to code more data than would be possible with human coders. For example, in a recent analysis we examined a sample of 50 learners engaging with one of MetaTutor's PAs during the subgoal setting phase of the learning episode (M=2m22s, SD=1m10s). During this short portion of the learning session, FaceReader was able to make 224,582 emotional state classifications, each corresponding to a different video frame of footage of a learner engaging with MetaTutor (Harley, Bouchet, & Azevedo, 2012b).

The preceding example highlights another FaceReader asset: the ability to act as a macro- and micro-measurement tool. In other words, FaceReader can be used to examine incremental transitions in emotional states that occur less than a second apart while also being able to summarize the prominence of different emotional states occurring over a time span that ranges for 2 h (in our application) without comprising its validity or reliability. Being able to examine emotions data continuously at multiple levels is crucial to examining emotions as a dynamic, rapidly changing psychological process (Ekman, 1992).

The primary disadvantage of using FaceReader is that its analyses of facial expressions is limited to basic, universal emotions (Ekman & Friesen 1978, 2003), which do not represent the whole scope of emotions relevant to learning with MetaTutor. Most notably, basic emotions exclude learning-centered emotions, such as boredom and confusion (D'Mello, Craig, & Graesser, 2009; Pekrun, 2006; McQuiggan, Robinson, & Lester, 2008). To capture these emotions, one would need to either develop a new coding scheme, add to an existing coding scheme (e.g., Craig, D'Mello, Witherspoon, & Graesser, 2007), or make use of additional emotional channels (Calvo & D'Mello, 2010, 2011; Mauss & Robinson, 2009; Zeng, Pantic, Roisman, & Huang, 2009), as we are doing. A potential additional disadvantage to FaceReader is the fact that the database is formed from acted, as opposed to naturally occurring, emotions. Given that humans are not able to control all their facial muscles efficiently (Ekman, 2003), it is possible that some subtle differences, such as artificially limited micro-motor muscle variance, may exist between posed and naturally embodied facial expressions. It should be noted, however, that capturing high-quality images of natural, unfolding emotions from multiple angles would be technically challenging without distracting participants and interfering with the emotions one is trying to measure. It should also be noted that these limitations might be more problematic for more subtle emotional states, such as boredom and curiosity, than higher intensity expressions, such as anger and sadness.

We conclude this section by identifying some of the specific features and opportunities regarding FaceReader through a guided tour of several components of FaceReader's online interface presented in Fig. 28.2. In the top left-hand corner of Fig. 28.2, the analysis visualization window, we can see the active appearance model FaceReader uses to model participants' faces, as well as the video quality bar, which is at an acceptable threshold. The top right-hand corner displays the emotional valence (experience of positive or negative emotions). One can see from this window that the learner has spent, from the duration of time shown, most of her visible learning session experiencing negatively valenced emotions (e.g., sadness, anger). The bottom right window illustrates the proportions of the different discrete emotions the learner has experienced, which tell us that she has embodied, during the time her video has been analyzed, a fairly equal proportion of surprise, anger, sadness, and neutrality. The bottom left expression window shows the onset and offset of the different discrete emotions, transitions between different emotional states, and that at times, different discrete emotional states that are co-occurring together (occurring simultaneously) (Harley et al., 2012a). The latter half of this window provides an example in which the learner suddenly embodies an intense surprised expression, which degrades slightly and is accompanied by a short accompanying peak of anger. We can interpret from these data that something in the learning environment (e.g., PA feedback) surprised the learner and also made her feel angry, though the experience of anger was fleeting (possibly because the learner successfully downregulated this negative emotion). FaceReader is a rich source of data, especially when combined with other data channels (e.g., log files), which allows us to identify the context in which learners are experiencing their emotions.

Summary and Conclusions

Early in this chapter we noted that MetaTutor is both a research tool and a learning tool. One of the objectives of this chapter has been to demonstrate the interconnectedness of these functions and the capacity for enhancing learning with MetaTutor. One of the chief strengths of MetaTutor is the multitude of different channels available for collecting and analyzing learners' interactions with the system. Going forward, we are exploring the addition of new channels as well as exploring new features of existing channels and how they can be aligned to provide an ever deeper and more contextualized understanding of students'

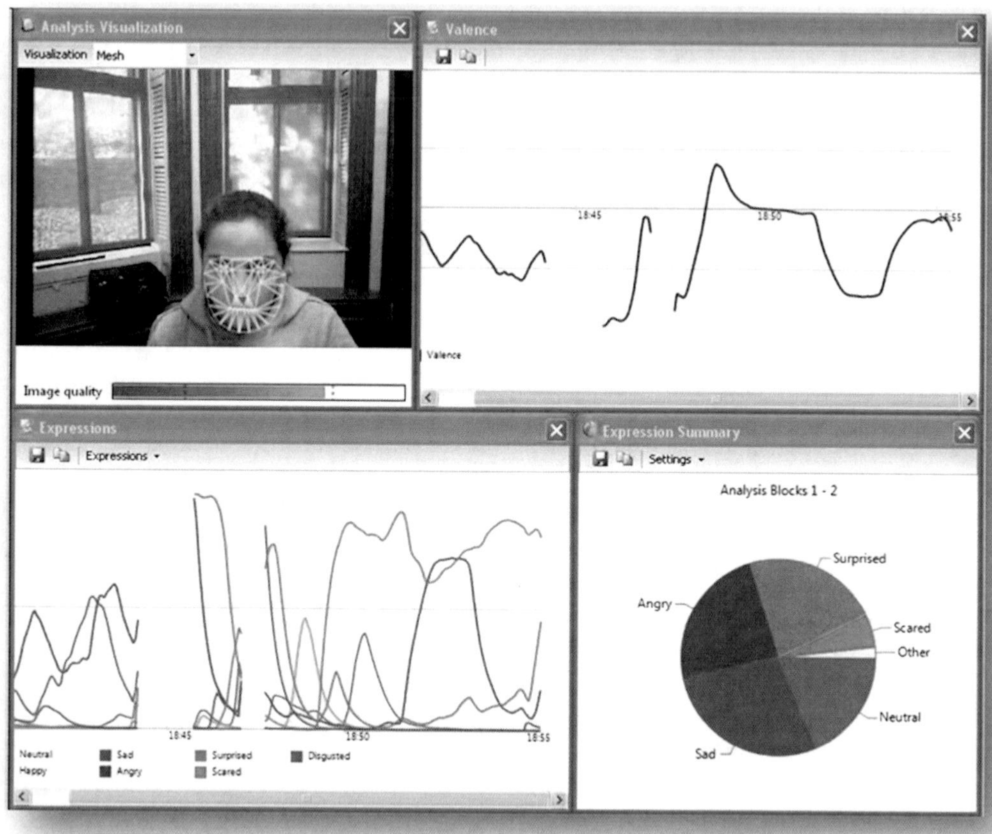

Fig. 28.2 FaceReader™ 4.0 interface

learning and co-regulation with MetaTutor. We conclude this chapter by outlining some of the future directions we are currently pursuing and have planned for MetaTutor.

Developments regarding measuring and understanding learners' experiences of affect and motivation represent one of the primary and broadest future directions for MetaTutor. Our analyses, which have focused on basic emotion facial expression analyses, are being expanded to include physiological measures of emotions (e.g., galvanic skin response and pupil dilation) as well as human-rater and self-report measures. These new methods for measuring emotion will provide us with the means to investigate convergent evidence for emotional states across a variety of different affective dimensions, including arousal, valence, discrete, and co-occurring emotions (Conati & Maclaren, 2009; Harley et al., 2012a; Hess & Polt, 1960; Lang, Greenwald, Bradley, & Hamm, 1993; Portala & Surakka, 2003). Some of these methods, including self-report and human-rater (based on a coding scheme that we are developing), will allow us to expand our analyses from basic emotions to include learner-centered ones. In addition, by having access to emotional data that are prospective, state (including trace), retrospective, and trait in nature, we will be able to explore dynamic fluctuations in emotions with a contextualized understanding of antecedents (e.g., co-regulation between PA and learner, trait emotions, motivations). Another component of our research that investigates the nature of emotions is analyzing (including pioneering ways to do so) learners' experience of co-occurring (i.e., simultaneous experience of) different discrete emotions (Harley et al., 2012a). These developments will be used to enhance learners' experience with MetaTutor by providing recommendations for adapting the system, such as PA's dialogue and behavior (e.g., facial expression) changes, as well as contributing to the development of a more comprehensive theory of SRL in terms of the role of affect and emotions.

Finally, as more channels of information become available, it will be even more crucial to align and merge them together in order to obtain an accurate overview of students' experience when learning with MetaTutor. Considering the richness of the collected data, educational data mining approaches will be particularly useful in order to (a) group students into different categories according to similarities in their browsing behavior and use of SRL processes; (b) extract from trace logs of the different data channels some patterns of browsing action, emotions, and/or eye movements that are characteristics of these categories of students; and (c) identify in which of those categories future students belong to in real time in order to provide them with the most relevant agents' feedback and scaffolding strategies (Bouchet, Harley et al., 2012).

In summary, we emphasized the importance of using multichannel trace data to examine the complex roles of CAM self-regulatory processes deployed by students during learning with multi-agent systems. We also argued that tracing these processes as they unfold in real time is key to understanding how they contribute both individually and together to learning. In addition, we described MetaTutor (a multi-agent, intelligent hypermedia system) and how it can be used to facilitate learning of complex biological topics and as a research tool to examine the role of CAM processes used by learners. We also provided a theoretical perspective and underlying assumptions of SRL as an event; we provided empirical evidence from five different trace data to exemplify how these diverse data sources can be used to understand the complexity of CAM processes and their relation to learning. Lastly, we provided implications for future research of ALTs that focus on examining the role of CAM processes during SRL with these powerful technological environments.

Acknowledgements The research presented in this chapter has been supported by funding from the National Science Foundation (DRL 0633918 and IIS 0841835) and the Social Sciences and Humanities Research Council of Canada (430-2011-0170) awarded to the first author and (DRL 1008282) awarded to the last author.

References

Albrecht, J. E., & O'Brien, E. J. (1993). Updating a mental model: Maintaining both local and global coherence. *Journal of Experimental Psychology: Learning, Memory, and Cognition, 19*, 1061–1069.

Aleven, V., Roll, I., McLaren, B. M., & Koedinger, K. R. (2010). Automated, unobtrusive, action-by-action assessment of self-regulation during learning with an intelligent tutoring system. *Educational Psychologist, 45*, 224–233.

Ames, C. (1992). Classrooms: Goals structures and student motivation. *Journal of Educational Psychology, 84*, 261–271.

Ames, C., & Archer, J. (1988). Achievement goals in the classroom: Students' learning strategies and motivation processes. *Journal of Educational Psychology, 80*, 260–267.

Arroyo, I., Woolf, B., Cooper, D., Burleson, W., Muldner, K., & Christopherson, R. (2009). Emotion sensors go to school. In V. Dimitrova, R. Mizoguchi, B. du Boulay, & A. Graesser (Eds.), *Proceedings of the International Conference on Artificial Intelligence in Education* (pp. 17–24). Amsterdam, The Netherlands: Ios Press.

Azevedo, R. (2007). Understanding the complex nature of self-regulated learning processes in learning with computer-based learning environments: An introduction. *Metacognition and Learning, 2*(2/3), 57–65.

Azevedo, R., & Chauncey-Strain, A. C. (2011). Integrating cognitive, metacognitive, and affective regulatory processes with MetaTutor. In R. A. Calvo & S. D'Mello (Eds.), *New perspectives on affect and learning technologies* (pp. 141–154). New York: Springer.

Azevedo, R., Cromley, J. G., Moos, D. C., Greene, J. A., & Winters, F. I. (2011). Adaptive content and process scaffolding: A key to facilitating students' self-regulated learning with hypermedia. *Psychological Testing and Assessment Modeling, 53*, 106–140.

Azevedo, R., Cromley, J. G., Winters, F. I., Moos, D. C., & Greene, J. A. (2005). Adaptive human scaffolding facilitates adolescents' self-regulated learning with hypermedia. *Instructional Science, 33*, 381–412.

Azevedo, R., & Feyzi-Behnagh, R. (2011). Dysregulated learning with advanced learning technologies. *Journal of e-Learning and Knowledge Society, 7*(2), 9–18.

Azevedo, R., Johnson, A., Chauncey, A., & Burkett, C. (2010). Self-regulated learning with MetaTutor: Advancing the science of learning with MetaCognitive tools. In M. Khine & I. Saleh (Eds.), *New science of learning: Computers, cognition, and collaboration in education* (pp. 225–247). Amsterdam: Springer.

Azevedo, R., Moos, D. C., Johnson, A. M., & Chauncey, A. D. (2010). Measuring cognitive and metacognitive regulatory processes during hypermedia learning: Issues and challenges. *Educational Psychologist, 45*, 210–223.

Azevedo, R., Johnson, A. M., Chauncey, A., & Graesser, A. (2011). Use of hypermedia to assess and convey self-regulated learning. In B. Zimmerman & D. Schunk (Eds.), *Handbook of self-regualtion of learning and performance* (pp. 102–121). New York: Routledge.

Azevedo, R., Feyzi-Behnagh, R., Duffy, M., Harley, J., & Trevors, G. (2012). Metacognition and self-regulated learning in student-centered leaning environments. In D. Jonassen & S. Land (Eds.), *Theoretical foundations of student-center learning environments* (2nd ed., pp. 171–197). New York: Routledge.

Azevedo, R., Landis, R. S., Feyzi-Behnagh, R., Duffy, M., Trevors, G., Harley, J., Hossain, G. (2012b). *The effectiveness of pedagogical agents' prompting and feedback in facilitating co-adapted learning with MetaTutor*. Paper presented at the 11th International Conference on Intelligent Tutoring Systems, Crete, Greece.

Azevedo, R., Bouchet, F., Feyzi-Behnagh, R., Harley, J., Duffy, M., & Trevors, G. (2012c). *MetaTutor as an innovative technology environment to assess students' self-regulatory processes*. Paper to be presented at a Symposium on Knowing What Students Know and Feel: Innovative Technology Rich Assessments at the annual meeting of the American Educational Research Association, Vancouver, British Columbia, Canada.

Azevedo, R., Moos, D. C., Greene, J. A., Winters, F. I., & Cromley, J. G. (2008). Why is externally-facilitated regulated learning more effective than self-regulated learning with hypermedia? *Educational Technology Research and Development, 56*(1), 45–72.

Azevedo, R., & Witherspoon, A. M. (2009). Self-regulated learning with hypermedia. In D. J. Hacker, J. Dunlosky, & A. C. Graesser (Eds.), *Handbook of metacognition in education* (pp. 319–339). Mahwah, NJ: Routledge.

Beatty, J. (1982). Task-evoked pupillary responses, processing load, and the structure of processing resources. *Psychological Bulletin, 91*(2), 276–292.

Beatty, J. (1988). Situational and predispositional correlates of public speaking anxiety. *Communication Education, 37*(1), 28–39.

Biswas, G., Jeong, H., Kinnebrew, J., Sulcer, B., & Roscoe, R. (2010). Measuring self-regulated learning skills through social interactions in a teachable agent environment. *Research and Practice in Technology-Enhanced Learning, 5*(2), 123–152.

Boekaerts, M. (2011). Emotions, emotion regulation, and self-regulation of learning. In B. Zimmerman & D. Schunk (Eds.), *Handbook of self-regulation of learning and performance* (pp. 408–425). New York: Routledge.

Boekaerts, M., Pintrich, P., & Zeidner, M. (2000). *Handbook of self-regulation*. San Diego, CA: Academic.

Bouchet, F., Harley, J., Trevors, G., & Azevedo, R. (2012). Clustering and profiling students according to their interactions with an intelligent tutoring system fostering self-regulated learning. *Journal of Educational Data Mining*.

Bouchet, F., Kinnebrew, J. S., Biswas, G., & Azevedo, R. (2012). Identifying students' characteristic learning behaviors in an intelligent tutoring system fostering self-regulated learning. Paper presented at the 5th International Conference on Educational Data Mining, Chania, Greece.

Bromme, R., Pieschl, S., & Stahl, E. (2010). Epistemological beliefs are standards for adaptive learning: A functional theory about epistemological beliefs and metacognition. *Metacognition and Learning, 5*(1), 7–26.

Butler, D., & Winne, P. (1995). Feedback and self-regulated learning: A theoretical synthesis. *Review of Educational Research, 65*(3), 245–281.

Calvo, R. A., & D'Mello, S. (2010). Affect detection: An interdisciplinary review of models, methods, and their applications. *IEEE Transactions on Affective Computing, 1*, 18–37.

Calvo, R. A., & D'Mello, S. K. (Eds.). (2011). *New perspectives on affect and learning technologies*. New York: Springer.

Chi, M. T. H. (1997). Quantifying qualitative analyses of verbal data: A practical guide. *Journal of Learning Sciences, 6*, 271–315.

Conati, C., & Maclaren, H. (2009). Empirically building and evaluating a probabilistic model of user affect. *User Modeling and User-Adapted Interaction, 19*, 267–303.

Conati, C., & Merten, C. (2007). Eye-tracking for user modeling in exploratory learning environments: An empirical evaluation. *Knowledge Based Systems, 20*(6), Elsevier Science Publishers B. V. Amsterdam, The Netherlands.

Cook, A. E., Halleran, J. G., & O'Brien, E. J. (1998). What is readily available during reading? A memory-based view of text processing. *Discourse Process, 26*, 109–129.

Craig, S., D'Mello, S., Witherspoon, A., & Graesser, A. (2007). Emote aloud during learning with AutoTutor: Applying the Facial Action Coding System to cognitive-affective states during learning. *Cognition and Emotion, 22*, 777–788.

D'Mello, K. S., Craig, S. D., & Graesser, A. C. (2009). Multimethod assessment of affective experience and expression during deep learning. *International Journal of Learning Technology, 4*(3/4), 165–187.

D'Mello, S., & Graesser, A. C. (2010). Multimodal semi-automated affect detection from conversational cues, gross body language, and facial features. *User Modeling and User-adapted Interaction, 20*(2), 147–187.

Dahl, T. I., Bals, M., & Turi, A. L. (2005). Are students' beliefs about knowledge and learning associated with their reported use of learning strategies? *British Journal of Educational Psychology, 75*, 257–273.

Dunlosky, J., & Lipko, A. R. (2007). Metacomprehension: A brief history and how to improve its accuracy. *Current Directions in Psychological Science, 16*(4), 228–232.

Efklides, A. (2011). Interactions of metacognition with motivation and affect in self-regulated learning: The MASRL model. *Educational Psychologist, 46*, 6–25.

Ekman, P. (1992). An argument for basic emotions. *Cognition and Emotion, 6*, 169.

Ekman, P. (2003). *The face revealed*. London: Weidenfeld & Nicolson.

Ekman, P., & Friesen, W. V. (1978). *Facial action coding system: A technique for the measurement of facial movement*. Palo Alto, CA: Consulting Psychologists Press.

Ekman, P., & Friesen, W. V. (2003). Unmasking the face. A guide to recognizing emotions from facial clues. Los Altos, CA: Malor Books. Retrieved from http://google.com/books (Original work published 1975).

Entwistle, N. J., & Peterson, E. R. (2004). Conceptions of learning and knowledge in higher education: Relationships with study behaviour and influences of learning environments. *International Journal of Educational Research, 41*, 407–428.

Feyzi-Behnagh, R., Khezri, Z., & Azevedo, R. (2011). An investigation of accuracy of metacognitive judgments during learning with an intelligent multi-agent hypermedia environment. In L. Carlson, C. Hoelscher, & T. Shipley (Eds.), *Proceedings of the 33rd Annual Conference of the Cognitive Science Society* (pp. 96–101). Austin, TX: Cognitive Science Society.

Greene, J. A., & Azevedo, R. (2007). A theoretical review of Winne and Hadwin's model of self-regulated learning: New perspectives and directions. *Review of Educational Research, 77*, 334–372.

Greene, J. A., & Azevedo, R. (2009). A macro-level analysis of SRL processes and their relations to the acquisition of sophisticated mental models. *Contemporary Educational Psychology, 34*, 18–29.

Greene, J. A., & Azevedo, R. (2010). The measurement of learners' self-regulated cognitive and metacognitive processes while using computer-based learning environments. *Educational Psychologist, 45*, 203–209.

Greene, J. A., Moos, D. C., & Azevedo, R. (2011). Self-regulated learning with computer-based learning environments. *New Directions for Teaching and Learning, 126*, 107–115.

Gross, J. J., Sheppes, G., & Urry, H. L. (2011). Emotion generation and emotion regulation: A distinction we should make (carefully). *Cognition and Emotion, 25*(5), 765–781.

Harley, J., Bouchet, F., & Azevedo, R. (2011). Examining learner's emotional responses to pedagogical agents' tutoring strategies. In H. Högni Vilhjálmsson, S. Koop, S. Marsella, & K. R. Thórisson (Eds.), *Lecture notes in artificial intelligence: subseries of lecture notes in computer science: Vol: 6895. Intelligent virtual agents (IVA)* (pp. 449–450). Berlin, Germany: Springer.

Harley, J., Bouchet, F., & Azevedo, R. (2012a). Measuring learners' co-occurring emotional responses during their interaction with a pedagogical agent in MetaTutor. In S. A. Cerri, W. J. Clancey, G. Papadourakis, & K. Panourgia. *Lecture notes in computer science: Vol: 7315. Intelligent tutoring systems* (pp. 40–45). Berlin, Heidelberg: Springer.

Harley, J., Bouchet, F., & Azevedo, R. (2012b). *Measuring learners' unfolding, discrete emotional responses to different pedagogical agents scaffolding strategies*. Paper presented at the annual meeting of the American Educational Research Association, Vancouver, British Columbia, Canada

Hess, E. H., & Polt, J. M. (1960). Pupil size as related to interest value of visual stimuli. *Science, 132*, 349–50.

Hulleman, C. S., Schrager, S. H., Bodmann, S. M., & Harackiewicz, J. M. (2010). A meta-analytic review of achievement goal measures: Different labels for the same constructs or different constructs with similar labels? *Psychological Bulletin, 136*, 422–449.

Hyönä, J. (1995). An eye-movement analysis of topic-shift effect during repeated reading. *Journal of Experimental Psychology: Learning, Memory, and Cognition, 21*, 1365–1373.

Johnson, A. M., Azevedo, R., & D'Mello, S. K. (2011). The temporal and dynamic nature of self-regulatory processes during independent and externally assisted hypermedia learning. *Cognition and Instruction, 29*(4), 471–504.

Just, M. A., & Carpenter, P. A. (1980). A theory of reading: From eye fixations to comprehension. *Psychological Review, 87*(4), 329–354.

Lang, P. J., Greenwald, M. K., Bradley, M. M., & Hamm, A. O. (1993). Looking at pictures: affective, facial, visceral, and behavioral reactions. *Psychophysiology, 30*(30), 261–273.

Lorch, R. E. J., & van den Broek, P. (1997). Understanding reading comprehension: Current and future contributions to cognitive science. *Contemporary Educational Psychology, 22*, 213–246.

Lundqvist, D., Flykt, A., & Öhman, A. (1998). *The Karolinska directed emotional faces* [KDEF, CD ROM]. Department of Clinical Neuroscience, Psychology section, Karolinska Institute. ISBN: 91-630-7164-9.

Malmberg, J., Jarvenoja, H., & Jarvela, S. (2010). Tracing elementary school students' study tactic use in gStudy by examining a strategic and self-regulated learning. *Computers in Human Behavior, 26*, 1034–1042.

Mauss, I. B., & Robinson, M. D. (2009). Measures of emotion: A review. *Cognition and Emotion, 23*, 209–237.

McQuiggan, S., Robinson, J., & Lester, J. (2008). Affective transitions in narrative-centered learning environments. *Educational Technology and Society, 13*(1), 40–53.

Metcalfe, J., & Dunlosky, J. (2008). Metamemory. In H. Roediger (Ed.), *Cognitive psychology of memory* (Vol. 2). Oxford: Elsevier.

Moos, D. C., & Azevedo, R. (2008). Self-regulated learning with hypermedia: The role of prior domain knowledge. *Contemporary Educational Psychology, 33*, 270–298.

Muis, K. R. (2007). The role of epistemic beliefs in self-regulated learning. *Educational Psychologist, 42*(3), 173–190.

Muis, K. R., & Franco, G. (2009). Epistemic beliefs: Setting the standards in self-regulated learning. *Contemporary Educational Psychology, 34*, 306–318.

O'Brien, E. J. (1995). Automatic components of discourse comprehension. In E. P. Lorch & E. J. O'Brien (Eds.), *Sources of coherence in reading* (pp. 156–176). Hillsdale, NJ: LEA.

Pekrun, R. (2006). The control-value theory of achievement emotions: Assumptions, corollaries, and implications for educational research and practice. *Educational Psychology Review, 18*, 315–341.

Pekrun, R., Goetz, T., Frenzel, A. C., Petra, B., & Perry, R. P. (2011). Measuring emotions in students' learning and performance: The achievement emotions questionnaire (AEQ). *Contemporary Educational Psychology, 36*, 34–48.

Pintrich, P. R. (2000). The role of goal orientation in self-regulated learning. In M. Boekaerts, P. Pintrich, & M. Zeidner (Eds.), *Handbook of self-regulation* (pp. 451–502). San Diego, CA: Academic.

Portala, T., & Surakka, V. (2003). Pupil size variation as an indication of affective processing. *International Journal of Human-Computer Studies, 59*(1–2), 185–198.

Rayner, K. (1998). Eye movements in reading and information processing: 20 years of research. *Psychological Bulletin, 124*(3), 372–422.

Scheiter, S., & van Gog, T. (2009). Using eye tacking in applied research to study and stimulate the processing of information from multi-representational sources. *Applied Cognitive Psychology, 23*(9), 1209–1214.

Schommer, M. (1998). The influence of age and education on epistemological beliefs. *British Journal of Educational Psychology, 68*(4), 551–562.

Schoor, C., & Bannert, M. (2012). Exploring regulatory processes during a computer-supported collaborative learning task using process mining. *Computers in Human Behavior, 28*(4), 1321–1331.

Schunk, D. (2001). Social cognitive theory of self-regulated learning. In B. Zimmerman & D. Schunk (Eds.), *Self-regulated learning and academic achievement: Theoretical perspectives* (pp. 125–152). Mahwah, NJ: Erlbaum.

Schunk, D. (2008). Attributions as motivators of self-regulated learning. In D. Schunk & B. Zimmerman (Eds.), *Motivation and self-regulated learning: Theory, research, and applications* (pp. 245–266). Mahwah, NJ: Erlbaum.

Schunk, D., & Usher, E. (2011). Assessing self-efficacy for self-regulated learning. In B. Zimmerman & D. Schunk (Eds.), *Handbook of self-regulation of learning and performance* (pp. 282–297). Mahwah, NJ: Routledge.

Terzis, V., Moridis, C. N., & Economides, A. A. (2010). Measuring instant emotions during a self-assessment test: The use of FaceReader. In A. J. Spink, F. Grieco, O. E. Krips, L. W. S. Loijens, L. P. J. J. Noldus, & P. H. Zimmerman (Eds.), *Proceedings of Measuring Behavior 2010* (pp. 192–195). Eindoven, The Netherlands: ACM.

Trevors, G., Duffy, M., & Azevedo, R. (2011). Are intelligent pedagogical agents effective in fostering students' note-taking while learning with a mutli-agent adaptive hypermedia environment? *Proceedings of the 11th Annual International Conference on Intelligent Virtual Agents* (pp. 475–476), Reykjavik, Iceland: Springer.

Van Kuilenburg, H., Wiering, M., & Den Uyl, M. J. (2005). A model based method for automatic facial expression recognition. *Proceedings of the 16th European Conference on Machine Learning, Porto, Portugal, 2005* (pp. 194–205). Springer-Verlag.

Van Someren, M. W., Reimann, P., Boshuizen, H. P. A., & de Jong, T. (Eds.). (1998). *Learning with multiple representations*. Oxford: Elsevier.

Weiner, B. (1985). An attributional theory of achievement motivation and emotion. *Psychological Review, 92*, 548–573.

Winne, P. H. (2001). Self-regulated learning viewed from models of information processing. In B. Zimmerman & D. Schunk (Eds.), *Self-regulated learning and academic achievement: Theoretical perspectives* (pp. 153–189). Mahwah, NJ: Erlbaum.

Winne, P. H. (2005). Key issues on modeling and applying research on self-regulated learning. *Applied Psychology: An International Review, 54*(2), 232–238.

Winne, P., & Hadwin, A. (1998). Studying as self-regulated learning. In D. Hacker, J. Dunlosky, & A. Graesser (Eds.), *Metacognition in educational theory and practice* (pp. 227–304). Mahwah, NJ: Erlbaum.

Winne, P., & Hadwin, A. (2008). The weave of motivation and self-regulated learning. In D. Schunk & B. Zimmerman (Eds.), *Motivation and self-regulated learning: Theory, research, and applications* (pp. 297–314). Mahwah, NJ: Erlbaum.

Winne, P. H., & Nesbit, J. C. (2009). Supporting self-regulated learning with cognitive tools. In D. J. Hacker, J. Dunlosky, & A. C. Graesser (Eds.), *Handbook of metacognition in education*. Mahwah, NJ: Erlbaum.

Zeng, Z., Pantic, M., Roisman, G., & Huang, T. (2009). A survey of affect recognition methods: Audio, visual, and spontaneous expressions. *IEEE Transactions on Pattern Analysis and Machine Intelligence, 31*(1), 39–58.

Zimmerman, B. J. (1989). Models of self-regulated learning and academic achievement. In B. J. Zimmerman & D. H. Schunk (Eds.), *Self-regulated learning and academic achievement: Theory, research and practice* (pp. 1–25). New York: Springer.

Zimmerman, B. (2000). Attaining self-regulation: A social cognitive perspective. In M. Boekaerts, P. Pintrich, & M. Zeidner (Eds.), *Handbook of self-regulation* (pp. 13–39). San Diego, CA: Academic.

Zimmerman, B. (2008). Investigating self-regulation and motivation: Historical background, methodological developments, and future prospects. *American Educational Research Journal, 45*(1), 166–183.

Zimmerman, B. J., & Schunk, D. H. (Eds.). (2001). *Self-regulated learning and academic achievement: theoretical perspectives*. New York, USA: Erlbaum.

Zimmerman, B. J., & Schunk, D. H. (Eds.). (2011). *Handbook of self-regualtion of learning and performance*. New York, USA: Routledge.

Zwann, R. A., & Singer, M. (2003). Text comprehension. In A. C. Graesser, M. A. Gernsbacher, & S. R. Goldman (Eds.), *Handbook of discourse processes* (pp. 83–121). Hillsdale, NJ: LEA.

29 Investigating Self-Regulated Learning in Teachable Agent Environments

John S. Kinnebrew, Gautam Biswas,
Brian Sulcer, and Roger S. Taylor

Abstract

We have developed a computer-based learning environment that helps students learn science by constructing causal concept map models. The system builds upon research in learning-by-teaching (LBT) and has students take on the role and responsibilities of being the teacher to a virtual student named Betty. The environment is structured so that successfully instructing their teachable agents requires the students to learn and understand the science topic for themselves. This learning process is supported through the use of adaptive scaffolding provided by feedback from the two agents in the system: the teachable agent, Betty, and a mentor agent, Mr. Davis. For example, if Betty performs poorly on a quiz, she may tell the student that she needs to learn more about the topics on which she is performing poorly. In addition, Mr. Davis may suggest that students ask Betty questions and get her to explain her answers to help them trace the causal reasoning chains in their map and find out where she may be making mistakes. Thus the system is designed to help students develop and refine their own knowledge construction and monitoring strategies as they teach their agent.

This chapter provides an overview of two studies that were conducted in fifth-grade science classrooms. A description of the analysis techniques that we have developed for interpreting students' activities in this learning environment is also provided. More specifically, we discuss the generation of hidden Markov models (HMMs) that capture students' aggregated behavior patterns, which form the basis for analyzing students' metacognitive strategies in the system. Our study results show that students who utilized LBT versions of our system performed better than students who used a non-teaching version of the system. Further, students' performances

J.S. Kinnebrew • G. Biswas (✉) • B.Sulcer • R.S. Taylor
Department of EECS & ISIS, Vanderbilt University,
Nashville, TN 37235, USA
e-mail: gautam.biswas@vanderbilt.edu

R. Azevedo and V. Aleven (eds.), *International Handbook of Metacognition and Learning Technologies*, Springer International Handbooks of Education 26, DOI 10.1007/978-1-4419-5546-3_29,

were strongest when the system explicitly provided support to help them develop self-regulated learning strategies. To gain further insight into the students' reactions to feedback from the two agents, we present results from a second study that employed a think-aloud protocol. Overall, the results from this study illustrated that students were more receptive to the explicit strategy-oriented feedback from the mentor agent. Interestingly, this study also suggested that students had difficulty in correctly applying Betty's feedback related to metacognitive monitoring activities.

Introduction

Cognitive scientists have established that metacognition and self-regulation are important components for developing effective learning in the classroom and beyond (Bransford, Brown, & Cocking, 2000; Zimmerman, 2001). The framework for self-regulated learning (SRL) originated from the social cognitive theory of learning proposed by Bandura (1997), who postulated that learning is governed by three interacting factors: (1) *personal* (e.g., learners attitudes and beliefs); (2) *behavioral* (e.g., the ability to invoke relevant prior knowledge, the ability to employ appropriate strategies to support learning); and (3) *environmental* (e.g., type of instruction, quality of feedback, nature of interactions with parents and peers). A number of researchers (e.g., Pintrich, 2000; Zimmerman, 2001; Zimmerman, Bandura, & Martinez-Pons, 1992) have demonstrated that students' SRL capabilities can play a significant role in high school academic achievement. In addition, studies by Brown and Palincsar [1989] have demonstrated that through instruction younger students can acquire and apply metacognitive skills, such as planning and monitoring. However, students in typical classrooms are rarely provided opportunities to learn and exercise these strategies (Paris & Paris, 2001; Zimmerman, 1990).

For about 8 years, our research team, the Teachable Agents Group, has been developing computer-based-learning environments that utilize the learning-by-teaching (LBT) approach to instruction in order to foster students' acquisition of knowledge and development of sophisticated metacognitive strategies. The system embodies the social cognitive learning framework and provides students with opportunities for self-directed, open-ended learning in the domains of science and mathematics (Biswas, Leelawong, Schwartz, Vye, & Vanderbilt, 2005; Blair, Schwartz, Biswas, & Leelawong, 2007; Leelawong & Biswas, 2008). In the system, students are given a *knowledge construction* task in which they engage in the iterative process of reading and building causal concept maps for a range of instructional topics (e.g., climate change, ecology, and thermoregulation). This process is enhanced through the *social interaction* component of the system in which students assume the role and responsibilities of being their agent's teacher. The environment is structured so that successfully instructing their teachable agent ("Betty") requires the students to learn and understand the topic for themselves. Our previous work has shown that students find the task of teaching and interacting with Betty to be motivating, and it also helps them enhance their own learning (Chase, Chin, Oppezzo, & Schwartz, 2009; Schwartz, Blair, Biswas, Leelawong, & Davis, 2007; Schwartz et al., 2009). The teachable agent's performance is a function of how well it has been taught by the student, which provides the student with a non-threatening way of assessing their own understanding and areas of confusion (e.g., "Ugh, Betty is so stupid, now I've got to figure out another way to help her learn this stuff," as opposed to "Why am I not able to get the correct answer?"). Based upon the student's level of progress and pattern of activities, the system triggers responses at appropriate times from Betty or Mr. Davis, the mentor agent, who provides guidance on problem-solving and metacognitive strategies. As a result, the students are more likely to increase their knowledge of the specific domain content and develop more sophisticated problem-solving and metacognitive strategies, which in turn helps their preparation for future learning (Biswas et al., 2005; Bransford & Schwartz, 1999; Schwartz & Martin, 2004; Schwartz et al., 2007).

This chapter presents analyses from several studies that were conducted in middle school science classrooms, in which students taught their agent about complex science topics, such as river ecosystems and global climate change. One of our goals was to determine the degree to which the agents' metacognitive and SRL prompts could help improve students' learning. Within this framework, we have developed analytical methods to identify and interpret students' learning strategies based on their activity traces in the system. Such analyses can shed light on students' underlying learning processes and the strategies they employ in achieving their learning tasks (Roscoe & Chi, 2007). To date there has been very little work on deriving students' SRL strategies from their activity sequences in computer-based learning environments (some exceptions are Hadwin, Nesbit, Jamieson-Noel, Code, and Winne (2007), Roll, Aleven, Mclaren, and Koedinger (2007), and Azevedo, Witherspoon, Chauncey, Burkett, and Fike (2009)). In this chapter, we present a novel methodology that derives HMMs (Li & Biswas, 2002; Rabiner, 1989) from student activity sequences to quantify and assess student learning and metacognition. In addition, we report the results of a second study, where we performed verbal protocol analyses to determine students' acceptance of the strategies discussed by the two agents, and how the feedback provided by the agents influenced their subsequent learning activities.

Measuring Self-Regulated Learning

To effectively design, test, and refine a system promoting SRL skills, it requires the ability to identify and measure metacognitive processes. The traditional approach to measuring students' SRL has been through the use of self-report questionnaires (e.g., Pintrich, Smith, Garcia, & McKeachie, 1993; Weinstein, Schulte, & Palmer, 1987; Zimmerman & Martinez-Pons, 1986). The underlying assumption in these questionnaires is that self-regulation is an aptitude that students possess. For example, the questionnaire items might attempt to assess students' inclination to elaborate as they read a passage or to determine their approach to managing available time resources (Perry & Winne, 2006; Zimmerman, 2008). This approach has been useful, as the self-report questionnaires have been shown to be good predictors of students' standard achievement test scores and they correlate well with achievement levels (Pintrich, Marx, & Boyle, 1993; Zimmerman & Martinez Pons, 1986). However, Hadwin and others (Azevedo & Witherspoon, 2009; Hadwin, Winne, Stockley, Nesbit, & Woszczyna, 2001; Hadwin et al., 2007; Perry & Winne, 2006) have argued that while the questionnaires provide valuable information about the learners' self-perceptions, they fail to capture the dynamic and adaptive nature of SRL as students are involved in learning, knowledge-building, and problem-solving tasks.

Increasingly, researchers have begun to utilize trace methodologies in order to examine the complex temporal patterns of SRL (Aleven, McLaren, Roll, & Koedinger, 2006; Azevedo & Witherspoon, 2009; Azevedo et al., 2009; Biswas, Jeong, Kinnebrew, Sulcer, & Roscoe, 2010; Hadwin et al., 2007; Jeong & Biswas, 2008; Zimmerman, 2008). Perhaps the most common type of data collected, and the focus of this chapter, is computer logs, which can record every action that the student performs in a computer-based learning environment. An example of computer trace log analysis is presented in Hadwin et al. (2007). They performed a study that collected activity traces of 8 students using the gStudy system (Perry & Winne, 2006). The activity traces were analyzed in four different ways: (1) frequency of studying events, (2) patterns of studying activity, (3) timing and sequencing of events, and (4) content analyses of students' notes and summaries. The results of this analysis were compared against students' self-reports on their SRL. One of the important findings was that many participants' self-reports of studying tactics, as determined by the MSLQ items, were not well calibrated with studying events traced in the gStudy system. The researchers found that the best matched item showed a 40% agreement, and the average agreement was 27%. The authors concluded from this study that trace data of student activity in e-learning environments are important for furthering our understanding of SRL.

More recently, trace data is being supplemented with other sources of data, such as concurrent verbal think-alouds (e.g., Azevedo & Witherspoon, 2009) and measures of effect (e.g., automatic recording of facial expression and posture) (Burleson, Picard, Perlin, & Lippincott, 2004; D'Mello, Craig, Witherspoon, Mcdaniel, & Graesser, 2008; D'Mello, Picard, & Graesser, 2007; Lester et al., 1997). Azevedo et al. (2009) have developed a hypermedia environment called MetaTutor to help students learn about complex and challenging science topics, such as the circulatory processes in human body systems. The system is also designed to train students in key SRL processes that relate to planning, metacognitive monitoring, learning strategies, and methods for handling task difficulties and demands. The authors used a combination of student trace data and think-aloud protocols to understand the nature of students' learning outcomes and their deployment of SRL processes. For example, one of their studies showed that students predominantly used strategies that pertained to acquiring knowledge from the multimedia resources, and they only occasionally employ monitoring strategies to check what they have learned (Azevedo & Witherspoon, 2009). Combining trace and think-aloud protocols provides more insight into the students' thought processes that govern the use of strategies. Furthermore, they can be used to validate the results of the trace data analysis.

Betty's Brain and Self-Regulated Learning

The Betty's Brain system, illustrated in Fig. 29.1, implements the LBT paradigm to help middle school students develop cognitive and metacognitive skills in science and mathematics domains (Biswas et al., 2005; Blair et al., 2007; Leelawong & Biswas, 2008; Schwartz et al., 2007). The system supports five primary types of activities:

- *Read*: The system contains a set of indexed, hypermedia resources that students can access and read at any time while working on the system. These resources contain all of the science information (and more) that students need to build their concept maps.
- *Edit*: Students explicitly teach Betty using a causal concept map representation (Jonassen & Ionas, 2008), where the relevant science concepts are nodes, and causal relations between the concepts are modeled as links. For example, fish eat (decrease) macroinvertebrates and this representation allows students to reason that an increase in fish causes a decrease in macroinvertebrates. Students teach Betty new concepts and links using a visual interface that includes menu selections and templates for adding and modifying information (e.g., the interface contains these four buttons: Teach Concept, Teach Link, Delete, and Edit).
- *Query*: Students use a template, illustrated in Fig. 29.1, to check their teaching by asking Betty questions, which she answers using causal reasoning through chains of links (Forbus, 1984; Leelawong & Biswas, 2008).
- *Explain*: Students can probe Betty's reasoning, by asking her to explain her answer to a query. She demonstrates the use of causal reasoning processes to derive her answer, and verbalizes her reasoning process using speech and simultaneous animation on the concept map.
- *Quiz*: Students can assess how much Betty has learned by having her take a quiz, which is made up of a set of questions chosen by the Mentor agent. Betty's inability to answer some of the questions correctly usually motivates the students to learn more so that they can make improvements to the concept map and help Betty do better on her quizzes.

Since our middle school students are novices in the science topics and the teaching tasks, we provide them with a variety of scaffolds to help them overcome obstacles they may face in learning and

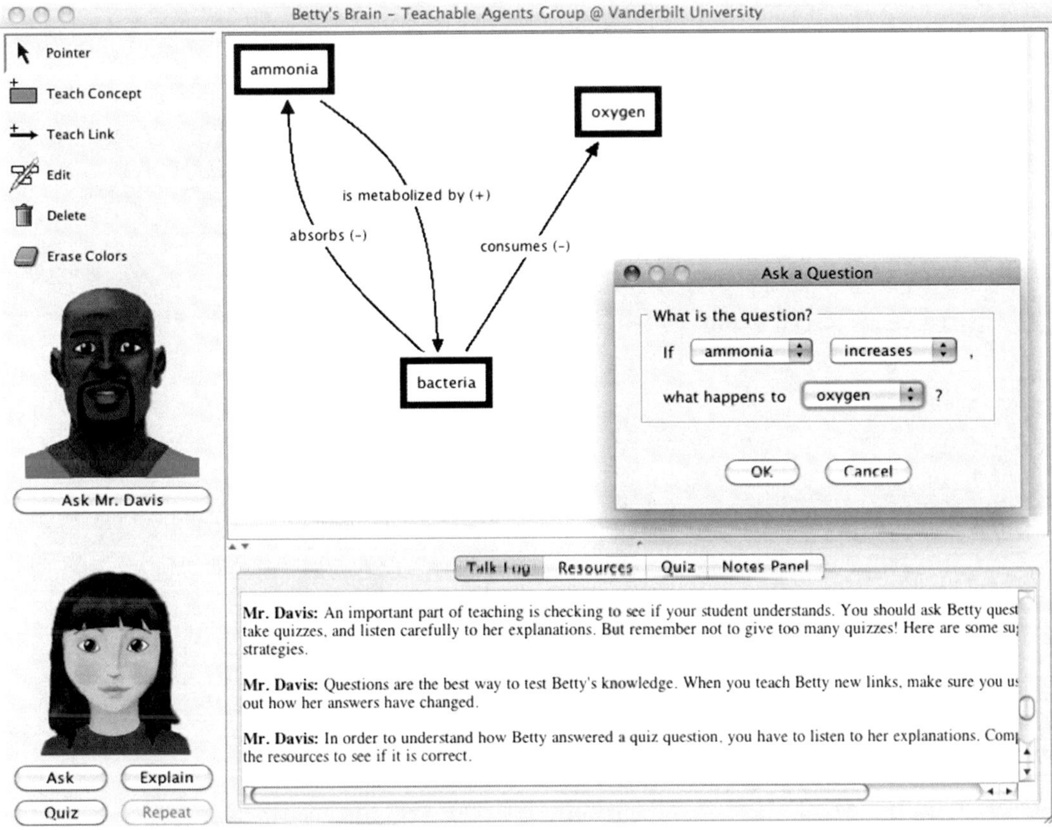

Fig. 29.1 Betty's Brain system with query window

teaching the domain material. In addition to answering queries and taking/administering quizzes, the agents also provide spontaneous feedback to the student on the relative effectiveness of their teaching performance. This feedback is designed to help students develop and employ more metacognitive learning strategies (Schwartz et al., 2007; Tan, Biswas, & Schwartz, 2006; Wagster, Tan, Wu, Biswas, & Schwartz, 2007).

Schunk and Zimmerman (1997) point out that the self-regulation profiles of novice learners are quite distinct from those of experienced learners. Novices are often poor at forethought, and their self-judgment abilities are not well developed. These strategies can be taught, but students in typical classrooms are rarely provided opportunities needed to learn and master them. Our system addresses this problem by adopting a SRL framework that promotes a set of comprehensive skills, such as setting goals for learning new materials and applying them to map building tasks; deliberating about strategies to enable this learning; monitoring one's learning progress; and revising one's knowledge, beliefs, and strategies as new material and strategies are learned (Azevedo, 2005; Schraw, Kauffman, & Lehman, 2002; Winne & Hadwin, 2008; Zimmerman, 2001).

Figure 29.2 illustrates our conceptual cognitive/metacognitive model that we have employed in designing the Betty's Brain system. Pintrich (2002) differentiates between two major aspects of metacognition for learners: (1) *metacognitive knowledge* that includes knowledge of general strategies and when they apply, as well as awareness of one's own abilities, and (2) *metacognitive control* and self-regulatory processes that learners use to monitor and regulate their cognition and learning. In our model, metacognitive control is illustrated in the monitoring and knowledge construction strategies in Fig. 29.2. In more detail,

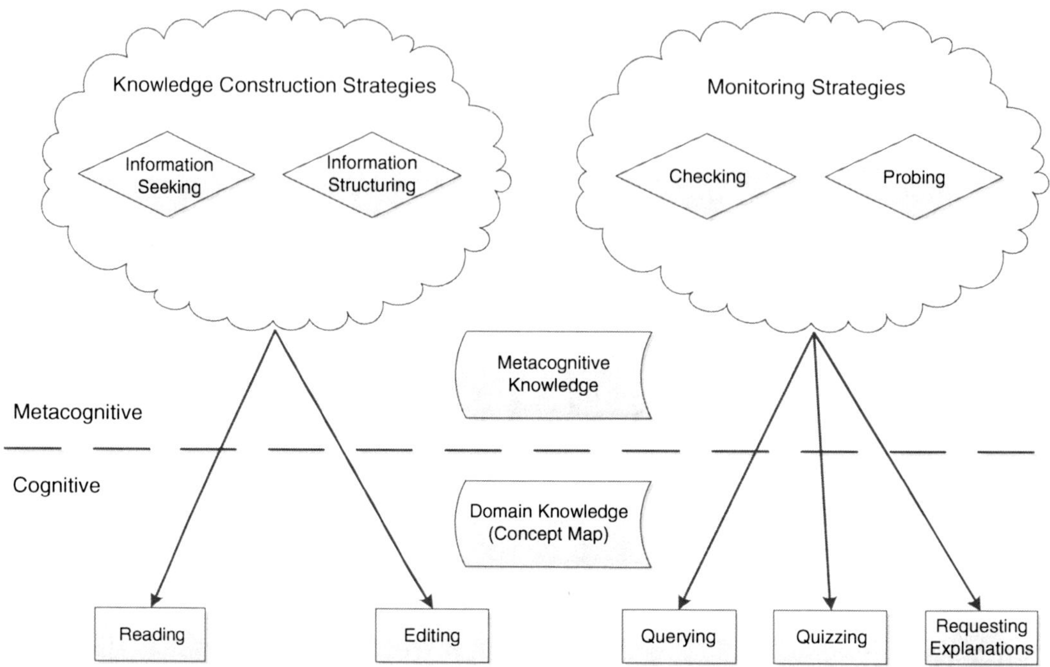

Fig. 29.2 Our model of self-regulated learning strategies and activities in the Betty's brain system linked to these strategies

Pintrich discusses a goal orientation framework for characterizing SRL that covers mastery and performance orientations to achieving goals (Pintrich, 2000). In our approach, feedback from the mentor promotes mastery orientation, e.g., focus on learning with understanding, and setting standards for checking and probing the map (asking queries and reflecting on the explanations generated by Betty) to make sure it has no errors. Betty's interactions with the student focus more on the avoidance aspect of mastery orientation, i.e., making sure students strive for self-improvement and work toward producing an error-free map.

For knowledge construction in the Betty's Brain system (i.e., building causal concept maps), we identify two key types of mastery-oriented self-regulation strategies: (1) *information seeking*, in which students study and search available resources in order to gain missing domain information or remediate existing knowledge, and (2) *information structuring*, in which students structure the information gained into causal and taxonomic relationships to build and revise their concept maps. Information seeking strategies are directed toward effective use of the resources in the system, whereas information structuring focuses on strategies for construction and revision of the concept map.

The model also posits two types of monitoring strategies: (1) *checking*, where students use the query or the quiz features to test the correctness of their concept map and (2) *probing*, a stronger monitoring strategy, where students systematically analyze their map in greater detail, by asking for explanations and following the causal reasoning steps generated by the agent to locate potential errors. Effective guidance (i.e., relevant and timely feedback) based on this SRL model makes students aware of their learning strategies and helps them develop better strategies, such as rereading the resources to check if there are errors in their concept maps (combining information seeking and checking strategies), and asking queries and checking explanations to find the source of an error (a probing strategy).

Table 29.1 provides examples of the agent feedback, which is triggered by students' activity patterns (see column 2) and linked to strategies for

Table 29.1 Examples of agent responses to observed student behavior patterns

SRL strategy	Triggering activities	Betty response	Mr. Davis response
Knowledge construction: information seeking	Student taught Betty several concepts, but has added only a few links.	*What do the resources say about that concept? Could we search the resources to learn more?*	*Reading is a very important part of learning. You should read the resources often to help you understand and double-check what you are teaching. Here are some strategies that you can use to improve your reading skills.*
Knowledge construction: information structuring	Student has just added a number of concepts but no links to the concept map.	*Can we read the resources to make sure we understand the relations between these concepts?*	*A good teacher explains to her students how concepts affect each other. Add links to the map to teach Betty how the concepts cause other concepts to change.*
Monitoring: checking	Betty has incorrect answers on the quiz she just took.	*Could you ask me some review questions to see how good my answers are?*	*Questions are the best way to test Betty's knowledge. When you teach Betty new links, make sure you ask her questions to find out how her answers have changed.*
Monitoring: probing	Betty has got some of her quiz answers wrong.	*These quizzes can be tough. Can we go over my explanations to see how well I understand?*	*After each quiz, try to review a few of Betty's answers and explanations. Follow each step in her explanations carefully to be sure that they make sense.*
Monitoring: pointing out a suboptimal strategy	Student asks Betty to take repeated quizzes without reading or asking questions.	*I want to do well on the quizzes. It would help if I learned more between each quiz instead of taking so many.*	*You have been asking Betty to take a lot of quizzes recently. Try asking her questions to see where she is making mistakes, and teach her more in between quizzes.*

knowledge construction and monitoring implied by our model.[1] The agents have different roles (and relationships with the student) in the system, which affects the wording and the content of the feedback they provide. Betty's persona and role as an engaged student "interested in learning and performing well," is influenced by the social cognitive framework. Betty's feedback incorporates metacognitive awareness that she conveys to the students at appropriate times to help them develop and apply monitoring and self-regulation strategies (Schwartz et al., 2009; Wagster et al., 2007). Mr. Davis, the mentor, and, therefore, the more knowledgeable persona in the system, provides help in the form of suggested activities linked to effective SRL strategies (e.g., "if you are not sure, check the resources to see if Betty is answering her questions correctly.").

[1] In the system, the same triggering conditions are used to generate Betty's and Mr. Davis' feedback. The system is designed so that the feedback is provided only after the triggering pattern is activated a certain number of times. This number is chosen randomly from a predefined range of values (e.g., [2, 5]) and recomputed after every instance of feedback. The numbers for Betty and Mr. Davis are chosen independently.

Experimental Studies

We have conducted several classroom studies where students use the teachable agents system to learn and gain a better understanding of a variety of science topics, such as river ecosystems, thermoregulation, and climate change. In these studies, the topics and specific science content provided by the system are closely linked to the middle school science curriculum. At the beginning of each study, the science teacher introduces students to the topic during regular classroom instruction. The intervention phase starts with an overview of causal relations and causal mapping during a 45-min class period. This is followed by a hands-on training session with the system the next day. Over the next 4 or 5 days, the students teach Betty by building a causal concept map for the science topic, which represents what Betty knows.

To assess students' acquisition of science domain knowledge and causal reasoning skills, we employ two measures. The first is a pretest to posttest gain score. These tests contain a mix of content-related multiple choice and free response items (Biswas et al., 2010; Leelawong & Biswas, 2008) that are administered before the students are introduced to causal reasoning, and at the end of the intervention. The second measure examines students' final maps, in terms of completeness and accuracy.

In this chapter, we analyze the results from two classroom studies. The first study compared the students' use of SRL strategies in three different conditions described below. We had two questions: (1) Would students who taught an agent use more SRL strategies in their learning and teaching tasks than students learning entirely for themselves? and (2) Would students who received SRL feedback from the agents use more sophisticated SRL strategies than students who did not? The second study used verbal protocol analysis to assess the effectiveness of different kinds of SRL strategies, and also checked whether the feedback provided by one agent was more effective than the feedback provided by the other agent. The results, and a discussion of these results, are presented in the remainder of this section.

Study 1: Modeling Students' SRL Strategies

In this study, our goal was to determine if teaching the Betty agent and providing metacognitive feedback would help students become better learners than those who did not teach or receive the feedback. Our participants were 56 students in 2 fifth-grade science classrooms taught by the same teacher. Students were assigned to one of three conditions using stratified random assignment based on standardized test scores. All students created river ecosystem concept maps over five 45-min sessions. Two of the conditions (1) the LBT group and (2) the self-regulated learning-by-teaching (SRL) group created their map to teach Betty so that she could pass a test on her own. In addition to the teachable agent, both groups had access to Mr. Davis, the mentor agent. As students taught Betty, they could ask her questions, get her to explain her answers to the questions, and take quizzes, which were sets of questions created by Mr. Davis. After Betty took a quiz, the mentor graded the quiz and displayed the results to the students. Both systems also provided feedback to students after a quiz.

The differences between the LBT and SRL groups were in the feedback provided. In the LBT version of the system, Mr. Davis provided *corrective* feedback after the quiz results were displayed. The corrective feedback was linked to a quiz question that produced an incorrect answer, and it included information about one of the following: (1) a missing concept that would be required to generate the correct answer; (2) a missing link that would be required to generate the correct answer, or (3) a link that was incorrectly represented in the map (e.g., one of the link effects was incorrect, or the direction of a link was reversed). The mentor's feedback would first pick on missing concepts, then missing links (i.e., if the student's map contained the relevant concepts to answer the question), and last, incorrect links (i.e., if all necessary concepts and links were on the map, but one or more links were incorrectly specified or extraneous).

In contrast, the SRL version of the system provided the SRL strategy feedback presented in Sect. 29. After seeing Betty's quiz results, the students could ask the mentor for suggestions. In response, Mr. Davis would suggest relevant SRL strategies, such as an information seeking strategy: he would point to keywords for finding relevant sections of the resources to learn more about concepts and relations that were missing/incorrect in the map. In addition to feedback after a quiz, Betty and Mr. Davis also generated spontaneous responses triggered by the activity patterns, such as the ones described in Table 29.1.

Our control condition for the study, the intelligent coaching system (ICS) group was told to create the map to learn for themselves. The Betty agent was removed from this version of the system, and the students interacted only with the mentor, Mr. Davis. Otherwise, the activities available in the ICS interface were identical to the two LBT systems. For example, students in the ICS group could also query their map and ask for explanations, but in this case, it was Mr. Davis, and not Betty, who responded to them. Similarly, ICS students took the quiz for themselves rather than having Betty take the quiz. The content and form of quizzes and explanations were identical for the ICS, LBT, and SRL groups. In the ICS group, Mr. Davis provided the same corrective feedback as in the LBT version of the system.

All student activities in the system were captured in log files. Each activity was assigned to one of five primary categories: (1) EDIT—add, edit, or delete concepts and links in the concept map; (2) QUER(y)—query Betty on a portion of the map; (3) QUIZ—ask Betty to take a quiz; (4) READ—read the resources; and (5) EXPL(anation)—ask Betty to explain her answer to a query. For each activity, the program captured additional information related to the activity. For example, when the student asked a question, the question and Betty's response to the question were also stored in the log file.

Analyses that do not take into account the sequential nature of student interactions with the system, such as counting the frequency of student activities, can provide only limited information for learning strategy models of student behavior (Biswas et al., 2010). We believe that a state-based representation that captures the sequential characteristics of students' activities provides a more powerful narrative of the student learning behaviors. HMMs (Rabiner, 1989), which contain a set of states and probabilistic transitions between those states (more likely transitions are assigned higher probabilities), provide such a representational scheme. The states in a HMM are hidden, meaning that they cannot be directly observed in the environment/system. Instead, they produce output (e.g., student activities in the Betty's Brain system) that can be observed. Deriving a HMM from activity traces requires simultaneous estimation of (1) the number of states; (2) the probabilities associated with transitions between states; (3) the probabilities associated with observing certain outputs (i.e., particular student activities, such as reading or querying activities); and (4) the probability of a state being the initial state in an activity sequence.

By providing a concise representation of student learning strategies and behaviors, HMMs have the potential for providing a high-level view of how students approach their learning tasks (e.g., what strategies they use and how they switch between strategies) (Biswas et al., 2010; Jeong & Biswas, 2008). Algorithms for learning an HMM from output sequences are well known but require appropriate configuration/initialization parameters for effective use (Rabiner, 1989). Specifically, HMM learning algorithms require an initial HMM description, whose parameters are then modified to maximize the likelihood of producing observed output sequences. In particular, the number of states in the HMM and their initial output probabilities can have a significant effect on the resulting, learned HMM.

We have developed an algorithm designed to generate HMMs from a set of student activity sequences (Jeong & Biswas, 2008; Li & Biswas, 2000, 2002). The first step in the analysis is to extract each students' activity sequences over the period of the study from the log files. Although all students had access to the full set of actions, not all of them used them effectively. Using queries to check whether recent revisions to the map were correct, or to locate errors in the concept map, is an example of effective use of queries. On the other hand, asking questions simply to make Betty speak, so that the student could make fun of her mechanical, computer-generated voice is clearly an ineffective use of queries for the learning task. When students generated questions that were not related to parts of the map they had worked on recently, it was unclear whether these queries were related to effective learning. We addressed this issue by developing a *relevance score* that took into account how much the current action could be linked to other recent actions.

Each student action was assigned a relevance score that depended on the number of relevant previous actions within a pre-specified window. This score provides a measure of *informedness* for knowledge construction activities and, similarly, a measure of *diagnosticity* for monitoring activities. Overall, the relevance score provides a rough measure of strategy consistency or coherence over a sequence of actions. For this analysis, a prior action was considered relevant to the current action if it was related to, or operated on, one

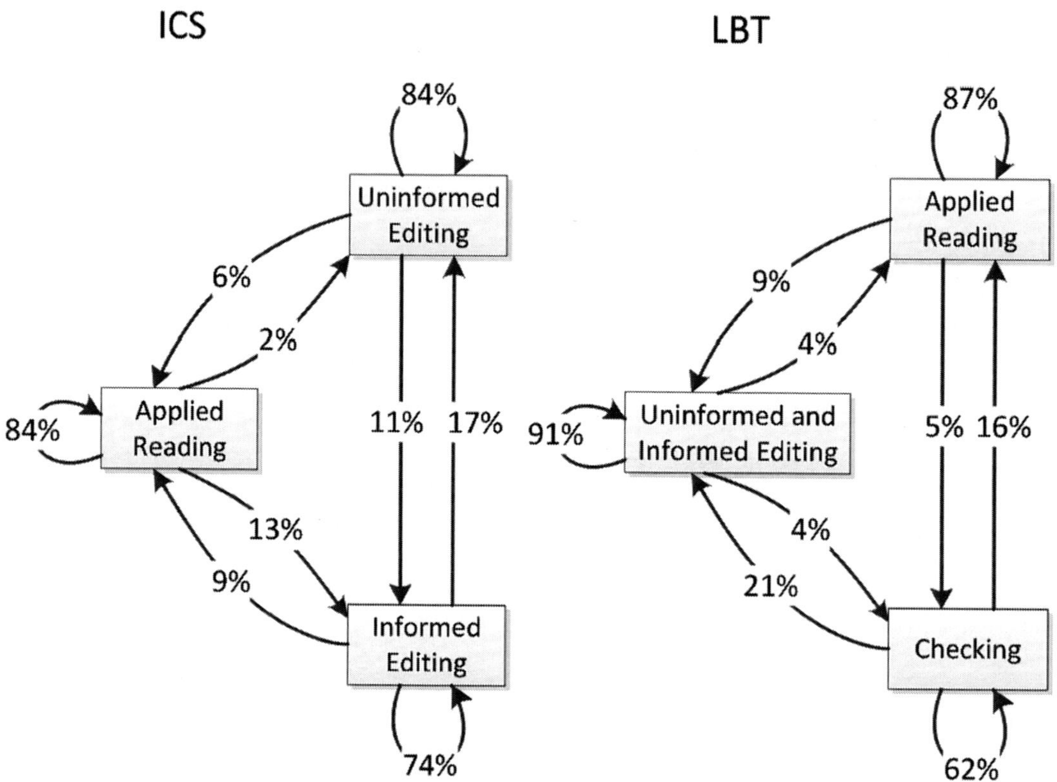

Fig. 29.3 ICS and LBT group HMMs derived from activity sequences

of the same map concepts or links. For example, if a student edited a link that was used to generate an answer in a recent query, the query action was counted in the edit's relevance score. The increased relevance score suggested a more informed edit action because it was related to a recent query.

The relevance score is employed in HMM generation by refining the classification of student activities. Each of the actions in an activity sequence is assigned a label, H (high) or L (low), based on its relevance score, in order to maintain the context and relevance information of the actions in the sequence. For example, a QUER-H activity implies that the query the student asked is related to other activities recently performed, while a QUER-L implies that the query activity is largely unrelated to the students' recent activities.

The HMM models derived for the ICS, LBT, and SRL groups are shown in Figs. 29.3 and 29.4. States in the models are named based on an interpretation of their outputs (activities) illustrated in Figs. 29.5 and 29.6. The possible transitions between states are shown as arrows, and the transition probabilities are expressed as percentages. For example, the ICS behavior model indicates an 84% likelihood that a student who just performed an applied reading action (i.e., one of the observable actions associated with the Applied Reading state described below) will next perform another applied reading action, but there is a 13% chance that the student will perform an informed editing action (i.e., an action produced by the Informed Editing state) next. The models for the ICS and LBT groups each have three states, but the activities associated with some of those states differ significantly. Therefore, the states are interpreted, and named, differently for those groups. Further, the derived model for the SRL group has five states instead of three and shows some interesting differences in the set of actions associated with those states.

We used the activities associated with a state to categorize the states of the three derived HMM

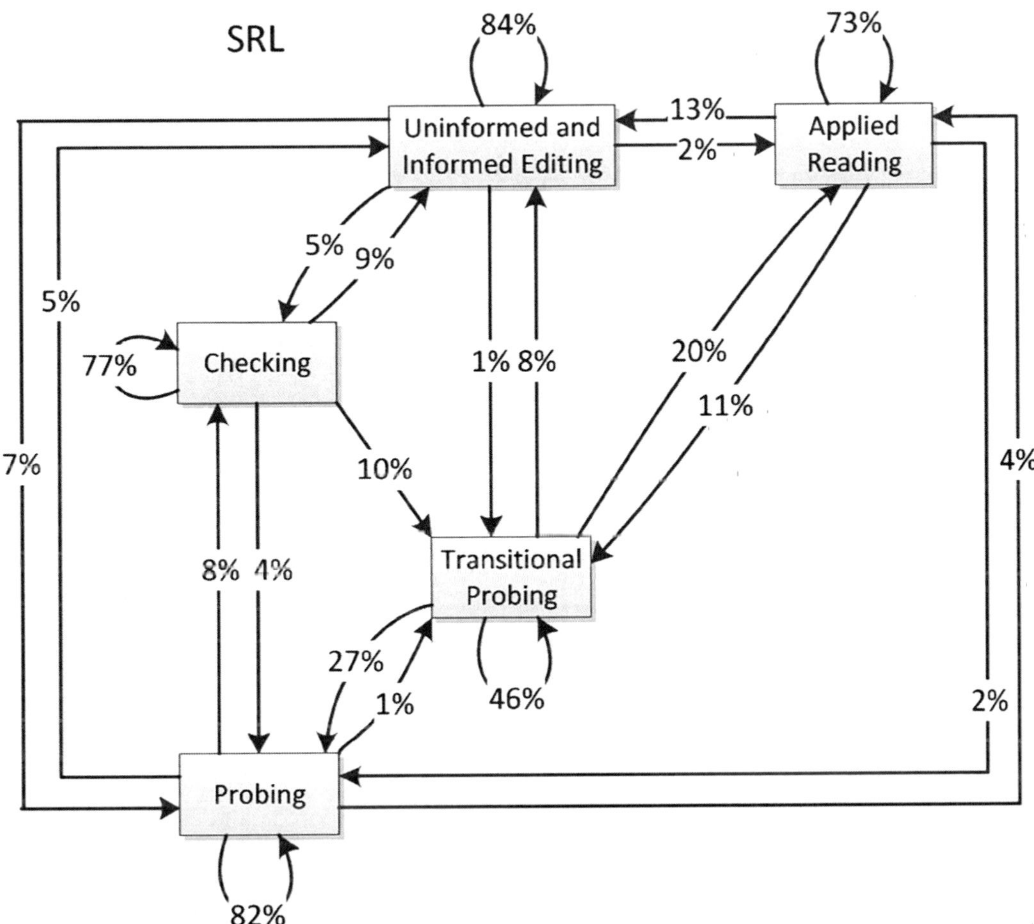

Fig. 29.4 SRL group HMM derived from activity sequences

models. This analysis produced seven different types of states that are described below.

1. *Applied reading*—students are primarily engaged in reading the resources and applying the knowledge gained from reading by editing their maps. This state combines information-seeking strategies with informed information structuring.
2. *Uninformed editing*—students are primarily making uninformed changes to their map, indicating the use of trial-and-error or guessing strategies for information structuring. Students may generate queries, but the queries generally do not relate directly to the editing activities. This represents a suboptimal information structuring strategy.
3. *Informed editing*—students are primarily making informed changes to their map (information structuring) based on relevant queries or quiz questions. As opposed to uninformed editing, the students are using queries and quizzes to guide their map editing actions.
4. *Uninformed and informed editing*—students are primarily making changes to their map, some of which are based on relevant queries or quizzes. This state combines the activities of the uninformed editing and informed editing states, including situations where students are making edits relevant to recent queries and quizzes, as well as situations in which students are making edits without focusing on a single area of the map.

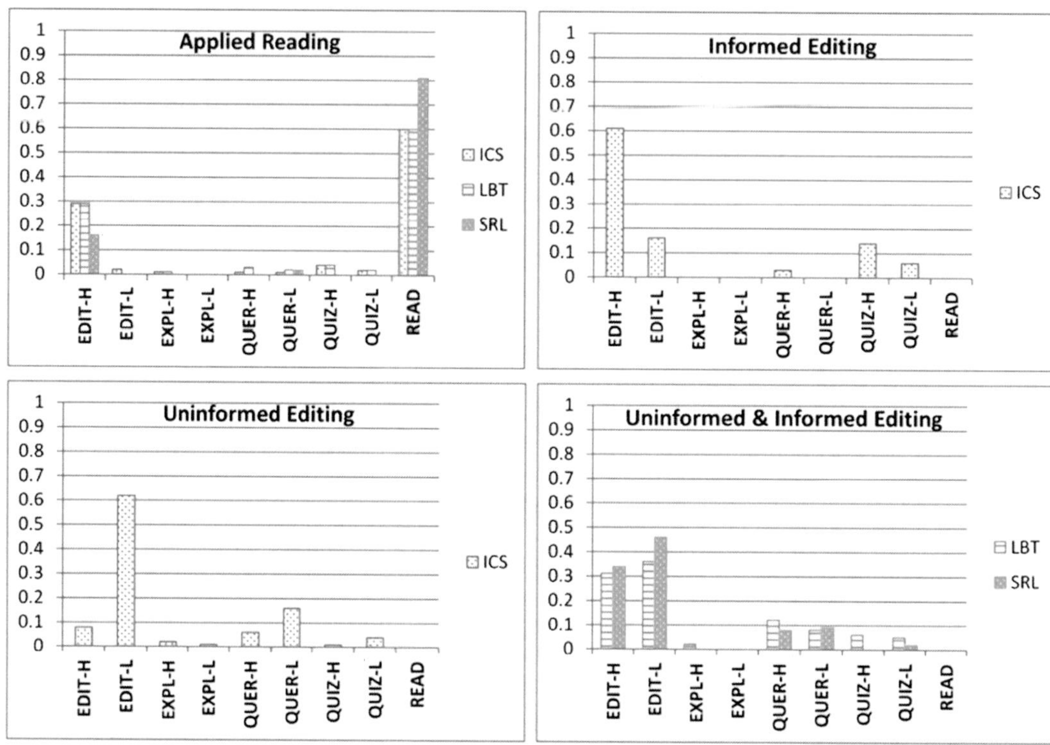

Fig. 29.5 Activities in knowledge construction states

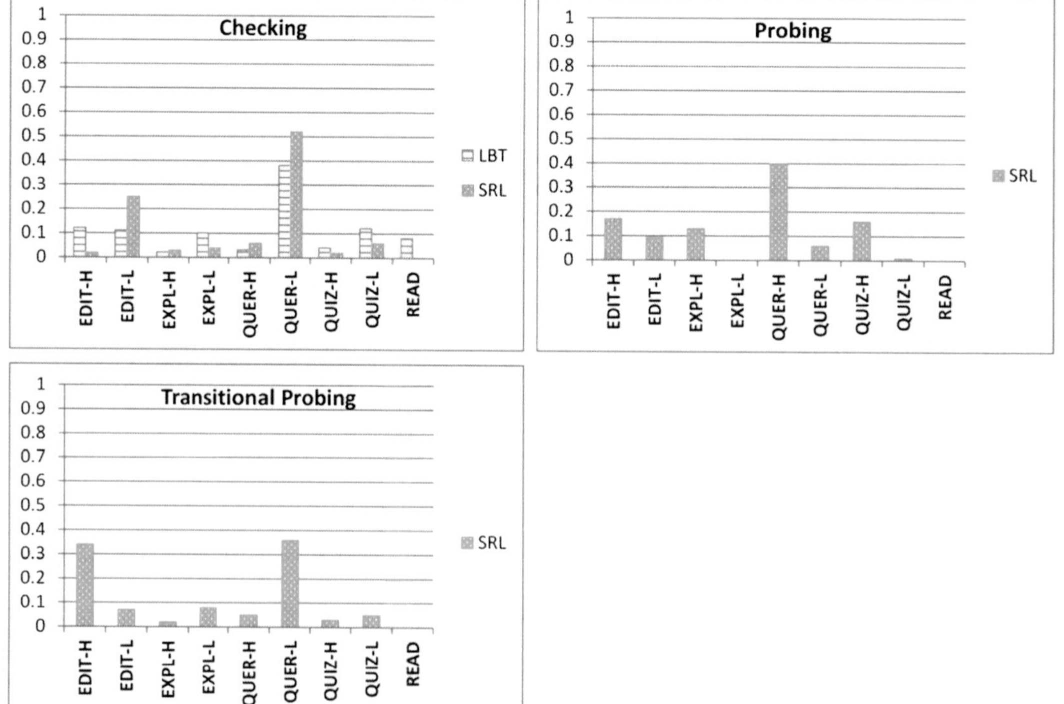

Fig. 29.6 Activities in monitoring states

Table 29.2 Proportion of expected state occurrences by condition

	ICS	LBT	SRL
Behaviors	Proportion (%)	Proportion (%)	Proportion (%)
Applied reading	33	30	17
Uninformed editing	36	–	–
Uninformed and informed editing	–	60	34
Informed editing	31	–	–
Checking	–	10	13
Transitional probing	–	–	7
Probing	–	–	29

5. *Checking*—students are querying and quizzing Betty to check the correctness of their concept maps. However, the use of queries and quizzes may be unfocused. For example, queries may not be related to recently edited areas of the map, and it is not clear that students are using the quiz results to focus on areas on the map where there are errors. Therefore, this state corresponds to a weak monitoring strategy.
6. *Probing*—students combine querying and quizzing with the explanation feature, which illustrates the chain of links that were followed to generate an answer to a question. Further, the queries, explanations, and quizzes are focused on a particular area of the map, and the results inform map editing. This combination implies a deeper, more focused monitoring strategy than the checking state and may be evidence of metacognitive reflection on the quality of the student's map/knowledge.
7. *Transitional probing*—students perform activities similar to the probing state, but generally with lower relevance scores, suggesting that they may be transitioning to probing a different area of the concept map.

As discussed above, each of the interpreted states can be mapped onto one or more knowledge construction and monitoring strategies outlined in our conceptual SRL model that was illustrated in Fig. 29.2. The HMMs provide evidence that the SRL condition uses more effective monitoring strategies (i.e., probing strategies in addition to checking strategies) than the LBT and ICS conditions.

We probed further to determine the prevalence of individual states suggested by a generated HMM. To do this, we calculated the proportion of *expected state occurrences* by condition in Table 29.2. This calculation uses the HMM to provide an *expected value* for the average frequency with which a state would occur when producing sequences of a given length. Specifically, the expected state occurrences measure employs state transition probabilities in the derived HMM and average activity sequence lengths from the trace data to calculate an expected value for the proportion of individual state occurrences (Biswas et al., 2010). Although states corresponding to knowledge construction behaviors account for a significant percentage of behaviors in all groups, the HMMs for the LBT and SRL groups also show use of monitoring strategies (10% for LBT and 49% for SRL). The SRL HMM also includes more states suggesting a greater number (and possibly greater complexity) in the types of strategies employed. Further, the activities involved in these additional states suggest use of *probing*, a more advanced monitoring behavior, which is absent from the ICS and LBT HMMs.

The results of the HMM analysis identify differences in strategies employed by the different groups of students, but do not directly indicate the effect of these behaviors on student learning. Therefore, Table 29.3[2] shows the learning gains measured by tests and map scores for each

[2] All statistical comparisons of means among conditions were made with ANOVA post-hoc (Tukey HSD) tests, and effect sizes are computed as Cohen's d. Further, since some of the differences falling outside of the significance cutoff of $p<0.05$ still had moderately large effect sizes, we report the results for multiple significance cutoff values ($p<0.1$ and $p<0.05$), allowing the reader to make their own determinations based on the reported results.

Table 29.3 Mean pre-to-post test and concept map score gains

	Conditions		
Gain score	ICS	LBT	SRL
Multiple choice	0.4 (2.4)	1.1 (3.1)	0.4 (1.5)
Free response	1.9 (3.0)	4.3 (3.2)	4.8 (4.7)
Map concepts	8.1 (2.4)	7.3 (2.7)	10.4 (3.1)
Map links	12.2 (3.8)	12.7 (5.3)	16.2 (4.4)

condition in the study. Results indicate that the two groups that taught Betty (LBT and SRL) outperformed the ICS group on gains in both test and map scores, although not all of these differences were statistically significant. In particular, differences on multiple choice test score gain were not statistically significant between any of the conditions. However, for the free response test questions, the SRL group showed greater gains than the ICS group ($p<0.1$ and a moderately large effect size of $\hat{d}=0.72$). For the gain in correct map concepts, the SRL group outperformed both the ICS group ($p<0.05$, $\hat{d}=0.81$) and the LBT group ($p<0.01$, $\hat{d}=1.05$). Similarly, for the gain in correct map links, the SRL group outperformed the ICS and LBT groups ($p<0.05$, $\hat{d}=0.97$ and $p<0.1$, $\hat{d}=0.72$, respectively).

Overall, these results indicate that the students who taught Betty (i.e., LBT and SRL groups) outperformed the other students (i.e., the ICS group), both in learning gains and the use of monitoring strategies. Although the SRL group received different feedback (SRL rather than corrective) from the mentor, the only difference between the LBT and ICS groups was whether students taught Betty or learned for themselves. The ICS students use of less effective learning strategies, as apparent in the HMMs, may explain their smaller learning gains. Further, the SRL group had higher free response and map score gains than the LBT group (although not all of the differences were statistically significant for the number of students in this study), suggesting that the SRL feedback promoted more effective learning and concept mapping performance. Moreover, while 60% of SRL students completed their concept maps during the five sessions, only 44% of LBT students and 31% of ICS students were able to complete their concept maps. The results of the HMM analysis, combined with the results on learning gains, suggest that the metacognitive feedback helped students implement SRL strategies, which allowed them to more effectively learn the science content. Although the HMM analysis illustrates the effectiveness of providing metacognitive feedback in Betty's Brain, it does not indicate which agent or types of feedback were most effective. This was the focus of the second study, which we describe next.

Study 2: Comparing the Mentor and Teachable Agent Feedback

In order to assess the effectiveness of different forms of feedback in our system (i.e., differences by (1) agent and (2) content of feedback: knowledge construction versus monitoring), we conducted a study, which included a think-aloud protocol to determine students' reactions to the agent feedback. The study was conducted in 3 fifth-grade science classrooms in the same school as study 1.[3] Two of the classrooms had the same science teacher as in study 1. The third classroom had a different teacher, but teacher 2 worked closely with teacher 1 for the unit taught in this study. All students worked on a newer version of the SRL system from study 1. In this version of the system, the feedback from the two agents was better organized into the categories described in Table 29.1.

Students worked in a total of 40 pairs chosen by the teachers to ensure that the paired students were at similar academic levels and had compatible personalities. Before the study began, the teachers instructed students on how to collaborate on the system. The students had to discuss with one another and come to a consensus before they performed an action on the system. Control of the keyboard and mouse alternated between the students (e.g., if one student had control of the input devices on day 1, then the partner was given control on day 2). The science teachers

[3] Study 1 and study 2 were conducted in different years.

Table 29.4 Student verbal response to agent feedback

Agent →	N	Referenced (%)	Affirmed (%)	Dismissed (%)	Deferred (%)
Betty	649	34	6	16	2
Mr. Davis	275	30	18	10	2

ran a brief practice session on working with the system before the students started this phase of the study. All students had worked individually with the Teachable Agent system on another science unit (ecosystems), so they were familiar with the system.

Students worked on the topic of pollution in river ecosystems for three 45-min periods. We recorded student conversations and interactions using webcams. After the study was concluded, two coders reviewed all of the video data and recorded students' responses to the feedback. For every instance in which the TA or the mentor provided feedback, the coders noted whether the students' subsequent discussion *affirmed, dismissed*, or *deferred* the agent's feedback. Inter-rater reliability for each category was over 85% with Cohen's kappa values over 0.6, and the results are summarized in Table 29.4.

Students explicitly referenced the feedback from the agents about a third of the time (34% for Betty and 30% for Mr. Davis). Even when students did not explicitly reference the feedback, they sometimes responded to the feedback by talking directly to the agent in response or suggesting a course of action directly indicated (or contra-indicated) by the feedback. All student discussions following feedback were coded in three categories of possible response to the feedback[4]: (1) affirm (e.g., "We should do that" or "We need to read more" responding to feedback suggesting the students read the resources), (2) dismiss (e.g., "No, I don't want to read" or "Let's just keep giving her quizzes" responding to feedback suggesting students teach Betty more between giving her quizzes), and (3) defer (e.g., "Hold on, we will get to that in a second").

[4]Many student discussions, including some that explicitly referenced the feedback, neither affirmed, dismissed, nor deferred the feedback.

As illustrated in Table 29.4, there were differences between how frequently the students affirmed or dismissed feedback from the two agents. Students were more likely to affirm feedback from Mr. Davis, and were more likely to dismiss feedback from Betty. This suggests that students paid less attention to the self-reflective feedback from Betty than to the more explicit, strategy-oriented feedback from Mr. Davis. Although one possible explanation for this difference is that Mr. Davis provided better feedback and advice, the tenor of student discussions indicated that they treated Betty like a less-knowledgeable peer, while according Mr. Davis the status of a knowledgeable authority figure and considering his advice more carefully.

To understand how students' verbal responses related to learning, we analyzed the study results for the two metacognitive categories of feedback from each agent: (1) knowledge construction strategies, and (2) monitoring strategies. Table 29.5 summarizes the percentages of each type of verbal reaction to the different forms of feedback, as well as their correlation with the student pair's final map score. Students who more frequently affirmed the knowledge construction strategy feedback from either the TA or the mentor had higher map scores, but the correlations were not statistically significant. Students who dismissed either the knowledge construction or the monitoring feedback from either agent had lower map scores (negative correlations). However, when the students affirmed the monitoring feedback, the results were surprising. Affirming Mr. Davis's monitoring feedback showed a positive correlation with map score (not statistically significant), but affirming Betty's monitoring feedback was negatively correlated with map score ($p<0.05$). We discuss this result in greater detail later, but overall the students seemed to affirm the knowledge construction feedback more, and affirming this feedback implied higher map scores.

Table 29.5 Verbal responses to feedback and corresponding map score correlations ($^{b}p<0.05$)

Agent→	Betty Percent verbal response (Correlation with map score)			Mentor Percent verbal response (Correlation with map score)		
Category ↓	Affirm	Dismiss	Defer	Affirm	Dismiss	Defer
Knowledge construction	9% (0.20)	27% (−0.45[b])	2% (−0.16)	20% (0.37)	22% (−0.31)	2% (0.24)
Monitoring	4% (−0.46[b])	11% (−0.35)	2% (0.04)	17% (0.28)	6% (−0.44[b])	2% (−0.16)

The verbal responses to feedback listed in Table 29.4 suggest a difference in the way students react to the feedback from the two agents, and these reactions affect their concept map building performance.[5] For example, those who affirmed Mr. Davis's knowledge construction and monitoring feedback seemed to do better in their map building task.

To determine whether the students' verbal responses to feedback matched their expected actions in the system, we analyzed student actions immediately following each agent feedback statement. For example, if Betty said "Can we go over my explanations to see if I am missing anything," we checked to see if the subsequent student actions included asking Betty to explain an answer. Table 29.6 reports for both Betty and Mr. Davis (1) the average number of feedback events by category per student, (2) the average proportion,[6] of subsequent activities that matched the actions advised by the feedback (using a window size of 3 actions)[7] and (3) the correlation between the percentage of matched actions and the students' final map scores.

Overall, the correlation between percentage of matching actions (out of the three student actions subsequent to the feedback) and the students' final map scores was positive (0.34 for Betty and 0.36 for the Mentor), but the correlations were not statistically significant. More detailed analysis by category of metacognitive feedback, showed a positive correlation between students' final map scores and their following Betty's and Mr. Davis's advice on knowledge construction feedback. Students were more likely to follow Betty's feedback suggestions than those of the Mentor, but the differences were small (28–24%). The more students' subsequent actions matched the feedback, the higher their map scores, as measured by the correlations: 0.52 for matching Betty's knowledge construction advice ($p<0.1$) and 0.11 for matching the Mentor's knowledge construction advice. These results differ from the verbal responses to feedback, where students affirmed Mr. Davis's knowledge construction feedback more than they did Betty's, and the corresponding correlations with map scores were also higher for the mentor (0.37 versus 0.2).

On the other hand, for monitoring feedback, Mr. Davis appears to have been more effective than Betty. Though the relative number of Betty monitoring feedback events was high compared to Mr. Davis's (13.1–5.5), student actions after Betty's feedback showed a poor match to the feedback content (only 0.5%). For the mentor feedback the match was 33%. Combining this information with the verbal response results indicates that the students were more dismissive of Betty's monitoring feedback, and at the same time they rarely followed up with activities that matched the feedback content. In addition, the correlation between the activity match percentage and students' map scores was negative, implying

[5] Agent role (and consequently relationship with the student) and the content of agent feedback are inextricably linked in this study, making it impossible to attribute student responses to one factor or the other. However, the correlation between students' responses to agent feedback has useful implications for future system design and experimental study opportunities discussed in this section and the next.

[6] We employed a proportion in a window of subsequent actions because agent feedback often suggested a course of action that could involve repeated actions (e.g., edits or reads), and it is not possible to determine precisely whether a student's action was an attempt to follow agent advice or not.

[7] We tested a variety of different window sizes, and all of them produced similar results.

Table 29.6 Action response to feedback and corresponding map score correlations ($^*p<0.1$)

Feedback category → Agent ↓	Measures	Knowledge construction	Monitoring
Betty	Feedback events	5.77	13.08
	Action (proportional) Match	28.2%	0.5%
	Map score correlation	0.52*	−0.41
Mr. Davis	Feedback events	2.46	5.54
	Action (proportional) Match	24.02%	33.0%
	Map score correlation	0.11	0.26

those who affirmed Betty's monitoring feedback or tried to apply it ended up with lower map scores. On the other hand, Mr. Davis's monitoring feedback had more affirmations and there were more attempts to follow his suggestion, and these correlated with higher map scores (though the correlations were not statistically significant).

Together the verbal and action response results show clear differences in the way students responded to the two agents. Overall, the students affirmed the mentor's feedback more than they did the teachable agent's, and in general, higher affirmation levels implied better final map scores. These results also indicate that the monitoring feedback was less effective than knowledge construction feedback. With the exception of Betty's monitoring feedback, the results showed positive correlations with map scores for both verbal and action response measures. Although there are many potential explanations for the negative correlation between Betty's monitoring feedback and map scores, the results suggest that her monitoring feedback was generally ineffective in helping students improve their concept maps. This could imply that students could not understand Betty's feedback and, therefore, they did not apply her suggestions during their learning and teaching tasks. The few who did, may have applied them inappropriately, and, therefore, used up time that could have been more productively spent in other activities. Alternatively, this could have been the result of self-selection, in which lower-performing students attempted to apply Betty's monitoring advice even though they did not understand it. However, those who followed similar feedback from Mr. Davis did better on their map. Overall, the results indicate that the metacognitive feedback had a generally positive effect on students' learning, but the more explicit strategy feedback from the Mentor agent was more effective than Betty's self-evaluative statements and suggestions.

Discussion and Conclusions

The Betty's Brain system is designed to leverage the benefits of learning by teaching and causal reasoning to help students learn science. The teaching interactions and agent feedback support students' engagement and promote the development and use of educationally productive cognitive and metacognitive processes. In study 1, students who utilized learning by teaching versions of our system (i.e., the LBT and SRL groups) constructed better concept maps than students who used the non-teaching ICS version of the system. Moreover, students' performances were strongest when the system explicitly supported their use of SRL strategies by having Betty model and prompt for such behaviors, and having the mentor provide additional strategy-oriented advice.

Our approach to analyzing students' activity sequences using HMMs produced good results. We were able to characterize students' activity patterns into a number of (good and bad) knowledge construction and monitoring strategies. The interpretation of SRL group behavior with the HMMs also matched the SRL feedback model we implemented in the Betty's Brain system, while the LBT group HMM showed only one of the two types of monitoring strategies (i.e., checking behaviors) and the ICS group HMM did not show either of the monitoring strategies.

Although the HMM analysis illustrated the effectiveness of providing metacognitive feedback in the Betty's Brain system, it did not indicate which agent or types of feedback were most effective in promoting SRL behaviors. Our second study included a think-aloud protocol to determine students' reactions to the agent feedback. We combined the think-aloud protocols with analysis of student activity traces to develop a more complete picture of how well students employed the feedback to their map building tasks. Overall, students' verbal responses to agent feedback suggested that they were more receptive to the explicit, strategy-oriented advice from the mentor agent, as opposed to the self-reflective, but less explicit, feedback from the teachable agent. Further, students were more likely to affirm the knowledge construction feedback from each agent than the monitoring feedback. This analysis also showed a positive correlation between affirming feedback and students' map scores, except in the case of Betty's monitoring feedback.

Additional analysis of student responses to feedback, in terms of actions taken following feedback events, showed a similar differentiation between knowledge construction and monitoring feedback. Students taking more actions consistent with an attempt to apply the knowledge construction feedback tended to have better map scores. However, students taking more actions advised by Betty's monitoring feedback tended to have lower map scores, suggesting they were unable to apply the strategies suggested by that feedback. This brings up a number of issues. It suggests that students find it easier to understand and apply knowledge construction strategies (e.g., read the resources to find the correct relation between two concepts or check the resources to see if all of the required concepts appear on the map) than monitoring strategies (e.g., ask a query to check if the map is correct or ask for an explanation to check an answer step-by-step to identify errors). Other studies, such as Azevedo et al. (2009) also suggest that students rarely employ monitoring strategies during learning and knowledge construction tasks, but frequently apply a variety of other metacognitive strategies.

It may also be true that students understand a monitoring strategy but do not know when to apply it, since the feedback only implicitly addressed this issue by advising strategies at appropriate times. For example, when constructing their concept map, students may not know when to switch from map building to map checking and back in an effective way. Moreover, they may have difficulty in formulating "good" queries that help them check a relevant part of their map. Therefore, monitoring strategy feedback may need to be presented in more elaborate detail with justification of its importance in the learning task and identification of applicable situations. For example, analysis of the context and details of advised actions (e.g., Betty's feedback "Can we go over my explanation step by step and check it with the resources?") suggests the use of explain-and-read actions, but effective application of the feedback involves reading sections of the resources related to the map concepts and links in the current query and explanation. Some of these details may need to be built into the feedback mechanisms, especially in the early stages, to help students learn *when* and *how* to apply strategies in an effective way.

Since students appeared to be more receptive to the explicitly strategy-oriented feedback from the more authoritative agent, i.e., the mentor, it may be especially fruitful to improve the mentor agent's feedback. We intend to continue analyzing the data from this and future studies in order to better understand how specific phrasing and different forms of metacognitive feedback affect student behavior. We have also been conducting studies to determine how to make the timing and content of strategy feedback more relevant to the student's current activities on the system.

In addition to analyzing and enhancing the agent feedback to promote metacognitive strategies and prepare students for future learning, we also plan to refine our HMM analysis technique. Enhanced HMM analysis could provide a better understanding of the different strategies employed by students when learning complex science topics and allow for more adaptive feedback suited to the current context of the students' activities. In particular, we intend to employ clustering of individual student HMMs to improve the accuracy of our HMM analysis and use sequence mining to pre-process the trace data in the HMM analysis to maintain more of the temporal information in the aggregated behaviors of HMM states.

Acknowledgments This work has been supported by Dept. of ED IES grant #R305H060089, NSF REESE Award #0633856, and NSF IIS Award #0904387.

References

Aleven, V., McLaren, B., Roll, I., & Koedinger, K. (2006). Toward meta-cognitive tutoring: A model of help seeking with a Cognitive Tutor. *International Journal of Artificial Intelligence in Education, 16*(2), 101–128.

Azevedo, R. (2005). Using hypermedia as a metacognitive tool for enhancing student learning? The role of self-regulated learning. *Educational Psychologist, 40*(4), 199–209.

Azevedo, R., & Witherspoon, A. M. (2009). Self-regulated use of hypermedia. In A. Graesser, J. Dunlosky, & D. Hacker (Eds.), *Handbook of metacognition in education*. Mahwah, NJ: Erlbaum.

Azevedo, R., Witherspoon, A., Chauncey, A., Burkett, C., & Fike, A. (2009). MetaTutor: A metacognitive tool for enhancing self-regulated learning. *Annual Meeting of the American Association for Artificial Intelligence, Symposium on Metacognitive and Cognitive Educational Systems* (pp. 4–19).

Bandura, A. (1997). *Self-efficacy: The exercise of control*. New York, NY: Freeman.

Biswas, G., Jeong, H., Kinnebrew, J. S., Sulcer, B., & Roscoe, R. (2010). Measuring self-regulated learning skills through social interactions in a teachable agent environment. *Research and Practice in Technology-Enhanced Learning (RPTEL), 5*(2), 123–152.

Biswas, G., Leelawong, K., Schwartz, D., Vye, N., & Vanderbilt, T. T. A. G. (2005). Learning by teaching: A new agent paradigm for educational software. *Applied Artificial Intelligence, 19*(3), 363–392.

Blair, K., Schwartz, D. L., Biswas, G., & Leelawong, K. (2007). Pedagogical agents for learning by teaching: teachable agents. *Educational Technology & Society: Special Issue on Pedagogical Agents, 47*(1).

Bransford, J. D., Brown, A. L., & Cocking, R. R. (Eds.) (2000). *How people learn*. Washington, DC: National Academy Press.

Bransford, J. D., & Schwartz, D. L. (1999). Rethinking transfer: A simple proposal with multiple implications. *Review of Research in Education, 24*(1), 61.

Brown, A. L., & Palincsar, A. S. (1989). Guided, cooperative learning and individual knowledge acquisition. In L. B. Resnick (Ed.), *Knowing, learning, and instruction: Essays in honor of Robert Glaser* (pp. 393–451). Hillsdale, NJ: Lawrence Erlbaum Associates.

Burleson, W., Picard, R. W., Perlin, K., & Lippincott, J. (2004) A platform for affective agent research. *Workshop on Empathetic Agents, International Conference on Autonomous Agents and Multiagent Systems, New York, NY*.

Chase, C. C., Chin, D. B., Oppezzo, M. A., & Schwartz, D. L. (2009). Teachable agents and the protégé effect: Increasing the effort towards learning. *Journal of Science Education and Technology, 18*(4), 334–352.

D'Mello, S. K., Craig, S. D., Witherspoon, A., Mcdaniel, B., & Graesser, A. (2008). Automatic detection of learners affect from conversational cues. *User Modeling and User-Adapted Interaction, 18*(1), 45–80.

D'Mello, S., Picard, R. W., & Graesser, A. (2007) Toward an affect-sensitive AutoTutor. *IEEE Intelligent Systems, 22*(4), 53–61.

Forbus, K. D. (1984) Qualitative process theory. *Artificial intelligence, 24*(1–3), 85–168.

Hadwin, A. F., Nesbit, J. C., Jamieson-Noel, D., Code, J., & Winne, P. H. (2007). Examining trace data to explore self-regulated learning. *Metacognition and Learning, 2*(2), 107–124.

Hadwin, A. F., Winne, P. H., Stockley, D. B., Nesbit, J. C., & Woszczyna, C. (2001) Context moderates students' self-reports about how they study. *Journal of Educational Psychology, 93*(3), 477–487.

Jeong, H., & Biswas, G. (2008). Mining student behavior models in learning-by-teaching environments. *Proceedings of the First International Conference on Educational Data Mining, Montreal, Quebec, Canada* (pp. 127–136).

Jonassen, D. H., & Ionas, I. G. (2008). Designing effective supports for causal reasoning. *Educational Technology Research and Development, 56*(3), 287–308

Leelawong, K., & Biswas, G. (2008). Designing learning by teaching agents: The Betty's Brain system. *International Journal of Artificial Intelligence in Education, 18*(3), 181–208.

Lester, J. C., Converse, S. A., Kahler, S. E., Barlow, S. T., Stone, B. A., & Bhogal, R. S. (1997). The persona effect: affective impact of animated pedagogical agents. *Proceedings of the SIGCHI conference on Human Factors in Computing Systems (CHI '97), Atlanta, GA* (pp. 359–366).

Li, C., & Biswas, G. (2000). A Bayesian approach to temporal data clustering using hidden Markov models. *Proceedings of the Seventeenth International Conference on Machine Learning* (pp. 543–550).

Li, C., & Biswas, G. (2002). A Bayesian approach for learning hidden Markov models from data. *Scientific Programming: Special Issue on Markov Chain and Hidden Markov Models, 10*(3), 201–219.

Paris, S. G., & Paris, A. H. (2001). Classroom applications of research on self-regulated learning. *Educational Psychologist, 36*(2), 89–101.

Perry, N. E., & Winne, P. H. (2006). Learning from learning kits: gStudy traces of students? Self-regulated engagements with computerized content. *Educational Psychology Review, 18*(3), 211–228.

Pintrich, P. R. (2000). An achievement goal theory perspective on issues in motivation terminology, theory, and research. *Contemporary Educational Psychology, 25*(1), 92–104.

Pintrich, P. R. (2002). The role of metacognitive knowledge in learning, teaching, and assessing. *Theory into Practice, 41*(4), 219–225.

Pintrich, P. R., Marx, R. W., & Boyle, R. A. (1993). Beyond cold conceptual change: The role of motivational beliefs and classroom contextual factors in the process of conceptual change. *Review of Educational Research, 63*(2), 167–199.

Pintrich, P. R., Smith, D. A. F., Garcia, T., & McKeachie, W. J. (1993). Reliability and predictive validity of the Motivated Strategies for Learning Questionnaire (MSLQ). *Educational and psychological measurement, 53*(3), 801-813.

Rabiner, L. R. (1989). A tutorial on hidden Markov models and selected applications in speech recognition. *Proceedings of the IEEE, 77*(2), 257–286.

Roll, I., Aleven, V., Mclaren, B. M., & Koedinger, K. R. (2007). Designing for metacognition: Applying cognitive tutor principles to the tutoring of help seeking. *Metacognition and Learning, 2*, 125–140.

Roscoe, R. D., & Chi, M. T. H. (2007). Understanding tutor learning: knowledge-building and knowledge-telling in peer tutors' explanations and questions. *Review of Educational Research, 77*(4), 534–574.

Schraw, G., Kauffman, D. F., & Lehman, S. (2002). Self-regulated learning theory. In L. Nadel (Ed.), *The encyclopedia of cognitive science* (pp. 1063–1073), London: Nature Publishing Company.

Schunk, D. H., & Zimmerman, B. J. (1997). Social origins of self-regulatory competence. *Educational Psychologist, 32*(4), 195–208.

Schwartz, D. L., Blair, K. P., Biswas, G., Leelawong, K., & Davis, J. (2007). Animations of thought: Interactivity in the teachable agent paradigm. In R. Lowe & W. Schnotz (Eds.), *Learning with animation: Research and implications for design* (pp. 114–140). Cambridge: Cambridge University Press.

Schwartz, D. L., Chase, C., Chin, D. B., Oppezzo, M., Kwong, H., Okita, S. et al. (2009) Interactive metacognition: Monitoring and regulating a teachable agent. In D. J. Hacker, J. Dunlosky, & A. C. Graesser (Eds.), *Handbook of metacognition in education* (pp. 340–358). New York: Routledge Press.

Schwartz, D. L., & Martin, T. (2004). Inventing to prepare for future learning: The hidden efficiency of encouraging original student production in statistics instruction. *Cognition and Instruction, 22*(2), 129–184.

Tan, J., Biswas, G., & Schwartz, D. (2006). Feedback for metacognitive support in learning by teaching environments. *Proceedings of the 28th Annual Meeting of the Cognitive Science Society, Vancouver, Canada* (pp. 828–833).

Wagster, J., Tan, J., Wu, Y., Biswas, G., & Schwartz, D. (2007). Do learning by teaching environments with metacognitive support help students develop better learning behaviors. *Proceedings of the 29th Annual Meeting of the Cognitive Science Society, Nashville, TN* (pp. 695–700).

Weinstein, C. E., Schulte, A. C., and Palmer, D. R. (1987). *The learning and study strategies inventory*. Clearwater, FL: H & H Publishing.

Winne, P., & Hadwin, A. (2008). The weave of motivation and self-regulated learning. In D. H. Schunk & B. J. Zimmerman (Eds.), *Motivation and self-regulated learning: Theory, research, and applications* (pp. 297–314). New York, NY: Taylor & Francis.

Zimmerman, B. J. (1990). Self-regulating academic learning and achievement: The emergence of a social cognitive perspective. *Educational Psychology Review, 2*(2), 173–201.

Zimmerman, B. J. (2001). Theories of self-regulated learning and academic achievement: An overview and analysis. In B. J. Zimmerman & D. H. Schunk (Eds.), *Self-regulated learning and academic achievement: Theoretical perspectives* (pp. 1–37). Mahwah, NJ: Erlbaum.

Zimmerman, B. J. (2008). Investigating self-regulation and motivation: Historical background, methodological developments, and future prospects. *American Educational Research Journal, 45*(1), 166–183.

Zimmerman, B. J., Bandura, A., & Martinez-Pons, M. (1992). Self-motivation for academic attainment: The role of self-efficacy beliefs and personal goal setting. *American Educational Research Journal, 29*(3), 663–676.

Zimmerman, B. J., & Martinez-Pons, M. (1986). Development of a structured interview for assessing student use of self-regulated learning strategies. *American Educational Research Journal, 23*(4), 614–628.

Supporting Self-Regulated Science Learning in Narrative-Centered Learning Environments

30

James C. Lester, Bradford W. Mott, Jennifer L. Robison, Jonathan P. Rowe, and Lucy R. Shores

Abstract

Narrative-centered learning environments provide engaging, story-centric virtual spaces that afford opportunities for discreetly embedding pedagogical guidance for content knowledge and problem-solving skill acquisition. Students' abilities to self-regulate learning significantly impact performance in these environments and are critical for academic achievement and lifelong learning. This chapter explores the relationship between narrative-centered learning environments and self-regulation for science learning. Connections are drawn between the salient characteristics of narrative-centered learning environments and principles for promoting self-regulation in science education. These relationships are further explored through an examination of the Crystal Island learning environment. The chapter investigates the hypothesis that narrative-centered learning environments are particularly well suited for simultaneously promoting learning, engagement, and self-regulation. Empirical support is provided by a summary of findings from a series of studies conducted with over 300 middle school students.

Narrative-centered learning environments have become the subject of increasing attention in the intelligent tutoring systems community (Aylett, Louchart, Dias, Paiva, & Vala, 2005; Johnson & Valente, 2008; McQuiggan, Rowe, Lee, & Lester, 2008). Narrative-centered learning environments are a class of educational games that contextualize educational content and problem solving with interactive story scenarios. By combining salient features of stories (rich settings, believable characters, and compelling plots) with key elements of digital game environments (agency, rewards, and multimedia feedback), narrative-centered learning environments show significant promise for increasing student motivation, supporting meaning making, and guiding complex problem solving. Narrative-centered learning environments tap into students' innate facilities for crafting and understanding stories (Bruner, 1990), and they

J.C. Lester (✉) • B.W. Mott • J.L. Robison • J.P. Rowe • L.R. Shores
North Carolina State University,
Raleigh, NC 27695, USA
e-mail: lester@ncsu.edu

R. Azevedo and V. Aleven (eds.), *International Handbook of Metacognition and Learning Technologies*, Springer International Handbooks of Education 26, DOI 10.1007/978-1-4419-5546-3_30,

encourage students to become active participants in ongoing narratives. By integrating technologies from intelligent tutoring systems, embodied conversational agents, and serious games into story-centric virtual environments, narrative-centered learning environments offer the promise of adaptive, situated learning experiences that are highly interactive and engaging for students. Narrative-centered learning environments have been studied in a range of domains, including anti-bullying education (Aylett et al., 2005), language learning (Johnson & Valente, 2008), and science education (Ketelhut, Dede, & Clarke, 2010; McQuiggan, Rowe et al., 2008).

Narrative-centered learning environments offer the potential to not only enhance students' content knowledge but also aid in problem solving and self-regulation. Self-regulated learning refers to students' ability to generate, monitor and control their cognitive, metacognitive, and motivational processes (Zimmerman, 1990). Self-regulation is particularly important in scientific inquiry where learning is guided by students' curiosity and motivation for acquiring knowledge through the application of efficient strategies (Graesser, McNamara, & VanLehn, 2005). Although narrative-centered learning environments can be designed for a broad range of subject matters, this chapter focuses on specific approaches to self-regulated learning in science education. Schraw, Crippen, and Hartley (2006) identify six pedagogical strategies that have been empirically shown to increase student self-regulation in science, including inquiry-based learning, collaboration, strategy instruction, construction of mental models, technology use, and the role of epistemological beliefs. Each of these strategies can be implemented within the motivating contexts of narrative-centered learning environments.

This chapter explores the benefits of narrative-centered learning environments for student self-regulated learning in science. Connections between pedagogical strategies for self-regulated learning in science and interactive narrative environments are drawn through an examination of CRYSTAL ISLAND, a narrative-centered learning environment for middle-school microbiology. Empirical support is provided by a summary of results drawn from several studies with CRYSTAL ISLAND investigating learning outcomes, engagement, and problem-solving activities.

Self-Regulation in Narrative-Centered Learning Environments

Narrative-centered learning environments offer significant promise for promoting guided discovery learning by leveraging the motivational characteristics of narrative and interactive game environments and providing a compelling context for developing and applying problem-solving skills. However, students' ability to pursue pedagogical and narrative goals is central to narrative-centered learning environments' efficacy, particularly in open-ended environments that feature inquiry-based scenarios and multiple problem-solving paths. As a consequence, self-regulation is often critical for students interacting with narrative-centered learning environments.

Self-Regulated Learning

Research suggests that individuals who are able to self-regulate their learning processes in intentional and reflective ways are more likely to achieve academic success (Butler, Cartier, Schnellert, & Gagnon, 2006). The term *self-regulated learning* can be used to describe learning that is guided by metacognition, strategic action, and motivated behavior (Zimmerman, 1990). Pintrich (2000) notes that although multiple models of self-regulated learning exist, most share four main assumptions: (1) learners actively construct knowledge during the learning process, (2) learners actively control, monitor, and regulate aspects of their learning environment, as well as facets of their own cognition, behavior, and motivation, (3) learning is goal-driven, and (4) goals are compared to standards or criteria in order to monitor progress and adapt facets of cognition, behavior, and motivation.

Self-regulation is particularly important in domains that emphasize inquiry. Inquiry activities typically permit multiple lines of investigation, feature both implicit and explicit goals, and require knowledge construction and critical thinking skills (Anderson, 2002). In order to effectively navigate inquiry scenarios, students must be able to identify and synthesize relevant background knowledge, iteratively formulate hypotheses and hypothesis-testing plans, and critically assess and augment their investigation strategies based on prior findings and current problem-solving contexts. Self-efficacy and motivation is important for students to sustain effort across hypothesis-testing-revision cycles and to adjust problem-solving strategies when necessary. Students who are self-regulated learners are likely to have many of the same skills needed to optimally benefit from inquiry-based learning methods.

Unfortunately, students often require explicit instruction in order to effectively self-regulate their learning, and may not develop these skills on their own. Boekaerts and Niemvirta (2000) note that teachers, and not students themselves, tend to have the responsibility of conveying information and procedures, monitor performance, provide feedback, and motivate learning. This assignment of responsibilities hinders the development of self-regulation by making learning the responsibility of the teacher rather than the student. It has been shown that although most teachers agree that one of the primary goals of education is to develop intrinsically motivated, self-regulated learners (Paris, Lipson, & Wixon, 1994), few students receive instruction in self-regulated learning in school and few have opportunities to regulate their own learning (Randi & Corno, 2000).

Scaffolding Self-Regulated Learning in Intelligent Tutoring Systems

Over the past several years, the education community has begun to investigate the role that learning technologies can play in detecting, scaffolding, and teaching effective self-regulatory processes. These attempts differ widely in the types of metacognitive phenomena with which they are concerned, the complexity of the environments used to support self-regulation, and the amount of support given to students to develop these skills. For example, work on the MetaTutor intelligent tutoring system has examined the role of self-regulatory strategies in hypertext science learning environments (Witherspoon, Azevedo, & D'Mello, 2008). This work has shown that providing students with prompts from a human tutor on appropriate types of self-regulatory strategies, such as goal setting, plan development, and summarizing learned materials can improve students' use of these strategies. In particular, their findings indicate that students who are able to offload their self-regulatory processes use more diverse sets of strategies than students who have not been given the same instruction. Alternatively, the Betty's Brain system implements *teachable agents*, where students instruct a virtual character from their own knowledge (Leelawong & Biswas, 2008). Students are then able to run queries on the knowledge of their virtual pupil and uncover errors in their own concepts and problem-solving approaches. This type of system encourages self-regulatory processes without providing explicit instruction about them, although providing additional scaffolding can lead to further benefits.

Other work has focused on specific student behaviors related to self-regulatory processes. Aleven, McLaren, Roll, and Koedinger (2004) examined how students use help-giving features of tutorial learning environments. They argue that there are appropriate uses of help-seeking behavior (e.g., during a problem-solving impasse) and also a variety of poor strategies of help seeking (e.g., using help instead of trying themselves, or never seeking help even when it is needed). With the emergence of help-providing systems, understanding the types of "help-seeking" bugs that students engage in is important for designing educational technologies that not only teach content but also teach effective learning strategies. In similar work, Litman and Forbes-Riley (2009) examined how well students are able to monitor their own learning and judge their own correctness during natural-language tutorial sessions.

They used measures of uncertainty and correctness to develop a unified concept of accuracy, and showed that the more accurate students are in their judgments of knowing, the more likely they are to learn.

Narrative-Centered Learning Environments

Narrative-centered learning environments offer several natural affordances for enhancing students' learning experiences and promoting self-regulatory processes. Stories draw audiences into plots and settings, thereby introducing engaging opportunities for situated learning. Fantasy contexts in educational games have also been shown to provide motivational benefits (Parker & Lepper, 1992). Although it is important to remain mindful of potential disadvantages, such as seductive details (Harp & Mayer, 1998), a carefully targeted narrative experience has the potential to be pedagogically compelling.

Recent work on narrative-centered learning environments has leveraged a range of techniques for providing effective, engaging learning experiences. Multiuser virtual environments, such as Quest Atlantis (Barab et al., 2009) and River City (Ketelhut et al., 2010) use rich narrative settings to contextualize inquiry-based science learning scenarios with prominent social and ethical dimensions. BiLAT (Kim et al., 2009) and the Tactical Language and Culture Training System (TLCTS) (Johnson & Valente, 2008) emphasize story-driven interactions with virtual characters to provide instruction on cross-cultural negotiation and foreign language learning, respectively.

Empirical studies have begun to yield promising results that support the potential of narrative-centered learning environments in the classroom. For example, Ketelhut and colleagues (2010) compared several large-scale implementations of River City to a *paper-based control* condition that taught equivalent content and skills. The study found that students who used River City experienced improved content learning gains, increased evidence of thoughtful scientific inquiry, and increased interest in science careers, although the findings failed to be reproduced across all implementations and assessment strategies. Students' diversity and quantity of data gathering behaviors also increased as they used River City over multiple sessions. Barab and colleagues (2009) compared the Taiga Park module of Quest Atlantis to an *expository text* equivalent (i.e., an electronic textbook), as well as a *simple framing* condition (i.e., the scenario was situated with a third person storyline, but the story was not interactive). Students who used Taiga Park outperformed the expository text condition on proximal post-test items. Students who used Taiga Park in dyads were also observed to outperform the expository text condition on distal post-test items. However, comparisons with the simple framing condition were equivocal; the dyad Taiga Park group outperformed the simple framing group on an open-ended transfer task, but there were no differences between groups on standardized post-test items. While evaluation methodologies are still the subject of ongoing research, River City and Quest Atlantis have yielded promising initial benchmarks for the expected efficacy of narrative-centered learning environments.

Related work has examined how artificial intelligence can be used to generate engaging interactive story experiences that are pedagogically effective and tailored to individual students' interactions. FearNot! uses affectively driven autonomous agents to generate dramatic, educational vignettes about bullying (Aylett et al., 2005). TLCTS uses a range of artificial intelligence techniques for speech recognition, dialogue modeling, and virtual human behavior across a suite of story-centric, serious games designed for language and culture learning (Johnson & Valente, 2008). BiLAT uses rule-based intelligent tutoring facilities that deliver individualized guidance in the form of hints and feedback, as well as structured after-action reviews (Kim et al., 2009). Extending intelligent tutoring systems to support self-regulated learning during narrative-centered learning experiences is a promising direction for this line of research. However, systematic investigation of narrative-centered learning environment features that best promote self-regulated learning processes is still in its infancy.

Leveraging Narrative Environments for Self-Regulated Learning

As noted above, Schraw and colleagues (2006) identify six areas of focus for improving self-regulated learning in science education: inquiry-based learning, collaboration, strategy instruction, construction of mental models, technology use, and epistemological beliefs. Narrative-centered learning environments present opportunities for discreetly implementing each of these strategies in motivating and effective ways. Incorporating these strategies may also provide students with important problem-solving guidance that simultaneously enhances student self-efficacy and engagement in the sciences.

Inquiry-Based Learning

Interactive narratives naturally support several key aspects of inquiry-based learning. For example, audiences interact with narrative in a way that resembles the steps of inquiry-based learning. Generally, narratives contain sequences of causally related events that contribute to an overarching plot, and most individuals appear to have inherent schemata for these structures (Bruner, 1990). Audiences naturally draw inferences about the narratives they encounter (Gerrig, 1993). As the plot of a narrative develops, audiences instinctively form hypotheses about possible future events. These hypotheses are actively tested as the story continues, and they are either supported or contradicted as the plot is revealed. Thus, each situation must be reevaluated in light of new information, and alternate hypotheses must be formulated.

The continuous cycle of forming and evaluating expectations has the benefit of keeping readers motivated and engaged. Furthermore, events, such as unexpected twists, humorous or empathetic characters, and fantasy are generally introduced to encourage reader engagement. This narrative inference process aligns well with the hypothesis generation-testing-revision cycles of inquiry-based learning, creating opportunities for the two processes to complement one another in effective and engaging manners. Of course, the alignment between narrative inference and inquiry-based learning depends upon tight integration between narrative content and science content. Tight integration between narrative and curriculum is one of the key features of narrative-centered learning environments. This integration is one of the primary characteristics distinguishing narrative-centered learning environments from other types of educational games with stories that are tangential to their primary instructional objectives. In the case of science learning, tight integration means that the inferences necessary for reasoning about the narrative are the same inferences necessary for scientific thinking.

Narrative-centered learning environments also support active participation in stories as students adopt the roles of characters. Students in narrative-centered learning environments carry out problem-solving actions in a manner similar to that of authentic inquiry. In authentic inquiry, students generate research questions and guide themselves through the problem-solving process (Anderson, 2002); however, in the case of narrative-centered learning environments, students' problem-solving activities can also be guided within the structure of the narrative. For example, in a medical mystery scenario, by establishing which actions serve as the narrative's desired resolution (e.g., determining the identity of a mysterious disease), the student is implicitly scaffolded to set an overall goal: it is the student with guidance from the narrative, rather than guidance from the instructor, who determines what actions to take in order to accomplish the task at hand (the desired plot resolution). Narrative-centered learning environments also offer means for supporting hypothesis formation and testing. Each action taken by a student (e.g., running a virtual lab experiment, gathering background information) is taken because the student believes it will bring her closer to the solution, based on her current understanding or hypothesis. Evidence that an action does not lead to the goal solution may indicate a flawed hypothesis, forcing the student to reconsider her hypotheses and problem-solving plans.

Collaboration

Given the importance of characters for engaging narratives, collaboration within narrative-centered learning environments is a natural technique for supporting self-regulated learning. Schraw and colleagues (2006) identify four distinct ways in which collaboration directly enhances SRL instruction: modeling partner behaviors, planning and evaluating discussion, utilizing the academic strengths of each student, and promoting classroom equity (Schraw et al., 2006).

A promising feature of narrative-centered learning environments is introducing a companion agent, a character that works closely with the student and can prompt discussion, reflection, and assistance in natural and subtle ways. Companion agents can assume the role of an apprentice, peer, or mentor to the student character. As an apprentice, the companion agent can ask the student to interpret and explain data gathered in the course of problem solving and to convey to the agent how this new information contributes to achieving the narrative's resolution. This method of forming explanations and teaching material to others has been shown to have beneficial effects on understanding and self-regulated learning (Chi, de Leeuw, Chiu, & LaVancher, 1994; Leelawong & Biswas, 2008).

A companion agent can serve as a peer by asking questions, such as "What should we do next?" in order to prompt student planning, monitoring, and self-reflection, which are three key metacognitive strategies. Companion agents subtly inform the student of oversights or discourage conceptual overconfidence while maintaining the student's sense of agency and responsibility. A companion agent that serves as a mentor to the student interacts in a similar fashion by modeling important behaviors and guiding the student through the environment. Because companion agents are personified as characters within a story, their presence yields a noninvasive mechanism for metacognitive prompting, which can also be used to collect metacognitive data about the student. Techniques for devising companion agents capable of delivering metacognitive prompts that are appropriate for a given narrative context and SRL phase is an open research question.

Strategy Instruction

A growing body of research suggests that explicit instruction in self-regulated learning strategies promotes academic achievement (Schunk & Zimmerman, 1998). Specifically, these skills include effective problem-solving and critical-thinking skills (Schraw et al., 2006). Utilizing engaging features of narratives, such as character interactions, can transition strategy instruction from explicit procedural steps provided by an instructor to an integral component of a compelling narrative.

Within the context of a narrative, a student can be assigned a specific role in conjunction with a target task. Particular skills appropriate for that role can be practiced in ways motivated by the narrative, rather than through direct instruction. For example, a student could be assigned the role of a scientist or examiner whose occupational requirements discreetly scaffold problem-solving processes, such as recording notes for reporting back to an authority figure, representing information in a physical model, or evaluating the relevance of information for a particular a task. Rather than providing explicit instruction to students to perform specific steps, the student's learning is scaffolded in a manner that has been engagingly incorporated into the story environment.

Additionally, critical thinking skills can be incorporated into narrative plots. As Schraw and colleagues (2006) observe, essential critical thinking skills are "identifying relevant information, constructing arguments, testing the credibility of information and hypotheses, and forming plausible conclusions" while consistently monitoring these activities (p. 124). Identifying relevant information and testing the credibility of information and hypotheses can be achieved through prompted reflection, which encourages students to formulate questions about a given task and extract the most important information. Characters can explicitly ask students questions throughout the learning interaction that encourages reflection on how information was attained and why it is vital for accomplishing the task at hand. Moreover, expert characters, as well as virtual posters and books in the environment, can be utilized to help the student practice how to decide what information is the most important when an abundance of information sources are available.

With respect to constructing arguments and forming plausible conclusions, students can benefit from interactions with other virtual characters in the narrative. These characters can be designed to probe students and suggest other subgoals to pursue. If a student finds these suggestions inadequate, he or she can be prompted to explain to the character why the advice will not be followed. As the student provides this explanation, a narrative-centered learning environment can dynamically probe the student until an adequate argument has been formulated. After the student provides an explanation for a desired learning goal, the system has an opportunity to detect what information the student understands, and what information the student should elaborate or further investigate.

Mental Models and Conceptual Change

Mental models are cognitive aids that enable students to mentally represent and reason about complex processes. Narrative-centered learning environments and virtual environments in general, can contribute to novel mental model construction and conceptual change. The graphical technology of narrative-centered learning environments allows animated, 3D representations of scientific processes to aid in student conceptual understanding. Moreover, since the structure of narrative builds upon sequences of events, models can be continuously created and refined as more information is gathered and events occur.

Student Personal Beliefs

Student epistemological beliefs and self-efficacy play an important role in self-regulation because of their effect on students' perceived personal abilities and motivation (Schraw et al., 2006). Students with high levels of science self-efficacy have been shown to be more motivated and more likely to undertake and persist on difficult tasks. It is plausible that virtual characters could be designed to provide appropriate feedback on student performance and enhance student self-efficacy during narrative-centered learning experiences. Further, as peer modeling has been shown to increase self-efficacy (Schunk & Hanson, 1985), virtual characters can be used to model desirable behaviors.

Students who hold the epistemological belief that academic ability is not static, and can be improved with effort, are more likely to be motivated when working on intellectually challenging tasks (Schommer, 1990). Virtual characters can be utilized to model and discuss desired epistemological beliefs. For instance, findings contradicting the student's initial beliefs can occur as the plot progresses; an agent in the environment can help the student to understand that these contradictions are natural and common. Character interactions are a natural element of narrative, and leveraging multimodal conversations with virtual characters is a promising vehicle for impacting student self-efficacy and epistemological beliefs.

An Implemented Narrative-Centered Learning Environment

Now in its fourth major iteration, CRYSTAL ISLAND is a narrative-centered learning environment built on Valve Software's Source™ engine, the 3D game platform developed for the popular Half-Life 2 series of games. The curriculum underlying CRYSTAL ISLAND's mystery narrative is derived from the North Carolina state standard course of study for eighth-grade microbiology. Students play the role of the protagonist, Alex, who is attempting to discover the identity and source of an infectious disease plaguing a research station. Figure 30.1 displays a screenshot from CRYSTAL ISLAND, in which the student learns about the infectious disease through a conversation with a virtual character.

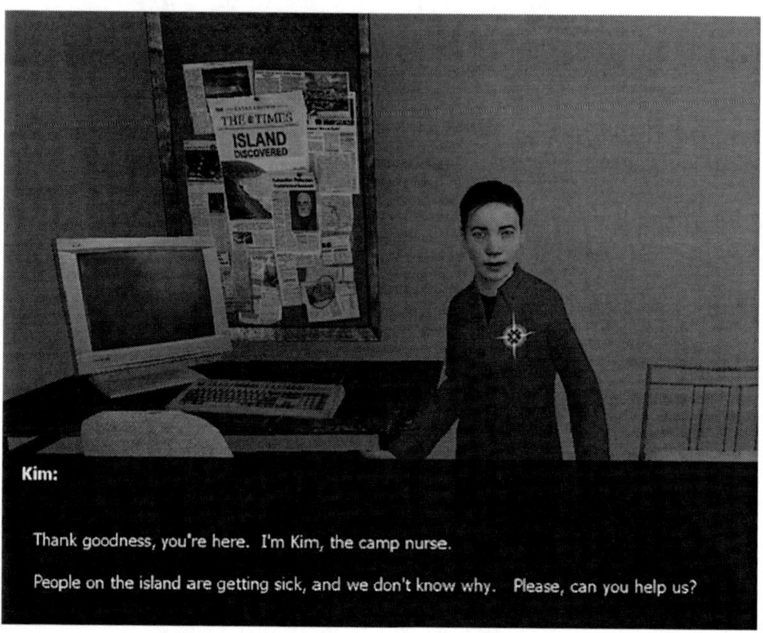

Fig. 30.1 CRYSTAL ISLAND narrative-centered learning environments

CRYSTAL ISLAND's narrative takes place in a small research camp situated on a recently discovered tropical island. As students explore the camp, they investigate the island's spreading illness by forming questions, generating hypotheses, collecting data, and testing hypotheses. Throughout their investigations, students interact with non-player characters offering clues and relevant microbiology facts via multimodal "dialogues" delivered by characters through student menu choices and characters' spoken language. The dialogues' content is supplemented with virtual books, posters, and other resources encountered in several of the camp's locations. As students gather information about the spreading illness, they have access to a personal digital assistant to take and review notes, consult a microbiology field manual, communicate with characters, and report progress in solving the mystery. To solve the mystery, students complete a *diagnosis worksheet* to manage their working hypotheses and record findings about patients' symptoms and medical history, as well as any findings from tests conducted in the camp's laboratory. Once a student enters a hypothesized diagnosis, cause of illness, and treatment plan into the diagnosis worksheet, the findings are submitted to the camp nurse for review and possible revision.

To illustrate how CRYSTAL ISLAND implements instructional strategies for self-regulated science learning, consider the following scenario. The student has been exploring the CRYSTAL ISLAND virtual environment and has been tasked by the camp nurse with researching the island's mysterious spreading illness. The student begins by consulting with the island's residents, as well as by reading nearby posters and books that discuss various microbiology concepts. Some of the island's characters help to identify objects and symptoms that are relevant to the scenario, while others provide pertinent microbiology information. However, not all of the camp's team members provide relevant information, so the student must critically evaluate the information she obtains. As the student gathers clues and progresses through the narrative, she begins to develop, test, and revise hypotheses about possible explanations for the disease (*inquiry-based learning*). This inquiry process emerges naturally in the course of solving the science mystery, and to organize her thoughts the student records her inferences about the symptoms and candidate causes of the outbreak in a diagnosis worksheet. The worksheet enables her to encode a simplified version of her mental model of the disease's spread (*mental models*). The student shares her diagnosis worksheet with the camp nurse, and they collaboratively review evidence that the student has collected, as well as the worksheet's proposed diagnosis, but discover a flaw (*collaboration*). The nurse, who serves as a virtual mentor to guide the student through the inquiry process, encourages the student to reflect on her current findings. The student and the nurse then discuss possible directions for establishing a revised hypothesis (*strategy instruction*). The student decides to test several partially consumed food items that the sick members recently ate, and after conducting a battery of tests in the laboratory, she discovers that a container of unpasteurized milk in the dining hall is contaminated with bacteria. By combining this discovery with information about the sick characters' symptoms, the student concludes that the team members' illness stems from an *Escherichia coli* infection. The student reports her findings back to the camp nurse, and together they discuss a plan for treatment of the sick team members.

Findings

Over the past few years, Crystal Island has been the subject of several studies conducted with North Carolina middle school students to investigate factors related to self-regulated learning, including learning gains, problem-solving, engagement, and off-task behavior (McQuiggan, Goth, Ha, Rowe, & Lester, 2008; McQuiggan, Rowe et al., 2008; Rowe, Shores, Mott, & Lester, 2010a, 2010b). Three categories of instruments have been used to collect data about student learning processes during interactions with Crystal Island: (1) direct prompts and self-report requests embedded within the virtual environment, (2) pre-intervention and post-intervention tests and subjective surveys, and (3) trace data logs of students' in-game actions. Embedded prompts and self-reports have asked students to report on their current goals, goal-achievement progress, confidence in their content knowledge, and reflections about the problem-solving strategies employed. Pre- and post-intervention measures have assessed students' content knowledge, knowledge transfer, goal achievement orientation, self-efficacy, game-playing experience, personality, situational interest, and presence. Student trace data logs have recorded students' problem-solving actions, on-task and off-task behaviors, goals, affective states, and help-seeking behaviors. These investigations have yielded several areas of empirical support for the promise of narrative-centered learning environments to promote engaging science learning and self-regulatory processes.

An experiment involving an early version of Crystal Island investigated the impact of story content on student learning in narrative-centered learning environments (McQuiggan, Rowe et al., 2008). The study compared two versions of Crystal Island—a full-narrative version featuring a poisoning scenario and rich character inter-relationships, and a minimal narrative-version featuring only story details necessary to support the problem-solving scenario—against a more traditional instructional approach, a narrated slideshow that conveyed the same curricular material. The results showed that students in the Crystal Island conditions exhibited learning gains, but that those gains were less than those produced by traditional instructional approaches. However, the motivational benefits of narrative-centered learning, particularly with regard to self-efficacy, presence, and interest, were substantial. Students reported the highest levels of presence in the full-narrative condition, a finding that bears important implications for motivation.

A follow-up study using an updated version of Crystal Island found improved learning gains compared to the prior study (Rowe et al., 2010a). Furthermore, it was found that several factors hypothesized to be related to student engagement (e.g., presence, in-game performance, and situational interest) were significantly associated with improved learning outcomes, independent of students' background knowledge and game-playing experience. These results contrast with the initial study's findings that placed learning and engagement variables at odds with one another. The updated version of CRYSTAL ISLAND incorporated a number of changes believed to contribute to the improved learning outcomes. The changes included the following: multimodal spoken character dialogues, an expanded diagnosis worksheet, a streamlined narrative (lacking the poisoning scenario and non-essential character relationships), tighter coupling between the narrative and microbiology curriculum, simplified controls, a revised laboratory testing device, a new sub-activity in which students labeled parts of cells, and an updated look-and-feel of the island. The findings indicate that story and gameplay features can be crafted such that engagement in the interactive narrative scenario can contribute to learning outcomes, rather than detract from learning.

Several analyses have been conducted to investigate students' problem-solving processes during interactions with CRYSTAL ISLAND. One version of CRYSTAL ISLAND maintained an in-game score to assess students' progress and efficiency in completing the science mystery. Score incorporated time taken to accomplish important narrative goals, students' ability to demonstrate microbiology content knowledge, and evidence of careful hypothesis formulation. Scores were decreased after any attempt to "game the system" by repeatedly submitting incorrect diagnoses to the camp nurse or guessing on content knowledge quizzes. A comparison of students who achieved high scores during gameplay versus low-scoring students found striking differences in their learning outcomes, self-efficacy for science, and gameplay profiles (Rowe et al., 2010b). High-scoring students scored significantly higher on a post-experiment content test, were significantly more self-efficacious for science, and performed more information gathering and offloading behaviors during gameplay, such as reading virtual books and accurately completing their diagnosis worksheets. Low-scoring students tended to spend more time engaged in dialogues with non-player characters and conducted more tests in the laboratory, including unnecessary tests. These findings may be symptomatic of low-scoring students being less effective at devising and following successful problem-solving and self-regulatory strategies in CRYSTAL ISLAND, as evidenced by inefficient inquiry behaviors and decreased diagnosis worksheet performance. Examples of inefficient inquiry behaviors include randomly guessing the mystery's solution, conducting an excessive number of redundant or irrelevant laboratory tests, and taking excessive amounts of time to complete the narrative's sub-goals.

An examination of students' note-taking behaviors during interactions with CRYSTAL ISLAND revealed that students who took notes about their hypotheses performed better on a post-experiment content test (McQuiggan, Goth et al., 2008). This observation reinforces inquiry-based learning findings suggesting the importance of scaffolding students' hypothesis generation activities. The study also found significant gender effects on note-taking, with females taking significantly more notes than males. Goal orientation and efficacy for self-regulated learning were also significantly correlated with note-taking behavior.

Findings from a study with CRYSTAL ISLAND indicated that gender and game-playing experience significantly impact variables related to student engagement, such as presence (Rowe et al., 2010b). It was found that male students reported being more present than female students during interactions with CRYSTAL ISLAND, and that experienced gamers tended to be more present than less-experienced gamers. An analysis of student off-task behavior within the virtual environment (i.e., students' attendance to non-essential environmental features) also found negative associations with science achievement; students with lower scores on pre-experiment and post-experiment content tests tended to perform more off-task behaviors than their higher-scoring counterparts (Rowe, McQuiggan, Robison, & Lester, 2009). Male students were also found to perform significantly more off-task behaviors. It was unclear to what extent these off-task behaviors consisted of students' disengaging from the learning activity versus engaging in behaviors that were inconsistent with effective problem-solving tactics. It may be that these off-task behaviors are symptomatic of inadequate self-regulatory processes, but additional investigation is necessary to confirm this hypothesis. While the rich details of virtual environments may draw some students away from learning-focused activities, they play a critical role in establishing a compelling narrative and virtual environment. Rather than remove such elements in the hope of avoiding off-task behaviors, a more promising approach is to devise adaptive scaffolding techniques that help students regulate their learning and return to productive problem-solving behaviors. Despite these open questions, the finding that students' gender and game-playing experience impact factors associated with student engagement is important for informing future research about the design of narrative-centered learning environments that seek to promote engagement as part of supporting self-regulated learning.

Discussion and Challenges

Findings indicate that narrative-centered learning environments can be effective platforms for inquiry-based learning that synergistically integrate learning and engagement in problem-solving scenarios. Although the potential for introducing seductive details is an important issue, the potential for narrative-centered learning environments to create engaging practice opportunities for self-regulatory skills and discreetly embed scaffolding for self-regulatory processes is a compelling potential benefit. Analyses of students' problem-solving performances in an implemented narrative-centered learning environment have revealed significant variations in self-regulatory skills, as evidenced by variations in problem-solving tactics, note-taking behaviors, learning and engagement outcomes, and off-task behaviors. Continued development of an empirical account of students' self-regulation in narrative-centered learning environments, and the efficacy of different techniques for subtly scaffolding self-regulatory processes, is an important direction for further investigation and will inform the design of future narrative environments.

Despite the considerable potential of narrative-centered learning environments to provide engaging inquiry support facilities for students, designing effective narrative-centered learning environments to enhance students' self-regulatory skills poses several challenges. First, narrative-centered learning environments' ability to deliver individualized and adaptive scaffolding for self-regulated behaviors is strongly dependent upon accurate assessments of the student's current knowledge and abilities. However, it can prove difficult to access information about students' self-regulatory processes due to their internal nature. While detailed records of students' behaviors during interactions with narrative-centered learning environments offer a window into students' self-regulatory skills, further investigation is needed to develop automated methods for dynamically diagnosing self-regulation skills in a manner that is not disruptive to learning.

Second, developing effective narrative-centered learning environments is currently highly resource-intensive. New authoring systems are needed to accelerate the development of narrative-centered learning environments, and professional development materials need to be created so that teachers can effectively integrate these new technologies into their classrooms.

Conclusions

Narrative-centered learning environments provide inquiry-based learning interactions through rich, immersive story worlds that charge students with effectively utilizing content knowledge and problem-solving skills to achieve plot resolutions. Success during interactions with narrative-centered learning environments is often dependent upon the degree to which students are self-regulated; it is the students, not instructors, that ultimately guide instruction by setting learning goals, monitoring goal progression, implementing strategies, and maintaining motivation. Narrative-centered learning environments offer the potential to supplement self-regulated learning processes by discreetly embedding such instruction within narrative structures. Self-regulatory instruction can then be provided through the narrative itself rather than through explicit prompts. While there are challenges to subtly integrating self-regulatory support, advances in intelligent tutoring systems and intelligent interactive narrative technologies hold significant promise for adaptive, real-time self-regulated learning scaffolding and assessment.

Acknowledgments The authors wish to thank members of the IntelliMedia Group of North Carolina State University for their assistance. Additional thanks go to Omer Sturlovich and Pavel Turzo for use of their 3D model libraries, and Valve Software for access to the Source™ engine and SDK. This research was supported by the National Science Foundation under Grants REC-0632450 and DRL-0822200. Any opinions, findings, and conclusions or recommendations expressed in this material are those of the authors and do not necessarily reflect the views of the National Science Foundation.

References

Aleven, V., McLaren, B., Roll, O., & Koedinger, K. (2004). Toward tutoring help seeking: Applying cognitive modeling to meta-cognitive skills. *Proceedings of the Seventh International Conference on Intelligent Tutoring Systems* (pp. 227–239). Maceiò, Alagoas, Brazil.

Anderson, R. D. (2002). Reforming science teaching: What research says about inquiry. *Journal of Science Teacher Education, 13*(1), 1–12.

Aylett, R., Louchart, S., Dias, J., Paiva, A., & Vala, M. (2005). FearNot! An experiment in emergent narrative. *Proceedings of the Fifth International Conference on Intelligent Virtual Agents* (pp. 305–316). Kos, Greece.

Barab, S., Scott, B., Siyahhan, S., Goldstone, R., Ingram-Goble, A., Zuiker, S., et al. (2009). Transformational play as a curricular scaffold: Using videogames to support science education. *Journal of Science Education and Technology, 18*(4), 305–320.

Boekaerts, M., & Niemvirta, M. (2000). Self-regulated learning: Finding a balance between learning goals and ego-protective goals. In M. Boekaerts, P. R. Pintrich, & M. Zeidner (Eds.), *Handbook of self-regulation* (pp. 417–450). San Diego, CA: Academic.

Bruner, J. (1990). *Acts of meaning*. Cambridge, MA: Harvard University Press.

Butler, D., Cartier, S., Schnellert, L., & Gagnon, F. (2006). *Secondary students' self-regulated engagement in "learning through reading": Findings from an integrative research project*. Paper presented at the annual conference of the Canadian Society for Studies in Education, Toronto, ON, Canada.

Chi, M., de Leeuw, N., Chiu, M., & LaVancher, C. (1994). Eliciting self-explanations improves understanding. *Cognitive Science: A Multidisciplinary Journal, 18*(3), 439–477.

Gerrig, R. (1993). *Experiencing narrative worlds: On the psychological activities of reading*. New Haven, CT: Yale University Press.

Graesser, A., McNamara, D., & VanLehn, K. (2005). Scaffolding deep comprehension strategies through point & query, autotutor, and iSTART. *Educational Psychologist, 40*(4), 225–234.

Harp, S., & Mayer, R. (1998). How seductive details do their damage: A theory of cognitive interest in science learning. *Journal of Educational Psychology, 90*(3), 414–434.

Johnson, W. L. & Valente, A. (2008). Tactical Language and Culture Training Systems: Using artificial intelligence to teach foreign languages and cultures. *Proceedings of the 20th National Conference on Innovative Applications of Artificial intelligence, 3* (pp. 1632–1639).

Ketelhut, D., Dede, C., & Clarke, J. (2010). A multi-user virtual environment for building higher order inquiry skills in science. *British Journal of Educational Technology, 41*(1), 56–68.

Kim, J., Hill, R. W., Durlach, P. J., Lane, H. C., Forbell, E., & Core, M. (2009). BiLAT: A game-based environment for practicing negotiation in a cultural context. *International Journal of Artificial Intelligence in Education, 19*(3), 289–308.

Leelawong, K., & Biswas, G. (2008). Designing learning by teaching agents: The Betty's Brain system. *International Journal of Artificial Intelligence in Education, 18*(3), 181–208.

Litman, D. & Forbes-Riley, K. (2009) Improving (meta) cognitive tutoring by detecting and responding to uncertainty. *Working notes of the 2009 AAAI Fall Symposium on Cognitive and Metacognitive Educational Systems*, Arlington, VA.

McQuiggan, S., Goth, J., Ha, E. Y., Rowe, J., & Lester, J. (2008). Student note-taking in narrative-centered learning environments: Individual differences and learning outcomes. *Proceedings of the Ninth International Conference on Intelligent Tutoring Systems* (pp. 510–519). Montreal, QC, Canada.

McQuiggan, S., Rowe, J., Lee, S., & Lester, J. (2008). Story-based learning: The impact of narrative on learning experiences and outcomes. *Proceedings of the Ninth International Conference on Intelligent Tutoring Systems* (pp. 530–539). Montreal, QC, Canada.

Paris, S., Lipson, M. Y., & Wixon, K. (1994). Becoming a strategic reader. In R. B. Ruddell, M. Ruddell, & H. Singer (Eds.), *Theoretical models and processes of reading* (4th ed., pp. 788–810). Newark, DE: International Reading Association.

Parker, L., & Lepper, M. (1992). Effects of fantasy contexts on children's learning and motivation: Making learning more fun. *Journal of Personality and Social Psychology, 62*(4), 625–633.

Pintrich, P. (2000). The role of goal orientation in self-regulated learning. In M. Boekaerts, P. Pintrich, & M. Zeidner (Eds.), *Handbook of self-regulation* (pp. 451–502). San Diego, CA: Academic.

Randi, J., & Corno, L. (2000). Teacher innovations in self-regulated learning. In M. Boekaerts, P. Pintrich, & M. Zeidner (Eds.), *Handbook of Self-regulation* (pp. 651–685). San Diego, CA: Academic.

Rowe, J., McQuiggan, S., Robison, J., & Lester, J. (2009). Off-task behavior in narrative-centered learning environments. *Proceedings of the Fourteenth International Conference on Artificial Intelligence in Education* (pp. 99–106). Brighton, UK.

Rowe, J., Shores, L., Mott, B., & Lester, J. (2010a). Integrating learning and engagement in narrative-centered learning environments. *To appear in Proceedings of the Tenth International Conference on Intelligent Tutoring Systems*, Pittsburgh, PA.

Rowe, J., Shores, L., Mott, B., & Lester, J. (2010b). Individual differences in gameplay and learning: A narrative-centered learning perspective. *To appear in Proceedings of the Fifth International Conference on Foundations of Digital Games*, Monterey, CA.

Schommer, M. (1990). Effects of beliefs about the nature of knowledge on comprehension. *Journal of Educational Psychology, 82*(3), 498.

Schraw, G., Crippen, K., & Hartley, K. (2006). Promoting self-regulation in science education: Metacognition as part of a broader perspective on learning. *Research in Science Education, 36*(1–2), 111–139.

Schunk, D., & Hanson, A. (1985). Peer models: Influence on children's self-efficacy and achievement. *Journal of Educational Psychology, 77*, 313–322.

Schunk, D., & Zimmerman, B. J. (1998). *Self-regulated learning: From teaching to self-reflective practice.* New York: Guilford.

Witherspoon, A., Azevedo, R., & D'Mello, S. (2008). The dynamics of self-regulatory processes within self- and externally-regulated learning episodes during complex science learning with hypermedia. *Proceedings of the Ninth International Conference on Intelligent Tutoring Systems* (pp. 260–269). Montreal, QC, Canada.

Zimmerman, B. J. (1990). Self-regulated learning and academic achievement: An overview. *Educational Psychologist, 25*, 3–18.

A Behavior Change Perspective on Self-Regulated Learning with Teachable Agents

31

Marily Oppezzo and Daniel L. Schwartz

Abstract

Producing lasting changes to metacognition, or the more encompassing construct of self-regulated learning (SRL), has strong parallels to producing behavior change. In the former case, the goal is to develop new "habits of mind," and in the latter, the goal is to develop new "habits of behavior." The techniques and theories of behavior change can inform the design of instruction intended to support the development and transfer of SRL. For example, we describe a set of studies in which teaching adolescents behavior change techniques improves their motivational control for both diet and homework goals. Behavior change theories often emphasize the stages of behavior change. We abstract from the various theories to present a four-stage model of behavior change. We then use the model to critique our own work on Teachable Agents. Teachable Agents are a software program where students learn by teaching a computerized pupil. We discuss the successes of the Teachable Agents in achieving SRL goals and improving learning for each stage of the model, but we also describe how Teachable Agents has missed possible opportunities to improve SRL outcomes based on the behavior change literature.

Producing lasting changes to metacognition, or the more encompassing construct of self-regulated learning (SRL), has strong parallels to producing behavior change. In SRL, through experience and maturation, children develop ways to manage their problem solving and learning. In behavior change, people develop ways to manage health-related behaviors that can range from safe sex to treatment compliance for diabetes and alcoholism. In the former case, the goal is to develop new "habits of mind," and in the latter, the goal is to develop new "habits of behavior." Behavior change is notoriously difficult and important, and the problem has spawned a vast literature that may be unknown to metacognitive researchers. For example, here is a small subset of the journals that include articles on behavior change: *Addictive Behaviors, American Journal of Health Promotion, Behaviour Change, Behavior*

M. Oppezzo, Ph.D. (✉) • D.L. Schwartz, Ph.D.
School of Education, Stanford University, Stanford, CA, USA
e-mail: moppezzo@gmail.com

R. Azevedo and V. Aleven (eds.), *International Handbook of Metacognition and Learning Technologies*, Springer International Handbooks of Education 26, DOI 10.1007/978-1-4419-5546-3_31,

Therapy, Drug and Alcohol Dependence, Health Psychology, and Journal of Obesity.

The behavior change literature comprises many theoretical approaches, some of which are familiar to SRL. One approach falls under the broad umbrella of utility theory. People weigh chances and costs of success against likely payoffs. When put into action, this approach can variously emphasize people's estimation of self-efficacy (Bandura, 2005), their perceptions of benefits and barriers to success (Janz & Becker, 1984), and their expectancy of the social and personal value of the outcomes (Ajzen & Fishbein, 1980). A completely different approach resides under the equally broad umbrella of capacity limits, which highlights that being worn down makes it harder for people to maintain motivation for difficult goals. People have limited psychological and material resources, rooted not just in motivation but also in physical energy stores (Gailliot et al., 2007). When these are depleted, people are more likely to fail at goals that require effort (Baumeister & Vohs, 2007), even if they do not feel depleted (Finkel et al., 2006). When put into action, this approach emphasizes how to help people conserve their motivational energy (Twenge & Baumeister, 2002), conserve their ego (Webb & Sheeran, 2003), reevaluate their resources (Dweck, 1996), amplify what resources they have by building up willpower (Corno, 2001), and enlist environmental and social support (Cohen, 1988). Yet a third approach to behavior change falls within the behaviorist tradition, where the goal is to arrange external conditions that shape people into new habits. When this approach is put into action, treatments range from desensitization of phobias (Bandura, Blanchard, & Ritter, 1969) to scheduling incentives and disincentives (Rowan-Szai, Joe, Chatham, & Simpson, 1994). There are other approaches as well.

To introduce the behavior change literature and show its possible relevance to SRL, we take an unusual approach. First, we do not review the SRL and metacognitive literature, which has many fine summaries within this volume. The second unusual move is that we critique our own work from the vantage of the behavior change literature. We show how this literature highlights the limitations of our own work on teachable agents. Teachable agents reside in a computer program where students teach virtual characters to help them learn science (see below for more details). While the software has been successful at teaching biology and causal reasoning, the behavior change literature points out missed opportunities and hopeful assumptions.

An Example of Where Behavior Change and SRL Meet

Before beginning our review of behavior change and relating it to teachable agents, we provide a brief example that shows how the line between behavior change and SRL is readily blurred. In a pair of studies, we taught adolescents processes for "maintaining motivation" that could then be applied to subsequent outcome goals, such as doing more homework or maintaining a healthful diet.

Several behavior change theories, including self-efficacy theories, assume that in dire straits people will use their heightened willpower and practiced self-management strategies (e.g., in weight-loss therapy, Foreyt & Goodrick, 1990). Weinstein (2007), for example, found that if people believe they can change a behavior, find it easy to do, worth it, and leading to desirable outcomes, they are more successful at changing their behavior. Our leading assumption coming into the studies was that adolescents also hold a similar set of beliefs that willpower and self-efficacy are the best ways to reenergize fading motivations. Unfortunately, it is exactly at those times when temptation is strongest that rationality is at its weakest. A number of behavior change theories (Cohen, 1988; Rowan-Szai et al., 1994) recognize this problem, and they provide guidance for what we will term "distributing motivation" to the environment. Therefore, we thought it might be useful to teach students strategies that involve manipulating the environment to support their abilities to stay motivated. In essence, we taught them to outsource their motivation.

In one study, 143 adolescents were assigned to one of two treatments. In the *self-control*

It's not my FAULT!
CONFIDENCE
Huge History Assignment
D+
Post-it
VISUALIZE IT
Open Your Mind's Eye
Cookies
200g
11. Edna just got a bad grade on her last history paper. She has another history paper due in four days and is not motivated. What can you tell her to do to motivate herself?

Fig. 31.1 "Edna" motivation item

treatment, students were taught how to improve their motivation by energizing themselves from within using techniques drawn from the behavior change literatures, including pep talks, attacking excuses, choosing proximal goals, and reframing failures. In the *context-control* treatment, students were taught techniques for outsourcing motivational supports to the environment; for example, prepare the environment ahead of time ("ask my parents to buy healthy foods instead of junk food"), change the context to facilitate success ("work in library" away from distractions), and create contextual triggers for goals ("put a post-it note of my goal on the mirror"). Both groups of students learned through a combination of brief lectures and short application activities.

At pre- and posttest, students were tested on their cognitive application of "internal" (self-control) and "distributed" (context-control) strategies. Students received Fig. 31.1 and were presented with Edna's motivational problem, "Edna just got a bad grade on her last history paper. She has another history paper due in 4 days and is not motivated. What can you tell her to do to motivate herself?" Figure 31.1 was designed to include equal numbers of cues for internal and distributed strategies. Figure 31.2 shows that at pretest, both treatments exhibited relatively high applications of internal strategies and relatively low applications of distributed strategies. At posttest, students in the context-control condition showed strong increases in distributed strategies, and the students in the self-control condition showed relatively little change. Thus, students already knew many strategies for self-control, but strategies of context-control were new to them. Multiple choice and open-ended questions exhibited similar results.

In a second study, 115 adolescents were assigned to the same two treatments. The pre- and posttest measures showed the same pattern as before. In this study, we further asked the students to pursue a challenging goal of personal interest after they completed the posttest. Their goals were

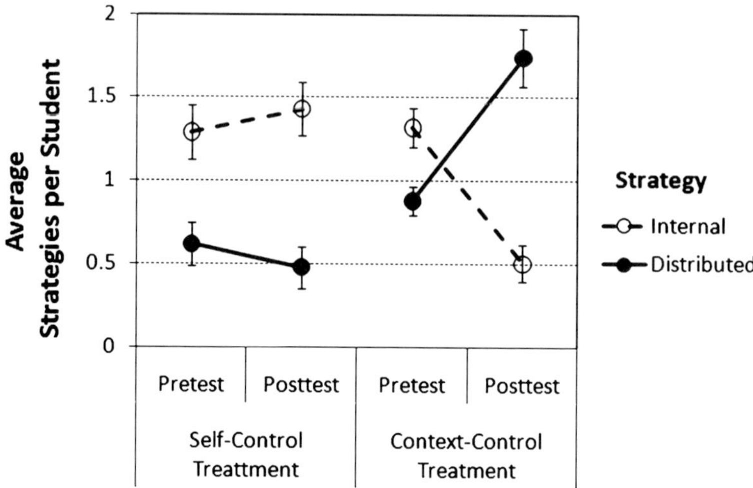

Fig. 31.2 Average number of strategies students listed to motivate Edna at pre- and posttest, broken out by condition (Error bars are the standard error of the mean)

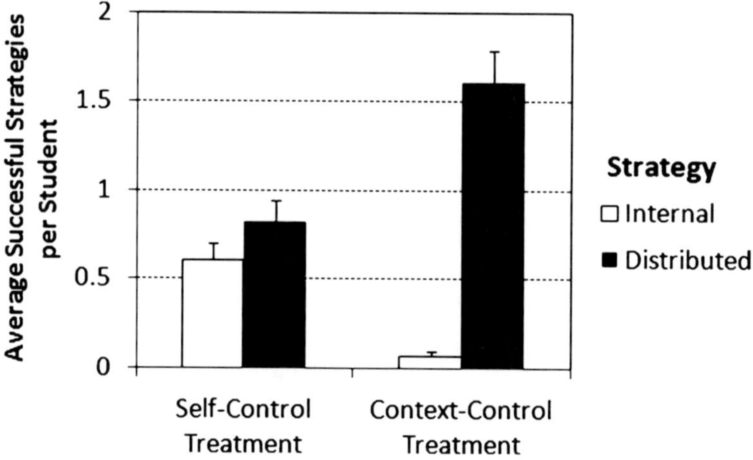

Fig. 31.3 Average number of self-reported successful strategies, broken out by condition, for a 2-week behavior change period where students pursued self-selected goals

nearly all academic (e.g., improving homework performance), which makes their behavior change goals synonymous with SRL. The students self-reported their progress over 2 weeks by recording their successful strategies and their perceived success at achieving their goals. Figure 31.3 shows that when asked to report successful strategies they used to motivate themselves, the context-control condition reported more distributed strategies. Moreover, those students who used distributed strategies exhibited more perceived success at achieving their goals, regardless of condition (not shown in Fig. 31.3).

Finally, a third study on 138 adolescents followed the same format, but we switched the final goal for the students from an SRL goal (increase homework completion) to a classic behavior change goal (increase the intake of fruits and vegetables). The results replicated the prior two studies. However, we went a step further in the data collection. We asked students to recall their previous day fruit and vegetable consumption for the 24-h just prior to receiving the goal of improving their diet and then again 3 weeks after receiving the behavior change goal (e.g. Buzzard et al., 1996). The context-control condition showed significant improvement (mean serving increase = 1.92, SD = 0.53) compared to the self-control condition (mean serving increase = 0.17, SD = 0.45). Moreover, the reported use of distributed strategies was significantly correlated with increased serving intake, ($r = 0.20$, $p < 0.05$), but internal strategies were not ($r = -0.044$, $p = 0.634$).

Collectively, these studies demonstrate that adolescents already know several internal motivation strategies, whereas distributed strategies are new to them, can be learned, and lead to greater changes. The studies also show that the same strategy training works for both classic behavior change goals (healthy living) and SRL goals (academic improvement). The barrier between behavior change and SRL interventions has points of permeability. Teaching students to use the environment to shape their own behavior appears to yield an effective SRL strategy, which may be seen as one possible contribution of the behavior change literature to SRL.

Stages of Behavior Change

One useful contribution of the behavior change literature is its emphasis on stages of change. For example, The Transtheoretical Model (TTM) of Behavior Change (Prochaska, DiClemente, & Norcross, 1992) is a popular approach that suggests matching the intervention strategy to an individual's stage and readiness to change. For example, interventions that support maintenance of a behavior will be ineffective when people do not yet know a change is possible for them to achieve. A focus on stages is relevant to SRL, because it suggests that different "treatments" may be better suited to different stages of SRL development. It provides more nuance than an overly uniform prescription that SRL should begin with scaffolds that are eventually faded.

Fig. 31.4 Abstraction of behavior change stages

The time course of change is an active area of research, so there are disagreements over the number of stages, whether they are discrete or continuous and whether they are best described as mutually exclusive or more or less active at any given time. TTM alone has 16 key constructs and five stages (Ferrer et al., 2009). Another stage model by Rothman, Baldwin, Hertel, and Fuglestad (2011) breaks behavior change into two distinct phases of initiation and maintenance and delineates two stages within each. We have abstracted from these debates into the model shown in Fig. 31.4 (see Horn, 1976). The figure shows that there are four primary stages, and people can move forward (good) and backward (bad) among the stages.

Pre-intend Stage

People are unsure if they should make an effort to change a behavior. The goal of a specific behavior change may be unknown or unmotivated. A simple example is a person who smokes and does not particularly want to quit, or in earlier times, the person did not know it was a good idea to quit. One solution comes from Protection Motivation Theory (Maddux & Rogers, 1983). It emphasizes the need for people to fully understand the deleterious consequences of poor behavior so they will protect themselves. This led to interventions that scared people about the consequences of risky behavior, for example, by showing the effects of sexually transmitted diseases in health class, or more recently, FDA legislation that requires cigarette packages to have graphic images of cancer and death after September 2012. Teachers and parents intuitively use Protection Motivation Theory to motivate learning goals, for example, by warning that such-and-such behaviors will not get students into college.

While Protection Motivation emphasizes "avoidance," other theories further incorporate "approach," for example, by showing the benefits of eating healthy and not just the risks of eating poorly. Instances include the theory of reasoned action (Ajzen & Fishbein, 1980), the theory of planned behavior (Ajzen, 1991), and the health belief model (Janz & Becker, 1984).

Intend Stage

People want to change or initiate a behavior, but they have not taken action. The intend stage exists between the pre-intend and implement stages as an acknowledgment that people often have good intentions, which they have learned, but which they have not yet turned into action. For instance, a review of health behaviors, including condom use, exercise, and cancer screening, found that people translate "good" intentions into action only 53% of the time (Sheeran, 2002). Thus, it is important to understand the characteristics of this stage and what it takes to move people along. There are multiple reasons people have good intents, but fail to take action. On the cognitive side, implementation intention theory proposes that people do not recognize opportunities for action (Gollwitzer & Sheeran, 2006). People may also lack knowledge for how to execute a behavior. On the motivation side, people may not believe they can achieve the behavior, and enhancing self-efficacy becomes an important goal of interventions (e.g., the Health Action Process Approach, Schwarzer, 2008).

Implement Stage

People take actions dedicated to behavior change. For example, smoking cessation programs provide social supports, clear metrics of progress, and alternative behaviors to supplant smoking. In the SRL literature, these may be interpreted as different types of scaffolds for new behaviors. A major goal is the prevention of relapse during implementation. Marlatt and Gordon (1985) proposed the relapse prevention model. They partitioned the main causes of relapse into (a) immediate determinants (e.g., high-risk situations, coping skills, outcome expectancies) and (b) covert antecedents (e.g., lifestyle factors, cravings). More relevant to SRL, problem-solving therapy (Perri et al., 2001) teaches people basic cognitive problem-solving skills to facilitate behavior maintenance.

Inhabit Stage

People maintain a new behavior, which no longer has to be motivated consciously. The inhabit stage is not necessarily the end of the behavior change process. In many instances of behavior change, there is always a risk of "falling off the wagon," despite having inhabited a new behavior for years. The long-term judicious application of new behaviors requires ongoing environmental support. It is often insufficient to simply tell people what they can do to maintain their new behaviors once the intervention or training is over. For instance, the Cochrane Review[1] conducted a meta-analysis on smoking cessation programs and found that training people on "necessary" skills for avoiding later relapse had no effects (Hajek, Stead, West, Jarvis, & Lancaster, 2009). One successful approach is to help people change their environments to support stability and repetition (Wood, Tam, & Witt, 2005).

In the following sections, we treat SRL as comprised of these stages. We apply the behavior change perspective to our work with teachable agents. Therefore, we first need to take a brief detour to explain the software and typical student activities.

Teachable Agents

With a teachable agent (TA), students learn by teaching a computer character. The students create the concept map that is the character's "brain,"

[1] Cochrane Reviews are systematic summaries of evidence of the effects of healthcare interventions intended to help people make practical decisions about therapy choices.

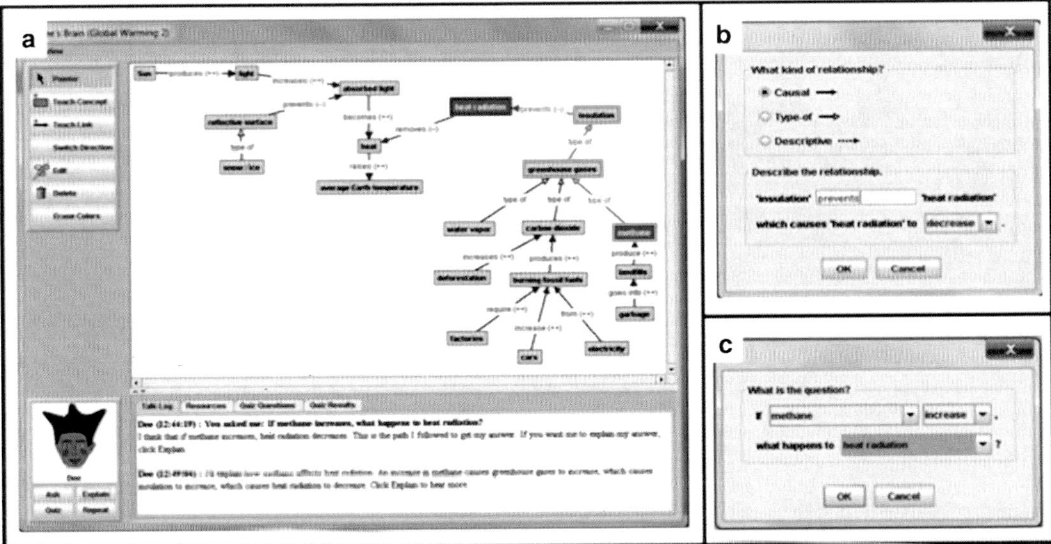

Fig. 31.5 The teachable agent interface. (**a**) The student has named her agent "Dee," customized Dee's look, and taught her about global warming. Dee has answered the question, "If 'methane' increases, what happens to 'heat radiation'?" both graphically and in text. (**b**) The "Teach Link" window where the student has taught Dee the causal proposition: "insulation" decreases "heat radiation." (**c**) The "Ask" window where the student can query Dee to test her understanding

and they receive feedback based on how well their computerized pupil can answer questions.

Figure 31.5a shows the main teaching interface. Students teach their agent by adding nodes and links using the "Teach" buttons. When students add a link, the palette in Fig. 31.5b appears. It requires students to name the link and specify the type of relationship the link represents, which can be "causal," "type-of," or "descriptive." If students choose a "causal" link, they must further specify whether an increase to the first node causes an increase or decrease to the second node (e.g., landfills increase methane).

To provide feedback and enhance the teaching metaphor, TA comes with a qualitative reasoning engine. The engine uses path traversal algorithms to reason through causal and hierarchical chains in the concept map (Biswas, Schwartz, Leelawong, Vye, & TAG-V, 2005). Figure 31.5c shows the palette that students can use to ask their agent a question. In this example, the student has asked the agent, "If 'methane' increases, what happens to 'heat radiation'?". Figure 31.5a shows how the agent highlighted successive nodes and links in the concept map to illuminate the chain of inference it used to answer the question. The agent also described the chain of inference in the lower text panel of Fig. 31.5a. In this manner, students can trace their agent's thinking, both as a model of causal reasoning and also as a way to see if the agent has learned what they think they taught it.

A second source of feedback compares an agent's answers against a hidden expert map entered by the teacher or curriculum developer. Students can submit their agent for testing by clicking on a "Quiz" button, and the students receive feedback on how their agent did. If the instructor desires, the feedback can further include tips on doing better, for example, "A link or more is missing from your map. The Resources is a good place for more information." Because TA is a server-side technology, a teacher can also project all the maps at the front of the class simultaneously and give the agents a simultaneous question that anchors classroom discussion and formative assessment.

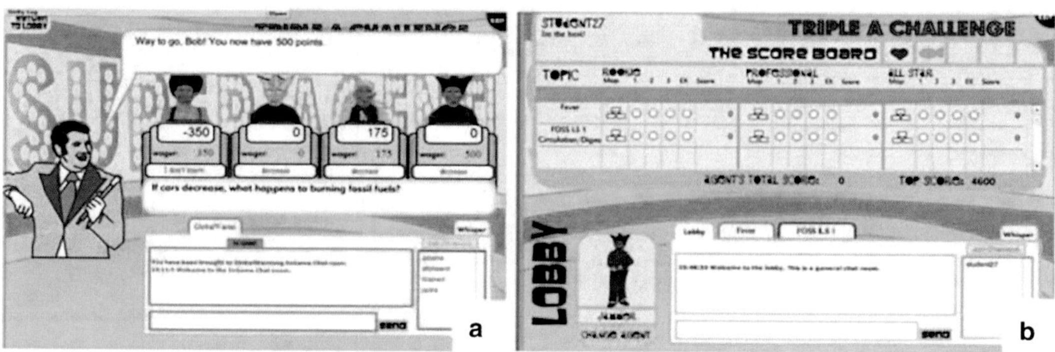

Fig. 31.6 Larger environment for TA. (**a**) Students can chat and have their agents compete in an online game show for homework. (**b**) Lobby: student portal to mapping, agent customization, chat, and game show

Figure 31.6 provides screenshots of an Internet homework system called the Triple-A Challenge. Students can log on from home or school to teach their agents, customize their look, chat with other students online, and have their agents participate in an online game with other students' agents. During a game, a host asks agents to answer questions on the material. Students "wager" on their agent, before it gives an answer. Further details about these features and others may be found in Kinnebrew et al. 2013, Chin et al. (2010), and at http://workingexamples.org/frontend/project/18, which includes a video tutorial and guest login. The teachable agents software, in varying forms, has been shown to motivate students to persevere after failure, increase student effort toward learning including reading more to learn, provide added value without adversely affecting the basic value of regular curriculum, increase students' causal understanding and reasoning, and better prepare students to transfer so they can better learn new science content even after the software has been removed (see Chase, Chin, Oppezzo, & Schwartz, 2009 and Chin et al., 2010, which also include further evidence on the active ingredients of the software).

From Pre-intention to Intention

To move people into the intend stage, behavior change interventions try to convince people that it is worth adopting the goal of achieving a certain outcome. The assumption is that understanding and intending a change is necessary, if not sufficient for behavior change. Therefore, researchers examine whether behavior change programs at least achieve the proximal goal of increasing intention (e.g., after an evening of instruction), if not the distal goal of actual change (e.g., when people go home). In general, the transition depends on developing (a) goal knowledge and (b) goal adoption. For example, one study employed ten 75-min sessions on safe sex (Gong et al., 2009). By using a set of questionnaires, the researchers found that the instruction (a) increased students' knowledge of HIV/AIDS and their knowledge of condom effectiveness. The instruction also (b) lowered their perceived costs to remaining abstinent and increased condom use intention, thus demonstrating successful pre-intend to intend transition. (Whether the students actually changed their behavior involves the implement stage not the intend stage.)

If we view metacognitive strategies as a behavioral goal to adopt, Pintrich (1999) summarizes the high-level issue, "The use of various cognitive and self-regulatory strategies involves a level of engagement that is often more demanding in terms of time and effort for students than their normal level of engagement. In order for them to invest the extra time and effort in self-regulated learning, they must be motivated to use these various strategies" (p. 467). The goal of instruction that targets the transition from pre-intend to intend is to provide this extra motivation by clarifying the intended goal and its effects.

The challenge then is to convince students of the merit of metacognitive goals, or at least provide a separate goal that will simultaneously reveal the merit of metacognition during the pursuit of the primary goal. The TA software does the latter. The TA software provides students with an understandable and readily adopted goal, namely, to teach a virtual agent. This moves them from the pre-intend to intend stage when working with the agent. For example, we have found a protégé effect, where students adopt the goal of reading on behalf of their agent more than when learning for themselves (Chase et al., 2009). We say more about this in the next section.

However, one of the limitations of the TA software is there are some possible goal misalignments that stem from the fact that the goal is to help the agent learn rather than help oneself learn. While this has worked to improve student learning as a side effect of teaching the agent, it also runs into some problems. For example, the outcome goal associated with the narrative of teaching the agent is to help the agent pass a test or do well in a quiz show. Health behavior change theories call this a "stealth intervention," where the outcome goal may not be ideal, but the path to get there reinforces the ideal behavior. In the TA system, the students' goal is for their agents to give correct answers rather than develop their own understanding. As an analogy, it is like having the goal to date somebody, which leads one to lose weight. But if it is possible to date the person without losing weight, then the adoption of the weight-loss goal disappears. In the TA software, this effect of this goal misalignment shows up in the form of shortcut links.

Consider an agent that has been taught about global warming, and the agent receives the question of how cars affect global warming. The correct answer is that an increase in cars causes an increase in global warming. If children see their agent give the wrong answer, a simple fix is to insert a direct link between cars and global warming. This is a shortcut link, because it skips important steps in the causal chain, for example, that cars produce carbon dioxide, which is a greenhouse gas, and greenhouse gasses are a type of insulation. Ideally, students would try to understand why cars increase global warming, but many students do not, because their agent can still answer some questions correctly with the shortcut link.

We have tried a number of ways to overcome this problem. We have included feedback mechanisms that indicate which questions the agent gets right for the wrong reasons (by using a shortcut link). We have also included feedback indicating how many steps should be in the causal chain for a given question. And we have also designed the game show and quizzes so they help students establish the intermediate links (by asking about them directly), before asking longer-chain questions that tempt students into introducing shortcut links. But, these fixes have not worked extremely well, in part, because many students simply maintain the more obvious goal—make the agent give the right answer. Moreover, once students have introduced multiple errors into their agent's brain, it becomes difficult to track them down, so students simply add in more and more shortcut links to get answers right rather than debug their agent.

One behavior change solution would be to instill disincentives. Students, for example, might lose points every time there is a shortcut link. However, even if students' started to avoid shortcut links, they would only develop deeper understanding of science content as a side effect, rather than an adopted goal of learning for themselves.

One might suggest changing the narrative of TA so it targets goals of understanding rather than agent performance goals. However, younger students may not know what it means to adopt a learning goal of understanding. For example, they may not know how to recognize consequences of understanding besides successful performance. In this case, performance rather than understanding will remain the primary goal. Moreover, younger students may not know what subgoals to adopt to achieve understanding. In this case, it takes a heavier hand than assuming that students will adopt the appropriate goals on their own.

Kinnebrew et al. 2013 have used shortcut links as an opportunity to directly teach SRL process goals to students. Sometimes a flaw in an instructional design can be a strength for teaching metacognition. For example, when the software detects a student making shortcut links, a mentor agent suggests the student should read more about the scientific concepts in a related resource. Conceivably, the software could be further modified to help students understand that the proper set of concepts (nodes) with just the right set of associations among them (links) is a model of understanding that they can take as an explicit goal for themselves rather than just focusing on performance.

To further enhance the effectiveness of providing students with metacognitive tips, the behavior change literature has some suggestions. The theory of planned behavior (Ajzen, 1991) proposes educating people about the costs and benefits of the behavior, as well as strengthening people's perception of the causal link between the behavior and the outcome expectancies. The TA system should provide children with simple-to-interpret evidence that helps them make the connection between achievable behaviors (reading a resource) and desirable goals (agent performance). For example, the system might include markers of incremental progress that show how adopting SRL process goals improves the larger outcome goal of their agent succeeding. For example, there could be "points" for process goal adoption, as well as points for outcomes, and the relation between the two could be made clear over time. Figuring out how to do this without undermining the fun aspects of the environment is nontrivial but worthwhile. Also, the system should show the disconnection between maladaptive behaviors (shortcut links) and outcome goals. For example, it should be possible to set up the quiz and game show so that getting the right answer by following a shortcut links makes the agents lose even more points than just giving the wrong answer.

From Intention to Implementation

To turn good intentions into action, people need to recognize situations where those intentions are relevant. For example, people need to learn to recognize situations that are likely to cause them to smoke. Implementation intentions are detailed "if-then" plans that specify the when, where, and how of goal implementation (Gollwitzer & Sheeran, 2006). For example, "if situation Y is encountered, then I will initiate my goal behavior 'x.'" Encouraging explicit development of implementation intentions enhances rates of goal attainment compared to just forming a goal intention. The performance enhancement occurs even when the participants are already highly motivated (Sheeran & Orbell, 2000) and when their self-control has been diminished by ego-depleting tasks (Webb & Sheeran, 2003). The effectiveness of implementation intentions is dissociable from self-efficacy changes (Milne, Orbell, & Sheeran, 2002). The benefit of implementation intentions is building a cognitive association between conditions and actions.

With respect to SRL, the move from intend to implement is not about helping students develop appropriate outcome and process goals for learning. This occurs in the pre-intend to intend stage. Instead, this transition focuses on getting students to recognize when it is useful to pursue those goals. Students often know the appropriate strategies, but they simply do not take action on them. They may not recognize their applicability, or students may not think they are worth the effort. In SRL, the if-then rules can be quite subtle, because they also include some estimate of effort and value. Students may know a particular strategy, and they may even know that it is applicable, but the cost of the strategy may not be worth the perceived value of the outcome. For example, most adults know that making a list simplifies shopping and reduces errors, but for many adults, it is simply not worth the effort to make a shopping list, because they can "get by" following a suboptimal process.

Appropriate experiences can help people recalibrate their estimates of effort to value for a particular SRL implementation. For example, Martin and Schwartz (2009) compared graduate and undergraduate students completing a diagnosis task. Both groups knew how to organize the relevant information, but only the graduate students chose to do so. The undergraduates were content to "get by" on this task, rather than spend the extra time. They did not recognize that the diagnosis task could benefit from up-front organization. In contrast, the graduate students, who had many experiences with the value of pre-organizing data for analysis and decision making, had learned that investing a little time up-front can yield great benefits later.

The TA software does well in moving students from intention to action. The teaching narrative triggers SRL behaviors to the extent the children know them. A pair of studies by Chase and colleagues (2009) demonstrated a protégé effect. In both studies, students interacted with identical software. The difference was whether they thought the graphical character on the screen was their virtual pupil (*teach* condition), or whether the character represented them (*self* condition). (Students in the self condition just thought they were using a new kind of software program intended to help them learn.) In a classroom study, 80 eighth graders learned the biological mechanisms of fever. A posttest indicated that students in the teach condition learned more, and the effect was especially pronounced for the hardest questions and the lower-achieving students. Students in the teach condition spent nearly twice as much time reading the relevant resources, and they spent more time revising their map instead of engaging in off-task activities like chatting online.

The second study took the same format, except it was conducted in a think-aloud protocol with fifth graders. It helped to reveal how the teaching narrative triggered productive behaviors. One reason is that it created an "ego-protective buffer." When a student's agent failed on a question, the students were very attentive to the failure and they showed high affect. For example, "Poor Diokki, I'm sorry" (Diokki is the name the student gave to her agent). Or "Whoa, I need to teach better." In contrast, in the self condition, the children tended to bury negative outcomes by not acknowledging them and showing minimal affect. The TA provided an ego-protective buffer so students could acknowledge their agents' failures without feeling themselves stupid. A second reason is that the TA provides clear ways to improve their TA through visual feedback and modifying the links. Children in the teach condition were much more likely to revise their agent upon the feedback from the system. The self students were less inclined to revise when the software indicated an error in the map. One hypothesis is that the self students did not have an obvious way to improve their own understanding. To their understanding, fixing the map was not equivalent to fixing their own thoughts. In contrast, the teach students could readily appreciate that fixing and testing the map was a direct path to improving their TA's performance, which had the side effect of helping them learn.

Given that the students already had some SRL knowledge for how to improve their understanding (read more, pay attention to mistakes, revise), the effect of the teaching narrative was to motivate the use of these goals, moving them into the implementation phase. So, in this regard the TA was successful in supporting implementation and improving learning. At the same time, one wonders whether students who use TA develop explicit implementation intentions that work beyond the space of the TA metaphor. The question of transfer is the topic of the next section.

From Implementation to Inhabitation

Implementing a behavior change is considered different from inhabiting a changed behavior. For example, behaviors involved in quitting smoking are different from those involved in being an ex-smoker. In SRL, the parallel would be developing SRL behaviors with scaffolds and then maintaining those behaviors once the scaffolds have faded. A difference between behavior change and SRL, however, is that recidivism is a major concern in behavior change. Regardless of whether an individual is stopping or starting a behavior, there is a high risk of relapse when put in novel or high-stress situations (Marlatt & Gordon, 1985). SRL theories do not normally view a failure to use SRL as regressing to bad habits, though it could be conceptualized that way. For example, students may slip back to the familiar routine of using flash cards to memorize, despite having been taught and experienced that making elaborative associations is a better route to improved memory.

Both behavior change and SRL theories need to confront the risk of regressing to a prior stage. This risk exists, in part, because the goal of behavior and SRL change is to produce adaptable habits rather than rigid behaviors. Adaptability makes it possible for people to flex with changing circumstances rather than being rigid and brittle, for example, when they go to a foreign country without their usual healthy foods. The adaptive aspect is also important for metacognition, because metacognition can sometimes interfere with performance and learning, and it should be avoided in those cases. For example, in sports people can overthink and overregulate proceduralized motor skills, such as shooting a free throw in a basketball game, which interferes with well-practiced motor patterns (i.e., choking, Beilock & Carr, 2001). In learning, it is sometimes better to allow implicit processes to guide induction rather than explicitly generating and checking hypotheses (Reber, 1989), a standard metacognitive tenet.

The challenge for the inhabit stage is that flexibility also increases the possibility of relapse. Therefore, behavior change interventions often follow people past implementation into the inhabit stage. For example, Baum, Clark, and Sandler (1991) examined a 12-week treatment for weight loss that included follow-up contacts that emphasized relapse prevention. This program led to a greater degree of maintenance or continued weight loss compared to control subjects who did not receive follow-up.

With TA, we have some evidence that the benefits of TA transfer beyond the time students spend in the environment—students spontaneously adapt their thinking when learning new content. We review this evidence, before returning to the question of what else we might do to ensure that these gains would not be lost in the future.

With technology-based instruction, there is always a concern that students will become too reliant on technological scaffolds. For example, there were many debates on whether calculators in school would hinder students' abilities to do math on their own. If calculators did hinder math performance when the calculators were not available, then the technology was not supporting adaptive habits of mind. Therefore, we wanted to know if this was the case with TA. In a pair of studies, Chin and colleagues (2010) examined the effects of TA on learning causal relations among elementary school students. The first study demonstrated that TA led to a superior causal understanding of global warming compared to using a commercial concept mapping tool (Inspiration). In the second study, six classes of fifth graders and their teachers participated in a several-month implementation. The school district had adopted the FOSS science kit as their primary method of instruction (Full Option Science System). In the first half of the study, three classes used the Living Systems science kit as usual. The other three classes used the science kit plus the TA software. The total time available for instruction was the same for both conditions, and the teachers using the TA software were asked to use it once a week for the 2-month unit. At the end of the unit, students took the test that came with the science kit. The students from both conditions did the same on most questions. Thus, the technology did not detract from the basic value of the curriculum. Notably, the TA condition did significantly better on the causal questions that came with curricular test, so it also provided added value. We also evaluated student learning with researcher-designed measures of casual understanding. The TA condition did better on these as well as shown on the left of Fig. 31.7.

Relevant to the question of transfer and maintenance of SRL, the study included a second phase. After completing the first kit on Living Systems (e.g., circulation in animals and plants), the classes crossed over for the very different unit on Water Planet (e.g., water cycle). The classes that had been using the TA returned to using just the kits. And the classes that had only been using the kits added in the TA software. Figure 31.7 shows the results from before and after the crossover. As may be seen, the classes that had not initially used TA improved in their causal understanding once they did use TA. This replicates the prior findings that TA supports a causal understanding of science content. More importantly,

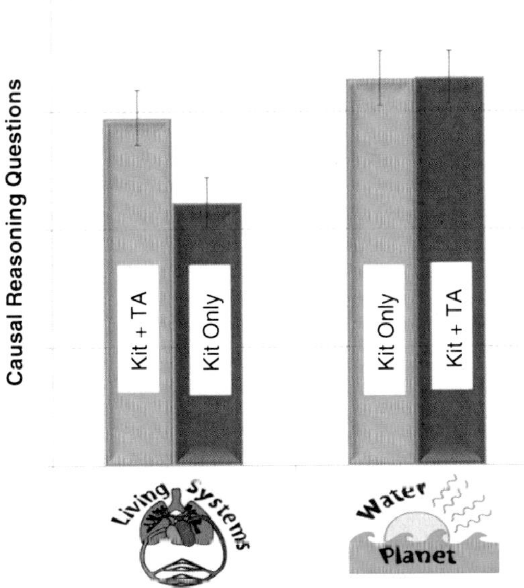

Fig. 31.7 Test of whether TA prepares students for future learning once the technology is no longer there

the classes that stopped using the TA software for the second kit did not drop in performance on the causal questions about the Water Planet unit. These classes did not receive any special instruction on making causal models of the content, and the teachers did not bring it up.

It appears that using the TA earlier had prepared the students to transfer for future learning (Bransford & Schwartz, 1999). Their experiences with the TA had taught them to connect up science ideas with causal relations (something not covered in the kits for this age group), and they spontaneously continued to do so for new science content without further scaffolding. In this sense, the students had learned to inhabit causal ways of understanding. So, rather than the students becoming dependent on the learning technology, the learning technology better prepared students to learn once it was removed.

What transferred that led to the improved causal learning even after TA was removed? Our current interpretation is that the students had learned to think about causal relations. They learned a powerful and natural schema for interpreting and organizing information in science class. We doubt that they had learned to think about their thinking in a general way, or that they had changes to their self-efficacy or motivational states once they left the TA environment. In other work, Kinnebrew et al. 2013 have developed ways to support transfer of metacognitive strategies within the environment. For example, a mentor agent provides tips to the students for how to study to be a more effective teacher. They have found that when the mentor agent is turned off in the software, the students persist in the strategies the mentor agent suggested. However, this feature was not "turned on" in the FOSS kit study, and we were looking at transfer beyond the software.

Considering the wisdom of behavior change during the inhabit stage, the TA environment does very little to support transfer or maintenance of behavior change beyond implementation within the TA environment. And the environment beyond TA rarely includes explicit supports to prevent "relapse." What changes might help improve the transition of SRL strategies to "everyday" life?

One obvious omission in the preceding study is that the teachers did not check in with the students to help them maintain the SRL behaviors they had done with TA, such as checking answers, seeking feedback, and revising understanding. Given the demands of the experimental design, we could not encourage this type of explicit maintenance. Nevertheless, it would be easy to do.

A second addition would help students develop implementation intentions that reach beyond the TA environment. For example, students might be taught that the SRL processes they use in TA are transferable and explicit goals. This would involve helping them understand which of their behaviors were and were not responsible for the gains in their agent, as mentioned earlier. Then, students could be helped to develop "if-then" associations to other formal or informal learning settings. The "if" conditions could refer to external conditions (e.g., "when learning science"), or the "if" triggers could refer to mental conditions (e.g., "when unsure of a causal chain"). The "then" side of the associations might include "draw and trace causal maps." Of course, these would need to be more precise and would need some narrative changes to fit within TA.

Simultaneously, it would be useful to develop avoidance implementation intentions as well. Adding "shortcut" links would be a behavior to avoid, but this situation is rather unique to TA. Therefore, it would be important to target more recurrent conditions that create high risk for relapse. For example, in conditions of low motivation and tight deadlines, students may just want to get it done and abandon SRL behaviors. One might take the approach described in the first study presented in this chapter. Teach children general behavior change strategies for maintaining their motivation toward goals they value, and then let them practice these goals in the context of teaching their agent, which we know they value. In this model, TA becomes a chance to practice or inhabit SRL goals taught by other means.

Conclusion

A common mistake many people make is that they do not consider behavior change to be an instance of learning, but rather see good learning outcomes as synonymous with deep understanding. If we remember that learning is adaptation, behavior change is a very powerful demonstration of learning. Approaching metacognition as an enduring beneficial behavior to instill, rather than merely knowledge we teach, allows for new ideas of how to approach metacognitive education, based in a literature that is not often applied to academic learning. We evaluated our own technology against the recommendations the behavior change research supports and highlighted the room for improvement found in our educational tool.

We found that TA has a goal misalignment for developing SRL because the goal of the TA narrative is to have the agent perform well, rather than have the students learn for themselves. Nevertheless, the goal of teaching does have beneficial side effects in that students do adopt better SRL behaviors and they learn for themselves. Thus, one possible move to improve SRL with teachable agents is to reconfigure the software so that students have to teach their agent SRL strategies and goals. For instance, an agent might complain that trying hard is not worth it, and the agent could introduce its own shortcut links. Students would have to teach their agent why it is important to try hard and how to go about it. This should help students develop more SRL knowledge and the conditions when it is most important. Perhaps, students would transfer these types of knowledge and strategies beyond the technology, much like they transferred causal reasoning schemas based on their interactions with the agents. This approach would neatly fit the premise behind the teachable agents, which is that learning by teaching is an effective and engaging approach to learning—in this case, learning behavior change and SRL strategies.

We suspect that many of the improvements we considered could be derived from pockets of the SRL literature. Therefore, one might grumble that behavior change has nothing new to offer to SRL. A better response is to recognize that these two fields of research overlap a great deal, despite differences in the specific problems they try to solve. Sharing research and ideas across the divide could be highly informative.

Acknowledgments This material is based upon work supported by the National Science Foundation under grants IIS-0904324 & REESE-0723795. Any opinions, findings, and conclusions or recommendations expressed in this material are those of the authors and do not necessarily reflect the views of the National Science Foundation.

References

Ajzen, I. (1991). The theory of planned behavior. *Organizational Behavior and Human Decision Processes, 50*(2), 179–211.

Ajzen, I., & Fishbein, M. (1980). *Understanding attitudes and predicting social behavior*. Englewood Cliffs, NJ: Prentice-Hall.

Bandura, A. (2005). The primacy of self-regulation in health promotion. *Applied Psychology: An International Review, 54*(2), 245–254.

Bandura, A., Blanchard, E. B., & Ritter, B. (1969). Relative efficacy of desensitization and modeling approaches for inducing behavioral, affective, and attitudinal changes. *Journal of Personality and Social Psychology, 13*(3), 173–199.

Baum, J. G., Clark, H. B., & Sandler, J. (1991). Preventing relapse in obesity through posttreatment maintenance systems: Comparing the relative efficacy of two levels of therapist support. *Journal of Behavioral Medicine, 14*(3), 287–301.

Baumeister, R. F., & Vohs, K. D. (2007). Self-regulation, ego depletion, and motivation. *Social and Personality Psychology Compass, 1*(1), 115–128.

Beilock, S. L., & Carr, T. H. (2001). On the fragility of skilled performance: What governs choking under pressure? *Journal of Experimental Psychology, 130*(40), 701–725.

Biswas, G., Schwartz, D. L., Leelawong, K., Vye, N., & TAG-V. (2005). Learning by teaching: A new agent paradigm for educational software. *Applied Artificial Intelligence, 19*, 363–392.

Bransford, J. D., & Schwartz, D. L. (1999). Rethinking transfer: A simple proposal with multiple implications. *Review of Research in Education, 24*, 61–100.

Buzzard, M., Faucett, C. L., Jeffery, R. W., McBane, L., McGovern, P., Baxter, J. S., et al. (1996). Monitoring dietary change in a low-fat diet intervention study: Advantages of using 24-hour dietary recalls vs food records. *Journal of the American Dietetic Association, 96*(6), 574–579.

Chase, C. C., Chin, D. B., Oppezzo, M. A., & Schwartz, D. L. (2009). Teachable agents and the protégé effect: Increasing the effort towards learning. *Journal of Science Education and Technology, 18*(4), 334–352.

Chin, D. B., Dohamen, I., Oppezzo, M., Cheng, B., Chase, C., & Schwartz, D. L. (2010). Preparation for future learning with Teachable Agents. *Educational Technology Research and Development, 58*, 649–669.

Cohen, S. (1988). Psychosocial models and the role of social support in the etiology of physical disease. *Health Psychology, 7*, 269–297.

Corno, L. (2001). Volitional aspects of self-regulated learning. In B. J. Zimmerman & D. H. Schunk (Eds.), *Self-regulated learning and academic achievement: Theoretical perspectives* (2nd ed., pp. 191–226). Mahwah, NJ: Lawrence Erlbaum Associates, Inc.

Dweck, C. S. (1996). Implicit theories as organizers of goals and behavior. In P. M. Gollwitzer & J. A. Bargh (Eds.), *The psychology of action: Linking cognition and motivation to behavior* (pp. 69–90). New York: The Guilford Press.

Ferrer, R. A., Amico, K. R., Bryan, A., Fisher, W. A., Cornman, D. H., Kiene, S. M., et al. (2009). Accuracy of the stages of change algorithm: Sexual risk reported in the maintenance stage of change. *Prevention Science, 10*, 13–21.

Finkel, E. J., Campbell, W. K., Brunell, A. B., Dalton, A. N., Scarbeck, S. J., & Chartrand, T. L. (2006). High-maintenance interaction: Inefficient social coordination impairs self-regulation. *Journal of Personality and Social Psychology, 91*(3), 456–475.

Foreyt, J. P., & Goodrick, G. K. (1990). Factors common to successful therapy for the obese patient. *Medicine and Science in Sports and Exercise, 23*(3), 292–297.

Gailliot, M. T., Baumeister, R. F., Dewall, C. N., Maner, J. K., Plant, E. A., Tice, D. M., et al. (2007). Self-control relies on glucose as a limited energy source: Willpower is more than a metaphor. *Journal of Personality and Social Psychology, 92*(2), 325–336.

Gollwitzer, P. M., & Sheeran, P. (2006). Implementation intentions and goal achievement: A meta-analysis of effects and processes. *Advances in Experimental Social Psychology, 38*, 69–119.

Gong, J., Stanton, B., Lunn, S., Deveaux, L., Li, X., Marshall, S., et al. (2009). Effects through 24 months of an HIV/AIDS prevention intervention program based on protection motivation theory among preadolescents in the Bahamas. *Pediatrics, 123*(5), e917–e928.

Hajek, P., Stead, L. F., West, R., Jarvis, M., & Lancaster T. (2009). Relapse prevention interventions for smoking cessation. *Cochrane Database of Systematic Reviews*, (1), Art. No.: CD003999. doi: 10.1002/14651858.CD003999.pub3.

Horn, D. A. (1976). A model for the study of personal choice health behavior. *International Journal of Health Education, 19*, 89–98.

Janz, N. K., & Becker, M. H. (1984). The health belief model: A decade later. *Health Education Quarterly, 11*(1), 1–47.

Kinnebrew, J. S., Biswas, G., Sulcer, B., & Taylor, R.S. (2013). Investigating self-regulated learning in teachable agent environments. In R. Azevedo & V. Aleven (Eds.). International handbook of metacognition and learning technologies. New York: Springer.

Maddux, J. E., & Rogers, R. W. (1983). Protection motivation and self-efficacy: A revised theory of fear appeals and attitude change. *Journal of Experimental Social Psychology, 19*, 469–479.

Marlatt, G. A., & Gordon, J. R. (1985). *Relapse prevention: Maintenance strategies in the treatment of addictive behaviors*. New York: Guilford Press.

Martin, L., & Schwartz, D. L. (2009). Prospective adaptation in the use of representational tools. *Cognition and Instruction, 27*(4), 370–400.

Milne, S., Orbell, S., & Sheeran, P. (2002). Combining motivational and volitional interventions to promote exercise participation: Protection motivation theory and implementation intentions. *British Journal of Health Psychology, 7*, 163–184.

Perri, M. G., Nezu, A. M., McKelvey, W. F., Shermer, R. L., Renjiliarr, D. A., & Viegener, B. J. (2001). Relapse prevention training and problem-solving therapy in the long-term management of obesity. *Journal of Consulting and Clinical Psychology, 69*(4), 722–726.

Pintrich, P. R. (1999). The role of motivation in promoting and sustaining self-regulated learning. *International Journal of Educational Research, 31*, 459–470.

Prochaska, J. O., DiClemente, C. C., & Norcross, J. C. (1992). In search of how people change: Applications to the addictive behaviors. *American Psychologist, 47*, 1102–1114.

Reber, A. S. (1989). Implicit learning and tacit knowledge. *Journal of Experimental Psychology. General, 118*, 219–235.

Rothman, A. J., Baldwin, A. S., Hertel, A. W., & Fuglestad, P. T. (2011). Self-regulation and behavior change: Disentangling behavioral initiation and behavioral maintenance. In R. F. Baumeister & K. D. Vohs (Eds.), *Handbook of self-regulation: Research, theory, and applications* (pp. 106–122). New York: Guilford Press.

Rowan-Szai, G., Joe, G. W., Chatham, L. R., & Simpson, D. D. (1994). A simple reinforcement system for methadone clients in a community-based treatment program. *Journal of Substance Abuse Treatment, 11*(3), 217–223.

Schwarzer, R. (2008). Modeling health behavior change: How to predict and modify the adoption and maintenance of health behaviors. *Applied Psychology: An International Review, 57*(1), 1–29.

Sheeran, P. (2002). Intention-behavior relations: A conceptual and empirical review. In W. Stroebe & M. Hewstone (Eds.), *European review of social psychology* (Vol. 12, pp. 1–36). Chichester, UK: Wiley.

Sheeran, P., & Orbell, S. (2000). Using implementation intentions to increase attendance for cervical cancer screening. *Health Psychology, 19*, 283–289.

Twenge, J. M., & Baumeister, R. F. (2002). Self-control: A limited yet renewable resource. In Y. Kashima, M. Foddy, & M. Platow (Eds.), *Self and identity: Personal, social, and symbolic* (pp. 57–70). Mahwah, NJ: Lawrence Erlbaum Associates, Inc.

Webb, T. L., & Sheeran, P. (2003). Can implementation intentions help to overcome ego-depletion? *Journal of Experimental Social Psychology, 39*, 279–286.

Weinstein, N. D. (2007). Misleading tests of health behavior theories. *Annals of Behavioral Medicine, 33*(1), 1–10.

Wood, W., Tam, L., & Witt, M. G. (2005). Changing circumstances, disrupting habits. *Journal of Personality and Social Psychology, 88*(6), 918–933.

Part VI

Individual and Collaborative Learning in Classroom Settings

Electronic Portfolio Encouraging Active and Reflective Learning

32

Philip C. Abrami, Eva M. Bures, Einat Idan, Elizabeth Meyer, Vivek Venkatesh, and Anne Wade

Abstract

At the Centre for the Study of Learning and Performance we have developed, tested, and disseminated to schools without charge, an Electronic Portfolio Encouraging Active and Reflective Learning (ePEARL). ePEARL is designed to be faithful to predominant models of self-regulation, scaffolding and supporting learners and their educators from grade one (level one) through grade twelve and beyond (level four). ePEARL encourages learners to engage in the cyclical phases and sub-phases of forethought, performance, and self-reflection. In a series of studies, including two longitudinal quasi-experiments, we have explored the positive impacts of ePEARL on the enhancement of students' self-regulated learning skills, their literacy skills and changes in teaching, while simultaneously researching classroom implementation fidelity and teacher professional development. This chapter briefly explains the development of ePEARL, our research program, and issues in the scalability and sustainability of knowledge tools.

This chapter is submitted for inclusion consideration in the *International Handbook of Metacognition and Learning Technologies*. The preparation of this chapter was aided by grants from the Social Sciences and Humanities Research Council of Canada and the *Fonds québécois de la recherche sur la société et la culture*.

P.C. Abrami (✉) • E. Idan • V. Venkatesh • A. Wade
Centre for the Study of Learning and Performance,
Concordia University, Montreal, QC, Canada
e-mail: abrami@education.concordia.ca

E.M. Bures
Centre for the Study of Learning and Performance,
Bishop's University School of Education, Lennoxville,
QC, Canada

E. Meyer
School of Education, California Polytechnic State
University, San Luis Obispo, CA, USA

R. Azevedo and V. Aleven (eds.), *International Handbook of Metacognition and Learning Technologies*, Springer International Handbooks of Education 26, DOI 10.1007/978-1-4419-5546-3_32,

An electronic portfolio (EP) is a digital container capable of storing and organizing visual and auditory content, including text, images, video, and sound. EPs may also be learning tools when they are designed to support a variety of learning processes and assessment purposes (Abrami & Barrett, 2005). Since they are web-based, they provide remote access that encourages anywhere, anytime learning and make it easier for peers, parents, and educators to provide input and feedback. EPs have three broad purposes: process, showcase, and assessment. They can be multipurposed, for example, supporting students' development of skills and their achievement. Our emphasis is on EPs used as *process portfolios* to support how users learn through embedded structures and strategies. A process EP is a purposeful collection of student work that tells the story of a student's effort, progress, and/or achievement in one or more subject areas. Process portfolios are personal learning management tools meant to encourage academic improvement, personal growth and development, and a commitment to lifelong learning.

Process EPs are gaining in popularity for multiple reasons. They provide multimedia display and assessment possibilities for school and work contexts allowing the use of a variety of means to develop, demonstrate, and assess understanding. They may also be advantageous for at-risk children whose competencies may be better reflected through more authentic tasks; EPs can serve as a form of differentiated instruction. At the same time, by engaging learners, their deficiencies in core competencies may be overcome. EPs are superior to print-based portfolios for cataloguing and organizing learning materials, and better at illustrating the process of learner development. Process EPs may scaffold attempts at knowledge construction by supporting reflection, refinement, conferencing, and other processes of self-regulation that are important skills for lifelong learning and learning how to learn. Students who are self-regulated are cognitively, motivationally, and behaviorally active participants in their own learning process (Zimmerman, 1989, 2000) and thus may demonstrate better academic performance (Rogers & Swan, 2004). These are the reasons we developed our EP tool, ePEARL.

Overview of the SRL Framework and the Design of ePEARL

The three cyclical phases of self-regulation (e.g., Zimmerman, 2000) include both metacognitive and motivational components, providing the foundation for better sustainability of learning and skill development. The *forethought phase* includes task analysis (goal setting and strategic planning) and self-motivation beliefs (self-efficacy, outcome expectations, intrinsic interest/value, and goal orientation). Tasks involved in the forethought phase are setting outcome goals, setting process goals, documenting goal values, planning strategies, and setting up a learning log. The next phase, the *performance phase*, includes self-control (self-instruction, imagery, attention focusing, and task strategies) and self-observation (self-recording and self-experimentation). Tasks involved in the performance phase are creating work and entering learning log entries. Finally, the *self-reflection phase* includes self-judgment (self-evaluation and casual attribution) and self-reaction (self-satisfaction/affect and adaptive-defensive responses). Tasks involved in the self-reflection phase are reflecting on work, reflecting on process, and thinking of new goal opportunities. ePEARL has been carefully designed to support each of these phases in age-appropriate ways, encouraging students and teachers to set goals, produce work, and reflect upon it with feedback from others.

ePEARL was developed at the Centre for the Study of Learning and Performance (CSLP) in collaboration with our partner LEARN and is programmed in PHP using a MySQL database. ePEARL is a bilingual (English–French), web-based, student-centered EP software that is designed to support the phases of self-regulation. ePEARL contains four developmentally appropriate levels for use in early elementary (Level 1), late elementary (Level 2), and secondary schools (Level 3), as well as for teachers and adult learners, especially preservice teachers (Level 4). To view a sample ePEARL environment, log on to http://grover.concordia.ca/ePEARL/promo/en/index.php.

ePEARL features include personalizing the portfolio; setting general or task-specific goals; creating new work via a text editor and/or audio recorder or linking to work created elsewhere; reflecting on work; sharing work; obtaining feedback from teachers, peers, and parents; evaluating personal motivation; editing work and saving revisions as a new version; and sending work to a presentation portfolio for archiving and exporting. ePEARL also contains a rich collection of video vignettes to assist students and teachers to understand and use both the tool and the self-regulated learning (SRL) processes it is designed to strengthen. ePEARL is intended for use in all school subjects; we are currently trialing a version for use by the Royal Conservatory of Music, called iSCORE, as part of piano studio teaching (Upitis, Abrami, Brook, Troop, & Varela, 2010).

ePEARL Level 4 Objectives and Audience

ePEARL Level 4 is a new project undertaken by the CSLP in 2009 as a way to support preservice and in-service teachers, as well as other postsecondary students in becoming self-regulated learners. Rather than make superficial modifications to the "look-and-feel" of Level 3, we chose to recreate the environment in a way that would tackle the particular opportunities and challenges presented by older students and the tasks they face. This allowed us to investigate the more complex and nuanced aspects of Zimmerman's (2000) self-regulation model.

For example, adult users should be more aware than children of the variety of elements influencing their learning experience and can more easily grasp them once they are made aware and are therefore more equipped to correctly assess their influence. Furthermore, adult students face topics and learning tasks that may greatly influence their intrinsic interest and performance (Pintrich, 2003). Tasks may also differ at this level; postsecondary students are often required to carry out tasks that are more complex, flexibly structured, and lengthier than those assigned to younger students. Tasks like these require finer planning and more precise monitoring, as well as more sophisticated reflection and adaptive inferences. They also demand that motivation be sustained for a longer period of time, as the final reward of achieving the goal may be substantially delayed. A critical aspect of self-regulation is the cyclical nature of learning and improvement, and adult learners should be more competent at adjusting their activities based on their continual self-monitoring and evaluation. These are some of the reasons we incorporated visual representations, sidebar design, and drill-down features into Level 4.

Visual Representations

Zimmerman (2000) stresses the importance of having an organized hierarchical system of goals "...such that process goals operate as proximal regulators of more distal outcome goals" (p. 17). ePEARL Level 4 supports this idea by allowing the breakdown of work into tasks and supporting tasks that are linked to each other and to distal goals in a hierarchical manner. This system of goals is shown as a graphic "map" that presents the learner with an overview of the self-planned forethought phase. The resulting visual hierarchy allows learners both to easily identify where in the system of goals s/he is currently working, as well as to understand the importance of completing the proximal goal as a step to achieving the final goal.

ePEARL Level 4 also displays certain information from individual work as a visual graph to provide a novel cross section of learning behaviors and to inspire new insight into one's own learning practice; for example, learners use, and subsequently rate, strategies during their continued use of ePEARL. One of the graphs presents the strategies based on how successful the learner has judged them to be. Another graph presents the number of works that the learner has associated with each distal goal, allowing him/her to realize which goals are being neglected. Presenting visual representations of accumulated data this way will help learners see patterns in their behaviors in a timely manner and take steps to correct unsuccessful practices.

Sidebar Design

In ePEARL Level 4 we have tried to reinforce the cyclical nature of learning and improvement, especially the need to adjust one's activity based on one's monitoring and evaluation, through our interface design. While the main area of the screen is dedicated to working on the current task, a right-hand column constantly displays pertinent supporting information. Whether through textual instructions, pedagogical explanations, or other parts of the work, the sidebar promotes consideration of elements that may have otherwise been overlooked.

In ePEARL Level 4 we encourage simultaneous performance, monitoring, and modification in the sidebar, while the main area focuses on the performance phase. We know that the temporal proximity of feedback makes an observation more effective (Zimmerman, 2000), and the sidebar allows learners to immediately record their impressions without interrupting their progress. In the sidebar, learners are constantly encouraged to monitor the effectiveness of the plan (through self-reporting, checklist completion, and rating scales) and to modify those aspects that are not effective (by removing unsuccessful strategies and selecting new ones if necessary). Viewing different aspects of the work simultaneously can help draw learners' attention to links that can inspire novel conclusions about their own learning habits.

Drill Down

As mentioned earlier, tasks at the postsecondary level are expected to be more complex and take longer to complete. They often include more procedures and components to be completed. ePEARL Level 4 is a tool that supports learners as they go through the process of creating work in a self-regulated manner. However, too much support delivered in an intrusive way may be distracting rather than helpful. Forcing learners through a lengthy and repetitive procedure does not allow for personal choice or a customized experience and thus fails to conform to the philosophy of SRL as the self-directive processes of a learner-driven practice (Zimmerman, 2008). Moreover, forcing learners to complete every part of an online interface, without regard for the task or the level of support needed by the learner and without giving the learner any sense of agency or choice, will most likely result in frustration and a loss of motivation (Pintrich, 2003).

For these reasons, the interface we developed for ePEARL Level 4 allows for flexible interaction with the tool. It allows learners to focus on the aspects in which they feel that they need most assistance by choosing to drill down for more support at that point in the process. For example, the self-reflection phase in ePEARL Level 4 is comprised of a single general reflection question. However, there are also additional "focused questions" that may be accessed if a learner wishes to tackle reflecting more deeply. The additional questions prompt the learner to relate specifically to a feature of self-regulation (such as task analysis or self-observation) or to examine his/her works in ePEARL (such as rating which professional skills were reinforced during the task).

In this manner, we not only avoid fatigue and avoidance of the tool but also support learners' evolving understanding and use of both the tool and SRL practice. While learners are familiarizing themselves with the process, a teacher might encourage students to focus on one phase and complete all tasks associated with that phase, completing only the basic questions for others. Learners might use only the general reflection question to initiate reflective thinking at the beginning of the year and eventually feel comfortable and secure enough to answer one or more of the focused questions.

Challenges

The main instructional design challenge is the balance of addressing the SRL components without creating frustration and apathy in the users, which would invariably lead to abandoning ePEARL altogether. We have put tremendous effort in designing a tool that will successfully support learners in self-regulating their learning. However, because the social and environmental influences are so great, there must be a simultaneous effort to support teachers and other stakeholders in creating the necessary environment and attitude that foster SRL. "Modeling and instruction serve as a primary vehicle through which parents, teachers, and communities socially convey self-regulatory skills, such as persistence, self-praise, and adaptive self-reactions…" (Zimmerman, 2000, pp. 25–26). Working collaboratively does not only mean sharing drafts of work and providing constructive comments on the work of peers but also mean creating a community that values, models, and rewards self-regulatory practices. Predetermined prompts from a computer, for example, may not effectively implement the motivational aspect of self-regulation. Regardless, one can solicit self-reported data about the motivational state of the learner and support the teacher in properly addressing the motivational issues. For this reason, work with teachers is essential, and, in addition to our work on the EP, much of our efforts are directed towards supporting teachers in fostering self-regulation in their classrooms. The online support the learner gains through ePEARL is only part of the self-regulation process. The social aspect of the model must also be experienced in the classroom or community, where learning is truly valued, errors are honestly examined, and progress is understood as personal success. We return to the larger challenges of the educational uses of ePEARL later in this chapter.

Effectiveness of ePEARL

Until recently, evidence on the impacts of EPs on educational outcomes was sparse (Barrett, 2007; Carney, 2005; Zeichner & Wray, 2001). In separate quasi-experiments we have established the positive impact of ePEARL on students' SRL and literacy skills using a standardized measure of achievement (e.g., Canadian Achievement Test, 4th edition).

The first yearlong nonequivalent pretest–posttest quasi-experiment conducted by Meyer, Abrami, Wade, Aslan, and Deault (2010) provides exciting evidence that EPs, specifically ePEARL, can be used in ways to promote significant gains in children's literacy skills. Participants in this study were from elementary schools (grades 4–6) in Quebec, Manitoba, and Alberta. The constructed response subtest of the Canadian Achievement Test (CAT-4) was administered along with a self-regulation questionnaire in both the fall and the spring. The student questionnaire data showed that students who used ePEARL reported higher levels of some SRL processes, including setting process goals, listing strategies, using comments from their teacher to improve, and understanding how they were being evaluated, than students who did not use ePEARL. Analyses of the CAT-4 data also showed that students using ePEARL made significant gains in writing skills. Students showed significant improvements in content management, which refers to the word choice, sentence structure, and conventions of print.

The 2008–2009 study (Abrami, Venkatesh, Meyer, & Wade, in press) included nine experimental classrooms, coded as medium or high implementation ($n=154$ students), and 12 control classrooms ($n=165$ students) in a second, yearlong nonequivalent pretest–posttest control group quasi-experiment. Students using ePEARL made significantly greater gains compared to controls in writing skills as assessed by the constructed response subtest of the CAT-4. Multivariate analyses also revealed that, over time, students who used ePEARL reported higher levels of SRL processes than those in the control group.

We further investigated how student enthusiasm for using ePEARL affected student performance as well as self-regulatory processes. Multivariate analyses of SRL and CAT-4 achievement scores were significantly different among high- and low-enthusiasm students suggesting that student enthusiasm may explain whether and to what extent using EPs in classrooms will have a positive impact.

This finding reinforces the instructional design concerns expressed about ePEARL Level 4 and is a topic we will return to later in this chapter. Not all students accept the use of EPs similarly, and this has a noticeable impact on classroom applications of EPs and other knowledge tools. As discussed later, the acceptance of EPs by teachers, and the pedagogical approach that underlies them, provides a similar set of challenges.

ePEARL Scoring Rubrics and Authentic Assessment

The use of EPs provides opportunities for learners to present multimedia learning artifacts related to both learning processes as well as their final products. EPs, therefore, present unique opportunities for authentic assessment of learning (Abrami & Barrett, 2005). Consequently, as part of the research and development of ePEARL, we attempted to score and analyze the content of students' EPs.

We developed scoring rubrics linked to outcomes for both SRL and literacy. We assigned a holistic score for both literacy and SRL, and we assigned an analytical score for each based on several measurable subskills. Our rubrics can be used to measure the processes and levels of engagement demonstrated within the portfolio when applied to the entire portfolio contents, or to measure the achievement and/or growth of students when applied to artifacts they chose.

Summary of Rubric Design and Links to Other Measures

Herman, Gearhart, and Baker (1993) and Herrington, Reeves, Oliver, and Woo (2004) argued that portfolios allow more authentic assessment than traditional paper-and-pen tests, which may not reflect the student's real abilities. Others (e.g., Frey & Schmitt, 2007; Stiggins, 2002) argued that portfolios allow learners to substantiate their abilities by selecting evidence, reflecting real-life practices. EPs additionally allow learners to represent their understandings in multiple ways, including through audio recordings, photographs, video, and drawings, fitting with evolving conceptions of literacy (Carbonara, 2005).

Numerous rubrics have been developed but inter-rater and validity are rarely explored. We explored whether we can develop assessment tools which provide consistent and valid results, both to help further triangulate our findings concerning whether ePEARL helps improve students' self-regulatory and literacy skills and also to explore whether EPs could be used as a form of alternative standardized assessment. We examined the inter-rater reliability of our tools and their validity, looking at whether our assessment measures correlated with other measures of literacy and self-regulatory skills.

Table 32.1 Assessment approaches to assess literacy and SRL through EPs

Assessment approach	Criteria
Analytic rubric assessing literacy	Ideas and details
	Sentences and organization
	Voice
	Conventions
	Purpose
	Creativity
	Perceptions
Holistic rubric assessing literacy	Draw on criteria above; comments
Analytic rubric assessing SRL	Goals
	Strategies
	Reflection
Holistic rubric assessing SRL	Draw on criteria above; comments

Design of Assessment Approaches

The literacy rubric design and criteria were inspired by the literacy competencies from the Quebec Education Program (Gouvernement du Québec, 2001) and the criteria used to assess the constructed response subtest of the CAT-4. The SRL component was largely based on Zimmermann's (2000) model of SRL and others that emerged during design. After several revisions, two complementary approaches were developed, applying first a holistic rubric and then an analytical rubric to assess SRL and literacy. See Table 32.1.

First, the coder assigns a mark ranging from 1 ("experimenting") to 5 ("extending"), following a holistic rubric that describes each level. Table 32.2 shows the holistic rubric to assess literacy. It has five levels.

Then, the coder applies an analytical rubric measuring subskills. Table 32.3 shows the seven subskills measured by the analytical rubric for writing and the descriptors for Level 5 ("extending").

Table 32.2 Holistic rubric for assessing writing in EPs

Writing: holistic judgment	
Evaluate the writing skills students demonstrate through the pieces in their portfolio using these criteria: ideas and details, voice, organization and sentences, conventions, purpose and meaning, creativity and imagination, and perceptions	
Please circle a holistic mark of 1, 2, 3, 4, or 5, evaluating the category as a whole where:	
Category	Description
5 is extending	Writing supports ideas that show evidence of thoughtful understanding of producing, extending, and enhancing meaning and information with thorough explanations, details, and reflection
4 is achieving	Writing and ideas are focused understandings that explain and demonstrate meaning and information achieving some good explanations, details, and reflection
3 is developing	Writing and ideas are developing and in progress with meanings and information that is in the process of gaining a more complete understanding and accurate method of self-expression
2 is beginning	Writing and ideas demonstrate some vague meanings and information that shows a superficial or vague understanding of information
1 is experimenting	Writing is inconsistent, incomplete, or very confused demonstrating the need for much more attention to details, explanations, ideas, and accuracy
Comments:	

Table 32.3 Analytical rubric for writing in the EPs

Writing	Indicators for extending 5
Ideas and details	The details show evidence of careful attention with elements selected to enhance the communication of central ideas that thoughtfully and thoroughly explore meaning and content by producing and extending the information to the reader
Voice	The writer's voice is consistent, compelling, and engaging while respecting the intended purpose and audience
Organization and sentences	Written messages and ideas are thoroughly and thoughtfully crafted with close attention to the intended purpose and audience illustrated through very well-written sentences and organized, effective paragraphing that conveys a very clear message to the reader
Conventions	Capitalization, punctuation, and spelling are thorough with excellent attention and adherence to editing and revision that enhances and extends communication with the reader
Purpose and meaning	Use of language, dialogue, and descriptive word choice is very appropriate for the intended purpose and/or audience with careful attention paid to crafting writing and an understanding of purpose and meaning is clearly conveyed to the reader
Creativity and imagination	Explanations and interpretations demonstrate original ideas with value that enhances and extends the writer's imaginative ideas painting a clear image for the reader
Perceptions	Writing shows a carefully crafted, thoughtful, and meaningful point of view that clearly and consistently expresses personal understanding, thoughts, feelings, and perceptions of the task, subject content, and world beyond
Comments: total score:/35	

Although only portfolios from classrooms labeled medium or high from the 2007–2008 study were included in the analyses, we found that effective integration was in its infancy—some teachers developed task goals and put time aside for reflection; others used the portfolios mostly as a place to store important activities (Bures, Abrami, & Bentley, 2007). In applying the tools this turned out to be problematic, and our final analyses drew only on the subset of three classes where we found both SRL and literacy to be assessable ($n=66$). During the second year of research, implementation was more successful, and we included all experimental classes in the analysis excluding some individual portfolios, leaving $n = 188$ portfolios in the analyses. The improved implementation was evident in the portfolios, which demonstrated much better integration of SRL and literacy.

Even in coding amongst these subsets, challenges existed. In particular, students posted a range of quality work, from very polished pieces to very "rough" work. How does one assign a consistent mark? Does one weigh the most thoughtful piece or the most edited? The arrangement of work and the order in which the artifacts were viewed by coders caused inherent issues in the scoring of the collection of work. In addition, some portfolio content was judged differently by assessors with different teaching perspectives. For example, coders trained as English teachers tended to be harsher with criteria, such as conventions, sentences, and organization. Another challenge was dealing with specific cases that were hard to agree on. For example, where one coder valued a creative writer and assigned a 5, another valued organization more and assigned a 4. For this reason, discussion of discrepant cases seems necessary and productive (Bures, Barclay, Abrami, Meyer, & Venkatesh, 2012).

Inter-rater Reliability of EP Assessment

We found a range of Cronbach alpha scores in the high 1970s for literacy and SRL in both years, with some improvement in the second year. In the first year the holistic assessment of literacy was the weakest, whereas the analytic rubric assessment of literacy was the strongest. In the second year, both the holistic and analytic approaches to literacy were the strongest.

Validity of EP Assessment of Literacy

How did our assessment tools relate to other measures of literacy? We double-coded the CAT-4s of our study's participants. Following the same assessment approaches as we do for the EPs, the coders assigned both a holistic literacy and a rubric literacy score to the CAT-4s. The experience of coding the CAT-4s where the task demands and time constraints were held constant was in sharp contrast to the experience of coding EPs. The time restraints and specific tasks created consistency within a group of students making coding more consistent for the CAT-4s. This was significantly different from our experiences coding EPs, which were typically a mixed bag of artifacts ranging from very weak to very strong.

For the first year, the holistic scores and rubric scores we gave to literacy in the portfolios correlated well with one another ($r = 0.84$). The holistic scores we gave to literacy in the portfolios correlated moderately with the holistic scores we gave to the CAT-4s ($r = 0.48$) but not to the rubric scores we gave to the CAT-4s. The holistic literacy scores also correlated moderately with the official scores (as a total) given to the pretest CAT-4s ($r = 0.38$). The rubric scores we gave to literacy in the portfolios correlated reasonably well with the holistic and rubric scores we gave to the CAT-4s ($r = 0.60$ and 0.48, respectively). The holistic and rubric scores we gave to the portfolios also correlated moderately well with the official scores given to the pretest CAT-4s ($r = 0.55$), but not with the posttest CAT-4s. Except for this later finding, which surprised us, we are reasonably satisfied that we have the foundation of usable, reliable, and valid scoring rubrics. With more and better quality data from year two, we hope to extend these findings.

Teacher Interviews and Qualitative Data

In our year one 2007–2008 longitudinal study, in 7 out of 16 classrooms (43%), ePEARL was barely implemented. These classrooms were labeled as "low" implementers. The portfolios in most of these classrooms had never been used, or were used quite minimally during the school year. Of the remaining nine classrooms, four were "medium" implementers (25%) and five were "high" (31%). The medium- and high-implementation classrooms were then combined for all analyses. In order to better understand the reasons for teachers' varying degrees of implementation, we designed a Teacher Exit Interview Protocol (TEIP). This 40–60 min semi-structured interview guide was written with the intent of better understanding the factors that facilitate or inhibit the teachers' ability to integrate ePEARL into their classroom teaching. The interview addressed teachers' general impressions of the tool as well as the external and internal factors that shaped their use of it, such as administrative and technical support, access to computers, time management and scheduling issues, knowledge of portfolios and SRL, familiarity with ePEARL, and reasons for participating in the research. Questions addressed the teachers' expectations surrounding their use of ePEARL, what they found valuable, and what they saw as obstacles to using ePEARL with their students.

Cost: Barriers to Implementation

In order to identify why so many teachers were low implementers, we examined the "cost" items coded in teacher interviews. These items were defined as "the perceived physical and psychological demands of implementation operating as a disincentive to applying the innovation (preparation time, effort, etc.)" (Wozney, Venkatesh, & Abrami, 2006, p. 178). The most common factors that teachers mentioned as impeding their ability to work with ePEARL were as follows: it was time consuming; it conflicted with other demands for their time; they had limited access to computers; and there were problems with the school's server.

Value: Motivators in Implementation

All teachers in this study experienced some barriers to their implementation of ePEARL. However, it is clear that some of the teachers were able to overcome these perceived obstacles and persist in their teaching with this tool. Value items were defined as "the degree to which the teacher perceived the innovation or its associated outcomes as worthwhile. These include benefits to the teacher (congruency with teaching philosophy, career advancement) and to the students (increased achievement, enhanced interpersonal skills)" (Wozney et al., 2006, p. 178). The most common factors that teachers identified as valuable and may have been motivators for their use were high level of student engagement/motivation/interest, teachers' personal enthusiasm for ePEARL, good pedagogical support to integrate the tool, the structure of the software that helped students plan and organize their work, accessibility of ePEARL from home or any Internet-connected computer, and the customize feature which allowed students to take ownership over their portfolio.

Impacts on Teaching

High-implementation teachers also reported that ePEARL provided good pedagogical support (9/9) through the embedded help feature, instructional videos, sample lessons, and training provided. It also had a positive impact on transforming their teaching practice (7/9). Only two low implementation teachers mentioned the pedagogical supports they received through working with ePEARL, and only one mentioned any positive impact on his/her teaching practice. It is possible that low implementers were not able to experience this level of engagement with the tool if the other issues in their schools limited their use of and familiarity with ePEARL.

On the other hand, the medium and high implementers described how certain features in ePEARL, such as the place to provide a description of an assignment and the criteria, helped them make their expectations for their students more explicit and gave them a better awareness of the students' level of understanding of a task or an assignment. They integrated the SRL-based language of planning, doing, and reflecting throughout classroom activities, and students in these classrooms showed increased levels of goal setting and reflecting on their work as compared to students in control classrooms (Meyer, Wade, Pillay, Idan, & Abrami, 2010). One teacher noted, "I've used it as a guiding tool for my teaching this year. I love the learning cycle and it's helped me to become a better teacher because I've used the prompts to make sure I'm setting the criteria, making sure they know what makes a good job, and so we use it often, just out of context, not necessarily going online. But the language and the whole process" (Teacher 9).

The fact that ePEARL provided clear step-by-step guidance that made explicit the steps of SRL was something that several teachers noted as beneficial. A second teacher who also appreciated the structure of ePEARL echoed this perspective: "I found that the way the template was set up, as far as getting the students to share what the criteria was for their work and to get them to reflect on their work; that really channeled me in my teaching. I found you really had to force yourself in every lesson to think about 'Okay, we really need to think about the end in mind'" (Teacher 10).

This teacher's statement indicates how the design of the software supports him/her in being more conscious of how they are designing and presenting lessons and activities. Although it was clear that they understand the value of having clear objectives in mind, this statement indicates that s/he did not always make it explicit for the students and ePEARL helped him/her to realize this and improve in this area. A third teacher mentioned how working with ePEARL has changed his/her approach to teaching and helped him/her to be more deliberate in how s/he introduces new projects in class. "That whole deliberate 'here are the steps of learning'—I was never that deliberate. I made way too many assumptions of what they understood in that process. So that has very much changed the way I approach all of our things now. Like setting the goals, strategies, and criteria—Yeah, you talk about it, but it was never that deliberate and that's where the changes are coming. So yes, very much it's changed my approach" (Teacher 11).

A fourth teacher had a similar experience in being more conscious of how s/he taught and provided instructional support for students' development of SRL skills: "I like that because I think it helped me also focus a bit more on their setting goals. It really made me focus on that and verbalize it more. Like I said, sometimes I have a tendency to take things for granted, whereas here, I realize that we have to talk about certain aspects a little bit more if we really want to be ensured that the kids know exactly what direction they should be taking. And for them to be able to think about what the final result should look like, it gives them a good idea of what are they gonna do to get there? That part I thought was good for me. Definitely" (Teacher 15).

These excerpts illustrate that the design and features of ePEARL provided added value to teachers' instructional practice which resulted in positive impacts on student learning (Meyer, Abrami, Wade, & Scherzer, 2011). These quotations also demonstrate how the structure of the ePEARL software and the pedagogical support tools embedded in it helped teachers be more conscious of how they are presenting information and how their students understand what is being taught. It also helped more experienced educators reflect on how they taught language arts and offered a new perspective to instruction that inspired them and allowed them to be more creative. The teachers talked about the power of the portfolio and the ability to see evidence that a student has understood an assignment or a class activity. It also helped teachers to recognize when a student was lost or confused because s/he was not able to enter a description of the task or explain the criteria in his/her own words.

Challenges

Our greatest challenges remain primarily implementation fidelity linked to teacher professional development and secondarily the orientation and engagement of some learners towards actively using ePEARL. To increase the efficacy of using ePEARL to enhance literacy and SRL strategies requires that the tool be used effectively and appropriately with engaged teachers who can support students through the multiple processes of SRL. Many teachers struggle to help students set goals, post their work and reflect upon it, and sustain the SRL cycle over time. We have explored expectancy theory (e.g., expectancy of success, value, and cost) as one means to explain differences among teachers in adoption and also considered the effects of contextual barriers (e.g., technical support and administrative encouragement) to implementation fidelity.

Especially for older students and adults, we are attempting to balance usability challenges with scaffolding more refined and in-depth SRL processes. We are paying particular attention to student and teacher motivational dispositions; realizing that tools like ePEARL, however powerful and flexible, may be poorly used, and we are trying to find ways to prevent that.

Abrami (2010) and Abrami, Bernard, Bures, Borokhovski, and Tamim (2011) considered several reasons why learners do not better utilize some knowledge tools. The first reason is based on the principle of least effort. Even the best strategic learners need to balance efficiency concerns with effectiveness concerns, as well as balance proximal goals with distal ones. Strategic learners need to find the middle ground between how much they can learn and how well they can learn, or between the quantity of learning and the quality of learning.

Second, strategic learners often have to find the balance between intrinsic interests and extrinsic requirements. Frankly, the educational system imposes its own restrictions on students that may not make effortful strategies uniformly appropriate.

Third, decades ago, McClelland and Atkinson illustrated the impact not only of individual differences in achievement strivings but the importance of perceived outcome to learners' task choices and persistence. Years later, Weiner showed how causal attributions for task outcomes varied among learners that these attributions affected thinking, behavior, and feelings and that attributions varied depending on subjective estimates of the likelihood of future success and later, perceived outcome.

When we ask students to take personal responsibility for their own learning, we may create an internal conflict for students. First, does a student believe s/he can succeed at this learning task? Second, does a student believe that this tool will help him/her succeed? Third, does a student want to take responsibility for his/her own learning? While McClelland and Atkinson (e.g., McClelland, Atkinson, Clark, & Lowell, 1953) showed that high-need achievers are drawn to moderately challenging tasks, we know that high-need achievers tend to avoid tasks which are low in the probability of success. Weiner and others (e.g., Weiner, 1980) showed that there are marked differences in causal attributions when learners perceive they have succeeded versus failed. Attributional bias means learners attribute success to internal causes and failure to external ones. Defensive attributions for failure (e.g., I failed because the exam was too hard or my teacher did not help) help protect a learner's sense of self-efficacy (i.e., keep a learner from concluding s/he failed because of lack of ability).

Therefore, there may be situations where increased personal responsibility for learning is not always beneficial to a learner's achievement strivings, causal attributions, and self-efficacy. These situations have mostly to do with the learner's perception of the likelihood of future success and/or perceived outcome. For example, in novel or very demanding situations, especially ones that are high in importance, learners may want to avoid taking responsibility for their learning (and the learning of others) until such time as they are confident of a positive outcome. In other words, it is likely that some learners will return the responsibility for learning to the instructor or, more generally, the instructional delivery system, rather than accept it themselves.

Fourth, related to the above is the importance of effort–outcome covariation. Productive learners come to believe that their efforts at learning lead to successful learning outcomes. These learners come to believe that "the harder and more that I try, the more likely I am to achieve a positive learning outcome." The opposite belief is when a learner believes that his/her efforts bear little, if any, relationship to learning outcomes. In behavioral terms, this is learning that outcomes are noncontingent on actions, called learned helplessness by Seligman (1975). Seligman demonstrated that after experiencing these noncontingencies learners made almost no effort to act even when the contingencies were changed. This passivity, even in the face of aversive stimuli, is difficult to reverse.

To summarize, the following factors may be at work in preventing more pervasive and persistent use of knowledge tools:

1. Teachers and students do not value the outcome(s) of tool use sufficiently to increase their efforts to use it for learn—it is not so important to do well.
2. Teachers and students believe that gains in learning from increased effort from tool use are inefficient—it takes too much effort to do a little bit better.
3. Learners do not want to become more responsible for their own learning—it is too risky unless the perceived chances of a positive outcome are increased.
4. Teachers and students believe that novel approaches to learning (use of unfamiliar knowledge tools) increase the likelihood of poor outcomes, not increase them—it is not of interest or too risky because they do not believe the tool will help students learn.

There are ways to overcome these challenges. First, knowledge tools must be structured so they increase the efficiency of learning as well as the effectiveness of learning. As such, instructional designers should pay more attention to *ease of use* as an overall design objective, where learners need even more guidance as to which features to use, how, and when. Time is one critical factor, and it may be dealt with in numerous ways, including structuring how tool activities are carried out (e.g., weekly) or making them part of the evaluation scheme. Simplicity of use may be important, avoiding the addition of time to learn how to use technology at the expense of time needed to learn the content. It would be interesting to know not only whether use of each tool resulted in increased achievement but also whether the quality and quantity of use related to learning gains—a form of cost/benefit ratio.

Second, students and teachers may need more guidance about *when to use* the tool and not only whether to use it. That is, the tool should be used when a learning task is both difficult and important. Advice and feedback from instructors and consultants may help, as well as queries and suggestions embedded in the tool. Not every learning task requires the use of a knowledge tool, and its use probably varies according to the skills and interests of each learner. Furthermore, even when a task warrants the use of a tool, not all features of the tool may need to be used. Some explanation, embedded within the tool, regarding when to use which feature would also be useful. As such, additional features should be designed to be used flexibly when appropriate to the learning task.

Third, like any tool, physical or cognitive, users need *practice* to use the tool well and wisely. You don't license a driver after one day's practice or ask a carpenter apprentice to build a cabinet after a single time using a band saw. Asking teachers and students to use a tool voluntarily, when performance matters, is stacking the deck against enthusiastic use. Requiring use may ameliorate the problem because it is fair to everyone. Nevertheless, learners may now face the dual challenge of not only learning complex and challenging material but doing so in a novel and effortful way. Therefore, the tool should be "well learned" before it becomes a required part of a course or program of study or course time allocated to learning how to use it. And teachers and students must be convinced that the tool helps students learn. In the latter regard, careful attention should be paid to feedback from students and instructors on success and failures stories, including the former as testimonials embedded in the tool.

Fourth, cognitive tools and learning strategies may work best when they are an integral feature of a course or program of study and not an add-on. This is the true meaning of *technology integration* or when the use of technology is not separate from the content to be learned but embedded in it. This integration may require forethought, performance, and self-reflection on the part of instructors to insure effective and efficient class use. In addition, instructors need training and experience with the use of tools to encourage scalability and sustainability.

References

Abrami, P. C. (2010). On the nature of support in computer-supported collaborative learning using gStudy. *Computers in Human Behavior, 26*, 835–839. doi:10.1016/j.chb.2009.04.007.

Abrami, P. C., & Barrett, H. (2005). Directions for research and development on electronic portfolios. *Canadian Journal of Learning and Technology, 31*(3),

1–15. Retrieved February 1, 2013 from http://www.cjlt.ca/index.php/cjlt/article/view/92/86.

Abrami, P. C., Bernard, R. M., Bures, E. M., Borokhovski, E., & Tamim, R. (2011). Interaction in distance education and online learning: Using evidence and theory to improve practice. *Journal of Computing in Higher Education*. doi:10.1007/s12528-011-9043-x.

Abrami, P. C., Venkatesh, V., Meyer, E., & Wade, A., (in press). Using electronic portfolios to foster literacy and self regulated learning skills in elementary students. *Journal of Educational Psychology*.

Barrett, H. (2007). Researching electronic portfolios and learner engagement: The REFLECT initiative. *Journal of Adolescent and Adult Literacy, 50*(6), 436–449.

Bures, E., Abrami, P., & Bentley, C. (2007). Assessing electronic portfolios—Now that we have them, what can we do with them? In G. Richards (Ed.), *Proceedings of World Conference on E-Learning in Corporate, Government, Healthcare, and Higher Education 2007* (pp. 7030–7038). Chesapeake, VA. AACE.

Bures, E., Barclay, A., Abrami, P. C., Meyer, E., & Venkatesh, V. (2012). Contextualizing assessment: Students demonstrating and developing literacy and self-regulated learning skills through electronic portfolios (Manuscript submitted for publication).

Carbonara, D. (2005). *Technology literacy applications in learning environments*. Hershey, PA: Idea Group Publishing.

Carney, J. (2005). *What kind of electronic portfolio research do we need*? Paper presented at the Society for Information Technology and Teacher Education International Conference, Phoenix, AZ.

Frey, B., & Schmitt, V. (2007). Coming to terms with classroom assessment. *Journal of Advanced Academics, 18*(3), 402–423. doi:10.4219/jaa-2007-495.

Gouvernement du Québec. (2001). *Quebec Education Program—English version*. Retrieved February 1, 2013 from Ministère de l'Éducation website: http://www.mels.gouv.qc.ca/dgfj/dp/programme_de_formation/primaire/educprg2001h.htm.

Herman, J. L., Gearhart, M., & Baker, E. L. (1993). Assessing writing portfolios: Issues in the validity and meaning of scores. *Educational Assessment, 1*(3), 201–224. doi:10.1207/s15326977ea0103_2.

Herrington, J., Reeves, T., Oliver, R., & Woo, Y. (2004). Designing authentic activities in web-based courses. *Journal of Computing in Higher Education, 16*(1), 3–29. doi:10.1007/BF02960280.

McClelland, D. C., Atkinson, J. W., Clark, R. A., & Lowell, E. L. (1953). *The achievement motive*. New York: Appleton.

Meyer, E., Abrami, P. C., Wade, A., Aslan, O., & Deault, L. (2010). Improving literacy and metacognition with electronic portfolios: Teaching and learning with ePEARL. *Computers in Education, 55*, 84–91. doi:10.1016/j.compedu.2009.12.005.

Meyer, E., Abrami, P. C., Wade, A., & Scherzer, R. (2011). Electronic portfolios in the classroom: Factors impacting teachers' integration of new technologies and new pedagogies. *Technology, Pedagogy and Education, 20*(2), 191–207.

Meyer, E., Wade, A., Pillay, V., Idan, E., & Abrami, P. C. (2010). Using electronic portfolios to foster communication in K-12 classrooms. In C. Black (Ed.), *The dynamic classroom: Engaging students in higher education* (pp. 125–133). Madison, WI: Atwood Publishing.

Pintrich, P. R. (2003). A motivational science perspective on the role of student motivation in learning and teaching contexts. *Journal of Educational Psychology, 95*, 667–686. doi:10.1037/0022-0663.95.4.667.

Rogers, D., & Swan, K. (2004). Self-regulated learning and internet searching. *Teachers College Record, 106*, 1804–1824.

Seligman, M. E. P. (1975). *Helplessness: On depression, development and death*. San Francisco: W.H. Freeman.

Stiggins, R. J. (2002). Assessment crisis. The absence of assessment FOR learning. *Phi Delta Kappan, 83*, 758–765.

Upitis, R., Abrami, P. C., Brook, J., Troop, M., & Varela, W. (2010, November). *Using ePEARL for music teaching: A case study*. Paper presented at the International Association for the Scientific Knowledge conference, Oviedo, Spain.

Weiner, B. (1980). *Human motivation*. New York: Holt-Rinehart and Winston.

Wozney, L., Venkatesh, V., & Abrami, P. C. (2006). Implementing computer technologies: Teachers' perceptions and practices. *Journal of Technology and Teacher Education, 14*(1), 173–207. Retrieved February 1, 2013 from http://www.editlib.org/f/5437.

Zeichner, K., & Wray, S. (2001). The teaching portfolio in US teacher education programs: What we know and what we need to know. *Teaching and Teacher Education, 17*, 613–621. doi:10.1016/S0742-051X(01)00017-8.

Zimmerman, B. J. (1989). A social cognitive view of self-regulated academic learning. *Journal of Educational Psychology, 81*, 329–339.

Zimmerman, B. J. (2000). Attaining self-regulation: A social cognitive perspective. In M. Boekaerts & P. R. Pintrich (Eds.), *Handbook of self-regulation* (pp. 13–39). New York: Academic.

Zimmerman, B. J. (2008). Investigating self-regulation and motivation: Historical background, methodological developments, and future prospects. *American Educational Research Journal, 45*(1), 166–183. doi:10.3102/0002831207312909.

Overcoming Deceptive Clarity by Encouraging Metacognition in the Web-Based Inquiry Science Environment

33

Jennifer L. Chiu, Jennifer King Chen, and Marcia C. Linn

Abstract

In our research we view metacognition and cognition as interacting processes that together promote coherent understanding. We propose that the use of the knowledge integration pattern to design instructional scaffolding encourages the interplay between these two processes. In this chapter, we present and discuss findings that indicate that instructional activities designed using the knowledge integration pattern promote student learning from dynamic visualizations by helping to overcome deceptive clarity.

Introduction

In our research we view metacognition and cognition as interacting processes that together promote coherent understanding. We propose that the use of the knowledge integration pattern to design instructional scaffolding encourages the interplay between these two processes. In this chapter, we present and discuss findings that indicate that instructional activities designed using the knowledge integration pattern promote student learning from dynamic visualizations by helping to overcome deceptive clarity.

Typical instruction encourages learners to focus primarily on the cognitive aspects of learning, such as adding new ideas or comprehending explanations of phenomena. However, we believe that designing curriculum that also supports students in being metacognitive by, for example, distinguishing among ideas using generated criteria or reflecting on potential alternatives as they engage in these and other cognitive activities results in overall greater benefits for student learning and understanding. In fact, much research points to the benefits of incorporating metacognitive activities to promote coherent understanding (e.g., Aleven & Koedinger, 2002; Azevedo, 2005; Graesser, McNamara, & VanLehn, 2005; Quintana, Zhang, & Krajcik, 2005; White & Frederiksen, 1998), especially with dynamic visualizations. We find that activities that promote metacognitive skills such as prompting self-monitoring and

J.L. Chiu (✉)
Science, Technology, Engineering and Math (STEM) Education, Curry School of Education, University of Virginia, Bavaro Hall, Charlottesville, VA 22904, USA
e-mail: jlchiu@virginia.edu

J.K. Chen • M.C. Linn
Education in Mathematics, Science, and Technology, University of California, Tolman Hall, Berkeley, CA 94720-1670, USA
e-mail: jykchen@berkeley.edu; mclinn@berkeley.edu

R. Azevedo and V. Aleven (eds.), *International Handbook of Metacognition and Learning Technologies*, Springer International Handbooks of Education 26, DOI 10.1007/978-1-4419-5546-3_33,

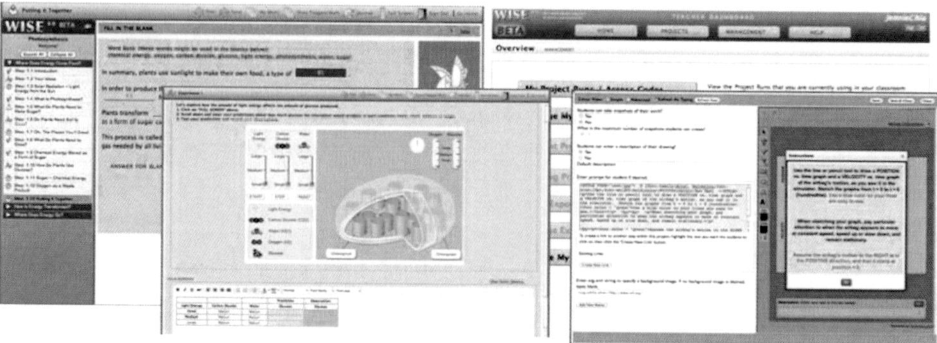

Fig. 33.1 WISE guides students' inquiry investigations through the use of a map of activities and various step types and tools, such as explanation prompts and dynamic visualizations. The WISE environment also offers tools for teachers and researchers to monitor student work and give feedback, as well as to author and customize instruction

supporting critique of one's understanding can help students to interpret and learn from visualizations more successfully. By incorporating metacognitive activities into curricula featuring visualizations, we can help learners develop coherent, normative understanding that builds upon their prior knowledge. This emphasis can also help students develop important metacognitive skills such as evaluating, distinguishing, and reflecting upon their understanding (Aleven & Koedinger, 2002; Azevedo, Moos, Greene, Winters, & Cromley, 2008; White & Frederiksen, 2005). Our perspective is consistent with research that advocates for less extraneous and more germane cognitive processing with dynamic visualizations (Wouters, Paas, & van Merrienboer, 2008). Although research points to the need for use of metacognitive skills and knowledge integration when learning from visualizations, few studies have focused on promoting or capturing students' use of metacognition when interacting with dynamic visualizations.

This chapter describes research conducted by the Technology-Enhanced Learning in Science (TELS) Center using the Web-based Inquiry Science Environment (WISE). Our work focuses on supporting student learning from dynamic visualizations using instructional scaffolding developed according to the knowledge integration pattern (Linn & Eylon, 2006). Research reports varied levels of effectiveness for instruction with visualizations (Hoffler & Leutner, 2007). We present evidence that the use of dynamic visualizations often results in *deceptive clarity*—students' overestimation of their understanding of the visualization after rote completion of the instructed steps or only a brief inspection (Tinker, 2009). The deceptive clarity of visualizations is highly problematic, in that it can short-circuit students' consideration of alternative ideas and limit more detailed interrogation with the visualization, producing the kinds of mixed results found in the literature. In this chapter we argue that instruction developed with the knowledge integration pattern that encourages both metacognitive *and* cognitive processes can help to overcome deceptive clarity and support student learning. We discuss how a variety of WISE instructional supports, such as prompting students to make predictions or asking them to explain their understanding, can help students develop skills to monitor their learning of complex science from dynamic visualizations.

WISE and Dynamic Visualizations

The Web-based Inquiry Science Environment (WISE; http://www.wise.berkeley.edu/) is a free online environment supported by the National Science Foundation (Fig. 33.1).

Projects created in WISE support effective inquiry learning and use interactive, research-based instruction in conjunction with engaging, dynamic visualizations (Slotta & Linn, 2009). Other instructional tools used in WISE projects in addition to dynamic visualizations include reflection notes, predict and revise prompts, student journals, drawing tools, online discussion forums, and concept maps. Projects present students with compelling inquiry questions embedded within relevant topics such as global climate change, airbag safety, and genetic inheritance. By making science accessible, and by providing instruction that encourages students to make their thinking visible to themselves and others, WISE projects promote the development of both integrated understanding as well as skills for autonomous, lifelong learning (Linn, Eylon, & Davis, 2004).

Dynamic visualizations refer to external representations used for learning that display processes of scientific phenomena that change over time. Basic forms of dynamic visualizations include animations, which consist of sets of frames that alter properties such as shape or size, depict motion, or make objects appear and disappear (Lowe, 2004; Moreno & Mayer, 2007). More sophisticated instructional simulations and computational models enable students to interact and experiment with phenomena on scales that are not directly observable such as molecular dynamics (Linn & Eylon, 2006) or with visualized concepts such as force (White & Frederiksen, 1998). These dynamic visualizations enable students to alter variables or settings to see different outcomes. Students can generate and test hypotheses by experimenting and interacting with the visualization, as well as synthesize and refine their hypotheses by reflecting upon observed outcomes as well as the effectiveness of their experimentation strategies for learning (Ertmer & Newby, 1996).

By incorporating dynamic visualizations, WISE projects offer students the opportunity to interact with complex scientific phenomena in ways that are difficult or impossible with traditional forms of instruction, such as lecture or text-based teaching. For instance, text-based instruction of chemical reactions typically focuses on rules or classification of chemical reactions, such as single-replacement or combustion reactions. With typical instruction, students might read that increasing the temperature of reactant molecules will increase the reaction rate because of increased collisions. In order to understand this concept more fully, however, students must visualize atoms and molecules interacting on a molecular scale. Thus a limitation of text-based instruction is that it requires students to rely solely on their own mental representations, which may be flawed or incomplete. Instruction featuring dynamic visualizations enables students not only to compare their existing mental representations with scientifically normative dynamic visualizations, but also to consider new ideas gleaned from interacting with the visualizations. *Chemical Reactions*, a weeklong WISE project for high school chemistry students, uses dynamic molecular visualizations of chemical reactions. Students can change parameters and variables and immediately observe what happens on an atomic level. For instance, students can add energy to reactants and watch product molecules form on the screen (Fig. 33.2). Similarly, the WISE *Static Electricity* project (Shen & Linn, 2010) incorporates dynamic visualizations of protons and electrons that students can use to investigate how the movement of electrons relates to the phenomenon of receiving an electric shock. In the WISE *Birds of a Feather Evolve Together* project, students explore how different traits and environments impact the survival of species with a dynamic visualization that models natural selection. The visualization enables students to experiment with various species over multiple generations.

Dynamic Visualizations and Deceptive Clarity

Research demonstrates that while dynamic visualizations have significant overall impact on learning (Hoffler & Leutner, 2007), students face difficulties when using them (Tversky, Morrison,

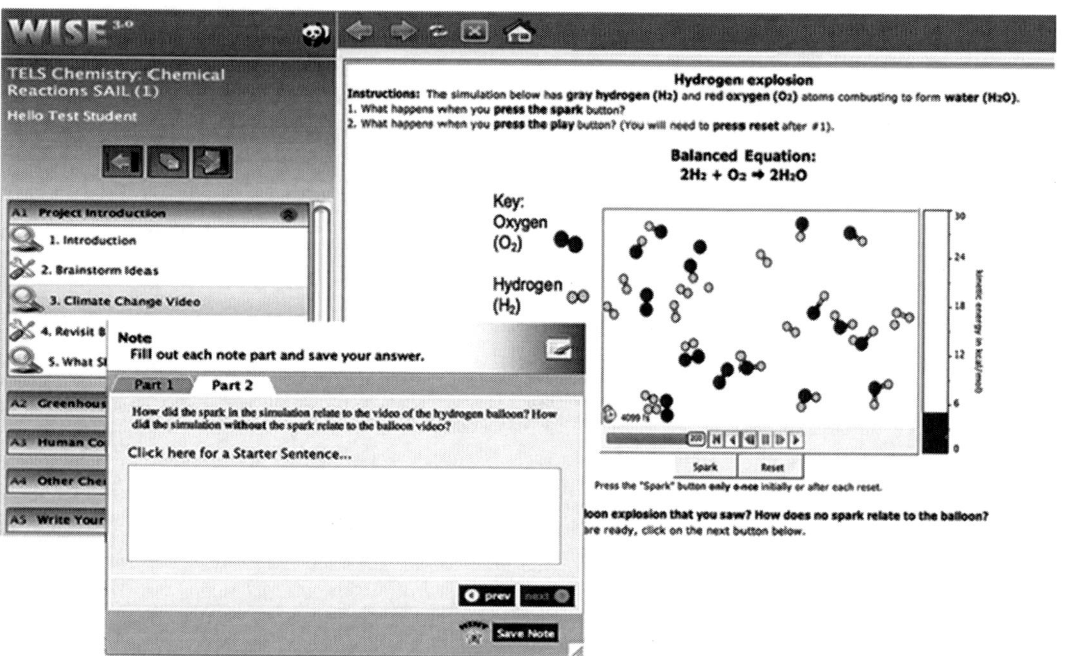

Fig. 33.2 *Chemical Reactions* uses dynamic molecular visualizations and pedagogical tools such as embedded prompts within WISE

& Betrancourt, 2002). For example, students tend to overestimate their own understanding of visualized systems (Rozenblit & Keil, 2002). This kind of deceptive clarity can be particularly detrimental for learning. For instance, Lowe (2004) investigated learning with animated weather maps. Subjects tended to focus on perceptually salient aspects of the visualization, such as isolated spatial or temporal features. Subjects had trouble building more coherent predictions of weather that integrated features across the visualization. Videos of subjects during the learning task revealed that learners did not know they should be looking at other important features of the visualization (i.e., *"Do I have to do all these lines as well?"*, p. 268). Other research reports similar illusions of understanding with other visualizations (Lewalter, 2003; Schnotz & Rasch, 2005).

Interactivity can encourage students to engage and revisit with visualizations, and can have a large impact on learning effectiveness (Moreno & Mayer, 2007). Interactive features allow students to pause, slow down, speed up or replay a visualization, or to change variables and inputs to observe different outcomes. Learners can revisit visualizations and focus upon concepts or aspects they may have missed upon initial interrogations. However, even with interactive features learners can fail to build integrated understanding from visualizations (Kalyuga, 2007). Students need to be aware of the important concepts upon which to focus, and they also need to know how to monitor their understanding to appropriately manipulate the visualization to address any gaps in knowledge (Lowe, 2004). For example, students using a chemical reaction visualization can focus on the impact of heat on molecular motion, manipulate settings to understand that relationship, think they understand it and move on to the next step. If students are not aware of other important aspects (such as bonding), or have a false sense of understanding, students will not fully utilize the functionalities of the visualization, such as replaying it or experimenting with other variables (Linn & Eylon,

2011). This kind of self-monitoring can have a large impact on how students interact with and how much students learn from dynamic visualizations (Azevedo, Guthrie, & Seibert, 2004).

Research into self-regulatory learning (SRL) in multimedia environments lends insight into deceptive clarity and visualizations (Azevedo, 2005). Self-regulated learning involves setting goals, determining and using learning strategies to meet those goals, monitoring one's learning, evaluating how well one is reaching those goals and responding by changing strategies (Zimmerman, 2008). Students interacting with visualizations may set different goals than students working with text. For example, visualizations may trigger students to set procedural goals to complete steps or run the visualization instead of setting learning goals to seek conceptual understanding of the underlying concepts. Students may then select strategies, monitor effectiveness and evaluate outcomes based on these different goals (Reiber, Tzeng, & Tribble, 2004). In this way, differences in how students perceive the task of learning with visualizations can result in students believing that they have understood the targeted concepts.

Overcoming Deceptive Clarity Through Knowledge Integration

The knowledge integration pattern builds upon research that learners have rich, diverse, and often conflicting ideas about scientific phenomena from various contexts and experiences (Davis & Linn, 2000; diSessa, 2000; Linn, Clark, & Slotta, 2003; Songer & Linn, 2006). Students' existing ideas are viewed as fruitful starting points for developing deep understanding.

The knowledge integration instructional pattern consists of four interleaved processes: Eliciting current ideas, adding new ideas, developing criteria for evaluating ideas, and sorting out ideas (Linn & Eylon, 2006). First, eliciting current ideas recognizes the diverse backgrounds and experiences that individual students bring with them into the classroom and acknowledges these experiences and ideas as rich starting points for learning (Davis & Linn, 2000; diSessa, 2000; Linn et al., 2003; Songer & Linn, 2006). Prompting learners to become aware of their pre-existing ideas prepares them to form connections between these ideas and new ones. Second, adding new ideas involves introducing normative ideas for students to consider against their existing ones. The careful design of effective visualizations can serve as a fertile source of useful and relevant ideas for students to evaluate and incorporate into their thinking. Third, supporting students in developing criteria for evaluating ideas helps them to readily distinguish between their own ideas and new ones. Fourth, in sorting out their ideas, learners are encouraged to reflect upon their ideas by using their developed criteria to evaluate, sort and consolidate their ideas into a revised and more coherent understanding. Using generated criteria to evaluate the connections among their ideas can help students to refine their knowledge based on these evaluations. The process of knowledge integration thus encourages students to consider their current networks of ideas, make judgments about their understanding, and seek ways to improve their understanding by going back and adding, sorting, or refining ideas. When learners sort out their ideas and use evidence to support their thinking, they strengthen their understanding. The knowledge integration instructional pattern thus helps students to gain a coherent, integrated understanding of a scientific topic.

Instruction that focuses on knowledge integration helps students overcome the deceptive clarity of visualizations because students engage in both cognitive and metacognitive processes that help them to more productively engage in monitoring their learning with the visualizations. The knowledge integration pattern encompasses a spectrum of activities that can be considered as more cognitive in nature (such as adding normative ideas) to processes that are more metacognitive in nature (such as distinguishing and reflecting upon ideas). Ideally, learners monitor and reflect upon their knowledge, find gaps or discrepancies in their understanding, and act to remedy these situations by building coherent networks of ideas.

Since traditional classroom instruction does not typically focus upon metacognitive skill development (Linn & Eylon, 2011), we focus on scaffolding to help students engage in the entire knowledge integration pattern, with a special focus on distinguishing, evaluating, and reflecting upon ideas and connections. Instructional prompting or scaffolds help learners develop more sophisticated skills and engage in more complicated activities than they could on their own (Bransford, Brown, & Cocking, 1999). Appropriate scaffolding in classroom environments can be especially challenging, with many students starting at varying levels of skills and knowledge. In order for scaffolding to be most effective, it needs to fall in the target zone of not giving too much or too little support (Vygotsky, 1978).

Prior research suggests that scaffolding in computer-enhanced environments can help learners engage in metacognitive activities with curriculum featuring visualizations (Azevedo et al., 2008). For instance, White and Frederiksen (1998, 2000) used reflective prompts in their ThinkerTools curriculum to encourage student self-evaluation at the end of each inquiry cycle during the project. Students were either prompted to engage in reflective self-assessment or not prompted to self-assess. Students with monitoring support who self-assessed understood scientific inquiry better than those who did not self-assess, and the support especially benefitted students with lower prior knowledge.

Davis and Linn (2000) investigated the effect of two different types of prompts—sentence starters that were either activity-focused or self-monitoring—on middle school students' integration of heat and light energy knowledge while working with the WISE *Aliens on Tour* and *All the News* projects. These projects required students to design houses and clothing for cold-blooded aliens with different climate requirements and critique news articles about energy and thermodynamics. Students responded to activity-focused prompts and self-monitoring prompts. The activity-focused prompts were aimed to help students think about the justification required to demonstrate the quality of their designs (e.g., *"Our design will work well because…"*) while the self-monitoring prompts encouraged students to reflect on the quality of their designs (e.g., *"Our design could be better if we…"*). Findings indicate that while the activity-focused prompts were effective for helping students to finish their project activities, students did not develop integrative knowledge. Self-monitoring prompts, however, encouraged knowledge integration by helping students to plan their activities, reminding them to reflect on their understandings, and encouraging them to explain and justify their design decisions. Additionally, students who used the self-monitoring prompts to evaluate their understanding and identify places of confusion had greater project scores (Davis & Linn, 2000).

In addition, prompting students to predict, distinguish, draw, or critique ideas also engages them in the process of knowledge integration (Linn, Chang, Chiu, Zhang, & McElhaney, 2010). These generative activities can be especially beneficial for learning with visualizations because learners can compare new ideas to their prior knowledge or existing mental models of phenomena (Chi, De Leew, Chiu, & Lavancher, 1994; Lombrozo, 2006). This gives students the opportunity to identify what they do not understand (Rozenblit & Keil, 2002) or to revise their views (Chi, 2000). Engaging students in the process of knowledge integration helps students refocus their learning goals on conceptual understanding and employ both cognitive and metacognitive strategies to reach those goals (e.g., Zimmerman, 2008).

Students may fail to revise their initial ideas and proceed with isolated views of the visualization if not prompted to distinguish ideas. For example, Chi (2000) describes how generating self-explanations while reading text helped a subject revise her mental model of the circulatory system. The student first used self-explanations to generate her existing network of ideas. During a later segment, the student distinguishes ideas when she comes across a piece of information that conflicts with her existing model of how the circulatory system works (that blood flows into the lungs). The student reveals her efforts to distinguish ideas by making many monitoring statements such as "I don't understand." Subsequently she revised her understanding of the circulatory system to include a loop from the heart to the lungs. This example demonstrates how prompting to distinguish ideas can help students overcome deceptive clarity. The prompts can help students realize what they do not understand, recognize conflicting ideas, and remedy these conflicts or gaps in their understanding.

Research suggests that distinguishing ideas also benefits those learning with visualizations. For instance, Cromley, Azevedo, and Olson (2005) investigated how people self-regulate when learning from a multimedia environment that included animations of the circulatory system. Learners engaged in relatively less self-regulation with the animation than other forms of instruction, supporting the notion of deceptive clarity. However, if the learners summarized their understanding as they watched the animation, the participants learned more. Similarly, in the WISE *Orbital Motion* project, students interact with a set of three dynamic visualizations to help them connect from their everyday ideas about projectiles to a more sophisticated understanding of orbital motion. In one visualization, students experiment with launching a cannonball using different initial horizontal speeds. Without the proper instructional scaffolding, students may interact with the visualization only briefly (such as launching the cannonball using just a few arbitrarily selected speeds) and believe their understanding to be sound or unproblematic. However, the use of predict and revise prompts before and after the visualization encourages students to reflect more carefully about their interactions with the visualization in order to achieve important key outcomes—such as determining appropriate launch speeds for getting the cannonball to hit the ground, achieve orbit, or escape into space. (King Chen, Tinker, & McElhaney, 2011).

Distinguishing ideas can also help students overcome deceptive clarity with visualizations because they encourage students to identify gaps in their understanding (Renkl & Atkinson, 2002; Rozenblit & Keil, 2002). For instance, Rozenblit and Keil (2002) conducted a number of experiments where subjects judged their understanding of certain concepts, explained their ideas about the concepts, and then re-rated their understanding. Rozenblit and Keil (2002) found that prompting students to generate their own ideas about concepts consistently helped subjects to recognize what they did not understand, especially for visualized phenomena. This approach was not as helpful for recognizing gaps in understanding of procedures, narratives, or facts. These findings suggest that if students fail to monitor their understanding while interacting with a visualization, having them generate their own ideas can help them to become aware of and identify what they may have missed in the visualization.

Generating predictions can also help students overcome deceptive clarity by identifying gaps in understanding. In one study, subjects asked to predict behavior of animated and static visualizations of devices had a better understanding than those who did not predict (Hegarty, Kriz, & Cate, 2003). The researchers suggest that predicting behavior helped the subjects recognize what they did and did not know about the mechanical device. This aligns with other studies that find that predicting answers benefits learning, even if these predictions are incorrect (Kornell, Hays, & Bjork, 2009).

Similarly, other activities that encourage students to articulate causal chains of events or sequences of states can help learners to identify and fill in gaps in their understanding. Examples of these kinds of activities include generating representations, drawing, or categorizing and sequencing. Chang, Quintana, and Krajcik (2010) studied students creating animations using *Chemation*, a program that enables students to make flipbook-style dynamic visualizations of chemical phenomena. They found that students had a better understanding of atom rearrangement than students using static visualizations and media because the students had to pay attention to the dynamic aspects of bonds breaking and bonds forming when creating their animations.

We report next on a collection of findings that point to the benefit of using the knowledge integration pattern for learning with dynamic visualizations. We present our results regarding deceptive clarity in more detail to demonstrate how generation activities can help students elicit, add, distinguish, sort out, reflect, and refine their ideas with visualizations. These results describe how the knowledge integration pattern encourages both cognitive and metacognitive processes and how this combination benefits learning with visualizations.

Empirical Findings

WISE provides a rich environment to research how instruction focused on knowledge integration can support students' development of self-knowledge and self-monitoring skills while interacting with dynamic visualizations. WISE logs students' work as they progress through the unit. These data logs capture exactly when and what students write, details about students' navigation through the project, and how students interact with the visualizations. We use these data logs combined with self-assessments, embedded explanations, and pre- and post-test measures to both research and promote students' self-monitoring in authentic classroom environments.

Addressing Deceptive Clarity with Explanations

The WISE *Chemical Reactions* project exemplifies how designing for and prompting knowledge integration processes can help students mindfully build, assess, critique and sort out their ideas with dynamic visualizations. *Chemical Reactions* guides students through an investigation of how chemical reactions relate to climate change. The project focuses on making connections among symbolic, molecular and observable levels of chemical reactions, as well as balanced equations, stoichiometric ratios, and limiting reagents. Students interact with visualizations of common hydrocarbon combustion reactions that contribute carbon dioxide to the atmosphere, use dynamic visualizations of hydrogen combustion to investigate hydrogen as an alternative fuel, and explore greenhouse visualizations to learn how greenhouse gases trap infrared radiation. Students reflect upon and synthesize the information they learn throughout the project in an electronic letter to their congressperson.

In *Chemical Reactions* students are asked to distinguish between two visualizations. One that shows the addition of energy and the resulting explosion and one that does not involve adding energy. While distinguishing among the two visualizations, the students' connections among existing ideas and ideas added from the visualization become visible. Many students initially notice that the atoms and molecules bounced around the container faster after the spark is added, but when asked to distinguish they realized they did not know *how* the spark caused the reaction to occur (i.e., *"I think the spark caused the molecules to move around faster, but I'm not sure"*). Using the interactive dynamic visualization, students can go back and test their current ideas to fill in gaps in understanding or see if their predictions or ideas are correct. They can inspect the visualization in greater detail to see that the spark caused the reaction to occur by adding energy that breaks bonds, creating free radicals that then form intermediate and product molecules.

To explore how students judged their understanding of concepts with these visualizations, we prompted for judgments of learning (Chiu & Linn, 2008). We asked one group of students to rate their understanding immediately after the visualizations, and another group to rate their understanding after writing an explanation of their understanding. We found that students judged themselves as more knowledgeable immediately after working with the visualizations. Students rated themselves as less knowledgeable after writing an explanation of their understanding. These results have replicated across later groups of students. Analysis and observations of students using the project revealed that when students initially interacted with the visualizations, they tended to focus on following the instructions or making the visualization "blow up." These kinds of interactions seemed to convince students that they understood the concepts underlying the visualizations simply by completing the visualization steps without deeper interrogation.

Prompting students to explain helped students realize gaps in their understanding. Analysis of log files revealed that students were likely to revisit the visualization after the explanation prompt. For instance, students would "blow up" the visualization, or make carbon dioxide and water product molecules and then judge their understanding of balanced equations as very good. After being prompted to explain how the balanced equation relates to the visualization, student pairs often asked one another, "I don't know, how did it relate?" Students would subsequently revisit the visualization before writing anything, in the middle of generating their explanation. Students would also revisit the visualizations after they had finished writing their explanation to check their work.

Prompting for explanations helped students engage with the full knowledge integration pattern, interacting with the visualizations in both cognitive and metacognitive ways. Not only did students successfully connect their existing ideas of balancing equations to new ideas from the visualizations, but they also developed more accurate self-knowledge and criteria for their ideas (as demonstrated by their realizations that their understanding was not as good as they first thought). Explaining also supported students' development of self-regulatory skills, such as sorting out and refining ideas and connections. Students acted upon their judgments of learning and revisited the visualization to repair gaps in their knowledge or to resolve conflicts with their understanding of the concepts.

Addressing Deceptive Clarity with Drawing

In addition to explanation, other generative activities such as drawing can promote knowledge integration with dynamic visualizations. Drawing can help students elicit and build upon their prior ideas, as well as sort and refine their existing ideas and the new ones conveyed by the visualization. In a progression of classroom studies, Zhang (Linn et al., 2010; Zhang & Linn, 2008) investigated how generating drawings can help students overcome the deceptive clarity of visualizations. In these studies, middle school students used a similar chemical visualization to the one in *Chemical Reactions*. Pilot testing indicated that students failed to understand bonds breaking and forming as part of the chemical reaction process. To investigate how drawing can help students learn from visualizations, Zhang compared students who drew sequences of chemical reactions to students prompted to spend more time with the visualization. The students in the drawing condition were asked to draw the reacting molecules before the reaction began, right after the reaction began, after the chemicals had reacted for some time, and after the chemicals had reacted for a very long time.

Zhang found that students in the drawing condition learned more overall than the students who only explored the visualization, as generating drawings helped students distinguish their ideas from the visualization. Prompting students to draw stages of the reaction helped focus the students on the chemical reaction in terms of bonds breaking and forming. Students could revisit the visualization and compare their drawings to the visualization. Similar to generating explanations, generating drawings helped students realize gaps in their understanding, or concepts they may have missed in their initial investigation of the visualization. Having students create representations of chemical reactions helped students become aware of their limited understanding and spurred them to sort out and refine their thinking by revising the visualization. These results resonate with other research studies demonstrating the benefit of having students create representations of chemical reactions (Chang, Quintana, & Krajcik, 2010; Schank & Kozma, 2002).

To further investigate the effect of generating drawings, Zhang compared students that drew pictures to students who selected screenshots of the model to represent four stages during the process of a chemical reaction (Linn et al., 2010). Zhang found that the students who generated their own drawings outperformed students who selected screenshots on posttest assessments, controlling for prior knowledge. The drawing group outperformed the selection group on assessment items that called for selecting and sequencing static pictures of chemical reactions, as well as items that called for the students to use their understanding in different contexts (i.e., different reactions). Zhang suggested that generating drawings helped students reflect and sort out their ideas, whereas the selection activity failed to encourage students to stop and refine their understanding. This suggests that activities such as generating drawings and explanations can help students overcome the deceptive clarity of visualizations and promote knowledge integration, whereas other activities such as selection may not be as beneficial because they do not encourage learners to revisit and refine their understanding of the visualization.

Discussion

The findings we presented point to the effectiveness of various instructional scaffolding techniques that can promote student self-monitoring and self-assessment. Engaging students in making predictions, generating explanations, or creating drawings or representations provides opportunities for them to identify weaknesses in their thinking, to evaluate, sort, connect and refine new and old ideas, or to verify their understandings. We view these types of scaffolding as examples of *desirable difficulties*—that is, instruction that enhances learning by introducing beneficial cognitive difficulties for the student to address (Bjork & Linn, 2006).

We believe the knowledge integration pattern helps learners succeed using visualizations because it promotes this blend of cognitive and metacognitive interaction with the learning environment. Indeed, recent research from various sources points to the benefit of combining cognitive and metacognitive support for instruction with visualizations (Ainsworth, 2008; Aleven & Koedinger, 2002; Azevedo, Winters, & Moos, 2004; Moos & Azevedo, 2008; Reiber et al., 2004). If learners are not aware of gaps in their understanding or aware of critical information to focus upon within the visualization, students can continue without further thought. Engaging students in the knowledge integration pattern thus helps students to interact with the visualizations both cognitively and metacognitively—they not only add ideas to their thinking but also revisit the visualizations to refine and sort out their understanding.

Other current research points to the importance of combining dynamic visualizations with the full knowledge integration pattern. Kombartzky, Ploetzner, Schlag, and Metz (2010) investigated how prompting learners to engage in strategies to elicit, distinguish, and reflect upon ideas could influence learning with a dynamic visualization about honeybees. Kombartzky et al. (2010) compared students in two groups: The essay group interacted with visualizations and then wrote an essay about what they learned; the strategy group made predictions about the visualization, explained the visualization, revisited the visualization, drew their understanding, and reflected upon their work. Students in the strategy condition outperformed the students in the essay condition. Similarly, recent work with self-regulatory learning in hypermedia environments found that learners who make large conceptual gains tend to engage in monitoring strategies such as summarizing and making inferences, and making judgments of understanding (Azevedo, 2005; Azevedo et al., 2004; Greene & Azevedo, 2007).

Design principles based on recent research from various perspectives also indicate the benefit of including knowledge integration activities (Plass, Homer, & Hayward, 2009). For instance, design principles based on the cognitive-affective theory of multimedia learning (CATLM) calls for activating prior knowledge and providing opportunities for students to examine and repair their understanding (Moreno & Mayer, 2007). Plass et al. (2009) highlight the importance of aligning interaction within visualizations with cognitive as well as metacognitive goals.

Current Challenges

For students to use visualizations most effectively, careful design of instruction that supports the use of metacognition is essential. However, there are still several challenges for moving this area of work forward. Examples of some outstanding issues include: Conducting research in authentic classroom settings, assessing students' use of metacognition, and investigating the role of collaboration in developing self-monitoring skills.

Conducting research in authentic classrooms: Conducting design experiments in authentic classrooms poses challenges for research on metacognition. Although we can implement particular types of instructional support and measure the impacts of those interventions on students, it is very difficult to identify, distinguish and assess the use of metacognitive processes by students. Research conducted within the real-life constraints of classrooms necessitates the careful design of studies that not only focus on what is best for the learner, but also will allow researchers to obtain useful and appropriate data that addresses the research questions of interest. Results from laboratory settings may or may not transfer to classroom environments where the concepts to be learned are integrated with the overall course instead of presented as an unrelated experiment (Richland, Linn, & Bjork, 2007). Conducting classroom refinement studies will help researchers find what kinds of metacognitive interventions work in classrooms, as well as contribute to learning theory (i.e., Brown, 1992). In general, more design experiments using visualizations in classrooms will help test and refine design principles and recommendations from experimental settings.

For instance, recent studies show benefit for iterative refinement of classroom instruction with visualizations to support both cognitive and metacognitive processes using the knowledge integration pattern (Chiu, 2010; Linn et al., 2010; Tate, 2009). In *Airbags: Too Fast, Too Furious?*, a WISE high school physics project investigating motion and airbag safety, students use a visualization that enables them to conduct car collision experiments and explore relations among speed, distance, and driver safety. Pilot testing revealed that students needed support to set goals and plan experimental trials before interacting with the visualization. In a revised version of the project, the visualization was accordingly modified so that students could select experimentation goals from a drop-down menu with options such as "driver height," "collision speed," "crumpling," or "just exploring" before proceeding to investigate the selected goal with the dynamic visualization. As a result, students could interact with and revisit the visualization by focusing on different research goals, helping students to elicit, integrate and refine their ideas in a more targeted manner (McElhaney, 2010).

Knowledge Community and Inquiry (KCI) instruction builds upon inquiry-based learning and knowledge communities approaches to encourage inquiry-based knowledge construction within classrooms (Slotta & Peters, 2008). KCI studies have also found that the knowledge integration pattern helps to refine instruction with visualizations. As part of an inquiry science lesson, students created and annotated their own wikipages using WISE visualizations of climate change (Najafi & Slotta, 2010). As a result of pilot testing, the researchers found that students needed help making and reflecting upon links from their co-constructed curriculum to the visualizations. Subsequent revisions will incorporate reflective self-assessments and self-monitoring guidance to enhance learning with the visualizations.

Assessing students' metacognitive activities: Students' use of metacognition can only be indirectly inferred by analyzing what the student does. Consequently, it is extremely difficult to know with any degree of certainty if certain actions are, from the student's perspective, truly cognitive or metacognitive. Research that can make these kinds of delineations more accurately usually occurs in lab settings with relatively small numbers of learners (i.e., Hegarty et al., 2003;

Lowe, 2004; Moos & Azevedo, 2008; Reiber et al., 2004). These studies provide valuable, fine-grained information about strategies and self-regulatory techniques used with visualizations. Future research needs to find ways to capture metacognitive processes accurately and reliably in classroom settings.

Using the knowledge integration instructional pattern provides particular utility in classroom settings to promote and assess both cognitive and metacognitive goals. In our studies with explanation and drawing we use self-ratings and prompts for explanation measures of learning and self-assessment as well as scaffolds for self-monitoring. We use the logging technologies of WISE to determine how students navigate through the environment. Although these measures may not distinguish strictly metacognitive from strictly cognitive activities, there are great learning benefits from using these tools in the classroom. Supplemented by data log files, we have insight into the actions that student pairs take during the inquiry units. More tools that work efficiently and effectively in classrooms would greatly benefit the field.

Investigating the role of collaboration in prompting self-monitoring: The complexity of the classroom limits the nuances that can be determined, since students working with WISE projects typically work in pairs. The decision to have students work in pairs is dictated by several factors, including: (1) Evidence that students learn from each other, (2) the limitations of classroom space and computers for students (class sizes are approaching 40 in the schools where we work), and (3) the availability of computers for all students. With students' varying levels of prior knowledge and skills, student work in pairs makes it challenging to accurately determine and distinguish cognitive and metacognitive actions for individual students. There is relatively little research that investigates collaborative learning with scientific visualizations, and the existing research provides mixed results (Ainsworth, 2008). More research is needed to explore how students learn from each other when working with visualizations.

Conclusion

These results support the importance of combining cognitive and metacognitive activities to promote knowledge integration. This is particularly evident in studies of student interactions with visualizations. Cognitive activities such as adding ideas are not sufficient to ensure that those ideas are coherently understood. Interactive dynamic visualizations can provide unique opportunities for learners to deeply engage in thinking about challenging scientific phenomena when instruction emphasizes metacognition. Students' interactions with visualizations need to be carefully scaffolded in order to support metacognitive activities such as distinguishing ideas and reflecting on alternative interpretations. Because students often do not monitor their understanding, they tend to incorrectly accept inaccurate interpretations of visualizations. These results suggest that metacognitive activities can strengthen the educative impact of visualizations.

Instruction designed according to the knowledge integration pattern can help learners to overcome the deceptive clarity of visualizations. This involves first eliciting student ideas, a common outcome of prompts for self-explanations or predictions. When students generate their own ideas they are prepared to look for confirmatory evidence and are often surprised when their expectations are not met. The second element of the pattern, adding ideas, is supported by interactive visualizations. The third element, distinguishing ideas, is often achieved by specific activities such as critique of alternatives, drawing ideas, selecting among alternatives, contrasting cases (such as comparing the case of using a spark or no spark in a chemical reaction visualization), or conducting experiments. The final element of the pattern, reflecting and sorting out ideas, is essential for success of the instruction. This is often accomplished by asking students to prepare a presentation, report, or poster and to pay attention to the way their ideas communicate to others.

The knowledge integration pattern emphasizes incorporating both cognitive and metacognitive activities into instructional scaffolding. When combined, students' learning from the cognitive activities is enhanced by the self-monitoring emphasized in the metacognitive activities. Consequently, students are guided to think more deeply about their interactions with a visualization, to evaluate their thinking and identify gaps in understanding, and to critique and revise their explanations.

Acknowledgments This material is based upon work supported by the National Science Foundation under grants No. ESI-0334199 and ESI-0455877. Any opinions, findings, and conclusions or recommendations expressed in this material are those of the authors and do not necessarily reflect the views of the National Science Foundation. The authors appreciate helpful comments from the Technology-Enhanced Learning in Science research group.

References

Ainsworth, S. (2008). How do animations influence learning? In D. Robinson & G. Schraw (Eds.), *Recent innovations in educational technology that facilitate student learning*. Charlotte, NC: Information Age Publishing.

Aleven, V., & Koedinger, K. (2002). An effective metacognitive strategy: Learning by doing and explaining with a computer-based Cognitive Tutor. *Cognitive Science, 26*, 147–179.

Azevedo, R. (2005). Using hypermedia as a metacognitive tool for enhancing student learning? The role of self-regulated learning. *Educational Psychologist, 40*, 199–209.

Azevedo, R., Guthrie, J. T., & Seibert, D. (2004). The role of self-regulated learning in fostering students' conceptual understanding of complex systems with hypermedia. *Journal of Educational Computing Research, 30*(1), 87–111.

Azevedo, R., Moos, D., Greene, J., Winters, F., & Cromley, J. (2008). Why is externally-facilitated regulated learning more effective than self-regulated learning with hypermedia? *Educational Technology Research and Development, 56*(1), 46–72.

Azevedo, R., Winters, F. I., & Moos, D. C. (2004). Can students collaboratively use hypermedia to learn about science? The dynamics of self- and other-regulatory processes in an ecology classroom. *Journal of Educational Computing Research, 31*, 215–245.

Bjork, R. A., & Linn, M. C. (2006). The science of learning and the learning of science: Introducing desirable difficulties. *APS Observer, 19*, 29.

Bransford, J. D., Brown, A. L., & Cocking, R. R. (Eds.). (1999). *How people learn: Brain, mind, experience and school*. Washington, DC: National Research Council.

Brown, A. L. (1992). Design experiments: Theoretical and methodological challenges in creating complex interventions in classroom settings. *The Journal of the Learning Sciences, 2*(2), 141–178.

Chang, H.-Y., Quintana, C., & Krajcik, J. (2010). The impact of designing and evaluating molecular animations on how well middle school students understand the particulate nature of matter. *Science Education, 94*(1), 73–94.

Chi, M. T. H. (2000). Self-explaining: The dual process of generating inference and repairing mental models. In R. Glaser (Ed.), *Advances in instructional psychology* (pp. 161–238). Mahwah, NJ: Lawrence Erlbaum Associates.

Chi, M. T. H., De Leew, N., Chiu, M.-H., & Lavancher, C. (1994). Eliciting self-explanations improves understanding. *Cognitive Science, 18*, 439–477.

Chiu, J. L. (2010). Supporting students' knowledge integration with technology-enhanced inquiry curricula (Doctoral dissertation). *Dissertation and Theses Database*. (UMI No. AAT 3413337).

Chiu, J., & Linn, M. C. (2008). Self-assessment and self-explanation for learning chemistry using dynamic molecular visualizations. In international perspectives in the learning sciences: Cre8ting a learning world. *Proceedings of the 8th International Conference of the Learning Sciences* (Vol. 3, pp. 16–17). Utrecht, The Netherlands: International Society of the Learning Sciences, Inc.

Cromley, J. G., Azevedo, R., & Olson, E. D. (2005). Self-regulation of learning with multiple representations in hypermedia. In C.-K. Looi, G. McCalla, B. Bredeweg, & J. Breuker (Eds.), *Artificial intelligence in education: Supporting learning through intelligent and socially informed technology* (pp. 184–191). Amsterdam, The Netherlands: IOS Press.

Davis, E. A., & Linn, M. C. (2000). Scaffolding students' knowledge integrations: Prompts for reflection in KIE. *International Journal of Science Education, 22*(8), 819–837.

diSessa, A. (2000). *Changing minds: Computers, learning and literacy*. Cambridge, MA: MIT Press.

Ertmer, P. A., & Newby, T. J. (1996). The expert learner: Strategic, self-regulated, and reflective. *Instructional Science, 24*, 1–24.

Graesser, A., McNamara, D., & VanLehn, K. (2005). Scaffolding deep comprehension strategies through Pint and Query, AuthTutor and iSTRAT. *Educational Psychologist, 40*(4), 225–234.

Greene, J., & Azevedo, R. (2007). Adolescents' use of self-regulatory processes and their relation to qualitative mental model shifts while using hypermedia. *Journal of Educational Computing Research, 36*(2), 125–148.

Hegarty, M., Kriz, S., & Cate, C. (2003). The roles of mental animations and external animations in understanding mechanical systems. *Cognition and Instruction, 21*(4), 325–360.

Hoffler, T., & Leutner, D. (2007). Instructional animations versus static pictures: A meta-analysis. *Learning and Instruction, 17*, 722–738.

Kalyuga, S. (2007). Enhancing instructional efficiency of interactive e-learning environments: A cognitive load perspective. *Educational Psychology Review, 19*(3), 387–399.

King Chen, J. Y., Tinker, R., & McElhaney, K. (2011). *Supporting student understanding of projectile and orbital motion with dynamic models*. Poster presented at the Annual Meeting of the American Educational Research Association, New Orleans, LA. http://www.telscenter.org.

Kombartzky, U., Ploetzner, R., Schlag, S., & Metz, B. (2010). Developing and evaluating a strategy for learning from animations. *Learning and Instruction, 20*, 424–433.

Kornell, N., Hays, M. J., & Bjork, R. A. (2009). Unsuccessful retrieval attempts enhance subsequent learning. *Journal of Experimental Psychology: Learning, Memory, and Cognition, 35*(4), 989–998.

Lewalter, D. (2003). Cognitive strategies for learning from static and dynamic visuals. *Learning and Instruction, 13*(2), 177–189.

Linn, M. C., Chang, H.-Y., Chiu, J. L., Zhang, H., & McElhaney, K. (2010). Can desirable difficulties overcome deceptive clarity in scientific visualizations? In A. Benjamin (Ed.), *Successful remembering and successful forgetting: A Festschrift in honor of Robert A. Bjork*. New York: Routledge.

Linn, M. C., Clark, D., & Slotta, J. D. (2003). WISE design for knowledge integration. *Science Education, 87*, 517–538.

Linn, M. C., & Eylon, B.-S. (2006). Science education. In P. A. Alexander & P. H. Winne (Eds.), *Handbook of educational psychology* (2nd ed.). Mahwah, NJ: Erlbaum.

Linn, M. C., & Eylon, B.-S. (2011). *Science learning and instruction: Taking advantage of technology to promote knowledge integration*. New York: Routledge.

Linn, M. C., Eylon, B. S., & Davis, E. A. (2004). The knowledge integration perspective on learning. In M. C. Linn, E. A. Davis, & P. Bell (Eds.), *Internet environments for science education* (pp. 73–83). Mahwah, NJ: Erlbaum.

Lombrozo, T. (2006). The structure and function of explanations. *Trends in Cognitive Sciences, 10*(10), 464–470.

Lowe, R. (2004). Interrogation of a dynamic visualization during learning. *Learning and Instruction, 14*, 257–274.

McElhaney, K. W. (2010). Making controlled experimentation more informative in inquiry investigations (Doctoral dissertation). *Dissertation and Theses Database*. (UMI No. AAT 3413549).

Moos, D. C., & Azevedo, R. (2008). Self-regulated learning with hypermedia: The role of prior knowledge. *Contemporary Educational Psychology, 33*, 270–298.

Moreno, R., & Mayer, R. (2007). Interactive multimodal learning environments. *Educational Psychology Review, 19*, 309–326.

Najafi, H., & Slotta, J. (2010). Analyzing equality of participation in collaborative inquiry: Toward a knowledge community. *Proceedings of the 9th International Conference of the Learning Sciences*, Chicago, IL.

Plass, J. L., Homer, B. D., & Hayward, E. (2009). Design factors for educationally effective animations and simulations. *Journal of Computing in Higher Education, 21*(1), 31–61.

Quintana, C., Zhang, M., & Krajcik, J. (2005). A framework for supporting metacognitive aspects of online inquiry through software-based scaffolding. *Educational Psychologist, 40*(4), 235–2244.

Reiber, L. P., Tzeng, S., & Tribble, K. (2004). Discovery learning, representation, and explanation within a computer-based simulation: Finding the right mix. *Learning and Instruction, 14*, 307–323.

Renkl, A., & Atkinson, R. K. (2002). Learning from examples: Fostering self-explanations in computer-based learning environments. *Interactive Learning Environments, 10*, 105–119.

Richland, L. E., Linn, M. C., & Bjork, R. A. (2007). Cognition and instruction: Bridging laboratory and classroom settings. In F. Durso, R. Nickerson, S. Dumais, S. Lewandowsky, & T. Perfect (Eds.), *Handbook of applied cognition* (2nd ed.). New York: Wiley.

Rozenblit, L. R., & Keil, F. C. (2002). The misunderstood limits of folk science: An illusion of explanatory depth. *Cognitive Science, 26*, 521–562.

Schank, P., & Kozma, R. (2002). Learning chemistry through the use of a representation-based knowledge building environment. *Journal of Computers in Mathematics and Science Teaching, 2*(3), 254–271.

Schnotz, W., & Rasch, T. (2005). Enabling, facilitating, and inhibiting effects of animations in multimedia learning: Why reduction of cognitive load can have negative results on learning. *Educational Technology Research and Development. Special Issue: Research on Cognitive Load Theory and Its Design Implications for E-Learning, 53*(3), 47–58.

Shen, J., & Linn, M. C. (2010). A technology-enhanced unit of modeling static electricity: Integrating scientific explanations and everyday observations. *International Journal of Science Education*. doi:10.1080/09500693.2010.514012.

Slotta, J., & Linn, M. C. (2009). *WISE Science: Web-based inquiry in the classroom*. New York: Teachers College Press.

Slotta, J. & Peters, V. (2008). A blended model for knowledge communities: Embedding scaffolded inquiry. *Proceedings of the International Conference of the Learning Sciences*. Utrecht, Netherlands.

Songer, N., & Linn, M. C. (2006). How do students' views of science influence knowledge integration? *Journal of Research in Science Teaching, 28*(9), 761–784.

Tate, E. (2009). Asthma in the community: Designing instruction to help students explore scientific dilemmas that impact their lives (Doctoral dissertation). *Dissertation and Theses Database*. (UMI No. AAT 3383554).

Tinker, R. (2009). In *Visualizing to integrate science understanding for all learners (VISUAL)*, NSF Discovery Research K-12 grant proposal, #0918743.

Tversky, B., Morrison, J. B., & Betrancourt, M. (2002). Animation: Can it facilitate? *International Journal of Human Computer Studies, 57*(4), 247–262.

Vygotsky, 1. S. (1978). *Mind in society: The development of higher psychological processes.* Cambridge, MA: Harvard University Press.

White, B., & Frederiksen, J. (1998). Inquiry, modeling and metacognition: Making science accessible to all students. *Cognition and Instruction, 16*(1), 3–118.

White, B., & Frederiksen, J. (2000). Has been deleted from the text and substituted with the 2005 reference.

White, B., & Frederiksen, J. (2005). A theoretical framework and approach for fostering metacognitive development. *Educational Psychologist, 40*(4), 211–223.

Wouters, P., Paas, F., & van Merrienboer, J. J. G. (2008). How to optimize learning from animated models: A review of guidelines based on cognitive load. *Review of Educational Research, 78*(3), 645–675.

Zhang, Z., & Linn, M. C. (2008). Using drawings to support learning from dynamic visualizations. In *International perspectives in the learning sciences: Creating a learning world.* Proceedings of the 8th International Conference of the Learning Sciences (Vol. 3, pp. 161–162). Utrecht, The Netherlands: International Society of the Learning Sciences, Inc.

Zimmerman, B. (2008). Investigating self-regulation and motivation: Historical background, methodological developments, and future prospects. *American Educational Research Journal, 45*, 166–183.

Investigating Text–Reader Interactions in the Context of Supported etext

34

Bridget Dalton and Annemarie Sullivan Palincsar

Abstract

We describe the empirical and theoretical roots of the *Reading to Learn* program of research, which was designed to investigate the metacognition and learning of upper elementary students in supportive etext environments. The results of study one, a think-aloud study in which children responded to narrative and informational texts, were used to inform the design of supports that were investigated in study two. Study two was an intervention study in which children read and responded to one of three etext versions: A *static* version, an *interactive diagram* version in which students could animate the graphic that corresponded with information presented in the prose and could manipulate the diagrams to explore ideas that were presented in the prose, or an *interactive diagram/coaching* version, which included two animated pedagogical agents, who provided both procedural and conceptual support. We critique the methods used in the intervention study and propose further research suggested by its findings.

Out-of-school, students' primary interaction with text is digital, multimodal, nonlinear, and interactive. The popularity of etext readers such Amazon's Kindle and the Apple iPad is fueled by crowd-innovation that drives the design and application potential of etext for learning, entertainment, and social networking. In contrast, etexts that are designed and supported for K-12 academic literacy and learning lags woefully behind its promise, especially in relation to the goals of access and equity for the substantial numbers of students who have difficulty understanding academic text required in high school (Kamil, 2003) and college (ACT, 2010).

There are numerous potential explanations for the lack of progress in this arena. From our perspective, there are two particularly compelling constraints. First, theoretical models of etext comprehension and design frameworks for creating supported etext are relatively underdeveloped,

B. Dalton (✉)
University of Colorado Boulder,
249 UCB, Boulder, CO 80309, USA
e-mail: bridget.dalton@colorado.edu

A.S. Palincsar
University of Michigan, Ann Arbor, MI, USA

R. Azevedo and V. Aleven (eds.), *International Handbook of Metacognition and Learning Technologies*, Springer International Handbooks of Education 26, DOI 10.1007/978-1-4419-5546-3_34,

especially in relation to students' understanding of domain-specific, multimodal etext. Second, there is limited practical knowledge about how teachers might effectively integrate etext into classroom curriculum and instruction in service of literacy and academic achievement.

The *Reading to Learn* (RTL) research program, which we feature in this chapter, was funded by an Institute of Educational Sciences Program of Research on Reading Comprehension development grant (awarded to Dalton and Palincsar). The ultimate goal of this grant was to develop and investigate a digital environment that would support students, especially those who struggle to read and comprehend text, to interpret and learn from challenging informational science text that was presented in an etext digital environment (Palincsar & Dalton, 2005). The ambitious agenda of this research program was designed in response to several important findings in the literature specific to children and youth learning with informational text. Furthermore, the research built upon earlier research conducted independently by the investigators.

In this chapter, we set the stage for the RTL program of research by describing the empirical and theoretical foundations for this work. We then turn to descriptions of how we designed the research to study the etext digital environment that we constructed, and conclude by identifying future research that is suggested by our work to date and that would be particularly informative to the issue of understanding the strengths and limitations of etext environments in promoting metacognition and learning.

Setting the Stage for the *RTL* Research Program: Empirical and Theoretical Roots

The "fourth-grade slump" was one source of impetus for this work. This term is used to characterize the phenomenon whereby children who are making adequate progress on reading measures before grade four demonstrate significant declines on reading achievement measures that are used in grade four and beyond. Literacy scholars have long speculated that one possible explanation for this phenomenon is the imbalance in the text types to which young children are exposed (Chall & Jacobs, 2003). While children are principally exposed to narrative text in the primary grades, they are assessed with the use of informational texts in the upper grades; texts with which they have had little support to learn to read. Duke's (2000) landmark study in which she investigated the genre of text used in 20 first-grade classrooms selected from very low- and very high-SES communities revealed that first-graders were typically being exposed to informational text for only 3.6 min a day if they were in high-SES communities and even less if they were in low-SES communities. This research suggested the importance of introducing informational text to young students and also the importance of identifying ways to support young children to learn from informational text.

In addition, we were aware that the preponderance of basic research that has been conducted to understand the processing in which young readers engage has been conducted using narrative text. One of our goals was to understand the resources young readers bring to the reading of informational text when compared with the processes in which they engage with narrative text. Furthermore, we were curious to understand how the affordances of etext (e.g., text-to-speech functionality) would enable us to get a more complete sense of these processes; if children were unencumbered by the demands of decoding words, what could we learn about how they interpret text, integrate ideas, and build new knowledge with text?

A final—and the most significant—goal of our work was to determine what role etext could play in "leveling the playing field" for children who struggle with the various demands of learning from text; we wanted to exploit the multiple affordances of digital text so that students who struggle with decoding, vocabulary, and/or comprehension might still have access to the ideas in text.

Empirical Roots

The RTL research built upon the long history of reading research in which both investigators had been independently involved. Palincsar and her colleagues had been studying ways of supporting students to be engaged in self-regulating activity as they read text. Dalton and colleagues shared this interest in improving students' comprehension, developing and studying universally designed etexts with embedded representational, strategic, and affective supports (Dalton & Proctor, 2007; Dalton, Proctor, Uccelli, Mo, & Snow, 2011). In the following sections, we describe how the results of our respective lines of inquiry led to the development and testing of the RTL etext enhanced with interactive diagrams and pedagogical agents to support students' reading of challenging science text.

Reciprocal teaching (Palincsar & Brown, 1984; 1988; 1989) was conducted as generic strategy instruction with little regard for domain-specific ways of using text; students read assorted texts derived principally from children's periodicals. Teachers modeled and supported students to learn how to self-question, summarize, clarify, and predict while reading through discussions in which these strategies were used to extract and co-construct the information in text (RRSG, 2002). While reciprocal teaching was effective at enhancing students' ability to read with comprehension, as assessed by both criterion-referenced and norm-referenced measures (Rosenshine & Meister, 1994), it was not designed to support the teaching of disciplinary learning, which builds understanding of how knowledge is produced in the disciplines (Moje, 2008; Shanahan & Shanahan, 2008).

With her colleague, science educator Shirley Magnusson, Palincsar began studying learning with science text. Their work began with descriptive studies of teachers enacting inquiry-based science teaching in grades K-5. One of the striking findings in these initial studies was that teachers avoided the use of text. This is problematic because NAEP data, measuring science achievement with nationally representative samples, indicate that 59 % of eighth-graders scored only at or above the *basic* level, while 29 % performed at or above the *proficient* level, and only 3 % scored at or above the *advanced* level[1] (Braun, Coley, Jia, & Trapani, 2009). Using multilevel analyses, ETS determined which instructional strategies explained student performance on the NAEP, after adjusting for both student and teacher characteristics. They found one of the distinguishing instructional features was that students whose teachers taught with the effective use of text attained higher performance on the NAEP assessment.

There were several explanations that teachers in Magnusson and Palincsar's research offered for not using text in their instruction. The first explanation was their concern that the text would usurp the students' own sense-making; the second was that the texts they were able to find were either vacuous (offering little in the way of explanation for phenomena) or too dense and, hence, impenetrable for the average reader in their classrooms. In response to these concerns, Palincsar, Magnusson, and their colleagues (Magnusson & Palincsar, 2005; Palincsar & Magnusson, 2001; Palincsar, Hapgood, & Magnusson, 2007) developed texts that were loosely modeled on a scientist's notebook.

The notebooks included the scientist's narrative descriptions of her investigations, as well as her developing arguments based on representations of data in the form of graphs and figures. The researchers argued that as students "follow and critique the path of reasoning of the scientist whose notebook they are reading, they are also learning how to construct scientific arguments from the data they collect in their own first-hand investigations" (Palincsar et al., 2007, p. 119). The skillful scaffolding of the teacher, through prompts and cues during discussions about the text, supported elementary students in gaining not only important scientific information, but also

[1] *Below Basic* (130 and below). *Basic* denotes partial mastery of prerequisite knowledge and skills that are fundamental for proficient work at each grade (131–166). *Proficient* represents solid academic performance. Students reaching this level have demonstrated competency over challenging subject matter (167–223). *Advanced* represents superior performance (224 and above).

knowledge of the practices in which scientists engage in order to develop that knowledge.

A number of the commitments that we made in the design work that was integral to the RTL research were informed by the research Palincsar and Magnusson (2001) conducted with the notebook texts. For example, we learned that it was possible to write the prose so that it encouraged an inquiry stance in the reading of text; we did this by identifying the phenomenon under study and raising questions that would elicit explanations (e.g., why objects sink and float; the scientific explanation for motion on an inclined Vs. horizontal plane; the explanation for the flow of electricity in series and parallel circuits). In the *Reading to Learn* project, we designed a text that explained the behavior of light interacting with solid objects.

We learned that our most effective teachers positioned their students to use the text in an inquiry fashion; the students were encouraged to think about how the information in the text was advancing their understanding of the phenomenon under study. The students were encouraged to identify the claims that the scientist was making in her notebook and to evaluate the warrant for those claims, based upon the evidence that the scientist had provided. In the *Reading to Learn* project, in one version of the environment, we animated the graphics so that readers could, in fact, manipulate the graphics and engage in their own investigation of the claims that were made in the prose. In a second version of the environment, an agent modeled and then guided the reader to use the graphics in an inquiry fashion; that is, to manipulate them and document what happened as a consequence.

Scholars have long argued that graphics are integral to communicating scientific information (e.g., Lemke, 2004). Magnusson and Palincsar (2005) included an array of graphics in their notebook texts, including data tables, diagrams, and illustrations. What they learned, however, was that readers needed support to interpret and use the information in those graphics. In the *Reading to Learn* project, graphics were integral to communicating information to the reader. To scaffold students' sense-making with those graphics, we designed several features. The first feature promoted the integration of the prose and graphic; by choosing a particular icon, the prose that was associated with a particular graphic would become highlighted; the reader could then look closely at the relationship between the information in the prose and how that information was communicated in the graphic. A second feature, as mentioned above, was the capacity to animate the graphic so that the graphic would illustrate the ideas in the prose and students could also check out their understanding by further manipulation of the graphic. For example, to communicate that what we see is a function of light reflected from an object to our eyes, the user could manipulate both the source of light, as well as the location of the object in relation to an eye.

We designed our RTL etexts in accordance with these key findings from the work of Palincsar and colleagues. At the same time, we were guided by Dalton and Proctor's (2008) research on the design of enhanced etexts for students with diverse learning needs. Integrating universal design for learning principles (Rose & Meyer, 2002) with Palincsar and Brown's (1984) research on reciprocal teaching, they created etext versions of chapter books that supported readers' access to the content through text-to-speech read aloud functionality, while focusing on their strategic reading of the text through embedded cognitive and metacognitive strategies support (Dalton, Pisha, Eagleton, Coyne, & Deysher, 2002). As students read, or listened, to the etext, they were prompted to "stop and think," applying reciprocal teaching strategies, as well as visualization, feeling, and metacognitive reflection strategies. They typed or audio-recorded their responses into an electronic work log that was available online to students and teachers, guided by pedagogical agents who provided think alouds, hints, and model strategy responses. The goal was to provide just-in-time support for students that would enhance their understanding of a particular etext, while also helping them develop a strategic approach to text that would transfer to other contexts. Providing affective support was another core aspect of the design, and was addressed primarily by offering students multiple options for choice of learning supports and modes of expression within the digital environment. This initial study showed the promise of this design approach for improving struggling readers' comprehension (Dalton et al., 2002).

Over the course of several studies, Dalton and colleagues continued to develop an etext design framework, expanding the role of pedagogical agents and multimedia support to develop comprehension and oral reading of young children with cognitive disabilities (Coyne, Pisha, Dalton, Zeph, & Cook Smith, 2010), and comprehension and vocabulary learning of fifth-grade monolingual and bilingual students (Dalton et al., 2011; Proctor et al., 2011).

Multiple modes of representation took on a more prominent role in Coyne and colleagues' (2010) study of universally designed picture books. Characters in the illustrations voiced thoughts and feelings that were often implicit in the text and students were able to view "real-life" videos and photos to build background knowledge and connect the imaginary world of the picture book with children's contemporary lives. These multiple representations were complemented by strategic support in the form of pedagogical agents who went beyond voicing think alouds and models to physically interacting with one another and the text to demonstrate how to echo read, partner read, and read independently with the audio-recording tool. These young children with significant learning difficulties were quite purposeful in their interactions with the various etext affordances. They engaged in a social relationship with the pedagogical agents, closely watching their actions and conversing with them as they tried out the read aloud option and responded to the strategy prompts. Across several studies, Dalton and colleagues explored how students used varied response options within the etexts, including visual multiple choice, written multiple choice, audio-recording, typing, interactive word webs, and American Sign Language video. While they did not test the differential effect of multiple modes of expression on student learning, data from observations and student interviews suggested that choice and variety were important to students, especially when they needed to persist with challenging text. Arguing that the whole is more than the parts, Dalton et al. (2011) suggest that students are able to engage productively with etexts enhanced to support text access, strategic reading, and vocabulary learning. In designing the RTL etexts, we integrated Dalton and colleagues' etext research with Palincsar and colleagues research on students' learning from science notebooks and hands-on science investigation to investigate the role of interactive graphics and pedagogical agents in supporting children's understanding of science etext. We predicted that children would benefit from reading etext with pedagogical agents that served as learning companions, modeling both thinking and actions as they interacted with animated diagrams. We also predicted that diagram animations explicitly connected to the prose and opportunities to manipulate the diagram to pursue questions would be helpful to students' learning and engagement with challenging science text.

Theoretical Framework for Supported etext Design

There is a growing research base demonstrating the positive learning effects of supported etext and multimedia learning (for reviews, see Dalton & Proctor, 2008; Mayer, 2005). With regard to etext, McKenna and Zucker (2009) suggest that Stanovich's (1980) interactive compensatory model of reading provides a theoretical foundation for the design of ebook features. The interactive compensatory model of reading emerged from Stanovich's close studies of how children with varying degrees of competence—specific to word recognition—made use of context in interpreting text. Prior to the studies by Stanovich and his colleagues (e.g., Stanovich, West, & Feeman, 1981), it was hypothesized that better readers (defined as readers who were more fluent with word recognition) paid more attention to context (i.e., the words surrounding challenging words or the topic of the text) to support their reading. However, Stanovich and his colleagues found just the opposite; the word recognition of more successful readers was, in fact, less influenced by context. The interactive compensatory model that arose from their empirical studies argued that how contextual variables interacted with reading skill depended on the level in the processing system that context was affecting. While other scholars (e.g., Rummelhart, 1977) were already propounding an interactive model of reading suggesting that readers draw on multiple levels of text processing (e.g., using prior knowledge of the topic, using semantic—or vocabulary—knowledge, using knowledge of syntax) to construct the meaning of text, Stanovich elaborated on this model by suggesting that limitations at any level of text processing could be compensated for by reliance on other levels of text processing.

A second theoretical perspective that undergirds our work is Kintsch's construction–integration model (Kintsch, 1988). This model draws a distinction between the *textbase* and the *situation model*. The textbase refers to the written words that are typically organized into sentences, paragraphs, and higher-order discourse units. The situation model, in contrast, refers to the meaning of the text that arises from the integration of the textbase with the reader's prior knowledge and goals. For most readers, constructing the textbase is much less a problem than is the process of constructing a good situation model. While the text is typically rich with resources to support the construction of the textbase (e.g., the organization of the words into sentence, text structure, graphic aids), the construction of the situation model is dependent upon a broader array of factors, including each individual's background knowledge, personal experiences, interests and purposes for reading. Furthermore, a "good" situation model must reflect the textbase.

The RTL Program of Research: Summary of Study One

These theoretical models set the stage well for thinking about the role of technology in supporting reading comprehension to the extent that etext offers multiple affordances that readers can draw upon depending upon their reading profiles; if students struggle with word recognition, they can use text-to-speech features to support their reading; if they struggle with the semantic demands of text, they can use synonym finders or linked glossaries to support their reading; and, if they are challenged by impoverished prior knowledge regarding a topic, the etext environment can be constructed in such a fashion that the reader can engage in activity that will support knowledge building as they read.

In our program of research, we were interested in how children would make sense of the etexts and monitor their comprehension if we offloaded some of the cognitive processing associated with text-based features that typically function as gatekeepers in reading. For example, many struggling readers lack the word recognition and fluency levels required to read academic texts with deep understanding. Therefore, we included a text-to-speech tool (TTS) that allows students to have words, sentences or passages read aloud with synchronized highlighting, and which offered them the option to customize their etext by choosing the font size, the voice of the narrator, and the rate of narration. We hypothesized that struggling readers would benefit from TTS if it—in fact—partially offloaded word recognition demands, thereby increasing cognitive capacity for developing understanding.

While we predicted that TTS would not be particularly useful to typically achieving readers, we anticipated that a second type of text-based processing support—multimedia vocabulary hyperlinks—would support both typically achieving and struggling readers' comprehension of these vocabulary intensive texts. Several words per screen of etext were hyperlinked to a multimedia glossary item that students could access by clicking on the link. Again, we predicted that this text-based scaffold would have a direct effect on students' vocabulary learning and an indirect effect on their overall understanding of the text.

Study one was designed as a think-aloud study. The participants were 43 ethnically diverse fifth-graders, including 21 typically achieving readers and 22 struggling readers (i.e., students who scored one-standard deviation below the mean on the Gates MacGinitie Reading Achievement Test). Students read both a narrative and two informational etexts. The narrative was a Native American "pourquoi" tale, "How Coyote Stole Fire" written by L. Poniatowski (CAST, Inc). The tale had a strong plot with a clear problem–solution, characters with explicit traits, and a richly detailed setting. Each screen of text included an illustration that communicated content that was important to the story. The two informational texts were written by our colleague, Shirley Magnusson, who is a science educator. Given the prominent role that prior knowledge plays in text comprehension, we chose to feature one science topic -light—across the two texts. One text focused on the refraction of light in creating rainbows and the second focused on how light enables us to see. Both etexts included features characteristic of science text: (a) The texts began by introducing a phenomenon (the presence of rainbows and the need for light to see), (b) the texts proceeded to explain these phenomena, accompanied by evidence in support of the explanation, and (c) the prose was accompanied by graphics that were integral to coming to a complete understanding of the ideas in the text. Icons signaled to the students when they were to stop and share their thinking with the researcher who sat beside them; there were at least three stopping places on each screen.

While both the struggling and typical readers showed evidence of conceptual learning from the informational texts, the struggling readers derived less from their interactions with the texts than did the typical readers. To investigate possible explanations for this difference, and to develop a profile of the text–reader interactions of these two groups of readers, the think-aloud data were coded guided by the following question: *How* did children comprehend the texts? That is, *what resources did they bring and what processes did they employ*? Through an iterative process of working with transcripts of struggling and typical readers for the two informational and one narrative etexts, we developed a coding scheme that—at the broadest level—included three categories:

1. *General codes* (such as no response, response not interpretable).
2. *Comprehension Monitoring* codes indicating that the reader attends to their comprehension of the text (e.g., rereads, makes a statement indicating general lack of understanding, or makes a statement regarding a specific point in the text that is not understood).
3. *Comprehension Fostering* codes reflecting attempts on the part of the reader to construct the meaning of the text, by, for example, paraphrasing the text or describing some feature in the text. Not all comprehension fostering moves were productive however; there were moves, such as inaccurate paraphrases that were not productive means of comprehension fostering. Given our interest not only in the students' sense making of continuous text, ("horizontal" integration), but also their engagement in "vertical" integration of the text, we also coded each comprehension fostering move to identify: (a) Intratextual moves (when the reader indicated that he or she was processing information across the larger text), and (b) moves that indicated the use of information outside the text. These moves were, in turn, coded to reflect whether the reader was working to construct the meaning of key ideas in the text, or of ideas that were not central to the text.

To summarize key findings, both struggling and typical readers engaged in many more comprehension monitoring and comprehension fostering moves when reading the narrative text than when reading the informational text. Furthermore, typical readers engaged in a significantly higher percentage of comprehension fostering and monitoring moves when reading the informational texts than did the struggling readers; specific examples included: evaluating ideas, making connections within and outside the text, and integrating text information. In general, students, regardless of reading achievement, tended not to connect or integrate graphics with other sources of information, suggesting this may be an unfamiliar skill for fourth-grade students. While it is less important for narrative, where the graphic seldom carries critical information that is not conveyed in prose, this is not the case for informational text, where graphics often carry unique information that is integral to knowledge building and comprehension (Lemke, 2004). This finding, in particular, influenced the design of the etext versions that we investigated in Study two (reported below). In addition, identifying and using a through-way in the interpretation of the text, even if the child did not have an accurate interpretation of the text, was more apparent in the reading of the narrative than expository text. That is, students who pursued ideas in their reading of the narrative (e.g., a character's motivation, or the unfolding of a series of events), were not observed to pursue ideas (e.g., how scientists have studied light, how ideas about the causes of color have changed over time), in their reading of the informational texts. This finding shaped our thinking about we could design etexts to support students to manipulate the text to enhance their sense-making with the text.

The RTL Program of Research: Critique and Summary of Study Two

The results of Study One informed the design of Study Two, which was an experimental study to investigate the effects of learning in one of three versions of the digital environment that culminated from the descriptive work described above. The three versions featured the same prose and graphics and addressed the topic of how our eyes use light to see (including: the reflection of light, the functioning of the eye, and how we see color). Version 1, which we labeled, the *static* version, offered text-to-speech and embedded vocabulary support. Version 2, the *interactive diagram* version, contained the same supports as the static version; in addition, students could access a *prose–diagram interaction feature* (PDI) that would animate the graphic that corresponded with information presented in the prose; furthermore, students in this condition were directed to use a *diagram manipulation feature* (DM) to explore ideas that were presented in the prose. Version 3, the *interactive diagram/coaching* version, contained the same features present in Version 2 and was further enhanced with the addition of two animated pedagogical agents, who provided both procedural and conceptual support. The procedural support was directed at using the features optimally, while the conceptual support was designed to provide metacognitive information as the agent shared his or her thinking about the information that was presented in the environment. (See Fig. 34.1 for a sample screen shot from the etext used in this study).

There were three questions guiding the experimental study: (1) What are the effects of using digital science text with interactive diagrams and pedagogical agents on students' vocabulary and concept knowledge?; (2) How do the effects vary for struggling readers versus their typically achieving peers?; and (3) How do student learning outcomes relate to their use of support features?

A total of 70 fifth-grade participants were assigned to one of three versions of the environment. One advantage of our method is that we yoked students based on a norm-referenced measure of reading comprehension and a researcher-designed assessment of subject-matter knowledge, and then randomly assigned them to one of the three conditions. This resulted in equivalent groups, at least as established by two indicators that are known to predict text comprehension (vocabulary knowledge and prior knowledge). A weakness of this approach is that we knew nothing about the participants' facility with—or interest in—learning in a digital environment, which might also be predictive of one's performance in this environment.

We conducted the experimental study as a researcher-implemented intervention; that is, a researcher sat with each child and—following a prescribed protocol—monitored the child's activity in the environment. The strength of this approach is that the investigators were able to gather extensive information regarding the students' engagement and activity in the environment; in addition, the researchers were able to scaffold the child's efforts to use the environment productively (were it necessary to provide support). Furthermore, one of the tasks that we asked the students to engage in was to respond to a writing prompt on most screen pages; children could elect to have the investigator enter their responses if they were concerned about the writing demands.

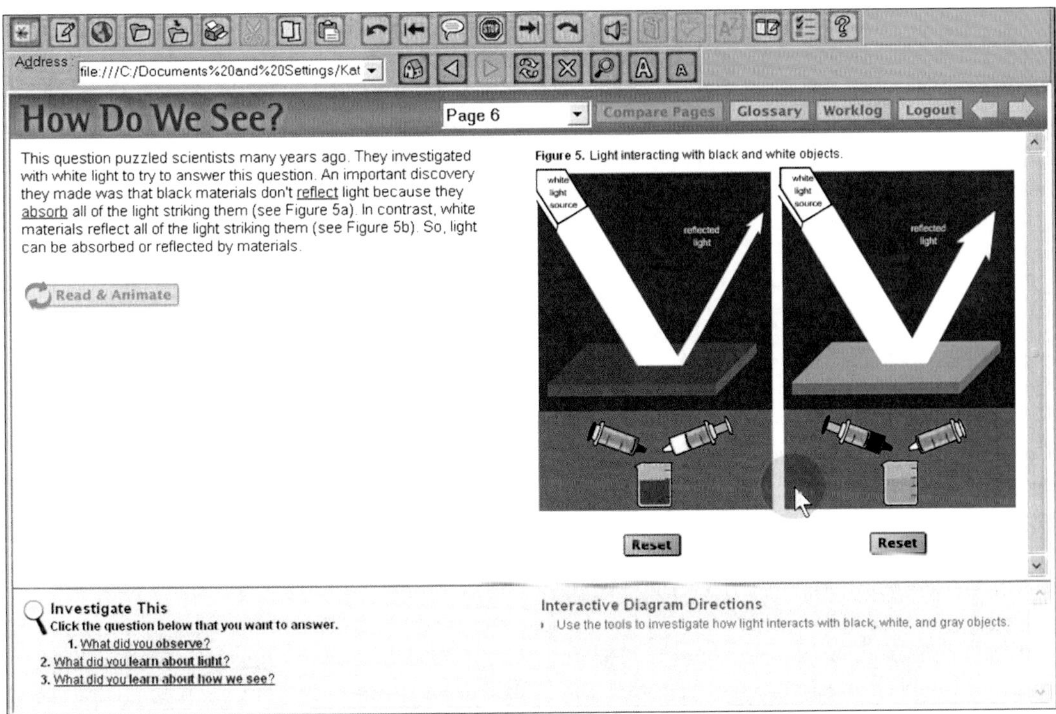

Fig. 34.1 This screenshot illustrates the investigate view. First, the student clicked on the paint tubes to color one block dark grey, and the other block light grey. Then, she clicked on the light source and observed the animation to learn how light interacts with differently colored objects.

None of this would have been possible if we had conducted this as a classroom-based intervention. On the other hand, the trade-off is that this was not a study of students' spontaneous use of the environment and we were not able to learn how the environment would lend itself to classroom use by large numbers of students. The first trade-off is relevant because one of the dilemmas that designers confront is the extent to which they extend an invitation to the user versus require the user to interact with the environment in particular ways. Given the phase of the development work, we believed it was important to learn what was possible if the user deployed the system in optimal ways.

Another methodological decision we made, again in the interest of optimizing the use of the environment, was to include an initial training session in which students learned how to use the various support features in a sample tutorial multimedia text on optical illusions that we designed specifically for this purpose. At the end of the training session, and prior to beginning the sessions in which the students used the environment, they were provided iconic representations of each feature and were asked to describe the feature. If a student was unsure or inaccurate in his or her recall of the feature's purpose and functionality, we reviewed this information. We regard this as a productive aspect of our design. This step provided us with information about the ease with which children acquired an understanding of the environment and its supports; it also ensured that our ability to assess the usefulness of the environment was not impeded by children's challenges with the tools.

All researchers are confronted with decisions about what to measure. This is both a theoretical and pragmatic challenge. It is a theoretical challenge to the extent that the researcher hypothesizes the relationship between the activity of the learner and the potential outcome of that activity;

this hypothesis guides the choice of what to measure. Measurement is a pragmatic challenge because time demands call for economical choices. We believe that our approach to measurement was a strength in our method, although there are revisions we would make in subsequent research. One advantage of our approach is that we designed an array of proximal and distal measures. The most proximal measure, intended to inform our understanding of the use of the environment, was an *event usage tracker*; features tracked included: accessing the glossary, synonyms, highlighting, and prose-diagram integration. This measure also documented the time that the student spent with each page (screen) of the environment. This measure enabled us to then analyze changes in vocabulary and content-knowledge scores in relationship to the use of the features.

Another measure on the proximal end of the continuum of measures were the responses that students made to the writing prompts that were embedded within the system; these prompts were designed to assess the children's understanding of the key ideas on each screen; we designed these prompts to require the students to apply the information that they had been introduced to on that screen.

Moving along the continuum to more distal measures, we included a pre- and post-assessment of *content-based subject-matter knowledge* and *content-based vocabulary knowledge*. Both of these were multiple-choice, researcher-designed, criterion-referenced measures. The strength of the design of these measures is that they could be scored easily and reliably; the limitation, of course, is that this format allows little access to children's thinking. One way to strengthen the use of these items would have been to include a think-aloud component, asking children to share with the researcher what they were thinking about as they considered each choice.

Finally, once students had completed the post-assessments, we included a *post-reading interview*. This interview was designed in the spirit of a "survey of consumer satisfaction." We were eager to learn what value the children ascribed to the various features; in fact, we asked the children to rate the features in terms of their helpfulness and to recommend revisions or additions to the environment. We regard this step as an advantage in our method; the students enjoyed taking on this role as informants and—in hand with their actual use of the environment—we gathered additional information useful to redesign efforts.

The findings from Study Two can be summarized in the following manner. The students in the interactive conditions (interactive diagram and interactive diagrams + pedagogical agents) significantly outperformed their peers in the static condition, demonstrating the benefit of going beyond providing typical hypertext access supports, such as read aloud functionality and glossary hyperlinks, to providing supports that make explicit linkages between prose and diagram information and which can be manipulated to reveal relationships and processes conveyed in diagrams. Further, the positive results were consistent for struggling and typically achieving readers, suggesting that flexible supports can benefit students across a range of reading skills. The fact that struggling readers in the interactive conditions did not close the gap with their typically achieving peers highlights the need for additional research. To close the gap, struggling readers may require additional support, different types of support, and/or more time working within supported digital environments.

While we did not find expected differences in favor of the pedagogical agent condition, this may have been due to our relatively small sample size, or may have been due to the design approach we employed, where we varied the type and level of pedagogical agent support across the screens so that we could explore how students responded to different kinds of agent support. Our observations revealed many instances where students, and especially those who were stronger readers, used the coaches productively. Clearly, more research is needed in this area, given the potential of agents to take on helpful peer learning or expert teaching roles.

Future Research

Influenced by di Sessa's (2004) notion of meta-representational competence, and curious about the challenges upper elementary students had productively using graphical information, we are interested in developing an assessment of meta-representational competence; such an assessment would aid us in determining what role metacognition versus skill might be playing in children's sense-making with graphics; that is, are the challenges students seem to demonstrate using and integrating information from the graphics a function of awareness or a function of their naivety regarding how to interpret graphics?

Spurred by the finding that including agents did not serve to enhance the activity or learning of our participants, we are keenly interested in conducting further research on the productive role of agents and determining how those roles can be tailored to the profiles of learners; for example, in relationship to their prior knowledge, metacognitive awareness, interest in the topic, and/or graphic literacy.

We believe that we would learn more about the students' metacognitive activity in this environment were they to work collaboratively in the environment. For example, recall that the dynamic versions of the etext encourage the students to investigate by manipulating the graphics to test out their understanding of the ideas in the prose. If students were to plan these simple investigations together and recap the results of their inquiry, we would have a richer sense of how they were making sense of the ideas in the text and drawing upon the multiple sources of information to construct meaning from the text.

Finally, a study conducted by DeFrance (2008) encourages us to conduct more systematic analyses of the use and outcome of the various features in this environment. DeFrance compared the effects of the *highlight and animate* feature in the RTL etexts with the use of the *manipulating graphics* feature, and found that, while there were no significant differences by condition in the amount of knowledge gained, there were significant differences in the quality of knowledge expressed. Transcripts revealed that understandings about light and vision, expressed by those who used the Highlight & Animate Feature, were more often conceptually and linguistically "complete." That is, their understandings included both a description of phenomena as well as an explanation of underlying scientific principles, which participants articulated using the vocabulary of the text. This kind of careful, systematic, and close study of children's use of these environments will support future development of etext environments and will also refine theory regarding knowledge building in these environments.

Acknowledgments The research reported here was funded by a grant from the Institute of Education Sciences, US Department of Education to CAST, Inc (Co-Principal Investigators B. Dalton, CAST, and A.S. Palincsar, University of Michigan). The opinions expressed are those of the authors and do not represent views of the Institute or the US Department of Education. The authors thank our research teams, especially S.J. Magnusson, Susanna Hapgood, Nancy DeFrance, Patrick Proctor, Debi Khasnabis, Ge Vue, Kristin Robinson, and E. Mo. We also thank the administrators, teachers, and, especially, the children who have contributed to this work. Finally, we thank the editors for their helpful feedback and their inexhaustible patience.

References

ACT (2010, October 23). *The condition of college and career readiness 2010*. Retrieved from http://www.act.org/research/policymakers/cccr10/pdf/ConditionofCollegeandCareerReadiness2010.pdf.

Braun, H., Coley, R., Jia, Y., & Trapani, C. (2009, May). *Exploring what works in science instruction: A look at the eighth-grade science classroom*. ETS Policy Information Report. Princeton, NJ: Educational Testing Service.

Chall, J. S., & Jacobs, V. A. (2003). Poor children's fourth-grade slump. *American Educator, 27*(1), 14–15, 44. Spring, 2003.

Coyne, P., Pisha, B., Dalton, B., Zeph, L., & Cook Smith, N. (2010). Literacy by design: A universally designed digital reading approach for young students with significant intellectual disabilities. *Remedial and Special Education*. doi:10.1177/0741932510381651. Advance online publication.

Dalton, B., & Proctor, C. P. (2007). Reading as thinking: Integrating strategy instruction in a universally designed digital literacy environment. In D. S. McNamara (Ed.), *Reading comprehension strategies: Theories, interventions, and technologies* (pp. 423–442). Mahweh, NJ: Lawrence Erlbaum.

Dalton, B., Pisha, B., Eagleton, M., Coyne, P., & Deysher, S. (January, 2002). *Engaging the text: reciprocal teaching and questioning strategies in a scaffolded digital learning environment*. Final report to US Department of Education, Office of Special Education Programs.

Dalton, B., & Proctor, C. P. (2008). The changing landscape of text and comprehension in the age of new literacies. In J. Coiro, M. Knobel, C. Lankshear, & D. Leu (Eds.), *Handbook of research on new literacies* (pp. 297–324). Mahweh, NJ: Lawrence Erlbaum.

Dalton, B., Proctor, C. P., Uccelli, P., Mo, E., & Snow, C. E. (2011). Designing for diversity: The role of reading strategies and interactive vocabulary in a digital reading environment for 5th grade monolingual English and bilingual students. *Journal of Literacy Research, 43*(1), 68–100.

DeFrance, N. (2008). *Struggling readers learning with graphic-rich digital science text: Effects of a highlight & animate feature and manipulable graphics*. Unpublished dissertation study. University of Michigan.

diSessa, A. A. (2004). Metarepresentation: Native competence and targets for instruction. *Cognition and Instruction, 22*(3), 293–331.

Duke, N. K. (2000). 3.6 Minutes per day: The scarcity of informational texts in first grade. *Reading Research Quarterly, 35*, 202–224.

Kamil, M. L. (2003). *Adolescents and literacy: Reading for the 21st century*. Washington, DC: Alliance for Excellent Education.

Kintsch, W. (1988). The role of knowledge in discourse comprehension: A construction-integration model. *Psychological Review, 95*(2), 163–182.

Lemke, J. L. (2004). The literacies of science. In E. W. Saul (Ed.), *Crossing borders in literacy and science instruction: Perspectives on theory and practice* (pp. 33–47). Arlington, VA: National Science Teachers Association Press.

Magnusson, S. J., & Palincsar, A. S. (2005). Teaching and learning inquiry-based science in the elementary school. In J. Bransford & S. Donovan (Eds.), *Visions of teaching subject matter guided by the principles of how people learn*. Washington, DC: National Academy Press.

Mayer, R. E. (Ed.). (2005). *The Cambridge handbook of multimedia learning*. New York: Cambridge University Press.

McKenna, M. C., & Zucker, T. A. (2009). Use of electronic storybooks in reading. In A. G. Bus & S. B. Neuman (Eds.), *Multimedia and literacy development: Improving achievement for young learners* (pp. 254–272). NY: Routledge.

Moje, E. B. (2008). Foregrounding the disciplines in secondary literacy teaching and learning: A call for change. *Journal of Adolescent and Adult Literacy, 52*(2), 96–107.

Palincsar, A. S., & Brown, A. L. (1984). Reciprocal teaching of comprehension-fostering and comprehension-monitoring activities. *Cognition and Instruction, 1*(2), 117–175.

Palincsar, A. S. & Brown, A. L. (1988). Teaching and practicing thinking skills to promote comprehension in the context of group problem solving. *Remedial and Special Education*, 9 (1), 53–59.

Palincsar, A. S., & Brown, A. L. (1989). Instruction for self-regulated reading. In L. Resnick & L. Kloepfer (Eds.), *Toward the thinking curriculum: Current cognitive research*. Alexandria, VA: Association for Supervision and Curriculum Development.

Palincsar, A. S., & Magnusson, S. J. (2001). The interplay of first-hand and text-based investigations to model and support the development of scientific knowledge and reasoning. In S. Carver & D. Klahr (Eds.), *Cognition and instruction: Twenty five years of progress* (pp. 151–194). Mahwah, NJ: Lawrence Erlbaum.

Palincsar, A., & Dalton, B. (2005). Speaking literacy and learning to technology; Speaking technology to literacy and learning. In B. Maloch, J. Hoffman, D. Schallert, C. Fairbanks, & J. Worthy (Eds.), *Invited annual research address, 54th yearbook of the National Reading Conference* (pp. 83–102). Oak Creek, WI: National Reading Conference, Inc.

Palincsar, A. S., Hapgood, S., & Magnusson, S. J. (2007). Examining "Expert Guidance" in the context of inquiry-based science teaching: Applying lenses that Ann Brown honed to the study of teachers' practice. In J. C. Campione, K. Metz, & A. S. Palincsar (Eds.), *Children's learning in the laboratory and in the classroom: Essays in honor of Ann Brown*. NY: Routledge.

Proctor, P., Dalton, B., Uccelli, P., Biancarosa, G., Mo, E., Snow, C. E., & Neugebauer, S. (2011). Improving comprehension online: Effects of deep vocabulary instruction with bilingual and monolingual fifth graders. *Reading and Writing: An Interdisciplinary Journal, 24*(5), 517–544.

Rand Reading Study Group (2002). Reading for Understanding. Santa Monica, CA: RAND.

Rose, D., & Meyer, A. (2002). *Teaching every student in the digital age: Universal design for learning*. Alexandria, VA: Association for Supervision and Curriculum Development.

Rummelhart, D. E. (1977). Toward an interactive model of reading. In S. Dornic (Ed.), *Attention and performance* (Vol. 6, pp. 573–603). New York: Academic.

Rosenshine, B., & Meister, C. (1994). Reciprocal teaching: A review of research. *Review of Educational Research, 66*, 181–221.

Shanahan, T., & Shanahan, C. (2008). Teaching disciplinary literacy to adolescents: Rethinking content-area literacy. *Harvard Educational Review, 78*(1), 40–59.

Stanovich, K. E. (1980). Toward an interactive-compensatory model of individual differences in development of reading fluency. *Reading Research Quarterly, 16*, 32–71.

Stanovich, K. E., West, R. F., & Feeman, D. J. (1981). A longitudinal study of sentence context effects in second grade children: Tests of an interactive compensatory model. *Journal of Experimental Child Psychology, 32*, 185–199.

35 Learning Functional Models of Aquaria: The ACT Project on Ecosystem Learning in Middle School Science

Ashok K. Goel, Spencer Rugaber, David A. Joyner, Swaroop S. Vattam, Cindy E. Hmelo-Silver, Rebecca Jordan, Suparna Sinha, Sameer Honwad, and Catherine Eberbach

Abstract

The ACT project is an ongoing collaboration among learning, cognitive, computing and biological scientists at Georgia Institute of Technology and Rutgers University, focusing on learning functional models of ecosystems in middle school science. In particular, ACT (for Aquarium Construction Toolkit) is an interactive learning environment for stimulating and scaffolding construction of Structure-Behavior-Function (SBF) models to reason about classroom aquaria. Initial results from deployment of ACT in several classrooms with a few hundred middle school children indicate statistically significant improvement in identification of the structure, behaviors and functions of classroom aquaria as well as appropriation of SBF modeling by some middle school teachers for modeling other natural systems. In this article, we summarize and review the main results from ACT on learning about SBF models of ecosystems in middle school science and describe self-regulated learning in ACT, while also looking ahead and outlining the design of a metacognitive ACT toolkit.

A.K. Goel (✉) • D.A. Joyner • S.S. Vattam
Design & Intelligence Laboratory, School of Interactive Computing, Georgia Institute of Technology, Atlanta, GA, USA
e-mail: ashok.goel@cc.gatech.edu

S. Rugaber
School of Computer Science, Georgia Institute of Technology, Atlanta, GA, USA

C.E. Hmelo-Silver
Graduate School of Education, Rutgers University, New Brunswick, NJ, USA

R. Jordan
Department of Ecology, Evolution, and Natural Resources, School of Environmental and Biological Sciences, Rutgers University, New Brunswick, NJ, USA

S. Sinha
Department of Educational Psychology, Rutgers University, New Brunswick, NJ, USA

S. Honwad, Ph.D.
Center for Play, Science and Technology Learning (SciPlay), Rutgers University, New Brunswick, NJ, USA

C. Eberbach
Rutgers University, New Brunswick, NJ, USA

R. Azevedo and V. Aleven (eds.), *International Handbook of Metacognition and Learning Technologies*, Springer International Handbooks of Education 26, DOI 10.1007/978-1-4419-5546-3_35,

Background, Motivations, and Goals

Modeling complex systems supports the development of important cognitive strategies and skills such as monitoring, measurement, sensemaking, troubleshooting, explanation, prediction, diagnosis, redesign, and design. Thus, learning about models of complex systems has been recognized as a key idea in science education in national science standards (National Research Council, 1996) as well as local standards (e.g., New Jersey Department of Education, 2006).

However, modeling complex systems is cognitively challenging because such systems are dynamical and cyclic. Further, although some components of a complex system may be visible, many components, relations and processes are typically invisible. Thus, modeling complex systems challenges cognitive resources such as attention, memory and perception. The juxtaposition of modeling complex systems as an educational goal and the cognitive difficulty of modeling complex systems in turn poses a practical challenge for cognitive and learning sciences. From a cognitive perspective, major questions in modeling complex systems include what is a useful classification of components, relations, and processes in complex systems; how can various entities in a complex system be identified in the vocabulary of this classification; how can the complex system be decomposed into subsystems and then recomposed from the subsystems; and how can all this knowledge be organized for easy access and use?

A common class of models of complex systems uses functions as abstractions for organizing knowledge of structural components and causal processes (e.g., Chandrasekaran, 1994; Kitamura, Sano, Namba, & Mizoguchi, 2002; Rasmussen, 1986). In structure–behavior–function (SBF) models (Bhatta & Goel, 1997; Goel et al., 1996; Goel, Rugaber, & Vattam, 2009) for example, *Structure* refers to components of a complex system as well as connections among the components; *Behaviors* describe mechanistic processes in the complex system; and *Functions* refer to abstractions that connect various structural components and causal behaviors Representations of structural components and causal processes refer to the functions they accomplish; representations of functions in turn act as indices into the components and processes that combine to accomplish them.

The ACT project is an ongoing collaboration among learning, cognitive, biological, computing, and artificial intelligence scientists at Georgia Institute of Technology and Rutgers University, focusing on learning about SBF models of ecosystems in middle school science (Goel et al., 2010; Hmelo-Silver et al., 2011; Honwad et al., 2010; Sinha et al., 2010). The ACT system (for Aquarium Construction Toolkit) is an interactive learning environment for stimulating, scaffolding and supporting construction and use of SBF models for reasoning about classroom aquaria (Vattam et al., 2011). Initial results from deployment of ACT in many classrooms with several hundred middle school children indicate statistically significant improvement in their understanding of SBF models of classroom aquaria (Goel et al., 2010) as well as appropriation of the SBF metamodels by some middle school teachers for modeling other natural systems (Sinha et al., 2010).

In particular, we (1) summarize and review some of the main results on learning SBF models of ecosystems in middle school science, situating ACT in the context of learning about models of complex systems in science education in general, and (2) describe self-regulated learning in ACT, while also looking ahead and outlining the design of a metacognitive ACT tool. Although metacognition and self-regulation were not major concepts in our thinking when we started on the ACT project, they gradually permeated our analysis and by now have become key ideas in our plans for future research.

Supporting Learning of Functional Models of Complex Systems

Since complex systems are all around us, in nature as well as society, supporting student learning about complex systems has been recognized as a key goal in science education (Sabelli,

2006). One common class of complex systems exhibits hierarchically organized structure (Simon, 1962, 1999). Systems that manifest hierarchically organized complexity typically are *nearly decomposable:* although causal processes at one abstraction level in these systems emerge out of interactions among components and processes at lower levels, the interactions among subsystems at any level are contained and can be organized hierarchically. Functions are abstractions of subsystems that enable such a hierarchical decomposition. This is an important cognitive feature because it implies that analyzing such systems entails decomposing them into the appropriate subsystems at different levels of functional abstraction and understanding interactions among the subsystems at a given level of functional abstraction.

For the ACT project, we selected fish-aquarium systems as the context in which middle-school students would learn about complex systems. This context was motivated in part by a growing focus on environmental education that necessitates an understanding of coupled earth and ecological systems (National Research Council, 1996). Given recent environmental stresses across the globe, ecosystem understanding is fast becoming a requisite for informed decision-making as citizens (Jordan, Singer, Vaughan, & Berkowitz, 2008), but students often have many misconceptions about ecological systems (Jordan, Gray, Demeter, Liu, & Hmelo-Silver, 2009).

Working with classroom aquaria engages students in its design, i.e., its establishment and maintenance. The notions of functions of systems and causal mechanisms that accomplish them are central to the act of designing. From the perspective of designing a classroom aquarium, students must decompose the tank into the relevant structures and their functions. For example, students identify the filter in an aquarium with respect to its role in maintaining healthy water quality. This may pave the way for discussion of mechanisms of the filter in the aquarium and perhaps facilitate analogical reasoning about the function of filtration in natural systems. Thus, the task of establishment and maintenance of a classroom aquarium has the potential to support deep understanding of causality and functionality at many levels of abstraction.

An aquarium, however, is not simply an engineered system; many complex ecological processes comprise the aquarium ecosystem. In fact, establishing and maintaining an aquarium system requires an understanding of biological, chemical, and physical properties and processes (Dawes, 2000; Stadelmann & Finley, 2003; Stansbury, 1999). Once the aquarium is set up in a classroom, complex patterns will begin to emerge as nutrients and energy flow, and organisms compete, reproduce, and self-organize into complex webs of interaction. Making sense of these patterns requires students to make connections between functions and mechanisms. Since students are particularly susceptible to misrepresenting causality in such systems (Jordan et al., 2009), cognitive scaffolding is particularly important for these systems.

There is a growing consensus in the science education community that engaging students in authentic science means introducing them to the central role of models in science (Duschl & Grandy, 2008; Gilbert, 2004; Lehrer & Schauble, 2006; Stewart, Cartier, & Passmore, 2005). While the word model has been applied to variety of simplified representations such as physical replicas, summative representations of datasets and "model organisms," we use the term model here as shorthand for *scientific* model. A scientific model is a scientist's interpretation of a target system, process or phenomenon that proposes or elaborates on the mechanisms that underlie it (Nersessian, 2008).

Depending on the discipline and the questions of interest, modeling can take a variety of external forms: words, equations, graphs, diagrams, or computer code. Each of these different forms of modeling has its own affordances and constraints, and a detailed review of different modeling forms is beyond our scope here. The power of functional modeling approaches such as SBF lies in the centrality of function in organizing knowledge of hierarchically organized complex systems. Decomposing a system in terms of function can direct the modeler's attention at the relevant structures and underlying mechanisms (called behaviors in the SBF language) that drive the function. That is, this approach provides a way to begin to analyze a complex system into meaningful subsystems each linked by their placement in a functional hierarchy.

The origin of SBF models lies in Chandrasekaran (1994) Functional Representation (FR) scheme. Goel et al. (2009) describe the evolution of SBF from FR. Briefly, (1) the structure portion of an SBF model of a complex system specifies the *what* of the system, namely, the components of the system as well as the connections among them. (2) Behaviors specify the *how* of the complex system, namely, the causal processes occurring in the system. A behavior typically comprises of multiple states and transitions among them. The transitions are annotated by causal explanations for them. (3) Functions specify understanding of the *why* of the system. A function is a teleological interpretation of the components and processes in the system. (4) A component of a complex system can itself comprise a system and thus have its own SBF model. (5) The behavior of a system specifies the composition of the functional abstractions of its subsystems into the system functions. Kitamura et al. (2002), among others, have described similar functional models of complex systems. Erden et al. (2008) provide a recent survey of functional models of complex systems and their use in design.

Since SBF models explicitly represent functions, they also differ from causal models of complex systems. The interactive tool called Betty's Brain (Biswas, Leelawong, Schwartz, & Vye, 2005) is a good representative of the use of causal models in interactive learning because it too works in the same general domain (ecology) and targets the same general audience (middle school students). The innovation in the system lies in transforming the role of students into teachers of problem-solving software agents (Betty). This role transformation is motivational and engaging to middle school students. The models that students help Betty build, however, are causal graphs, with no mention of function and only implicit specification of structure. Although SBF models also represent behaviors in the form of causal graphs, the behavioral representations are grounded in the structure and indexed by their functional abstractions.

ACT: Interactive Construction of SBF Models

Socio-cultural theories of learning suggest engaging learners in the knowledge building practices of scientists (e.g., Edelson, 1997). Clement (2008) has argued that learning in science is fundamentally a process of model construction, critiquing and revision. The ACT project has focused on supporting and scaffolding interactive and collaborative construction of SBF models of aquaria. The ACT toolkit supports four tools: SBFAuthor, RepTools, NetLogo, and Electronic Notebook. (In this chapter, we describe only the most recent version of ACT called ACT3.)

Software Architecture

The ACT architecture is decomposed into the data model, which holds the current model in active memory, and the model view, which displays the current SBF model to the user. The data model is itself split into two parts: the SBF model and the visual model. An SBF model exists separately from any kind of visualization. It is comprised solely of nodes and connections between nodes. In order to preserve the simplicity of the model on its own, the visual information needed to present the model to the user is stored separately, linked to the SBF model by the names of nodes and edges. When a model is manipulated, the pertinent information of the manipulation is passed along to the appropriate portion of the data model: modifications to literal relationships are saved in the SBF model, while modifications to the visual layout are saved to the visual model.

The model view is broken into three primary parts: the Model Graph view, the Model Table view, and the Electronic Notebook. The Model Graph and Model Table will be described more in

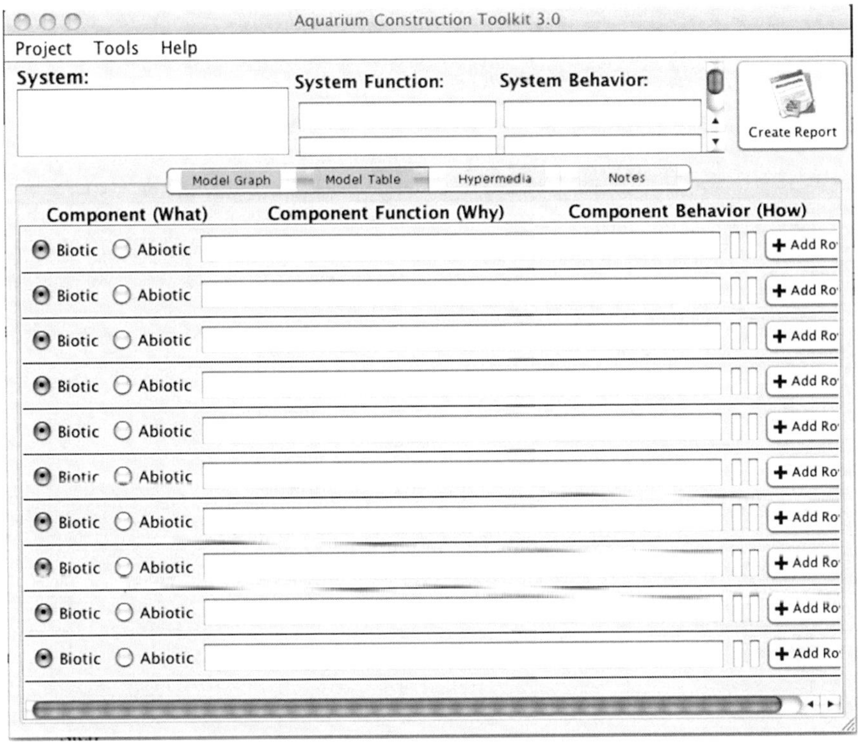

Fig. 35.1 Model table view

the following sections. The Notebook tab provides students with a time log where they can write notes about model construction, observations or other pertinent information that should be saved along with the model. The model view also supports a Create Report function, which prints the model to a PDF file for transportation to computers without the ACT software.

Model Table

The Model Table and Model Graph are dual views of an SBF model in that entering information in one view automatically enters the appropriate information in the other view. Figure 35.1 illustrates the Model Table view. The Model Table features three columns for Structure, Behavior, and Function, respectively. A structural component may be linked to many Behaviors (a one-to-many association), but a specific Behavior is linked to a specific Functions (a one-to-one association). Adding structures to the Model Table automatically result in their creation as nodes on the Model Graph. Similarly, adding Functions of a component in the Model Table results in entries in the Model Graph through the component's pop-up dialog menu. The control works both ways: new structures, behaviors, and functions added on the Model Graph automatically appear on the Model Table.

Model Graph

The Model Graph is a dual view of the Model Table. Figure 35.2 illustrates the Model Graph view including the palette on the left. Model Graph enables students to create a portion of an SBF model represented as a graph. The nodes in the graph represent biotic and abiotic components in the structural part of the mode. The links in the

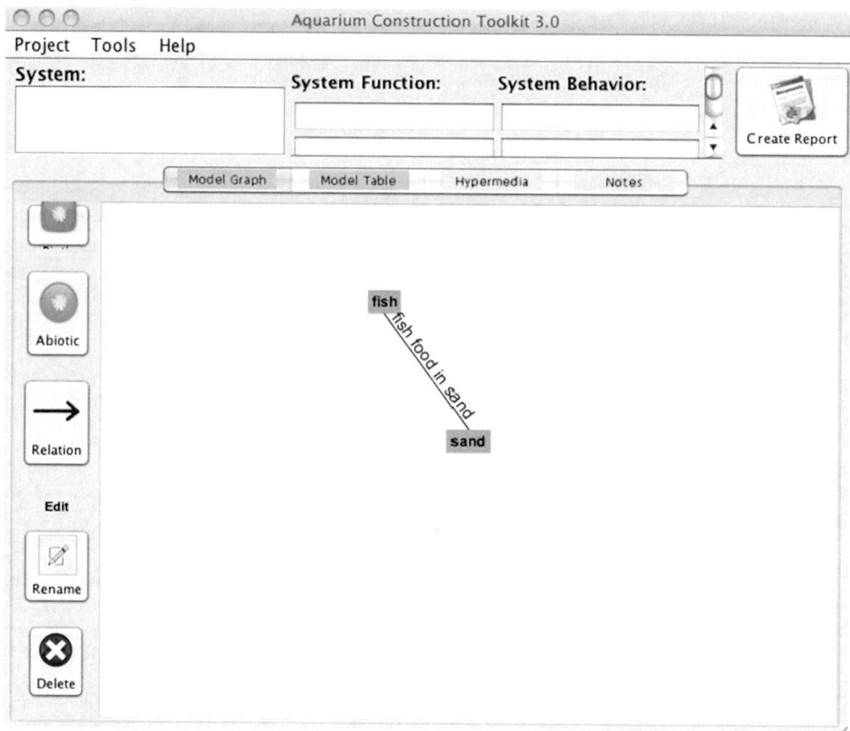

Fig. 35.2 Model graph view

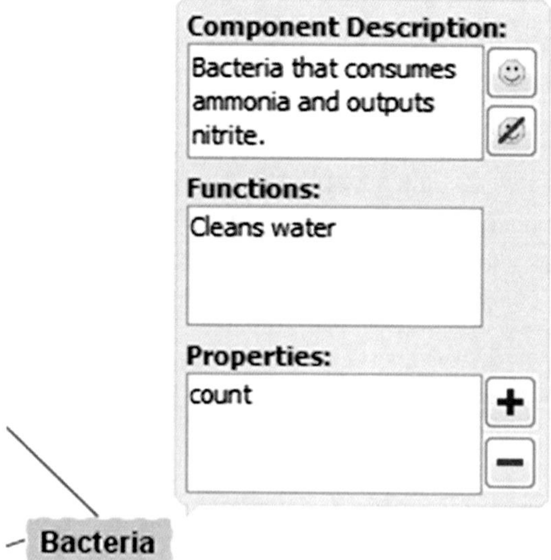

Fig. 35.3 Dialog for adding details to the structure in the model graph

graph represent relations among the components. Although the annotations on the links were intended to capture behaviors, in practice we found that students annotated the links with several kinds of relations. Dialog boxes associated with the nodes (illustrated in Fig. 35.3) enable a student to enter information about the functions of the structural components represented by the nodes. Figure 35.4 illustrates a Model Graph of an SBF model actually constructed by a student in a seventh grade classroom.

RepTools

ACT also incorporates the RepTools. RepTools was designed to accompany a physical aquarium installed in each classroom. It provides digital tools that feature function-centered hypermedia from which students can read about the structures, behaviors, and functions occurring within an aquarium system (Liu & Hmelo-Silver, 2009). Figure 35.5 illustrates a screen shot from the hypermedia in RepTools. RepTools also includes a micro and macro-level NetLogo-based simulations (Wilensky, 1999; Wilensky & Resnick, 1999)

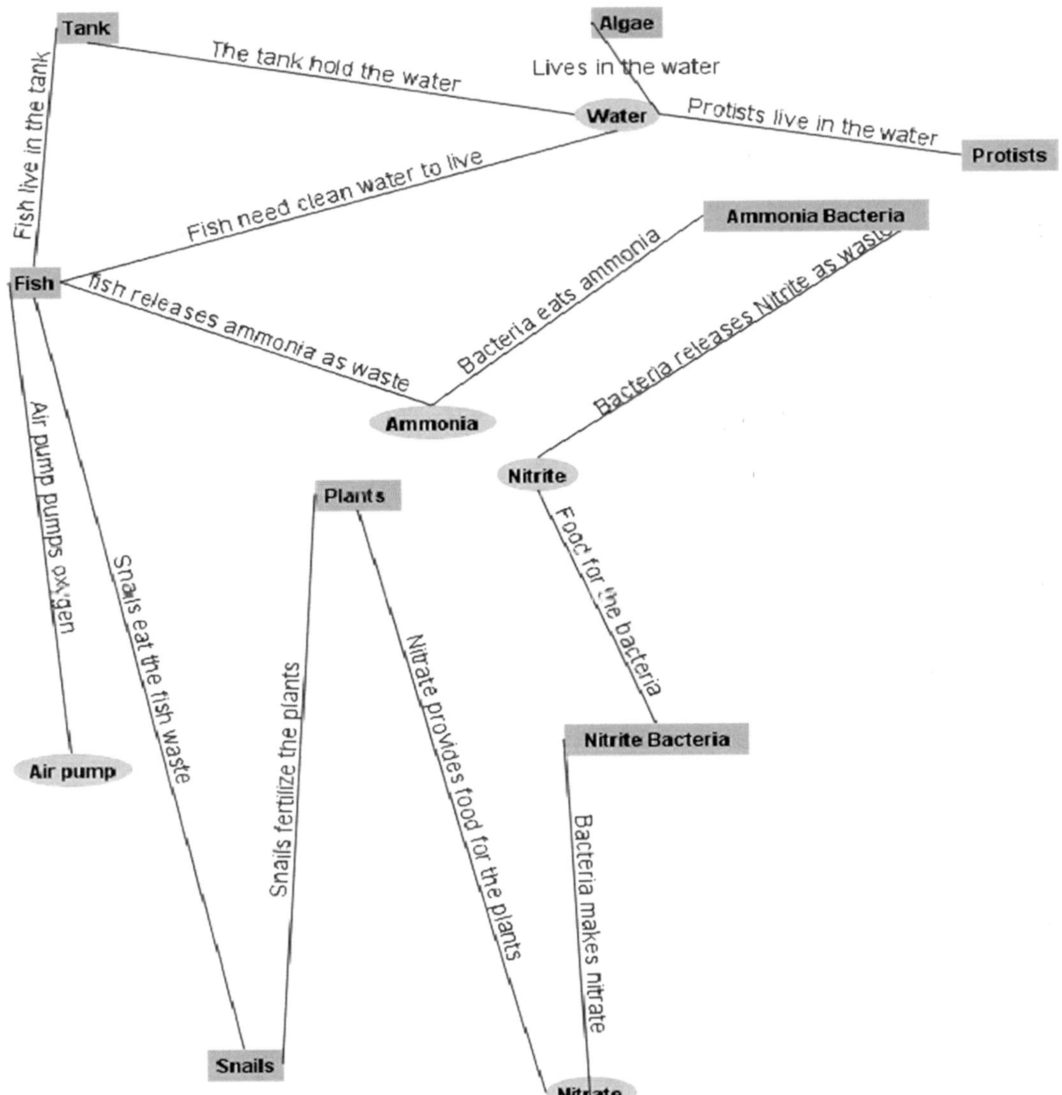

Fig. 35.4 Model graph of the nitrification process designed by a seventh grade student using ACT3

developed by experts. The macro-level simulation enables students to test ideas about fish spawning and water quality, and the micro-level simulates the nitrification process that occurs within an aquarium as part of its biological filtration (Hmelo-Silver, Liu, Gray, Finkelstein, & Schwartz, 2007). Figure 35.6 illustrates the screenshot of a NetLogo simulation in ACT3.

Finally, ACT3 contains an Electronic Notebook for recording notes. In combination, this suite of tools enable students to not only test ideas about the aquarium system but also gain insight into the processes and outcomes that occur at multiple levels within the aquarium.

Learning SBF Models in the Classroom

Since 2008, ACT has been used by several hundred middle school students in central New Jersey. In this chapter, we describe pre- and post-test results in four classrooms obtained in 2009.

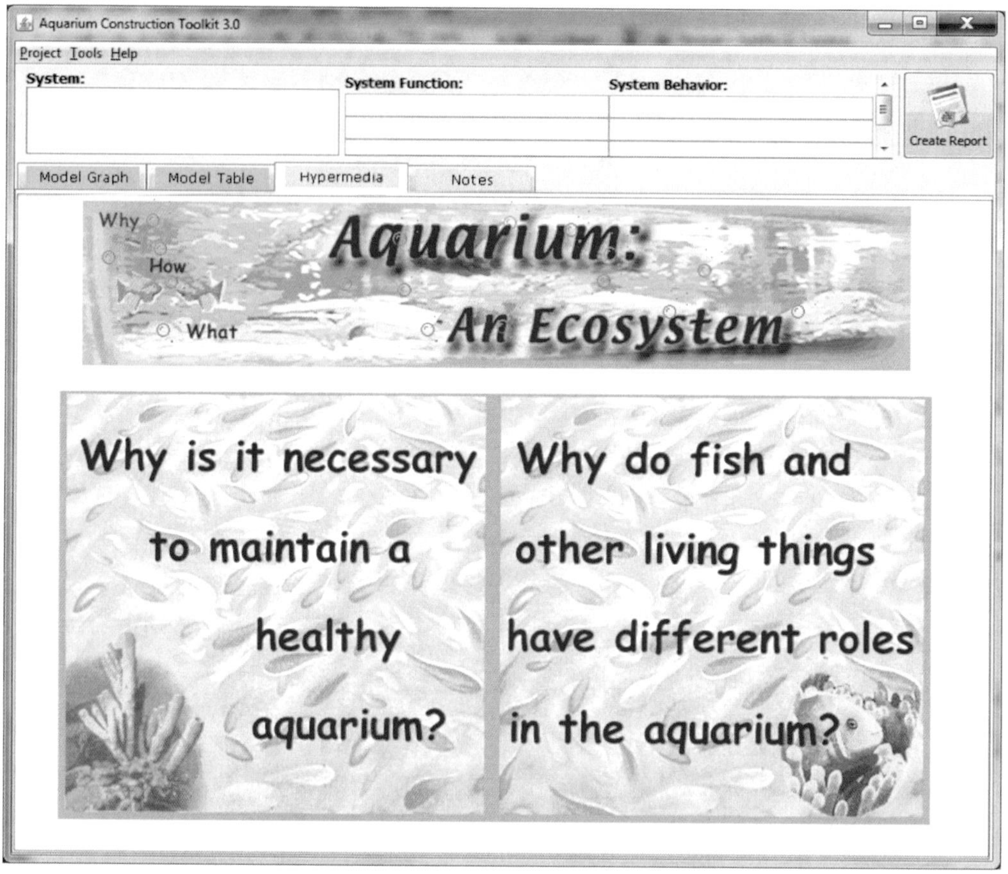

Fig. 35.5 A screen shot of function-oriented hypermedia in RepTools

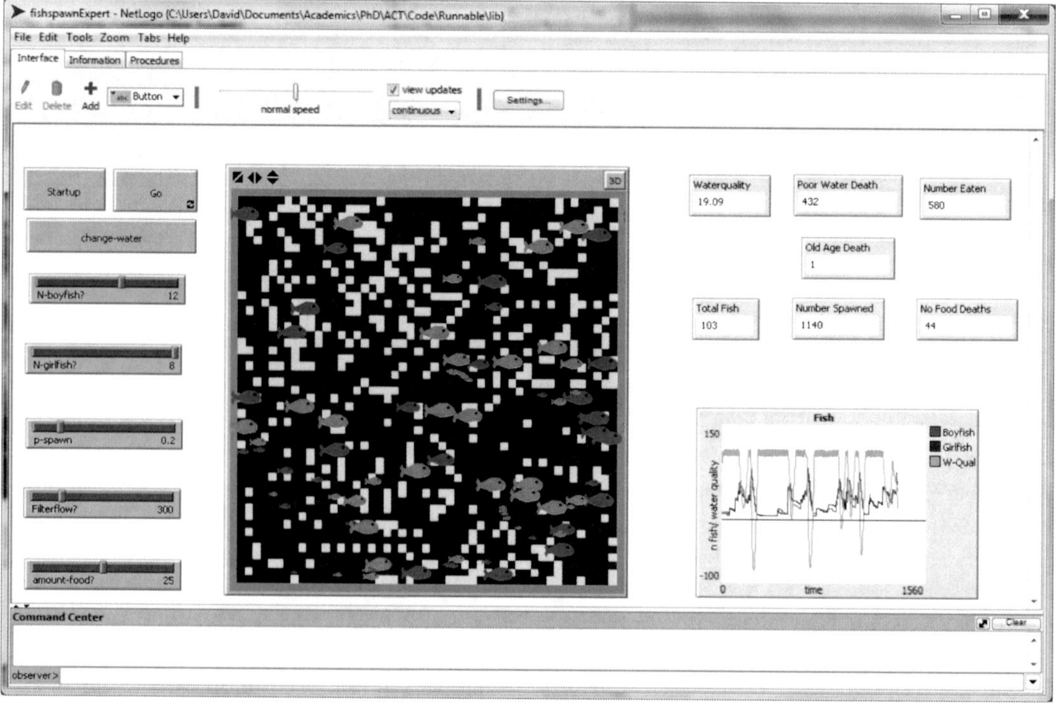

Fig. 35.6 A screen shot from a NetLogo simulation in ACT

Learning Context

Overall two hundred and seventy three (273) students participated in this 2009 study from four middle schools classrooms in central New Jersey—three from seventh grade and one from the eighth grade. In each case, the curriculum unit pertained to learning about ecosystems and lasted from 1–2 weeks. Their science teachers integrated the unit on ecosystems as a part of their regular science instruction. Prior to beginning the study, none of the students were familiar with SBF as a modeling tool for complex systems. All four teachers attended an evening workshop where they were introduced to these digital tools prior to implementation in the classroom. To prepare for the unit, the research team worked with the cooperating teachers to set up aquariums in the classrooms. Students used ACT on laptops while working in small groups, which varied from 2 to 6 students per computer, to generate SBF models.

Classroom Instruction

The four science teachers appropriated the curriculum and implemented it based on their individual scientific knowledge and teaching styles. While all the teachers used SBF modeling to organize their thinking about complex systems, there were variations within actual implementations of the curriculum.

SBF Introduction

Two teachers decided to begin the instruction with a discussion on the aquarium and focus on SBF as an initial activity using the ACT Model Table. The other teachers adopted the reverse strategy. Their introduction of the unit began with description of SBF while illustrating it in terms of the students' immediate environment (for e.g., the classroom as a complex system). This top-down effect was intended for the students to think about the SBF from a micro to macro level.

Modeling Aquatic Ecosystem

While some teachers emphasized the importance of the models as a means to represent ideas in summative fashion, other teachers chose to use the modeling task throughout implementation of the curriculum as a means to continually formulate and refine ideas. Additionally, some teachers chose to have students model the entire system, while other teachers had students generate a model based on a portion of the system that corresponded quite closely to one of the NetLogo simulations.

Again, Fig. 35.4 illustrates a model graph created in ACT by a seventh grade student as part of an SBF model-construction activity. This figure shows one of the systems frequently modeled in the classrooms: the nitrification process described previously. Structures are shown as nodes (purple for biotic structures, blue for abiotic structures), while relations link together structures that directly and relevantly influence one another. Although not depicted in the figure, inside the structure boxes are statements about a component's function as indicated in the dialog box of Fig. 35.3; these functions can also be seen in the Model Table in Fig. 35.1. In this way, students are encouraged to recognize and explicitly state the functions of the system.

Pre- and Posttest Results

To assess the effectiveness of the SBF-driven curriculum and technology, identical tests were administered before and after engagement in the aquarium unit. These tests asked about the structures, behaviors, and functions of the aquaria, and students were also given problems to solve regarding aquarium processes. To examine learning with respect to SBF, we coded the pre- and posttests using an SBF coding scheme (Hmelo, Holton, & Kolodner, 2000). Structural components, such as fish, plants, filter, were coded as structure. A reference to the mechanisms of how the components worked was coded as behavior. Example behaviors include absorbing carbon dioxide and producing oxygen through photosynthesis. Reference to the outcome of a behavior was coded as function. For example, a function of the filter could be to clean and circulate water. All tests were coded blind to condition by one rater.

Table 35.1 Pre- and posttest results

	Structure	Behavior	Function
Pretest mean (SD)	8.08 (2.624)	3.80 (2.107)	4.78 (2.924)
Posttest mean (SD)	9.33 (2.347)	6.20 (2.766)	8.12 (3.241)
$t(273)$	5.60[a]	11.65[a]	12.55[a]
Effect size	0.24	0.44	0.47

[a]All $p<0.05$

In this preliminary study, the objective was to ensure that SBF modeling in the ecosystem unit described here is successfully increasing understanding of functions and behaviors of classroom aquaria. Since students already are generally familiar with the structure of aquaria, increases in understanding of structure are considered a baseline for comparison of how the curriculum enhances understanding of functions and behaviors. Table 35.1 shows initial results from the pre- and posttests collapsed across the four middle school classrooms consisting of 273 students. The first number in the first two rows refers to the Mean and the second number in parentheses to the Standard Deviation. As indicated by the effect sizes, gains in structural understanding were small, while we saw moderate effect sizes for increase in understanding behaviors and functions. These tests suggest that the ecosystem curriculum unit and SBF modeling scaffolded by the ACT tool effectively increased understanding in terms of the deeper understanding of functions and behaviors of aquaria. Thus, these results replicate the findings from our initial study using ACT2.

Summary of Other Results

In addition to pre- and posttests, we have collected and analyzed several other kinds of data. For example, we have used an SBF coding scheme to analyze written answers by students to specific questions. We have found (Hmelo-Silver et al., 2011) that partly as a result of SBF modeling in the class (scaffolded in part by the ACT system) students are able to draw connections between different levels of abstraction in the aquaria ecosystem.

We have also examined (Honwad et al., 2010) drawings generated by middle school students as part of their SBF modeling (scaffolded in part by the ACT software). Building from several years of data, there is preliminary evidence that the ecosystem curriculum, SBF modeling and the ACT tool helps draw students away from focusing on linear relationships and visible components, and toward identifying invisible components and nonlinear relationships.

In addition, we have examined (Sinha et al., 2010) increase in understanding of SBF modeling in some of the middle school teachers with whom we work. One of the teachers in the initial study took the initiative to appropriate SBF modeling for teaching an entirely different domain: the human digestive system. In this analysis, we examined the growth of the teacher's understanding of SBF modeling over a few years, culminating in her eventual transfer of the SBF meta-model to an entirely new domain, without any prompting from us as researchers.

Metacognition and Self-Regulated Learning in ACT

Over the last several years, there have been several efforts at using interactive learning environments to support self-regulated learning. For example, Azevedo and colleagues have examined the cognitive strategies students use to learn about complex systems from hypermedia and how hypermedia can be designed to facilitate self-regulated learning (Azevedo, Guthrie, & Seibert, 2004; Azevedo & Hadwin, 2005). Similarly, Aleven and colleagues have studied how students seek help in interactive tutoring systems and how help systems can be designed to enable better self-regulated help-seeking behavior (Aleven, McLaren, Roll, & Koedinger, 2004; Aleven, Stalh, Schworm, Ficher, & Wallace, 2003).

According to Azevedo (2005), an interactive learning environment as a metacognitive tool should require students to make decisions about cognitive strategies, support students' cognitive and metacognitive processes, support task-, domain-, or activity-driven inquiry, and reside in a context in which tutors and peers can serve as external regulating agents. ACT clearly meets several of these requirements. For example, students' interaction with ACT typically is inquiry-driven, often starting with a question that a teacher may pose. During the course of learning, students may additional questions that drive parts of their subsequent reasoning. Further, students using ACT are confronted with the need to select, organize and combine several cognitive strategies to learn many different concepts and skills. They must learn how to use the variety of tools comprising ACT (SBFAuthor, RepTools, NetLogo, Electronic Notebook); they must learn about SBF modeling; they must learn about aquaria, and, more generally, about complex systems; finally, they must learn about the scientific method and how to apply it to understanding a complex situation. Furthermore, students using ACT receive feedback from their teachers as well as from the other members of their collaborative teams.

Nevertheless, questions arise as to what sorts of metacognitive reinforcement ACT could itself provide and how? ACT, like any other software tool, provides, usually negative, feedback to users if they misuse it: such feedback takes the form of error messages. Could ACT also provide positive feedback? In fact, ACT already provides several forms. Most simply, ACT comes supplied with a small library of SBF models. This library provides several examples from which the students can begin construction of their own models, should a teacher chose to make them available. Furthermore, learning about aquaria is supported by the hypermedia content available via ACT's built-in Web browser and RepTools functionally indexed hypermedia content.

At a much higher level, a NetLogo simulation of an SBF model in ACT2 (Vattam et al., 2011), when compared against student expectations or existing data, can serve a normative role in student learning. While seeing that their SBF model fails to perform up to their expectations can serve as negative reinforcement to some students, trying to modify the model to match expectations, can act as an incentive. Finally, learning about how science is typically done is indirectly supported by the complementary roles played by the theoretical and experimental parts of ACT2. Empirically, students can use ACT to record data from a physical aquarium, if one is available, and they can run experiments using NetLogo.Student theories take the form of SBF models. Falsifiability is provided when a model is auto-matically turned into a simulation and then run. Thus, ACT2 clearly affords self-regulated learning.

Unfortunately, as we discussed in Sect. 4, our middle school students did not use ACT2 the way we had intended. Apparently they found it too difficult to construct the detailed SBF models in a 1- or 2-week curriculum unit on ecosystems that are needed for purposes of simulation. The simpler SBF models in ACT3 do not permit simulation. Nevertheless, ACT3 too affords self-regulated learning as students must make decisions about how to classify objects that they are creating. This kind of collaborative decision making is another manifestation of self-regulated learning (Roschelle, 1996). From the early use of ACT in classrooms, our observations have indicated that the tool has forced teachers and students alike to grapple with their understanding of structures, behaviors, and functions of complex systems. Use of ACT3 leads to discussions about how to classify an object or which column in the Model Table the object goes into, as the students work in a joint space to collaboratively construct, revise, and refine their models.

Towards a Metacognitive ACT

In the next version of ACT, tentatively named EMT for Ecological Modeling Toolkit, we intend to provide more active metacognitive reinforcement in the form of guides and critics. A *guide*, sometimes also called a *wizard*, is a user-interface mechanism to provide the ability to describe a complex activity in the form of a series of steps. Individual steps enable the user to answer specific questions, enter parameters, or select options. Usually, only meaningful interactions are allowed, so reinforcement takes the form of a successfully specified activity. Examples of guides are easily found in commercial software, such as the process of importing data from a text file into Microsoft Excel.

While guides are proactive, critics are reactive. A *critic* is a software device that spontaneously provides feedback to the user when some user action fails to conform with one of a configurable set of rules. An example of critics can be found in the Argo/UML software modeling tool (Robbins & Redmiles, 1999). In Argo/UML, a subset of 30 rules can be selected for critiquing as users build UML models. Criticisms take the form of alert messages at the time that a rule is violated. However, in other systems, interactions can also take the form of questions, which, while indicating that a problem exists, encourages users to figure out the nature of a problem themselves.

We plan to add guides and critiques to EMT. To do this requires that EMT have a metacognitive architecture. By metacognitive, we mean that EMT itself is aware of what a user is trying to accomplish, can notice any deviations and provide appropriate feedback. We will build on the REM metacognitive architecture that is capable of diagnosing and repairing faults in software agents (Murdock & Goel, 2008, 2001, 2003).

The major element of EMT's metacognitive architecture will be an SBF model of SBF modeling; that is, a meta-model. With respect to supporting critics, the SBFAuthor tool will be intended to report on all user changes to a model being constructed. The changes will be compared with EMT's expectations of the form such a model should take, and any deviation will be reported. Like Argo/UML, the exact rules to be enforced will be configurable, as will the form that the feedback messages take.

The SBF meta-model can also support guides. That is, by its very nature, the meta-model specifies the form of any constructed model. A guide can then traverse the meta-model suggesting to the user appropriate next steps. Note that different traversal strategies (e.g., top-down and bottom-up modeling) and allowed deviations are possible, and EMT's guides will be configurable to take advantage of this freedom. In this architecture, the user initiates a request. The guide recognizes the request and initiates a dialog with the user. The dialog structure is based on the SBF meta-model. The dialog consists of a series of steps, each of which may communicate with the user and the editor.

Note that several interesting research questions arise from the metacognitive approach. While experience with Argo/UML was positive, applying critics to more abstract subject matter, such as the scientific method, will be challenging. Also, the degree of specificity in student feedback needs to be tunable to support different teaching styles and students' backgrounds. Finally, there will no doubt be technical challenges in applying the metacognitive approach across a suite of separately built tools. We should think that the work of Aleven et al. (2004, 2003) should provide a basis for addressing some of these questions. In particular, their analysis of how students use (and abuse) helps in interactive learning systems should inform our design of the guides and critics in metacognitive EMT.

Summary and Conclusions

In this chapter, we have presented a brief review of the ACT project. Our conclusions are correspondingly large-grained; our technical papers describe more fine-grained analysis of the results from the ACT project. Here, we summarize our main conclusions in the form of answers to questions that our colleagues in the learning and cognitive sciences often have asked us:

1. *What do you mean by a complex system?* The term "complex system" is ambiguous and open to multiple interpretations. We use the term to refer to hierarchically organized complex systems that nearly decomposable. In such systems, while causal processes at one abstraction level in these systems emerge out of interactions among components and processes at lower levels, the interactions among subsystems at any level of abstraction are contained and can be organized hierarchically.
2. *What do you mean by a model?* Like the term complex system, the term "model" too is ambiguous and can have multiple interpretations. We use the term model to signify a scientific model, i.e., a scientific interpretation

of a target system that proposes mechanisms underlying the system. Since a model provides a mechanistic explanation of the system, a model is fundamentally an explanatory construct.

3. *What is a function and a behavior in an SBF model? How does an SBF model differ from other mechanistic causal models?* The term behavior in an SBF model refers to a mechanism. The term function refers to an interpretation of a mechanism (or behavior). Functions provide a scheme for decomposing a hierarchically organized system into subsystems. SBF models represent functions explicitly, and use them as indices into causal mechanisms to organize knowledge of hierarchically organized systems.
4. *How may a science curriculum teach about complex systems?* Our experience with the ACT project suggests four dimensions of learning about complex systems (the 4Cs): *cognition, concepts, connections,* and *content*. First, learning about complex systems provides opportunities for learning about cognitive strategies such as decomposing a system into subsystems at various level of abstraction and then composing them into a functional model. Second, learning about complex systems foregrounds important concepts such as mechanism, abstraction, hierarchy, feedback, cycles, and emergence. Third, learning about complex systems enables understanding of connections among different elements such as structural components and causal mechanisms, making connections among mechanisms at different scales, and noticing similarities between complex systems in different domains. Finally, we believe that significant portions of science curriculum can be recast as learning about complex systems.
5. *What are some opportunities for metacognition and self-regulation in learning about functional models of complex systems?* The first three of our 4C's—*cognition, concepts,* and *connections*—not only provide ample opportunities for metacognition and self-regulation in learning about functional models of complex systems, but also provide some challenges that appear unique to functional models of complex systems. For example, on the one hand, learning about functional models provides opportunities for learning about the cognitive strategies of model construction, model use, model evaluation, and model revision. On the other, it also provides the cognitive challenge of learning about decomposing a complex system into subsystems, and about recognizing connections among structural components, causal mechanisms, and functional abstractions.
6. *In what ways does the ACT tool support self-regulated learning?* Although metacognition and self regulation were not major concerns in our initial design of the ACT system, on reflection it appears that ACT supports self-regulated learning in several ways, some of which worked well in practice and others that we need to rethink. For example, students must learn how to match the variety of tools comprising ACT to different tasks; they must learn about SBF modeling; they must learn about aquaria, and, more generally, about complex systems; finally, they must learn about the scientific method and how to apply it to understanding a complex situation. ACT presently provides help in the form of a video tutorial, a library of already built SBF models, and hypermedia content through RepTools.

Acknowledgments This paper has benefited from discussions with Julia Svoboda. We also thank Steven Gray at Rutgers University for his contributions to early parts of this work. We are grateful to the United States National Science Foundation [Grant (#0632519)] and the United States Institute for Education Sciences (Grant #R305A090210) for their support of their work.

References

Aleven, V., McLaren, B., Roll, I., & Koedinger, K. (2004). Toward tutoring help seeking: Applying cognitive modeling to meta-cognitive skills. *Proceedings of the 7th International Conference on Intelligent Tutoring Systems (ITS 2004)* (pp. 227–239). Berlin: Springer Verlag.

Aleven, V., Stalh, E., Schworm, S., Ficher, F., & Wallace, R. (2003). Help seeking and help design in interactive learning environments. *Review of Educational Research, 73*(3), 277–320.

Azevedo, R. (2005). Computer environments at metacognitive tools for enhancing learning. *Educational Psychologist, 40*(4), 193–197.

Azevedo, R., Guthrie, J. T., & Seibert, D. (2004). The role of self-regulated learning in fostering students' conceptual understanding of complex systems with hypermedia. *Journal of Educational Computing Research, 30*(1), 87–111.

Azevedo, R., & Hadwin, A. F. (2005). Scaffolding self-regulated learning and metacognition: Implications for the design of computer-based scaffolds. *Instructional Science, 33*, 367–379.

Bhatta, S., & Goel, A. (1997). Learning generic mechanisms for innovative design adaptation. *The Journal of the Learning Sciences, 6*(4), 367–396.

Biswas, G., Leelawong, K., Schwartz, D., & Vye, N. (2005). Learning by teaching: A New agent paradigm for educational software. *Applied Artificial Intelligence, 19*(3–4), 363–392.

Chandrasekaran, B. (1994). Functional representations and causal processes. In M. Yovits (Ed.), *Advances in computers* (pp. 73–143). Waltham, MA: Academic Press.

Clement, J. (2008). *Creative Model Construction in Scientists and Students: The Role of Imagery, Analogy, and Mental Simulation*. Dordrecht: Springer.

Dawes, J. (2000). Tropical aquarium fish: A step by step guide to setting up and maintaining a freshwater or marine aquarium. Sterling publishing, New York City.

Duschl, R., & Grandy, R. (2008). *Teaching scientific inquiry: Recommendations from research and implementation*. Rotterdam, Netherlands: Sense Publications.

Edelson, D. (1997). Realizing authentic scientific learning through the adaptation of scientific practice. In K. Tobin & B. Fraser (Eds.), *International Handbook of Science Education*. Dordrecht, NL: Kluwer.

Erden, M., Komoto, H., van Beek, T., D'Amelio, V., Echavarria, E., & Tomiyama, T. (2008). A review of function modeling: Approaches and applications. *Artificial Intelligence for Engineering Design Analysis and Manufacturing, 22*(2), 147–169.

Gilbert, J. (2004). Models and modelling: Routes to more authentic science education. *International Journal of Science and Mathematics Education, 2*(2), 115–130.

Goel, A., Gomez, A., Grue, N., Murdock, W., Recker, M., & Govindaraj, T. (1996). Towards design learning environments—Explaining how devices work. In *Proceedings of International Conference on Intelligent Tutoring Systems*. Springer, Cognitive Science Society, ACM, International Society of the learning Sciences, Montreal, Canada.

Goel, A., Rugaber, S., & Vattam, S. (2009). Structure, behavior and function of complex systems: The SBF modeling language. *International Journal of AI in Engineering Design, Analysis and Manufacturing, 23*, 23–35. Special Issue on Developing and Using Engineering Ontologies.

Goel, A., Vattam, S., Rugaber, S., Joyner, D., Hmelo-Silver, C., Jordan R, et al. (2010) Learning functional and causal abstractions of classroom Aquaria. In *Proceedings of 32nd Annual Meeting of the Cognitive Science Society*. Springer, Cognitive Science Society, ACM, International Society of the learning Sciences, Portland, Oregon.

Hmelo, C., Holton, D., & Kolodner, J. L. (2000). Designing to learn about complex systems. *The Journal of the Learning Sciences, 9*, 247–298.

Hmelo-Silver, C., Jordan, R., Honwad, S., Eberbach, C., Sinha, S., Goel, A, et al. (2011). Foregrounding behaviors and functions to promote ecosystem understanding. In *Proceedings of 9th Hawaii International Conference on Education*. London: Routledge.

Hmelo-Silver, C., Liu, L., Gray, S., Finkelstein, H., & Schwartz, R. (2007). *Enacting things differently: Using NetLogo models to learn about complex systems*. Paper presented at biennial meeting of European Association for Research on Learning and Instruction. Budapest, Hungary.

Honwad, S., Hmelo-Silver, C., Jordan, R., Eberbach, C., Gray, S., Sinha, S, et al. (2010). Connecting the visible to the invisible: Helping middle school children understand complex ecosystem processes. In *Proceedings of 32nd Annual Meeting of the Cognitive Science Society*. Springer, Cognitive Science Society, ACM, International Society of the learning Sciences, Portland, Oregon.

Jordan, R., Gray, S., Demeter, M., Liu, L., & Hmelo-Silver, C. (2009). An assessment of Students' understanding of ecosystem concepts: Conflating ecological systems and cycles. *Applied Environment Education and Communication: an International Journal, 8*, 40–48.

Jordan, R., Singer, F., Vaughan, J., & Berkowitz, A. (2008). What should every citizen know about ecology? *Frontiers in Ecology and the Environment, 7*, 495–500. Ecological Society of America.

Kitamura, Y., Sano, T., Namba, K., & Mizoguchi, R. (2002). A functional concept ontology and its application to automatic recognition of functional structures. *Advanced Engineering Informatics, 16*(2), 145–163.

Lehrer, R., & Schauble, L. (2006). Cultivating model-based reasoning in science education. In R. Sawyer (Ed.), *The Cambridge handbook of the learning sciences*. New York: Cambridge University Press.

Liu, L., & Hmelo-Silver, C. (2009). Promoting complex systems learning through the use of conceptual representations in hypermedia. *Journal of Research in Science Teaching, 46*, 1023–1040.

Murdock, J. W., & Goel, A. (2001). Learning about constraints by reflection. In Procs. Fourteenth Canadian Conference on Artificial Intelligence (AI-01). In Stroulia and S. Matwin (Eds.), LNAI 2056, (pp. 131–140). Berlin: Springer-Verlag.

Murdock, J. W., & Goel, A. (2003). Localizing planning with functional process models. In Procs. Thirteenth International Conference on Automated Planning and Scheduling (ICAPS-03), (pp. 73–81). Menlo Park, CA: AAAI.

Murdock, J. W., & Goel, A. (2008). Meta-case-based reasoning: Self-improvement through self-understanding. *Journal of Experimental & Theoretical Artificial Intelligence, 20*(1), 1–36.

National Research Council (NRC). (1996). *National science education standards*. Washington, DC: National Academy Press.

Nersessian, N. (2008). *Creating scientific concepts*. Cambridge, MA: MIT Press.

New Jersey Department of Education. (2006). Core Curriculum Content Standards. In State of New Jersey Department of Education. Retrieved June 19, 2008, from http://www.state.nj.us/education/cccs/.

Rasmussen, J. (1986). *Information processing and human-machine interaction*. New York: North-Holland.

Robbins, J., & Redmiles, D. (1999). Cognitive Support, UML Adherence, and XMI Interchange in Argo/UML. In *Proceedings of Conference on Construction of Software Engineering Tools (CoSET 99)* (pp. 61–70). Springer, Cognitive Science Society, ACM, International Society of the learning Sciences, Los Angeles, California.

Roschelle, J. (1996). Designing for cognitive communication: Epistemic Fidely or mediating collaborative inquiry. In D. Day & D. Kovacs (Eds.), *Computer, communication and mental models*. London, UK: Taylor & Francis.

Sabelli, N. (2006). Complexity, technology, science, and education. *The Journal of the Learning Sciences, 15*, 5–9.

Simon, H. (1962). The architecture of complexity. *Proceedings of the American Philosophical Society, 106*(6), 467–482.

Simon, H. (1999). Can there be a science of complex systems? In Y. Bar-Yam (Ed.), *Unifying themes in complex systems* (pp. 3–14). Cambridge, MA: Perseus.

Sinha, S., Gray, S., Hmelo-Silver, C., Jordan, R., Honwad, S., Eberbach, C, et al. (2010). Appropriating conceptual representations: A case of transfer in a middle school science teacher. In *Proceedings of 9th International Conference of the Learning Sciences*. Springer, Cognitive Science Society, ACM, International Society of the learning Sciences, Chicago. June 28–29, 2010.

Stadelman, P., & Finley, L. (2003). *Tropical fish: setting up and taking care of aquariums made easy: Expert advice for new aquarists*. Hauppauge, New York: Barron's Educational Series.

Stansbury, E. (1999). *The simplified classroom aquarium: A teacher's guide to operating and maintaining a small classroom aquarium*. Springfield: Charles C. Thomas publisher.

Stewart, J., Cartier, J., & Passmore, C. (2005). Developing understanding through model-based inquiry. In M. S. Donovan & J. Bransford (Eds.), *How people learn*. Washington, DC: National Research Council.

Vattam, S., Goel, A., Rugaber, S., Hmelo-Silver, C., Jordan, R., Gray, S., et al. (2011). Understanding complex natural systems by articulating structure-behavior-function models. *Special issue on Creative Design, 14*(1), 166–181.

Wilensky, U. (1999). NetLogo. http://ccl.northwestern.edu/netlogo/. Center for Connected Learning and Computer-Based Modeling, Northwestern University. Evanston, IL.

Wilensky, U., & Resnick, M. (1999). Thinking in levels: A dynamic systems approach to making sense of the world. *Journal of Science Education and Technology, 8*, 3–19.

Dynamic Computerized Scaffolding of Metacognitive Activities in Small Groups

36

Inge Molenaar, Carla van Boxtel, and Peter Sleegers

Abstract
This chapter describes a new method for the computerized scaffolding of self-regulated learning in computer-based learning environments. The system works with an attention management system that registers the attentional focus of learners with the intention to adjust scaffolding to students' current activities. As the support is related to students' current activities, structuring scaffolds that support students' activities and problematizing scaffolds that elicit students' activities can both be used. We found evidence that this scaffolding system enhances group performance and students' metacognitive knowledge. Moreover, different forms of scaffold had differential effects on learning. Problematizing scaffolds resulted in higher group performance, transfer of domain knowledge and metacognitive knowledge than structuring scaffolds. These differential effects are most likely explained by a combination of quantitative and qualitative differences in the metacognitive activities triggered by problematizing scaffolds compared with structuring scaffolds.

Introduction

In the Netherlands, as in other countries, students in elementary education often learn in small groups in computer-based learning environments (CBLEs), such as the Internet, e-learning, and CSCL environments and games. This is important because students will be learning in small groups with computers throughout their life (Simons, van der Linden, & Duffy, 2000). Moreover, students need to be able to control and monitor their learning in multiple settings to become successful lifelong learners in the global knowledge society. Learners

I. Molenaar (✉)
Behavioural Science Institute, University of Amsterdam, Postbus 94208, Amsterdam 1090 GE, The Netherlands
e-mail: i.molenaar@uva.nl

C. van Boxtel
Radboud University Nijmegen, Postbus 9104, 6500 HE Nijmegen, The Netherlands
e-mail: i.molenaar@pwo.ru.nl

P. Sleegers
Department of Education Organization and Management, University of Twente, Enschede, The Netherlands

R. Azevedo and V. Aleven (eds.), *International Handbook of Metacognition and Learning Technologies*, Springer International Handbooks of Education 26, DOI 10.1007/978-1-4419-5546-3_36,

in computer-based learning environments are asked to set learning goals, apply strategies, and select activities to pursue these goals and monitor and control their progress towards achieving these goals (Azevedo & Hadwin, 2005; Kalyuga, Chandler, & Sweller, 2001; Kirschner, Sweller, & Clark, 2006). Research has abundantly shown that students are unable to self-regulate their learning without additional help (Azevedo & Cromley, 2004; Azevedo, Moos, Johnson, & Chauncey, 2010; Bannert, 2006; Bannert, Hildebrand, & Mengelkamp, 2009).

Scaffolding supports learners to perform tasks they are unable to fulfill successfully themselves (Hmelo-Silver & Azevedo, 2006; Sharma & Hannafin, 2007; Wood, Bruner, & Ross, 1976). Scaffolding is defined as providing assistance to students when it is needed and fading the support as the learner competences increase (Wood et al., 1976). Scaffolding by human tutors supporting self-regulated learning in computer-based learning environments improves learning and motivation (Azevedo & Cromley, 2004; Azevedo et al., 2010 Bannert, 2006; Land & Greene, 2000; Veenman, Kok, & Blote, 2005). However, most scaffolding research has, to date, been directed at individual learners supported by human tutors in college and high school. There is some evidence that scaffolding is also helpful for small groups (Azevedo, Cromley, Winters, Moos, & Greene, 2005; Winters & Alexander, 2011), but it has never been explored among young learners in elementary school.

Furthermore, until now few computerized scaffolding systems have been designed for ill-structured domains, due to the difficulty of automatically interpreting students' activities and adjusting scaffolding accordingly (Woolf, 2009). In the AtGentive project,[1] a computerized scaffolding system entitled AtGentSchool was developed to support self-regulated learning in an e-learning environment (Ontdeknet) used in ill-structured domains. The aim of the project was to investigate the effect of 3D embodied agents supporting young learners to manage their attention in CBLEs. The appropriate allocation of attention is key to successful learning in CBLEs and is explained in more detail in this chapter; it is closely related to students' self-regulated learning (Molenaar & Roda, 2008; Roda, 2011). Attention management systems are used to monitor student focus of attention, i.e., what is the student attention directed at (Roda, 2011; Roda & Thomas, 2006). The first question addressed is: How can an attention management system facilitate the scaffolding of self-regulated learning? Additionally, scaffolding that adjusts to students' current focus of attention can take on different forms (structuring or problematizing) as they are attuned to the students' activities. There is, to date, little knowledge about the effects of different forms of scaffolds on the learning outcomes of collaborating students. Research has shown that problematizing scaffolds elicit more explanations from individual students, which support the articulation of their thinking and thereby leading to increased knowledge development (Chi, Siler, Jeong, Yamuachi, & Hausmann, 2001; Davis & Linn, 2000; King, 1998, 2002). Therefore, the second question addressed is: What are the effects of computerized scaffolding and of different forms of scaffold on the learning outcomes of collaborating students?

We contribute to this handbook by expanding on the existing work on scaffolding for self-regulated learning by describing the design of a computerized scaffolding system with an attention management system and its effects on the learning of collaborating students in elementary education. We first briefly describe the constructs of self-regulated learning, metacognition, and collaborative learning that informed our design and research. We then describe how the attention management system detects, traces, and models students' focus of attention and selects the appropriate scaffolds. The distinction between the two different forms of scaffolds is also described. Thirdly, we discuss the effects of our scaffolding system on the group's learning and activities. And finally, we discuss how elaborated process analysis can enhance our limited ability to trace self-regulated learning to support the design of future computerized scaffolding systems.

[1] The AtGentive project was a European under the sixth Framework program. AtGentive stands for "Attentive Agents for Collaborative Learners."

Theoretical Framework

As described above, learners in CBLEs need scaffolding to support their self-regulated learning and their metacognitive activities in particular in order to control and monitor their learning (Azevedo & Green, 2010; Azevedo & Hadwin, 2005; Zimmerman, 2002). However, the boundaries between the constructs of self-regulated learning and metacognition are unclear (Dinsmore, Alexander, & Loughlin, 2008). We therefore briefly introduce the theoretical definitions and models used in our research. Self-regulated learning was originally defined as an integrated theory of learning (Corno & Mandinach, 1983; Dinsmore et al., 2008), focusing on the interaction of cognitive, motivational, and contextual factors to explain learning. Today, we picture self-regulating learners as those who successfully use cognitive activities (read, process, elaborate) to study a topic and control and monitor their learning with metacognitive activities (orientate, plan, monitor, and evaluate their actions) and who are able to motivate themselves (Azevedo, Moos, Greenee, Winters, & Cromley, 2008; Zimmerman, 2002). We have used Zimmerman's model (2002) as the basis for designing our scaffolding system. What is important in this model is the cyclical clarification of the interaction between cognitive, metacognitive, and motivational activities. As we are to design and evaluate computerized scaffolding that supports students to control and monitor their learning, we focus on the interaction between the cognitive and metacognitive activities.

The construct of metacognition originates from cognitive information processing theory. It was originally defined as "cognition over cognition" or "knowledge about knowing," which learners need to control and monitor their learning. A distinction is made between metacognitive knowledge, i.e., the knowledge students have about the interaction between person, task, and strategy characteristics (Flavell, 1979), and metacognitive skills, i.e., the skills students have to apply metacognitive activities to control and monitor cognitive activities (Veenman, 2005). In order to make a clear distinction between cognitive and metacognitive activities, Nelson (1996) defined the object-level and the meta-level of learning. Cognitive activities are those activities that deal with the content of the task (the object-level), and metacognitive activities are those activities that control and monitor cognitive activities (the meta-level), such as orientation, planning, monitoring, evaluation, and reflection activities (Meijer, Veenman, & van Hout-Wolters, 2006). We therefore follow Veenman (2011) in viewing self-regulated learning as the major theoretical construct and metacognition as one of its components. We assume that metacognitive activities are a manifestation of students' metacognitive knowledge and skills.

As discussed above, we investigate the role of metacognitive activities in the context of a computer-based learning environment in which students learn collaboratively. To date, few researchers have applied the constructs of self-regulated learning and specifically metacognitive activities in collaborative learning research (Dillenbourg, Järvelä, & Fischer, 2009; Iiskalla, Vauras, Lehtinen, & Salonen, 2011). Evidently, learners in small groups need to regulate their own and the group learning (Hadwin & Oshige, 2007). This means that the groups need to use the appropriate cognitive activities to achieve their goals and apply metacognitive activities to control and monitor their learning (Hadwin & Oshige, 2007; Iiskalla et al., 2011; Volet, Vauras, & Salonen, 2009). To understand how students learn from scaffolding in a small group, we draw on the socio-cognitive perspective on collaborative learning. This perspective offers a framework to analyze how individuals learn in interaction with others emphasizing the individual development of the students and of the group as a whole as a result of the interaction (Hadwin & Oshige, 2007; Iiskala, Vauras, & Lehtinen, 2004; Vauras, Iiskala, Kajamies, Kinnunen, & Lehtinen, 2003; Volet et al., 2009). Learning is considered to take place through reciprocal activities among students. Consequently, peers are expected to play a mediating role in the learning of others (Salomon, 1993; Volet et al., 2009; Vygotsky, 1978). Elaboration on each others' contributions, such as giving feedback, asking questions and receiving answers, and discussing and exhanging ideas, is expected to enhance student learning (Chi, 2009; Webb, 2009). Learners contribute knowledge and skills to the social system, which elicits new activities from other group members. As a result, group members influence each other in a spiral-like fashion. This gives individual students the opportunity to practice skills and appropriate knowledge and consequently develop group and individual skills and knowledge (Salomon, 1993; Volet et al., 2009). This means that scaffolding collaborative learners can affect both group and individual learning.

Dynamic Scaffolding with an Attention Management System

The essential elements in the process of scaffolding are diagnosis, calibration, and fading (Puntambekar & Hubscher, 2005). Effective human tutors select their scaffolds by carefully diagnosing student behavior and reducing their support when student competences increase (Chi, 2009; Wood et al., 1976). However, as briefly mentioned above, the automatic diagnosis of student behavior is problematic. Therefore, in contrast to human tutors, most computerized scaffolding systems use *static* scaffolding. Static scaffolding is the same for all students and does not adjust to student activities, for example, a preset list of instructions that helps learners perform a learning assignment. *Dynamic* scaffolding, on the other hand, analyzes the student behavior in order to select the appropriate scaffold to support current student activities, for example, how to plan a learning task when the learner starts working on this particular task.

As indicated in Zimmerman's model (2002) of self-regulated learning, it is important to support cognitive, metacognitive, and motivational activities at the appropriate time during learning. Students need to learn not only *how* to regulate their learning but also *when* to regulate their learning. Consequently, a computer system that enables the dynamic scaffolding of self-regulated learning needs to diagnose current behavior and select the appropriate scaffolds to foster cognitive, metacognitive, and motivational activities when appropriate. Attention management research aims to determine the benefit of given information for a learner in a specific context and the cost associated with presenting information in a certain way (Roda & Nabeth, 2007; Roda & Thomas, 2006). The utility of attention management systems for educational sciences is to detect the students' attentional focus and interpret this information to select scaffolds that can support student learning (Molenaar & Roda, 2008). Below we describe how the attention management system supports scaffolding in the diagnosis, calibration, and fading phases.

In the diagnosis phase, the attentional focus is assessed based on the students' activities and progress. The system tracks the students' current activities based on the location, actions in the e-learning system, keystrokes, and mouse movements. For example, when a student browses through a text, AtGentSchool registers both the viewing of the particular text as well as the browsing behavior. This provides a real-time description of the students' current activities. The current and past activities combined indicate the students' progress on the learning assignment (Molenaar & Roda, 2008). For example, when students have not read any text before it indicates that the learners started to search for new information. Additionally, keyboard strokes and mouse movements also provide information. For example, no keyboard strokes or mouse movement registration in a certain timeframe indicates that the student is idle. This traced and tracked information is used to determine the students' attentional focus.

This information is used in real time by the system in the calibration phase to determine the appropriate scaffold. This scaffold can either support the students' current attentional focus or provide suggestions to change the focus when the current focus is inappropriate for the learning assignment. We use Zimmerman's model of self-regulated learning as a theoretical model to determine when cognitive, metacognitive, and motivational activities should be supported during learning (Zimmerman, 2002). There are three phases in this model: forethought, performance, and self-reflection. In the forethought phase, preparatory activities are done at the start of a new learning task; in the performance phase, executive activities are performed; and in the self-reflection phase, closing activities to finish the task are performed. In test runs with AtGentSchool, we found that when students' focus of attention changes in our e-learning environment, it is almost always also linked to a transition to a new phase (Molenaar & Roda, 2008; Molenaar, van Boxtel, Sleegers, & Roda, 2011). For example, when a group changes its focus from reading text to writing a summary, it moves from the performance to the forethought phase. This finding is particularly interesting for scaffolding metacognitive activities as the students' focus and progress provide enough information to determine useful metacognitive scaffolds. For example, when the students start to write a summary, it can be useful to scaffold them to plan how to write their summary. Below we discuss the relationship between changes in attentional focus, the phases, and metacognitive scaffolding.

The preparatory activities include task analysis which involves processes, such as orientation and planning. Therefore, when the learner is selecting a new task, it is useful to perform an orientation activity to determine the alignment of the overall learning goal and the new task. A scaffold supporting the orientation process can therefore be helpful here. For example, a scaffold supports the orientation activity for the concept map task: "*We advise you to make a mind map to sum up topics you want to learn more about when studying a foreign country.*" The second preparatory activity is to plan the task-setting goals and ensure there is alignment between the task execution and the overall learning assignment. Accordingly, a metacognitive planning scaffold at the start of a new task can help the learner to make a plan. For example, "*In a concept map you sum up all the topics you find important for studying another country.*" The execution activities entail self-control and self-observation. Self-observation supports the monitoring of the planned methods and strategies. Self-control ensures that students, based on the observation of their task advancement, align their activities with their plan. Consequently, metacognitive monitoring scaffolds appear during execution of a task. An example of a monitoring scaffold while working on the mind map is: "*Did you proceed on the concept map as you planned in advance?*" Finally, the closing activities entail self-judgment, which is done by evaluating against some standard or causal attribution. In the reflection phase, students determine whether their activities were performed in the most effective and efficient manner. They reflect on their activities to determine whether, in future instances, the same line of activities would be appropriate. Students can be supported in this by asking them to reflect on their actions after task completion, for example, "*Will you proceed to make the concept map in the same way in the future?*" These examples help us understand how, in the calibration phase, the diagnosed changes in the attentional focus of the student determine the metacognitive scaffolds.

The final element of scaffolding is fading, which is the gradual reduction of scaffolds leading to full transfer of control to the learner (Wood et al., 1976). The system determines whether the selected scaffold is actually needed for the students' progress. For example, if the group has successfully finished the concept map task before, the system will not send a planning scaffold until it traces information that indicates that the students are having problems proceeding with this task.

To summarize, AtGentSchool supports students with metacognitive scaffolds when the students' attentional focus changes. This is done through the continuous assessment of the focus (diagnosis) followed by selection of the appropriate metacognitive scaffold (calibration), which is only sent when the student needs support (fading). An additional benefit of dynamic scaffolding is that different forms of scaffold can be used, in other words, scaffolding is attuned to the learners' activities. In the next section, we introduce the different forms of scaffolds used in our system.

Fig. 36.1 An example of structuring and problematizing scaffolds

Mechanism of Scaffolding: The Form of the Scaffolds

There are different forms of scaffolds that can simply show context suitable examples of metacognitive activities (i.e., examples that are appropriate for the group's current activity) that directly help the group control and monitor their learning. Alternatively, scaffolds can problematize the metacognitive aspects of the task, posing questions that elicit metacognitive activities from the group members. This difference is based on a distinction made by Reiser (2004) between structuring and problematizing mechanisms of scaffolding. Structuring simplifies the learning assignment by reducing its complexity, clarifying the underlying components, and supporting planning and performance (i.e., providing the students with an example of a plan for the assignment). Problematizing increases the complexity of the learning assignment by emphasizing certain aspects of the assignment and asking learners to clarify the underlying components and perform activities to plan and construct their own strategies (i.e., asking students to make their own plan for the assignment).

Figure 36.1 shows an example of each form of scaffold used for an introduction task in which students must introduce themselves. Structuring scaffolds support metacognitive activities and stimulate students to elaborate on this example. For example, a structuring scaffold shows students an example plan of a task: "*Here you introduce yourself, for example, I am David, 15 years old and I like playing games and listening to music.*" Students can then elaborate and reformulate the specifications of the plan. Problematizing scaffolds, on the other hand, stimulate students' metacognitive activities, i.e., their verbal responses to the questions asked which address issues on the meta-level. An example of a problematizing scaffold is as follows: "*How are you going to introduce yourself?*" This scaffold asks students to verbalize and plan how to approach the introduction task. Research showed that problematizing scaffolds, such as question prompts, elicit individual students' explanations and support the articulation of their thinking (Chi et al., 2001; Davis & Linn, 2000; King, 1998, 2002). Therefore, different forms of scaffolds foster metacognitive activities differently, possibly leading to differential effects on learning.

The Effects of Scaffolding

The goal of scaffolding is twofold: (1) to *support* learners in activities they are unable to accomplish successfully by themselves and (2) to *develop* knowledge and skills needed to perform future learning (Hmelo-Silver & Azevedo, 2006; Pea, 2004; Sharma & Hannafin, 2007). The goal of scaffolding metacognitive activities of collaborating students is to stimulate metacognitive activities to improve group performance and students' domain and metacognitive knowledge. The rationale behind the first goal is that metacognitive activities monitor and control the cognitive activities (Nelson, 1996). This improves the cognitive activities through planning, prior knowledge activation and monitoring, and evaluation (Veenman, 2011). We therefore expect to find improved group performance. The socio-cognitive perspective on collaborative learning emphasizes that group performance also affects individual knowledge, which supports our expectation with respect to improved individual domain knowledge. With respect to the second goal, scaffolds develop metacognitive knowledge and skills through modeling and stimulating metacognitive activities. Consequently, we expect students to gain more metacognitive knowledge, i.e., the knowledge students have about the interaction between person, task, and strategy characteristics (Flavell, 1979).

The Studies

We conducted two experiments in elementary schools in order to assess the effects of dynamic scaffolding on the learning of collaborating students. The small groups worked on one computer in the e-learning environment Ontdeknet on an assignment "*where do I want to live?*" for six lessons. In Ontdeknet students had access to an inhabitant of their country of choice, their expert. Students could consult the expert by asking questions and reading information about the country written by the expert. In both studies, the teachers formed heterogenic groups, i.e., different gender, reading, and computer abilities. These groups were randomly assigned to the experimental or a control condition in school classes. The first study was conducted in the Czech Republic (67 dyads) and focused on the effects of scaffolding on self-regulated learning (also including metacognitive, cognitive, and motivational scaffolds) on group performance and students' domain knowledge. The second study was done in the Netherlands (52 triads) and focused on the effects of metacognitive scaffolding on group performance, the groups' metacognitive activities, and students' domain and metacognitive knowledge. In the first study, the dyads received scaffolding throughout the entire experiment, whereas in the second study, the triads only received scaffolding in the first two lessons. Moreover, in the second study, two different forms of scaffolds were used, i.e., structuring and problematizing scaffolds. We summarize the most important findings from these two studies below. For more detailed descriptions of the method and the results, see Molenaar, van Boxtel, and Sleegers (2010, 2011).

Design and Instruments

In both studies, we measured group performance analyzing the quality of the group paper and individual student's domain knowledge with scores on knowledge tests (Molenaar et al., 2010). In the second study, the transfer of domain knowledge, metacognitive knowledge, and metacognitive activities during learning was also assessed. The transfer of domain knowledge was determined by asking students to sum up all the important topics needed when considering moving to a new country. We measured metacognitive knowledge with a contextual reproduction test; students were asked to imagine that they were going to do the same assignment again and write down all the activities they would perform to control and monitor their learning in this assignment. The answers were scored against a full list of the metacognitive activities ideally performed to control and monitor working on this assignment drawn up by the researchers. The groups' metacognitive activities were analyzed using discourse analysis. All utterances of the small group were coded exclusively with one main code and one subcode. The analysis instrument was based on different think-aloud and discourse instruments (Azevedo & Cromley, 2004; Meijer et al., 2006; Veldhuis-Diermanse, 2002). The main categories were metacognitive, cognitive, relational, procedural, and off-task activities; see Table 36.1 for an overview (Molenaar et al., 2010). The following metacognitive sub-activities were coded: orientation, planning, monitoring, evaluation, and reflection; see Table 36.2 (Lu & Lajoie, 2008; Molenaar et al., 2010; Veenman, Van Hout-Wolters, & Afflerbach, 2006).

Table 36.1 Main categories of our coding scheme

Main category	Description
Metacognitive activities	Turns that deal with the regulation of the cognitive activities in the learning process
Cognitive activities	Turns about the content of the task and the elaboration of this content
Relational activities	Turns that deal with the social interaction between the students in the triad
Procedural activities	Turns that deal with the procedures to use the learning environment
Teacher/researcher	Turns that are made by the teacher or the researcher
Off-task	Turns that are not relevant to the task
Not codable	Turns that are too short or unclear to interpret

Table 36.2 Subcategories of metacognitive activities

Subcategory	Description	Examples
Orientation	Orientation on prior knowledge, task demands, and feelings about the task	What do we need to do?
		Do you know what a learning goal is?
Planning	Planning the learning process, for instance, sequencing activities or choice of strategies	How are we going to do this?
		Now we are going to ask questions
Monitoring	Monitoring the learning process: checking progress and comprehension of the task	I do not understand
		You are doing it wrong
		Wait, please just leave it like that
Evaluation	Evaluation of the learning process; checking the content of the learning activities	We posed a good question
		These are the most important issues
Reflection	Reflection on the learning process and strategies through elaboration of the learning process	Let me think, this is more difficult than I thought
		Why do we have the most difficult task?

Effects of Scaffolding on Performance and Learning Achievements

As mentioned above, we measured group performance and student' domain knowledge in both studies. In the first study, we found a positive effect of scaffolding on group performance, but no effect on the domain knowledge students acquired. In the second study, the groups receiving scaffolds scored, on average, higher than the control groups, but there was no significant effect on group performance. Again no significant effect on the students' domain knowledge was found. The absence of effects of metacognitive scaffolding on the students' domain knowledge is in line with other scaffolding studies, which also failed to find an effect of scaffolding on the quantity of domain knowledge (Bannert, 2006; Bannert et al., 2009; Lin & Lehman, 1999). One argument given for these findings is that metacognitive scaffolding does not affect the quantity, but does enhance the quality of domain knowledge (Bannert, 2006; Bannert et al., 2009). Therefore, in our second study, we included a measurement of transfer of domain knowledge. However, we did not find a significant effect of scaffolding on the transfer of domain knowledge.

The second study also investigated the effects of different forms of scaffolds on learning. We found a significant positive effect of problematizing scaffolds compared with structuring scaffolds on group performance and transfer of domain knowledge. Different forms of scaffolds have a differential effect on learning, the problematizing scaffolds are more effective at enhancing the group product and the transfer of individual domain knowledge. So, even though students did not acquire more knowledge, they could apply it better in their paper and transfer it to new situations.

Effects of Scaffolding on Groups' Metacognitive Activities and Students' Metacognitive Knowledge

The second purpose of scaffolding is to develop knowledge for future learning, in this case metacognitive knowledge. Moreover, many scaffolding studies assume that scaffolding stimulates learning activities and leads to lasting changes in student behavior (Pea, 2004). We therefore analyzed the effects on metacognitive knowledge and on group metacognitive activities during learning in the second study. We found a slight, but significant, positive effect of scaffolding on the metacognitive knowledge students acquired. The results of the discourse analysis that looked at the stimulation of metacognitive activities during scaffolding showed a significant positive effect of scaffolding on the number of metacognitive activities performed. The analysis of different metacognitive activities specified that orientation and monitoring activities were significantly more frequent in triads receiving scaffolding, and a trend in the expected direction was found for planning and evaluation. Finally, we found that triads receiving scaffolds (experimental groups) continued to perform significantly more metacognitive activities once the scaffolding had stopped compared with the triads in the control group. This provides empirical evidence for the assumptions of scaffolding research that scaffolding indeed stimulates metacognitive activities and contributes to lasting changes in the groups' metacognitive activities.

With respect to the effect of different forms of scaffolds on the metacognitive activities, there was also a significant positive effect on the metacognitive knowledge acquired. Students in the problematizing condition acquired significantly more metacognitive knowledge compared with students in the structuring condition. Furthermore, we found no significant difference in the number of metacognitive activities performed by the triads receiving different forms of scaffolds (problematizing structuring). Again the trend was as expected. Finally, the form of scaffolds (structuring vs. problematizing) did not affect the quantity of metacognitive activities after scaffolding ceased, but again the trend was as anticipated.

Link Between Learning Activities and The Individual Knowledge

These results indicate that scaffolding stimulates group metacognitive activities, has a lasting effect on group behavior, and increases students' metacognitive knowledge. However, we did not find an explanation for the differential effects on learning of different forms of scaffolds. There was no significant difference in the number of metacognitive activities fostered by the structuring and problematizing condition. However, we did find enhanced group performance, more transfer of domain knowledge, and more metacognitive knowledge in the problematizing condition. This raises the following question: How do problematizing scaffolds support better learning achievements than structuring scaffolds, even though they do not stimulate more metacognitive activities? In our view, the following reasons may explain these unexpected results. Firstly, the qualitative differences in metacognitive activities might possibly be an explanation indicating that some metacognitive activities are better than others and consequently have more effect on the learning achievements of students. Secondly, differences in students' collaborative discourse around metacognitive activities caused by the different forms of scaffolds might lead to different learning results. Successful collaborative discourse in which students exchange, share, and co-construct knowledge enhances learning (Chi, 2009; Teasley, 1997; Webb, 2009; Weinberger & Fischer, 2006). Problematizing scaffolds may possibly have improved the collaborative discourse. Thirdly, in line with the interdependence between metacognitive activities, the answer could be sought in differences in the sequential relations between the different metacognitive sub-activities (the optimal mix) or the positioning of the metacognitive activities over time. These directions will be explored in future research. In the last section, we discuss the challenges we face in building more effective dynamic systems that support metacognitive scaffolding in complex open learning environments.

Challenges for New Developments

The main limitation for the development of dynamic computerized scaffolding systems is the limited ability to measure metacognitive activities during learning (Azevedo et al., 2010; Greene & Azevedo, 2010; Schraw, 2010; Winne, 2010). In order to enhance the diagnostic, calibrating, and fading functions of computerized scaffolding systems, we need to be able to measure metacognitive activities concurrently during learning. The measurement of metacognitive activities with think-aloud and discourse protocols are performed retrospectively (Azevedo et al., 2010; Veenman, 2011). They are time consuming and can therefore only be applied to a limited dataset. Trace methods based on the log-file information of student's activities, eye tracking, or linguistic analysis are not yet sufficiently well developed to replace think-aloud analysis or discourse analysis concurrently during learning activities. A possible way to proceed is to develop our understanding of the temporal and sequential characteristics of self and social regulation. A better understanding of these aspects would support recognition of patterns as opposed to individual activities.

To date most researchers have analyzed the effect of scaffolding on student activities on a holistic level (Reimann, 2009). Holistic analyses consider the learning process as one whole unit, which restricts our understanding of temporal or sequential aspects within the process (Azevedo et al., 2010; Reimann, 2009; Wampold, 1992). Attention for temporal aspects can help us understand the positioning of metacognitive activities over time, e.g., is more planning at the beginning of a task more useful for learning (Kapur, 2011)? Concentration on sequential aspects supports more insights into the relationship between learning activities, e.g., are planning activities followed by monitoring activities? Accordingly, process analysis that looks at the temporal and sequential aspects would further support our understanding of how metacognitive activities influence learning. Moreover, these analyses provide evidence for theoretical assumptions in models of self-

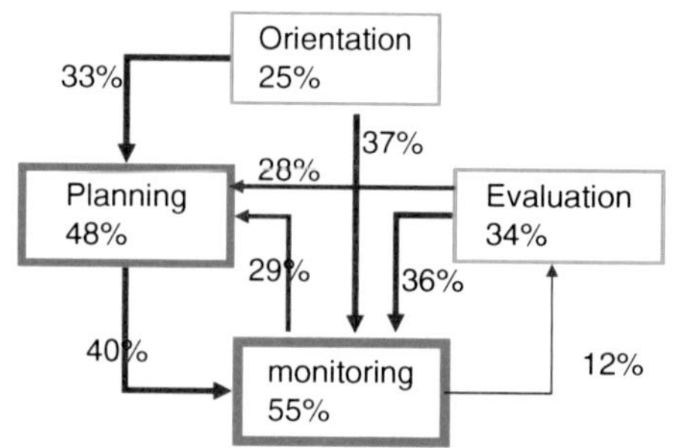

Fig. 36.2 Sequential diagram of sub-metacognitive activities

regulated learning in empirical data. We will illustrate this with an example taken from a sequential analysis. We were looking at the relationship between the different metacognitive activities to assess the assumption that metacognitive activities are cyclical.

We start by briefly introducing sequential analysis (Wampold, 1992). The relationship between metacognitive activities was analyzed as follows: firstly, the number of transitions between the different activities is counted, for example, an orientation activity is followed 300 times by a planning activity. Secondly, the expected transitional frequency is calculated. This is the number of times orientation activities would be followed by planning activities based on chance, for example, 150 times. This means that the likelihood of transition from orientation to planning is greater than expected by chance. Based on a *Z*-test, it is possible to determine whether this transition is significantly more or less likely to occur than expected by chance. Finally, the transaction frequencies indicate the likelihood of an orientation activity to be followed by a planning activity. For example, as shown in Fig. 36.2, 33% of the orientation activities are followed by a planning activity. Note that the percentages in the figure cannot be compared with each other as they are relative to the number of activities that occur.

Figure 36.2 is based on the discourse analysis of metacognitive activities in our second study. It includes over 50,000 activities analyzed and displays all significant transactions that have a transaction likelihood greater than 10% between the different metacognitive activities. Significant positive transaction probabilities indicate that a transition occurs significantly more than chance. In this case, we found that all activities are more likely to follow themselves as shown by the Greene blocks. Significant negative transaction probabilities indicate that a transition occurs significantly less than chance. In this case, all transactions between metacognitive activities occur less than chance as indicated by the red arrows. The percentages shown in the picture are the transaction likelihood; as explained above, an orientation activity has a 33% probability of being followed by a planning activity.

This analysis provided evidence that the metacognitive activities indeed follow each other in a cyclical manner. The transaction likelihood between orientation and planning activities is 33%, and between planning and monitoring activities, it is 40%. Yet the transaction likelihood between monitoring and evaluation activities is rather small—12%. Evaluation activities are unlikely to be followed by orientation activities but do lead to monitoring activities (36%) and planning activities (28%). We can therefore observe the cyclical process between orientation, planning, and monitoring activities, but evaluation activities are more isolated. The unexpected position of evaluation activities could possibly be explained by the development of metacognitive knowledge. The students who participated in our studies were between 10 and 12 years of age. Moreover, we did not scaffold evaluation activities, which might also explain their rather isolated position. These findings support the assumptions made for the design of our scaffolding system and indicate that for learners of this age the scaffolding of evaluation activities is important. Moreover, these analyses partially confirm the assumptions about the cyclical nature of metacognitive activities in the Zimmerman model (2002). This can be helpful for developing new methods to measure metacognitive activities during learning as it shows that we do not necessarily need to focus on single metacognitive activities, but can also look at metacognitive patterns. We used this example to illustrate that new insights can be arrived at with process analysis that focuses on the sequential aspects. Finally, as learning technologies move forward, they face a number of challenges that are not related to the core development of these systems: privacy-related challenges which raise questions about the ethics of registering and interpreting student behavior, financial challenges dealing with cost-effectiveness, and implementation challenges involving integration in the educational system.

Conclusion

In sum, our studies suggest that the dynamic computerized scaffolding of metacognitive activities in small groups can be successfully performed with an attention management system. The AtGentSchool system succeeded in stimulating metacognitive activities of small groups both during and after scaffolding ended. Students who received scaffolds had more metacognitive knowledge compared with students in the control group. With respect to different forms of scaffolds, we found that problematizing scaffolds support group performance and the transfer of domain knowledge more than structuring scaffolds. This indicates that scaffolding in small groups is most effective for learning when problematizing scaffolds are used. We expect that these differential effects of problematizing scaffolds can be explained by qualitative differences in group metacognitive activities.

Furthermore, we expect that metacognitive activities in a group setting seem to contribute to more metacognitive knowledge. However, our current theoretical understanding of metacognitive activities in social settings is derived from theories of individual learning. It is important that we develop our understanding how metacognitive activities are embedded in the groups' interaction. There is a strong emphasis in collaborative learning research on the quality of the interaction between the group members as it has high-quality interaction that positively contributes to learning (Chi, 2009; Webb, 2009; Weinberger & Fischer, 2006). It is therefore important in future research to examine how metacognitive activities embedded in different types of interaction facilitate group learning. Additionally, attention should also be given to the question how scaffolding influences the quality of the interaction and if different forms of scaffolds influence the collaboration between students differently, which can possibly explain differential learning results.

Overall our computerized scaffolding system supports the metacognitive activities of small groups in computer-based learning environments and equips learners with metacognitive knowledge and possibly skills for future learning. Although our system has a positive effect on metacognitive activities and knowledge, there is ample room for improvement. To enhance our computerized scaffolding, it is of great importance to develop concurrent measurement methods to track and trace metacognitive activities during learning. Process analysis with a sequential and temporal focus can increase our understanding of the positioning of metacognitive activities over time and in relation to other learning activities. This would help find new ways to measure metacognitive activities during learning.

References

Azevedo, R., & Cromley, J. G. (2004). Does training on self-regulated learning facilitate students' learning with hypermedia? *Journal of Educational Psychology, 96*(3), 523–535.

Azevedo, R., Cromley, J. G., Winters, F. I., Moos, D. C., & Greene, J. A. (2005). Adaptive human scaffolding facilitates adolescents' self-regulated learning with hypermedia. *Instructional Science, 33*, 381–412.

Azevedo, R. & Green, J. A. (2010). The Measurement of Learners' Self-Regulated Cognitive and Metacognitive Processes while Using Computer-based Learning Enviroments. *Educational Psychologist, 45*, 203–209.

Azevedo, R., & Hadwin, A. F. (2005). Scaffolding self-regulated learning and metacognition—Implications for the design of computer-based scaffolds. *Instructional Science, 33*(5–6), 367–379.

Azevedo, R., Moos, D. C., Greenee, J. A., Winters, F. I., & Cromley, J. G. (2008). Why is externally-facilitated regulated learning more effective than self-regulated learning with hypermedia? *Educational Technology Research and Development, 56*(1), 45–72.

Azevedo, R., Moos, C. D., Johnson, A. M., & Chauncey, A. D. (2010). Measuring cognitive and metacognitive regulatory processes during hypermedia learning: Issues and challenges. *Educational Psychologist, 45*, 210–223.

Bannert, M. (2006). Effects of reflection prompts when learning with hypermedia. *Journal of Educational Computing Research, 35*(4), 359–375.

Bannert, M., Hildebrand, M., & Mengelkamp, C. (2009). Effects of a metacognitive support device in learning environments. *Computers in Human Behavior, 25*(4), 829–835.

Chi, M. (2009). Active-constructive-interactive: A conceptual framework for differentiating learning activities. *Topics in Cognitive Science, 1*(1), 73–105.

Chi, M., Siler, S., Jeong, H., Yamuachi, T., & Hausmann, R. (2001). Learning from human tutoring. *Cognitive Science, 25*, 471–533.

Corno, L., & Mandinach, E. B. (1983). The role of cognitive engagement in classroom learning and motivation. *Educational Psychologist, 18*, 88–108.

Davis, E. A., & Linn, M. (2000). Scaffolding students' knowledge integration: Prompts for reflection in KIE. *International Journal of Science Education, 22*(8), 819–837.

Dillenbourg, P., Järvelä, S., & Fischer, F. (2009). The evolution of research on computer-supported collaborative learning: From design to orchestration. In N. Balacheff, S. Ludvigsen, T. de Jong, T. A. Lazonder, & S. Barnes (Eds.), *Technology-enhanced learning principles and products* (pp. 3–19). Paris: Springer.

Dinsmore, D. L., Alexander, P. A., & Loughlin, S. M. (2008). Focusing the conceptual lens on metacognition, self-regulation, and self-regulated learning. *Educational Psychology Review, 20*, 391–409.

Flavell, J. H. (1979). Metacognition and cognitive monitoring: A new area of cognitive-developmental inquiry. *American Psychologist, 34*(10), 906–911.

Hadwin, A., & Oshige, M. (2007). Self-regulation, co-regulation and socially shared regulation: examining many faces of social in models of SRL. *Paper presented at the EARLI.*

Hmelo-Silver, C. E., & Azevedo, R. (2006). Understanding complex systems: Some core challenges. *The Journal of the Learning Sciences, 15*(1), 53–61.

Iiskala, T., Vauras, M., & Lehtinen, E. (2004). Socially-shared metacognition in peer learning? *Hellenic Journal of Psychology, 1*(2), 147–178.

Iiskala. T., Vauras, M., Lehtinen, E., & Salonen, P. (2011). Socially Shared Metacognition within Primary School Pupil Dyads' Collaborative Processes. Learning and Instruction, 21, 379–393.

Kalyuga, S., Chandler, P., & Sweller, J. (2001). Learner experience and efficiency of instructional guidance. *Educational Psychology, 21*(1), 5–23.

Kapur, M. (2011). Temporality matters: Advancing a method for analyzing problem-solving processes in a computer-supported collaborative environment. *International Journal of Computer-Supported Collaborative Learning, 6*(1), 39–56.

King, A. (1998). Transactive peer tutoring: Distributing cognition and metacognition. *Educational Psychology Review, 10*(1), 57–74.

King, A. (2002). Promoting thinking through peer learning. *Theory into Practice, 41*(1), 33–39.

Kirschner, P. A., Sweller, J., & Clark, R. E. (2006). Why minimal guidance during instruction does not work: An analysis of the failure of constructivist, discovery, problem-based, experiential, and inquiry-based teaching. *Educational Psychologist, 41*(2), 75–86.

Land, S. M., & Greene, B. A. (2000). Project-based learning with the World Wide Web: A qualitative study of resource integration. *Educational Technology Research and Development, 48*(1), 45–67.

Lin, X., & Lehman, J. D. (1999). Supporting learning of variable control in a computer-based biology environment: Effects of prompting college students to reflect on their own thinking. *Journal of Research in Science Teaching, 36*(7), 837–858.

Lu, J., & Lajoie, S. P. (2008). Supporting medical decision making with argumentation tools. *Contemporary Educational Psychology, 33*(3), 425–442.

Meijer, J., Veenman, M. V., & van Hout-Wolters, B. H. (2006). Metacognitive activities in text-studying and problem solving: Development of a taxonomy. *Educational Research and Evaluation, 12*(3), 209–237.

Molenaar, I., & Roda, C. (2008). Attention management for dynamic and adaptive scaffolding. *Pragmatics and Cognition, 16*(2), 224–271.

Molenaar, I., van Boxtel, C., & Sleegers, P. (2010). The effects of scaffolding metacognitive activities in small groups. *Computers in Human Behavior, 26*(6), 1727–1738.

Molenaar, I., van Boxtel, C., & Sleegers, P. (2011). Metacognitive scaffolding in an innovative learning arrangement. *Instructional Science, 39*(6), 785–803. doi:10.1007/s11251-010-9154-1.

Molenaar, I., van Boxtel, C., Sleegers, P., & Roda, C. (2011). Atgentschool: Dynamic scaffolding with attention management. In C. Roda (Ed.), *Human attention in digital environments* (pp. 259–280). Cambridge, MA: Cambridge University Press.

Nelson, T. O. (1996). Consciousness and metacognition. *American Psychologist, 51*, 102–116.

Pea, R. D. (2004). The social and technological dimensions of scaffolding and related theoretical concepts for learning, education and human activity. *The Journal of the Learning Sciences, 13*(3), 423–451.

Puntambekar, S., & Hubscher, R. (2005). Tools for scaffolding students in a complex learning environment: What have we gained and what have we missed? *Educational Psychologist, 40*(1), 1–12.

Reimann, P. (2009). Time is precious: Variable- and event-centred approaches to process analysis in CSCL research. *International Journal of Computer-Supported Collaborative Learning, 3*, 239–257.

Reiser, B. J. (2004). Scaffolding complex learning: The mechanisms of structuring and problematizing student work. *The Journal of the Learning Sciences, 13*(3), 273–304.

Roda, C. (2011). *Attention support in digital systems.* Cambridge, MA: Cambridge University Press.

Roda, C., & Nabeth, T. (2007). *Supporting attention in learning environments: Attention support services, and information management.* Paper presented at the Creating new experiences on a global scale. Second European Conference on Technology Enhanced Learning, EC-TEL 2007, Crete, Greece (pp. 277–229).

Roda, C., & Thomas, J. (2006). Attention aware systems: Theories, applications, and research agenda. *Computers in Human Behavior, 22*(4), 557–587.

Salomon, G. (1993). *Distributed cognitions: Psychological and educational considerations.* Cambridge, MA: Cambridge University Press.

Schraw, G. (2010). Measuring self-regulation in computer-based learning environments. *Educational Psychologist, 45*, 258–266.

Sharma, P., & Hannafin, M. J. (2007). Scaffolding in technology-enhanced learning environments. *Interactive Learning Environments, 15*(1), 27–46.

Simons, P. R. J., van der Linden, J., & Duffy, T. (Eds.). (2000). *New learning*. Dordrecht, Netherlands: Kluwer Academic Publishers.

Teasley, S. (1997). Talking about reasoning: How important is the peer in peer collaboration? In L. B. Resnick, R. Säljö, C. Pontecorvo, & B. Burge (Eds.), *Discourse, tools and reasoning. Essays on situated cognition* (pp. 361–384). Berlin: Springer.

Vauras, M., Iiskala, T., Kajamies, A., Kinnunen, R., & Lehtinen, E. (2003). Shared-regulation and motivation of collaborating peers: A case analysis. *Psychologia, 46*(1), 19–37.

Veenman, M. V. J. (2005). The assessment of metacognitive skills: What can be learned from multimethod designs? In C. Artelt & B. Moschner (Eds.), *Lernstrategien und Metakognition: Implikationen für Forschung und Praxis* (pp. 75–97). Berlin: Waxmann.

Veenman, M. V. J. (2011). Learning to self-monitor and self-regulate. To appear In R. Mayer & P. Alexander (Eds.), *Handbook of research on learning and instruction*. New York: Routledge.

Veenman, M. V. J., Kok, R., & Blote, A. W. (2005). The relation between intellectual and metacognitive skills in early adolescence. *Instructional Science, 33*(3), 193–211.

Veenman, M. V. J., Van Hout-Wolters, B. H. A. M., & Afflerbach, P. (2006). Metacognition and learning: Conceptual and methodological considerations. *Metacognition and Learning, 1*(1), 3–14.

Veldhuis-Diermanse, A. E. (2002). *CSC Learning? Participation, learning activities and knowledge construction in computer-supported collaborative learning in higher education.* Wageningen, Netherlands: University of Wageningen.

Volet, S., Vauras, M., & Salonen, P. (2009). Self- and social regulation in learning contexts: An integrative perspective. *Educational Psychologist, 44*(4), 215–226.

Vygotsky, L. S. (1978). *Mind in society*. Cambridge, MA: Harvard University Press.

Wampold, B. E. (1992). The intensive examination of social interaction. In T. R. Kratochwill & J. R. Levin (Eds.), *Single-case research design and analysis: New directions for psychology and education* (pp. 93–133).

Hillsdale, NJ: Lawrence Erlbaum Associates, Publishers.

Webb, M. (2009). The teacher's role in promoting collaborative dialogue in the classroom. *British Journal of Educational Psychology, 79*, 1–28.

Weinberger, A., & Fischer, F. (2006). A framework to analyze argumentative knowledge construction in computer-supported collaborative learning. *Computers in Education, 46*, 71–95.

Winne, P. H. (2010). Improving measurements of self-regulated learning. *Educational Psychologist, 45*, 267–276.

Winters, F. I., & Alexander, P. A. (2011). Peer collaboration: The relation of regulatory behaviours to learning in hyperspace. *Instructional Science, 39*, 407–427.

Wood, D., Bruner, J., & Ross, G. (1976). The role of tutoring in problem solving. *Journal of Child Psychology and Psychiatry, 17*, 89–100.

Woolf, B. (2009). *Building intelligent interactive tutors*. Burlington, VT: Morgan & Kaufmann.

Zimmerman, B. J. (2002). Becoming a self-regulated learner: An overview. *Theory into Practice, 42*(2), 64–70.

37 Metacognitive Knowledge About and Metacognitive Regulation of Strategy Use in Self-Regulated Scientific Discovery Learning: New Methods of Assessment in Computer-Based Learning Environments

Hubertina Thillmann, Jill Gößling, Jessica Marschner, Joachim Wirth, and Detlev Leutner

Abstract

The aim of this chapter is to present new assessment methods for different aspects of metacognition that are relevant for self-regulated learning (SRL). In the theoretical part, two assumptions on the assessment of different aspects of metacognition are presented. Firstly, we argue that metacognitive knowledge about strategies and metacognitive regulation of strategies are two distinct components of metacognition that make different demands on their respective assessment method. Secondly, we argue that metacognitive knowledge about and metacognitive regulation of strategy use should be assessed with regard to the same strategies, in order to be able to relate both measures and to localize specific deficiencies. In the methods part, the theoretically driven development of two computer-based learning environments (CBLEs) for scientific discovery learning is presented. Based on these, two kinds of assessment methods are presented, a test format that intends to assess metacognitive knowledge about scientific discovery strategies and logfile-based measures that intend to assess metacognitive regulation of the use of these strategies during SRL with the CBLEs. In the empirical part, three studies are presented that investigated

H. Thillmann, Ph.D. (✉) • J. Marschner, Ph.D.
• J. Wirth, Ph.D.
Department of Research on Learning and Instruction,
Ruhr-University Bochum, GA 2/133, Universitätsstraße 150,
Bochum 44801, Germany
e-mail: hubertina.thillmann@rub.de

J. Gößling, Ph.D., M.Sc. • D. Leutner, Ph.D.
Department of Instructional Psychology, Duisburg-Essen
University, P.O. Box 45117, Essen, Germany

R. Azevedo and V. Aleven (eds.), *International Handbook of Metacognition and Learning Technologies*, Springer International Handbooks of Education 26, DOI 10.1007/978-1-4419-5546-3_37,

the test quality of these new assessment methods as well as the relationship between metacognitive knowledge about and metacognitive regulation of the same strategy. In sum, results speak in favor of a good test quality of the new assessment methods. Based on this, results revealed that the relationship between metacognitive knowledge about and metacognitive regulation of the actual use of the same strategy is moderated by current motivation. Finally, results are discussed with respect to the development of further instruments as well as with respect to approaches of SRL support.

SRL and Metacognition

Models of self-regulated learning (SRL) agree that self-regulated learners need to have metacognitive knowledge about strategies (Flavell, 1979) and need to metacognitively regulate the use of these strategies (Brown, 1987) (e.g., Boekaerts, 1997; Pressley, Borkowski, & Schneider, 1987; Winne & Hadwin, 1998; Zimmerman, 2000). Like in Boekaerts' (1997) six-component model of SRL, most models of SRL implicitly assume that what learners know, i.e., their metacognitive knowledge about strategies, should influence what they do, i.e., their metacognitive regulation of strategy use, which in turn should influence learning outcome. Only few models make explicit assumptions about the relationship between learners' metacognitive knowledge about and their metacognitive regulation of strategy use. For example, Pressley and colleagues (e.g., Pressley, 1995; Pressley et al., 1987) assume that there is no direct relationship but that there are rather several variables, such as prior knowledge and motivation that moderate the relationship between what learners know about strategies and what they actually do. Except metamemory research that focuses on the metacognitive knowledge about and metacognitive regulation of memory strategies (e.g., Körkel & Schneider, 1992; Schneider, Körkel, & Weinert, 1987), still little is known about the relationship between these two components of metacognition. We assume that this research deficit is due to a lack of assessment methods that differentially assess what self-regulated learners know about strategies and what they actually do. Thus, in order to empirically investigate this relationship, there is a need to develop objective, reliable, and valid measures for these components of metacognition in SRL. For developing appropriate measures, we assume that the following methodological demands need to be clarified: First, the methodological demands of assessing different components of metacognition, namely, metacognitive knowledge about strategies and metacognitive regulation of strategy use, should be taken into account. Second, also the objectives of metacognition, namely, the specific kinds of strategies that have to be known and regulated in the specific learning situation, should be taken into account. The latter demand might seem to be somehow trivial, but a look at the literature shows it is not. For example, in the German extension of PISA 2000, both metacognitive knowledge about reading strategies and the use of reading strategies were assessed with separate tests. However, the strategies assessed by each test were not the same. Consequently, results of this study seemed to be somehow unintuitive, as metacognitive knowledge about and the use of reading strategies were only weakly correlated and metacognitive knowledge about reading strategies turned out to better predict reading competency as compared to reading strategy use (cf. Artelt, Demmrich, & Baumert, 2001). This unintuitive result might be due to the fact that the metacognitive knowledge about reading strategies and the use of reading strategies was measured with different tests, but these tests did not focus the same strategies.

Components of Metacognition in SRL

According to the first point, we suggest that metacognitive knowledge needs different methods of assessment from metacognitive regulation. Following Flavell (1979), metacognitive knowledge can be divided into metacognitive knowledge about the task, about the person, and about strategies. He further assumed that a learner needs the interaction of these three kinds of knowledge in order to decide which kind of available strategies are appropriate in order to solve the specific task. Paris, Lipson, and Wixson (1983) further divided metacognitive knowledge about strategies into declarative knowledge about what the strategy is, procedural knowledge about how the strategy is performed, and conditional knowledge about when and why the strategy should be effective in a certain situation. Referring to cognitive models about knowledge acquisition (e.g., Anderson, 1983), they assumed that learners can only verbalize their declarative knowledge explicitly, while their procedural and conditional knowledge about strategies is stored in implicit memory. Based on this assumption, that can be regarded as a constraint for assessing metacognitive knowledge about strategies. Schlagmüller and Schneider (2007) developed a new test format for assessing learners' explicit as well as implicit metacognitive knowledge about strategies. The Würzburger Lesestrategie wissenstest (Würzburger reading strategy knowledge test, WLST 7-12; Schlagmüller & Schneider, 2007; see also Schneider, Schlagmüller, & Visé, 1998) is the first test with this specific test format. It presents typical learning situations with reading tasks combined with a list of strategies that are more or less appropriate in order to effectively solve the specific task. Learners have to rate the situation-specific appropriateness of each given strategy by giving school grades. Their strategy knowledge score is calculated as the degree of agreement between the learner's individual rating and an aggregated expert rating. Due to the closed answering format, the test is objective. Furthermore, it showed good reliability and hints of validity (Ramm et al., 2006; Schlagmüller & Schneider, 2007). Beyond that, the test has already been successfully adapted for assessing metacognitive knowledge about mathematical strategies in the German extension of PISA 2003 (see Ramm et al., 2006).

Following Brown (1987), metacognitive regulation can be divided into three subprocesses, namely, metacognitive planning, monitoring, and evaluating one's own cognitive processes. According to Winne (1996), "... [metacognitive] monitoring is the fulcrum upon which SRL pivots" (p. 331). If learners do not monitor at all or incorrectly monitor their use of learning strategies, they will not notice if their strategy use does not lead them towards their learning goals. Because metacognitive monitoring of strategy use like strategy use itself is a behavioral process, Winne and Perry (2000) as well as Veenman (2005) and Wirth (2008) argue that concurrent or online measures are needed to assess the ongoing process. Compared to offline measures, like retrospective questionnaires or interviews, online measures like think-aloud protocols or logfile measures should be more appropriate to assess SRL as an event (cf. Winne & Perry, 2000). Consequently, only under specific circumstances, namely, when the measures for metacognitive regulation of strategy use as well as for learning outcome are directly related to a specific learning situation (regarding time and content), positive correlations can be found between metacognitive regulation of strategy use and learning outcome (cf. Spörer & Brunstein, 2006). Thus, we want to put the focus on online measures of metacognitive regulation. The most common online measures for assessing metacognitive regulation of strategy use are think-aloud protocols and logfile-based measures (cf. Veenman, 2005). On the one hand, think-aloud protocols have a good reliability and validity, but they are a relatively time-consuming assessment method (e.g., Azevedo, Moos, Johnson, & Chauncey, 2010; Bannert & Mengelkamp, 2008; Cromley & Azevedo, 2006; Greene, Muis, & Pieschl, 2010; Veenman, 2005; Veenman, van Hout-Wolters, & Afflerbach, 2006; Vollmeyer & Rheinberg, 2000; Winne & Perry, 2000; Wirth, 2008). First, they require single-person testing because the learner has to speak out everything that comes to his or her mind. Second, the recorded verbalizations have to be transcribed into protocols which then can be analyzed by coding schemes. On the other hand, logfile-based measures of metacognitive regulation are based on the use of CBLEs. Within these CBLEs, learners' actions are automatically recorded into logfiles, which can then be analyzed with respect to action patterns that indicate metacognitive regulation. Logfile-based measures of metacognitive regulation of strategy use also show hints of validity (e.g., Hadwin, Nesbit, Code, Jamieson-Noel, & Winne, 2007; Perry & Winne, 2006; Thillmann, Künsting, Wirth, & Leutner, 2009; Veenman, 2005; Winne & Jamieson-Noel, 2002). Furthermore, they are less time consuming due to two features. First, logfile-based measures can be assessed in group testing. Second, the recording as well as the coding is automated because the algorithms are implemented once and can be applied unlimitedly.

Thus, in order to investigate different components of metacognition in SRL, we argue for using different assessment methods for assessing metacognitive knowledge about strategies and metacognitive regulation of strategies. In more detail, we suggest to use a test format analogous to the WLST 7-12 (Schlagmüller & Schneider, 2007) in order to assess metacognitive knowledge about strategies and to use logfile-based measures in order to assess metacognitive regulation of actual strategy use (e.g., Winne & Perry, 2000; Wirth, 2008).

Objectives of Metacognition in SRL

According to the second point, we suggest that it is necessary to assess metacognitive knowledge and metacognitive regulation concerning the same strategies, in order to be able to relate learners' knowledge about and their actual use of the same strategies to another. Based on the assumption that the kinds of learning strategies that have to be metacognitively known and regulated depend on the specific kind of learning task in the specific learning situation (e.g., Flavell, 1979; Winne & Hadwin, 1998), a detailed task analysis is needed in order to identify relevant strategies that have to be metacognitively known and regulated. As in the following studies, the focus will be on SRL within scientific discovery learning environments; the strategic demands of this kind of SRL will be analyzed in the following: Scientific discovery learning environments or inquiry learning environments enable learners to actively construct their knowledge by systematically experimenting within a domain and inferring the underlying relationships and rules from the results of the experiments (de Jong & van Joolingen, 1998; Klahr & Dunbar, 1988; Kuhn, Black, Keselman, & Kaplan, 2000; Njoo & de Jong, 1993; van Joolingen & de Jong, 1993). The Scientific Discovery as Dual Search (SDDS) model by Klahr and Dunbar (1988) describes scientific discovery learning as a systematic search in two representational "spaces." In the hypothesis space, learners have to choose between all possible hypotheses that can be stated about the learning environment at hand. In the experiment space, learners have to choose between all possible experiments that can be run in the given learning environment. The core assumption of the SDDS model is that successful scientific discovery learning can be described as the synchronized search in both representational spaces by relating the content of one's stated hypotheses to one's own experiments and vice versa. Translating the assumptions of the SDDS model into terms of SRL, scientific discovery learning environments enable learners to strategically generate and process information by interacting with the learning environment in order to understand the domain presented by the learning environment (e.g., Thillmann et al., 2009; Wirth & Leutner, 2006). Within this theoretical frame, the learning process can be described as self-regulating the use of strategies for stating and refining hypotheses and for running systematic experiments. A prominent strategy for running systematic experiments is the control-of-variables strategy (CVS; e.g., Klahr & Dunbar, 1988). The CVS can be defined as testing the effect of an independent variable on a dependent variable by varying only this independent variable and keeping all other independent variables constant. Stating and refining hypotheses can be realized by different strategies, for example, by writing a verbal protocol about one's ideas (Klahr & Dunbar, 1988) or by using a more structured hypothesis scratch pad (van Joolingen & de Jong, 1993).

Thus, in order to investigate the relationship between different components of metacognition in SRL with scientific discovery learning environments, we argue for developing different assessment methods for learners' metacognitive knowledge about and metacognitive regulation of two kinds of the same cognitive strategies, namely, for running systematic experiments as well as for stating and refining hypotheses.

Research Questions

We want to investigate whether (1) metacognitive knowledge about cognitive strategies for SRL with scientific discovery learning environments can be assessed in an objective, reliable, and valid manner by a strategy knowledge test with an analogous test format to the Würzburger reading strategy knowledge test (WLST 7-12; Schlagmüller & Schneider, 2007). Additionally, we want to investigate whether (2) metacognitive regulation of cognitive strategies for SRL with scientific discovery learning environments can be assessed in an objective, reliable, and valid manner by logfile-based measures. Beyond that, we want to investigate (3) the relationship between metacognitive knowledge about and metacognitive regulation of cognitive strategies in SRL with scientific learning environments.

Methods

Computer-Based Scientific Discovery Learning Environments

In order to investigate SRL with scientific discovery learning environments, two computer-based scientific discovery learning environments were developed (Fig. 37.1). The theoretically driven conception of these CBLEs was based on the SDDS model (Klahr & Dunbar, 1988).

Therefore, both CBLEs have an analogous formal structure comprising an external representation of the experiment space which is called the "lab" (on the left side of the computer screen) and of the hypothesis space which is called the "notepad" (on the right side of the computer screen). The lab consists of an interactive tool for running simulated experiments. Therefore, it offers the opportunity to choose values for the independent variables for running experiments and to observe the effects on the values of the dependent variables. These effects are produced by the underlying algorithm of the simulation, which is determined by the relationships and regularities of the respective content of the CBLE. The notepad consists of an interactive graphical tool for stating and refining hypotheses. It offers the opportunity to draw concept maps by choosing between all concepts that are presented in the lab, independent and dependent variables, as well as between different arrows and labels that can be used for connecting the concepts. All actions within the CBLEs can be conducted by drag and drop with the computer mouse and are automatically recorded into logfiles. For every action that is recorded, the logfile contains a time stamp, the kind of action that was conducted as well as the variables and variable values that were used. Thus, the logfiles build the basis for analyzing individual learning behavior or more specifically metacognitive regulation of strategy use.

With respect to the content structure, the two CBLEs are located within two science domains, namely, physics and chemistry, and were developed in collaboration with physics and chemistry educationalists. As Fig. 37.1 shows, one CBLE presents "buoyancy in liquids" and the other CBLE presents "acids and bases." Referring to the German school curriculum, these learning topics are intended for the 9th to 10th grade of science education in secondary school. Thus, in order to have learners to discover the topics of the CBLEs, they should have no systematic prior knowledge due to school education. Thus, the samples of our studies consisted of students from 8th to 10th grades of secondary school who are about 15 years old. Both CBLEs are introduced by short interactive tutorials that explain all functions and train all actions that are later needed for SRL with the CBLE.

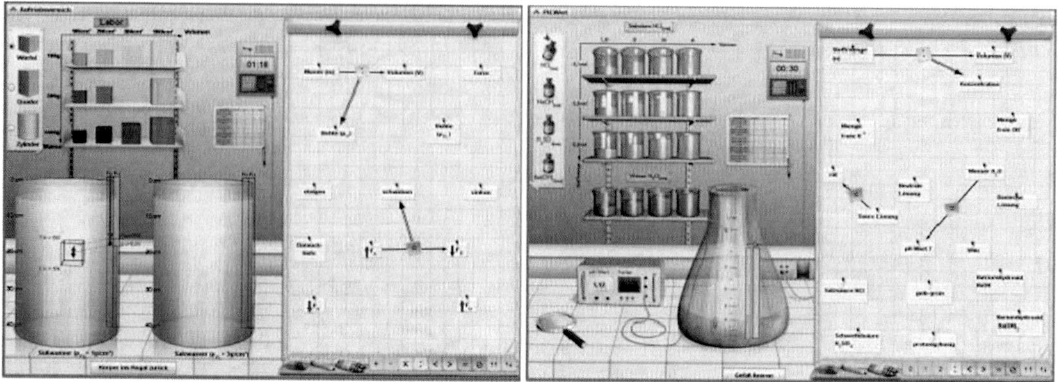

Fig. 37.1 Screenshots of the CBLEs "buoyancy in liquids" and "acids and bases"

Logfile-Based Measures of Metacognitive Regulation of Strategies

Based on the automatically recorded logfiles, different behavioral indicators of metacognitive regulation of strategy use were calculated. First, metacognitive regulation of the use of the CVS was detected in a logfile when learners had run two successive experiments in the experiment space and when all independent variables except one were kept constant across both experiments. The score for metacognitive regulation of the use of the CVS is based on the frequency of run experiments with CVS during SRL. Second, metacognitive regulation of stating or refining hypotheses was detected in a logfile when learners had stated or refined a hypothesis in the hypotheses space by connecting at least two concepts by a labeled link. The score for metacognitive regulation of stating or refining hypotheses is based on the frequency of stated or refined hypothesis during SRL.

Test on Metacognitive Knowledge About Strategies

In order to assess learners' metacognitive knowledge about strategies for SRL with scientific discovery learning environments, two versions of a new strategy knowledge test were developed.

The content of the Essener experimenting strategy knowledge test (EEST) focuses on metacognitive knowledge about the CVS. The test format is analogous to the WLST 7-12 (Schlagmüller & Schneider, 2007). As Fig. 37.2 shows, it consists of drafted scientific discovery learning situations each combined with a list of given action alternatives which describe the more or less elaborated use of the CVS. Learners have to rate the situation-specific utility of these action alternatives. The score on metacognitive knowledge about the CVS is based on quasi-pair comparisons between action alternatives. For example, if the experts agree that alternative (c) is better than alternative (b), learners get one point if their rating is in the same direction. Furthermore, learners get a half point when they rated (b) equally good as (c), and they get no point when they rated (b) better than (c). Thus, the score on metacognitive knowledge about the CVS is calculated as the amount of congruence between the learners' rating and an aggregated expert rating.

The EEST-2 includes three variations compared to the EEST. First, in order to better integrate the test administration into a computer-based testing, we switched from a paper-pencil-based test format to a computer-based test format. Second, in order to directly assess what will be analyzed afterwards, namely, paired comparisons of action alternatives, we changed from a rating answer format to a forced-choice answer format. Third, we extended the test from metacognitive

	School grades					
You want to find out, whether the room temperature changes when the fridge is opened. The following approaches for testing your idea come to your mind. Please score them with school grades (1=very good to 6=insufficient):	(A) 1	(B) 2	(C) 3	(D) 4	(E) 5	(F) 6
a) I compare the temperature within the fridge with the temperature outside the fridge.	□	□	□	□	□	□
b) I measure the room temperature when the fridge is opened.	□	□	□	□	□	□
c) I measure the room temperature before and after the fridge is opened.	□	□	□	□	□	□
d) I measure the room temperature repeatedly before and after the fridge is opened.	□	□	□	□	□	□
e) I measure the room temperature not until window and door are closed.	□	□	□	□	□	□

Fig. 37.2 Example item of the EEST on metacognitive knowledge about the CVS

knowledge about the CVS to metacognitive knowledge about stating and refining hypotheses. Thus, the EEST-2 also presents short sketches of scientific discovery learning situations each combined with three pairs of action alternatives that differ in their situational appropriateness. For each pair of action alternatives, learners had to decide which is the more appropriate one. A metacognitive strategy knowledge score is calculated as the number of correct answers.

Further Instruments

For validation of the new measures of metacognitive knowledge about and metacognitive regulation of strategies, further variables were assessed within the empirical studies. First, learners' content-specific knowledge about the learning contents of the CBLEs was assessed by two multiple-choice tests, one on "buoyancy in liquids" and one on "acids and bases." Both tests were administered computer based. Furthermore, both tests were administered twice, before and after SRL with the respective CBLE. The score on learning outcome was calculated as the standardized residual of a linear regression analysis predicting content-specific knowledge after learning (post) by content-specific knowledge before learning (pre). Second, learners' current motivation right before SRL was assessed by the subscales "challenge" and "interest" from the Questionnaire on Current Motivation (QCM; Rheinberg, Vollmeyer, & Burns, 2001). This motivation questionnaire was also administered computer-based. The motivation score was calculated as the mean of agreement. Third, learners' demographic data, like age, gender, and school grades, were assessed by a short demographic questionnaire that was administered paper-pencil-based.

Empirical Findings

Study 1

In order to investigate the first and the second research question on the test quality of the newly developed measures on metacognitive knowledge about and metacognitive regulation of scientific discovery strategies, we conducted a correlation study. In this first study, we investigated metacognitive knowledge about scientific discovery strategies and metacognitive regulation of the use of these strategies during SRL with the CBLEs on "buoyancy in liquids" and on "acids and bases."

Methods

Two hundred sixty-nine 8th- and 9th-grade students from upper secondary schools took part in this study. Their mean age was 14.2 years (SD=0.80) with 40.2% female. The study took place on two sessions during regular school lessons, each lasting about 90 min. In the first session, students filled in the demographic questionnaire, the pretest on content-specific knowledge according to the first CBLE (either "buoyancy in liquids" or "acids and bases") and the EEST-2 (day 1-pre). After the tutorial for the first CBLE and the instruction to learn, students answered the motivation questionnaire (day 1). During 15 min of SRL with the CBLE, all actions were recorded automatically into a logfile. After learning, students filled in the posttest on content-specific knowledge according to the first CBLE. The second session began with the pretest on content-specific knowledge according to the second CBLE. After the tutorial for the second CBLE and the instruction for SRL, students answered the motivation questionnaire (day 2). During 15 min of SRL with the CBLE, all actions were recorded automatically into a logfile. After learning, students filled in the posttest on content-specific knowledge according to the second CBLE.

Results

Because the CBLE on "acids and bases" turned out to put too high demands on learners, the following results will concentrate on the CBLE on "buoyancy in liquids." With regard to the first research question, results of the test on metacognitive knowledge about scientific discovery strategies showed acceptable reliability at least for the post-version, with Cronbach's alpha=0.57 (pre) and Cronbach's alpha=0.74 (post). Positive correlations were found between metacognitive knowledge about scientific discovery strategies and learning outcome (metacognitive knowledge pre: $r=0.11$; n.s.; metacognitive knowledge post: $r=0.31$; $p<0.01$). Finding only a significant correlation between metacognitive strategy knowledge-assessed post and learning outcome is in line with theoretical assumptions on the activation of metacognitive strategy knowledge in the learning phase and can be interpreted as a hint of construct validity of the EEST-2. Furthermore, positive correlations between metacognitive knowledge about scientific discovery strategies and the school grades ($0.16 \leq r \leq 0.27$; $p<0.05$), especially in the science courses physics, chemistry, and biology gave further hints of validity. With regard to the second research question, Fig. 37.3 shows a path model with different logfile-based measures of metacognitive regulation of strategy use predicting learning outcome. As can be seen from the path model, metacognitive regulation of CVS use ($\beta=0.15$; $p<0.05$) as well as of stating or refining hypotheses ($\beta=0.12$; $p<0.05$, one-tailed) and current motivation ($\beta=0.20$; $p<0.05$) show a small but significant effect on learning outcome, whereas running unsystematic experiments without CVS ($\beta=0.00$; n.s.) did not. This model has an acceptable fit ((X^2 3)=0.83; $p=0.842$; CFI=1.00; FMIN=0.003; RMSEA=0.00). This result can be regarded as a first hint of validity of the logfile-based measures of metacognitive regulation of strategy use.

In sum, results of the first study show that the newly developed test on metacognitive knowledge about the scientific discovery strategies, especially when administered after learning, has an acceptable reliability and shows the expected positive correlations with learning outcome and school grades. Regarding the logfile-based measures on the use of these strategies, results show the expected pattern of correlations with learning outcome that can be interpreted as first hints of validity.

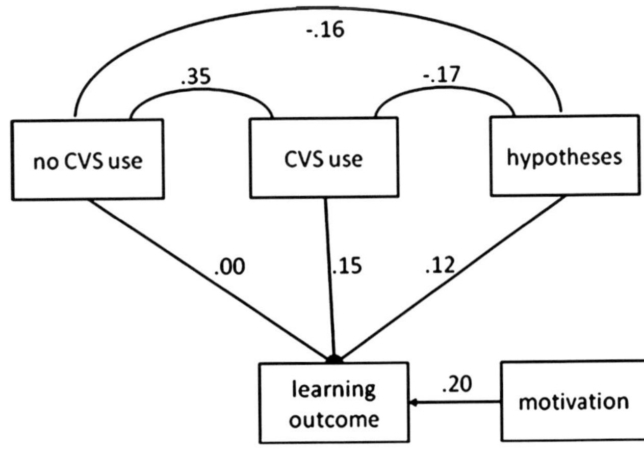

Fig. 37.3 Path model of Study 1

Study 2

In order to further investigate the test quality of the logfile-based measures on metacognitive regulation of scientific discovery strategies, we conducted a second correlation study. We used a multi-method approach in order to validate our logfile-based measures for stating and refining hypotheses as well as for using CVS. Both strategies were assessed computer-based using the CBLE on "buoyancy in liquids." The resulting logfile data were analyzed afterwards by the computer using the same algorithms described above. Additionally, learners were asked to think aloud while learning with the CBLE, and protocols of these think-aloud processes were analyzed and coded afterwards by a trained human coder. Furthermore, we recorded every event on the computer screen into video streams. We used these videos as a separate source of data. These video data, of course, should highly correlate with the logfile data since both kinds of data result from the same learner-computer interaction. However, it includes all data available, whereas logfile data only include data the computer was told to log. Thus, it could happen that the logfiles miss systematically specific information because they were systematically not logged. Comparing video data with logfile data can help in identifying such systematic missing data. Furthermore, the video data were analyzed by a human coder using high inferential ratings which could not be implemented into a computer algorithm.

Methods

Sixteen 9th-grade students from an upper secondary school took part in this correlation study. Their mean age was 14.4 years (SD=0.62) with 44% male. Each of them was tested separately during their regular school time. After the tutorial for the CBLE, students were trained to think aloud for about 10 min. Afterwards, students learned for 15 min with the CBLE. During this time, their mouse clicks were written into logfiles, and every event was video-recorded. Furthermore, students were asked to think aloud.

Results

Results reveal that logfile measures are highly suitable for assessing the use of CVS. The correlation between think-aloud and logfile data is, in fact, quite low (Spearman's rho=0.385). However, the respective correlation with video data is quite high (Spearman's rho=0.846). The low correlation with think-aloud data results from the fact that students verbalized what they did only at the beginning of the learning process. But they ceased verbalizing their experimental behavior very soon, although they were continuously instructed to talk out loud what they thought. Thus, think-aloud data underestimated the number of experiments and the use of CVS leading to low variance and low covariances, respectively.

Concerning stating and refining hypotheses, it turns out that, on the one hand, hypotheses can be identified in logfile data and that the hypotheses found in the logfile data were validated by think-aloud data and video data. On the other hand, logfile data contained much less indicators of hypotheses than think-aloud or video data. That means that logfile data underestimated the frequency of stating and refining hypotheses resulting in zero correlations with think-aloud and video data. This is probably due to the specific way students had to state hypotheses in the computer-based notepad. Although they were trained to use the notepad in advance, it was obviously much easier for the students to verbalize their hypotheses than expressing them in the notepad.

In sum, results of the second study show that logfile-based measures can be valid indicators for the use of the CVS and that they identify controlled experiments even more reliable than indicators based on think-aloud data. However, concerning stating and refining hypotheses, logfile-based measures often fail to identify hypotheses. It seems that logfile data are especially suitable for measures that indicate the use and the regulation of strategies that usually result in overt behavior. But if students are forced to express cognitive strategies in some kind of overt behavior they are not sufficiently familiar with, then logfile data tend to underestimate the occurrence of these strategies.

Study 3

In order to investigate the relationship between metacognitive knowledge about and metacognitive regulation of the one and the same strategy, we conducted a third correlation study in which we put the focus on metacognitive knowledge about the CVS and metacognitive regulation of the use of the CVS during SRL with the CBLE on "buoyancy in liquids."

Methods

Two hundred eighty-six 8th- to 10th-grade students from all types of German secondary schools took part in this correlation study. Their mean age was 15.1 years (SD = 0.90) with 51% female. The study took about 90 min during regular school lessons. Students began with answering the questionnaire on demographic data. Next, students filled in the test on metacognitive knowledge about the CVS and the pretest on content-specific knowledge about buoyancy. After the CBLE tutorial and the instruction for SRL, students had to answer questions on their motivation. During the 20 min of SRL with the CBLE, all actions were recorded automatically into a logfile. After learning, students filled in the posttest on content-specific knowledge about buoyancy.

Results

Again, with regard to the first research question, results revealed an acceptable reliability of the test on metacognitive knowledge about the CVS with Cronbach's alpha = 0.75. A positive correlation between metacognitive knowledge about the CVS and learning outcome ($r = 0.19$; $p < 0.01$) revealed a hint of construct validity. Regarding the second research question, again results revealed a positive correlation between metacognitive regulation of the use of the CVS and learning outcome ($r = 0.20$; $p < 0.01$) as a hint of construct validity.

With regard to the third research question, a correlation analysis revealed a positive correlation of $r = 0.21$ ($p < 0.01$) between metacognitive knowledge about the CVS and metacognitive regulation of its actual use. At a first glance, this correlation seems to be significant but small. Therefore, we tested the assumption stated by Pressley and colleagues (Pressley, 1995; Pressley et al., 1987) who assumed motivation to be one potential moderator on this relationship. An ANCOVA with current motivation and metacognitive knowledge about the CVS predicting metacognitive regulation of CVS use revealed an interaction effect, $F(1,279) = 2.91$; $p < 0.05$; partial

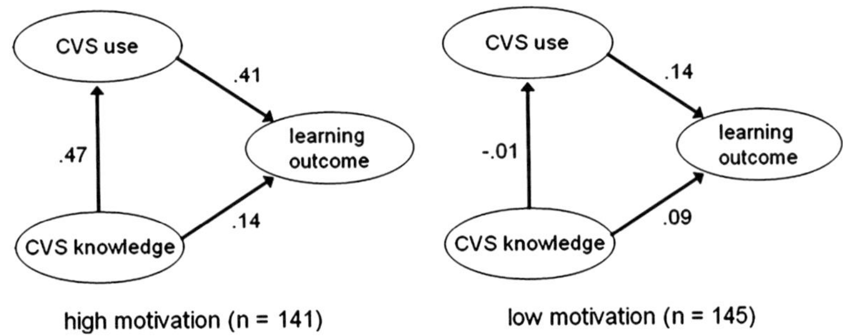

Fig. 37.4 Structural equation models of Study 3

$eta^2=0.01$. Thus, at a second glance, current motivation turned out to moderate the relationship between metacognitive knowledge about the CVS and metacognitive regulation of its actual use. In order to illustrate this moderation effect, we calculated two linear structural equation models on the basis of splitting the sample by the median of current motivation. A chi²-difference test showed that it is worth to allow for two different path coefficients instead of restricting to one ($\Delta X^2=7.68$; $\Delta df=1$; $p=0.006$). As can be seen in Fig. 37.4, while highly motivated students made use of their metacognitive knowledge about the CVS, less motivated students did not make use of it.

In sum, results of the third study confirmed the good test quality of the test on metacognitive knowledge about the CVS and of the logfile-based measure on metacognitive regulation of the same strategy. Furthermore, results show that it is worthwhile to measure metacognitive knowledge about and metacognitive regulation of the same strategy because this makes it possible to observe the relationship between those two. Lastly, results emphasize the role of motivation during SRL with scientific discovery learning environments, revealing a moderating role of current motivation on the relationship between metacognitive strategy knowledge and metacognitive regulation of the CVS.

Overall Discussion and Implications

To sum up, with respect to the first and the second research question, our results speak in favor of a good test quality of the newly developed test on metacognitive knowledge about scientific discovery strategies and the logfile-based measures of metacognitive regulation of these strategies. Thus, in order to develop assessment methods for investigating further kinds of SRL, we suggest the following steps: (1) to draft a theoretical model of the strategic demands of the specific kind of SRL, (2) to develop a CBLE that operationalizes the strategic demands of this specific kind of SRL, and (3) to develop a test on metacognitive knowledge about appropriate strategies and logfile-based measures for the metacognitive regul ation of strategy use. With respect to the third research question, our results empirically confirm the assumptions by Pressley and colleagues (Pressley, 1995; Pressley et al., 1987), revealing a moderating role of current motivation on the relationship between metacognitive knowledge about and metacognitive regulation of strategies in SRL.

With respect to limitations of the presented results, there are three points to highlight. First, we could not report any data about the CBLE on “acids and bases” because demands were too high for learners. We assume that this is due to the formal complexity of the chemical content of the CBLE that does not only include linear relationships between variables like the physics CBLE. Thus, we assume that exploring these nonlinear relationships was too difficult for our sample. Second, we could neither report any data on the reliability of the logfile-based measures because until now there are no adequate reliability coefficients available. Because the values of the logfile-based measures are assumed to vary across time, it does not make sense to generate scales based on time segments and to calculate their split-half reliability or their internal consistency. Thus, as reliability is a precondition for validity, so far we have to rely on the results on validity. Third, although results on the validity of our new measures are always consistent with our hypotheses and statistically significant, correlation coefficients are small. We assume that this is mainly due to the specific focus on the CVS. As successful self-regulated learners should choose from a repertoire of scientific discovery strategies, the CVS should only be one strategy in their repertoire. Thus, assessing metacognitive knowledge about and metacognitive regulation of the CVS is expected to explain only a small amount of variance of learning outcome. In sum, we conclude that the results of the presented studies should be replicated in further studies. Additionally, the relationship that was found between metacognitive knowledge about and metacognitive regulation of strategies should be tested for further strategies and in further learning environments in order to test its generalizability.

Finally, our results have implications for developing support for metacognition in SRL. Referring to Flavell (1979), the first challenge would be to have a comprehensive diagnostic assessment of learners' competencies first in order to design adequate, effective, and efficient support for SRL afterwards. Thus, according to Veenman et al. (2006), strategy trainings would be indicated only in case of a mediation deficiency. Accordingly, support methods like prompting (e.g., Azevedo, Cromley, & Seibert, 2004; Chi, De Leeuw, Chiu, & LaVancher, 1994; Davis, 2003; Thillmann et al., 2009; Wichmann & Leutner, 2009) would be indicated in case of a production deficiency. Referring to Azevedo and colleagues (2004), the second challenge lies in the development of individually adaptive online support during SRL. Based on the presented logfile-based measures for metacognitive regulation of strategy use, we argue for going one step further by assessing and analyzing logfiles not only after SRL but also concurrently during SRL. This should be the prerequisite for designing individually adaptive online support that is aligned to learners' actual needs. Referring to Wolters (2003), a final challenge for future SRL research lies in investigating motivation not only as a precondition or product of SRL but also as a subject of regulation within SRL.

References

Anderson, J. R. (1983). *The architecture of cognition*. Cambridge: Harvard University Press.

Artelt, C., Demmrich, A., & Baumert, J. (2001). Selbstreguliertes Lernen. [Self-regulated learning.]. In J. Baumert, E. Klieme, M. Neubrand, M. Prenzel, U. Schiefele, W. Schneider, P. Stanat, K.-J. Tillmann, & M. Weiß (Eds.), *PISA 2000. Basiskompetenzen von Schülerinnen und Schülern im internationalen Vergleich [PISA 2000. School students' basic competencies in the international comparison]* (pp. 271–298). Opladen: Leske & Budrich.

Azevedo, R., Cromley, J. G., & Seibert, D. (2004). Does adaptive scaffolding facilitate students' ability to regulate their learning with hypermedia? *Contemporary Educational Psychology, 29*, 344–370.

Azevedo, R., Moos, D. C., Johnson, A. M., & Chauncey, A. D. (2010). Measuring cognitive and metacognitive regulatory processes during hypermedia learning: Issues and challenges. *Educational Psychologist, 45*, 210–223.

Bannert, M., & Mengelkamp, C. (2008). Assessment of metacognitive skills by means of instruction to think aloud and reflect when prompted. Does the verbalisation method affect learning? *Metacognition & Learning, 3*, 39–58.

Boekaerts, M. (1997). Self-regulated learning: a new concept embraced by researchers, policy makers, educators, teachers, and students. *Learning and Instruction, 7*, 161–186.

Brown, A. (1987). Metacognition, executive control, self-regulation, and other more mysterious mechanisms. In F. E. Weinert & R. H. Kluwe (Eds.), *Metacognition, motivation, and understanding* (pp. 65–116). Hillsdale, New Jersey: Lawrence Erlbaum Associates.

Chi, M. T. H., De Leeuw, N., Chiu, M.-H., & LaVancher, C. (1994). Eliciting self-explanations improves understanding. *Cognitive Science, 18*, 439–477.

Cromley, J. G., & Azevedo, R. (2006). Self-report of reading comprehension strategies: What are we measuring? *Metacognition & Learning, 1*, 229–247.

Davis, E. A. (2003). Prompting middle school science students for productive reflection: Generic and directed prompts. *The Journal of the Learning Sciences, 12*, 91–142.

De Jong, T., & van Joolingen, W. R. (1998). Scientific discovery learning with computer simulations of conceptual domains. *Review of Educational Research, 68*, 179–201.

Flavell, J. H. (1979). Metacognition and cognitive monitoring. A new area of cognitive-developmental inquiry. *American Psychologist, 34*, 906–911.

Greene, J. A., Muis, K. R., & Pieschl, S. (2010). The role of epistemic beliefs in students' self-regulated learning with computer-based learning environments: Conceptual and methodological issues. *Educational Psychologist, 45*, 245–257.

Hadwin, A. F., Nesbit, J. C., Code, J., Jamieson-Noel, D. L., & Winne, P. H. (2007). Examining trace data to explore self-regulated learning. *Metacognition & Learning, 2*, 107–124.

Klahr, D., & Dunbar, K. (1988). Dual space search during scientific reasoning. *Cognitive Science, 12*, 1–48.

Körkel, J., & Schneider, W. (1992). Domain-specific versus metacognitive knowledge effects on text recall and comprehension. In M. Carretero, M. Pope, R.-J. Simons, & J. I. Pozo (Eds.), *Learning and instruction—European research in an international context* (pp. 311–323). Oxford. Pergamon Press

Kuhn, D., Black, J., Keselman, A., & Kaplan, D. (2000). The development of cognitive skills to support inquiry learning. *Cognition and Instruction, 18*, 495–523.

Njoo, M., & De Jong, T. (1993). Exploratory learning with a computer simulation for control theory: Learning processes and instructional support. *Journal of Research in Science Teaching, 30*, 821–844.

Paris, S. G., Lipson, M. Y., & Wixson, K. K. (1983). Becoming a strategic reader. *Contemporary Educational Psychologist, 8*, 293–316.

Perry, N. E., & Winne, P. H. (2006). Learning from learning kits: gStudy traces of students' self-regulated engagements with computerized content. *Educational Psychology Review, 18*, 211–228.

Pressley, M. (1995). What is intellectual development about in the 1990s? Good information processing. In F. E. Weinert & W. Schneider (Eds.), *Memory performance competencies. Issues in growth and development* (pp. 375–404). Mahwah, NJ: Lawrence Erlbaum Associates.

Pressley, M., Borkowski, J. G., & Schneider, W. (1987). Cognitive strategies: Good strategy users coordinate metacognition and knowledge. In R. Vasta & G. Whilehurst (Eds.), *Annals of child development* (Vol. 4, pp. 80–129). Greenwich, CT: JAI Press.

Ramm, G., Prenzel, M., Baumert, J., Blum, W., Lehmann, R., & Leutner, D. (Eds.). (2006). *PISA 2003: Dokumentation der Erhebungsinstrumente. [PISA 2003: Documentation of the assessment instruments]*. Münster: Waxmann.

Rheinberg, R., Vollmeyer, R., & Burns, B.D. (2001). FAM: Ein Fragebogen zur Erfassung aktueller Motivation in Lern- und Leistungssituationen [QCM: A questionnaire to assess current motivation in learning situations]. *Diagnostica, 47*, 57–66.

Schlagmüller, M., & Schneider, W. (2007). Würzburger Lesestrategiewissenstest für die Klassen 7-12 (WLST 7-12). [Wuerzburger reading strategy knowledge test for classes 7-12]. In M. Hasselhorn, H. Marx, & W. Schneider (Eds.), *Deutsche Schultests. [German school tests*]. Göttingen: Hogrefe.

Schneider, W., Körkel, J., & Weinert, F. E. (1987). The effects of intelligence, self-concept, and attributional style on metamemory and memory behaviour. *International Journal of Behavioral Development, 3*, 281–299.

Schneider, W., Schlagmüller, M., & Visé, M. (1998). The impact of metamemory and domain-specific knowledge on memory performance. *European Journal of Psychology of Education, 13*, 91–103.

Spörer, N., & Brunstein, J. C. (2006). Erfassung selbstregulierten Lernens mit Selbstberichtsverfahren [Assessing self-regulated learning with self-report methods]. *Zeitschrift für Pädagogische Psychologie, 20*, 147–160.

Thillmann, H., Künsting, J., Wirth, J., & Leutner, D. (2009). Is it merely a question of "what" to prompt or also "when" to prompt? The role of point of presentation time in self-regulated learning. *Zeitschrift für Pädagogische Psychologie, 23*, 105–115.

Van Joolingen, W. R., & de Jong, T. (1993). Exploring a domain with a computer simulation: Traversing variable and relation space with the help of a hypothesis scratchpad. In D. Towne, T. de Jong, & H. Spada (Eds.), *Simulation-based experiential learning* (pp. 191–206). Berlin, Germany: Springer.

Veenman, M. V. J. (2005). The assessment of metacognitive skills: What can be learned from multi-method designs? In B. Moschner & C. Artelt (Eds.), *Lernstrategien und Metakognition: Implikationen für Forschung und Praxis [Learning strategies and metacognition: Implications for research and practice]* (pp. 77–99). Berlin: Waxmann.

Veenman, M. V. J., van Hout-Wolters, B. H. A. M., & Afflerbach, P. (2006). Metacognition and learning: Conceptual and methodological considerations. *Metacognition & Learning, 1*, 3–14.

Vollmeyer, R., & Rheinberg, F. (2000). Does motivation affect performance via persistence? *Learning and Instruction, 10*, 293–309.

Wichmann, A., & Leutner, D. (2009). Inquiry learning: Multilevel support with respect to inquiry, explanations and regulation during an inquiry circle. *German Journal of Educational Psychology, 23*, 117–127.

Winne, P. H. (1996). A metacognitive view of individual differences in self-regulated learning. *Learning and Individual Differences, 8*, 327–353.

Winne, P. H., & Hadwin, A. F. (1998). Studying as self-regulated learning. In D. J. Hacker, J. Dunlosky, & A. C. Graesser (Eds.), *Metacognition in education theory and practice* (pp. 277–304). Mahwah, NJ: Lawrence Erlbaum.

Winne, P. H., & Jamieson-Noel, D. (2002). Exploring students' calibration of self reports about study tactics and achievement. *Contemporary Educational Psychology, 27*, 551–572.

Winne, P. H., & Perry, N. E. (2000). Measuring self-regulated learning. In M. Boekaerts, P. Pintrich, & M. Zeidner

(Eds.), *Handbook of self-regulation* (pp. 531–566). Orlando, FL: Academic.

Wirth, J. (2008). Computer-based tests: Alternatives for test and item design. In J. Hartig, E. Klieme, & D. Leutner (Eds.), *Assessment of competencies in educational contexts* (pp. 235–252). Göttingen: Hogrefe.

Wirth, J., & Leutner, D. (2006). Selbstregulation beim Lernen in interaktiven Lernumgebungen [Self-regulation of learning in interactive learning environments]. In H. Mandl & H. F. Friedrich (Eds.), *Handbuch Lernstrategien [Handbook learning strategies]* (pp. 172–184). Göttingen: Hogrefe.

Wolters, C. A. (2003). Regulation of motivation: Evaluating an underemphasized aspect of self-regulated learning. *Educational Psychologist, 38*, 189–205.

Zimmerman, B. J. (2000). Attaining self-regulation: A social cognitive perspective. In M. Boekaerts, P. R. Pintrich, & M. Zeidner (Eds.), *Handbook of self-regulation* (pp. 13–39). San Diego: Academic.

Model-Based Diagnosis for Regulative Support in Inquiry Learning

38

Wouter van Joolingen and Ton de Jong

Abstract

We discuss the use of models of inquiry processes, such as SDDS and the inquiry cycle for the generation of support on the regulation of these processes. It is argued that such scaffolding must be adaptive as too much scaffolding can actually hinder learning. A major problem encountered is the "paradox of adaptive scaffolding". In order to make scaffolding adaptive, the system needs to gather information about the learners' progress. In order to collect this information, often many learner actions are made explicit in the environment, a measure that is a scaffold itself. We discuss a few means of minimizing this unintended scaffolding, using less obtrusive methods for obtaining learner information, and present an example of how such information can be used to support learners in monitoring their progress.

Introduction

The learning and teaching of Science has a dual nature. On the one hand science teaching and learning needs to address the main insights that the sciences have produced, such as Newton's laws, the periodic system of the elements, and the way these insights can be applied to solve scientific and technical problems. On the other hand, an important goal of science learning is to induce an image of the processes of scientific work and research, as well as basic scientific skills, such as the framing of research questions and the scientific methods for pursuing their answers. In other, more compact wording, learners should learn both scientific knowledge and scientific skills.

In the last two decades scientific inquiry learning has been studied as an attempt to address both goals of science teaching. In inquiry learning learners work on a scientific task in which they need to answer a research question. In most cases the question concerns the relations that govern a given domain, such as the relation between height and energy of a falling body or the dependency of chemical reaction speed on temperature. By stating hypotheses and testing those by designing and performing experiments learners are expected to learn about the domain through the things they discover

W. van Joolingen (✉) • T. de Jong
Institute for Teacher Education and Science Communication, Faculty of Behavioral Sciences, University of Twente, Enschede, The Netherlands
e-mail: w.r.vanjoolingen@utwente.nl; a.j.m.dejong@utwente.nl

R. Azevedo and V. Aleven (eds.), *International Handbook of Metacognition and Learning Technologies*, Springer International Handbooks of Education 26, DOI 10.1007/978-1-4419-5546-3_38,

and about the scientific skills by practicing them in their pursuit for answers on the research questions.

The main argument for introducing inquiry learning, apart from reaching both main learning goals in one activity, is that the resulting scientific knowledge is assumed to be better structured and better rooted in learners' existing knowledge. This argument stems from constructivism (Jonassen, 1991), which sees learners as active agents who construct their own knowledge. Learning by performing scientific activities fits perfectly in this paradigm. The catch is of course that in this way learning scientific knowledge becomes dependent on the success of learning scientific skills. If learners fail to perform the scientific inquiry processes well, students may acquire little or no scientific knowledge, or worse, may acquire incorrect knowledge. For instance, learners may bring naïve conceptions to the learning experience, and by using experimentation strategies aimed at confirming their ideas, these conceptions, however wrong, may be strengthened. Alternatively, by using unproductive inquiry strategies, learners may not be able to distill the right variables and relations from the available data.

These considerations have lead to the idea that learners need support in inquiry learning (e.g., Alfieri, Brooks, Aldrich, & Tenenbaum, 2011; de Jong & van Joolingen, 1998). By offering support they will receive scaffolds for the inquiry processes. This should ensure that they perform the inquiry processes at a level at which they will be able to acquire scientific knowledge about the domain, and at the same time can practice inquiry processes themselves. Support can be directed at providing relevant information about the domain, on the performance of the inquiry processes, and on the *regulation* of these processes, in other words on the planning, monitoring, and evaluation of the inquiry endeavor (Manlove, Lazonder, & de Jong, 2006, 2009). In this chapter we will focus on the latter, but in order to be able to do so, we first introduce environments for inquiry learning, as well as models of the inquiry process.

Inquiry Learning Environments

Inquiry learning environments aim at enabling and supporting inquiry learning by offering a research question, one or more resources that can be explored to answer the question and tools to assist the learner in carrying out the right processes for doing so (van Joolingen & Zacharia, 2009). A resource for obtaining data can have multiple forms, ranging from field observations or experimental equipment to computer simulations, online databases, and video measurements. Theoretically, these different kinds of resources are similar in the sense that they all allow for measurement and/or observation and in many cases also manipulation of variables. Zacharia (2007) found in a comparison that students using virtual labs can perform equally well or even better on a conceptual knowledge posttest than students using real labs. In practice different resources have different affordances creating qualitative differences in experimentation behavior. For instance, changing a variable in a simulation may be done with a click on a button, whereas it may require advanced physical operations or physical labor in a real experiment. Also simulations can manipulate the time scale, allowing for a large number of simulated experiments to be done within the time of a single real life run. Moreover, simulations can provide a modified reality, for example, a simplification of a real system or some kind of alternative reality, such as a world without friction. In such a way inquiry processes can be focused on a domain that is completely known by the designer, which has the advantage that all possible actions and outcomes are known in advance. A disadvantage is the resulting closed nature of the environment, taking away the possibility of outcomes that are unexpected, even for the designer of the environment, such as outcomes stemming from faulty equipment. The recognition of such unexpected events may be an important skill in itself. Building them into a simulation may be hard and appear artificial for the students.

Models of Inquiry Learning

To define the nature of learning processes involved in inquiry learning, the process of inquiry needs to be modeled. Models of inquiry learning are often based on the *inquiry cycle* that has been described by many authors in varying forms, and was summarized by Löhner, van Joolingen, Savelsbergh, and van Hout-Wolters (2005) in terms of the processes *orientation*, *hypotheses generation*, *experimentation*, and *evaluation*. Although other authors use varying terminology and sometimes make refinements, the basic shape of the cycle remains intact, although the place for performing experiments requires special attention. An influential model into the use of experiments in scientific reasoning has been that of Klahr and Dunbar (1988), who approached inquiry as a problem solving process in their Scientific Discovery as Dual Search (SDDS) theory. They defined two search spaces, called *hypothesis space* and *experiment space*. The first of these spaces consist of all possible rules that could describe the domain, whereas the second contains all possible experiments that can be performed within the domain. Important in the SDDS theory is that it models when hypotheses and experiment space searches are needed. Experiment space search can take place to inspire new hypotheses, to fill in values for a prediction and to test hypotheses. Hypothesis space searches are triggered when prior knowledge is inadequate to explain observed phenomena. Although Klahr and Dunbar themselves found that learners do not always behave according to the model (e.g., hypotheses can be rejected without conflicting evidence or retained in spite of such evidence), SDDS provides a useful descriptive framework for the processes of inquiry learning, especially with respect to the role of experimentation, which occurs not only for the purpose of testing hypotheses but also helps in shaping them. For instance, when linear relation is hypothesized to exist between two variables, an experiment can be used to determine the proportionality factor (i.e., further specify the hypothesis). Further experiments can be used to test the hypothesis (e.g., by comparing experimental outcomes to the predictions generated by the hypothesis).

Van Joolingen and de Jong (1997) extended Klahr and Dunbar's model with a detailed analysis of the hypothesis space for the case of simulation-based learning in which the domain can be described in terms of variables and relations between them. As a result their model can handle moves in the hypothesis space, such as generalization, specification, and precision. Also, their model can be used to model learners' prior knowledge, by means of identifying subspaces in the hypothesis space that model whether the learner knows them and to what extent the learner considers them relevant for the current inquiry problem. It makes a difference whether learners do not find a hypothesis because they do not know a relation or because they do know it, but do not think it is appropriate. Different kinds of support would be appropriate for either case.

Hakkarainen and colleagues take a different stance towards inquiry and acknowledge the importance of discussion and argumentation in inquiry (Hakkarainen, Lipponen, & Järvelä, 2001; Hakkarainen & Sintonen, 2002). In their *interrogative model of inquiry* they focus on the development of research questions and their subdivision into sub questions by means of dialog and argumentation. Similar approaches are found in work by Scardamelia and colleagues on knowledge building environments (Hewitt & Scardamalia, 1998; Scardamalia & Bereiter, 1993)

The processes that compose the inquiry cycle, including the search for the most appropriate hypothesis and evidence to support it are what Njoo and De Jong (1993) call *transformative learning processes*. In addition to these processes, *regulative* learning processes are relevant in the process of inquiry and hence in constructing and executing the inquiry cycle. Regulative learning processes represent the learners' metacognitive strategies, and are used to exert control over the transformative processes. In other words, using regulative processes, the learner decides whether it is time to state a new hypothesis, to collect more data for the current one, or for something else. Regulative processes combine domain independent and domain dependent aspects. In most descriptions they include *planning*, *monitoring*, and *evaluation*. For planning, some general, domain independent notions of what a good plan is do exist. The plan itself will be formulated in terms of the domain investigated (e.g., "first check whether X relates to Z, then check Y"). This stresses that regulative skills are partly domain dependent. Relevant domain knowledge is needed to formulate and check the learning activities at the level of transformative processes.

Scaffolding Metacognitive Inquiry Processes

It has been recognized for a long time that inquiry without support for the learner, also referred to as *discovery learning* is not effective (de Jong & van Joolingen, 1998; Klahr & Nigam, 2004; Mayer, 2004). Hence there is a need for providing the learner with support in order to perform the learning processes in a productive manner.

Tools to assist the inquiry process range from general purpose tools, such as spreadsheets, word processors, and the like, to dedicated tools, such as experiment design tools or hypothesis scratchpads (van Joolingen & de Jong, 1991, 1993). Such tools can be integrated in the learning environment; others may be available as an add-on. In essence tools allow and assist learners in acquiring and expressing knowledge, a property that coined the term *cognitive tools* (Lajoie & Derry, 1993; van Joolingen, 1999). Tools can be directed at the transformative processes that deal with the generation of knowledge or with regulative processes for planning and controlling inquiry activities.

Any of the tools that help learners in materializing the inquiry process can offer several kinds of scaffolding (e.g., see Lajoie & Derry, 1993):

- Providing just-in-time information needed for a specific learning process. For instance, the tool can provide learners with names of variables to consider for investigation, or provide how-to information on performing an experiment.
- Providing templates to support learning processes. For instance, a template could be a partially stated hypothesis for which only a value or a relation needs to be filled in. Or a partial plan for the inquiry process can be provided.
- Automating learning processes. Tools can automate parts of the processes allowing learners to focus on other parts. For instance, tools can provide a step-by-step walkthrough of the transformative processes, relieving learners of the necessity to provide their own plans.
- Constraining behavior. By reducing the number of possible actions in the learning environment, e.g., by limiting the number of variables that a learner can manipulate, learners' transformative and regulative processes are simplified.
- Providing feedback. Tools (or agents in the learning environment) can provide feedback on learner's performance. For instance, by providing comments on the set of experiments as to what extent they are adequate to test a hypothesis.
- Increasing awareness of own behavior. A specific kind of feedback that can be provided is echoing learners' own behavior by presenting a visual representation of that behavior, such as a image showing the proportions of different kind of behavior (Anjewierden, Kolloffel, & Hulshof, 2007).

Often more than one kind of scaffolding is combined in one learning environment. Scaffolds can take over cognitively demanding parts of a complex task, freeing up cognitive resources, allowing learners to focus on other parts the of the task (van Merriënboer, Kirschner, & Kester, 2003). For inquiry learning several environments have been developed that provide such scaffolding for regulation. WISE (Slotta, 2004) provides learners with a menu structure that can be traversed from top to bottom, taking the planning of the inquiry out of the hands of the learners, so they can focus on other processes, such as collecting data to test a hypothesis.

Manlove et al. (2006) used a *process coordinator*, a tool that helped learners to plan by offering a default plan that could be fine-tuned by the learner. The tool also supported monitoring by requiring students to link the plan to products in the learning environment (such as empirical data) as evidence for completion of plan elements. In such away, monitoring was made an explicit activity.

In earlier work, Veermans, van Joolingen, and de Jong (Veermans, de Jong, & van Joolingen, 2000; Veermans, van Joolingen, & de Jong, 2006) introduced a tool that supports monitoring by allowing students to record the results of experiments. These results were subsequently used in generating feedback to learners' experimental behavior.

SimQuest (van Joolingen & de Jong, 2003) is an authoring system that allows to develop multiple kinds of scaffolding that include regulative support for planning. Its "assignments" provide small micro-plans for inquiry subtasks, such as investigating the influence of a variable or predicting the outcome of an experiment. Assignments can be chained and branched to create plans at a more global level. Assignments can be offered in a completely fixed sequence, offered all at once for the learner to choose from, or offered in a manner in between these extremes. Offering assignments in this way wholly or partly automates the planning process for the learner. Moreover, SimQuest offers model progression in a similar vein as devised by (White et al., 2002; White & Frederiksen, 1990). In model progression, models of increasing complexity are offered to the student, supporting planning by constraining the learners' freedom.

Adaptive Support for Regulating Inquiry Processes

The examples of regulative support for inquiry learning provided above have in common that they are not adaptive or at best they are partly adaptive to learners' behavior. For instance, the menu structure in WISE is fixed and all learners need to go through the same sequence. In other environments, the results of assignments (e.g., SimQuest) or answers to quizzes sometimes can be used to provide some adaptivity, for instance by varying the collection of assignments offered to learners based on the answers given. However, the main questions, whether learners need support or not and, if so, what is the right level of support, is usually answered in a fixed way for all students targeted with the learning environment.

This would not be a problem if offering regulative support would never have negative effects. But as a matter of fact such negative effects can occur. There is such a thing as too much scaffolding (Koedinger & Aleven, 2007). First of all, the purpose of scaffolding is that it can *fade* at the time the learners are capable of performing the scaffolded task on their own. As this moment will vary for individual learners, adaptive fading is necessary.

Moreover, one may expect that learners who receive support that they do not need will not achieve at a level that they would be able to reach otherwise. A hint of this effect can be found in a study by Wecker and colleagues (2007), who found that more computer literate learners learned less from a WISE course than less computer literate learners. A possible explanation is that advanced learners are more successful in bypassing the WISE menu structure, changing the focus from learning about the topic to getting to the end of the menu through the shortest route. Of course, computer literacy cannot be equated to the possession of inquiry skills, but one may expect that learners with more advanced regulative skills will also try to manage their way around the scaffolds, rather than focusing on the content.

Finally, scaffolds can be misused, even by less-advanced students. Especially when scaffolds ultimately lead to automating the process or providing answers to questions, learners may be tempted to *game* the system (Baker et al., 2006; Baker, Corbett, Koedinger, & Wagner, 2004), meaning that they will exploit all support options until the system does the task for them. In order to prevent this, the maximum level of scaffolding should be adapted to what a learner can and should do him- or herself within the learning environment.

Another danger of nonadaptive support is that learners and also teachers may confuse means and goals. Environments that offer a fixed support structure may reinforce the notion that the goal is to "go through" that structure or fill in all the blanks of the templates, instead of performing the processes that are supposed to be supported and learn from them. Support that changes and that adapts to learners' ability would less likely to reinforce that notion.

Providing adaptive support requires several levels of processing: diagnosis, intervention selection, and intervention. Diagnosis is necessary to identify the parts of the learning processes that need to be scaffolded and potentially how this scaffolding should be shaped. Intervention is actually providing the scaffold. In order to create truly adaptive support, it is necessary that these two parts are separated, that is, the scaffold should not do its own diagnosis. This is necessary because there is no one-to-one relation between problem and support. For a given problem, for instance lack of monitoring experiments and their resulting data, several ways of scaffolding may exist in the different scaffolding categories (e.g., automatic recording of experiments, or a fill-in table as template). The choice of action may depend not only on the problem detected but also on other factors, such as learner characteristics, previously used scaffolds, as well as whether a certain process is the focus of learning. If there is more than one process that requires support, it may be useful to automate one and scaffold the other in order to allow the learner to focus on one process at a time. Consequently, it is necessary to have a stage in between diagnosis and intervention.

As a result, providing adaptive support requires three kinds of processing: *diagnosis* to detect problems with regulative learning processes, *intervention selection* to choose between available interventions and *intervention implementation*, to actually provide the scaffolds to the learner. These processes need to be managed in the learning environment at a technical and conceptual level.

On a technical level, a good solution is to use *agents* that work in the background of the learning environment. Bollen, Giemza, and Hoppe (2008) present an agent architecture based on a blackboard architecture, based on *Tuple Spaces* (Weinbrenner, Giemza, & Hoppe, 2007). Three types of agents are introduced that correspond to the three processes mentioned above: analyzing agents, processing agents, and notifying agents. The analyzing agents analyze the stream of learner actions and convert these actions into meaningful units representing the processes that learners perform. For instance, Anjewierden and colleagues (Anjewierden et al., 2007; Anjewierden & Gijlers, 2008) created a tool that, after a human-assisted learning period, can automatically distinguish between regulative and transformative processes, based on chat utterances between two collaborating learners. An agent based on such an algorithm can write its results to the common memory (the tuple space). Processing agents can use such information, for several purposes, such as computing the way the learner distributes time between processes, or relate the information of one agent to that of another. This results in more information written to the tuple space. Notifying agents can be triggered by specific states in the tuple space, set by processing agents. For instance, the processing agent can note that the level of regulative processes is low and decide that the learner needs to be stimulated in regulating the work. The notifying agent can then activate one or more scaffolds that provide such stimulation. The implementation of the scaffold will be stored in the tuple space, and any resulting interaction with the learner will be logged and processed by analyzing agents. As a result, analyzing agents, processing agents, and notification agents can work together, but are loosely coupled.

Although the technical architecture for scaffolding inquiry learning can be provided this way, conceptual issues are still abundant. Questions such as "How to extract relevant information from a stream of log actions" and "How to determine the right level of scaffolding" are still open and largely unanswered. In the remainder of this chapter, we will focus on the first of these questions, corresponding to the diagnosis stage. As the options we will discuss are based on having a model of the inquiry process, they are labeled "Model-based regulative support."

Model-Based Diagnosis and the Paradox of Adaptive Scaffolding

As mentioned above, existing models of inquiry learning honor the inquiry cycle. Some of them add more, such as modeling a hypothesis space and an experiment space (Klahr & Dunbar, 1988; van Joolingen & de Jong, 1997) or heuristics for experimentation and data interpretation. Such models can help both in analyzing the logs of learners' actions, as well as in deciding whether intervention is necessary. For instance, Veermans (Veermans et al., 2000, 2006) used a model based on the inquiry cycle and a set of heuristics for experimentation, such as "vary one thing at a time" and "use easy values in varying input variables." In these studies, learners record the experimental data that they collect on their "monitoring tool," a scaffold that is offered to monitor experimentation. The experiments are interpreted using the heuristics from the model, e.g., for data points it is checked whether one or more variables are changed from one point to the other, and how the values of the input variables are changed. For instance, in order to test for linearity of a relation a good heuristic is to choose round numbers for variable values, choose equal intervals for the various values chosen, and use at least three, but preferably more data points. Moreover, learners had chosen a SimQuest assignment to investigate a given hypothesis before experimenting, meaning that the system could check whether their data was relevant to test that hypothesis. This results in a segmentation of the set of experiments according to these heuristics. A segment could be a series of data points in which just one variable was varied, or a set of points in which the data points are ordered according to regular intervals for the changing input variable. A second scaffold was then constructed echoing back the relevant segments allowing learners to draw conclusions from the data that was presented in that way, or reconsidering their experimental strategy if no relevant data segments could be found. Figure 38.1 presents an example of the resulting feedback that lists the experiments performed and suggests a conclusion that may be drawn based on these experiments.

This example illustrates the principle of model-based regulative support. Each action (a manipulation of the simulation), is interpreted (as a new data point) and abstracted (into data segments representing experiments). The segments are processed, meaning that they are matched to a current hypothesis, resulting in one or more segments that could be fed back to the learner. Finally, the feedback is actually implemented, in Veermans' case as a commented table. Although Veermans did not implement an agent architecture, the elements of the three agent types (analysis, processing, and notifying) are clearly present. The same heuristics have later been implemented, using such an architecture in the context of the SCY project (de Jong et al., 2010) by Weinbrenner and colleagues (2010) albeit with a different kind of feedback.

In order to generalize this way of providing support, a firm basis is needed in diagnosing learners' behavior. The basic source for such diagnosis is the logs of learners' actions with the learning environments. The approach to diagnosis presented here uses a two-stage process: detection and analysis. In order to detect learning processes from the learners' action, process definitions need to be given in terms of the detailed actions themselves. For instance, following Anjewierden (Anjewierden et al., 2007) an<experimental manipulation>can be defined as a sequence, such as<set value>[<set value>], <run simulation>, and <record data point>. Hierarchical constructs are possible, such as<experiment>=<experimental manipulation><experiment>. Wildcards, recursion, and parameterized actions (such as the names and values of the manipulated variables) allow for a flexible way of parsing the log files and extract relevant processes.

In order to be successful, it is important that processes have an explicit representation in the learning environment. It must be possible to map learners' actions to learning processes. For some actions this is unproblematic, as in the case of manipulations of a simulation, where changes in variable values and running the simulation are straightforwardly interpreted in terms of experimental manipulations.

Whereas processes that have direct effect on the state of the learning environment, such as experimentation, are relatively easy to detect, other processes, such as hypothesis generation and drawing conclusions, may not be directly visible in terms of actions in the learning environment. For instance, a hypothesis may be formulated

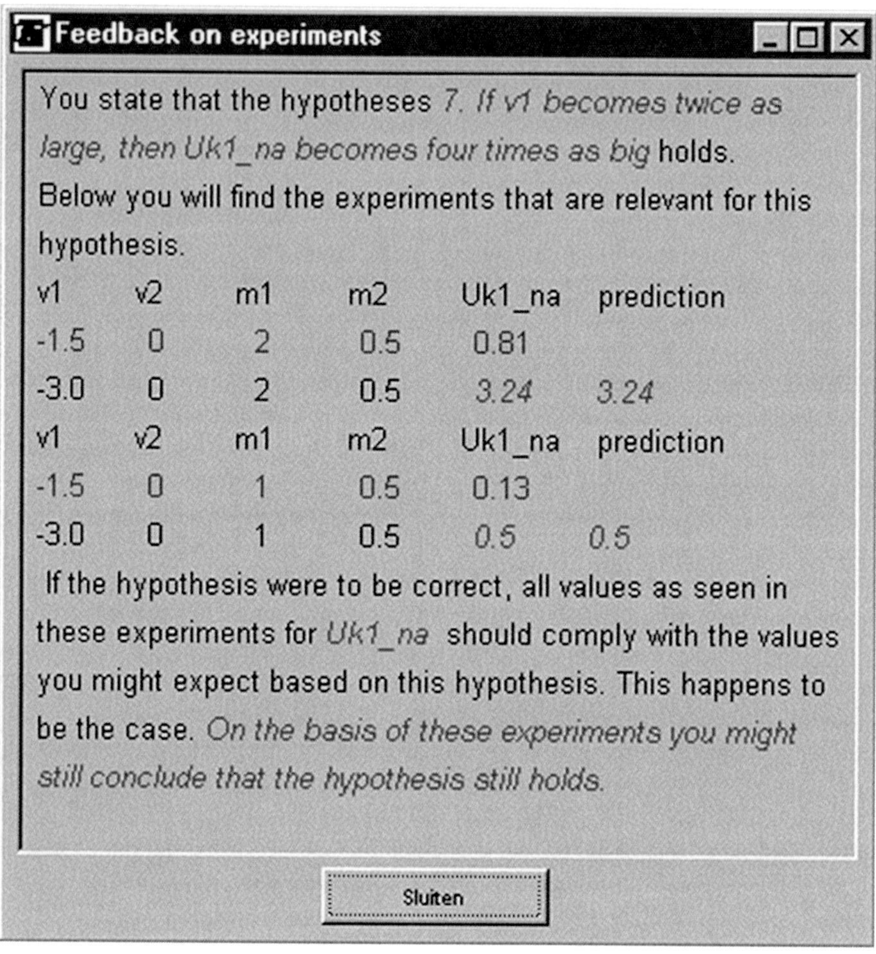

Fig. 38.1 Example of feedback generated on the basis of a learner's experiments, from the study by Veermans and colleagues (2000). The set of data points is divided into two groups, based on the values of the variables chosen. A conclusion is suggested

in the learner's minds, written down on paper, or discussed face to face with a peer. The system will not have access those kinds of information. In such cases, other means of extracting the learning processes from the learner's action logs need to be used. We see the following possibilities:

- Analyzing learner generated text, if the environment requires or stimulates learners to enter textual information. This can be done when learners collaborate via chat, but also when they are stimulated to make notes or answer questions in textual format. Current text mining techniques are powerful enough to extract meaning in terms of keywords and syntax. For instance, Anjewierden succeeded in extracting process information from chat messages (Anjewierden & Gijlers, 2008) as well as weblogs (Anjewierden & Efimova, 2006). Syntactical analysis can yield information whether a certain text fragment can be classified as hypothesis, plan, monitoring action, etc. Entering text is a natural part of approaches that focus on knowledge building (Hewitt & Scardamalia, 1998) or center around argumentation and discussion (Hakkarainen & Sintonen, 2002).
- Building processes into the loop of learners' work with the environment. By shaping the environment in such a way that learners need to perform explicit actions representing the

main processes, they can be recognized and used for analysis, an idea that goes back to the work on cognitive tutors (Anderson, Corbett, Koedinger, & Pelletier, 1995). For instance, Veermans' (2000) monitoring tool in a sense serves three functions: a prompt and template for the learner to record and monitor experiments, a way of externalizing the monitoring process itself as well as a source of information for the learning environment. By creating a loop of actions that learners will go though, the system can always "know" in which process the learner is engaged.

- Analyzing learners' products. In many inquiry learning environments, learners explicitly or implicitly create products, such as sets of data, reports, and concept maps. By analyzing the creation history of such objects as well as their contents, the performance of processes may be detected. This approach is taken in the SCY project (de Jong et al., 2010), where the whole learning process is represented as the creation of artifacts, so-called Emerging Learning Objects. Examples are agents that analyze texts collected by a learner and match them to a concept map that the learner is constructing. If one or more concepts are underrepresented, the learner receives a suggestion with some concepts that can or should be included.

All three ways of detecting require that the learning environment provides an explicit representation of processes in one form or another. Here we encounter a paradox; as such measures in a sense are scaffolds as well. It seems that in order to provide adaptive scaffolds, we need to provide some level of static scaffolding to gather the information for the detecting processes. For instance, if we ask learners to create a plan, so as to detect whether planning support is needed, merely asking is already providing some support. If we offer some kind of planning tool for this purpose, the support is even at a higher level. It seems we need to provide support in order to determine if support is necessary. This paradox cannot completely be avoided, but, depending on the detection goal, the intervention to collect data may be kept to a minimum level.

For the second stage of diagnosis, *analysis*, we need a model of inquiry as a reference. Two kinds of models can be distinguished labeled *process models* and *state space models*. The first is oriented towards the learning process itself, whereas the second focuses on changes of learners' and system's state as a result of applying these processes.

In process models, a notion exists of an "ideal process" for inquiry, such as the inquiry cycle at large, or a more detailed division into subprocesses. The processes detected can be matched to such a model, by counting the processes as they occur, and by matching the order in which the processes occur. In doing so it can be detected whether processes are under- or over-represented in the learners' activities, and regulative support can be activated. Van den Brock and Van Joolingen (2008) studied a modeling task in the domain of human resource management and compared experts with novices and collected think aloud protocols. The task was to create a model that explains why highly qualified personnel in the research department leave a company. They plotted the way experts and novices divided their processes over time, and found that experts stayed longer in the process of "orientation," which encompasses collecting information and identifying the main variables. This is similar to what Chi found in expert-novice comparisons in problem solving (Chi, Glaser, & Farr, 1988). Whereas novices moved to "implementing the model," meaning drawing the model's variables and relations, after a short orientation phase, experts kept orienting and adding new information throughout the whole task. Using such data, typical expert and novice behavior can be characterized and detected—not only post-hoc from think aloud data but also online using log file data. Processes, such as orientation and implementation, can be characterized by actions in the learning environment, such as searching for information and note taking (orientation) and modeling actions such as adding variables and relations (implementation).

In state space models, the focus is not on the processes themselves but on the results of their application. For instance, whenever the value of a variable is changed on a simulation, this can be recorded yielding a map overlay of the space of all possible variable value assignments. This can be used to assess whether the learner has seen relevant events in the simulation. If not, as before, action can be taken. In effect the problem spaces of SDDS (Klahr & Dunbar, 1988) and its extension (van Joolingen & de Jong, 1997) can be used as state models. The extended model captures how the hypothesis space and the experiment space can be constructed from domain descriptions (variables, relations, value spaces), which in fact form domain *ontologies*, and captures how the various actions can be mapped to the space. In this it is essential that processes, such as hypothesis generation and experimentation, can be detected and, even more importantly, that their parameters (which hypotheses, which values are manipulated) are known. Each action can then be added to one of the maps that overlay both search spaces. It should be noted that the result is not a traditional overlay learner model, as it is not a knowledge model that is overlaid but a search space.

In this SDDS mapping procedure we can thus detect what the learners' search spaces are: hypothesis spaces are based on relations and variables they mention and hence are aware of, and their experiment spaces are determined by variable manipulations. Of necessity, the detected spaces are always smaller than what a learner really knows, which also makes clear that the resulting model is not a model of knowledge but of activities.

In the SDDS case with two search spaces, the two maps can even be combined to yield further results. Each hypothesis actually splits the experiment space into two or three parts: (1) experiments that contradict the hypothesis, (2) experiments that could contradict the hypothesis but do not, e.g., because a relevant variable has been changed in the experiment, and the result is not contradicting the hypothesis, and (3) experiments that do not provide information about the hypothesis, because no relevant variable has been changed. The resulting overlay over experiment space can be matched with a learner's actual behavior. If there is a mismatch, supportive measures can be taken. This approach was used in the study by Veermans (2006), described above. For each experiment that learners performed it was determined in which part of experiment space it could be located according to the division above. The feedback that was given to students was determined based on this location in experiment space.

Discussion

We discussed ways to adaptively support inquiry learning, with a focus on the detection of problems in the regulation of learning processes. The detection process was subdivided into two parts: the detection of basic processes from log files and the automatic interpretation of these basic processes in terms of their regulation. With respect to the detection of basic processes we discussed the paradox of adaptive support. In order to detect basic processes in some cases we need to insert measures in the environment that help make processes explicit. This in itself is a form of support.

With respect to the interpretation of basic processes in terms of regulation, we introduced two kinds of model-based interpretive models: process models and state space models. Whereas in process models, a sequence of processes is matched to an ideal sequence or to ideal proportions of time spent on the various processes, in a state space model the focus is on the result of the processes in terms of mappings on search spaces. The first have as advantage that they stay close to models of inquiry that are commonly used and mostly based on the inquiry cycle. Potential feedback and support cane directly matched to such models. For instance, the support system could notify the learner of a lack of hypotheses while doing experiments. A drawback is that the model is heavily dependent on the accurate detection of basic log actions. For instance, if learners' hypotheses are missed, the result may be that the learner is diagnosed as performing undirected experiments, and the resulting support may be out of place. Especially if the model hinges around a precise order in which processes must be performed, errors are likely.

In the case of state space models, such a drawback is less apparent, as the focus is not on counting the processes, but on keeping track of their results. Of course this is also dependent of the information that can be retrieved from learners' activities, but it is less error prone as there is no sequence dependency and as the results of missing an action may be a state space overlay that is too small. This could lead to learners being asked to investigate parts that were already visited, but this may be not too severe. As a result, state space models can be more robust and may need less information to maintain. A great advantage of state space models is that support for regulation may be more directed towards the contents of learning. Support can then be tailored not only to the fact *that* learners need to regulate and plan but also on *what* they need to plan. And, if indeed state space models can be built using less information, the adaptive support paradox can be avoided. State space models do not detect the sequence in which the state space has been covered. This does not prevent the system to advise learners what to do next, namely address a part of state space that has remained undisclosed and may be of interest. However, detailed feedback based on the exact sequence of actions is not possible based on a state space model.

For this all to work, more research is needed to investigate the main parts of the approach. Although we did not discuss it discusses into detail in this chapter, the approach clearly depends on the detection of basic processes from raw data. In order to fine-tune the interpretive models for model-based analysis, agents need to be developed that match a stream of log file data onto a mapping on a process or state space model. Another level of mapping is that from the model-based maps to the choice of intervention: which interventions can be used to support problems that are detected in the models. And finally, the proof of the pudding will be in the eating, as the resulting environments need to be tested as to whether they lead to better learning.

References

Alfieri, L., Brooks, P. J., Aldrich, N. J., & Tenenbaum, H. R. (2011). Does discovery-based instruction enhance learning? *Journal of Educational Psychology, 103*, 1–18.

Anderson, J. R., Corbett, A. T., Koedinger, K. R., & Pelletier, R. (1995). Cognitive tutors: Lessons learned. *The Journal of the Learning Sciences, 4*, 167–207.

Anjewierden, A., & Efimova, L. (2006). Understanding weblog communities through digital traces: A framework, a tool and an example. In R. Meersman, Z. Tari, & P. Herrero (Eds.), *International workshop on community informatics (COMINF 2006)* (pp. 279–289). Berlin: Springer.

Anjewierden, A., & Gijlers, H. (2008). *An exploration of tool support for categorical coding*. Paper presented at the International Conference for the Learning Sciences (ICLS 2008), Utrecht.

Anjewierden, A., Kolloffel, B., & Hulshof, C. (2007). Towards educational data mining: Using data mining methods for automated chat analysis to understand and support inquiry learning processes. *International Workshop on Applying Data Mining in e-Learning (ADML 2007)*, Crete, pp. 27–36, 2007 (September).

Baker, R., Corbett, A., Koedinger, K., Evenson, S., Roll, I., Wagner, A., et al. (2006). Adapting to when students game an intelligent tutoring system. *Proceedings of the 8th International Conference on Intelligent Tutoring Systems* (pp. 392–401). Berlin: Springer.

Baker, R., Corbett, A. T., Koedinger, K. R., & Wagner, A. Z. (2004). *Off-task behavior in the cognitive tutor classroom: When students "Game the System"*. Paper presented at the ACM CHI 2004: Computer-Human Interaction. Berlin: Springer.

Bollen, L., Giemza, A., & Hoppe, H. U. (2008). *Flexible analysis of user actions in heterogeneous distributed learning environments*. Paper presented at the ECTEL 2008. Berlin: Springer.

Chi, M. T. H., Glaser, R., Farr, M., & Farr, M. (Eds.). (1988). *The nature of expertise*. Hillsdale, NJ: Lawrence Erlbaum Associates.

de Jong, T., & van Joolingen, W. R. (1998). Scientific discovery learning with computer simulations of conceptual domains. *Review of Educational Research, 68*, 179–202.

de Jong, T., van Joolingen, W. R., Anjewierden, A., Bollen, L., d'Ham, C., Dolonen, J., et al. (2010). Learning by creating and exchanging objects: The SCY experience. *British Journal of Educational Technology, 41*, 909–921.

Hakkarainen, K., Lipponen, L., & Järvelä, S. (2001). Epistemology of inquiry and computer-supported collaborative learning. In T. Koschmann, R. Hall, & N. Miyake (Eds.), *CSCL: Carry forward the conversation* (pp. 129–156). Mahwah, NJ: Lawrence Erlbaum Associates.

Hakkarainen, K., & Sintonen, M. (2002). The interrogative model of inquiry and computer-supported collaborative learning. *Science Education, 11*, 25–43. doi:10.1023/A:1013076706416.

Hewitt, J., & Scardamalia, M. (1998). Design principles for distributed knowledge building processes. *Educational Psychology Review, 10*, 75–96.

Jonassen, D. (1991). Objectivism versus constructivism: Do we need a new philosophical paradigm? *Educational Technology Research and Development, 39*, 5–14.

Klahr, D., & Dunbar, K. (1988). Dual space search during scientific reasoning. *Cognitive Science, 12*, 1–48.

Klahr, D., & Nigam, M. (2004). The equivalence of learning paths in early science instruction: Effects of direct instruction and discovery learning. *Psychological Science, 15*, 661–667.

Koedinger, K., & Aleven, V. (2007). Exploring the assistance dilemma in experiments with cognitive tutors. *Educational Psychology Review, 19*, 239–264.

Lajoie, S. P., & Derry, S. J. (1993). *Computers as cognitive tools*. Mahwah, NJ: Lawrence Earlbaum Associates, Inc.

Löhner, S., van Joolingen, W. R., Savelsbergh, E. R., & van Hout-Wolters, B. H. A. M. (2005). Students' reasoning during modeling in an inquiry learning environment. *Computers in Human Behavior, 21*, 441–461.

Manlove, S., Lazonder, A. W., & de Jong, T. (2006). Regulative support for collaborative scientific inquiry learning. *Journal of Computer Assisted Learning, 22*, 87–98.

Manlove, S., Lazonder, A. W., & de Jong, T. (2009). Trends and issues of regulative support use during inquiry learning: Patterns from three studies. *Computers in Human Behavior, 25*, 795–803.

Mayer, R. E. (2004). Should there be a three-strikes rule against pure discovery learning? *American Psychologist, 59*, 14–19.

Njoo, M., & de Jong, T. (1993). Exploratory learning with a computer simulation for control theory: Learning processes and instructional support. *Journal of Research in Science Teaching, 30*, 821–844.

Scardamalia, M., & Bereiter, C. (1993). Technologies for knowledge-building discourse. *Communications of the ACM, 36*, 37–41.

Slotta, J. D. (2004). The web-based inquiry science environment (WISE): Scaffolding knowledge integration in the science classroom. In M. Linn, E. A. Davis, & P. Bell (Eds.), *Internet environments for science education* (pp. 203–233). Mahwah, NJ: Lawrence Erlbaum Associates.

van den Broek, T., & Van Joolingen, W. R. (2008). *Exploring experts' reasoning during modeling an illdefined domain*. Unpublished Master thesis. Enschede: University of Twente.

van Joolingen, W. R. (1999). Cognitive tools for discovery learning. *International Journal of Artificial Intelligence in Education, 10*, 385–397.

van Joolingen, W. R., & de Jong, T. (1991). Supporting hypothesis generation by learners exploring an interactive computer-simulation. *Instructional Science, 20*, 389–404.

van Joolingen, W. R., & de Jong, T. (1993). Exploring a domain through a computer simulation: Traversing variable and relation space with the help of a hypothesis scratchpad. In D. Towne, T. de Jong, & H. Spada (Eds.), *Simulation-based experiential learning* (pp. 191–206). Berlin: Springer.

van Joolingen, W. R., & de Jong, T. (1997). An extended dual search space model of scientific discovery learning. *Instructional Science, 25*, 307–346.

van Joolingen, W. R., & de Jong, T. (2003). SimQuest: Authoring educational simulations. In T. Murray, S. Blessing, & S. Ainsworth (Eds.), *Authoring tools for advanced technology educational software: Toward cost-effective production of adaptive, interactive, and intelligent educational software* (pp. 1–31). Dordrecht: Kluwer Academic Publishers.

van Joolingen, W. R., & Zacharia, Z. C. (2009). Developments in inquiry learning. In N. Balacheff, S. Ludvigsen, T. de Jong, A. Lazonder, & S. Barnes (Eds.), *Technology-enhanced learning, principles and products* (pp. 21–37). Netherlands: Springer.

van Merriënboer, J. J. G., Kirschner, P. A., & Kester, L. (2003). Taking the load off a learner's mind: Instructional design for complex learning. *Educational Psychologist, 38*, 5–13.

Veermans, K. H., de Jong, T., & van Joolingen, W. R. (2000). Promoting self directed learning in simulation based discovery learning environments through intelligent support. *Interactive Learning Environments, 8*, 229–255.

Veermans, K. H., van Joolingen, W. R., & de Jong, T. (2006). Using heuristics to facilitate discovery learning in a simulation learning environment in a physics domain. *International Journal of Science Education, 28*, 341–361.

Wecker, C., Kohnle, C., & Fischer, F. (2007). Computer literacy and inquiry learning: When geeks learn less. *Journal of Computer Assisted Learning, 23*, 133–144.

Weinbrenner, S., Engler, J., Wichmann, A., & Hoppe, H. U. (2010). *Monitoring and analysing students' systematic behaviour—The SCY pedagogical agent framework*. Paper presented at the Fifth European Conference on Technology Enhanced Learning 2010. Berlin: Springer.

Weinbrenner, S., Giemza, A., & Hoppe, H. U. (2007). *Engineering heterogeneous distributed learning environments using tuple spaces as an architectural platform*. Paper presented at the The 7th IEEE International Conference on Advanced Learning Technologies ICALT 2007, Los Alamitos, CA.

White, B. Y., & Frederiksen, J. R. (1990). Causal model progressions as a foundation for intelligent learning environments. *Artificial Intelligence, 42*, 99–157.

White, B. Y., Frederiksen, J., Frederiksen, T., Eslinger, E., Loper, S., & Collins, A. (2002). *Inquiry Island: Affordances of a multi-agent environment for scientific inquiry and reflective learning*. Paper presented at the Fifth International Conference of the Learning Sciences (ICLS). MahWah, NJ: Erlbaum.

Zacharia, Z. C. (2007). Comparing and combining real and virtual experimentation: An effort to enhance students' conceptual understanding of electric circuits. *Journal of Computer Assisted Learning, 23*, 120–132.

Research on Self-Regulated Learning in Technology Enhanced Learning Environments: Two Examples from Europe

39

Roberto Carneiro and Karl Steffens

Abstract

Digital technologies have entered almost all spheres of our lives and they are believed to be the motor of innovation in our societies. While these technologies offer an almost unlimited access to information and a wide variety of tools for information processing and communication, it has also become clear that managing these resources requires a new kind of literacy, digital literacy, and that part of this digital literacy is the capacity to regulate one's own learning.

Introduction

Digital technologies have entered almost all spheres of our lives and they are believed to be the motor of innovation in our societies. While these technologies offer an almost unlimited access to information and a wide variety of tools for information processing and communication, it has also become clear that managing these resources requires a new kind of literacy, digital literacy, and that part of this digital literacy is the capacity to regulate one's own learning.

R. Carneiro (✉)
Institute for Distance Learning,
Universidade Católica Portuguesa, Lisbon, Portugal
e-mail: robertocarneiro@netcabo.pt

K. Steffens
Department of Didactics and Educational Research,
University of Cologne, Cologne, Germany
e-mail: Karl.Steffens@uni-koeln.de

In the present contribution, we have a short look at recent theoretical approaches to self-regulated learning with digital technologies. We then focus on research and implementation policies for technology enhanced learning in Europe. Finally, we present two examples of research on self-regulated learning in technology enhanced learning environments: Taconet, a community of European researchers that grew out of a project on this topic, and the New Opportunities Initiative (NOI), a large scale programme implemented by the Portuguese government to empower low skilled workers in which the use of digital technologies and self-regulated learning play a vital role.

Self-Regulated Learning and Digital Technologies

Self-regulated learning refers to learners' ability to plan, monitor and evaluate their learning processes. While a number of models for self-regulated

R. Azevedo and V. Aleven (eds.), *International Handbook of Metacognition and Learning Technologies*, Springer International Handbooks of Education 26, DOI 10.1007/978-1-4419-5546-3_39,

learning were proposed in the past, the model that is probably best-known is the one developed by Zimmerman (1998a, 1998b, 2000). According to this model, self-regulation is achieved in cycles consisting of (1) forethought, (2) performance or volitional control, and (3) self-reflection.

There is a close relationship between self-regulated learning and metacognition. "Students can be described as self-regulated to the degree that they are metacognitively, motivationally, and behaviourally active participants in their own learning process" (Zimmerman, 1998a, p. 4). Azevedo (2009), in discussing theoretical, conceptual, methodological, and instructional issues in research on metacognition and self-regulated learning, states "Learning typically involves the use of numerous self-regulatory processes, such as planning, knowledge activation, metacognitive monitoring and regulation, and reflection" (Azevedo, 2009, p. 87) suggesting that self-regulated learning is a concept which embraces metacognitive monitoring and regulation. Beishuizen & Steffens (2011) have compared the concept of self-regulated learning with related concepts like self-directed learning, personalised learning, and self-directed personalised learning.

The idea that computers may be considered as tools which facilitate metacognitive skills and self-regulated learning has been explored in a number of studies. Azevedo (2005a, 2005b) suggested that computer-based learning environments may be viewed as metacognitive tools to enhance SRL. Zimmerman and Tsikalis (2005, p. 270) reviewed the contributions to a special issue of Educational Psychologist on the effect of computer-based learning environments (CBLE) on SRL and learning outcome and concluded: "CBLEs that support self-regulatory processes in all three phases [i.e. forethought, performance, and self-reflection] are more likely to produce positive, self-sustaining cycles of learning". They point out, however, that most of the TELEs studied in the special issue only support students during one or two of the three phases and that most of them did not address motivational aspects of self-regulation. Winters, Green, and Costich (2008) reviewed 33 empirical studies on SRL in CBLEs. They conclude that the studies in their review "provided evidence that different learner and task characteristics (e.g. prior knowledge, goal orientation, learner control) and types of learner support are related to students' SRL when using CBLEs. However, the studies reviewed do not constitute a large body of evidence from which to draw set conclusions about these relationships. Consequently, future research is needed to bolster the trends and relations we have identified in this review" (Winters et al., 2008, p. 440).

Technology Enhanced Learning: Research and Implementation Policies in Europe

During the last two decades, the use of the digital media in educational institutions as well as in industry has markedly increased in many parts of the world, supported by policy measures of national governments and by transnational political bodies. In Europe, the European Council and the European Commission have played an important role. In 1996, the European Council issued a resolution on educational multimedia software in the fields of education and training which was "to help improve the quality and effectiveness of education and training systems and provide access to the information society for teachers, students and apprentices by giving them an insight into the use of these new tools and into training in the subject". (European Council, 1996). Based on this resolution, a programme on "Learning in the information society, action plan for a European education initiative" was developed.

Following the Lisbon European Council meeting in March 2000, the European Commission issued a paper on "eLearning—Designing tomorrow's education" (European Commission, 2000). In the paper, the Commission argued that globalisation and the new knowledge-driven economy confronted the European Union with grave problems which they had to tackle. The Commission therefore proposed an eLearning programme with four main lines of action. (1) Equipment, (2) Training at all levels, (3) Development of good quality multimedia services and contents, and (4)

Development and networking of centres for acquiring knowledge. The proposal was implemented as the eLearning Initiative from 2001 to 2003 (elearningeuropa, n.d.) and the eLearning Action Plan for the years 2001–2004 (European Commission, 2001).

In 2002, the European Commission proposed to adopt for the time period of 2004–2006 a multi-annual programme for the effective integration of Information and Communication Technologies (ICT) in education and training systems in Europe (European Commission, 2002a). In 2006, the Education, Audiovisual and Culture Executive Agency (EACEA) was founded as an institution of the European Commission. It was the EACEA's task to implement and pursue the Commission's Lifelong Learning Programme (LLP). The LLP with a budget of nearly seven billion Euros for 2007–2013 was a successor to a number of programmes the Commission had implemented before: (1) Comenius for schools, (2) Erasmus for higher education, (3) Leonardo da Vinci for vocational education and training, and (4) Grundtvig for adult education.

The main goal of the Lifelong Learning Programme is to enable "individuals at all stages of their lives to pursue stimulating learning opportunities across Europe. It is an umbrella programme integrating various educational and training initiatives". (EACEA, n.d.). The European Commission is, however, also funding European research on the use of ICT in education and training through various sub-programmes of its Lifelong Learning Programme. At the same time, it regularly issues calls for proposals for projects in its transversal programme. These are projects that cut across two or more of the LLP sub-programmes. The transversal programme includes four Key Activities: KA1 (Studies and Comparative Research), KA2 (Languages), KA3 (ICT), and KA4 (Valorisation).

In parallel to eLearning activities, the European Commission also implemented framework programmes (FPs) to cover activities of the European Community in the field of research, technological development, and demonstrations (RTD). Technology-enhanced learning has been a flagship priority in all FPs to date. (FP 6 from 2002 to 2006, European Commission, 2002b; FP 7 from 2007 to 2013, European Commission Research, n.d.).

SRL in TELEs: Two Examples from Europe

In this section, we present two large-scale European projects which focused on SRL in TELEs.

TACONET: From a Research Project to a Community of Researchers

In Europe, learning in the information society has become an important topic. It was in the context of the Sixth Framework Programme that the present authors collaborated in a European project on self-regulated learning in technology enhanced learning environments (TELEPEERS) from 2004 to 2006.[1] Altogether, 12 TELEs were evaluated (Table 39.1). In order to evaluate the TELEs, we developed two instruments, one to be used by experts (teachers and researchers: TELE-SRL) and one to be used by students who actually worked in these TELEs (TELESTUDENTS-SRL). Item construction was based on the three-phase cyclic model of self-regulated learning proposed by Zimmerman (1998a, 1998b, 2000): (1) forethought, (2) performance or volitional control, and (3) self-reflection. Across these phases, we distinguished between four dimensions of SRL: cognitive, motivational, emotional, and social.

Looking at the results of the evaluation, a very interesting pattern emerged. While the TELEs in category one (container systems with tutor) were evaluated quite well in total as well as with respect to all the different dimensions, the TELEs of the second group (content systems with tutors)

[1] "Self-regulated Learning in Technology Enhanced Learning Environments at University Level: a Peer Review" (TELEPEERS)".The project was being carried out with the support of the European Commission (Grant agreement 2003-4710-/001-001 EDU-ELEARN).

Table 39.1 TELES which were evaluated in the TELEPEERS project

TELE/home	Description
Container systems with tutor	
Digital Portfolio/Vrije Universiteit Amsterdam	A Web-based collection of student's work to demonstrate his/her efforts, progress and achievements in one ore more areas
DiViDU/Vrije Universiteit Amsterdam	A Web-based digital video used in teacher training to help student reflect on professional skills and attitudes
ILIAS/Universität zu Köln	An Internet-based authoring environment for course designers as well as an Internet-based learning environment for students at university level
Weblogs/Universitetet i Bergen	A personal, but public Web space for self-expression
Content systems with tutor	
ICT-based teacher training/Universidade Católica Portuguesa	An ICT-based teacher training master course to improve ICT knowledge and skills
Cognitive psychology course/ Nottingham Trent University	A Web-based support for an undergraduate course on cognitive psychology
Digital video course/Universidad de Barcelona	A blended learning course aimed at helping students acquire appropriate skills to use digital video and increase awareness of the media
Teacher training course on ET/CNR Istituto per le Tecnologie Didattiche Genoa	A computer mediated communication systems (CMCS) used in teacher training to improve knowledge and skills in Educational Technology
Content systems without tutor	
Sunpower/Universität zu Köln	A CD-ROM programme to improve communication strategies in English for business purposes targeted at adults with an intermediate level of English
Databases/Université de Technologie de Compiègne	An online tutorial on databases with topics ranging from design issues to practical aspects
Programming Tutorial/Université de Technologie de Compiègne	An online tutorial algorithms and programming based on Pascal
SWIM/Aalborg Universitet	A streaming Web-based information module which serves as an online tutorial to help students acquire adequate strategies for information seeking

also did quite well in total, but the evaluation of their potential to foster SRL was high only on the emotional and social dimensions, while the TELEs in the third group (content systems without tutor) seemed to support SRL more with respect to its cognitive and motivational dimension. In interpreting these results, it might be helpful to remind ourselves that a TELE is the whole of the technology enhanced learning environment, not just the digital tool which is being used. Bearing this is mind, it does not come too much of a surprise that TELES which are provided with a tutor or teacher seem to support the emotional and social dimension to a greater extent than TELEs without tutors. Where tutors are absent, the cognitive and motivational dimensions seem to play a more important role.

More detailed analyses and results and further studies were first published by each of the TELEPEERS partners, either individually or in collaboration with other partners in a special issue of the European Journal of Education in 2006 (Carneiro & Steffens, 2006; Steffens, 2006). Beishuizen and his team from Vrije Universiteit Amsterdam, together with colleagues from Nottingham Trent University, compared the introduction of portfolios in higher education in the UK and the Netherlands (Beishuizen et al., 2006). Carneiro (2006) explored the question whether ICT would help to motivate teachers in a teacher training programme at the Universidade Católica Portuguesa. Christiansen and Nyvang analysed why a specific TELE was not adopted by students at Aalborg University on the basis of Bateson's ecological epistemology of mind according to which learners, tools, and environment constitute a thinking system (Christiansen & Nyvang, 2006). Dettori, Giannetti, and Persico (2006) at

CNR Istituto per le Tecnologie Didattiche studied the role of SRL in online cooperative learning and its implications for pre-service teacher training. Underwood and her colleagues from Nottingham Trent University explored the important question whether the new ICTs inhibit or facilitate SRL (Banyard, Underwood, & Twiner, 2006). Bartolomé and his colleagues (Willem, Aiello, & Bartolomé, 2006) from Universitat de Barcelona report on a blended learning course they ran on the image of ethnic minorities and immigrants in the Spanish media, focusing on the question of whether the acquisition of SRL skills in a TELE would promote media literacy. Trigano (2006) from Université de Technologie de Compiègne had different versions of an ICT-supported course on algorithms and programming evaluated by experts and students where results showed that both groups of evaluators felt that the TELEs did seem to foster SRL. Baggetun and Wasson (2006) from Universitetet i Bergen studied Weblogs of their students with respect to their potential to foster SRL.

Soon after having started to work together in 2004, the participating researchers decided to initiate a Targeted Cooperative Network on Self-Regulated Learning in Technology Enhanced Learning Environments (TACONET).[2] Since then, the network has organised four international conferences on the topic of SRL in TELEs, the first one at the Universitat de Barcelona in 2004, the second at Universidade Católica Portuguesa in 2005 (Carneiro, Steffens, & Underwood, 2005), the third at Vrije Universiteit Amsterdam in 2007[3] (Beishuizen et al., 2007), and most recently at Universitat de Barcelona in 2010[4] (Bartolomé et al., 2011). While members of the TACONET network have contributed to other international conferences and workshops individually or in collaboration, they also have published their research results jointly (Bartolomé et al., 2007; Carneiro, Lefrere, Steffens, & Underwood, 2011). At the same time, they have initiated important projects in their countries. As a concrete example currently under implementation, we would like to report on the NOI in Portugal in which the first author had a leading role.

SRL and the NOI in Portugal

In this section we shall process empirical results of an extensive evaluative research conducted during the years 2008–2010[5] on NOI, a flagship programme implemented by the Portuguese government to accredit prior learning (APL) and to upgrade low-skilled adults to secondary levels of qualifications. NOI[6]—New Opportunities Initiative—is an innovative approach to motivate low-skilled adults to embark in a system of informal and non-formal skills recognition, accreditation and certification, with complements of formal learning, to achieve 4th, 6th, 9th and 12th grades education diplomas or/and a vocational certification. These complements of formal learning can be achieved through one of two paths: (1) enrolling in a school adult education programme, or (2) undergoing flexible modular training often offered through the New Opportunity Centre (NOC) itself. In one or another format of additional training, ICT occupies a significant place both as a subject of learning and most importantly as a means to collect information and to access knowledge.

NOI is a public sponsored programme which is generously funded by POPH (Programa Operacional de Potencial Humano) one of the three key nation-wide operational programmes co-financed by the structural funds under the

[2] See http://www.lmi.ub.es/taconet/ and http://www.taconet.org.

[3] As part of a seed project on SRL in TELEs with the financial support from the KALEIDOSCOPE Network of Excellence "Concepts and methods for exploring the future of learning with digital technologies" (2004–2006). http://www.noe-kaleidoscope.org/telearc/.

[4] As part of a Theme Team project on SRL in TELEs with the financial support from the STELLAR Network of Excellence "*S*ustaining *T*echnology *E*nhanced *L*earning at a *LAR*ge scale" (2009–2012). http://www.stellarnet.eu/.

[5] The text of this introduction is based on Carneiro (2010).

[6] Iniciativa Novas Oportunidades, http://www.en.anq.gov.pt/ and http://www.novasoportunidades.gov.pt/, Accessed December 31, 2010

Community Supported Framework 2007–2013. NOI targets the entire Portuguese adult population of low-skilled (estimated at around 72% of the labour force below secondary studies, or circa 3.5 million adults according to the 2001 Population Census). Its strategic objective is to reverse centuries of disinvestment in human capital and to endow the population with a minimum threshold of upper secondary qualifications. Barely five years after its announcement, about 450 New Opportunity Centres (NOCs) were put in place to operationalise the Initiative at field level. These NOCs hired over 10,000 adult education experts, register a record 1.6 million enrolments and have topped the impressive figure of 500,000 certifications (9th and 12th grades, equivalent to lower and upper secondary, respectively).[7] The Initiative addresses, by design, two distinct areas of intervention:

- The qualification of youth, curbing the high rates of failure and dropout from initial education and training systems.
- The qualification of adults, improving access and encouraging participation of the labour force into training programmes and vocational education.

Our research question addresses the adult qualification challenge. The quest consists in finding out to what extent NOI graduates have developed SRL skills epitomised along three key dimensions: metacognitive, metasocial, and metamotivation skills. The answer to this question may provide relevant clues to address effectively a window of strategic issues, burdened with heavy social consequences, which is lacking empirically supported policies: Is it possible to develop SRL competences in the low-skilled groups, those who constitute, as a rule, the population segments that present the greatest resilience to learning? Would it be feasible to design a quality lifelong learning system attractive to early school dropouts, capable of equipping the least qualified with metalearning motivations and competences? Could we dream of and realise an all-inclusive lifelong learning model that addresses the century old utopia of overcoming a persistent dichotomy between *haves and have nots*? (Carneiro, 2010).

NOI Metalearning Outcomes

Mapping learning outcomes and gains in competences constituted one of the priorities pursued in the comprehensive evaluative research undertaken on NOI. The overt aim was to support an evidence-based policy that would remain open to continuous improvement based on a comprehensive evaluative research. The empirical evidence gathered this far (two full years of field work and case studies, focus-groups and in-depth interviews, quantitative telephone surveys, and online surveys) allows us to focus in this section on meta-learning or learning to learn outcomes. Enhanced metalearning acquisitions are translated into augmented SRL capacities. One overall consequence of increased SRL competences is measured by the individual's propensity to undertake lifelong learning activities and strategies. Thus, a first integrated birds eye view provides evidence on accrued foundation skills for lifelong learning acquired by the average NOI graduate, with particular reference to:

(a) Literacy and eSkills (reading, writing, speaking, computer use, and Internet use) and evidence of changing daily habits after certification especially among the low skilled.
(b) Learning to learn skills (self-image and self-esteem, critical thinking, motivation for learning, learning strategies and participation in education and training): especially improved self-esteem and motivation for learning among the low skilled.
(c) Improved soft skills—personal and social skills, civic competences, and cultural awareness and expression.
(d) Less progress in basic skills: science and technology and foreign languages.

The methodology followed to evaluate NOI outcomes resorted to the European key competences framework which was for this purpose broken down into specific skills narratives and descriptors (Table 39.2). In the following sections we

[7] Latest figures available for 30 April 2011.

Table 39.2 Based on Portuguese key competencies frameworks for basic and secondary level of education (adult education)

Literacy skills	e.Skills	Science and technology basic skills	Language skills	Communication and cross-cultural skills	Personal and interactional social skills	Civic and ethic skills	Learning to learn skills
Reading and writing	Computer	Science	Mother tongue	Cultural diversity and expression	Self-direction and initiative	Diversity and responsibility	Self-concept and self-esteem
Listening and speaking	Internet	Technology	Foreign languages	Cultural participation	Change and adaptability	Civic participation	Thinking skills
Arithmetic and maths	Information	Systems			Interaction and collaboration		Learning motivation
	Media				Communication and influence		Learning strategies
Hard skills				*Soft skills*			*Meta skills*

shall probe into the broad database that was collected and organised as a result of the evaluative research undertaken. The purpose will be to dig out a further understanding on how low-skilled adults are able to consolidate a consistent set of self-regulated learning aptitudes and skills as a by-product of a APL/RPL type of certification. In particular, we shall interpret existing data addressing the three domains that were previously referred: metacognitive skills, metasocial skills, and metamotivation skills.

Metacognitive Skills

Learning to Learn

The generality of field observations leads us to conclude that the autonomy of the learning adult benefits from NOI processes. As an illustration, most adults are led to find their own solutions and to construct their self-reflections from the very first phase of producing a personal portfolio. Persons involved in NOI are required to develop a personal skills scorecard that leads adults into a better awareness of their strengths and weaknesses: what one knows, what one does not know, and also what one needs to learn to achieve a certain target in personal development. Concurrently, introduction to and familiarisation with the Internet ignites research skills that are potent levers of continuing learning and training.

Skills for Lifelong Learning

Anecdotal descriptions bear witness on NOI graduates' quantum improvements in task planning and management, including sustainable commitments to learning events (Valente, 2010):

> The person before me (juror of final appraisal session) is not the one I knew at the beginning.
> Ladies would come in (at NOC) low spirited, insecure; a few months later we notice an abyss of differences in these persons.

Learning to learn skills were among the highly ranked key competences and a path toward personal transformation. Effective learning to learn abilities include self-image and self-esteem, critical thinking, motivation for learning, learning strategies and participation in education and training. Although all of them appear to have progressed, the most significant gains were registered on self-esteem and motivation for learning among adults at lower secondary education.

It is most telling to observe the skills summary in the form of radar plotting that brings together in one same representation three sets of skills: before certification, after certification, and skills in use (actual job environment). This is done separately for lower secondary and for secondary education NOI graduates (Figs. 39.1 and 39.2). While lower secondary individuals reported a higher progress in almost all key competences particularly in hard skills—an expected outcome considering their lower levels of departure—those in upper secondary still reported considerable gains around the entire spectrum of appraised skills. Soft skills, such as personal and social skills, civic competences, and cultural awareness and expression undergo improvement but in a smaller and less consistent scale.

Curiously, when zooming into the job place one understands that hard skills are much less used in work contexts than soft and meta skills. Workers, regardless of their educational attainment, seldom use writing skills or basic skills in science and technology, and foreign languages and, when they get to use them, they do so at rather low complexity levels.

Enhanced ICT Skills

ICT is a domain that merits a special focus, grounded on the fact that research ascertains a maximum gain in competences by NOI graduates, including the former info-excluded. Indeed, over 80% of graduates regard themselves regular Internet users, a number that is at least 30% over the national average (Lopes, 2010). Our data show that there is a profound difference (sig $\chi^2=0.000$) in Internet use by educational level. Controlling for variables concerning NOI itineraries, while upper secondary achievers are close to 100% digital persons, those who have not gone beyond grade 6 (basic education) are handicapped at below

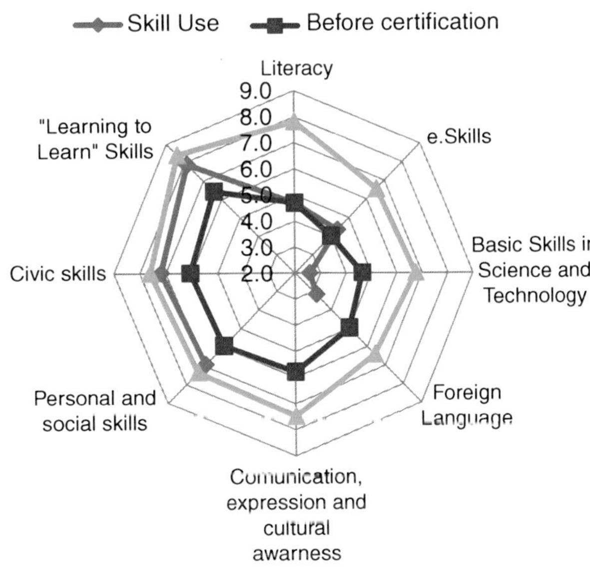

Fig. 39.1 Skills at lower secondary level

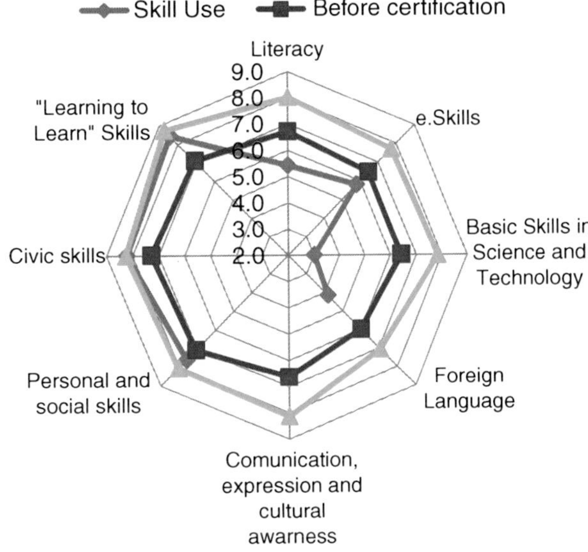

Fig. 39.2 Skills at upper secondary level

average utilisation rates. Two thirds of those interviewed declared to be non-Internet users before NOI. In other words, the successful completion of NOI, having experienced its unique processes, enhances regular individual Internet use in the order of threefold. The scope of this gain runs inversely to the initial level of education. While 80% of lower secondary persons report having access to the Internet for the first time, only 40% of those with upper secondary education did so.

Metasocial Skills

Above average social participation rates touch upon five categories. Albeit minimal in all five items one witnesses gains attributable to a successful conclusion of NOI. The biggest improvement is in category "talking about the world", a category covering topics as politics, society and economy. When analysing the polarity of responses the NPI (Negative Polarity Index) barely touches 6% while the PPI (Positive Polarity Index) increases to 47.8%. Likewise, when interrogated on attention devoted to politics on TV, radio or newspapers, while NPI is 15.4% PPI reaches 31.6%.

Two of these categories—"participation in environmental groups" and "social work volunteering"—struck a much more balanced polarisation: NPI 33.1% and 27.8%; PPI 23.7% and 25.9%, respectively. On the negative side one registers a high polarisation coupled with diminishing interests in unionisation (PPI 9.7% and NPI 49%) and to a lesser extent in political affiliation (PPI 8.4% and NPI 57%). These extreme polarisation values hint at the prevalence of strong emotional feelings whose main effect would be to hide social self-regulatory acquisitions. It is worth adding that statistical indicators of intergroup segregation are modest (sig $\chi^2=0.051$ to 0.730). Moreover, our survey shows a neat increase of social skills that are instrumental to the exercise of active citizenship and good parenting.

In summary, numerous participants underscored the "group spirit", ranking this item high in the list of NOI achievements. Collaboration, team work, intergenerational shared learning, participatory debate sessions, open discussions on contemporary issues and study visits were highlighted as strong points in the NOI methodology. These NOI learning styles were deemed extremely beneficial in support of awareness building and in providing confident routes to knowledge construction and co-construction. Social learning became prevalent at all moments, in the testimonies of NOI graduates, who praised the extended relational experiences reaching out to local communities, local authorities, teachers, and employers. Regardless of the respect owed to personal itineraries the NOI experiences are invariably seen as rich and rewarding social interactions by the heavy majority of participants.

Metamotivation Skills

Trust, Confidence, and Security: Self-Efficacy and Social Roles

Generally speaking the impacts on the self stand out as a primal acquisition by NOI graduates. The most salient aspect is the notion of mastering augmented levels of "general culture", a benefit mentioned by 55.5% of the surveyed. Significantly above the 25% bar, respondents single out the increase in knowledge concerning informatics, enhanced technical knowledge and the will to continue studying. Self-improvement scores worth underlining are: "I have a greater capacity to seek information" (21.4%), "My will to carry out further studies" (24.6%), "I realised that I have to know more" (36.3%). A most interesting fact is that 0.5% of NOI graduates with an upper secondary education certificate have enrolled in higher education while 3.5% intend to do so in the near future. Those who report little or no objective impacts on their formative self were 18%. Once again, following the already mentioned trend, upper secondary graduates reach higher levels of knowledge acquisition (sig $\chi^2=0.001$ to 0.055 differentiation indicators) while the lower skilled exhibit major gains in the area of informatics (sig $\chi^2=0.016$ to 0.052 differentiation indicators).

We observed extremely strong advancements regarding a number of important personality traits that feed into self-esteem namely (on a 1–10 scale): pride (8.13–8.86), capacity to share and discuss ideas (7.23–8.51), better social skills (7.10–8.32), happier and fulfilled (7.48–8.59 and 7.76–8.57, respectively). The evolution in "perceived self-security" before and after NOI confirms these findings.

An identical pattern is found when comparing levels of extroversion/introversion. Notwithstanding a more thorough analysis, this particular piece of data brings us to another interesting discovery. At the outset one sees clear intergroupal differences, with secondary graders scoring higher extroversion than the lower skilled (sig $\chi^2=0.025$). However, this situation is reversed (sig $\chi^2=0.308$) after NOI because the latter achieve much higher increases in extroversion than the former in relative terms, demonstrating a remarkable catching-up trajectory. Furthermore, our survey shows a notorious mastery and use of core social skills as a consequence of personal gains (developing a robust self). This mix of personal and social competences is instrumental to the exercise of both active citizenship and good parenting.

To summarise the main findings, we can say that NOI adults seem to benefit from an enhanced motivation to learn and from an increased awareness toward the relevance of lifelong learning. They remain attentive to the available opportunities for advanced learning and embark frequently in further training. Moreover, they report accrued self and informal learning outcomes and tend to keep strong links (alumni-type) with their NOC felt as a precious door to enable access to a whole new world of learning. It is now commonplace to ascertain that successful lower secondary graduates move forward enrolling in higher secondary processes combining APL and formal education requirements. A similar trend is observable concerning instrumental skills that explain higher demands in short technical or career oriented training courses: foreign language, ICT, accounting, job specific skills.

Grounded on observable behaviours, we can ascertain that NOI adults have gained a "thirst" for learning and are now prepared to define future ambitions, dreams and goals (FTP—future time perspective). FTP goals are an essential foundation of personal motivation to engage in effort learning insofar as they enable delaying short-term gratification stemming from a determination to arrive at longer term objectives.

Changing Perceptions of Learning

This section deals with transformative learning outcomes, those that enable access to a second loop of generative learning and knowledge acquisition strategies. There is ample evidence that NOI processes may produce profound changes in the entire perception of adults vis-à-vis education institutions, "reconciling them with the school" (Valente, 2010). Most of the participants were early school dropouts who carried a prejudiced view towards a school that they disliked and abandoned in their youth days and shared negative memories of the educational establishment. Having completed NOI provides them with both a feeling of atonement and a fresh inward look that reveals and releases a learning ambition to move life upward (Liz, Machado, & Portugal, 2010).

One relevant aspect that enables this transformation is the unique learning environment offered by NOI which is often alluded to as its major strength. It is like "discovering" the other side of the school where learning is practical, experiential, even magically enjoying, while intertwined with the formal recognition and certification of prior informal learning, a proud personal asset that was previously regarded useless and grossly valueless before NOI came into practice. Perceiving the value of one's learning experience and the resulting increase in self-esteem creates a sense of personal responsibility which equips the person to face the future and to engage in lifelong learning which in turn allows her/him to settle "unfinished business" and to get closure on the past which in turn will result in investing real effort directed at the transformation of daily routines (see Fig. 39.3). Thus, it is relevant to speak of transformational cycles of the self with distinct achievements at lower secondary and upper secondary certifications through NOI procedures.

Outlook

During the last decade, lifelong learning has become an important issue in many countries around the globe, and digital literacy, as well as learning to learn or self-regulated learning are

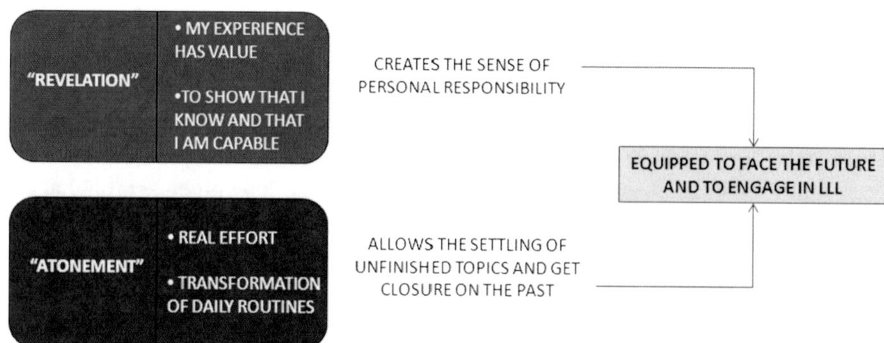

Fig. 39.3 Personal transformation cycles

being considered essential competencies (Delors et al., 1996; European Council, 2006; Steffens, 2011). In Europe, policy measures have aimed at implementing ICT in education in order to support the acquisition of these competencies. As we have shown in our report on TACONET activities, there is empirical evidence that TELEs do have the potential to support SRL. But as Kirkwood and Price stated after having reviewed a large number of studies on technology enhanced learning: "… although ICT can enable new forms of teaching and learning to take place, they cannot ensure that effective and appropriate learning outcomes are achieved" (Kirkwood & Price, 2005; p. 257). We should be aware that the implementation of ICT is not sufficient to achieve a change in learning that takes place in institutions of education and training. As Salomon noted almost 20 years ago: "If nothing significant changes in the classroom save the introduction of a tool, few if any important effects can be expected" (Salomon, 1993, p. 189).

The NOI is a good example of a significant change in the educational and training system of a country. ICT did play an important role, but the scope of change that was reached encompassed much more dimensions than a simple enhancement in the utilisation of digital technologies. NOI empirical evidence brings into life a much sought aim: that of singling out ways and strategies to bring down the barriers that have excluded low-skilled adults both from the effective participation in continuing learning and from the acquisition of the minimum self-regulating skills that characterise a competent lifelong learner—a very promising approach.

References

Azevedo, R. (2005a). Computer environments as metacognitive tools for enhancing learning. *Educational Psychologist, 40*, 193–197.

Azevedo, R. (2005b). Using hypermedia as a metacognitive tool for enhancing student learning? The role of self-regulated learning. *Educational Psychologist, 40*(4), 199–209.

Azevedo, R. (2009). Theoretical, conceptual, methodological, and instructional issues in research on metacognition and self-regulated learning: A discussion. *Metacognition and Learning, 4*, 87–95.

Baggetun, R., & Wasson, B. (2006). Self-regulated learning and open writing. *European Journal of Education, 41*(3/4), 453–472.

Banyard, P., Underwood, J., & Twiner, A. (2006). Do enhanced communication technologies inhibit or facilitate self-regulated learning? *European Journal of Education, 41*(34), 473–490.

Bartolomé, A., Beishuizen, J., Carneiro, R., Hansen, C., Lefrere, P., Lenné, D., et al. (2007). *Self-regulated learning in technology enhanced learning environments: A European review*. http://www.telearn.org/open-archive/browse?resource=1603_v1. Retrieved 29 December, 2010.

Bartolomé, A., Bergamin, P., Persico, D., Steffens, K., & Underwood, J. (Eds.). (2011). *Self-regulated learning in technology enhanced learning environments: Problems and promises. Proceedings of the STELLAR-*

TACONET Conference, Barcelona, Oct. 1, 2010. Aachen: Shaker.

Beishuizen, J., Carneiro, R., & Steffens, K. (2007). *Self-regulated learning in technology enhanced learning environments: Individual learning and communities of learners. Proceedings of the Kaleidoscope-Taconet conference Amsterdam*. Aachen: Shaker.

Beishuizen, J., & Steffens, K. (2011). A conceptual framework for research on technology enhanced learning. In R. Carneiro, P. Lefrere, K. Steffens, & J. Underwood (Eds.), *Self-regulated learning in technology enhanced learning environments: A European perspective* (pp. 3–19). Rotterdam: Sense Publishers.

Beishuizen, J., van Boxel, P., Banyard, P., Twiner, A., Vermeij, H., & Underwood, J. (2006). The introduction of portfolios in higher education: a comparative study in the UK and the Netherlands. *European Journal of Education, 41*(3/4), 491–508.

Carneiro, R. (2006). Motivating school teachers to learn: Can ICT add value? *European Journal of Education, 41*(3/4), 415–436.

Carneiro, R. (Ed.). (2010). *New opportunities—How Portugal catches-up with adult qualifications: What research tells us*. CEPCEP, UCP: Lisboa.

Carneiro, R., Lefrere, P., Steffens, K., & Underwood, J. (Eds.). (2011). *Self-regulated learning in technology enhanced learning environments: A European perspective*. Rotterdam: Sense Publishers.

Carneiro, R., & Steffens, K. (2006). Self-regulated learning in technology-enhanced learning environments: Studies in European higher education. Editorial. *European Journal of Education, 41*(3/4), 345–352.

Carneiro, R., Steffens, K., & Underwood, J. (Eds.). (2005). *Self-regulated learning in technology enhanced learning environments. Proceedings of the TACONET Conference in Lisbon, Sept.23*. Aachen: Shaker.

Christiansen, E., & Nyvang, T. (2006). Understanding the adoption of TELEs—The importance of management. *European Journal of Education, 41*(3/4), 509–519.

Delors, J., et al. (1996). *Learning: The treasure within. Report to UNESCO of the International Commission on Education for the Twenty-first Century*. Paris: UNESCO.

Dettori, G., Giannetti, T., & Persico, D. (2006). SRL in online cooperative learning: Implications for pre-service teacher training. *European Journal of Education, 41*(3/4), 379–414.

EAEAC. (n.d.). About lifelong learning programme. http://eacea.ec.europa.eu/llp/about_llp/about_llp_en.php. Retrieved 28 December, 2010.

eLearningeuropa. (n.d.). DOSSIER: eLearning programme 2000–2006: The Legacy. http://www.elearningeuropa.info/directory/index.php?page=doc&doc_id=17521&doclng=6. Retrieved 28 December, 2010.

European Commission. (2000). e-Learning—Designing tomorrow's education. http://ec.europa.eu/education/archive/elearning/comen.pdf. Retrieved 28 December, 2010.

European Commission. (2001). The eLearning action plan, Designing tomorrow's education. http://europa.eu/legislation_summaries/other/c11050_en.htm. Retrieved 28 December, 2010.

European Commission. (2002a). Proposal for a decision of the European Parliament and of the council adopting a multi-annual programme (2004–2006) for the effective integration of Information and Communication Technologies (ICT) in education and training systems in Europe. http://ec.europa.eu/education/archive/elearning/doc/dec_en.pdf. Retrieved 28 December, 2010.

European Commission. (2002b). The sixth framework programme in brief. http://ec.europa.eu/research/fp6/pdf/fp6-in-brief_en.pdf. Retrieved 28 December, 2010.

European Commission Research. (n.d.). What is FP7? The basics. http://ec.europa.eu/research/fp7/understanding/fp7inbrief/what-is_en.html. Retrieved 28 December, 2010.

European Council. (1996). Council resolution of 6 May 1996 relating to educational multimedia software in the fields of education and training. Official Journal C 195, 6 July 1996, http://europa.eu/legislation_summaries/other/c11031_en.htm. Retrieved 28 December, 2010

European Council. (2006). Recommendation of the European Parliament and of the Council of 18 December 2006 on key competences for lifelong learning http://eurlex.europa.eu/LexUriServ/LexUriServ.do?uri=OJ:L:2006:394:0010:0018:en:PDF. Retrieved 11 April, 2010.

Kirkwood, A., & Price, L. (2005). Learners and learning in the twenty-first century: what do we know about students' attitudes towards and experiences of information and communication technologies that will help us design courses? *Studies in Higher Education, 30*, 257–274.

Liz, C., Machado, M., & Portugal, J. (2010). Brand modelling the citizen perception of a Public Policy. In R. Carneiro (Ed.), *New opportunities—How Portugal catches-up with adult qualifications: what research tells us*. Lisboa: CEPCEP, UCP.

Lopes, H. (2010). Discussing new opportunities inside S-D Logic. In R. Carneiro (Ed.), *New opportunities—How Portugal catches-up with adult qualifications: what research tells us*. Lisboa: CEPCEP, UCP.

Salomon, G. (1993). On the nature of pedagogic computer tools: The case of writing partner. In S. P. Lajoie & S. J. Derry (Eds.), *Computers as cognitive tools* (pp. 179–196). Hillsdale, NJ: Lawrence Erlbaum.

Steffens, K. (2006). Self-regulated learning in technology enhanced learning environments: Lessons of a European peer review. *European Journal of Education, 41*(3/4), 353–379.

Steffens, K. (2011). Can schools produce lifelong learners? In R. Carneiro (Ed.). (2012). *New learning and educational innovation: The role of Information and Communication Technologies*. São Paulo: Vanguarda Educação Editora.

Trigano, P. (2006). Self-regulated learning in a TELE at the Université de Technologie de Compiègne: An analysis from multiple perspectives. *European Journal of Education, 41*(3/4), 381–396.

Valente, A. (2010). Bringing lifelong learning into low skilled adults' life. In R. Carneiro (Ed.), *New opportunities—How Portugal catches-up with adult qualifications: what research tells us*. Lisboa: CEPCEP, UCP.

Willem, C., Aiello, M., & Bartolomé, A. (2006). Self-regulated learning and new literacies: An experience at the University of Barcelona. *European Journal of Education, 41*(3/4), 437–490.

Winters, F. I., Greene, J. A., & Costich, C. A. (2008). Self-regulation of learning within computer-based environments: A critical analysis. *Educational Psychology Review, 20*, 429–444.

Zimmerman, B. J. (1998a). Developing self-fulfilling cycles of academic regulation: an analysis of exemplary instructional models. In D. H. Schunk & B. J. Zimmerman (Eds.), *Self-regulated learning from teaching to self-reflective practice* (pp. 1–19). New York: Guildford.

Zimmerman, B. J. (1998b). Models of self-regulated learning and academic achievement. In B. J. Zimmerman & D. H. Schunk (Eds.), *Self-regulated learning and academic achievement. Theory, research and practice* (pp. 1–25). New York: Springer.

Zimmerman, B. J. (2000). Attaining self-regulation: a social cognitive perspective. In M. Boekaerts, P. Pintrich, & M. Zeidner (Eds.), *Handbook of self-regulation* (pp. 13–39). New York: Academic Press.

Zimmerman, B. J., & Tsikalis, K. E. (2005). Can computer-based learning environments (CBLEs) be used as self-regulatory tools to enhance learning? *Educational Psychologist, 40*(4), 267–271.

Self-Observation and Shared Reflection to Improve Pronunciation in L2

40

Giuliana Dettori and Valentina Lupi

Abstract

This study concerns the use of audio technology and metacognition to improve pronunciation in the learning of a second language (L2). It describes a methodological approach to guide L2 learners to observe their utterances and become aware of their pronunciation errors, with the support of peer collaboration and metacognitive prompts. Identifying pronunciation errors is not easy because it requires good self-observation, evaluation and reflection skills. A meaningful episode from a pilot test of our methodological approach is presented, together with some reflections on the potential implications of our work.

Introduction

In the past couple of decades, metacognition has been increasingly considered a valuable support to the learning of a second language (L2) (Cotteral & Murray, 2009; Victori & Lockhardt, 1995; Wenden, 1998). Its application in this field has concerned several aspects in language learning, in particular: the conscious use of learning strategies (Rivera-Mills & Plonsky, 2007), the development of metalinguistic reflection (Gombert, 1992; Simard, 2004; Suzuki & Itagaki, 2007), and instruction for listening comprehension (Goh, 2008; Graham & Macaro, 2008; Valiente, 2008; Vandergrift & Tafaghodtari, 2010). Effective language learning strategies mainly concern memory development, work organization, and evaluation of personal language-related outcomes. Metalinguistic reflection consists in learner's conscious attention to the nature and function of linguistic elements; it can be carried out either within a single language or through the comparison of different languages. Finally, improving listening comprehension involves practicing core skills, such as listening selectively, e.g., for details or for gist, making inferences, and predicting the content of the following sentences, yet always keeping the attention on the development of effective communication; in this process, it is important that the learners develop awareness of task requirements as well as of their own strengths and weaknesses as listeners.

G. Dettori (✉)
Institute for Educational Technology—CNR,
Via De Marini 6, 16149 Genoa, Italy
e-mail: dettori@itd.cnr.it

V. Lupi
Junior High School "Don Milani-Colombo",
Salita Carbonara 51, 16125 Genoa, Italy

R. Azevedo and V. Aleven (eds.), *International Handbook of Metacognition and Learning Technologies*, Springer International Handbooks of Education 26, DOI 10.1007/978-1-4419-5546-3_40,

We focus on applying metacognition to a different step in L2 learning, namely, helping learners improve their pronunciation. This is a very important aspect, because good pronunciation and the ability to apply it in oral production are crucial to successful language use. The difficulty of improving pronunciation is evidenced by the fact that learners are often unable to identify their own errors, unless they are trained to do so (Dlaska & Krekeler, 2008). This is particularly true with young students, who are often barely aware of their learning outcomes. Disregarding these points contributes to low achievement in L2 for many learners.

Learning to pronounce effectively is usually viewed as a process in which rules are learned by heart and automated, and hence not as a typical application domain for metacognition. In our opinion, however, improving this aspect involves metacognition to a substantial degree, in that it requires that learners have a high level of awareness of their own utterances and the ability to evaluate them in comparison with those of others. This ability entails acquiring nontrivial observation/self-observation and reflection abilities, which in turn require the selection and application of regulatory strategies to plan, monitor, and evaluate the activity.

Audio files can be used to help students become aware of sound nuances, especially since current technology allows much more precise and flexible use of audio than was possible when language learning was relying on cassette recordings and the like. As with any other technology employed in education, however, we cannot expect the tool to be effective if not paired with a suitable methodology of use (Domine, 2009). In order to meet these learning needs, we have designed a methodological approach to the use of audio technology and have tested it in a junior secondary school to check if it is actually feasible and apt to put into play metacognitive processes suitable to improve L2 pronunciation.

Conceived in the context of task-based language teaching and learning (Ellis, 2003) and based on the theoretical framework of metacognition (see Sect. "Metacognition" below), our proposal consists of a number of short tasks of increasing difficulty to be carried out over a few months, in parallel to regular classes, so as to complement the usual curricular activities on grammar, lexicon, and civilization, yet running independently of them. We intentionally avoided the typical devices proposed in phonetics studies, such as analysis of larynx and tongue movements or diagrams of sound pitches, because our aim is not to give learners phonetics competence but rather to help them become able to use precisely and in a natural way the sounds of a second language by gaining awareness of what they actually utter. Introducing technical notions in this respect would only add cognitive load and make learners (especially teenagers, who are our main target population) look at oral production in L2 as an artificial activity.

In the next section we present the theoretical framework of metacognition that is at the basis of our work. In Sect. "Applying Metacognition and Audio Technology to Improve L2 Pronunciation", we describe the main issue, the technology applied and our methodological approach. We also describe and comment on a representative episode of its pilot implementation. Some reflections on possible implications of our work conclude the chapter.

Metacognition

Metacognition was initially addressed in the seventies of the past century in the area of developmental and cognitive psychology and has subsequently attracted the attention of an ever-growing number of researchers and practitioners in several fields. This diversity has given rise to a large amount of literature analyzing metacognition from a variety of perspectives that are not always in complete agreement with each other; as a consequence, a complete and consistent conceptualization of metacognition is still object of study (Veenman, van Hout-Wolters, & Afflerbach, 2006). Here, we limit our theoretical framework to the main characteristic aspects and to those that are relevant for our work.

The Nature of Metacognition

According to Flavell, to whom the birth of this field of inquiry is usually credited, metacognitive knowledge is "knowledge concerning one's own cognitive processes or products or anything related to them … For example, I am engaging in metacognition … if I notice that I am having more trouble learning A than B … if I think to ask someone about E to see if I have it right" (1976, p. 232).

In a later paper, Flavell deepens the concept and defines metacognitive knowledge as "knowledge and beliefs about what factors or variables act and interact in what ways to affect the course and outcome of cognitive enterprises" (1979, p. 907). He identifies three different types of metacognitive knowledge, which correspond respectively to focusing on the learner, on the learning task and on the process of learning: *person knowledge* (knowledge about oneself and others as cognitive processors), *task knowledge* (knowledge about the information and resources needed to undertake a task), and *strategy knowledge* (knowledge regarding the strategies which are likely to be effective to support tasks development and goal achievement).

Numerous studies from other authors have contributed to increasingly detailed characterizations. The three kinds of knowledge highlighted by Flavell helped identify two main aspects of metacognition: knowledge about knowledge (What is my knowledge gap?) and regulation of knowledge (What should I do to overcome it?) (Schraw & Moshman, 1995). These aspects are at the root of the widely accepted distinction between metacognitive knowledge, on one side, and strategies (Wenden, 1998) or skills (Veenman et al., 2006) on the other.

Differentiating cognition and metacognition is an important and difficult question. In general, knowledge that is used to solve problems and accomplish tasks is cognitive, while knowledge that enables learners to influence their own mental activity is considered metacognitive. Despite the clear distinction between these two kinds of knowledge from a theoretical point of view, separating them is not easy in practice, because it appears that learners move back and forth between metacognitive and cognitive processes frequently and rapidly (Larkin, 2010). Cognitive and metacognitive activities usually form a circular process in which it is difficult to completely separate the two components (Veenman et al., 2006). The ratio between cognition and metacognition in leaning activities varies over time, while learners acquire expertise, because regulation strategies, which initially need to be consciously applied and involve metacognition, gradually become internalized and automated, hence turning into cognitive skills, whose application does not require metacognitive processing (Larkin, 2010; Williams & Atkins, 2009).

It has been documented that learners of any age can have metacognitive knowledge (Wenden, 1998). It is recognized that this knowledge can appear rather early in childhood (Desoete, 2008; Larkin, 2010), under the influence of interaction with the environment, and then can continue to develop through adolescence (Schraw & Moshman, 1995), and even throughout life (Veenman et al., 2006). Strategies, on the other hand, are the basis of intentional and purposeful action, and must be selected consciously from among alternatives in order to attain some intended goal (Griffith & Ruan, 2005). Strategies develop later than knowledge, and usually need training and practice to improve (Schraw & Moshman, 1995).

Learning Metacognition

Even though research clearly indicates that metacognition can be improved through instruction (Schraw, 1998; Kramarski, 2008), there does not seem to be a single way apt to facilitate metacognitive development in any situation. We report just a few examples.

Based on a large analysis of the literature, Veenman and colleagues (2006) summarize three fundamental principles to favor metacognitive development: embed metacognitive instruction in the content matter; inform learners about the usefulness of metacognitive activities; provide extensive training opportunities. Larkin (2010) points out the need to organize learning situations that expressly require careful, highly conscious thinking and to provide learners with environments allowing metacognition to develop. Desoete (2009) suggests that educators stimulate self-reflection through reflective discourse and pay attention to whether learners correctly attribute success in relation to the use of strategies. Carr (2010) recommends explicit metacognitive instruction by means of self-explanation prompts and social interaction, two activities that also appear to support the transfer of learned skills to different tasks. Williams and Atkins (2009) remark that the effectiveness of strategy instruction does not appear to depend much on the particular strategies that are taught but on the fact that strategy instruction forces the students to pay attention and reflect on the task at hand.

A problem to be tackled during metacognitive instruction is to avoid inert knowledge. It is not rare that learners are aware of metacognitive knowledge and strategies and yet do not attempt, or are not able, to apply them (Hoffman & Spatariu, 2008; Roll, Aleven, & Koedinger, 2008; Schraw & Moshman, 1995). In order to avoid such situations, many authors suggest that learners be supported with metacognitive prompts, that is, questions that activate reflective cognition or recall strategy use. Prompting aims to stimulate awareness of task characteristics, regulation strategies, and evaluation of outcomes; it may influence both the accuracy and the efficiency of a learning activity (Hoffman & Spatariu, 2008). Providing students with metacognitive prompts appears to be more fruitful than showing them how to do an intended task (Roll et al., 2008). It is necessary, however, to avoid prompts that students feel are unnecessary, irrelevant, superfluous or redundant, because being too directive may hinder learners' cognitive activity instead of stimulating it, hence resulting in lower performance (Davis, 2003; Hoffman & Spatariu, 2008).

A different way to overcome the problem of inert metacognitive knowledge is described by Schraw and Moshman (1995), who suggest that learners should integrate their knowledge about cognition and regulatory strategies within a unified conceptual framework. Such integration is called a (personal) metacognitive theory and can take different forms, and gradually changes over time under the influence of personal experience and self-reflection. These authors characterize three different kinds of such metacognitive theories, which depend on the learner's level of awareness of his/her own cognitive functioning as well as of the constructive nature of knowledge: tacit or implicit; explicit and informal; explicit and formal. Awareness appears to be the necessary condition for the learner to be able to apply her/his knowledge and strategies to regulate cognition and learning. Schraw and Moshman also suggest three factors that appear to support learner's construction of a metacognitive theory: cultural learning (internalizing cultural elements via social interaction), individual construction (reflectively analyzing one's cognition and systematizing cognitive skills), and peer interaction (engaging in collective reasoning with a group of peers). Peer interaction is particularly relevant in that learners are reported to engage in more sophisticated reasoning while working as a group than when working alone (Schraw & Moshman, 1995).

The importance of collaborative work to foster metacognition is also highlighted by other authors; Larkin (2010) for instance, points out that metacognition is socially constructed during joint engagement with a task, not only through reflection after completing the task.

Metacognition for Learning

The literature reports on ways of supporting metacognition in general domains, such as memory, writing, and reading understanding, as well as in a variety of subjects, besides language learning, as already mentioned in the introduction: mathematics, science, chemistry, physical education and sport, religious education, ICT, history, geography, art, music and drama, in all cases with a positive influence on subject-matter learning (Hacker, Dunlosky, & Graesser, 2009b; Israel, Collins Block, Bauserman, & Kinnucan-Welsch, 2005; Kaberman & Dori, 2009; Larkin, 2010; Salatas Waters, & Schneider, 2010;Veenman et al., 2006).

Metacognition appears to influence learning outcomes by affecting how learners approach a task (Larkin, 2010). Many authors also claim that metacognitive activities have an impact on learning skills, beyond subject learning, even across domains that have little in common (Kaberman & Dori, 2009). White and colleagues (2009), for instance, argue that metacognition helps people to take charge of their own learning and supports the transfer of learning capabilities from one domain to others. Hacker and colleagues (2009a) assert that the basic components of metacognition can apply to almost any task that a student wants to perform. Larkin (2010) explains the transfer of learning skills across domains based on the fact that repeated application of metacognition leads learners to build a base of metacognitive knowledge about themselves in relation to tasks.

Despite the many voices in favor of the transferability of metacognitive skills across tasks and domains, clearly understanding how and to what extent this transfer takes place is still an open issue. Veenman and colleagues (2006) observe that studies focused on multiple tasks or domains have so far been in limited number and have had inconclusive or contradictory results, so that more investigation would be necessary in this respect. It appears, however, that general metacognition skills actually exist, can be fostered in parallel in different learning situations and are likely flexible enough to transfer to different domains and learning environments (Roll, Aleven, McLaren, & Koedinger, 2007; Veenman et al., 2006).

An important point in favor of giving attention to metacognition in formal learning is that metacognitive competence is, at least partially, independent of intelligence (Larkin, 2010). Intellectual abilities can boost a learner's formation of an initial core of metacognitive knowledge, but do not appear to influence, positively or negatively, its developmental course (Veenman et al., 2006). This means that metacognitive activities can fruitfully be proposed to all students in a class, independent of their proficiency. Also students with poor academic outcomes can take advantage of them. In fact, many authors claim that such activities appear to be particularly beneficial for weaker students (e.g., Goh, 2008; Vandegrift & Tafaghodtari, 2010), since they help them raise their performance to levels closer to those of their academically stronger peers (Kaberman & Dori, 2009). Moreover, the literature reports that metacognition can successfully be used with students with learning disabilities (Desoete, 2009; Larkin, 2010).

Supporting metacognition is a way to favor conceptual change (Larkin, 2010), because this support facilitates reflection on the difference between what learners think is true and newly acquired information that supports or disconfirms the original beliefs (Carr, 2010).

Metacognition appears to be important not only to favor academic achievement, but also in a wider life context. Focusing on this aspect provides an opportunity to look at the learners in all their complexity, as self-aware agents able to construct their understanding of the world (Hacker et al., 2009a). Larkin (2010) points out that learners' ability to reflect upon how they think and act can help them to make wiser decisions in other aspects of life, as well as to understand if they are getting closer or further away from their goals. For this reason, the positive influence of developing metacognition goes far beyond the school context and helps learners gain knowledge about themselves and others in relation to the world (Larkin, 2010).

Applying Metacognition and Audio Technology to Improve L2 Pronunciation

The Key Issue Being Considered

Correctly pronouncing the sounds of a foreign language requires that learners overcome the automatism to pronounce alphabet letters always as in their mother language (Dlaska & Krekeler, 2008), and start to associate letters or groups of letters with possibly different sounds in different contexts. (This last concept is familiar to native speakers of some languages, like English, but is rather surprising to native speakers of many other languages.) This task, hence, requires conceptual change and the use of efficient memorization strategies, both of which benefit from a metacognitive approach.

L2 learners, moreover, need to become able to articulate sounds that may not exist in their language. This entails clearly perceiving their own utterances and those of others and detecting similarities and differences. This ability, which becomes automatic over time, requires the acquisition of self-awareness, the conscious application of strategies and often also the detection of models that can help the learners to evaluate the correctness of their own productions. This again indicates that the learning of L2 pronunciation is a task that benefits from a metacognitive approach.

Spotting pronunciation errors is much less trivial than it might seem, in that students (and people in general) are mostly not used to closely monitoring their own and other's utterances and often keep repeating the same errors because they never really become aware of them despite being repeatedly corrected by their teachers. Effective help in this respect may come from collaboration with peers, in that the literature reports good reliability for peer assessments of pronunciation (Dlaska & Krekeler, 2008).

Working on learners' pronunciation may be supported by means of audio files. These types of files are currently used in school much less often than texts and pictures, and when they are used (which takes place especially in language learning or history) they mostly consist of original documents to be listened to. Students' productions and teacher's corrections, on the other hand, are usually limited to texts (on paper or files), regardless of the topic under study, at the expense of oral production.

The Technology Applied

We tackle the above task by relying on audio technology. In particular, we make use of a program to record and reproduce sounds and of multimedia exercises to practice sound observation.

The software we have been using for recording and playing audio files in the experience described below is Audacity, a free, open source program which is easy to use and to learn and is available, in several languages, for the three most widely used operating systems for personal computers. We considered the possibility of using widely available small recording devices, like portable phones, mp3 or digital recorders, but we found the use of Audacity on a personal computer preferable because of the better (and uniform) quality of sound and the more efficient management of files.

As for the multimedia exercises used to stimulate sound observation, we chose those proposed by the free Web site http://phonetique.free.fr, which require the user to discriminate between similar sounds whose incorrect pronunciation may alter a word's meaning. In this site, the listening exercises are proposed in groups of several items related to similar sounds; when all items in a group have been completed, the learner has the possibility to check the correctness of her/his answers, to correct the errors possibly made and finally to get the right answer in case she/he is unable to work it out. The possibility to see the mistakes made and try to correct them is very important in the context of our approach, because it helps to raise learners' awareness of their weakness and strengths.

Other technological tools for sound recording and observation might obviously be used instead of the mentioned ones, provided they offer the same functionalities.

The Proposed Methodological Approach

Any technology suggested to support education should be paired with a suitable methodology of use, especially in the case of tools of wide applicability, like audio files, which do not embody any educational orientation. To this end, we worked out a methodological approach based on a sequence of increasingly difficult tasks, with the aim to guide learners to observe their own utterances so as to notice pronunciation errors, with the support of group work and of metacognitive prompts provided by the teacher to stimulate perception, reflection, and memorization.

Our target audience are L2 learners, especially young, novice language speakers, who need to acquire a correct method and attitude towards language learning, as well as to become familiar with the sounds of the new language and with the application of suitable strategies to carry out the task. It is important to act at the beginning of language study, before (bad) pronunciation habits are already consolidated. There is no reason, however, to exclude the application of this approach with adult learners who are first tackling, or improving, a foreign language.

Prerequisite to the application of our approach is that the learners be already familiar with the pronunciation rules of the target language, so that they are able to read aloud simple sentences in L2, even if with uncertainties and errors. An initial base of domain-specific knowledge is an essential condition for learners to start the acquisition and use of metacognition, gaining awareness of their learning needs and developing suitable strategies to cope with them (Hoffman & Spatariu, 2008; Veenman et al., 2006). It must be noted, however, that the reverse is not true, i.e., high levels of domain knowledge are not sufficient to guarantee that learners will use metacognitive knowledge and strategies (Schraw, 1998), which stresses the need to plan educational activities stimulating metacognition.

The overall learning path starts with some exercises to help the learners to "sharpen their ears," trying to discriminate between similar sounds that should not be confused with each other. This activity is carried out individually and aims to consolidate the learners' initial base of knowledge on pronunciation. At the end of the exercises the learners are asked to answer a small number of written questions about the difficulties they encountered, so as to help them notice which sounds are more difficult for them to discriminate, hence improving awareness of their own strengths and learning needs. Such self-knowledge is part of metacognitive knowledge, as pointed out by Flavell (1976).

Then the typical tasks start. Each task consists of (individually) recording a short text followed by work in small groups on these audio files. Each group listens to and compares the recordings of all its members, trying to detect all pronunciation errors, discussing what the right pronunciation should be, looking for help from a variety of sources in case of need. Sources to be used should be planned by the teacher according to the learners' general competence and cognitive maturity; they may differ from task to task and range from *ad hoc* recordings provided by the teacher, to audio files on the Web suggested by the teacher, to (on or off line) dictionaries with audio facilities, and up to Web sites (typically videos) autonomously retrieved by the learners themselves. Finally the text is recorded again by each group member, possibly more than once if pronunciation errors are still made, until the group evaluates that a correct version has been obtained. Some general metacognitive prompts are given with the task assignment, to provide some basic guidance for the activity, such as "what do you check to make sure if the words are pronounced correctly?" and "Where can you get help to check which is the correct pronunciation?" Moreover, the teacher keeps an eye on the development of the activity, intervening with other guiding questions when the students seem to be at an impasse and need suggestions to choose a suitable strategy or encouragement to carry on the task. The teacher also pays attention to pronunciation errors possibly overlooked by all group members, so as to call attention on further corrections that are still necessary.

Activities of this kind are repeated several times over a few months, with increasingly complex recordings, until pronunciation confidence and a satisfactory level of proficiency are reached. The texts to be recorded range from short free talks, with basic sentences and a limited variety of words, to more complex free texts, to simple readings, and up to more complex readings requiring attention also to intonation and rhythm.

Each student collects all her/his recordings in a sort of audio portfolio witnessing her/his improvement. This portfolio may be used both for evaluation and to help him/her reflect on his/her progress. At the end of the learning path, each student is asked to write (in his/her native language) a report pointing out the difficulties met, the strategies used and what he/she thinks to have learned in the task. Sharing and discussing these reports with the whole class, under teacher's guidance, aims to further stimulate reflection and self-awareness.

A Practical Implementation

We have tested our approach with Italian pupils in the first year of lower secondary school (11–12 year-olds), who were in their first year of learning French. French pronunciation presents several difficulties for Italian learners because of some letters that are pronounced differently in the two languages (e.g., *e*, *ch*, *u*), the presence of sounds that do not exist in Italian (e.g., nasal vowels, *ll*, *eu*, *e*), groups of letters that sound differently in different contexts (e.g., *ent* at the end of a word, as in *souvent* or in *mangent*) and different groups of letters that sound the same (e.g., *eau*, *au*, and *o*). We now discuss one session of group work on pupils' recordings, to illustrate how the methodological approach works in practice.

The group involved was formed by two girls and one boy, all having average or average-to-low grades in French and in all subjects. This was the first time they met to work on French recordings. They met in school, and had at their disposal a PC with Audacity installed, as well as paper and pencil to take notes. They worked on this task for about 40 min. The whole session was recorded to provide data for analysis.

All pupils had already completed five groups of phonetic exercises assigned by the teacher on the Web site http://phonetique.free.fr, focused on the distinction of [y]—[u]; [e]—[ə]—[ɛ]; [o]—[ø]; [o]—[œ] and nasal vowels, with average results (from zero errors in the [o]-related exercises up to 4 out of 10 concerning the sounds [e]—[ə]—[ɛ]). Moreover, each of them had individually prepared an audio file of 20–30 s, with a short self-presentation in French (name, school, family composition), freely following a pattern recorded by the teacher. Hence, the presentations were similar enough to be comparable, even though they were not exactly equal. The three presentations were of different quality; all of them had pronunciation errors.

The pupils started by listening to the three recordings one after the other, then listened to them again, but did not seem to have an idea how to compare them, so the teacher asked "*Do you remember how all the words were pronounced, when you reach the end of a recording*?" This comment made the pupils realize that they were listening to too much of the recorded speech at once, and started listening the recordings a short piece at a time, alternating between the three files on similar parts, which facilitated discerning single words and how they had been pronounced by the three of them. They started taking notes on paper on the problems they were spotting (which did not include all pronunciation errors).

At the end of this part of the activity, the teacher reminded them that they were supposed to record their presentations again and without errors; hence the pupils decided to concentrate on a presentation at a time, and started listening the same one several times, pointing out what they did not find right, in a happy way as though they were taking part in a game: "*I heard an* e *too much in that word*"—"*You said* italienne, *which is feminine, but you are a boy*" "*the* t *should be heard in that word*", etc., and concluding "*So many mistakes!*". When detecting an error, all the pupils kept trying to pronounce the word correctly, repeating it several times with some variations, as though they had to check if it sounded right, obviously attempting to help the group mate who had pronounced it wrong to correct the pronunciation. This activity sometimes required the intervention of the teacher who helped them notice that there was still a problem and asked how they could get help to fix it: "*we should go to France and listen to native speakers*"—"*well, this is not very practical, we cannot do so now*"—"*we need to find an example*"—"*where can you find an example?*"—"*on the web*"—"*good, where on the web? what do you look for?*"—"*oh, but we can listen the teacher's example!*".

After examining each presentation, its author recorded it again trying to make it right, and the new recording was checked to determine if it was well done. All pupils had to record more than once before they produced a satisfactory version, because some errors were repeated even if they had been recognized in the previous recording. This led them to notice some memory problems, and therefore the teacher asked the group "*what can she do to remember? can you give her a suggestion?*" which prompted the pupils to propose some strategies: "*write it on paper*"—"*repeat it until she remembers*"—"*think of how it is written*". In this rerecording phase all errors were spotted by some of the pupils, and often it was the speaker herself/himself who commented on them. The boy, whose presentation was analyzed last, had made the most errors in the initial recording; in this final phase, he was able to correct himself several times while recording, probably taking advantage of the experience of the session work.

At the end, the teacher asked the pupils to share their impressions of the experience. They had found the activity to be difficult, and also found French difficult, but they thought that working with peers had been helpful, had fun doing the task and were happy to have been able to record a completely correct presentation in the end.

Discussion

The above description of an implementation session gives a good idea of the kinds of behavior that are induced by the proposed methodological approach to the use of audio technology.

At the beginning, the pupils were not able to tackle the task autonomously; they clearly needed guidance in order to focus on the elements to observe and to decide how to proceed and detect sources of help. They reacted positively to the teacher's questions and managed to successfully go through the task. An increasing ability to detect errors is evident if we compare the pupils' behavior at the beginning and at the end of the session: while at the beginning they were simply listening the recordings as a whole, later they learned to concentrate on small portions, where it was easier to notice details, and during the final rerecording they managed to remember all necessary corrections after only a few attempts. In this respect, the teacher crucially helped to boost the metacognitive process with suitable questions, paying attention to the learners' needs at each moment so as to shape and adjust her/his interventions as necessary.

Even though the activation of metacognitive processes is not made explicit in pupils' dialogues, it can be inferred from the cognitive activities carried out; this typically occurs in practical situations, according to the literature (Veenman et al., 2006). The improvement of self-observation and of strategic behavior strongly suggests that metacognition was actually put into play through joint engagement in the task.

The pupils' satisfaction with their improved productions helps build self-confidence in personal pronunciation skills, which in turn is likely to enhance the learner's confidence in being able to communicate in foreign language. This is important from the point of view of our study, since self-confidence is rooted in person-related knowledge and beliefs (Flavell, 1979), so much so that it is reported in the literature that confidence in one's knowledge is a form of metacognition important in academic settings (Lundberg & Mohan, 2009).

Obviously we cannot expect that new skills were acquired in just one session, as the literature underlines the need for repeated practice before learners internalize strategies and automate them into skills (Larkin 2010; Schraw & Moshman, 1995; Veenman et al., 2006). This is the reason why our methodological approach requires that learners repeat the activity several times over a few months, varying the content and complexity of the recordings, so as to help them to develop a habit of mind through a range of stimulating experiences.

Implications and Conclusions

The literature review presented in Sect. "Metacognition" points out that learners' global metacognitive development can be favored, among others, by the following:

- Providing opportunities for active and constructive collaboration with peers.
- Diversifying metacognitive activities across subjects and topics.

Active learning is widely recognized to make learners feel responsible for their activity and induce positive effects on learning outcomes and learners' global development. Moreover, constructive collaborative activity is reported to positively influence metacognitive development, more than individual study, by engaging learners in reasoning more deeply (Schraw & Moshman, 1995). The proposed approach contributes in this respect by engaging learners in active collaboration on meaningful tasks.

Metacognitive skills are reported to initially develop in separate domains, to later become generalized across domains (Veenman et al., 2006). Fostering the use of metacognition on a wide front is useful not only by helping learners to improve their learning outcomes and understanding in several subjects and topics, but also by providing them with a large variety of metacognitive facets, which will possibly give rise to a more composite and effective competence when learners' metacognitive skills merge to become generalized across domains. The proposed approach concerns an unusual but effective field in which learners may develop metacognitive skills, hence contributing to a meaningful diversification of their global metacognitive competence.

Focusing on a novel domain for learners' metacognitive activity also represents a contribution to the development of this research field, as the literature points out the need to explore metacognitive processes in new domains and across domains (Veenman et al., 2006).

Despite their simplicity, the technological tools used were crucial to implement the activity, which could hardly have been run so smoothly with traditional means. Their use was essential to call pupils' attention on their way to utter the different sounds of the new language, and hence to support the subsequent effort to improve personal performance. The use of free and widely available technology makes it feasible to apply this methodological approach also in schools that have limited funds and cannot afford sophisticated and expensive technological tools.

References

Afflerbach, P., & Meuwissen, K. (2005). Teaching and learning self-assessment strategies in middle school. In S. E. Israel, C. Collins Block, K. L. Bauserman, & K. Kinnucan-Welsch (Eds.), *Metacognition in literacy learning* (pp. 141–164). Mahwah, NJ: LEA.

Carr, M. (2010). The importance of metacognition for conceptual change and strategy use in mathematics. In H. Salatas Waters & W. Schneider (Eds.), *Metacognition, strategy use and instruction* (pp. 176–197). New York & London: Guilford.

Cotteral, S., & Murray, G. (2009). Enhancing metacognitive knowledge: structures, affordances and self. *System, 37*, 34–45.

Davis, E. A. (2003). Prompting middle school science students for productive reflection: Generic and directed prompts. *The Journal of the Learning Sciences, 12*(1), 91–142.

Desoete, A. (2008). Multi-metod assessment of metacognitive skills in elementary school children: How you test is what you get. *Metacognition and Learning, 3*, 189–206.

Desoete, A. (2009). The enigma of mathematical learning disabilities: Metacognition or STICORDI, that's the question. In D. J. Hacker, J. Dunlosky, & A. C. Graesser (Eds.), *Handbook of metacognition in education* (pp. 206–218). New York & London: Routledge.

Dlaska, A., & Krekeler, C. (2008). Self-assessment of pronunciation. *System, 36*, 506–516.

Domine, V. E. (2009). *Rethinking technology in schools.* New York: Peter Lang.

Ellis, R. (2003). *Task-based language learning and teaching*. Oxford: Oxford University Press.

Flavell, J. H. (1976). Metacognitive aspects of problem solving. In B. Resnik (Ed.), *The nature of intelligence* (pp. 231–235). Hillsdale, NY: LEA.

Flavell, J. H. (1979). Metacognition and cognitive monitoring: A new area of cognitive development inquiry. *American Psychologist, 34*, 906–911.

Goh, C. (2008). Metacognitive instruction for second language listening development. Theory, practice and research implications. *RELC Journal, 39*, 188–213.

Gombert, J. M. (1992). *Metalinguistic development.* Chicago, IL: The University of Chicago Press.

Graham, S., & Macaro, E. (2008). Strategy instruction in listening for lower-intermediate learners of French. *Language Learning, 58*(4), 747–783.

Griffith, P. L., & Ruan, J. (2005). What is metacognition and what should be its role in literacy instruction? In S. E. Israel, C. Collins Block, K. L. Bauserman, & K. Kinnucan-Welsch (Eds.), *Metacognition in literacy learning* (pp. 3–18). Mahwah, NJ: LEA.

Hacker, D. J., Dunlosky, J., & Graesser, A. C. (2009a). A growing sense of agency. In D. J. Hacker, J. Dunlosky, & A. C. Graesser (Eds.), *Handbook of metacognition in education* (pp. 1–4). New York & London: Routledge.

Hacker, D. J., Dunlosky, J., & Graesser, A. C. (2009b). *Handbook of metacognition in education*. New York & London: Routledge.

Hoffman, B., & Spatariu, A. (2008). The influence of self-efficacy and metacognitive prompting on math problem-solving efficacy. *Contemporary Educational Psychology, 33*, 875–893.

Israel, S. E., Collins Block, C., Bauserman, K. L., & Kinnucan-Welsch, K. (2005). *Metacognition in literacy learning*. Mahwah, NJ: LEA.

Kaberman, Z., & Dori, Y. J. (2009). Metacognition in chemical education: question posing in the case-based computerized learning environment. *Instructional Science, 37*, 403–436.

Kramarski, B. (2008). Promoting teachers algebraic reasoning and self-regulation with metacognitive guidance. *Metacognition and Learning, 3*(2), 83–99.

Larkin, S. (2010). *Metacognition in young children* New York & London: Routledge.

Lundberg, M., & Mohan, L. (2009). Context matters: Gender and cross-cultural differences in confidence. In D. J. Hacker, J. Dunlosky, & A. C. Graesser (Eds.), *Handbook of metacognition in education* (pp. 221–239). New York & London: Routledge.

Rivera-Mills, S. V., & Plonsky, L. (2007). Empowering students with language learning strategies: A critical review of current issues. *Foreign Language Annals, 40*(3), 535–548.

Roll, I., Aleven, V., & Koedinger, K. R. (2008). *Instruments and challenges in assessing help-seeking knowledge and behaviour. Proceedings of the 3rd workshop on metacognition and self-regulated learning in educational technologies* (pp. 41–50). Montreal: CND.

Roll, I., Aleven, V., McLaren, B. M., & Koedinger, K. R. (2007). Designing for metacognition—Applying cognitive tutor principles to the tutoring of help seeking. *Metacognition and Learning, 2*(2–3), 125–140.

Salatas Waters, H., & Schneider, W. (Eds.). (2010). *Metacognition, strategy use and instruction*. New York & London: Guilford.

Schraw, G. (1998). Promoting general metacognitive awareness. *Instructional Science, 26*, 113–125.

Schraw, G., & Moshman, D. (1995). Metacognitive theories. *Educational Psychology Review, 7*(4), 351–371.

Simard, D. (2004). Using diaries to promote metalinguistic reflection among elementary schools students. *Language Awareness, 13*(1), 34–48.

Suzuki, W., & Itagaki, N. (2007). Learner Metalinguistic reflection following output-oriented and reflective activities. *Language Awareness, 16*(2), 131–146.

Valiente Jiménez, M. J. (2008). Régulation métacognitive du contrôle de la compréhension orale en FLE [Metacognitive regulation of the monitoring of oral comprehension of French as a foreign language]. *Porta Linguarum, 9*, 79–91.

Vandergrift, L., & Tafaghodtari, M. H. (2010). Teaching L2 learners how to listen does make a difference: An empirical study. *Language Learning, 60*(2), 470–497.

Veenman, M. V. J., van Hout-Wolters, B. H. A. M., & Afflerbach, P. (2006). Metacognition and learning: Conceptual and methodological considerations. *Metacognition and learning, 1*, 3–14.

Victori, M., & Lockhardt, W. (1995). Enhancing metacognition in self-directed language learning. *System, 23*, 223–234.

Wenden, A. L. (1998). Metacognitive knowledge and language learning. *Applied Linguistics, 19*(4), 515–537.

White, B., Frederiksen, J., & Collins, A. (2009). The interplay of scientific inquiry and metacognition: more than a marriage of convenience. In D. J. Hacker, J. Dunlosky, & A. C. Graesser (Eds.), *Handbook of metacognition in education* (pp. 175–205). New York & London: Routledge.

Williams, J. P., & Atkins, J. G. (2009). The role of metacognition in teaching reading comprehhension to primary students. In D. J. Hacker, J. Dunlosky, & A. C. Graesser (Eds.), *Handbook of metacognition in education* (pp. 26–43). New York & London: Routledge.

Part VII

Motivation and Affect: Key Processes in Metacognition and Self-Regulated Learning

41

Fine-Grained Assessment of Motivation over Long Periods of Learning with an Intelligent Tutoring System: Methodology, Advantages, and Preliminary Results

Matthew L. Bernacki, Timothy J. Nokes-Malach, and Vincent Aleven

Abstract

Models of self-regulated learning (SRL) describe the complex and dynamic interplay of learners' cognitions, motivations, and behaviors when engaged in a learning activity. Recently, researchers have begun to use fine-grained behavioral data such as think aloud protocols and log-file data from educational software to test hypotheses regarding the cognitive and metacognitive processes underlying SRL. Motivational states, however, have been more difficult to trace through these methods and have primarily been studied via pre- and posttest questionnaires. This is problematic because motivation can change during an activity or unit and without fine-grained assessment, dynamic relations between motivation, cognitive, and metacognitive processes cannot be studied. In this chapter we describe a method for collecting fine-grained assessments of motivational variables and examine their association with cognitive and metacognitive behaviors for students learning mathematics with intelligent tutoring systems. Students completed questionnaires embedded in the tutoring software before and after a math course and at multiple time points during the course. We describe the utility of this method for assessing motivation and use these assessments to test hypotheses of self-regulated learning and motivation. Learners' reports of their motivation varied across domain and unit-level assessments and were differently predictive of learning behaviors.

Self-regulated learning (SRL) is a complex process in which learners have been described to "personally activate and sustain cognitions, affects, and behaviors that are systematically oriented toward the attainment of personal goals" (Zimmerman & Schunk, 2011, p. 1). Multiple theories of SRL (Pintrich, 2000; Winne & Hadwin, 1998; Winne, 2011; Zimmerman, 2000, 2011) describe this process and each acknowledges that

M.L. Bernacki (✉) • T.J. Nokes-Malach
Learning Research and Development Center, University of Pittsburgh, Room 819, Pittsburgh, PA 15260, USA
e-mail: bernacki@pitt.edu; matthew.bernacki@gmail.com

V. Aleven
Human-Computer Interaction Institute, Carnegie Mellon University, Pittsburgh, PA, USA

R. Azevedo and V. Aleven (eds.), *International Handbook of Metacognition and Learning Technologies*, Springer International Handbooks of Education 26, DOI 10.1007/978-1-4419-5546-3_41,

motivational constructs play an influential role. The methodologies used to research SRL have primarily focused on behaviors that can be related to cognitive and metacognitive processes such as think aloud protocols in which learners verbalize their thoughts (Azevedo, Moos, Johnson, & Chauncey, 2010; Ericsson & Simon, 1984; Greene, Robertson, & Costa, 2011) and log analyses in which the educational software logs learners' interactions with the system (Aleven, Roll, McLaren, & Koedinger, 2010). However, little work has used these methods to assess motivation because less is known about how such behaviors relate to various motivational constructs.

Prior research that has examined learners' motivational states has primarily relied on construct-, context-, and task-specific questionnaires administered before and after learning activities or classes. This method has yielded interesting results, but is problematic for two reasons. First, recent research suggests that pre-/post-assessment may be insufficient to accurately capture the dynamics of various motivational constructs that vary over the course of a learning activity or unit (e.g., achievement goals; Fyer & Elliot, 2007; Muis & Edwards, 2009). Second, a critical component of SRL theory is that the underlying processes are interactive suggesting that motivational states, like cognitive and metacognitive processes, should interact with each other in real time to affect learning outcomes. Measuring a motivational state prior to and separate from this process eliminates the opportunity to observe both dynamic changes in the construct and its influence within the SRL process. As a result, the use of pre-/post-measurement can lead one to draw conclusions about the role of motivation in SRL that are, at best, insufficient to capture the dynamic complexity of SRL and, at worst, inaccurate.

In this chapter, we describe a project in which we take the first step towards developing fine-grained assessments of motivational constructs in an SRL context. We pose questions to students at varying points during learning to capture self-reports of their motivational state with respect to the domain and the unit or problem they have just completed. Our focus is on motivational constructs that are hypothesized to vary much more rapidly on the order of minutes to hours (e.g., self-efficacy for specific math problems; Pajares, 1997), although we also acknowledge that learners likely have some stable motivational characteristics such as domain-level achievement goals that change relatively slowly over the course of months to years (Ames, 1992). For this reason, we investigate motivation at multiple grain sizes, examining the variability of a learner's motivational state when construed with respect to both the domain and at finer-grained levels such as the unit or problem. By repeatedly evaluating one's motivational state, we can observe variation or stability of specific constructs (e.g., self-efficacy), examine the task variables (e.g., unit or problem difficulty) that might affect such a state, and identify the associated learning behaviors. Our theoretical approach is analogous to Mischel (1968, 1973), Cervone (Cervone & Shoda, 1999) and others who, in questioning the stability of personality constructs, conducted productive programs of research examining the dynamics of personality and developed a deeper understanding of those constructs; one's personality is both coherent across situations and influenced by situational factors. The methodology we describe, especially when combined with online traces of behavior, can enrich our understanding of SRL as well as improve our ability to predict (and promote desirable) learning outcomes.

While our approach is not an online method like the log-files, eye tracking, or verbal protocols that continuously collect data, our repeated sampling of self-reports are considerably finer than traditional methods that only measure motivation at pre- or posttest. So, while our data do not provide a continuous measure of learners' motivational states, the frequency of our sampling (as often as every 1–2 min) does provide a series of snapshots of motivational variables that can be used to examine the relationship between motivation, learning behaviors, and learning outcomes, all of which are specific to a particular learning context. Furthermore, these finer-grained snapshots can be used more productively than simple pre-/posttest assessments when relating motivational data to other streams of trace data such as those mentioned above.

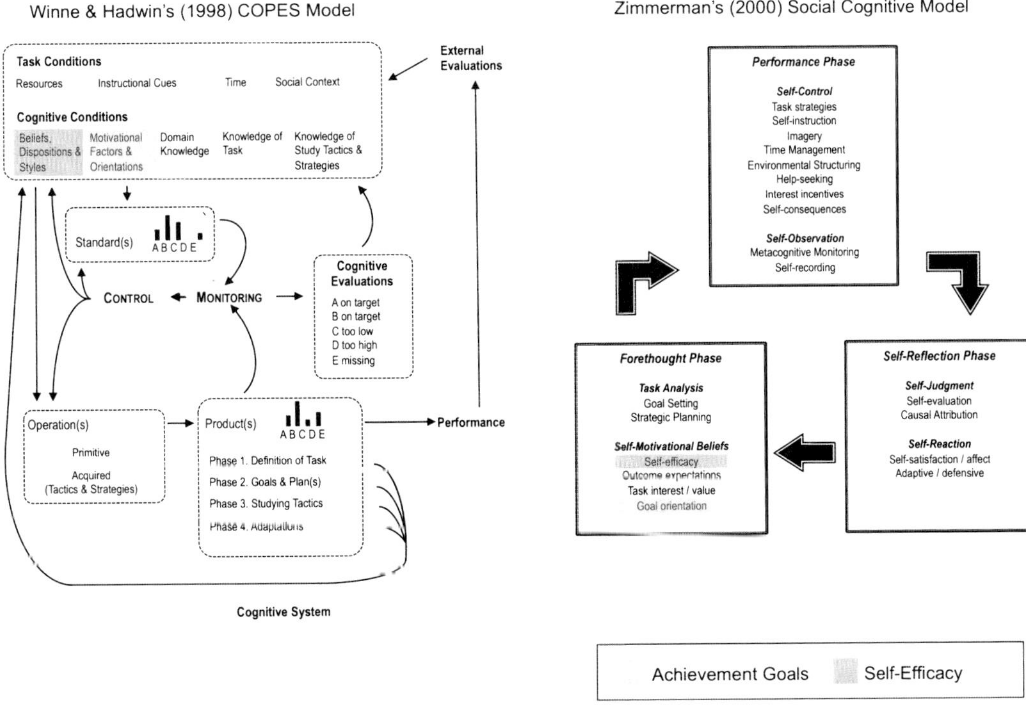

Fig. 41.1 Motivational constructs embedded in process models of self-regulated learning

In this chapter, we first describe the Cognitive Tutor, the intelligent tutoring system with which we conduct our research, and then summarize two theoretical frameworks that describe the SRL process, paying special attention to the motivational components included in each. We next describe the methods others have used to capture traces of SRL and the questionnaire methods typically used to assess motivation. In light of this review, we argue that motivation needs to be assessed using finer-grained methods that are more sensitive to the changes in motivation that occur during learning. The remainder of the chapter describes a microgenetic approach to assess motivation in SRL and illustrate the benefits and challenges of this approach with both hypothetical examples and empirical data.

First, however, we describe our interest in motivation as it relates to metacognition. We agree with the perspective of Veenman (Veenman, Bernadette, Hout-Wolters, & Afflerbach, 2006) who suggests that metacognition cannot be studied in "splendid isolation" (p. 10). In the inaugural issue of *Metacognition and Learning*, Veenman states that "we need to know more about how individual differences and contextual factors interact with metacognition and its components" (p. 4). Motivational constructs can operate as individual difference variables or can be influenced by contextual factors and should be examined concurrently with metacognitive processes as components of the dynamic models SRL theorists propose.

While there are dozens of motivational constructs that we might examine, we focus our work on achievement goals and self-efficacy for three reasons. First, each of these factors is explicitly referenced in one or more of the central theories of SRL (see Fig. 41.1). Changes in these factors are theorized to influence metacognitive processes. Second, these constructs have been associated with particular patterns of learning behavior in empirical studies, some of which are metacognitive in nature. Third, prior research has illustrated that learners' level of self-efficacy (Pajares, 1997) and achievement goals (Muis & Edwards, 2009) change during learning. In order to observe these changes and to investigate their influence on learners' metacognitive monitoring and acts of metacognitive control, we propose an approach that supports analysis of fine-grained behavioral data. In order to establish the context in which we conduct our research, we present an intelligent tutoring system that traces learners' behaviors, the Cognitive Tutor, which we use to assess students' motivational state while learning mathematics.

The Cognitive Tutor

Cognitive tutors are a family of intelligent tutoring systems (c.f. Koedinger & Aleven, 2007) that combine the disciplines of cognitive psychology and artificial intelligence to construct computational cognitive models of learners' knowledge (Koedinger & Corbett, 2006). Cognitive tutors are unique in that they monitor student's performance and learning by model tracing and knowledge tracing. That is, the cognitive tutor runs step-by-step through a hypothetical *cognitive model* (which represents the current state of the learner's knowledge) as the learner progresses through a unit. This allows the tutor to provide real-time feedback and context-specific advice. Learning in the tutor is defined as the acquisition of *knowledge components*, which are the mental structures that learners use, alone or in combination with other knowledge components, to accomplish steps in a problem.

The cognitive tutor combines a series of structured learning tasks (i.e., math problems) along with opportunities for self-regulation of learning. In most cognitive tutor environments, learners are given access to a unit which includes an introductory text and a problem set, as well as tools they can choose to access to support their learning. These include a hint button that provides context-specific hints, a glossary of terms relevant to the content and, at times, a worked example of a problem similar to those they are to complete. Students can also assess their own progress towards mastery (as assessed by the tutor) by clicking on the *skillometer*, a menu that presents skill bars indicative of the progress towards mastery for each skill in the unit. Bars are green in color and increase when steps are completed accurately; they turn gold when mastery is met.

While the tutor chooses the problems, the learner chooses how long to spend on the introductory reading, when to begin the problem set, as well as whether or not to request hints, access the glossary, check the skill bars, review the introductory text or view worked examples and in general, how deliberately to approach to tutor problem (versus superficial processing or guessing strategies). The inclusion of these resources creates the opportunity for the learner to self-regulate learning. For example, a learner, who while completing a problem encounters an unfamiliar term, can access a glossary to obtain a definition. Another learner who begins a problem set and does not understand a step can request a hint that provides directions on that step. Students' metacognitive monitoring is supported by the provision of the skillometer, as well as feedback about the accuracy of answers submitted per step. When tutor feedback indicates that a step is incorrect, a student might try to self-explain why that step is incorrect. After reading the hints, the student could try to reconstruct for himself/herself the line of reasoning presented in the hint (typically, a principle-based explanation of what to do next and how, and perhaps why). Access to the worked examples, glossary and introductory text also provide opportunities for metacognitive monitoring; learners can click on these features to make metacognitive judgments about their understanding of the concepts or mastery of a skill. This metacognitive monitoring may be aided by tutor feedback. For instance, the decision to ask for a hint may be based on self-assessment of whether a step is familiar (Aleven et al., 2010).

In addition to providing instruction and opportunities for self-regulation, the cognitive tutor collects fine-grained behavioral data of students' interactions with the tutor. This data is logged at the *transaction level*, whenever a learner attempts a step in a tutor problem, requests a hint, accesses a glossary item, etc. The tutor records this data as log-files that serve as a database for conducting microgenetic analyses of learning, using an open repository called DataShop (Koedinger, Baker, Cunningham, Skogsholm, Leber, & Stamper, 2010). Microgenetic approaches (c.f. Siegler & Crowley, 1991) involve the logging of frequent observations of individuals' behavior and allow for examination of change at a fine-grained level (e.g., eye-tracking, verbal protocols, log-files, etc.).

Analyses of transaction data have made it possible for researchers to identify when learners seek help in tutoring environments (Aleven & Koedinger, 2000) and when they abuse help features (Baker, Corbett, Koedinger, & Wagner, 2004). As a result of these investigations, researchers have attempted to scaffold help seeking by modifying the cognitive tutor design and creating a Help Tutor (Aleven, McLaren, Roll, & Koedinger, 2006). Transaction level data also allows for examination of behaviors as they relate to specific learning outcomes (e.g., Ritter, Anderson, Koedinger, & Corbett, 2007; Koedinger et al., 2010). In their present form, cognitive tutors provide a useful environment for studying facets of students' SRL behaviors like help seeking.

Building on the basic functionality of the Cognitive Tutor, we have implemented an additional component that, when added to the tutor, allows for the consideration of motivational constructs as they affect learning. Before we outline how this questionnaire component is integrated to capture self-reports of learner motivation, we first define the motivational constructs on which we focus, learners' achievement goals and perceived self-efficacy for mathematics, and highlight their role in SRL theories.

Motivational Factors: Achievement Goals and Self-Efficacy

Achievement Goal Orientation

Elliot (Elliot & McGregor, 2001; Elliot & Murayama, 2008) posits a 2×2 framework describing one's achievement goals in terms of definition (mastery vs. performance) and valence (approach vs. avoidance). Those with mastery approach goals engage in a task with the purpose of developing competence and define success with respect to intrapersonal standards of improvement over previous levels of competence, or as focused on meeting a self-imposed criterion of task-mastery (Ames, 1992; Elliot, 1999). Performance approach oriented learners define success interpersonally by measuring competence normatively against the competence of peers and aim to demonstrate their competence by outperforming peers. Mastery avoidance goals denote an orientation towards avoiding failure as defined by "avoiding self-referential or task-referential incompetence" (Elliot, 1999, p. 181). A performance avoidance oriented learner engages in a task to demonstrate that they are not any less competent than their peers.

Research on achievement goal theory has shown that individuals' goal orientations are related to learning behaviors and performances. Mastery-oriented individuals employ effective problem-solving practices (Elliott & Dweck, 1988), are more likely to expend effort, persist in the face of failure, and engage in deep processing (Elliot, McGregor, & Gable, 1999). Performance approach goals have also been positively related to effort (Harackiewicz, Barron, Pintrich, Elliot, & Thrash, 2002) but their processing tends to be more superficial (Elliot et al., 1999). Research has shown that performance avoidance goals are positive predictors of surface processing and negative predictors of deep processing (Elliot et al., 1999), and performance avoidant learners demonstrate disorganization and low interest (Elliot & Harackiewicz, 1996; Elliot & Church, 1997). One's goal orientation has also been associated with employment of SRL processes. Research has shown that mastery approach goals predict increased cognitive engagement and performance (Greene & Miller, 1996; Greene, Miller, Crowson, Duke, & Akey, 2004) and that performance goals have been found to predict study strategies (Archer, 1994) and metacognitive strategy use (Bouffard et al., 1995; Meece, Blumenfeld, & Hoyle, 1988).

With respect to performance, both mastery and performance approach goals have been found to relate positively to achievement

(Linnenbrink-Garcia, Tyson, & Patall, 2008) and students who pursue mastery goals show evidence of transferring past learning experiences to new tasks (Belenky & Nokes, 2012). Performance avoidance goals have consistently been shown to predict poor performance (Elliot & Church, 1997; Elliot et al., 1999; Harackiewicz et al., 2002).

In sum, we are interested in assessing achievement goals with fine-grained measures and examining their relations to behaviors in the tutoring system. We do so in order to further explore how achievement goals are influenced by task context (as theorized by Ames, 1992 and demonstrated by Horvath, Herleman, & McKie, 2006), how these changes in goals might alter the behaviors learners employ, and whether these context-specific factors might explain some of the conflicting results summarized by Linnenbrink-Garcia et al. (2008) who found that mastery and performance goals are only predictive of achievement in some cases.

Self-Efficacy

Bandura (1994) defined perceived self-efficacy as the belief about one's ability to perform at a particular level on a task. Self-efficacy is theorized to influence cognitive, metacognitive, motivational, and affective processes. Learners with high levels of self-efficacy are willing to engage in difficult tasks, set challenging goals, and maintain strong commitments to achieving their goals. High self-efficacy is theorized to support effort regulation and to influence one's attribution of failure (Bandura, 1991; Weiner, 1986). When individuals do fail to achieve, those high in self-efficacy are more likely to attribute their failure to insufficient effort, knowledge or skills and reengage to correct this insufficiency. In addition to influencing attribution to self or environmental factors, self-efficacy influences persistence and performance in learning tasks (Bandura, 1997). This association suggests that simultaneous examination of learners' efficacy and learning behaviors might be an important methodological approach to further our understanding of the influence self-efficacy has on other components of SRL.

Role of Motivation in Theories of Self-Regulated Learning

We describe our method in relation to the two most prominent theories of SRL, both of which depict SRL as a cyclical process involving cognitive, metacognitive and motivational components. We summarize each below and draw particular attention to Zimmerman's (2011) recent focus on motivational processes as they occur at each phase of the SRL process.

Winne and Hadwin's COPES Model

Winne and Hadwin (1998; Winne, 2011) offer a description of SRL as an event-based phenomenon that occurs in weakly sequenced phases. Learners, when self-regulating their learning (1) define the task, (2) set goals they would like to attain and develop a plan for their attainment, (3) enact tactics, and (4) monitor their progress towards goals against a preconceived set of internal standards. Within each phase, self-regulatory behaviors are governed by both cognitive and situative factors in which learners generate behaviors that are evaluated in light of their self-imposed standards. In this framework, motivation governs SRL processes beginning with the assessment of task conditions. We illustrate this relationship (see Fig. 41.1) using achievement goals and self-efficacy as examples, given their prominence in models of SRL.

The conditions that affect how students engage in a learning task include environmental conditions (e.g., time limits, environmental affordances) and learner characteristics such as cognitive and metacognitive capacities like prior knowledge, domain knowledge, metacognitive knowledge of tactics that could be employed, and motivational conditions including interest and goal orientation (see Fig. 41.1). These factors influence the type of goals learners set, the tactics they enact, and the standards by which they judge their learning and performance. Winne and Hadwin (1998) provide the following example:

> For example, students with a performance motivational orientation that view tasks as just jobs to complete may judge that the goal they understood their teacher set is at too high a level or requires too much effort. Therefore, they adjust or alter standards for summarizing the science chapter to levels where 'just getting by' is adequate. In light of this re-framed goal, the student now builds a plan to approach it. This student will probably plan simplistic tactics, such as paraphrasing headings and monitoring surface features of typography to insure that every bold phrase and every scientist's name (standards) is reproduced in the finished product (p. 281)

Similarly, one's level of self-efficacy influences the goal setting and evaluation processes. Efficacious learners are theorized to have greater expectations for what they can achieve in a task and set goals accordingly (Bandura, 1991). Their level of efficacy for carrying out the plan to achieve the goal can influence their persistence, and recurring efficacy judgments will influence their strategies during learning. This process has implications for future cycles through learning phases. The evaluation of learning leads to adaptations of learning processes. These adaptations are based on one's sensitivity to feedback, which can be internally or externally generated, and which is interpreted in the light of one's goals. One's level of self-efficacy affects the way such feedback is interpreted. Negative feedback can be a useful tool for a highly efficacious learner who uses the feedback as a cue that his or her performance is insufficient and continued or greater effort is required, while a learner with low self-efficacy may interpret negative feedback as indicative of deficits that cannot be overcome, and lead to disengagement or frustration.

Zimmerman's Social Cognitive Model

Zimmerman (2000) defines self-regulation as referring to "self-generated thoughts, feelings and actions that are planned and cyclically adapted to the attainment of personal goals" (p. 14). Individuals are theorized to engage in planning (i.e., forethought), volitional control, and self-reflection (see Fig. 41.1). This process occurs within a larger self-regulatory context in which learners regulate their behaviors, adjust performance processes, and adapt to their environment by managing the environmental factors that might inhibit goal attainment. By monitoring the success of their strategies and using feedback about potential barriers to goal attainment, learners can adapt to changing environments and regulate processes en route to attaining their goals.

Focusing on the cycle described in Zimmerman's framework, individuals first plan in which they analyze the task in order to identify the desired goal and develop a strategy to obtain this goal. This plan is then evaluated for its potential success, which Zimmerman (2000) describes as being mediated by one's self-motivational beliefs, including "self-efficacy and goal orientation" (p. 17). In the forethought stage, self-regulation can break down if an individual cannot clearly determine a goal, or cannot develop a strategy for reaching it. It can also stagnate if the individual cannot motivate himself or herself to seek such a goal or carry out the selected strategy. Once a goal has been identified and the individual intends to carry out a strategy to attain the goal, the individual acts. This stage is referred to as the performance or volitional control phase. Here, individuals critique their own strategy use in an attempt to maximize the efficiency of their efforts while carrying out a chosen strategy. After having completed an action and monitored the process and outcome, an individual engages in self-reflection by evaluating the performance and attributing the success or failure of the performance to causal factors.

In a more recent conceptualization of his sociocultural model, Zimmerman (2011) provides an elaborated description of motivation as catalyst at each SRL stage. During forethought, a learner's goal orientation dictates a goal to increase his competence, which may involve greater persistence in a difficult task, or a goal to perform well, which may involve avoiding challenges. Additionally, his perceived self-efficacy for a task will dictate the strategies he chooses to employ. In the performance phase, self-efficacy beliefs motivate his time management and self-monitoring practices (Bandura, 1997).

Zimmerman (2011) underscores the importance of assessing motivation not as "person measures" (p. 60) at pre- and posttest due to subjects' inaccurate recall and poor calibration, and praises event-based measurement of cognitive and metacognitive processes by way of trace and think-aloud methodologies. We share Zimmerman's views that a learner's motivation is an active and dynamic part of the self-regulatory process and that data collected during learning is necessary to capture the "dynamic interactive relations among these variables during successive SRL cycles" (p. 60). We next summarize the methods that have been used to capture evidence of cognitive, metacognitive, and motivational components of SRL, then describe our method for administering prompts to elicit self-reports of learners' motivational state during the learning tasks in which metacognitive and cognitive processes are traced.

Measurement of Self-Regulated Learning with Learning Technologies

Increasingly, research conducted in technology enhanced learning environments reflects the process view of SRL espoused by the most prominent theorists. Data is collected online and the analysis that ensues is conducted under the assumption that the learning process is iterative and learners' actions are dependent upon learning that has taken place earlier in the task or during prior learning tasks. At present, however, learning technologies that capture SRL data conduct no online measurement of motivational constructs. Instead, motivational constructs tend to be assessed before or after the learning task.

With only two data points, this method can only detect linear change. For example, when measuring learners' self-efficacy before and after the task, we cannot determine the point at which a learner's self-efficacy began to change or how it changed (linear, stepwise, etc.) over the course of a learning task. We can only measure whether it rose, fell or stayed the same from pre- to posttest. This limits our understanding of self-efficacy to coarse-grained associative relationships with learning behaviors. In contrast, if learners respond to efficacy prompts repeatedly throughout a unit, we can examine fine-grained changes from one data point to the next, concurrent with changes in behavior and identify patterns in log-files where reports of efficacy trend higher or lower, or when they follow an initiation of a behavior or a change in performance. Next we summarize measures and procedures typically employed to assess achievement goals, as well as recent evidence outlining elements of stability and change in achievement goals. This evidence demonstrates a need to employ more frequent, fine-grained assessment than is typical.

Assessment of Motivational Constructs

Instruments and Methods

When researchers aim to assess achievement goals, they employ questionnaires that include items that gauge the learner's endorsement of performance approach, performance avoidance, mastery approach, and mastery avoidance goals. The two most common questionnaires employed are the Achievement Goals Questionnaire (Elliot & McGregor, 2001 and a revised version, the AGQ-R; Elliot & Murayama, 2008) and the Patterns of Adaptive Learning Scale (PALS; Midgley et al., 2000). Each are composed of a series of items that pose a statement meant to reflect a specific achievement goal. For instance, an AGQ-R item reflecting a performance approach orientation reads, "My goal is to perform better than the other students." A PALS item reflecting the same orientation reads, "It's important to me that I look smart compared to others in my class." Respondents select a number from a Likert scale reflecting their level of agreement with the statement and mean scores per achievement goal are derived.

These questionnaires tend to be given once prior to or after the learning task. Recent studies that have administered achievement goal questionnaires repeatedly have reported both stability, but also some change over time and with respect to task conditions. Fryer and Elliot (2007) found rank-order stability across achievement goals and that mean levels of performance approach goals were stable across three time points (reported in conjunction with exams) while mastery approach increased and performance avoidance decreased over time. Examining self-reported achievement goals for two exams and two writing assignments, Muis and Edwards (2009) found a similar pattern of results and describe the extent the changes that occurred as moderate to large. These findings conform to theories of achievement goals (Ames, 1992; Dweck, 1986; Fryer & Elliot, 2007) that suggest an individual's achievement goal orientation is consistent to the extent that it reflects the cognitive framework the individual uses to guide behavior. At the same time, learners are theorized to set goals in light of task conditions (Pintrich, 2000, Winne & Hadwin, 1998). Because task conditions are often outside the scope of learners' control (i.e., the content of a task is prescribed) and because they tend to change over the course of a task when learning occurs in the context of adaptive learning technologies (i.e., tutors concentrate problems requiring yet-to-be-mastered skills), learners' task-specific goals can differ from their typical goal orientation. Muis and Edwards' (2009) finding that endorsement of achievement goals varied from exam to exam and differed between assessment types suggests that variation in the content of a task may influence individuals' adoption of achievement goals. A number of research studies have assigned participants to conditions in which task conditions have successfully elicited achievement goals (c.f. Linnenbrink-Garica et al., 2008, Table 2), which demonstrates the extent to which task conditions can influence achievement goals. Because learners' achievement goals have been shown to be contingent upon task conditions, repeated measurement is necessary to understand how task conditions might influence one's task-level achievement goals and the behaviors they motivate.

Achievement goals are not unique among motivational constructs in their capacity for change during the course of learning. Perceived self-efficacy has been shown to build upon prior efficacy judgments (Bandura, 1997) and, during the course of learning, self-efficacy judgments are adjusted in light of actual performance and feedback. Learners' self-efficacy is theorized to influence the goals learners set, the tactics they enact and the attributions they make about feedback when judging their progress towards goals. Exploration of this dynamic relationship between motivational state and metacognitive process requires fine-grained assessment of both constructs.

Factors like achievement goals and self-efficacy represent the motivational dimension of learning that Winne and Hadwin (1998) and Zimmerman (2000) identified as germane to SRL and as influential over metacognitive processes. However, methods to capture fine-grained evidence of these and other motivational constructs have not been incorporated into educational software prior to our study. We next present our methodological approach to address this situation, followed by some preliminary results.

Fine-Grained Sampling: A Microgenetic Approach to Assessing Motivation in SRL

We have added a component to the Cognitive Tutor that collects fine-grained motivational data to concurrently examine the dynamic and interactive metacognitive *and* motivational factors that influence learning. Using the items from questionnaires traditionally used to assess motivation pre- or posttest, we embed single items as prompts after problems and small, task-specific questionnaires after units to capture more fine-grained changes in motivational states (Fig. 41.2). We employ these prompts at multiple grain sizes and repeatedly over time in order to develop a rich understanding of how factors such as learners' goal orientation and level of self-efficacy affect SRL in specific contexts and at specific points during the use of the tutor. The following section serves as an overview of our first year-long investigation in which this microgenetic and longitudinal approach is employed.

A Microgenetic and Longitudinal Approach to Questionnaire Use

We collected automated self-report (questionnaire) data in multiple classrooms of students via

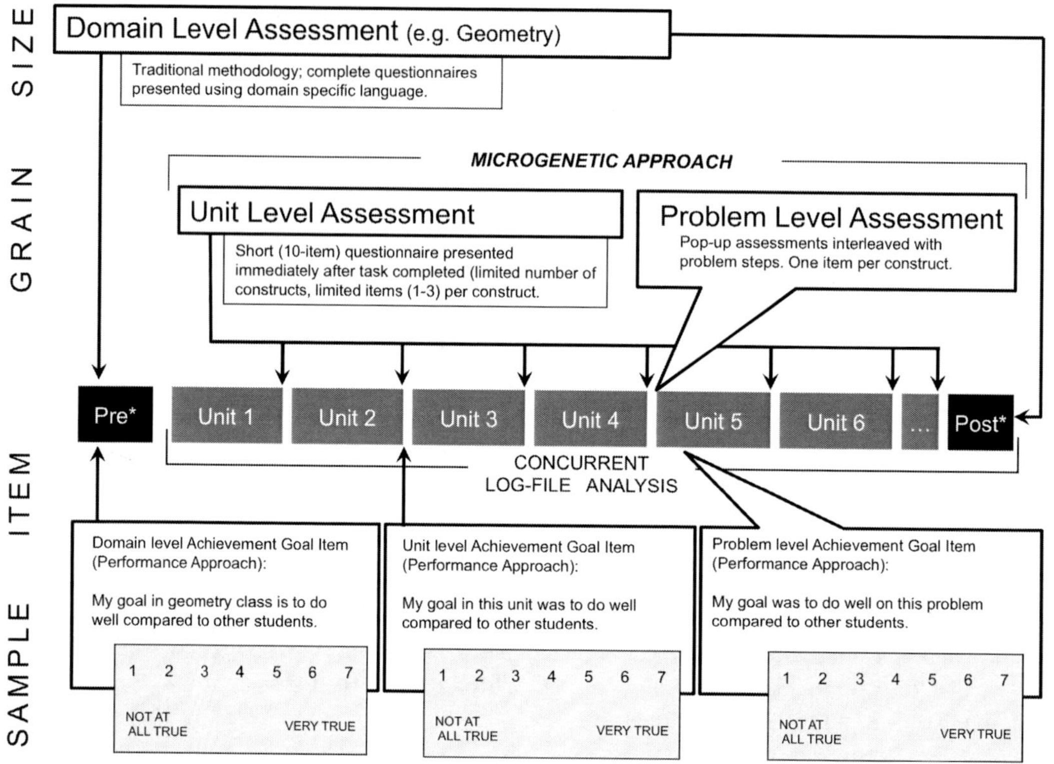

Fig. 41.2 Microgenetic approach to assessment of motivational constructs in the cognitive tutor

cognitive tutors for a range of variables. These students use the cognitive tutor software across the whole school year as part of their regular mathematics instruction. This effort has two components. First, we take a microgenetic approach to collect questionnaire data with a small number of prompts that are administered frequently (i.e., dense data collection over a range of time periods, providing motivational tracking from minutes to hours to weeks). These prompts are embedded in the learning software and therefore can be administered at the end of a unit and between problems. At these finer-grained levels, a small, specific set of constructs are sampled in order to limit the proportion of time students spend completing measures when engaging with the tutor. This method of data collection is applied to motivational variables that are expected to vary over the course of a semester or unit). Second, two or three times a year, we administer questionnaires focused on constructs that are theorized to be stable over time (i.e., these include domain-level achievement orientation, domain-level self-efficacy, and theory of intelligence; Dweck, 1999).

Key to the current approach is that this traditional pre-/post-data can be related to the more fine-grained prompts as well as traces of the behaviors in the tutor log data. Concurrent collection of these multiple streams of data allow for testing of theoretical assumptions that would not be testable using traditional methods of measurement. Additionally, students use the tutor for the duration of the school year (and often multiple years), making this platform uniquely suited for longitudinal data collection and evolution. In the next section, we expand on the benefits associated with employing a microgenetic approach including opportunities for (1) testing theories of SRL and (2) improving our understanding of motivational constructs. We then provide some initial results from a study of geometry learners' achievement goals at domain and unit levels.

Benefits of a Microgenetic Approach

Testing Theories of Self-Regulated Learning

A microgenetic approach allows us to isolate a particular component of a learning theory and use transaction level data to determine if the theorized process plays out as expected when individuals engage in the learning activity. In SRL theories, metacognition is described in a fine-grained manner and many parameters are theorized to affect metacognitive processes in ways that influence learning. Each of these parameters is also theorized to change dynamically over time. Microgenetic methods allow us to focus on a specific metacognitive process and test whether it occurs as theorized, as well as whether the presence of, absence of, or change in another parameter might influence how the metacognitive process works.

For example, Winne theorizes that learners evaluate their learning against a self-set standard (Winne & Hadwin, 1998, 2008; Winne, 1997, 2011). Zimmerman (2011) suggests that such standards are influenced by a learner's achievement goals, which have been found to vary when measured repeatedly (Fryer & Elliot, 2007; Muis & Edwards, 2009). As an illustration, consider a learner who consistently evaluates performances with respect to a standard over the course of the unit. If we find that his standard changes over time as evidenced by a change in the strength or prominence of one achievement goal over others, then we can explore the implications of this change on the learner's behavior. To do so, we would examine log-file data prior to and after a shift in goal endorsement (i.e., when a learner who previously rated mastery approach goals as strongest now rates performance avoidance goals as strongest; Muis & Edwards) and examine the time elapsed between hint requests and the next transaction. Perhaps we notice that when his goals shift from a stronger desire to master a skill to a stronger desire to perform just well enough to complete the unit, the learner also spends less time reading hints (smaller durations of time between a hint request and the next click) and a pattern of hint abuse (i.e., rapid clicking to a final hint that provides the answer to a problem step, but where the speed of clicks suggests minimal consideration of the conceptual scaffolding provided). We would expect such behavior to produce poor learning and can test this by analyzing the students' learning curve of various knowledge components traced by the tutor. Learning curves show the change in a performance metric (e.g., accuracy, time) over successive opportunities to apply a given skill, based on the performance of a group of students on problem steps that require that skill. The slope of the curves indicates the rate of learning. If our hypothesis is accurate, a learner who switches from a mastery approach goal to a performance avoidance goal should have a learning curve with a slope that flattens when the goal changes and a new pattern of behavior emerges (Koedinger et al., 2010).

This hypothetical example illustrates how a microgenetic approach allows us to isolate one element of a theory and determine whether a change in motivation precipitates a change in behavior. This approach opens new dimensions of investigation for testing the role of motivational constructs in SRL theories. A better specification of the dynamic role of motivation in SRL theories will further improve both the explanatory power of these models as well as improving the predictions for individuals' learning.

Investigating Motivational Constructs at Different Grain Sizes

Collecting traditional pre/post and fine-grained prompts allows for comparison of motivational constructs at different levels of granularity. With this data, we can determine whether the influence of a motivational construct on a learning process changes when the construct is investigated at domain, unit, and problem (see Fig. 41.2). This multilevel depiction of phenomena like achievement goals and self-efficacy enables scientists to examine patterns of stability and change and improve theoretical models to account for this change.

For instance, we might seek to test Bandura's (1997) hypothesis that learners' level of self-efficacy is related to their level of performance on problems. We could measure this construct (self-efficacy) at pretest or at posttest and test correlation with course grades. However, it is possible that students might feel confident in their understanding of some concepts but not others and may excel on problems testing some skills and struggle on problems testing others. When learners are asked to make domain-level judgments, they must take an 'average,' so to speak, of their distinct self-efficacy judgments. In this self-reported averaging – or perhaps they simply use the last episode they can remember—some variation and precision is likely to be lost. Similarly, using student grades as a measure of performance can oversimplify scenarios where a learner performs well on one type of problem and poorly on another. In our method, we also prompt students to make efficacy judgments immediately after a unit in the tutor and compare them to measures of performance on the unit. At a finer grain still, we also prompt learners' to judge self-efficacy immediately after problems that align to one of the unit's learning objective (see problem-level assessment in Fig. 41.2). By sampling self-efficacy at this grain size, we could determine whether Bandura's hypothesis holds at both the domain level (as evidenced by a significant correlation between domain-level self-efficacy collected as a pretest to math performance represented by grades) and at the problem level (correlation between problem-level efficacy judgments and performance on problems). If we were to find that the correlation between students' self-efficacy and performance is lower at the problem level than at the domain level, we would have discovered that self-efficacy judgments are associated with performance at more general levels of specificity, but this relationship weakens in the context of an actual task. We could then examine what other factors might inform students' self-efficacy judgments by looking at behaviors, performances, or motivational factors that may also predict variance in problem level self-efficacy judgments.

Investigating Associations Between Motivation and Metacognition

We can also use these fine-grained samplings of efficacy to examine the effect of an attempt at metacognitive control on a motivational variable. For example, we might test whether efficacy increases after students view a conceptual hint by identifying all learners who requested a hint and examine their efficacy judgments on problems testing a skill before and after the hint request. When a learner identifies that she does not understand a concept, she might seek help from the tutor and request a hint. This represents a cognitive judgment (i.e., that she needed help) and by isolating instances of this action and the students' responses to self-efficacy prompts, we can test theoretical assumptions about relationships between help seeking and self-efficacy. The additional inclusion of performance data (available in the log-file data) allows us to examine how a motivational state and an action spurred by a metacognitive control process affect learning. We next provide an empirical example of our work employing embedded questionnaires to examine the dynamic nature of motivational variables when learning with the cognitive tutor.

An Empirical Example of the Dynamic Nature of Motivation and Its Effect on Learning Behaviors

An abundance of studies have demonstrated the knowledge tracing capabilities of the cognitive tutor (e.g., Ritter, Anderson, Koedinger, & Corbett, 2007), and additional studies have demonstrated that the tutor is also an effective platform for identifying learning behaviors, scaffolding those that are adaptive (e.g., help-seeking: Aleven, Roll, MacLaren, & Koedinger, 2010), and discouraging those that are maladaptive (e.g., gaming; Baker et al., 2006).

To determine whether the tutor can be adapted to assess student motivation, we examined 72 high school geometry students' responses to domain-level questionnaires administered at the beginning and end of a semester and a series of unit-level questionnaires administered immediately after the final problem set of the unit was completed (Bernacki, Nokes-Malach, & Aleven, 2012). Our goal was to examine the relationship between domain and unit-specific motivation, the influence of task conditions on motivation, and relationship between motivation and learning behaviors in an intelligent tutoring system.

We tested the stability of achievement goals across levels of specificity by determining whether domain and unit-level achievement goals correlate (indicating stability), or if achievement goals for specific units differed from domain-level achievement goals. We also examined individuals' self-reported achievement goals across five units to determine whether learners endorse similar achievement goals across units despite known differences in content (e.g., task difficulty and duration). Students used the software two days per week during scheduled math classes and some worked with the software as homework. Units varied in the number of problems students completed per unit (medians ranged from 20 to 40 problems), total time spent per unit (medians ranged 34–73 min). The content of these units included multiple geometry principles such as the Pythagorean theorem, calculation of area, and properties of triangles and trapezoids.

In the first analysis, students reported different achievement goals (i.e., mastery-approach, performance-approach, and performance avoidance) when they are measured at different levels of specificity (domain and unit level). In all but one case, correlations between students' self-reported achievement goals for math versus achievement goals for the unit they just completed were nonsignificant, and in some cases, the correlation was actually negative. We take this to mean that students are pursuing different goals in the mathematics units they just completed compared with those they report when they reason abstractly about their goals in math.

When we examined the stability of achievement goals across units, unit-level achievement goals were highly correlated. Correlation coefficients across all pairs of units per construct ranged from $r=0.30$ to 0.71 (mean $r=0.58$). However, achievement goals were variable within learners. When averaging the proportion of students who report increases, decreases and no change in achievement goals across all pairs of units, we found that approximately one third of students increased in their endorsement of each achievement goal, one third decreased and the third reported no change in their goals. This within-learner variability confirms that fine-grained measurement is important, so long as these differences in achievement goals have implications for the behaviors learners conduct in the tasks.

When we examined the relationship between domain-level and unit-level achievement goals and learning behaviors (by comparing the coefficient of determination (R^2) for regression equations where learning behaviors were regressed on a set of domain-level or unit-level achievement goals in a single unit), results indicated that for some behaviors (help seeking, error rate and accuracy) domain-level achievement goals were better predictors of behavior, whereas for others (problems needed to achieve competence, seconds needed to complete problem) unit-level achievement goals were better predictors. Collectively, these findings indicate that when students self-report their domain-level and unit-level achievement goals, they reflect different aspects of learners' motivational states, and these aspects are useful for predicting different learning behaviors.

Because achievement goals were found to vary by level of specificity and across units, and because they can be used to predict the behavior of learners, we confirmed that there are benefits to assessing achievement goals at a fine-grained level. Additional studies are underway that prompt students to endorse their achievement goals *after a problem and within a unit* (i.e., between math problems) so that we might be able to examine how a change in one's achievement goals might instantiate a change in one's approach to solving math problems. We are also examining self-reports of self-efficacy for math tasks after units and between problems to confirm that such measures can provide information about the learning behaviors common to students with particular perceptions of their efficacy.

Conclusion

Our approach takes the first step towards the development of fine-grained assessments of motivation as learners engage in SRL processes. The preliminary evidence suggested that learners' unit-specific motivations may differ from their domain-level motivations, that learners' motivations change along with changes in task conditions, and that motivational data collected in conjunction with a unit can better predict a set of learners' behaviors as they engaged with the tutor. For these reasons, the approach appears to be fruitful for testing theories that posit interactions between motivation, cognition, metacognition, and learning outcomes. Despite these benefits, the approach has its limitations, and measurement challenges remain. We need to assess the reliability of students' responses to items to determine the degree to which variation in responses can be attributed to true differences in a motivational state versus variation due to measurement error. Similarly, we need to find ways to validate these questionnaires through behavioral or observational measures. We must also be wary of the influence that interrupting students' learning with prompts to answer questionnaire items may have on their learning. A long-term goal of this project is to validate students' responses to questionnaire items and then use existing log-file data and questionnaire responses to develop machine learned detectors for motivational variables. If this can be accomplished, we can then move past embedded questionnaires and assess motivation using the same unobtrusive methods used to trace behaviors representing the cognitive and metacognitive processes characteristic of SRL.

References

Aleven, V., & Koedinger, K. R. (2000). Limitations of student control: Do student know when they need help? In G. Gauthier, C. Frasson, & K. VanLehn (Eds.), *Proceedings of the 5th international conference on intelligent tutoring systems, ITS 2000* (pp. 292–303). Berlin: Springer Verlag.

Aleven, V., McLaren, B. M., Roll, I., & Koedinger, K. R. (2006). Toward meta-cognitive tutoring: A model of help seeking with a Cognitive Tutor. *International Journal of Artificial Intelligence in Education, 16*, 101–130.

Aleven, V., Roll, I., MacLaren, B. M., & Koedinger, K. R. (2010). Automated, unobtrusive, action-by-action assessment of self-regulation during learning with an intelligent tutoring system. *Educational Psychologist, 45*(4), 224–233.

Ames, C. (1992). Achievement goals and the classroom motivational climate. In D. Schunk & J. Meece (Eds.), *Student perceptions in the classroom* (pp. 327–348). Hillsdale, NJ: Erlbaum.

Archer, J. (1994). Achievement goals as a measure of motivation in university students. *Contemporary Educational Psychology, 19*, 430–446.

Azevedo, R., Moos, D. C., Johnson, A. M., & Chauncey, A. D. (2010). Measuring cognitive and metacognitive regulatory processes during hypermedia learning: Issues and challenges. *Educational Psychologist, 45*(4), 210–223.

Baker, R. S. J. D., Corbett, A. T., Koedinger, K. R., Evenson, E., Roll, I., Wagner, A. Z., et al. (2006). *Adapting to when students game an intelligent tutoring system. Proceedings of the 8th international conference on intelligent tutoring systems* (pp. 392–401).

Baker, R. S., Corbett, A. T., Koedinger, K. R., & Wagner, A. Z. (2004). *Off-task behavior in the cognitive tutor classroom: when students "game the system". Proceedings of the SIGCHI conference on human factors in computing systems (CHI '04)* (pp. 383–390). New York, NY, USA: ACM.

Bandura, A. (1991). Self-regulation of motivation through anticipatory and self-regulatory mechanisms. In R. A. Dienstbier (Ed.), *Perspectives on motivation: Nebraska symposium on motivation* (Vol. 38, pp. 69–164). Lincoln: University of Nebraska Press.

Bandura, A. (1994). Self-efficacy. In V. S. Ramachaudran (Ed.), *Encyclopedia of human behavior* (Vol. 4, pp. 71–81). New York: Academic.

Bandura, A. (1997). *Self-efficacy: The exercise of control*. New York: Freeman.

Belenky, D. M., & Nokes-Malach, T. J. (2012). Motivation and transfer: The role of mastery-approach goals in preparation for future learning. *Journal of the Learning Sciences, 21*(3), 399–432. doi:10.1080/10508406.2011.651232.

Bernacki, M. L. Nokes-Malach, T. J., & Aleven, V. (2012). Investigating stability and change in unit-level achievement goals and their effects on math learning with intelligent tutors. Paper to be presented at the Annual

Meeting of the American Educational Research Association, Vancouver, BC.

Bouffard, T., Boisvert, J., Vezeau, C., & Larouche, C. (1995). The impact of goal orientation on self-regulation and performance among college students. *British Journal of Educational Psychology, 65*, 317–329.

Cervone, D., & Shoda, Y. (1999). Beyond traits in the study of personality coherence. *Current Directions in Psychological Science, 8*, 27–32.

Dweck, C. S. (1986). Motivational processes affecting learning. *American Psychologist, 41*, 1040–1048.

Dweck, C. S. (1999). *Self-theories: Their role in motivation, personality, and development*. Philadelphia, PA: Psychology Press.

Elliot, A. J. (1999). Approach and avoidance motivation and achievement goals. *Educational Psychologist, 34*, 149–169.

Elliot, A. J., & Church, M. A. (1997). A hierarchical model of approach and avoidance achievement motivation. *Journal of Personality and Social Psychology, 72*, 218–232.

Elliot, A. J., & Harackiewicz, J. M. (1996). Approach and avoidance achievement goals and intrinsic motivation: A mediational analysis. *Journal of Personality and Social Psychology, 70*, 461–475.

Elliot, A. J., & McGregor, H. A. (2001). A 2 X 2 achievement goal framework. *Journal of Personality and Social Psychology, 80*(3), 501–519.

Elliot, A. J., McGregor, H. A., & Gable, S. (1999). Achievement goals, study strategies, and exam performance: A mediational analysis. *Journal of Educational Psychology, 91*(3), 549–563.

Elliot, A. J., & Murayama, K. (2008). On the measurement of achievement goals: Critique, illustration, and application. *Journal of Educational Psychology, 100*(3), 613–628.

Elliott, E. S., & Dweck, C. S. (1988). Goals: An approach to motivation and achievement. *Journal of Personality and Social Psychology, 54*, 5–12.

Ericsson, K. A., & Simon, H. A. (1984). *Protocol analysis: Verbal reports as data*. Cambridge, MA, USA: The MIT Press.

Fryer, J. W., & Elliot, A. J. (2007). Stability and change in achievement goals. *Journal of Educational Psychology, 99*(4), 700–714.

Greene, B. A., & Miller, R. B. (1996). Influences on achievement: Goals, perceived ability, and cognitive engagement. *Contemporary Educational Psychology, 21*, 181–192.

Greene, B. A., Miller, R. B., Crowson, H. M., Duke, B. L., & Akey, K. L. (2004). Predicting high school students' cognitive engagement and achievement: Contributions of classroom perceptions and motivation* 1. *Contemporary Educational Psychology, 29*(4), 462–482. doi:10.1016/j.cedpsych.2004.01.006.

Greene, J. A., Robertson, J., & Costa, L. J. C. (2011). Assessing self-regulated learning using think-aloud methods. In B. J. Zimmerman & D. H. Schunk (Eds.), *Handbook of self-regulation of learning and performance* (pp. 313–328). New York: Routledge.

Harackiewicz, J. M., Barron, K. E., Pintrich, P. R., Elliot, A. J., & Thrash, T. M. (2002). Revision of achievement goal theory: Necessary and illuminating. *Journal of Educational Psychology*. doi:10.1037//0022-0663.94.3.638.

Harackiewicz, J. M., Barron, K. E., Tauer, J. M., & Elliot, A. J. (2002). Predicting success in college: A longitudinal study of achievement goals and ability measures as predictors of interest and performance from freshman year through graduation. *Journal of Educational Psychology, 94*, 562–575.

Horvath, M., Herleman, H. A., & Lee McKie, R. (2006). Goal orientation, task difficulty, and task interest: A multilevel analysis. *Motivation and Emotion, 30*(2), 169–176. doi:10.1007/s11031-006-9029-6.

Koedinger, K. R., & Aleven, V. (2007). Exploring the assistance dilemma in experiments with Cognitive Tutors. *Educational Psychology Review, 19*(3), 239–264.

Koedinger, K. R., Baker, R. S. J. D., Cunningham, K., Skogsholm, A., Leber, B., & Stamper, J. (2010). A data repository for the EDM community: The PSLC DataShop. In C. Romero, S. Ventura, M. Pechenizkiy, & R. S. J. D. Baker (Eds.), *Handbook of educational data mining* (pp. 43–56). Boca Raton, FL: CRC.

Koedinger, K., & Corbett, A. (2006). Cognitive tutors: Technology bringing learning science to the classroom. In K. Sawyer (Ed.), *The Cambridge handbook of the learning sciences* (pp. 61–78). Cambridge, MA: Cambridge University Press.

Linnenbrink-Garcia, L., Tyson, D. F., & Patall, E. A. (2008). When are achievement goal orientations beneficial for academic achievement? A closer look at main effects and moderating factors. *Revue Internationale De Psychologie Sociale, 21*(1–2), 19–70.

Meece, J. L., Blumenfeld, P. C., & Hoyle, R. H. (1988). Students' goal orientations and cognitive engagement in classroom activities. *Journal of Educational Psychology, 80*, 514–523.

Midgley, C., Maehr, M. L., Hnida, L. Z., Anderman, E., Anderman, L., Freeman, K. E., et al. (2000). *Manual for the patterns of adaptive learning scales (PALS)*. Ann Arbor: University of Michigan.

Mischel, W. (1968). *Personality and assessment*. New York: Wiley.

Mischel, W. (1973). Towards a cognitive social learning theory reconceptualization of personality. *Psychological Review, 80*, 252–283.

Muis, K. R., & Edwards, O. (2009). Examining the stability of achievement goal orientation. *Contemporary Educational Psychology, 34*, 265–277.

Pajares, F. (1997). Current directions in self-efficacy research. In M. Maehr & P. R. Pintrich (Eds.), *Advances in motivation and achievement* (Vol. 10, pp. 1–49). Greenwich, CT: JAI.

Pintrich, P. R. (2000). The role of goal orientation in self-regulated learning. In M. Boekaerts, P. R. Pintrich, & M. Zeidner (Eds.), *Handbook of self-regulation* (pp. 451–502). San Diego, CA, USA: Academic.

Ritter, S., Anderson, J. R., Koedinger, K. R., & Corbett, A. (2007). Cognitive tutor: applied research in mathematics education. *Psychonomic Bulletin and Review, 14*(2), 249–255.

Siegler, R. S., & Crowley, K. (1991). The microgenetic method: A direct means for studying cognitive development. *American Psychologist, 46*, 606–620.

Veenman, M. V. J., Bernadette, H. A. M., Hout-Wolters, V., & Afflerbach, P. (2006). Metacognition and learning: conceptual and methodological considerations. *Metacognition & Learning, 1*, 3–14. doi:10.1007/s11409-006-6893-0.

Weiner, B. (1986). *An attributional theory of motivation and emotion*. New York: Springer-Verlag.

Winne, P. H. (1997). Experimenting to bootstrap self-regulated learning. *Journal of Educational Psychology, 89*(3), 397.

Winne, P. H. (2011). A cognitive and metacognitive analysis of self-regulated learning. In B. J. Zimmerman & D. H. Schunk (Eds.), *Handbook of self-regulation of learning and performance* (pp. 15–32). New York: Routledge.

Winne, P. H., & Hadwin, A. F. (1998). Studying as self-regulated learning. In D. J. Hacker, J. Dunlosky, A. C. Graesser, D. J. Hacker, J. Dunlosky, & A. C. Graesser (Eds.), *Metacognition in educational theory and practice* (pp. 277–304). Mahwah, NJ US: Lawrence Erlbaum Associates Publishers.

Winne, P. H., & Hadwin, A. F. (2008). The weave of motivation and self-regulated learning. In D. H. Schunk & B. J. Zimmerman (Eds.), *Motivation and self-regulated learning: Theory, research, and applications* (pp. 297–314). Mahwah, NJ: Erlbaum.

Zimmerman, B. J. (2000). Attaining self-regulation: A social cognitive perspective. In M. Boekaerts, P. R. Pintrich, & M. Zeidner (Eds.), *Handbook of self-regulation* (pp. 13–39). San Diego, CA, USA: Academic.

Zimmerman, B. J. (2011). Motivational sources and outcomes of self-regulated learning and performance. In B. J. Zimmerman & D. H. Schunk (Eds.), *Handbook of self-regulation of learning and performance* (pp. 49–64). New York: Routledge.

Zimmerman, B. J., & Schunk, D. H. (2011). *Handbook of self-regulated learning and performance*. New York: Routledge.

Affective Learning Companions and the Adoption of Metacognitive Strategies

42

Winslow Burleson

Abstract

Understanding the affective state of a learner is an important element in determining when and how best to provide appropriate support. We advanced an Affective Learning Companion built upon an Affective Agent Research Platform with the goal of discovering when, at various points in the problem solving process a student encounters optimal Flow experiences or non-optimal Stuck experiences (Burleson 2006; Burleson and Picard 2007). We employed the theories of Carol S. Dweck and John H. Flavell, to help students become aware of their emotional states, and to develop metacognitive strategies to use this awareness to persevere in the face of frustration. We wanted to know when and how an intelligent computer tutoring system could provide personally tailored intervention to prompt a student to find the best way to continue to engage in challenging experiences. The findings argue that there are important opportunities to increase girls' meta-affective skills, increase their experience of Flow and decrease their experience of Stuck, increase their mastery orientation, and increase their intrinsic-motivation. This holds true not only for the further development of affective support and its benefits for girls, but also for the appropriate "coordination" of the elements of the character's emotional intelligence for boys.

Introduction

Strategies and technologies for automated support for student learning, through tutoring strategies, peer tutoring, and learning companions, are central themes of research advanced by the Intelligent Tutoring Systems community. The approach of the investigation presented here is the use of multimodal real-time sensing coupled with an ALC that engages in verbal affective support and nonverbal social mirroring in ways that provide adaptive help to empower students to persist in the face of frustration.

W. Burleson (✉)
Arizona State University,
Tempe, AZ 85281, USA
e-mail: winslow.burleson@asu.edu

Our approach combines Dweck's theories on trait and incremental self-theories of intelligence with Flavell's research on metacognitive knowledge, experience, and skill to inform our own research goals to find ways to help students realize

R. Azevedo and V. Aleven (eds.), *International Handbook of Metacognition and Learning Technologies*, Springer International Handbooks of Education 26, DOI 10.1007/978-1-4419-5546-3_42,

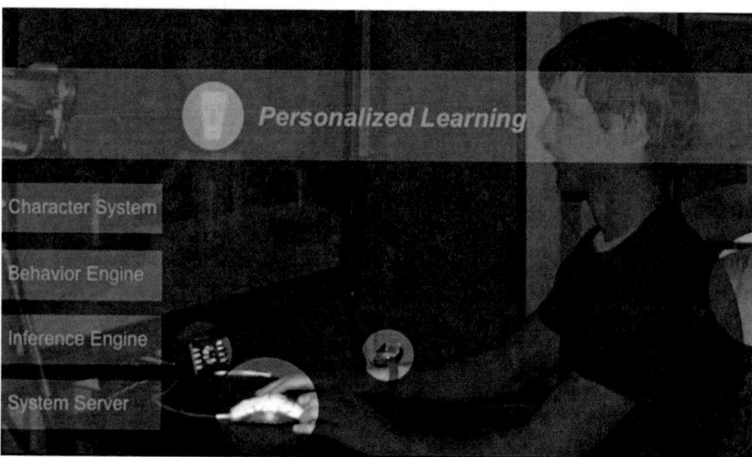

Fig. 42.1 Affective Agent Research Platform consisting of the Affective Learning Companion (ALC), the Character System, Behavior Engine, Inference Engine, and the System Server, which collects data from four sensors: the pressure mouse, skin conductance sensor, posture chair, and blue-eyes camera

their potential and navigate through frustration. Such researchers as Tak-Wai Chan theorized that an ITS—through a nonthreatening Learning Companion—can act as a kind of peer (Chan & Baskin, 1988). Peer tutors and learning companions have been shown to be good role models and supportive to learners because they can put a learner at ease. In the case of peer tutors, students may not believe they can ever equal an adult or teacher; a peer tutor can promote the idea of a level playing field, which in turn gives the learner a sense that success is attainable. On the emotional front, with or without tutoring, a learning companion, embedded with metacognitive strategies might serve as a social reflective agent that can empower students to combat anxiety and other negative feelings that often hinder successful learning.

Other researchers, such as Schank and Neaman (2001), theorized that a fear of failure may block learning. They urged ITS developers to provide the kinds of motivation that outweighs or distracts feelings of failure. However, this approach fails to appreciate that often, it is OK or even productive (providing important learning, reflection, insight, and even at times, motivation) to fail. We sought to support learners' ability to persevere in the face of failure and to fight through frustration, e.g., to foster their ability to fail fearlessly so that they might go on to greater successes. We believe a productive strategy for ITS is to foster metacognitive skills that help students manage the negative feelings that often come with a sense of failure, so that they don't quit or avoid challenging growth opportunities in the future. To this end, our affective agent research platform used sensors (see, Fig. 42.1) to sense elements of student affect and use this to study ways to help them to persevere through frustration.

The affective agent research platform was used to present the Towers of Hanoi,[1] with an affective learning companion in each of the four conditions of a 2×2 empirical investigation. The study contrasted, in one dimension, verbal affective support with verbal task support and in the other dimension, sensor-based social nonverbal mirroring (NVM; see Section "Theoretical/Conceptual Framework"), e.g., as empathetic facial expression and postural interaction, with prerecorded nonverbal interactions. This was achieved with a real-time multimodal sensing

[1] Towers of Hanoi is an nineteenth century mathematical challenge. Its apparent difficulty, to a user that does not understand recursion, can be adjusted by presenting the activity with a fewer or greater number of disks. This puzzle and the number of disks were selected so that the challenge could be set at a level that would frustrate users. Pilot studies indicated that seven disks was suitably challenging for 11–13-year-old participants.

system that also allowed the logging and subsequent classification of behavior events, e.g., selection of a "quit" button. This was achieved by developing the system using a modular architecture including a system server, data logger, inference engine, behavior engine, and character engine. The character engine employs scripted character attributes and uses multimodal real-time sensing to capture diverse elements of learners' affective expression. The character scripts are used to deliver the affect and task-based support, and are augmented by real-time sensor-based instructions that enable the ALC to display social NVM or prerecorded nonverbal events. It was hypothesized that the affective support and the NVM would improve student's persistence, intrinsic motivation, and measures of Flow/Stuck and self-reported meta-affective skill (see below for descriptions of these measures).

Trait and Incremental Self-Theories of Intelligence

Dweck's work shed light on the role of feelings in learning and their interaction with self-theories of intelligence. She developed a strategy of metacognitive knowledge for how to think about one's own intelligence and one's ability to "grow" one's own intelligence. She demonstrated that if students can embrace the concept that the mind is like a muscle that can grow stronger, then too, they can believe their intelligence can grow stronger. Throughout this chapter we refer to this concept as Dweck's message—encouraging students to think of their mind as a muscle that, even when challenges are frustrating, grows stronger through their efforts. Dweck's message was used as the affective verbal intervention. What students believe about their own intelligence profoundly affects their motivation, learning and behavioral strategies—especially when they perceive failure (Dweck, 1999). This research identified two predominant groups of people—incrementalists, who believe their own intelligence can be enhanced, and trait learners, who figure their intelligence is largely fixed. When incrementalists fail at a task, they are motivated to try harder to get better and smarter. On the other hand, people who hold trait-based beliefs may lack the motivation to continue. They may quit in order to avoid confirmation of an inability based on previous failure of the task. Our work, expands on the delivery of Dweck's interventions, opening the way to sensing and responding to students on a personal level in real-time by assessing when a learner becomes frustrated, and then trying and evaluating different interventions; ultimately the aim is that these will be suited specifically for that student's needs.

Studies of expert tutor's interaction strategies have found that nearly half of an expert tutor's interactions with students are affective in nature (Lepper, Woolverton, Mumme, & Gurtner, 1993) and that interactions are adapted to respond to individuals needs (Lehman, Matthews, D'Mello, & Person, 2009). Expert tutors might be empathetic and encourage a student to use such a strategy as a mind-is-like-a-muscle in times of frustration, or when the student looks ready to quit. Or, the expert tutor will feel when it's right to stand back when he or she senses the likelihood of quitting is low and the student can figure it out on his or her own. We wanted our platform to be able to sense when to intervene and when to let the student learn to face and overcome challenges as they engage in personally motivated effort and learning.

Metacognitive Knowledge, Experience, and Skill

Dweck's theories build on Flavell's theories of metacognition to describe how students can use strategies and self-awareness to improve their thinking processes (Efklides & Vauras, 1999; Flavell 1979). Flavell's theory of Metacognition comprised three elements: metacognitive knowledge, metacognitive experience and metacognitive skill. Metacognitive knowledge is about a person knowing strategies that might be effective. Metacognitive experience is an awareness of what's going on with one's thinking at any given time, and metacognitive skill is the ability to coordinate the application of metacognitive knowledge in the context of one's metacognitive experience, applying the knowledge in a situation in which it will be effective.

In particular our research focuses on the realm of metacognition based on affect, or meta-affect, which comprises meta-affective knowledge, meta-affective experience and meta-affective skill. This aligns with the affective elements of: phase 2, monitoring; phase 3, control; and phase 4, reaction and reflection; in Pintrich's conceptual framework for assessing motivation and self-regulated learning (Pintrich, 2004).

Meta-affective knowledge is knowing how affect impacts one's thinking ability. For example, does a person's thinking processes become more rigid and less flexible when frustrated (leading to a negative impact on progress), or does that thinking process grow, in line with Dweck's theory that "the mind is like a muscle and through exercise and effort you can grow your intelligence?"

Meta-affective experience, then, is a conscious reflection of one's own feelings and how they steer one into action, or inaction. For example, there is an affective self-awareness when a person becomes frustrated and is aware that this frustration is impeding their progress.

Finally, *meta-affective skill* is the ability to synthesize meta-affective knowledge and meta-affective experience: to, at a time of meta-affective experience, apply one's meta-affective knowledge. For instance, instead of letting frustration lead to quitting, a person might calm him or herself down and consider alternate strategies to resolve the problem. They might apply their knowledge that sticking with the task at hand, even though it is frustrating, may better help them achieve their desired goal.

Section "Theoretical/Conceptual Framework" discusses how Flow and Stuck theory is used to help students through affective and nonverbal social interactions from an ALC. Section "Effectiveness of Tool/Empirical" discusses the detection of "frustration" using an array of multimodal real-time affective sensors. In "Discussion" section, we discuss the challenges that persist across the development of our theories, methods, analysis and instructional contexts. Finally, in Section "Design Implications," we look at the design implications in terms of the compelling opportunities to further advance investigation of nonverbal mirroring (NVM), longitudinal adaptive support, and self-actualized learning and creativity.

Theoretical/Conceptual Framework

Now that we have discussed Dweck's work on Trait and Incremental Self-Theories of Intelligence and how we situate these with Flavel's Metacognitive Knowledge, Experience, and Skill framework, in this section we discuss Flow/Stuck Theory and NVM.

Flow/Stuck Theory

When it comes to developing ITS, there is a distinction between manipulating the environment, or task, to keep flow going versus empowering the student through self-awareness to self-regulate their own motivational strategies (Hill et al., 2001; Kapoor et al., 2007; Malone, 1984). A student's perception of the challenge at hand and their belief in their own abilities to match it can determine whether he or she experiences Flow or Stuck (See Table 42.1). Flow is the theory of optimal experience. Stuck is a state of nonoptimal experience encountered when a student is frustrated during a learning activity (Burleson, 2006). So, instead of the positive experience of Flow, which is when a learner believes his or her skill matches the challenge at hand and there's a feeling of being in control and being able to concentrate, focus and enjoy an activity for its own sake, Stuck represents the opposite. It is a negative or nonoptimal experience in learning, that goes beyond just being frustrated; it is accompanied by feelings of lack of control, lack of concentration and focus, mental fatigue and distress. Stuck has the potential to sap students' endurance because they perceive tasks as taking longer than they actually do. Several researchers have linked a participant's overestimation of how long it took to complete a task with self-reported levels of frustration (Czerwinski,

Table 42.1 Flavell's Meta-Experience or feelings of experience include Csikszentmihalyi's Flow or Optimal Experience and Stuck or nonoptimal experience

Flow: optimal experience—Csikszentmihalyi	*Stuck*: nonoptimal experience—Burleson
All encompassing	All encompassing
A feeling of being in control	A feeling of being out of control
Concentration and highly focused attention	A lack of concentration and inability to maintain focused attention
Mental enjoyment of the activity for its own sake	Mental fatigue and distress caused by engagement with the activity
A distorted sense of time	A distorted sense of time (Weybrew, 1984; Czerwinski et al., 2001)
A match between the challenge at hand one's skills	A *perceived* mismatch between the challenge at hand and one's skill
Frequently associated with positive affect	Frequently associated with negative affect

Meta-Experience: feelings of experience (Flavell, 1979; Efklides, 2002)

Horvitz et al., 2001; Liu & Picard, 2005; Weybrew, 1984; Zeigarnik, 1967).

Negative affect has been shown to have a disproportional impact as compared to positive affect, a phenomenon called "negative asymmetry." Because of its negative asymmetry and the detrimental consequences of negative affect (Giuseppe & Brass, 2003), mitigating negative affect may have a significant effect. Our goal is to work with students through an ITS to help them become self-aware of Stuck and metacognitive strategies they can apply to overcome it. Their affective awareness coupled with their meta-affective skill may improve their overall attitude toward and experience with learning opportunities.

We, along with others working on emotional intelligence, contend that an awareness of affective states (in our case, feelings of frustration and Stuck) can influence the ability to alter that state. Within the theory of Flow, feelings of awareness can have a negative impact on Flow experiences as they can interrupt the state and tend to diminish happiness and the sense of optimal experience (Csikszentmihalyi, 1990). When it comes to Stuck, however, feelings of awareness that serve as interruptions can actually be used to help users, as indicators of when to apply their metacognitive knowledge (e.g., Dweck's message), to lessen the effects of Stuck on learning.

Learners in Stuck may be thinking "I can't do this" or "arrrghh, this isn't working," and feeling helpless or hopeless. They often internalize these feelings of difficulty and become Stuck. Our strategy is to help the students to interrupt their Stuck experience, more productively. We do this within an ITS by first detecting frustration and then providing an external interruption with content that has been shown in prior work to help students persist through frustration (Dweck, 1999). Eventually we intend to fade this support, developing better learning strategies, e.g., learners who can work through frustration and avoid the detrimental impact of Stuck.

To pursue this research challenge we constructed an ALC that recognized different indicators of failure/frustration and then help the student become aware of and work through a state of Stuck (e.g., to apply Dweck's message and preserver). When things are humming along and a student continues to progress through a task, feeling confident he or she will get to the next step and the next, and so forth, he or she is literally going with the flow. It's when students get stuck—or frustrated—that progress on a challenge can be negatively impacted and the pursuit of the challenge abandoned. An effective computer tutor must recognize frustration and react accordingly to encourage the student to develop their self-efficacy, so that they may persevere through frustration and overcome and succeed at greater and greater challenges.

Nonverbal Social Interaction

NVM, the synchronicity between two or more individuals' facial expressions and head and body movements, serves important functions in human social interactions. Recently, NVM between a human and an embodied agent (a virtual character) has been shown to increase the persuasive ability of the agent and increase the social bond with the agent (Bailenson & Yee, 2005). How an agent within the learning system acts or reacts to a student can be informed by a learner's facial expressions, gestures, postural shifts, and arousal state. Agent's expressive behaviors also can promote useful outcomes such as making agents likeable (Elliott, Rickel & Lester, 1999; Johnson, Rickel, Lewis & Lester, 2000; Koda & Maes, 1996; Lester, Towns & Fitzgerald, 1999). For instance, if the agent cracks a joke and one student smiles while another frowns, then it likely would be fine for that agent to flash a smile back to the first student. However, the second student might perceive that smile as rude. Depending on the agent's goals, one response might be more intelligent than another. If whatever the agent is doing increasingly irritates that student, then it might be helpful for the agent to see the student's response and act in a way that acknowledges its failure (that is, if the goal includes wanting the student to have a favorable impression). We know that individuals' opinions of the competence, trustworthiness, and likeability, of others are colored by how the other—human or intelligent agent—chooses to respond to their emotion.

Beyond overt facial expression, we know that some types of body movement, such as mirroring of body position, are important to interpersonal relationships as nonverbal ways of expression, interpretation, and communication (Bull, 1983). So, while we don't assume that human–human interaction is the same as human–computer interaction, we recognize there is much to be learned from findings, e.g., those of Reeves, Nass and Moon, (Moon, 2000; Reeves & Nass, 1996), that show that person-to-person interaction can help us design human–computer interaction. Bailenson used social mirroring in his work on Transformed Social Interactions to show that an agent mirroring a user's head movement is perceived as more persuasive and likeable than one responding with prerecorded head motions (Bailenson & Yee, 2005). In another nonverbal channel, Marci and Gottman found that skin conductance, a measure of arousal, from couples in counseling sessions could indicate the strength of their relationships and predict divorce (Gottman & Levenson, 1992; Marci & Riess, 2005).

To advance Lepper's and Winslet's findings on the importance of the social and motivational bonds between instructor and student, within and ITS, we employed NVM in a multimodal real-time affective agent platform. Based on Bailenson's implementation of NVM we used data from the four sensors to mirror (with a four second delay, to avoid the awkward experience of real-time mirroring yet maintain the beneficial social experience) (Bailenson & Yee, 2005): with the pressure mouse, tension or agitation, presented as rapid body movement; skin conductance, which can be interpreted as levels of arousal, adjusting skin tone, to present the character as pail, neutral, or flush; with the chair, leaning forward and sitting or slumping back; with the camera, head nod and shake behaviors and mouth fidget (asymmetric mouth movement) and smile (symmetric upward movement of the sides of the mouth). While, we recognize that—to date—there are not yet any intelligent tutoring systems that can sense natural (both verbal and nonverbal) human communication of emotion and respond as well as or equal to another person, (Burleson et al., 2004) we have built an ITS that was capable of recognizing and responding to elements of student affect (verbally and nonverbally) to mitigate Stuck and promote Flow, and in this respect can be considered a "relational agent," an ALC.

Effectiveness of Tool/Empirical

In this section we discuss the detection of "frustration" using an array of multimodal real-time affective sensors. This discussion also includes an introduction to the measures, methods, and findings on fostering Flow and mitigating Stuck; the efficacy of NVM; and students' belief in their ability to use metacognitive strategies.

Fig. 42.2 Images showing some of the diverse expressive abilities of the Affective Learning Companion (ALC) controlled by the Character System, which, during Nonverbal Mirroring (NVM), is driven by sensor input

Measures and Methods

Our Affective Agent Research Platform collected data in relation to the student's affective states through NVM. In this system, the student sits in front of a wide screen plasma display showing an agent and a 3D environment. The student interacts with the agent and can manipulate objects and tasks within the environment. Besides nonverbal interactions, our character interacts with the user through an asymmetric voice/text selection dialogue (Burleson et al., 2004) in which the characters speaks using Microsoft's "Eddie" voice scripted with Text-Aloud, a text-to-speech application and the student responds by clicking on one of multiple text response options. The chair is outfitted with a high-density array of force-sensitive resistors (FSR); the mouse detects use through pressure on similar resistors; and, a wireless skin conductance sensor with two electrodes on a wristband was worn by the student. A video camera for off-line coding and the Blue-Eyes camera (Kapoor et al., 2007) to record elements of facial expressions were also used. While game state or task state is not a traditional sensor, it is gathered by our system as a source of data and is treated as a sensor channel in a manner similar to each of the other sensors.

Data is collected by the system server and stored in the data logger to be processed off-line using a classifier that can determine affective state, i.e., when a student will (or will not) express their desire to quit by selecting an onscreen button (Kapoor et al., 2007). The server coordinates user interface, activity, and behavior engine and character interactions. The behavior engine processes the real-time data from the sensors to interpret nonverbal interactions to be displayed by the character engine. The character's behaviors include speaking (affective and task-based messages), nodding, smiling or fidgeting the mouth, shifting its posture forward or backward, changing its color and fidgeting very slightly. (These are the character behaviors controlled in this experiment, although the character is capable of much more the NVM was presented as a 4 s delayed response to the sensor input) (see Fig. 42.2 for a range of character expressions).

We conducted a series of pilot studies and experiments. The first of the two most important studies predicted frustration and provided an opportunity to try out the system, i.e., the affective support dialogue and the NVM. The second was the 2×2 empirical study investigating Dweck's affective message promoting meta-affective strategies (thinking of the mind as a muscle even though you may be frustrated) vs. task-based support and NVM vs. prerecorded nonverbal behaviors, with respect to the four conditions' impact on Flow and Stuck. These two studies included twenty-four 12- to 13-year-old middle school students and seventy-six 11- to 13-year-old girls and boys, respectively. They interacted with the agent and sensing system, for 16 and 25 min periods while trying to solve a Towers of Hanoi activity with seven disks. Subsequent to the Towers of Hanoi activity, the students in the first study spent an additional 10 min interacting with the system while trying to solve another puzzle. The research platform and architecture senses and analyzes signals related to affect with the ability to interpret and respond through an agent that is both scriptable and expressive in real-time. We applied techniques from psychophysiology, emotion communication, signal processing, pattern recognition, and machine learning.

In the first study, prior to applying the sensors to students, we conducted a pretest to determine the students' self-theory of intelligence and how they approach reaching their goals (Dweck, 1999). The agent appeared and presented to participants a 7-min slide show based on a similar presentation Dweck has used to shift children's beliefs about their own intelligence. Then, the learning companion introduced the Towers of Hanoi activity. Two buttons prominent at the top of the screen with text, "I'm frustrated" and "I need some help," were available to the student, although he or she was free to choose or ignore the buttons. These were used as self-labeled affect by the offline classification algorithms. If a student clicked on one of the buttons, or after 16 min passed, whichever occurred first, the student was presented with a supportive dialogue by the character during which he or she is encouraged to continue. After 16 min from the beginning of the activity, or when he or she finished the activity, a post-activity survey asked about the experience. A second activity was administered and followed by the post-test self-theory of intelligence and goal mastery orientation surveys. Then, the students were given a debriefing and a chance to ask questions.

In the second study we wanted to contrast ITS traditional task-based support with the alternative of affective support. T, the ALC provided either task-based guidance (discussing the benefit of moving large or small disks) or affective support based on Dweck's message, at the mean time of quitting (174 s into the activity, as determined in the first study). Students were then asked if they thought they would be able to use the strategy and were encouraged to do their best; which was measured in terms of perseverance (measured as the duration a student continues to engage in the activity before quitting). Additional dependent measures for post-activity frustration, self-reported meta-affective ability, and stuck/flow, were derived from the pretest and posttest instruments.

Sensing Student Frustration

We used technologies developed by members of the MIT Media Lab's Affective Computing Group and the data from the first study to predict with 79% accuracy whether a participant would quit at a given time; the time window that provided the most accurate classification was 3 s (Kapoor et al., 2007). This was conducted through the data from the 24 participants. A Support Vector Machine (SVM) was developed and validated using "leave-one-out cross-validation." Using data from 150 s from each subject we classified the data observed through the sensors as "pre-frustration" or "not pre-frustration" behavior based on probabilistic machine learning techniques. Our system allowed students to report how they were feeling by being able to click on a button labeled "I'm frustrated," or another labeled "I need some help." The student could ignore them or click one of them. When a student clicks the "I'm frustrated" button, we label the segment leading up to that click as "frustration." We know that students might be feeling frustration and still not click the button, but studies from human–computer interactions suggest a kind of comfort zone in which people are more willing to share negative information about themselves with a computer than with a trained person (Card et al., 1974; Lucas et al., 1977; Robinson & West, 1992) so this approach is likely to work better within an ITS than within a non-ITS setting. We use the user's self-labeling as an indication of them being frustrated and aware of it, and then went back and collected their behavioral data leading up to that button click. The data was compared with comparable data from the students who did not indicate frustration, (i.e., those who either did not click on a button or those who clicked on "I need some help" since even though they had the opportunity to, they chose not to express frustration). These two sets of data were then used to construct an automated system to discriminate between frustrated versus other. Then, the system was tested on a set of data that was not used to train the system, e.g., leave-one-out cross-validation. The classification system was not used in real-time, during the second study.

Findings on Flow, Stuck, Meta-Affective Skill, and NVM

We now summarize some of the results of our understanding of the impact of NVM and of the affect vs. task-based support of an ALC's intervention, as these relate to frustration, meta-affective skill, and Flow/Stuck. Our findings showed that gender had a significant effect on students' experience with the ALC (Burleson & Picard, 2007). It is possible that differences in the social and emotional skill developments of girls and boys at these ages (11–13 year olds), with girls typically maturing earlier than boys, may have contributed to these differences. For example, it was found that the girls who were more frustrated at the time of intervention showed higher levels of intrinsic motivation, regardless of intervention. A possible explanation for this may be related to how much a participant cares about the activity. Girls who care more about doing this activity (or activities in general) may also find it more frustrating. Independent of the frustration and independent of the type of intervention they receive, the caring may also lead to their increased intrinsic motivation. To assess intrinsic motivation, following a recommendation from Dweck, we provided students a short break to do anything that they wanted and observed weather they reengaged in the activity on their own accord.

To further explore this, we developed a measure of congruence as a function of frustration and intervention type that we used to encode what we believed to be the appropriateness of the intervention (Affective vs. Task) provided with respect to a participant's self-reported level of frustration at the time of intervention (174 s into the activity, the mean time of quitting as determined in the first study). For example, affective interventions for those with higher levels of frustration and task interventions for those with lower levels of frustration were coded as more congruent. While boys and girls who received interventions that had lower congruence had similar levels of post activity frustration, we found that boys who received interventions that had higher congruence had higher levels of post activity frustration and girls who received interventions with higher congruence had substantially less post activity frustration. While there was not a main effect for the type of intervention, in contrast to the girls, boys showed a strong difference in their levels of frustration due to the type of intervention, with much lower levels of frustration occurring in the task support conditions.

One of the biggest gender differences was found in the relationship between self-reported meta-affective skill and Flow/Stuck in the pre/post activity instruments (Burleson, 2006). In contrast to the result that no significant correlation between meta-affective skill and Flow/Stuck was present when assessed across both genders, the assessment with only girls shows a strong correlation between meta-affective skill and more Flow/less Stuck, while for boys, these measures show a strong correlation in the opposite direction. This is a clear instance where the grouping of the genders clearly mixes different gender effects, yielding no significance when assessed together. One possible hypothesis for the discrepancy in gender at this age is that girls aged 11–13 may be better able to assess their own emotions than boys. If girls are better at assessing their emotions then they may be better able to use their meta-affective skill to lead themselves to more Flow/less Stuck. Boys on the other hand may report that they have meta-affective skill but may actually be less able to recognize their own emotions; thus, even though they may have reported having some meta-affective skill, they may not be as capable at applying it to their own experiential benefit, leaving them to experience less Flow/more Stuck.

While girls showed no main effect difference in the level of frustration based on the type of intervention, a further analysis indicated that this masked a more complex relationship that showed significant differences, due to the interaction of the type of intervention and the presence of mirroring (NVM). These differences can be explained in terms of the "coordination" of the different elements of the character's emotional intelligence. Girls who experienced an affective support intervention in conjunction with NVM (Condition 1) had lower levels of self-reported post activity frustration than girls who received either affective support without NVM (Condition 3) or girls who received task support with NVM (Condition 2). Condition 1 is an experience in which the mirroring and intervention are "coordinated" so that the character displays higher levels of emotional intelligence (as defined in this experiment as the presence of intervention, congruence, and mirroring) than participants receiving Condition 2 and Condition 3 experiences.

One might argue that girls who received task support without mirroring (Condition 4) were also in a "coordinated" condition that presents a character with higher levels of emotional intelligence; they could also argue that in this condition girls experienced similar low levels of frustration when compared to the girls in condition 1. Extending this argument one might then argue that the existing capabilities of Intelligent Tutoring Systems, to provide task support without mirroring have similar benefits to girls, and the effort to develop affect support and mirroring are unwarranted. However the importance of affect support for girls is bolstered by further analysis showing that girls that receive affective support self-report having higher levels of meta-affective skill and more Flow/less Stuck (these relationships were not found for boys). Meta-affective skill correlated significantly with beneficial changes in goal/mastery orientation and there was a trend toward significance in the positive relationship between Flow/Stuck and intrinsic-motivation. The findings from this analysis, taken together, support an argument not only for the further development of affective support and its benefits for girls, but also for the appropriate "coordination" of the elements of the character's emotional intelligence.

These findings indicate that there are important opportunities to increase girls' meta-affective skills, increase their experience of Flow and decrease their experience of Stuck, increase their mastery orientation, and increase their intrinsic-motivation. Data from the boys also supports the argument for coordinating the elements of the character's emotional intelligence. A significant interaction between congruence and NVM indicates that the boys that experience more congruent intervention without mirroring also experienced twice as much post activity frustration as boys in the other three mirroring × congruence conditions. This particular form of discordant emotional intelligence displayed by the character seems to have had a negative impact on these boys.

Discussion

In this section we'll discuss a few of the challenges that persist across the development of our theories, methods, analysis and how these relate to diverse instructional contexts.

While Dweck's work and her theories are substantial, and there is recent work from Person and Greasser (D'Mello et al., 2010) and Lehman (Lehman et al., 2009), overall little is known about expert human tutors and their methods. A deep understanding of the complex role that affect plays within the dynamic process of learning is also incomplete (Picard et al., 2004). Likewise, NVM is not fully understood and its effects while reproducible are not always reliably so (Bull, 1983). Many subtleties may yet be discovered.

When we conduct research that combines tutoring, affective learning, and NVM these uncertainties are compounded. For example, many challenges facing the development of affective tutoring systems can be seen when results are compared to results of human–human interaction studies. From human–human interaction, we know that human expression is not necessarily affectively congruent with the task. There are different conditions for smiles, including nervousness, humor, and success. We can expect such interactions to be similarly complex for human–agent interactions, so it is unclear what the agent expression should be for it to be perceived empathetically. However, we'll need new advances in real-time technology to allow us to recognize these deeper nuances of interactions. As we move toward training multimodal sensor systems in multiple sessions, across larger and more diverse populations, we expect that we will generate new approaches. Currently the development, deployment, maintenance, and configuration of novel multimodal sensors are one of the most significant challenges that need to be overcome to elucidate these deeper phenomena.

Methodologically, since our ITS is quite complex and requires advanced instrumentation, moving from the laboratory settings that were employed in the studies presented here to real world classroom environments presents further challenges. There have been some recent advances (Arroyo et al., 2009; Arroyo et al., Accepted) and we are hopeful that these will continue to lead to advancing understanding across diverse population. For example, students with learning disabilities seem to respond particularly well to our current ALC interventions and we are now engaged in a new series of studies involving high school and college students with mathematics disabilities. We are also beginning studies across diverse cultural settings and exploring ways to provide support in activities that extend beyond the desktop.

Analysis of affective sensor data is an ongoing research frontier, with some, but not enough, consensus on the best practices and gold standards. Issues include the data sampling rate, the timeframe to use for analysis, and the relative merit of self-report and consensual coding. We continue to favor behavioral events, such as the decision-making and related actions involved in activating a quit button, as salient events and meaningful elements that are useful for grounding our understanding of participants' affective states and the investigation of how these behaviors and their underlying cognitive and affective processes affect participants' ongoing learning activities.

Only a very few instructional settings have been studied in conjunction with affective sensing and even fewer with affective learning companions or response systems. Understanding how to provide interventions and when the best time to intervene might be continues to be an open challenge and research opportunity, across most learning settings. While we have developed and evaluated an initial set of interventions, we are finding that interventions need to be specifically tailored to the learning settings. This process can require extensive pilot testing and experiments. The work presented here did not specifically address learning metrics within the Towers of Hanoi context, but rather individuals' perseverance (for which there was no main-effect from the interventions) and meta-affective strategies. Separately, we have aimed our research at advancing combinations of learning and affect (Arroyo et al., 2009) in real world settings.

Design Implications

In conclusion we discuss how the design implications of our work and findings, in terms of the opportunities to further advance investigation of Affective Agent Research Platforms and agents that employ theory-based design and incorporate NVM, longitudinal adaptive affective support, are informing our future work. We have shown the ability to provide adaptive metacognitive support that relates to affect (meta-affective support). We have also shown that coupling this with NVM has the potential to reduce learners' frustration. Right now there are many ways to implement NVM and further work is needed to determine the most effective approaches and benefits. It is an open question as to whether, ultimately, it might be possible to mirror without as many sensors once agents are trained (some elements of NVM could be implemented using widely available built in cameras). More recently, using similar range of sensors, we have shown the ability to reliably detect frustration and several additional affective states (Arroyo et al., 2009; Kapoor, Burleson, & Picard, 2007). We have also moved our investigations out of laboratory settings into computer classroom settings showing the ability to use multimodal sensors in real-time in classroom settings to detect and respond to students' affective states in learning contexts.

If our findings are confirmed by further studies and if they can be more broadly applied across diverse populations, then we believe that the ITS community can effectively advance the use of ALC by incorporating deeper levels of emotional intelligence that are better correlated to the complex dynamics and interactions of both learners' affective and cognitive experiences. However, as our initial results demonstrate, developers and researchers need to make sure they are carefully coordinating (consider coupling mirroring with verbal affective support, for girls, and abandoning mirroring when providing task support, for boys) the diverse elements of emotional intelligence appropriately for any given population, learning setting, to individual learners.

While the strategies and algorithms for this careful coordination are not yet fully understood and a great deal of research remains to be conducted to address the multiple challenges of long-term adaptive support, these approaches may 1 day foster a new generation of personalized learning (Gardner, 2009). Even in the near-term we are exploring the use of nonverbal social–emotional communication and relational agents in areas as diverse as engineering design teams and therapeutic care giving. In the long term, we see the potential to expand the range of learning opportunities from the current desktop implementation into a vast array of everyday situations. Ultimately, we see these situations involving individual and social activities, life-long learning, and the promotion of self-actualized learning and creativity (Burleson 2005).

References

Arroyo, I., Burleson, W., Tai, M., Muldner, K., & Woolf, B. (Accepted). Gender differences in the use and benefit of advanced learning technologies for mathematics [Special issue on Advanced Learning Technologies]. *Journal of Educational Psychology*. V. Aleven & C. Beal (guest editors).

Arroyo, I., Cooper, D. G., Burleson, W., Woolf, B. P., Muldner, K., Christopherson, R. (2009). Emotion sensors go to school. *International Conference on Artificial Intelligence and Education*, IOS Press, pp. 17–24.

Bailenson, J. N., & Yee, N. (2005). Digital chameleons: Automatic assimilation of nonverbal gestures in immersive virtual environments. *Psychological Science, 16*, 814–819.

Bull, P. (1983). *Body movement and interpersonal communication*. New York, NY: John Wiley & Sons.

Burleson, W. (2005). Opportunities for creativity, motivation, and self-actualization in learning systems. *International Journal of Human-Computer Studies, 63*, 436–451. Special Issue on Creativity and Computational Support. ISSN 1071–5819.

Burleson, W. (2006). *Affective learning companions: Strategies for empathetic agents with real-time multimodal affective sensing to foster meta-cognitive and meta-affective approaches to learning, motivation, and perseverance*. MIT PhD Thesis, September 2006. (http://affect.media.mit.edu/publications.php)

Burleson, W., & Picard, R. (2007). Evidence for gender specific approaches to the development of emotionally intelligent learning companions. *IEEE Intelligent Systems Journal, 22*(4), 62–69.

Burleson, W., Picard, R. W., Perlin, K., & Lippincott, J. (2004 July). A platform for affective agent research. *Workshop on Empathetic Agents, 3rd International Joint Conference on Autonomous Agents and Multi-Agent Systems*, New York, NY.

Card, W. I., Nicholson, M., Crean, G. P., Watkinson, G., Evans, C. R., Wilson, J., et al. (1974). A comparison of doctor and computer interrogation of patients. *International Journal of Bio-Medical Computing, 5*, 175–187.

Chan, T. W., & Baskin, A. B. (1988). *Studying with the prince: the computer as a learning companion* (pp. 194–200). Canada: Montreal.

Csikszentmihalyi, M. (1990). *Flow: The psychology of optimal experience*. New York, NY: Harper & Row.

Czerwinski, M., Horvitz, E., & Cutrell, E. (2001). Subjective duration assessment: An implicit probe for software usability. *Proceedings of IHM-HCI 2001 Conference, 2*, 167–170. Lille, France.

D'Mello, S., Jackson, T., Craig, S., Morgan, B., Chipman, P., White, H., et al. (2010). *AutoTutor detects and responds to learners affective and cognitive states*. Cambridge, MA: MIT Media Lab.

Dweck, C. (1999). *Self-theories: their role in motivation, personality and development*. Philadelphia, PA: Psychology Press.

Efklides, A. (2002). Feelings as subjective evaluations of cognitive processing: How reliable are they?

Psychology: *The Journal of the Hellenic Psychological Society, 9*, 163–184.

Efklides, A., & Vauras, M. (1999). Introduction. *European Journal of Psychology of Education, 14*, 455–459.

Elliott, C., Rickel, J., & Lester, J. (1999). Lifelike pedagogical agents and affective computing: An exploratory synthesis. In M. Woodridge & M. Veloso (Eds.), *Artificial intelligence today* (pp. 195–212). Chicago, IL: Springer. 1600 of Lecture Notes in Computer Science.

Flavell, J. H. (1979). Metacognition and cognitive monitoring: A new area of cognitive developmental inquiry. *The American Psychologist, 34*, 906–911.

Gardner, H. (2009, May/June). The next big thing: personalized education. *Foreign Affairs Magazine*.

Giuseppe, L., & Brass, D. (2003). Exploring the social ledger: negative relationships and negative asymmetry in social networks in organizations. *Academy of Management Review. Special issue: Building Effective Networks, Academy of Management*. Chicago, IL.

Gottman, J. M., & Levenson, R. W. (1992). Marital processes predictive of later dissolution. *Journal of Personality and Social Psychology, 63*(2), 221–233. ABSTRACT. Behavior, Physiology, and Health.

Hill, R., Gratch, J., Johnson, W. L., Kyriakakis, C., LaBore, C., Lindheim, R., et al. (2001). *Toward the holodeck: integrating graphics, sound, character and story*. In *Proceedings of the Fifth International Conference on Autonomous Agents*. (pp. 409–416). Montreal, QC, Canada.

Johnson, L., Rickel, J., Lewis J., & Lester, J. (2000). Animated pedagogical agents: Face-to-face interaction in interactive learning environments. *International Journal of Artificial Intelligence in Education, 11*, 47–78.

Kapoor, A., Burleson, W., & Picard, R. (2007). Automatic prediction of frustration. *International Journal of Human Computer Studies, 65*(8), 724–736. August, 2007.

Koda, T., & Maes, P. (1996). Agents with faces: The effect of personification. HCI'96.

Lehman, B., Matthews, M., D'Mello, S., & Person, N. (2009). What are you feeling? Investigating student affective states during expert human tutoring sessions. *Proceedings of the 9th International Conference on Intelligent Tutoring Systems* (2008)

Lepper, M. R., Woolverton, M., Mumme, D. L., & Gurtner, J.-L. (1993). Motivational techniques of expert human tutors: lessons for the design of computer-based tutors: lessons for the design of computer-based tutors. In S. P. Lajoie & S. J. Derry (Eds.), *Computers as cognitive tools* (pp. 75–105). Erlbaum, NJ: Hillsdale.

Lester, J., Towns, S. G., & Fitzgerald, P. (1999). Achieving affective impact: Visual emotive communication in lifelike pedagogical agents. *International Journal of Artificial Intelligence in Education, 10*, 278–291.

Liu, K., & Picard, R. W. (2005). *Embedded empathy in continuous. Interactive health assessment*. Portland, Oregon: CHI Workshop on HCI Challenges in Health Assessment.

Lucas, R. W., Mullen, P. J., Luna, C. B. X., & McInroy, D. C. (1977). Psychiatrists and a computer as interrogators of patients with alcohol-related illness: A comparison. *The British Journal of Psychiatry, 131*, 160–167.

Malone, T. W. (1984). *Heuristics for designing enjoyable user interfaces: lessons from computer games*. Norwood, NJ: Ablex Publishing Corporation.

Marci, C., & Riess, H. (2005). The clinical relevance of psychophysiology: Support for the psychobiology of empathy and psychodynamic process. *American Journal of Psychotherapy, 59*, 213–226.

Moon, Y. (2000). Intimate exchanges: Using computers to elicit self-disclosure from consumers. *The Journal of Consumer Research, 26*, 323–339.

Picard, R. W., Papert, S., Bender, W., Blumberg, B., Breazeal, C., Cavallo, D., et al. (2004). Affective learning a manifesto. *BT Technology Journal, 22*(4), 253–269.

Pintrich, P. R. (2004). A conceptual framework for assessing motivation and self-regulated learning in college students. *Educational Psychology Review, 16*(4), 385–407.

Reeves, B., & Nass, C. (1996). *The media equation*. Cambridge, MA: Cambridge University Press.

Robinson, R., & West, R. (1992). A comparison of computer and questionnaire methods of history-taking in a genito-urinary clinic. *Psychology and Health, 6*, 77–85.

Schank, R., & Neaman, A. (2001). Motivation and failure in educational systems design. In K. Forbus & P. Feltovich (Eds.), *Smart machines in education* (pp. 37–70). Cambridge, MA: AAAI Press and MIT Press.

Weybrew, B. B. (1984). The Zeigarnik phenomenon revisited: Implications for enhancement of morale. *Perceptual and Motor Skills, 58*, 223–226.

Zeigarnik, B. (1967). *On finished and unfinished tasks. A sourcebook of Gestalt psychology*. New York, NY: Humanities Press. W. D. Ellis.

43 How Mastery and Performance Goals Influence Learners' Metacognitive Help-Seeking Behaviours When Using Ecolab II

Amanda Carr (nee Harris), Rose Luckin, Nicola Yuill, and Katerina Avramides

Overview

The Ecolab software is an interactive learning environment for 10–11-year-old learners designed to help children learn about food chains and food webs. This area of Ecology forms part of the Key Stage 2 (7–11 years old) UK National Science Curriculum. In a large programme of work, we have used the software to explore the design of metacognitive tools to support learning. In the current chapter, we discuss the results of our recent work on achievement goal orientation and help seeking within the Ecolab environment. We situate these results within the broader landscape of our previous studies and discuss the evolutionary approach we have adopted to develop a methodology to support the design of metacognitive learning tools. This methodology has been built up over a series of empirical studies with the Ecolab software that have demonstrated that children who achieved above average learning gains use a high level of system help. Each study adds more evidence and detail to increase our understanding of children's help-seeking behaviour. We can therefore use this foundation to situate and interpret our findings and to extend our investigations to encompass different aspects of learner help seeking. In the empirical work that we focus upon in this chapter, we investigate the relationships between young learners' metacognition: specifically their help-seeking behaviour and their achievement goal orientations towards learning. This work draws together and extends two strands of our previous research: metacognitive software scaffolding (Luckin & Hammerton, 2002) and the influence of goal orientation on children's learning (Harris, Yuill, & Luckin, 2008). In a series of studies, we have evaluated children's help-seeking behaviour and achievement goal orientation in classroom settings and then assessed the relationship between learning outcomes and help-seeking behaviour during interactions with the Ecolab II software. Our research with Ecolab shows how tracking metacognitive behaviours—choice and use of more or less specific help—in the light of children's goal orientations and having the software adapt the type of help according to learners' motivation can be used to support learning. This work shows the value of including learner motivation in the design of metacognitive scaffolding.

A. Carr (nee Harris) (✉)
Department of Applied Social Sciences, Canterbury Christ Church University, CT1 1QU, Canterbury, UK
e-mail: amanda.carr@canterbury.ac.uk

R. Luckin • K. Avramides
The London Knowledge Lab, Institute of Education, London WC1N 3QS, UK
e-mail: r.luckin@ioe.ac.uk; k.avramides@ioe.ac.uk

N. Yuill
School of Psychology, University of Sussex, Falmer, Brighton BN1 9QH, UK
e-mail: nicolay@sussex.ac.uk

R. Azevedo and V. Aleven (eds.), *International Handbook of Metacognition and Learning Technologies*, Springer International Handbooks of Education 26, DOI 10.1007/978-1-4419-5546-3_43,

Theoretical Background

Metacognition and Help Seeking

Our work with Ecolab addresses help seeking as a metacognitive activity. Metacognition refers both to an awareness of cognitive processes and the ability to regulate them (Flavell & Wellman, 1977). Planning, monitoring, checking and error detection and correction are all key processes involved in metacognitive regulation. Students who engage in these activities regularly are those who typically show the greatest learning gains and deep-level processing (Goos, Galbraith, & Renshaw, 2002). Help seeking involves both an awareness of difficulty or error and the ability to use an appropriate strategy in order to overcome the problem detected. Seeking appropriate help is generally considered an adaptive strategy that promotes task mastery and comprehension (Newman, 1990). However, learners' behaviour varies a great deal in relation to help seeking. For example, some learners do not always request help when it would be most useful, while others consistently seek help even though they are able to undertake a task independently (Butler, 2006). Students vary in the quality, as well as the quantity, of the help they request, and a distinction has been made between instrumental and executive help (Nelson-Le Gall & Glor-Scheib, 1985). Instrumental help involves using methods that clarify and support understanding, such as helpful hints or clues, which lead to independent task mastery. Executive help involves seeking solutions that lead to task completion without necessarily increasing comprehension, such as requesting a solution. In previous work, differences in help-seeking behaviour have been shown to relate to different types of achievement goals (Butler, 2006; Harris et al., 2008).

Achievement Goal Theory

Goal theorists argue that people approach learning in distinct ways depending on their beliefs about and attitudes towards a particular task (Ames, 1992; Dweck, 2000; Dweck & Legget, 1988; Nichols, 1984). Those who are focused on understanding new material, mastering skills and developing competence are said to hold mastery goals: learning and improvement are assessed using self-referenced standards where the quality of one's work is judged relative to one's previous achievement. Mastery goals are associated with the use of adaptive learning strategies and deep-level learning (Ames, 1992). For example, mastery-motivated children tend to expend more effort, are more persistent, show a preference for challenging tasks and use instrumental help-seeking strategies (Newman, 1990). In contrast, learners who are focused on demonstrating their knowledge and gaining favourable judgements of ability are said to hold performance goals: learning is judged by how well one is performing relative to others and involves social comparisons (Elliot & Dweck, 1988). With a greater concern for evaluation of performance by others, help seeking tends to be viewed as an indication of low ability within a performance orientation. Performance-motivated children tend to show a preference for tasks they feel they can complete without challenge, and if they do seek help, they tend to choose executive-type help (Aleven, McLaren, & Koedinger, 2006). In general, performance goals are associated with less adaptive strategies and consequently surface-level learning (Elliot & Dweck, 1988; Ryan & Pintrich, 1997).

The Ecolab Software

The Ecolab software is an adaptive interactive learning environment that provides 10–11-year-old children with a virtual ecology laboratory that can be viewed as a simulated world of animals and plants, as a food web or as an energy histogram (see Fig. 43.1). The Ecolab also provides an artificial collaborative learning partner that offers adaptive assistance based on a detailed learner model. It was built as a research tool to investigate how the zone of proximal development (ZPD, Vygotsky, 1978, 1986) could be used to inform software design and has been the subject of several iterations of participatory design activity that have produced Ecolab II.

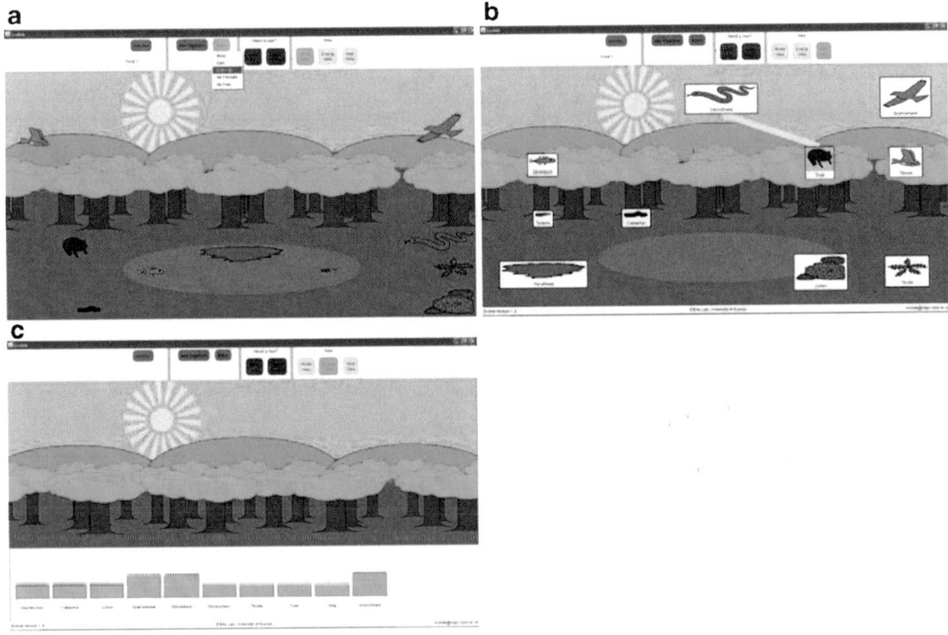

Fig. 43.1 Ecolab II screen views. (**a**) world view, (**b**) webview, (**c**) energy view

The original version of the Ecolab software called Ecolab I provided "help" at the domain level, that is, at the level of individual actions, such as when an animal moved or ate another animal or plant. This help was available when the learner was completing these specific actions and made an error. Findings from the Ecolab I evaluation demonstrated that offering learners a combination of challenging activities and appropriate support could improve test scores, which may indicate learning. A further important finding from the Ecolab I evaluation was that help-seeking behaviour amongst learners varied in its efficacy and was an important factor for learning outcomes. Ecolab II offered different qualities and quantities of prompt to try to get the child to consider what they should do next: be it selecting a task or selecting how much help to ask for.

The Ecolab II system builds a software-based model of the learner and scaffolds their interactions with timely interventions. This learner model represents the system's interpretation of the learner's understanding of a small curriculum of knowledge about food chains and webs and the learner's ability in two metacognitive processes: help seeking and task selection. In relation to help seeking, the child can select help from the system at one of four levels of specificity. Clue levels were developed using Wood, Bruner and Ross's (1976) levels of scaffolding as a guide. Clues increase in specificity from low-level instrumental help at clue levels 1 and 2, to more specific executive help including part or all of the solution at clue levels 3 and 4 (see Luckin, 2010 for a full description of the Ecolab software).

Using the Ecolab II Software to Explore Learners' Goal Orientation

At the start of our exploration of mastery- and performance-oriented learners' interactions with Ecolab II, we conducted an initial classroom study with thirty-five 10-year-old children. The aim of the study was to explore how mastery and performance goals might influence learners' help-seeking behaviour when using Ecolab II. Previous work had highlighted the importance of observing behaviour *and* the context in which it occurs in order to assess accurately the role that mastery and performance goals play in learning (Harris et al., 2008; Martinez-Miron, Harris, Du Boulay, Luckin & Yuill, 2005). We therefore began our study by constructing detailed learner profiles in relation to the children's achievement goal orientation and help-seeking behaviour. This method enabled us to identify 27 children who displayed clear preferences for either mastery goals (seven male, six female) or performance goals (nine male, five female). We then observed their interactions with Ecolab II and used system logs to measure help-seeking behaviour (Harris, Bonnett, Luckin, Yuill, & Avramides, 2009 for full details).

We found several important differences between mastery- and performance-oriented children in the type of help they used and also in whether that help was effective in moving them forward with the task. Firstly, performance-oriented children tended to select clues at the higher end of the scale (i.e. clues that offered more help) more frequently than their mastery-oriented counterparts. This suggested that within the Ecolab II environment, performance-oriented children were pursuing more executive-type help, a pattern of results which replicates findings from other domains (e.g. Aleven et al., 2006). Secondly, we found that although the performance-oriented children were selecting higher-level clues more frequently, this level of help was proving less useful to them. Level 4 clues provided a single, generic example of a relationship hierarchy within the ecosystem (e.g. "stickleback eats tadpole and is eaten by heron"). Performance learners had significant difficulty in generalising from the generic example to the specific organisms they were working on at the time (e.g. "vole eats blackberries and is eaten by grass snake"). We found that mastery children were better able to generalise these generic clues to their own food chains. On the other hand, performance-oriented children seemed less able to do this and tended to repeat their earlier mistakes after selecting clue level 4. These children were also significantly more likely to move on to another problem if the clue had not helped them immediately. This usually involved a less challenging action such as linking two organisms rather than three organisms.

These results suggested important differences in metacognitive behaviour between mastery- and performance-oriented children. In addition, we were able to monitor and track these differences using system logs. This suggests the potential for modelling learners' motivation and therefore providing scaffolding structures that can dynamically support learners of differing goal orientations. However, before these developments can be explored, a deeper understanding of the role of goal orientation in help seeking and their impact on learning gains is needed.

Goal Orientation, Help Seeking and Learning Using Ecolab II

We addressed the question of how goal orientation and different patterns of help-seeking impact on learning outcomes in a second large-scale classroom study. The differences evident between mastery and performance learners in our previous study led us to implement some software revisions. The first revision was an alteration to the content of the help offered at the highest help level (i.e. greatest amount of assistance from the software; level 4) to address the difficulty that performance learners experienced with generalising assistance from an example to the specifics of their particular problem. In this study, we changed the content of level 4 help so that it reflected more directly the specific problem at hand rather than a generic example. The second change we made was the addition of audio prompts. This was implemented to address the way in which learners seemed to miss learner model prompts in preference for clicking through to the next problem without reading the prompts. Including audio slowed down the rate at which learners could click through and also allowed us to eliminate differences in reading ability, which may have disadvantaged some children.

Twenty-nine 10-year-old children (13 males and 16 females) participated in this study, which took place over a 4-week period. We followed the same procedure as the first study, but this time children completed an Ecolab pre- and posttest before and after their two Ecolab sessions (Luckin

& Hammerton, 2002). Again, we used system logs to analyse help-seeking behaviour and we calculated the difference between children's scores on the pre- and posttest assessment as a measure of learning outcome. We describe our results here in more detail under the following two sections

Learning Outcomes

First we analysed children's pretest scores to measure their initial level of domain knowledge. We then used a median split to divide the sample into two groups indicating children of higher and lower initial ability. The group mean for the whole sample was 40.38 (SD = 14.39) out of a possible 75. Although there were equal numbers of mastery- and performance-oriented children in the higher ability group, performance-oriented children were over-represented in the lower ability group. As a result the performance group mean at pretest (M = 36.33, SD = 13.05) was significantly lower than the mastery group mean (M = 47, SD = 14.05) at pretest. After two sessions of exploration with the Ecolab environment we administered the same test again to measure any changes in the children's domain knowledge. At posttest the group mean had increased to 46.13 (SD = 12.96) out of a possible 75 which represented a significant change. However, closer examination of these scores showed that improvement was not evident across the whole sample and in fact some children showed no change or even a slight regression in their test scores. Figure 43.2 shows the breakdown of improvement by initial ability level and achievement goal orientation. There are two points to make about this graph. First, *children initially categorised as lower ability were the ones who showed the most improvement*. This may not seem that surprising given that the potential for improvement was greatest in this group. However, there was no ceiling effect in the higher ability group, as pretest scores were on average 23 points below the maximum. This suggests that although there were opportunities for learning, these had not been realised by the higher ability group. This result is also consistent with previous Ecolab evaluations during which lower ability learners frequently made greater learning gains (see Luckin, 2010 for detail). Second, *there are interesting differences between mastery and performance children particularly for the high ability group*. In fact the pattern of improvement for these groups is qualitatively different. While the high ability performance children made some improvement, their mastery-oriented peers showed a regression in their test scores from pre- to posttest. Closer examination of the posttest result showed that the mastery-oriented group did make improvements but only on the final section of the test. This section was by far the most challenging as it represented a significant degree of transfer in which children had to translate hierarchical food chain relationships into algebraic representations. The mastery-oriented group significantly outperformed the performance group at posttest on this part of the test, while the performance-oriented group made greater learning gains on the less challenging parts of the test. This suggests that the level of challenge experienced, or perceived, by the learner has an important role to play in their level of engagement and improvement.

Metacognitive Behaviour

The next stage in our analysis was to examine whether improvement scores were related to particular patterns of help-seeking behaviour during children's interaction with the Ecolab. Given the qualitative difference between mastery and performance-oriented children in patterns of learning outcome, we examined log data for each group separately. Analysis of the logs revealed that in this study, mastery and performance children's preferences for help at the four levels of specificity were broadly similar. In a similar pattern to that observed in our previous study, performance-oriented children showed a greater preference for clues at the highest level of specificity. This reflects a performance tendency towards executive-type help in which the whole or part of the correct solution is provided.

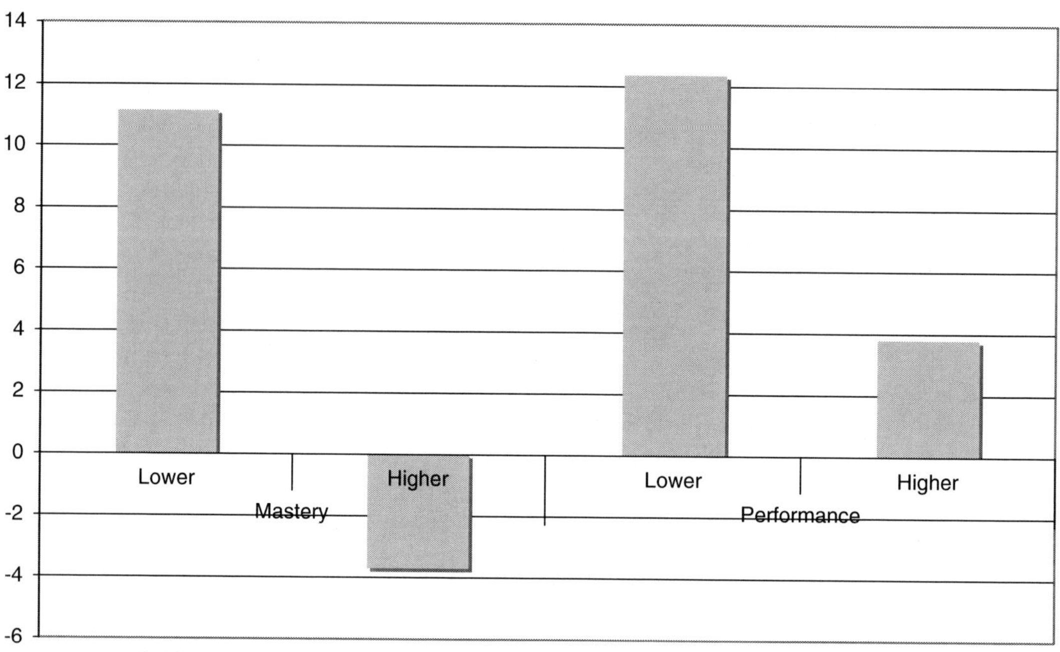

Fig. 43.2 Pre- to posttest improvement

Next we were interested in the usefulness of help at the different levels of specificity both in the immediate term (i.e. during task) and in the longer term (i.e. during posttest). In order to do this, we calculated the number of times each clue was followed by an attempt to complete the action (e.g. complete a food chain) to which the clue referred. Instances where clues were not followed by an attempt to complete the current activity or that were followed by selecting another clue were excluded for this part of the analysis. Of the food chains that were attempted, we calculated the proportion of actions, which were correct or incorrect directly following the use of the clue.

We found a general increase in the proportion of correct actions with the increase in clue specificity. This was expected, provided the child followed the advice offered by the clue, because higher clues provided help that was focused on the particular action and organisms the child was working with when the clue was selected. In fact, level 4 help provides the complete answer to the problem. Interestingly however this did not always lead to the child reproducing the correct answer, a point we return to below. We did observe a difference between mastery- and performance-oriented groups in the immediate usefulness of higher and lower-level help. For mastery-oriented children, the proportion of correct actions following a clue steadily increased in line with clue specificity; help levels 1 and 2 led to correct actions around 50% of the time while levels 3 and 4 led to correct actions around 60% of the time. However, there appears to be more of a step change in the usefulness of higher versus lower end clues for the performance-oriented children. For these children, less than 40% of help at levels 1 and 2 led to correct actions, but this rose to almost 70% correct for levels 3 and 4. It seems therefore that clue specificity made a bigger difference to the performance-oriented children. These children choose clues at the higher level more often, and these clues led to producing a greater number of correct food chains.

These results stand in contrast to our first study in which the generic higher-level clues were least useful and suggest the revision we made to the software in increasing the specificity of level 4 help proved useful, for performance-oriented learners at least. However, increasing the specificity of these clues meant that they now contained the correct solution, which would reduce the need for children to work this out on their own. Our next question therefore concerned the longer-term effect on learning this behaviour may have. Here we found another important difference between mastery- and performance-oriented learners. For the mastery-oriented group, there were no associations between their use of help and improvement scores. However, for the performance-oriented group, a very clear pattern emerged in relation to their use of higher-level help. *Improvement scores were positively correlated with the proportion of incorrect actions following high level clues* ($r\ (17) = 0.49,\ p < 0.05$) *and negatively correlated with the proportion of correct actions following high-level clues* ($r\,(17) = 0.51,\ p < 0.05$). This means that the more mistakes performance children made after receiving high-level help, the greater their learning gains at posttest. This is a particular interesting result in the light of the profiles of learning behaviour associated with mastery and performance goals. For example, performance goals are typically associated with a desire not to make mistake, while mastery goals orient learners towards "learning from mistakes." However, our results suggest that performance-oriented learners do in fact learn from their mistakes even if they try to avoid making them by selecting executive-type help. This is a particularly interesting finding in the light of the revisions we made to this level of help (i.e. increased specificity) and the tendency for performance-oriented learners to show a preference for level 4 help. It is not clear from our data why level 4 help did not always lead to a correct action given that it explicitly stated the correct solution. However, it does suggest that merely repeating the solution provided in the clue is not effective at promoting learning. This is consistent with research into "gaming the system" (Baker, Corbett, Koedinger, & Wagner, 2004), which refers to behaviour aimed at exploiting system help in order to obtain a correct answer. If performance-oriented learners were using level 4 help for this purpose, they would not have needed to reflect on the content of the clue unless the solution was not followed correctly. We might speculate therefore that getting an incorrect answer after level 4 help violates the expectation that performance-oriented learners hold of the purpose and usefulness of this level of help (i.e. it contains the correct answer). The effect of this may cause the learner to stop and reflect when they would not otherwise have done. While further empirical investigation of this effect is needed, the data does suggest that adaptations to level 4 help, which use a "violation of expectation" approach, may be particularly effective for performance-oriented learners.

Discussion

In this section of this chapter, we reflect upon our learning technology: the Ecolab software, our theoretical framework, the zone of proximal development and software scaffolding, offer a critique of our methodology and discuss the implications of the results reported and the challenges we face for the further development of the goal-oriented Ecolab II software and the design of metacognitive tools to support learning more generally:

1. The context for learning with the Ecolab.
   The Ecolab software is designed for use with learners aged 10–11 years within the formal education classroom. It encompasses subject matter about food chains and food webs, which is a part of the national curriculum within the United Kingdom for children of this age. It was built as a research tool to investigate how the ZPD could be used to inform software design. The Ecolab was designed for a single learner to use on a laptop or desktop computer. The software constructs a software-based model of the learner and scaffolds their interactions with timely interventions. Initially, in the Ecolab I software, this learner model represented the system's interpretation of the learner's understanding of a small curriculum of domain knowledge. Subsequently, in Ecolab II, this model also includes the learner's ability in two metacognitive processes: help seeking

and task selection. The Ecolab software in its various versions has provided a test rig for the empirical exploration of scaffolding these metacognitive processes for over 10 years.

2. The zone of proximal development and the theoretical framework that underpins the Ecolab approach.
   The ZPD provides the theoretical underpinning for the work conducted with the Ecolab. It specifies that what is important when considering a child's learning and development is their ability to achieve a solution when they are offered assistance. However, Vygotsky (1978, 1986) does not prescribe the exact nature of the instructional assistance that is to be offered to learners. The scaffolding approach (Wood, Bruner & Ross, 1976) represents one way of pinning down the nature of the assistance that more able others, including teachers and intelligent tutoring systems can provide for children as they learn and has been used in much subsequent research. The scaffolding approach informed the interpretation of the ZPD upon which the Ecolab design framework, and specifically the learner model, is based. It is a design framework that explores the relationship between the identification of a learner's collaborative capability and the specification of the assistance that needs to be offered to the learner in order for them to succeed at a particular task. This assistance is offered by the Ecolab software itself based upon the model of the learner it maintains: it is the software that acts as the learner's more able partner. Through a range of empirical studies, some of which are described in this chapter, we have been able to vary the learner model and the scaffolding assistance offered to the learner by the Ecolab. In particular we have been able to explore the manner in which the metacognitive processes of help seeking and task selection might be scaffolded and the impact that individual differences in a learner's goal orientation might have upon the interventions that are effective for learning.
3. Learning from the empirical findings of the Ecolab studies about learner goal orientation and metacognitive processes.
   The methodology used for the studies we report in this chapter has been built upon previous experience. All three learning measures use, or use and extend, previous approaches: the goal-orientation profiling has been previously validated with learners of this age, the learning outcomes are measured using an assessment that has been used for every Ecolab evaluation to date, and the log analysis uses techniques developed through previous Ecolab evaluations. We are now building into the software improved logging functionality in an attempt to automate some of the analysis that we have previously needed to complete "by hand." This evolutionary approach to methodology design also means that we have a wealth of data about the way learners use the Ecolab software in which to situate each new study.
   For example, children who achieved above average learning gains during previous evaluations of the Ecolab II software used a high level of help: In one study, 73% used a high level of system assistance, and 82% of these learners with above average learning gains used an above average amount of system assistance, and in a second evaluation study, 87% used a high level of system assistance, and 62% used an above average amount system assistance. Whilst the numbers involved in these studies are small (26 in each of these two studies), each extra study adds more evidence and detail to increase our understanding of children's help-seeking behaviour. We can therefore use this foundation to situate and interpret our findings with respect to the relationships between help seeking and learner goal orientation.
   We know that effective help seeking supports increased learning gains, and if we are to develop software that encourages such effective help seeking, then we need to understand more about what motivates learners' help-seeking behaviours. The work reported here once again offers evidence that children who were initially categorized as lower ability showed the most improvement in their learning gains. In addition, we can see that the patterns of improvement for mastery-oriented and perfor-

mance-oriented children, particularly for the high ability groups, are qualitatively different. The high ability performance-oriented children make modest improvements, but their mastery-oriented peers show a regression in their test possibly due to a lack of perceived challenge and subsequent engagement. Performance-oriented learners used more level 4 help (the greatest amount of help offered by the system), than mastery-oriented learners, and more interestingly we saw a step change in the usefulness of higher- versus lower-level help for the performance-oriented children, as compared to their mastery-oriented peers. This usefulness was not restricted to the performance-oriented children's performance, whilst using the Ecolab II software, it also extended to their learning gains, as measured by the change in their scores from pre to post system use. For performance-oriented learners, the more mistakes made after receiving high-level help whilst using the software, the greater their learning gains at posttest.

4. Challenges, limitations and implications.
The findings we report here support the proposal that it is possible to use software scaffolding, such as that offered by Ecolab II, and to adapt it to meet the needs of learners with different goal orientations so that they can achieve more effective help seeking. Performance-oriented learners' help-seeking skills have been demonstrated to be an area that needs improvement and our findings therefore represent valuable progress. However, there is evidence to suggest that the needs of the mastery-oriented learners were less well supported by the adaptations made to the Ecolab II software. It is therefore worth reflecting upon what might be changed in future evaluation studies to meet the challenge for mastery-oriented learners and to overcome the limitations in the current software implementation.

One possible explanation for the mastery group's lack of progress or even regressed outcomes might lie in their experience of the challenge provided by the software. We know that mastery-oriented learners are motivated by challenging tasks that test their capabilities and drive them towards new levels of understanding and task mastery (Dweck & Leggert, 1988). If they did not experience this sort of motivation whilst using the Ecolab II, their engagement with and interest in the task would have been low. Future Ecolab developments oriented towards mastery learners may therefore consider ways of adapting to learners' challenge seeking behaviour in order to maintain motivation, interest and engagement.

The software scaffolding adaptations made for this study were informed by empirical work with learners: we altered the content of the help offered at the highest help level (level 4) in order to try to address the difficulty that performance-oriented learners experienced with generalising from an example to their specific problem, and we added audio prompts to ensure learners were not able to click through important prompts or were not disadvantaged by reading ability. The results from the latest study suggest that these adaptations have offered support to performance-oriented learners, but have been less helpful to mastery-oriented learners. This finding suggests that a fruitful course of investigation would be to consider how the learner model might reflect learner goal orientation. Initially, two versions of the Ecolab II software are needed. The version used in the study reported here might be considered to be the performance-oriented version. A version without the changes to the content of level 4 help, so that learners are required to make the generalisation from the example to their particular problem, might be one feature of a more challenging mastery-oriented version.

For all learners, the lack of use of level 2 and level 3 help, which is more instrumental, is a concern. In future studies, we need to test the extent to which when learners do use these intermediate levels of help, they are sufficient to help learners to achieve success. We also need to evaluate differences in the behaviour of performance and mastery-oriented learners with these intermediate help levels. This might perhaps be explored through adaptations to the learner model so that it reflects a bias towards suggesting that learners use these intermediate help levels. Subsequently this bias would need to be tuned towards any differences found between performance-oriented and master-oriented learners. Evaluations of the two version of the Ecolab II could offer data to inform the manner in which the learner model is adapted in order to better tailor scaffolding interventions to the goal orientations being displayed by each individual learner.

Our programme of work with Ecolab uses a combination of automatically logged data on, e.g. help choices, dispositional measures of learners (learning goal orientation) and learning outcome measures, to make inferences about why learners choose the help they do, and then we manipulate the design of adaptive software so that it best fits the metacognitive needs of learners with different goal orientations. We anticipate that this multi-method approach can be adapted and extended by us and others to develop new, better-adapted versions of software such as Ecolab and that the approach could be developed to look at other aspects of motivation in learning.

References

Aleven, V., McLaren, B., & Koedinger, K. (2006). Towards computer-based tutoring of help-seeking skills. In S. A. Karabenick & R. S. Newman (Eds.), *Help seeking in academic settings*. London: Lawrence Erlbaum.

Ames, C. (1992). Classroom: goals, structures and student motivation. *Journal of Education and Psychology, 84*(3), 261–271.

Baker, R., Corbett, A. T., Koedinger, K. R., & Wagner, A. Z. (2004). Off-task behavior in the cognitive tutor classroom: When students "game the system". *Proceedings of CHI 2004: Computer-Human Interaction*, (pp. 383–390). ACM.

Butler, R. (2006). An achievement goal perspective on student help-seeking and teacher help-giving in the classroom. In S. A. Karabenick & R. S. Newman (Eds.), *Help seeking in academic settings*. London: Lawrence Erlbaum.

Dweck, C. (2000). *Self-theories: Their role in motivation, personality and development*. Hove: Psychology Press.

Dweck, C., & Leggert, E. (1988). A social-cognitive approach to motivation and personality. *Psychological Review, 95*, 256–273.

Elliot, A., & Dweck, C. (1988). Goals: An approach to achievement and motivation. *Journal of Personality and Social Psychology, 54*(1), 5–12.

Flavell, J. H., & Wellman, H. M. (1977). Metamemory. In R. V. Kail & J. W. Hagen (Eds.), *Perspectives on the development of memory and cognition Hillsdale*. NJ: Erlbaum.

Goos, M., Galbraith, P., & Renshaw, P. (2002). Socially mediated metacognition: Creating collaborative zones of proximal development in small group problem solving. *Educational Studies in Mathematics, 49*, 193–223.

Harris, A., Bonnett, V., Luckin, R., Yuill, N., & Avramides, K. (2009). Scaffolding effective help-seeking behaviour in mastery and performance oriented learners. In V. Dimitrova, R. Mizogucji, B. du Boulay, & A. Graesser (Eds.), *Artificial intelligence in education* (pp. 425–432). Amsterdam, Netherlands: Ios Press.

Harris, A., Yuill, N., & Luckin, R. (2008). The influence of context-specific and dispositional achievement goals on children's paired collaborative interaction. *British Journal of Educational Psychology, 78*(3), 355–374.

Luckin, R. (2010). *Re-designing learning contexts: Technology-rich, learner-centred ecologies*. Abingdon: Routledge.

Luckin, R., & Hammerton, L. (2002). Getting to know me: Helping learners understand their own learning needs through metacognitive scaffolding. In S. A. Cerri, G. Gouardères, & F. Paraguaçu (Eds.), *Lecture notes in computer science* (Vol. 2363, pp. 759–771). Berlin: Springer Verlag.

Martinez-Miron, E., Harris, A., Du Boulay, B., Luckin, L., & Yuill, N. (2005). The role of learning goals in the design of ILEs: Some issues to consider. *12th International Conference on Artificial Intelligence in Education (AIED)*. (pp. 427–434). IOS Press.

Nelson-Le Gall, S., & Glor-Scheib, S. (1985). Help-seeking in elementary classroom: An observational analysis. *Contemporary Educational Psychology, 10*, 58–71.

Newman, R. S. (1990). Children's help-seeking in the classroom: The role of motivational and factors and attitudes. *Journal of Education and Psychology, 82*(1), 71–80.

Nichols, J. G. (1984). Achievement motivation: Conceptions of ability, subjective experience, task choice, and performance. *Psychological Review, 91*, 328–346.

Ryan, A. M., & Pintrich, P. R. (1997). Should I ask for help? The role of motivation and attitudes in adolescents' help seeking in math class. Journal of Educational Psychology, 89, 329–341.

Vygotsky, L. S. (1978). *Mind in Society: The Development of Higher Psychological Processes*. (M., Cole, V., John-Steiner, S., Scribner, & E., Souberman, Trans.). Cambridge, MA: Harvard University Press.

Vygotsky, L. S. (1986). *Thought and language*. Cambridge, MA: MIT Press.

Wood, D., Bruner, J., & Ross, G. (1976). The role of tutoring in problem solving. *Journal of Child Psychology and Psychiatry, 17*, 89–100.

Affect, Meta-affect, and Affect Regulation During Complex Learning

44

Sidney K. D'Mello, Amber Chauncey Strain, Andrew Olney, and Art Graesser

Abstract

Complex learning of difficult subject matter with educational technologies involves a coordination of cognitive, metacognitive, and affective processes. While extensive theoretical and empirical research has examined learners' cognitive and metacognitive processes, research on affective processes during learning has been slow to emerge. Because learners' affective states can significantly impact their thoughts, feelings, behavior, and learning outcomes, inquiry into how these states emerge and influence engagement and learning is of vital importance. In this chapter, we describe several key theories of affect, meta-affect, and affect regulation during learning. We then describe our own empirical research that focuses on identifying the affective states that spontaneously emerge during learning with educational technologies, how affect relates to learning outcomes, and how affect can be regulated. The studies that we describe incorporate a variety of educational technologies, different learning contexts, a number of student populations, and diverse methodologies to track affect. We then describe and evaluate an affect-sensitive version of AutoTutor, a fully-automated intelligent tutoring system that detects and helps learners regulate their negative affective states (frustration, boredom, confusion) in order to increase engagement, task persistence, and learning gains. We conclude by discussing future directions of research on affect, meta-affect, and affect regulation during learning with educational technologies.

S.K. D'Mello (✉)
University of Notre Dame, Notre Dame, UN 46556, USA
e-mail: sdmello@nd.edu

A.C. Strain • A. Olney • A. Graesser
University of Memphis, Memphis, TN, USA

R. Azevedo and V. Aleven (eds.), *International Handbook of Metacognition and Learning Technologies*, Springer International Handbooks of Education 26, DOI 10.1007/978-1-4419-5546-3_44,

Affect, Meta-affect, and Affect Regulation During Learning

Though affect is usually relegated to the sidelines as a perennially present but low-impact mood state, when triggered by the right event, emotions quickly claim the spotlight in our theater of consciousness. Anger and rage rapidly consume us when we perceive that we have been wronged, elation fills an uneventful day when a much anticipated grant is funded, and we are enveloped in sadness upon hearing of the death of a loved one. Anger, joy, fear, sadness, disgust, surprise, angst, contempt, envy, grief, pride, shame, and ecstasy, are some of the everyday feelings that are familiar to us all. It could be argued that such affect states interact with every thought, modulate every decision, and influence every action, from the mundane to the elaborate.

Given the pervasiveness of affect in our daily lives (Scherer, Wranik, Sangsue, Tran, & Scherer, 2004), what should not come as a surprise to most, is that learning at deeper levels of comprehension is essentially an affectively charged experience (Calvo & D'Mello, 2011). During learning with educational technologies like multimedia, hypermedia, and intelligent tutoring systems, learners may experience frustration when they have to manage a multitude of topic-related hyperlinks, confusion when illustrative figures and graphs seem to contradict the corresponding text, anger when a knowledgeable pedagogical agent withholds helpful guidance, boredom when the environment lacks stimulation, and perhaps even hopelessness or despair when their efforts seem unlikely to help them reach their goals. This negative portrait of the emotional experiences that accompany learning has a complementary positive side. Learners experience curiosity when they encounter novel and unfamiliar topics, eureka moments when insights are unveiled and major discoveries made, delight when challenges are conquered, and flow states (Csikszentmihalyi, 1990) when they are so engaged in learning that time and fatigue disappear. In agent-based learning technologies, learners can even experience feelings of companionship when the agent appears helpful and supportive, and gratitude when the agent provides scaffolding to help them resolve an impasse or get them out of a stuck state.

In general, emotion and cognition are inextricably bound in educational technologies that require learners to generate inferences, demonstrate causal reasoning, diagnose and solve problems, make conceptual comparisons, produce coherent explanations, and show application and transfer of acquired knowledge. Contemporary theories of emotion and cognition assume that cognitive processes such as memory encoding and retrieval, causal reasoning, deliberation, and goal appraisal are modulated and facilitated by affect (Bower, 1981; Mandler, 1999; Ortony, Clore, & Collins, 1988; Scherer, Schorr, & Johnstone, 2001; Stein & Levine, 1991). The inextricable link between affect and cognition is sufficiently compelling that some claim the scientific distinction between emotion and cognition is artificial, arbitrary, and of limited value (Lazarus, 2000).

Although the twentieth century has been ripe with emotion theory along with models of emotion and cognition, research investigating the links between emotions and learning is much more recent. Some of the most exciting research has emerged from the interdisciplinary arena that spans psychology (Dweck, 2002; Stein & Levine, 1991), education (Meyer & Turner, 2006; Pekrun, Elliot, & Maier, 2006), computer science (Arroyo et al., 2009; Conati & Maclaren, 2009), and neuroscience (Immordino-Yang & Damasio, 2007). Some of this research has focused on student emotions in classrooms, where a broad array of affective responses are elicited in a number of contexts. Research in the context of learning technologies has focused on in-depth analysis of a smaller set of emotions (boredom, flow, confusion, frustration, anxiety, curiosity, delight, and surprise) that arise during deep learning over short time spans of 1–2 h (Baker, D'Mello, Rodrigo, & Graesser, 2010; Conati & Maclaren, 2009; Craig, Graesser, Sullins, & Gholson, 2004; D'Mello, Craig, Sullins, & Graesser, 2006; Graesser et al., 2006).

This chapter discusses such research by providing a synthesis of affect–learning connections that we and our collaborators have explored over the past few years. We also discuss meta-affect and affect regulation as two related and equally significant phenomena. *Meta-affect* pertains to "thinking about affect" and using this information to guide thought and action. *Affect regulation*, a relatively new and exciting field of research (Gross, 2008), addresses how people regulate their emotions either before or after they occur. After discussing these phenomena, we describe novel learning technologies that aspire to promote engagement and learning by modeling and externally regulating learner affect. We conclude by reflecting on some of the key findings and propose some avenues for further research.

Affect During Learning

The affect–learning theories that have emerged highlight the contributions of academic risk taking, motivation, mood states, flow, goals, and cognitive disequilibrium. They also describe how affect can play a role in learners' metacognitive processes and self-regulation. This section provides a brief overview of some of these theories followed by a discussion of some empirical research aimed at testing their critical hypotheses.

Theories of Affect and Learning

The academic risk theory and intrinsic motivation literature address how individual differences in risk taking behavior and motivation influence learners' emotional states and behavior choices. The academic risk theory contrasts (a) adventuresome learners who want to be challenged with difficult tasks, take risks of failure, and manage negative emotions when they occur, with (b) cautious learners who tackle easier tasks, take fewer risks, and minimize failure and its resulting negative emotions (Clifford, 1988).

The intrinsic motivation literature has identified affective states such as curiosity as indicators of motivation level and learning (Harter, 1992; Stipek, 1988). Intrinsically motivated learners derive pleasure from the task itself (e.g., enjoyment from problem solving), while learners with extrinsic motivation rely on external rewards (e.g., praise from a pedagogical agent after successfully solving the problem).

Whereas these theories address individual differences, mood theories and flow theory are concerned with how mood states impact emotions and performance. Mood theories highlight the role of baseline mood states (positive, negative, or neutral) in learning, particularly for creative problem solving. In particular, flexibility, creative thinking, and efficient decision-making in problem solving have been linked to experiences of positive affect (Isen, 2001), while negative affect has been associated with a more methodical approach to assessing the problem and finding the solution (Schwarz & Skurnik, 2003). According to flow theory, learners are in a state of flow (Csikszentmihalyi, 1990) when they are so deeply engaged in learning the material that time and fatigue disappear. The zone of flow occurs when the structure of the learning environment matches a learner's zone of proximal development (Brown, Ellery, & Campione, 1998), so that the learner is presented with just the right sort of materials, challenges, and problems to the point of being totally absorbed.

Goal theory and cognitive disequilibrium theory specify how particular events predict emotional reactions and are pitched at a finer temporal resolution than theories that highlight individual differences and mood states. Goal theory is consistent with contemporary appraisal theories (Scherer et al., 2001), arguably the most widely accepted account of emotion. Appraisal is a presumably unconscious (but can also be consciously mediated) process that produces emotions by evaluating an event along a number of dimensions such as novelty, urgency, ability to cope, consistency with goals, etc. Goal theories emphasize interruptions of goals as the key appraisal dimension (Stein & Levine, 1991). In particular, the arousal level (intense/weak) of an emotional episode is dependent upon how great the interruption is to the person's goal whereas the valence (positive/negative) depends on the person's evaluation of the interruption (Lazarus, 1991; Mandler, 1999). Hence, outcomes that achieve challenging goals result in positive emotions, whereas outcomes that jeopardize goal accomplishment result in negative emotions (Dweck, 2002; Stein & Levine, 1991).

The cognitive disequilibrium theory postulates an important role for impasses (VanLehn, Siler, Murray, Yamauchi, & Baggett, 2003) in comprehension and learning processes. Cognitive disequilibrium is a state that occurs when learners face obstacles to goals, contradictions, incongruities, anomalies, uncertainty, and salient contrasts (Graesser, Lu, Olde, Cooper-Pye, & Whitten, 2005; Piaget, 1952). Cognitive equilibrium is restored after thought, reflection, problem solving, and other effortful deliberations. This theory states that the complex interplay between external events that trigger impasses, and the resultant cognitive disequilibrium, are the key to understanding the cognitive-affective processes that underlie deep learning. In particular, the affective states of confusion and perhaps frustration are likely to occur during cognitive disequilibrium because confusion indicates an uncertainty about what to do next or how to act.

Because emotions have the potential to impact motivation, attention, thoughts, and behavior, students should be equipped with strategies for regulating the emotions that arise during learning. However, theories of how emotional processes are regulated during learning with educational technologies have been slow to emerge. The cognitive-affective model of learning (Moreno & Mayer, 2007) highlights the role of affect and motivation by suggesting that learners' emotions have the potential to direct energy and attentional resources to the learning task. The dual-processing model of emotion (Boekaerts, 2007) suggests that students' emotions can help direct the strategies they use during learning. For example, in the face of stress, some students may select nonproductive strategies such as avoidance or distraction that redirect their attention away from their learning goals. Other students may see stress as an opportunity to improve and will tend to use coping strategies to help them deal with their emotions and stay focused on their learning goals. Although these theories underscore the importance of emotion on self-regulation during learning with educational technologies, many questions remain to be answered regarding the intricate relationship between emotion and self-regulation.

Identifying the Affective States That Occur During Complex Learning

The theoretical perspectives described above make a number of predictions about the affective experiences that arise during learning with educational technologies. We have tested some of these predictions in our analysis of emotion-learning connections in a variety of learning contexts, with a number of student populations, and with diverse methodologies. Table 44.1 presents an overview of 18 studies that we and our collaborators have conducted over the past 6 years.

The "learning context" column in Table 44.1 refers to the educational technology used, and the educational task including computer tutoring, problem solving, text comprehension, and essay writing. The numbers in parentheses beside each learning context refer to the number of studies involving that context. As evident from Table 44.1, seven of the studies involved learning computer literacy with *AutoTutor* (Graesser et al., 2004), an intelligent tutoring system with conversational dialogues (described in more detail in a subsequent section). Other computer learning systems include *Aplusix* (Nicaud & Saidi, 1990), an ITS for mathematics, the *Incredible Machine* (Ryan, 2001), a simulation environment for logic puzzles, and a version of Operation ARIES!, a game-like ITS for critical thinking.

Emotions are notoriously difficult to measure because they are fuzzy, ill-defined, noisy, and compounded with individual differences in experience and expression. Methodological artifacts usually have an undesirable influence on the measured emotions, so it is imperative to obtain convergence across methodologies. This is precisely the approach we have adopted in our research, as illustrated by the diverse research protocols depicted in Table 44.1.

The studies have yielded a number of insights into student affective experiences during deep learning and effortful problem solving with edu-

Table 44.1 Synopsis of studies investigating affect during learning with educational technologies

Learning context	Domain	Population	Method	References
AutoTutor(7)	Computer literacy	College students	Observational, emote-aloud, cued-recall	Craig et al. (2004), D'Mello et al. (2006), Graesser et al. (2006)
Aplusix (1)	Algebra	High school	Observational	Baker et al. (2010)
Incredible Machine (1)	Logic puzzles	High school	Observational	(Baker et al. (2010)
LSAT problem solving on computer (1)	Analytical reasoning	Aspiring lawyers	Cued-recall	(D'Mello, Lehman and Person (2011)
Reading illustrated digital texts (2)	Mechanical reasoning	College students	Delayed self-report	D'Mello & Graesser (in review)
Online course (1)	Statistics	College students	Online self-report, and cued-recall	
Operation ARIES! (3)	Critical thinking	College	Cued-recall	Lehman et al. (2011)
Writing essays on computer interface (2)	Various topics	College	Cued-recall	

cational technologies. One finding is that confusion, frustration, boredom, and flow/engagement are the dominant affective states that students experience irrespective of the learning environment, the learning task, the student population, and the emotion measurement methodology. In contrast to these states that are consistently observed with high frequencies, some emotions are consistently observed, but with lower frequencies. Others are observed with relatively high frequencies, but only in some contexts. In particular, delight and surprise occur in many contexts, but the frequency of occurrence of these states is low. Curiosity occurs with high frequency, but it is only observed in some contexts; when students are intrinsically motivated with respect to the task, as was the case when aspiring law school students solved analytical reasoning problems from the LSAT. Similarly, anxiety is observed in high-stakes situations as was the case with the LSAT. Despite differences in patterns of occurrence, confusion, frustration, boredom, flow/engagement, delight, surprise, curiosity, and anxiety are the major emotions that students experience during learning and problem solving; we refer to these as "learning-centered" states.

In contrast to the learning-centered emotions, the "basic" emotions consisting of anger, joy, surprise, disgust, happiness, and sadness (Ekman, 1992), are comparatively rare (one exception is happiness, which does occur in some contexts). These emotions are considered to be "basic" by some who claim that they are innate, universally experienced and recognized, and cross cultural boundaries (Ekman, 1992; Izard, 1994), but others dispute this view (Barrett, 2006; Russell, Bachorowski, & Fernandez-Dols, 2003). Although these six basic emotions have claimed center-stage of most emotion research in the last four decades, our results suggest that they might not be relevant to lerning, at least for the short learning sessions of these studies. It is possible that they might be more relevant during learning in more extended time spans (such as completing a dissertation) or high stakes tests (e.g., final exams in courses). However, this hypothesis needs to be substantiated with some empirical evidence.

Relationship Between Affect and Learning

In addition to specifying the emotions that are expected to occur during learning, the theories also predict specific relationships between emotions and learning gains. According to flow theory, the state of flow should also show a positive correlation with learning gains (Csikszentmihalyi, 1990), while boredom should be negatively correlated with learning gains. If constructivist theory and the claims about cognitive disequilibrium are correct, we should observe a positive relationship between confusion and learning gains if the learning environment productively helps the learners regulate their confusion. Similarly, a negative correlation is predicted between frustration and learning gains.

These predictions were tested by correlating the proportional occurrence of boredom, confusion, flow, and frustration with measures of deep learning collected in the studies with AutoTutor (see Table 44.1). Perhaps the most important and consistent finding was that confusion was positively correlated with learning gains (Craig et al., 2004; D'Mello & Graesser, 2011; Graesser, Chipman, King, McDaniel, & D'Mello, 2007). This relationship is consistent with the model discussed earlier that claims that cognitive disequilibrium is one precursor to deep learning (Graesser et al., 2005) and with theories that highlight the merits of impasses during learning (VanLehn et al., 2003). According to these models, confusion itself does not cause learning gains, but the cognitive activities that accompany confusion and impasse resolution are linked to learning, a finding that has received some empirical support (D'Mello & Graesser, in review).

One study confirmed the prediction that boredom was negatively correlated to learning while flow was positively correlated (Craig et al., 2004). However, we have not been able to replicate this finding in subsequent studies. It might be the case that these states operate on longer time-scales, so their effects on learning could not be observed in short 30–35 min learning sessions. Longer learning sessions would be required before the effects of these states can be observed.

One surprising finding was that frustration was not correlated with learning gains in any of the studies with AutoTutor. Frustration is a state that occurs when learners fail to resolve an impasse, they get stuck, and goals are blocked. The apparent lack of a relationship between frustration and learning might be attributed to the fact that the ITS used in these studies does not let a learner perseverate in a stuck state. Typical learning situations with educational technologies are fraught with such stuck states, since learners must often manage an abundance of information with little direction or guidance (especially in multimedia and hypermedia contexts). In comparison, AutoTutor offers explanations and hints in order to advance the learning session. Withholding assertions and preventing a student from proceeding until they provide an appropriate response would presumably increase frustration and possibly impact learning.

There is some evidence to support this claim. For example negative affect (amalgamation of frustration, anxiety, and annoyance) was negatively correlated with posttests scores when the task was to read a passage in physics without any interference from a tutor (Linnenbrink & Pintrich, 2002). Frustration was also negatively linked to performance outcomes when students solved analytical reasoning problems in the absence of a tutor (D'Mello et al., 2010).

Meta-affect During Learning

So far we identified the emotions that are relevant to learning with educational technologies, but the story does not end here. There is the question of how learners think about the emotions they experience. The *feelings-as-information* theory (Schwarz, 2012) provides some useful insights into meta-affective processes (outside of learning contexts) that can be applied to learning with educational technologies. A central tenet of this theory is that affect has an informational function and different feelings (in context) convey different types of information. For example, a learner experiencing hopeless confusion while solving a physics problem might infer that there is a knowledge deficiency. Surprise, feelings of knowing (i.e., familiarity), and boredom are three states that inform learners about their knowledge levels (Ortony et al., 1988).

Another principle of the theory is that the impact of a given feeling is proportional to its perceived information values with respect to the current situation. Feelings that are considered to be directly related to the task provide more information than feelings considered to be purely incidental. For example, being sad because a pedagogical agent expressed disappointment in one's failure to comprehend a topic is relevant to the learning task and is of some value. However, sadness because it is a gloomy day is purely incidental to learning physics and is less informational in this context.

The final postulate of the theory is that when feelings are used as an information source, they are used as any other information source. Feelings can be used to modulate learning, help with decisions, and influence processing strategies. For example, experiencing confusion during problem solving might facilitate the deployment of analytical processing strategies (D'Mello & Graesser, in review; Schwarz, 2012) that are focused on identifying and resolving the source of the confusion. Feeling that the learning goal has not been reached (i.e., the learner has not gained an understanding of the topic at hand) may lead to an increased use of learning strategies like summarizing or attempting to make inferences (Azevedo, 2009) or investing more time in learning the topic (Metcalfe, 2002).

Although the feeling-as-information theory postulates a significant role for meta-affect, confirmatory empirical data from learning contexts is sparse. We do know that learners' identify confusion, frustration, boredom, flow/engagement, delight and surprise when they are asked to emote-aloud (i.e., articulate their emotions) during learning or when they view videotapes of their tutoring sessions and judge their emotions at different points in time (D'Mello et al., 2006; Graesser et al., 2006). However, we do not know how reliably different classes of learners can identify these emotions. We suspect from 150 years of psychological research on emotions that some learners lack sensitivity to their own emotions, that other learners are hypersensitive, and that there is a large continuum of possibilities in between. We also know that people do not always accurately identify the source of their feelings (Schwarz, 2012), thereby limiting its informational values.

Research is conspicuously absent on how the learners perceive the causes, consequences, and information value of each affect state. The negative emotions are particularly in need of research. When a learner is frustrated from being stuck, the learner might attribute the frustration to either themselves ("I'm not at all good at physics"), the computer tutor ("The tutor doesn't understand this either"), or the materials ("There are too many hyperlinks here to even begin to synthesize"). As the theory suggests, the information value derived from the feeling of frustration would presumably depend on these attributions of cause (Weiner, 1986). When a student is confused, some students may view this as a positive event to stimulate thinking and attempt to show their ability by conquering the challenge; other students will attribute the confusion to their poor ability, an inadequate tutor, or poorly designed educational technology. When students are bored, they are likely to blame the tutor or material rather than themselves.

Affect Regulation During Learning

Once learners experience an emotion and are aware of the emotion, there is the question of how they might regulate the emotion. The goal of emotion regulation is presumably to downregulate negative emotions and upregulate positive emotions, although it is never quite this straightforward. For example, during collaborative online learning, one student might suppress happiness from receiving praise from a pedagogical agent when in the presence of a friend who has just received negative feedback from that agent. Regulation of emotions during learning with educational technologies is yet another area with considerably little empirical research. However, Gross (2008) has proposed an important process model of emotion regulation that is applicable in everyday situations. Perhaps this model can yield some insights into how learners might regulate their affective states.

The model assumes that an emotion arises when an emotion-eliciting situation is experienced, attended to, and cognitively appraised (these different phases are a critical component of the model). The model proposes five broad emotion regulation strategies; four of these strategies can be deployed before the emotion (to be regulated) is experienced, while the onset of the emotion governs deployment of the fifth strategy. The first two strategies, situation selection and situation modification, are regulatory strategies aimed at selecting and modifying contexts (situations) that minimize or maximize the likelihood of experiencing certain emotions. For example, a learner who perceives that he or she has low computer skills may choose to use Wikipedia to gather information about a topic rather than using a more complex information source like PsychInfo in order to avoid the negative emotions (e.g., frustration in this case) associated with organizing a search, conducting a literature review, and synthesizing information. This is an example of situation selection, because the learner has opted out of a negative affect-induction situation (i.e., the complex information source).

Eventually, this learner may find that using a more complex information source is necessary in order to obtain the resources which are needed gain a full understanding of a given topic. If the learner has no choice in selecting the situation (i.e., the student has to use PsychInfo rather than Wikipedia), the learner can reduce his or her negative emotions by asking a peer or teacher to demonstrate the proper way use a complex search engine. Here, an emotion-inducing situation (i.e., using PsychInfo) has been alleviated by modifying the situation (i.e., seeking help from a peer or teacher).

Affect can also be regulated when a situation cannot be selected or modified. In these cases, a person can avoid attending to situational elements that might induce negative emotional reactions. For example, after receiving negative feedback from a pedagogical agent, a learner might try to keep frustration levels down by focusing on the instances where he or she received positive feedback, while ignoring negative feedback; this strategy is referred to as *distraction* (Gross, 2008). Alternately, *rumination* involves explicitly attending to the emotion-elicitation situation and can lead to a heightened intensity and increased duration of an emotional reaction (Bushman, 2002). Rumination would occur when a learner perseverates on the negative feedback, thereby increasing these negative emotions.

Affect can be regulated even when a person's attention is focused on an event that has the potential to elicit a particular emotional reaction. One such strategy is *cognitive reappraisal* (Dandoy & Goldstein, 1990), which involves changing the perceived meaning of a situation in order to alter its emotional content. For example, negative yet constructive feedback can actually be transformed into a more positive experience if the learner perceives the feedback in a different way. This would occur if the learner believes that the agent is only giving feedback in an attempt to help the learner resolve a misconception and understand the material more clearly. In essence, *cognitive reappraisal* occurs when the learner switches from a mindset of "the agent is trying to embarrass me" to "the agent just wants what's best for me."

Finally, *response modulation* is a strategy that can only be applied after the emotion is experienced. Perhaps the most widely studied form of response modulation is *expressive suppression*, which involves a sustained effort to minimize the expression of emotional behavior. Hence, a student in the throes of anger as a result of an agent's feedback can attempt to alleviate the anger by relaxing the body and taking slow deep breaths.

At this point in science, there is insufficient research documenting whether and to what extent students engage in these affect regulation strategies during learning with educational technologies. This leaves the door wide open for researchers to conduct more research in this area and propose models and theories that are more specific to educational technologies. For example, we have recently conducted one preliminary study that tested the effect of cognitive reappraisal on alleviating boredom. Learners were asked to study 18 pages of the US Constitution and Bill of Rights (this can be quite a dull read) from a Web-based digital text over a 30–60 min session. Learners who were instructed to use a cognitive reappraisal strategy (experimental group) reported more arousal, valence, attentiveness, and demonstrated enhanced comprehension of the material than those in the control group, who were not instructed to reappraise their emotions (Strain & D'Mello, 2011). Indeed, emotion regulation strategy training does have some benefits, at least within the context of this laboratory study. The pertinent question is whether this intervention is equally effective in more authentic learning contexts and with more advanced educational technologies.

Affect, Meta-affect, and Affect Regulation with an Affective Tutor

After exploring the affective, meta-affective, and affect-regulatory processes during learning we turn our attention to an affect-sensitive version of an intelligent tutoring system (ITS) called AutoTutor. AutoTutor helps students learn topics in Newtonian physics, computer literacy, and critical thinking via a natural language conversational dialogue (Graesser et al., 2004). AutoTutor's dialogues are organized around difficult questions and problems that require reasoning and explanations in the answers. AutoTutor actively monitors learners' knowledge states and engages them in a turn-based dialogue as they attempt to answer these questions. It adaptively manages the tutorial dialogue by providing feedback (e.g., "good job," "not quite"), pumping the learner for more information (e.g., "What else"), giving hints (e.g., "What about X"), prompts (e.g., "X is a type of what"), identifying and correcting misconceptions, answering questions, and summarizing answers.

While the existing AutoTutor system is sensitive to learners' cognitive states, the affect-sensitive version is dynamically responsive to learners' affective states as well (D'Mello et al., 2010). It detects and responds to boredom, confusion, and frustration because appropriate responses to these negative states could potentially have a positive impact on engagement and learning outcomes.

Design of the Affect-Sensitive AutoTutor

The affect-sensitive tutor embeds the learner and the tutor into an affective loop that involves *detecting* the learner's affective states, *responding* to the detected states, and *synthesizing* emotional expressions via animated pedagogical agents. The affect detection system monitors conversational cues, gross body language, and facial features to detect boredom, confusion, frustration, and neutral (no affect). Affect-detection accuracy is not perfect but is reasonably accurate (affect diagnosis is correct about 50% of the time compared to a 25% chance baseline).

Once the learner's affect has been detected, the tutor attempts to regulate the sensed affective state with an emotional statement. AutoTutor's strategies to respond to learner's emotions were derived from attribution theory (Weiner, 1986), cognitive disequilibrium during learning (Graesser et al., 2005; Graesser & Olde, 2003; Piaget, 1952), politeness theory (Brown & Levinson, 1987; Wang et al., 2008), and recent statements about the role of empathy in regulating negative emotions (Dweck, 2002; Lepper & Chabay, 1988). In addition to theoretical considerations, the assistance of experts in tutoring was enlisted to help create the set of tutor responses.

The affect-sensitive responses attempt to regulate negative emotions by attributing the source of the learners' emotion to the material or the tutor instead of the learners themselves. So the affective AutoTutor might respond to mild boredom with "This stuff can be kind of dull sometimes, so I'm gonna try and help you get through it. Let's go." A response to confusion would include attributing the source of confusion to the material ("Some of this *material* can be confusing. Just keep going and I am sure you will get it") or the tutor itself ("I know I do not always convey things clearly. I am always happy to repeat myself if you need it. Try this one").

In addition to detecting and regulating learner affect, the affective tutor also synthesizes affect with facial expressions and emotionally modulated speech. These affective expressions include: approval, mild approval, disapproval, empathy, skepticism, mild enthusiasm, and high enthusiasm.

Evaluating the Affect-Sensitive AutoTutor

We have recently conducted an experiment that evaluated the pedagogical effectiveness of the affective AutoTutor when compared to the original tutor (D'Mello et al., 2010). This original AutoTutor has a conventional set of fuzzy production rules that are sensitive to the cognitive states of the learner, but not to the learner's emotions. The obvious prediction is that learning gains should be superior for the affective AutoTutor.

The results of the experiment indicated that the affective AutoTutor was significantly more effective ($d = 0.713$) than the regular tutor for low-domain knowledge students, during the second half of the interaction. This suggests that it is inappropriate for the tutor to be supportive to these students before there has been enough context to show there are problems. Simply put, it may not be wise to be supportive until the students need support. Second, the students with more knowledge never benefited from the affective AutoTutor. These students do not need the emotional support, but rather they need to concentrate on the content. Third, there are conditions when emotional support is detrimental, if not irritating to the learner. There appears to be a liability to quick support and empathy compared to no affect-sensitivity for students who have high domain knowledge and are being tutored early in the learning session. In summary, the evaluation of the affective AutoTutor has yielded some important insights; however, these findings are tentative and merit replication in a broader set of contexts.

Conclusions

This chapter has discussed the affective, meta-affective, and affect-regulatory processes that accompany deep learning and problem solving with educational technologies. We have identified a set of learning-centered affective states (confusion, frustration, boredom, flow/engagement, delight, surprise, anxiety, and curiosity) that were prominent in our analyses of affect during learning. Complimentary research validating this set of states with different learning environments, diverse student populations, and with alternate methodologies would represent an important advancement in this area. Of equal importance is the need for research studies that track emotions in the wild (i.e., in classrooms, school labs, and online courses) (Arroyo et al., 2009; Baker et al., 2010) and for extended periods of time. In particular, longitudinal studies that model how emotions emerge from interactions between affective traits, moods, and external events will represent a significant advancement in modeling the diffusive, elusive, fuzzy, and dynamic nature of emotions during learning.

Our discussions of meta-affect and affect regulation were unfortunately brief, mainly due to the paucity of research that has tracked these processes during learning sessions. This does not come as a surprise; however, because with the exception of anxiety, systematic research into affect–learning connections is still in its infancy. In our view, identifying the emotions that are relevant to learning with educational technologies is the first step in such a research program. The next steps involve understanding the critical meta-affect and affect regulation processes that are active during learning. The time is ripe for exciting research along these fronts.

Finally, we described and evaluated an ITS that detects, regulates, and synthesizes affect. The idea of having a fully automated affect-sensitive tutor has been proposed only recently (Picard, 1997), so these affective tutors are indicators of the astonishing progress being made in this area. Although our initial experiment with the affect-sensitive AutoTutor yielded some positive effects, it should be noted that a one size fits all approach to affective feedback is not likely to adequately regulate all the emotional experiences that accompany learning. What is needed is a bold innovative approach that optimally coordinates cognition and emotions in a manner that is dynamically adaptive to the knowledge, goals, traits, moods, and styles of each individual learner. In addition to augmenting next-generation learners with cutting-edge technologies, such a research program will undoubtedly sustain significant discoveries bridging affect and learning for several decades.

Acknowledgement This research was supported by the National Science Foundation (ITR 0325428, HCC 0834847, DRL 1235958) and Institute of Education Sciences, US Department of Education (R305A080594 and R305B070349). Any opinions, findings and conclusions, or recommendations expressed in this paper are those of the authors and do not necessarily reflect the views of NSF.

We thank our research colleagues in the Emotive Computing Group and the Tutoring Research Group (TRG) at the University of Memphis (http://emotion.autotutor.org). We gratefully acknowledge our partners in the Affective Computing group at the MIT Media Lab.

Requests for reprints should be sent to Sidney D'Mello, 384 Fitzpatrick, University of Notre Dame, Notre Dame, IN 46556, USA. sdmello@nd.edu.

References

Arroyo, I., Woolf, B., Cooper, D., Burleson, W., Muldner, K., & Christopherson, R. (2009). Emotion sensors go to school. In V. Dimitrova, R. Mizoguchi, B. Du Boulay, & A. Graesser (Eds.), *Proceedings of 14th International Conference on Artificial Intelligence In Education* (pp. 17–24). Amsterdam: Ios Press.

Azevedo, R. (2009). Theoretical, methodological, and analytical challenges in the research on metacognition and self-regulation: A commentary. *Metacognition and Learning, 4*, 87–95.

Baker, R., D'Mello, S., Rodrigo, M., & Graesser, A. (2010). Better to be frustrated than bored: The incidence and persistence of affect during interactions with three different computer-based learning environments. *International Journal of Human Computer Studies, 68*(4), 223–241.

Barrett, L. (2006). Are emotions natural kinds? *Perspectives on Psychological Science, 1*, 28–58.

Boekaerts, M. (2007). Understanding Students' affective processes in the classroom. In P. Schutz & R. Pekrun

(Eds.), *Emotion in Education* (pp. 37–56). San Diego, CA: Academic.

Bower, G. (1981). Mood and memory. *The American Psychologist, 36*, 129–148.

Brown, A., Ellery, S., & Campione, J. (1998). Creating Zones of Proximal Development Electronically in Thinking Practices in Mathematics and Science Learning. In J. Greeno & S. Goldman (Eds.), *(pp* (pp. 341–368). Mahawah, NJ: Lawrence Erlbaum.

Brown, P., & Levinson, S. (1987). *Politeness: Some universals in language usage*. Cambridge: Cambridge University Press.

Bushman, B. J. (2002). Does venting anger feed or extinguish the flame? Catharsis, rumination, distraction, anger, and aggressive responding. *Personality and Social Psychology Bulletin, 28*(6), 724–731.

Calvo, R., & D'Mello, S. (Eds.). (2011). *New perspectives on affect and learning technologies*. New York, NY: Springer.

Clifford, M. (1988). Failure tolerance and academic risk-taking in ten- to twelve-year-old students. *The British Journal of Educational Psychology, 58*(15–27).

Conati, C., & Maclaren, H. (2009). Empirically building and evaluating a probabilistic model of user affect. *User Modeling and User-Adapted Interaction, 19*(3), 267–303.

Craig, S., Graesser, A., Sullins, J., & Gholson, J. (2004). Affect and learning: An exploratory look into the role of affect in learning. *Journal of Educational Media, 29*, 241–250.

Csikszentmihalyi, M. (1990). *Flow: The psychology of optimal experience*. New York, NY: Harper and Row.

D'Mello, S., Craig, S., Sullins, J., & Graesser, A. (2006). Predicting affective states expressed through an emote-aloud procedure from AutoTutor's mixed-initiative dialogue. *International Journal of Artificial Intelligence in Education, 16*(1), 3–28.

D'Mello, S. K., Lehman, B. A., & Person, N. (2011). Monitoring affect states during effortful problem solving activities. *International Journal of Artificial Intelligence in Education, 20*(4), 361–389.

D'Mello, S., Lehman, B., Sullins, J., Daigle, R., Combs, R., Vogt, K., et al. (2010). A time for emoting: When affect-sensitivity is and isn't effective at promoting deep learning. In J. Kay & V. Aleven (Eds.), *Proceedings of 10th International Conference on Intelligent Tutoring Systems* (pp. 245–254). Berlin: Springer.

D'Mello, S. K., & Graesser, A. C. (in review). Inducing and tracking confusion and cognitive disequilibrium with breakdown scenarios

D'Mello, S., & Graesser, A. C. (2011). The half-life of cognitive-affective states during complex learning. *Cognition and Emotion, 25*(7), 1299–1308.

Dandoy, A. C., & Goldstein, A. G. (1990). The Use of Cognitive Appraisal to Reduce Stress Reactions—a Replication. *Journal of Social Behavior and Personality, 5*(4), 275–285.

Dweck, C. (2002). Messages that motivate: How praise molds students' beliefs, motivation, and performance (in surprising ways). In J. Aronson (Ed.), *Improving academic achievement: Impact of psychological factors on education* (pp. 61–87). Orlando, FL: Academic.

Ekman, P. (1992). An argument for basic emotions. *Cognition & Emotion, 6*(3–4), 169–200.

Graesser, A., Chipman, P., King, B., McDaniel, B., & D'Mello, S. (2007). Emotions and learning with AutoTutor. In R. Luckin, K. Koedinger, & J. Greer (Eds.), *13th International Conference on Artificial Intelligence in Education* (pp. 569–571). Amsterdam: Ios Press.

Graesser, A., Lu, S., Olde, B., Cooper-Pye, E., & Whitten, S. (2005). Question asking and eye tracking during cognitive disequilibrium: Comprehending illustrated texts on devices when the devices break down. *Memory and Cognition, 33*, 1235–1247.

Graesser, A., Lu, S. L., Jackson, G., Mitchell, H., Ventura, M., Olney, A., et al. (2004). AutoTutor: A tutor with dialogue in natural language. *Behavioral Research Methods, Instruments, and Computers, 36*, 180–193.

Graesser, A., McDaniel, B., Chipman, P., Witherspoon, A., D'Mello, S., & Gholson, B. (2006). *Detection of emotions during learning with AutoTutor.* Paper presented at the 28th Annual Conference of the Cognitive Science Society, Vancouver, Canada.

Graesser, A., & Olde, B. (2003). How does one know whether a person understands a device? The quality of the questions the person asks when the device breaks down. *Journal of Educational Psychology, 95*(3), 524–536.

Gross, J. (2008). Emotion regulation. In M. Lewis, J. Haviland-Jones, & L. Barrett (Eds.), *Handbook of emotions* (3rd ed., pp. 497–512). New York, NY: Guilford.

Harter, S. (1992). The relationship between perceived competence, affect, and motivational orientation within the classroom: Process and patterns of change. In A. Boggiano & T. Pittman (Eds.), *Achievement and motivation: A social-developmental perspective* (pp. 77–114). New York, NY: Cambridge University Press.

Immordino-Yang, M. H., & Damasio, A. R. (2007). We feel, therefore we learn: The relevance of affective and social neuroscience to education. *Mind, Brain and Education, 1*(1), 3–10.

Isen, A. (2001). An influence of positive affect on decision making in complex situations: Theoretical issues with practical implications. *Journal of Consumer Psychology, 11*, 75–85.

Izard, C. (1994). Innate and universal facial expressions: Evidence from developmental and cross-cultural research. *Psychological Bulletin, 115*(288–299).

Lazarus, R. (1991). *Emotion and adaptation*. New York, NY: Oxford University Press.

Lazarus, R. (2000). The cognition-emotion debate: A bit of history. In M. Lewis & J. Haviland-Jones (Eds.), *Handbook of Emotions* (2nd ed., pp. 1–20). New York, NY: Guilford Press.

Lehman, B. A., D'Mello, S. K., Strain, A., Gross, M., Dobbins, A., Wallace, P., Millis, K., & Graesser, A. C. (2011). Inducing and tracking confusion with contradictions during critical thinking and scientific reasoning.

In G. Biswas, S. Bull, J. Kay, & A. Mitrovic (Eds.), *Proceedings of 15th International Conference on Artificial Intelligence in Education* (pp. 171–178). Berlin: Springer-Verlag.

Lepper, M., & Chabay, R. (1988). Socializing the intelligent tutor: Bringing empathy to computer tutors. In H. Mandl & A. Lesgold (Eds.), *Learning Issues for Intelligent Tutoring Systems* (pp. 242–257). Hillsdale, NJ: Erlbaum.

Linnenbrink, E., & Pintrich, P. (2002). The role of motivational beliefs in conceptual change. In M. Limon & L. Mason (Eds.), *Reconsidering conceptual change: Issues in theory and practice* (pp. 115–135). Dordretch, Netherlands: Kluwer Academic Publishers.

Mandler, G. (1999). Emotion. In B. M. Bly & D. E. Rumelhart (Eds.), *Cognitive science. Handbook of perception and cognition* (2nd ed., pp. 367–382). San Diego, CA: Academic.

Metcalfe, J. (2002). Is study time allocated selectively to a region of proximal learning? *Journal of Experimental Psychology: General, 131*, 349–363.

Meyer, D., & Turner, J. (2006). Re-conceptualizing emotion and motivation to learn in classroom contexts. *Educational Psychology Review, 18*(4), 377–390.

Moreno, R., & Mayer, R. (2007). Interactive multimodal learning environments. *Educational Psychology Review, 19*(3), 309–326.

Nicaud, J. F., & Saidi, M. (1990). Explanation of Algebraic Reasoning: The APLUSIX System. In S. Ramani, R. Chrandrasekar, & K. Anjaneyulu (Eds.), *Knowledge Based Computer Systems* (pp. 145–154). Berlin Heidelberg: Springer.

Ortony, A., Clore, G., & Collins, A. (1988). *The cognitive structure of emotions*. New York, NY: Cambridge University Press.

Pekrun, R., Elliot, A., & Maier, M. (2006). Achievement goals and discrete achievement emotions: A theoretical model and prospective test. *Journal of Educational Psychology, 98*(3), 583–597.

Piaget, J. (1952). *The origins of intelligence*. New York, NY: International University Press.

Picard, R. (1997). *Affective Computing*. Cambridge, Mass: MIT Press.

Russell, J. A., Bachorowski, J. A., & Fernandez-Dols, J. M. (2003). Facial and vocal expressions of emotion. *Annual Review of Psychology, 54*, 329–349.

Ryan, K. (2001). The incredible machine: Even more contraptions [Computer Software]: Sierra Entertainment.

Scherer, K., Schorr, A., & Johnstone, T. (Eds.). (2001). *Appraisal processes in emotion: Theory, methods, research*. London: London University Press.

Scherer, K. R., Wranik, T., Sangsue, J., Tran, V., & Scherer, U. (2004). Emotions in everyday life: Probability of occurrence, risk factors, appraisal and reaction patterns. *Social Science Information, 43*(4), 499–570.

Schwarz, N. (2012). Feelings-as-information theory. In P. Van Lange, A. Kruglanski & T. Higgins (Eds.), *Handbook of theories of social psychology* (pp. 289–308). Thousand Oaks, CA: Sage.

Schwarz, N., & Skurnik, I. (2003). Feeling and thinking: Implications for problem solving. In J. Davidson & R. Sternberg (Eds.), *The Psychology of Problem Solving* (pp. 263 290) New York: Cambridge University Press.

Stein, N., & Levine, L. (1991). Making sense out of emotion. In O. W. Kessen & F. Kraik (Eds.), *Memories, thoughts, and emotions: Essays in honor of George Mandler* (pp. 295–322). Hillsdale, NJ: Erlbaum.

Stipek, D. (1988). *Motivation to learn: From theory to practice*. Boston, MA: Allyn and Bacon.

Strain, A. C., & D'Mello, S. K. (2011). Emotion regulation during learning. In G. Biswas, S. Bull, J. Kay, & A. Mitrovic (Eds.), *Proceedings of 15th International Conference on Artificial Intelligence in Education* (pp. 566–568). Berlin: Springer-Verlag.

VanLehn, K., Siler, S., Murray, C., Yamauchi, T., & Baggett, W. (2003). Why do only some events cause learning during human tutoring? *Cognition and Instruction, 21*(3), 209–249.

Wang, N., Johnson, W. L., Mayer, R. E., Rizzo, P., Shaw, E., & Collins, H. (2008). The politeness effect: Pedagogical agents and learning outcomes. *International Journal of Human Computer Studies, 66*(2), 98–112.

Weiner, B. (1986). *An attributional theory of motivation and emotion*. New York, NY: Springer.

45 Self-Regulated Learning with Hypermedia: Bringing Motivation into the Conversation

Daniel C. Moos and Christopher A. Stewart

Abstract

Despite its popularity in the classroom, hypermedia learning is challenging, as empirical research has shown. The inherent design of the hypermedia structure requires students to engage in a variety of metacognitive monitoring processes, which provides feedback that facilitates the process of adaptation during learning. The Self-Regulated Learning Theory (SRL) has provided a theoretical lens to examine these processes during hypermedia learning. While a myriad of theoretical approaches to SRL exist, the Information Processing model has been widely used in the context of hypermedia learning. This article outlines the contributions of this theory to field of hypermedia learning, while also highlighting the need for additional empirical research that systematically considers theoretically-grounded constructs of motivation within SRL. The premise of this chapter is that motivation offers a potential explanation of individual differences in how students respond to negative feedback loops during hypermedia learning. Methodological and theoretical challenges are examined, including the identification of specific motivation constructs (e.g., outcome expectations, incentives, efficacy expectations, attributions, and utility) that align with existing SRL theoretical frameworks.

Introduction

The ever-evolving landscape of technology has produced environments that offer interactive forums to uniquely facilitate the acquisition of knowledge. Hypermedia, for example, represents a type of computer-based learning environment (CBLE) that offers an augmentation of multimedia and earlier forms of hypertext. Multimedia environments present information through a variety of

D.C. Moos (✉)
Department of Education, Gustavus Adolphus College, Mattson Hall, 800 West College Avenue, Saint Peter, MN 56082, USA
e-mail: dmoos@gustavus.edu

C.A. Stewart
North Lakes Academy Charter School, 255 7th Ave NW # B Forest Lake, MN 55025, USA

R. Azevedo and V. Aleven (eds.), *International Handbook of Metacognition and Learning Technologies*, Springer International Handbooks of Education 26, DOI 10.1007/978-1-4419-5546-3_45,

formats, including audio, animation, and/or still images. Richard Mayer's long line of research has identified the potential benefit of providing students with multiple representations of information. Aside from engaging the student, multiple representations can facilitate knowledge acquisition in a manner that is consistent with cognitive principles of learning (Mayer, 2005). However, multimedia environments lack the interactivity found in other types of CBLEs, such as hypertext.

Students can experience a certain level of interactivity when learning with hypertext through hyperlinked nodes of textual information. This design feature in hypertext allows students to make decisions with respect to the instructional path (Shapiro & Niederhauser, 2004). Hypermedia takes the design features from both multimedia and hypertext by integrating multiple representations within hyperlinked nodes. Research has suggested that this combination of interactivity and rich, multiple forms of information provides a powerful learning context for a diverse group of students (Jacobson, 2008). Despite the promises of these design features, hypermedia can present significant challenges to students. Multiple representations necessitate the coordination of information, while nonlinear access through hyperlinked nodes requires students to constantly monitor the relevancy of content and their emerging understanding. These challenges have attracted a significant body of research, which has provided evidence of processes that facilitate learning with hypermedia (see Azevedo, 2007, 2009; Greene & Azevedo, 2009; Moos & Azevedo, 2008c; Schraw, 2006; Veenman, 2007; Winne & Nesbit, 2009; Zimmerman, 2008). Take, for example, the following excerpt from a study that used a think-aloud protocol to capture how students learn about conceptually complex topics such as the circulatory system within the context of a hypermedia environment (Moos & Azevedo, 2008a). A portion of the student's thoughts and actions during a 30-min hypermedia learning task is provided below.

> I am going to start with the circulatory system just because I am already there…
>
> …and I'm just reading the introduction…circulatory system…also known as the cardiovascular system and it deals with the heart…it transports oxygen and nutrients and it takes away waste… um, it does stuff with blood and I'm kind of remembering some of this from bio in high school, but not a lot of it.
> **Reads:** *The heart and the blood and the blood vessels are the three structural elements and the heart is the engine of the circulatory system, it is divided into four chambers.*
> I knew this one, two right and two left…the atrium, the ventricle and the left atrium, and the left ventricle…okay start the introduction [of the heart], just kind of scout it out real quick…and there's a section called function of the heart…and it looks like it will give me what I need to know…um…introduction, oh that's just basic stuff that we've been doing…
> **Reads:** *Structure of the heart has four chambers…*
> We did that…
> **Reads:** *The atria are also known as auricles. They collect blood that pours in from veins…*
>
> So, it looks like the first step is atria in the system and then the veins.

This segment illustrates the richness that some students experience while learning with hypermedia. In the excerpt, the student monitored the relevancy of the hypermedia content and her emerging understanding while also using strategies to build relevant domain knowledge. This active engagement of the learning process included nonlinear navigation. This student began with the introduction of the circulatory system in the hypermedia environment but then navigated to another section (the Heart) in response to a monitoring activity (i.e., "…I knew this one…"). Furthermore, she limited reading of text when metacognitive activities reveal an adequate understanding (i.e., "We did that…"). This excerpt represents how self-regulation can positively affect learning with hypermedia due to its inherent design features, both in terms of its nonlinearity and provision of multiple representations. However, while some students actively engage in the design features of hypermedia while self-regulating their learning, empirical research has demonstrated significant variability between students. For example, take the excerpt from another participant in the same study (Moos & Azevedo, 2008a).

> I am going to the introduction…
>
> **Reads:** *Circulatory system, or cardiovascular system, in humans, the combined function of the heart, blood, and blood vessels to transport oxygen and*

nutrients to organs and tissues throughout the body and carry away waste products...
I'm going to take notes...transport oxygen...nutrients...to organs and tissues and carry away waste products.
Reads: *Among its vital functions, the circulatory system increases the flow of blood to meet increased energy demands during exercise and regulates body temperature. In addition, when foreign substances or organisms invade the body, the circulatory system swiftly conveys disease-fighting elements of the immune system, such as white blood cells and antibodies to regions under attack...*
I'm writing down the structural elements...
Reads: *The heart is the engine of the circulatory system. It is divided into four chambers: The right atrium, the right ventricle, the left atrium, and the left ventricle. The walls of the chambers are made of a special muscle called myocardium, which contract continuously and rhythmically to pump blood.*
...okay, the heart...engine...the chambers...right and left atrium...right and left ventricle. Okay... special muscle...myocardium...mmmm...
Reads: *The human heart has four chambers, the upper two chambers...the right side of the heart is responsible for pumping oxygen-poor blood to the lungs...This oxygen-poor blood feeds into two large veins, the superior vena cava and inferior vena cava. The right atrium conducts blood to the right ventricle, and the right ventricle pumps blood into the pulmonary artery. The pulmonary artery carries the blood to the lungs, where it picks up a fresh supply of oxygen and eliminates carbon dioxide.*

Unlike the first example, this student read substantially more information and progressed through the environment in a linear progression. That is, while the first student navigated to a different section (the Heart) once she identified an adequate understanding, the second student began in the introduction and proceeded to read linearly. Furthermore, the second student relied on a much less diverse set of learning processes. The first student monitored the relevancy of the content and her emerging understanding, while the second student used the environment in a much more linear fashion and relied on a small subset of strategies (namely, note-taking and summarizing). The discrepancy between how these two students engaged in the learning process with hypermedia reflects the substantial individual differences found in empirical research. The following section will first discuss the theoretical frameworks that have been used to explain how students learn with hypermedia, highlighting how these theoretical approaches have provided the foundation for research concerning individual differences in hypermedia learning. Following this section, the chapter will discuss the empirical and methodological approaches that are grounded in the aforementioned theoretical frameworks. Next, the chapter will identify possible explanations for individual differences with an emphasis on the need for research to more fully explore the role of theoretically grounded motivation constructs. Lastly, this chapter concludes by exploring the methodological and theoretical challenges to considering motivation in SRL with hypermedia.

Theoretical and Conceptual Framework

Learning with hypermedia requires students to engage in a variety of cognitive (i.e., use of learning strategies and activation of prior knowledge), metacognitive (i.e., identifying the relevancy of content and monitoring emerging understanding), and motivational (i.e., self-efficacy) processes (Azevedo, 2005, 2008, 2009; Azevedo, Moos, Witherspoon, & Chauncey, 2010; Greene & Azevedo, 2007, 2009; Moos & Azevedo, 2008c; Moos & Marroquin, 2010; Moos, 2009, 2010, 2011; Veenman, 2007; Winne & Nesbit, 2009; Zimmerman, 2008). As such, the inherent nature of hypermedia calls for a theoretical explanation of learning that is robust enough to account for a diverse set of factors. Self-regulated learning (SRL) theories offer a natural fit for this line of research. While SRL consists of many camps and perspectives that sometimes focus on different constructs (Boekaerts, Pintrich, & Zeidner, 2000; Zimmerman & Schunk, 2001), these perspectives share four common assumptions that have been used to guide hypermedia research (Pintrich, 2000). First, it is assumed that students actively construct their own meaning from an interaction between prior knowledge and information available in the context. Second, it is also assumed that students can potentially monitor and regulate their cognition, behavior, and motivation. Third, it is assumed that all behavior is goal directed and self-regulated students modify their behavior to achieve a desired goal. Lastly, it is assumed that self-regulation results from an interaction of contextual factors, personal characteristics of the student, and the student's performance.

While these basic assumptions highlight the guiding principles of SRL, there are distinct theoretical perspectives that guide specific areas of research. Winne (2001) and Winne and Hadwin's (1998) information processing theory (IPT) of SRL has received considerable attention within hypermedia learning research. This theoretical approach outlines four phases of SRL: (1) understanding the task, (2) goal setting and planning how to reach the goal(s), (3) enacting strategies, and (4) metacognitively adapting studying. Though phases may suggest that SRL is linear, an underlying assumption is that there is a recursive nature because of a feedback loop. Information processed in one phase can become an input to subsequent information processing. Additionally, students may adapt their *planning* and/or *strategies* in order to meet the goal based on discrepancies revealed by *monitoring* activities. Students may experience this cyclical process a number of times throughout a hypermedia learning session. Take the student presented in the earlier example, which illustrated how self-regulation manifests itself in hypermedia learning. This student read the text and used strategies such as note-taking (stage 3). A monitoring activity (stage 4) revealed that, in fact, she had previously learned the material in that particular section of the hypermedia environment. As a result of this monitoring activity, she developed a new plan (to learn about the direction of blood flow, stage 2) and then enacted a strategy (summarizing, stage 3). Thus, truly self-regulated students will proceed through a number of cycles in the four phases of SRL.

The first phase of SRL consists of the student constructing a perception of the learning task. These perceptions are derived from information about the task, such as learning goals, as well as information from long-term memory. Task definition and performance is facilitated when a student draws prior domain knowledge into working memory from long-term memory. The next phase of self-regulated learning concerns the development of goals and plans (Butler & Winne, 1995; Winne & Hadwin, 1998). Processes associated with this stage are dynamic as students can modify the goals through the process of learning. In phase 3, the student applies tactics and/or strategies (Winne, 2001; Winne & Hadwin, 1998), which facilitate knowledge acquisition. Lastly, phase 4 consists of cognitive evaluation and monitoring activities. These processes reveal any discrepancy between the current knowledge state and a goal (Winne, 2001; Winne & Hadwin, 1998). In other words, phase 4 reflects metacognition, commonly referred to as the knowledge of one's thinking and the ability to reflect and modify processes and strategies related to this knowledge (Flavell, 1979, 1985; Schraw & Dennison, 1994). According to Winne (2001) and Winne and Hadwin's (1998) model of SRL, these metacognitive processes assume a foundational role in self-regulated learning because they produce information that facilitates the adaptation of planning and/or strategies to more effectively meet the learning goal(s) (Butler & Winne, 1995; Winne, 1997; Winne & Hadwin, 2008).

Empirical Evidence and Methodological Approaches

Some methodological approaches consider SRL as a relatively enduring trait (i.e., *aptitude*), while others assume that SRL is a dynamic process that unfolds within particular contexts (i.e., *event*). The IPT approach to SRL lends itself to the view that SRL is a sequence of dynamic *events*, a view that has distinct implications for methodologies. Perhaps the most relevant implication of this ideological position is that SRL processes are cyclical in nature and dynamically unfold during a learning task (Azevedo & Witherspoon, 2009; Winne, 2001; Winne & Perry, 2000; Zimmerman, 2008). Thus, SRL needs to be measured in real time so that the dynamic nature of the complex processes can be captured. Several approaches have emerged that offer methodologies consistent with the assumption that SRL is an event. For example, *error detection tasks* are designed to measure SRL processes related to monitoring and control as they unfold within a specific context (Winne & Perry, 2000). This methodological approach induces errors in the learning task, which allows the researcher to observe (a) when and whether the student detects the error and (b) what the student does once the error is detected. Students may or may not be told that errors exist in the instructional material prior to the learning task. Several methodologies exist, including asking students to mark the errors (e.g., by underlining) and/or the use of eye tracking to determine eye fixations (Schneider et al., 2008). Methodologies that use eye tracking assume that students will attend longer to errors in the instructional material. Another approach that has been used to examine SRL in real time is *traces* or observable indicators of cognitive activities (Winne, 1982). For example, measuring note-taking and underlining during learning provides real-time information about the student's cognitive activities. In these trace methodologies, it is assumed that students mark text (such as underlining) and/or attend to information longer when they are discriminating between content (Winne, 2005). Thus, these behaviors (underlining and/or extended eye fixations) represent cognitive and metacognitive activities, which are consistent with some SRL theories. For example, Winne and Hadwin's (1998) model suggests that metacognitive monitoring leads to adaptation, possibly in the form of enacted strategies (such as underlining) and/or changes in behavior (such as attending to information). Given these assumptions, studies that use trace methodologies, such as error detection tasks and/or eye tracking, typically focus on specific processes related to SRL, namely, metacognition and strategies.

Another approach to measuring SRL during learning is the use of the think-aloud method. This protocol is an on-line trace methodology that offers a means through which researchers can examine SRL *during* learning (Azevedo, 2005). The think-aloud protocol has an extensive history in cognitive psychology and cognitive science (see Ericsson, 2006; Ericsson & Simon, 1994). Cognitive psychology and cognitive science have used both concurrent and retrospective think-aloud protocols as data sources for cognitive processes (Anderson, 1987). While the think-aloud protocol has been most popular in reading comprehension (Dreher & Guthrie, 1993; Pressley & Afflerbach, 1995), it has been shown to be an excellent tool to gather verbal accounts of SRL and map out self-regulatory processes during learning (e.g., Azevedo & Cromley, 2004; Boekaerts et al., 2000). A concurrent think-aloud protocol assumes that thought processes are a sequence of states and that information in a state is relatively stable (Ericsson, 2006; Ericsson & Simon, 1994). Consequently, verbalizing thoughts during learning will not disrupt the learning process. It should be noted "that subjects verbalizing their thoughts while performing a task do *not* describe or explain what they are doing (Ericsson & Simon, 1994, pg. xiii)" during concurrent think-aloud protocols. If subjects are not asked to reflect, describe, and/or explain their thoughts during learning, but rather are asked to simply verbalize thoughts entering their attention, then it is assumed that the sequence of thoughts will not be disrupted.

Research in the field of hypermedia learning has used a concurrent think-aloud protocol to explore how different developmental groups use SRL processes. For example, Azevedo, Moos, Greene, Winters, and Cromley (2008) examined adolescents' ability to use SRL processes while learning about the circulatory system with hypermedia. A portion of this sample had access to a tutor who assisted in the use of SRL, while the other group did not have access. In the absence of support, adolescents tended to use ineffective strategies and few monitoring activities. However, adolescents who worked with a tutor during the hypermedia learning task engaged in a variety of SRL processes, including effective strategies, a myriad of monitoring activities, and adaptive help-seeking behavior.

Greene, Bolick, and Robertson (2010) considered the role of SRL in hypermedia environments for high school students. This study, which was guided by Winne and Hadwin's (1998) SRL model, found that high school students tended to rely on strategy use (phase 3) while learning with hypermedia. Interestingly, though, it was planning processes, and not strategy use, that were most predictive of hypermedia learning. Research has also used this methodology to examine how adult students self-regulate their learning with hypermedia. Moos (2010), for example, considered the extent to which various SRL processes (learning strategies, monitoring, and planning) were predictive of hypermedia learning outcomes for undergraduate students. Results indicate that while these SRL processes were predictive of learning outcomes, there was also substantial individual variability in how frequently participants self-regulated their learning.

The results from these studies reflect some commonalities in research examining SRL with hypermedia. First, processes related to SRL are predictive of learning outcomes with hypermedia. For example, De Jong (1992) found that a significant amount of the variance in learning outcomes (19–60%) was explained by students' use of regulation strategies, results that have also been found in the context of hypermedia learning (Moos, 2011). Second, despite the documented importance of these processes in hypermedia learning, there is significant variability in how students self-regulate in this context, differences that can only be partially explained by developmental level. The following section discusses possible explanations of these individual differences and the need to more fully explore the role of motivation in these differences.

Individual Differences in SRL with Hypermedia

Empirical evidence that explicitly attempts to identify stable individual differences with respect to SRL, and metacognition in particular, continues to be scarce. From a theoretical standpoint, Winne (1997) suggested that a wide range of potential individual differences should be examined to further our understanding of self-regulated learning and metacognition. Keleman, Frost, and Weaver (2000) agreed, highlighting the importance of collecting a robust body of research guided by theoretically driven data on individual differences. To narrow the search for potential factors that affect metacognition and self-regulation in general, a wide array of individual differences must be assessed and if appropriate, dismissed. Keleman et al. (2000) challenged the notion that individual differences in metacognitive accuracy reflect differences in participants' metacognitive ability, seeking to disprove the existence of a *general* metacognitive ability. Using four common metacognitive tasks, (JOL, FOK, text comprehension monitoring, and ease of learning judgments), this study found that individual differences with respect to memory and confidence were stable across learning tasks and produced consistent and reliable correlations with self-regulation. However, individual differences in metacognitive accuracy did not reveal a similar robustness across learning tasks as they were much less stable. These data question whether individual differences in metacognitive accuracy for particular tasks represent a more general metacognitive ability. Thus, this finding suggests that measures of general metacognitive ability may not be a valid explanation of individual differences that have an impact on self-regulated learning ability and/or metacognitive abilities (Keleman et al., 2000).

Other studies have considered additional variables over and beyond that of general metacognitive ability, taking a different approach and focusing on the role of developmental differences in metacognition. According to Bartsch and Estes (1996), who investigated and explained the "theory of mind" approach, an adolescent's initial understanding of mental states serves as the groundwork for an eventual ability to engage in processes related to metacognition. It is at this developmental stage, Bartsch and Estes (1996) argued, that children's ability to engage in and/or develop metacognitive abilities is most vulnerable to individual differences. For example, they suggest qualitative conditions like various developmental needs (e.g., autism spectrum disorder (ASD)), or an individual's cultural approach to the theory of mind can alter one's metacognitive development.

Vukman (2005) supported the claim that adolescence is a critical developmental stage for metacognitive abilities. In this study, 57 individuals from four developmental groups ("adolescents," "young adults," "mature adults," and "older adults") solved both logical interpolation and relativistic/dialectic problems. A think-aloud protocol was used to assess the participants' metacognitive accuracy. The findings indicated that development into adulthood increases the capability to be aware of and be able to accurately reflect on one's own abilities. Younger adults demonstrated significantly lower metacognitive accuracy, and findings regarding the participants' awareness of and reflection on one's own mental processes were consistent with previous research: There is an increase into early adulthood, followed by a peak in mature adulthood, and then a slight decline in older adults.

Developmental differences, however, offer only a partial explanation for individual differences in metacognition. Even adults demonstrate substantial individual differences (e.g., Azevedo et al., 2008; Greene & Azevedo, 2009), a finding that has been explained by differences in prior domain knowledge. Moos and Azevedo (2008a), for example, used a think-aloud protocol to examine how undergraduate students used SRL processes while learning about a complex science topic with a hypermedia environment. Differences in the extent to which these participants used SRL were significantly explained by their prior domain knowledge of the science topic. Those who came into the learning task with lower prior domain knowledge tended to rely on learning strategies and rarely planned nor did they engage in metacognitive monitoring processes. On the other hand, participants who had higher prior domain knowledge used fewer strategies and more metacognitive monitoring processes during the hypermedia learning task. This finding is consistent with the IPT explanation of factors that affect metacognition.

According to Winne (1996), there are five areas in which individual differences may affect students' ability to self-regulate their learning: domain knowledge, knowledge of tactics and strategies, performance of tactics and strategies, regulation of tactics and strategies, and global dispositions. This theoretical explanation highlights the role of prior domain knowledge in the process of self-regulation, which was supported by Moos and Azevedo (2008a). Their findings suggest that those with higher prior knowledge have an existing knowledge structure that enables them to effectively monitor the nonlinear nature of hypermedia and their emerging understanding. Thus, they can engage in "knowledge verification" (Moos & Azevedo, 2008a), where they regulate their learning by using planning process to activate relevant prior domain knowledge and monitor their learning by comparing information in hypermedia with their current understanding. Students with lower prior knowledge, however, do not initially have access to this prior domain knowledge and thus do not have the knowledge base to engage in such monitoring processes. Rather, they engage in "knowledge acquisition" (Moos & Azevedo, 2008a), whereby they need to rely on strategies to develop a well-established knowledge base of the topic. However, this explanation does not address individual differences with respect to students' *willingness* to use SRL processes, including metacognitive processes, during hypermedia learning.

Closely considering the IPT approach to SRL may account for this largely unexplored area of hypermedia learning. This theory has been cited as having provided substantial contributions to the field and most notably for its explanation of the role of self-monitoring processes in terms of feedback loops (Zimmerman & Schunk, 2001). An underlying assumption of this theoretical approach is that students are compelled to self-adjust their learning in the face of negative discrepancies between feedback and self-evaluative standards. However, while this theoretical approach offers a powerful explanatory lens, it currently does not offer a full explanation of individual differences in response to negative feedback loops (Zimmerman & Schunk, 2001). In other words, while maturation and prior domain knowledge may offer students the capacity to engage in self-regulation, their willingness to engage in these processes varies. Furthermore, individual reactions to negative feedback loops differ, and differences may be magnified in contexts that require the use of dynamic adaptation of strategies and tactics. Hypermedia offers an example of such an environment; the nonlinear access to information requires students to constantly monitor their emerging understanding and relevancy of the content, while making adaptations based on the feedback loop of these monitoring processes. A challenge for the IPT approach to SRL is to explain differences in how individuals respond to negative feedback loops. A promising direction for this issue is to explore the relationship between motivation and SRL within the hypermedia environment.

The importance of motivation in the context of active participation in one's learning is not a new concept within the SRL theory (e.g., Pintrich & De Groot, 1990), though there has been less empirical attention in the context of hypermedia learning (see Moos & Marroquin, 2010 for a review). SRL theories identify the role of motivational beliefs in the student's task perception. Zimmerman's (1995) social-cognitive perspective of SRL, for example, highlights the role of personal agency and self-efficacy in behavioral processes. Complete explanations of individual differences with respect to SRL need to be driven by theoretical frameworks that account for SRL as complex, dynamic interaction between social, behavioral, *and* motivational components (Zimmerman, 1995). These theoretical considerations have been supported by empirical research that has examined various constructs of motivation and different components of SRL (e.g., Bartels, Magun-Jackson, & Joseph, 2010; Eflides, 2011; Moos, 2010, 2011).

For example, Hong, Peng, and Rowell (2009) compared the use of self-regulation and metacognitive strategies on homework between 7th- and 11th-grade Chinese students, studying the effects of grade differences, achievement levels, and gender. Amongst the 7th-grade students, high achievers used self-regulation and metacognition strategies more frequently when compared to low achievers. However, these results were not duplicated for 11th-grade students. In fact, Hong et al. (2009) found that older students in general used self-regulation and metacognitive strategies less often, which they identified as a function of motivation. Specifically, these researchers found a positive relationship between intrinsic motivation and use of SRL processes. The older students experienced diminished intrinsic motivation, which, in turn, resulted in decreased use of SRL processes. This finding of declining intrinsic value placed in schoolwork has been corroborated for Western culture students as well (Wigfield & Guthrie, 1997).

Research has explored other theoretically grounded constructs of motivation, including goal orientation. For example, Bartels and Magun-Jackson (2009) examined the relationship between approach-avoidance motivation and self-regulation for 145 undergraduates. Regression analyses revealed that participants' reported use of two cognitive strategies (organization and elaboration) was significantly predicted by their approach-avoidance motivation. Specifically, those classified as approach motivated used these cognitive strategies significantly more frequently (Bartels & Magun-Jackson, 2009). This study furthers the argument that motivation constructs play a key role in explaining individual differences in SRL by noting the cyclical nature of this complex relationship. According to this line of research, motivation (i.e., approach goal orientation) can lead to the use of strategies such as elaboration and organization, which will lead to higher learning outcomes. As a result, a positive feedback loop encourages the student to use additional strategies, which further increases academic performance. Thus, the initial individual difference between those students with different levels of motivation is magnified as they progress through the task due to feedback loops and responses to these loops. While this study highlights the dynamic impact of motivation on use of cognitive strategies during learning, it should be noted that this study used a self-report questionnaire to measure SRL and hypothesized the relationship between cognitive strategies and learning outcomes.

Vollmeyer and Rheinberg (2006) provided additional empirical support through examining motivation at the initial point of learning (in the form of challenge, probability of success, interest, and anxiety), as well as motivation during learning (in the form of flow), in a number of contexts including hypermedia. Results supported a model in which initial motivation significantly affects motivation during learning, as well as the use of learning strategies and overall performance. This study highlights the importance of extensively measuring motivation and its effect on cognitive strategies related to SRL with hypermedia. Research has also examined the relationship between motivation and other SRL processes with hypermedia learning, including monitoring and planning. For example, Moos and Azevedo (2009) measured undergraduates' self-efficacy, use of metacognitive monitoring processes, prior knowledge, and learning outcomes. Results indicated that self-efficacy was a significant predictor of the participants' monitoring of their understanding, environment, and progress towards the learning goal. These lines of research have begun to address the dynamic relationship between motivation and various processes of SRL with hypermedia. Continued examination of these complex relationships requires a careful consideration of methodological and analytical challenges associated with this line of research. Furthermore, the recent focus on event-based methodological approaches to capture SRL, such as think-aloud protocols (see Azevedo and colleagues' research) and other trace methodologies (see Winne and colleagues' research), has provided the means to better address theoretical questions concerning SRL.

Methodological and Analytical Challenges

The challenges of measuring motivation during hypermedia learning are not distinct from that of capturing cognitive and metacognitive processes related to SRL. The chosen methodology of measuring these processes is directly aligned with the assumption that motivation is either an event or aptitude. When motivation is considered an aptitude, stability is assumed, and thus, it is further assumed that a single measurement aggregates a motivation construct based on multiple events (Winne & Perry, 2000). As such, self-perceptions of motivation are considered valid measures, with self-report questionnaires being the most typical protocol for measuring motivation. Several self-report questionnaires are used most frequently including the *Learning and Study Strategies Inventory* (LASSI; Weinstein, 1987). This self-report questionnaire, which is composed of 77 items, was "designed to measure use of learning and study strategies" (Weinstein, 1987, p. 2) by undergraduate students. Another frequently used self-report questionnaire the *Motivated Strategies for Learning Questionnaire* (MSLQ) was developed to additionally assess "college students' motivational orientations and their use of different learning strategies for a college course" (Pintrich, Smith, Garcia, & McKeachie, 1991; p. 3). The motivation section in the MSLQ was designed to measure the broad areas of affect, expectancy, and value, while the learning strategies section was designed to measure cognitive, metacognitive, and resource management strategies.

While self-reports are relatively easy to administer and score, their alignment with key assumptions of the IPT approach to SRL comes into question. Self-reports assume that motivation is an aptitude, while measurements guided by the IPT approach generally categorize all processes related to SRL, including motivation, as events. This theoretical assumption perceives self-regulation in terms of dynamic, constant interaction between self-evaluative standards, self-monitoring relative to those standards, and adjustments geared towards addressing discrepancies between these standards. These dynamic processes can result in recursive updates to "cognitive conditions" (Winne & Hadwin, 1998), including motivational factors and orientations. For example, take a hypothetical student who uses information from resources, instructional cues, time, and/or the social context and comes to the decision that the task is difficult (Winne, 2001). This preconceived conceptualization of the task might create initial feelings of low self-efficacy. This student's motivation could be measured through a typical self-report questionnaire administered after the provision of information that sufficiently identifies the task conditions, but before the student actually engages in the learning task. Such a methodological approach would be effective in identifying the student's *initial* motivation. However, empirical evidence has demonstrated that self-efficacy, along with other cognitive and metacognitive processes related to SRL, are apt to fluctuate, even during relatively short learning tasks (Moos & Azevedo, 2008b). This fluctuation may be magnified in learning contexts that require self-regulation, such as hypermedia. Students typically report higher levels of self-efficacy immediately prior to using hypermedia, possibly because they are not fully aware of the cognitive and metacognitive challenges presented by this environment (Moos & Azevedo, 2008b).

There is a methodological need to capture motivation at various points during the learning process. The challenge of this approach is identifying when to administer motivation measures. Research has used time intervals to collect motivation (see Moos & Azevedo, 2008b), a methodological approach that calls for administering self-report questionnaires (i.e., MSLQ) at set time intervals during the hypermedia learning task (i.e., every 10 min). This approach provides an analytical benefit because it allows for a systematic collection of data points that are consistent across participants. However, while this approach may be attractive from a methodological standpoint, there are some theoretical concerns. It is assumed that adaptations to SRL processes, including motivational beliefs, are a function of the feedback loop generated by metacognitive monitoring (Winne & Hadwin, 1998). Thus, it would stand to reason that the most appropriate time to measure the fluctuation of motivation during hypermedia learning is immediately following metacognitive monitoring as this process is responsible for adaptations to motivational beliefs. Previous empirical research, though, has demonstrated significant variability in the timing and frequency with which students engage in metacognitive monitoring during hypermedia learning. A challenge for future research is to develop methodologies that allow for highly individualized measurements of motivation fluctuation in hypermedia learning. Empirically identifying circumstances that trigger adaptations of motivational beliefs is an important first step.

This step has been taken by research that has used production rules to model fluctuations of learning processes (see Aleven, Roll, McLaren, & Koedinger, 2010; Winne & Nesbit, 2009). Current work has focused on "state-transition" analyses (e.g., Witherspoon, Azevedo, & D'Mello, 2008) so that data can be mined to better understand the evolvement (and triggers) of cognitive and metacognitive processes during hypermedia learning. These data mining techniques are leading to production rules that can be embedded in intelligent hypermedia environments, which have the potential to identify, model, and foster cognitive and metacognitive processes during learning (see Azevedo et al., 2008, 2010). However, this line of research heavily focuses on the "cold" cognitive structures of SRL, with the "hot" components (i.e., motivation) receiving much less attention. Methodological approaches that also consider state-transition analyses with respect to motivation will enable the creation of more robust production rules that encompass all aspects of SRL (see Baker, Rodrigo, & Xolocotzin, 2007).

Theoretical Challenges

The challenge of determining when to measure motivation is magnified by the importance of identifying which theoretically grounded motivation constructs are most appropriate to consider. Earlier theoretical frameworks suggested that *outcome expectations, incentives, efficacy expectations,* and *attributions* are the motivation constructs that best explain students' definition of the task and development of plans to reach goals and critical phases in SRL (Byrnes, 1998; Winne, 1997). Winne (1997) further argued that *utility* is a critical motivation construct to consider, particularly if it is assumed that individuals may have their own idiosyncratic view of the task and plan. These views may drastically differ from the experimenter set goals, and thus it is important to account for this motivation construct. While such theoretical approaches articulate the role of some motivation constructs in SRL, they are faced with the challenge of explaining individual differences with respect to adaptation in the face of negative feedback loops. Some students may adjust their strategies, adapt different learning goals, and increase their effort in the face of negative discrepancies between goals and current knowledge state, but other students may not make any adjustments and/or simply lower standards. Why do these individual differences exist, and how can IPT provide a theoretical explanation, particularly in the context of hypermedia learning? Why might some students be willing to make adaptations in the face of negative feedback loops, while others choose not to do so? Answers to these questions can be considered by examining the motivation constructs already identified in the IPT theory of SRL: *outcome expectations, incentives, efficacy expectations, attributions,* and *utility*. Take efficacy expectations, for example. A student who is efficacious is bound to respond differently to a negative feedback when compared to a student who has low efficacy. However, the theoretical explanation is complicated by the consideration of multiple motivation constructs. How might a student respond if he or she were efficacious, but saw little value in the learning task (Wigfield & Eccles, 2000)? These questions are line with the evolving field of academic motivation. Different intellectual traditions (Weiner, 1992) have given rise to various motivation theories, and as a consequence, a number of conceptually distinct motivation constructs have been identified. As highlighted by several researchers (see Murphy & Alexander, 2000 for a review), research interested in explaining individual differences in the learning process would be well served to systematically examine various, theoretically grounded constructs of motivation.

Conclusion

In the context of hypermedia, the vast majority of research has focused on the "cold" cognitive structure (Pintrich, Marx, & Boyle, 1993) involved learning. As a result, a growing but rich body of research has provided process data on the cognitive and metacognitive processes that facilitate hypermedia learning. However, this research has been limited in explaining individual differences in the use of SRL processes, particularly metacognition. Individual differences tend to be explained by maturation and/or prior domain knowledge, with less empirical work focusing on the motivationally "hot" information that is critical in the adaptation of SRL during hypermedia learning. The IPT approach to SRL offers a powerful, theoretical lens to examine the role of adaptation during hypermedia learning. Increased empirical attention to theoretically grounded constructs of motivation will strengthen the explanation of individual differences in how students react in the presence of negative feedback loops.

References

Aleven, V., Roll, I., McLaren, B. M., & Koedinger, K. R. (2010). Automated, unobtrusive, action-by-action assessment of self-regulation during learning with an intelligent tutoring system. *Educational Psychologist, 45*(4), 224–233.

Anderson, J. R. (1987). Methodologies for studying human knowledge. *Behavioral and Brain Sciences, 10*, 467–505.

Azevedo, R. (2005). Using hypermedia as a metacognitive tool for enhancing student learning? The role of self-regulated learning. *Educational Psychologist, 40*(4), 199–209.

Azevedo, R. (2007). Understanding the complex nature of self-regulated learning processes in learning with computer-based learning environments: An introduction. *Metacognition and Learning, 2*(2/3), 57–65.

Azevedo, R. (2008). The role of self-regulation in learning about science with hypermedia. In D. Robinson & G. Schraw (Eds.), *Recent innovations in educational technology that facilitate student learning* (pp. 127–156). Charlotte, NC: Information Age Publishing.

Azevedo, R. (2009). Theoretical, methodological, and analytical challenges in the research on metacognition and self-regulation: A commentary. *Metacognition and Learning, 4*(1), 87–95.

Azevedo, R., & Cromley, J. G. (2004). Does training on self-regulated learning facilitate students' learning with hypermedia? *Journal of Educational Psychology, 96*(3), 523–535.

Azevedo, R., Moos, D. C., Greene, J. A., Winters, F. I., & Cromley, J. C. (2008). Why is externally-regulated learning more effective than self-regulated learning with hypermedia? *Educational Technology Research and Development, 56*(1), 45–72.

Azevedo, R., Moos, D. C., Witherspoon, A. M., & Chauncey, A. D. (2010). Measuring cognitive and metacognitive regulatory processes used during hypermedia learning: Theoretical, conceptual, and methodological issues. *Educational Psychologist, 45*(4), 1–14.

Azevedo, R., & Witherspoon, A. M. (2009). Self-regulated use of hypermedia. In D. J. Hacker, J. Dunlosky, & A. C. Graesser (Eds.), *Handbook of metacognition in education* (pp. 319–339). Mahwah, NJ: Erlbaum.

Azevedo, R., Johnson, A., Chauncey, A., & Burkett, C. (2010). Self-regulated learning with MetaTutor: Advancing the science of learning with MetaCognitive tools. In M. Khine & I. Saleh (Eds.), *New science of learning: Computers, cognition, and collaboration in education* (pp. 225–247). Amsterdam: Springer.

de Baker, R. S. J., Rodrigo, M. T., & Xolocotzin, U. E. (2007). The dynamics of affective transitions in simulation problem-solving environments. In A. C. Paiva, R. Prada, & R. W. Picard (Eds.), *Proceedings of the 2nd International Conference on Affective Computing and Intelligent Interaction* (pp. 666–677). Berlin: Springer.

Bartels, J., & Magun-Jackson, S. (2009). Approach-avoidance motivation and metacognition self-regulation: The role of need for achievement and fear of failure. *Learning and Individual Differences, 19*, 459–463.

Bartels, J. M., Magun-Jackson, S., & Joseph, R. (2010). Dispositional approach-avoidance achievement motivation and cognitive self-regulated learning: The mediation of achievement goals. *Individual Differences Research, 8*(2), 97–110.

Bartsch, K., & Estes, D. (1996). Individual differences in children's developing theory of mind and implications for metacognition. *Learning and Individual Differences, 8*(4), 281–304.

Boekaerts, M., Pintrich, P., & Zeidner, M. (2000). *Handbook of self-regulation*. San Diego, CA: Academic.

Butler, D. L., & Winne, P. H. (1995). Feedback and self-regulated learning: A theoretical synthesis. *Review of Educational Research, 65*(3), 245–281.

Byrnes, J. (1998). *The nature and development of decision making: A self-regulation model*. Mahwah, NJ: Erlbaum.

De Jong, F. P. C. M. (1992). *Independent learning: Regulation of the learning process and learning to regulate: a process approach*. Doctoral dissertation, University of Brabant.

Dreher, M. J., & Guthrie, J. T. (1993). Searching for information. *Contemporary Educational Psychology, 18*(2), 127–179.

Eflides, A. (2011). Interactions of metacognition with motivation and affect in self-regulated learning: The MASRL model. *Educational Psychologist, 46*(1), 6–25.

Ericsson, K. A. (2006). Protocol analysis and expert thought: Concurrent verbalizations of thinking during experts' performance on representative tasks. In K. A. Ericsson, N. Charness, R. R. Hoffman, & P. J. Feltovich (Eds.), *The Cambridge handbook of expertise and expert performance* (pp. 223–242). Cambridge, MA: Cambridge University Press.

Ericsson, K. A., & Simon, H. A. (1994). *Protocol analysis: Verbal reports as data* (2nd ed.). Cambridge, MA: MIT Press.

Flavell, J. H. (1979). Metacognition and cognitive monitoring: A new area of cognitive-developmental inquiry. *American Psychologist, 34*, 906–911.

Flavell, J. H. (1985). *Cognitive development*. Englewood Cliffs, NJ: Prentice Hall.

Greene, J. A., & Azevedo, R. (2007). Adolescents' use of self-regulatory processes and their relation to qualitative mental model shifts. *Journal of Educational Computing Research, 26*(2), 125–148.

Greene, J. A., & Azevedo, R. (2009). A macro-level analysis of SRL processes and their relations to the acquisitions of a sophisticated mental model of a complex system. *Contemporary Educational Psychology, 34*(1), 18–29.

Greene, J. A., Bolick, C. M., & Robertson, J. (2010). Fostering historical knowledge and thinking skills using hypermedia learning environments: The role of self-regulated learning. *Computers in Education, 54*, 230–243.

Hong, E., Peng, Y., & Rowell, L. L. (2009). Homework self-regulation: Grade, gender, and achievement-level differences. *Learning and Individual Differences, 19*(2), 269–272.

Jacobson, M. (2008). A design framework for educational hypermedia systems: Theory, research, and learning emerging scientific conceptual perspectives. *Educational Technology Research and Development, 56*, 5–28.

Keleman, W. L., Frost, P. J., & Weaver, C. A. (2000). Individual differences in metacognition: Evidence against a general metacognitive ability. *Memory & Cognition, 28*(1), 92–107.

Mayer, R. E. (2005). Cognitive theory of multimedia learning. In R. E. Mayer (Ed.), *The Cambridge handbook of multimedia learning* (pp. 31–48). New York: Cambridge University Press.

Moos, D. C. (2009). Note-taking while learning with hypermedia: Cognitive and motivational considerations. *Computers in Human Behavior, 25*, 1120–1128.

Moos, D. C. (2010). Self-regulated learning with hypermedia: Too much of a good thing? *Journal of Educational Multimedia and Hypermedia, 19*(1), 59–77.

Moos, D. C. (2011). Self-regulated learning and externally generated feedback with hypermedia. *Journal of Educational Computing Research, 43*(3), 261–294.

Moos, D. C., & Azevedo, R. (2008a). Self-regulated learning with hypermedia: The role of prior domain knowledge. *Contemporary Educational Psychology, 33*, 270–298.

Moos, D. C., & Azevedo, R. (2008b). Exploring the fluctuation of motivation and use of self-regulatory processes during learning with hypermedia. *Instructional Science, 36*, 203–231.

Moos, D. C., & Azevedo, R. (2008c). Monitoring, planning, and self-efficacy during learning with hypermedia: The impact of conceptual scaffolds. *Computers in Human Behavior, 24*(4), 1686–1706.

Moos, D. C., & Azevedo, R. (2009). Self-efficacy and prior domain knowledge: To what extent does monitoring mediate their relationship with hypermedia? *Metacognition and Learning, 4*(3), 197–216.

Moos, D. C., & Marroquin, L. (2010). Multimedia, hypermedia, and hypertext: Motivation considered and reconsidered. *Computers in Human Behavior, 26*, 265–276.

Murphy, K., & Alexander, P. (2000). A motivated exploration of motivation terminology. *Contemporary Educational Psychology, 25*(1), 3–53.

Pintrich, P. (2000). The role of goal orientation in self-regulated learning. In M. Boekaerts, P. Pintrich, & M. Zeidner (Eds.), *Handbook of self-regulation* (pp. 452–502). San Diego, CA: Academic.

Pintrich, P. R., & De Groot, E. (1990). Motivational and self-regulated learning components of classroom academic performance. *Journal of Educational Psychology, 82*(1), 33–50.

Pintrich, P., Marx, R. W., & Boyle, R. A. (1993). Beyond cold conceptual change: The role of motivational beliefs and classroom contextual factors in the process of conceptual change. *Review of Educational Research, 63*(2), 167–199

Pintrich, P., Smith, D. F., Garcia, T., & McKeachie, W. J. (1991). *The manual for the use of the Motivated Strategies for Learning Questionnaire (MSLQ) (Tech. Rep. No. 91-B-004).* Ann Arbor, MI: University of Michigan, School of Education.

Pressley, M., & Afflerbach, P. (1995). *Verbal protocols of reading: The nature of constructively responsive reading*. Hillsdale, NJ: Erlbaum.

Schneider, M., Heine, A., Thaler, V., Torbeyns, J., De Smedt, B., Verschaffel, L., et al. (2008). A validation of eye movement as a measure of elementary schools children's developing number sense. *Cognitive Development, 23*(3), 424–437.

Schraw, G. (2006). Knowledge: Structures and processes. In P. Alexander & P. Winne (Eds.), *Handbook of educational psychology* (pp. 245–263). Mahwah, NJ: Erlbaum.

Schraw, G., & Dennison, R. S. (1994). Assessing metacognitive awareness. *Contemporary Educational Psychology, 19*(4), 460–475.

Shapiro, A., & Niederhauser, D. (2004). Learning from hypertext: Research issues and findings. In D. H. Jonassen (Ed.), *Handbook of research on educational communications and technology* (2nd ed., pp. 605–620). Mahwah, NJ: Erlbaum.

Veenman, M. (2007). The assessment and instruction of self-regulation in computer-based environments: A discussion. *Metacognition and Learning, 2*, 177–183.

Vollmeyer, R., & Rheinberg, F. (2006). Motivational effects on self-regulated learning with different tasks. *Educational Psychology Review, 18*(3), 239–253.

Vukman, K. B. (2005). Developmental differences in metacognition and their connections with cognitive development in adulthood. *Journal of Adult Development, 12*(4), 211–221.

Weiner, B. (1992). *Human motivation: Metaphors, theories, and research*. Clearwater, FL: H & H Publishing.

Weinstein, C. E. (1987). *LASSI user's manual*. Clearwater, FL: H & H Publishing.

Wigfield, A., & Eccles, J. S. (2000). Expectancy-value theory of achievement motivation. *Contemporary Educational Psychology, 25*, 68–81.

Wigfield, A., & Guthrie, J. T. (1997). Relations of children's motivation for reading to the amount and breadth or their reading. *Journal of Educational Psychology, 89*(3), 420–432.

Winne, P. H. (1982). Minimizing the black box problem to enhance the validity of theories about instructional effects. *Instructional Science, 11*, 13–28.

Winne, P. H. (1996). A metacognitive view of individual differences in self-regulated learning. *Learning and Individual Differences, 8*, 327–353.

Winne, P. H. (1997). Experimenting to bootstrap self-regulated learning. *Journal of Educational Psychology, 89*, 1–14.

Winne, P. H. (2001). Self-regulated learning viewed from models of information processing. In B. Zimmerman & D. Schunk (Eds.), *Self-regulated learning and academic achievement: Theoretical perspectives* (pp. 153–189). Mahwah, NJ: Erlbaum.

Winne, P. (2005). Key issues on modeling and applying research on self-regulated learning. *Applied Psychology: An International Review, 54*(2), 232–238.

Winne, P. H., & Hadwin, A. F. (1998). Studying self-regulated learning. In D. J. Hacker, J. Dunlosky, & A. Graesser (Eds.), *Metacognition in educational theory and practice* (pp. 277–304). Hillsdale, NJ: Erlbaum.

Winne, P., & Hadwin, A. (2008). The weave of motivation and self-regulated learning. In D. Schunk & B. Zimmerman (Eds.), *Motivation and self-regulated learning: Theory, research, and applications* (pp. 297–314). Mahwah, NJ: Erlbaum.

Winne, P. H., & Nesbit, J. C. (2009). Supporting self-regulated learning with cognitive tools. In D. J. Hacker, J. Dunlosky, & A. C. Graesser (Eds.), *Handbook of metacognition in education*. Mahwah, NJ: Erlbaum.

Winne, P. H., & Perry, N. E. (2000). Measuring self-regulated learning. In M. Boekaerts, P. Pintrich, & M. Zeidner (Eds.), *Handbook of self-regulation* (pp. 531–566). Orlando, FL: Academic.

Witherspoon, A., Azevedo, R., & D'Mello, S. (2008). The dynamics of self-regulatory processes within self- and externally-regulated learning episodes. In B. Woolf, E. Aimeur, R. Nkambou, & S. Lajoie (Eds.), *Proceedings of the International Conference on Intelligent Tutoring Systems: Lecture Notes in Computer Science (LNCS 5091)* (pp. 260–269). Berlin: Springer.

Zimmerman, B. (1995). Self-regulation involves more than metacognition: A social cognitive perspective. *Educational Psychologist, 30*(4), 217–221.

Zimmerman, B. (2008). Investigating self-regulation and motivation: Historical background, methodological developments, and future prospects. *American Educational Research Journal, 45*(1), 166–183.

Zimmerman, B. J., & Schunk, D. H. (Eds.). (2001). *Self-regulated learning and academic achievement: Theoretical perspectives* (2nd ed.). Mahwah, NJ: Erlbaum.

The Role of Motivation in Knowledge Acquisition

46

Regina Vollmeyer and Falko Rheinberg

Abstract

As our research is based on so called dynamic systems or microworlds we first describe and discuss this paradigm. We give a short overview on the huge variety of tasks that are subsumed under this label. In particular, we reflect on advantages of our biology-lab task.

Subsequently, we introduce our cognitive-motivational process model which specifies variables that help to describe self-regulated learning. Initial motivation (probability of success, interest, anxiety, and challenge) affects performance through mediating variables, for example strategies and motivation during learning. Metacognition especially planning could be included as a further mediating variable.

This theoretical model has already been studied with our biology-lab task (Vollmeyer & Rheinberg, 2006). In this study, motivation influenced performance (initial motivation and motivation during learning could both predict knowledge acquisition). Initial motivation influenced which strategy was chosen (more motivated participants chose more systematic strategies and were more motivated during learning). Participants with a systematic strategy and more motivation during learning performed better. With the aid of this study we discuss which aspects of metacognition could be integrated into the model without risking an overlap with the construct of motivation.

In the beginning of the 1990s, I started my research on knowledge acquisition in cooperation with Bruce Burns (University of Sydney, Australia) and Keith Holyoak (University of California, Los Angeles, USA). The aim of our research was to investigate in how people learn about relations between variables in an unknown system. This question is very important, as people have to act in complex environments, like the

R. Vollmeyer (✉)
Institute of Psychology, Johann Wolfgang Goethe-University Frankfurt, P.O. Box 11 19 32, Frankfurt 60054, Germany
e-mail: R.Vollmeyer@paed.psych.uni-frankfurt.de

F. Rheinberg
University of Potsdam, Postdam, Germany

R. Azevedo and V. Aleven (eds.), *International Handbook of Metacognition and Learning Technologies*, Springer International Handbooks of Education 26, DOI 10.1007/978-1-4419-5546-3_46,

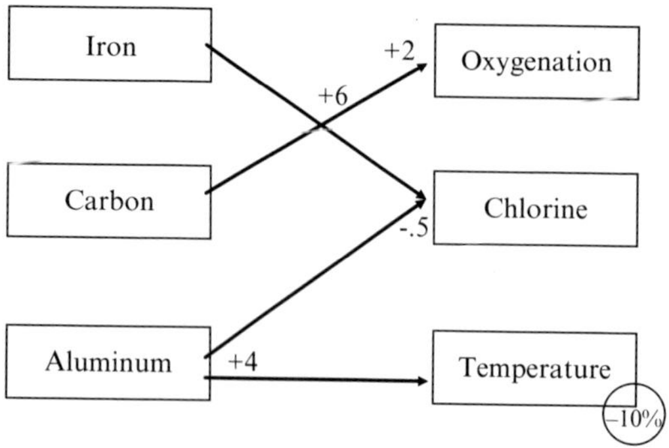

Fig. 46.1 Structure of a biology-lab system

world climate or an oil rig explosion in the Gulf of Mexico. Such complex systems have in common that people do not know exactly which variables are affected if one condition is changed. In real life, it is not possible to run experiments and watch what happens. However, researchers have created so-called microworlds which make it possible to study how people acquire knowledge and/or solve problems in artificial microworlds.

After having started studying cognitive processes, Falko Rheinberg and I integrated motivation into this research in the end of the 1990s. In this chapter, we will argue that integrating motivation into a theory of problem-solving represents progress, as we think that with this variable we can predict the performance in problem-solving tasks more precisely. However, before we introduce our theoretical framework (see "The Cognitive-Motivational Process Model"), we describe the technology, which we call "microworlds" or complex dynamic systems, and its advantages.

Microworlds

Osman (2010) gives a review of research on human behavior in microworlds or complex dynamic systems. With these microworlds, researchers studied mainly cognitive processes, for example, decision-making, implicit learning, or planning. Microworlds are used not only in psychology but also in other domains (e.g., economics, management, or engineering). Figure 46.1 illustrates a simple microworld that we used in our research on problem-solving (e.g., Burns & Vollmeyer, 2002; Vollmeyer, Burns, & Holyoak, 1996).

In a cover story, the participants were told that they were in a biology lab in which there is a tank with three water quality factors (oxygenation, chlorine, and temperature). These quality factors were the output variables of this system, affected by three input variables (iron, carbon, and aluminum). On each trial, a participant can change one, two, three, or none of the input variables. One output is relatively simple to manipulate because it is influenced by only one input (carbon→oxygenation). The other two outputs are more complex, because each is influenced by two inputs. One output (chlorine) is affected by two inputs, and the other (temperature) is affected by a decay factor (marked with a circle connected to the output) in addition to a single input variable. The decay factor was implemented by subtracting a percentage (10%) of the output's previous value on each trial. Decay is a dynamic aspect of the system, because it yields state changes even if there is no input (i.e., all inputs are set to zero). The system is therefore complex in that it involves multiple input variables that must be manipulated to control multiple output variables.

In the research in which microworlds are used to study cognitive processes, our biology lab is a rather simple system, as it includes six variables in total, three inputs and three outputs. There are even microworlds with more than 2,000 variables like the simulation of the town Lohhausen (Dörner, Kreuzig, Reither, & Stäudel, 1983). In this microworld, participants take over the role of the mayor of the town Lohhausen, and their goal was to take care of the future prosperity of the town over the short and long term. A 10-year period was simulated, and participants had eight 2-h sessions in total. However, it was not clear which variable was a good indicator for prosperity. Was it the town's capital, the bank's capital, or the factory's capital? Were social indicators important (number of unemployed, number of apartments)? As there were so many variables, participants were in an uncertain situation. In smaller systems, it is possible to learn the structure of the whole system, whereas in microworlds with many variables and complicated relations between variables, participants are not able to detect all variables and their relations. These more complex microworlds have a high intransparency, and participants have to deal with uncertainty as

```
exp15                                ROUND 1
TRIAL...            1        2        3        4        5
ACTUAL STATE...

oxygenation..     100      100      100      300      300
Cl concentrat     500      450     1050     1050     1050
temperature..    1000     1300     1170     1053      948

INPUTS...

iron.......         0      100        0        0        0
carbon.....       100        0        0        0
aluminum...         0        0      100        0
```

Fig. 46.2 Screenshot of a biology-lab system

to how to solve problems with these systems. However, some microworlds mirror real-world problems (i.e., have higher ecological validity) as, for example, radar tracking (Kozlowski & Bell, 2006). It depends on the research question what kind of microworld researchers choose. An early overview of mainly European microworlds is presented by Funke (1991).

Two different phases can be distinguished with such microworlds: (1) the exploration phase and (2) the application phase. If the microworld is presented with a nonspecific goal (e.g., "Learn how the inputs and outputs are connected"), learners explore the system. A screenshot of such a microworld is depicted in Fig. 46.2. Participants start with the actual state on Trial 1 in which they can choose numbers for the three inputs. The result of their manipulation is presented on Trial 2 under actual states. As the participants know that they have to find out the rules how the system works, they are free to choose values for the inputs. Through hypothesis testing, they need to formulate and test the rules. However, as soon as specific goals appear (e.g., "Bring oxygenation to 50"), learners need to apply their knowledge. If participants know the exact weights for each link, they can calculate the correct input. Another method is the means-ends analysis already described for problem-solving. Participants have to enter values for the inputs and watch how close they are to the goals. They then push the inputs closer and closer to the goals. Therefore, with microworlds, it is possible to study different cognitive processes.

Advantages of Using Microworlds

Microworlds have the advantage that they are presented on a computer, and therefore, it is easy to collect log files. These log files contain information about which inputs a participant manipulated. Microworlds also make it easy to exercise control over experimental procedures, as they can keep track of the amount of time each participant works with the system. Also, the presentation of questionnaires can be controlled by the system. Thus, it is unproblematic to compare participants in an identical situation.

Another advantage is that prior knowledge about the content does not interfere with the learning behavior because no participant has ever learned how, for example, iron affects chlorine. Therefore, it is a complete new situation for a novice. Normally, prior knowledge is a good predictor for learning (Hattie, 2008). Thus, when running experiments with verbal material (e.g., as in a study with a hypermedia system on World

War I, Vollmeyer & Burns, 2002), researchers need to take into account that learners with more prior knowledge acquire more knowledge about this material. In novel domains, control of prior knowledge is not necessary with microworlds.

A third advantage is that besides log files other research methods can be used. For example, it is possible to use research methods to capture the participants' thoughts with the thinking-aloud technique (Burns & Vollmeyer, 2002; Ericsson & Simon, 1993). This is particularly interesting because with think-aloud protocols researchers can study how participants plan and monitor their actions, which are aspects of metacognition (see below).

The above-mentioned advantages render dynamic systems especially suitable for research questions that can be tested experimentally in the laboratory or in the classroom. To develop theories, such a system can be varied in small steps (e.g., task difficulty, goal specificity, implementing feedback). This may be the reason why researchers use them for many different research questions; one research question is self-regulated learning.

Self-Regulated Learning

In the last 15 years, several theories that describe self-regulated learning were put forward in educational psychology, but Rheinberg, Vollmeyer, and Rollett (2000) defined a self-regulated learner as someone who learns without being forced or without external tutoring. Other authors add components to describe what exactly such a learner is regulating. In their model, Schunk and Zimmerman (1994) and Zimmerman (1995) specified self-regulated learning strategies, self-monitoring of effectiveness, and self-motivation. Boekaerts (1996) and Pintrich (2000) described how learners use cognitive strategies, metacognition, volition, and motivation to monitor their learning process. In the literature on organizational psychology, researchers more often use Kanfer and Ackerman's (1989) model of self-regulation, which comprises self-monitoring, self-evaluation, and self-reaction. Thus, different theories of self-regulation explain the learning process, but each one specifies different variables.

In line, we (Vollmeyer & Rheinberg, 1998, 2006) formulated a theoretical framework in which several psychological constructs describing learning can be put in order. The model emphasizes motivation and cognitive processes during learning, and therefore, we called it the cognitive-motivational process model.

The Cognitive-Motivational Process Model

The starting point of our cognitive-motivational process model is that people have a certain initial motivation when they encounter a certain task, for example, a dynamic system as our biology lab. The initial motivation has an impact on the learning outcome, not in a direct but in an indirect way. Between initial motivation and the learning outcome are mediating variables. To be more concrete, we will explain the different parts of the model in Fig. 46.3.

Initial Motivation

As there are many different motivational constructs in psychology, we first had to reduce the number of motivational constructs. We did this on a theoretical and empirical level (see Rheinberg, Vollmeyer, & Burns, 2001) and postulated four aspects of initial motivation: (1) *probability of success*, (2) *anxiety*, (3) *interest*, and (4) *challenge*.

Probability of success is an aspect discussed as early as the models of Lewin, Dembo, Festinger, and Sears (1944), as well as that of Atkinson (1957, 1964). It is also part of newer theories such as those by Bandura (1997), Anderson (1993), and Wigfield and Eccles (2002). Learners at least implicitly calculate the probability of success in that they take into account their ability and the perceived difficulty of the task.

The second aspect is *anxiety*, which we partly interpret as fear of failure in a specific situation (Atkinson, 1957, 1964). However, this aspect is not intended to be the opposite of high probability

Initial Motivation	Mediators	Performance
Probability of success	Persistence	Knowledge acquisition
Anxiety	Strategy systematicity	Goal achievement
Interest	Motivational state	
Challenge	Metacognition (planning)	

Fig. 46.3 Variables of the cognitive-motivational process model

of success, because it can be high for learners who, for example, are in a social situation in which they do not want to fail even though they expect to succeed.

The third aspect is *interest*. For learning, the topic of the learning material is important as has been shown in theories on interest (e.g., Krapp, Hidi, & Renninger, 1992). If learners are interested, they have positive affect and positive evaluations regarding the topic.

The last aspect we included in the model is *challenge*. Challenge is experienced among others if learners accept the situation as an achievement situation in which they want to have success (value component from expectancy-value models).

Mediators for the Influence of Initial Motivation on Performance

Researchers often study the relationship between motivation and performance. However, they seldom explain exactly how positive motivation leads to a good learning outcome. Does this effect occur because motivated learners persist longer on the task? Or do they put more effort into the task to process the material deeper? To answer these questions, we identified some potential mediators, but of course the list is not exhaustive. We first describe which mediators we have studied, and then we will discuss how metacognition could be integrated as a mediator. Our research inspired by this model will be presented in the section entitled "Our Results on Self-Regulatory Behavior Gained with Microworlds."

Duration and Frequency of the Learning Activity

An indicator for high motivation is a high persistence for a task, which is measured as time on task (i.e., *duration*). If initial positive motivation prolongs time on task, then people might acquire more knowledge. Indeed, researchers (e.g., Fisher, 1996; Helmke & Schrader, 1996; Volet, 1997) have found that the longer students study a certain topic at school the higher is their level of academic achievement. As it is not clear what people exactly do when they learn longer, time on task is a vague measure. However, the use of microworlds makes available a second indicator of persistence, namely, the *total number of times* with which participants manipulate the inputs. We studied persistence with the help of the microworld biology lab (Vollmeyer & Rheinberg, 2000).

Systematic Learning Strategies

Learning strategies are regarded as an important predictor of learning outcomes. Craik and Lockhart (1972) described why deep processing of the learning material leads to better knowledge than shallow strategies. However, it seems to be a problem to find indicators of deep processing or good strategies. For example, Artelt (2000) and

Jamieson-Noel and Winne (2003) showed that there is no relationship between learners' self-reported strategies and their actual use. Thus, researchers need other methods than self-reported questionnaires. More specifically, they need objective data to describe learners' strategies. As an example, we describe how we operationalized strategy systematicity when using a microworld (e.g., Vollmeyer et al., 1996). Based on Tschirgi's (1980) classification, participants who vary only one input at a time and hold the other inputs constant are called systematic (e.g., iron 10, carbon 0, aluminum 0). In contrast, participants could change all inputs haphazardly which is highly unsystematic (e.g., iron 10, carbon 10, aluminum 10). Using systematic strategies leads to more knowledge acquisition.

Motivational State During Learning

As a third mediator, Vollmeyer and Rheinberg (1998) suggested the *motivational state* of the learner. Whereas the already described *initial motivation* refers to participants' appraisals, affect, and interpretations of the whole situation *before* starting to learn, the motivational state refers to the participants' motivation *during* the exploration phase. In our questionnaire, we ask how much fun people are having during learning and whether or not people clearly know what to do next. The latter aspect refers to expectancies: If learners do not know how to handle a task, they are less motivated and may give up. As people experience success and/or failure during learning, their motivational state can vary over the learning period, and therefore, it is informative to measure it several times. When using microworlds, it is possible to interrupt the learners after manipulating the system for a certain number of trials.

Metacognition

In most self-regulation theories, metacognition is an important variable (see "Self-Regulated Learning"). Although metacognition is a "fuzzy concept" (Flavell, 1981), in our own work on learning with microworlds, we followed Simon's idea (1996) that metacognition is mainly used for executive control like planning (Vollmeyer & Rheinberg, 1999), a cognitive process which is mainly used in the exploration phase. In the area of problem-solving, Davidson, Deuser, and Sternberg (1994) instead described four metacognitive processes: problem identification, representation, planning how to proceed, and solution evaluation. This definition is similar to the one used in Winne's model of self-regulated learning (e.g., Winne, 2001; Winne & Hadwin, 1998).

To point out that different researchers use the term metacognition to mean different cognitive processes, we want to refer to a recent study by Güss, Tuason, and Gerhard (2010). They studied how different cultures (the USA, Brazil, India, Germany, Philippines) solve problems with two microworlds. Therefore, they asked their participants to think aloud while they were a commanding officer of a fire brigade (microworld: WINFIRE) or a supermarket manager controlling the temperature of a cold storage depot (microworld: COLDSTORAGE). In the coding system for their thinking-aloud protocols, they had one category for metacognition. This category was used when general goals or strategies were expressed ("I'm going to prioritize the towns over the forest"). Hence, in this study on problem-solving, metacognition was restricted to planning.

Another aspect of metacognition is monitoring, that is, controlling one's learning. Nelson and Narens (1994) divided monitoring into three categories: (1) ease of learning, (2) judgments of learning, and (3) feeling of knowing.

However, as Weinert (1984) had discussed earlier, metacognition, or more concretely, monitoring, and motivation are sometimes defined and operationalized the same way (e.g., ease of learning maps to probability of success, feeling of knowing maps to "motivational state"). Therefore, if both constructs (motivational state and metacognition) were included in one study, we would expect a correlation between these two mediators, because their operationalization overlaps. The same problem occurs with the construct of *flow* by Csikszentmihalyi (1975). Flow is a pleasant state, in which the following characteristics occur: (1) a challenge-skill balance, (2) merging of action and awareness, (3) unambiguous feedback, (4) concentration on the task at hand, (5) time transformation, and (6) fluency of action. We added the construct *flow* as mediating variable into our cognitive-motivational process model (Vollmeyer & Rheinberg, 2006). However, as motivational state and flow overlap in their definition as well as in their operationalization (i.e., among other items both questionnaires ask for self-reported ability), it is unclear how to disentangle these concepts. As flow is theoretically better defined, we decided to use only flow in further investigations. Adding metacognition (especially monitoring) into the cognitive-motivational process model would even enlarge the problem because all measures are self-reported and some questionnaire items express similar meaning. The aspect of planning, however, should capture new information about the cognitive process.

Performance

The cognitive-motivational process model leaves open how many indicators for performance should be conceptualized. In terms of validity, it is better to use more indicators. When using microworlds, researchers can measure what the participants learned of the system's structure in the exploration phase. Knowledge acquisition is gathered in that a diagram as in Fig. 46.1 without the links and weights is presented to the participants. After every round, they have to fill in which link exists and which weight they assume. The more they know about the links between the inputs and the outputs, the better is their knowledge acquisition. If specific goals are presented in the application phase (e.g., "Oxygenation should be on 50"), then goal achievement could measure the transfer of knowledge. The latter is true for participants who discovered the system's links and the weights. They only have to use their knowledge to calculate the inputs.

Our Results on Self-Regulatory Behavior with Microworlds

In a prior article (Vollmeyer & Rheinberg, 2006), we summarized our results of how motivational effects influence self-regulated learning. Therefore, a test of our cognitive-motivational process model has been published in detail. The published study was based on 109 students. In the current chapter, we present a short version with more emphasis on the results' limitations and challenges.

The general aim of our research was to demonstrate the importance of motivation in the learning process. Even before participants start acquiring knowledge about a microworld, positive initial motivation (high probability of success, high interest, and high challenge) should help in choosing a more systematic and maybe a more effortful strategy. Positive initial motivation should also support motivation during learning. A systematic strategy and positive motivation during learning should foster knowledge acquisition. We exploited the microworld's advantages in that we could use the log files to define strategies. Thus, we had a category system consisting of three categories: the highly systematic strategy (change one input variable at a time, Tschirgi, 1980), the highly unsystematic strategy (change all inputs at a time), and a category in between (change two variables). We interrupted our participants three times (Rounds 1 to 3) after six trials to measure their motivation with a questionnaire. Finally, we had two measures of performance, namely, knowledge acquisition and goal achievement. For knowledge acquisition, we asked our participants to fill in the links and weights in the empty structure diagram (see Fig. 46.1) (measured three times during participants' activity with the microworld). We then counted how many correct links and weights the participant had discovered. Goal achievement was the score calculated as difference between the goal state and the actual score of each output variable. With the help of a path analysis, we could support these theoretical assumptions through an empirical model (see Fig. 46.4).

The structural equation model (see Fig. 46.4) shows that with high motivation (high interest, high challenge, and high probability of success), participants chose a more systematic strategy and experienced more positive motivation during learning. A highly systematic strategy and positive motivation during learning led to better knowledge acquisition. When participants had to apply their knowledge, good knowledge of the system's structure and high motivation helped them reach goal states more accurately (high goal achievement).

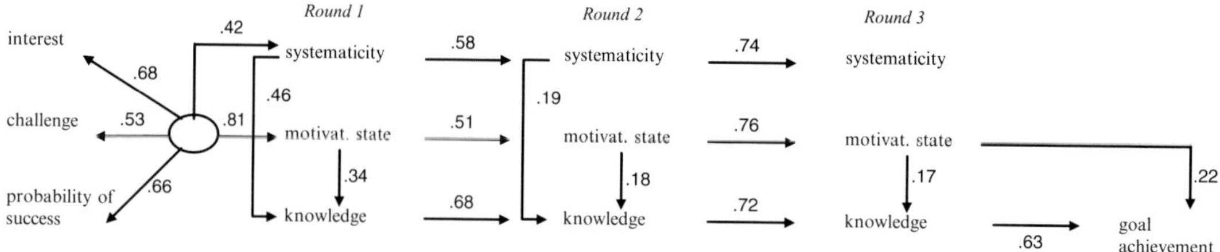

Fig. 46.4 Path analysis of the task-specific model for the microworld *biology lab*

Limitations and Challenges

Comparing the theoretical model in Fig. 46.3 and the empirical model in Fig. 46.4 makes it obvious that we could not include all possible mediating variables. To study the role of *persistence*, we would need a different design, in which it is left open how often a participant wants to manipulate our microworld. We realized such a design (Vollmeyer & Rheinberg, 2000) and found that indeed motivation affects persistence: Whereas initial motivation had an influence on persistence (i.e., more motivated participants were more persistent), the relationship between persistence and learning was disrupted because learners with more knowledge stopped earlier. However, learners with low knowledge but high motivation were more persistent and hence accumulated more knowledge over time. Thus, motivation had its most measurable impact on the learning outcomes of slow learners.

More problematic is the inclusion of the mediating variable metacognition. Although it would be possible to have participants think aloud to measure their problem identification, planning, and so on, adding these aspects of metacognition into the path analysis would lead to methodological problems. For each additional variable, we need more participants to have enough power to run the path analysis. Another limitation of the path analysis is that it is based on correlations, and thus, we cannot claim causality. The model in Fig. 46.4 is based on the procedure that initial motivation was measured before participants entered their first change to an input. Strategy systematicity was coded from the first trial to the first interruption, and knowledge acquisition and motivational state were both measured during the interruption. Therefore, the path model could be criticized on the grounds that the relation between knowledge acquisition and motivational state could be turned around. Even if we added only a single indicator for metacognition, we would enlarge the problem of causality. As the verbal protocols would be measured at the same time as the strategy systematicity, it could be argued that metacognition in the exploration phase (i.e., planning, solution evaluation) influences strategy systematicity, or vice versa. Depending on how we choose the direction of the arrows, we will obtain different effects on the dependent variables (i.e., knowledge acquisition and goal achievement). Even if we compared all plausible models and their model fits, we might find the best empirical model but still be left with doubts as to whether the best theoretical model was detected.

To integrate metacognition into our model, it is necessary to first study all aspects that Davidson et al. (1994) mentioned for problem-solving via verbal protocols. Then maybe we could find a way to reduce the four aspects if they are correlated. Thus, one aggregated score for metacognition in the exploration phase could be added into our model. However, monitoring will be even more difficult to integrate methodologically because this concept is already close to motivational state (see above) and it is measured through a questionnaire at the same time point as motivational state and knowledge acquisition (problem of causality).

Analyzing our data through structural equations offers another interesting question: What happens during the learning process? With the help of our microworld, we can study, with significant precision and in a longitudinal way, what participants feel after they manipulated the inputs for a certain number of trials. Did some participants lose interest? Or was there an increase in some participants' belief that they could manage the task (i.e., probability of success)? For these questions, we also need more participants to study subpopulations.

Up to now, we have not really analyzed our data as a process model for self-regulated learning. Self-regulation means that learners supervise their own learning and change their behavior and/or their motivation if, for example, a strategy does not work or an unexpected result occurs. In the path analysis in Fig. 46.4, systematicity and motivational states between Rounds 1 and 2 are not as high as between Rounds 2 and 3. Between the first rounds it seems that some learners changed their behavior and/or their motivation. Although theoretically we expect a feedback loop, the empirical model cannot depict these assumptions. More analyses are needed to explain this self-regulation process.

Final Remarks

So far we used microworlds only for research questions as opposed, for example, to diagnostic questions (Wirth & Klieme, 2003). We gained insight into how motivation affects the learning process. However, previously we started manipulating single variables of the model. For example, Vollmeyer and Burns (1996) presented correct, wrong, or no hypotheses about the structure of the system. The result was that even a wrong hypothesis helped students better predict the outcomes for the output variables. In a study by Vollmeyer, Püttmann, and Imhof (2009), we increased the (self-reported) probability of success through instruction related to stereotype threat (Schmader, Johns, & Forbes, 2008). In this study, we did not use a microworld but a physics task because we manipulated girls' stereotype threat. (Instruction: "It is important to keep in mind that if you are feeling anxious while working with the program, this anxiety could be the result of these negative stereotypes that are widely held in society and have nothing to do with your actual ability to do well on the task.") As expected, the girls' probability of success increased. As a consequence, the girls started with better learning strategies and experienced more flow during learning than the girls without this instruction. Finally, they even acquired the same amount of knowledge as males did.

If even such small manipulations can foster the formulation of hypotheses (Vollmeyer & Burns, 1996) or probability of success (Vollmeyer et al., 2009), the next step in our research could be to develop a program to support students' self-regulated learning. Our results have demonstrated that a more positive motivation before starting to learn and more systematic strategies improved learning.

References

Anderson, J. (1993). *Rules of the mind.* Hillsdale, NJ: Erlbaum.

Artelt, C. (2000). Wie prädiktiv sind retrospektive Selbstberichte über den Gebrauch von Lernstrategien für strategisches Lernen? [How predictive are self-reported strategies for their actual use?]. *Zeitschrift für Pädagogische Psychologie, 14,* 72–84.

Atkinson, J. W. (1957). Motivational determinants of risk-taking behavior. *Psychological Review, 64,* 359–372.

Atkinson, J. W. (1964). *An introduction to motivation.* Princeton, NJ: Van Nostrand.

Bandura, A. (1997). *Self-efficacy: The exercise of control.* New York: Freeman.

Boekaerts, M. (1996). Self-regulated learning at the junction of cognition and motivation. *European Psychologist, 1,* 100–122.

Burns, B. D., & Vollmeyer, R. (2002). Goal specificity and dual-space search theories of problem solving. *The Quarterly Journal of Experimental Psychology, 55A,* 241–261.

Craik, F. I. M., & Lockhart, R. S. (1972). Levels of processing: A framework for memory research. *Journal of Verbal Learning and Verbal Behavior, 11,* 671–684.

Csikszentmihalyi, M. (1975). *Beyond boredom and anxiety.* San Francisco, CA: Jossey-Bass.

Davidson, J. E., Deuser, R., & Sternberg, R. J. (1994). The role of metacognition in problem solving. In J. Metcalfe & A. P. Shimamura (Eds.), *Metacognition in educational theory and practice* (pp. 25–45). Mahwah, NJ: Erlbaum.

Dörner, D., Kreuzig, H. W., Reither, F., & Stäudel, T. (1983). *Lohhausen. Vom Umgang mit Unbestimmtheit und Komplexität [Lohhausen. On dealing with uncertainty and complexity].* Bern, Switzerland: Huber.

Ericsson, K. A., & Simon, H. A. (1993). *Protocol analysis (revised ed.).* Cambridge, MA: MIT Press.

Fisher, C. W. (1996). Academic learning time. In E. de Corte & F. E. Weinert (Eds.), *International encyclopedia of developmental and instructional psychology* (pp. 675–694). Oxford, England: Elsevier.

Flavell, J. H. (1981). Cognitive monitoring. In W. P. Dickson (Ed.), *Children's oral communication skills* (pp. 35–60). New York: Academic.

Funke, J. (1991). Solving complex problems: Exploration and control of complex systems. In R. J. Sternberg & P. A. Frensch (Eds.), *Complex problem solving: Principles and mechanisms* (pp. 185–222). Hillsdale, NJ: Erlbaum.

Güss, C. D., Tuason, M. T., & Gerhard, C. (2010). Cross-national comparisons of complex-solving strategies in two microworlds. *Cognitive Science, 34*, 489–520.

Hattie, J. (2008). *Visible learning*. New York: Routledge.

Helmke, A., & Schrader, F. W. (1996). Kognitive und motivationale Bedingungen des Studierverhaltens: Zur Rolle der Lernzeit [Cognitive and motivational conditions of study behavior: The role of learning time]. In J. Lompscher & H. Mandl (Eds.), *Lehr- und Lernprobleme im Studium [Teaching and learning problems in university courses]* (pp. 39–53). Bern, Switzerland: Huber.

Jamieson-Noel, D. L., & Winne, P. H. (2003). Comparing self-reports to traces of studying behavior as representations of students' studying and achievement. *Zeitschrift für Pädagogische Psychologie, 17*, 159–171.

Kanfer, R., & Ackerman, P. L. (1989). Motivation and cognitive abilities: An integrative aptitude-treatment interaction approach to skill acquisition. *Journal of Applied Psychology, 74*, 657–690.

Kozlowski, S. W. J., & Bell, B. S. (2006). Disentangling achievement orientation and goal setting: Effects on self-regulatory processes. *Journal of Applied Psychology, 91*, 900–916.

Krapp, A., Hidi, S., & Renninger, K. A. (1992). Interest, learning and development. In K. A. Renninger, S. Hidi, & A. Krapp (Eds.), *The role of interest in learning and development* (pp. 3–25). Hillsdale, NJ: Erlbaum.

Lewin, K., Dembo, T., Festinger, L., & Sears, P. S. (1944). Level of aspiration. In J. McHunt (Ed.), *Personality and the behavior disorders* (Vol. 1, pp. 333–378). New York: Ronald Press.

Nelson, T. O., & Narens, L. (1994). Why investigate metacognition? In J. Metcalfe & A. P. Shimamura (Eds.), *Metacognition in educational theory and practice* (pp. 1–25). Mahwah, NJ: Erlbaum.

Osman, M. (2010). Controlling uncertainty: A review of human behaviour in complex dynamic environments. *Psychological Bulletin, 136*, 65–86.

Pintrich, P. R. (2000). The role of goal-orientation in self-regulated learning. In M. Boekaerts, P. R. Pintrich, & M. Zeidner (Eds.), *Handbook of self-regulation* (pp. 452–502). San Diego, CA: Academic.

Rheinberg, F., Vollmeyer, R., & Burns, B. D. (2001). FAM: Ein Fragebogen zur Erfassung aktueller Motivation in Lern- und Leistungssituationen [A questionnaire to assess current motivation in learning situations]. *Diagnostica, 47*, 57–66.

Rheinberg, F., Vollmeyer, R., & Rollett, W. (2000). Motivation and action in self-regulated learning. In M. Boekaerts, P. Pintrich, & M. Zeidner (Eds.), *Handbook of self-regulation* (pp. 503–529). San Diego, CA: Academic.

Schmader, T., Johns, M., & Forbes, C. (2008). An integrated process model of stereotype threat effects on performance. *Psychological Review, 115*, 336–356.

Schunk, D. H., & Zimmerman, B. J. (1994). *Self-regulation of learning and performance*. Hillsdale, NJ: Erlbaum.

Simon, H. A. (1996). Metacognition. In E. De Corte & F. E. Weinert (Eds.), *International encyclopedia of developmental and instructional psychology* (pp. 436–441). New York: Elsevier.

Tschirgi, J. E. (1980). Sensible reasoning: A hypothesis about hypotheses. *Child Development, 51*, 1–10.

Volet, S. E. (1997). Cognitive and affective variables in academic learning: The significance of direction and effort in students' goals. *Learning and Instruction, 7*, 235–254.

Vollmeyer, R., & Burns, B. D. (1996). Hypotheseninstruktion und Zielspezifität: Bedingungen, die das Erlernen und Kontrollieren eines komplexen Systems beeinflussen [Hypothesis instruction and goal specificity: Conditions that influence the learning and control of a complex system]. *Zeitschrift für Experimentelle Psychologie, 43*, 657–683.

Vollmeyer, R., & Burns, B. D. (2002). Goal specificity and learning with a hypermedia program. *Experimental Psychology, 49*, 98–108.

Vollmeyer, R., Burns, B. D., & Holyoak, K. J. (1996). The impact of goal on strategy use and the acquisition of problem structure. *Cognitive Science, 20*, 75–100.

Vollmeyer, R., Püttmann, A., & Imhof, M. (2009). How to improve women's performance in physics through stereotype threat. In N. A. Taatgen & H. van Rijn (Eds.), *Proceedings of the 31st Annual Conference of the Cognitive Science Society* (pp. 1471–1476). Austin, TX: Cognitive Science Society.

Vollmeyer, R., & Rheinberg, F. (1998). Motivationale Einflüsse auf Erwerb und Anwendung von Wissen in einem computersimulierten System [Motivational influences on the acquisition and application of knowledge in a simulated game]. *Zeitschrift für Pädagogische Psychologie, 12*, 11–23.

Vollmeyer, R., & Rheinberg, F. (1999). Motivation and metacognition when learning a complex system. *European Journal of Psychology of Education, 14*, 541–554.

Vollmeyer, R., & Rheinberg, F. (2000). Does motivation affect performance via persistence? *Learning and Instruction, 10*, 293–309.

Vollmeyer, R., & Rheinberg, F. (2006). Motivational effects on self-regulated learning with different tasks. *Educational Psychology Review, 18*, 239–253.

Weinert, F. E. (1984). Metakognition und Motivation als Determinanten der Lernaktivität: Einführung und Überblick [Metacognition and motivation as determinants for learning activity: Introduction and overview].

In F. E. Weinert & R. H. Kluwe (Eds.), *Metakognition, Motivation und Lernen [Metacognition, motivation, and learning]* (pp. 9–21). Stuttgart, Germany: Kohlhammer.

Wigfield, A., & Eccles, J. S. (2002). The development of competence beliefs. In A. Wigfield & J. S. Eccles (Eds.), *Development of achievement motivation* (pp. 91–122). San Diego, CA: Academic.

Winne, P. H. (2001). Self-regulated learning viewed from models of information processing. In B. J. Zimmerman & D. H. Schunk (Eds.), *Self-regulated learning and academic achievement: Theoretical perspectives* (pp. 153–189). Hillsdale, NJ: Erlbaum.

Winne, P. H., & Hadwin, A. F. (1998). Studying as self-regulated learning. In D. J. Hacker, J. Dunlosky, & A. C. Graesser (Eds.), *Metacognition in educational theory and practice* (pp. 277–304). Hillsdale, NJ: Erlbaum.

Wirth, J., & Klieme, E. (2003). Computer-based assessment of problem solving competence. *Assessment in Education: Principles, Policy & Practice, 10*, 329–345.

Zimmerman, B. J. (1995). Self-regulated learning and academic achievement: An overview. *Educational Psychologist, 25*, 3–17.

Index

R. Azevedo and V. Aleven (eds.), *International Handbook of Metacognition and Learning Technologies*, Springer International Handbooks of Education 26, DOI 10.1007/978-1-4419-5546-3,

D

E

S

Printed by Publishers' Graphics LLC